Lecture Notes in Computer Science 7459

Commenced Publication in 1973
Founding and Former Series Editors:
Gerhard Goos, Juris Hartmanis, and Jan van Leeuwen

Sara Foresti   Moti Yung   Fabio Martinelli (Eds.)

Computer Security – ESORICS 2012

17th European Symposium
on Research in Computer Security
Pisa, Italy, September 10-12, 2012
Proceedings

 Springer

Volume Editors

Sara Foresti
Università degli Studi di Milano
Dipartimento di Informatica
Via Bramante 65, 26013 Crema, Italy
E-mail: sara.foresti@unimi.it

Moti Yung
Google Inc. and
Columbia University, Computer Science Department
1214 Amsterdam Avenue, New York, NY 10025, USA
E-mail: moti@cs.columbia.edu

Fabio Martinelli
National Research Council (CNR)
Institute of Informatics and Telematics (IIT)
Information Security Group
Pisa Research Area
Via G. Moruzzi 1, 56125 Pisa, Italy
E-mail: fabio.martinelli@iit.cnr.it

ISSN 0302-9743   e-ISSN 1611-3349
ISBN 978-3-642-33166-4   e-ISBN 978-3-642-33167-1
DOI 10.1007/978-3-642-33167-1
Springer Heidelberg Dordrecht London New York

Library of Congress Control Number: 2012945787

CR Subject Classification (1998): K.6.5, E.3, D.4.6, K.4.4, C.2.0, J.1, H.4, D.2.4, H.2.7

LNCS Sublibrary: SL 4 – Security and Cryptology

Typesetting: Camera-ready by author, data conversion by Scientific Publishing Services, Chennai, India

Printed on acid-free paper

Springer is part of Springer Science+Business Media (www.springer.com)

Preface

This volume contains the papers selected for presentation at the 17th European Symposium on Research in Computer Security (ESORICS 2012), held during September 10–12, 2012, in Pisa, Italy.

In response to the symposium's "call for papers," 248 papers were submitted to the conference from 43 countries. These papers were evaluated on the basis of their significance, novelty, technical quality, as well as on their practical impact or their level of advancement of the field's foundations.

The Program Committee's work was carried out electronically, yielding intensive discussions over a period of a few weeks. Of the papers submitted, 50 were selected for presentation at the conference (resulting in an acceptance rate of 20.16%). We note that many top-quality submissions were not selected for presentation because of the high technical level of the overall submissions, and we are certain that many of these submissions will, nevertheless, be published at other competitive forums in the future. Besides the technical program composed of the papers collated in these proceedings, the conference included three invited talks.

An event like ESORICS 2012 depends on the volunteering efforts of a host of individuals and support of numerous institutes. There is a long list of people who volunteered their time and energy to put together and organize the conference, and who deserve special thanks. Thanks to all the members of the Program Committee and the external reviewers for all their hard work in evaluating the papers. We are also very grateful to all the people whose work ensured a smooth organization process: the ESORICS Steering Committee, and its Chair Pierangela Samarati in particular, for their support; Giovanni Livraga, for taking care of publicity; Daniele Sgandurra, for maintaining the website; and the Local Organizing Committee, for helping with organization and taking care of local arrangements. We would also like to thank everyone who organized the workshops co-located with ESORICS. Special thanks are due to the keynote speakers, Gilles Barthe, Christian Cachin, and Ahmad-Reza Sadeghi, who enhanced the conference's program by delivering illuminating talks in their respective research areas. A number of institutes deserve thanks as well: the Institute of Informatics and Telematics of National Research Council (CNR) for its support and for hosting the event, and the Dipartimento di Informatica of the Università degli Studi di Milano for its support.

Last but certainly not least, our thanks go to all the authors who submitted papers and all the symposium's attendees. We hope you find the proceedings of ESORICS 2012 stimulating and a source of inspiration for your future research and education programs.

September 2012

Sara Foresti
Moti Yung
Fabio Martinelli

Organization

General Chair

Fabio Martinelli — National Research Council - CNR, Italy

Program Chairs

Sara Foresti — Università degli Studi di Milano, Italy
Moti Yung — Google Inc. and Columbia University, USA

Program Committee

Claudio A. Ardagna	Università degli Studi di Milano, Italy
Alessandro Armando	Università di Genova, Italy
Mikhail J. Atallah	Purdue University, USA
Michael Backes	Saarland University, Germany
David A. Basin	ETH Zurich, Switzerland
Kevin Bauer	Massachusetts Institute of Technology, USA
Joachim Biskup	University of Dortmund, Germany
Marina Blanton	University of Notre Dame, USA
Carlo Blundo	Università degli Studi di Salerno, Italy
Kevin R.B. Bulter	University of Oregon, USA
Srdjan Čapkun	ETH Zurich, Switzerland
Liqun Chen	HP Labs, UK
Seung-Geol Choi	University of Maryland, USA
Véronique Cortier	LORIA, France
Marco Cova	University of Birmingham, UK
Jason Crampton	University of London, UK
Frédéric Cuppens	Télécom Bretagne, France
Anupam Datta	Carnegie Mellon University, USA
Sabrina De Capitani di Vimercati	Università degli Studi di Milano, Italy
Claudia Diaz	K.U. Leuven, Belgium
Sven Dietrich	Stevens Institute of Technology, USA
Roberto Di Pietro	Università di Roma Tre, Italy
Josep Domingo-Ferrer	Universitat Rovira i Virgili, Spain
Wenliang (Kevin) Du	Syracuse University, USA
Riccardo Focardi	Università Ca' Foscari di Venezia, Italy
Simon Foley	University College Cork, Ireland
Keith B. Frikken	Miami University, USA
Dieter Gollmann	TU Hamburg-Harburg, Germany

Local Organizing Committee

Patrizia Andronico	National Research Council - CNR, Italy
Raffaella Casarosa	National Research Council - CNR, Italy
Adriana Lazzaroni (Chair)	National Research Council - CNR, Italy
Ilaria Matteucci	National Research Council - CNR, Italy
Paolo Mori	National Research Council - CNR, Italy
Marinella Petrocchi	National Research Council - CNR, Italy
Daniele Sgandurra	National Research Council - CNR, Italy

ESORICS Steering Committee

Michael Backes	Saarland University, Germany
Joachim Biskup	University of Dortmund, Germany
Frédéric Cuppens	Télécom Bretagne, France
Sabrina De Capitani di Vimercati	Università degli Studi di Milano, Italy
Yves Deswarte	LAAS, France
Dieter Gollmann	TU Hamburg-Harburg, Germany
Sokratis Katsikas	University of Piraeus, Greece
Miroslaw Kutylowski	Wroclaw University of Technology, Poland
Javier Lopez	University of Malaga, Spain
Jean-Jacques Quisquater	UCL Crypto Group, Belgium
Peter Ryan	University of Luxembourg, Luxembourg
Pierangela Samarati (Chair)	Università degli Studi di Milano, Italy
Einar Snekkenes	Gjøvik University College, Norway
Michael Waidner	TU Darmstadt, Germany

External Reviewers

Isaac Agudo
Everaldo Aguiar
Hadi Ahmadi
Mihhail Aizatulin
Sadia Akhter
Joseph A. Akinyele
Massimiliano Albanese
Mehrdad Aliasgari
José Bacelar Almeida
Mashael Alsabah
Elena Andreeva
Ero Balsa
Adam Bates
David Bernhard
Clara Bertolissi

Jeffrey Bickford
Norbert Bißmeyer
Daniel Bleichenbacher
Jeremiah Blocki
Eric Bodden
Andrey Bogdanov
Christian Broser
Sven Bugiel
Shakeel Butt
Stefano Calzavara
Roberto Carbone
Boaz Catane
Aldar C-F. Chan
Kai Yuen Cheong
Tom Chothia

Sherman Chow
Cheng-Kang Chu
Michael Clarkson
Gabriele Costa
Cas Cremers
Nora Cuppens
Paolo D'Arco
Duc Dang Nguyen
Luca Davi
Alessandra De Benedictis
Emiliano De Cristofaro
Stéphanie Delaune
Hua Deng
Rinku Dewri
Alexandra Dmitrienko
Stelios Dritsas
Francois Dupressoir
Tariq Elahi
Nicholas Farnan
Oriol Farràs
Gerardo Fernandez
William Fitzgerald
Andrea Forte
Cedric Fournet
Christoph Fritsch
Andreas Fuchs
Ludwig Fuchs
Kazuhide Fukushima
William Garrison
Geri Georg
Wesley George
Marco Ghiglieri
Yossi Gilad
Oliver Gmelch
Stefano Guarino
Stuart Haber
Marit Hansen
Sabri Hassan
Mitsuhiro Hattori
Jens Hermans
Michael Herrmann
Shoichi Hirose
Yoshiaki Hori
Siv Hilde Houmb
Jingyu Hua

Xinyi Huang
Marian Kamal Iskander
Takamasa Isohara
Mohammad Jafari
Limin Jia
Jun Jiang
Xing Jin
Zachery Jorgensen
Miltos Kandias
Yoshiaki Kasahara
Dilsun Kaynar
Aggelos Kiayias
Felix Klaedtke
Marek Klonowski
Steve Kremer
Łukasz Krzywiecki
Dennis Kügler
Jean Lancrenon
Hoi Le
Fagen Li
Giovanni Livraga
Shoufu Luo
Tongbo Luo
Weiliang Luo
Matteo Maffei
Krzysztof Majcher
Pasquale Malacaria
Keith Martin
Takahiro Matsuda
Toshihiko Matsuo
Damon McCoy
Stefan Meier
Florian Mendel
Alessio Merlo
Hooman Mohajeri Moghaddam
Prashanth Mohan
Benjamin Mood
Charles Morisset
Francisco Moyano
Dieudonne Mulamba
Alexios Mylonas
Jasvir Nagra
Toru Nakanishi
Michael Netter
Takashi Nishide

Yuan Niu
David Nuñez
Kazumasa Omote
Jose A. Onieva
Kenneth Paterson
Constantinos Patsakis
Thea Peacock
Riccardo Pelizzi
Olivier Pereira
Cristina Pèrez Solá
Betram Poettering
Serena Elisa Ponta
Hannah Pruse
Bo Qin
Silvio Ranise
Paul Ratazzi
Alfredo Rial
Moritz Riesner
Ruben Rios
Rodrigo Roman
Moustafa Saleh
Benedikt Schmidt
Thomas Schneider
Dominique Schroeder
Divya Sharma
Entong Shen
Haya Shulman
Hervais Simo
Arunesh Sinha
Yannis Soupionis
Deian Stefan
Martin Stopczynski
Mikhail Strizhov
Pierre-Yves Strub
Chunhua Su
Nik Sultana
Kun Sun
Wenhai Sun
Nikhil Swamy

Qiang Tang
Isamu Teranishi
Marianthi Theoharidou
Manachai Toahchoodee
Mohammad Torabi Dashti
Bill Tsoumas
Jalaj Uphadyay
Anthony Van Herrewege
Serge Vaudenay
Antonio Villani
Nick Virvilis
Jose L. Vivas
Bing Wang
Huaqun Wang
Lusha Wang
Wenhao Wang
Yifei Wang
Bogdan Warinschi
Michael Weber
Wei Wei
Joel Weinberger
Szymon Wilczek
Qianhong Wu
Shuang Wu
Haixia Xu
Jia Xu
Peng Xu
Rui Xue
Filip Zagórski
Santiago Zanella Béguelin
Lei Zhang
Ning Zhang
Rui Zhang
Tongjie Zhang
Xiao Zhang
Xin Zhang
Xianfeng Zhao
Yao Zheng

Table of Contents

Counteracting Man-in-the-Middle Attacks

Network Security

Users Privacy and Anonymity

Location Privacy

Voting Protocols and Anonymous Communication

Private Computation in Cloud Systems

Formal Security Models

Identity Based Encryption and Group Signature

Authentication

Encryption Key and Password Security

Malware and Phishing

Software Security

Modeling and Enhancing
Android's Permission System

Elli Fragkaki, Lujo Bauer, Limin Jia, and David Swasey

Carnegie Mellon University, Pittsburgh, PA, USA

Abstract. Several works have recently shown that Android's security architecture cannot prevent many undesired behaviors that compromise the integrity of applications and the privacy of their data. This paper makes two main contributions to the body of research on Android security: first, it develops a formal framework for analyzing Android-style security mechanisms; and, second, it describes the design and implementation of SORBET, an enforcement system that enables developers to use permissions to specify secrecy and integrity policies. Our formal framework is composed of an abstract model with several specific instantiations. The model enables us to formally define some desired security properties, which we can prove hold on SORBET but not on Android. We implement SORBET on top of Android 2.3.7, test it on a Nexus S phone, and demonstrate its usefulness through a case study.

1   Introduction

Recent years have witnessed an explosion in the use of mobile computing thanks to the proliferation of feature-rich smartphones, and associated app stores and easy-to-install applications. Smartphones have powerful hardware, with many useful sensors (e.g., GPS, camera, microphone, accelerometer) exposed via rich APIs, and enough computing power to run complex applications. Applications take advantage of these rich APIs to perform convenient and useful, but potentially privacy-sensitive tasks such as accessing address-book or location information; accessing online banking and medical accounts; and controlling home security systems. App stores make it easy for users to install and run applications, while providing few guarantees about their provenance or behavior.

To protect sensitive resources from applications, and applications from each other, Android and other mobile OSes implement security mechanisms such as permission systems and strong isolation between applications. These mechanisms, however, have in practice proved insufficient, with an increasing number of malicious applications starting to target smartphones [15,23,16].

A number of works have investigated these weaknesses from various perspectives, including demonstrating how applications can communicate through covert channels [24,18], developing tools to detect information leaks [8,5,14], and implementing more powerful protection mechanisms (e.g., [22,20,7,2]).

This paper adds to the body of research on Android security in two main ways: first, by developing a formal framework for analyzing Android-style security mechanisms, including defining properties desired of those, and verifying

S. Foresti, M. Yung, and F. Martinelli (Eds.): ESORICS 2012, LNCS 7459, pp. 1–18, 2012.

whether these properties hold; and, second, by designing and implementing an enforcement system that provides application developers with simple language constructs to specify flexible secrecy and integrity policies, and provably exhibits desirable security properties. To remain practically relevant, we constrain our enforcement system, which we call SORBET, to be easily retrofittable into Android's current architecture. The design and implementation of SORBET improves existing Android permission system in the following aspects: (1) we formally state the properties that we wish our new mechanisms to achieve, and formally prove that our system design supports them; (2) we enhance Android's permission system to support coarse-grained secrecy and integrity policies; and (3) we provide more flexible support for fine-grained and scope-limited delegation of permissions.

Formal analysis. One of our main goals is to improve our understanding of the security properties that we desire of Android-like permission systems, and to verify that specific systems are capable of specifying and enforcing desired properties. We pursue this goal by building a generalized, abstract model of the Android permission system, and stating a set of desirable properties in terms of the model. We then develop instantiations of this model both for the current Android permission system and for SORBET. Based on this formal account, we study the properties of the current system; our investigation reveals both design and implementation flaws, which guide the design of SORBET. We also prove that SORBET's design is sufficient to support the properties that we have defined.

Coarse-grained secrecy and integrity policies. SORBET's key innovation is coarse-grained mechanisms that allow developers to protect their applications against privilege escalation and undesired information flows (e.g., [6,8]). Android's permission system only prevents applications that do not have the correct permissions from directly calling a protected component. This is inadequate to protect against a malicious application that reaches a protected component indirectly, via a chain of calls to innocent applications. To protect against such attacks, we enrich Android's permission system with the ability to specify information-flow constraints and explicit declassification permissions, and implement a lightweight calling-context tracking and checking mechanism. A key challenge here is to support *local* specification of *global* properties.

Flexible and fine-grained delegation. Run-time delegation of URI permissions is a key feature in Android, and allows applications to use third-party components (e.g., a viewer activity) to manipulate content that those components normally would not be permitted to access. On examination, we discovered that Android's implementation of permission delegation is plagued by a number of flaws and questionable design decisions. SORBET supports more flexible and principled permission delegation and revocation, and allows developers to specify constraints that limit the lifespan and redelegation scope of the delegated permissions. Developing a mechanism that correctly enforces lifetime and scope constraints turns out to be unexpectedly tricky, due to redelegation and the dynamic nature of Android applications and components, including application installation and uninstallation, and instantiation and termination of components.

Contributions and Roadmap. This paper makes the following contributions:

- We develop a formal model that generalizes Android-style permissions (§2.2). We show how Android's current permission system can be represented as an instantiation of our abstract model (§2.3).
- Building on this model, we define a set of security properties that one may desire of Android-style permission systems (§3.1). We show that Android currently obeys some of the desired security properties, but not others, and expose several design inconsistencies and implementation flaws (§3.2).
- We describe SORBET, a set of improvements to Android's permission system that supports developer-specified coarse-grained information-flow and privilege-escalation policies. We formalize SORBET as an instantiation of our model and show that it better supports the desired security properties (§4).
- Finally, we implement SORBET on top of Android 2.3.7, test it on a Nexus S phone, and demonstrate several new scenarios that it enables (§5).

2   Preliminaries

We first review the Android architecture as it pertains to permissions (§2.1). We then develop an abstract model of Android-style permission systems (§2.2), and an instantiation of it that captures details of Android's implementation (§2.3).

2.1   Android Overview

Android is a Linux-based open-source OS designed for smartphones. Android applications are written in Java and compiled to Dalvik bytecode. Each application is executed in a separate Dalvik Virtual Machine (DVM) instance.

Android applications are composed of four types of components:

Activities define the user interface. Only one activity interacts with the user at a time. Users typically interact with a sequence of activities to perform a task.

Services run in the background and have no user interface. Unlike activities, services remain active regardless of which application is in the foreground.

Broadcast receivers listen for system-wide broadcasts, and inform other application components upon the receipt of a broadcast.

Content providers store data and are the main way to share data between applications. Each provider exposes a public URI that uniquely identifies its data set. Components and applications can access or update the data via SQL queries.

Activities, services, and broadcast receivers communicate via *intents*, asynchronous messages that deliver data and, if needed, cause a new instance of the recipient component to be created. The OS mediates both cross- and intra-application communications via intents. The recipient of an intent can be specified explicitly by its package and class name, or implicitly via the *action* the intent attempts to initiate. We will often write that a component *calls* another component in lieu of explaining that the communication is via an intent.

Static Constructs

Components	C	$::= C_{code} \mid C_{data}$

Code Components $C_{code} ::= (name, \mathcal{A}, \varphi_{ckCallee}, \varphi_{ckCaller}, \mathcal{P}_{decl}, \mathcal{P}_{req}, \mathcal{P}_{grnt})$
Data Components $C_{data} ::= (name, \varphi_{ckCaller}, \mathcal{P}_{decl})$

Component Groups $\widehat{C}$ $::= (name, \varphi_{ckCallee}, \varphi_{ckCaller}, \mathcal{P}_{decl}, \mathcal{P}_{req}, \mathcal{P}_{grnt}, \{C_1, \cdots, C_n\})$

Run-time Constructs

Run-time Instances Ins $::= iC \mid i\widehat{C}$

Comp Instances iC $::= (name_r, C, \mathcal{P}_{grnt})$
Comp Group Instances $i\widehat{C}$ $::= (name_r, \widehat{C}, \mathcal{P}_{grnt}, \{iC_1, \cdots, iC_n\})$

Principals $Prin ::= Ins \mid user$
Targets $Tgt ::= Ins \mid C \mid \widehat{C}$
Events $E \quad ::= x = E_1; E_2 \mid \mathsf{call}\ iC_1\ iC_2\ I \mid \mathsf{return}\ iC_1\ iC_2\ I \mid \mathsf{resolve}\ iC\ \varphi$
      $\mid\ \mathsf{grant}\ Prin\ Tgt\ P\ \mathcal{F} \mid \mathsf{revoke}\ Prin\ (\{Tgt_1, \cdots, Tgt_n\})\ P$
      $\mid\ \mathsf{checkguard}\ iC\ Tgt\ \varphi \mid \mathsf{exit}\ Ins \mid \mathsf{install}\ Prin\ \widehat{C} \mid \mathsf{uninstall}\ Prin\ \widehat{C}$

Fig. 1. Syntax of permission model

Android uses *(application) permissions* to protect components and sensitive APIs. Permissions are strings (e.g., android.permission.INTERNET) defined by the system or declared by applications. A component or API protected by a permission can be accessed only by applications that hold this permission. Applications acquire (application) permissions only at install time, with the user's consent.

Additionally, content providers can use *URI permissions* to grant ad-hoc access to specific pieces of data that they control (records, tables, or databases). URI permissions can be dynamically granted and revoked.

2.2 Abstract Model

To be able to formally state the properties desired of a permissions architecture, we develop an abstract, formal model of Android-style permissions systems. The model comprises: (1) static elements, which are the code and data we want to protect; (2) run-time elements, such as system events and component instances; and (3) a transition system that captures the behavior of the protection mechanisms. The model is more general than Android's implementation as its purpose is to encompass a wider design space of permission systems, including previously suggested extensions (e.g., [22]). We only sketch the model here; see our technical report [13] for details. Fig. 1 shows the model's static and run-time elements.

Static Constructs. Following Android, applications in our model are built from components. We distinguish between *code components* (C_{code}) and *data components* (C_{data}). Code components—activities, services, and broadcast receivers—may act both as callers and as callees; data components—content providers—are passive and only receive calls. A code component is comprised of a name ($name$), the actions $\mathcal{A}$ to which the component is willing to respond, permissions ($\mathcal{P}_{decl}$, $\mathcal{P}_{req}$, and $\mathcal{P}_{grnt}$), and guards ($\varphi_{ckCallee}$, $\varphi_{ckCaller}$).

In Android, calls to a component are guarded by a permission check. We generalize this check to an abstract guard modeled by a boolean function $\varphi_{ckCaller}$. For now, we specify only that $\varphi_{ckCaller}$ takes as arguments a component and the calling context and returns true or false. A second general guard, $\varphi_{ckCallee}$, specifies when outgoing calls should be allowed.

We distinguish between permissions that are declared ($\mathcal{P}_{decl}$), requested from the user ($\mathcal{P}_{req}$), and granted ($\mathcal{P}_{grnt}$). This allows us to model behaviors such as dynamic delegation of permissions.

We model applications, $\widehat{C}$, as a set of components ($\{C_1, \cdots, C_n\}$) with guards and permissions that apply to all. This is consistent with Android, where permissions are typically declared, requested, and granted at the application level, but individual components can protect themselves with additional permissions.

Run-Time Constructs. It is important to distinguish static components from run-time instances, and run-time instances from each other. A static component C may have multiple run-time instances iC, composed of a unique identifier (e.g., pointer), $name_r$, and the permissions $\mathcal{P}_{grnt}$ granted to this instance. We similarly model run-time component groups $i\widehat{C}$ (e.g., a running application).

Principals $Prin$ are entities that can grant and revoke permissions: run-time components and component groups, and the user (i.e., human who installs applications). Targets Tgt are the objects of such operations, and can be either run-time or static components or component groups.

Abstracting detail, we focus on system events that concern permissions, such as component communication via intents (call iC_1 iC_2 I), and granting (grant) and revoking permissions (revoke). We discuss these further in §2.3 and §4.1 when we focus on the Android and SORBET instantiation of the abstract model.

Transition System. We capture the dynamics of the model as a transition system. We model a system state Σ as a tuple composed of a set of entities (run-time and static) and auxiliary data structures Aux. We write $\mathcal{E}$ to denote a sequence of events to be processed by the system. We assume that each event is associated with a unique event ID n. The evolution of the system is a series of transitions ($\Sigma; \mathcal{E} \xrightarrow{o} \Sigma'; \mathcal{E}'$), where o records whether the evaluation of event n is successful ($o = \mathsf{ok}(n)$) or fails ($o = \mathsf{fail}(n)$). Evaluation of a call event will fail, for example, if the appropriate guards don't evaluate to true. A trace, denoted by $\mathcal{T}$, is a sequence of transitions: $\Sigma_0; \mathcal{E}_0 \xrightarrow{o_1} \Sigma_1; \mathcal{E}_1 \cdots \xrightarrow{o_k} \Sigma_k; \mathcal{E}_k$.

The specific rules in the transition system depend on the concrete implementations being modeled. Here we show the rule schema for a successful call event. The call succeeds only if both guards evaluate to true.

CALL-T $(\Sigma; \mathcal{E}, n :: \mathsf{call}\ iC_1\ iC_2\ I) \xrightarrow{\mathsf{ok}(n)} (\Sigma'; \mathcal{E})$ where $\Sigma' = updateCall(\Sigma, \mathsf{call}\ iC_1\ iC_2\ I)$
    if $iC_2.\varphi_{ckCaller}(\Sigma, iC_1) = \mathsf{true}$ and $iC_1.\varphi_{ckCallee}(\Sigma, iC_2) = \mathsf{true}$

A parallel rule, CALL-F, specifies that a call fails if either guard returns false.

2.3   Android Model

We instantiate our abstract model to describe the key behaviors of Android's permission system[1]. This has helped us to identify flaws in its implementation

---

[1] When we refer to Android, we mean version 2.3.7, which was the newest version available while we were carrying out our investigation. The behaviors we describe generally hold in 4.0 as well.

and peculiarities in its design. We omit a full description, but show example instantiations of guards ($\varphi_{\mathcal{P}}^{uri}$) and transition rules for granting permissions.

Guards. The guard $\varphi_{\mathcal{P}}^{uri}$ checks whether a component has the URI permissions specified in $\mathcal{P}$. $\varphi_{\mathcal{P}}^{uri}$ can be used as $\varphi_{ckCaller}$ when $\mathcal{P}$ is the set of URI permissions protecting a component.

We first define functions to look up the permissions associated with a run-time component from the current state. Function $grantedByUsrPerm(iC, \Sigma)$ returns permissions granted at install time, and function $URIPerm(iC, \Sigma)$ returns the URI permissions dynamically granted to iC; $URIPerm$ in turn relies on a data structure $\mathcal{M}$ to track the URI permissions granted to each application. Then, we define $\varphi_{\mathcal{P}}^{uri}$ as follows.

$$\varphi_{\mathcal{P}}^{uri} \triangleq f(iC, \Sigma) = \mathcal{P} \subseteq grantedByUsrPerm(iC, \Sigma) \cup URIPerm(iC, \Sigma)$$

Granting Permissions. URI permissions can be granted temporarily, via an intent, or permanently, via grantUriPermission. We model the former as:
  grant iC_1 iC_2 P $\mathcal{F}_{tmp}$; call iC_1 iC_2 I.

Here, iC_1 grants permission P with flag $\mathcal{F}_{tmp}$ to iC_2 before transferring control to iC_2. Granting permanently we model as grant iC_1 $\widehat{C}$ P $\mathcal{F}_{prm}$. Flags $\mathcal{F}_{tmp}$ and $\mathcal{F}_{prm}$ constrain the lifetime of the delegation of P and the scope of its potential redelegation by iC_2. Mirroring Android, the lifetime of permissions granted with $\mathcal{F}_{tmp}$ is confined to the lifetime of the recipient (iC_2) of the grant operation. When granting with $\mathcal{F}_{prm}$, the recipient will have the permission until the system reboots or the permission is revoked. Neither flag restricts the scope of redelegation. The following rule shows how grant currently works in Android.

$$(\Sigma; \mathcal{E}, n :: \mathsf{grant}\ iC_1\ iC_2\ P\ \mathcal{F}_{tmp}) \xrightarrow{\mathsf{ok}(n)} (\Sigma'; \mathcal{E}) \quad \text{if } \varphi_{\{P\}}^{uri}(iC_1, \Sigma) = \mathsf{true}$$
$$\text{where } \Sigma' = updateGrant(\Sigma, iC_1, iC_2, P, \mathcal{F}_{tmp})$$

Granting succeeds only if the granter has permission P. Afterwards, *updateGrant* updates state, by recording in $\mathcal{M}$ that the enclosing application of iC_2 now has permission P with flag $\mathcal{F}_{tmp}$, and that the instance iC_2 has P in $\mathcal{P}_{grnt}$.

The rule for granting with $\mathcal{F}_{prm}$ (omitted here) differs only in its update function: $\mathcal{M}$ records that now $\widehat{C}$ has permission P with the flag $\mathcal{F}_{prm}$. These rules make explicit that Android does not distinguish between $\mathcal{F}_{tmp}$ and $\mathcal{F}_{prm}$ when deciding whether a component can grant permissions. This causes problems when components redelegate permissions, as we discuss in §3.2.

3   Security Properties

We define several properties that one might desire of an Android-style security architecture (§3.1) and investigate whether they currently hold (§3.2).

3.1   Specifying Desired Security Properties

We formulate the properties desired of Android's security architecture based on the resources that need protection. These are typically interfaces that allow access to functionality that could cause harm or inconvenience (e.g., sending expensive text messages) and to sensitive data that should not leave the possession of components that legitimately require it (e.g., financial information in a banking application; location information). We abstractly define access-control properties that specify when and how a protected interface can be called and information-flow properties that specify when and what information can flow to or from a component. We also investigate lower-level, functional-correctness properties concerning granting and revoking permissions, since these directly affect the access-control and information-flow properties.

Local Properties.   The following two properties state that the immediate restrictions specified by a component on its callers or callees are always obeyed.

PROPERTY 1. (Local callee protection)   *If a component A is called by another component B, then A's guard $\varphi_{ckCallee}$ evaluates to* true.

PROPERTY 2. (Local caller protection)   *If a component A calls another component B, then A's guard $\varphi_{ckCaller}$ evaluates to* true.

It is easy to show that Prop. 1 and 2 hold on any instantiation that includes rules like CALL-T and CALL-F (see §2.2).

Delegation and Revocation Properties.

PROPERTY 3. (Delegation)   *A component A has a permission P if A owns P, or there is a delegation chain from a component B to A such that A satisfies the scope and lifetime constraints imposed by every component on the chain, and that every component on the chain also has P.*

Intuitively, Prop. 3 ensures that the use of a redelegated permission is confined by the lifetime and scope constraints specified by the original granter. For instance, if an email component gives to a viewer component the URI permission P for displaying an attachment, two sensible constraints are that P is confined to a specific instance of the viewer, and that the viewer cannot redelegate P.

PROPERTY 4. (Revocation)   *If A revokes P from B, then there is a delegation chain from A to B, or A owns P.*

This is a basic correctness property for revocation. Allowing arbitrary components to revoke permissions is likely to be disruptive; hence, only the owner or granter should be allowed to revoke a permission.

Global Properties.   The next two properties are simplified noninterference. We customize the general notion that secret inputs cannot affect public outputs and tainted inputs cannot affect endorsed outputs to fit the permission-based Android model.

PROPERTY 5. (Privilege escalation)   *Given any component B protected by permission P, and any component A that does not have that permission, if S_{AB} is a system that contains A and B (and other components), and S_B is the same system without A, then a call chain ending with B exists in S_{AB} if and only if it exists in S_B. Additional call chains ending with B may exist in S_{AB} if explicitly allowed by policy.*

In other words, with respect to accessing B, a system with unprivileged component A should behave the same as a system without A. The only exception is if additional policy explicitly allows A to affect B. Without such exceptions, this property would likely be too restrictive.

For example, let B be the interface, guarded by permission P, for rebooting the phone. Suppose that component C has P (which allows it to call B), and a public interface, such that any calls to that interface will cause C to call B. Then, a component A that does not have P can indirectly cause B to be invoked by calling C. C's indiscriminate invocation of B is an example of the confused-deputy problem. Since a trace culminating in that invocation of B cannot exist in a system without A, Prop. 5 prohibits this behavior.

In the other direction, we may want to prevent sensitive information from being leaked, which permission systems typically cannot specify directly. We leverage permissions to state an undesired information flow as follows. Suppose that permission P_1 guards the source of some information and permission P_2 guards the sink. Then, an undesired information flow can be specified as a call chain from a component that uses P_1 to a component that uses P_2. A system that has no undesired information flows should then obey the following property.

PROPERTY 6. (Information flow)   *Given an undesired information flow from a component A guarded by P_1 to a component B guarded by P_2, a call chain that ends with B exists in a system with A if and only if the same call chain exists in a system without A. Additional call chains ending with B may exist in the system with A only if explicitly allowed by policy.*

Without a more expressive policy specification language, these properties cannot be specified precisely.

3.2   Analyzing Android Permissions

We investigated the extent to which Android's current permission system, as represented by our model, supports the properties defined in §3.1.

Local Properties Hold.   Android's permission system implements the CALL-T and CALL-F rules, and the guards specified by the components are checked at run time; hence, Prop. 1 and 2 hold. However, Prop. 2 holds trivially, because callers cannot state useful guards on callees.

Delegation and Revocation Properties Do Not Hold.   Prop. 3 requires that a permission does not outlive the lifespan specified by its granter. Android's implementation, however, does not distinguish between $\mathcal{F}_{tmp}$ and $\mathcal{F}_{prm}$ when deciding whether a component can grant permissions. This violates Prop. 3 and causes several bugs (see our companion technical report [13]), e.g., a component that gained temporary permission can redelegate the permission permanently, including to itself.

Android's revokeURIPermission revokes a URI permission from all components to which it was dynamically granted, and can be called by any component that was granted the permission at install time. This violates Prop. 4, which requires that a component A can revoke only from entities to which it granted permission (unless A owns the permission). Such violations can easily cause confusion, as unrelated applications can revoke each other's permissions.

Global Properties Do Not Hold. Previous work has pointed out that Android suffers from privilege-escalation flaws (e.g., [6]); i.e., Prop. 5 does not hold. Prop. 6 also does not hold, as Android does not have a mechanism for preventing, or even specifying, undesired information flows. An application can access any component for which it has the permission to do so, regardless of whether it had previously accessed protected information. Previous work has shown that this results in various specific undesired information flows [24,18,8].

Examining Android in light of these properties also revealed several design and implementation bugs, which we reported to Google. These include the ability of components that received a temporary permission to redelegate that permission permanently, and improper bookkeeping of granted permissions during application uninstallation and installation that can lead to privilege escalation. These flaws are discussed in more detail in our companion technical report [13].

4   Sorbet: Android Permissions++

Motivated by the properties of §3.1, we develop SORBET, an improved permission system that supports (1) developer-defined policies to mitigate undesired information flows and privilege-escalation attacks; and (2) well-behaved permission delegation and revocation. Our goals were to enable developers and users to specify richer policies on their applications without dramatically altering Android, and to construct an enforcement system that is provably well behaved.

Some of the mechanisms we use have been discussed previously [10,22,14,7]; we integrate these and other ideas into a system that we can formally show satisfies interesting security properties and enables new use cases.

4.1   New Features in Sorbet

Coarse-Grained Information-Flow Protection. SORBET extends Android's permission labels to make them suitable for specifying coarse-grained information-flow policies, and enforces such policies at component and application boundaries. By reusing permission labels, this approach requires little new syntax.

In SORBET, a component A guarded by P_1 (e.g., the contacts permission) can specify (in the application manifest) information-flow policies of the form disallow-flow(P_1, P_2). This indicates that any component B that made use of P_1 to access A cannot (including transitively) use permission P_2. A component can also request at install time the permission allow-declassify(P_1, P_2) to declassify sensitive information, i.e., to escape the restriction imposed by disallow-flow(P_1, P_2). We formalize this mechanism and the property it enforces in §4.2 and §4.3.

Our mechanism can be used by programmers to strengthen their own code by separating trusted information that should remain internal to an application from untrusted flows that may be communicated to the outside, thereby decreasing the chance of the application being misused by malicious ones. The mechanism can also be used to defend against malicious applications or developers, by specifying policies that should hold between applications.

Coarse-Grained Privilege-Escalation Protection.   To mitigate the confused-deputy problem, SORBET tracks the permissions of all components on the call stack. When a component A is called, and A is protected by permission P, SORBET checks if every component on the call stack has P. However, this is too restrictive for practical use; e.g., an email app, which needs to use the INTERNET permission to send email, could do so only when started by applications that have the INTERNET permission. To address this, SORBET allows components to request a privileged permission $\hat{P}$. When a component B has the permission $\hat{P}$, it is permitted to call A even when other components on its call stack do not have P. $\hat{P}$ is similar to the *enable privilege* operation in Java stack inspection. Other works have also tracked the call stack for similar purposes (e.g., [7]); SORBET's novelty here is in allowing developers to specify policies, and in enabling proofs that this and other design features allow the system to exhibit desired properties.

As with information flow, SORBET protects against privilege escalation at both component level and application level. To account for Android's inability to completely mediate communication (e.g., via public static fields) between components within

Flag	Recipient	Redelegation scope	Lifetime
$\mathcal{F}_{comp}$	activity	no redelegation	activity exit
$\mathcal{F}_{task}$	activity	activities in the same task	activity exit
$\mathcal{F}_{appTmp}$	activity	activities in the same app	activity exit
$\mathcal{F}_{allTmp}$	activity	any component	activity exit
$\mathcal{F}_{app}$	app	no redelegation	app uninstall
$\mathcal{F}_{all}$	app	unrestricted	app uninstall

Fig. 2. Flags for constraining delegation. Columns show the recipient scope, the scoping constraints of redelegation, and the lifetime of the granted permission.

an application, the policy enforced at the application level assumes that component boundaries within an application are not respected.

Principled Redelegation and Revocation.   SORBET also addresses Android's problems with indiscriminate redelegation. The challenge here is to design a (correct) mechanism to allow programmers to predictably control delegation lifetime and redelegation scope. Building on Android's notion of temporary and persistent permissions, we enable the **grant** operation to precisely convey the intended scope of the recipient (a component or an application), the scope of redelegation (none, components in the same task, components in the same application, and unrestricted), and the lifetime of the permission (until the recipient activity exits, or is uninstalled). For simplicity, we converge on six combinations of these constraints (summarized in Fig. 2), which the programmer can specify via flags passed as arguments to **grant**. The enforcement mechanism enforces the transitive properties that the constraints implicitly require.

SORBET allows a component A to revoke a permission P from component B only if A granted P to B (or A owns P). In other words, the act of delegating creates a new link in a delegation chain, and revocation removes that link.

4.2   Implementation of Improvements in Abstract Model

We now briefly describe SORBET as an instantiation of the abstract model. We focus on mechanisms for enforcing information flow, and briefly discuss privilege escalation. Delegation and revocation are discussed in our technical report [13].

Information-Flow Protection.   To enforce information-flow policies specified by disallow-flow(P_1, P_2) and allow-declassify(P_1, P_2), we augment the model with an auxiliary data structure $\mathcal{N}$, which keeps track of information-flow constraints. More concretely, $\mathcal{N}$ maps a component instance iC to the set of information-flow constraints that includes all such policies specified by components in the call chain before and including iC.

We define $forbidP(\mathcal{N}, iC)$ to return the set of permissions that are forbidden from being used by constraints in $\mathcal{N}(iC)$. For instance, if $\mathcal{N}(iC) = \{\text{disallow-flow}(P_1, P_2)\}$, then $forbidP$ returns $\{P_2\}$. Function $guardP(\Sigma, iC)$ returns the set of permissions that guards the calls to component iC. A successful call between components in the same group can now be defined as follows.

$$\text{CALL-T } (\Sigma; \mathcal{E}, n :: \text{call } iC_1 \ iC_2 \ I) \xrightarrow{\text{ok}(n)} (updateCall(\Sigma, \text{call } iC_1 \ iC_2 \ I); \mathcal{E})$$
$$\text{if } iC_2.\varphi_{ckCaller}(\Sigma, iC_1) = \text{true and } iC_1.\varphi_{ckCallee}(\Sigma, iC_2) = \text{true}$$
$$\text{and } guardP(\Sigma, iC_2) \cap forbidP(\mathcal{N}, iC_1) = \emptyset$$

The last line is the added check for information-flow policies. The call succeeds only if the permission required to access the callee is not forbidden by the policy.

If the call succeeds, information will flow from the caller to the callee, and constraints need to be similarly propagated. In addition, the callee has its own constraints that need to be incorporated in $\mathcal{N}$. For this, we define two new functions. $updFlow(\mathcal{N}, iC, Fl)$ returns a new mapping $\mathcal{N}'$, where $\mathcal{N}'(iC) = \mathcal{N}(iC) \cup Fl$. $updDeclassify(\mathcal{N}, iC, \text{allow-declassify}(P_1, P_2))$ returns a new mapping $\mathcal{N}'$, which removes disallow-flow(P_1, P_2) from $\mathcal{N}$ for iC. Hence, after a declassification permission allow-declassify(P_1, P_2) is encountered, the constraint that forbade access to components guarded by P_2 is lifted. E.g., if the user explicitly allows access to the Internet after private data is read, then this will be allowed.

We define function $flowP(\Sigma, iC)$ to return the set of information-flow constraints that guard the calls to iC, and $getDeclassify(iC)$ to return the set of declassification permissions of iC. The function $updateCall$ first computes $\mathcal{N}' = updFlow(\mathcal{N}, iC_2, flowP(\Sigma, iC_1))$, then $\mathcal{N}'' = updFlow(\mathcal{N}', iC_2, \mathcal{N}(iC_1))$, and finally $\mathcal{N}''' = updDeclassify(\mathcal{N}'', iC_2, getDeclassify(iC_2))$.

Android does not mediate all communications between components within the same application (e.g., via shared static fields). SORBET conservatively assumes that components within an application have communicated, and treats cross-application calls differently. We write $\mathcal{N}_A(iC)$ to be the union of sets of information-flow constraints $\mathcal{N}(iC')$, for each iC' that is in the same application as iC. We define $forbidPA(\mathcal{N}, iC) = \mathcal{N}_A(iC)$. We define function *guardPA*(Σ, iC) to return the set of permissions that guards the calls to all components in the same application as component iC. In the rule for cross-application calls, $\mathcal{N}_A$ takes the place of $\mathcal{N}$, and *guardPA* takes the place of *guardP*. This means that if any component in an application has accessed private data protected by disallow-flow(P_1, P_2), then no component in that application can use permission P_2. The update function similarly accumulates all constraints in the entire application, rather than just one component.

Returns are treated similarly to calls, with the caller and callee designations switched. We omit the definitions here for space reasons.

Privilege-Escalation Protection. To prevent privilege escalation, we use auxiliary tree-like data structures to keep track of the full call history. We define a call forest $\mathcal{T}_S$ as a list of call trees $\mathcal{T}$, as follows:

$$\textit{Call Forest } \mathcal{T}_S ::= [\mathcal{T}_1, \cdots, \mathcal{T}_n] \qquad \textit{Call Tree } \mathcal{T} ::= (\mathcal{T}_S, (iC, \mathcal{P}))$$

We use $\mathcal{MT}_S$ to denote a mapping from run-time components to call forests. Each call tree represents a call chain, and the root of the tree is the last component on the call chain. The child of the root is a call forest, which is a list of call chains, each representing a past call chain to the root component. If component A (which has permissions P_A) calls B (with permissions P_B), and C (with permissions P_C) also calls B, and B has only one run-time instance, then $\mathcal{MT}_S(B) = [([], (A, P_A)), ([], (C, P_C))]$. In other words, each call tree in the call forest $\mathcal{MT}_S(B)$ records the full context of the call stack. If B now calls D, the call tree $([([], (A, P_A)), ([], (C, P_C))], (B, P_B))$ will be stored in $\mathcal{MT}_S(D)$.

A call from component A to component B is allowed only when for any permission P that guards the access to B, either A has $\hat{P}$; or A has P and for every call chain recorded in $\mathcal{MT}_S(A)$, either (1) all the components have permission P; or (2) there exists a component C that has permission $\hat{P}$, and all the components in the call stack after C have P.

As with information flow, the rule for cross-application calls assumes that all components within an application have communicated with each other.

4.3   Properties

We prove SORBET obeys Prop. 1–6. Here we show only the more concrete restatements of Prop. 5 and 6 made possible by SORBET's new policy statements (disallow-flow, allow-declassify, and $\hat{P}$). For brevity, details and proof sketches are relegated to our companion technical report [13].

We first define an indirect call chain.

DEFINITION 1. (Indirect call chain)   *Given components A and B, there exists an* indirect call chain *from A to B if there exist*

1. *components $D_1, \cdots, D_k$; and*
2. *call chains from A to D_1, from D_1 to D_2, $\cdots$, and from D_k to B.*

We say that a component A can *influence* another component B if there is an indirect call chain from A to B. For example, A can affect the behavior of

B (i.e., the intents that B sends) if either (1) A is part of a call chain to B, or (2) A appears in a call chain to some component D, and this chain shares a component with a different call chain to B. The shared component carries A's influence to B.

PROPERTY 5*. (Privilege escalation (2))   *Given a component B protected by permission P, and a component A that does not have P and belongs to a different application than B, if S_{AB} is a system that contains A and B (and other components), and S_B is the same system without A, then a (possibly indirect) call chain that ends in B exists in S_{AB} if and only if it exists in S_B. Additional (possibly indirect) call chains may exist in S_{AB} only if each such chain has a common suffix with a (possibly indirect) call chain from A to B, and there exists a component between A and B that has permission $\hat{P}$; or there is a component B' between A and B, the path between B and B' contains components of the same application, and B' is not protected by permission P but communicated to B via unmonitored channels.*

PROPERTY 6*. (Information flow (2))   *Suppose a component A is guarded by permission P_1 and an information-flow policy* disallow-flow(P_1, P_2), *and a component B is guarded by P_2, and A and B belong to different applications. Then, a (possibly indirect) call chain that ends with B, in a system with A, exists if and only if the same call chain exists in a system without A. Additional (possibly indirect) call chains may exist in the system with A only if each such chain has a common suffix with a (possibly indirect) call chain from A to B, and there exists a component between A and B that has permission* allow-declassify(P_1, P_2).

5   Implementing and Evaluating Sorbet

We implemented SORBET on top of Android 2.3.7. This section describes the most salient implementation details, including the syntactic additions for expressing SORBET's policies, and a case study that illustrates SORBET's features.

Syntactic Additions. We extended Android's manifest file syntax to support information-flow and integrity policies. The component protected by P_1 can specify disallow-flow(P_1, P_2) by adding `android:forbiddenPermissions=["`P_2`"]` to the permissions by which this component is protected. allow-declassify(P_1, P_2) is specified as `<declassified-info source=["`P_1`"] destination=["`P_2`"]/>`. A permission is labeled as privileged $\hat{P}$ by the addition of a "privileged" attribute to its declaration: `<uses-permission android:name="`P`" android:privileged="true"/>`.

Implementation Overview. SORBET's keystone is a reference monitor built on top of Android's ActivityManager (Fig. 3). ActivityManager already mediates inter-component communication, which includes preventing calls that are illegal by Android's policy; SORBET modifies it so that mediation of relevant calls is handled by SORBET instead of by the legacy parts of ActivityManager. Enforcing SORBET's policies also requires additional bookkeeping, including of instance data (e.g., to recognize that a particular application has accessed a resource protected by a "forbidden" permission), and richer static policy specified in application manifests. Hence, a significant component of SORBET's implementation is the data structures that implement this bookkeeping. The bookkeeping includes keeping track of individual files accessed by applications; for enforcement purposes, these are treated as components.

The most challenging part in implementing SORBET was to identify not just which application invoked a protected resource (which Android typically already does) but which specific component instance was responsible for the call; we accomplished this by enhancing Android's IPC data structures to carry more information about the caller. Another challenge was to capture operations not mediated by ActivityManager, such as opening a socket or a file. Android enforces permission-based policies on such operations by Linux-level checks based on the (Linux) group ID of the calling application; applications are assigned group IDs at installation time by the package manager. To mediate access to these operations, we

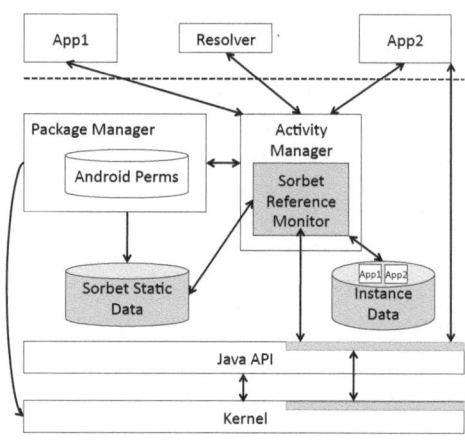

Fig. 3. SORBET architecture: additions to Android are shaded; arrows indicate interactions between system components

used TOMOYO Linux [21], a set of Linux kernel patches that replaces scattered, ad-hoc access-control checks with centralized ones.[2] We further extended TOMOYO Linux so that access attempts for which policy was enforced at Linux level (e.g., to open a socket or a file) trigger a call to SORBET's reference monitor. This also allows SORBET to mediate security-relevant behaviors implemented in native code that may be included in Android applications.

Case Study. To test SORBET and illustrate its usefulness, we used it to implement several policies; some that can be implemented (sometimes partially) by previously proposed mechanisms (e.g., [2,7]), and some that require SORBET's features. Our main case study involves four applications: a file manager for storing and manipulating private files (e.g., a diary or list of account numbers); a text editor; an encryption application; and an email application. The high-level policy we focus on is to prevent private files from being leaked on the Internet, but to allow them to be manipulated by various applications at the user's behest (e.g., by using the private file manager to launch an editor). Private files are kept in a content provider implemented by the file manager, and protected by separate permissions that allow read and write access. Applications can access private files only when dynamically delegated the appropriate permissions by the file manager. We next describe several specific scenarios (summarized in Fig. 4) that examine variants of this policy and show how they could be implemented.

---

[2] TOMOYO Linux has similarly been used by other researchers [2].

Scenario			Private File Manager	Editor	Encryption App	Email App	PE	IF
1	Private files cannot be sent over the network	a	protected by R/W perms	–	–	–	–	–
		b	protected by R/W perms	use Internet	use Internet	use Internet	✓	–
		c	protected by R/W perms forbid Internet	use Internet	use Internet	use Internet	–	✓
2	Private files sent over network only via email	a	protected by R/W perms	use Internet	use Internet	use Internet	✓	–
		b	protected by R/W perms forbid Internet	use Internet	use Internet	use Internet declassify R/W→Internet	–	✓
3	Private files sent over network only via email and if encrypted		protected by R/W perms forbid Internet	use Internet	use Internet declassify R/W→Internet	use Internet	✓	✓

Fig. 4. Three scenarios from our case study. Columns indicate the permissions assigned to each application, and whether enforcement is via protection from privilege escalation (PE), or information flow prevention (IF).

Scenario 1. We start from a base case in which private files must not be sent over the network (Fig. 4, Scenario 1). In Android, the only way to prevent one of these applications from leaking files to the network is to avoid granting any of the applications the Internet permission (Scenario 1a). In SORBET, this policy can be enforced by either the mechanism that prevents privilege escalation or the one that prevents undesired information flows. In the first case, all other applications can be granted the Internet permission, but will no longer be able to use it if the file manager, which does not have this permission, is on the call stack (Scenario 1b). In the second case, the file manager declares the Internet permission as forbidden, with the same effect (Scenario 1c).

Scenario 2. We now extend the desired policy to allow only the email client to send a private file (an activity that the user explicitly initiates), while other applications can use the Internet for other purposes. This cannot be implemented in stock Android, but can still be done with either of SORBET's protection mechanisms. For enforcement via the privilege-escalation mechanism, the email app must declare and be granted the privileged version of the Internet permission. To enforce the same policy via SORBET's information-flow mechanism, the file manager would declare the Internet permission as forbidden (as in Scenario 1), and the email would declare the permission to declassify from R/W to Internet.

Scenario 3. Finally, we extend the policy from Scenario 2 to allow emailing private files only if they are encrypted. Enforcing this without limiting reasonable uses of the email app requires both the information-flow and privilege-escalation mechanisms. As in Scenario 2a, the email app is given the privileged Internet permission, so that it can send email even if indirectly invoked by the file manager, which does not have the Internet permission. In addition, the file manager declares the Internet permission forbidden, and the encryption app is allowed to declassify. Now, the only path to emailing private files is via the encryption app, which is trusted to invoke the email app only with encrypted data.

The last scenario shows that SORBET allows easy specification of useful policies significantly beyond what Android offers. Our case study used minimally modified off-the-shelf applications: Open Manager v2.1.8, Qute Text Editor v0.1, Android Privacy Guard v1.0.9, Email v2.3.4. We modified manifest files, added sending functionality to some, and added a content provider to Open Manager. SORBET's overhead was sufficiently small to be unobservable by the user.[3]

6   Related Work

Researchers have analyzed the security of Android's permission system [5,10], developed analysis tools for Android applications [11], and proposed new protection mechanisms (e.g., [20,22]). Many works studied Android's attack surface (e.g., [19]), including covert channels [24], DoS [1] and web attacks [17], and unauthorized application repackaging [27].

Several works have pointed out flaws in Android's permission system. One weakness is the lack of global properties: Android's permission system does not prevent privilege escalation or information leakage. Davi et al. [6] and Felt et al. [12] have studied privilege-escalation attacks in detail. Bugiel et al. developed a system that monitors interactions between applications at run time and mitigates a wide range of privilege-escalation attacks [2]. Our mechanism has many similarities, but we focus on allowing developers to specify policies on a per-application basis, and emphasize formal analysis of mechanisms. Dietz et al. proposed a framework, Quire, for provenance tracking to mitigate the confused deputy problem [7]. Our goals overlap, but SORBET differs in several ways: We do not track full provenance information, but instead focus on flexible, application-level policy specification based on permissions; we rely on the Android runtime for bookkeeping, rather than using digital signatures. We also support declassification, and formally investigate SORBET's properties. Another approach to mitigating application collusion is through domain isolation. Bugiel et al. assigned trust levels to applications, allowing them to communicate only if they are at the same level [3]. They focus on defining policy for a set of applications at the same trust level, whereas we let applications define policy individually.

Several works have investigated privacy leaks in Android [8,24,4,9]. We provide a formal framework that allows such flaws to be seen as violations of desired security properties. Projects such as TaintDroid [8] and AppFence [14] aim to automatically detect and prevent dangerous information leaks. Our work is in several ways complementary. TaintDroid and AppFence operate at a much finer granularity, tracking tainting at the level of variables, and enforce fixed policies. In contrast, our enforcement is at the component level, and allows developers to specify policies, including, e.g., declassification, which is key to enabling applications that have legitimate reason to send tainted data to operate. We also formally prove that our design enforces desired high-level security properties.

---

[3] We ran microbenchmarks, but, as common in this setting, the small changes—and sometimes improvements—in latency were dwarfed by the variances between runs.

Systems such as Saint [22] and Apex [20] also improve Android's permission system, e.g., by protecting callers with guards that consider context beyond just permissions, while staying generally close to the original design. We focus on deeper revisions to the permission model and enforcing transitive properties.

Formal analysis of Android-related security issues has received less attention. Shin et al. [25] developed a formal model in order to verify functional correctness properties of Android, which revealed a flaw in the naming scheme for permissions and a possible attack [26]. In contrast, our work develops a more abstract model suitable for reasoning about extensions to Android's permission system.

7   Conclusion

This paper develops a framework for formally analyzing Android-style permission systems, and shows how to enhance Android's permission system to support rich policies while maintaining convenient, application-centric policy specification. We have proved the design of our enforcement system satisfies a set of security properties, showed its feasibility by implementing and running it on a Nexus S phone, and demonstrated its usefulness through a case study. In doing so, we discover that Android's inability to provide strong isolation between components constrains the expressiveness of our system and complicates its implementation. Our system successfully provides both application- and component-level protections, but it would need to resort to application-level protection less often if Android's component-level abstractions were more robust.

Acknowledgments. This research was supported by NSF grants 0917047 and 1018211; by CyLab at Carnegie Mellon under grants DAAD19-02-1-0389 and W911NF-09-1-0273 from the Army Research Office; and by a gift from KDDI R&D Laboratories Inc.

References

1. Armando, A., Merlo, A., Verderame, M.M.: Would you mind forking this process? A denial of service attack on Android (and some countermeasures). In: Proc. IFIP SEC (2012)
2. Bugiel, S., Davi, L., Dmitrienko, A., Fischer, T., Sadeghi, A.R., Shastry, B.: Towards taming privilege-escalation attacks on Android. In: Proc. NDSS (2012)
3. Bugiel, S., Davi, L., Dmitrienko, A., Heuser, S., Sadeghi, A.R., Shastry, B.: Practical and lightweight domain isolation on Android. In: Proc. SPSM (2011)
4. Chaudhuri, A.: Language-based security on Android. In: PLAS Workshop (2009)
5. Chin, E., Felt, A.P., Greenwood, K., Wagner, D.: Analyzing inter-application communication in Android. In: Proc. MobiSys (2011)
6. Davi, L., Dmitrienko, A., Sadeghi, A.R., Winandy, M.: Privilege Escalation Attacks on Android. In: Burmester, M., Tsudik, G., Magliveras, S., Ilić, I. (eds.) ISC 2010. LNCS, vol. 6531, pp. 346–360. Springer, Heidelberg (2011)
7. Dietz, M., Shekhar, S., Pisetsky, Y., Shu, A., Wallach, D.S.: Quire: Lightweight provenance for smart phone operating systems. In: Proc. USENIX Security (2011)

8. Enck, W., Gilbert, P., Gon Chun, B., Cox, L.P., Jung, J., McDaniel, P., Sheth, A.N.: TaintDroid: An information-flow tracking system for realtime privacy monitoring on smartphones. In: Proc. USENIX OSDI (2010)
9. Enck, W., Octeau, D., McDaniel, P., Chaudhuri, S.: A study of Android application security. In: Proc. USENIX Security (2011)
10. Enck, W., Ongtang, M., McDaniel, P.D.: On lightweight mobile phone application certification. In: Proc. CCS (2009)
11. Felt, A.P., Chin, E., Hanna, S., Song, D., Wagner, D.: Android permissions demystified. In: Proc. CCS (2011)
12. Felt, A.P., Wang, H., Moshchuk, A., Hanna, S., Chin, E.: Permission re-delegation: Attacks and defenses. In: Proc. USENIX Security (2011)
13. Fragkaki, E., Bauer, L., Jia, L.: Modeling and enhancing Android's permission system. Tech. Rep. CMU-CyLab-11-020, CyLab, Carnegie Mellon University (2011)
14. Hornyack, P., Han, S., Jung, J., Schechter, S., Wetherall, D.: These aren't the droids you're looking for: Retrofitting Android to protect data from imperious applications. In: Proc. CCS (2011)
15. Lineberry, A., Richardson, D.L., Wyatt, T.: These aren't the permissions you're looking for (2010), www.defcon.org/images/defcon-18/dc-18-presentations/Lineberry/DEFCON-18-Lineberry-Not-The-Permissions-You-Are-Looking-For.pdf (accessed April 10, 2012)
16. Loftus, J.: DefCon dings reveal Google product security risks (2011), gizmodo.com/5828478 (accessed April 10, 2012)
17. Luo, T., Hao, H., Du, W., Wang, Y., Yin, H.: Attacks on WebView in the Android system. In: Proc. ACSAC (2011)
18. Marforio, C., Francillon, A., Čapkun, S.: Application collusion attack on the permission-based security model and its implications for modern smartphone systems. Tech. Rep. 724, ETH Zurich (2011)
19. Mylonas, A., Dritsas, S., Tsoumas, B., Gritzalis, D.: Smartphone security evaluation – The malware attack case. In: Proc. SECRYPT (2011)
20. Nauman, M., Khan, S., Zhang, X.: Apex: extending Android permission model and enforcement with user-defined runtime constraints. In: Proc. ASIACCS (2010)
21. NTT Data Corporation: TOMOYO Linux (2012), tomoyo.sourceforge.jp/ (accessed April 10, 2012)
22. Ongtang, M., McLaughlin, S.E., Enck, W., McDaniel, P.D.: Semantically rich application-centric security in Android. In: Proc. ACSAC (2009)
23. Passeri, P.: One year of Android malware (full list) (2011), hackmageddon.com/2011/08/11/one-year-of-android-malware-full-list/ (accessed June 20, 2012)
24. Schlegel, R., Zhang, K., Zhou, X., Intwala, M., Kapadia, A., Wang, X.: Soundcomber: A stealthy and context-aware sound Trojan for smartphones. In: Proc. NDSS (2011)
25. Shin, W., Kiyomoto, S., Fukushima, K., Tanaka, T.: A formal model to analyze the permission authorization and enforcement in the Android framework. In: Proc. SocialCom/PASSAT (2010)
26. Shin, W., Kwak, S., Kiyomoto, S., Fukushima, K., Tanaka, T.: A small but non-negligible flaw in the Android permission scheme. In: Proc. POLICY (2010)
27. Zhou, W., Zhou, Y., Jiang, X., Ning, P.: Detecting repackaged smartphone applications in third-party Android marketplaces. In: Proc. CODASPY 2012 (2012)

Hardening Access Control and Data Protection in GFS-like File Systems

James Kelley[1], Roberto Tamassia[1], and Nikos Triandopoulos[2,3]

[1] Brown University, Providence, Rhode Island, USA
[2] RSA Laboratories, Cambridge, Massachusetts, USA
[3] Boston University, Boston, Massachusetts, USA

Abstract. The Google File System (GFS) is a highly distributed, fault-tolerant file system designed for large files and high throughput batch processing. We consider the first complete security analysis of GFS systems. We formalize desirable security properties with respect to the successful enforcement of access control mechanisms and data confidentiality by considering a threat model that is much stronger then in previous works. We propose extensions to the GFS protocols that satisfy these properties, and provide a comprehensive analysis of the extensions, both analytically and experimentally. In a proof-of-concept implementation, we demonstrate the practicality of the extensions by showing that they incur only a 12% slowdown while offering higher-assurance guarantees.

1 Introduction

As more companies adopt the cloud computing framework, an increasing amount of sensitive and mission-critical data will be placed in the cloud. Thus, it is necessary to develop and deploy strong security controls in the underlying cloud framework to protect this data. This necessity is underscored by the work several researchers have done demonstrating various weaknesses in current commercial cloud offerings (e.g., [23,24]).

The Google File System (GFS) is the file system developed in-house by Google to support their storage needs [12]. GFS is a distributed file system utilizing a single server for managing file metadata and (up to) legions of data servers for storing file data. A file is split into blocks (typically tens or hundreds of megabytes in size) which are spread out over the data servers. The servers are assumed to be running on commodity hardware, and the system is meant to scale to thousands of machines. So, machine failures are assumed to be a frequent, and entirely normal, occurrence.

The paradigm ushered in by GFS has since seen deployment in cloud computing infrastructures—notably, HDFS in Hadoop [14]—as the underlying storage mechanism for the large quantities of data. The architecture of GFS lends itself to supporting a MapReduce computing framework, and, indeed, they were developed together. As such, GFS sees use in large data centers for performing computations on enormous data sets (e.g., tens and hundreds of terabytes or more) with already great efficiency and several efforts to further improve its

S. Foresti, M. Yung, and F. Martinelli (Eds.): ESORICS 2012, LNCS 7459, pp. 19–36, 2012.

performance (e.g., [5,8,15]). The usefulness of the MapReduce framework has made the use of data warehouses highly desirable, but potentially costly—due to the large setup and maintenance costs. Given this, companies are increasingly outsourcing these MapReduce needs to the cloud (such as Amazon's EC2 and Elastic MapReduce services). GFS has thus inspired several copy-cat cloud-centric implementations, including the Hadoop File System, CloudStore, and TPlatform [4,6,22], all of these falling under the banner of *GFS-like file systems*.

1.1   Security Issues and Challenges

In a GFS-like system, files are broken up into blocks which are replicated and distributed across multiple *data servers* to achieve fault-tolerance. The system is managed by a central *metadata server* that handles all metadata operations and tracks the placement of blocks, seeking to balance the load across all servers and maintain enough replicas of blocks. Figure 1 shows the basic architecture in GFS-like systems. For example, to create a file, a user contacts the metadata server who records the metadata and replies with a list of data servers; then, the user contacts the data servers to upload the data. Also, the metadata server manages access control information for each file, but here things become problematic.

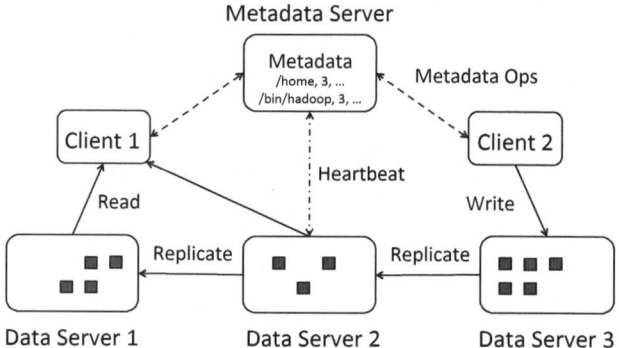

Fig. 1. Basic architecture of a GFS-like system

The design of GFS assumes a benevolent environment: the users are assumed to behave well and not interfere with each other. For example, in the Hadoop File System (HDFS) (and others, see [6,22]), by default the data servers service any request from any user. An assumption of total user benevolence has little justification in the real-world. Thus, it is necessary to integrate security controls into GFS-like file systems to make attacks by malicious users much more difficult.

As an example attack, when accessing a file, a user will contact the metadata server M to learn the location of the file blocks and then contact the individual servers to read the blocks. Since access control checks are performed only at M, they can be bypassed by contacting data servers directly. In a more sophisticated attack, the attacker could register their own machine as a data server. GFS does not authenticate any data server registrations, so any machine may complete the registration protocol. Once registered, the attacker can simply wait to be given users' data blocks. Ideally, a GFS-like system should achieve a holistic security posture guaranteeing that no attacker can compromise the secure functionality of the system with respect to the integrity and confidentiality of its stored files, nor compromise the system's access control mechanisms.

A key step in adding robust security to these file systems is to extend responsibility of access control checking to the data servers themselves. In addition to stronger access control enforcement, all access control checks, and data structures holding the access control information, must be very efficient. GFS-like file systems are performance oriented, with data intensive applications and hundreds to thousands of parallel tasks. A related concern is that one must also endeavor to avoid putting an undue burden on system administrators. Complex security controls are much more likely to be ignored if they make administration much more difficult and/or negatively impact the job-efficiency of normal users.

The initial paper describing GFS states that no security was built into the system, other than rudimentary checks at the metadata server: no access control checks at servers and no protection of data in flight [12]. Yahoo! has instrumented the Hadoop File System (HDFS) with additional access controls to address some of the security concerns of its users [29]. Their architecture uses Kerberos for user authentication and message integrity, and uses a token-based access control scheme (similar to Kerberos tickets). As with GFS, there are no protections for network traffic and no method to prevent unauthorized servers from registering as data servers. An outline of many more attacks against the Hadoop MapReduce framework, of which HDFS is a part, is given in [1]. Some work was done in [7,28] to harden Hadoop against a worst-case-scenario adversary, putting HDFS on top of the least-authority file system Tahoe, but this resulted in rather severe performance penalties. Moreover, the system does not protect against an attacker bypassing the metadata server to read a block directly from a data server.

1.2   Our Contributions and Approach

In this work, we present the first formal definitions of security for a GFS-like file system. The adversary considered in the work is also a great deal stronger than in previous work and the first to be formally defined. The work by Yahoo! in [29] had an adversarial model, but the adversary was given in terms of its abilities relative to system privileges (e.g., could not be root) rather than any general abilities. Our main result is in proving that our modified GFS architecture is secure, given our formal definition of security, against our more powerful adversary.

From a practical perspective, the contributions of this work are several. Yahoo!'s work on securing HDFS relied on integrating it with Kerberos to provide message authentication and integrity, but not confidentiality. In this work message integrity, authentication, and confidentiality are built into the GFS protocols themselves, without adding a central key distribution center. Another contribution is the integration of stronger, pervasive access control enforcement. It is worth noting that Yahoo!'s work also has pervasive access control enforcement via tokens; however, forging the tokens becomes trivial if the adversary is permitted to have root access on their machine. There is no such restriction on our adversary. Finally, we deployed a proof-of-concept implementation of these protocols using the Hadoop File System as our starting point. We then performed several experiments to show the practicality of our architecture, showing an overall slowdown of 12%: a reasonable price for stronger, provable security.

In our approach, the metadata server has an asymmetric key pair, with the public key distributed to all data servers. The system administrator also has an asymmetric key-pair which is used to authenticate the start up of each data server; the public half is known to the metadata server. Next, the data servers are brought online. Each data server generates two random keys to be shared with the metadata server for authenticating and encrypting subsequent messages. The keys are encrypted using the metadata server's public key, grouped with some registration information, and the bundle is signed by the administrator. Upon receiving the message, the metadata server verifies the signature, then decrypts and saves the keys while recording the registration information and then replies to the server with some start-up information. All future messages between these two servers are authenticated via a MAC using one of the keys sent during registration. The server periodically sends a heartbeat to the metadata server to attest to its liveness. Once the data servers have started and registered, the cluster can begin to service clients. When a client first starts to use the cluster, it must create a session with the metadata server. The client creates two random session keys and sends them to the metadata server encrypted with public key of the server. The metadata server stores the keys and replies with an acknowledgment of the registration. All further communication will be authenticated by using a MAC with one of the keys associated with the client.

Access control for the files is maintained through tokens: a token (similar to a Kerberos ticket) is issued by the metadata server to a client to read/write a file block. Each token is specific to the server that is holding the block. When returning the token and block location to the client, the metadata server also sends a pair of random secret keys to be used in authenticating messages to/from the data server and encrypting any file data transmitted. These keys are only valid for the duration of the client's request to the data server. The metadata server also prepares and returns a ciphertext to be passed to the data server by the client which contains the information needed for the data server to interact with the client. When a client is finished with their session, they inform the metadata server, who then deletes the session keys. If the client crashes, the session information expires after a given interval of inactivity.

The rest of this paper is organized as follows. Section 2 presents our formal security definitions. In Section 3, we describe our security-enhanced GFS protocols and their asymptotic efficiency. Section 4 provides the security analysis. Section 5 reports on an experimental evaluation on our proof-of-concept implementation in Hadoop, comparing it to the insecure default Hadoop. Section 6 discusses related work and Section 7 presents concluding remarks.

2   Definitions and Model

The GFS protocols have a fixed set of roles that can be assumed by principals: (a) the metadata server M, (b) a data server D, (c) a client C, (d) or the system administrator SA. A principal not conforming to exactly one of these roles when executing a protocol will produce an invalid execution of the protocol and all messages sent in the protocol will be ignored by the other principal.

In the following security definitions, we consider a polynomially bounded adversary: bounded in both time and space. The adversary is also subject to a few more restrictions, detailed below. We will later prove that, subject to standard cryptographic assumptions and the definitions in this section, the adversary has only a negligible probability of successfully violating the security guarantees.

At a high level, GFS is a collection of protocols implementing a network-facing file system API. We will define this API to be synonymous with the collection of protocols and it will be this collection that we will secure.

Definition 1. *The* GFS API *is the suite of protocols covering all client–server and server–server communication in the GFS file system.*

As a first step in setting up a GFS-like system, the system administrator SA must determine which machines are to constitute the cluster. The metadata server M is chosen as part of the configuration of the cluster by the administrator, so we assume M to be given and fixed. The first property we wish the cluster to have is that only those servers chosen by SA to be data servers can become part of the cluster. That is, we want to guarantee that SA has full control over which servers may be data servers. Moreover, we want to ensure that, with overwhelming probability, a data server can only possess the data blocks that have been assigned to it by M.

Definition 2. *A data server D exporting the GFS API is* authorized, *if D has successfully completed the registration protocol with M at the behest of the system administrator SA. Moreover, we say that a data server D is* authorized with respect to a block b *if D is authorized and M chooses D as a location for b.*

In a similar vein to the above definition, we next define correct behavior for a client. A client's interactions with the cluster revolves around reading and writing blocks. Naturally, we would like to restrict clients to only accessing blocks for which they are "authorized" (defined below). We define *accessing a block* to be either a read or a write operation on the block.

Definition 3. *A client C of the GFS API is* authorized *to access a block b, if that C is permitted, by the access control policy P associated with b, to access b.*

The policy P could be any type of access control policy (e.g., capability-based, mandatory access control, etc.). In GFS-like systems, the enforcement of an access control policy is performed solely at the metadata server with data servers blithely servicing any arriving request. This work provides a secure means to extend policy enforcement to the data servers via unforgeable (except with negligible probability) access tokens. Note, however, that the initial policy check is still only performed at M.

As a final, basic term we define the notion of "completing a protocol." A protocol is considered complete if each principal believes that the other is authorized and if all messages are received and verify correctly. For example, if a client tries to read a block from a server, the client has completed the protocol when they receive the block from the server and the message containing the block passes all security checks ("verifies"). The server has completed the protocol upon sending the data block and having it verify at the client. If either party sends an incorrect/malformed message, and it is detected by the recipient, then they have *not* completed the protocol.

We begin the security definitions by first defining what it means for the GFS API to be secure with respect to server-to-server interactions. Following that definition, we define security with respect to clients and passive adversaries. The term "server" will be used as a shorthand for a data server and/or the metadata server. Whenever a statement applies to only one of the two, the type of server will be made explicit.

Definition 4. *The GFS API is* server-secure *if, with overwhelming probability, only authorized servers can complete the server-to-server protocols. Moreover, the GFS API is* client-secure, *if with overwhelming probability, only authorized servers and clients can complete the client–server protocols.*

That is, the GFS API is *server-secure* if for any unauthorized server U, it cannot successfully complete any of the server-to-server protocols, except with negligible probability (similarly for *client-security*). Later, we will show that our modifications achieve these properties. Note that, here, "authorized" covers both meanings of a server being authorized: authorized to be a data server, and with respect to a block. These definitions encompass the behaviors of an active adversary, but we must not neglect a passive adversary.

Definition 5. *The GFS API, is* passive-secure *if, with overwhelming probability, an adversary A, given a polynomially bounded number of messages from GFS protocol instances, cannot learn the contents of any data block.*

Later we will prove that our modifications to the GFS protocols achieve this property. We can now define what it means for a GFS API to be "secure."

Definition 6. *The GFS API, G, is* secure *if, with overwhelming probability, it holds that G is: (i)* server-secure, *(ii)* client-secure, *and (iii)* passive-secure.

No current GFS implementation achieves any of these properties, except against much more limited adversaries than the one considered here. For example, the work done by Yahoo! is *client-secure* for adversaries that cannot read arbitrary network traffic, but, since no file is encrypted, it is not *passive-secure*.

We assume that the adversary is polynomially bounded in both space and time and is allowed start any protocol, at any time, with any party that recognizes that protocol. The adversary may try to impersonate another user or server, or use his own identity. The adversary *cannot* subvert known "good" servers or clients. As an additional power, we allow the adversary to observe any instance of any protocol at will (i.e., read arbitrary data on the network). As an example, a malicious user that has obtained root access on their machine fits our model; a malicious user breaking into another user's machine (or a data server) does not. Denial of service attacks are beyond the scope of this work.

We consider only the GFS protocols, all other communication is considered out-of-band. We also assume that there is some reliable, secure mechanism available to the metadata server (but not necessarily to data servers) for determining a user's identity (e.g., Kerberos). Finally, we will assume reliable message delivery, but the adversary is permitted to manipulate messages while in transit.

3   Proposed Architecture

In securing GFS-like file systems, we modify the constituent protocols to be provably secure against the adversary defined above. Messages between clients and servers, and among servers, must be authenticated to protect integrity and, in some instances, encrypted to maintain confidentiality of data. The data servers will need to register with the metadata server and clients will need to start sessions with the metadata server. The proposed architecture uses public-key cryptography to bootstrap itself to a place where it can use symmetric cryptography for greater efficiency. This section contains high-level descriptions of the secured protocols along with an asymptotic analysis of each protocol. Exact message parameters are omitted both for brevity and clarity. For notation, symmetric keys are denoted with a lower case k and the public and private halves of an asymmetric key used by principal P are denoted PK_P and SK_P, respectively. A message authentication code created with a key k will be denoted m_k. Variables that represent a name are capitalized. The metadata server will be denoted by M. It is assumed that M can securely determine the identity of a client, but data servers do not have this ability.

Client–Metadata Server. When a client C first interacts with M in a session, C sends the server two keys k_1 and k_2 (along with a nonce) encrypted with the public key of M and a MAC appended for integrity, created with k_1. The key k_1 is used to authenticate all subsequent messages while k_2 is used to encrypt some of the responses from M (e.g., an encryption key for sending file data). Upon receiving the message, M decrypts the keys and verifies the MAC, then M replies with the nonce and a MAC of the nonce using k_1. Efficiency-wise, this protocol requires $O(1)$ asymmetric encryption operations, each on input of size $O(1)$, and $O(1)$ symmetric operations, each on an input of size $O(l)$ and requiring $O(l)$ time, where l is the length of the message. All subsequent metadata requests and replies simply contain the request/response, a nonce, and a MAC.

When the client wishes to read/write a file block, they must first contact M to find the location(s) of the block. Along with the block's location, say server D,

M also sends back a ciphertext containing the access token and ephemeral keys for encrypting and authenticating the messages between C and D. Each key and token is valid for a single request. A copy of the ciphertext is encrypted with the long-term encryption key shared between the M and D, to be passed along to D by C. If there are multiple locations for the block, then there is a ciphertext and token for each location, as the client could potentially access any or all of them. If the replication factor is r and the file has n blocks, M must create rn tokens and send a message of size $O(rn)$. Note, according to [27], while files can be quite large, at Yahoo! the average file has 1.5 blocks. With a replication factor of 3 this gives an average of 4.5 tokens created when opening a file.

For a write request, the client contacts M each time it wants to add a block to the file. M picks locations for the r replicas and determines the "pipeline" of servers: where the client sends the data to the first server, who forwards it to the next, etc., rather than have the client communicate with each server individually. As noted above, when writing a block, the receiving data server will need to receive from the client an access token and a ciphertext created by M. Thus, M creates r tokens and r ciphertexts, one for each data server in the pipeline. Each ciphertext contains the necessary information (and ciphertexts) for the corresponding data server to continue the pipeline (detailed below). Note that each subsequent encryption is performed on an incrementally longer message. For simplicity, assume that the increment i is fixed. Then we have that $i + 2i + \cdots + ri = O(ir^2)$ bytes must be encrypted to produce a ciphertext of length $O(r)$. Overall the cost to M is $O(ir^2)$. Note, however, that the message generated by M is typically just a few hundred bytes; so these operations are not a significant cost. The overall message size for writing a block is $O(r)$, as in the original GFS.

Client–Data Server. The interactions between clients and data servers consist entirely of requesting and serving read/write operations. The response from the metadata server to the client (when it starts a request) contains two ephemeral keys k_a and k_e that will be used to authenticate and encrypt (respectively) messages between C and D.

Read and write requests, though similar, require slightly different protocols. For a read request, C receives a list of tuples L from M containing all of the information needed by C to read any block of the file (e.g., access token, encryption key, etc.). Suppose C wishes to read the block b located at data server D. C contacts D and sends the read request along with a nonce and the ciphertext c from b's tuple in L. C also creates and sends a ciphertext c' containing the nonce, the access token t for b, and the client's identity C, encrypted with k_e. Once D receives the request, it decrypts c to obtain the keys and C's identity. D then decrypts c' and checks the access token t. If t is valid, D sends back b encrypted with the same ephemeral key k_e. Both messages are authenticated via a MAC computed with k_a. Note that only $O(1)$ encryption and MAC operations are performed in both sending and receiving b, but the computational cost for each is proportional to the length of the message.

To write a block, C first sends the request to M who replies with the name of the server D (who will hold the block), an access token, two ephemeral keys (as above), and a ciphertext c_D constructed for D. Here, c_D contains the information needed by D to verify the client's identity and authorization, as well as information about the next server in the pipeline so that D can forward the data. M also sends a ciphertext c for C containing essentially the same information as c_D. Each message between M and C, again, is authenticated with a MAC.

C then contacts D to write the block. First, C generates a nonce and encrypts it along with the block data d, using k_e. C then constructs a message containing the write request, the encrypted data, the nonce, the ciphertext c_D, and a (newly created) ciphertext c_2 containing the access token t, all of which is authenticated with m_{k_a}. D decrypts c_D to obtain the ephemeral keys and verify m_{k_a}. Following this, D decrypts c_2 to obtain t and verifies it. D subsequently forwards the data to the next server, D', then decrypts and writes the data to disk. Note that the data is not reencrypted with a new key as each server in the pipeline has a copy of k_e, given to it in the ciphertext created by M. Finally, D replies with final status s of the write, authenticated with m'_{k_a}.

Related to efficiency, we see that the initial message sent by C to D is of size $O(r + l)$—as in the original GFS—where r is the replication factor and l is the length of the block. Part of the message sent is a ciphertext of size $O(r)$, which was constructed by M for D. The encryption requires $O(l)$ time and the MAC computation takes $O(r + l)$ time. Each data server in the pipeline verifies the MAC of the data and then forwards it to the next node in the pipeline before decrypting it—avoiding a possible decryption-reencryption bottleneck. Thus, each data server needs to perform a MAC calculation on a message of size $O(r + l)$ and a single decryption operation on a ciphertext of length l.

Data Server–Metadata Server. An essential part of maintaining data security and integrity is preventing a malicious user from spoofing or manipulating any communication between data servers and M. The first step in ensuring security is to prevent any spurious data servers (i.e., those started and controlled by the attacker) from registering as data servers. To effect this, the system administrator possesses an asymmetric key pair $(\mathrm{PK}_A, \mathrm{SK}_A)$, with M possessing the public half. M itself has its own asymmetric key pair $(\mathrm{PK}_M, \mathrm{SK}_M)$, which will be utilized by the data servers.

When a data server D starts, it seeks to register with M. Part of the registration message is a pair of symmetric keys k_a^D and k_e^D to be shared with M. The key k_a^D is used to create a MAC for each subsequent message between D and M, as well as for creating the access tokens for blocks hosted by D. The key k_e^D is used for encrypting messages from M to D. The keys themselves are encrypted with PK_M, along with a nonce, to produce the ciphertext, which is added to the registration message. The administrator then signs the message and D sends it to M. Upon receiving the message, M verifies the signature, decrypts c, then saves the keys k_a^D and k_e^D. M then sends some start-up information to D, authenticated with $m_{k_e^D}$. Note that the efficiency of the registration protocol is near optimal, as there are $O(1)$ symmetric and asymmetric cryptographic operations. The asymmetric operations are all on $O(1)$-sized input, while the symmetric operations require $O(l)$ time, where l is the length of the message.

After registration, D periodically sends heartbeat and "block report" messages (usually combined together) to M. The heartbeat attests to D's liveness while the block report is simply an update on any block state changes (e.g., added or deleted). When receiving either of these, M replies with a (possibly empty) list of commands for D to execute. The heartbeat message is typically a fixed size and so D requires $O(1)$ time to compute the MAC. But, with the block report, if the report is of length l', then the MAC takes $O(l')$ time to compute (but still only requires $O(1)$ space).

Data Server–Data Server. Data servers must also interact with each other, but only in limited circumstances: as part of a pipeline when writing a file block and transferring blocks during load balancing. In both situations, the sender appears to the receiver to be just another client writing a block. Thus the sending data server must have enough information to emulate a client in the client–data server protocol for writing blocks.

Suppose we have a pipeline of n servers, $D_1, \ldots, D_n$, where D_i is the i-th server in the pipeline. The D_i will need to forward the data to D_{i+1}. D_n simply receives the data and does not forward it further. For each D_i, the metadata server M creates a ciphertext c_{D_i} containing the information necessary for D_i to continue the data pipeline. The c_{D_i}'s are nested within each other, so that c_{D_1} contains c_{D_2}, which contains c_{D_3}, etc. Each server D_i removes the i-th layer of encryption and obtains, along with other information, the ciphertext $c_{D_{i+1}}$. The "other information" includes: a nonce, two ephemeral keys, an access token, and the identity of D_{i+1}. The keys and access token play the same role here as they do in the client–data server protocol. Transferring blocks during load balancing is essentially identical to the client–data server protocol for writing a block. For more details, see the above section describing client–data server interactions. Note that these inter-server interactions have the same efficiency as the client–data server protocol for writing a block.

As part of increasing the security of GFS-like file systems, we have the data server become a point of enforcement for the access controls. Suppose a client wants to access a file consisting of blocks $b_1, \cdots, b_n$. The metadata server M first checks that C has access rights, then creates a token t_i for each block b_i. Each t_i is valid only at the corresponding data server that holds a copy of b_i, call it D. The token itself is a simply a MAC created from the token information and the long-term key k_a^D (described above). When a request to operate on b_i arrives, D will check the token t_i before servicing the request.

4   Security

To prove the security of the protocols, we will define a "game" for the adversary to play. The game simply encapsulates a standard cryptographic reduction: we will reduce the security of the protocols to the security of the cryptographic primitives used (i.e., MACs and signatures). The setup for the reduction is a bit unusual, but, as shown below, the formulation is equivalent to the standard reduction framework. We assume that the encryption schemes are semantically secure and the MAC and signature schemes are existentially unforgeable under chosen-plaintext attacks. All keys are assumed long enough to be computationally infeasible to brute-force.

4.1 Security Game

We wish to accurately model the adversary, the system, and their interactions with each other, while giving the adversary as much flexibility as possible. We define a *message-creation game* where A has access to a simulator S that maintains a simulation of the cluster. A dictates all the events in S. Each event details a protocol to be executed with principals and parameters chosen by A. A may submit each message in a protocol as separate events with an arbitrary (but polynomially bounded) number of events inbetween. We do not allow parallel executions of the protocols, e.g. multiple instances of server registration initiated by the same server. Cryptographic keys are chosen by A only when the adversary's role in the protocol generates the keys. Otherwise the keys are generated and maintained by the simulator and are hidden from A.

After an event e is submitted to S and the internal state of S is updated, S outputs a transcript of the (full or partial) protocol execution dictated by e. The adversary wins the game if, after some polynomial number of steps, he produces a message that is unique, well-formed, and correctly verifies at the intended recipient (i.e., a principal in the simulator). We restrict the output message such that it must be for a protocol of which A is *not* one of the principals—otherwise A can win trivially. Note that each protocol consists of exactly two messages: an initiation message and the response. If the output of the adversary is a response message, then, for A to win, there must have been an event detailing the initiation message for that protocol. This setup gives A much more power over the cluster than would be possible in the real world. However, we will prove that the protocols are secure against even this more powerful adversary.

4.2 Security Proofs

The following proofs will use the game described above to reduce the security of the protocols to the security of a cryptographic primitive: whether it is a digital signature or a message authentication code. The registration protocol is the only protocol that involves an asymmetric signature for integrity and authentication; all other protocols use MACs to provide the same protections. As such, the security of the registration protocol's initial message reduces to the security of the digital signature, while the security of every other message reduces to the the MAC. The next two parts give outlines of formal proofs demonstrating these reductions.

Data Server Registration. Assume there exists a probabilistic polynomial-time adversary A, taking as input the public key of the metadata server PK_M, and the public key of the system administrator PK_{SA}, who can win the message-creation game with non-negligible probability. Moreover, assume A's output is the initial message of the registration protocol. We will construct an algorithm B that uses A as a subroutine to break the signature scheme. B takes as input the public key PK of the signature oracle $\mathcal{O}$ and the security parameter 1^k.

To use the adversary A, B will need to emulate the simulator. For each event e output by A, B will run the protocol with the given parameters, update the state s of the cluster, and return a transcript t to A. Whenever e dictates the registration of a new data server, B forms the registration message m in the usual way and then queries $\mathcal{O}$ on m to get the signature σ. The signature σ is used in place of the administrator's signature. All other protocols are executed normally with B exactly mimicking the simulator. Eventually, A outputs a message m. If the message is anything other than the initial message of the registration protocol, B fails. Otherwise, B extracts the signature $\tilde{\sigma}$ and the data d that was signed and outputs the pair $(d, \tilde{\sigma})$. If A won the game, then m verifies at its intended recipient: the metadata server. This implies that $\tilde{\sigma}$ was a valid signature for d even though A had no access to the key, i.e. A produced a forgery.

Since B outputs, essentially, the output of A, B succeeds exactly when A succeeds. Thus, if the transcripts given to A are distributed properly, B inherits the success probability of A. Note that B runs exactly the protocols in GFS, with the parameters and principals determined by A each time. Furthermore, the signature oracle $\mathcal{O}$ outputs signatures using a key that is from the same scheme as the key of the system administrator. Thus, since (almost) all protocols are run exactly as in the simulator and the signatures are from a distribution identical to the expected distribution, we have that the input to A is distributed *exactly* as expected. This implies that if A has a non-negligible probability of winning the game, then B has a non-negligible probability of producing a forgery. However, this contradicts the security of the signature scheme. Thus, it must be that A has only a negligible probability of winning the game when attacking the initial message of the registration protocol.

General Proof of Security. We now prove the security of the remaining protocols as a group. First, it is important to notice that each of the other protocols have the same structure: principal P_1 sends a message μ with a MAC m, and then principal P_2 replies with a message μ' and a MAC m'. We can exploit this structure and use an adversary A that can complete one of these protocols to create an adversary B that can break the security of the MAC scheme. Note that here we are assuming that the protocols, and the confidential values transferred therein, are secure against a passively observing adversary—we will prove this property later. In this reduction, B will have access to polynomially many oracles for the MAC scheme, each independently instantiated (i.e., the key in each oracle is chosen at random). B is successful if it can forge a message for *any* of the instantiated oracles.

Note that having polynomially many oracles is equivalent in power to having a single oracle. Briefly, given a single oracle $\mathcal{O}$ of polynomially-bounded power (e.g., a signature oracle) and an adversary who succeeds against polynomially many oracles, we can "guess," with non-negligible probability, which oracle will be attacked by the adversary. Using this guess, we can then use $\mathcal{O}$ to satisfy queries to the "to-be-attacked" oracle and simulate the remaining oracles. If the adversary succeeds with non-negligible probability and we made a correct guess, then we succeed with non-negligible probability.

Since we do not know how many oracles will be needed by B, we give B access to a meta-oracle $\mathcal{MO}$ that will manage the oracle instances. $\mathcal{MO}$ has three operations: *start*, *stop*, *query*. The command *start* takes no parameters, instantiates a new MAC oracle with a randomly chosen key, and returns a unique identifier for the oracle. The *stop* operation takes an oracle identifier as input and "destroys" the indicated oracle instance, making further queries under that identifier invalid. The *query* operation takes as input the identifier for an oracle and the input to the oracle, and then returns the output from the selected oracle.

As before, B emulates the simulator as closely as possible when interacting with A. Whenever an event e starts a new protocol instance, B determines whether or not a new oracle must be instantiated or if previously instantiated oracle must be used. For instance, if a client C is reading a block from a data server D, then B must ask $\mathcal{MO}$ to start a new oracle, since a unique MAC key is used in each block transfer. B would use a previously instantiated oracle for, say, a data server sending a heartbeat to the metadata server. However, if A is one of the principals in the protocol, then, since A knows the keys, B must itself compute the MAC for the message, all other MACs are computed by the oracles. Note that this does not affect B's chance of success as A is forbidden from attacking protocols in which it is a principal.

One difficulty in this reduction is what to do when the key for the MAC is sent as part of the message or in a previously executed protocol (e.g., the ephemeral keys for reading a block). Since the oracles are used for (almost) all MAC generation, B does not have access to the keys and cannot include them in any messages. The solution is to choose the keys in the message at random—except for those instances where A is a principal. While substituting in a random key does not perfectly mimic the simulator, we show next that the distribution of messages is computationally indistinguishable from the ideal distribution.

Suppose that A can distinguish the distribution of messages produced by B from the expected distribution, and that we have access to an encryption oracle for the cipher used to encrypt the keys. Then there exists an A' that, given a sample from one distribution or the other, distinguishes the distributions with a non-negligible advantage over $\frac{1}{2}$. Construct C that generates two random keys k_0 and k_1, and then constructs two messages m_0 and m_1 (both conforming to one of the protocols). C then submits m_0 and m_1 to the oracle to get $\mathcal{O}(m_b) = c_b$ for a random $b \in \{0, 1\}$. Once it has c_b, C finishes constructing the protocol message M and computes the MAC using k_0. C submits M with the MAC to A' and outputs whatever A' does. C is correct exactly when A' is correct. Thus C has a non-negligible chance to distinguish the encryptions of m_0 and m_1, contradicting the semantic security of the cipher. Thus, the view of A is computationally indistinguishable from the expected view. Since B succeeds exactly when A

succeeds, if A wins non-negligiblely often, then so does B, contradicting the security of the MAC scheme. Thus, it must be that there *does not* exist an A that can win the game with non-negligible probability. This, combined with the previous result, implies that A cannot win the game for any of the protocols.

Proof of Security of the Access Token. The definition of security for the access token is most naturally existential unforgeability under chosen-plaintext attacks. That is, with overwhelming probability, any token created by the adversary will not verify at any of the data servers. Note that since the token itself is simply a MAC of a few specific parameters, the security of the token is exactly the security of the MAC scheme. Thus, since we assumed that the MAC is secure, we have that the access tokens are also secure.

Proof against the Passive Adversary. To prove passive security, we must ensure that the adversary A cannot learn the contents of any data block. Since A is not interacting with any other principals, the only way for A to learn the contents a block is for A to capture the block intransit. File blocks only travel between and among clients and data servers and, as stated above, the file blocks are always encrypted before being transmitted. It is worth noting that in several instances, the key used to encrypt a file block is also sent with the block. However, the key is also encrypted with a semantically secure cipher. This layer of encryption should stymie the adversary A, unless A can acquire the key(s) or compute a non-negligible amount of information about the key(s).

The semantic security of the cipher implies that the passive adversary, with overwhelming probability, can only learn a negligible amount of information about any transmitted key (likewise for any key used to encrypt the transmitted key). Similarly, since the cipher used to encrypt the block data is also semantically secure and—it was assumed—the key is too long to brute-force in a reasonable amount of time, with overwhelming probability, the passive adversary A can only learn a negligible amount of information about the contents of the block. This is exactly the definition of being *passive-secure*, as desired.

Security Properties Proven. Overall, the above proofs give us the fact that an adversary (as described in Section 2), with overwhelming probability, cannot complete *any* of the protocols in the GFS API, giving us the *server-secure* and *client-secure* properties. Additionally, we demonstrated that with overwhelming probability the system is also secure against a passive adversary. Thus we have that the extensions given in this work give a GFS API that is *secure*.

5   Experimental Results

To demonstrate the practicality of this secured architecture, a proof-of-concept implementation was created by modifying the open-source Hadoop platform [14] to implement the above secured protocols. The changes were made to version 0.20.104.2 of the Yahoo! branch of the code (which has since been merged into mainline Hadoop). This branch was chosen because it contains all of the Kerberos integration work performed by Yahoo!. This allows a more direct comparison of the efficiency of previous security work with the efficiency of this work.

Our implementation uses 2048 RSA for the asymmetric keys, and UMAC128 for the message authentication codes [18]. The stream cipher Salsa20/12 from [2] is used for all data encryption—chosen for both its speed and strong security. The experiments were performed on a cluster of 40 Dell PowerEdge 1855s each running a dual-core 2.8GHz Intel Xeon with 8 GB of memory and 300GB of disk space—for a total of 12TB of disk space in the cluster. The operating system used on each is 64-bit Debian Linux. The metadata server was run on a quad-core Intel Core2 Q6600 at 2.4GHz with 4GB of memory. While the processor has 64-bit instructions, the OS was 32-bit Debian Linux with PAE.

We used standard benchmarks of Hadoop: Gridmix2, NNThroughputBench-mark, and TestDFSIO. Gridmix2 is a mix of various MapReduce jobs designed to stress HDFS in a number of ways while emulating a real-world workload and is regarded as the standard macro-benchmark for Hadoop clusters. NNThrough-putBenchmark is used to test the throughput, and hence scalability, of the meta-data server (called the NameNode in Hadoop). The TestDFSIO utility measures the raw read and write speed of the cluster. We summarize the results in Table 1.

Table 1. Comparison of our work against default Hadoop. The first column is in seconds, the second and third in MB/s and the remaining in operations per second.

	Gridmix2	Avg Read IO	Avg Write IO	Open	Create	BlockReport
Default Hadoop	23997s	58.6 MB/s	20.2 MB/s	45871	324	8333
Sec-Hadoop	26819s	27.9 MB/s	10.8 MB/s	6711	331	7821
% Slowdown	11.8	52.4	46.5	85.4	-2.1	6.1

Overall Performance. The Gridmix2 column in Table 1 shows that, overall, this work produces a 12% slow down of Hadoop. The work by Yahoo! in comparison achieves a 3% slowdown of the Gridmix2 benchmark, but none of the file data is encrypted. The remaining columns give the average IO rates for reads and writes when creating 40 files of 2048MB each with a replication factor of 3. Average IO is defined as the average the individual IO rates for the created files. We can see that the average IO rates for the secured Hadoop are a bit less than half of the rates for the default Hadoop. While this is a significant drop in performance, the effect of this is attenuated by the fact that cluster performance is not solely IO-bound. For example, even though our work has half the read/write performance, the overall impact was just a 12% slowdown for the cluster.

Scalability. GFS-like file systems are designed to rapidly scale upward, but growth is often limited by the capacity of the metadata server. Shvachko in [27] performs a detailed estimation of the practical limits of a Hadoop cluster assessing memory and computational costs. Looking at the same metrics, the memory overhead in our work is at most in the tens of kilobytes as only a few dozen bytes are stored per server and client. The real cost of our modifications is computational: an increase in both the time spent processing messages from data servers and handling metadata operations from clients. Table 1 shows that the throughput of the metadata server decreases between 6.1% and 85.4%, depending on the action performed. While this reduces the scalability of the cluster, the limit would only affect very large Hadoop deployments. In particular, our rather modest metadata server is still able to handle several thousand operations per second. Thus, a secured cluster could easily scale to hundreds of servers and even to a few thousand. But, as the "Open" metric shows, a secured Hadoop will have trouble scaling past a few thousand nodes.

6   Other Related Work

Yahoo! has released their own version of Hadoop, an open source implementation of the Map-Reduce framework, including a security-enhanced HDFS [29]. This version incorporates Kerberos authentication into all communication: all servers and users are registered as principals in the Kerberos database and must authenticate before sending any messages. Their work provides message integrity and authentication, but not confidentiality. Recent work has been done on distributed file systems that operate as the underlying cloud storage. However, security is rarely, if ever, mentioned. The efforts in [11] give a file system that is similar to GFS but uses a collection of metadata servers instead of a single central server and finer-grained resource control. User authentication is the only security feature. The work in [17] provides a flexible and modular cloud storage system where components can be swapped in/out to provide customized levels of reliability, efficiency, and consistency semantics, but security is not discussed.

Previous work on security in GFS-like file systems is sparse. Airavat modifies Hadoop to support mandatory access controls and store the security labels with the blocks [25]. However, MAC policies are often unwieldy, difficult to set up, and time-consuming to maintain. Also, the implementation results in a slow-down of up to 25%. TPlatform [22] has the same access control limitations as the original Hadoop. CloudStore, another implementation of GFS, does not have any access controls [6]. Another effort by [16] builds fine-grained access controls on top of the Hadoop file system (HDFS), but it assumes that HDFS is inherently secure.

SUNDR is a network file system that seeks to reduce the amount of trust clients must give to the file servers—the converse of our goal: reducing the trust given to clients—and implements fork-consistency [19]. GPFS is another distributed file system that provides efficient, fault-tolerant storage [26]. Access control checks are performed at the storage servers and users are assumed to be relatively benevolent. The Panache file system is designed to be fully parallel in all read/write operations, utilizing GPFS to store file data and metadata and uses parallel NFS on the client-side for reading/writing data [10]. SFS aims to provide a secure file system over an untrusted network (e.g., the Internet) using "self-certifying paths" via public-key based client-server authentication [20]. Related work on the integrity verification of outsourced file systems includes authenticated data structures (e.g., [13,21]) and proofs of data possession (e.g., [9]).

7   Conclusion and Future Work

This work demonstrates the feasibility of greatly enhancing the security of GFS-like file systems, while maintaining a reasonable overhead. However, a 12% slowdown is not insignificant and could be improved through various avenues. One avenue would be to add more flexibility in the architecture (e.g., choosing to encrypt block data but not use a MAC) so that administrators can more finely tune the trade-off in security and efficiency. Additional experimentation with other cipher suites and MAC schemes could be helpful to reduce the overhead from the security. Another avenue to explore would be utilizing the work of [3] to provide transport-level encryption for all traffic, transparently to the Hadoop cluster itself. One weakness of our secured system is the lack of confidentiality protections for file metadata. While the data itself could not be pilfered, metadata such as file names can contain sensitive information. Protecting metadata is a logical next step in increasing the assurance of GFS-like file systems.

Acknowledgments. Research supported in part by the National Science Foundation under grants CNS–1012060, CNS–1012798, and CNS–1012910 and by a NetApp Faculty Fellowship. We thank James Lentini for useful discussions.

References

1. Becherer, A.: Hadoop Security Design: Just Add Kerberos? Really? (2010), http://media.blackhat.com/bh-us-10/whitepapers/Becherer/BlackHat-USA-2010-Becherer-Andrew-Hadoop-Security-wp.pdf
2. Bernstein, D.J.: The Salsa20 Family of Stream Ciphers. In: Robshaw, M., Billet, O. (eds.) New Stream Cipher Designs. LNCS, vol. 4986, pp. 84–97. Springer, Heidelberg (2008)
3. Bittau, A., Hamburg, M., Handley, M., Mazières, D., Boneh, D.: The case for ubiquitous transport-level encryption. In: USENIX Security, pp. 26–42 (2010)
4. Borthakur, D.: HDFS Architecture, http://hadoop.apache.org/hdfs/docs/current/hdfs_design.html
5. Borthakur, D., Gray, J., Sarma, J.S., Muthukkaruppan, K., Spiegelberg, N., Kuang, H., Ranganathan, K., Molkov, D., Menon, A., Rash, S., Schmidt, R., Aiyer, A.: Apache Hadoop goes realtime at Facebook. In: SIGMOD, pp. 1071–1080 (2011)
6. CloudStore, http://code.google.com/p/kosmosfs/
7. Cordova, A.: MapReduce over Tahoe–a least-authority encrypted distributed file system (2009), http://www.cloudera.com/videos/hw09_mapreduce_over_tahoe
8. Dittrich, J., Quiané-Ruiz, J., Jindal, A., Kargin, Y., Setty, V., Schad, J.: Hadoop++: Making a yellow elephant run like a cheetah (without it even noticing). PVLDB 3(1), 518–529 (2010)
9. Erway, C., Küpçü, A., Papamanthou, C., Tamassia, R.: Dynamic provable data possession. In: CCS, pp. 213–222 (2009)
10. Eshel, M., Haskin, R., Hildebrand, D., Naik, M., Schmuck, F., Tewari, R.: Panache: A parallel file system cache for global file access. In: USENIX FAST (2010)
11. Fesehaye, D., Malik, R., Nahrstedt, K.: A Scalable Distributed File System for Cloud Computing. Tech. rep., University of Illinois at Urbana-Champaign (2010), http://www.ideals.illinois.edu/handle/2142/15200

12. Ghemawat, S., Gobioff, H., Leung, S.: The Google file system. In: SOSP, pp. 29–43 (2003)
13. Goodrich, M.T., Papamanthou, C., Tamassia, R., Triandopoulos, N.: Athos: Efficient Authentication of Outsourced File Systems. In: Wu, T.-C., Lei, C.-L., Rijmen, V., Lee, D.-T. (eds.) ISC 2008. LNCS, vol. 5222, pp. 80–96. Springer, Heidelberg (2008)
14. Hadoop, http://hadoop.apache.org
15. Jiang, D., Ooi, B.C., Shi, L., Wu, S.: The performance of MapReduce: An in-depth study. PVLDB 3(1-2), 472–483 (2010)
16. Kantarcioglu, M., Khan, L., Thuraisingham, B., Gupta, A., Vyas, M., Khadilkar, V., Mishra, N.: Fine-grained Access Control using HIVE (September 2010), http://cs.utdallas.edu/secure-cloud-repository/Hive-AC/hive-ac.html
17. Kossmann, D., Kraska, T., Loesing, S., Merkli, S., Mittal, R., Pfaffhauser, F.: Cloudy: A modular cloud storage system. PVLDB 3(2), 1533–1536 (2010)
18. Krovetz, T.: UMAC: Message Authentication Code using Universal Hashing. RFC 4418 (Informational) (March 2006), http://www.ietf.org/rfc/rfc4418.txt
19. Li, J., Krohn, M., Mazières, D., Shasha, D.: Secure untrusted data repository. In: USENIX OSDI, pp. 91–106 (2004)
20. Mazières, D., Kaminsky, M., Frans Kaashoek, M., Witchel, E.: Separating key management from file system security. In: SOSP, pp. 124–139 (1999)
21. Papamanthou, C., Tamassia, R., Triandopoulos, N.: Authenticated hash tables. In: CCS, pp. 437–448 (2008)
22. Peng, B., Cui, B., Li, X.: Implementation Issues of a Cloud Computing Platform. IEEE Data Engineering Bulletin (2009)
23. Ristenpart, T., Tromer, E., Shacham, H., Savage, S.: Hey, you, get off of my cloud: Exploring information leakage in third-party compute clouds. In: ACM CCS, pp. 199–212 (2009)
24. Rocha, F., Correia, M.: Lucy in the sky without diamonds: Stealing confidential data in the cloud. In: IEEE/IFIP DNSW, pp. 129–134 (2011)
25. Roy, I., Ramadan, H.E., Setty, S.T.V., Kilzer, A., Shmatikov, V., Witchel, E.: Airavat: Security and privacy for MapReduce. In: USENIX NSDI, pp. 297–312 (2010)
26. Schmuck, F., Haskin, R.: GPFS: A shared-disk file system for large computing clusters. In: USENIX FAST, pp. 231–244 (2002)
27. Shvachko, K.V.: HDFS scalability: the limits of growth. USENIX; Login 35(2), 6–16 (2010)
28. Wilcox-O'Hearn, Z., Warner, B.: Tahoe: The least-authority filesystem. In: ACM StorageSS, pp. 21–26 (2008)
29. Yahoo! Distribution of Hadoop, http://developer.yahoo.com/hadoop/

Attack of the Clones: Detecting Cloned Applications on Android Markets

Jonathan Crussell[1,2], Clint Gibler[1], and Hao Chen[1]

[1] University of California, Davis
{jcrussell,cdgibler}@ucdavis.edu, hchen@cs.ucdavis.edu
[2] Sandia National Labs*, Livermore, CA
jcrusse@sandia.gov

Abstract. We present DNADroid, a tool that detects Android appli-cation copying, or "cloning", by robustly computing the similarity be-tween two applications. DNADroid achieves this by comparing program dependency graphs between methods in candidate applications. Using DNADroid, we found at least 141 applications that have been the vic-tims of cloning, some as many as seven times. DNADroid has a very low false positive rate — we manually confirmed that all the applications detected are indeed clones by either visual or behavioral similarity. We present several case studies that give insight into why applications are cloned, including localization and redirecting ad revenue. We describe a case of malware being added to an application and show how DNADroid was able to detect two variants of the same malware. Lastly, we offer examples of an open source cracking tool being used in the wild.

1 Introduction

In the past few years, mobile phones sales have grown explosively. As of Novem-ber 2011, Android has dominant smart phone marketshare [9], with phone sales recently reaching 850,000 activations per day [24]. The Android operating system provides the core smartphone experience, but much of the user experience relies on third-party applications. To this end, Android has numerous marketplaces where users can download third-party applications that enable easy access to social networking, games, and more. As with traditional desktop applications, there is a need to protect users from malicious applications and developers from plagiarists who wish to benefit from a legitimate developer's hard work.

Developers can release applications on the official Android Market and/or on any one of a number of third-party markets. They can charge directly for their applications, but many choose to instead offer free applications that are ad-supported or contain in-game billing for additional content. Some applications have both a premium (paid) and free, ad-supported version.

---

* Sandia National Laboratories is a multi-program laboratory managed and operated by Sandia Corporation, a wholly owned subsidiary of Lockheed Martin Corporation, for the U.S. Department of Energys National Nuclear Security Administration under contract DE-AC04-94AL85000.

S. Foresti, M. Yung, and F. Martinelli (Eds.): ESORICS 2012, LNCS 7459, pp. 37–54, 2012.

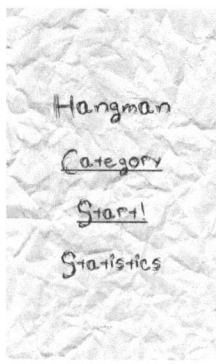 

(a) Google Market
br.com.passeionaweb...
Ads: googleads

(b) EoeMarket
com.ttmobilegame...
Ads:: wooboo

Fig. 1. A pair of cloned applications. This paper detects cloning based on code similarity only, as an application's UI may be easily changed. Caption lists the market, package name and ad library associated with each application.

It is important to maintain a healthy market environment to encourage developers to continue creating applications. One important aspect of a healthy market is that developers are financially compensated for their work, an issue we investigate in this paper. There are several ways developers may lose potential revenue: a paid application may be "cracked" and released for free or a free application may be copied, or "cloned", and re-released with changes to the ad libraries that cause ad revenue to go to the plagiarist. In the latter case, the plagiarist may modify an existing library in an application, replacing the developer's client ID[1] with her own, or she may insert a new ad library that gives revenue to the plagiarist. Unfortunately, the openness of Android markets and the ease of repackaging Android applications contribute to the ability of plagiarists to clone applications and resubmit them to markets. Unlike Apple's App Store, where applications must pass a review process, applications on most Android markets are distributed without review. The official Android Market, however, recently added a service that scans new applications [35]. Although Google claims Bouncer drastically reduced the amount of malware installed by users, its effects on clones, which may not be malicious towards the user, is unknown.

Android application cloning has been reported by developers and the academic community [22, 23, 41]. An example we discovered, Fig. 1, shows the screenshots of two applications that are similar both in their UI and code, but were uploaded to different markets by different developers. Our analysis found the two to have significant code overlap, suggesting that at least one is a clone[2]. Since

---

[1] A client ID is a developer-unique string or number used by advertisers to determine who should be compensated when an ad is displayed or clicked.

[2] Potentially they could both be clones of an application we have not analyzed.

it is straightforward to detect directly copied code, we expect plagiarists to disguise their code to evade detection. To combat these disguises, we need robust techniques for detecting Android application cloning. We develop a technique based on program dependence graphs (PDGs) because it is has been shown to be effective in resisting many types of detection evasion techniques, such as statement reordering, insertion, and deletion [34]. Additionally, since it is uncommon for PDGs to be the same for independently developed code, our technique has a very low false positive rate.

Our contributions in this paper are as follows: (1) We have designed and implemented DNADroid, a tool for detecting cloned Android applications. DNADroid detects code clones based on PDGs and therefore resists common program transformations. (2) We ran DNADroid on applications downloaded from thirteen Android markets. DNADroid detected at least 141 applications that have been cloned. We show examples of applications being cloned multiple times by different developers, in one case up to seven times. (3) We demonstrate the very low false positive rate of DNADroid — we have manually verified, through UI or functionality comparisons, that all applications detected by DNADroid are in fact clones. (4) We present five case studies that illustrate different goals of mobile application plagiarists.

2 Background

Android Markets. As Android has increased in popularity, the number of applications has rapidly increased [21]. Developers can publish in the official Android market for a one-time $25 dollar fee, or use alternative markets such as SlideMe [14] and GoApk [10] which often only require an email address to publish applications. Unlike Apple's App Store, Android markets tend not to vet applications but rather rely on user feedback. This relaxed policy makes it easier for people to clone, modify, and redistribute applications. Finding these clones is important to protect developers' intellectual property and revenue streams and to alert users of potentially malicious clones.

Android Application Structure. Applications are distributed in Android Packages (APKs). These packages contain everything that the application needs to run- from resources like images and XML files specifying UI layouts to the application code. APKs also include a *manifest* XML that specifies a number of aspects about the application, including its name, version information, the package (or namespace) of the code, the permissions it requires to execute, and much more. Android applications are primarily developed in Java, though native code may be used. The Java source code is compiled to Java byte code and then converted into the Dalvik executable (DEX) format. Although similar to Java byte code, DEX byte code is incompatible with the Java virtual machine and instead runs on the Dalvik virtual machine. The conversion of Java byte code to DEX byte code is largely reversible and there are several tools that handle this conversion. We analyze only the DEX byte code and leave native code analysis for future work.

3   Threat Model

Our goal is to find cloned Android applications. We assume that the plagiarist has access to the compiled APK file that has been uploaded to an Android market. We also assume that the plagiarist will change some part of the file in order to change its cryptographic hash, as detecting identical applications is trivial.

Definition of "Clone". Clones occur when two applications (1) have similar code but (2) have different ownership. Therefore, clone detection differs from code reuse detection because the latter is concerned with only the first criterion. Because of the second criterion, DNADroid ignores (1) third-party libraries (for advertising, additional functionality, etc.), since they are intended to be reused and (2) multiple versions of the same application if they have the same ownership. Every Android application is signed by the owner's private key before being uploaded to a market. We determine two applications to have the same owner if they are signed by the same key.

We use the term owner rather than developer to describe the entity which published the application because a plagiarist illegitimately claims ownership of an application by publishing it under her own name without having developed the core functionality. Additionally, it is the owner that receives the revenue generated by the application, not the original developer.

Resistance to Evasion Techniques. A plagiarist will most likely modify the cloned code to evade detection. We design DNADroid to resist all the following evasion techniques: (1) *High level modifications*: Modify package, class, method and variable names as well as add or delete classes and methods. Create, change, or delete constants. (2) *Method Restructurings*: Move methods between classes, split a large method into multiple smaller methods, or combine multiple methods into a larger one. (3) *Control Flow Alterations*: Swap the *if* and *else* branches after negating the truth value. Change *for* loops to infinite *while* loops with a *break* statement or vice versa. Rewrite loops using *goto* statements. *Switch* and *if/else* statements may be swapped and individual cases may be reordered, created or removed. (4) *Addition/Deletion*: Insert code that does not affect the value of computed results or delete existing code. (5) *Reordering*: Reorder any code segments that are data and control independent.

Non Goals. We do not attempt to find cloning in native code in an application. As only a small percentage (7%) of the 75,000 applications we analyzed include native code, this is currently acceptable. Additionally, it is significantly more difficult for a plagiarist to understand and modify native code than DEX byte code. If a plagiarist does copy native code from an application, there is a good probability that she will steal DEX byte code as well, which DNADroid would find.

DNADroid does not attempt to determine which applications are the victims and which are clones. Without external knowledge, this is difficult to do in general based on the code alone. Simple solutions like comparing application release dates or file sizes do not work in all cases, for example when a plagiarist steals beta releases [23] or when a plagiarist replaces an advertising library with a different, smaller one.

4   Clone Detection Approaches and Related Work

We describe several approaches for statically detecting cloned code, explaining their strengths and weaknesses, and conclude with the method used by DNADroid. As Android applications are largely interactive, dynamically detecting cloned code would face the same scalability limitations as TaintDroid [28], where authors had to manually interact with each application. This eliminates techniques such as [32, 37] for detecting similar Android applications. We also list and categorize related work, motivating the need for DNADroid.

Feature Based. Feature based approaches analyze a program and extract a set of features. Plagiarism between two programs is detected by comparing the extracted features from the programs. The features chosen can vary significantly, from number or size of classes, methods, loops, or variables to included libraries. This approach is limited because it discards so much information about the structure of the programs. Feature based systems are highly susceptible to having a low detection rate or high false positive rate.

Structure Based. Structure based systems convert programs into a stream of tokens and then compare the streams between two programs. By converting programs into a stream of tokens and ignoring easily changed constructs such as comments, whitespace, and variable names, structure based systems detect plagiarism more robustly than feature based systems. Examples of this approach include JPLAG [38], Winnowing [40] and MOSS [18]. Comparing DEX byte code streams could be a quite quick and scalable method to find *exactly* or *near exactly* copied code.

Unfortunately, the byte code streams contain no higher level semantic knowledge about the code, making this approach vulnerable to code modifications. For example, structure based approaches cannot determine if one or more instructions in the stream have been spuriously added and do not contribute to the outcome of the program. Winnowing [40] attempts to find plagiarism with modifications using *k-grams*, by finding common token substrings of length k. If the differences between the programs are relatively infrequent or tend to be greater than k tokens apart then the comparison will find many k-length token streams in common. However, a wily plagiarist could simply insert a random instruction every few instructions to utterly break the stream comparison.

Program Dependency Graph (PDG) Based. A Program Dependence Graph (PDG) represents a method in a program, where each node is a statement and each edge shows a dependency between statements. There are two types of dependencies: data and control. A data dependency edge between statements s_1 and s_2 exists if there is a variable in s_2 whose value depends on s_1. For example, if s_1 is an assignment statement and s_2 references the variable assigned in s_1 then s_2 is data dependent on s_1. A control dependency between two statements exists if the truth value of the first statement controls whether the second statement executes.

The evasion techniques discussed in our threat model (Sect. 3) hardly change a method's PDG. If the copied parts of the program behave the same as their original counterparts, they should have the same dependencies between the input and output variables. Since these dependencies do not change even after significant disguises have been applied to the copied code, PDG-based plagiarism detection is much more robust than structure based systems [34]. As we expect plagiarists to actively try to hide their work to various extents, this robustness is essential.

Android Clone Detection. There have been several recent papers which apply some of the above techniques to Android, here we briefly describe their approaches. We note that all these approaches are structure based or structure based approximations (using hashing).

Androguard [19] supports several standard similarity metrics including normal compression distance (NCD) and the comparison of the SHA256 hash of methods and basic blocks. NCD utilizes compressibility as a measure of similarity as two similar strings are more compressible than each on its own. DEXCD [27] tokenizes the opcodes in a decompiled APK and then attempts to find similar streams of opcodes between applications. DroidMOSS [41] computes fuzzy hashes of each method in the APK and combines them to form a hash for the entire APK. It then compares the fuzzy hashes of APKs to detect similarity based on the individual method hashes that both APKs share.

None of these tools use any semantic information to aid in detecting plagiarism. This makes them susceptible to evasion techniques discussed in Sect. 3. As such, we created DNADroid to more robustly detect the plagiarism of Android applications.

5   Methodology

DNADroid, as depicted in Fig. 2, proceeds in two stages. First, pairs of potentially cloned applications are selected based on their attributes. Then, the code of each pair of applications is examined to determine similarity.

5.1   Selecting Potentially Cloned Applications

The goal of an application plagiarist is to entice unwary users to choose her cloned application instead of the original. Since users find most applications through search, the plagiarist wishes to construct the name and description of her cloned application to resemble those of the original application so that both applications appear together in queries. Based on this observation, the first step of DNADroid is to select similar applications based on their attributes. As mentioned in Section 3, we do not consider pairs of applications signed by the same key, as they share a developer.

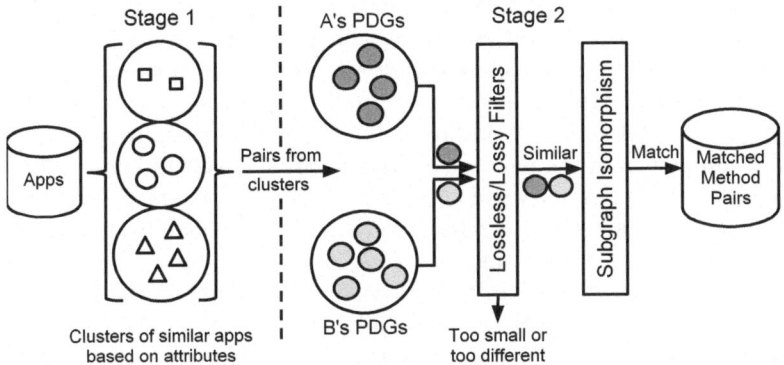

Fig. 2. Overview of DNADroid

Determining Application Similarity Based on Attributes. A plagiarist's goal is to have users install her clone so she will often use meta information that is similar to the victim application to describe the clone. By using similar meta information, a clone is more likely to appear in search queries with the victim. To mimic the search engines on Android markets, we use Solr [20], an open source enterprise-grade search platform from the Apache Lucene project, to index all the attributes of the applications, including name, package, market, owner, and description. In order to find clone candidates, we use Solr's fuzzy search on the meta information of one application to determine which applications are similar. These similar applications are fed into the second stage of DNADroid.

Although we found Solr effective in finding similar applications, DNADroid could use other tools for the same purpose, including using the markets' search and recommendation features directly.

5.2   Detecting Code Clones

The second stage of DNADroid determines the code similarity of a pair of applications.

Constructing PDGs. We convert both applications' code from the DEX format to a JAR using *dex2jar* [39]. [3] We then utilize WALA [25] to construct PDGs for each method in every class of the applications. We create the PDGs with only data dependency edges so that our detection is more robust against statement reordering, insertion and deletion

Comparing PDGs. DNADroid detects similarity between two applications by finding semantically similar code at the method level.

    Excluding Common Libraries Many applications include third-party libraries, such as the ad library Admob or the Facebook API. As these libraries

---
[3] There are other tools available to convert from DEX to JAR, however, we found that *dex2jar* worked the best in practice. If a better tool became available, we could easily replace *dex2jar* with it.

are not written by the owners of the applications, they should not be included in the clone detection. Libraries tend to have a common package name, like *com.admob.android* or *com.facebook.android*. However, we cannot simply filter classes based on package name alone, as a malicious owner could reuse a popular package name for her code or could insert malicious functionality into the library itself. We dumped both the package name and SHA-1 hash of known library files for thousands of applications and recorded the most frequent SHA-1 hashes for each library. This allows us to exclude common library code from analysis while remaining resistant to tampering.

`Lossless and Lossy Filters` Once we have constructed the PDGs for each method in A and B, we apply two fast filters to exclude method pairs that are unlikely to be clones [34]. We first apply the *lossless* filter, which removes PDGs from consideration that are smaller than a specified size (< 10 nodes). Small matches between methods are more likely to occur by chance and these matches are often from trivial, boilerplate code.

Next we apply the *lossy* filter, which discards method pairs that are unlikely to match due to a difference in the distribution of types of nodes in the two PDGs. For example, a PDG that contains many method invocation nodes is unlikely to match one with none. First, we calculate a frequency vector for each of the methods in the pair. This vector counts how many times a specific node type occurs in the PDG. A method with five arithmetic operations would have a five in the dimension of the vector corresponding to arithmetic operations. We then compare these two vectors using hypothesis testing which calculates how likely one distribution is an observation from the first. Specifically, the hypothesis test we use is the G-test, which is a log likelihood ratio test. If the likelihood is below some significance threshold, α, then we exclude the pair because the graphs have a low probability of being similar. Even though this filter may exclude similar PDGs in theory (hence the name *lossy*), we demonstrate experimentally that these cases are rare in practice with an α value of 0.05 (Sect. 6.4).

`Subgraph Isomorphism` If a pair of PDGs survives the above filters, the final test for similarity is subgraph isomorphism, which attempts to find a mapping between nodes in PDG_A and nodes in PDG_B. Subgraph isomorphism is NP-Complete; however, when used for comparing PDGs, empirical evidence shows that it is often efficient because a PDG represents a single method, which developers tend to keep within a maintainable size. Additionally, PDGs are comprised of different statement types, which greatly reduces the possible mappings between two PDGs, as only nodes of the same statement type will match. We use the VF2 algorithm to compute subgraph isomorphisms, which is a backtracking algorithm geared towards matching large graphs [26]. VF2 takes advantage of the fact that PDGs contain a variety of node types, which restricts the total number of possible pairs of nodes for testing.

`Computing Similarity Scores` We determine the similarity of a pair of applications based on their matched PDG pairs. For each method f (excluding the methods in known libraries) in application A, let $|f|$ be the number of nodes in this method's PDG. Find the best match of this PDG in B's PDGs and denote

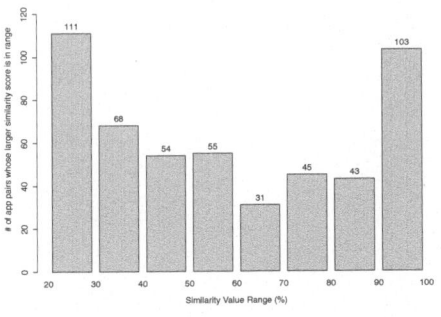
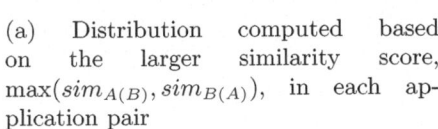
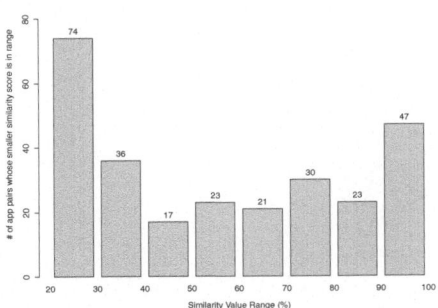

(a) Distribution computed based on the larger similarity score, $\max(sim_{A(B)}, sim_{B(A)})$, in each application pair

(b) Distribution computed based on the smaller similarity score, $\min(sim_{A(B)}, sim_{B(A)})$, in each application pair

Fig. 3. Distribution of similarity scores among application pairs. Each bar represents the number of application pairs whose similarity scores are in the range on the x-axis

it as $m(f)$. Our metric, *similarity score*, is the ratio between the sums of the $|f|$ values and the $|m(f)|$ values:

$$sim_{A(B)} = \frac{\sum\limits_{f \in A} |m(f)|}{\sum\limits_{f \in A} |f|} \tag{1}$$

Equation 1 shows the portion of application A that is matched by code in application B.

6   Evaluation

We collected 75,000 free applications from thirteen Android markets: the official Android market [31] and a number of third party markets [1, 3, 2, 5–7, 10–14]. From these applications, we randomly selected 9,400 pairs from the potential clones identified by the first stage of DNADroid based on their attributes (Sect. 5.1). The second stage of DNADroid determined which of these pairs were indeed clones based on code similarity (Sect. 5.2).

We used the Hadoop [4] MapReduce framework to parallelize DNADroid and HDFS to share data across a small cluster of one server-class and three desktop machines. The average throughput of DNADroid on this small cluster is 0.71 application pairs per minute.

6.1   Similarity between Applications

We define application clones as a pair of applications that have similar code but different ownership. The comparison of each pair of applications A and B

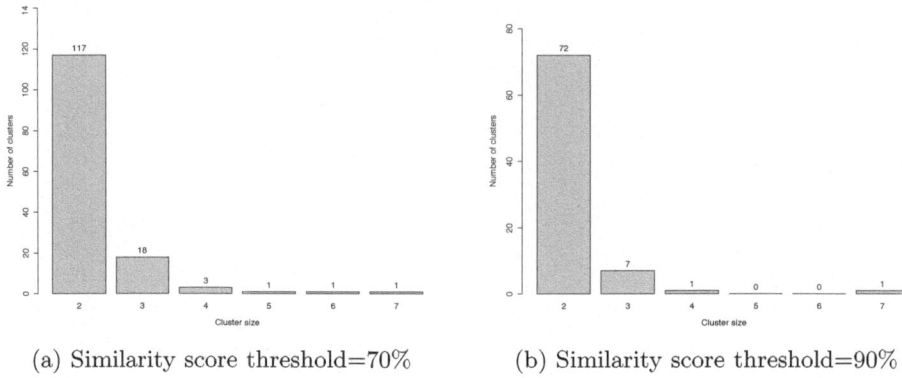

(a) Similarity score threshold=70%   (b) Similarity score threshold=90%

Fig. 4. Distribution of clone cluster sizes

produces two similarity scores, $sim_{A(B)}$ and $sim_{B(A)}$, as defined in Equation 1. $sim_{A(B)}$ is the percentage of code in A that is matched by code in B. A high similarity score shows that a substantial portion of one application is present in another, providing evidence of code cloning.

Figure 3 show the distributions of the similarity scores among all the pairs of applications analyzed: Fig. 3a uses the larger similarity score in each application pair while Fig. 3b uses the smaller score. Figure 3a shows that 103 application pairs have similarity scores above 90%, 43 application pairs between 80% and 90%, and 45 application pairs between 70% and 80%.

In this paper, we define two applications to be clones when at least one of the applications has a similarity score over 70% ($\max(sim_{A(B)}, sim_{B(A)}) \geq 70\%$). We choose to use the max similarity score of the pair to avoid the following problem: a malicious developer may add a significant amount of code to the cloned application, causing the original application code to match a small percent of the cloned application. However, she cannot influence the content of the original application, which has already been released. The original application will still be highly matched by the cloned application, causing DNADroid to identify the clone pair. Using a 70% similarity score threshold, DNADroid found at least 191 application pairs in which one or both of the applications are clones.

6.2   Clustering Cloned Applications

Are many Android applications cloned a small number of times or are a relatively few cloned many times? We attempt to gain insight into this question by clustering applications based on their computed similarities. Clusters are computed using the following algorithm: for each pair of applications, A and B, if either $sim_{A(B)}$ or $sim_{B(A)}$ is above the threshold, then A and B are in the same cluster. After running this algorithm over all pairs of applications, we have a set of clusters, each of which contains at least 2 applications.

Figure 4 shows the distribution of the sizes of clone clusters at two different similarity score thresholds. The majority of the clone clusters have just two applications; however, there are larger clusters with the largest having seven applications. Figure 4a illustrates that, at a 70% threshold, DNADroid found at least 141 applications that are victims of cloning. As each clone cluster of applications has at least one victim application, the number of clusters is a lower bound on the number of victim applications.[4]

It is instructive to examine the clone clusters. Figure 5 shows two clusters. Figure 5a shows a cluster of six applications. The bottom three applications (21*ad*, *aa*87, and *f*59*d*) are signed by the same private key (i.e., written by the same author) and have the same package name (com.bwx) but have different version numbers. The top application (714*a*) has a different package name (com.zhanghuisns) and is signed by a different private key. Finally, the middle two applications are signed by the same private key and have the same package name (com.mybooft). Based on the key signatures, we can split the graph into three families - top, middle and bottom. Using the similarity scores and the version information, it appears that the middle family most likely cloned from an ancestor of the bottom family and that the top family may have cloned from the middle or bottom family.

Figure 5b shows similar relationships between different families of applications, where a seed family appears to have been cloned multiple times by different developers. These figures demonstrate that clustering is an effective tool in analyzing relationships between cloned applications.

6.3   Visual and Behavioral Verification

To confirm that the application pairs identified by DNADroid are indeed similar, we examined their GUI and user interactions. Figure 7 shows the screenshots of some of the application pairs that were detected by DNADroid as clones. It takes only a quick glance to determine that both screenshots in each application pair are indeed very similar. For application pairs whose initial screen shots are drastically different, we manually ran and interacted with them to verify that they have similar functionality. Manual verification confirmed that every application pair found by DNADroid were in fact clones, yielding an experimental false positive rate of 0%.

6.4   Filter Performance

Filter Effectiveness. DNADroid uses several filters to improve its speed and scalability by excluding method pairs that are unlikely to match. A naive approach would require $O(n * m)$ method comparisons, where n and m are the number of methods in each application. To reduce the number of method pair comparisons, DNADroid uses three filters (Sect. 5.2). The library class filter excludes on average 27.16% of each application's classes. The *lossless* and *lossy* filters on average exclude 33.88% and 2.62% of the methods in an application,

---

[4] The victim application may or may not be a member of the clone cluster. The latter case arises if we downloaded only the clones of the victim application but not the victim itself.

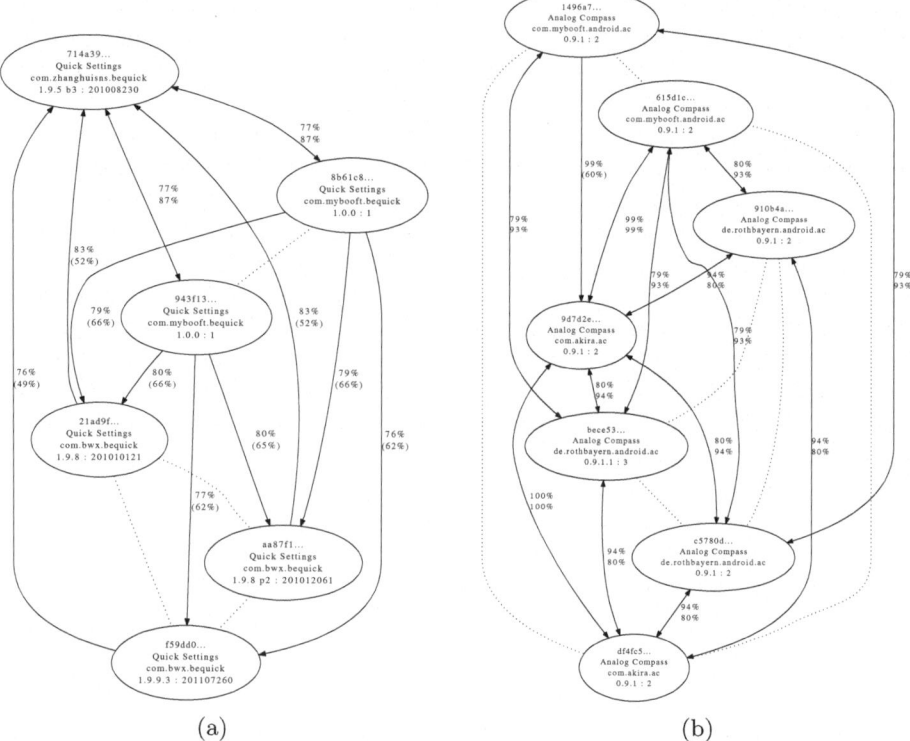

(a)   (b)

Fig. 5. Application Clone Clusters. Each node represents an application. The label in each node contains the SHA-1 hash prefix, name, package, version name, and version code of the application. Each solid edge from Application A to Application B means that a large percentage (> 70%) of A is found in B, where the top number on the edge is the similarity score of A in B, and the bottom number (in parentheses) is the similarity score of B in A. A dotted line links two applications by the same author (have the same public key signature).

respectively. Combined, these three filters reduce DNADroid's search space by 90.04%.

Filter Accuracy. Of the three filters, only the *lossy* filter may exclude interesting methods pairs that would have matched[5]. We wish to ensure that our *lossy* filter rarely rejects similar method pairs, as this would cause DNADroid to underreport the similarity of applications and potentially miss clone pairs.

To measure the accuracy of the *lossy* filter, we randomly selected 250 application pairs already examined by DNADroid and reran them without the *lossy* filter. Figure 6a is a CDF of the application similarity scores, both with and without the *lossy* filter. The figure shows that the *lossy* filter has negligible

---

[5] The class filter excludes known common libraries and the lossless filter excludes small methods, neither of which constitute interesting code reuse.

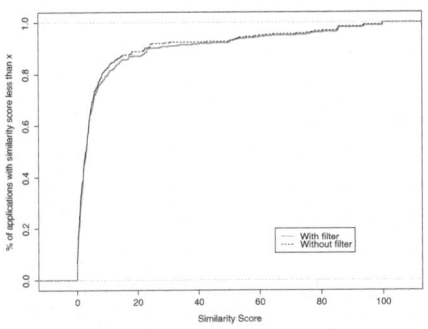
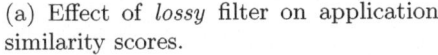
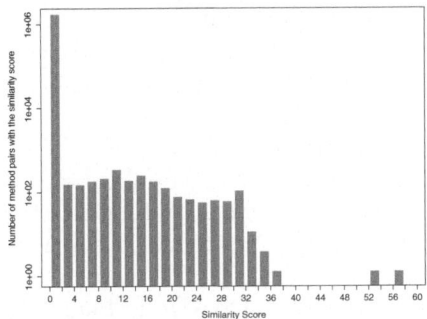

(a) Effect of *lossy* filter on application similarity scores.

(b) Distribution of similarity scores of method pairs excluded by the *lossy* filter in log-y scale.

Fig. 6. Examining *lossy* filter effectiveness

impact on similarity scores. Therefore, the *lossy* filter does not cause DNADroid to miss clone pairs it would otherwise have found.

Figure 6a explored the macro effects of the *lossy* filter, in Fig. 6b we examine its effect on individual method pairs. Figure 6b shows the histogram of the similarity scores of the method pairs excluded by the *lossy* filter on a *log-y* scale. As expected, more than 99.86% of these similarity scores are zero (The similarity score of A in B, $sim_{A(B)}$, is zero if the PDG A is not subgraph isomorphic to the PDG B). Only a few similarity scores exceed 40%, and no score exceeds 60%.

This experiment demonstrates that the *lossy* filter is highly accurate: it seldom excludes method pairs that are likely clones and it negligibly affects the similarity scores of application pairs.

7   Case Studies

"Benign" Cloning. DNADroid found 30 pairs that both have a 100% similarity score using our matching algorithm. For the few that we manually reviewed, we found that the applications were indeed identical, apart from having String values in the application translated. Since these strings are constants, changing them doesn't change the PDGs. There seems to be no incentive for the plagiarist apart from providing an application to an otherwise excluded audience. For the latter reason, we believe these pairs to be cases of "benign" cloning, since there appears to be no benefit to the plagiarist. However, without manual review, we cannot confirm that they are all "benign."

Changes to Advertising Libraries. A number of clone pairs involved applications that had changes to their advertising libraries. As stated in Sect. 5, DNADroid can discern application from library code in APKs. Using this and our coverage values, we can see when an application has most likely been cloned for monetary gain.

An example of such cloning is a download manager, XWind Downloader, which we have found on three different markets: the official Android Market [31], GoApk [10], and Freeware Lovers [8]. The versions available from the official Market and Freeware Lovers have the same SHA-1 hash and were both published by the same developer account name, which leads us to believe that the author has officially published his application in both markets. The GoApk version, however, has a different SHA-1 hash and is signed with a different developer key. The GoApk version has removed the Youmi [17] advertising library present in the application from two other markets and has replaced it with the WooBoo [16] advertising library. DNADroid found 99.9% of the official Android Market version within the GoApk version, an almost sure sign of cloning.

For the 141 applications that we believe to be the victims of cloning, we compared the libraries that DNADroid detected in the victim with those in the clone. We found that 91 (65%) of these pairs had different libraries, all of which included changes to advertising libraries. This number suggests that plagiarists are often fiscally motivated, attempting to siphon ad revenue from popular applications.

Malware Added to an Application. "HippoSMS" is a malicious application recently discovered by [33] that we downloaded and compared to our collection of applications.

We found that it shares the same package name as a Chinese video player we crawled from GoApk. Both applications require a surprising number of sensitive permissions; the video player requires 11 permissions while the malware requires 10. According to Stowaway [29], a tool for detecting over privileged applications, the seemingly benign video player requires 6 permissions that it doesn't use, whereas the malware only requires 1 extra. Given the number of permissions the video player requires, we conjecture that its developer may have intended to insert malware into the application at a later time, or that the video player is a clone itself. When compared with DNADroid we discovered that 98.57% of the video player code is in the malicious application, a near certain indicator of cloning.

Two Variants of the Same Malware. This case study consists of two malicious applications that are identified by VirusTotal [15] as being variants of the "BaseBridge" malware family. Both applications have been stripped of meaningful class and method names. However, this obfuscation did not fool DNADroid — DNADroid found coverages of 35% and 28% between the two variants. Manual review confirmed that the methods matched between the applications perform the malware functionality. This demonstrates the potential of DNADroid to aid markets in automatically detecting similar variants of the same malware, though significant transformations could subvert DNADroid's current implementation.

Use of Freeware Cracking Tool in the Wild. During our exploration of public work in Android application cloning we encountered the cracking tool AntiLVL [36]. AntiLVL attempts to automatically subvert several types of license protection mechanisms used in Android applications including the Android

License Verification Library (LVL), Amazon Appstore DRM and Verizon DRM. We found applications cracked by AntiLVL hosted on several markets.

AntiLVL has several primary mechanisms for subverting license protections. After decompiling an application with *baksmali* [30], AntiLVL attempts to subvert common license enforcement checks by rewriting them to always return successfully. AntiLVL also inserts a new file, *SmaliHook.class* in the applications it rewrites. This class contains methods to spoof the device ID, make fake license checks which always return true, and hide AntiLVL's modifications from the application itself by returning the original applications file size, MD5, and signatures for the original application. We also found that the cracked applications occasionally show evidence of AntiLVL use in their CERT.SF, a signature file included in applications that lists the digital signatures of every file in the application.

We found 189 applications containing SmaliHook.class and 235 containing references to AntiLVL in their signature files for a total of 310 unique applications. Given the nature of AntiLVL, it's almost certain that these applications are clones of paid applications. Interestingly, even though only 8% of our total applications were acquired from Chinese markets, 88% of the applications including AntiLVL traces were from Chinese markets. Only four applications containing AntiLVL were obtained from the official Android market, despite it being the source of 65% of our applications. Two of the four applications were different versions of the same application which Google has since removed. Of the remaining two applications on the Android market, both are live and have "50,000 to 100,000" installs as of March 2012.

8   Discussion

False Positive. Since it is a serious allegation to claim an application is a clone, we design DNADroid to have a very low false positive rate. We manually verified that *all* the application pairs that DNADroid identified as clones are indeed similar, with either similar start-up screens or similar user interactions (Sect. 6.3).

False Negative. DNADroid may overlook cloned applications due to a few reasons. First, DNADroid uses Solr to select candidate cloned applications based on their attributes, such as name and description (Sect. 5.1). This is based on the observation that cloned applications often have similar attributes as the original so that they appear together in market search results. Therefore, if the plagiarist crafts the attributes of her application to avoid being identified as having similar attributes to the original application (e.g., by using a different language), it can avoid detection by DNADroid. However, by attempting to evade initial similarity detection, a plagiarist may jeopardize the chances of her clone being installed. This is not a fundamental limitation, as DNADroid would still find a high code similarity between the two if compared. If a better tool to identify similar applications becomes available, DNADroid could easily leverage it.

Another source of false negatives is program obfuscation. By using PDG-based clone detection, DNADroid can resist common program transformations (Sect. 3). However, there exist advanced program transformations that can evade PDG-based clone detection. This is a fundamental limitation of DNADroid. Even though these advanced transformations are feasible, they require much more effort by the plagiarist (ultimately, the plagiarist can reimplement the application, which is not cloning in the strict sense).

Comparison to Other Approaches. We ran Androguard [19] against the same 191 pairs that DNADroid identified as clones. Androguard performed well in some cases, but crashed on 24 pairs and found very low coverage values for 10 pairs, causing it to miss 18% of the pairs DNADroid found. We intended to compare DNADroid to DEXCD [27] and DroidMOSS [41] but DEXCD had problems running on the pairs DNADroid identified and DroidMOSS is not currently publicly available. We hope to compare results in the future.

Performance. There exist more efficient algorithms for detecting code clones, however, these algorithms trade robustness for speed. Robust techniques, such as those utilized by DNADroid are more expensive but result in fewer false positives and false negatives. Fortunately, we can take advantage of inexpensive meta information clustering and the inherent parallelism in clone detection to make DNADroid practical.

9 Conclusion

The explosive growth of Android devices over the past few years has led to a booming mobile application community. Unfortunately, with increased incentives and low barriers to entry, plagiarists and clones have followed. To combat cloning, markets need robust techniques to identify these clones, as application clones harm the market ecosystem. We present DNADroid, a tool for finding clones on a large scale. DNADroid selects likely clone candidates based on their attributes and then robustly compares their code for significant overlap. We evaluated DNADroid on applications crawled from thirteen Android markets. DNADroid identified at least 141 applications that have been cloned and an additional 310 applications that were cracked with AntiLVL, an open source Android cracking tool. We describe five case studies which provide insight into different motivations for plagiarists. DNADroid has a very low false positive rate — we have confirmed that all the applications detected by DNADroid are indeed clones via visual or behavioral verification. Our findings indicate that DNADroid is an effective tool to aid in the fight against mobile application cloning.

Acknowledgments. The authors would like to thank Ben Sanders and Justin Horton for helping us obtain Android applications and our anonymous reviewers for their input. This paper is partially based upon work supported by the National Science Foundation (NSF) under Grant No. 0644450 and 1018964. Any opinions, findings, and conclusions or recommendations expressed in this material are those of the author and do not necessarily reflect the views of the National Science Foundation.

References

1. Amazon appstore (May 2012), http://www.amazon.com/mobile-apps/
2. Android soft 4 u market (May 2012), http://www.androidsoft4u.com/
3. Androidonline market (May 2012), http://www.androidonline.net/
4. Apache hadoop (May 2012), http://hadoop.apache.org/
5. App china market (May 2012), http://www.appchina.com/
6. Brother soft market (May 2012), http://www.brothersoft.com/
7. Eoemarket (May 2012), http://www.eoemarket.com/
8. Freeware lovers market (May 2012), http://freewarelovers.com
9. Gartner says sales of mobile devices grew 5.6 percent in third quarter of 2011; smartphone sales increased 42 percent (May 2012), http://www.gartner.com/it/page.jsp?id=1848514
10. Goapk market (May 2012), http://market.goapk.com
11. Handango market (May 2012), http://www.handango.com/
12. M360 market (May 2012), http://app.m.360.cn/
13. One mobile market (May 2012), http://www.1mobile.com/
14. Slideme: Android community and application marketplace (May 2012), http://slideme.org/
15. Virustotal (May 2012), http://virustotal.com
16. Wooboo advertising library (May 2012), http://www.wooboo.com.cn/
17. Youmi advertising library (May 2012), http://www.youmi.net
18. Aiken, A.: Moss (measure of software similarity) plagiarism detection system (1998)
19. Androguard: Androguard: Manipulation and protection of android apps and more... (May 2012), http://code.google.com/p/androguard/
20. Apache. Solr (May 2012), http://lucene.apache.org/solr/
21. AppBrain. Number of available android applications (May 2012), http://www.appbrain.com/stats/number-of-android-apps
22. BajaBob. Smalihook. java found on my hacked application (May 2012), http://stackoverflow.com/questions/5600143/android-game-keeps-getting-hacked
23. Beard, S.: Market shocker! iron soldiers xda beta published by alleged thief (May 2012), http://androidheadlines.com/2011/01/market-shocker-iron-soldiers-xda-beta-published-by-alleged-thief.html
24. Burns, M.: 850k daily android activations, 300m total devices, says andy rubin (May 2012), http://techcrunch.com/2012/02/27/850k-android-activations-daily-300m-total-devices-says-andy-rubin/
25. IBM T. J. Watson Research Center. Watson libraries for analysis (wala) (May 2012), http://wala.sourceforge.net/wiki/index.php/Main_Page
26. Cordella, L.P., Foggia, P., Sansone, C., Vento, M.: A (sub) graph isomorphism algorithm for matching large graphs. IEEE Transactions on Pattern Analysis and Machine Intelligence 26(10), 1367–1372 (2004)
27. Davis, I.: Dexcd (May 2012), http://www.swag.uwaterloo.ca/dexcd/index.html
28. Enck, W., Gilbert, P., Chun, B.G., Cox, L.P., Jung, J., McDaniel, P., Sheth, A.N.: Taintdroid: an information-flow tracking system for realtime privacy monitoring on smartphones. In: Proceedings of the 9th USENIX Conference on Operating Systems Design and Implementation, pp. 1–6. USENIX Association (2010)

29. Felt, A.P., Chin, E., Hanna, S., Song, D., Wagner, D.: Android permissions demystified. In: Proceedings of the 18th ACM Conference on Computer and Communications Security, pp. 627–638. ACM (2011)
30. Freke, J.: smali: An assembler/disassembler for android's dex format (May 2012), https://code.google.com/p/smali/
31. Google. Android market (May 2012), http://market.android.com
32. Jhi, Y.C., Wang, X., Jia, X., Zhu, S., Liu, P., Wu, D.: Value-based program characterization and its application to software plagiarism detection. In: Proceeding of the 33rd International Conference on Software Engineering, pp. 756–765. ACM (2011)
33. Jiang, X.: Security alert: New android malware – hipposms – found in alternative android markets (May 2012),
    http://www.cs.ncsu.edu/faculty/jiang/HippoSMS/
34. Liu, C., Chen, C., Han, J., Yu, P.S.: Gplag: detection of software plagiarism by program dependence graph analysis. In: Proceedings of the 12th ACM SIGKDD International Conference on Knowledge Discovery and Data Mining, pp. 872–881. ACM (2006)
35. Lockheimer, H.: Android and security (April 2012),
    http://googlemobile.blogspot.com/2012/02/android-and-security.html
36. lohan: Antilvl - android license verification library subversion (May 2012),
    http://androidcracking.blogspot.com/p/antilvl.html
37. Myles, G., Collberg, C.: Detecting software theft via whole program path birthmarks. In: Information Security, pp. 404–415 (2004)
38. Prechelt, L., Malpohl, G., Philippsen, M.: Finding plagiarisms among a set of programs with jplag. J. UCS 8(11), 1016 (2002)
39. pxb1988, dex2jar: A tool for converting android's .dex format to java's .class format (May 2012), https://code.google.com/p/dex2jar/
40. Schleimer, S., Wilkerson, D.S., Aiken, A.: Winnowing: local algorithms for document fingerprinting. In: Proceedings of the 2003 ACM SIGMOD International Conference on Management of Data, pp. 76–85. ACM (2003)
41. Zhou, W., Zhou, Y., Jiang, X., Ning, P.: Detecting repackaged smartphone applications in third-party android marketplaces. In: Proceedings of 2nd ACM Conference on Data and Application Security and Privacy, CODASPY 2012 (2012)

A   Screenshots

(a)   (b)

Fig. 7. Screenshots of pairs of cloned applications

Boosting the Permissiveness of Dynamic Information-Flow Tracking by Testing

Arnar Birgisson, Daniel Hedin, and Andrei Sabelfeld

Chalmers University of Technology, 412 96 Gothenburg, Sweden

Abstract. Tracking information flow in dynamic languages remains an open challenge. It might seem natural to address the challenge by runtime monitoring. However, there are well-known fundamental limits of dynamic flow-sensitive tracking of information flow, where paths *not* taken in a given execution contribute to information leaks. This paper shows how to overcome the permissiveness limit for dynamic analysis by a novel use of testing. We start with a program supervised by an information-flow monitor. The security of the execution is guaranteed by the monitor. Testing boosts the permissiveness of the monitor by discovering paths where the monitor raises security exceptions. Upon discovering a security error, the program is modified by injecting an annotation that prevents the same security exception on the next run of the program. The elegance of the approach is that it is sound no matter how much coverage is provided by the testing. Further, we show that when the mechanism has discovered the necessary annotations, then we have an accuracy guarantee: the results of monitoring a program are at least as accurate as flow-sensitive static analysis. We illustrate our approach for a simple imperative language with records and exceptions. Our experiments with the QuickCheck tool indicate that random testing accurately discovers annotations for a collection of scenarios with rich information flows.

1 Introduction

In a dynamically loaded *web mashup* that involves sensitive information from several parties, how do we prevent information leakage? A web mashup consolidates independent web services, potentially by mutually distrusting providers, into an integrated web service. For example, a web mashup to display the location of secret objects (say vehicles collecting cash from ATMs) might make use of a map service (such as Google Maps) for enhanced visualization. The map service code needs access to the secrets in order to display them. At the same time, the map service needs access to its servers to load new map components on demand. How do we ensure that the map service does not leak secrets back to its servers?

The state of the art in web mashup security [24] leaves the question open. A range of approaches from separation to full integration has been suggested, tailored to web mashup scenarios such as online ads, where access-control policies

S. Foresti, M. Yung, and F. Martinelli (Eds.): ESORICS 2012, LNCS 7459, pp. 55–72, 2012.

are sufficient. However, the problem of tracking information in mashups after access has been granted remains largely unsolved. Of particular challenge is handling the dynamic nature of programming languages like JavaScript that manipulate information in web mashups.

With the above scenario as our long-term motivation, the goal of this paper is a practical mechanism for tracking information flow in dynamic languages.

It might seem natural to address dynamic languages with dynamic analysis. Dynamic enforcement of secure information flow can be done similarly to dynamic type checking: values are decorated with labels representing the security of each value, and for each operation the labels are checked at runtime. The data labels may change over time, which means that the analysis is *flow-sensitive*.

Flow-sensitive enforcement is one where an assignment such as $x := e$ propagates the security level of the expression e to the variable x. On the other hand, a flow-insensitive system assigns security levels that do not change. Such a system disallows the assignment if the level of the expression is not at least as restrictive as the level of the variable. Flow-sensitivity allows an information-flow policy to be specified in terms of sources, where information enters the system, and sinks, where information exits the system, rather than on syntactic variables inside the program. This frees the programmer from explicitly managing security levels of local variables. Since variables can be reused for different purposes, flow-sensitivity also has the potential of accepting more programs that are secure.

However, there are well-known fundamental limits of dynamic flow-sensitive tracking of information flow [9,29,5,22]. Flow-sensitivity introduces a channel for leaking information though the labels themselves, which is possible to exploit even though labels may not be observable in the language.

Consider the program in Figure 1, assuming *secret* to hold 0 or 1 initially. The program copies *secret* into *public*. However, a purely dynamic monitor faces challenges to detect this flow. Indeed, when *secret* is 1, then *public* is never accessed after branching on *secret*. When *secret* is 0, then the assignment of 0 to *public* takes place inside of a conditional that branches on a variable *temp* that has not been touched since its initialization. In both cases, the problem is the branches that are *not* executed, which are missed by purely dynamic analysis. In general, it is not possible to have sound dynamic flow-sensitive information-flow enforcement that is strictly more permissive than flow-sensitive static analysis [22].

```
public = 1; temp = 0;
if (secret) temp = 1;
if (!temp) public = 0;
```

Fig. 1. Flow-sensitivity attack

This implies that a purely dynamic information-flow monitor must be either unsound (i.e., there are *false negatives*) or imprecise (i.e., there are *false positives* that are accepted by static analysis). In this design space, the *no-sensitive-upgrade* [32,2] discipline shows how to achieve soundness. This discipline states that the original label of a variable under assignment must be taken into account, and if it is not at least as restrictive as the level of the control-flow context, upgrading its level is disallowed. With this discipline, the program above is stopped if it reaches the assignment to *temp* because it attempts an upgrade in the *secret* control-flow context.

Hence, no-sensitive-upgrade provides soundness at the price of permissiveness. Of particular concern is that for programs like one in Figure 1, the permissiveness of monitoring is worse than that of static analysis. Indeed, flow-sensitive static analysis [12] is able to detect the flow in the program above, and ensure that both *temp* and *public* become secret after the conditional. On the other hand, secure programs with flow-sensitive manipulation of dynamic data structures are out of reach for static analysis, implying that many interesting programs are rejected due to the crude approximation by static analysis. This means that neither static nor dynamic analysis as is provide a satisfactory solution to the problem of false positives.

This paper shows how to achieve the best of the two worlds without resorting to full-scale static analysis. We overcome the permissiveness limit for dynamic analysis by a novel use of testing. We show that testing boosts the permissiveness of dynamic information-flow enforcement by discovering places in code for automatic injection of upgrade annotations. Upon discovering a security error, the program is modified by injecting an annotation that prevents the same security exception on the next run of the program. Further, we show that when the mechanism has discovered the necessary annotations, then we have an accuracy guarantee: the results of monitoring a program are at least as accurate as flow-sensitive static analysis. The process leads to a program that is never blocked by the monitor because sensitives upgrades have been "tested away". Importantly, eradicating sensitive upgrades is not at the price of unnecessarily pushing up security levels for data: we show that the levels are never pushed above what is demanded by the static approach. This allows us significant reduction of false positives while in total absence of false negatives.

The elegance of the approach is that it is sound no matter how much coverage is provided by the testing. In contrast to fuzzing or vulnerability and penetration testing, it is not the original program that is tested but its monitored counterpart. This guarantees security, thanks to the soundness of the monitor. As discussed above, we gain permissiveness in the sense that the monitor stops less programs and accuracy in the sense that the results of monitoring a program are at least as accurate as flow-sensitive static analysis.

We illustrate our approach for a simple imperative language with references and exceptions. Our experiments with the random testing tool QuickCheck [7] indicate that random testing accurately discovers annotations for a collection of scenarios with rich information flows. We are able to further enhance the permissiveness by *delayed upgrades*, which records the reference to be upgraded but does not perform the actual upgrade until just before entering sensitive context.

We envision that our method can be applied most productively during the software development and testing phase, when our approach can help discovering upgrade annotations before the code is shipped.

2   Background

The dynamic features of languages like JavaScript offer on their own a compelling argument for dynamic information-flow enforcement. In addition, independent of language features, functionality provided by the execution environment may pose challenges for static analyses. Consider, for instance, the API provided by the DOM [11] in combination with Google maps. When creating a new Google map we need to pass the part of the page where the map should be drawn. Typically, this is done by assigning an id to the element and fetching it with getElementById as illustrated below.

```
<script type="text/javascript" label="google">
  new google.maps.Map(document.getElementById("map_canvas"));
  ...
<div id="map_canvas" label="google"></div>
<form>
```

From an information-flow perspective we want to enforce that the Google code is only allowed send back the parts of the page labeled 'google'. This entails that the analysis must treat getElementById differently depending on which element is fetched (something which cannot be statically decided in general — in particular since the page may be dynamically changing). For a dynamic analysis this poses no problem, since the elements are tagged with their labels.

Speaking more generally, dynamic analysis has the ability to handle data with dynamic structure, e.g., heaps, with high precision. Consider the following example, where l_1 and l_2 are aliases.

$$l_1 = \text{new } \{\}; \ l_1.f = 1; \ l_2 = l_1; \ l_2.f = h;$$

A flow-sensitive static analysis must take the alias into account and update the type of both l_1, and l_2. In general aliasing is not decidable, and the program would be rejected by static analyses like Jif [19]. Dynamic analyses do not have this problem, since the label of f is stored with the value of f.

However, as shown in the introduction, dynamic enforcement of secure information flow has fundamental limits for flow-sensitivity under secret control. *Secret control* or *secret context* refers to the commands inside conditionals and loops with guards that contain secrets. Promising steps in the direction of overcoming these limits are *privatization operations* [3] or *upgrade* [10] commands that enable the upgrade of labels before entering secret contexts. This work makes use of upgrade commands for the security levels of values (upg), the structure of heap objects (upgs) and exceptions (upge), all explained below.

Values. Consider the following example, where the public variable l is assigned to under secret control. This causes the monitor to block on a sensitive upgrade.

```
        if (h) l = 1;
```

By inserting an upgrade that upgrades the label of l before the execution of the conditional we make sure that execution is not stopped.

```
        l = upg(l,secret); if (h) l = 1;
```

Structure. If structured data, like records, is changed under secret control the structure of the data may encode secrets. In general, the security labels associated with the different parts of structured data might not be enough to model the security level of the structure. The reason for this is that not only the presence of certain data may encode secrets but also the absence, and it's not necessarily the case that the security level of the absence of data can be read from the security level of the presence of other data. In such cases, if the absence is visible to the program, the security model of the structured data must be extended to model absence.

Using records as an example, consider for instance the following program, where the field f is added to o depending on the secret h.

```
o = new {}; if (h) o.f = 1;
```

Following the general explanation above, after execution, the presence or absence of f encodes the value of h. In the case h is true the field f will be present, and the fact that its presence is secret is recorded in the security label of the value of f. However, in the case h is false the field f will not be present and its absence encodes information about h. Since the absence of fields is visible via record projection, as is explained in Section 3, records are equipped with a structure label. The structure label of records can be understood as an upper bound of the context in which the record may have been modified, or in the terms of absent fields as the upper bound on the security level of the non-existence of the absent fields.

Returning to the example above, o has public structure, which causes the execution of the secret conditional of the example to be stopped — adding a field would require upgrade of the structure label under secret control. In order to allow for the addition, the structure of the record can be upgraded before the secret context.

```
o = new {}; upgs(o,secret); if (h) o.f = 1;
```

Exceptions. Exceptions pose a significant challenge for secure information flow due to the non-local transfer of control. In the example below the value of h is copied into l.

```
try { if (h) throw; l = 0; } catch { l = 1; }
```

The standard static solution to this is to type commands following a potential exception in a secret context as under secret control [20,18]. Since the majority of commands in languages like JavaScript can cause exceptions and due to the possibility of non-local transfer of control this can cause a significant amount of code to be typed under secret control. Following [10] we adopt a more permissive discipline and introduce a special exception label that tracks the level at which exceptions are allowed to be thrown. Initially, the exception label is public, which allows the body of the try above to execute in public context (in the case $h = 1$ the monitor will stop with a security violation). To allow for exceptions in secret contexts the language provides an upgrade, which can be inserted before the secret context as follows.

```
try { l = upg(l, secret); upge(secret);
      if (h) throw; l = 0; }
catch { l = 1; }
```

This upgrade causes the subsequent commands of the try, and of the handler to be considered to be a secret context. After the try, the exception label is once again lowered.

Manual upgrade annotations open the possibility of improving the permissiveness of the monitored program. However, they come at a price of placing the heavy annotation burden on the programmer. It forces the programmer to be aware of the monitor the programs will run under. As this is undesirable, and sometimes impossible (e.g., with legacy code), our goal is to fully relieve the programmer from the annotation burden. With the background set, we proceed to describe a method that applies testing for automatically discovering and injecting upgrade instructions to boost the permissiveness of the monitor.

3   Monitor and Rewriting

This section introduces the language — a simple JavaScript-inspired language with records and exceptions, its monitor semantics, which is essentially a distilled version of the monitor of [10], and establishes the soundness of the monitor.

3.1   Syntax and Semantics

Figure 2 shows the syntax of expressions and commands, as well as supporting structures. Values v consist of strings, numbers, a special value undefined, together with the pointers. Records are maps from values to values, and the heap μ is a partial map from pointers to records. A reference is a pair of a pointer and a value, referring to a particular field in a record.

Values stored in records, as well as the components of a reference, are decorated with a security label σ; the structure label of records is written after the semicolon inside the curly braces.

As is common [8,31] we assume that the labels form a predefined lattice, and do not consider the case where labels are not know a priori or where the structure of the lattice can be modified dynamically. Without loss of generality, we will use a simple two-level lattice described by public $\sqsubseteq$ secret, where $\sqsubseteq$ denotes the lattice order. Let $\sqcup$ and $\sqcap$ denote least upper bound, and greatest lower bound, and let $\perp$ and $\top$ denote public and secret labels.

Expressions consist of literals for the primitive values, variables, projections of records, and pure binary operators. Lefthand sides make up a subset of expressions that can be assigned to, and will evaluate to references. Righthand sides of assignments can be expressions or record allocations, optionally annotated with an explicit upgrade of the value or structure label.

The commands are standard, apart from the upge command, which upgrades the current exception label. Variables represent string-keyed fields in a distinguished record $\mu(0)$. This record, referred to as the *global record*, is in line with how variables are handled in JavaScript and simplifies the semantics.

Expressions	$e ::= n \mid \text{'s'} \mid x \mid e[e] \mid \texttt{undefined} \mid e * e$
Pointers	$p \in \mathbb{N}_0$
Values	$v, w ::= n \mid \text{'s'} \mid \texttt{undefined} \mid p$
References	$\rho ::= (p^\sigma, v^\sigma)$
Lefthand sides	$l ::= x \mid l[e]$
Righthand sides	$r ::= e \mid \texttt{new } \{\} \mid \text{upg}(r, \sigma) \mid \text{upgs}(r, \sigma)$
Records	$o ::= \{v \mapsto v^\sigma, \ldots, v \mapsto v^\sigma ; \sigma\}$
Heap	$\mu \; : \; \text{Pointers} \hookrightarrow \text{Records}$
Commands	$c ::= \texttt{skip} \mid l := r \mid c; c \mid \text{upge}(\sigma)$
	$\mid \; \texttt{if } e \texttt{ then } c \texttt{ else } c \mid \texttt{while } e \texttt{ do } c \mid \texttt{try } c \texttt{ catch } c \mid \texttt{throw}$

Fig. 2. Notation and syntax

Evaluation and dereferencing is detailed in Figure 3. We write $[\![\cdot]\!]_\mu$ for the evaluation of expressions and lefthand sides in a heap μ. This evaluation returns either a labeled value or a reference and is free of side-effects. Dereferencing a reference further resolves it to a value by looking it up in the heap. The dereferenced value has a label that takes into account also the security labels of the expressions used to build the reference itself. This ensures that values that are reached via secret pointers have a secret label. Dereferencing is written $(\cdot)^*_\mu$, and for convenience we define it for values as identity and write $[\![e]\!]^*_\mu$ instead of $([\![e]\!]_\mu)^*_\mu$.

Dereferencing a non-existing field succeeds with the $\texttt{undefined}$ value. This means that the existence of fields can be probed by record projection.

Note that evaluation and dereferencing are not total functions. In particular, the expression $e_1[e_2]$ is not valid if $[\![e_1]\!]^*$ is not a pointer value. In our formalization such cases cause the evaluation to get stuck, while in practice they might result in throwing reference exceptions.

Let E denote *environments*, consisting of pairs of a heap and an exception label. We define the semantics of the language and the monitor as a big step relation $\rightarrow$. An initial configuration $\langle c \mid pc, E \rangle$ consists of a command c, a security label pc, and an environment E. The label pc represents the level of the current control context, and is updated by conditional branches and iteration.

The relation $\rightarrow$ relates an initial configuration to an execution result, if one exists. A terminating execution of a command c in an environment E may result in one of the following: (i) In the case of successful termination, the term Ok E', where E' is the resulting environment. (ii) In the case of an uncaught exception, the term Throw E', where E' is then environment in which the exception was thrown. (iii) A security stop $\text{Stop}(t, \sigma)$, where t is either a reference to a field (p, w), the term $\text{struct}(p)$ representing the structure label of a record, or exception representing the runtime exception level.

A stop indicates that the program has reached a point, where the corresponding entity requires at least the security level σ for the monitor to be sound. For instance, attempting to write to a public field under secret control results in a $\text{Stop}((p, w), \top)$, where (p, w) identifies the field, and $\top$ signifies that the field must be at least $\top$ for the write to be accepted. Similarly, attempting to add a field to a record with public structure under secret control results in $\text{Stop}(\text{struct}(p), \top)$, where p identifies the record that must be have secret structure for the addition to

$$[\![n]\!]_\mu = n^\perp \qquad [\![s]\!]_\mu = s^\perp \qquad [\![\texttt{undefined}]\!]_\mu = \texttt{undefined}^\perp \qquad [\![x]\!]_\mu = (0^\perp, x,^\perp)$$

$$[\![e_1 * e_2]\!] = (v_1 * v_2)^{\sigma_1 \sqcup \sigma_2} \quad \text{where } v_1^{\sigma_1} = [\![e_1]\!]^* \text{ and } v_2^{\sigma_2} = [\![e_2]\!]^*$$

$$[\![e_1[e_2]]\!]_\mu = (p^{\sigma_1}, v^{\sigma_2}) \quad \text{where } p^{\sigma_1} = [\![e_1]\!]_\mu^*, \text{ and } v^{\sigma_2} = [\![e_2]\!]_\mu^*$$

$$(v^\sigma)_\mu^* = v^\sigma \qquad (p^{\sigma_p}, w^{\sigma_w})_\mu^* = \begin{cases} v^{\sigma_p \sqcup \sigma_w \sqcup \sigma_v} & \text{if } \mu(p) = \{\dots, w \mapsto v^{\sigma_v}, \dots; \sigma_s\} \\ \texttt{undefined}^{\sigma_p \sqcup \sigma_w \sqcup \sigma_s} & \text{otherwise and } \mu(p) = \{\dots; \sigma_s\} \end{cases}$$

Fig. 3. Evaluation and dereferencing

be accepted. Finally, attempting to throw an exception under secret control with a public exception level results is Stop(exception, $\top$), indicating that the exception level must be $\top$ for the exception to be accepted. From such a stop and its corresponding execution tree, we determine a location in the source program where an explicit upgrade command needs to be inserted to avoid that particular stop. This process is described in Section 4.

Unlike expressions, the evaluation of righthand sides can have side-effects, and we use the same relation notation $\rightarrow$ as for commands for the evaluation of righthand sides. Evaluation of a configuration $\langle r \mid pc, E \rangle$ can result in a labeled value and an updated environment $\mathsf{Ok}(v^\sigma, E')$, or a security stop $\mathsf{Stop}(t, \sigma)$, which carries the same meaning as above. Evaluation of a righthand side can never throw an exception.

For space reasons, the full set of inference rules defining the semantics can be found in the full version of this paper [4]. To give the reader an insight into the monitor, we exemplify with the rule for successful execution of the internal #put operator, which handles record updates.

$$\text{PUT} \frac{\begin{array}{c} [\![l]\!]_\mu = (p^{\sigma_p}, w^{\sigma_w}) \qquad \mu(p) = \{\dots, w \mapsto v_0^{\sigma_0}, \dots; \sigma_s\} \\ (pc \sqcup \epsilon \sqcup \sigma_p) \sqcap \sigma_w \sqsubseteq \sigma_s \qquad pc \sqcup \epsilon \sqcup \sigma_p \sqcup \sigma_w \sqsubseteq \sigma_0 \\ o' = \mu(p)[w \mapsto v^{\sigma_v \sqcup pc \sqcup \epsilon \sqcup \sigma_p \sqcup \sigma_w}; \sigma_s \sqcup \sigma_w] \end{array}}{\langle \#\mathtt{put}(l, v^{\sigma_v}) \mid pc, \mu, \epsilon \rangle \rightarrow \mathsf{Ok}(\mu[p \mapsto o'], \epsilon)}$$

$\#\mathtt{put}(l, v)$ is an internal command that performs the writing part of assignments, writing a value v to a field represented by the lefthand side l. The evaluation is split into three cases: one succeeding and two stopping. To allow the update we require that σ_0, the previous label of the value, is above the control context, as well as above the combined labels of the reference from l. In addition, since writing with a secret key can affect the structure, the key's security label σ_w must be added to the structure label of the record. For this reason we demand that if σ_w is secret then either $pc \sqcup \epsilon \sqcup \sigma_p$ is public, or the structure label of the record σ_s is secret. These conditions ensure that the label of the value is independent of secrets. When they are satisfied, the record is updated with the new labeled value, its label raised to include the control context and the reference labels. The cases where the conditions are not satisfied correspond to the two stopping cases: one demanding the upgrade of the value of the field, and one demanding the upgrade of the structure label.

3.2 Soundness

As is common [31], we use *termination-insensitive noninterference* (TINI) as our semantic security condition. TINI offers the possibility of liberal enforcement well suited for dynamic monitors, while only allowing low-bandwidth leaks. Like other typical semantic security conditions TINI is undecidable.

Noninterference can be stated as the preservation of a family of low-equivalence relations under execution. For languages with heaps, the family is indexed over a *bijection* on low-reachable pointers ensuring that the low-reachable parts of low-equivalent heaps are isomorphic. Low-equivalence guarantees that low-reachable public values are equal — for the secret parts no demands are made. In addition it guarantees that the labeling is independent of secrets. For space reasons, the low-equivalence relation $\sim$ can be found in the full version of this paper [4].

TINI states that successful execution in low-equivalent environments results in low-equivalent environments. Let $\mathcal{C}$ denote any non-Stop configuration.

Theorem 1 (TINI). *For any program c, β, and two heaps μ_1 and μ_2 such that $\mu_1 \sim_\beta \mu_2$, we have that if $\langle c \mid \perp, \mu_i, \perp \rangle \to \mathcal{C}_i$ for $i = 1, 2$ then there is a β' such that $\mathcal{C}_1 \sim_{\beta'} \mathcal{C}_2$.*

This means that the resulting (low-reachable) public parts of the heap are independent of secrets; whatever choice of secret values in the initial heaps, the produced results are equal in their public values. The proof of this and further theorems are contained in the full version of the paper [4].

4 Rewriting

To improve the permissiveness of the dynamic monitor, executions resulting in stops (found by, e.g., testing) are used to patch the program with explicit upgrades to prevent the stop from occurring again.

A heap is called *initial* if it contains no records other than the global record, itself containing only primitive (non-pointer) values. Let μ_0 range over initial heaps. Given a derivation tree of an execution $\langle c \mid \perp, \mu_0, \perp \rangle \to \mathsf{Stop}(t, \sigma)$, the different cases for t dictate how the program needs to be rewritten in order to prevent that particular stop.

case $t = (p, w)$**:** This stop indicates that the program attempted to assign to the field w of the record at heap location (with pointer) p, which would have resulted in upgrading its existing security level in secret context, or over a secret reference. In order to make this run succeed, the field must be explicitly upgraded.

In the case that $p = 0$, i.e., the upgrade refers to a variable in the program. The execution tree is used to see where the program entered the secret context in order to insert an upgrade command just before that point. In this case w is a string value with the name of the variable, which is converted to an identifier x and the command $x := \mathsf{upg}(x, \sigma)$ is inserted before the secret context.

```
if (h) l = 1;  ⟿  l = upg(l,secret); if (h) l = 1;
```

If $p \neq 0$ however, the reference is to a field in a record other than the global record, and may be built from a lefthand side containing arbitrary expressions. Building an upgrade command that refers to the same field at a different place in the program requires complex tracking of heap mutations. Instead of inserting an upgrade command before an enclosing conditional, the execution tree is used to find an assignment to the field in a public context and over public pointers. Such an assignment exists, because the record is not in the initial heap, and the stop indicates that the field of the record must already exist with a public label. This implies that the field was added in a public context over a public pointer. The assignment is converted to an upgrade, by wrapping its righthand side with upg and the label σ. This ensures that the field is labeled as secret from that point in the program.

```
o = new {}; o.f = 0; if (h) o.f = 1;  ↷
            o = new {}; o.f = upg(0, secret); if (h) o.f = 1;
```

case $t = \mathsf{struct}(p)$**:** This stop indicates that an upgrade of a record's structure label was needed in secret context, or over a secret pointer. Similar to the second case above, the structure of the record must be upgraded in a public context over a public pointer. The execution tree is used to find the last assignment satisfying these properties where p was the value of the assignment's righthand side, and wrap that righthand side with upgs and the appropriate label. Such an assignment must always exist, as the only record existing in the initial heap is the global record which always has secret structure. Hence p must point to an allocated record, and it must have been allocated in a public context—otherwise the structure of the record would already be public.

```
o = new {}; if (h) o[h] = 1;  ↷  o = upgs(new {}); if (h) o[h] = 1;
```

case $t = \mathsf{exception}$**:** This stop is generated when the program attempts to throw an exception in a context where the exception label ϵ is not above the pc. To make this execution succeed, the exception label must be upgraded whether the secret branch is entered or not. The execution tree is used to determine the syntactic if or while command in which we enter secret control, and the program is patched by inserting an $\mathsf{upge}(\sigma)$ before this command.

```
        if (h) throw;  ↷  upge(secret); if (h) throw;
```

In what follows, we will refer to one step of the above process as a rewriting relation on programs. If $\langle c \mid \bot, \mu, \bot \rangle \rightarrow \mathsf{Stop}(t, \sigma)$, then we say $c \curvearrowright_\mu c'$ where the program c' is obtained by applying the above rules on the proof of the stopped execution. If $\langle c \mid \bot, \mu, \bot \rangle \rightarrow \mathcal{C}$ let $c \curvearrowright_\mu c$.

The process above describes how to rewrite the program to make one failing run succeed. Of course, there may be other failing runs so this process is iterated. Let $\mathcal{S}$ be a set of initial heaps and let $\curvearrowright_\mathcal{S}$ be a relation on programs such that $c \curvearrowright_\mathcal{S} c'$ iff there exists a heap $\mu \in \mathcal{S}$ such that $c \curvearrowright_\mu c'$ and $c \neq c'$.

Theorem 2 (Termination). *For any set $\mathcal{S}$ of initial heaps, any sequence*

$$c_0 \curvearrowright_\mathcal{S} c_1 \curvearrowright_\mathcal{S} c_2 \curvearrowright_\mathcal{S} \cdots$$

terminates, i.e., there is an n such that $c_n \curvearrowright_\mu c_n$ for all $\mu \in \mathcal{S}$.

The theorem is straightforward, considering that the number of possible upgrade commands, as well as the number of locations they may be inserted are bounded given the rewriting procedure above in a finite lattice of security levels.

For a given set S of initial heaps rewriting will produce a program that the monitor will not stop when run in any of the heaps in S. A program is *non-stopping* if the monitor does not stop execution for any initial environment. Under the assumption that all values, including strings, have finite domains (which is the case in all practical settings, due to hardware limitations) rewriting can be used to find non-stopping programs.

Theorem 3. *Let $\mathcal{T}$ be the set of all initial heaps. The result of rewriting based on $\mathcal{T}$ is non-stopping, i.e., for $c \rightsquigarrow_{\mathcal{T}}^{*} c'$, it holds that c' is non-stopping.*

5 Accuracy

Consider the security labeling of the execution environment under execution. We say that a labeling is more accurate than another if is at least as permissive, and it is not more secret. In this section we establish that upgrade injection does not result in a security labeling that is less accurate than that of a standard flow-sensitive static type system; the contrary, however, is possible.

To show accuracy we adapt a standard flow-sensitive information-flow type system [18,19] to the language in Figure 2 and establish its soundness. For space reasons the development of the type system and its soundness can be found in the full version of this paper [4].

The type language consists of two different types: *primitive* types, and *record* types. Primitive types are security labels or security labeled record type *names*. The use of names to make recursive record types inductive is common practice, and their meaning in terms of record types is given by a map ρ from record type names C to record types. Finally, record types are maps from values to primitive types. Let $\Gamma, \Delta ::= (C, \epsilon)$ denote environment types and exception environment types respectively, where C is the type of the global record, and ϵ is the exception level.

The type judgments for commands are of the form $pc, \Gamma_1 \vdash_\Delta c \Rightarrow \Gamma_2$. The judgment is read: the command c is well-typed in security context pc, environment type Γ_1 and exception environment type Δ yielding environment type Γ_2. The intuition is that if c is run in environments that correspond to Γ_1 the result will correspond to either Γ_2 or Δ depending on whether the execution was successful or resulted in an exception.

With this we can formulate the accuracy result: rewriting executions of well-typed programs results in well-typed programs w.r.t. the same entry and exit environment types.

Theorem 4 (Accuracy). *For any program c_1 and initial heap μ such that $\bot, C, \bot \vdash_\Delta c_1 \Rightarrow \Gamma$ and $\delta \vdash \mu : C, \bot$ we have that if $c_1 \rightsquigarrow_\mu c_2$ then $\bot, C, \bot \vdash_\Delta c_2 \Rightarrow \Gamma$.*

The result implies that the rewriting process produces programs that will be at least as accurate as a standard static type system. In many cases the upgrade injection together with dynamic monitoring will be more accurate. This is due to the possibility of flow-sensitive heap entities, the presence of dead code, or the possibility of value dependent labels as an example in the next section will show.

6   Implementation

We have implemented the monitor from Section 3 in Haskell. The implementation uses QuickCheck [7] to generate random initial heaps and perform the iterative process of finding stopping executions and automatically injecting upgrade commands into the input program.

When the monitor encounters the situation that an upgrade is needed but the control-flow context, the exception label or the reference used does not allow it, it stops the execution and conveys this information back to the test runner. The test runner uses this, together with an execution trace collected during the run, to determine a syntactic location in the original program where an upgrade command is inserted.

QuickCheck uses *generators* to perform random testing of Haskell code, by generating test cases and checking if user-supplied *properties* hold for it. Our implementation allows for descriptions of generators of initial heaps, where both existence, value and labeling of initial variables can be randomized. The monitor is then tested against the property that running a given program does not result in a security stop. When QuickCheck finds a stopping case, the test harness rewrites the program and restarts the testing process.

Our experiments have shown that performing this iterative process yields a rewritten program where enough upgrades have been inserted so that no initial heap results in a stopped execution. Below we present some of the more illustrative experiments which run using an initial heap description that labels h as secret boolean (i.e., a number with values 0 or 1) and l as public.

Experiment 1: Consider the example of Section 1; the implementation discovers the stopped runs where t and l are upgraded in secret context, and inserts the needed upgrades immediately before each conditional. The resulting program is shown in Figure 4, where the two upgrades have been inserted where secret context may be entered.

```
l = 1; t = 0;
t = upg(t,secret);
if (h)  t = 1;
l = upg(l,secret);
if (!t) l = 0;
```

Fig. 4. Consistent labeling

Experiment 2: As described in previous sections, the existence of a field may encode secret information. For this reason the monitor tracks the security level of the structure of a record. Thus the program o = new {}; if (h) o[0] = 1; is stopped by the monitor, and the rewriter turns this stop into the program shown in Figure 5. Adding the upgs makes adding a field in secret context safe, since any later projections of non-existing fields will be labeled as secrets.

Experiment 3: When writing to a field, it is not sufficient to consider only the control context to determine if its value or the structure of the containing record. The choice of field and record, which is written to, may depend on se-

```
o = upgs(new {}, secret);
if (h) o[0] = 1;
```

Fig. 5. Secret structure

cret information in the lefthand side used to refer to it. This is reflected in the security labels of the reference built from the lefthand side, and is taken into account when updating the record. Consider the following program.

```
o = new {}; o[0] = 0; o[1] = 0; o[h] = 1;
```

First a new record is allocated and initialized to contain two zero-valued fields with keys 0 and 1 resp. Thereafter, one of the fields is modified depending on the secret value h. The assignment would label the modified field as secret, but this would constitute an upgrade which itself depends on the value of h. Thus, the implementation stops the assignment. Since h is a secret number with values 0 or 1 both fields (but not the structure) will be upgraded, resulting in the following program.

```
o = new {}; o[0] = upg(0, secret); o[1] = upg(0, secret); o[h] = 1;
```

Experiment 4: The rewriter is also able to inject upgrades of the exception label. Recall the program from Section 2, which attempts to leak h through the use of exceptions. The implementation detects this and inserts an upgrade of the exception label before entering secret context. This alone is not enough to make the program run, since this upgrade now makes the assignments to l be under secret control (recall that

```
try {
    l = upg(1, secret);
    upge(secret);
    if (h) throw;
    l = 0;
} catch { l = 1; }
```

Fig. 6. Throw under secret control

the exception label is considered part of the control context). Thus, another iteration of rewriting is required to upgrade the variable l itself as well. The result is shown in Figure 6.

Experiment 5: When a variable needs to be upgraded, the upgrade is inserted at the closest point in the program, where the context is strictly lower than the target level. For lattices with more than two levels there is a risk that this upgrade will trigger another stop, since the label of the value of the variable may be lower than the label of the context at this point. This is intentional; instead of moving the upgrade up, the stop is allowed to trigger another rewrite in the next iteration. This results in a stepwise upgrade of the variable with the possibility of a more accurate labeling.

Consider the left program of Figure 7, in which the variables pub, cls and sec have corresponding security labels from a lattice with public $\sqsubseteq$ classifed $\sqsubseteq$ secret. Here, the last assignment requires x to be upgraded to secret. If this is done at the assignment x = 0, then the runs where cls is true will unnecessarily force cls to be upgraded as well. However, x cannot be directly upgraded from public to secret in the else branch, because that upgrade would be under classified

```
x = 0;                              x = 0;
if (cls) {                          x = upg(x, classified);
    if (x) cls = x;                 if (cls) {
} else {                                if (x) cls = x;
    if (sec) x = sec;               } else {
}                                       x = upg(x, secret);
                                        if (sec) x = sec;
                                    }
```

Fig. 7. Cascading upgrades

control. This in turn creates an upgrade of x to classified before entering the outer if-command. The resulting program is shown on the right in Figure 7.

It is worth noting that this example improves on the precision of a static type system. As seen from an observer at the classified level, it is a safely visible decision which branch is taken in the outer conditional, but that decision depends on the value. Standard type-systems for information flow are not value-sensitive, and infers that x needs to be secret because of the potential assignment in the else-branch. In a dynamic setting however, there is no need to upgrade x further than to classified if that branch is not taken.

Delayed upgrades. Upgrading a record field at the point of its last public assignment may be premature. For example, consider the following program.

```
o = new {}; o[0] = 1; x = o[0]; if (h) o[0] = 42;
```

Labeling o[0] with secret right in the public assignment to it will unnecessarily cause the variable x to have a secret value as well. It is therefore too early to upgrade o[0] before entering the secret control context. Instead, the upgrade should be inserted before the conditional. However, note that o[0] may be any lefthand side, involving arbitrary expressions, and it may not even be the same one in both assignments. To build a syntactic lefthand side that refers to the same field as o[0] at a different program point is not possible in general.

Instead, the implementation uses a technique that avoids premature upgrading via *delayed upgrades*. We insert the upgrade command in the last public assignment, including a program label which refers to the conditional command where it should actually be upgraded. The se-

```
o = new {};
o[0] = upg(1, secret, L1);
x = o[0]; // still public
L1: if (h) o[0] = 42;
```

Fig. 8. Delayed upgrade

mantics of such a delayed upgrade command resolves the righthand side to a reference and stores it along with the label L1 in a list of pending upgrades. An actual upgrade of the reference is only performed just before, and if, a command with that label is reached. If the labeled command appears in a conditional block itself, the field in question is not even upgraded at all if that command is never reached. We note that the stepwise upgrading seen in Figure 7 extends to non-variables also when delayed upgrades are enabled.

7   Related Work

A large body of work targets language-based methods for information-flow security [25]. We discuss dynamic methods for information-flow enforcement, which are most closely related to the focus of this paper. For a general survey of dynamic information-flow techniques, we refer to Le Guernic's thesis [15].

Fenton [9] discusses purely dynamic monitoring for information flow but does not prove noninterference. Volpano [30] considers a purely dynamic monitor to prevent explicit (but not implicit) flows. Languages like Perl and PHP support *taint mode* to dynamically track explicit flows.

Shroff et al. [27] discuss a purely dynamic monitor that in addition to tracking explicit flows, provides limited support to discovering implicit flows. The monitor is based on recording dependencies discovered at runtime and propagating them to subsequent runs of the code. While this method does not guarantee noninterference, it fits a scenario of tracking common flows in a trusted application.

In a flow-insensitive setting, Sabelfeld and Russo [26] show that a monitor similar to Fenton's enforces termination-insensitive noninterference without losing in precision to classical static information-flow checkers. This line of work has progressed further to extend the monitor to a language with dynamic code evaluation, communication, and declassification [1], as well as timeout instructions [21]. Further, Russo et al. [23] investigate the impact of dynamic tree structures like the DOM on information flow. Their monitor prevents attacks based on navigating and deleting DOM tree nodes. The monitor derives the security level of presence for each node from the context of its creation. It keeps invariants such as the presence level of a parent may not exceed the presence level of a child.

As discussed earlier, Austin and Flanagan [2,3] suggest a purely dynamic monitor for information flow with a limited form of flow sensitivity. They discuss two disciplines: *no sensitive-upgrade*, where the execution gets stuck on an attempt to assign to a public variable in secret context, and *permissive-upgrade*, where on an attempt to assign to a public variable in secret context, the public variable is marked as one that cannot be branched on later in the execution. Austin and Flanagan [3] discuss inserting *privatization operations*, which are akin to our upgrade commands. The insertion takes place when a variable that was previously upgraded in secret context is about to be branched upon.

Stefan et al. [28] present a library for dynamic information-flow control in Haskell using a notion of *floating labels*, related to the concept of program counter, to restrain the side effects of computations. Even though they do not allow labels of references (c.f. variables) to change, their primitives allow for the manipulation of labels that causes related problems. Their solution to this is to demand the programmer to annotate the program, which is comparable to the use of upgrades. Magazinius et al. [16] show how to inline a no-sensitive upgrade monitor into programs in a language with dynamic code evaluation.

Russo and Sabelfeld [22] show that purely dynamic flow-sensitive monitors do not subsume the permissiveness of flow-sensitive security type systems. They also provide a framework for hybrid monitors that allows expressing a range of hybrid monitors as one by Le Guernic et al. [14].

Hedin and Sabelfeld [10] propose dynamic information-flow control for a core of JavaScript that includes objects, higher-order functions, exceptions, and dynamic code evaluation. They discuss the usefulness of upgrade annotations but do not provide methods to generate them. Our paper shows how to relieve the programmer from the burden of upgrade annotations, making dynamic information-flow control more practical.

Chugh et al. [6] present a hybrid approach to handling dynamic execution. Their work is staged where a dynamic residual is statically computed in the first stage, and checked at runtime in the second stage.

Masri et al. [17] develop a method for detecting and debugging information flows for restricted Java bytecode (no exceptions, multithreading, or exit statements). The method is a form of dynamic program slicing that allows detecting explicit flows. They also show that static analysis and a preprocessing transformation can be used to include implicit flows into consideration.

Kang et al. [13] consider taint analysis for implicit flows in trusted code. They enhance a purely dynamic analysis to propagate selected information about control-flow dependencies, hitting a middle ground between ignoring implicit flows and propagating taint along all control dependencies indiscriminately.

Compared to the previous work, a key novelty of this paper is the usage of testing (rather than static analysis) to boost the permissiveness of dynamic enforcement.

8   Conclusion

While dynamic information-flow enforcement might seem to be a natural fit for tackling languages with dynamic data structures, there are fundamental limits of permissiveness of purely dynamic techniques. This paper demonstrates how to overcome these limits by testing. We show that testing boosts the permissiveness of dynamic information-flow enforcement by discovering places in code for automatic injection of upgrade annotations. The inference of upgrade annotations ensures that the dynamic analysis is more permissive than the static counterpart, without losing soundness. Our experiments with the QuickCheck tool suggest that we achieve the permissiveness of hybrid monitors without static analysis on a collection of scenarios with rich information flows.

Future work includes extending the formalization with functions (which we have already implemented in our prototype). The upgrade injection mechanism allows setting the upgrades before functions are called, which enables smooth integration with third-party libraries. Based on the prototype reported in Section 6 and our approach to tackling the core JavaScript features [10], we pursue the implementation of information-flow monitor enhanced with upgrade instruction injection for the full JavaScript language.

Acknowledgments. This work was funded by the European Community under the ProSecuToR and WebSand projects and the Swedish research agencies SSF and VR. Arnar Birgisson is a recipient of the Google Europe Fellowship in Computer Security, and this research was supported in part by this Google Fellowship.

References

1. Askarov, A., Sabelfeld, A.: Tight enforcement of information-release policies for dynamic languages. In: Proc. IEEE Computer Security Foundations Symposium (July 2009)
2. Austin, T.H., Flanagan, C.: Efficient purely-dynamic information flow analysis. In: Proc. ACM Workshop on Programming Languages and Analysis for Security (PLAS) (June 2009)
3. Austin, T.H., Flanagan, C.: Permissive dynamic information flow analysis. In: Proc. ACM Workshop on Programming Languages and Analysis for Security (PLAS) (June 2010)
4. Birgisson, A., Hedin, D., Sabelfeld, A.: Boosting the permissiveness of dynamic information-flow tracking by testing (June 2012) (full version),
   http://www.hvergi.net/arnar/publications/pdf/testing-full.pdf
5. Cavallaro, L., Saxena, P., Sekar, R.: On the Limits of Information Flow Techniques for Malware Analysis and Containment. In: Zamboni, D. (ed.) DIMVA 2008. LNCS, vol. 5137, pp. 143–163. Springer, Heidelberg (2008)
6. Chugh, R., Meister, J.A., Jhala, R., Lerner, S.: Staged information flow for JavaScript. In: Proc. ACM SIGPLAN Conference on Programming Language Design and Implementation (2009)
7. Claessen, K., Hughes, J.: Quickcheck: a lightweight tool for random testing of haskell programs. In: Proc. ACM International Conference on Functional Programming, pp. 268–279 (2000)
8. Denning, D.E., Denning, P.J.: Certification of programs for secure information flow. Comm. of the ACM 20(7), 504–513 (1977)
9. Fenton, J.S.: Memoryless subsystems. Computing J. 17(2), 143–147 (1974)
10. Hedin, D., Sabelfeld, A.: Information-flow security for a core of JavaScript. In: Proc. IEEE Computer Security Foundations Symposium (June 2012)
11. Hors, A.L., Hegaret, P.L.: Document Object Model Level 3 Core Specification. Tech. rep., The World Wide Web Consortium (2004)
12. Hunt, S., Sands, D.: On flow-sensitive security types. In: Proc. ACM Symp. on Principles of Programming Languages, pp. 79–90 (2006)
13. Kang, M.G., McCamant, S., Poosankam, P., Song, D.: DTA++: Dynamic taint analysis with targeted control-flow propagation. In: Proc. Network and Distributed System Security Symposium (February 2011)
14. Le Guernic, G., Banerjee, A., Jensen, T., Schmidt, D.: Automata-Based Confidentiality Monitoring. In: Okada, M., Satoh, I. (eds.) ASIAN 2006. LNCS, vol. 4435, pp. 75–89. Springer, Heidelberg (2008)
15. Le Guernic, G.: Confidentiality Enforcement Using Dynamic Information Flow Analyses. Ph.D. thesis, Kansas State University (2007)
16. Magazinius, J., Russo, A., Sabelfeld, A.: On-the-fly Inlining of Dynamic Security Monitors. In: Rannenberg, K., Varadharajan, V., Weber, C. (eds.) SEC 2010. IFIP AICT, vol. 330, pp. 173–186. Springer, Heidelberg (2010)

17. Masri, W., Podgurski, A., Leon, D.: Detecting and debugging insecure information flows. In: Proc. of the 15th International Symposium on Software Reliability Engineering (ISSRE), pp. 198–209 (2004)
18. Myers, A.C.: JFlow: Practical mostly-static information flow control. In: Proc. ACM Symp. on Principles of Programming Languages, pp. 228–241 (January 1999)
19. Myers, A.C., Zheng, L., Zdancewic, S., Chong, S., Nystrom, N.: Jif: Java information flow (July 2001), http://www.cs.cornell.edu/jif
20. Pottier, F., Simonet, V.: Information flow inference for ML. ACM TOPLAS 25(1), 117–158 (2003)
21. Russo, A., Sabelfeld, A.: Securing timeout instructions in web applications. In: Proc. IEEE Computer Security Foundations Symposium (July 2009)
22. Russo, A., Sabelfeld, A.: Dynamic vs. static flow-sensitive security analysis. In: Proc. IEEE Computer Security Foundations Symposium (July 2010)
23. Russo, A., Sabelfeld, A., Chudnov, A.: Tracking Information Flow in Dynamic Tree Structures. In: Backes, M., Ning, P. (eds.) ESORICS 2009. LNCS, vol. 5789, pp. 86–103. Springer, Heidelberg (2009)
24. De Ryck, P., Decat, M., Desmet, L., Piessens, F., Joosen, W.: Security of Web Mashups: A Survey. In: Aura, T., Järvinen, K., Nyberg, K. (eds.) NordSec 2010. LNCS, vol. 7127, pp. 223–238. Springer, Heidelberg (2012)
25. Sabelfeld, A., Myers, A.C.: Language-based information-flow security. IEEE J. Selected Areas in Communications 21(1), 5–19 (2003)
26. Sabelfeld, A., Russo, A.: From Dynamic to Static and Back: Riding the Roller Coaster of Information-Flow Control Research. In: Pnueli, A., Virbitskaite, I., Voronkov, A. (eds.) PSI 2009. LNCS, vol. 5947, pp. 352–365. Springer, Heidelberg (2010)
27. Shroff, P., Smith, S., Thober, M.: Dynamic dependency monitoring to secure information flow. In: Proc. IEEE Computer Security Foundations Symposium, pp. 203–217 (July 2007)
28. Stefan, D., Russo, A., Mitchell, J., Mazières, D.: Flexible dynamic information flow control in haskell. In: Proceedings of the 4th ACM Symposium on Haskell, pp. 95–106. ACM (2011)
29. Vogt, P., Nentwich, F., Jovanovic, N., Kirda, E., Kruegel, C., Vigna, G.: Cross-site scripting prevention with dynamic data tainting and static analysis. In: Proc. Network and Distributed System Security Symposium (February 2007)
30. Volpano, D.: Safety Versus Secrecy. In: Cortesi, A., Filé, G. (eds.) SAS 1999. LNCS, vol. 1694, pp. 303–311. Springer, Heidelberg (1999)
31. Volpano, D., Smith, G., Irvine, C.: A sound type system for secure flow analysis. J. Computer Security 4(3), 167–187 (1996)
32. Zdancewic, S.: Programming Languages for Information Security. Ph.D. thesis, Cornell University (July 2002)

Effective Symbolic Protocol Analysis via Equational Irreducibility Conditions*

Serdar Erbatur[1], Santiago Escobar[2], Deepak Kapur[3], Zhiqiang Liu[4],
Christopher Lynch[4], Catherine Meadows[5], José Meseguer[6],
Paliath Narendran[1], Sonia Santiago[2], and Ralf Sasse[6]

[1] University at Albany-SUNY, Albany, NY, USA
{se,dran}@cs.albany.edu
[2] DSIC-ELP, Universitat Politècnica de València, Spain
{sescobar,ssantiago}@dsic.upv.es
[3] University of New Mexico, Albuquerque, NM, USA
kapur@cs.unm.edu
[4] Clarkson University, Potsdam, NY, USA
{liuzh,clynch}@clarkson.edu
[5] Naval Research Laboratory, Washington DC, USA
meadows@itd.nrl.navy.mil
[6] University of Illinois at Urbana-Champaign, USA
{meseguer,rsasse}@illinois.edu

Abstract. We address a problem that arises in cryptographic protocol analysis when the equational properties of the cryptosystem are taken into account: in many situations it is necessary to guarantee that certain terms generated during a state exploration are in *normal form* with respect to the equational theory. We give a tool-independent methodology for state exploration, based on unification and narrowing, that generates states that obey these irreducibility constraints, called *contextual symbolic reachability analysis*, prove its soundness and completeness, and describe its implementation in the Maude-NPA protocol analysis tool. Contextual symbolic reachability analysis also introduces a new type of unification mechanism, which we call *asymmetric unification*, in which any solution must leave the right side of the solution irreducible. We also present experiments showing the effectiveness of our methodology.

1 Introduction

There has been an increasing amount of research in recent years in building tools for cryptographic protocol analysis where the equational properties of the

* S. Escobar and S. Santiago have been partially supported by the EU (FEDER) and the Spanish MEC/MICINN under grant TIN 2010-21062-C02-02, and by Generalitat Valenciana PROMETEO2011/052. The following authors have been partially supported by NSF: S. Escobar, J. Meseguer and R. Sasse under grants CCF 09-05584, CNS 09-04749, and CNS 09-05584; D. Kapur under grant CNS 09-05222; C. Lynch, Z. Liu, and C. Meadows under grant CNS 09-05378, and P. Narendran and S. Erbatur under grant CNS 09-05286.

S. Foresti, M. Yung, and F. Martinelli (Eds.): ESORICS 2012, LNCS 7459, pp. 73–90, 2012.
© Springer-Verlag Berlin Heidelberg 2012

cryptosystems are taken into account. This allows one to retain the advantages of a Dolev-Yao style [14] analyzer, such as ease of reasoning about concurrency and ability to construct counterexamples, while allowing for greater expressiveness.

With the above in mind, a number of approaches have been explored in the literature for analyzing protocols when equational theories are involved. These include equational unification techniques for unification-based tools such as Maude-NPA [17], equational constraint solving techniques for constraint based tools, e.g. [12,11], and equational deducibility procedures for checking whether one term is deducible from a given set of terms, e.g. [2,5,9,13].

In many cases, equational reasoning is integrated with syntactic reasoning. There are a number of reasons for doing this, which we describe in more detail in Section 1.1, but one reason is that optimizations that are done to eliminate redundant or nonsensical states may need to be done via syntactic checking, as in Maude-NPA. We illustrate the issues that can arise with the following protocol, which we will use as a running example. It uses an exclusive-or operator $\oplus$, which is associative and commutative (AC) and self-canceling with identity 0, and a function pk, where $pk(A, X)$ stands for encryption of message X with $A's$ (standing for Alice's) public key; below, B stands for Bob.

Example 1. Upon receiving the final message, Alice verifies that she received $X \oplus N_A$ for some X received in the first message $pk(A, X)$. The protocol is seen differently by Bob and Alice, as shown in the second and third columns.

Alice and Bob	Bob	Alice
1. $B \to A : pk(A, N_B)$	1. $B \to A : pk(A, N_B)$	1. $B \to A : pk(A, X)$
2. $A \to B : pk(B, N_A)$	2. $A \to B : pk(B, Z)$	2. $A \to B : pk(B, N_A)$
3. $B \to A : N_A \oplus N_B$	3. $B \to A : Z \oplus N_B$	3. $B \to A : N_A \oplus X$

We find an instance of the protocol from Alice's perspective by applying the substitution $X \mapsto N_A \oplus Y$ to achieve the left-hand column of Example 2. Maude-NPA could identify this instance as infeasible and discard it, since Alice cannot receive a message $N_A \oplus Y$ before she generates the nonce N_A.

Example 2. But further instantiating Y (perhaps as a result of further unifications elsewhere) to $N_A \oplus N_B$ causes problems.

Alice after $X \mapsto N_A \oplus Y$	Alice after $Y \mapsto N_A \oplus N_B$.
1. $B \to A : pk(A, N_A \oplus Y)$	1. $B \to A : pk(A, N_A \oplus N_A \oplus N_B) = pk(A, N_B)$
2. $A \to B : pk(B, N_A)$	2. $A \to B : pk(B, N_A)$
3. $B \to A : N_A \oplus N_A \oplus Y$	3. $B \to A : N_A \oplus N_A \oplus N_A \oplus N_B = N_A \oplus N_B$

This makes $N_A \oplus Y$ reduce to N_B and $N_A \oplus N_A \oplus Y$ reduce to $N_A \oplus N_B$, giving the right-hand side of Example 2: the intended legal execution of the protocol! Thus, Maude-NPA's syntactic check inadvertently could have ruled out a legal execution.

We avoid this problem as follows. We first decompose the $\oplus$ theory into (R, E), where E is the AC theory and R is a set of rewrite rules for the properties $\{X \oplus 0 = X, X \oplus X = 0\}$. We then divide the possible instantiations of $\{pk(A, X), N_A \oplus X\}$ into two cases, each of which are constrained to remain irreducible under substitution. One is $\{pk(A, X), N_A \oplus X\}$, and the other is $\{pk(A, Y \oplus N_A), Y\}$ obtained by the substitution $X \mapsto Y \oplus N_A$. Every other reduced instantiation of $N_A \oplus X$ is an instance of either one or the other modulo AC. The case obtained by $X \mapsto Y \oplus N_A$ can now be safely deleted, because due to the irreducibility constraint that Y cannot contain N_A and 0, the N_A will never vanish from $N_A \oplus Y$ under any substitution.

This strategy works for several reasons. One is that Maude-NPA syntactic checks require that irreducibility constraints only be put on received messages. Another, and more important, is that the exclusive-or theory has the *finite variant property* [10] modulo AC. Thus, for every term s there is a finite set $s_1', \ldots, s_k'$ of reduced instances of s such that any other reduced instance of s is equal modulo AC to a substitution instance of one of the s_i'. These two features mean that it is possible to integrate syntactic checks that are invariant under AC together with unification-based reachability modulo a richer theory, allowing us to improve efficiency without sacrificing soundness and completeness. Indeed, this is vital for Maude-NPA and other tools, because almost all of the checks used for optimization require the received messages to be in normal form.

Another capability that is needed for our strategy to work opens up a new area of research, namely, developing a sound and complete, tool-independent symbolic state exploration algorithm that preserves irreducibility constraints. In Maude-NPA state exploration is implemented via equational unification of sent messages with received messages, which means that the equational unification algorithm used should preserve the irreducibility of the received messages. Indeed, it was experimentation with a unification algorithm that did *not* have this property, the algorithm of [24], that produced the example we described above. Variant narrowing unification (the algorithm currently used by Maude-NPA) has the properties that we need, but our search of the literature has produced no other examples. This has led us to define a class of unification algorithms known as *asymmetric unification algorithms* modulo a theory (R, E), which produce a most general set of unifiers which leave the right hand side irreducible. We are working on techniques for converting standard equational unification algorithms into asymmetric algorithms, and have produced an asymmetric version of the exclusive-or algorithm in [24].

We are not the only ones to use an approach that integrates syntactic and equational reasoning: this has also been done by other researchers for other reasons, as we describe in Section 1.1. However, most work in this area has concentrated on specific applications of this approach, and not on how to implement the approach itself. This paper is devoted to providing a general procedure for doing this, called *contextual symbolic reachability analysis* modulo a theory (R, E), where R is a set of rewrite rules. This employs a technique called *contextual unification* in which some subterms of the two terms being unified are constrained to be irreducible. In Maude-NPA these are input terms, which, since they are unified with output terms, create the opportunity for exploiting asymmetric unification. However, this is not the only way contextual symbolic reachability analysis could be implemented. For example, we could follow the

approach of OFMC [4] which requires that both input and output terms are irreducible. Thus, our tool-independent framework should have many applications
beyond Maude-NPA, allowing for experimentation with different techniques.

The rest of the paper is organized as follows. In Section 2 we give some preliminary definitions used in rewriting and unification. In Section 3 we give a general
procedure for symbolic reachability via narrowing. In Section 4 we introduce
contextual symbolic reachability analysis, prove its soundness and completeness,
and illustrate its use in Maude-NPA. In Section 5, we show experiments illustrating the benefits, in Maude-NPA, of using contextual symbolic reachability
and asymmetric unification to integrate reachability analysis modulo exclusive-
or with optimizations based on syntactic checks. In Section 6 we discuss some
future directions.

1.1 Related Work

Although our specific approach has not, to the best of our knowledge, been exploited in cryptographic protocol analysis tools outside of Maude-NPA, there
are a number of similar cases. For example, ProVerif [6] (detail in [8, Sec. 5])
and OFMC [4] (detail in [29, Sec. 10]) both compute the variants of intruder
and/or protocol rules, modulo the free theory for ProVerif, and modulo the
free theory or AC for OFMC. This has the effect of computing the variants of
both sides of the unification problem. More recently, variants have been applied
to expanding the capacity of ProVerif to deal with AC theories. Thus, in [23],
Küsters and Truderung implement a special case of the exclusive-or theory in the
ProVerif tool by expressing it as a rewrite theory with the finite variant property
with respect to the free theory ($E = \emptyset$) and computing variants that are unified syntactically. This requires some restrictions on the syntax of the protocol,
however. Similar approaches have been applied by Küsters and Truderung for
modular exponentiation [22], and Arapinis et al. [3] for commuting encryption
and AC theories.

The main differences between this work and what we propose here are twofold.
First of all, unlike [8,23,22,3] we do not restrict ourselves to the case in which
E is the free theory ($E = \emptyset$), but allow it to be AC, or, potentially, any other
theory for which finitary unification algorithms exist. Secondly, unlike ProVerif,
OFMC, and [23,22,3] we do not necessarily require that irreducible variants be
computed for both sides of a unification problem, but we allow for example the
possibility that variants are computed for only one side, allowing for potentially
more efficient special-purpose asymmetric unification algorithms.

2 Preliminaries

We follow the classical notation and terminology from [32] for term rewriting, and
from [27] for rewriting logic and order-sorted notions. We assume an order-sorted
signature $\Sigma = (S, \leq, \Sigma)$ with poset of sorts $(S, \leq)$. We also assume an S-sorted
family $\mathcal{X} = \{\mathcal{X}_s\}_{s \in S}$ of disjoint variable sets with each $\mathcal{X}_s$ countably infinite.

$\mathcal{T}_\Sigma(\mathcal{X})_s$ is the set of terms of sort s, and $\mathcal{T}_{\Sigma,s}$ is the set of ground terms of sort s. We write $\mathcal{T}_\Sigma(\mathcal{X})$ and $\mathcal{T}_\Sigma$ for the corresponding order-sorted term algebras. For a term t, $Var(t)$ denotes the set of variables in t.

A *substitution* $\sigma \in \mathcal{S}ubst(\Sigma, \mathcal{X})$ is a sorted mapping from a finite subset of $\mathcal{X}$ to $\mathcal{T}_\Sigma(\mathcal{X})$. Substitutions are written as $\sigma = \{X_1 \mapsto t_1, \ldots, X_n \mapsto t_n\}$ where the domain of σ is $Dom(\sigma) = \{X_1, \ldots, X_n\}$ and the set of variables introduced by terms $t_1, \ldots, t_n$ is written $Ran(\sigma)$. The identity substitution is *id*. Substitutions are homomorphically extended to $\mathcal{T}_\Sigma(\mathcal{X})$. The application of a substitution σ to a term t is denoted by $t\sigma$ or $\sigma(t)$.

A Σ-*equation* is an unoriented pair $t = t'$, where $t, t' \in \mathcal{T}_\Sigma(\mathcal{X})_s$ for some sort $s \in S$. An *equational theory* (Σ, E) is a pair with Σ an order-sorted signature and E a set of Σ-equations.

An E-*unifier* for a Σ-equation $t = t'$ is a substitution σ such that $t\sigma =_E t'\sigma$. For $Var(t) \cup Var(t') \subseteq W$, a set of substitutions $CSU_E^W(t = t')$ is said to be a *complete* set of unifiers for the equality $t = t'$ modulo E away from W iff: (i) each $\sigma \in CSU_E^W(t = t')$ is an E-unifier of $t = t'$; (ii) for any E-unifier ρ of $t = t'$ there is a $\sigma \in CSU_E^W(t = t')$ such that $\sigma|_W \sqsupseteq_E \rho|_W$ (i.e., there is a substitution η such that $(\sigma\eta)|_W =_E \rho|_W$); and (iii) for all $\sigma \in CSU_E^W(t = t')$, $Dom(\sigma) \subseteq (Var(t) \cup Var(t'))$ and $Ran(\sigma) \cap W = \emptyset$.

A *rewrite rule* is an oriented pair $l \to r$, where $l \notin \mathcal{X}$ and $l, r \in \mathcal{T}_\Sigma(\mathcal{X})_s$ for some sort $s \in S$. An *(unconditional) order-sorted rewrite theory* is a triple (Σ, E, R) with Σ an order-sorted signature, E a set of Σ-equations, and R a set of rewrite rules. The rewriting relation on $\mathcal{T}_\Sigma(\mathcal{X})$, written $t \to_R t'$ or $t \to_{p,R} t'$ holds between t and t' iff there exist $p \in Pos_\Sigma(t)$, $l \to r \in R$ and a substitution σ, such that $t|_p = l\sigma$, and $t' = t[r\sigma]_p$. The relation $\to_{R/E}$ on $\mathcal{T}_\Sigma(\mathcal{X})$ is $=_E; \to_R; =_E$. The transitive (resp. transitive and reflexive) closure of $\to_{R/E}$ is denoted $\to_{R/E}^+$ (resp. $\to_{R/E}^*$). A term t is called $\to_{R/E}$-irreducible (or just R/E-irreducible) if there is no term t' such that $t \to_{R/E} t'$. For $\to_{R/E}$ confluent and terminating, the irreducible version of a term t is denoted by $t\downarrow_{R/E}$.

A relation $\to_{R,E}$ on $\mathcal{T}_\Sigma(\mathcal{X})$ is defined as: $t \to_{p,R,E} t'$ (or just $t \to_{R,E} t'$) iff there is a non-variable position $p \in Pos_\Sigma(t)$, a rule $l \to r$ in R, and a substitution σ such that $t|_p =_E l\sigma$ and $t' = t[r\sigma]_p$. $\to_{R/E}$-reducibility is undecidable in general since E-congruence classes can be arbitrarily large. Therefore, R/E-rewriting is usually implemented [21] by R, E-rewriting under some conditions on R and E such as confluence, termination, and coherence (see [21]). We call (Σ, E, R) a *decomposition* of an order-sorted equational theory (Σ, G) if $G = R \uplus E$ and R and E satisfy the conditions for $\to_{R,E}$ to implement $\to_{R/E}$.

Given a decomposition (Σ, E, R) of an equational theory, (t', θ) is an R, E-*variant* [19] (or just a variant) of term t if $t\theta\downarrow_{R,E} =_E t'$ and $\theta\downarrow_{R,E} =_E \theta$. A *complete set of R, E-variants* [19] (up to renaming) of a term t is a subset, denoted by $[\![t]\!]_{R,E}$, of the set of all R, E-variants of t such that, for each R, E-variant (t', σ) of t, there is an R, E-variant $(t'', \theta) \in [\![t]\!]_{R,E}$ such that $(t'', \theta) \sqsupseteq_{R,E} (t', \sigma)$, i.e., there is a substitution ρ such that $t' =_E t''\rho$ and $\sigma|_{Var(t)} =_E (\theta\rho)|_{Var(t)}$. A decomposition (Σ, E, R) has the *finite variant property* [19] (also called a *finite* *variant decomposition*) iff for each Σ-term t, a complete set $[\![t]\!]_{R,E}$ of its most general variants is finite.

3   Symbolic Reachability Analysis by Narrowing

In this section we recall basic facts about narrowing modulo equations of [28] using topmost rewriting as a tool-independent semantic framework for symbolic reachability analysis of protocols under algebraic properties. We first define reachability goals.

Definition 1 (Reachability goal). *Given an order-sorted rewrite theory* (Σ, G, T), *a reachability goal is defined as a pair* $t \xrightarrow{?}{}^*_{T/G} t'$, *where* $t, t' \in \mathcal{T}_{\Sigma}(\mathcal{X})_\mathsf{s}$. *It is abbreviated as* $t \xrightarrow{?}{}^* t'$ *when the theory is clear from the context;* t *is the* source *of the goal and* t' *is the* target. *A substitution* σ *is a* T/G-*solution of the reachability goal (or just a solution for short) iff there is a sequence* $\sigma(t) \to_{T/G} \sigma(u_1) \to_{T/G} \cdots \to_{T/G} \sigma(u_{k-1}) \to_{T/G} \sigma(t')$.

A set Γ *of substitutions is said to be a* complete set of solutions *of* $t \xrightarrow{?}{}^*_{T/G} t'$ *iff (i) every substitution* $\sigma \in \Gamma$ *is a solution of* $t \xrightarrow{?}{}^*_{T/G} t'$, *and (ii) for any solution* ρ *of* $t \xrightarrow{?}{}^*_{T/G} t'$, *there is a substitution* $\sigma \in \Gamma$ *more general than* ρ *modulo* G, *i.e.,* $\sigma|_{Var(t) \cup Var(t')} \sqsupseteq_G \rho|_{Var(t) \cup Var(t')}$.

If in a goal $t \xrightarrow{?}{}^*_{T/G} t'$, terms t and t' are ground, then goal solving becomes a standard rewriting reachability problem. However, since we allow terms t, t' with variables, we need a mechanism more general than standard rewriting to find solutions of reachability goals. *Narrowing* generalizes rewriting by performing *unification* at non-variable positions instead of the usual matching. Specifically, narrowing instantiates the variables in a term by a G-unifier that enables a rewrite modulo G with a given rule and a term position.

Definition 2 (Narrowing modulo G). *Given an order-sorted rewrite theory* (Σ, G, T), *the narrowing relation on* $\mathcal{T}_{\Sigma}(\mathcal{X})$ *modulo* G *is defined as* $t \overset{\sigma}{\leadsto}_{T,G} t'$ *(or* $\overset{\sigma}{\leadsto}$ *if* T, G *is understood) iff there is* $p \in Pos_{\Sigma}(t)$, *a rule* $l \to r$ *in* T *such that* $Var(t) \cap (Var(l) \cup Var(r)) = \emptyset$, *and* $\sigma \in CSU_G^V(t|_p = l)$ *for a set* V *of variables containing* $Var(t)$, $Var(l)$, *and* $Var(r)$, *such that* $t' = \sigma(t[r]_p)$.

The reflexive and transitive closure of narrowing is defined as $t \overset{\sigma}{\leadsto}^*_{T,G} t'$ *iff either* $t = t'$ *and* $\sigma = id$, *or there are terms* $u_1, \ldots, u_n$, $n \geq 1$, *and substitutions* $\sigma_1, \ldots, \sigma_{n+1}$ *s.t.* $t \overset{\sigma_1}{\leadsto}_{T,G} u_1 \overset{\sigma_2}{\leadsto}_{T,G} u_2 \cdots u_n \overset{\sigma_{n+1}}{\leadsto}_{T,G} t'$ *and* $\sigma = \sigma_1 \cdots \sigma_{n+1}$.

Soundness and completeness of narrowing for solving reachability goals is proved in [21,28] for order-sorted *topmost* rewrite theories, i.e., rewrite theories were all the rewrite steps happened at the top of terms.

3.1   Search in Maude-NPA

In this section we give a high-level summary of the general narrowing-based approach implemented in Maude-NPA. For further information, please see [15,17]. Note that our treatment of symbolic reachability analysis modulo equations by narrowing is completely general and *tool-independent*. We only use Maude-NPA for illustration purposes to give examples, and also because it supports the irreducibility conditions discussed in this paper. Multiset rewrite rules, used as a model for protocol analysis [30,7], is another example of topmost rewrite theories where reachability properties are checked.

Given a protocol $\mathcal{P}$, states are modeled as elements of an initial algebra $T_{\Sigma_\mathcal{P}/E_\mathcal{P}}$, where $\Sigma_\mathcal{P}$ is the signature defining the sorts and function symbols (for the cryptographic functions and for all the state constructor symbols) and $E_\mathcal{P}$ is a set of equations specifying the *algebraic properties* of the cryptographic functions and the state constructors. Therefore, a state is an $E_\mathcal{P}$-equivalence class $[t] \in T_{\Sigma_\mathcal{P}/E_\mathcal{P}}$ with t a ground $\Sigma_\mathcal{P}$-term. However, we explore *symbolic state patterns* $[t(x_1, \ldots, x_n)] \in T_{\Sigma_\mathcal{P}/E_\mathcal{P}}(X)$ on the free $(\Sigma_\mathcal{P}, E_\mathcal{P})$-algebra over a set of sorted variables X.

In Maude-NPA [15,17], a *state pattern* in a protocol execution is a term t of sort State, $t \in T_{\Sigma_\mathcal{P}/E_\mathcal{P}}(X)_{\mathsf{State}}$, which is a term of the form $\{S_1 \& \cdots \& S_n \& \{IK\}\}$ where $\&$ is an associative-commutative union operator with identity symbol $\emptyset$. Each element in the set is either a *strand* S_i or the *intruder knowledge* $\{IK\}$ at that state.

The *intruder knowledge* $\{IK\}$ also belongs to the state and is represented as a set of facts. There are two kinds of intruder facts: positive knowledge facts (the intruder knows m, i.e., $m \in \mathcal{I}$), and negative knowledge facts (the intruder *does not yet know* m but *will know it in a future state*, i.e., $m \notin \mathcal{I}$), where m is a message expression.

A *strand* [20] represents the sequence of messages sent and received by a principal executing the protocol and is represented as a sequence of messages $[msg_1^-, msg_2^+, msg_3^-, \ldots, msg_{k-1}^-, msg_k^+]$ such that msg_i is a term of sort Msg, msg^- (also written $-msg$) represents an *input* message, and msg^+ (also written $+msg$) represents an *output* message. Strands are used to represent both the actions of honest principals (with a strand specified for each protocol role) and the actions of an intruder (with a strand specified for each intruder action). In Maude-NPA, strands evolve over time; the symbol | is used to divide past and future. Also, we keep track of all the variables of sort Fresh generated by a concrete strand. That is, all the variables $r_1, \ldots, r_j$ of sort Fresh generated by a strand are made explicit right before the strand, as follows: $:: r_1, \ldots, r_j :: [\, m_1^\pm, \ldots, m_i^\pm \mid m_{i+1}^\pm, \ldots, m_k^\pm \,]$ where $msg_1^\pm, \ldots, msg_i^\pm$ are the past messages, and $msg_{i+1}^\pm, \ldots, msg_k^\pm$ are the future messages ($msg_{i+1}^\pm$ is the immediate future message). The nils are present so that the bar may be placed at the beginning or end of the strand if necessary, but we often remove them, except when there is nothing else between the vertical bar and the beginning or end of a strand. A strand $:: r_1, \ldots, r_j :: [msg_1^\pm, \ldots, msg_k^\pm]$ is a shorthand for $:: r_1, \ldots, r_j :: [nil \mid msg_1^\pm, \ldots, msg_k^\pm, nil]$.

Example 3. For the protocol of Example 1, the strand specification of the protocol is as follows:

(Bob)   :: r_1 :: [$+(pk(A, n(B, r_1)))$, $-(pk(B, Y))$, $+(Y \oplus n(B, r_1))$]
(Alice) :: r_2 :: [$-(pk(A, X))$, $+(pk(B, n(A, r_2)))$, $-(n(A, r_2) \oplus X)$]

Intruder strands are also included for each function. For example, application of exclusive-or by the intruder is described by the strand $[(X)^-, (Y)^-, (X \oplus Y)^+]$.

The protocol analysis methodology of Maude-NPA is then based on the idea of *backward reachability analysis*, where we begin with one or more state patterns corresponding to *attack states*, and want to prove or disprove that they are *unreachable* from the set of initial protocol states. In order to perform such a reachability analysis we must describe how states change as a consequence of principals performing protocol steps and of the intruder actions. This can be done by describing such state changes by means of a set $T_{\mathcal{P}}$ of *rewrite rules*, so that the rewrite theory $(\Sigma_{\mathcal{P}}, G_{\mathcal{P}}, T_{\mathcal{P}})$ characterizes the behavior of protocol $\mathcal{P}$ modulo the equations $G_{\mathcal{P}}$.

The following rewrite rules describe the general state transitions, where each state transition implies moving the vertical bar of one strand:

$$\{SS \;\&\; [L \mid M^-, L'] \;\&\; \{M{\in}\mathcal{I}, IK\}\} \rightarrow \{SS \;\&\; [L, M^- \mid L'] \;\&\; \{IK\}\} \qquad (1)$$

$$\{SS \;\&\; [L \mid M^+, L'] \;\&\; \{IK\}\} \rightarrow \{SS \;\&\; [L, M^+ \mid L'] \;\&\; \{IK\}\} \qquad (2)$$

$$\{SS \;\&\; [L \mid M^+, L'] \;\&\; \{M{\notin}\mathcal{I}, IK\}\} \rightarrow \{SS \;\&\; [L, M^+ \mid L'] \;\&\; \{M{\in}\mathcal{I}, IK\}\} \qquad (3)$$

where variables L, L' denote lists of input and output messages of the form m^+ or m^- within a strand, IK denotes a set of intruder facts ($m{\in}\mathcal{I}, m{\notin}\mathcal{I}$), and SS denotes a set of strands. In a *forward execution* of the protocol strands, Rule (1) synchronizes an input message with a message already learned by the intruder, Rule (2) accepts output messages but the intruder's knowledge is not increased, and Rule (3) accepts output messages and the intruder's knowledge is positively increased. For an unbounded number of sessions, we have extra rewrite rules (one for each positive message in a protocol or intruder strand) that dynamically introduce additional strands into a state.

The way to analyze *backwards* reachability is then relatively easy, namely, to run the protocol "in reverse." This can be achieved by using the set of rules $T_{\mathcal{P}}^{-1}$, where $v \longrightarrow u$ is in $T_{\mathcal{P}}^{-1}$ iff $u \longrightarrow v$ is in $T_{\mathcal{P}}$.

Example 4. The protocol of Example 1 can be modeled as a rewrite theory (Σ, G, T) where T is the reversed version of the generic rewrite rules (1)–(3) plus the rewrite rules for introducing new strands. The final pattern used as an input to the backwards symbolic reachability analysis could, for example, be as follows:

{ :: r_2 :: [$nil, -(pk(A, X)), +(pk(B, n(A, r_2))), -(X \oplus n(A, r_2)) \mid nil$] &
  :: r_1 :: [$nil, +(pk(A, n(B, r_1))), -(pk(B, Y)), +(Y \oplus n(B, r_1)) \mid nil$] & SS & $\{IK\}$}

This pattern does not require the intruder to have learnt anything, so it is very general and could lead to a regular execution and to an attack. Indeed, this protocol has the following attack reachable from that final pattern, where the intruder starts a protocol session with B but uses B's nonce to start a protocol session with A, so finally the intruder is able to learn both B's nonce and A's nonce:

1. $B \rightarrow I : pk(i, N_B)$
2. $I \rightarrow A : pk(a, N_B)$
3. $A \rightarrow B : pk(B, N_A)$
4. $B \rightarrow A, I : N_A \oplus N_B$

4 Contextual Symbolic Reachability Analysis

As we have explained in the Introduction, the symbolic reachability approach presented in the previous section does not really work in practice, since the particular way that a representative is chosen for each equivalence class may be crucial for the correct behavior, and in many cases the termination of a tool crucially depends on state space reduction techniques based on checking such representatives, as we illustrated for the case of nonces that *cannot* have been generated yet at a given point. Therefore, we now present a general, tool-independent framework for symbolic reachability analysis which refines narrowing modulo equations by imposing *irreducibility conditions* on representatives of equivalence classes. First, we give a way of imposing these irreducibility conditions on a rewrite theory, expressed by the notion of *contextual rewrite theory*.[1]

Definition 3 (Contextual Rewrite Theory). *A* contextual rewrite theory *is a tuple* (Σ, E, R, T, ϕ) *where* $(\Sigma, E \cup R, T)$ *is an order-sorted topmost rewrite theory,* (Σ, E, R) *is a decomposition of the equational theory* $(\Sigma, E \cup R)$, *and* ϕ, *called the* irreducibility requirements, *is a function mapping each* $f \in \Sigma$ *to a set of its arguments, i.e.,* $\phi(f) \subseteq \{1, \ldots, ar(f)\}$, *where* $ar(f)$ *is the number of arguments of* f. *The set of maximal irreducible positions of a term* t *is denoted by* $\phi(t)$.

A term t *is called* ϕ, R, E-irreducible *(or just* ϕ-irreducible*) if for each* $p \in \phi(t)$, $t|_p \downarrow_{R,E} =_E t|_p$, *and* strongly ϕ-irreducible *if for any* R, E-normalized sub-stitution σ, $t\sigma$ *is* ϕ-irreducible.

Example 5. For the protocol of Examples 1 and 3, the contextual rewrite theory (Σ, E, R, T, ϕ) is formed of T containing the reversed version of the generic rewrite rules (1)–(3) plus the rewrite rules for introducing new strands, and the equational theory $(\Sigma, E \cup R)$ for exclusive-or is decomposed into (Σ, E, R) where E is the associativity and commutativity axioms for $\oplus$ and R is as follows:[2]

$$X \oplus 0 \rightarrow X \quad X \oplus X \rightarrow 0 \quad X \oplus X \oplus Y \rightarrow Y$$

---

[1] Our use of "contextual" should be distinguished from : (i) "contextual rewriting," e.g., [34], and (ii) "context-sensitive rewriting," e.g., [26]. Our use is unrelated to contextual rewriting, which is a form of conditional rewriting with constraints, but is closely related to context-sensitive rewriting, where the rewritable argument positions of a function symbol f are specified by a function $\mu(f) \subseteq \{1, \ldots, ar(f)\}$ similar to our irreducibility requirements function $\phi(f) \subseteq \{1, \ldots, ar(f)\}$. However, ϕ-irreducibility is a *strictly stronger* requirement than μ-irreducibility when $\phi = \mu$.

[2] Note that the two first equations are not AC-coherent, but adding the last equation is sufficient to recover that property (see [33]).

The irreducibility requirements ϕ are imposed on two operators: $-(\_)$ for *input messages* in a strand, and $\_\in\mathcal{I}$ for each *positive fact* in the intruder knowledge. That is, $\phi(-(\_)) = \{1\}$, $\phi(\_\in\mathcal{I}) = \{1\}$, and $\phi(f) = \emptyset$ otherwise.

We extend the notion of a reachability goal to the contextual case.

Definition 4 (Contextual Reachability goal). *Given a contextual rewrite theory* (Σ, E, R, T, ϕ), *we define a contextual reachability goal as* $t \stackrel{?}{\rightarrow}{}^{*}_{T,R,E,\phi} t'$, *where* $t, t' \in \mathcal{T}_{\Sigma}(\mathcal{X})_{\mathsf{s}}$. *We write* $t \stackrel{?}{\rightarrow}{}^{*}_{\phi} t'$ *when the theory is clear. A substitution* σ *is a solution of the contextual reachability goal* $t \stackrel{?}{\rightarrow}{}^{*}_{T,R,E,\phi} t'$ *iff there is a sequence* $\sigma(t) \rightarrow_{T,(E\cup R)} \sigma(u_1) \rightarrow_{T,(E\cup R)} \cdots \rightarrow_{T,(E\cup R)} \sigma(u_{k-1}) \rightarrow_{T,(E\cup R)} \sigma(t')$ *such that* $\sigma(t), \sigma(u_1), \ldots, \sigma(u_{k-1}), \sigma(t')$ *are all* ϕ, R, E-*irreducible.*

As for reachability goals, a contextual version of narrowing provides a mechanism to find solutions to contextual reachability goals. However, we have to first define a new equational unification mechanism, called *contextual unification*, as the basis for contextual narrowing, where the $E \cup R$-unification is extended to the contextual case, which has some asymmetry due to the irreducibility restrictions only on the right hand side.

Definition 5 (Contextual Unification). *Given a contextual rewrite theory* (Σ, E, R, T, ϕ), *a substitution* σ *is a* contextual R, E-*unifier of a set* P *of contextual equations of the form* $P = \{t_1 =_{\downarrow_\phi} t'_1, \ldots, t_n =_{\downarrow_\phi} t'_n\}$ *iff for every contextual equation* $t_i =_{\downarrow_\phi} t'_i$ *in* P, *the substitution* σ *is an* $(R \cup E)$-*unifier of the equation* $t_i = t'_i$ *and, furthermore,* $\sigma(t'_i)$ *is* ϕ, R, E-*irreducible.*

    A set of substitutions Ω *is a* complete set of contextual R, E-*unifiers of* P, *denoted by* $CSU_{R,E,\phi}(P)$, *iff: (i) every member of* Ω *is a contextual* R, E-*unifier of* P, *and (ii) for every contextual* R, E-*unifier* θ *of* P *there exists* $\sigma \in \Omega$ *such that* $\sigma \sqsupseteq_E \theta$.

Example 6. Consider the protocol of Example 1. The contextual unification problem found by Maude-NPA is $t =_{\downarrow_\phi} t'$ where t is $\{SS\ \&\ [L, M^+ \mid L']\ \&\ \{M\in\mathcal{I}, IK\}\}$ i.e., the right-hand side of Rule (3), and t' is the following state, found by Maude-NPA after one backwards narrowing step from the state pattern of Example 4:

$$\{ :: r_2 :: [nil, -(pk(A, X)), +(pk(B, n(A, r_2)))] \mid -(X \oplus n(A, r_2)), nil] \ \&$$
$$:: r_1 :: [nil, +(pk(A, n(B, r_1))), -(pk(B, Y)), +(Y \oplus n(B, r_1)) \mid nil] \ \&$$
$$SS\ \&\ \{(X \oplus n(A, r_2))\in\mathcal{I}, IK\}\}$$

The two key terms are $Y \oplus n(B, r_1)$ and $X \oplus n(A, r_2)$. Note that term $X \oplus n(A, r_2)$ appears in two positions in t', under symbols $-(\_)$ and $\_\in\mathcal{I}$, both required to be irreducible by ϕ. The singleton most general contextual unifier is $\sigma_1 = \{Y \mapsto X \oplus n(B, r_1) \oplus n(A, r_2)\}$, whereas the substitution $\sigma_2 = \{X \mapsto Y \oplus n(B, r_1) \oplus n(A, r_2)\}$ is *not* a valid contextual unifier: term $X \oplus n(A, r_2)$ is under the irreducibility condition of symbol $-(\_)$ and the substitution σ_2 would make it reducible, whereas term $Y \oplus n(B, r_1)$ is under symbol $+(\_)$, which does not have any irreducibility condition and the substitution σ_1 makes it reducible.

Contextual unification can be reduced to the simpler notion of *asymmetric unification*.

Definition 6 (Asymmetric Unification). *Given a decomposition (Σ, E, R) of an equational theory $(\Sigma, E \cup R)$, a substitution σ is an* asymmetric R, E-unifier *of a set P of asymmetric equations $\{t_1 =_\downarrow t_1', \ldots, t_n =_\downarrow t_n'\}$ iff for every asymmetric equation $t_i =_\downarrow t_i'$ in P, σ is an $(E \cup R)$-unifier of the equation $t_i = t_i'$ and $(t_i' \downarrow_{R,E})\sigma$ is in R,E-normal form.*

A set of substitutions Ω is a complete set of asymmetric R,E-unifiers *of P iff: (i) every member of Ω is an asymmetric R,E-unifier of P, and (ii) for every asymmetric R,E-unifier θ of P there exists a $\sigma \in \Omega$ such that $\sigma \sqsupseteq_E \theta$ (over $Var(P)$).*

A special-purpose asymmetric unification algorithm for exclusive-or has been developed for this paper and is used in the experiments reported in Section 5. A detailed discussion of this algorithm will be presented elsewhere. The reduction of contextual unification to the simpler asymmetric unification is provided by the following lemma.

Lemma 1. *Given a contextual rewrite theory (Σ, E, R, T, ϕ) and a set of contextual equations $P = \{t_1 =_{\downarrow_\phi} t_1', \ldots, t_n =_{\downarrow_\phi} t_n'\}$, σ is a contextual R, E-unifier of P iff there is a substitution θ such that θ is an asymmetric R, E-unifier of $\Gamma(P)$ and $\sigma =_E \theta|_{Var(P)}$, where*

$$\Gamma(P) = \{t_i =_\downarrow X, t_i' =_\downarrow X \mid t_i =_{\downarrow_\phi} t_i' \in P, X \text{ fresh variable}\} \cup$$
$$\{t_i'|_{p.j} =_\downarrow t_i'|_{p.j} \mid t_i =_{\downarrow_\phi} t_i' \in P, f \in \Sigma, p \in Pos_f(t_i'), j \in \phi(f)\}$$

Using a contextual unification algorithm, we can modify the standard notion of narrowing so that it uses contextual unification to solve symbolic contextual reachability goals. Note that the following definition differs from Definition 2 only in using contextual unification $CSU_{R,E,\phi}(l =_{\downarrow_\phi} t|_p)$ instead of regular unification $CSU_{R\cup E}(l = t|_p)$ and and carrying a set of irreducible terms Π passed to the contextual unification algorithm, where Π is the set of irreducible terms that have been computed earlier in the narrowing sequence.

Definition 7 (Contextual Narrowing modulo R, E). *Given a contextual rewrite theory (Σ, E, R, T, ϕ), the contextual narrowing relation modulo R, E on pairs $\langle t, \Pi \rangle$ for t a term and Π a set of irreducible terms is defined as $\langle t, \Pi \rangle \overset{\sigma}{\leadsto}_{T,R,E,\phi} \langle t', \sigma(\Pi) \rangle$ (or $\overset{\sigma}{\leadsto}_\phi$ if T, R, E are understood) iff there is $p \in Pos_\Sigma(t)$, a rule $l \to r$ in T such that $Var(t) \cap (Var(l) \cup Var(r)) = \emptyset$, a substitution $\sigma \in CSU_{R,E,\phi}^V(P)$ for $P = \{l =_{\downarrow_\phi} t|_p\} \cup \{u =_{\downarrow_\phi} u \mid u \in \Pi\}$ and a set V of variables containing $Var(t)$, $Var(l)$, and $Var(r)$, and $t' = \sigma(t[r]_p)$.*

The essential equivalence between contextual reachability analysis and standard narrowing-based reachability analysis is proved as follows: given a standard goal $t \overset{?}{\to}_{T,R\cup E}^* t'$, any solution to it can be computed by contextual narrowing $\leadsto_{T,R,E,\phi}$ under some extra conditions involving *variants*. Let us motivate the issues involved by an example.

Example 7. Let us consider the state pattern shown in Example 4 with an extra requirement that the intruder learns $n(A, r_2)$:

$$\{ :: r_2 :: [nil, -(pk(A, X)), +(pk(B, n(A, r_2))), -(X \oplus n(A, r_2)) \mid nil] \ \&$$
$$\quad :: r_1 :: [nil, +(pk(A, n(B, r_1))), -(pk(B, Y)), +(Y \oplus n(B, r_1)) \mid nil] \ \&$$
$$\quad SS \ \& \ \{n(A, r_2) \in \mathcal{I}, IK\}\}$$

This attack pattern should be possible in Maude-NPA by just applying the substitution $X \mapsto 0$, where 0 is the identity symbol of $\oplus$. However, the term $X \oplus n(A, r_2)$ becomes reducible under such substitution and the attack would not be reachable because of our irreducibility condition on $X \oplus n(A, r_2)$. To solve this problem, the key idea is that the pattern $X \oplus n(A, r_2)$ should be replaced by its *variants* before each contextual narrowing step, i.e., by the possible instance patterns of it which are irreducible, namely: (i) the pattern $X \oplus n(A, r_2)$ itself, (ii) the pattern Y, which is the normal form after applying substitution $X \mapsto Y \oplus n(A, r_2)$, (iii) the pattern 0, which is the normal form after applying substitution $X \mapsto n(A, r_2)$, and (iv) the pattern $n(A, r_2)$, which is the normal form after applying substitution $X \mapsto 0$. Only after replacement of the original term by these variants, can we impose the irreducibility conditions for reducing the search space. That is, for contextual reachability analysis, we need to first compute what we call the ϕ, R, E-variants of a term.

Definition 8 (ϕ, R, E-variants). *Given a contextual rewrite theory (Σ, E, R, T, ϕ), the set of R,E,ϕ-variants of a pair $\langle t, \Pi \rangle$ for t a term and Π a set of irreducible terms is defined as $[\![\langle t, \Pi \rangle]\!]_{R,E}^{\phi} = \{(\sigma(t)[v_1, \ldots, v_n]_{p_1, \ldots, p_n}, \sigma) \mid (g(v_1, \ldots, v_n), \sigma) \in [\![g(t|_{p_1}, \ldots, t|_{p_n})]\!]_{R,E} \land \forall u \in \Pi : \sigma(u) \text{ is } \phi, R, E\text{-irreducible}\}$ where $\phi(t) = \{p_1, \ldots, p_n\}$ and g is an auxiliary function symbol not appearing in R and E. For readability, we write $\langle t, \Pi \rangle \twoheadrightarrow_{R,E}^{\theta} \langle w, \overline{\Pi} \rangle$ to denote that $(w, \theta) \in [\![\langle t, \Pi \rangle]\!]_{R,E}^{\phi}$ and $\overline{\Pi} = \theta(\Pi) \cup \{w\}$.*

Example 8. Let us consider the state t' shown in Example 6:

$$\{ :: r_2 :: [nil, -(pk(A, X)), +(pk(B, n(A, r_2))) \mid -(X \oplus n(A, r_2)), nil] \ \&$$
$$\quad :: r_1 :: [nil, +(pk(A, n(B, r_1))), -(pk(B, Y)), +(Y \oplus n(B, r_1)) \mid nil] \ \&$$
$$\quad SS \ \& \ \{(X \oplus n(A, r_2)) \in \mathcal{I}, IK\}\}$$

We generate the four variants associated to $X \oplus n(A, r_2)$ in subterms rooted by $-(\_)$ and $\_\in\mathcal{I}$, since these are the symbols with irreducibility constraints: (i) the original one but with the assumption that X will never contain either $n(A, r_2)$ or 0, (ii) the pattern $n(A, r_2)$ where $X \oplus n(A, r_2)$ has been collapsed into the nonce, (iii) the pattern Z where $X \oplus n(A, r_2)$ has been collapsed into a new variable Z by assuming $X \mapsto Z \oplus n(A, r_2)$, and (iv) the term 0 where $X \oplus n(A, r_2)$ has been collapsed into 0 by assuming $X \mapsto n(A, r_2)$:

$$\{ :: r_2 :: [nil, -(pk(A, X)), +(pk(B, n(A, r_2))) \mid -(X \oplus n(A, r_2)), nil] \ \&$$
$$\quad :: r_1 :: [nil, +(pk(A, n(B, r_1))), -(pk(B, Y)), +(Y \oplus n(B, r_1)) \mid nil] \ \&$$
$$\quad SS \ \& \ \{(X \oplus n(A, r_2)) \in \mathcal{I}, IK\}\}$$

$\{ :: r_2 :: [nil, -(pk(A, 0)), +(pk(B, n(A, r_2))) \mid -(n(A, r_2)), nil] \ \& $
$\quad :: r_1 :: [nil, +(pk(A, n(B, r_1))), -(pk(B, Y)), +(Y \oplus n(B, r_1)) \mid nil] \ \& $
$\quad SS \ \& \ \{n(A, r_2) \in \mathcal{I}, IK\}\}$

$\{ :: r_2 :: [nil, -(pk(A, Z \oplus n(A, r_2))), +(pk(B, n(A, r_2))) \mid -(Z), nil] \ \& $
$\quad :: r_1 :: [nil, +(pk(A, n(B, r_1))), -(pk(B, Y)), +(Y \oplus n(B, r_1)) \mid nil] \ \& $
$\quad SS \ \& \ \{Z \in \mathcal{I}, IK\}\}$

$\{ :: r_2 :: [nil, -(pk(A, n(A, r_2))), +(pk(B, n(A, r_2))) \mid -(0), nil] \ \& $
$\quad :: r_1 :: [nil, +(pk(A, n(B, r_1))), -(pk(B, Y)), +(Y \oplus n(B, r_1)) \mid nil] \ \& $
$\quad SS \ \& \ \{0 \in \mathcal{I}, IK\}\}$

The reader can check that only the variants of the terms in the intruder knowledge (which are indeed coming from messages of the form $-(M)$) are generated.

The key idea to achieve the desired semantic equivalence between contextual narrowing and ordinary narrowing is to precede each contextual narrowing step by a ϕ-variant computation step.

Theorem 1 (Contextual Soundness and Completeness). *Given a contextual rewrite theory* (Σ, E, R, T, ϕ), *a reachability goal* $t \overset{?}{\rightarrow}{}^* t'$, *and a solution* σ *of it, there are a set of terms* $u_1, \ldots, u_n, w_1, \ldots, w_{n+1}, t''$ *and a set of substitutions* $\theta_1, \ldots, \theta_{n+1}, \theta'_1, \ldots, \theta'_{n+1}$ *such that*

$$\langle t, \Pi_0 \rangle \twoheadrightarrow^{\theta_1}_{R,E} \langle w_1, \Pi_1 \rangle \qquad \overset{\theta'_1}{\rightsquigarrow}_{T,R,E,\phi} \langle u_1, \overline{\Pi_1} \rangle$$
$$\twoheadrightarrow^{\theta_2}_{R,E} \langle w_2, \Pi_2 \rangle \qquad \overset{\theta'_2}{\rightsquigarrow}_{T,R,E,\phi} \langle u_2, \overline{\Pi_2} \rangle$$
$$\vdots$$
$$\twoheadrightarrow^{\theta_n}_{R,E} \langle w_n, \Pi_n \rangle \qquad \overset{\theta'_n}{\rightsquigarrow}_{T,R,E,\phi} \langle u_n, \overline{\Pi_n} \rangle$$
$$\twoheadrightarrow^{\theta_{n+1}}_{R,E} \langle w_{n+1}, \Pi_{n+1} \rangle \overset{\theta'_{n+1}}{\rightsquigarrow}_{T,R,E,\phi} \langle t'', \overline{\Pi_{n+1}} \rangle$$

and also: (i) $\Pi_0 = \emptyset$, $\Pi_1 = \{w_1\}$, $\overline{\Pi_1} = \theta'_1(\Pi_1)$, $\Pi_2 = \theta_2(\overline{\Pi_1}) \cup \{w_2\}$, $\overline{\Pi_2} = \theta'_2(\Pi_2)$, ..., $\Pi_{n+1} = \overline{\Pi_n} \cup \{w_{n+1}\}$, $\overline{\Pi_{n+1}} = \theta'_{n+1}(\Pi_{n+1})$, *(ii) for each* $i \in \{1, \ldots, n+1\}$, *the term* $w_i \theta'_i \theta_{i+1} \theta'_{i+1} \cdots \theta_{n+1} \theta'_{n+1}$ *is* ϕ, R, E-*irreducible, (iii) there is a substitution* τ *such that* $\sigma =_E \theta_1 \theta'_1 \theta_2 \theta'_2 \cdots \theta_{n+1} \theta'_{n+1} \tau$, *and (iv)* $t' =_E t'' \tau$.

Conversely, any substitution σ *for which there is a sequence as above satisfying conditions (i)-(iv) is a solution of* $t \overset{?}{\rightarrow}{}^* t'$.

Example 9. Continuing Example 8, we have four state patterns after variant generation. Contextual narrowing follows from the first variant state pattern as described in Example 10 below. The second variant state pattern will lead to an initial state where the intruder provides message $pk(A, 0)$ and the vertical bar of Bob's strand is never touched. And the third and the fourth variant state patterns will be discarded by Maude-NPA, since they do not satisfy the syntactic check explained in the Introduction discarding states sending a nonce before it is generated. The state space reduction achieved in Maude-NPA is huge by using the irreducibility conditions on symbols $-(\_)$ and $\_\in\mathcal{I}$ and other state space reduction techniques based on such conditions (we further discuss experiments on this topic in Section 5).

Condition (ii) in Theorem 1 for terms w_i to be (ϕ-)irreducible after substitution application ensures that variants are not computed more than once for each irreducible subterm in term t or irreducible subterms introduced by right-hand sides of rules. This is very important to further reduce the search space.

Example 10. Let us consider the state t' shown in Example 6. After several variant generation and contextual narrowing steps using the reversed form of rewrite rules (1)–(3), the following state is found

$$\{ :: r_2 :: [nil, -(pk(A,X)), +(pk(B,n(A,r_2)))] \mid -(X \oplus n(A,r_2)), nil] \ \& $$
$$:: r_1 :: [nil, +(pk(A,n(B,r_1)))] \mid -(pk(B, X \oplus n(A,r_2) \oplus n(B,r_1))), $$
$$+(X \oplus n(A,r_2) \oplus n(B,r_1) \oplus n(B,r_1), nil] \ \& $$
$$SS \ \& \ \{ \ pk(B, X \oplus n(A,r_2) \oplus n(B,r_1)) \in \mathcal{I}, \ (X \oplus n(A,r_2)) \notin \mathcal{I}, \ IK \ \}\}$$

We can check that there is no contextual unifier that allows terms $pk(B, n(A, r_2))$ and $pk(B, X \oplus n(A, r_2) \oplus n(B, r_1))$ to be unifiable according to the reversed form of rewrite rule (3), since the second term is under a symbol with irreducibility restrictions and the substitution $X \mapsto n(B, r_1)$ would make it reducible.

However, another protocol session can be used, since the term $pk(B, X \oplus n(A, r_2) \oplus n(B, r_1))$ can be unified with term $pk(B, n(A', r_2'))$ coming from another session, using the contextual unifier $X \mapsto n(A', r_2') \oplus n(A, r_2) \oplus n(B, r_1)$. The resulting state is as follows

$$\{ :: r_2' :: [nil, -(pk(A', X')) \mid + (pk(B, n(A', r_2'))), -(X' \oplus n(A', r_2')), nil] \ \& $$
$$:: r_2 :: [nil, -(pk(A, n(A', r_2') \oplus n(A, r_2) \oplus n(B, r_1))), $$
$$+(pk(B, n(A, r_2))) \mid $$
$$-(n(A', r_2') \oplus n(A, r_2) \oplus n(B, r_1) \oplus n(A, r_2)), nil] \ \& $$
$$:: r_1 :: [nil, +(pk(A, n(B, r_1))) \mid $$
$$-(pk(B, n(A', r_2') \oplus n(A, r_2) \oplus n(B, r_1) \oplus n(A, r_2) \oplus n(B, r_1))), $$
$$+(n(A', r_2') \oplus n(A, r_2) \oplus n(B, r_1) \oplus n(A, r_2) \oplus n(B, r_1) \oplus n(B, r_1), nil] \ \& $$
$$SS \ \& \ \{ \ pk(B, n(A', r_2') \oplus n(A, r_2) \oplus n(B, r_1) \oplus n(A, r_2) \oplus n(B, r_1)) \notin \mathcal{I}, $$
$$(n(A', r_2') \oplus n(A, r_2) \oplus n(B, r_1) \oplus n(A, r_2)) \notin \mathcal{I}, \ IK \ \}\}$$

However, although the two contextual narrowing steps have computed contextual unifiers, the combination of both unifiers does not satisfy the irreducibility conditions of the original term $-(X \oplus n(A, r_2))$, since now it is reducible, i.e., the term $-(n(A', r_2') \oplus n(A, r_2) \oplus n(B, r_1) \oplus n(A, r_2))$ is reducible. Therefore, this narrowing sequence is discarded, since it does not fulfill the conditions for solutions of contextual reachability goals given in Theorem 1, further reducing search.

Table 1. Experiments with standard reachability analysis using regular XOR unification algorithm vs contextual reachability analysis using asymmetric XOR unification algorithm. A pair n/t means: n = number of states, and t = time in seconds.

states/seconds	1 step	2 steps	3 steps	4 steps	5 steps
RP - Standard	2/0.08	5/0.16	13/0.86	49/3.09	267/17.41
RP - Contextual	1/0.03	45/1.08	114/2.26	1175/37.25	13906/4144.30
WEPP - Standard	5/0.09	9/0.42	26/1.27	106/5.80	503/ 34.76
WEPP - Contextual	4/0.05	9/0.12	26/0.64	257/144.65	2454/612.08
TMN - Standard	5/0.11	15/ 0.55	99/3.82	469/ 25.68	timeout
TMN - Contextual	4/0.06	24/0.53	174/3.63	1079/170.29	9737/1372.55

5 Experiments

We have performed several experiments to compare the contextual symbolic reachability approach presented in this paper with other approaches. We have used three protocols using exclusive-or: (i) the running protocol (RP) of Example 1, (ii) the Wired Equivalent Privacy Protocol (WEPP) of [1], and (iii) the TMN protocol of [31,25]. For all three protocols, we are able to find the associated attacks in Table 2 below. We have run the experiments in this Section in an Intel Xeon machine with 4 cores and 24GB of memory, using Maude 2.7.

In Table 1, we compare the standard reachability analysis of Section 3, which uses the XOR unification algorithm developed in [24], and the contextual reachability analysis of Section 4, which uses the asymmetric XOR unification algorithm developed for this paper. A detailed discussion of this asymmetric XOR unification algorithm will be presented elsewhere. We show the number of states generated from one level to the next one of the backwards reachability tree with the indicated number of steps as the maximum depth. We also include the execution time from one level to the next one. We write "timeout" when the tool did not finish within a time interval of two hours.

As shown in Table 1, contextual reachability analysis is not better than the standard reachability analysis because of variant generation, which creates many more states than may be necessary for rule application. However, although typically many more states are created, the use of variants and irreducibility constraints is crucial (as explained in the Introduction) for further optimizations of the search space, as shown in Table 2, which shows that contextual reachability analysis enables several Maude-NPA optimizations, including grammars (see [16,18] for details) and drastically reduces the search space.

Table 2 shows that, although, due to the extra computations needed for the optimization, the execution time without optimization is sometimes better than with optimizations, this only happens up to Step 3. The important point is that from Step 2 on, the total number of states is *drastically reduced* when optimizations are added (the only exception at Step 1 is RP, due to some differences on how variants are generated). In fact, the crucial point is not just the great reduction in the number of states, but the *finiteness of the analysis* for all the examples with optimization, whereas no such finiteness is even theoretically possible without optimizations. This is particularly important when an attack does

Table 2. Experiments for contextual reachability analysis using asymmetric XOR unification algorithm with and without optimizations

states/seconds	1 step	2 steps	3 steps	4 steps	5 steps	Finite Analysis?
RP - w/o Opt.	1/0.03	45/1.08	114/2.26	1175/37.25	13906/4144.30	No, timeout with 6 steps
RP - with Opt.	4/0.59	7/0.59	7/1.92	7/1.89	7/3.02	Yes, at step 10
WEPP - w/o Opt.	4/0.05	9/0.12	26/0.64	257/144.65	2454/612.08	No, timeout with 7 steps
WEPP - with Opt.	2/0.36	2/0.20	1/0.80	2/1.42	1/0.03	Yes at step 5
TMN - w/o Opt.	4/0.06	24/0.53	174/3.63	1079/170.29	9737/1372.55	No, timeout with 7 steps
TMN - with Opt.	3/0.42	6/9.85	9/1.78	9/4.43	8/3.20	Yes, at step 21

not exist, since then finiteness of the analysis *proves* that the protocol is secure against such an attack. Therefore, the above performance results validate experimentally the main thesis of this paper, namely that: (i) support of irreducibility conditions in symbolic reachability is essential for *effective* protocol analysis, since crucial optimizations depend on such conditions; and (ii) contextual reachability analysis supports irreducibility conditions in a sound and complete way and makes such optimizations possible.

The integration of this framework into Maude-NPA is still under testing and optimization, and further work is needed to increase performance. Indeed, the current experiments have been performed with a version of the contextual narrowing simpler than the conditions of Theorem 1 (irreducibility constraints on Π are not enforced), but is still valid for the benchmarked protocols, i.e., in these protocols, each strand contains only one expression using the xor operator, and thus Π remains irreducible by default.

6   Conclusions and Future Directions

We are only at the beginning of exploring contextual symbolic reachability analysis as a general approach, and there are many paths that can be followed. One is exploring the different types of irreducibility constraints and their effect on efficiency. It would appear that an approach that requires fewer constraints would be more efficient than one that applies more; e.g. that modifying a tool such as OFMC that requires constraints on both sent and received messages to use constraints only on input messages, as does Maude-NPA, would lead to reduced state space size and greater efficiency, but this needs to be verified.

Using one-sided constraints also potentially allows us to gain greater efficiency through special-purpose asymmetric unification algorithms. We are now investigating this with respect to asymmetric exclusive-or unification, and plan to develop and investigate other such algorithms in the future. Asymmetric unification is a subject about which currently very little is known; as it is explored further, we expect to find out a lot more about it and how it can be optimized.

Finally, we believe that cryptographic protocol analysis is not the only potential application for symbolic contextual reachability analysis. Indeed, it should be applicable to any state exploration problem in which symbolic states obey equational theories. Future work in this area should involve an investigation of these other problems and the ways in which contextual symbolic reachability analysis could be applied to them.

References

1. IEEE 802.11 Local and Metropolitan Area Networks: Wireless LAN Medium Access Control (MAC) and Physical (PHY) Specifications (1999)
2. Abadi, M., Cortier, V.: Deciding knowledge in security protocols under equational theories. Theor. Comput. Sci. 367(1-2), 2–32 (2006)
3. Arapinis, M., Bursuc, S., Ryan, M.: Privacy Supporting Cloud Computing: ConfiChair, a Case Study. In: Degano, P., Guttman, J.D. (eds.) Principles of Security and Trust. LNCS, vol. 7215, pp. 89–108. Springer, Heidelberg (2012)
4. Basin, D., Mödersheim, S., Viganò, L.: An On-the-Fly Model-Checker for Security Protocol Analysis. In: Snekkenes, E., Gollmann, D. (eds.) ESORICS 2003. LNCS, vol. 2808, pp. 253–270. Springer, Heidelberg (2003)
5. Baudet, M., Cortier, V., Delaune, S.: YAPA: A Generic Tool for Computing Intruder Knowledge. In: Treinen, R. (ed.) RTA 2009. LNCS, vol. 5595, pp. 148–163. Springer, Heidelberg (2009)
6. Blanchet, B.: An efficient cryptographic protocol verifier based on prolog rules. In: CSFW, pp. 82–96. IEEE Computer Society (2001)
7. Blanchet, B.: Using horn clauses for analyzing security protocols. In: Cortier, V., Kremer, S. (eds.) Formal Models and Techniques for Analyzing Security Protocols. IOS Press (2011)
8. Blanchet, B., Abadi, M., Fournet, C.: Automated verification of selected equivalences for security protocols. J. Log. Algebr. Program. 75(1), 3–51 (2008)
9. Ciobâcă, Ş., Delaune, S., Kremer, S.: Computing Knowledge in Security Protocols under Convergent Equational Theories. In: Schmidt, R.A. (ed.) CADE-22. LNCS (LNAI), vol. 5663, pp. 355–370. Springer, Heidelberg (2009)
10. Comon-Lundh, H., Delaune, S.: The Finite Variant Property: How to Get Rid of Some Algebraic Properties. In: Giesl, J. (ed.) RTA 2005. LNCS, vol. 3467, pp. 294–307. Springer, Heidelberg (2005)
11. Comon-Lundh, H., Delaune, S., Millen, J.: Constraint solving techniques and enriching the model with equational theories. In: Cortier, V., Kremer, S. (eds.) Formal Models and Techniques for Analyzing Security Protocols. Cryptology and Information Security Series, vol. 5, pp. 35–61. IOS Press (2011)
12. Comon-Lundh, H., Shmatikov, V.: Intruder deductions, constraint solving and insecurity decision in presence of exclusive or. In: LICS, pp. 271–280. IEEE Computer Society (2003)
13. Ciobâcă, Ş.: Knowledge in security protocols
14. Dolev, D., Yao, A.C.-C.: On the security of public key protocols (extended abstract). In: FOCS, pp. 350–357 (1981)
15. Escobar, S., Meadows, C., Meseguer, J.: A rewriting-based inference system for the NRL protocol analyzer and its meta-logical properties. Theoretical Computer Science 367(1-2), 162–202 (2006)
16. Escobar, S., Meadows, C., Meseguer, J.: State Space Reduction in the Maude-NRL Protocol Analyzer. In: Jajodia, S., Lopez, J. (eds.) ESORICS 2008. LNCS, vol. 5283, pp. 548–562. Springer, Heidelberg (2008)
17. Escobar, S., Meadows, C., Meseguer, J.: Maude-NPA: Cryptographic Protocol Analysis Modulo Equational Properties. In: Aldini, A., Barthe, G., Gorrieri, R. (eds.) FOSAD 2007. LNCS, vol. 5705, pp. 1–50. Springer, Heidelberg (2009)

18. Escobar, S., Meadows, C., Meseguer, J., Santiago, S.: State space reduction in the maude-nrl protocol analyzer. Information and Computation (in press, 2012)
19. Escobar, S., Sasse, R., Meseguer, J.: Folding variant narrowing and optimal variant termination. J. Log. Algebr. Program (in press, 2012)
20. Thayer Fabrega, F.J., Herzog, J., Guttman, J.: Strand Spaces: What Makes a Security Protocol Correct? Journal of Computer Security 7, 191–230 (1999)
21. Jouannaud, J.-P., Kirchner, H.: Completion of a set of rules modulo a set of equations. SIAM J. Comput. 15(4), 1155–1194 (1986)
22. Küsters, R., Truderung, T.: Using ProVerif to analyze protocols with Diffie-Hellman exponentiation. In: CSF, pp. 157–171. IEEE Computer Society (2009)
23. Küsters, R., Truderung, T.: Reducing protocol analysis with xor to the xor-free case in the horn theory based approach. Journal of Automated Reasoning 46(3-4), 325–352 (2011)
24. Liu, Z., Lynch, C.: Efficient General Unification for XOR with Homomorphism. In: Bjørner, N., Sofronie-Stokkermans, V. (eds.) CADE 2011. LNCS, vol. 6803, pp. 407–421. Springer, Heidelberg (2011)
25. Lowe, G., Roscoe, B.: Using csp to detect errors in the tmn protocol. IEEE Transactions on Software Engineering 23, 659–669 (1997)
26. Lucas, S.: Context-sensitive computations in functional and functional logic programs. J. Functl. and Log. Progr. 1(4), 446–453 (1998)
27. Meseguer, J.: Conditional rewriting logic as a united model of concurrency. Theor. Comput. Sci. 96(1), 73–155 (1992)
28. Meseguer, J., Thati, P.: Symbolic reachability analysis using narrowing and its application to verification of cryptographic protocols. Higher-Order and Symbolic Computation 20(1-2), 123–160 (2007)
29. Mödersheim, S.: Models and methods for the automated analysis of security protocols. PhD thesis, ETH Zurich (2007)
30. Mödersheim, S., Viganò, L., Basin, D.A.: Constraint differentiation: Search-space reduction for the constraint-based analysis of security protocols. Journal of Computer Security 18(4), 575–618 (2010)
31. Tatebayashi, M., Matsuzaki, N., Newman Jr., D.B.: Key Distribution Protocol for Digital Mobile Communication Systems. In: Brassard, G. (ed.) CRYPTO 1989. LNCS, vol. 435, pp. 324–334. Springer, Heidelberg (1990)
32. TeReSe (ed.): Term Rewriting Systems. Cambridge University Press, Cambridge (2003)
33. Viry, P.: Equational rules for rewriting logic. Theor. Comput. Sci. 285(2), 487–517 (2002)
34. Zhang, H., Remy, J.-L.: Contextual Rewriting. In: Jouannaud, J.-P. (ed.) RTA 1985. LNCS, vol. 202, pp. 46–62. Springer, Heidelberg (1985)

Deciding Epistemic and Strategic Properties of Cryptographic Protocols

Henning Schnoor

Institut für Informatik, Christian-Albrechts-Universität zu Kiel, 24098 Kiel, Germany
`schnoor@ti.informatik.uni-kiel.de`

Abstract. We propose a new, widely applicable model for analyzing knowledge-based (epistemic) and strategic properties of cryptographic protocols. We prove that the corresponding model checking problem with respect to an expressive epistemic strategic logic is decidable. As corollaries, we obtain decidability of complex security properties including coercion-resistance of voting protocols, accountability of protocols using a trusted third party, and abuse-freeness of contract signing protocols.

Introduction

In design and verification of cryptographic protocols, symbolic techniques [1] have proven very successful. A breakthrough result in this area is that secrecy properties of protocols can be decided in coNP, even if the adversary is allowed to send arbitrarily complex terms [2]. Recently, game-based properties of cryptographic protocols have been studied [3]. Such properties are relevant e.g., for contract signing [4–6] and non-repudiation [7] protocols, and can naturally be expressed in Alternating-Time Temporal Logic (ATL, [8]), a logic explicitly designed to reason about strategies. Decidability results for such properties have been obtained in [9, 10]. However, existing symbolic approaches for strategic analysis have the following limitations:

(i) The models and logics that have been applied cannot express *epistemic* properties, i.e., properties concerned with knowledge of principals as, e.g., abuse-freeness of contract-signing protocols [11] or anonymous broadcast [12]. Similarly, they only consider *complete-information strategies*: Honest principals and the adversary base their decisions on complete knowledge about the current state, including private messages between other principals and cryptographically hidden secrets. Thus, capabilities of all parties are over-approximated, potentially leading to both "false positives" and "false negatives" in the security analysis.

(ii) They do not handle *probabilistic* protocols that allow random *decisions*. These are essential for some security goals [13] and can be used to model random routing in anonymity protocols.

We propose an approach overcoming these shortcomings by a thorough treatment of knowledge and probabilism. To express security properties, we use QAPI [14],

S. Foresti, M. Yung, and F. Martinelli (Eds.): ESORICS 2012, LNCS 7459, pp. 91–108, 2012.

a very expressive extension of ATL*. In addition to epistemic and probabilistic aspects, QAPI allows explicit reasoning and quantification of strategies similarly to strategy logic [15]. This allows to express dependencies between strategies of different coalitions, as for example knowledge that one coalition has about the behavior of others. Our contributions are as follows:

1. We define a symbolic model for protocol analysis treating explicit knowledge, incomplete information, and probabilistic protocols.
2. We show that the question whether a protocol satisfies a security property (specified by a QAPI-formula) is decidable for active and passive adversaries.

Our decidability result holds for finitely many parallel sessions, it is well-known that even very simple security properties are undecidable for the unbounded session case [16]. Our proof implies that relevant strategies can always be finitely represented, hence can be implemented in software.

As a toy example, we consider a coin-flipping protocol: Bob randomly chooses a bit $b_1 \in \{0, 1\}$ and a random string N, and sends $hash(\langle b_1, N \rangle)$ to Alice. Alice randomly chooses $b_2 \in \{0, 1\}$ and sends b_2 to Bob. He then sends N and b_1 to Alice, who verifies that these match the hash. The security property is that neither Alice nor Bob can dictate the outcome of the protocol, which is the bit $b_1 \oplus b_2$. This is only true since Alice's b_2 may not depend on the secret value b_1, hence security of the protocol can only be shown with an epistemic approach. In addition to this toy example, we give the following applications:

1. We show how accountability and verifiability of protocols that involve a trusted third party and coercion-resistance of voting protocols can be expressed in our model, implying decidability of these properties.
2. We prove that abuse-freeness of contract-signing protocols can be formalized in our model, and obtain decidability as a corollary. This resolves an open question from [11].
3. We show how coercion-resistance of voting protocols can be expressed in our model. In addition to the epistemic and strategic properties, this property has a probabilistic aspect. Again, we obtain decidability as a corollary.

Related Work. In the above-mentioned [9], a decision algorithm for (non-epistemic, complete-information, non-probabilistic) strategic properties of protocols is given. In [10] a decidability result for a strategic property (balance) of contract-signing protocols was established. This result follows from our decidability result. In the very influential paper [17], a logic for authentication protocols was introduced, which models knowledge gained during the run of an authentication protocol. Among the many follow-ups are [18–20].

[13] defines a symbolic model for probabilistic protocols, however no decidability result is proven. We significantly generalize that model: First, we treat security goals that involve epistemic aspects. Second, we treat arbitrary term signatures with equational theories instead of only nonces and signatures as in [13]. Further, we allow arbitrarily complex terms.

Organization. In Sections 1 and 2, we define the protocol model. In Section 3, we recall the semantics of the logic QAPI. Section 4 contains our main result: The question whether a given protocol satisfies a given security property (i.e., a formula) is decidable. Section 5 contains the applications. Due to the page limit, the proof of our main result as well as a more detailed discussion of the applications are omitted and can be found in the full version of the paper [21].

1   Syntax: Specifying a Protocol

1.1   Two Examples

The Coin-Flipping Protocol. In the coin-flipping protocol (cp. Introduction), Bob chooses his bit first and thus cannot dictate the outcome of the protocol (as Alice verifies consistency with the hash value). We therefore consider the more interesting case of dishonest Alice: Only the hash function prevents her from dictating the result unilaterally. Hence we first consider the case that Alice is the adversary, and assume that only Bob follows the protocol, his specification is presented in the left-hand side of Figure 1. Dashed lines represent messages received by Bob, solid ones are messages sent by him. The message $\langle \alpha, N \rangle$ is a pair containing the bit α and the ran-

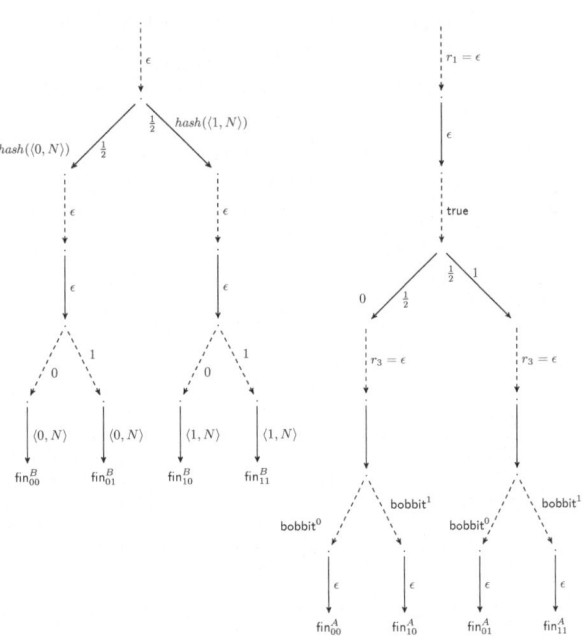

Fig. 1. Coin-Flipping Protocol: Specification

dom string N. The probabilities $\frac{1}{2}$ express that Bob chooses the bits 0 and 1 with probability $\frac{1}{2}$ each. Omitted probabilities are 1. Different messages from Alice (0 or 1) lead to different follow-up states for Bob. We omit error states for syntactically incorrect incoming messages, etc. Since our model is concurrent, we add a dummy sequence for the step when Alice is active.

In our formalism, the security property of the coin-flip protocol is expressed as $\forall_3 S \neg \langle\langle \mathcal{A} : S \rangle\rangle^{>0.5} \Diamond \left(\mathsf{fin}_{00}^B \vee \mathsf{fin}_{11}^B \right)$. The formula expresses that for every strategy S (that cannot break the hash function, this is specified by the index 3), if the adversary Alice follows S, she only has a probability of $\frac{1}{2}$ to reach a state in which both random bits are the same and hence the result bit is 0; the 1-case is symmetric.

As a further example, we also show how Alice's role can be specified in our model. For simplicity, the graphical representation in the right-hand side of Figure 1 uses the terms r_i for the message Alice received in the i-th protocol step (our general notation will be introduced below). The final receive step made by Alice is the most important one: Here she receives the pair $\langle b_1, N \rangle$ from Bob. Alice now checks that Bob did not cheat (i.e., that this pair is indeed consistent with the hash value received earlier in the protocol run), and computes the result of the coinflip. For this, she uses the following test: For $\alpha \in \{0, 1\}$, the "test" bobbit$^\alpha$ is the conjunction $(r_2 = hash(r_4)) \bigwedge (\Pi_1(r_4) = \alpha)$, this test is true iff the pair sent by Bob in step 4 matches the hash value sent earlier and the bit contained in Bob's commitment is α. Here the operator Π_1 denotes extraction of the first element of a pair. Depending on this test and on her own previously chosen bit, Alice then moves into one the states fin_{00}^A, fin_{01}^A, fin_{10}^A, fin_{11}^A, where the bit combinations $\alpha\beta$ denote the 4 possible choices of bits by Alice and Bob (the first bit is Bob's random choice, the second one Alice's).

The test **true** used in the first receive step when the hash value of Bob's pair $\langle b_1, N \rangle$ is received always returns true: At this point of the protocol run, no tests are performed, the value is merely stored for later reference.

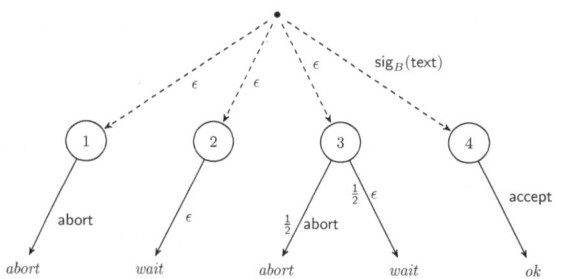

Fig. 2. Protocol State Example

Wait State in a Contract Signing Protocol. Consider the protocol excerpt in Figure 2. There are two possible incoming messages: The empty term ϵ and a cryptographic signature of some text. If ϵ is received, there are three possible reactions: 1. send an **abort**-message, and move to an "aborted" state, 2. move into a waiting state, 3. randomly choose between the first two alternatives. If the signature is received, an ok-state is reached and an **accept** message sent. The random choice in the example is clearly contrived, however there are protocols where randomized decisions are essential, e.g., the contract signing protocol introduced in [13], the coin-flipping protocol discussed above, and random routing.

1.2 Formalizing Protocol States

Our formal protocol definition is the natural one. The most important aspect is how principals react to incoming messages. These reactions depend on observable properties of the message. Such properties are modeled as *tests*. Let IDs be a set of identities in a PKI. Let $\mathcal{N}$ be the disjoint union of the infinite sets $\mathcal{N}_A$ and $\mathcal{N}_i$ for each $i \in$ IDs (nonces generated by the adversary and honest participants). Let $X = \{x_1, x_2, \ldots\}$ be an infinite set of variables. Let Σ^t be a term signature containing function symbols with assigned arities representing cryptographic primitives. The set of terms $\mathcal{T}_{\Sigma^t}$ is defined as usual inductively on $\mathcal{N}$, X, and symbols from Σ^t. We assume that for each $i \in \text{IDs}$, there are terms i, pk_i and sk_i, denoting the name, public and private key of i, and that Σ^t contains operations $\langle .,. \rangle$ to construct tuples and Π_i to access their components. For $C \subseteq \text{IDs}$, the set T_C is the set of terms constructable from Σ^t and $X \cup \bigcup_{i \in C} \mathcal{N}_i \cup \mathcal{N}_{\mathcal{A}}$ where no sk_i for $i \notin C$ appears. We call these terms C-terms. These can be constructed with access to the secret keys and nonces of members of C. We write $T_{\mathcal{A}}$ instead of T_C if C is clear from the context, to highlight that these terms can be constructed by the adversary when the identities in C are corrupted.

We write $t[t_1'/x_1, \ldots, t_n'/x_n]$ for the term obtained from t by simultaneously replacing every occurrence of the variable x_i with the term t_i'.

We assume a convergent equational theory E. See Figure 3 for an example theory with public-key encryption, signatures, and pairing; in the equations x_i refers to an identity, x_t is a term, and x_r represents randomization nonces. The (uniquely determined) *normal form* of a term t, denoted with $[[t]]$,

$$\text{dec}_{\text{sk}_{x_i}}\left(\text{enc}_{\text{pk}_{x_i}}(x_t)^{x_r}\right) = x_t$$

$$\text{verify}\left(\text{sig}_{\text{sk}_{x_i}}(x_t)^{x_r}, x_t, \text{pk}_{x_i}\right) = \text{ok}$$

$$\text{for } i \in \{1,2\}, \Pi_i\langle t_1, t_2 \rangle = t_i$$

Fig. 3. Example equational theory

is obtained by exhaustive application of equations from E. In the example, if $t = \text{dec}_{\text{sk}_A}\left(\text{enc}_{\text{pk}_A}(\text{abort})^r\right)$, then $[[t]] = \text{abort}$.

Formally, an *equation* over Σ^t is a pair of Σ^t-terms (l, r), written as $l = r$ (our equations are "oriented," where intuitively, we write the "more complicated" term on the left-hand side). An *equational theory* E over Σ^t is a set of equations over Σ^t. For example, the equation $\text{dec}_{\text{sk}_{x_i}}\left(\text{enc}_{\text{pk}_{x_i}}(x_t)^{x_r}\right) = x_t$ in the theory from Figure 3 models that when encrypting a term x_t with the public key of an identity x_i with randomness x_r, and decrypting the term with the private key of the same identity, then the result is x_t again. This equation is a "simplification rule," transforming a complex term (the ciphertext) into a simpler term (the plaintext). E induces a *rewrite relation* $\rightarrow_E$ on terms, where $t_1 \rightarrow_E t_2$ if t_2 can be obtained from t_1 by applying a rule in E in the natural way.

With $\twoheadrightarrow_E^*$, we denote closure of $\rightarrow_E$ under transitivity, reflexivity, and application of function symbols (i.e., rules can be applied in subterms); $\equiv_E$ is the closure of $\twoheadrightarrow_E^*$ under symmetry and transitivity. Terms t_1 and t_2 are called E-*equivalent*, if $t_1 \equiv_E t_2$. The relation $\rightarrow_E$ is *confluent*, if for all t, t_1, t_2 with $t \twoheadrightarrow_E^* t_1$ and $t \twoheadrightarrow_E^* t_2$, there is some t' with $t_1 \twoheadrightarrow_E^* t'$ and $t_2 \twoheadrightarrow_E^* t'$. The relation $\rightarrow_E$ is *terminating* if there is no infinite sequence of terms t_1, t_2, ... such that for all i we have $t_i \neq t_{i+1}$ and $t_i \rightarrow_E t_{i+1}$. The theory E is *convergent* if $\rightarrow_E$ is both confluent and terminating.

E is a *convergent subterm theory* [22] if for each $(l, r) \in E$, r is a subterm of l or a constant, and E is convergent. Convergent subterm theories cover many interesting applications including the behavior of usual cryptographic primitives. Many decision problems for such theories are decidable [22].

A term $t \in \mathcal{T}_{\Sigma^t}$ is in *normal form* or a *message* if $t \twoheadrightarrow_E^* t'$ implies $t = t'$. If $\twoheadrightarrow_E$ is convergent, then for each term t there is a unique term t' in normal form such that $t \twoheadrightarrow_E^* t'$, we denote this term with $[[t]]$. If $\twoheadrightarrow_E$ is convergent, then terms are equivalent if and only if they have the same normal form.

Definition 1. *[11] For a set C of identifies, an* atomic C-test *is a pair (M, M') of C-terms where exactly one variable x appears in M and M'. A message m satisfies (M, M'), if $M[m/x] \equiv_E M'[m/x]$. A C-test is a Boolean combination of atomic C-tests, with the obvious semantics. Messages m and m' are C-indistinguishable if there is no C-test that exactly one of them satisfies.*

The definition extends to sequences of messages. Indistinguishibility is also known as *static equivalence* [23]. We now define protocol states. These specify how an incoming message is handled in a protocol: Depending on properties of the message (modeled with tests), there are different possible choices how a principal can react. In randomized protocols, these choices are probability distributions over actions, where an action consists of a reply message and a state change. In the definition below, the parsing sequence corresponds to the dashed lines in the example above; the send sequence formalizes the solid lines. A state hence consists of the dashed lines originating at the same point plus their solid successors. The dashed lines are labeled with tests (the example also uses ϵ as the test satisfied by the empty message only), the solid lines are labeled with terms sent as replies and the probabilities with which they are chosen. In Section 2 below, we will explain the semantics of the protocol execution.

Definition 2. *A protocol state w is a special symbol* Finished *or consists of*

- *a parsing sequence $t_1, \ldots, t_k$, where each t_i is a test,*
- *a send sequence $(s_{1_1}, \alpha_{1,1}), \ldots, (s_{1,l}, \alpha_{1,l}), (s_{2,1}, \alpha_{2,1}), \ldots, (s_{k,l}, \alpha_{k,l})$, where each $s_{i,j}$ is a term, and $\alpha_{i,j} \geq 0$ is a rational number with $\sum_{j=1}^{l} \alpha_{i,j} = 1$ for all $i \in \{1, \ldots, k\}$.*

If w is not Finished*, then a number $i \in \{1, \ldots, k\}$ is a* choice *in w, and l is the* randomization degree *of w. We also call such states* regular protocol states.

A protocol role is a program for a principal (see Figure 1). It combines states into a tree, with different possible actions in each state. We assume sufficiently many copies of Finished, so that a protocol role may have different final states. We model a single protocol session, a finite number of concurrent sessions can be implemented by expressing the resulting interleaving protocol in our model.

Definition 3. *A protocol role $\mathcal{R}$ consists of a finite directed tree (V, E), where V is a set of protocol states and E is a set of labeled edges such that:*

- *If $w \in V$ has k choices and randomization degree l, then w has $k \cdot l$ successors with edges labeled with (i, j) for $i \in \{1, \ldots, k\}$ and $j \in \{1, \ldots, l\}$.*
- *If $w \in V$ is a copy of* Finished*, then w does not have any successor.*
- *There is an identity $i \in$ IDs such that every subterm appearing in $\mathcal{R}$ is an i-term, i is also called the* identity *of $\mathcal{R}$.*

Requiring an identify for each role ensures it uses a single private key only. A *k-roles protocol* is a tuple $Pr = (\mathcal{R}_1, \ldots, \mathcal{R}_k)$, where each $\mathcal{R}_i$ is a protocol role.

2   Semantics: Executing a Protocol

We first informally describe the execution of protocols. Again, k is the number of honest protocol participants. Principals send and receive messages consisting of $(k+1)$-ary tuples. An incoming message contains in component i the message from principal $i \in \{1, \ldots, k\}$ or the adversary if $i = k + 1$. Analogously, the message sent in each round is a tuple with $(k + 1)$ entries, where the i-th entry is intended to be sent to principal i, or to the adversary if $i = k + 1$.

An honest principal $h \in \{1, \ldots, k\}$ operates as follows: In each state, h analyzes the incoming message tuple, and checks for each test from the parsing sequence whether the message satisfies it. The test takes the history of the protocol run into account, i.e., is applied to the sequence of messages received so far by h. If test t_c is satisfied, a number $d \in \{1, \ldots, l\}$ is chosen randomly using the distribution specified by $\alpha_{c,1}, \ldots, \alpha_{c,l}$, and the term $s_{c,d}$ is the reply sent by h. Using a variable referring to the sequence of previously received messages, the reply may depend on previously received messages. The local successor state is determined by the outgoing edge (c, d) of the current one. If the incoming message satisfies more than one of the tests, the principal makes a *strategic choice* by choosing the one to apply. This occurs in the above contract-signing example if the incoming message is the empty term. To avoid cumbersome case distinctions, we require that for every message, there must be a test that it satisfies.

The adversary may send arbitrary terms that he can construct using the secret keys from *corrupted* identities.

2.1   Formal Protocol Model as a Concurrent Game Structure

The formal model combines a set of global states of a protocol run (containing the protocol state of every participant) with the possible actions (*"moves"*) and consequences thereof for every party. A usual way to specify strategic situations as this one are concurrent game structures (CGS). We use the definition from [24], which models probabilistic games and incomplete information:

Definition 4. *A concurrent game structure is a tuple* $\mathcal{C} = (\Sigma, Q, \mathbb{P}, \pi, \Delta, \delta, \mathsf{eq})$:
- Σ *and* $\mathbb{P}$ *are non-empty, finite sets of* players *and* propositional variables, Q *is a non-empty set of* states,
- $\pi \colon \mathbb{P} \to 2^Q$ *is a* propositional assignment *(p is true in all states from* $\pi(p)$*),*
- Δ *is a* move function *assigning to each state* q *and player* a *a nonempty set* $\Delta(q, a)$ *of* moves *available at state* q *to player* a*. For* $A \subseteq \Sigma$ *and* $q \in Q$*, an* (A, q)-move *is a function* c *mapping each* $a \in A$ *to a move* $c(a) \in \Delta(q, a)$*.*
- δ *is a* probabilistic *transition function which for each state* q *and* (Σ, q)-move c *specifies a discrete probability distribution* $\delta(q, c)$ *on* Q *(the distribution of the follow-up state of* q *if all players perform their move as specified by* c*),*
- eq *is an* information function $\mathsf{eq} \colon \{1, \ldots, n\} \times \Sigma \to \mathcal{P}(Q \times Q)$*, where* n *is a natural number, and for each* $i \in \{1, \ldots, n\}$ *and* $a \in \Sigma$*,* $\mathsf{eq}(i, a)$ *is an equivalence relation on* Q*. Each* $i \in \{1, \ldots, n\}$ *is called a* degree of information.

A subset $A \subseteq \Sigma$ is a *coalition of* $\mathcal{C}$. We write $q_1 \sim_{\mathsf{eq}_i(A)} q_2$ for $(q_1, q_2) \in \cap_{a \in A} \mathsf{eq}(i, a)$. If $q_1 \sim_{\mathsf{eq}_i(a)} q_2$, then player a cannot distinguish states q_1 and q_2 (if i denotes the degree of information available to him). Multiple degrees of information allow to dynamically specify the information available to principals, e.g., whether they are regarded as being able to break cryptography, etc.

We define the protocol execution as CGS, which formalizes the mechanisms described earlier. In the state description below, C is the set of corrupted identities, each honest principal $h \in \{1, \dots, k\}$ is in protocol state w_h. For each principal $i \in \{1, \dots, k, \mathcal{A}\}$, the sequence $\mathcal{M}_i$ contains the messages received so far. The sequence $\mathrm{moves}_{\mathcal{A}}$ records the moves performed by the adversary. The numbers c_h and d_h are the strategic and random choices made by h. The propositional variables allow to reason about the local state of honest principals.

Definition 5. *Let* $Pr = (\mathcal{R}_1, \dots, \mathcal{R}_k)$ *be a protocol. The* CGS *induced by* Pr *is* $\mathcal{C}_{Pr} = (\Sigma, Q, \mathbb{P}, \pi, \Delta, \delta, \mathsf{eq})$, *where*

- $\Sigma = \{1, \dots, k, \mathcal{A}\}$,
- Q *consists of tuples of the form* $q = (C, w_1, \mathcal{M}_1, \dots, w_k, \mathcal{M}_k, \mathcal{M}_{\mathcal{A}}, \mathrm{moves}_{\mathcal{A}})$, *where* $C \subseteq \mathrm{IDs}$, *for each* $i \in \{1, \dots, k\}$, w_i *is a protocol state of* $\mathcal{R}_i$, $\mathcal{M}_i$ *and* $\mathcal{M}_{\mathcal{A}}$ *are sequences of messages, and* $\mathrm{moves}_{\mathcal{A}}$ *is a sequence of terms.*
- *for each protocol state* w *occurring in* Pr *and each* $h \in \{1, \dots, k\}$ *there is a propositional variable* st^h_w *which is true in a state* q *as above iff* $w_h = w$,
- *for a state* q *as above where for all* $h \in \{1, \dots, k\}$, w_h *has* k_h *choices, randomization degree* l_h, *parsing sequence* $t^h_1, \dots, t^h_{k_h}$ *and send sequence* $(s^h_{1,1}, \alpha^h_{1,1}), \dots, (s^h_{k_h, l_h}, \alpha^h_{k_h, l_h})$, *the available moves are as follows: For* $\mathcal{A}$, *every term* $m_{\mathcal{A}} \in T_{\mathcal{A}}$ *is a move, for an honest principal* $h \in \{1, \dots, k\}$, *the number* $c_h \in \{1, \dots, k_h\}$ *is a move if and only if* $\mathcal{M}_h$ *satisfies the test* $t^h_{c_h}$. *The transition function* δ *is defined as follows: For the move determined by the adversary move* $m_{\mathcal{A}}$ *and the principal moves* $c_1, \dots, c_k$ *and numbers* $d_1, \dots, d_k$, *where* $1 \le d_h \le l_h$, *there is a successor state* $q' = (C, w'_1, \mathcal{M}'_1, \dots, w'_k, \mathcal{M}'_k, \mathcal{M}'_{\mathcal{A}}, \mathrm{moves}_{\mathcal{A}} \circ m_{\mathcal{A}})$, *where*

  - w'_h *is the successor of* w_h *in* $\mathcal{R}_h$ *connected with the edge labeled* (c_h, d_h),
  - *to define* $\mathcal{M}'_j$, *we denote with* M_i *for* $i \in \{1, \dots, k, \mathcal{A}\}$ *the message sent by* i, *which is* $[[s^i_{c_i, d_i}[\mathcal{M}_i / x]]]$ *if* $i \le k$, *or* $[[m_{\mathcal{A}}[\mathcal{M}_{\mathcal{A}} / x]]]$ *if* $i = \mathcal{A}$,
  - *for all* $i \in \{1, \dots, k, \mathcal{A}\}$, *the new sequence* $\mathcal{M}'_i$ *is obtained by adding to* $\mathcal{M}_i$ *a* $(k+1)$-*ary tuple containing in its* j-*th component the* i-*th component of* M_j *(i.e., the term that* j *sends to* i*),*
  - *the probability of this successor state is* $\prod_{h=1}^{k} \alpha^h_{c_h, d_h}$.

  If a principal is in a copy of **Finished**, *he only has dummy moves.*
- *We define three information degrees: For a player* $a \in \Sigma$,

  1. $\mathsf{eq}(1, a)$ *is the equality relation—this models complete information modulo* $\equiv_{\mathrm{E}}$ *(since the states only contain normal forms of terms),*

2. *in* eq$(2, a)$, *two states are equivalent if and only if principal a is in the same local state[1], and the component $\mathcal{M}_a$ is the same in both states (this models local information with ability to break cryptography[2])*

3. eq$(3, a)$ *is the equivalence relation where states are equivalent if and only if the principal is in the same local state[1], and components $\mathcal{M}_a$ are a-indistinguishable (C-indistinguishable if $a = \mathcal{A}$).*

The message received by a principal in each step is a tuple containing messages from every protocol principal, allowing simultaneous processing of messages. Messages are immediately delivered to the intended recipients using secure channels. Realistically, use of such channels can be restricted by using *buffer principals* which the adversary may instruct to delay/drop messages.[3] These are modeled as ordinary protocol roles relaying messages, allowing flexible "implementations" of channels and various levels of "adversary activeness:" If a protocol does not use buffers at all, but principals only communicate via the adversary, the adversary is active without restriction. If all communication uses secure channels (with copies sent to the adversary), the adversary is passive. Intermediate degrees can express secure channels to trusted third parties, etc.

For each $C \subseteq$ IDs, there is an *initial state* $q_{init}^C = (C, r_1, \epsilon, r_2, \epsilon, \ldots, r_k, \epsilon, \epsilon, \epsilon)$, where r_i is the root of $\mathcal{R}_i$. In this state, no message has been sent, every principal is in its initial state, and the adversary knows the keys of all identities in C. This models *static corruption*, where a set of identities (fixed before the protocol run) as adversarial. See Section 5.3 for an example of dynamic corruption. We remove all states from $\mathcal{C}_{Pr}$ that cannot be reached from one of the initial states.

We note that there are two ways in which probabilism is relevant in our model: First, protocol specifications may use random decisions as in the coin-flipping protocol. Second, some security properties contain success probabilities. In the coin-flipping protocol, the adversary has a success probability of $\frac{1}{2}$ but not higher, we will sketch a less trivial application in Section 5.4.

3   Probabilistic, Epistemic ATL with Strategy Quantification

To express security goals, we use the ATL*-variant QAPI [14, 24]. QAPI is not security-specific, but a logic for reasoning about strategic and epistemic properties of general multi-agent systems. QAPI is very expressive and generalizes several related logics. We only discuss the subset of QAPI relevant for this paper, however our results hold for the complete logic. [14] contains detailed discussions and comparisons as well as references to many related logics.

---

[1] The local state of $\mathcal{A}$ consists of the set C and the sequence moves$_\mathcal{A}$.

[2] This only allows the *knowledge* and *decisions* of principals to depend on "hidden" information, but does not allow e.g., the adversary to send a hidden plaintext as part of a message on his own. The latter can be expressed in our model with letting the adversary corrupt the corresponding identities.

[3] In order to avoid infinite protocol runs, we forbid rounds in which the adversary delays every available channel in the obvious way.

3.1   Formulas

QAPI extends ATL* with epistemic features, probabilities, and explicit strategies. Formulas may contain variables $S_1, \ldots, S_n$ referring to strategies, these will
be bound by quantifiers. This allows explicit reasoning about strategies.

Definition 6. *The set of* QAPI-*formulas for a CGS* $\mathcal{C}$ *is defined as follows:*

- *A propositional variable of* $\mathcal{C}$ *is a state formula, conjunctions and negations
  of state (path) formulas for* $\mathcal{C}$ *are state (path) formulas for* $\mathcal{C}$,
- *every state formula is a path formula,*
- *if* $A_1, \ldots, A_n$ *are coalitions,* ◀ *is one of* $\leq, <, \geq, >$, ψ *is a path formula, and*
  $S_1, \ldots, S_n$ *are variables for strategies, then* $\langle\langle A_1 : S_1, \ldots, A_n : S_n \rangle\rangle^{\blacktriangleleft \alpha} \psi$ *is
  a state formula,*
- *if* A *is a coalition,* i *is a degree of information, and* ψ *is a state formula,
  then* $\mathcal{K}_i^A \psi$ *is a state formula,*
- *If* φ_1 *and* φ_2 *are path formulas, then so are* $\mathsf{X}\varphi_1$, $\mathsf{P}\varphi_1$, $\mathsf{X}^{-1}\varphi_1$, *and* $\varphi_1 \mathsf{U} \varphi_2$.

Intuitively, $\langle\langle A_1 : S_1, \ldots, A_n : S_n \rangle\rangle^{\blacktriangleleft \alpha} \psi$ expresses that if the coalitions $A_1, \ldots,$
A_n play the strategies referred to by $S_1, \ldots, S_n$, then for every possible behavior
of the remaining players, the probability that the resulting sequence of states
satisfies the formula ψ is ◀ α. The formula $\mathcal{K}_i^A \psi$ expresses "coalition A *knows*
that ψ is true (with information degree i)." We use standard abbreviations like
$\varphi \vee \psi = \neg(\neg\varphi \wedge \neg\psi)$, $\varphi \rightarrow \psi = \neg\varphi \vee \psi$, $\Diamond\varphi = \mathsf{true}\,\mathsf{U}\varphi$, and $\Box\varphi = \neg\Diamond\neg\varphi$.

3.2   Strategies and Semantics

An a-*strategy* for a player a is a function s assigning a move from $\Delta(q, a)$ to
each state q. It is i-*uniform*, if $q_1 \sim_{\mathsf{eq}_i(a)} q_2$ implies $s(q_1) = s(q_2)$: In states
that a player cannot tell apart with information degree i, he performs the same
move. For a coalition A, an A-*strategy* is a family $(s_a)_{a \in A}$, where each s_a is an
a-strategy, it is i-uniform if every s_a is. We only consider *memoryless* strategies,
since each state contains complete information about the preceding protocol run.
Formulas are evaluated on states or on paths, where a *path* is a sequence λ of
states in a CGS $\mathcal{C}$. With $\lambda[i]$ we denote the i-th state in λ.

Definition 7. *Let* $\mathcal{C} = (\Sigma, Q, \mathbb{P}, \pi, \Delta, \delta, \mathsf{eq})$ *be a CGS, let* φ *be a state formula,
let* ψ_1 *and* ψ_2 *be path formulas, let* $S_1, \ldots, S_n$ *be strategies instantiating the
variables* $S_1, \ldots, S_n$, *let* λ *be a path, let* $t \in \mathbb{N}$, *let* $q \in Q$ *be a state, let* $\overrightarrow{S}$ *be an
abbreviation for* $(S_1, \ldots, S_n)$. *Then*

- $\mathcal{C}, \overrightarrow{S}, q \models p$ *iff* $q \in \pi(p)$ *for* $p \in \mathbb{P}$,
- *negation and conjunction are treated as usual,*
- $(\lambda, t), \overrightarrow{S} \models \varphi$ *iff* $\mathcal{C}, \overrightarrow{S}, \lambda[t] \models \varphi$,
- $(\lambda, t), \overrightarrow{S} \models \mathsf{X}\psi_1$ *iff* $(\lambda, t + 1), \overrightarrow{S} \models \psi_1$,
- $(\lambda, t), \overrightarrow{S} \models \mathsf{P}\psi_1$ *iff* $(\lambda, t'), \overrightarrow{S} \models \psi_1$, *for some* $t' \leq t$,
- $(\lambda, t), \overrightarrow{S} \models \mathsf{X}^{-1}\psi_1$ *iff* $t \geq 1$ *and* $(\lambda, t - 1), \overrightarrow{S} \models \psi_1$,

- (λ, t), $\overrightarrow{\mathsf{S}} \models \psi_1 \mathsf{U} \psi_2$ *iff there is some* $i \geq t$ *such that* (λ, i), $\overrightarrow{\mathsf{S}} \models \psi_2$ *and* (λ, j), $\overrightarrow{\mathsf{S}} \models \psi_1$ *for all* $t \leq j < i$,
- $\mathcal{C}$, $\overrightarrow{\mathsf{S}}$, $q \models \mathcal{K}_i^A \varphi_1$ *iff* $\mathcal{C}$, $\overrightarrow{\mathsf{S}}$, $q' \models \varphi_1$ *for all* $q' \in Q$ *with* $q' \sim_{\mathsf{eq}_i(A)} q$,
- $\mathcal{C}$, $\overrightarrow{\mathsf{S}}$, $q \models \langle\langle A_{i_1} : \mathsf{S}_{i_1}, \ldots, A_{i_k} : \mathsf{S}_{i_k} \rangle\rangle^{\blacktriangleleft \alpha} \psi$ *iff when coalition* A_{i_j} *plays*[4] *the* A_{i_j}*-strategy* S_{i_j} *for all* j, *then the resulting path satisfies* ψ *with probability* $\blacktriangleleft \alpha$, *for every possible behavior of the players in* $\Sigma \setminus (A_{i_1} \cup \cdots \cup A_{i_k})$.

This definition treats formulas where strategies instantiating the variables S_i are given. A *quantified strategy formula* is a state formula prefixed by a quantifier block where each strategy variable S_i is quantified with $\exists_i$ or $\forall_i$ for an information degree i. This expresses "there is (for all) i-uniform strategies," with the obvious semantics: $\exists_{i_1} \mathsf{S}_1 \forall_{i_2} \mathsf{S}_2 \ldots \exists_{i_n} \mathsf{S}_n \varphi$ is true in state q if there is a i_1-uniform strategy S_1 such that for all i_2-uniform strategies S_2, ..., there is an i_n-uniform strategy S_n such that this choice of strategies satisfies φ according to the definition above.

3.3 Modeling of Knowledge

The knowledge operator used in QAPI (see above) has the usual semantics from epistemic logics. For security settings, this is often unsuitable: If a party "knows" a fact to be true with probability significantly larger than $\frac{1}{2}$, is often enough for a protocol to be insecure. This, however, is not captured in the standard definition. Also, a party's knowledge may sometimes take other principals' strategies into account, which also cannot be expressed with the standard epistemic knowledge operator. However, QAPI's quantified strategies can be used to address these issues. As an example, "(with information degree i) there is a strategy s_A such that B knows whether φ holds with probability at least $\frac{4}{5}$, if B knows that A follows s_A," can be expressed as follows: We modify the protocol for B to allow an "announcement" proclaiming that B believes φ to be true.[5] Let bel_φ be a formula true in all states in which B has made this announcement (see also [25]). Then the above can be expressed as

$$\exists_i \mathsf{S}_A \exists_i \mathsf{S}_B \, \langle\langle A : \mathsf{S}_A, B : \mathsf{S}_B \rangle\rangle^{\geq \frac{4}{5}} \, (\varphi \iff \Diamond \mathsf{bel}_\varphi).$$

Here it is crucial that the strategy chosen for S_B may depend on the one chosen for S_A. Our discussion of coercion-resistance (Section 5.4) contains an example of a security analysis where such considerations are relevant. The above discussion shows that explicit *uniform* strategies are strong enough to express the knowledge operator, although at the cost of modifying the game structure (in our case, the protocol). Hence the basic knowledge operator can be seen as "syntactic sugar," which we however keep in the language as it can increase readability. We are grateful to anonymous reviewers pointing out these issues.

---

[4] If a appears in more than one A_{i_j}, he follows strategy S_{i_j} with $j = \min \{ j \mid a \in A_{i_j} \}$.

[5] This can be done by e.g., introducing a dedicated party who receives messages saying "I believe φ is true/false," or with several other natural mechanisms

4 Main Result

Security of protocols in our model is decidable for convergent subterm theories:

Theorem 1. *Assume that* E *is a convergent subterm theory. There is an algorithm which, given a protocol Pr, a set C of corrupted identities, and a quantified strategy formula φ, decides whether $\mathcal{C}_{Pr}, q_{init}^{C} \models \varphi$.*

The challenge in the proof is that active adversaries can send arbitrarily complex messages, leading to an infinite structure $\mathcal{C}_{Pr}$. We show that it suffices to consider "bounded strategies:" Protocols only parse terms up to a bounded depth; rewriting rules resulting from convergent subterm theories also have "bounded" effects. It follows that one can restrict the adversary to send terms of bounded depth. This [2]-style argument only directly covers reachability properties; more involved arguments apply to strategic and epistemic properties.

5 Applications

We now show several examples of applications of our result. In addition to our running coin-flipping example, we also treat abuse-freeness of contract signing protocols. We briefly mention that standard anonymous broadcast protocols as the dining cryptographers can be expressed in our model in the straight-forward way. We also treat two applications that use our framework in a less obvious way, namely 1. accountability and verifiability, and 2. coercion-resistance of voting protocols. An in-depth discussion of these properties is out of the scope of this paper, we treat these properties in as much detail as required to highlight the features of our approach. In particular, our treatment uses direct reasoning about strategies, epistemic and probabilistic aspects in an essential way.

5.1 The Coin-Flipping Protocol

The coin-flipping protocol satisfies its previously-mentioned security property:

Proposition 1. *The state $q_{init}^{\{Alice\}}$ of the CGS induced by the coin-flipping protocol satisfies the formula $\forall_3 S \neg \langle\langle \mathcal{A} : S \rangle\rangle^{>0.5} \Diamond \left(fin_{00}^{B} \vee fin_{11}^{B} \right)$.*

The formula is satisfied because the messages $hash(\langle 0, N \rangle)$ and $hash(\langle 1, N \rangle)$ are indistinguishable for Alice, since she does not know N. Therefore, a 3-uniform strategy has to choose the same action for both of Bob's possible messages.

5.2 Abuse-Freeness of Contract Signing Protocols

If Alice and Bob want to exchange a contract, abuse-freeness requires that there is no situation where Bob can prove to an outsider Charly that the current state is *unbalanced*, i.e., Bob can unilaterally decide whether the contracts are successfully exchanged or not. A straight-forward definition of abuse-freeness is "there is no point in the execution of the protocol where Bob has a strategy to ensure that Charly knows that the protocol is in an unbalanced state." This can be expressed in our model in the obvious way. In the full version of this paper [21], we show how the more complex definition of abuse-freeness given in [11] can be expressed in our framework. As a consequence, we obtain decidability of abuse-freeness. This resolves an open question from [11].

5.3 Accountability and Verifiability

Accountability and verifiability are properties relevant for protocols involving trusted third parties, e.g., voting [26], auctions [27], contract signing [5], identity-based encryption etc. In [28], a formal definition of accountability is given that is independent of the specific application.

Accountability requires that if a protocol run "fails" (i.e., does not achieve some goal), then a party J (the "judge") can determine which one of the participants in the protocol "misbehaved," i.e., did not follow the protocol.

Up to now, we modeled principals either as honest, or as part of the adversary. Accountability is concerned with principals who have a "wanted" behavior (the protocol), but can start "misbehaving" during the protocol run (i.e., abandon the protocol and behaving adversary-like from that point on).

To express this we use our model in a different way: We modify every honest principal of the protocol except J to run an "adversary program" at any time. This is a new sub-branch of the protocol, and forwards received messages to the adversary, lets the adversary dictate messages to be sent to the other principals, and provides an oracle for operations involving the private key of the "misbehaving" identity, e.g., decrypts ciphertexts and signs messages as instructed by the adversary (the exact set of services provided depends on the involved cryptographic primitives).[6] Since the variables in $\mathcal{C}_{Pr}$ indicate the current state of honest principals, for each i we have a formula φ_i^{adv} that is true iff i runs the adversary program. Forwarding and oracle access causes delay in the protocol execution, to account for this we introduce "wait cycles" into the protocol. The adversary program essentially models dynamic corruption.

In [28], *individual accountability* is defined as follows: At the end of every protocol run in which a goal φ is not satisfied, J announces the identity of some party that did not follow the protocol (using a distinguished state for each output). Let blame_i be a formula that is true if J announced that i "misbehaved." Let φ be a goal. Then a protocol provides individual accountability for φ if the following formula is satisfied ($\forall_1 S_\emptyset \langle\langle \emptyset : S_\emptyset \rangle\rangle$ quantifies over all reachable states):

$$\forall_1 S_\emptyset \langle\langle \emptyset : S_\emptyset \rangle\rangle \, \square \left((\neg\varphi \rightarrow \Diamond(\bigvee_{i \in I} \mathrm{blame}_i)) \wedge \square(\bigwedge_{i \in I} \mathrm{blame}_i \rightarrow \varphi_i^{\mathsf{adv}}) \right).$$

---

[6] Usually, the adversary only accesses the oracle a finite number of times: Decryptions and signatures are only necessary for encryptions done by, or signature verifications performed by, honest principals; these only perform a finite number of operations. Hence the "oracle" can be implemented in a finite protocol role.

This expresses that if φ is not satisfied, then at the end of the run J will correctly announce one identity from I that did not follow the protocol, and all announcements of J are indeed "correct."

The above does not use epistemic or strategic properties: We merely expressed that J works "correctly." Epistemic features come into play when the situation is less clear than above, i.e., when there is no existing judge procedure that we can use. We can ask whether a party J has enough information[7] to serve as a judge, and derive an implementation. The following expresses that if φ is false, then J will know, for some party i, that i did not follow the protocol:

$$\forall_1 S_\emptyset \, \langle\langle \emptyset : S_\emptyset \rangle\rangle \, \Box(\neg\varphi \to \Diamond(\bigvee_{i \in I} (\mathcal{K}_3^J \varphi_i^{\text{adv}}))).$$

If the formula is true, J has enough knowledge to serve as judge (the index 3 states that J's knowledge is limited by cryptography). We obtain an "implementation" of J in a straight-forward way: We allow J (in addition to other instructions that J follows in the original protocol) to perform "blame" announcements as earlier. We now ask whether there is a strategy for J to "blame correctly:"

$$\exists_3 S_J \, \langle\langle J : S_J \rangle\rangle \, (\Box(\neg\varphi \to \Diamond(\bigvee_{i \in I} \text{blame}_i)) \wedge \bigwedge_{i \in I} (\text{blame}_i \to \varphi_i^{\text{adv}})),$$

in the positive case the strategy for J then encodes a verification program. Finally, verifiability can be seen as a weaker form of accountability. In [28], it is defined as follows: A goal φ of a protocol Pr is verifiable by J if J knows whether φ holds when the protocol run is over. This can be easily expressed in our model: Let end be a propositional variable that is true at the end of the protocol run. Then the formula

$$\forall_1 S_\emptyset \, \langle\langle \emptyset : S_\emptyset \rangle\rangle \, \Box(\text{end} \to (\mathcal{K}_3^J \varphi \vee \mathcal{K}_3^J \neg\varphi))$$

expresses that J knows whether φ holds at the end of every possible protocol run. Theorem 1 now implies decidability of accountability and verifiability.

5.4   Coercion-Resistance of Voting Protocols

Coercion-resistance requires that no voter Alice can prove to a party Charly that she voted as instructed by him, precluding selling of votes. In [29], coercion-resistance is defined[8] as follows: For every "coercer strategy" of Charly, there is a "counter-strategy" for Alice such that Alice's vote is counted as she wants to vote, but Charly believes that he controlled her voting process.

---

[7] Clearly, the protocol must specify which information J has, i.e., which messages J receives—if J has complete information, accountability trivial.

[8] Their definition is given in a cryptographic model, we present an analogous formulation in our symbolic model. Other definitions [30] are expressed in epistemic terms close to our model. However the game-based definition from [29] covers probabilistic aspects that we want to model.

Clearly, we cannot require Charly to *always* fail to "catch" Alice—if Charly's chosen candidate receives zero votes, then Charly knows that Alice did not obey him. We thus allow Charly to correctly guess that Alice voted differently than promised with some probability, possibly larger than $\frac{1}{2}$. See [29] for a discussion of suitable values for the involved probabilities. We model Charly's belief as the probability to successfully "guess" whether Alice followed his instructions. This mirrors the approach of [25] to consider probabilistic knowledge as strategies for a betting game, see also Section 3.3.

We express coercion-resistance in our model. We note that our model requires that the number of communication rounds between Alice and Charly is bounded by a constant, since this has to be encoded into Alice's protocol description. A generalized model with no bounds on the protocol length can be defined, however, such a model will be undecidable (cp. [10]). We stress that neither the complexity nor the structure of the messages are restricted in our model.

In coercion-resistance, two principals may deviate from the protocol: Charly uses a *coercer strategy* to influence Alice, and Alice runs a *counter-strategy* to vote as she intends[9]. Our model allows arbitrary behavior only for the adversary, hence we model *both* the coercer and the counter strategy as adversary-strategies. We introduce a test principal T whose goal it is to determine whether Alice follows Charly's instructions (the adversary plays the "coercer strategy") or uses the "counter-strategy." Since both of these strategies are played by the adversary, we need a way to distinguish them. To this end, the strategies have to "announce themselves:" We let Alice expect, in the first message from the adversary, a bit signaling the performed strategy, she changes local state accordingly. She runs a copy of the adversary program (see Section 5.3) from then on. We use formulas $\varphi^{A-\mathsf{coerc}}$ and $\varphi^{A-\mathsf{counter}}$ to express that the running strategy signaled coercion or counter, respectively. A T-strategy is *successful* if T announces "coercion" iff the running strategy signaled coercion, and "counter" iff the strategy signals "counter." Since T's epistemic capabilities should match Charly's, T has access to the same messages that Charly would see in a protocol run.

To express that the counter-strategy lets Alice vote as she wants, we introduce a principal V (vote) choosing Alice's (sincere) vote, which he sends to Alice. V's strategies then correspond to Alice's possible votes. Coercion-resistance for a probability δ is now (semi-formally) expressed as follows[10]:

> for all $\mathcal{A}$-strategies s_{coerc} signaling coerce
> there is an $\mathcal{A}$-strategy s_{counter} signaling counter s.t.
> s_{counter} lets Alice vote as chosen by V
>   AND no T-strategy is successful with probability $\geq \delta$.

---

[9] Clearly, in many protocols there will be a fixed counter-strategy that Alice can use which we could directly "implement" into our modeling of Alice; this would simplify the modeling of coercion-resistance significantly.

[10] For readability, we omit the universal quantification over V's strategy.

This expresses that for every coercer strategy, there is a counter-strategy letting Alice vote as she wants, and the test principal (with information as available to Charly) cannot identify the performed strategy with probability $\geq \delta$.

To express this in QAPI, let φ^{V} express that Alice voted as instructed by V (this formula depends on the voting system), let $\varphi^{\mathsf{A\text{-}coerc}}$ and $\varphi^{\mathsf{A\text{-}counter}}$ express that coercion (counter) is signaled. Let $\varphi^{\mathsf{T\text{-}suc}}$ indicate that T guesses correctly.

$$\varphi^{\mathsf{T}<\delta} = \neg\left((\langle\langle\mathsf{T}:\mathsf{S_T}, \mathcal{A}:\mathsf{S_{counter}}\rangle\rangle^{\geq\delta}\,\varphi^{\mathsf{T\text{-}suc}}) \wedge (\langle\langle\mathsf{T}:\mathsf{S_T}, \mathcal{A}:\mathsf{S_{coerce}}\rangle\rangle^{\geq\delta}\,\varphi^{\mathsf{T\text{-}suc}}) \right)$$

expresses that T's success probability is less that δ for one of the strategies.

$$\varphi^{\mathsf{sig\text{-}coerce}} = (\langle\langle\mathcal{A}:\mathsf{S_{coerc}}\rangle\rangle^{\geq 1}\,\Diamond\varphi^{\mathsf{A\text{-}coerc}})$$

expresses that $\mathsf{S_{coerc}}$ signals coercing correctly, analogously let $\varphi^{\mathsf{sig\text{-}counter}}$ express that $\mathsf{S_{counter}}$ signals counter. Finally,

$$\varphi^{\mathsf{vote}} = \langle\langle\mathcal{A}:\mathsf{S_{counter}}\rangle\rangle^{\geq 1}\,\Diamond\varphi^{\mathsf{V}}$$

expresses that the strategy $\mathsf{S_{counter}}$ lets Alice vote as she wants to. We now express coercion-resistance as follows:

$$\forall_3\mathsf{S_{coercer}}\exists_3\mathsf{S_{counter}}\forall_3\mathsf{S_V}\forall_3\mathsf{S_T}\varphi^{\mathsf{sig\text{-}coerce}} \rightarrow (\varphi^{\mathsf{sig\text{-}counter}} \wedge \varphi^{\mathsf{vote}} \wedge \varphi^{\mathsf{T}<\delta}).$$

We stress that the coercer- and counter-strategies are played by the adversary $\mathcal{A}$ and not by Alice. Several key features of our approach are used in the above modeling: It is clearly necessary to consider only uniform strategies. We also made extensive use of quantification: Letting the strategy of T depend on the $\mathcal{A}$-strategies is crucial for the approach, as is the ability to directly reason about specific strategies in formulas. Finally, reasoning about success probabilities of strategies was required to express the probabilistic notion of coercion-resistance.

Variations of coercion-resistance can be expressed similarly: One can exchange the order of quantification of the counter-strategy and the strategy of T to only demand that for every fixed test strategy there is a counter-measure, one can require only that Alice's counter-strategy is successful with some given probability, etc. The above implies decidability of coercion-resistance.

6   Conclusion and Future Research

We introduced a decidable model that treats epistemic and strategic properties of probabilistic cryptographic protocols. We demonstrated that the expressiveness of the logic QAPI allows to express complex epistemic and probabilistic security properties. Advanced features as quantification, explicit strategies, and probabilistic reasoning were central in our modeling of the treated security properties. Open questions are a complexity analysis of the model checking problem, and extending decidability to a larger class of equational theories.

Acknowledgments. We are grateful to the anonymous referees and to Thomas Wilke for suggestions which lead to significant improvement of the paper.

References

1. Dolev, D., Yao, A.C.C.: On the security of public key protocols. IEEE Transactions on Information Theory 29(2), 198–207 (1983)
2. Rusinowitch, M., Turuani, M.: Protocol insecurity with a finite number of sessions, composed keys is NP-complete. Theoretical Computer Science 1-3(299), 451–475 (2003)
3. Kremer, S., Raskin, J.F.: Game analysis of abuse-free contract signing. In: CSFW, p. 206. IEEE Computer Society (2002)
4. Ben-Or, M., Goldreich, O., Micali, S., Rivest, R.L.: A fair protocol for signing contracts. IEEE Transactions on Information Theory 36(1), 40–46 (1990)
5. Asokan, N., Shoup, V., Waidner, M.: Asynchronous protocols for optimistic fair exchange. In: Proceedings of the IEEE Symposium on Research in Security and Privacy, pp. 86–99. IEEE Computer Society Press (1998)
6. Garay, J.A., Jakobsson, M., MacKenzie, P.D.: Abuse-Free Optimistic Contract Signing. In: Wiener, M. (ed.) CRYPTO 1999. LNCS, vol. 1666, pp. 449–466. Springer, Heidelberg (1999)
7. Kremer, S., Raskin, J.F.: A game-based verification of non-repudiation and fair exchange protocols. Journal of Computer Security 11(3), 399–430 (2003)
8. Alur, R., Henzinger, T.A., Kupferman, O.: Alternating-time temporal logic. Journal of the ACM 49(5), 672–713 (2002)
9. Kähler, D., Küsters, R., Truderung, T.: Infinite state AMC-model checking for cryptographic protocols. In: LICS, pp. 181–192. IEEE Computer Society (2007)
10. Kähler, D., Küsters, R., Wilke, T.: Deciding properties of contract-signing protocols. Transactions on Computational Logic (2009)
11. Kähler, D., Küsters, R., Wilke, T.: A Dolev-Yao-Based Definition of Abuse-Free Protocols. In: Bugliesi, M., Preneel, B., Sassone, V., Wegener, I. (eds.) ICALP 2006, Part II. LNCS, vol. 4052, pp. 95–106. Springer, Heidelberg (2006)
12. Chaum, D.: The dining cryptographers problem: Unconditional sender and recipient untraceability. J. Cryptology 1(1), 65–75 (1988)
13. Aizatulin, M., Schnoor, H., Wilke, T.: Computationally Sound Analysis of a Probabilistic Contract Signing Protocol. In: Backes, M., Ning, P. (eds.) ESORICS 2009. LNCS, vol. 5789, pp. 571–586. Springer, Heidelberg (2009)
14. Schnoor, H.: Explicit strategies and quantification for ATL with incomplete information and probabilistic games. Technical Report 1008, Institut für Informatik, Christian-Albrechts-Universität zu Kiel (2010)
15. Chatterjee, K., Henzinger, T.A., Piterman, N.: Strategy Logic. In: Caires, L., Vasconcelos, V.T. (eds.) CONCUR 2007. LNCS, vol. 4703, pp. 59–73. Springer, Heidelberg (2007)
16. Even, S., Goldreich, O.: On the security of multi-party ping-pong protocols. In: FOCS, pp. 34–39. IEEE (1983)

17. Burrows, M., Abadi, M., Needham, R.M.: A logic of authentication. ACM Trans. Comput. Syst. 8(1), 18–36 (1990)
18. Abadi, M., Tuttle, M.R.: A semantics for a logic of authentication (extended abstract). In: PODC, pp. 201–216 (1991)
19. Boyd, C., Mao, W.: On a Limitation of BAN Logic. In: Helleseth, T. (ed.) EUROCRYPT 1993. LNCS, vol. 765, pp. 240–247. Springer, Heidelberg (1994)
20. Halpern, J.Y., Pucella, R., van der Meyden, R.: Revisiting the foundations of authentication logics (manuscript)
21. Schnoor, H.: Deciding epistemic and strategic properties of cryptographic protocols. Technical Report 2012/340, Cryptology ePrint Archive (2012)
22. Abadi, M., Cortier, V.: Deciding knowledge in security protocols under equational theories. Theoretical Computer Science 367(1-2), 2–32 (2006)
23. Abadi, M., Fournet, C.: Mobile values, new names, and secure communication. In: POPL, pp. 104–115 (2001)
24. Schnoor, H.: Strategic planning for probabilistic games with incomplete information. In: van der Hoek, W., Kaminka, G.A., Lespérance, Y., Luck, M., Sen, S. (eds.) AAMAS. IFAAMAS, pp. 1057–1064 (2010)
25. Halpern, J.Y., Tuttle, M.R.: Knowledge, probability, and adversaries. J. ACM 40(4), 917–962 (1993)
26. Kremer, S., Ryan, M., Smyth, B.: Election Verifiability in Electronic Voting Protocols. In: Gritzalis, D., Preneel, B., Theoharidou, M. (eds.) ESORICS 2010. LNCS, vol. 6345, pp. 389–404. Springer, Heidelberg (2010)
27. Parkes, D.C., Rabin, M.O., Shieber, S.M., Thorpe, C.: Practical secrecy-preserving, verifiably correct and trustworthy auctions. Electronic Commerce Research and Applications 7(3), 294–312 (2008)
28. Küsters, R., Truderung, T., Vogt, A.: Accountability: Definition and relationship to verifiability. In: Al-Shaer, E., Keromytis, A.D., Shmatikov, V. (eds.) ACM Conference on Computer and Communications Security, pp. 526–535. ACM (2010)
29. Küsters, R., Truderung, T., Vogt, A.: A game-based definition of coercion-resistance and its applications. In: CSF, pp. 122–136. IEEE Computer Society (2010)
30. Küsters, R., Truderung, T.: An epistemic approach to coercion-resistance for electronic voting protocols. In: IEEE Symposium on Security and Privacy, pp. 251–266. IEEE Computer Society (2009)

Satisfiability and Feasibility
in a Relationship-Based Workflow Authorization Model

Arif Akram Khan and Philip W.L. Fong

Department of Computer Science
University of Calgary
Calgary, Alberta, Canada
{arikhan,pwlfong}@ucalgary.ca

Abstract. A workflow authorization model is defined in the framework of Relationship-Based Access Control (ReBAC), in which the protection state is a social network. Armed with this model, we study a new decision problem called workflow feasibility. The goal is to ensure that the space of protection states contains at least one member in which the workflow specification can be executed to completion. We identify a sufficient condition under which feasibility can be decided by a refutation procedure that is both sound and complete. A formal specification language, based on a monotonic fragment of the Propositional Dynamic Logic (PDL), is proposed for specifying protection state spaces. The adoption of this language renders workflow feasibility NP-complete in the general case but polynomial-time decidable for an important family of workflows.

Keywords: Relationship-based access control, workflow authorization model, workflow satisfiability, workflow feasibility, graph homomorphism, refutation procedure, propositional dynamic logic, model checking.

1 Introduction

In a workflow authorization system [1, 2, 3, 4, 5, 6], permissions are encapsulated in tasks, such that users acquire permissions by executing a task in a workflow. This design achieves permission abstraction [7] in the context of business processes in enterprise-level systems. Access control policies are usually specified in the form of constraints over who can execute which tasks in the workflow. An instantiation of the workflow (i.e., an assignment of tasks to users) must honour the constraints in order to be considered valid.

Research on workflow authorization models focus on the issue of *availability*: i.e., are the permissions encapsulated in a workflow *available* when needed? Early studies explored the problem of *workflow satisfiability* [3, 5]: i.e., can a workflow be instantiated such that all constraints are satisfied in the current protection state? In a recent study pursued by Wang and Li [8, 6], a higher degree of availability is analyzed. Specifically, they [8, 6] studied the problem of

S. Foresti, M. Yung, and F. Martinelli (Eds.): ESORICS 2012, LNCS 7459, pp. 109–126, 2012.

workflow resiliency[1]. Suppose an emergency makes some users unavailable, can the workflow still be completed? A (statically) k-resilient workflow remains satisfiable even after any k users are removed from the current state.

In this work, we study the problem of ***workflow feasibility*** where we ask whether the permissions can be made available in any "*reasonable*" protection state or not. Although the permissions may not be available in the current protection state (i.e., the workflow is not currently satisfiable), there should be at least one protection state in a known state space where the workflow is satisfiable. This notion can been seen as the dual of resiliency, as explained in Sect. 2.

We envision that the policy developer has *a priori* knowledge of what the protection state space looks like. When she is to author a new workflow (or revise an existing one), she wants to evaluate the workflow, to determine whether the specification may be overly restrictive with respect to her understanding of what protection states are known to be in the state space. If the workflow is not satisfiable in any of the known protection states (i.e., infeasible), then constraints in the workflow specification must be relaxed.

While previously proposed workflow authorization models are built on top of a Role-Based Access Control framework [11, 3, 12, 13, 4], recent authors did recognize that many constraints in a workflow specification are binary relations over executors of tasks [5, 6]. To facilitate the modelling of interpersonal relationships, we ground our workflow authorization model in the recently proposed framework of ***Relationship-Based Access Control (ReBAC)*** [14, 15, 16]. In ReBAC, authorization decisions are based on the interpersonal relationships among users, and the protection state is a social network of users. As we will be studying satisfiability in the midst of evolving interpersonal relationships, we find ReBAC to be a natural theoretical basis.

Our specific contributions are the following:

1. We formulate a ReBAC workflow authorization model (Sect. 3). With this model, we offer a novel characterization of the workflow satisfiability problem based on graph homomorphism [17] (Sect. 4). This new perspective forms the basis for the rest of our results.
2. We propose a new decision problem, workflow feasibility, for assessing the availability of permissions encapsulated in a workflow against a known space of protection states (Sect. 5).
3. We propose to decide workflow feasibility using a refutation procedure, and we identify the exact conditions under which refutation is both sound and complete (Sect. 6).
4. We propose to specify a ReBAC protection state space using a fragment of ***Propositional Dynamic Logic*** [18]. When state spaces are specified in this way, workflow feasibility is NP-complete in the general case, but polynomial-time decidable for an important class of workflow specifications in which constraints are conjunctive (Sect. 7).

---

[1] Resiliency was also studied in a context not related to workflow authorization systems [9, 10].

2   Related Works

Workflow Authorization Models. Workflow authorization has received a lot of attention from the security research community. Early works on workflow authorization focus on synchronizing authorization decisions with the progression of workflow [2, 1]. These works do not concentrate on workflow constraints [12, 19, 20, 21, 22]. Role Based Access Control (RBAC) is widely used to model such constraints [11, 3, 12, 13, 4]. Our work instead focuses on relationship-based constraints.

Consistency. Bertino *et al.* developed a sophisticated constraint specification language [11, 3], in which constraints are clauses in logic programming. A desired characteristic of a set of constraints is that there should be at least one way to complete the workflow without breaching any of them. Bertino *et al.* called this **consistency**. They proposed a planning algorithm for assigning users and roles to tasks in such a way that the workflow constraints are satisfied (i.e., deciding consistency). The complexity of this algorithm is exponential. Tan *et al.* defined consistency in a stricter sense by requiring one complete plan for each authorized user and role [4]. Their algorithm for deciding consistency is again exponential.

Satisfiability. Although the concept was implicit in the work of Bertino *et al.* [11, 3], Crampton first coined the term **workflow satisfiability**, and gave a precise, solution-independent definition for it [5]. Specifically, satisfiability refers to the existence of an instantiation of a workflow specification such that all the constraints are satisfied. Satisfiability is defined with respect to a fixed protection state (e.g., for an RBAC system, the protection state consists of a role hierarchy and a user-role assignment). Wang and Li showed that workflow satisfiability is NP-complete [8, 6], and NP-completeness remains even by considering only the simplest types of constraints (i.e., user-step authorization and user-inequality constraints). They further proved that the problem is fixed-parameter tractable, meaning that there is a decision procedure for satisfiability which is exponential only to the number of tasks (but not the size of the protection state). Assuming the number of tasks is bounded by a small value, the problem is tractable. Workflow satisfiability is the building block of the feasibility problem. We offer a novel characterization of satisfiability in terms of graph homomorphism, which is instrumental in establishing our results.

Resiliency. Wang and Li pointed out availability to be the essence behind the pursuit of workflow satisfiability, and took it into a higher degree [8, 6]. While workflow satisfiability examines availability in the current protection state, they extended the notion to examine availability in any bleak future state when some users might be absent. They call the new problem **workflow resiliency**. In other words, resiliency deals with availability in a state space that includes all possible protection states reachable from the current one by removing users.

This paper is related to their work in three ways. First, we follow the lead of Wang and Li in considering availability in the midst of a changing protection state. Second, the problem of workflow feasibility can be seen as the dual of the resiliency problem. While resiliency is concerned with availability in *every* state of a state space induced by *adversarial transitions*, feasibility is concerned with availability in *at least one* state of a state space induced by *normal transitions*. Third, we consider not only the change of personnel, but also the evolution of their interpersonal relationships.

Relationship Based Access Control. We base our workflow authorization model on Relationship-Based Access Control (ReBAC) [14, 15, 16], which uses interpersonal relationships among users as the basis of authorization decisions. These relationships induce a social network that is explicitly tracked by a ReBAC system. A ReBAC access control policy specifies how a resource requester shall be topologically related to the resource owner in the social network in order for access to be granted. Sect. 3 shows that our ReBAC workflow authorization model can capture all constraint types previously discussed in [4, 5, 8, 6].

3   A ReBAC Workflow Authorization Model

Notation. We write $dom(f)$ and $ran(f)$ respectively for the domain and the range of a function f. We write $f : A \rightharpoonup B$ whenever $dom(f) \subseteq A$ and $ran(f) \subseteq B$. If $X \subseteq dom(f)$ then we write $f(X)$ for $\{f(x) \mid x \in X\}$. We write 2^X for the power set of X (i.e., the set of all subsets of X).

Protection System. A **ReBAC protection system** (or simply a **system**) is parameterized by two sets, $\mathcal{U}$ and $\mathcal{L}$. The set $\mathcal{U}$ is a *countably infinite* set of **user identifiers** of the system. At run time, only a finite subset of $\mathcal{U}$ is active (see below). We write u and v for typical members of $\mathcal{U}$. The set $\mathcal{L}$ is a *finite* set of **relation identifiers**. Each member of $\mathcal{L}$ identifies a type of interpersonal relationship tracked by the system: e.g., "parent", "doctor", etc. It is assumed that these relations are binary. Note that a relation and its inverse may be named differently: e.g.,"patient" and "doctor". We write l for a typical member of $\mathcal{L}$. In the following, we fix the sets $\mathcal{U}$ and $\mathcal{L}$.

Protection State. The **state** of a ReBAC protection system is characterized by a **social network**, which is essentially an edge-labelled directed graph. The vertices of a social network represent the *active* users of the system. The directed edges are labelled with relation identifiers from $\mathcal{L}$. There is a directed edge from u to v with label l whenever the two participate in the binary relation named by l. We make these notions formal in the following.

A **relational structure** (or simply a **graph** for brevity) is a pair $\langle V, \{R_l\}_{l \in \mathcal{L}}\rangle$, where $V \subseteq \mathcal{U}$ is a non-empty, finite set of vertices, and $\{R_l\}_{l \in \mathcal{L}}$ is a family of binary relations, indexed by the set $\mathcal{L}$. Each binary relation $R_l \subseteq V \times V$ specifies the vertex pairs that are related in a type-l relationship. Given a relational structure G, $V(G)$ is the vertex set of G, and $R_l(G)$ is the binary relation with index l. Given a *finite or countably infinite* set X, $\mathcal{G}(X)$ denotes the set of all relational structures for which the vertex set is a *nonempty, finite* subset of X.

Workflow Specification. Fixing a ReBAC system with a set of relation identifiers $\mathcal{L}$, a **workflow specification** $\mathcal{W}$ is a 3-tuple $\langle \mathcal{T}, \leq, \mathcal{C} \rangle$, where:

- $\mathcal{T}$ is a *finite* set of **task identifiers**. A typical member of $\mathcal{T}$ is denoted by t. When a workflow is instantiated, a user $u \in \mathcal{U}$ will be assigned to execute each task $t \in \mathcal{T}$. User u is said to be the **executor** of task t.
- $\leq$ is a partial order over $\mathcal{T}$. It is required that the partial order has both a least element and a greatest element. Intuitively, if $t_1 \leq t_2$ then t_2 must not be executed before t_1. If t_1 and t_2 are incomparable, then their relative ordering is not restricted.
- $\mathcal{C}$, the **constraint expression**, is a *positive* boolean combination of **primitive constraints**. A primitive constraint has the form $l(t_i, t_j)$, where $l \in \mathcal{L}$ and $t_i, t_j \in \mathcal{T}$. The constraint requires that the executor of t_i must be related to the executor of t_j in a type-l relationship.

An example of a constraint expression is the following: $\big(l_1(t_1, t_2) \vee l_2(t_1, t_2) \big) \wedge l_3(t_1, t_2)$. Intuitively, the constraint expression is satisfied iff $l_3(t_1, t_2)$ as well as one of $l_1(t_1, t_2)$ or $l_2(t_1, t_2)$ are satisfied. Formally, each primitive constraint is interpreted as a proposition symbol in the propositional formula $\mathcal{C}$. A truth assignment to the propositional symbols can be represented as a family of binary relations $\{C_l\}_{l \in \mathcal{L}}$ (where each $C_l \subseteq \mathcal{T} \times \mathcal{T}$), such that $l(t_i, t_j)$ receives an assignment of true iff $(t_i, t_j) \in C_l$. Note that, as $\mathcal{C}$ does not contain negation, there is always at least one truth assignment that satisfies $\mathcal{C}$.

A constraint expression is **conjunctive** if it does not contain disjunctions.

Workflow Instances. Given a workflow specification $\mathcal{W} = \langle \mathcal{T}, \leq, \mathcal{C} \rangle$, a function $\pi : \mathcal{T} \rightharpoonup \mathcal{U}$ is called a **workflow instance** (or simply a **plan**). Intuitively, π is an assignment of executors to tasks. If $dom(\pi) = \mathcal{T}$ (i.e., there is an user assignment for every task), then π is said to be **complete**. Otherwise, π is **partial**. If $dom(\pi) = \emptyset$ then π is **empty**. Given a protection state $G = \langle V, \{R_l\}_{l \in \mathcal{L}} \rangle$, a workflow instance π is **valid for** $\mathcal{W}$ **in** G (or simply **valid**) if the partial ordering and the constraint expression of $\mathcal{W}$ are both satisfied. Formally, π is valid if the following three conditions are all satisfied: (i) $ran(\pi) \subseteq V$; (ii) if $t_1 \leq t_2$ and $t_2 \in dom(\pi)$ then $t_1 \in dom(\pi)$ (such that no preceding task is left out); (iii) there exists a *satisfying* truth assignment $\{C_l\}_{l \in \mathcal{L}}$ for the constraint expression $\mathcal{C}$, such that for every $(t_1, t_2) \in dom(\pi) \times dom(\pi)$, if $(t_1, t_2) \in C_l$ then $(\pi(t_1), \pi(t_2)) \in R_l$.

Example 1. A hypothetical *Assignment Evaluation Workflow* needs to be run against a social network (Fig. 1) of an academic institution. Bob is teaching a class in which both Alice and Elham are enrolled, and for which both Charlene and Daniel are Teaching Assistants (TAs). In the social network, two vertices are related by a Not-Equal relationship iff they are distinct. Such edges are not displayed in Fig. 1 to preserve cleanliness.

Consider the workflow specification $\mathcal{W}$ with tasks and constraints depicted in Fig. 2. The tasks are ordered as in the following:

$$\text{Submission} < \text{Marking} < \text{Reviewing} < \text{Grading}$$

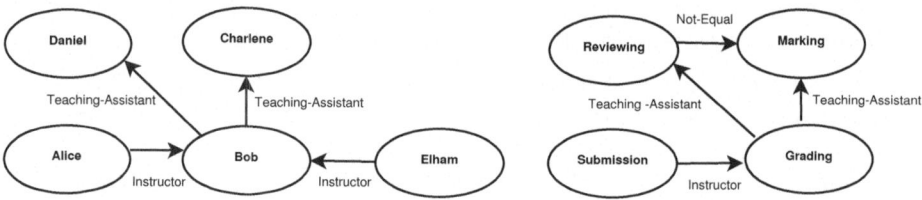

Fig. 1. Social Network without $\neq$ edges   **Fig. 2.** Tasks and Constraints

The constraint expression is the conjunction of the following four primitive constraints:

1. The submitted assignment is graded by the instructor of the submitter:

$$\text{Instructor}(\text{Submission}, \text{Grading})$$

2. The assignment is marked by a TA assisting the instructor:

$$\text{Teaching-Assistant}(\text{Grading}, \text{Marking})$$

3. Reviewing is performed by a TA of the instructor:

$$\text{Teaching-Assistant}(\text{Grading}, \text{Reviewing})$$

4. The TA who reviews the marking is different from the TA who performs the marking:

$$\text{Not-Equal}(\text{Reviewing}, \text{Marking})$$

The four edges in Fig. 2 denote these four primitive constraints. The following workflow instance is complete and valid for $\mathcal{W}$ in G:

$$[\text{Submission} \mapsto \text{Alice}, \text{Grading} \mapsto \text{Bob}, \text{Marking} \mapsto \text{Charlene}, \text{Reviewing} \mapsto \text{Daniel}]$$

Expressiveness. We compare our workflow authorization model with those of Crampton *et al.* [4, 5] and Wang and Li [8, 6]. The goal is to point out that, the present formulation of ReBAC workflow authorization is sufficient for expressing all constraints that appeared in the literature.

The first kind of constraints we discuss about is ***role-step authorization constraints*** (what Wang and Li later called ***user-step authorization constraints***). The idea is to associate with a task a unary predicate specifying the set of users who can carry out that task. This can be captured readily in our model, as every unary user predicate P can be represented by a binary relation R_P, such that $P(u)$ holds whenever $(u, u) \in R_P$.

A second kind of constraints in [4, 5] (called ***entailment constraints***) has the form (D, t_1, t_2, ρ), where $D \subseteq V(G)$, $(t_1, t_2) \in \mathcal{T} \times \mathcal{T}$, and ρ is a binary relation. Such a constraint is simply a binary relation between the executors of t_1 and t_2 which can be encoded by a dedicated binary relation in ReBAC.

A third kind of constraints in [4] is **cardinality constraints**, which come in two variants: local and global. A **local cardinality constraint** can be encoded as a number of entailment constraints [23]. A global cardinality constraint demands that at least k distinct executors must be involved in the execution of some n tasks. Such a constraint can be expressed as a disjunction of $\binom{n}{k}$ conjunctive constraints. Each of the conjunctive constraints demands that k of the n tasks are assigned distinct executors.

Wang and Li [8, 6] have **simple binary constraints** $\rho(t_1, t_2)$, which is identical to our primitive constraints. Their **universal constraints** $\rho(\forall X, t)$ can be expressed as a conjunction of primitive constraints (one for each task in X). The **existential constraints** $\rho(\exists X, t)$ can be encoded as a disjunction of primitive constraints (one for each task in X).

4   Workflow Satisfiability as Graph Homomorphism

Workflow satisfiability is the building block of workflow feasibility. In this section, we point out a novel connection between workflow satisfiability and graph homomorphism that will be used extensively in the sequel.

A workflow specification $\mathcal{W}$ is **satisfiable** in a protection state G if there is a complete workflow instance π that is valid for $\mathcal{W}$ in G.

Given a workflow specification $\mathcal{W} = \langle \mathcal{T}, \leq, \mathcal{C} \rangle$, a relational structure $\langle \mathcal{T}, \{C_l\}_{l \in \mathcal{L}} \rangle$ is a **task network** whenever $\{C_l\}_{l \in \mathcal{L}}$ is a *satisfying* truth assignment for the constraint expression $\mathcal{C}$. A task network is **minimal** if no proper subgraph corresponds to a satisfying truth assignment for $\mathcal{C}$. Let $TN(\mathcal{W})$ be the set of all *minimal* task networks for $\mathcal{W}$. Note that if $\mathcal{C}$ is conjunctive, then $TN(\mathcal{W})$ contains exactly one minimal task network. Fig. 2 shows the minimal task network for the workflow in Example 1.

A **homomorphism** from a relational structure $G = \langle V, \{R_l\}_{l \in \mathcal{L}} \rangle$ to another relational structure $G' = \langle V', \{R'_l\}_{l \in \mathcal{L}} \rangle$ is a function $h : V \to V'$ such that $(u, v) \in R_l$ implies $(h(u), h(v)) \in R'_l$. If such a function h exists, then G is **homomorphic to** G', and we write $G \to G'$. If, in addition, the function h is a bijection, and h^{-1} is a homomorphism from G' to G, then h is called an **isomorphism**, and G is **isomorphic to** G'. In this case we write $G \cong G'$. We also write $h(G)$ for the **homomorphic image** of G, which is defined as the relational structure $\langle h(V), \{R''_l\}_{l \in \mathcal{L}} \rangle$ such that $R''_l = \{(h(u), h(v)) \mid (u, v) \in R_l\}$. Note that $h(G)$ is a subgraph of G'. Specifically, the homomorphic image $h(G)$ consists of only those vertices and edges in G' to which vertices and edges of G are mapped. Obviously, $G \to h(G)$ via h. The following proposition relates workflow satisfiability and homomorphism.

Proposition 1. *A workflow specification $\mathcal{W}$ is satisfiable in protection state G iff there exists a task network in $TN(\mathcal{W})$ that is homomorphic to G.*

The proposition is simply a corollary of (a) the definition of valid complete workflow instances as well as (b) the observation that a workflow is satisfiable iff it is satisfiable via a *minimal* task network (i.e., a member of $TN(\mathcal{W})$).

Deciding if one graph (or relational structure in general) is homomorphic to another is known to be NP-complete [17]. Thus workflow satisfiability for ReBAC is NP-hard even if the constraint expression is conjunctive. Moreover, the general problem is NP-complete since a nondeterministic Turing Machine can decide a problem instance in two steps: (i) guess a satisfying truth assignment for the constraint expression and a homomorphic mapping from the corresponding task network to the social network; (ii) verify the guesses (which takes polynomial time). This lower bound is not a new result [6]. The purpose here is to establish the connection between workflow satisfiability and graph homomorphism.

5   Workflow Feasibility

Workflow satisfiability assesses availability against the current protection state. We examine an alternative way of evaluation in this section by determining availability in the presence of state changes. We ask, is the workflow specification reasonably formulated, such that it can be instantiated in *some* protection state (among all possible states in the state space)? If yes, we say that the workflow specification is **feasible**. As relationships change over time, a workflow that is unsatisfiable in one protection state can become satisfiable after a period of time. So the lack of availability in the current state does not necessarily mean that the permissions encapsulated in the workflow can not be made *available* ever. That is why we need to assess feasibility.

Not every possible social network is in the state space. Generally there are some topological restrictions governing the articulation of relationships in the social networks of a given business domain. These restrictions render some states (i.e., social networks) illegitimate. Social networks containing such an inconsistency do not belong to the state space. So, the definition of feasibility considers satisfiability with respect to a well-defined family of legitimate social networks. As we shall see, such a family is specified in terms of what we call a graph predicate.

Example 2. The following are examples of topological restrictions.

1. **Antitransitivity**. Consider a relational structure describing the relationships among manufacturers, distributors and retailers. Suppose that there is a single relation supply, which relates a supplier to a consumer. A manufacturer shall not compete with its distributors. So we demand supply to be an **antitransitive** relation. That is, there shall not be x, y and z for which x supplies goods to y, y supplies goods to z, but x also supplies goods directly to z.
2. **Acyclicity**. Suppose the supervise relation relates a supervisor to a person under her supervision. We expect this relation to be **acyclic**. That is, the social network induced by this relation shall not contain a directed cycle.
3. **Bipartiteness**. Say the vertices of a social network are firms. To prevent conflicts of interests, the firms that any firm deals with shall not deal with one another. To ensure this, the deals-with relation shall form a bipartite

graph (assuming **deals-with** is symmetric). A bipartite graph is a graph in which vertices can be divided into two disjoint partitions, such that no two vertices in the same partition are adjacent.

5.1 Graph Predicates

A *graph predicate* is a boolean function P with type $\mathcal{G}(\mathbb{N}) \rightarrow \{0,1\}$, where $\mathbb{N}$ is the set of natural numbers. That is, given a relational structure G with vertices labelled by natural numbers, the predicate $P(G)$ returns a boolean value. In the following, we consider only graph predicates that are *topology based* [24]: i.e. $G \cong G'$ implies $P(G) = P(G')$. A topology-based graph predicate ignores vertex labelling. As vertex labelling is not important, we overload our notation such that graph predicates can be applied to either social networks or task networks. The *negation* of a graph predicate P, denoted by $\neg P$, is the graph predicate defined such that $(\neg P)(G) = 1$ iff $P(G) = 0$.

5.2 Families of Social Networks

The family of relational structures induced by a graph predicate P is defined as follows: $\mathcal{G}_P(X) = \{G \in \mathcal{G}(X) \mid P(G) = 1\}$. Intuitively, $\mathcal{G}_P(X)$ is the set of all relational structures from $\mathcal{G}(X)$ that satisfy the graph predicate P. When the state space is defined in this way, the graph predicate is called a *characteristic predicate* of the state space. Similarly, a family of relational structures can also be induced by a *violation predicate* (which is the negation of the characteristic predicate) as $\mathcal{G}_P^-(X) = \{G \in \mathcal{G}(X) \mid P(G) = 0\}$. Intuitively, a relational structure is excluded from the family iff it satisfies the violation predicate. We will make extensive use of violation predicates in the next section.

5.3 Workflow Feasibility Defined

A workflow specification $\mathcal{W}$ is said to be *feasible for* the family of social networks induced by a characteristic predicate P, iff there is a social network $G \in \mathcal{G}_P(\mathcal{U})$ such that $\mathcal{W}$ is satisfiable in G. We require P to be decidable in the following definition of workflow feasibility as a decision problem.

WORKFLOW FEASIBILITY
Instance: Workflow specification $\mathcal{W}$ and decidable graph predicate P.
Question: Is $\mathcal{W}$ feasible for graph family $\mathcal{G}_P(\mathcal{U})$?

A problem instance can also be specified with a decidable *violation predicate*. The reason is that the negation of a decidable graph predicate is also decidable.

Formulated in its full generality, workflow feasibility is recursively enumerable[2]. By placing further constraints on the choice of characteristic predicates, workflow feasibility can be rendered decidable, a topic to which we now turn.

---

[2] Feasible workflows can be enumerated as follows. Enumerate all pairs $(\mathcal{W}, G)$, where $\mathcal{W}$ is a workflow specification and $G \in \mathcal{G}(\mathcal{U})$. For each pair, check that (i) $P(G)$ and (ii) $\mathcal{W}$ is satisfiable in G. Output $\mathcal{W}$ if both checks succeed.

6   Feasibility via Refutation

While we have argued that feasibility is an important criterion of availability, the feasibility of a given workflow is not known to be decidable in the general case. In this section, we propose a **refutation procedure** to decide feasibility. We motivate our approach as follows. Under some special conditions to be stated below, if a task network satisfies a violation predicate P, then every social network that it is homomorphic to will also satisfy P. Therefore, if every task network in $TN(\mathcal{W})$ satisfies the violation predicate, then we can safely conclude that the workflow is infeasible. The refutation procedure is summarized below:

> To determine if $\mathcal{W}$ is feasible for $\mathcal{G}_P^-(\mathcal{U})$, evaluate $P(G)$ for every task network $G \in TN(\mathcal{W})$. If the test is positive in every case, then declare $\mathcal{W}$ *"infeasible"*; otherwise declare $\mathcal{W}$ *"maybe feasible"*.

The procedure always terminates because there is only a finite number of truth assignments and P is decidable. It is a refutation procedure because it employs a *violation predicate* to detect if $\mathcal{W}$ is *unsatisfiable* for any member of $\mathcal{G}_P^-(\mathcal{U})$.

The examples below show that the refutation procedure is not always sound.

Example 3. Here are two violation conditions that can cause refutation to make unsound judgement.

1. **Connectedness.** Consider the (irreflexive, symmetric) colleague relation in an organizational setting where it is an integrity requirement that the graph induced by the colleague relation must be connected. It would be an unsound decision by the refutation procedure to declare a task network infeasible when two tasks are found to be disconnected, as the two tasks could be assigned to users that are connected in the social network by other ways.

2. **Quasi-reflexivity.** Suppose clerk is a unary predicate over users, marking off those users who are in the role of an administrative assistant. Suppose further that we would like to impose clerk as a role-step authorization constraint. Sect. 3 suggests that we can do so by encoding clerk as a binary relation. Such a relation must be **quasi-reflexive** (i.e., xRy implies $x = y$). It would be an unsound decision by the refutation procedure to declare a task network infeasible when two distinct tasks are found to be related by the clerk relation, as the two tasks could be assigned to the same user.

Therefore, some special conditions must be met in order for refutation to be sound. Sect. 6.1 specifies these conditions. Sect. 6.2 then considers the issue of **completeness**: when the refutation procedure fails to declare that a workflow specification $\mathcal{W}$ is infeasible, can we then conclude that $\mathcal{W}$ is feasible?

6.1   Soundness

A graph predicate P is **invariant over homomorphism** if, for every relational structures G and H, $P(G)$ and $G \to H$ jointly imply $P(H)$. Now we can express the condition under which refutation is sound.

Theorem 1 (Soundness). *The refutation procedure is sound if the violation predicate P is invariant over homomorphism.*

The process of establishing that a violation predicate is invariant over homomorphism can be tedious. We therefore streamline this process by decomposing invariance over homomorphism into two easily checkable conditions: (a) **monotonicity** and (b) **invariance over vertex contraction**. We define these two conditions in the sequel, and give examples of how they can be used for demonstrating that a violation predicate is invariant over homomorphism.

Monotonicity. A graph predicate P is monotonic if, when P is evaluated to true for a relational structure G, adding vertices and edges to G will not cause P to be evaluated to false. Formally, a graph predicate P is **monotonic** iff, for every relational structure G and H, $G \subseteq H$ implies $P(G) \Rightarrow P(H)$. In Example 3.1, the violation predicate is *not* monotonic, causing refutation to become unsound.

Invariance over Vertex Contraction. Intuitively, vertex contraction is an operation that merges two vertex in a relational structure. Formally, given a relational structure $G \in \mathcal{G}(X)$ and two vertices $u, v \in V$, we denote by $VC(G, u, v)$ the graph $G' = \langle V', \{R'_l\}_{l \in \mathcal{L}} \rangle$, where: $V' = V(G) \setminus \{ v \}$ and $R'_l = \{(h_{u,v}(x), h_{u,v}(y)) \mid (x, y) \in R_l(G)\}$. Here, the function $h_{u,v} : V \to V'$ is defined as follows: $h_{u,v}(x) = u$ if $x = v$, otherwise $h_{u,v}(x) = x$. In summary, $VC(G, u, v)$ is obtained from G by "folding" v into u. All the edges previously joining v now join u instead.

A graph predicate P is **invariant over vertex contraction** iff $P(G) \Rightarrow P(VC(G, u, v))$. Example 3.2 shows a violation predicate that is *not* invariant over vertex contraction, thereby causing refutation to become unsound.

Invariance over Homomorphism. To show that a graph predicate P is invariant over homomorphism, one could instead demonstrate that P is both monotonic and invariant over vertex contraction.

Theorem 2. *A graph predicate P is invariant over homomorphism iff it is both monotonic and invariant over vertex contraction.*

Proving invariance over homomorphism is usually tedious. Monotonicity, however, is usually quite trivial to establish. Similarly, invariance over vertex contraction is also quite manageable, as one only focuses on the effect of "merging" a pair of vertices.

Example 4. Consider the violating predicates for the restrictions in Example 2.

1. **Antitransitivity.** The violation predicate detects if there exist vertices x, y and z (not necessarily distinct), for which supply holds between x and y, y and z, as well as x and z.
2. **Acyclicity.** The violation predicate returns true whenever the graph contains a directed cycle.

3. **Bipartiteness**. The violation predicate returns true whenever the graph contains an odd-length cycle [25, Theorem 1.2].

These violation predicates are monotonic and invariant over vertex contraction. In each case, violation corresponds to the presence of a specific graph structure, and thus monotonicity follows immediately. The violation of antitransitivity is invariant over vertex contraction: since the vertices x, y and z are not necessarily distinct, merging two of them preserves violation. A similar argument applies to the violation of acyclicity (resp. bipartiteness): contracting two vertices in a cycle (resp. odd cycle) produces a shorter cycle (resp. a shorter cycle of odd length).

6.2   Completeness

When the refutation procedure declares a workflow to be *"infeasible"*, soundness guarantees that the declaration must be correct. Another possible declaration is *"maybe feasible"*. If the declaration of *"maybe feasible"* always implies that the workflow is feasible, then we say that the refutation procedure is **complete**. In a technical sense, the refutation procedure is complete.

Theorem 3 (Completeness). *The refutation procedure is complete if the violation predicate P is invariant over homomorphism.*

In practice, a violation predicate that precisely characterizes the state space may be highly complex, and thus it needs not be invariant over homomorphism. A pragmatic policy developer will be wise to use another predicate P' to approximate P, in such a way that (a) $P'(G) \Rightarrow P(G)$ for every $G \in \mathcal{G}(\mathcal{U})$, and (b) P' is invariant over homomorphism. In this case, the refutation procedure will be sound but not complete, as $\neg P'(\mathcal{W})$ does not guarantee $\neg P(\mathcal{W})$.

7   Using PDL for Violation Specification

This section examines the specification of violation predicates using a formal specification language. We have two design objectives for this language. The first objective concerns the appropriateness of the specified predicates. In order for the refutation procedure to be sound, violation predicates shall be invariant over homomorphism. We therefore demand the specification language to express only graph predicates that are invariant over homomorphism. The second objective concerns the efficiency of evaluating the specified predicates. We demand that the specification language captures only polynomial-time checkable graph predicates.

To meet both objectives, we adopt a monotonic fragment of the Propositional Dynamic Logic (PDL) [18] for specifying violation predicates. As we shall see, our PDL-based specification language is invariant over homomorphism, and has a polynomial-time model checking algorithm [26].

We have also introduced minor adaptations to the PDL for our purposes. Specifically, we observe in Example 4 that many violation predicates detect the presence of cyclic substructures. Our adaptation of PDL can be used for specifying the existence of such substructures.

7.1 Syntax and Semantics of PDL

We provide here a brief introduction to the syntax and semantics of the PDL fragment on which our specification language is based.

Suppose there is a finite or countably infinite set *Prop* of propositional symbols. The monotonic PDL fragment involves two types of constructs: **formulas** and **relations**. The syntax of formulas (ϕ, ψ) and relations (α, β) are defined inductively in the following:

$$\alpha, \beta ::= l \mid -\alpha \mid \alpha \cup \beta \mid \alpha; \beta \mid \alpha^*$$
$$\phi, \psi ::= \top \mid p \mid \phi \vee \psi \mid \phi \wedge \psi \mid \langle \alpha \rangle \phi$$

where $l \in \mathcal{L}$ is a relation identifier, and $p \in$ *Prop* is a propositional symbol. Informally, relations are regular expressions with the relation identifiers as the alphabet. Specifically, our regular expression language offers the following relation combinators: converse ($-$), alternation ($\cup$), concatenation (;) and Kleene star (*). Lastly, formulas are modal logic formulas with relations as modalities. Note that we only consider monotonic constructs in the language. Note also that we do not include the "ϕ?" relation in PDL (originally for constructing conditional relations). As we shall see, this last design decision has a significant impact on the complexity of model checking.

The formulas and relations are interpreted over a relational structure $G = \langle V, \{R_l\}_{l \in \mathcal{L}} \rangle$ and a labelling function $L : Prop \rightarrow 2^V$. The labelling function specifies for each propositional symbol the set of vertices for which the propositional symbol is true. Two interpretation functions μ_G and $\rho_{G,L}$ respectively provide the interpretations of relations and formulas (for the specific G and L). Specifically, $\mu_G(\alpha) \subseteq V \times V$ is a binary relation over the vertex set of G. Similarly, $\rho_{G,L}(\phi) \subseteq V$ identifies the set of vertices in G for which the formula ϕ is satisfied. When the choice of G and L is clear, we simply write $\mu(\alpha)$ and $\rho(\phi)$ for brevity. The semantics of the language is defined as follows.

$$\mu(l) = R_l \qquad\qquad \rho(\top) = V$$
$$\mu(-\alpha) = \mu(\alpha)^{-1} \qquad\qquad \rho(p) = L(p)$$
$$\mu(\alpha \cup \beta) = \mu(\alpha) \cup \mu(\beta) \qquad \rho(\phi \vee \psi) = \rho(\phi) \cup \rho(\psi)$$
$$\mu(\alpha; \beta) = \mu(\alpha) \circ \mu(\beta) \qquad \rho(\phi \wedge \psi) = \rho(\phi) \cap \rho(\psi)$$
$$\mu(\alpha^*) = \mu(\alpha)^* \qquad \rho(\langle \alpha \rangle \phi) = \{u \in V \mid \exists v \in \rho(\phi) . (u, v) \in \mu(\alpha)\}$$

In words, l is interpreted simply as the binary relation R_l in G. The converse $-\alpha$ is interpreted as the inverse of the relation represented by α. Alternation $\alpha \cup \beta$ is interpreted as the union of the relations represented by α and β. The concatenation $\alpha; \beta$ is the relational composition of the relations represented by α and β. The Kleene star α^* is interpreted as the reflexive transitive closure of the relation represented by α. The constant formula $\top$ is satisfied by all vertices in G. The propositional symbol p is satisfied by the vertices in $L(p)$. Disjunction and conjunction are interpreted as set union and intersection. The formula $\langle \alpha \rangle \phi$ is satisfied by those vertices with an α-neighbor that in turn satisfies ϕ.

We write $G, L, u \models \phi$ whenever $u \in \rho_{G,L}(\phi)$. When this is the case, the graph pattern specified by ϕ is satisfied in G at vertex u with labelling function L.

7.2 Specifying Violation Predicates with PDL

Without using propositional symbols (i.e., $Prop = \emptyset$), the above language allows us to write formulas that represent path patterns (with $\top$ as the pattern for the empty path). Recall we observe from Example 4 that many practical violation predicates detect cyclic structures in the social network. We therefore customize the monotonic PDL fragment above for representing cyclic structures. Specifically, we adopt exactly one propositional symbol org, called the **anchor**. That is, we set $Prop = \{\mathsf{org}\}$. The anchor proposition org names the vertex from which the search for cyclic pattern begins[3]. In this way, we can write formulas that detect if the initial vertex is revisited, and thus a cycle is found. Formally, let $[\mathsf{org} \mapsto u]$ denote the labelling function $L : \{\mathsf{org}\} \to \mathcal{U}$ for which $L(\mathsf{org}) = u$. Then the following checks if the cyclic structure specified by ϕ exists in G by initiating the search from the vertex u.

$$G, [\mathsf{org} \mapsto u], u \models \phi$$

We write $[\![\phi]\!]$ to denote the graph predicate that takes a graph G as argument and returns true iff:

there exists $u \in V(G)$ such that $G, [\mathsf{org} \mapsto u], u \models \phi$.

That is, $[\![\phi]\!]$ searches for a vertex $u \in V(G)$ at which ϕ is satisfied. The space of protection states induced by ϕ is therefore $\mathcal{G}^-_{[\![\phi]\!]}(\mathcal{U})$.

Example 5. The formulas below specify the violation predicates in Example 4.

1. **Antitransitivity**. Note the use of converse $(-)$ in this example.

   $$\langle \mathsf{supply}; \mathsf{supply}; -\mathsf{supply} \rangle \mathsf{org}$$

2. **Acyclicity**. Note the use of Kleene star $(^*)$ in this example.

   $$\langle \mathsf{supervise}; \mathsf{supervise}^* \rangle \mathsf{org}$$

3. **Bipartiteness**. Let l be a shorthand for **deals-with**. Note the use of alternation $(\cup)$ in this example.

   $$\langle (l \cup -l); ((l \cup -l); (l \cup -l))^* \rangle \mathsf{org}$$

The following is a corollary of a well-known result [28, Chapter 2].

Theorem 4. *For every formula ϕ in the above monotonic fragment of PDL, $[\![\phi]\!]$ is invariant over homomorphism.*

Invariance is due to our choice of a monotonic fragment of PDL. Therefore, specifying violation predicates with our PDL fragment preserves the soundness of refutation.

---

[3] A propositional symbol that names a specific vertex is called a **nominal** in hybrid logic [27, 16].

7.3 Model Checking

We show that evaluating a graph predicate $[\![\phi]\!]$ takes polynomial time. This involves testing the $\models$ relation at every vertex of the graph argument. To this end, we describe an adaptation of Lange's PDL model checking algorithm [26].

Suppose $G = \langle V, \{R_l\}_{l \in \mathcal{L}} \rangle$. Let $n = |V|$. We represent a binary relation over V as a boolean square matrix (i.e., an $n \times n$ matrix with boolean entries). Specifically, $\mu(\alpha)$ returns such a matrix. We also represent a subset of V by a boolean column vector of size n. Specifically, $\rho(\phi)$ returns such a column vector.

With this data representation, μ can be evaluated inductively using matrix operations. As the base case, $\mu(l)$ is simply the boolean matrix representation of R_l. Now, $\mu(-\alpha)$ involves transposing a matrix, and $\mu(\alpha \cup \beta)$ involves bitwise-or. Both operations take $O(n^2)$ time. Next, $\mu(\alpha; \beta)$ involves (boolean) matrix multiplication, while $\mu(\alpha^*)$ involves reflexive transitive closure. Both operations are $O(n^3)$. In summary, $O(n^3)$ time is needed for each relation subexpression.

In a similar fashion, ρ can be evaluated inductively. The picture, however, is sightly more complex. The evaluation of $\rho_{G,[\text{org} \mapsto u]}$ must be performed for every $u \in V$. The first base case $\rho_{G,[\text{org} \mapsto u]}(\top)$ is a column vector with all entries set to 1. The second base case $\rho_{G,[\text{org} \mapsto u]}(\text{org})$ is a column vector with a 1 in u's row, and 0 everywhere else. The evaluation of $\rho_{G,[\text{org} \mapsto u]}(\phi \vee \psi)$ and $\rho_{G,[\text{org} \mapsto u]}(\phi \wedge \psi)$ involve bitwise-or and bitwise-and respectively, both are $O(n)$ operations. The evaluation of $\rho_{G,[\text{org} \mapsto u]}(\langle \alpha \rangle \phi)$ involves the multiplication of the $n \times n$ matrix $\mu_G(\alpha)$ with the column vector $\rho_{G,[\text{org} \mapsto u]}(\phi)$, which is an $O(n^2)$ operation. In summary, evaluating $\rho_{G,[\text{org} \mapsto u]}(\phi)$ for a single $u \in V$ is an $O(n^2)$ operation. Therefore, evaluating $\rho_{G,[\text{org} \mapsto u]}(\phi)$ for every $u \in V$ takes $O(n^3)$ time.

Since the processing of each subexpression or subformula takes $O(n^3)$ time, and there are all together $|\phi|$ subexpressions and subformulas, the evaluation of $[\![\phi]\!]$ takes $O(|\phi| \times n^3)$ time. Although a third-degree polynomial is involved, the complexity is actually quite reasonable, as the refutation procedure evaluates the violation predicate against task networks rather than social networks. While the latter typically have an intimidating size, the former have a much more manageable size. This same assumption regarding the small number of tasks in a typical workflow has been used by other authors also [6].

Our design choice of not including the "ϕ?" construct from PDL pays dividend in the time complexity of model checking. Had we included that construct, the interpretation function μ_G would be parameterized not only by G, but also the labelling function (as in $\mu_{G,L}$). As a result, we would have to perform an $O(n^3)$ operation for every relation subexpression *and* for every labelling function $[\text{org} \mapsto u]$, where $u \in V$. The final tally for the time complexity of model checking would then be $O(|\phi| \times n^4)$ instead of our current $O(|\phi| \times n^3)$.

7.4 Complexity of Refutation

When the constraint expression is conjunctive, *the* minimal task network can be readily constructed from the constraint expression, and thus refutation can be conducted in polynomial time by applying the above model checking algorithm over the minimal constraint network. But with this restriction of expressiveness, certain constraints such as global cardinality constraints [4] and existential constraints [8, 6] can not be expressed.

The following theorem asserts that refutation using PDL formulas is computationally hard for general constraint expressions.

Theorem 5. *Given a workflow $\mathcal{W}$ and a PDL formula ϕ, deciding if $[\![\phi]\!](G)$ is true for every task network $G \in TN(\mathcal{W})$ is coNP-complete.*

This result implies that workflow feasibility, of which refutation is a co-problem, is NP-complete when the violation predicate is specified in PDL. Intuitively, feasibility is hard in the general setting because it involves a search for a non-violating task network among all task networks. In contrast, there is only one minimal task network when the constraint expression is conjunctive, and it takes only polynomial time to check if this minimal task network satisfies a graph predicate that is specified in PDL.

8   Conclusion and Future Work

We introduced a workflow authorization model in the framework of ReBAC. The model offers a fresh characterization of the workflow satisfiability problem in terms of graph homomorphism. Armed with this new understanding, we studied a new decision problem called workflow feasibility, which is the dual of workflow resiliency. A refutation procedure was proposed for deciding feasibility. The refutation procedure was shown to be sound and complete if the space of protection states can be characterized by a violation predicate that is invariant over graph homomorphism. To facilitate verification, we proposed two verification conditions that jointly imply invariance over homomorphism. We also proposed the adoption of a monotonic fragment of PDL as a language for specifying the violation predicate. We showed that with this specification language the time complexity of refutation is polynomial for conjunctive constraints, and coNP-complete for general constraint expressions.

We highlight some possible extensions of this work. The monotonic fragment of PDL used in this paper employs the anchor nominal org for detecting revisited vertices. A possible extension of this feature involves the hybridization of the monotonic fragment of PDL [27, 16]. This extension will allow us to capture complex graph patterns while maintaining invariance over homomorphism. It is unknown how this extension will impact the time complexity of model checking.

We pointed out that feasibility can be seen as the dual of resiliency. This perspective generates a new form of resiliency problem, in which deformative transitions do not remove users (as in [8, 6]), but instead remove relationships (i.e., the social network is evolving). This problem has not been studied in existing literature. As user removal can be simulated via relationship removal (i.e., presence of users can be captured by a unary predicate present, which in turn can be encoded using a binary relation), such a problem is a generalization of Wang and Li's notion of resiliency in [8, 6].

Acknowledgments. This work is supported in part by an NSERC Discovery Grant and a Canada Research Chair.

References

1. Thomas, R.K., Sandhu, R.S.: Task-based Authorization Controls (TBAC): A Family of Models for Active and Enterprise-Oriented Autorization Management. In: Proceedings of the 11th IFIP WG11.3 Working Conference on Database and Application Security (DAS 1998), Lake Tahoe, California, USA, pp. 166–181 (1998)
2. Atluri, V., Huang, W.K.: An Authorization Model for Workflows. In: Martella, G., Kurth, H., Montolivo, E., Bertino, E. (eds.) ESORICS 1996. LNCS, vol. 1146, pp. 44–64. Springer, Heidelberg (1996)
3. Bertino, E., Ferrari, E., Atluri, V.: The specification and enforcement of authorization constraints in workflow management systems. ACM Transactions on Information and System Security 18(1), 65–104 (1999)
4. Tan, K., Crampton, J., Gunter, C.A.: The consistency of task-based authorization constraints in workflow systems. In: Proceedings of the 17th IEEE Workshop on Computer Security Foundations (CSFW 2004), pp. 155–169. IEEE Computer Society, Washington, DC (2004)
5. Crampton, J.: A reference monitor for workflow systems with constrained task execution. In: Proceedings of the tenth ACM Symposium on Access Control Models and Technologies (SACMAT 2005), Stockholm, Sweden, pp. 38–47 (2005)
6. Wang, Q., Li, N.: Satisfiability and resiliency in workflow authorization systems. ACM Transactions on Information and System Security 13(4), 40:1–40:35 (2010)
7. Baldwin, R.W.: Naming and grouping privileges to simplify security management in large databases. In: Proceedings of the 1990 IEEE Symposium on Security and Privacy (S&P 1990), Oakland, CA, USA, pp. 116–132 (May 1990)
8. Wang, Q., Li, N.: Satisfiability and Resiliency in Workflow Systems. In: Biskup, J., López, J. (eds.) ESORICS 2007. LNCS, vol. 4734, pp. 90–105. Springer, Heidelberg (2007)
9. Li, N., Tripunitara, M.V., Wang, Q.: Resiliency policies in access control. In: Proceedings of the 13th ACM Conference on Computer and Communications Security (CCS 2006), Alexandria, VA, USA, pp. 113–123 (October 2006)
10. Li, N., Wang, Q., Tripunitara, M.: Resiliency policies in access control. ACM Transactions on Information and System Security 12(4) (April 2009)
11. Bertino, E., Ferrari, E., Atluri, V.: A flexible model supporting the specification and enforcement of role-based authorization in workflow management systems. In: Proceedings of the Second ACM Workshop on Role-based Access Control (RBAC 1997), Fairfax, Virginia, United States, pp. 1–12 (1997)
12. Ahn, G.J., Sandhu, R., Kang, M., Park, J.: Injecting RBAC to secure a web-based workflow system. In: Proceedings of the Fifth ACM Workshop on Role-Based Access Control (RBAC 2000), Berlin, Germany, pp. 1–10 (2000)
13. Kandala, S., Sandhu, R.: Secure role-based workflow models. In: Proceedings of IFIP WG11.3 Working Conference on Database and Application Security (DAS 2001), Niagara, Ontario, Canada, pp. 45–58 (2001)
14. Fong, P.W.L.: Relationship-based access control: protection model and policy language. In: Proceedings of the First ACM Conference on Data and Application Security and Privacy (CODASPY 2011), San Antonio, TX, USA, pp. 191–202 (February 2011)

15. Fong, P.W.L., Siahaan, I.: Relationship-based access control policies and their policy languages. In: Proceedings of the 16th ACM Symposium on Access Control Models and Technologies (SACMAT 2011), Innsbruck, Austria, pp. 51–60 (June 2011)

16. Bruns, G., Fong, P.W.L., Siahaan, I., Huth, M.: Relationship-based access control: Its expression and enforcement through hybrid logic. In: Proceedings of the 2nd ACM Conference on Data and Application Security and Privacy (CODASPY 2012), San Antonio, TX, USA (February 2012)

17. Hell, P., Nešetřil, J.: Graphs and Homomorphisms. Oxford University Press (2004)

18. Fischer, M.J., Ladner, R.E.: Propositional dynamic logic of regular programs. Journal of Computer and System Sciences 18(2), 194–211 (1979)

19. Casati, F., Castano, S., Fugini, M.: Managing workflow authorization constraints through active database technology. Information Systems Frontiers 3(3), 319–338 (2001)

20. Crampton, J., Huth, M.: Synthesizing and verifying plans for constrained workflows: Transferring tools from formal methods. In: Proceedings of the 2011 Workshop on Verification and Validation of Planning and Scheduling Systems (June 2011)

21. Huang, W.K., Atluri, V.: Secureflow: a secure Web-enabled workflow management system. In: Proceedings of the Fourth ACM Workshop on Role-based Access Control (RBAC 1999), Fairfax, Virginia, United States, pp. 83–94 (1999)

22. Warner, J., Atluri, V.: Inter-instance authorization constraints for secure workflow management. In: Proceedings of the Eleventh ACM Symposium on Access Control Models and Technologies (SACMAT 2006), Lake Tahoe, California, USA, pp. 190–199 (2006)

23. Crampton, J.: On the satisfiability of constraints in workflow systems. Technical Report RHUL-MA-2004-1, Department of Mathematics, Royal Holloway, University of London (2004)

24. Fong, P.W.L., Anwar, M., Zhao, Z.: A Privacy Preservation Model for Facebook-Style Social Network Systems. In: Backes, M., Ning, P. (eds.) ESORICS 2009. LNCS, vol. 5789, pp. 303–320. Springer, Heidelberg (2009)

25. Bondy, J.A., Murty, U.S.R.: Graph Theory with Applications. North-Holland (1976)

26. Lange, M.: Model checking propositional dynamic logic with all extras. Journal of Applied Logic 4(1), 39–49 (2006)

27. Areces, C., ten Cate, B.: Hybrid logics. In: Blackburn, P., van Benthem, J., Wolter, F. (eds.) Handbook of Modal Logic. Elsevier (2007)

28. Blackburn, P., de Rijke, M., Venema, Y.: Modal Logic, Cambridge (2002)

Deciding Security for a Fragment of ASLan*

Sebastian Mödersheim

DTU Informatics, Denmark
samo@imm.dtu.dk

Abstract. ASLan is the input language of the verification tools of the AVANTSSAR platform, and an extension of the AVISPA Intermediate Format IF. One of ASLan's core features over IF is to integrate a transition system with Horn clauses that are evaluated at every state. This allows for modeling many common situations in security such as the interaction between the workflow of a system with its access control policies.

While even the transition relation is undecidable for ASLan in general, we show the security problem is decidable for a large and useful fragment that we call TASLan, as long as we bound the number of steps of honest participants. The restriction of TASLan is that all messages and predicates must be in a certain sense unambiguous in their interpretation, excluding "type-confusions" similar to some tagging results for security protocols.

1 Introduction

It is well-understood how to automatically verify small security protocols that consist of the exchange of a few messages. Less well understood is the automated verification of complex distributed systems that we see today in practice, where the logic of a component comprises more than a few message exchanges. An example is a web server that maintains a database (e.g. of keys, of electronic orders, or of electronic applications). This database may be accessed or modified by different transactions the server can perform. These transactions themselves may be embedded into a larger workflow of a company that runs the server, e.g., how employees of the company process requests posted by customers via the server. Finally, there may be access control policies specifying who is allowed to perform which actions or has access to certain information.

Modeling such complex systems requires an expressive specification language. We consider in this paper the AVANTSSAR [2] Specification Language ASLan [4] that was designed in exactly this spirit—to model complex systems like the ones just sketched. At the core, an ASLan specification describes an infinite-state transition system where every state is a set of (ground, first-order) predicates

---

* The author thanks Luca Viganò, Alberto Calvi, Marco Rocchetto, and the anonymous reviewers for many helpful comments. The research presented in this paper has been partially supported by MT-LAB, a VKR Centre of Excellence for the Modelling of Information Technology.

S. Foresti, M. Yung, and F. Martinelli (Eds.): ESORICS 2012, LNCS 7459, pp. 127–144, 2012.

that express, for instance, the local state of honest agents (or uncorrupted components), what messages are known to the intruder, the state of databases shared by agents, or facts related to the security goals such as which messages are supposed to be secret. The transition relation is expressed by *set rewriting rules* (similar to multi-set rewriting [9], only the repetition of predicates does not make a difference). Additionally, ASLan allows for negative conditions in rules.

A powerful feature of ASLan on top of this transition system is the specification of Horn clauses over state predicates. These Horn clauses are evaluated locally in every state and give rise to a set of *implicit* consequences. These consequences are used in matching the next transition rule. For instance, we may express a Horn theory that models access control rules such as "If file F belongs to group G and A is a member of G then A has access to F." or "If A is a deputy of B, then A has all access rights that B has." Membership in a group, or being a deputy are predicates that may change upon state transitions. The Horn clauses thus allow us to formulate immediate consequences of a state, and after each transition, they are automatically updated. Vice-versa, the Horn clauses may themselves be used as conditions in a transition rule, e.g. A may perform a certain action only in a state from which the necessary access rights can be derived by the Horn clauses. More generally, the Horn theories allow for modeling all kinds of internal computations, expressed as such immediate consequences.

Even though we have chosen here the particular language ASLan, we believe that the concepts that we deal with are of general relevance for the modeling of complex systems, in particular the immediate evaluation of consequences in every state of a state transition system. (As an example, recall that the common Dolev-Yao model of an intruder is represented as the least closure of the messages that the intruder has seen under a set of deduction rules.)

The expressivity of ASLan however comes at a price for automated verification: since first-order Horn clauses allow for logic programming, the transition relation is in general undecidable. In fact it is common that specification languages give rise to undecidable problems, and the challenge is to find fragments for which feasible decision procedures are possible.

Contributions. We first review the syntax and semantics of ASLan and make some conceptual simplifications. We exclude at this point some features of ASLan that are in our opinion less essential, but difficult to handle; we briefly discuss how to (partially) support them in section 5.

Next, we define the fragment TASLan forbidding certain kinds of ambiguities in the formats of messages and predicates. TASLan requires, that all messages are annotated with an intended type such that all messages, and their non-variable subterms, that occur in the specification have no unifier unless they have the same intended type. We also extend this restrictions to other predicates. We then show that a TASLan specification has an attack iff it has a well-typed attack, so restriction to a typed model is no restriction for TASLan.[1]

---

[1] For space reasons, we give here only proof sketches; the full proofs can be found in the extended version [14].

This result is in the spirit of several tagging results [11,7,1], and generalizes them: we do not require a particular way to avoid ambiguities (such as tagging) and do not limit ourselves to particular analysis technique (such as ProVerif); and, most importantly, our result works for full TASLan, including non-atomic keys, negative conditions (such as those needed for authentication), and the additional Horn theories.

This result allows for a number of simplifications of the model, in particular bounding the size of terms without restriction. We develop a decision procedure for bounded-length TASLan: given a bound l, can we reach an attack state in l steps or less? This procedure is generalizing the popular constraint-based approach that we refer to as the *lazy intruder* [13,15,6]. In fact, this procedure is part of our argument for the typing result on TASLan. For the theoretical closure, we show that the problem whether an attack is reachable in at most l steps for a TASLan specification is NEXPTIME complete.

Organization. In section 2 we review the ASLan syntax and semantics. In section 3 we introduce a symbolic transition system that is the basis for the later decision procedure. In section 4 we introduce the fragment TASLan and give the decision procedure for bounded length traces. From this procedure we also derive our typing result and conclude with the result on the complexity. In section 5 we briefly discuss aspects of ASLan that we have excluded. We conclude with a discussion of related work in section 6.

2 ASLan

Syntax. Table 1 shows the syntax of ASLan (where we have left out some features that are in our opinion less crucial, and support for which we discuss in section 5). We use the following conventions: we introduce syntactic categories by $C ::=$, where the symbol C represents our notation of elements of that category. Each following line represents one alternative for that category. Further, we write v for a vector $v_1, \ldots, v_n$ (where the lengths n of the vectors may be 0, and different vectors may have different lengths). Similarly, we write $\hat{\phi}$ for a conjunction of the form $\phi_1 \wedge \ldots \wedge \phi_n$.

Example 1. To illustrate the concepts of ASLan, we give a toy example in Table 2. Note that in this example we use a notational convention of ASLan that we do not enforce in the treatment of this paper: constant, function and predicate symbols are identifiers that start with a lower-case letter, while variable symbols are all identifiers that start with an upper-case letter. In this example we specify as Horn clauses the access control example from the introduction, together with an initial state and two transition rules. The first transition rule is applicable if A is a member of group $G1$ and A is not the deputy of anybody. Upon the transition, we generate a fresh value of type gid—in the rule referred to by the variable $G2$. Then A will be a member of $G2$ (actually the only member so far). Also the left-hand side predicate $mem(A, G1)$ will no longer hold. The second rule is an example how attack states can be defined. Here, we derive an attack

Table 1. Syntax of ASLan

$D ::=$	Declarations		$F ::=$	Facts
$c : \beta$	Constant Symbol		P	Predicate
$X : \tau$	Variable Symbol		$t_1 = t_2$	Equality
$f : \tau$	Function Symbol		$\exists \boldsymbol{X} : F$	Existential quantification
$p : \mathsf{pred}\ \tau$	Predicate Symbol		$L ::=$	Literals
$\tau ::=$	Types		F	Fact
β	Basic type		$\neg F$	Negated Fact
$f(\boldsymbol{\tau})$	Composed type		$S ::=$	States
untyped	Untyped		$\hat{P}$	Conjunction of predicates
$s, t ::=$	Terms		$R ::=$	Transition Rules
c	Constant		$\hat{L} \exists [\boldsymbol{X}] \Rightarrow S$	
X	Variable		$H ::=$	Horn Clauses
$f(\boldsymbol{t})$	Composed Terms		$\forall \boldsymbol{X} : S \rightarrow P$	
$P ::=$	Predicates		$\mathcal{P} ::=$	ASLan Specification
$p(\boldsymbol{t})$			$(\boldsymbol{D}, S, \boldsymbol{R}, \boldsymbol{H})$	

whenever in a state an agent A has access to files $F1$ and $F2$ (note $F1 = F2$ is allowed) that belong to groups $G1$ and $G2$, respectively, where $G1 \neq G2$ is required; thus when A has a the same time access to files of different groups, the specification has an attack. Note that the specification is infinite state as the first transition rule can be applied any number of times.   □

Type Declarations. The declarations section of an ASLan specification is by default only an annotation of intentions of the modeler; we do *not* assume that an intruder always sends well-typed messages, and our semantics will thus be ignoring the type declarations by default. The declarations give a means to statically type-check a specification (i.e., checking in the behavior of honest agents the typing is consistent) and later are relevant for our typing result.

A particularity of our type system is that for functions we do not allow the specification of a return type—the resulting type is always a composed type as follows. If f is declared as a function symbol of type $\tau_1, \ldots, \tau_n$ and $t_1 : \tau_1, \ldots, t_n : \tau_n$ are terms of the appropriate types, then $f(t_1, \ldots, t_n) : f(\tau_1, \ldots, \tau_n)$. Thus the type of a term reflects its composition, and only atomic terms can be of an basic type. The only way to escape this tight typing system is using the "type" untyped. Let Γ be a mapping from all declared symbols to a type. We require that every symbol that occurs in the specification has a unique type-definition. We define a general type judgment relation $t : \tau$ (read: t is of type τ) as follows:

$$\frac{}{s : \tau}\ \Gamma(s) = \tau \qquad \frac{t_1 : \tau_1 \quad \cdots \quad t_n : \tau_n}{f(t_1, \ldots, t_n) : f(\tau_1, \ldots, \tau_n)}\ \Gamma(f) = (\tau_1, \ldots, \tau_n)$$

$$\frac{s : \tau}{s : \mathsf{untyped}} \qquad \frac{t_1 : \tau_1 \quad \cdots \quad t_n : \tau_n}{p(t_1, \ldots, t_n) : p(\tau_1, \ldots, \tau_n)}\ \Gamma(p) = (\tau_1, \ldots, \tau_n)$$

Table 2. Toy example of an ASLan specification

Declarations:

    mem : pred $(agent, gid)$ own : pred (gid, fid)

    $deputy$: pred $(agent, agent)$ xs : pred $(agent, fid)$

    $attack$: pred $()$ $A, B, a, b : agent$

    $G, G1, G2, g1, g2 : gid$ $F, F1, F2, f1, f2 : fid$

Initial State:

    $mem(a, g1) \wedge mem(b, g2) \wedge own(g1, f1) \wedge own(g2, f2)$

Transition Rules:

    $mem(A, G1) \wedge \neg \exists B : deputy(A, B) \Rightarrow[G2]\!\!\Rightarrow mem(A, G2)$

    $xs(A, F1) \wedge xs(A, F2) \wedge own(A, G1) \wedge own(A, G2) \wedge G1 \neq G2 \Rightarrow attack()$

Horn clauses:

    $mem(A, G) \wedge own(G, F) \rightarrow xs(A, F)$

    $deputy(A, B) \wedge xs(B, F) \rightarrow xs(A, F)$

We require that all terms and predicates in the specification have a type according to this specifications, and for equation $t_1 = t_2$, t_1 and t_2 have a type in common.

2.1 Further Context Sensitive Properties

We give further conditions about ASLan specifications that are not definable by a context-free grammar. Let $fv(t)$ denote the free variables of t (for terms, predicates, facts, states). Let $Pos(\hat{L})$ denote the positive facts in a conjunction $\hat{L}$ of literals.

- For a rule $\hat{L} =[\boldsymbol{X}] \Rightarrow S$ we require that $fv(\hat{L}) \uplus \boldsymbol{X} \supseteq fv(S)$. Moreover, $fv(Pos(\hat{L})) = fv(\hat{L})$.
- For a Horn clause $H = \forall \boldsymbol{X} : S \rightarrow P$, we require $fv(H) = \emptyset$ and $fv(P) \subseteq fv(S)$.
- The initial state is ground. Together with the previous two conditions, all reachable states are ground (except in the symbolic approach we define later).
- There are two distinguished predicate symbols ik (for intruder knowledge) and attack with $\Gamma(\text{ik}) = $ (untyped) and $\Gamma(\text{attack}) = ()$. Both symbols are *persistent*: they never get deleted on transitions.
- We call a non-persistent predicate *explicit* if it occurs on the right-hand side of a transition rule and *implicit* if it occurs on the right-hand side of a Horn clause. All predicate symbols except ik and attack must be either explicit or implicit. Denote with $PosE(\hat{L})$ the positive explicit predicates of a rule and with $PosI(\hat{L})$ both the positive implicit and the positive persistent predicates.
- Horn clauses in which ik occurs can only have one of the following two forms:
  - Generate: $\forall X_1, \ldots, X_n : \text{ik}(X_1) \wedge \ldots \wedge \text{ik}(X_n) \rightarrow \text{ik}(f(X_1, \ldots, X_n))$
  - Analyze: $\forall \boldsymbol{X} : \text{ik}(t) \wedge \text{ik}(t_1) \wedge \ldots \wedge \text{ik}(t_n) \rightarrow \text{ik}(s)$ where s and the t_i are proper subterms of t.

- Implicit and persistent predicates (see Section 2.1) cannot occur negatively in the specification.

2.2   Semantics

Model Relation. An interpretation $\mathcal{I}$ maps from all variables to ground terms. ϕ,ψ range over all logical constructions above. We define a relation $\mathcal{I}, S \models \phi$ that says whether a pair of an interpretation $\mathcal{I}$ and a state S is a *model* of the formula ϕ:

$$\mathcal{I}, S \models P \qquad \text{iff } \mathcal{I}(P) \in \mathcal{I}(S)$$
$$\mathcal{I}, S \models t_1 = t_2 \text{ iff } \mathcal{I}(t_1) = \mathcal{I}(t_2)$$
$$\mathcal{I}, S \models \phi \wedge \psi \quad \text{iff } \mathcal{I}, S \models \phi \text{ and } \mathcal{I}, S \models \psi$$
$$\mathcal{I}, S \models \neg \phi \qquad \text{iff } \mathcal{I}, S \not\models \phi$$
$$\mathcal{I}, S \models \exists X.\phi \quad \text{iff exists ground } t : \mathcal{I}[X \mapsto t], S \models \phi$$

We also say ϕ is satisfiable iff it has a model. Other constructs are defined as syntactic sugar as standard, e.g. $\forall X : \phi$ as $\neg \exists X : \neg\phi$. For a statement $\mathcal{I}, S \models \phi$ we may omit $\mathcal{I}$ if ϕ is closed (i.e. $fv(\phi) = \emptyset$), and we may omit S if ϕ does not contain predicates.

As standard, define $\phi \models \psi$ if all models of ϕ are also models of ψ; and $\phi \vDash\!\dashv \psi$ if both $\phi \models \psi$ and $\psi \models \phi$.

Least Herbrand Models. For the semantics of transition rules, we need to define the least closure of a state under the Horn clauses. Let $\hat{H}$ be the conjunction of the Horn clauses of a given ASLan specification. This induces the following closure operation on states: for any ground state S, $HC(S)$ is the least set $S' \supseteq S$ such that: $P \in S'$ if $\hat{H} \wedge S' \models P$. Note that here and in the following, we treat a conjunction $S = P_1 \wedge \ldots \wedge P_n$ of predicates also as a set of predicates $S = \{P_1, \ldots, P_n\}$.

With our definition of the $\models$ relation and the least Horn closure we have chosen one interpretation of first-order terms that are often referred to as *free models* or *least Herbrand models*, which are the semantical basis for logic programming languages like Prolog. In particular, all terms are interpreted in the Herbrand universe (which is here the free algebra) and, in a given state S, all predicate symbols are interpreted by the least relations that are consistent with the Horn clauses and S. This relation is uniquely defined for Horn clauses.

Transition Relation. Define $S \Rightarrow S'$ if there is a rule $\hat{L} = [\boldsymbol{X}] \Rightarrow S_R$ and interpretation $\mathcal{I}$ such that $\mathcal{I}, HC(S) \models \hat{L}$ and $\mathcal{I}(\boldsymbol{X})$ are fresh constants and $S' = S \setminus \mathcal{I}(PosE(\hat{L})) \cup \mathcal{I}(S_R)$.

Several notes are in order. The implicit consequences $HC(S) \setminus S$ of a state S are never "explicified", i.e. they are not carried over to S'. Recall that $PosE(\cdot)$ does not include the persistent predicates, so all persistent predicates of S are still contained in S'. Further, this definition does not care about type specifications. As a consequence of the ASLan conditions, all reachable states $\{S \mid S_0 \Rightarrow^* S\}$ (for initial state S_0 of the specification) are ground.

Example 2. In the specification of Table 2, the Horn closure of the initial state contains $xs(a, f1) \wedge xs(b, f2)$. If we take the first transition rule form the initial state for $A = a$, this removes the predicate $mem(a, f1)$ and thus the Horn closure of that state no longer contains $xs(a, f1)$. So in each state, the Horn closure is computed anew; all consequences that are no longer derivable simply vanish.   □

A state is called an *attack state* if $S \models$ attack. A specification is called *secure* if it has no reachable attack state.

Security in ASLan (and even just the transition relation $S \Rightarrow S'$) is undecidable, since the Horn clauses (using untyped arguments) capture logical programming. It is still semi-decidable, because we do not allow negated implicit predicates in transition rules.

Definition 1 (Typed Model). *We say $\mathcal{I}$ is a* well-typed interpretation *if $\mathcal{I}(X) : \Gamma(X)$ for all variables X. We define a* typed model *of an ASLan specification as a variant of the above semantics where all notions are restricted to well-typed interpretations.*

In other words, our default semantics ignores all type information (because an intruder in reality is always able to send ill-typed terms) but we can choose to restrict the interpretation to well-typed terms. We show below that for all TASLan specifications it holds that, if an attack exists, then also an attack in the typed model exists. Thus in TASLan, the restriction to a typed model is sound.

3   A Symbolic Representation

We now introduce a symbolic representation of the infinite transition system that will pave the way for an effective decision procedure for the TASLan fragment when bounding the length of traces.

Symbolic States. A symbolic state is generalization of a normal state, which may contain variables and constraints. We define its syntax as follows:

$\phi ::=$	Symbolic state
P	Predicate
$S \vdash P$	Deduction constraint
$\neg \exists \boldsymbol{X} : s_1 = t_1 \wedge \ldots \wedge s_n = t_n$	Negated substitution
$X = t$	Substitution
$\phi \wedge \psi$	Conjunction

We conservatively extend the model relation w.r.t. the Horn theory $\hat{H}$ of the specification (note this case does not depend on a state S):

$$\mathcal{I}, S \models S_0 \vdash P \text{ iff } \mathcal{I}(S_0) \wedge \hat{H} \models \mathcal{I}(P)$$

Thus, the constraint $S_0 \vdash P$ is true in all those interpretation in which the predicate P can be derived from the predicates in S_0 by the Horn theory $\hat{H}$.

This is a generalization of the *lazy intruder* technique [13,15,6] where these constraints are limited to messages in the intruder knowledge.

Thus, by the relation $\mathcal{I}, S \models \phi$, symbolic states have a semantics as representing a set of ground states (and related interpretations). Usually, this set will be infinite, but is may also be finite or even empty. We say that a symbolic state is *satisfiable* if it has a model. For ASLan this satisfiability is not decidable in general (because the Horn clauses allow for logic programming).

Symbolic Transition Relation. To define a transition relation, let us first make two simplifications to transition rules. Without changing the semantics of a rule, we can remove all existential quantifiers in positive facts of a transition rule, if we just ensure by renaming that it does not occur freely in the rule. Moreover we can get rid of positive equations of the form $s = t$ as follows: compute the most general unifier σ of s and t and apply σ to the entire rule as expected.

We also use the following notations. For a rule R let $\alpha(R)$ denote a renaming of all variable symbols in R with fresh variable symbols (that do not occur previously). This is necessary in the symbolic model to keep variables of different rule applications apart. Moreover for a substitution $\sigma = [X_1 \mapsto t_1, \ldots, X_n \mapsto t_n]$ where the X_i are disjoint from the variables in t_i, let $[\sigma]$ be the logical formula $X_1 = t_1 \wedge \ldots \wedge X_n = t_n$ describing σ.

We define the symbolic transition relation (with a long arrow as compared to the ground transition relation) as follows: $\phi \Longrightarrow \psi$ iff there is a transition rule R with $\alpha(R) = \hat{L} = [X] \Rightarrow S$, and a substitution σ such that all the following conditions hold:

- σ is a most general substitution such that $\sigma(PosE(L)) \subseteq \sigma(PosE(\phi))$. (Note that in contrast to term unification, for subset unification we get finitely many most general unifiers that are pairwise incomparable.)
- Extend σ such that the variables of X (that are freshly created in the transition) are replaced by fresh constants.
- For every implicit predicate $P \in PosI(L)$ let $\chi_P = Pos(\sigma(\phi)) \vdash \sigma(P)$; denote with $\hat{\chi}$ their conjunction.
- Let Φ be the least conjunction of negated substitutions such that
  - for every negative fact $\neg \exists X : P$ of $\sigma(\hat{L})$ and every positive fact P' of $\sigma(\phi)$, if τ is the most general unifier of P and P', then $(\neg \exists X.[\tau]) \in \Phi$.
  - every negative equation of $\sigma(\phi)$ is also contained in Φ.
- $\psi = \sigma(\phi) \setminus \sigma(PosE(L)) \wedge \sigma(S) \wedge \Phi \wedge \hat{\chi} \wedge [\sigma]$.

Example 3. Extending our toy example from Table 2, we model that our system can process signed commands from an administrator (who would be modeled using similar rules). In this simplistic example we omit replay and eavesdropping protections:

$$admin(A, K) \wedge ik(sign(K, [add, A, B, G]_4)) \wedge A \neq B \wedge \neg mem(A, G)$$
$$\Rightarrow mem(B, G) \tag{1}$$

Suppose here $admin(A, K)$ expresses that A is an administrator who can issue commands with private signature key K. The command in this example is to add an agent B to group G and has the format $[add, A, B, G]_4$ where $[\cdot]_4$ represents a 4-tuple and add is a tag/command name. We discuss this way of modeling plaintext structures in Section 4.1. The rule excludes both that A can add her/himself to a group and that A can add somebody to a group he/she belongs to.

Consider now that the intruder is one of the system administrators; then he can form any kind of commands himself and send them to the service—this choice of commands is infinite. Rules with $ik(\cdot)$ on the left-hand side often give rise to an infinite ground state space, and even with typing restrictions to a very large space. In contrast, the symbolic transition system has only one successor state per rule application. Consider for instance the state:

$$\phi = admin(i, ki) \wedge mem(a, g1) \wedge mem(i, adm) \wedge$$
$$ik(ki) \wedge ik(a) \wedge ik(b) \wedge ik(i) \wedge ik(g1) \wedge ik(g2) \wedge ik(adm)$$

We can apply the symbolic transition relation for rule (1) under the unifier $\sigma = [A \mapsto i, K \mapsto ki]$ to match the positive explicit fact $admin(A, K)$ (in general the rule variables have to be renamed in order to avoid collisions with variables in the given state, but here we started with a ground state). From the $ik(\cdot)$ fact of the rule, we obtain the constraint $\phi \vdash ik(sign(ki, [add, a, B, G]_4))$. Note that the rule variables B and G remain uninstantiated. From the negative conditions of the rule we obtain the constraints $a \neq B \wedge G \neq adm$. The symbolic successor state consists of $\sigma(\phi)$ together with the noted constraints and the (uninstantiated) right-hand side fact $mem(B, G)$. This single symbolic state comprises all the infinitely many choices of the intruder (any messages for B and G that satisfy the constraints). This includes choices where B is not an agent name and G is not a group name, but as we later show, such ill-typed solutions are never interesting for the intruder when the specification satisfies the type-unambiguity rules of TASLan. $\qquad\square$

The following lemma shows that the symbolic transition system is a correct representation of the ground transition system:

Lemma 1. *Let* $\llbracket\phi\rrbracket = \{S \mid \exists \mathcal{I} : \mathcal{I}, S \models \phi\}$. *Then for all symbolic states* ϕ:

$$\{S' \mid \exists \psi : \phi \Longrightarrow \psi \wedge S' \in \llbracket\psi\rrbracket\} = \{S' \mid \exists S : S \in \llbracket\phi\rrbracket \wedge S \Rightarrow S'\} .$$

As a consequence, a satisfiable symbolic state that contains the predicate attack *is reachable using* $\Longrightarrow$ *from initial state* S_0 *in* l *steps iff a ground attack state is reachable using* $\Rightarrow$ *from* S_0 *in* l *steps.*

The proof in [14] shows that every construction in the symbolic transition relation has a counter-part in the ground definition.

We now distinguish several kinds of constraints in a symbolic state and we tackle each of them in isolation and before we look at their interaction:

– Intruder deduction constraints $S \vdash P$ where P and all predicates in S are of the form $ik(t)$ for some term t.

- Other deduction constraints $S \vdash P$ where no predicate is of the form $ik(t)$.
- Negated substitutions $\neg \exists \boldsymbol{X} : s_1 = t_1 \wedge \ldots \wedge s_n = t_n$.
- Substitutions $X = t$. Our constructions will ensure that the variable X does not occur elsewhere, and this kind of (always satisfiable constraint) is just to remember partial solutions, i.e. all models of the containing symbolic state must satisfy $\mathcal{I}(X) = \mathcal{I}(t)$.

The satisfiability of negative equalities is straightforward to check: for $L = \neg \exists \boldsymbol{X} :$ $s_1 = t_1 \wedge \ldots \wedge s_n = t_n$ check the unification problem $\tau((s_1, t_1), \ldots, (s_n, t_n))$ for a substitution τ that replaces all free variables L (i.e. those that are not quantified in $\boldsymbol{X}$) with fresh constants (of the appropriate type). There is a unifier iff L is unsatisfiable.

We show below that satisfiability of intruder deduction constraints is also decidable, slightly extending known results. However, satisfiability of other constraints is not decidable for ASLan in general, since we can use Horn clauses for logic programming.

4   Type Ambiguity-Free Specifications

We now introduce a fragment of ASLan, called TASLan: basically the format of messages (and predicates) must be different whenever their intended type is different. We show that security is decidable for TASLan if the length of traces is bounded; more precisely, this problem is NEXPTIME complete. Note that the restriction in TASLan is not a typed model directly, but rather a generalization of the tagging principle; however we do not prescribe a particular way of disambiguating messages. We show—as a side result of our decision procedure for bounded-length TASLan—that a typed model is sound (even without any bounds on the length of traces).

We proceed as follows. We first introduce the fragment TASLan, and then show that for symbolic states in TASLan, we can decide the satisfiability of all constraints. This gives an effective procedure for bounded-length traces. Finally we give the typing result (that the typed model is "relatively sound" for TASLan), and show how this can be used for different kinds of automatic verification methods other than our symbolic method.

Definition 2. *TASLan is the fragment of ASLan specifications with the following additional requirements/modifications:*

- *Every predicate except* ik *has a type in which* untyped *does not occur.*
- *For every predicate* ik(t) *in the transition rules, t is non-atomic and has a type in which* untyped *does not occur.*
- *Let SMP be the non-atomic subterms of all terms t that occur in a predicate* ik(t) *in the transition rules, α-renamed so that two distinct elements of SMP have no variables in common. Whenever there is a unifier for two $t_1, t_2 \in$ SMP, then t_1 and t_2 must have the same type.*

We also assume that the intruder can always generate fresh elements of any type in any state, so that for instance the constraint $\mathsf{ik}(X) \wedge \mathsf{ik}(Y) \wedge X \neq Y$ is always satisfiable. While it is natural to "grant" this to the intruder, it is tricky to formulate this, because we actually need transition rules to freshly generate new intruder constants. We silently assume such rules, and note that our lazy treatment of constraints below gives this property for free: a constraint like the above is simply considered as a solved form (without making actual transitions for creating two concrete values for X and Y).

4.1 How Restrictive Is TASLan?

As indicated in the add command in Example 3 (which of course falls into the TASLan fragment), we model concatenation by the family $[\cdot]_n$ of n-tuple operators (for $n > 1$). This model abstracts from several implementation details, such as field lengths or special tags that mark the beginning and end of fields— we simply assume that the implementation has a unique way to decompose every acceptable message into its components. This is a reasonable requirement to the implementation that excludes many low-level attacks. Tags like *add* in the example then are an easy way to disambiguate messages. (Alternatively, one can instead introduce new functions, e.g. $add(A, B, G)$ in example, and give the intruder rules for composing/decomposing them.)

Basically, we thus see every kind of plaintext message like a *paper form* that has a well-defined set of fields. Many ASLan specifications are already written in this style—independent of our work. With this "form approach", almost all specifications meet the requirements of TASLan. This is because we exclude with a single tag any confusions between different forms that carry similar information but with different meaning.

Many ASLan specifications, and even more protocols, do not use this regime and thus do not immediately fall into the TASLan fragment. To use the most cited example, the encrypted content of the first two messages of NSPK—the pairs NA, A and NA, NB—already violate our requirements because NA and NB are random numbers while A is an agent name. (In fact, this ambiguity gives rise to a type-flaw attack [12].) Our approach would be to identify the ambiguities and resolve them; the messages may then be $[nspk1, NA, A]_3$ and $[nspk2, NA, NB]_3$ for instance, and this variant falls into the TASLan fragment.

We propose that in this way every protocol can be transformed into a reasonable TASLan model, but in doing so one may exclude some potential low-level type-flaw or parsing attacks. However the transformation process gives clear indications where problems could arise and what we require from the implementation. Thus one could say that TASLan requires, and exploits, what good engineering practice demands in the first place.

4.2 Symbolic Horn Closure

Let $\hat{H}$ be the conjunction of Horn clauses without intruder deduction (which we handle separately). We want to consider the Horn closure under $\hat{H}$ for symbolic states. In general, this closure is infinite in ASLan (due to instantiation of variables), but we will show it is finite in TASLan. For that, we define the following evaluation relation over symbolic states:

Definition 3. *Let $\hat{H}$ be the conjunction of Horn clauses without intruder deduction. $\phi \hookrightarrow \psi_1 \vee \psi_2$ if there is a Horn clause $H_R \in \hat{H}$ such that*

- $\alpha(H_R) = \forall \hat{X} : S \to P$ *for a renaming α of variables in H_R,*
- *S unifies with a subset of $Pos(\phi)$ under the most general unifier σ,*
- $\psi_1 = \sigma(\phi \wedge P)$ *and $\psi_2 = \neg[\sigma]$,*
- $\sigma(P) \notin \phi$ *(so the predicate is indeed newly derived)*
- *The negative equation constraints in ψ_1 are satisfiable.*

We extend $\hookrightarrow$ to a relation on disjunctions of symbolic states as expected. We say $\phi_1 \vee \ldots \vee \phi_n$ is a normal form *(for Horn theory $\hat{H}$) if it has no successor modulo $\hookrightarrow$.*

The $\hookrightarrow$ can be understood as follows: at every reduction step we check whether a new predicate (that is not yet present in ϕ) is derivable in one step under a substitution σ. Note that we are not forced to take the substitution σ, because this only represents a subset of the ground states represented by ϕ in which the new predicate $\sigma(S)$ is derivable. All the other states are represented by $\neg[\sigma]$ (and in those, $\sigma(S)$ is in general not derivable). Thus each $\hookrightarrow$ step makes a case split into states that satisfy σ and those that do not. In order to have a notion of normal form without enforcing any substitution σ, we have the condition that requires that the negative equalities in ϕ_1 are satisfiable: if we have entered a case with $\neg[\sigma]$, then we cannot actually apply σ to that symbolic state anymore.

Example 4. Consider the Horn clauses from Table 2 and the following symbolic state (which can occur in a specification with more transition rules):

$$\phi = mem(a, g1) \wedge own(g1, f1) \wedge mem(A2, G2) \wedge own(g2, f2) \wedge deputy(a, A3)$$

Note that here for instance $G2$ is a variable, and $g2$ a constant. One possible derivation with $\hookrightarrow$ is as follows:

$$\phi \hookrightarrow \underbrace{(\phi \wedge xs(a, f1))}_{\phi_1} \vee (\phi \wedge false)$$

$$\phi_1 \hookrightarrow \underbrace{(\phi_1[G2 \mapsto g1] \wedge xs(A2, f1))}_{\phi_2} \vee \underbrace{(\phi_1 \wedge G2 \neq g1)}_{\phi_3}$$

$$\phi_3 \hookrightarrow \underbrace{(\phi_3[G2 \mapsto g2] \wedge xs(A2, f2))}_{\phi_4} \vee \underbrace{(\phi_3 \wedge G2 \neq g2)}_{\phi_5}$$

$$\phi_4 \hookrightarrow \underbrace{(\phi_4[A2 \mapsto A3] \wedge xs(a, f2)) \vee (\phi_4 \wedge A2 \neq A3)}_{\phi_6}$$

We thus have $\phi \hookrightarrow^* \phi_2 \vee \phi_5 \vee \phi_6$ which is a normal form—for instance if we try in ϕ_2 to apply the second Horn clause (under $A2 = a$ or under $A2 = A3$) we get only the already present fact $xs(a, f1)$. □

Lemma 2. $\hookrightarrow$ *is convergent modulo* $\bumpeq$ *for TASLan, while for ASLan in general it is not terminating (but confluent).*

Proof sketch. (Full proof in [14]) Confluence is immediate because $\phi \hookrightarrow \psi$ implies $\phi \bumpeq \psi$. Termination for TASLan follows from the fact that unification between predicates cannot introduced ill-typed substitutions, and thus the set of derivable symbolic predicates (modulo renaming) is finite.

Combining the previous results (for the detailed proof see [14]), we get:

Lemma 3. *Satisfiability of symbolic states* ϕ *of TASLan without considering intruder deduction constraints is decidable.*

The proof in fact gives us a procedure to obtain from ϕ an equivalent disjunction $\psi_1 \vee \ldots \vee \psi_n$ of symbolic states where all $S \vdash P$ constraints (except intruder deduction) are eliminated and the remaining inequalities constraints are all satisfiable.

4.3 Lazy Intruder Constraint Reduction

We now turn to checking the satisfiability of intruder constraints of the form $S \vdash P$ where all predicates of S and P are of the form $\mathsf{ik}(t)$. An important property for the lazy intruder deduction is that they are well-formed:

Definition 4. *A conjunction of intruder deduction constraints is called* well-formed *if we can order them as* $S_1 \vdash P_1 \wedge \ldots \wedge S_n \vdash P_n$ *such that*

- $S_{i+1} \implies S_i$ *for* $0 \leq i < n$, *i.e. the intruder knowledge grows monotonically.*
- $fv(S_i) \subseteq \bigcup_{0 \leq j < i} fv(P_j)$, *i.e. all variables in the constraints first occur from a message the intruder generated.*

We call an intruder constraint $S \vdash \mathsf{ik}(t)$ simple *if* t *is a variable. A simple constraint is always satisfiable (because the intruder can generate fresh terms of any type as discussed before).*

In a symbolic state that is reachable from a ground initial state, we order the constraints in the order they have been created. The intruder knowledge grows monotonically because $\mathsf{ik}(\cdot)$ is persistent. The condition on variable occurrence however does not hold for reachable symbolic states in general: variables may as well be "introduced" by other (non-intruder) constraints of the form $S \vdash P$. However, after performing the symbolic Horn closure, these constraints are all gone, and the respective variables can be substituted by terms that can only contain variables that occur elsewhere in the state—i.e. introduced by intruder constraints.

Theorem 1 (Adaption of [15]). *Satisfiability of well-formed intruder deduction constraints is NP-complete. Moreover, there is a procedure that transforms a well-formed ϕ into a finite disjunction of well-formed intruder deduction constraints $\psi_1 \vee \ldots \vee \psi_n \models \phi$ ($n \geq 0$) such that every ψ_i is simple.*

Proof sketch. (Full proof in [14]) The proof follows the standard lazy intruder idea, using a calculus of rules of the form "if ϕ is satisfiable then also ψ is". This set of rules is shown sound, complete, and terminating. The length of deductions is polynomial, so a non-deterministic machine can decide satisfiability in polynomial time. Vice-versa we can encode satisfiability of Boolean formulae into intruder deduction constraints.

Together we now have:

Lemma 4. *Satisfiability is decidable for reachable symbolic states of TASLan specifications, and thus whether an attack state is reachable in l steps or less.*

4.4   Organizing Search

With this, we have generalized the symbolic, constraint-based decision procedures for bounded-length verification—the lazy intruder—to support Horn clauses. There are now several choices how to coordinate the different aspects of constraint reduction. When solving the constraints of a symbolic state ϕ, we usually get into a finite case split $\psi_1 \vee \ldots \vee \psi_n$ of symbolic states where each ψ_i has only constraints in a solved form. If $n = 0$ we know that ϕ is unsatisfiable and can be discarded from the search. When constructing the successor states of ϕ we can either continue with ϕ or compute the successor states of each of the ψ_i. It is in general unclear which is preferable: continuing on ϕ requires that we repeat a lot of constraint reduction work in the successor states, while continuing on ψ_i can mean a large case split into similar cases. Our current prototype is based on the ψ_i expansion, but we see room for optimization in finding a middle ground between the two extremes: sometimes being more lazy and leaving some choices open once we have established that there exists at least one solution.

4.5   Typed Model for TASLan

It is crucial that all results so far do *not* require the restriction to a typed model (Definition 1), but merely exploit the fact that TASLan requires distinct formats for messages of distinct types (Definition 2). We now use these results, in particular Theorem 1, to show that the restriction to a typed model comes without loss of attacks for TASLan specifications:

Lemma 5. *If there is an attack against a TASLan specification, then there is an attack in the typed model, i.e. where every variable of transition and Horn rules is instantiated with a term of the desired type.*

Proof sketch. (Full proof in [14]) We inspect all parts of the satisfiability check for symbolic states that introduce substitutions of variables, and show that they cannot induce ill-typed substitutions. In particular for intruder deduction constraints, we have only a substitution when unifying a term s is the intruder knowledge with a term t he needs to generate. This unification is only applied when neither s nor t are variables; by the condition of TASLan, non-variable subterms s and t of message can only have a unifier if they have the same type.

Theorem 2 (Completely typed model is no restriction). *Every TASLan specification $\mathcal{S}$ can effectively be transformed into a specification $\mathcal{S}'$ such that*

- *In $\mathcal{S}'$ also the variables in intruder rules are typed.*
- *$\mathcal{S}$ has an attack iff $\mathcal{S}'$ has an attack (and the same holds when bounding traces to length l or less).*
- *$|\mathcal{S}'|$ is polynomial in the size of $\mathcal{S}$.*

Proof. Instantiate all intruder rules with types that can ever occur when honest agents are sending and receiving. □

There is another way to see this: since every variable now has a completely determined type, we can turn this into a problem without function symbols: consider a predicate $p(t)$ for $t : f(\tau)$, then we could replace this with a predicate $p_f(t')$ for $t' : \tau$. This is because even if t is a variable, the typed model dictates it can only be instantiated with a term of the form $f(t')$ for $t' : \tau$, i.e. we can equivalently replace t with $f(x)$ where $x : \tau$ is a new variable. Applying this to the whole specification, we obtain a specification without function symbols. However note that we hereby replace ik($\cdot$) with a family of predicates that represent intruder knowledge of certain functions—and they must be treated accordingly as persistent predicates that are allowed on the right-hand side of both Horn clauses and transition rules. This reflects that with the typed model we essentially turn the logic programming problem of the Horn clauses into a Datalog problem [5].

We now prove NEXPTIME completeness of TASLan insecurity when we are given a bounded length of traces ("bounded number of sessions" in the security protocol parlance):

Theorem 3. *The following problem is NEXPTIME-complete: Given a bound $l \in \mathbb{N}$, and a TASLan specification S, is an attack state reachable in l state transitions or less? Here the problem size N is the length in bits of the description of S and l together (thus $l \leq 2^N$).*

Proof sketch. (Full proof in [14]) We can bound the size of the universe U of predicates that can be constructed (using the fresh constants generated in the l transitions) by $|U| = 2^{poly(N)}$ for $poly(N)$ some polynomial of N. (The state space being bounded by $2^{|U|}$.) The Horn closure is in $O(|U|)$ and we can thus have a machine non-deterministically generate each trace of length up to l in time $O(l \cdot |U|)$ and accepting if that trace contains attack. This shows containment in NEXPTIME. Vice-versa we can give a polynomial encoding of an NEXPTIME-complete Tiling problem into TASLan for bounded steps.

5   Towards a Full ASLan

We have so far neglected some features of the original ASLan that seem less central to us. Here we briefly discuss how to (partially) support these features as well.

"Wildcard" Horn Clauses   For Horn clauses $\forall \boldsymbol{X} : S \rightarrow P$ we had previously required $fv(P) \subseteq fv(S)$ (and $fv(S) \subseteq \boldsymbol{X}$) so the right-hand side cannot introduce new variables. Thus prevents clauses like $\forall X :\rightarrow p(X, X)$. Dropping this restriction causes a slight problem for the symbolic approach, because this may lead to non-termination of Horn closure (since this introduces new variables). Further this can destroy the well-formedness condition for the symbolic intruder deduction (because the new variables are not depending on a choice of the intruder). This limitation can be overcome with a special predicate $isBeta(\cdot)$ for new variables of type β. An example is found in the proof of NEXPTIME-hardness in Theorem 3.

Subtypes.   The original ASLan allows the declaration of subtypes, e.g. honest as a subtype of agent. Such an example could be modeled in TASLan by having only the basic type agent, and a special predicate honest (of type agent) that holds true for all those agents that are honest. A similar encoding is possible for two composed types τ_1 and τ_2 that differ only in an basic subtype.

Mappings.   For many problems it is helpful to have some function symbols to express mappings such as $sk(A, B)$ to denote the shared key between agents A and B, but of course the resulting key is then of type $sk(agent, agent)$ and thus with terms of a basic type $symkey$ to represent symmetric keys. More generally, the problem is to model a function f of type $\boldsymbol{tau} \rightarrow \tau_0$ where $\tau_0 \neq f(\boldsymbol{tau})$. A way to achieve this is the use of a new predicate to represent the function, e.g. in the example $sk' : (agent, agent, symkey)$. We then need to take care of an appropriate constant for the function result, e.g. the symmetric key here. Also this encoding has its limitations: for instance a function like $s : \beta \rightarrow \beta$ cannot be injective (as this would lead to an infinite type).

Algebraic Properties.   One may consider algebraic properties to support some cryptographic primitives. This quickly rules out many methods, e.g. when the equivalence class of a term gets infinite. We just hint that for some algebraic properties the symbolic methods work [10].

FOLTL Goals.   We have considered only state-based safety properties, while ASLan allows for the specification of FOLTL goals, i.e. first-order logic extended with the temporal operators of linear temporal logic. Again this logic gives rise to undecidable problems in general. Borrowing from the arguments of Theorem 3, we can however identify a decidable fragment that fits with the TASLan approach. The idea is that typed TASLan for a bounded-length trace gives a finite universe of predicates (because also the number of fresh constants that can be created is bounded). When checking safety properties, considering finite traces is no restriction. When checking non-safety properties (e.g. for resilient channels [3]) common methods also need to consider finite state spaces (so that all infinite traces go in loops through the state space), in which case it is also not a restriction to limit the number of fresh constants. When we have a finite universe, then we can reduce problem into a propositional LTL problem.

We have left this out of our main presentation since many verification methods based on abstract interpretation and symbolic constraints do not combine well with FOLTL goals, for instance a goal like $G(\mathsf{ik}(s) \to \mathsf{ik}(t))$ implies negative intruder knowledge constraints that cannot be directly handled.

6 Conclusions

ASLan is a specification language that integrates Horn clauses with transition systems, and this combination in the specification language gives a particular expressive power: we can formulate a transition system with immediate evaluations for every state. The typical application is the interaction between the work-flow of a distributed system and its access control policies, see the AVANTSSAR case studies for a large class of security-relevant systems [2]. A completely different application to combine immediate evaluations with transitions is in our recent work to analyze security of virtualized infrastructures [8]. Here we model a network representing a virtualized infrastructure that can change due to actions of honest agents and intruder. The Horn clauses can be used to make evaluations on the network in each state, e.g. between which nodes information flow is possible.

In this paper we have reviewed the syntax and semantics of ASLan, giving a conceptually simpler account than previous definition [4]. We have extended the concepts of symbolic transition systems to ASLan as a logically sound basis for constraint-based model-checking.

We have defined the fragment TASLan by the requirement that messages and predicates of different intended types must have sufficiently different formats so they cannot be confused. To a large extend, such disambiguations are good engineering practice anyway, and we can exploit this to obtain a class of specifications that is better to tackle with automated methods, while maintaining the powerful concept of combining transition systems with immediate evaluations.

We have built a decision procedure for bounded-length TASLan (or a semi-decision procedure for unbounded length) extending the constraint-based "lazy intruder" approach [13,15,6] to support the combination with Horn deduction constraints.

We show that, when an attack exists, the lazy intruder will find a well-typed attack, and thus we have a generalization of several typing-results [11,7,1]: for TASLan specification, we can safely restrict the verification to a typed model. This enables methods that cannot deal with an infinite universe of intruder-generated messages or only under great difficulty. Seen another way, the typed model simplifies the undecidable logic-programming problem induced by the Horn clauses to a decidable Datalog problem.

On the conceptual side, we show that the problem whether a TASLan specification has an attack for a bounded number of transitions is NEXPTIME complete.

Despite the high complexity class, first experiments with extending the tool OFMC [6] demonstrate that the method is feasible for many practically relevant problems: a first prototype successfully analyzes 70 of the 142 ASLan specifications of the AVANTSSAR library [2] in under 8 minutes.

References

1. Arapinis, M., Duflot, M.: Bounding Messages for Free in Security Protocols. In: Arvind, V., Prasad, S. (eds.) FSTTCS 2007. LNCS, vol. 4855, pp. 376–387. Springer, Heidelberg (2007)
2. Armando, A., Arsac, W., Avanesov, T., Barletta, M., Calvi, A., Cappai, A., Carbone, R., Chevalier, Y., Compagna, L., Cuéllar, J., Erzse, G., Frau, S., Minea, M., Mödersheim, S., von Oheimb, D., Pellegrino, G., Ponta, S.E., Rocchetto, M., Rusinowitch, M., Torabi Dashti, M., Turuani, M., Viganò, L.: The AVANTSSAR Platform for the Automated Validation of Trust and Security of Service-Oriented Architectures. In: Flanagan, C., König, B. (eds.) TACAS 2012. LNCS, vol. 7214, pp. 267–282. Springer, Heidelberg (2012)
3. Armando, A., Carbone, R., Compagna, L.: LTL Model Checking for Security Protocols. In: Proceedings of CSF20. IEEE Computer Society Press (2007)
4. The AVANTSSAR Project: Deliverable 2.3: ASLan (2010) (final version), www.avantssar.eu
5. Bancilhon, F., Maier, D., Sagiv, Y., Ullman, J.D.: Magic sets and other strange ways to implement logic programs. In: PODS, pp. 1–15 (1986)
6. Basin, D., Mödersheim, S., Viganò, L.: OFMC: A symbolic model checker for security protocols. International Journal of Information Security 4(3), 181–208 (2005)
7. Blanchet, B., Podelski, A.: Verification of cryptographic protocols: tagging enforces termination. Theor. Comput. Sci. 333(1-2), 67–90 (2005)
8. Bleikertz, S., Groß, T., Mödersheim, S.: Automated verification of virtualized infrastructures. In: CCSW, pp. 47–58 (2011)
9. Cervesato, I., Durgin, N.A., Mitchell, J.C., Lincoln, P., Scedrov, A.: Relating strands and multiset rewriting for security protocol analysis. In: CSFW, pp. 35–51 (2000)
10. Chevalier, Y., Küsters, R., Rusinowitch, M., Turuani, M.: Deciding the Security of Protocols with Diffie-Hellman Exponentiation and Products in Exponents. In: Pandya, P.K., Radhakrishnan, J. (eds.) FSTTCS 2003. LNCS, vol. 2914, pp. 124–135. Springer, Heidelberg (2003)
11. Heather, J., Lowe, G., Schneider, S.: How to prevent type flaw attacks on security protocols. In: Proceedings of CSFW 2000. IEEE Computer Society Press (2000)
12. Meadows, C.: Analyzing the Needham-Schroeder Public-Key Protocol: A Comparison of Two Approaches. In: Martella, G., Kurth, H., Montolivo, E., Bertino, E. (eds.) ESORICS 1996. LNCS, vol. 1146, pp. 351–364. Springer, Heidelberg (1996)
13. Millen, J.K., Shmatikov, V.: Constraint solving for bounded-process cryptographic protocol analysis. In: Proceedings of CCS 2001, pp. 166–175. ACM Press (2001)
14. Mödersheim, S.: Deciding Security for a Fragment of ASLan (Extended Version). Technical Report IMM-TR-2012-06, DTU Informatics (2012), imm.dtu.dk/~samo
15. Rusinowitch, M., Turuani, M.: Protocol insecurity with a finite number of sessions, composed keys is NP-complete. Theor. Comput. Sci. 1-3(299), 451–475 (2003)

A Probabilistic Framework for Localization of Attackers in MANETs⋆

Massimiliano Albanese[1], Alessandra De Benedictis[2],
Sushil Jajodia[1], and Paulo Shakarian[3]

[1] Center for Secure Information Systems
George Mason University, Fairfax, VA, USA
{malbanes,jajodia}@gmu.edu
[2] Department of Computer Science
University of Naples "Federico II", Naples, Italy
alessandra.debenedictis@unina.it
[3] Department of Electrical Engineering and Computer Science
United States Military Academy, West Point, NY, USA
paulo@shakarian.net

Abstract. Mobile Ad Hoc Networks (MANETs) represent an attractive and cost effective solution for providing connectivity in areas where a fixed infrastructure is not available or not a viable option. However, given their wireless nature and the lack of a stable infrastructure, MANETs are susceptible to a wide range of attacks waged by malicious nodes physically located within the transmission range of legitimate nodes. Whilst most research has focused on methods for detecting attacks, we propose a novel probabilistic framework for estimating – independently of the type of attack – the physical location of attackers, based on the location of nodes that have detected malicious activity in their neighborhood. We assume that certain countermeasures can be deployed to capture or isolate malicious nodes, and they can provide feedback on whether an attacker is actually present in a target region. We are interested in (i) estimating the minimum number of countermeasures that need to be deployed to isolate all attackers, and (ii) finding the deployment that maximizes either the expected number of attackers in the target regions or the expected number of alerts *explained* by the solution, subject to a constraint on the number of countermeasures. We show that these problems are NP-hard, and propose two polynomial time heuristic algorithms to find approximate solutions. The feedback provided by deployed countermeasures is taken into account to iteratively re-deploy them until all attackers are captured. Experiments using the network simulator NS-2 show that our approach works well in practice, and both algorithms can capture over 80% of the attackers within a few deployment cycles.

Keywords: Attacker localization, MANET, probabilistic framework.

⋆ This research was funded in part by the US Army Research Office under MURI grant W911NF-09-1-0525 and DURIP grant W911NF-11-1-0340. Part of the work was performed while Sushil Jajodia was a Visiting Researcher at the US Army Research Laboratory.

S. Foresti, M. Yung, and F. Martinelli (Eds.): ESORICS 2012, LNCS 7459, pp. 145–162, 2012.

1 Introduction

Mobile Ad Hoc Networks (MANETs) connect mobile devices without an underlying fixed infrastructure. The topology of the network keeps changing over time as nodes move or leave, and new nodes join the network. These intrinsic features make MANETs an attractive and cost effective solution for providing connectivity in areas where a fixed infrastructure is not available or deploying one is not a technically or financially viable alternative [4]. Current applications of ad hoc networks cover a variety of areas, ranging from tactical networks for military communications to smart sensor networks for environmental monitoring. For instance, in the scenario depicted in Fig. 1(a), troops deployed on a battlefield are equipped with mobile devices forming a tactical MANET that enables them to communicate with commanders at the headquarters.

On the downside, their wireless nature and the lack of a stable infrastructure make MANETs vulnerable to a wide range of attacks, both active and passive, that can be waged by malicious nodes physically located within the transmission range of one or more legitimate nodes. In the scenario of Fig. 1(a), enemies equipped with wireless devices may be hiding in the field (e.g., attackers A_1 and A_2), or they may have simply planted wireless sensors at certain locations.

In the last couple of decades, considerable research effort has been devoted to the problem of detecting various types of attacks against wireless networks. However, despite an increasing interest in attacker localization, in both wireless sensor networks and ad-hoc mobile networks, no general solution has been devised yet. Instead, ad-hoc solutions based on the specific nature of certain attacks have been widely investigated. In particular, many different jammer localization approaches have been proposed in recent years [3,9,10].

In order to address this important problem, we propose a novel and more general approach to attacker localization in MANETs, based on a probabilistic model of the attacker's location. Specifically, we can estimate the location of

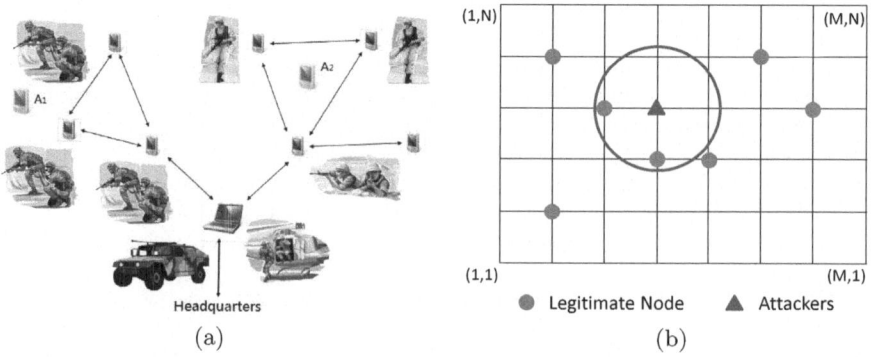

(a)   (b)

Fig. 1. Examples of (a) tactical MANETs, and (b) nodes in a discrete space

malicious nodes based on the location of all attacks detected in the network, or, more generally, the location of legitimate nodes that have detected malicious activity in their neighborhood. For the purpose of our analysis, we assume that alerts are given. Additionally, our model assumes that malicious nodes are in the neighborhood of nodes generating an alert. This assumption is justified by extensive work in the area of activity detection for MANETs. For instance, Watchdog [11] is an intrusion detection system running on each node of the network. By listening to its neighbors, each node can detect routing misbehavior. In [12], Patwardhan et al. present a similar technique. The main difference is that in Watchdog a node monitors the traffic it sends to its neighbors, whereas in [12] a node monitors the traffic between neighbors which are in range of each other.

The proposed framework does not rely on attack-specific assumptions, such as those typically used in the literature on jammer localization, namely, static wireless nodes and single attacker scenario [3]. For ease of presentation, we assume that attackers are static, but extending our framework to take mobility of malicious nodes into account is quite straightforward, and it is part of our furure plans. Additionally, we assume that a number of countermeasures are available to capture or isolate malicious nodes. Such countermeasures might include sending a patrol to physically capture malicious nodes, or running a specialized algorithm to identify and isolate malicious nodes in the regions selected by our framework. We are interested in optimally deploying available countermeasures. Specifically, we are interested in addressing the following classes of problems:

(i) Estimating the minimum number of countermeasures that need to be deployed to capture all attackers.
(ii) Finding the deployment that maximizes either the expected number of attackers in the target regions or the expected number of alerts *explained* by the solution, subject to a constraint on the number of countermeasures.

We show that these problems are NP-hard, and propose two polynomial time heuristic algorithms to find approximate solutions. Experiments show that our approach works well in practice, and both algorithms can capture over 80% of the attackers within 10-12 deployment cycles, in most scenarios.

The remainder of the paper is organized as follows. Section 2 discusses related work. Section 3 introduces the proposed framework, and provides a formal statement of the problems addressed in our work. Heuristic algorithms are presented in Section 4, and experimental results are reported in Section 5. Finally, Section 6 gives concluding remarks, and indicates future research directions.

2   Related Work

In recent years, there has been increasing interest in the localization of attackers in both wireless sensor networks and ad-hoc mobile networks. The vast majority of current approaches focus on specific types of attacks, most notably jamming attacks [3,9,10]. Cheng et al. [3] offer a comprehensive study of the jammer localization problem, and propose a simple yet effective algorithm called *Double*

Circle Localization (DCL). They assume all nodes in the network (i) are deployed randomly; (ii) are static; (iii) have the same capability (e.g. transmission power); (iv) know their own location; and (v) can recognize whether they are jammed. They consider a single-jammer scenario, and apply the free-space propagation model, according to which jamming signals attenuate with distance. The proposed algorithm calculates the minimum bounding circle and the maximum inscribed circle of the convex hull of the set of jammed nodes, and combines their centers to estimate the location of the jammer. They show that their algorithm outperforms three existing geometry-based algorithms, namely, Centroid Localization (CL), Weighted Centroid Localization (WCL), Virtual Force Iterative Localization (VFIL) [10]. The CL algorithm estimates the position of the jammer by simply averaging the coordinates of all jammed nodes. The WCL algorithm [2] weights the contribution of each jammed node when computing the centroid. One way of assigning weights is based on the distance between the jammer and the affected node, which can be estimated by measuring the strength of the incoming radio signal. VFIL tries to improve CL by adjusting its estimation based on the distribution of jammed nodes.

Other approaches focus on identifying nodes or subnetworks that are affected by attacks, but they provide a very coarse grained estimate of the attacker's position. Kim and Song [8] present a simple approach for fast detection of attacks using CCA (Clear Channel Assessment) values – a measure of the availability of a communication medium. If a node tries to send a message and finds the channel busy, its CCA value is increased and the node will retry to retransmit later. If the CCA value of a node exceeds a given threshold, this mechanism judges that the node is attacked, or otherwise affected by nearby attacks.

Han et al. [6] address the problem of attackers intentionally hiding or falsifying their position in order to decrease the accuracy of the localization process, which is traditionally executed by multiple observers (usually Access Points) which can simultaneously observe the intruder's transmissions and use time delays, angle of arrival, or signal strength information to localize the intruder. They propose a proactive technique, named Access Point Coordinated Localization (APCL), that forces the attacker to reveal undistorted signal features unintentionally, in order to subsequently use traditional localization techniques.

Our approach significantly differs from existing literature, in that it seeks a more general solution to the problem of attacker localization in MANETs. Research in this area has mostly focused on specific types of attacks, requiring several simplifying assumptions. We drop most such assumptions, and show that our framework can deal with different types of attacks, including jamming.

3   Probabilistic Framework

In this section, we present our probabilistic framework for attacker localization in MANETs. We first provide some technical preliminaries in Section 3.1, and then present the framework in detail (Section 3.2). We conclude in Section 3.3 by providing a formal statement of the problems addressed in this paper.

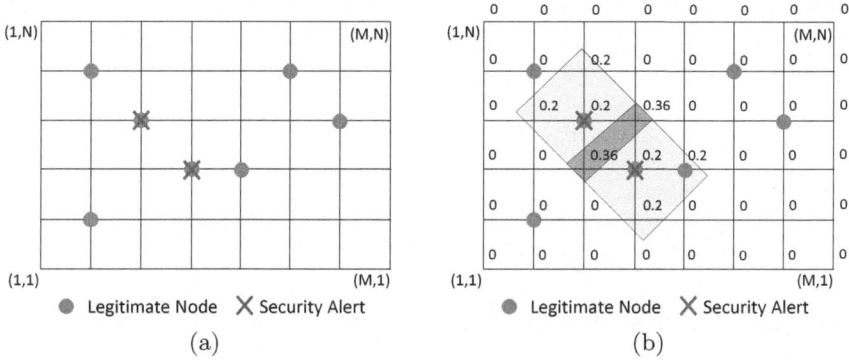

Fig. 2. Examples of (a) security alerts, and (b) computation of $\Pr(attacker(p))$

3.1 Technical Preliminaries

Without loss of generality we assume a discrete notion of space, as formalized by Definition 1, and assume that, at any time, both legitimate and malicious nodes are at one of a finite number of discrete locations.

Definition 1 (Space). *Given two integers $M, N \in \mathbb{N}$, a space $\mathcal{S} = \{1, \ldots, M\} \times \{1, \ldots, N\}$ is a finite subset of points of $\mathbb{N}^2$.*

For ease of modeling, the above definition assumes that a space is a rectangular region within $\mathbb{N}^2$. Fig. 1(b) shows a discrete space for $M = 8$ and $N = 6$. In this example, legitimate nodes are located at points $(2, 2)$, $(2, 5)$, $(3, 4)$, $(4, 3)$, $(5, 3)$, $(6, 5)$, and $(7, 4)$, and an attacker is located at point $(4, 4)$.

Associated with the space is a distance function $dist : \mathcal{S} \times \mathcal{S} \to \mathbb{R}$ that satisfies the normal distance axioms:

- Positive definiteness: $\forall p_1, p_2 \; dist(p_1, p_2) \geq 0$ and $dist(p_1, p_2) = 0 \Leftrightarrow p_1 = p_2$
- Symmetry: $\forall p_1, p_2 \; dist(p_1, p_2) = dist(p_2, p_1)$
- Triangle inequality: $\forall p_1, p_2, p_3 \; dist(p_1, p_2) + dist(p_2, p_3) \geq dist(p_1, p_3)$

Given the above notion of space, a MANET $\mathcal{M}$ at time t can be represented, for the purpose of our analysis, as a subset of $\mathcal{S}$ including all the points where a mobile node is deployed at time t. A set $\mathcal{A}$ of alerts can be represented as a set of pairs $a = (p, t)$, where t is the time at which an alert a was generated and p is the location at time t of the node triggering the alert.

3.2 Framework

Given an alert, we first need to define the probability that an attacker located within range of the alert's location is responsible for causing the alert. We use the binary predicate $causes : \mathcal{S} \times \mathcal{A} \to \{true, false\}$ to specify if there is an attacker at point $p \in \mathcal{S}$ causing an alert $a \in \mathcal{A}$. We assume that the transmission range $r \in \mathbb{R}$ is fixed and equal for all legitimate nodes and attackers.

Definition 2 (Attacker's Probability Distribution). *Let $a \in \mathcal{A}$ be an alert. The attacker's probability distribution for a, denoted θ_a, is a probability distribution over $\mathcal{S}$ defined as follows:*

$$\theta_a(p) = \Pr(causes(p, a)) \tag{1}$$

s.t.

$$\theta_a(p) \begin{cases} \geq 0, & \text{if } dist(p, a) <= r \\ = 0, & \text{if } dist(p, a) > r \end{cases} \tag{2}$$

where $dist : \mathcal{S} \times \mathcal{S} \to \mathbb{R}$ is the distance associated with the space $\mathcal{S}$.

Note that, for all $a \in \mathcal{A}$, $\sum_{p \in \mathcal{S}} \theta_a(p) = 1$, i.e., the attacker who caused a must be in $\mathcal{S}$. Intuitively, if a node in the MANET has been attacked, this node must be within an attacker's transmission range r. Given an alert $a \in \mathcal{A}$, we use S_a to denote the set of points $S_a = \{p \in \mathcal{S} \mid \theta_a(p) \geq 0\}$. In other words, the attacker who caused a must in S_a. We do not assume a specific distribution $\theta_a(p)$. Any distribution can be used in our framework, as long as the properties described by Equation 2 are satisfied. The choice of a specific distribution depends on a number of factors, including the radio propagation model, and the information available to nodes triggering an alert. In the simplest case, we can assume that the attacker's probability is uniformly distributed in a circular region of radius r centered at the alert's location. If more information is available, we can add constraints to possible attacker locations. For instance, when signals propagate according to the free space model and receivers can measure the received signal power the attacker's probability is uniformly distributed in an annulus of radius $d \pm \epsilon$, where d is the estimated distance of the attacker and ϵ is a tolerance parameter. The free space propagation model assumes the ideal propagation condition that there is only one clear line-of-sight path between the transmitter and receiver. In [5], H. T. Friis presented the following equation to calculate the received signal power in free space at distance d from the transmitter.

$$P_r(d) = \frac{P_t \cdot G_t \cdot G_r \cdot \lambda^2}{(4 \cdot \pi)^2 \cdot d^2 \cdot L} \tag{3}$$

Where P_t is the transmitted signal power, G_t and G_r are the antenna gains of transmitter and receiver respectively, L is the system loss, and λ is the wavelength. The free space model basically represents the communication range as a circle around the transmitter.

We now introduce the notion of an *explanation*. Intuitively, an explanation is a set of points such that the presence of an attacker at each of these points would *explain* all the alerts that were generated.

Definition 3 (Explanation). *Let $\mathcal{S}$ be a space, and let $\mathcal{A}$ be a set of alerts triggered by nodes of a MANET $\mathcal{M}$ deployed over $\mathcal{S}$. An explanation E for $\mathcal{A}$ is a subset of $\mathcal{S}$ s.t. for all $a \in \mathcal{A}$, $E \cap S_a \neq \emptyset$. We use $\mathcal{E}$ to denote the set of all possible explanations. An explanation is said to be minimal iff $\nexists E' \in \mathcal{E}$ s.t. $|E'| < |E|$.*

In Definition 2, we introduced the probability $\theta_a(p)$ that an attacker in p is responsible for a single alert a. Given a set of alerts, we are interested in finding the probability that any given point $p \in \mathcal{S}$ hosts an attacker. We use the unary predicate $attacker : \mathcal{S} \rightarrow \{true, false\}$ to specify if there is an attacker at a point $p \in \mathcal{S}$. If we assume that, given any two points $p_1, p_2 \in \mathcal{S}$ and any two alerts $a_1, a_2 \in \mathcal{A}$, $causes(p_1, a_1)$ and $causes(p_2, a_2)$ are independent, then the following result can be proved. We refer to this assumption as *causality independence*.

Proposition 1. *Given a space $\mathcal{S}$, and a set of alerts $\mathcal{A}$, the following property holds under causality independence:*

$$(\forall p \in \mathcal{S}) \left(\Pr(attacker(p)) = 1 - \prod_{a \in \mathcal{A}} (1 - \theta_a(p)) \right) \tag{4}$$

Example 1. Consider the scenario of Fig. 2(a), and assume that $r = 1.1$ and θ_a is uniformly distributed over $S_a = \{p \in \mathcal{S} \mid dist(p, a) \leq r\}$. By computing the value of $\Pr(attacker(p))$ according to Equation 4, we obtain the result shown in Fig. 2(b). The light-shaded region comprises all points $p \in \mathcal{S}$ s.t. $\Pr(attacker(p))$ is greater than 0. In other words, the attacker(s) must be in that region. The dark-shaded region only contains points with $\Pr(attacker(p)) > 0.3$.

Definition 4 (Expected Number of Attackers). *Given a set of points $D \subseteq \mathcal{S}$, the number of attackers in D is a random variable N_a^D which can assume value $|E \cap D|$ for any $E \in \mathcal{E}$. The expected number of attackers in D is*

$$\mathrm{Ex}\left[N_a^D\right] = \sum_{E \in \mathcal{E}} \Pr(E) \cdot |E \cap D| \tag{5}$$

where $\Pr(E)$ is the probability of explanation E.

Intuitively, the expected number of attackers is the weighted average, over all possible explanations, of the number of attackers in an explanation, where the weight of an explanation is its probability. The expected numbers of attackers in $\mathcal{S}$ is $\mathrm{Ex}\left[N_a^{\mathcal{S}}\right] = \sum_{E \in \mathcal{E}} \Pr(E) \cdot |E|$. In the example of Fig. 2(b), $E\left[N_a^{\mathcal{S}}\right] = 1.92$, meaning that, although most explanations include two attackers, single-attacker explanations also exist (e.g., $E_1 = \{3, 3\}$). The following result shows that, under *causality independence*, calculating $\mathrm{Ex}\left[N_a^D\right]$ is computable in polynomial time.

Proposition 2. *Let $D \subseteq \mathcal{S}$ be a set of points in $\mathcal{S}$ and let N_a^D denote the number of attackers in D. The following property holds.*

$$\mathrm{Ex}\left[N_a^D\right] = \sum_{E \in \mathcal{E}} \Pr(E) \cdot |E \cap D| = \sum_{p \in D} \Pr(attacker(p)) \tag{6}$$

3.3   Problem Statement

Given an ad-hoc network deployed over a space $\mathcal{S}$, and a set of alerts $\mathcal{A}$, we are interested in optimally deploying a limited number of resources in order to capture the attackers responsible for the alerts. We assume that a deployed resource can capture all malicious nodes within a capture range defined as a circle of radius l – with $l \ll r$ – centered at the location of the resource. We use the term *deployment* to refer to a set of points in $\mathcal{S}$ where resources are deployed. We can define the following three optimization problems.

Problem 1 (Minimize deployment size). Given a space $\mathcal{S}$, a set of alerts $\mathcal{A}$ over $\mathcal{S}$, and a probability threshold $\tau \in [0,1]$, find a deployment $D \subseteq \mathcal{S}$ of minimum size that *sufficiently* explains all the alerts in $\mathcal{A}$.

$$\textbf{minimize}_{D \in 2^{\mathcal{S}}} |D|$$
$$\textbf{subject to} \tag{7}$$
$$(\forall a \in \mathcal{A}) \ \sum_{p \in D} \theta_a(p) \geq \tau$$

In this optimization problem, the constraints require that D be an explanation (see Definition 3), and each alert be explained with probability equal to or greater than a threshold τ. We wish to minimize the number of resources deployed.

Problem 2 (Maximize expected number of attackers). Given a space $\mathcal{S}$, a set of alerts $\mathcal{A}$ over $\mathcal{S}$, a positive integer $k \in \mathbb{N}^+$, and a probability threshold $\tau \in [0,1]$, find a deployment $D \subseteq \mathcal{S}$ of size k or less that *sufficiently* explains all the alerts in $\mathcal{A}$, and maximizes the expected number of attackers in D under causality independence.

$$\textbf{maximize}_{D \in 2^{\mathcal{S}}} \sum_{p \in D} \Pr(attacker(p))$$
$$\textbf{subject to}$$
$$|D| \leq k \tag{8}$$
$$(\forall a \in \mathcal{A}) \ \sum_{p \in D} \theta_a(p) \geq \tau$$

In this problem, the first constraint limits the number of resources that can be deployed, whereas the second set of constraints, similarly to Problem 1, require that D be an explanation (see Definition 3), and each alert be explained with probability equal to or greater than a threshold τ. The objective function is the expected number of attackers in D, which, based on Proposition 2, can be computed as the sum over $p \in D$ of $\Pr(attacker(p))$.

Problem 3 (Maximize expected number of explained alerts). Given a space $\mathcal{S}$, a set of alerts $\mathcal{A}$ over $\mathcal{S}$, a positive integer $k \in \mathbb{N}^+$, and a probability threshold $\tau \in [0,1]$, find a deployment $D \subseteq \mathcal{S}$ of size k or less that *sufficiently* explains all the alerts in $\mathcal{A}$, and maximizes the expected number of alerts that would be explained by attackers located at each point in D.

$$\textbf{maximize}_{D \in 2^{\mathcal{S}}} \sum_{a \in \mathcal{A}} \sum_{p \in D} \theta_a(p)$$
$$\textbf{subject to}$$
$$|D| \leq k \tag{9}$$
$$(\forall a \in \mathcal{A}) \ \sum_{p \in D} \theta_a(p) \geq \tau$$

In this problem, the constraints are the same as in the previous problem, but the objective is to maximize the expected number of alerts that the presence of an attacker in each point of D would explain. Note that, unlike Problem 2, Problem 3 does not use any independence assumptions.

Algorithm 1. MIN-K$(S, \mathcal{A}, \tau, l)$

Input: set of points S, set of alerts $\mathcal{A}$, threshold τ, and capture radius l
Output: deployment $D \subseteq S$

1: $D \leftarrow \emptyset$
2: $\mathcal{A}^* \leftarrow \emptyset$ // Alerts covered
3: **while** $\mathcal{A}^* \neq \mathcal{A} \wedge S \neq \emptyset$ **do**
4:     $S' \leftarrow \{p_i \in S \setminus D \mid |\mathcal{A}_i^* \setminus \mathcal{A}^*| \text{ is maximum}\}$ // $\mathcal{A}_i^*$: set of alerts covered by p_i
5:     $S'' \leftarrow \{p_j \in S' \mid \Pr(attacker(p_j)) \text{ is maximum}\}$
6:     $p \leftarrow$ randomly selected point from S''
7:     $D \leftarrow D \cup \{p\}$
8:     $S \leftarrow S \setminus \{p_k \in S \mid dist(p_k, p) \leq l\}$
9:     $\mathcal{A}^* \leftarrow \mathcal{A}^* \cup \{a_k \in \mathcal{A} \mid \sum_{q \in D} \Pr(causes(q, a_k)) \geq \tau\}$
10: **end while**
11: **return** D

---

4 Algorithms

In this section, we first show that all the three problems defined in the previous section are NP-Hard, and then presents two polynomial heuristic algorithms that offer good approximation guarantees. The first of these two algorithm solves Problem 1, whereas the second algorithm solves both Problem 2 and Problem 3.

Theorem 1. *Problems 1, 2, and 3 are NP-Hard.*

Proof. Problem 1 can be shown to be NP-Hard by reduction from the set cover problem, which is known to be NP-Hard. Specifically, the universe in the set cover problem can be treated as the set of alerts $\mathcal{A}$ to be covered (*explained*) and the several subsets of the universe can be treated as the candidate locations explaining subsets of $\mathcal{A}$. As Problem 1 is NP-Hard, the corresponding decision problem, where there is some cardinality constraint of k on the solution, is also NP-Hard (and easily shown to be NP-Complete). Therefore, finding any solution that meets the constraints of Problems 2 and 3 is NP-Hard as well.

4.1 Algorithm MIN-K

Algorithm MIN-K (Algorithm 1) approximates Problem 1, and it is inspired by the heuristic algorithm for solving the set covering problem [7]. Given a set of elements, called the universe, and n sets whose union comprises the universe, the set cover problem is to identify the smallest number of sets whose union still contains all elements in the universe. In our case, given a set of alerts, we are interested in identifying the smallest number of locations that can explain all the alerts, where each location explains one or more alerts.

    The algorithm takes as input a set $S \subseteq \mathcal{S}$ of candidate points, a set of alerts $\mathcal{A}$, a threshold τ, and a capture radius l, and returns a deployment $D \subseteq \mathcal{S}$. Lines 4-9 are iterated until either all the alerts are covered ($\mathcal{A}^* = \mathcal{A}$) or there

---

Algorithm 2. MULT-UPD$(S, \mathcal{A}, k, \tau, l)$

Input: set of points S, set of alerts $\mathcal{A}$, integer k, threshold τ, and capture radius l
Output: deployment $D \subseteq S$
1: $D \leftarrow \emptyset$
2: $\lambda \leftarrow e^{k-\tau} \cdot (1 + |\mathcal{A}|)$
3: $\mathcal{A}^* \leftarrow \emptyset$ // Alerts covered
4: **for all** $a_i \in \mathcal{A}$ **do**
5:     $w_i \leftarrow \frac{1}{(k-\tau)}$
6: **end for**
7: **while** $|D| < k \wedge \mathcal{A}^* \neq \mathcal{A} \wedge S \neq \emptyset$ **do**
8:     $S' \leftarrow \{p_i \in S \setminus D \mid \frac{\sum_{a_i \in \mathcal{A}} (w_i - w_i \cdot \theta_{a_i}(p_j))}{f(D \cup \{p_j\}) - f(D)}$ is minimum$\}$
9:     $p \leftarrow$ randomly selected point from S'
10:     $D \leftarrow D \cup \{p\}$
11:     $S \leftarrow S \setminus \{p_k \in S \mid dist(p_k, p) \leq l\}$
12:     $\mathcal{A}^* \leftarrow \mathcal{A}^* \cup \{a_k \in \mathcal{A} \mid \Pr(causes(p, a_k)) \geq \tau\}$
13:     **for all** $a_i \in \mathcal{A}$ **do**
14:         $w_i \leftarrow w_i \cdot \lambda^{(1-\theta_{a_i}(p_j))/(k-\tau)}$
15:     **end for**
16: **end while**
17: **return** D

---

are no more candidate points to examine ($S = \emptyset$). The algorithm first considers the set $S' \subseteq S$ such that the number of additional alerts covered by each point $p_i \in S'$ – w.r.t. the set $\mathcal{A}^*$ of alerts covered so far – is maximum (Line 4). Then, a point p is randomly selected from the set S'' of points p_j in S' having maximum value of $\Pr(attacker(p_j))$ (Lines 5-6). Finally, p is added to the solution and all points with a radius l from p are excluded from further consideration (Lines 7-8). All the alerts a_k that are sufficiently explained by D are added to $\mathcal{A}^*$ (Line 9).

Proposition 3. *MIN-K runs in $O(r^2 \cdot |\mathcal{A}|^2)$ time.*

Proof. The outer loop of the algorithm takes no more than $|\mathcal{A}|$ steps. The bound on the inner loop is $O(r^2 \cdot |\mathcal{A}|)$ iterations, as the number of points to consider at each step is proportional to a node's transmission area, that is $\pi \cdot r^2$.

4.2   Algorithm MULT-UPD

Algorithm MULT-UPD (Algorithm 2) is a multiplicative-updates algorithm that can be used to approximate solutions to Problems 2 and 3. It is based on the multiplicative-updates algorithm of [1], which is designed to find approximate solutions to the maximization of a submodular function with respect to packing constraints. We show in Proposition 5 that this algorithm runs in polynomial time, though we do not guarantee it provides optimal solutions (Theorem 1 suggests that an efficient polynomial algorithm that provides optimal solutions is unlikely). We apply the algorithm of [1] by embedding Problem 2 or 3 into a packing problem. As this algorithm is used for both problems, we will use the notation $f : 2^{\mathcal{S}} \to \mathbb{R}$ to denote a generic objective function. The definition of f depends on which problem is being solved. For Problem 2, it is:

$$f(D) = \sum_{p \in D} \Pr(attacker(p)) \qquad (10)$$

For Problem 3, it is defined as follows:

$$f(D) = \sum_{a \in \mathcal{A}} \sum_{p \in D} \theta_a(p) \qquad (11)$$

As stated earlier, the algorithm of [1] is designed to find a solution to maximize a *submodular* function. As f above is additive under either problem, submodularity follows trivially.[1] What remains to be shown is that our problems can be re-written as packing problems. We prove this in the following proposition.

Proposition 4. *The constraints of Problems 2 and 3 can be re-written as:*

$$\begin{aligned} |D| &= k \\ (\forall a \in \mathcal{A})\ \textstyle\sum_{p \in D}(1 - \theta_a(p)) &\leq k - \tau \end{aligned} \qquad (12)$$

Proof. For any $a \in \mathcal{A}$, we can re-write the original constraint as $k - \sum_{p \in D} \theta_a(p) \leq k - \tau$. We also note that the size of D must be k (except in a degenerate case). Therefore, we can re-write the constraint again as $\sum_{p \in D}(1 - \theta_a(p)) \leq k - \tau$.

With this embedding in mind, the algorithm functions by associating a weight with each alert (corresponding to the constraint that the alert must be explained with probability τ). The algorithm then proceeds in a generally greedy fashion – but every time an element is added to D, the weights for all constraints that are not met increase. When the algorithm makes a greedy selection, these weights are considered in addition to the increase experienced by the objective function. Though the algorithm of [1] provides an approximation ratio, this ratio does not apply to our embedding as the original algorithm allows solutions of less than size k (this is because Proposition 4 does not necessarily hold for approximate solutions). As a consequence, some of the alerts are not explained within probability τ. These alerts can be thought of as "difficult to explain" given the resource constraint (k). However, this is acceptable for our application as we look to provide iterative deployments of the resources (see algorithm ITER-DEP in the next section) so unexplained alerts will likely be covered in a subsequent deployment. We show that this algorithm runs in polynomial time.

Proposition 5. *MULT-UPD runs in $O(k \cdot r^2 \cdot |\mathcal{A}|^2)$ time.*

Proof. The outer loop of the algorithm takes no more than k steps. The bound on the inner loop is $O(r^2 \cdot |\mathcal{A}|)$ iterations, as the number of points to consider for each alert is proportional to the a node's transmission area, that is $\pi \cdot r^2$, and the calculation at Line 8 requires $O(|\mathcal{A}|)$ time.

---

[1] As does some other requirements such as monotonicity and that $f(\emptyset) = 0$.

Algorithm 3. ITER-DEP$(\mathcal{S}, \mathcal{A}, M, \tau, l)$

Input: space $\mathcal{S}$, set of alerts $\mathcal{A}$, max number of deployment cycles M, threshold τ, and capture radius l

1: $\mathcal{A}' \leftarrow \mathcal{A}$ // Alerts to explain
2: $count \leftarrow 0$ // Iteration counter
3: **for all** $p \in \mathcal{S}$ **do**
4:     compute $\Pr(attacker(p))$
5: **end for**
6: $S \leftarrow \{p \in \mathcal{S} \mid \Pr(attacker(p)) > 0\} = \bigcup_{a \in \mathcal{A}} S_a$
7: **while** $S \neq \emptyset \wedge count < M \wedge \mathcal{A}' \neq \emptyset$ **do**
8:     $D \leftarrow computeDeployment(S, \mathcal{A}', k, \tau, l)$
9:     **for all** $p \in D$ s.t. p is a hit **do**
10:       **for all** $q \in S$ s.t. $dist(p, q) < l$ and q is an attacker **do**
11:         **for all** $a \in \mathcal{A}'$ s.t. $\Pr(causes(q, a)) \geq \tau$ **do**
12:           $S \leftarrow S \setminus \{s \in S \mid \Pr(causes(s, a)) \geq 0\}$
13:         **end for**
14:         $\mathcal{A}' \leftarrow \mathcal{A}' \setminus \{a \in \mathcal{A}' \mid \Pr(causes(q, a)) \geq \tau\}$
15:       **end for**
16:     **end for**
17:     **for all** $p \in \mathcal{S}$ **do**
18:       compute $\Pr(attacker(p))$
19:     **end for**
20: **end while**

4.3 Algorithm ITER-DEP

Algorithms MIN-K and MULT-UPD both compute a single deployment of countermeasures. As the number of countermeasures deployable at each step may be limited (Problems 2 and 3), and some of the deployed countermeasures may result in false positives, it may not be possible in practice to capture all malicious nodes in a single deployment.

Algorithm ITER-DEP (Algorithm 3) takes as input a space $\mathcal{S}$, a set of alerts $\mathcal{A}$, the maximum number of deployment cycles M, a threshold τ, and a capture radius l, and iteratively redeploys countermeasures taking into account feedback from countermeasures deployed in the previous cycle. The algorithm first computes the initial values of $\Pr(attacker(p))$ under causality independence (Lines 3-5), and, based on those, a set S of candidate locations (Line 6). It then iterates until there are no more locations to consider, or all the alerts have been explained, or the maximum number of iterations has been reached (Lines 7-20). During each iteration, a deployment is computed using any of the algorithms presented earlier (Line 8). For each true positive, the set of alerts is updated by removing those that are sufficiently explained by the captured attacker, and the set of candidate points is updated accordingly (Lines 9-16). Lastly, the values of $\Pr(attacker(p))$ are updated.

Proposition 6. *ITER-DEP runs in* $O(M \cdot r^2 \cdot |\mathcal{A}|^2)$ *time when MIN-K is used, and* $O(M \cdot k \cdot r^2 \cdot |\mathcal{A}|^2)$ *time when MULT-UPD is used.*

Proof. The outer loop of the algorithm (Lines 7-20) takes no more than M steps. The complexity of Lines 8-19 is dominated by the complexity of Line 8, that is the complexity of the deployment algorithm – $O(r^2 \cdot |\mathcal{A}|^2)$ and $O(k \cdot r^2 \cdot |\mathcal{A}|^2)$ for MIN-K and MULT-UPD respectively. In fact, the bound on the loop at Lines 9-16 is $O(r^2 \cdot |\mathcal{A}|^2)$, as Line 13 is executed $|\mathcal{A}| \cdot \pi \cdot r^2 \cdot |\mathcal{A}|$ times, in the worst case.

5   Experiments

This section reports on the experiments we conducted to validate our framework. Additional experiments, showing how our approach can be used to localize jammers, are reported in Appendix A. We used NS-2 to simulate different network scenarios, with nodes moving according to a Random Way Point model[2], and attackers randomly choosing one or more of their neighbors as their targets.

We implemented a prototype of the proposed framework as a Java application that takes as input log files generated by NS-2 and containing detailed information about all the alerts. We studied algorithms MIN-K and MULT-UPD in terms of (i) number of deployment cycles needed to capture all the attackers, and (ii) time to compute a deployment as the number of alerts increases.

5.1   Experimental Setup

In our experiments, we considered a $20km \times 20km$ field, using a 10-meter granularity, and deployed 4,000 network nodes and about 600 attackers, both uniformly distributed in this area. Overall, attackers triggered more than 1,000 alerts. For the purpose of these experiments, we assumed that deployable countermeasures are physical resources, such as patrols, that can capture attackers within a 30-meter radius l. After a resource has been deployed, points within a radius l are assumed to be free of malicious nodes. With this assumption, all resources can be reused in the next deployment cycle.

As discussed in Section 3.2, several models can be use to compute the *attacker's probability distribution* of Definition 2. In our experiments, we assume all nodes are compatible with the free space radio propagation model and have a transmission range of 250 meters. Assuming that we can link an alert to a specific communication attempt from the attacker node, and that attackers are not able to falsify their beam direction and radio parameters to distort signal features, we can use the received signal power to estimate the distance d between the attacker and the victim, based on the selected radio propagation model. In this case, the probability distribution θ_a for an alert a can be assumed to be uniform in a annulus of radius $d \pm \epsilon$ centered at the alert's location (we set $\epsilon = 0.1 \cdot r$, where r is the transmission range). Fig. 3 shows the result of computing $\Pr(attacker(p))$ for a simple scenario, based on assumptions discussed above. Different colors denote different levels of probability values, with darkest areas being more likely to contain attackers. Points in high probability areas may explain multiple alerts.

---

[2] However, any mobility and radio propagation model can be used in our framework.

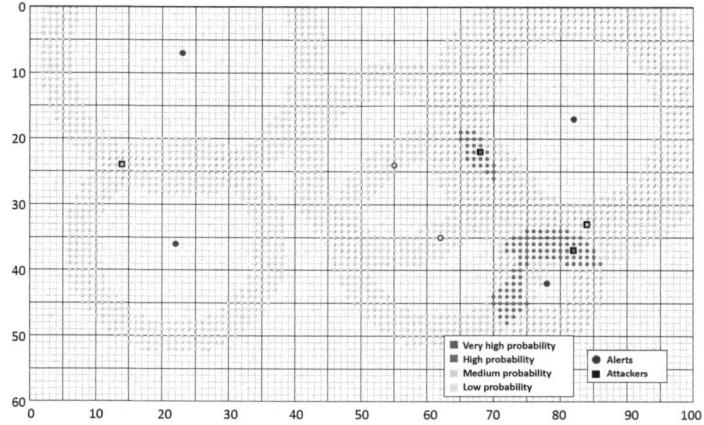

Fig. 3. Values of $\Pr(attacker(p))$ for a simple scenario

In order to compare the two algorithms, we first run MIN-K and found the minimum number of resources needed to cover all the alerts in a single deployment cycle, and then used this number as the value of k in MULT-UPD. To cover all the alerts in the scenario described above, we need about 500 resources.

5.2   Experimental Results

We analyzed the convergence of the proposed approach with respect to *recall*[3], which we measured as the fraction of attackers *captured* in each deployment cycle. Specifically, we use a notion of *cumulative recall*, as for each deployment cycle we count the total number of attackers captured since start.

Fig. 4 shows the cumulative recall function for the algorithms proposed: MIN-K, and the two versions of MULT-UPD maximizing expected number of attackers (MULT-UPD $v1$ in figure) and expected number of explained alerts (MULT-UPD $v2$) respectively. As shown, all the algorithms can capture 80% of the attackers in a very few deployment cycles, even in unfavorable scenarios, such as low network density. Indeed, convergence is influenced by network configuration and density: if an attacker triggers more alerts, it will be localized in a higher probability area and will be captured faster.

We also studied how the time for computing a single deployment varies when the number of alerts increases. As shown in Fig. 5, MIN-K performs significantly better than the two versions of MULT-UPD: it takes about 200 seconds to process around 1,000 alerts, while both versions of MULT-UPD take more then 700 seconds (about 12 minutes). However, both algorithms run in time quadratic in the number of alerts, as shown by the trend lines in Fig. 5. This confirms the theoretical results presented earlier in Section 4.

---

[3] Recall is a widely adopted measure in the information retrieval and pattern recognition fields, indicating the fraction of relevant instances retrieved by an algorithm.

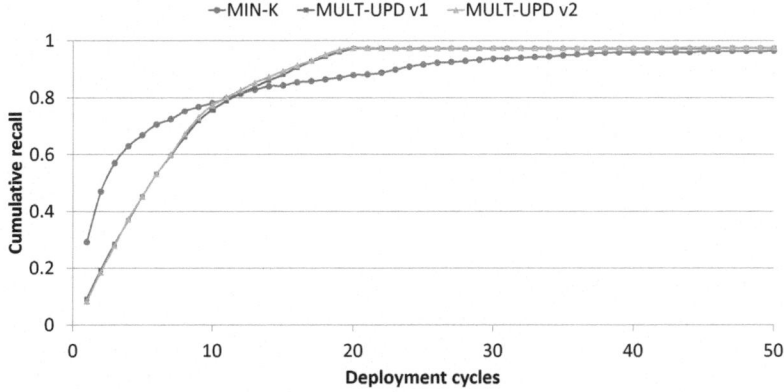

Fig. 4. Cumulative recall over subsequent deployment cycles

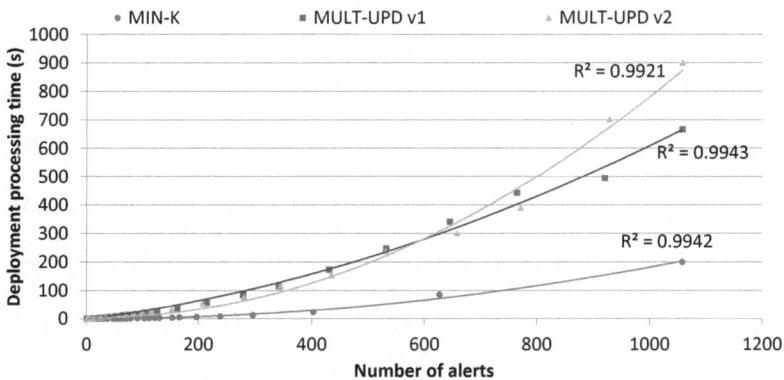

Fig. 5. Deployment processing time vs. number of alerts

6   Conclusions

In this paper, we have presented a probabilistic framework for the localization of attackers in Mobile Ad Hoc Networks (MANETs). Prior to our work, no general solution was devised to address this important problem, and most proposed approaches focused on specific types of attacks, most notably jammer attacks. The proposed framework can estimate the physical location of attackers, based on the location of nodes that have detected malicious activity in their neighborhood.

We assume that certain countermeasures can be deployed to capture or isolate malicious nodes, and they can provide feedback about the actual presence of an attacker in the target regions. We presented different variants of the localization problem, and we showed that all of them are NP-hard. We then proposed two polynomial heuristic algorithms that can compute approximate solutions. The feedback provided by deployed countermeasures is taken into account to iteratively re-deploy countermeasures until all attackers are captured. Experiments showed that our approach works well in practice, and both algorithms can capture over 80% of the attackers within a few deployment cycles.

Our future plans include removing the assumption that attackers are static, and extending our framework to be able to track moving attackers.

References

1. Azar, Y., Gamzu, I.: Efficient submodular function maximization under linear packing constraints. The Computing Research Repository (CoRR) (July 2010)
2. Blumenthal, J., Grossmann, R., Golatowski, F., Timmermann, D.: Weighted centroid localization in zigbee-based sensor networks. In: Proceedings of the IEEE International Symposium on Intelligent Signal Processing (WISP 2007) (October 2007)
3. Cheng, T., Li, P., Zhu, S.: An algorithm for jammer localization in wireless sensor networks. In: Proceedings of the 26th IEEE International Conference on Advanced Information Networking and Applications (AINA), Fukuoka, Japan (March 2012)
4. Datta, R., Marchang, N.: Security for Mobile Ad Hoc Networks. In: Handbook on Securing Cyber-Physical Critical Infrastructure, pp. 147–190. Morgan Kaufmann (January 2012)
5. Friis, H.T.: A note on a simple transmission formula. Proceedings of the IRE 34(5), 254–256 (1946)
6. Han, C., Zhan, S., Yang, Y.: Proactive attacker localization in wireless LAN. SIG-COMM Computer Communication Review 39(2), 27–33 (2009)
7. Johnson, D.S.: Approximation algorithms for combinatorial problems. Journal of Computer and System Sciences 9, 256–278 (1974)
8. Kim, Y.-J., Song, S.: The Feasibility Study of Attacker Localization in Wireless Sensor Networks. In: Kim, T.-h., Adeli, H., Robles, R.J., Balitanas, M. (eds.) UCMA 2011, Part II. CCIS, vol. 151, pp. 180–190. Springer, Heidelberg (2011)
9. Liu, H., Liu, Z., Chen, Y., Xu, W.: Determining the position of a jammer using a virtual-force iterative approach. Wireless Networks 17(2), 531–547 (2011)
10. Liu, H., Xu, W., Chen, Y., Liu, Z.: Localizing jammers in wireless networks. In: Proceedings of the IEEE International Conference on Pervasive Computing and Communications (PerCom 2009), Galveston, TX, USA (March 2009)
11. Marti, S., Giuli, T.J., Lai, K., Baker, M.: Mitigating routing misbehavior in mobile ad hoc networks. In: Proceedings of the 6th Annual International Conference on Mobile Computing and Networking (MobiCom 2000), Boston, MA, USA, pp. 255–265 (August 2000)
12. Patwardhan, A., Parker, J., Iorga, M., Karygiannis, T.: Secure routing and intrusion detection in ad hoc networks. In: Proceedings of the Third IEEE International Conference on Pervasive Computing and Communications (PerCom 2005), Kauai Island, HI, USA, pp. 191–199 (March 2005)

A   Localizing Jammers

In this appendix, we study the performance of our framework with respect to jamming attacks. Although many countermeasures have been proposed against jamming attacks, mostly based on frequency manipulation, it would be desirable to capture and deactivate jammers upon detection, as their activity heavily affects power consumption.

In the following, we first compare MIN-K and MULT-UPD w.r.t. localization error for a complex scenario involving multiple jammers, and show that MIN-K guarantees lower error. We then compare MIN-K with the Double Circle Localization (DCL) algorithm [3], and show that MIN-K offers better performance and lower sensitiveness to network density.

We considered a $20km \times 20km$ field and randomly placed 185 jammers, which jammed 445 nodes; we run MIN-K and MULT-UPD 100 times and recorded, for each jammer, the minimum distance from a deployed resource in the first deployment cycle. The cumulative distribution function of the error is shown in Fig. 6. As expected, the localization error of MIN-K is much smaller than MULT-UPD. In fact, the mechanism used by MIN-K to choose deployment points, unlike MULT-UPD, is aimed at covering all the alerts: this means that each resource will be deployed within distance r from an alert. As the attacker is also be within distance r from the alert, the maximum possible error is twice the transmission range. When running MULT-UPD, an alert might not be covered in the first deployment cycle, so the responsible jammer could be very far from any deployed resource.

We now compare MIN-K with the Double Circle Localization (DCL) algorithm [3]. The authors of DCL considered a square field of $100m^2$ with uniformly distributed nodes having a transmission range of 10 meters; they placed the jammer at the center of the field and evaluated the accuracy of jammer localization for two different network densities, 1 and 3 nodes per m^2 respectively, showing that the algorithm is able to achieve a very small error. In fact, 100% of the results were computed with an error smaller than 10 meters for the lowest density

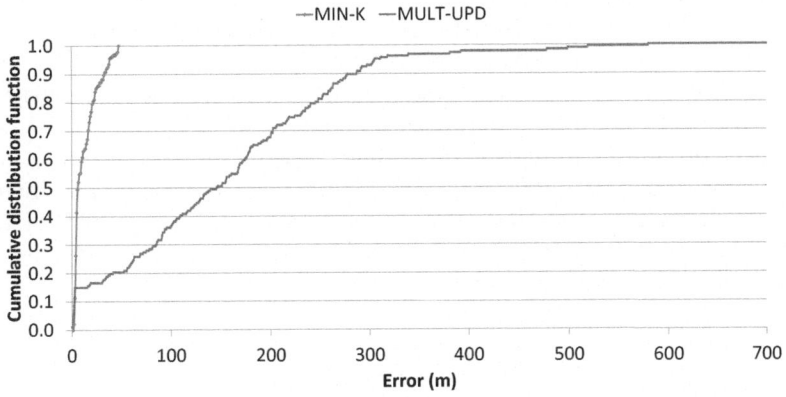

Fig. 6. CDF of the localization error for MIN-K and MULT-UPD

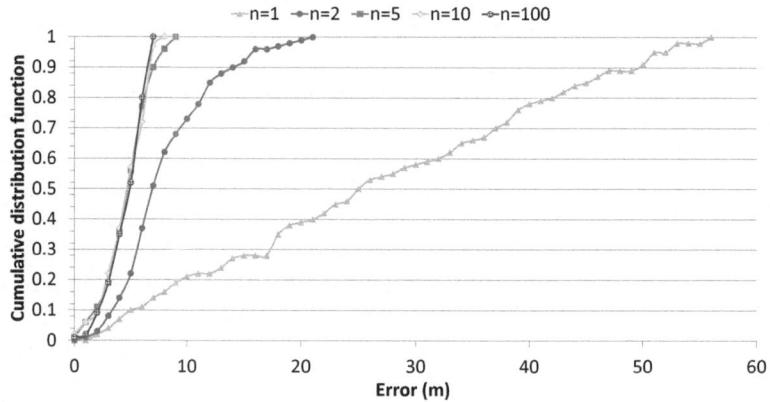

Fig. 7. CDF of the localization error for MIN-K for several node densities

and smaller than 5 meters for the highest density. It should be noted that this algorithm – similarly to other algorithms based on geometric considerations – achieves good accuracy only when network density is sufficiently high. Moreover, DCL, in its current form, can be applied only to one-jammer scenarios. Not only our framework is able to deal with multiple jammers, but it is also less sensitive to network density, as we show next.

We first considered the same network scenario used in [3], and run both MIN-K and MULT-UPD. Due to the high node density of this scenario and the resulting values of $\Pr(attacker(p))$, our framework – using a 1-meter resolution – was always able to find the correct position of the jammer in the first deployment cycle. To evaluate our framework's performance for jamming attacks in more general scenarios, we considered a $100m \times 100m$ field, with the jammer placed at the center of the field, and deployed networks having different densities. Specifically, we deployed 1, 2, 5, 10, and 100 nodes respectively, with a 71 meter transmission range (the whole field is jammed), and evaluated the accuracy for MIN-K over 1,000 independent runs. Fig. 7 shows the cumulative distribution function of the error. When considering a single node in the jammed area, the maximum error is high. As network density slightly increases, performance dramatically increases: it takes only a few nodes in the jammed area to bound the error within 10% of the transmission range. At this point, further increasing node density has a very small impact on localization error.

Robust Probabilistic Fake Packet Injection for Receiver-Location Privacy in WSN

Ruben Rios[1], Jorge Cuellar[2], and Javier Lopez[1]

[1] Network, Information and Computer Security (NICS) Lab,
University of Malaga, Spain
{ruben,jlm}@lcc.uma.es
[2] Siemens AG, Munich, Germany
jorge.cuellar@siemens.com

Abstract. The singular communication model in wireless sensor networks (WSNs) originate pronounced traffic patterns that allow a local observer to deduce the location of the base station, which must be kept secret for both strategical and security reasons. In this work we present a new receiver-location privacy solution called HISP (Homogenous Injection for Sink Privacy). Our scheme is based on the idea of hiding the flow of real traffic by carefully injecting fake traffic to homogenize the transmissions from a node to its neighbors. This process is guided by a lightweight probabilistic approach ensuring that the adversary cannot decide with sufficient precision in which direction to move while maintaining a moderate amount of fake traffic. Our system is both validated analytically and experimentally through simulations.

1 Introduction

Wireless Sensor Networks (WSNs) [1] can be seen as an extension of ordinary computers that allow them to sense and react over the environment surrounding them. These networks are composed of battery-powered devices, the sensor nodes, which are capable of measuring the physical phenomena in their vicinity and wirelessly transmit these data to a central node called base station or sink. The base station gathers the packets from different sources and processes them in order to gain insight about the area being monitored.

This technology has raised a tremendous interest in the academia and is finally drawing the attention of companies because of their potential integration into many diverse application scenarios. The criticality of many of these applications together with the hardware limitations of sensor nodes require the development of tailored security mechanisms to guarantee the proper operation of the network in the presence of adversaries [2]. Most of the countermeasures found in the literature have been built on top of cryptographic primitives in order to protect the information traversing the network. However, even when secure encryption algorithms are used to protect message content, traffic analysis reveals sensitive contextual information about the network and the application scenario [3].

S. Foresti, M. Yung, and F. Martinelli (Eds.): ESORICS 2012, LNCS 7459, pp. 163–180, 2012.
© Springer-Verlag Berlin Heidelberg 2012

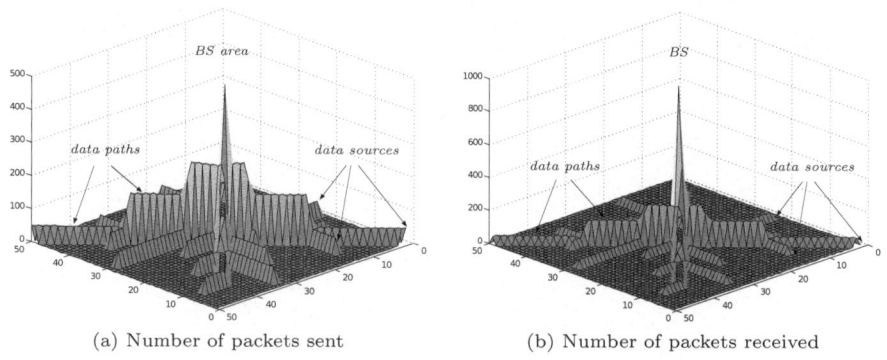

(a) Number of packets sent   (b) Number of packets received

Fig. 1. Communication pattern in a typical WSN

A noteworthy problem related to contextual privacy is the protection of the location of relevant network nodes. In particular, the location of source nodes is important because it provides the attacker with information about the area where special events occur. Consider, for example, a WSN deployed to control the transportation of hazardous materials into and out of a nuclear or chemical plant. If an attacker obtains the location of source nodes he might be able to approximate the location and movements of the trucks carrying these materials. Moreover, this information might allow the adversary to deduce sensitive information about the distribution of the plant or even the presence of problems in the industrial processes. On the other hand, protecting the location of the base station is tremendously important because if it gets compromised or even destroyed, the whole system is rendered useless. Besides the physical protection of the network, the location of the base station is strategically critical because this key device is most likely housed in a relevant facility within the plant.

The aforementioned privacy problems are extensible to any application scenario because they are caused by the particular way of operation of WSNs. In a typical configuration, packets containing event data are generated at various locations from where they are forwarded in the shortest possible path towards the sink. Fig. 1 represents a WSN consisting of 50 × 50 nodes where 15 nodes are reporting event data using a shortest-path routing protocol. Although this is the most suitable configuration for preserving the limited energy budget of sensor nodes, it produces pronounced traffic patterns that reveal the location of both the source nodes and the base station.

Most of the research so far has focused on the source-location privacy problem while the protection of receiver-location privacy has received much less attention. The main reason is that hiding the base station is a especially difficult task because all the traffic is addressed to this single node with the consequent increase of traffic in its vicinity. These features are exploited by adversaries who may monitor the direction of packet flows or the amount of traffic being transmitted to uncover the location of the sink. To counter these strategies several works have focussed on the use of random routing protocols [4,5] and the injection of fake traffic [6,7,8]. Many of these solutions fail to provide a sufficient protection level or they impose prohibitive energy costs and message delivery delays.

The main contribution of this work is the HISP (Homogenous Injection for Sink Privacy) protocol. HISP is based on the idea of locally homogenizing the amount and direction of the packets forwarded from the sensor nodes to their neighbors. Besides, this protection mechanism ensures that event data reach the base station without incurring in significant delays or excessive energy costs. To achieve this, HISP sends real packets using a random walk algorithm and introduces controlled amounts of fake traffic in such a way that the distribution of real packets remains probabilistically hidden.

The rest of this paper is organized as follows. Sec. 2 describes the network and threat model. A detailed description of the HISP protocol is presented in Sec. 3. Subsequently, in Sec. 4, we evaluate and analyze the main features and potential limitations of our approach. Moreover, Sec. 5 presents a discussion about the privacy protection level provided by the proposed solution. Sec. 6 compares this work with previous solutions in the area of location privacy in WSNs. Finally, Sec. 7 concludes the paper.

2 Problem Statement

This section presents the main features of WSNs as well as the adversarial model under consideration. Moreover, it introduces the main assumptions applicable to the rest of this work.

2.1 Network Model

We consider WSNs used for monitoring purposes. Usually, this type of networks follow an event-driven model, which means that the decision of transmitting data to the base station is made by individual sensor nodes upon the occurrence of special events. Consequently, this implies a many-to-one communication model where all the information flows from source nodes to a single base station.

Also, we assume that the deployed WSN is comprised of numerous sensor nodes which are deployed in a vast area. This prevents the adversary from controlling the communications in a large portion of the network as well as having all sensors within easy reach. Moreover, sensor nodes could be hidden or placed out of the visual field of the adversary. Sometimes this is not a strong assumption, for instance if we consider application scenarios such as under-water or under-ground sensor networks.

We focus on highly-connected sensor networks composed of n sensor nodes, where every node is aware of its adjacent neighboring nodes and the direction towards the sink. We require sensor nodes to have relatively high connectivity, that is, every node has several neighbors with which they share keys in order to be able to transmit to or receive packets from various locations. Note that, in sparse WSNs, an adversary can identify the route followed by messages more easily because the number of potential senders or receivers is rather limited.

Finally, we assume that sensor nodes make use of secure encryption algorithms that prevent an adversary from obtaining any identifiable information from packet payloads. In other words, the encryption mechanism under consideration must be robust to cryptanalysis attacks and also provide indistinguishability between real and fake transmissions. The key management scheme is beyond the scope of this paper. A survey can be found in [9].

2.2   Adversarial Model

The adversarial model considered is external, passive and mobile. An *external* adversary does not control sensor nodes and thus has no access to the key material. A *passive* attacker does not interfere with the communications or the normal operation of the network. In general, passive adversaries limit their actions to performing traffic analysis attacks. These attacks depend on the hearing range of the adversary, which is typically equivalent to that of an ordinary sensor node[1]. Moreover, a *mobile* adversary is capable of moving in the field based on his observations according to a particular strategy.

First, we define adversaries based on their eavesdropping capabilities. In particular, we take into consideration both the hearing range and the ability to retrieve packet header information. With respect to the hearing range, we might find adversaries capable of observing the transmissions of a single and adversary capable of monitoring all the communications in the network. On the other side, we distinguish between adversaries who, by observing a message, are capable to recognize the addressee of the next hop and those unable to retrieve this information. This information is contained in the header of the packets but it might be protected by means of some pseudonyms mechanism[11]. Next, we provide a formal definition of the adversarial model:

Definition 1 ($\mathcal{ADV}$). *Let $X = \{x_1, x_2, \cdots, x_m\}$ be the set of sensor nodes comprising the network and let x_i be an ordinary sensor node in the proximity of the adversary. We define the following adversaries:*

- *$\mathcal{ADV}_n$ chooses first a node x_i, and then observes the transmissions of node x_i and all its neighbors within distance n. On the next round he may choose a different node $x_{i'}$. The choice of the next $x_{i'}$ depends on the movement strategy, see for instance time-correlation and rate monitoring, below.*
- *$\mathcal{ADV}_n^a$ is similar to the previous one: he observes the transmissions of node x_i and all its neighbors within distance n, but this observation includes also the addressees of all those transmissions.*

Fig. 2 provides a visual representation of the different adversarial models at distances no larger than 1. The central node, x_i, broadcasts a message that is

---

[1] The hearing range of current sensor nodes operating outdoors is around 100 meters for low power configurations [10]. However, these values might be altered by many factors such as the signal frequency or the presence of obstacles.

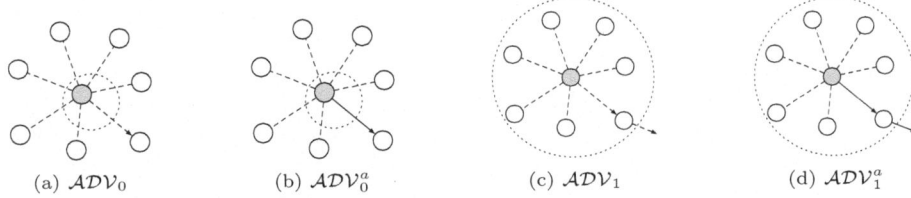

(a) $\mathcal{ADV}_0$ (b) $\mathcal{ADV}_0^a$ (c) $\mathcal{ADV}_1$ (d) $\mathcal{ADV}_1^a$

Fig. 2. Adversarial Model Examples

received by all its immediate neighbors. Transmissions are depicted by means of lines and arrows. An arrow represents that the packet is addressed to that particular node while dashed lines represent that these nodes are passive observers. When the arrow is dashed we mean that the node identifier cannot be retrieved by the attacker while the ordinary arrow represents that the identifier is accessible. Finally, the dotted circles represent the hearing range of the adversary.

We can define other types of attackers that are not able to see all the neighbors within a certain distance but a partial set of them. These type of attackers and their analysis will be left for future work. The attacker model considered in this work has a limited hearing range, similar to those depicted in Fig. 2. This is the typical hearing range considered in the literature, which focusses on adversaries with eavesdropping capabilities equivalent to an ordinary sensor node. Based on his observations and the peculiarities of the communication model, the adversary decides in which direction to move in order to reach the sink. Also, we are consistent with the two potential strategies proposed in the literature.

The adversary might perform two types of attacks to decide on the next move. In the *time-correlation* attack, the adversary observes the transmission times of a node and its neighbors. Based on the assumption that a node forwards a received packet shortly after receiving it, the adversary is able to deduce the direction to the sink and move accordingly. In the *rate-monitoring* attack, the adversary moves in the direction of the nodes transmitting a higher number of packets. This attack is based on the fact that nodes in the vicinity of the base station must transmit their own data as well as forward the traffic from remote sources. This strategy is less efficient because it requires the adversary to capture a sufficient number of packets before moving. Additionally, this attack is not effective when there are very few data sources or the adversary is not close to the sink.

3 Homogenous Injection for Sink Privacy

This section provides a detailed description of the HISP protocol. We present an overview of its main features as well as some fundamental properties that must be hold to ensure a robust privacy-preserving transmission protocol and the arrival of packets to the sink. Also, the neighbor discovery process is described since it is crucial for the subsequent data transmission stage.

3.1 System Overview

The HISP protocol is basically a biased random routing reinforced with the injection of controlled amounts of fake traffic. Upon the reception of a real message, the sensor node decides the next hop in the route based on some probability, which is dependent on the connectivity of the node. Fake packets are incorporated to prevent the adversary from being able to determine the direction to the sink when observing the number of packets being forwarded in his vicinity. In this way, messages are evenly distributed among all the neighbors of a node without introducing significant delays in the delivery of packets.

We devised a computationally inexpensive approach to determine the recipients of fake and real messages. Whenever a node has to transmit event data it picks a pair of neighbors. This pair is obtained from the combination of two elements without repetitions from all neighbors in its routing table. The routing table of the sensor is sorted incrementally (see Fig. 3), such that neighbors closer to the base station are placed first, then neighbors at the same distance, and finally neighbors in the opposite direction. This arrangement give rise to combinations of neighbors where nodes closer to the sink are more likely to appear in the first position of the pair while the second position contains equally distant or further neighbors. Thus, the random selection of these pairs leads to an homogeneous distribution of messages among all the neighbors of the node. HISP takes advantage of these features to send real packets to the first element and fake packets to the second.

3.2 Neighbor Discovery Process

Shortly after the deployment of the network, a network discovery protocol is launched to allow every sensor node to be aware of a routing path to the base station. This information is usually obtained by means of a discovery message broadcast by the base station. This message contains a hop count that is initially set to zero and is incremented at every hop by its recipients. On reception, every node stores the minimum distance value received from all of its neighbors. In this way, every node generates a routing table that contains its neighbors at distance $n - 1$, n, and $n + 1$, where n is the number of hops from the node to the base station. The result of this process is depicted in Fig. 3. The numbers represent the minimum distance of the node to the base station, the arrows indicate the direction towards the sink and the dashed lines indicate links to neighbor at the same distance. In the following, we will refer to nodes closer, equal, and further or $neigh_{n-1}$, $neigh_n$, and $neigh_{n+1}$ to mention these groups of neighbors.

The neighbor discovery process is essential to the rest of protocol. The reason is that the number and distribution of neighbors affects to both the privacy-protection level and the delivery of event messages to the base station as we will show in the following sections.

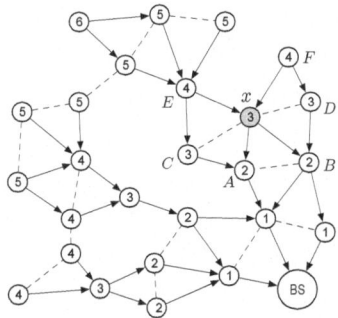

neighs(x)	distance
A	$n-1$
B	$n-1$
C	n
D	n
E	$n+1$
F	$n+1$

Fig. 3. Routing table of shaded node x

3.3   Data Transmission Properties

This section presents several key properties which are intended to limit the information gain of a local adversary during the transmission of data. Moreover, the fulfillment of these properties ensures the timely delivery of event data.

The protocol we are aiming at uses both real and fake messages. The source node, as well as any node that receives a real message, sends a real and a fake message, which should be indistinguishable to the intruder but not to the addressees. Property 2 aims to balance the amount of traffic being delivered by a node among its neighbors. By doing this, a local adversary cannot make a decision on which direction to follow based on the number of packets forwarded to neighboring nodes. While the paths of fake messages have relatively short length (this is a parameter of the solution), the path of real messages is intended to converge to the sink. This is established by Property 1: real messages must be transmitted to nodes closer to the base station with a high probability. These two properties together ensure that both real packets reach the base station and also that the flow of real messages is hidden by fake messages since they are indistinguishable. An additional technical property ensures that the transmission of every pair of messages is sent to *two* different nodes.

Property 1 (Convergence). *Let x be an arbitrary sensor node and BS be the base station. Also, let $neigh(n)$ be the set of immediate neighbors of a particular node n. Then we say that a path is convergent if x chooses the next node $x' \in neigh(x)$ such that:*

$$E(dist(x', BS)) < E(dist(x, BS))$$

where E is the mathematical expectation and dist is the distance between two particular nodes.

Property 2 (Homogeneity). *Let x be an arbitrary sensor node and $neigh(n)$ be the set of immediate neighbors of a particular node n. We say that the transmissions of a node x hold the homogeneity property if:*

$$\forall y, z \in neigh(x) \quad Frec_m(x, y) \simeq Frec_m(x, z)$$

where $Frec_m(x, y)$ represents the number of messages (real and fake) transmitted by node x to node y.

Property 3 (Exclusion). Let m and m' be a pair of messages and t be a particular transmission time. Let $send(m, x, y, t)$ denote that x sends to y the message m at time t. The exclusion property states that:

$$\forall m, m', x, y, t \quad send(m, x, y, t) \wedge m \neq m' \Rightarrow \neg send(m', x, y, t)$$

3.4   Transmission Protocol

We devised a message transmission protocol that is consistent with the properties defined in Sec. 3.3. This protocol introduces insignificant computational and memory overhead because it is based on straightforward operations. More precisely, it requires a simple sorting operation and a pseudo-random number generator [12].

Since we send two messages, the combinations of two elements without repetitions from all neighbors in the routing table is an elegant and lightweight mechanism for the selection of neighbors that is consistent with the provisions of Property 3. Moreover, if the routing table is incrementally ordered in terms of the distance of its neighbors to the base station (i.e., $[neigh_{n-1}, neigh_n, neigh_{n+1}]$) we achieve that most of the resulting combinations have a closer or equally distant neighbor in the first position of the tuple. Therefore, Property 1 is satisfied because the real packet is transmitted always to the first neighbor. Also Property 2 holds provided that we randomly select any pair from all possible combinations.

In Algorithm 1 we describe the behavior of a node upon the reception of a packet. The algorithm uses as input the received packet, a data structure which contains the combinations of two neighbors once sorted, and a network parameter that controls the durability of fake packets in the network. Initially, the algorithm decides the random pair of neighbors to whom packets will be addressed (line 1). Subsequently, if the received packet is real then it is be forwarded to $neigh1$ while $neigh2$ receives a fake packet whose time-to-live is set to MAX_TTL (line 3). This parameter is dependent on the hearing range of the adversary and provides a trade-off between energy consumption and privacy. Also, note that the packets are sent in random order to prevent the adversary from trivially learning which is the real message. The described behavior is identical in case that the node, rather than being an intermediary, is a source node which signals the occurrence of an event in the field.

On the contrary, if the received packet is fake, the node first obtains the time-to-live (TTL) of the packet and decrements its value by one (line 5). This prevents fake messages from flooding the network. In case the new TTL is greater than zero, the node sends two fake messages with the current TTL value (line 7).

Algorithm 1. Transmission strategy

Input: $packet \leftarrow receive()$
Input: $combs \leftarrow combinations(sort(neighs), 2)$
Input: MAX_TTL
1: $\{neigh1, neigh2\} \leftarrow select\_random(combs)$
2: **if** $isreal(packet)$ **then**
3:      $send\_random(neigh1, packet, neigh2, fake(MAX\_TTL))$
4: **else**
5:      $TTL \leftarrow get\_time\_to\_live(packet) - 1$
6:      **if** $TTL > 0$ **then**
7:          $send\_random(neigh1, fake(TTL), neigh2, fake(TTL))$
8:      **end if**
9: **end if**

Since we consider adversaries with a hearing range similar to an ordinary sensor nodes (i.e., the family $\mathcal{ADV}_1$), fake messages might be forwarded only once but still exceed the reach of the adversary.

4 Protocol Analysis

This section presents a detailed analysis on the potential limitations that might hinder the successful deployment of the HISP scheme in WSNs. First, we explore the impact of the network topology and the expected number of hops for real messages to reach the base station. Finally, we analyze the overhead introduced by our solution in terms of fake packet transmissions.

4.1 Bounding the Number of Neighbors

The distribution of real and fake messages is clearly impacted by the number of the neighbors in each of the groups of the routing table. In other words, Property 1 could be unsatisfied in case the number of neighbors in $neigh_{n-1}$ is significantly lower than the number of neighbors in $neigh_{n+1}$.

This problem is dependent on the topology of the network and the hearing range of the nodes. To have a clearer picture of how much this poses a real limitation to our protocol, we provide a numerical analysis on the number of $neigh_{n+1}$ that any sensor node can withstand without sacrificing any of the properties defined in Sec. 3.3.

Definition 2. *A real message converges to the base station if for any node in the route it traverses $\mathbb{P}_c > \mathbb{P}_f$, where $\mathbb{P}_c$ is the probability of transmitting the message to a node closer to the base station, and $\mathbb{P}_f$ is the probability of sending the message to a further node.*

In order to yield this property, several conditions must be met. In particular, let S be the total number of neighbors of an arbitrary node such that $S = C + E + F$, where C, E, and F are the number of neighbors in $neigh_{n-1}$, $neigh_n$, and $neigh_{n+1}$, respectively. The theorem below gives a sufficient condition on C, F and S to ensure the desired property.

Theorem 1 *Real messages reach the base station if $F < \sqrt{2C(S - C)}$ for any sensor sensor in the route.*

Proof. We want to show that if $F < \sqrt{2C(S - C)}$ then $\mathbb{P}_c > \mathbb{P}_f$, such that $\mathbb{P}_c$ and $\mathbb{P}_f$ are the probabilities of sending a correct message to a node in $neigh_{n-1}$ and $neigh_{n+1}$, respectively.

The number of combinations of two neighbors where at least the first element belongs to $neigh_{n+1}$ is:

$$\binom{F}{2} = \frac{F(F - 1)}{2}$$

while the number of combinations of two neighbors where the first element of the duple is a node in $neigh_{n-1}$ is:

$$\binom{C}{2} + C(E + F)$$

Consequently, the probability of selecting a closer neighbor is higher than the probability of selecting a further neighbor iff the number of combinations with a closer neighbor in the first position of the duple is larger than those with the first element being a further neighbor. Formally:

$$\mathbb{P}_c > \mathbb{P}_f \Leftrightarrow C(C - 1) + 2C(E + F) > F(F - 1)$$

In order to simplify the analysis we make some generalizations which are less restrictive but still provide a sufficient condition for the proof.

$$2C(E + F) > F^2 \Rightarrow C(C - 1) + 2C(E + F) > F(F - 1)$$

Provided that $C + E + F = S$, the previous equation can be expressed as:

$$F < \sqrt{2C(S - C)} \tag{1}$$

Therefore, we might say that if equation 1 is satisfied, then the following implication holds:

$$F < \sqrt{2C(S - C)} \Rightarrow \mathbb{P}_c > \mathbb{P}_f$$

Intuitively, the imposed restriction can be satisfied in networks deployed by hand following a particular topology (e.g., grid or mesh). Still, we deem necessary to validate the feasibility of our restriction in randomly deployed networks by means of experimental simulations. In particular, Fig. 4 depicts the average results over 50 repetitions of our network discovery protocol for various network sizes. We considered the following network parameters: (i) a square field area of side 1,

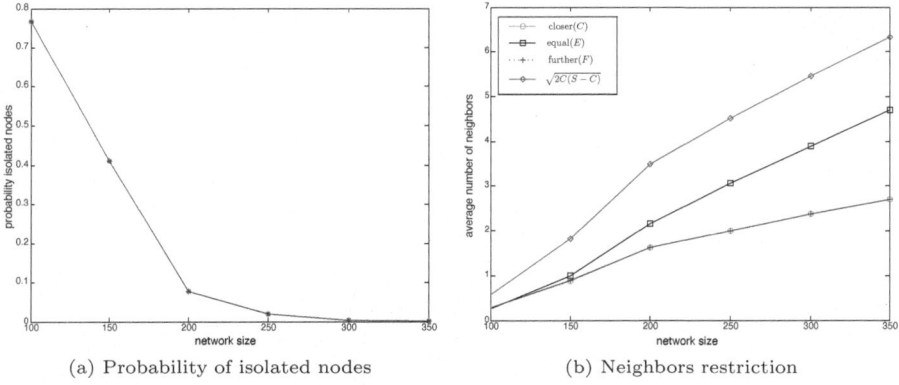

(a) Probability of isolated nodes   (b) Neighbors restriction

Fig. 4. Node connectivity in randomly deployed networks

(ii) the transmission radius of the nodes is set to 0.1, and (iii) networks ranging in size from 100 to 700 nodes randomly located. In Fig. 4a we show that the probability of isolated nodes drops significantly when the network size is over 200 nodes. Moreover, Fig. 4b presents the average number of neighbors closer, equal and further for any node in the network. In this figure we also show that the restriction imposed by Equation (1) on the maximum number of further neighbors is satisfied at all times.

Note that the results shown in Fig. 4b are average values and there might be some particular nodes not satisfying the restriction. However, this would only pose some additional delay unless there are network regions with a high concentration of nodes unable to fulfill the imposed condition. This issue might cause network packets to continuously move back and forth impeding their progress towards the base station. This is not the case when the node density is sufficient.

In general, we can state that when the number of nodes in a randomly deployed network is over 350 per square kilometer there is a high probability of full connectivity considering a transmission range of 100 meters. Also, in this case, the restriction on the number of neighbors is always satisfied.

4.2 Message Delivery Time

The probabilistic nature of our protocol introduces some uncertainty on the delivery of messages to the sink. This issue has some implications both on the reaction time of the network and the energy consumption of the nodes. Therefore, we provide some insights on the expected number of hops to reach the base station for a packet originated n hops away.

Let x_n be the expected number of hops for a packet originated at distance n. The proposed transmission protocol can be modeled by the following recurrence equation:

$$x_n = 1 + px_{n-1} + qx_n + rx_{n+1} \qquad (2)$$

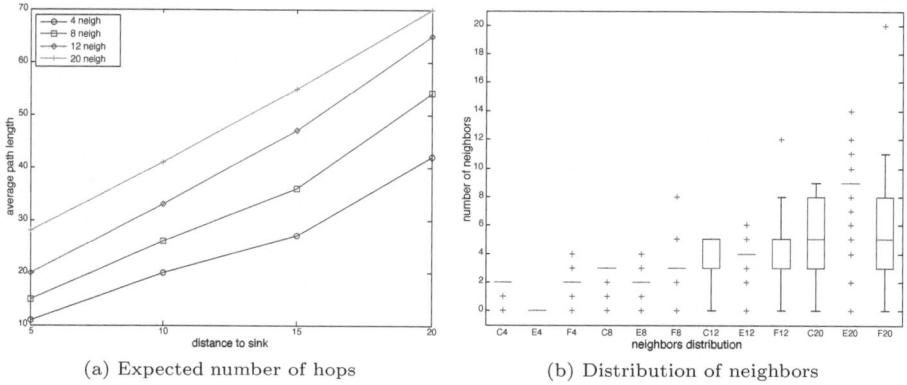

(a) Expected number of hops   (b) Distribution of neighbors

Fig. 5. Protocol performace for various network configurations

This equation represents a biased random walk where, after sending the packet and increasing the number of hops by one, the packet will be forwarded to a neighbor. At each hop, we have a probability p of delivering the packet to a node closer to the base station, a probability q of staying at the same distance, and a probability r of moving in the opposite direction. Therefore, the average speed towards the base station is $p - r$.

In general, the above result is true for constant values of p and r but this is not always the case in sensor networks. The reason is that not all sensor nodes present the same distribution of neighbors. This is dependent on the hearing range of the nodes, the network topology and their location in the network. In Fig. 5 we present the performance of our protocol for WSNs deployed in a grid with equal transmission power for all nodes. We consider various configurations by increasing the transmission power, which in turn changes the connectivity of the network. On average, every node has 4, 8, 12 or 20 neighbors. Also, for every configuration we place the source at various distances from the base station: 5, 10, 15 and 20 hops. Several source nodes are selected for each distance and every single source node generates 500 data packets to be received by the base station.

The results show that the expected number of hops increases with the distance to the sink as well as with the connectivity of the nodes. As the number of neighbors available to a node increases, the more difficult it is for the adversary to make a decision on which of the recipients is actually closer to the base station. However, a significant increase in the number of neighbors has also implications on the delivery time because as the transmission range grows, more nodes will be in the equal list of the node. This issue is shown in Fig. 5b, where we provide a box-plot representation of the number of neighbors closer (C), equal (E), and further (F) for the simulated network configurations. For example, C_4 indicates closer neighbors in the $4neigh$ network configuration.

Additionally, note from Fig. 5a that, for all the configurations, the average speed of the packets decreases when they are close to the sink. Consider, for example, the $4neigh$ configuration. When the distance to the sink is 5, the expected delivery time is 11, while a packet at distance 20 will be delivered after 42 hops. This means that the time difference from distance 20 to 5 is 31 and thus, the average speed is $15/31 = 0.484$. However, in the proximities of the base station (from distance 5 to 0) the speed drops to $5/11 = 0.454$. The reason is that the distribution of neighbors for nodes around the base station is different from distant nodes. More precisely, the nodes in close vicinity of the base station have very few nodes in the closer list but the number of nodes at the same distance or further away is high. The imbalance between the lists of neighbors grows with the transmission range of the nodes, being more significant for the $20neigh$ configuration. In this case, the speed drops from 0.358 to 0.179 in the vicinity of the sink.

4.3   Fake Traffic Overhead

The injection of fake traffic is a fundamental feature of the HISP protocol since it covers the flow of real messages. However, the amount of fake traffic must be kept as low as possible in order to extend the lifetime of the nodes. To control the propagation of fake messages, HISP defines a system parameter, MAX_TTL, which depends on the hearing range of the adversary.

Instead of transmitting fake messages at regular intervals, which would provide the best privacy protection but would deplete sensors' batteries rapidly, the devised protocol injects fake traffic triggered by the presence of real messages. The scope of fake messages is conditioned by the eavesdropping capabilities of the adversary. Thus, if the adversary under consideration belongs to the $\mathcal{ADV}_0$ family, the value of the system parameter can be set to zero, while if the adversary is a global observer, this value is to be as large as the diameter of the network. In the latter case, the energy cost would be similar to transmitting at regular intervals with the difference that fake messages will remain in the network only in the presence of events.

In Fig. 6 we illustrate the fake traffic overhead imposed by HISP for different values of the MAX_TTL parameter in the various network configurations considered. More precisely, we show the ratio of fake over real messages that is introduced to balance the transmissions in a band around the real path. When MAX_TTL is set to zero the ratio is 1 because every real packet is transmitted in conjunction with a fake packet, which is no longer propagated. As the time-to-live grows, the ratio increase is on the order of $\mathcal{O}(2^{n+1})$ where n is the hearing range of the adversary. In any case, given the adversarial model considered in this work the overhead imposed by this approach is moderate.

The overhead imposed by fake messages might be reduced by half if we introduce a slight modification. Instead of sending two packets upon the reception of traffic, we might send a single packet with two identifiers. In this way, and assuming that the identifiers are hidden to potential observers, the two recipients receive the packet and continue with the forwarding process. The first identifier indicates the real recipient and the second indicates the fake recipient.

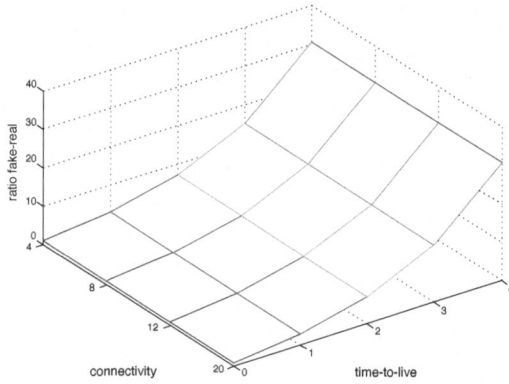

Fig. 6. Overhead of fake messages

This improvement is possible due to the broadcast nature of wireless transmissions, which allows all the neighbors from a node to overhear its messages.

Finally, as shown in Fig. 6, the ratio is not affected by different network topologies. This is not surprising since the number of transmissions performed by the protocol is independent of the connectivity of the sensor nodes.

5   Discussion

The devised receiver-location privacy mechanism is aimed to protect from local adversaries capable of performing various traffic analysis attacks. The strategy of the adversary is to repeatedly move closer to the base station by observing the transmissions along the communication path. Starting at any point of the network he eventually finds a data sender. From this location, the adversary attempts to determine the direction to the base station by observing the communications of the data sender and its neighbors.

Firstly, the adversary might perform a time-correlation attack and move in the direction of the neighbor forwarding the first message transmitted by the data sender. Given the features of our solution several cases may occur depending on whether the packet is real or fake. If the packet is real, the adversary is highly likely to reduce by one his distance to the base station. However, this is not necessarily the case because real traffic might be also forwarded in other directions. Moreover, the probability of following a real packet is lower than the probability of following a fake packet. The reason is that, as real messages move, they generate pairs of messages, one real and one fake, while fake messages trigger the transmission of pairs of fake messages. Also, note that the adversary can only be certain of whether he made the right choice when he follows a fake packet that is no longer propagated. In fact, this issue provides the adversary with no information about the direction to the base station because fake messages are forwarded in any direction.

Alternatively, the adversary might choose to perform a sufficient number of observations before making a decision on the next move. In that case, the adversary will move towards the neighbor with the higher transmission rate. To reduce the success of this strategy, the HISP protocol makes nodes to evenly distribute messages among their neighbors, thus locally homogenizing the number of packets being observed by a potential adversary. Again, the adversary cannot determine which packets are real and which are fake unless he observes a node that after receiving a packet does not forward it. This implies that he is at the edge of the band of fake messages surrounding the path of real data. Being able to precisely determine the limits of the band of fake messages could provide the adversary with information on how to reach the base station. However, the number and behavior of events being reported by the sensor nodes may be extremely dynamic, which hinders the process of bounding the aforementioned band. Moreover, real packets are sent following a random walk which causes the band to be rather arbitrary. Consequently, even if the adversary was capable of delimiting the edges of the band at some point, this information does not necessarily lead him to the base station.

Defining a sound strategy is rather difficult even when the adversary is fully aware of the protection mechanism in place. The highly dynamic nature of events in the field results in irregular communication flows which greatly complicates the definition of the most effective strategy to reduce the distance to the target.

6 Related Work

This section compares the HISP scheme with previous solutions developed to protect both source- and receiver-location privacy in WSNs.

6.1 Source-Location Privacy

The source-location privacy problem was introduced in [13]. This work proposes the Phantom Routing protocol to counter adversaries tracing back packets to the source node. This protocol sends every message on a random or directed walk to a phantom source, which finally forwards the packet to the sink using a flooding-based or a single-path routing. In this way, every packet appears to be originated from a different source. This protocol presents several drawbacks specially in the walking phase, which tends to stay close to the original source. New solutions [14] concentrated on guiding this walking phase, while in other solutions [15] the phantom sources are placed in a ring where the messages are mixed with fake traffic.

To hide the presence of events to adversaries with a global hearing range, [16] makes all sensors to transmit messages at a fixed rate regardless of the existence of real events. This provides perfect privacy but the cost is unacceptable for battery-powered devices. Several authors concentrated on reducing the energy implications of this approach. In [17] a filtering scheme is proposed to reduce the amount of fake traffic at various network locations. Also, some statistical approaches [18,19] were devised to modify the real and fake transmission frequency without arousing suspicion on the attacker.

In general, the presented solutions are based the randomization of the routes and the injection of fake traffic, which misleads the adversary or hides the presence of real packets.

6.2   Receiver-Location Privacy

Receiver-location privacy was originally investigated in [4,6] where various load balancing techniques were designed. They proposed a multi-parent routing technique that randomly selects the next hop in the path from all available nodes closer to the sink instead of sending packets always to the same node. To further complicate traffic analysis, this technique is complemented with random walks in any direction and the injection of fake packets with a given probability distribution.

Other approaches [6,8] concentrated on the creation of hot-spots, which are areas with high volumes of fake traffic that aim to attract adversaries performing rate-monitoring attacks. The authors in [7] propose to make all nodes transmit the same number of packets so that the traffic rate is homogenized regardless of the proximity to the base station. This strategy provides the best protection but it also imposes the highest energy requirements. Besides, in [20] the base station mimics the behavior of ordinary nodes (i.e. forward some of the packets it receives) to enhance its privacy. Additionally, the authors propose to move the base station to a safer location based on its own measured privacy level.

The work closest to ours is [5] because it makes use of a path diversification and fake packet injection. In this work, the authors propose to forward packets to nodes closer to the base station with some probability $1 - p_f > 0.5$ and to nodes further with probability $p_f < 0.5$. These probabilities ensure that packets eventually reach the sink but, after a sufficient number of observations, the adversary is able to deduce the direction to the sink. To reduce this problem, fake packets are injected in the opposite direction based on a certain probability p_{fake} only after the reception of a real packet. In general, the adversary cannot distinguish real from fake traffic, however, if he observes that a node that receives a packet does not forward it, he can be certain that this is fake packet whose time-to-live has expired. Since fake packets are only sent to further nodes, the must move in the opposite direction to find the sink.

We propose a packet transmission protocol also based on random route generation and fake packet transmissions that is capable of circumventing the problems presented by the previous works.

7   Conclusions

This work presents a new receiver-location privacy scheme for WSNs called HISP. The proposed solution is based on the injection of fake traffic to hide the flow of real traffic which is sent to the base station using a random walk. The goal is to probabilistically homogenize the overall number of packets that a node distributes among its neighbors. More precisely, the devised protocol preserves three critical properties (i.e., convergence, homogeneity, and exclusion), which ensure the delivery of event data to the base station as well as the robustness of receiver-location privacy against local adversaries.

The feasibility of the HISP protocol has been validated both analytically and experimentally. In particular, we have analyzed the impact of the connectivity of the network on the convergence of the packets to the base station and the privacy protection level. Also, we have investigated on the expected convergence time of packets in order to gain insights on the potential applicability of our solution to time-critical applications. Finally, we have explored the overhead imposed in terms of fake traffic injection for adversaries with different eavesdropping capabilities.

As future work we consider investigating new ways of reducing the fake traffic overhead required to protect against adversaries with a large hearing range. Also, we will explore the robustness of our scheme against more skilled adversaries. To that end, we first need to define a set of strategies based on the knowledge of the adversary about the network and the privacy protection protocol in use. The adversary may change his strategy depending on the context of the network. Countering such powerful adversaries may also require the development of new and more sophisticated protection mechanisms not considered so far.

Acknowledgments. This work has been partially funded by the European Commission through the FP7 project NESSoS (FP7 256890) and the Spanish Ministry of Science and Innovation through the ARES (CSD2007-00004) and SPRINT (TIN2009-09237) projects. SPRINT is co-financed by FEDER (European Regional Development Fund). The first author is supported by the Spanish Ministry of Education through the F.P.U. Program. Also, special thanks to Martín Ochoa for his valuable comments in preliminary versions of this work.

References

1. Yick, J., Mukherjee, B., Ghosal, D.: Wireless sensor network survey. Computer Networks 52(12), 2292–2330 (2008)
2. Walters, J., Liang, Z., Shi, W., Chaudhary, V.: Wireless Sensor Network Security: A Survey. In: Security in Distributed, Grid, and Pervasive Computing, pp. 367–409. Auerbach Pub. (2007)
3. Pai, S., Bermudez, S., Wicker, S., Meingast, M., Roosta, T., Sastry, S., Mulligan, D.: Transactional Confidentiality in Sensor Networks. IEEE Security & Privacy 6(4), 28–35 (2008)
4. Deng, J., Han, R., Mishra, S.: Countermeasures Against Traffic Analysis Attacks in Wireless Sensor Networks. In: 1st International Conference on Security and Privacy for Emerging Areas in Communications Networks (SECURECOMM 2005), pp. 113–126 (2005)

5. Jian, Y., Chen, S., Zhang, Z., Zhang, L.: Protecting receiver-location privacy in wireless sensor networks. In: 26th IEEE International Conference on Computer Communications (INFOCOM 2007), pp. 1955–1963 (2007)
6. Deng, J., Han, R., Mishra, S.: Decorrelating wireless sensor network traffic to inhibit traffic analysis attacks. Pervasive and Mobile Computing 2(2), 159–186 (2006)
7. Ying, B., Gallardo, J.R., Makrakis, D., Mouftah, H.T.: Concealing of the Sink Location in WSNs by Artificially Homogenizing Traffic Intensity. In: 1st International Workshop on Security in Computers, Networking and Communications, pp. 1005–1010 (2011)
8. Chang, S., Qi, Y., Zhu, H., Dong, M., Ota, K.: Maelstrom: Receiver-Location Preserving in Wireless Sensor Networks. In: Cheng, Y., Eun, D.Y., Qin, Z., Song, M., Xing, K. (eds.) WASA 2011. LNCS, vol. 6843, pp. 190–201. Springer, Heidelberg (2011)
9. Zhang, J., Varadharajan, V.: Wireless sensor network key management survey and taxonomy. J. Netw. Comput. Appl. 33(2), 63–75 (2010)
10. Gómez, C., Paradells, J., Caballero, J.E.: Sensors Everywhere: Wireless Network Technologies and Solutions. Fundación Vodafone España (2010) ISBN 978-84-934740-5-8.
11. Misra, S., Xue, G.: Efficient anonymity schemes for clustered wireless sensor networks. Int. J. Sen. Netw. 1(1/2), 50–63 (2006)
12. Latif, R., Hussain, M.: Hardware-Based Random Number Generation in Wireless Sensor Networks(WSNs). In: Park, J.H., Chen, H.-H., Atiquzzaman, M., Lee, C., Kim, T.-h., Yeo, S.-S. (eds.) ISA 2009. LNCS, vol. 5576, pp. 732–740. Springer, Heidelberg (2009)
13. Ozturk, C., Zhang, Y., Trappe, W.: Source-Location Privacy in Energy-Constrained Sensor Network Routing. In: 2nd ACM Workshop on Security of Ad Hoc and Sensor Networks (SASN 2004), pp. 88–93 (2004)
14. Wang, H., Sheng, B., Li, Q.: Privacy-aware routing in sensor networks. Computer Networks 53(9), 1512–1529 (2009)
15. Li, Y., Ren, J.: Preserving Source-Location Privacy in Wireless Sensor Networks. In: 6th Annual IEEE Communications Society Conference on Sensor, Mesh and Ad Hoc Communications and Networks (SECON 2009), pp. 493–501 (2009)
16. Mehta, K., Liu, D., Wright, M.: Location Privacy in Sensor Networks Against a Global Eavesdropper. In: IEEE International Conference on Network Protocols (ICNP 2007), pp. 314–323 (2007)
17. Yang, Y., Shao, M., Zhu, S., Urgaonkar, B., Cao, G.: Towards Event Source Unobservability with Minimum Network Traffic in Sensor Networks. In: 1st ACM Conference on Wireless Network Security (WiSec 2008), pp. 77–88 (2008)
18. Shao, M., Yang, Y., Zhu, S., Cao, G.: Towards Statistically Strong Source Anonymity for Sensor Networks. In: 27th IEEE Conference on Computer Communications (INFOCOM 2008), pp. 466–474 (2008)
19. Alomair, B., Clark, A., Cuellar, J., Poovendran, R.: Statistical Framework for Source Anonymity in Sensor Networks. In: IEEE Global Telecommunications Conference (GLOBECOM 2010), pp. 1–6 (2010)
20. Acharya, U., Younis, M.: Increasing base-station anonymity in wireless sensor networks. Ad Hoc Networks 8(8), 791–809 (2010)

Privacy-Aware Message Exchanges for Geographically Routed Human Movement Networks

Adam J. Aviv[1], Micah Sherr[2], Matt Blaze[1], and Jonathan M. Smith[1]

[1] University of Pennsylvania
[2] Georgetown University

Abstract. This paper introduces a privacy-aware geographic routing protocol for *Human Movement Networks* (HumaNets). HumaNets are fully decentralized opportunistic and delay-tolerate networks composed of smartphone devices. Such networks allow participants to exchange messages *phone-to-phone* and have applications where traditional infrastructure is unavailable (*e.g.*, during a disaster) and in totalitarian states where cellular network monitoring and censorship are employed. Our protocol leverages self-determined *location profiles* of smartphone operators' movements as a predictor of future locations, enabling efficient geographic routing over metropolitan-wide areas. Since these profiles contain sensitive information about participants' *prior movements*, our routing protocol is designed to minimize the exposure of sensitive information during a message exchange. We demonstrate via simulation over both synthetic and real-world trace data that our protocol is highly scalable, leaks little information, and balances privacy and efficiency: messages are 30% more likely to be delivered than similar random walk protocols, and the median latency is only 23-28% greater than epidemic protocols while requiring an order of magnitude fewer messages.

1 Introduction

The ubiquity of smartphones enable new communication models beyond those provided by cellular carriers. While standard cellular communication uses a centralized infrastructure that is maintained by the service provider, smartphones have communication interfaces such as ad-hoc WiFi and Bluetooth that allow direct communication between devices. Since smartphone owners often carry their devices, leave them constantly on, and encounter other individuals (and their smartphones) in their daily routines, *smartphones enable fully decentralized store-and-forward networks that completely avoid the cellular infrastructure.*

Human Movement Networks (HumaNets) [1] fit this model and are designed to allow participants to exchange messages phone-to-phone without using any centralized infrastructure. HumaNets' "out-of-band" message passing is applicable when cellular networks are unavailable or if the networks are untrusted (*i.e.*, operated by a totalitarian state that censors, shuts down, or otherwise leverages its communication systems to restrict its citizenry).

S. Foresti, M. Yung, and F. Martinelli (Eds.): ESORICS 2012, LNCS 7459, pp. 181–198, 2012.

Rather than rely on network addresses, HumaNets route messages using *geocast* – an addressing scheme that directs messages towards a particular geographic region. Such a messaging system could be used, for example, to notify a group of people in a targeted area of an upcoming event, or to warn them of some impending crisis. To cope with mobility, HumaNet routing protocols route messages based on message carriers' predicted *future* locations. This is accomplished by leveraging self-determined *location profiles* that approximate the smartphone owners' routine movements. The patterns of human mobility – for example, the daily commute to and from work – serve as predictors of future locations. HumaNets take advantage of this observation by greedily forwarding messages to smartphones whose owners' location profiles indicate that they are good candidates for delivery.

Privacy issues must be central when designing a HumaNet routing protocol since location profiles contain sensitive information about participants' *prior movements*. The disclosure of such information is particularly dangerous when HumaNets are used for covert communication in totalitarian regimes. Existing decentralized routing approaches that do not consider privacy [2,3], rely on trusted third parties [4], or assume *a priori* trust relationships [5] are also unsuitable for HumaNets.

This paper proposes a novel routing protocol for HumaNets that protects participants' location profiles from an adversary who wishes to learn previous movements and/or determine "important" locations of network users (*e.g.*, home, work, or the location of underground activist meetings). Our technique, which we call *Probabilistic Profile-Based Routing* (PPBR), balances performance and privacy by efficiently routing messages in a manner that minimizes the exposure of users' location profiles. We demonstrate through trace-driven simulations using both real-world and synthetic human movement data that our PPBR protocol is highly scalable, efficiently routes messages, and preserves the privacy of profile information. In summary, the contributions of this paper are: (1) The introduction and design of a fully decentralized, privacy-preserving, geographic-based HumaNet message routing protocol for smartphones; (2) An analysis of the privacy and security properties offered by our routing protocol; and, (3) A trace-driven simulation study (using both real-world and synthetic data) that evaluates our method's scalability and efficiency.

2 Network Assumptions and Goals

To achieve reasonable performance, HumaNets leverage humans' tendency to follow *routines*: The locations that people frequented in the past are predictors of their future locations [1]. However, a device's location history may be extremely sensitive, and moreover, combining multiple nodes' location histories may allow an adversary to discover social networks and enumerate participants' movements. Hence, the high-level goal of our PPBR protocol and the central challenge of this paper is to enable *efficient geographic-based messaging that limits the exposure of important location information at message exchanges*.

Importantly, however, our HumaNet routing protocol does not conceal the identities of the network's participants. An adversary who intercepts a PPBR message can reasonably conclude that the sender is participating in a HumaNet. Participating in a HumaNet inherently carries risk if used as an anti-censorship technology: This is unfortunately true of any system that may be deemed "subversive". However, when other means of communication are impossible (either due to global monitoring or blocked connectivity), HumaNets provide a *means* to exchange information in a manner that is efficient, scalable, difficult to surveil, and privacy-aware.

Requirements. HumaNets routing protocols are designed for location-aware mobile devices. We assume that network participants can learn their locations (*e.g.*, via GPS[1]) without relying on the cellular service provider's network, and that devices contain sufficient storage to record their movement histories. We note that current generation smartphones meet HumaNets' modest storage and processing requirements.

We additionally assume that participants have knowledge of the routing area. Since HumaNets enable geocast routing, a message that is targeted at specific receivers requires the sender to have some knowledge about the receivers' likely future locations (*e.g.*, their home or work); this requirement is similar to that imposed by traditional networking where users need knowledge of a service's hostname or IP address. We also assume that participants know some coarse-grain information about general movement statistics over the routing area. In particular, nodes should be capable of estimating the "popularity" of city areas – *e.g.*, that the upper west side of Manhattan is more densely traveled than Far Rockaway, Queens. This information can be obtained from census data, other public source of information, or personal experience. Such information can be shipped with the HumaNets software and is assumed to be known to an adversary.

Threat Model. We envision both passive and active adversaries. A passive adversary may have any number of confederates and is able to observe message exchanges at a fixed number of locations throughout the HumaNet routing area. An active adversary may additionally participate in HumaNets by generating fake messages, accepting messages, and/or dropping or misrouting messages.

We do not provide protection against a *mobile targeting adversary*. An adversary that can physically follow a node can trivially learn about its whereabouts and discover its routine movements. Such a "stalker" adversary is also very costly to deploy. In this paper, we focus on less targeted attackers and assume an adversary who monitors, intercepts, or participates in local exchanges that occur in its presence. The adversary is aware of the participants and their locations at the time of an exchange, and thus we do not claim that our system provides traditional location-privacy [6] for ad hoc networks, although such extensions may be relevant here.

---

[1] GPS is a unidirectional protocol and requires only the reception of signals from U.S.-operated satellites.

The adversary's goals are as follows:

- DISRUPTION: Inject failures into the network such that messages can no longer be reliably delivered.
- DE-ANONYMIZATION: Determine the originating sender of intercepted messages.
- PROFILING: Infer movement patterns of a targeted individual or learn his/her "important" locations (*e.g.*, home, work, underground meeting place).

Performance and Security Goals. The goal of our routing protocol is to provide the following properties in the presence of active and passive adversaries:

- RELIABILITY: Messages should reach their intended destinations with high probability.
- EFFICIENCY: Messages should reach their intended destinations with reasonable latency and overhead.
- SCALABILITY: HumaNets should be able to scale to a large number of participants with many concurrent messages.
- POINT-TO-POINT: Messages should be exchanged only point-to-point and avoid any centralized routing structures.
- PRIVACY-PRESERVATION: The protocol should not leak the sender's identity, nor should it reveal information about participants' previous locations. We do not distinguish between locations that should or should not remain private (e.g., secret meeting place vs. place of work). The treatment of *all* prior locations as private simplifies our protocol design, and more importantly, improves usability by preventing configuration errors that may lead to accidental exposure of private locations.

At first blush, it may seem that naïve flooding and random walk strategies are sufficient to achieve the above goals. Although these strategies achieve the POINT-TO-POINT and PRIVACY-PRESERVATION properties, they are lacking with respect to SCALABILITY, EFFICIENCY, and/or RELIABILITY. In particular, flooding achieves optimal latency and delivery rates because all paths are explored, but scales poorly since all transfers that do not occur along the optimal path constitute a wasted effort (and, consequently, wasteful power consumption). Moreover, since several senders may use HumaNets to disseminate their messages, flooding requires that nodes store (and worse, communicate) a large fraction of all messages. At the other extreme, random walk protocols in which messages are transferred (as opposed to copied) upon node contacts scales well but incurs poor RELIABILITY and EFFICIENCY.

It may also seem that traditional cryptographic solutions would be applicable here. However, the decentralized and highly dynamic nature of HumaNets make their deployment difficult. In particular, many cryptographic solutions require centralized services or trusted third parties. Such approaches are problematic in our setting since a strong (*e.g.*, nation-state) adversary could either compromise or prevent access to centralized services. Routing techniques that rely on complex key distribution schemes or expensive cryptographic operations (for example,

SMC [7]) are incompatible with HumaNets' distributed architecture and use of power-constrained devices. A significant advantage of PPBR is that it provides PRIVACY-PRESERVATION using simple probabilistic techniques, and avoids the key management and computation issues present in protocols that provide more traditional cryptographic protections [4,5,8].

Finally, we note that a non-goal of our system is authentication of message senders and message content. PPBR is a content-agnostic service that routes packets, whether they be sent by dissidents trying to organize a rally or a totalitarian state that wishes to provide misinformation. However, as with standard networking protocols, PPBR may be combined with other techniques – for example, the use of pseudoidentities and digital signatures – to provide stronger authenticity guarantees.

3   Privacy-Preserving Routing

At a high level, the *Probabilistic Profile-Based Routing* (PPBR) protocol requires participants (nodes) to *estimate* whether they are good candidates for delivering a message. Upon receiving a message from a *carrier* — *i.e.*, a node that announces a message — the receiving node makes a local determination as to whether it is well positioned to deliver the message to the addressed destination. The node either *accepts* or *discards* the message, and in either case, *does not notify the current carrier as to its choice*. If the message is accepted, the receiving node becomes a carrier and begins to announce the message. However, unlike flooding techniques in which messages are continuously duplicated, leading to an exponential number of message copies, each message carrier in PPBR announces the message to only k contacts, of which only one out of the k receiving nodes should accept it. The main task is thus for a receiver to locally determine whether it is best suited to deliver the message out of the $k - 1$ other nodes that received the message.

3.1   HumaNet Preliminaries

Addressing. HumaNets provide a basic addressing primitive, *geocast*, in which messages are addressed to a geographic location (*e.g.*, a city square). Messages are routed to nodes who are likely to travel towards the destination address and are then locally flooded within the confines of the specified destination. We do not consider temporal features in addressing or routing – *i.e.*, addressing a message to a location for a specific time – but the protocol described herein can be easily expanded to meet temporal specifications[2]. Additionally, HumaNets do not provide message confidentiality; however, message payloads can be protected using standard encryption techniques.

---

[2] One method for delivering messages at a targeted time of day is for nodes to maintain multiple location profiles, each representing movement information collected at different times of day. The message exchange algorithm is as described later; however, each node now uses the location profile most relevant to the addressed time and location.

HumaNets interpret the routing area as a grid, the dimensions of which are assumed to be known *a priori* to all nodes (for example, based on latitude and longitude). Messages are addressed to a particular grid square. In the remainder of the paper, when describing a message address or destination, we refer to the index of the corresponding grid square.

Finally, HumaNets are fully decentralized, delay tolerate networks, and as such, deliver messages according to a "best-effort" policy. Importantly, PPBR does not utilize message delivery acknowledgments; the omission of ACKs and NACKs *increases* privacy since it prevents an observer from trivially discovering whether or not a message was accepted by the receiver.

Message Exchanges. Messages are exchanged between smartphone devices when they come into wireless contact with one another. We consider a contact to occur when two nodes are within wireless transmission range, *e.g.*, the range of Bluetooth or a point-to-point 802.11 transmission in ad hoc mode. At set time intervals, nodes awaken and begin the routing protocol. If a contact is made, messages can be exchanged. Otherwise, if there are no other participants nearby, the node returns to normal activity.

HumaNets require coarse time synchronization (*i.e.*, within a few seconds) to ensure message exchanges occur at the appropriate times. Such synchronicity could be achieved using NTP servers, but this would require nodes to send messages over centralized networks. Fortunately, smartphone devices are already highly synchronized as a requirement of participating in the centralized cellular network [9,10] (a network which HumaNets do not use to send messages). If cellular services are disabled or are untrusted to provide correct time information, nodes could alternatively obtain the timing information from GPS satellite timestamps.

3.2   Routing Overview and Constructions

PPBR consists of two phases: a *passing phase* and a *holding phase* (see Figure 1). In the passing phase, a carrier of a message attempts to pass the message to the first k nodes that it encounters. A node that receives a message will locally estimate whether it has the highest similarity to the message address (a grid square) out of the $k - 1$ other nodes who also received (or will receive) the message. If the node perceives itself to be the best candidate for delivery, it accepts the message, becomes a carrier, and prepares to transition to the passing phase. Otherwise, the message is dropped. A node transitions from the passing phase to the holding phase once it has announced the message to k other neighbors.

The challenge of PPBR is enabling each node to accurately predict whether it is the best of k candidates to accept a message *without conferring with other nodes*. The intuition behind our approach is that a node can compute a *similarity score* to a message's destination using its *location profile* – a compact representation of its movement history. To populate its location profile, a node periodically records its GPS location and determines the fraction of time spent within each grid square. Using its location profile along with background knowledge of the movement patterns of an "average" node, the node can estimate how well it is positioned to deliver the message relative to the $k - 1$ other participants who will receive the message.

An important characteristic of PPBR's passing phase is that message reception is not acknowledged. An eavesdropper therefore cannot determine whether a message was accepted or declined by a nearby node. This makes it difficult for an adversary to conduct PROFILING attacks against a receiver, since it has no information to form a judgment as to whether the receiver's profile is well-suited for delivering the message. (We explore the effectiveness of PROFILING attacks against a carrier who announces a message in Section 5.) To further aggravate PROFILING attacks, if a node accepts a message and becomes a carrier, it does not announce the message until it has moved a distance d away from its current location, preventing the eavesdropper from observing the transition.

After a carrier has performed k message announcements, it transitions to the holding phase. In the holding phase, the carrier maintains the message for some time period, during which the node, hopefully, enters the message's addressed grid square and starts the local flood (restricted to the destination grid square). If the node does not reach the addressed grid square within a *local timeout*, the carrier drops the message. A message also has an associated *global timeout* after which all carriers drop the message.

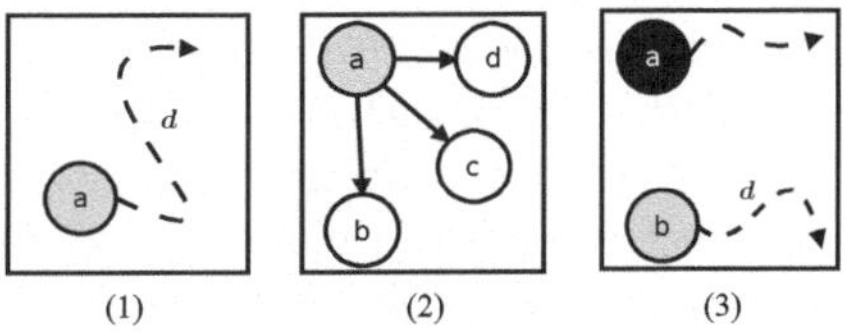

Fig. 1. Overview of PPBR routing. (1) The initial message carrier (node a) enters the passing phase (grey shading). (2) The carrier encounters three nodes. (3) Node b considers itself the best of k candidates and accepts the message, becoming a carrier and initiating its passing phase. After advertising k messages, node a enters the holding phase (black shading).

Location Profiles. Nodes compute *location profiles* based on their movement histories.[3] Although long term collection could be useful in constructing a profile, HumaNets rely on shorter historical windows to minimize the effects from non-repeated movements, *e.g.*, vacations.

Each node periodically polls its location (*e.g.*, via GPS) to update its location profile. The profile is a matrix indexed by geographic grid square such that the value at position $\langle x, y \rangle$ is the normalized number of location readings in which the node was located at position $\langle x, y \rangle$ in the grid. That is, the value at position $\langle x, y \rangle$ in the location profile corresponds to the frequency that the node visited location $\langle x, y \rangle$ in the physical world over some time window. Following our heuristic, we assume that the matrix value at $\langle x, y \rangle$ (which is defined based on past behavior) approximates the node's future likelihood of visiting location $\langle x, y \rangle$ in the physical topology.

More formally, consider a current window of location entries $W = (\langle x_i, y_i \rangle, \langle x_j, y_j \rangle \ldots)$ that are already mapped to grid square references.

---

[3] News reports suggest that popular smartphones may already collect such information [11].

The profile p, indexed by grid squares, contains the values:

$$p[\langle x, y \rangle] = \begin{cases} \frac{|W_{\langle x,y \rangle}|}{|W|} & \text{if } \langle x, y \rangle \in W \\ 0 & \text{otherwise} \end{cases} \quad , \qquad (1)$$

where $W_{\langle x,y \rangle}$ is the sub-list containing location entries occurring within the grid square $\langle x, y \rangle$, $p[\cdot]$ is the index function returning the associated value, and $|\cdot|$ indicates the length of the list.

General Node Profile. An advantage of PPBR is that it does not require nodes to share their location profiles. However, the technique assumes some globally shared information which we call the *general node profile*. The general node profile is a model of the "average" node's movement, and has the same structure and features as the standard location profile. Rather than representing the frequented locations of a single node, the general profile expresses the patterns of the general population. We assume that the general node profile is included with HumaNet software.

As we demonstrate in Section 4, the general node profile does not have to be a perfect model and can be based on a rough estimate of population densities. In practice, we posit that a sufficient general node profile could be constructed using public data such as population densities from census data, transportation studies, or common knowledge.

Marginal Similarity. A node determines if it is the best of $k-1$ other message recipients by comparing its similarity with the message's destination to the "average" node's similarity calculated using the general node profile. If the node's similarity is a factor greater, the message is accepted.

More precisely, a node must first be able to calculate the similarity of a location profile to a message address (grid square). We consider not only the value in the profile at the addressed grid-point, but also the values at nearby grid-points, discounted by their square distance. Formally, we define the similarity of a node n to a message m addressed to a_m to be:

$$\mathsf{sim}(p, a_m) = p[a_m] + \sum_{\substack{a_p \in p \\ a_p \neq a_m}} \frac{p[a_p]}{\mathsf{dist}(a_p, a_m)^2} \quad , \qquad (2)$$

where p is a location profile and $\mathsf{dist}(a_p, a_m)$ denotes the Euclidean distance between grid-points a_p and a_m. This computation captures the desired property that a node that more frequently visits the message's targeted destination (and nearby areas) will have higher similarity than a node that visits the destination region less often[4].

A similarity score computed with the general node profile, rather than an individual node's profile, represents an estimate of the "average" node's similarity to the message address. We define the relationship between a node n's

---

[4] We have additionally experimented with other decay functions, and found that they produce similar (but slightly degraded) performance.

similarity and that of the general node's similarity as the *marginal similarity* σ. It is calculated as $\sigma = \frac{\text{sim}(p_n, a_m)}{\text{sim}(p_g, a_m)}$, where p_n is the profile of node n and p_g is the general node profile. The marginal similarity speaks to how well a node is suited to become a carrier of a message addressed to a_m as compared to a node on average: higher values indicate the node would make a good message carrier, while lower values indicate a poor carrier. The next challenge is selecting a threshold value for σ at which point only one of the k nodes that received the message will accept it and become a carrier.

Threshold Selection. We define τ as the *threshold marginal similarity score* at which a node accepts a message and becomes a carrier. Intuitively, τ should be the marginal similarity such that $1/k$ marginal similarity calculations are greater than τ. The threshold is calculated locally (and privately) by each node. First, a node computes σ for every grid square in p_g:

$$\bar{\sigma} = \left\langle \left. \frac{\text{sim}(p_n, a)}{\text{sim}(p_g, a)} \; \right| \; \forall \, a \in p_g \right\rangle \tag{3}$$

The computations are arranged in a sorted list $\bar{\sigma}$, where $\bar{\sigma}_i < \bar{\sigma}_j$ if $i < j$. $\bar{\sigma}$ represents marginal similarity calculations for all likely message addresses, and we wish the node to accept a message for $1/k$ of those addresses. To do this, a node chooses τ such that $1/k$ values in $\bar{\sigma}$ are greater than τ; more precisely, $\tau = \bar{\sigma}_i$ and $i = \lfloor |\bar{\sigma}| * (k - 1)/k \rfloor$, where $| \cdot |$ denotes the length function. τ must be updated whenever the node's location profile changes. To conserve battery, such a computation could occur nightly while the device is charging.

It should be noted that the threshold computation assumes a uniform distribution of message addresses. Although this assumption does not likely hold in practice, our experimental results indicate that our approach is sufficiently accurate to cause approximately $1/k$ messages to be accepted by potential carriers. In particular, using our tested datasets (see Section 4) in which messages are addressed non-uniformly, between 8.5%-9.5% of messages are accepted.

4   Performance Evaluation

To evaluate the performance of PPBR, we constructed a discrete event-driven HumaNets simulator. Our simulator takes as input a trace of human (cellphone) movement and overlays the PPBR routing algorithm. In all simulations, we choose k to be 10 and conduct 300 independent runs. Message senders are selected randomly across participants, and message addresses (grid squares) are randomly chosen by selecting a (different) node and addressing the message to its most frequented grid square as defined by its location profile. Our simulation was concerned with measuring the effectiveness of PPBR over metropolitan areas, and as such, we did not simulate local flooding. We considered a message successfully delivered if it reaches the destination address. The grid overlay consists of 200 m × 200 m grid squares, roughly the size of a city block, and we chose d — the requisite travel distance of a node before transitioning to the passing phase — to be the size of a grid square (200 m).

Table 1. Characteristics of the movement data sets

	Nodes	Length	Area	Contact Rate	Waypoints
SLAW [12]	1000	7 days	100 km²	12.62 per hour	150
Cabspotting [13]	536	20 days	326 km²	1.17 per hour	n/a

Datasets. Due to privacy constraints, the number of realistic datasets that are suited for evaluation is unfortunately small. We require that the data contain not only a large number of nodes, but also that the movement of the nodes should express regular routines over an extended collection time (*i.e.*, many days). To demonstrate the feasibility of PPBR, we utilize a suitable real-world data trace as well as a synthetic trace of human movement (summarized in Table 1):

- **Cabspotting:** The **Cabspotting Dataset** [13] contains GPS coordinates and timestamps of 536 taxicabs in the San Francisco area. The dataset spans 20 days: from May 20, 2008 until June 7, 2008. It should be noted that although the movements of taxis are not representative of the general population (taxis are arguably more mobile than the average person), simulations using this dataset can be interpreted as representing a network composed of the taxi drivers' smartphones.
- **SLAW:** We require a synthetic model that (i) accurately represents human *flight patterns*, (ii) contact rates, (iii) *waypoints* (popular places), and (iv) routines. The closest model to meeting our needs is **Self-similar Least Action Walk** (SLAW) [12]. Based in part on Levy walks [14], SLAW introduces a protocol called *Least Action Trip Planning* (LATP) that produces human-like trips between fractal waypoints, that are themselves determined by finding hotspots in actual GPS traces.

Node Contacts. For two nodes to make contact, they must be in the same location at the same time. However, the periodicity of location entries in the Cabspotting dataset is not consistent across nodes (or for the same node). We consider two nodes to have made contact if they are within 10 meters in a 10 second window. In SLAW, a location entry is generated every 60 seconds consistently across all nodes; we consider a contact to occur if two nodes are within 10 meters at the same minute mark.

Timeouts. We use a 12 hour local timeout with both traces. For the shorter, more dense SLAW movement trace, a three day global timeout is used. The longer, more sparse Cabspotting trace uses a seven day global timeout. Finally, simulations begin after an initial delay so that node profiles can be well seeded; delays of three and seven days are used for SLAW and Cabspotting, respectively.

Location Profiles. Each node constructs its location profile using a three day window of location histories. Location profiles are updated daily, and the current day's profile represents the location history of the three previous days.

Table 2. Median and Average Latencies (first and third quartiles in braces) and Delivery Rate

	Cabspotting [13]		**SLAW** [12]	
	Med/Avg Latency (hrs)	Rate	Med/Avg Latency (hrs)	Rate
PPBR	3.6/6.8 [1.2,4.6]	62.6%	4.2/4.8 [2.6,6.2]	61.8%
Walk-10%	4.4/6.0 [1.6,8.1]	43.4%	5.1/5.5 [2.9,5.2]	48.0%
Flood-10%	2.8/4.1 [1.6,4.4]	99.4%	3.4/3.3 [2.2,4.2]	100.0%

To generate the general node profile, we select a 10% sample of nodes from each dataset and use three days worth of movement data. The 10% sample is excluded from all simulation experiments. A visualization of the resulting general node profile are shown in Figures 4 and 5 in the Appendix.

4.1   Simulation Results

To measure the efficiency of PPBR, we compare our strategy against two probabilistic protocols that do not use location information: *probabilistic random walk* and *probabilistic flooding*. The probabilistic random walk routing scheme also has passing and holding phases; however, unlike PPBR, the random walk does not use location profiles. Instead, a node accepts a carrier's advertised message with a fixed probability of $1/k$ (*i.e.*, 10%). We also compare PPBR to a 10% probabilistic flood in which nodes duplicate the message to a contacted node with probability 0.1. The flood provides insight into a worst case for network load – *i.e.*, exponential growth in the number of duplicate messages. The global and local timeouts for both random protocols are identical to those used by PPBR.

Threshold Estimation. As described in Section 3.2, each node computes its threshold marginal similarity score (τ) based on the general node profile and its knowledge of the routing area. To determine if our local, per-node threshold calculations were generating good thresholds, we looked at the variance of thresholds calculated at each node for one day in the simulation. The average value for τ was 1.557 and 1.353 for SLAW and Cabspotting, respectively. We found that there is very low variance among the nodes' thresholds: 0.011 for SLAW and 0.085 for Cabspotting. Further, we observed that thresholds were effectively limiting message acceptance to $1/k$; with $k = 10$ the probability of message retention was 9.5% and 8.5% for SLAW and Cabspotting, respectively.

Performance Metrics. We evaluate our routing performance using the following metrics: *delivery rate* is the percentage of messages that reach the destination address (a grid square); *latency* is the amount of time it takes for a message to be delivered; and *network load* is the number of messages in the network at a given time. Ideally, the routing protocol should deliver messages with a high delivery rate, low latency, and low network load.

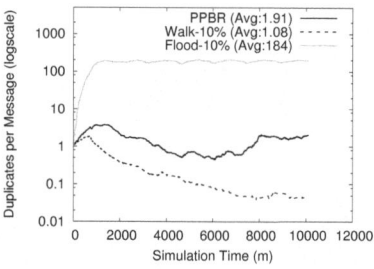 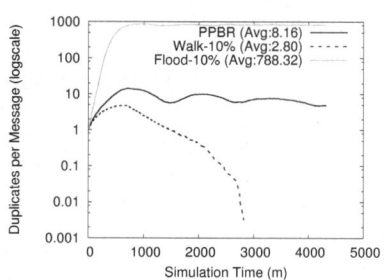

Fig. 2. The number of message copies ("duplicates") of each message for (**left**) Cab-spotting and (**right**) SLAW, and inset, the average

Delivery Rate and Latency. Table 2 lists the delivery rates and latencies for PPBR, random walk, and probabilistic flooding[5]. Unsurprisingly, flooding offers both the best latency and delivery rates. (As we show later, it also incurs a very high network load, making it impractical for networks of battery-constrained smartphone devices.) PPBR routing outperforms random walk for both median latency and delivery rate. Although the average latency for PPBR using the Cabspotting dataset is 0.8 hours slower, the median latency is nearly an hour faster and within 28% of probabilistic flooding. The skew in the average latency is caused in part by the higher delivery rate, and that some messages were delivered after random walk was no longer delivering messages.

Network Load. The load on the network is measured as the average number of message duplicates in the system across all simulations runs. PPBR does not guarantee that only a single copy of a given message is present in the system. Carriers announce a message to k other nodes; ideally, only one node *should* accept it. If the message is accepted, the carrier retains the message until either it is delivered or a local timeout occurs. Hence, each message could potentially have multiple (or zero) duplicates.

Figure 2 plots the number of messages that persist in the system over time, normalized to the number of senders in the system (which, in our simulation experiments is always 300). The average number of message copies, computed over the entire simulation, is shown in the Figure's key. Note that the number of message duplicates may be less than one if either some messages are not accepted by any of the k encountered nodes, or if all message copies are delivered to their destinations. As expected, flooding incurs significant network load, resulting in approximately two orders of magnitude more message copies than PPBR. Although the number of duplicates is slightly larger for PPBR than our naïve random walk protocol, the load is easily manageable.

---

[5] The delivery rates reported in Table 2 result from single attempted transmissions.

5 Security Properties

Profiling. All message exchanges in PPBR occur in the open, and an adversary can observe any exchange in its presence. However, PPBR offers strong privacy protections against PROFILING attacks for both the node announcing a message as well as the node who receives, and possibly accepts, the message announcement.

Message Exchange Carrier Protections: An adversary can determine that a carrier node who advertises a message has a high marginal similarity to the message's address; otherwise, the node would not be advertising the message. The adversary knows that the marginal similarity for the carrier is lower bounded by the threshold τ, and that nodes choose τ such that they should expect to accept messages addressed to $1/k$ of the grid squares. Hence, *the acceptance of a message does not necessarily indicate that the message's address is particularly important to the node that accepted it.* Depending upon the value of k, a node may be expected to accept messages targeted at hundreds of grid squares across the routing area.

Larger values of k decrease privacy since nodes accept messages for fewer locations, and, thus, an adversary could deduce that these locations are more likely relevant to the victim node. Conversely, smaller values of k increase privacy since nodes accept messages to more locations, further obscuring which are important. Smaller values of k also incur higher power consumption and network load as more nodes will likely accept (and transfer) the message. In our simulation studies, we found that $k = 10$ achieves reasonable privacy while restraining the number of message transfers.

To study this tradeoff further, we compared the set of addresses (grid squares) that would result in a node a accepting a message to the node's most frequented locations as defined in the location profile. Although nodes accepted messages addressed to $1/k$, many of those locations correspond to grid square that are uninteresting to an adversary who wishes to learn the most frequented grid squares. This relationship is depicted in Figure 3 (left). The curves represent the averages across all nodes in the Cabspotting and SLAW datasets. The x-axis denotes the number of points an adversary is interested in (*i.e.*, the x grid squares most frequented by the node). The y-axis plots the fraction of the locations that are accepted by the node which are of interest to the adversary. Generally, the more specific the adversary's interest, the more difficult it is for him to distinguish the pertinent message addresses that are announced by a node, and consequently, the more difficult it is to discover the node's most frequented locations.

The adversary's ability to discern profile information is further diminished due to our algorithm's willingness to discard announcements that are targeted at highly frequented areas. Recall that the marginal similarity is the ratio of the node's similarity score to the general node profile's similarity score. Hence, if a message is addressed to a grid square that is often frequented by the node *but also highly frequented according to the general node profile*, then the ratio will

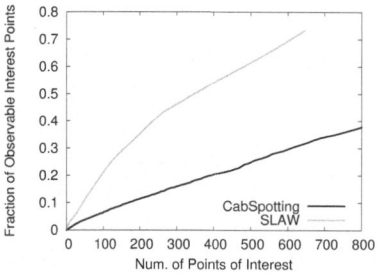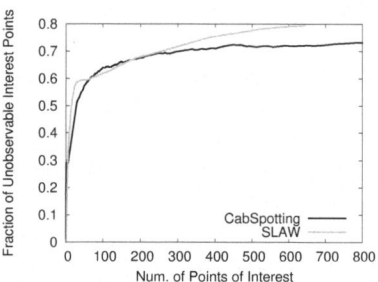

Fig. 3. Fraction of Safe Interest Points (**left**) and Fraction of Interesting Observations (**right**)

not exceed the τ threshold, and the node will *never* accept a message addressed there. Consequently, such interesting locations are unobservable and *safe* from adversarial analysis. Figure 3 (right) visualizes this relationship. Again, the x-axis considers the number of grid squares an adversary would find interesting for a victim node. The y-axis represents the fraction of those interesting grid squares a node would *never* accept a message for, averaged across all nodes.

Message Exchange Receiver Protections: During the passing phase, receivers do not acknowledge acceptance (or rejection) of a message, and hence an adversary cannot directly determine its similarity to the message's destination address. An adversary who is able to follow the node for a distance of at least d can determine whether the message has been accepted by observing whether or not it is re-advertised by the node. Such a stalking attack inherently leaks the victim's location information regardless of the particular routing protocol being used. Regardless, if the node *is* followed, or if a separate colluding eavesdropper discovers that the node later advertised the message, then the adversary can only conclude that the node accepted the message. In such cases, the effectiveness of a PROFILING attack against the receiver is identical to the effectiveness against a carrier advertising a message (see above).

De-Anonymization. The standard addressing primitive of HumaNets is geocast, and thus all participants at the addressed location at the time of delivery should receive the message. Receiver anonymity is trivially exposed in HumaNets because an adversary located in the address location learns the identities of the message recipients simply by observing them. However, PPBR provides in-transit anonymity for message originators (or senders). An intercepted message, past the initial hop, cannot be traced to the original sender without completely retracing the message's path. If an adversary is witness to the initial hop of a message, the originating sender may be exposed. We note, however, that this is similar to the level of protection provided by many Internet-based anonymity systems (*e.g.*, Crowds [15]) in which an adversary on the first hop may infer with some probability that it has identified the sender (since the sender may have originated upstream). It is also worth noting that message replay attacks in which an attacker re-injects a message in hopes of discovering its path are also infeasible. It is highly unlikely a message will take the same path due to variability in human movement.

Disruption. PPBR also provides protection against DISRUPTION attacks in which an adversary attempts to intercept messages in the network. If the attacker is able to infiltrate the network and receive a large portion of the k handoffs for each message, then the probability that the message will be transferred to an honest node is reduced. However, such an attack may also be prohibitively expensive for an adversary since message exchanges occur whenever two participants have a chance encounter. Additionally, such an attack may be mitigated by adjusting the number of passing attempts (*i.e.*, k) to compensate.

6 Related Work

The ability to leverage geographic information to efficiently route packets has been well explored in the literature [2,16]. In many instances, these techniques require participants to announce their locations. For example, Last Encounter Routing (LER) [2] and ProPHET [16] expose location information; LER assumes that the network is sufficiently connected to allow stable and longstanding paths. Although these techniques may efficiently route messages, they are not well-suited for settings in which the disclosure of location histories and/or social relationships may be cause for government-imposed punishment.

There are a number of approaches that attempt to preserve *location privacy*. Here, the goal is often to prevent an adversary from either identifying the source of an intercepted communication or tracking a node over time. Several protocols (cf. [17,18]) achieve location privacy by relying on ephemeral pseudoidentities. Such approaches provide *unlinkability* by impeding an adversary's ability to associate different broadcasts with the same node. Although these techniques can be used in conjunction with our PPBR protocol, we assume an adversary who is physically present at various (but not all) locations in the network and can identify individuals and associate broadcasts with their senders (*e.g.*, through physical identification). Similarly, anti-localization techniques [19] that are designed to prevent an adversary from determining a sender's location [20] are ineffective since our adversary can physically observe nodes.

A number of location privacy protocols (cf. [4,21]) are loosely based off of AODV [22], a popular routing protocol for decentralized mobile networks (*e.g.*, MANETs). However, such techniques assume a highly connected and mostly static network in which messages can be quickly forwarded between nodes. These protocols assume that nodes are mostly stationary, communication can occur with low latency, and anonymous paths can be reused for multiple exchanges, and as such, are therefore not well-suited for networks of mobile smartphones.

There are a number of existing delay tolerant network (DTN) protocols that are similar to HumaNets, but either have limited functionality or lack HumaNets' privacy protections. For instance, Zebranet [23] uses local information to efficiently exchange information between sensor nodes in order to track wildlife.

However, the network can route messages only towards fixed basestations. GeoDTN+Nav [24] is a vehicular ad-hoc network routing scheme that, like HumaNets, relies on location profiles to deliver messages in a DTN. However, GeoDTN+Nav requires that at least some nodes follow fixed paths (*e.g.*, bus routes) or provide their destinations before travel (*e.g.*, via a car navigation system). And in previous work, we applied *polygon-intersection algorithm* [1] to HumaNets; however, this protocol does not consider privacy.

The work that perhaps most closely resembles ours is Shifka *et al.*'s protocol [8]. Here, the authors use the heuristic that nodes that share more *contexts* are more likely to encounter one another. Like our approach, participants construct profiles that describe frequented locations, but Shifka *et al.* relies on searchable encryption schemes (namely, PEKS) to limit the adversary's ability to enumerate the contents of a profile. Additionally, their approach assumes a trusted third party that assigns attribute values (*e.g.*, a frequented location) to nodes.

7 Conclusion

This paper presents *probabilistic profile based routing* (PPBR), a novel privacy preserving geographic messaging protocol for HumaNets. Designed for networks of smartphone devices, our PPBR routing protocol avoids the use of the cellular network — or any other centralized infrastructure — and is well-suited for environments in which traditional communication is subject to monitoring and/or censorship. PPBR leverages self-determined location profiles to assist routing while minimizing the disclosure of location information to outside observers as well as adversaries who infiltrate the network. In particular, we demonstrate using simulations over real-world and synthetic movement data that PPBR is resistant to disruption, de-anonymization, and location-leakage attacks, while achieving reasonable delivery rates and latency.

Acknowledgments. This work is partially supported by NFS grants CNS-1064986, CNS-1149832 and CNS-0905434, and ONR grant N00014-09-1-0770. This material is based upon work supported by the Defense Advanced Research Project Agency (DARPA) and Space and Naval Warfare Systems Center Pacific under Contract No. N66001-11-C-4020. Any opinions, findings and conclusions or recommendations expressed in this material are those of the author(s) and do not necessarily reflect the views of the Defense Advanced Research Project Agency and Space and Naval Warfare Systems Center Pacific.

References

1. Aviv, A.J., Sherr, M., Blaze, M., Smith, J.M.: Evading Cellular Data Monitoring with Human Movement Networks. In: USENIX Workshop on Hot Topics in Security (HotSec) (August 2010)
2. Grossglauser, M., Vetterli, M.: Locating mobile nodes with ease: learning efficient routes from encounter histories alone. IEEE/ACM Trans. Netw. 14(3), 457–469 (2006)

3. Hui, P., Chaintreau, A., Scott, J., Gass, R., Crowcroft, J., Diot, C.: Pocket Switched Networks and Human Mobility in Conference Environments. In: ACM SIGCOMM Workshop on Delay-Tolerant Networking, WDTN (2005)
4. El Defrawy, K., Tsudik, G.: PRISM: Privacy-friendly Routing in Suspicious MANETs (and VANETs). In: International Conference on Network Protocols, ICNP (2008)
5. Boukerche, A., El-Khatib, K., Xu, L., Korba, L.: An Efficient Secure Distributed Anonymous Routing Protocol for Mobile and Wireless Ad Hoc Networks. Computer Communications 28(10), 1193–1203 (2005)
6. Gruteser, M., Grunwald, D.: Anonymous Usage of Location-Based Services Through Spatial and Temporal Cloaking. In: ACM International Conference on Mobile Systems, Applications, and Services, MobiSys (2003)
7. Yao, A.C.: Protocols for Secure Computations. In: Symposium on Foundations of Computer Science, FOCS (1982)
8. Shikfa, A., Onen, M., Molva, R.: Privacy and Confidentiality in Context-Based and Epidemic Forwarding. Computer Communications 33(13), 1493–1504 (2010)
9. 3rd Generation Partnership Project: Universal Mobile Telecommunications System (UMTS); Synchronization in (UTRAN) Stage 2. Technical Specification Group Services and System Aspects 3GPP TS25.402 v8.1.0, 3rd Generation Partnership Project (July 2009)
10. Mann, P.: Timing Synchronization for 3G Wireless. EE Times Asia (December 2004)
11. Bilton, N.: Tracking File Found in iPhones. The New York Times (April 20, 2011)
12. Lee, K., Hong, S., Kim, S.J., Rhee, I., Chong, S.: SLAW: A New Mobility Model for Human Walks. In: IEEE International Conference on Computer Communications, INFOCOM (2009)
13. Piorkowski, M., Sarafijanovoc-Djukic, N., Grossglauser, M.: A Parsimonious Model of Mobile Partitioned Networks with Clustering. In: Conference on COMmunication Systems and NETworkS, COMSNETS (2009)
14. Rhee, I., Shin, M., Hong, S., Lee, K., Chong, S.: On the Levy-Walk Nature of Human Mobility. In: IEEE International Conference on Computer Communications, INFOCOM (2008)
15. Reiter, M.K., Rubin, A.D.: Crowds: Anonymity for Web Transactions. ACM Transactions on Information and System Security 1(1), 66–92 (1998)
16. Lindgren, A., Doria, A., Schelén, O.: Probabilistic Routing in Intermittently Connected Networks. In: Dini, P., Lorenz, P., de Souza, J.N. (eds.) SAPIR 2004. LNCS, vol. 3126, pp. 239–254. Springer, Heidelberg (2004)
17. Freudiger, J., Manshaei, M.H., Hubaux, J.P., Parkes, D.C.: On Non-cooperative Location Privacy: A Game-theoretic Analysis. In: ACM Conference on Computer and Communications Security, CCS (2009)
18. Zhang, Y., Liu, W., Lou, W., Fang, Y.: MASK: Anonymous On-Demand Routing in Mobile Ad Hoc Networks. IEEE Transactions on Wireless Communications 5(9), 2376–2385 (2006)
19. Lu, X., Hui, P., Towsley, D., Pu, J., Xiong, Z.: Anti-localization Anonymous Routing for Delay Tolerant Network. Computer Networks 54(11), 1899–1910 (2010)
20. Husted, N., Myers, S.: Mobile Location Tracking in Metro Areas: Malnets and Others. In: ACM Conference on Computer and Communications Security, CCS (2010)
21. Sy, D., Chen, R., Bao, L.: ODAR: On-Demand Anonymous Routing in Ad Hoc Networks. In: IEEE International Conference on Mobile Adhoc and Sensor Systems, MASS (2006)

22. Perkins, C., Belding-Royer, E., Das, S.: Ad hoc On-Demand Distance Vector (AODV) Routing. RFC 3561, IETF (2003)
23. Juang, P., Oki, H., Wang, Y., Martonosi, M., Peh, L.S., Rubenstein, D.: Energy-efficient computing for wildlife tracking: design tradeoffs and early experiences with ZebraNet. In: Conference on Architectural Support for Programming Languages and Operating Systems (ASPLOS-X) (October 2002)
24. Cheng, P., Weng, J., Tung, L., Lee, K., Gerla, M., Haerri, J.: GeoDTN+Nav: A Hybrid Geographic and Dtn Routing with Navigation Assistance in Urban Vehicular Networks. In: Symposium on Vehicular Computing Systems (2008)

Appendix: General Node Profile Heatmaps

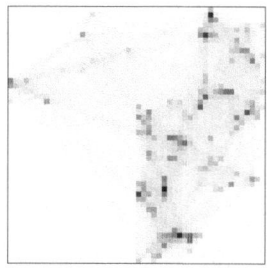

Fig. 4. Heatmap of the General Node Profiles for the SLAW dataset. Darker shades indicate regions with higher node densities.

Fig. 5. Heatmap of the General Node Profiles for the Cabspotting dataset. Darker shades indicate regions with higher node densities.

Trust No One Else: Detecting MITM Attacks against SSL/TLS without Third-Parties

Italo Dacosta, Mustaque Ahamad, and Patrick Traynor

Converging Infrastructure Security (CISEC) Laboratory
Georgia Tech Information Security Center (GTISC)
Georgia Institute of Technology
{idacosta,mustaq,traynor}@cc.gatech.edu

Abstract. The security guarantees provided by SSL/TLS depend on the correct authentication of servers through certificates signed by a trusted authority. However, as recent incidents have demonstrated, trust in these authorities is not well placed. Increasingly, certificate authorities (by coercion or compromise) have been creating forged certificates for a range of adversaries, allowing seemingly secure communications to be intercepted via man-in-the-middle (MITM) attacks. A variety of solutions have been proposed, but their complexity and deployment costs have hindered their adoption. In this paper, we propose Direct Validation of Certificates (DVCert), a novel protocol that, instead of relying on third-parties for certificate validation, allows domains to *directly and securely vouch* for their certificates using previously established user authentication credentials. By relying on a robust cryptographic construction, this relatively simple means of enhancing server identity validation is not only efficient and comparatively easy to deploy, but it also solves other limitations of third-party solutions. Our extensive experimental analysis in both desktop and mobile platforms shows that DVCert transactions require little computation time on the server (e.g., less than 1 ms) and are unlikely to degrade server performance or user experience. In short, we provide a robust and practical mechanism to enhance server authentication and protect web applications from MITM attacks against SSL/TLS.

1 Introduction

The Secure Sockets Layer (SSL) protocol and its successor, Transport Layer Security (TLS), have become the de facto means of providing strong cryptographic protection for network traffic. Their near universal integration with web browsers arguably makes them the most visible pieces of security infrastructure for average users. While vulnerabilities are occasionally found in specific implementations, SSL/TLS are widely viewed as robust means of providing confidentiality, integrity and server authentication. However, these guarantees are built on tenuous assumptions about the ability to authenticate the server-side of a transaction by using digital certificates signed by a *trusted* third-party certification authority (CA).

S. Foresti, M. Yung, and F. Martinelli (Eds.): ESORICS 2012, LNCS 7459, pp. 199–216, 2012.
© Springer-Verlag Berlin Heidelberg 2012

The security community has long been critical of the Public Key Infrastructure for X.509 (PKIX) and its CA-based trust model [13,19]. Much of the concern has focused on the role of the CAs and their ability and motivation to not only correctly verify and attest the coupling between an identity and a public key, but also to protect their own resources. Browsers and operating systems determine what CAs users should trust by default (i.e., trust anchors). However, this model has resulted in *hundreds of CAs, all equally trusted and from more than 50 different countries* [11]. Due to this excessive trust, CAs can forge certificates for any domain that will be accepted as valid by most browsers. Thus, adversaries can obtain forged certificates by coercing or compromising any CA and use them to execute man-in-the-middle (MITM) attacks against SSL/TLS connections. Last year, the number of reported attacks against CAs increased considerably [18, 22, 23, 34]. In some cases, adversaries were able to forge certificates for important web domains (e.g., google.com, yahoo.com and live.com). Even worse, it has been estimated that a forged certificate was used to intercept close to 300,000 Gmail sessions in Iran [26]. Furthermore, there is evidence that governments and private organizations are using forged certificates as part of their surveillance and censorship efforts [27, 35, 36]. The frequency of these incidents is likely to increase in the future, as more and more web applications rely on SSL/TLS to protect all their communications.

Multiple solutions have been proposed to deal with the threat imposed by forged certificates and MITM attacks. The most popular approach is the use of additional third-parties to extend or replace the rigid CA trust model (e.g., network notaries [30,38], public audit logs [12,25] and secure DNS (DNSSEC) [20]). In this approach, users can select one or more third-parties to vouch for the authenticity of a certificate, improving the chances of detecting a MITM attack. However, depending only on third-parties for certificate validation has several shortcomings such as: significant deployment and operational costs (e.g., additional infrastructure with high availability requirements), more complex trust model for users, privacy concerns and more complex revocation procedures. Therefore, *the inherent complexity and costs associated with third-party solutions have prevented their widespread deployment*. As a result, most users still rely on weak certificate validation checks to detect MITM attacks.

In this paper we propose Direct Validation of Certificates (DVCert), an efficient and easy to deploy protocol that provides stronger certificate validation and effective detection of MITM attacks without using third-parties. Our mechanism comes from a simple observation – users have already established secrets (e.g., passwords) with their most important web applications. *DVCert allows web applications to use these secrets to directly and securely attest for the authenticity of their certificates without exposing those secrets to offline attacks*. After a single round-trip DVCert transaction, a browser receives the information required to validate all the certificates that could be used during a session with the web application, including certificates from other domains. As a result, to execute a MITM attack, an adversary not only needs to compromise a CA but also each targeted web domain. A DVCert transaction uses a modified Password

Authenticated Key Exchange (PAKE) protocol known as PAK [8, 28]. However, we are not simply applying a known protocol; rather, we modified PAK to provide *only* server authentication and integrity protection instead of mutual authentication and generation of encryption keys (i.e., traditional use of PAKE protocols). These changes allow better performance and simplify deployment without affecting PAK's formal security proofs. Our experimental evaluation shows that an optimized DVCert transaction requires little computation time on the server (e.g., < 1 ms) and on the browser. More importantly, DVCert transactions are executed at most once per session; thus, their impact on server performance or user experience is negligible. DVCert's design also provides multiple advantages over third-party solutions: simpler trust model, lower deployment and operational costs (e.g., no additional infrastructure is required) and no privacy risks. Finally, DVCert is a readily available mechanism designed to improve the current CA trust model and be compatible with third-party solutions such as DNSSEC, once these solutions are deployed in the future. In so doing, we make the following contributions:

– **Designing and implementing an efficient and easy to deploy mechanism to detect MITM attacks against SSL/TLS without third-parties:** We develop a protocol that provides more robust certificate validation and detects MITM attacks, even if the adversary uses forged certificates. By allowing web applications to attest directly for their certificates, our mechanism avoids many of the challenges hindering the deployment of third-party solutions. We implemented a proof-of-concept extension for Firefox and Firefox for mobile browsers and a PHP-based server component to demonstrate the deployability of our solution.

– **Conducting an extensive performance analysis in multiple platforms:** We characterize DVCert's performance using our prototype implementation in both desktop and mobile browsers. Our results show that an optimized DVCert transaction requires 0.54 ms of computation time on the server and 12.03 and 97.70 ms on a laptop and on a smartphone respectively. Compared to a naïve implementation, these results represent a 94.96%, 55.07% and 77.82% improvement on the server, laptop and smartphone correspondingly. Furthermore, we apply ProVerif [6] to formally verify DVCert's resilience to offline attacks.

– **Making our DVCert implementation available to the community:** The DVCert extension for Firefox and Firefox for mobile as well as the server PHP code are available for evaluation at: http://www.cc.gatech.edu/~idacosta/dvcert/index.html.

The remainder of this paper is organized as follows: Section 2 offers important background information on SSL/TLS and MITM attacks and presents our motivation; Section 3 provides the design and formal description of DVCert; Section 4 presents our security analysis of DVCert; Section 5 shows our experimental analysis and results; Section 6 offers additional analysis and discussion of our proposed protocol; Section 7 provides an overview of important related work; and Section 8 presents our conclusions.

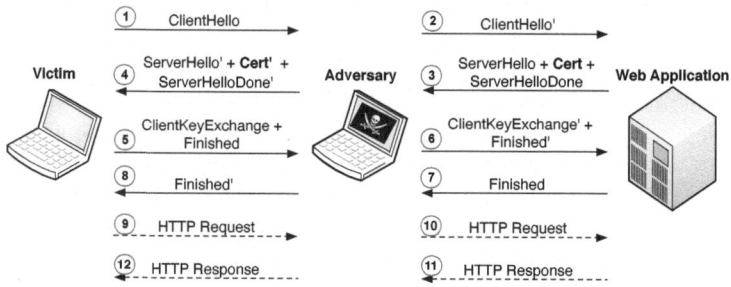

Fig. 1. Example of a MITM attack against SSL/TLS

2   Background and Motivation

2.1   The SSL/TLS Protocols and Web Applications

The SSL/TLS protocols [10, 17] are the main security mechanisms used to protect the communications between browsers and web applications. By providing a transparent encryption layer, SSL/TLS guarantee the confidentiality and integrity of the data traveling across the Internet. Moreover, SSL/TLS allow browsers to authenticate web application's servers via X.509 digital certificates [2]. A digital certificate binds the server's identity (i.e., domain name) to the server's public key and it is signed by a Certification Authority (CA) trusted by both the server and the browser. Initially, due to performance considerations, most web applications used SSL/TLS only to protect requests carrying private data (e.g., passwords, credit card numbers). However, due to the increasing number of attacks against web sessions (e.g., session hijacking), many applications have been forced to protect all their communications with SSL/TLS. For this reason, is common that during a session, a browser establishes multiple SSL/TLS connections not only with web application's servers but also with servers from third-party domains (e.g., CDNs and ads networks). Through a short survey from the Alexa Top 20 US sites and popular online banking sites (15 in total), we determined that an average of 12 certificates per domain were validated by the browser, with a minimum of 4 and a maximum of 22. Moreover, most sites included at least one certificate from a third-party domain.

2.2   MITM Attacks against SSL/TLS

The security guarantees offered by SSL/TLS rely on the correct authentication of the server. All such guarantees are rendered ineffective if an adversary is able to convince users to accept an illegitimately generated certificate, as shown in Figure 1. First, the adversary positions herself in the network path between the victim's computer and the server. When the victim sends a request for establishing a new SSL/TLS connection with the server (message 1), the adversary intercepts and responds to it (message 4) using a forged certificate (Cert'). If the victim accepts this certificate, then she completes the SSL/TLS setup with the adversary (messages 5 and 8), who has, as a result, successfully masqueraded as the server. Simultaneously, the adversary establishes a new SSL/TLS connection with the server (messages 2, 3, 6, and 7). At this point, the adversary has two active SSL/TLS connections: one with the victim and one with the server. However, from the victim's and server's perspectives, there is only one secure connection in place. The adversary can now decrypt, re-encrypt and forward all the messages exchanged between the victim and the server (messages 9 to 12). As a result, the adversary can access private information (e.g., passwords) or even modify it (e.g., code injection).

2.3   Problems with Third-Party Solutions

A considerable number of mechanisms have been proposed to improve server-side authentication and protect against MITM attacks (see Section 7). The most popular approach is the use of additional third-party entities that can also vouch for the authenticity of server certificates. Third-party solutions provide a number of benefits: protection of the first connection to a new domain, scalable attestation of certificates for all public domains and minimal requirements for web applications. Unfortunately, this approach also faces several critical challenges. First, *these mechanisms have significant deployment and operational costs.* The additional infrastructure needed can be expensive to deploy and operate due to requirements such as high-availability, data consistency, performance and security. Even web applications can be affected by the operational overheads required by these mechanisms. Second, *the resulting trust model is more complex.* The use of multiple trusted entities to choose from can make the trust model more complex to evaluate and understand. Thus, average users are likely to rely on default trust configurations. Moreover, trust is dynamic – a trusted entity today may become an adversary tomorrow. Third, *these mechanisms introduce new privacy risks.* Users' browsing activity is disclosed to third-party entities. Preventing this problem can add complexity to these solutions. Fourth, *certificate revocation procedures become more complex.* The use of multiple entities make revocation more difficult because of the additional overhead required to revoke multiple proofs of authenticity (e.g., signatures). Finally, *captive portals typically interfere with these mechanisms.* In places such as airports and hotels, captive portals can block requests for certificate validation to external entities before user registration. Thus, captive portals need to be modified to allow additional certificate validation mechanisms.

3   Direct Validation of SSL/TLS Certificates

We present Direct Validation of SSL/TLS Certificates (DVCert), an efficient and practical mechanism that improves certificate validation and provides stronger protection against MITM attacks. Instead of relying on third-parties, DVCert uses the existing shared secrets between the user and the web application to directly validate server certificates. DVCert overcomes the limitations of third-party solutions while also reducing the risks associated with using low-entropy keys in network protocols.

3.1   Scenario and Threat Model

Our scenario assumes a large, highly distributed web application. The application uses SSL/TLS to protect all the communications with its users (i.e., always-on HTTPS). To establish SSL/TLS connections, the application has multiple certificates signed by a trusted CA. In addition, the application's web pages include content from third-party servers. These servers also communicate using SSL/TLS and have their own valid certificates. We assume that SSL/TLS are correctly configured in the application's servers as well as in the third-party servers. Furthermore, users share a password with the application and use HTML forms for authentication. Instead of plaintext passwords, the application stores password salted hashes using public salt values. Finally, we assume that users follow a robust password policy that is enforced by the application.

We consider a polynomial-time (PPT) adversary that has access to all the communication between the web application and its users. The adversary's goal is to eavesdrop and tamper with this communication by executing MITM attacks against SSL/TLS. To perform such attacks, we assume that it is possible for the adversary to obtain forged certificates for any domain that are signed by some trusted CA. However, the adversary does not have access to users' passwords, password salted hashes or server's private keys. Moreover, we do not consider attacks against user computers or application servers to obtain such information and attacks that exploit SSL/TLS implementation or configuration errors.

3.2   Desired Protocol Properties

We identified properties required to achieve an effective and practical defense against MITM attacks and use them to design DVCert. (1) *Effective detection of MITM attacks*: the proposed mechanism must provide robust server authentication and effective detection of MITM attacks against SSL/TLS, even if illegitimately obtained certificates are used. (2) *Robustness against offline attacks*: the proposed mechanism should not leak information about the user's authentication credentials and must be resilient to offline attacks such as dictionary and cryptanalytic attacks. (3) *Deployability*: the proposed mechanism should not require additional hardware or software, only small changes to the browser and web application. In addition, it should be simple to configure in both the browser and the web application. (4) *Performance*: the proposed mechanism must be efficient. It must not affect the overall performance and scalability of the web application. Moreover, it should not introduce risks of DoS attacks. (5) *Privacy*: the proposed mechanism should not disclose user information to third-parties and adversaries. (6) *Compatibility*: the proposed mechanism must not interfere with existing functionality in the browser and web application. Browsers not

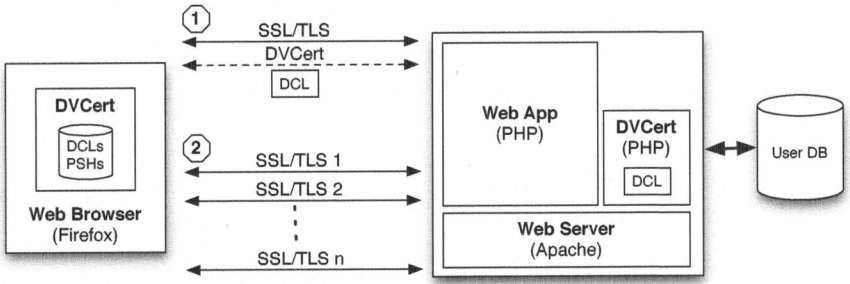

Fig. 2. High level overview of DVCert. (1) The browser uses a DVCert transaction to obtain a fresh DCL (Domain Certificate List); (2) it uses the DCL to validate certificates used in all the SSL/TLS connections with the application.

supporting the proposed mechanism should still be able to access the web application. Moreover, the proposed mechanism must be compatible with other certificate validation protocols. (7) *Usability*: the proposed mechanism should require minimal user intervention and have minimal impact on user experience. (8) *Simple trust model*: the proposed mechanism should have an easier to understand trust model in comparison to third-party solutions. Users must not be required to make additional trust assessments.

3.3 Protocol Description

MITM attacks against SSL/TLS connections are possible because server certificates are validated using only a single third-party signature and mutual authentication is weak. DVCert addresses these problems by allowing web applications to use already available shared secrets to *vouch directly* for the authenticity of certificates instead of relying only on third-parties. Figure 2 shows a high level description of the DVCert protocol. First, the browser establishes a SSL/TLS connection with the web application and then executes a DVCert transaction based on the user's password and a modified PAKE protocol (step 1). In this transaction, the browser authenticates the web application and receives its latest certificate information. The certificate information is shared using a Domain Certificate List (DCL), a data structure maintained by the web application that contains the *fingerprints*[1] *of all the certificates* that could be used during a session with the application. The DCL not only includes the fingerprints of the application's certificates but also of third-party's certificates used in the application (e.g., CDNs and ads networks). Second, the browser stores the DCL temporarily and uses it to validate the certificates of each SSL/TLS connection with the application (step 2), including the SSL/TLS channel established in step 1. If a certificate is not found in the DCL, then the corresponding SSL/TLS connection is flagged as untrusted (i.e., probable MITM attack). Once the DCL expires, a

---

[1] A certificate fingerprint is the cryptographic hash of the binary representation (e.g., DER encoding) of the certificate.

Shared information: g, p, $d = domain$, $s = H(u|d)$. Hash functions H, H_1, H_2, H_3, H_4
Information held by Browser: $u = username$, $pw = password$
Information held by Server: $P = H(pw|s)$, $DCL = domain\ certificate\ list$

Browser	Server
$a \in Z_q$	
$P = H(pw|s)$	
$m_1 = g^a \times H_1(u|d|P)(\mathrm{mod}\ p)$ (1) $\xrightarrow{\ u,\ m_1\ }$	$m_1\ \mathrm{mod}\ p \overset{?}{\neq} 0$
	$b \in Z_q$
	$g^{ab} = (\frac{m_1}{H_1(u|d|P)})^b (\mathrm{mod}\ p)$
	$m_2 = g^b \times H_2(u|d|P)(\mathrm{mod}\ p)$
	$r = (u|d|P|g^a|g^b|g^{ab})$
	$h_1 = H_3(r|H(DCL))$
$g^{ab} = (\frac{m_2}{H_2(u|d|P)})^a (\mathrm{mod}\ p)$ (2) $\xleftarrow{\ m_2,\ h_1,\ h_2,\ DCL\ }$	$h_2 = H_4(r)$
$r = (u|d|P|g^a|g^b|g^{ab})$	
$h_1 \overset{?}{=} H_3(r|H(DCL))$	
$h_2 \overset{?}{=} H_4(r)$	

Operations:
$x|y$: concatenation of strings x and y
$H^i(x)$: *i-th* standard cryptographic hash of x
$H_i(x)$: special agreed-on cryptographic hash of x [9, 21]

Fig. 3. Detailed description of a DVCert transaction. On each transaction, the server is authenticated and the browser securely receives a new DCL.

new DVCert transaction is executed (step 1) to update it. Finally, to avoid asking for the user's password on each transaction, the browser securely stores the password salted hash (PSH) together with the DCL.

DVCert achieves our goals by building on a significantly modified version of PAK [8, 9, 21, 28]. PAK (and the PAKE family of protocols) is based on the Diffie-Hellman (DH) key exchange and allows the use of low entropy secrets such as passwords to securely establish a session secret (i.e., authenticated Diffie-Hellman). PAK was selected as a starting point for our work because of its formal security proof and its ability to use shorter exponents [29] for better performance when compared to other related PAKE-based protocols. The major difference in our approach is that DVCert uses PAK *only* for server authentication instead of mutual authentication and generation of encryption keys (standard use of PAKE protocols), and include features to protect the integrity of the DCL and distinguish between tampering of the DCL and password errors. In other words, only the browser verifies the session secret established during the transaction. By not providing user authentication, DVCert requires fewer messages and, more importantly, avoids changes to the browser login user interface – a major challenge for the deployment of PAKE protocols in web applications [15]. Hence, DVCert is compatible with current user authentication mechanisms (e.g., HTML form-based authentication).

Figure 3 shows the details of a DVCert transaction (step 1 on Figure 2). First, the browser establishes a SSL/TLS connection with the server. This connection is used to protect protocol information (e.g., usernames) from eavesdroppers. Next, the browser generates a random exponent a (browser's DH secret), computes the

DH value g^a and uses it and the password salted hash P to compute m_1. If the password salted hash is not available for this domain (e.g., first DVCert transaction with this domain), then the browser prompts the user for her username u and password pw, computes the password salted hash P and stores it in a secure location for future transactions (i.e., the user is prompted only once for her password). Once m_1 has been calculated, the browser sends it and the username u to the server using a special header field in a HTTP request (message 1) over SSL/TLS. After receiving the DVCert request, the server verifies that $m_1 \neq 0$ to prevent a known attack, uses the username u to retrieve the password salted hash P from the server's database, generates the random exponent b (server's DH secret) and computes the DH value g^b. The server now obtains the browser's DH value g^a from m_1, calculates the session secret g^{ab} and computes m_2 and h_2. In addition, the server uses the latest version of the DCL to compute h_1. Next, the server sends m_2, h_1, h_2 and the DCL to the browser in the HTTP response (message 2). Then, the browser uses the received values to obtain the server's DH value g^b and to calculate the session secret g^{ab}. Next, the browser uses the session secret g^{ab} and other protocol state information to compute new h_1 and h_2 values. The browser now compares the computed h_1 with the one received from the server. If the values match, then the DVCert transaction was successful. Thus, the DCL file is trusted (i.e., has not been tampered with) and can be used to validate certificates. In addition, the successful verification of h_1 also proves the server's identity. If the h_1 values do not match, then the browser proceeds to verify h_2. If this verification succeeds, then the DCL has been modified and there is a high probability that a MITM is in progress. Therefore, neither the DCL nor any communication with the server can be trusted. The browser displays a warning to the user and halts the communications with the server. If the h_2 values are different, then the transaction could have failed due to a password error (e.g., user typed the wrong password) or a MITM attack. Thus, the browser displays a warning and prompts the user for a new password for a limited number of attempts. If the protocol still fails after several attempts, then the browser halts all communications with the server. In other words, h_2 is used to differentiate between protocol failures due to a MITM attacks or due to password errors.

After a successful DVCert transaction, the browser stores the DCL and the password salted hashes in a secure location isolated from other browser components. The browser stores one DCL per domain for a limited period of time according to a domain policy (e.g., once per session). Thus, the total number of DVCert requests per user is significantly lower than the total number of SSL/TLS connections. When a SSL/TLS connection is established with a server, the browser checks that the certificate is in the corresponding DCL (step 2 in Figure 2). If the certificate is not in the DCL, then a MITM attacks is likely to be in progress. Thus, the browser displays a warning to the user and halts the communications with the server. Once a DCL expires, the browser sends an automatic request (i.e., no user intervention) for a new DVCert transaction to update the DCL.

Finally, DVCert assumes that PAK constants, the prime number p and the generator g, are publicly known. For example, they can be hardcoded in DVCert's browser and server components. This measure is important to prevent an adversary from sending bogus p and g values and tricking the user into an improper DVCert exchange that could leak password information. Moreover, DVCert assumes that the web application stores password salted hashes ($P = H(pw|s)$) and that salt values (s) are also publicly known. If the salt is not known in advance, the browser can send an additional request to the server to obtain it.

4 Security Analysis

DVCert main's goal is to detect MITM attacks against SSL/TLS. DVCert achieves this by effectively binding the SSL/TLS layer to the application layer (i.e., channel binding [4, 39]). As a result, a MITM adversary trying to avoid detection by modifying the DCL is not only forced to compromise a CA to obtain a forged certificate but also to compromise each of the targeted domains to obtain users' authentication credentials.

An adversary can try to capture DVCert messages and use offline attacks to obtain user authentication credentials. However, the attacker needs to execute a MITM attack first to access DVCert messages. Thus, such attempts will be detected by DVCert. Furthermore, PAK's formal proofs of security for standard [8] and short exponents [29] (i.e., 384 bits) provide strong guarantees that the adversary will not learn password information from DVCert messages. DVCert modifications to PAK do not affect these proofs. For example, PAK and DVCert transmit the same number of hash values (2) over the network. The main difference is that DVCert uses one message less and uses the DCL as part of the computation of h_1.

We used ProVerif [6], an automatic cryptographic protocol verifier, to formally characterize DVCert. *Using ProVerif, we successfully demonstrated that DVCert does not leak password information (i.e., resilience to offline attacks).* Due to space limitations, ProVerif configuration details and results are available in DVCert's web site.

DVCert information stored in the browser or the server cannot be used to impersonate the user because DVCert does not provide user authentication. Therefore, DVCert offers resilience to server compromise similar to augmented PAKE protocols. The adversary can still use offline dictionary attacks against the stolen credentials, but the use of strong passwords can mitigate this risk.

The DCL includes fingerprints of certificates from third-party domains because these certificates cannot be validated directly (users do not share secrets with these domains). This is important because a MITM attack against a third-party SSL/TLS connection could be used to compromise the session with the web application (e.g., code injection attacks). The web application is responsible for maintaining the latest certificate information from third-party domains in the DCL. For example, the web application could rely on existing secure connections with third-party domains to obtain their certificate information. Alternatively, the application could rely on third-party validation mechanisms.

A concern with PAKE protocols is the risk of denial of service attacks due to the cost of public key operations. DVCert mitigates this risk by optimizing such operations without reducing security. For example, DVCert can use shorter exponents for better performance without affecting formal proofs of security. PAK allows the use of exponents with a minimum size of 384 bits (1024 bits DH group) [29] while maintaining a similar level of security. Another suggested optimization is the use of static parameters in the server (i.e., b, g^b and m_2) to reduce the number of operations (see Section 5). This technique affects the protocol's perfect forward secrecy property; however, DVCert does not require it (i.e., the session secret is not used for encryption). Finally, the web application could also monitor and limit the number of DVCert requests a user can make per day according to a domain policy.

5   Experimental Analysis

We implemented DVCert browser and server components (see Figure 2) to evaluate their performance and deployability. The DVCert browser component was implemented as an extension for Firefox 10.0.x and Firefox for mobile (Fennec) 4.03b. The extensions were written mainly in Javascript, but we also used C code for modular exponentiation operations through Firefox's js-ctypes API and the GMP library[2]. Approximately 500 lines of code were required for both extensions. The DVCert server component was implemented in PHP and required approximately 400 lines of code. More importantly, the DVCert server component is completely independent of the web application code; only access to the user database is required. PAK implementation details as well as test vectors were obtained from the RFC 5683 [9] and the ITU-T Recommendation X.1035 [21]. The experiments used a laptop (Apple MacBook Pro with dual core 2.53 GHz processor, 4GB of memory and Mac OS X 10.6) and a smartphone (Samsung Galaxy S 4G with a 1 GHz Cortex-A8 processor, 512 MB of memory and Android 2.2.1) as our clients. On the server side, we used a Ubuntu 10.10 server with 2 quad-core 2.00 GHz processors, 16 GB of memory and Gigabit Ethernet. The server was configured with Apache 2.2, PHP 5.3 and a 2048 bits RSA certificate. Finally, our prototype DVCert implementation is currently available for evaluation at http://www.cc.gatech.edu/~idacosta/dvcert/index.html.

Certificate validation operations using the DCL are inexpensive. For example, for each SSL/TLS connection, the browser executes one hash operation and one search operation. Assuming an ordered DCL, binary search is used to determine if a certificate is in the DCL with time $O(\log n)$, where the DCL's size n is in the order of tens of certificates. In addition, the size of the DCL is small (e.g., a SHA-1 certificate fingerprint requires only 160 bits). Hence, the impact on network bandwitdh due to the DCL is negligible. Therefore, our experimental

---

[2] Javascript-only DVCert add-ons for Firefox required an execution time at least one order of magnitude higher than add-ons using C native code for modular exponentiation, particularly in the smartphone. Ultimately, we envision DVCert to be implemented directly in the browser and using native code for its operations.

evaluation focused on the costs associated with DVCert transactions where more complex operations take place.

First, we measured the time required to generate a DVCert request (t_g) and the time required to verify the corresponding response (t_v) in the browser for different exponent sizes: 2048, 1024 and 384 bits. Morevoer, we used a DCL with one certificate fingerprint in all the experiments. Table 1 shows the results for 100 DVCert transactions per configuration using a laptop and a smartphone, including 95% confidence intervals. The results show that for 2048 bits exponents, an often recommended size for standard key exchange protocols [7], the browser required 26.78 ms and 440.58 ms of total computation time $(t_g + t_v)$ on the laptop and on the smartphone respectively. While these computation times should not affect the user experience due to the low frequency of DVCert transactions, we can see that using 384 bits exponents decreased these times to 12.03 ms on the laptop (55.07% improvement) and 97.70 ms on the smartphone (77.82% improvement); thus, such delays are unlikely to be noticed by users.

Second, we measured the server response time using network traces for single HTTPS requests (i.e., our baseline) and HTTPS requests with DVCert. Each request retrieved a small HTML page ($\approx$ 500 bytes. We chose this small size to measured only the overhead added by SSL/TLS and DVCert). Moreover, our measurements did not include SSL/TLS setup times. For HTTPS request with DVCert, we evaluated different exponent sizes (2048, 1024 and 384 bits) and the use of dynamic (t_r) and static (t_{rsp}) server parameters. Based on these measurements, we estimated how much time the server spent on DVCert operations $(t_d$ and $t_{dsp})$ by subtracting the baseline time from the HTTPS+DVCert server response times. The results for 100 DVCert transactions per configuration are shown in Table 2, including 95% confidence intervals. The most robust configuration, 2048 bits and dynamic parameters, required 10.71 ms of additional server computation time, while the most efficient configuration, 384 bits and static parameters, required around 0.54 ms (94.96% improvement). Thus, the most efficient DVCert configuration requires less time than serving a HTTPS request (1.17 ms) and it is smaller than the average network jitter in the US (0.67 ms [5]). Also, Table 2 shows how static parameters can reduce DVCert processing time on the server by at least 38%. Overall, these results show that DVCert operations have similar processing requirements to other server operations (e.g., SSL/TLS setup, HTTPS requests processing) while still maintaining robust security guarantees. Thus, DVCert should not degrade performance or increase the risk of DoS attacks.

Finally, we evaluated the overall impact of DVCert on server throughput in the hypothetical scenario where each SSL/TLS connection includes a DVCert transaction (i.e., upper bound). For this purpose, we measured the rate of HTTPS requests (using one SSL/TLS connection per request) and the rate of HTTPS+DVCert requests that the server can handle. As before, we evaluated DVCert with different exponent sizes (2048, 1024 and 384 bits) and one setup with static parameters and 384 bits exponents. The test load was generated with *httperf*, a HTTP traffic generator tool. Figure 4 shows the results of this

Table 1. DVCert request generation time (t_g) and response verification time (t_v), including 95% confidence intervals, on a laptop and on a smartphone for different exponent sizes.

Exp. Size	Laptop t_g (ms)	Laptop t_v (ms)	Phone t_g (ms)	Phone t_v (ms)
2048 bits	10.36 ($\pm$0.09)	16.42 ($\pm$0.29)	171.92 ($\pm$1.79)	268.66 ($\pm$9.64)
1024 bits	3.95 ($\pm$0.07)	9.55 ($\pm$0.14)	48.68 ($\pm$2.11)	71.88 ($\pm$7.87)
384 bits	3.26 ($\pm$0.09)	8.77 ($\pm$0.14)	33.58 ($\pm$0.72)	64.12 ($\pm$7.44)

Table 2. Server response time (t_r) for a HTTPS request and a HTTPS request with DVCert using dynamic and static parameters (t_{rsp}) and different exponent sizes. By subtracting the time of a single HTTPS request, we estimated the cost of DVCert operations with dynamic (t_d) and static (t_{dsp}) parameters and determined the percentage of improvement (% Imp.) due to static parameters.

Request Type	t_r (ms)	t_d (ms)	t_{rsp} (ms)	t_{dsp} (ms)	% Imp. (t_{dsp})
HTTPS only	1.17 ($\pm$0.01)	–	1.17 ($\pm$0.01)	–	–
DVCert 2048 bits	11.88 ($\pm$0.01)	10.71	6.66 ($\pm$0.01)	5.49	48.74%
DVCert 1024 bits	3.02 ($\pm$0.01)	1.85	2.20 ($\pm$0.01)	1.03	44.32%
DVCert 384 bits	2.04 ($\pm$0.01)	0.87	1.71 ($\pm$0.01)	0.54	37.93%

experiment for 10 measurements per point (300 in total), including 95% confident intervals. This figure shows that, even if every SSL/TLS connection uses a DVCert transaction, using 384 bits exponents allows a maximum throughput close to the one obtained using single HTTPS requests. Moreover, 1024 bit exponents could also allow a similar performance if static parameters are used (based on the results shown in Table 2). Thus, using 1024 bits exponents or shorter and static parameters reduces the risk of DoS attacks, eliminating the need for additional DoS defenses (e.g., client puzzles).

6 Discussion

6.1 DVCert Benefits

In addition to meeting the design goals described in Section 3.2, DVCert solves most of the problems hindering the deployment of third-party defenses against MITM attacks (see Section 2.3). First, *DVCert is easier to deploy and maintain*. In most scenarios, DVCert should not require additional infrastructure due to its low processing costs. Only minor modifications are required to add DVCert support to the web application and the browser (see Figure 2). For example, DVCert only needs access to the application's user database and certificate information (i.e., the DCL). Hence, DVCert can be deployed as an independent service without modifying any existing functionality in the application. In the browser, DVCert can also be implemented as an independent component that

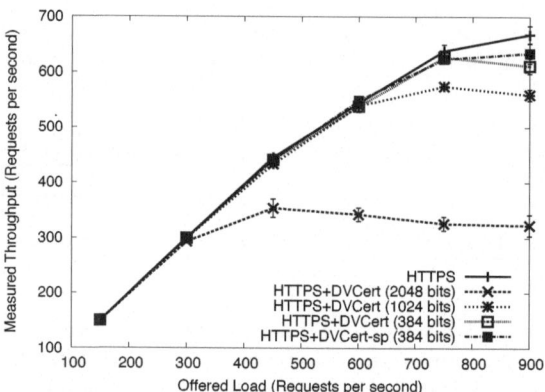

Fig. 4. Comparison of the web server throughput for single HTTPS request and HTTPS requests with DVCert in the hypothetical case that DVCert transactions are executed per SSL/TLS connection (i.e., upper bound). HTTPS+DVCert configurations used different exponent sizes and one configuration used static parameters (HTTPS+DVCert-sp).

only requires the certificate information used on each SSL/TLS connection and secure storage for the password salted hashes and DCL data. Moreover, by relying on passwords, users do not need to deal with additional secrets or devices and can benefit from DVCert on a wider range of platforms. Second, *DVCert has a simpler trust model.* It relies on existing trust relationships between users and web applications; hence, users do not need to assess and establish new trust relationships with third-parties. Third, *DVCert does not introduce new privacy risks.* User browsing activity is not revealed to third-parties when a certificate is validated using DVCert. This property is particularly important for users with high privacy and anonymity requirements (e.g., Tor users). Fourth, *certificate revocation is simpler.* For instance, a certificate can be revoked by just removing it from the DCL. Thus, there is no need for mechanisms such as CRLs and OCSP, both criticised due to their ineffectiveness [24]. Fifth, *DVCert is more resilient to compromise than third-party approaches.* Third-party solutions can vouch for certificates belonging to a large number of domains. However, if compromised, then all the protected domains could be affected by MITM attacks. In contrast, DVCert is deployed independently per domain; thus, attacks against one domain will not affect other domains. Finally, *DVCert is compatible with captive portals in certain scenarios.* For instance, DVCert could verify the certificates of captive portals that already share a secret with the user (e.g., Wi-Fi provider account) or where the user receives a shared secret via a secondary channel (e.g., a receipt).

6.2   DVCert Limitations

DVCert allows web applications to vouch for their certificates using existing authentication credentials. Thus, DVCert can only protect web applications where the user has an account and a shared secret. However, this is not a major limitation because most of the web applications that are likely to be targeted by adversaries (e.g., sites with private information) require authentication credentials. A related case are web applications that rely on federated identity management (e.g., OpenID) or Single sign-on (SSO) systems. Here, users share a password with an identity provider instead of the web application. Still, DVCert can be extended to validate certificates in such scenarios. For instance, the web application can provide its DCL to the identity provider during the login process. Then, the browser can execute a DVCert transaction to obtain not only the DCL of the identity provider but also of the targeted application. We plan to explore this idea in our future work. Another limitation is that DVCert cannot be used to protect the first connection to a web application. DVCert is by design a trust-on-first-use (TOFU) [38] mechanism such as the SSH protocol. Therefore, when registering to a web application for the first time, users can only rely on CA signatures and other third-party mechanisms to validate certificates. However, for most scenarios, it is unlikely that adversaries will be monitoring users before they have created an account with a web application. Moreover, applications with high security requirements could also use secondary channels to protect the user registration process.

7   Related Work

Multiple browser-based mechanisms have been proposed to detect forged certificates. For instance, browser extensions can keep track of the certificates used by the browser and can detect certificate changes [1, 36]. While simple, the effectiveness of this approach is affected by false positives and lack of user training. A related technique, known as certificate pinning [16], uses a white-list of certificates for important domains that are hardcoded in the browser. This solution is less prone to false positives; however, it is neither flexible nor scalable. A more robust approach is the use of secondary channels such as cellular networks [33] and Tor [3] to obtain additional copies of the server certificate. Unfortunately, this approach is difficult to deploy and can introduce significant delays.

Most research in the area of MITM defenses focuses on using additional third-parties to improve or replace the CA trust model. For example, mechanisms such as Perspectives [38] and Convergence [30] allow users to choose multiple network notaries that can complement or replace CAs signatures. The Mutually Endorsing CA Infrastructure (MECAI) [14] proposes a similar approach, but instead of introducing new notaries, MECAI uses existing CAs as notaries. A different technique is presented by the Electronic Frontier Foundation (EFF) Sovereign Keys (SK) project [12]. In SK, domain certificates include an additional integrity signature created with the domain's sovereign key. To verify this signature, browsers can obtain the corresponding sovereign key from a semi-centralized, append-only public data structure. Google's Certificate Transparency (CT) [25] proposal also relies on a similar data structure, but instead of storing keys, it stores records of each certificate emitted by a CA; thus, browsers can check this public audit log to validate they are using the correct certificate. The IETF DNS-based Authentication of Named Entities (DANE) working group [20] is developing protocols that use secure DNS (DNSSEC) extensions to bind certificates to domain names. Finally, while third-party based solutions offer several benefits, their adoption has been hindered by multiple problems such as deployment and operational costs, lack of user training, false positives and others (see Section 2.3).

To a lesser degree, researchers have also explored the use of shared secrets (e.g., passwords) to defend against MITM attacks. For example, the TLS-SRP protocol [37] uses SRP [40] for mutual authentication and SSL/TLS key derivation based on the user's password (i.e., certificates and CAs are not required). However, TLS-SRP requires inter-layer communication between the application and the SSL/TLS stack, breaking SSL/TLS transparency. A different technique is to use shared secrets for channel binding [39], as proposed in the Session Aware (TLS-SA) user authentication protocol [32]. To detect MITM attacks, TLS-SA uses authentication codes based on user credentials and SSL/TLS session information, effectively binding the application and SSL/TLS layers. TLS-SA, however, requires client certificates and hardware tokens to resist offline dictionary attacks, affecting its adoption. Finally, the Mutual Authentication Protocol for HTTP [31] also combines user authentication with SSL/TLS channel binding, but it relies on the user's password instead of client certificates. To provide mutual authentication and prevent offline guessing attacks, this mechanism relies on the direct implementation of a PAKE protocol. However, this mechanism requires additional server state, only protects the login connection and requires changes to the browser and web application login UI (a significant challenge for deploying PAKE-based protocols [15]).

8   Conclusions

As recent incidents have demonstrated, adversaries are exploiting weaknesses in the CA trust model to compromise communications protected by SSL/TLS via MITM attacks. This trend is likely to accelerate as more and more web applications adopt SSL/TLS to protect all their communications. Currently proposed solutions face multiple challenges due to their complexity and deployment and operational costs; thus, they are unlikely to be widely available in the near future. We present DVCert, a practical mechanism that relies on previously established shared secrets to allow the web application to directly and securely vouch for the authenticity of its certificates. By using a single round-trip transaction with the web application, based on a modified PAK protocol, the browser learns the information required to locally verify all the certificates that could be used during a session with the application. Our experimental analysis shows that DVCert transactions require little execution time on the server and the browser; therefore, they should not have a serious impact on server performance or user experience. Finally, DVCert could be extended to protect not only the integrity of SSL/TLS certificates but also other application's resources such as Javascript code and binary objects. We intend to explore this approach in our future work.

Acknowledgments. This work was supported in part by the US National Science Foundation (CAREER CNS-0952959). Any opinions, findings, conclusions or recommendations expressed in this publication are those of the authors and do not necessarily reflect the views of the National Science Foundation. We would also like to thank William Enck for his helpful comments.

References

1. Certificate Patrol (2010), http://patrol.psyced.org/
2. Adams, C., Farrell, S.: RFC 2510 - Internet X.509 Public Key Infrastructure Certificate Management Protocols (1999), https://tools.ietf.org/html/rfc2510
3. Alicherry, M., Keromytis, A.D.: DoubleCheck: Multi-path Verification Against Man-in-the-Middle Attacks. In: Proceedings of the IEEE Symposium on Computers and Communications (2009)
4. Altman, J., Williams, N., Zhu, L.: RFC 5929 - Channel Bindings for TLS (2010), http://tools.ietf.org/html/rfc5929
5. AT&T: Network Averages (2012), http://ipnetwork.bgtmo.ip.att.net/pws/averages.html
6. Blanchet, B.: ProVerif: Cryptographic Protocol Verifier in the Formal Model, http://www.proverif.ens.fr/
7. BlueKrypt: Cryptographic Key Length Recommendation (2012), http://www.keylength.com/
8. Boyko, V., MacKenzie, P.D., Patel, S.: Provably Secure Password-Authenticated Key Exchange Using Diffie-Hellman. In: Preneel, B. (ed.) EUROCRYPT 2000. LNCS, vol. 1807, pp. 156–171. Springer, Heidelberg (2000)
9. Brusilovsky, A., Faynberg, I., Zeltsan, Z., Patel, S.: RFC 5683 - Password-Authenticated Key (PAK) Diffie-Hellman Exchange (2010), http://tools.ietf.org/html/rfc5683
10. Dierks, T., Rescorla, E.: RFC 5246 - The Transport Layer Security (TLS) Protocol Version 1.2 (2008), http://tools.ietf.org/html/rfc5246
11. Eckersley, P., Burns, J.: The (Decentralized) SSL Observatory. In: USENIX Security Symposium (2011) (Invited Talk)
12. Electronic Frontier Foundation (EFF): The Sovereign Keys Project (2011), https://www.eff.org/sovereign-keys
13. Ellison, C., Schneier, B.: Ten Risks of PKI: What You're Not Being Told About Public Key Infrastructure. Computer Security Journal 16(1), 1–7 (2000)
14. Engert, K.: MECAI (2011), http://kuix.de/mecai/
15. Engler, J., Karlof, C., Shi, E., Song, D.: Is It Too Late for PAKE? In: Proceedings of the IEEE Web 2.0 Security and Privacy Workshop (2009)
16. Evans, C., Palmer, C.: Certificate Pinning Extension for HSTS (2011), http://www.ietf.org/mail-archive/web/websec/current/pdfnSTRd9kYcY.pdf
17. Freier, A., Karlton, P., Kocher, P.: RFC 6101 - The Secure Sockets Layer (SSL) Protocol Version 3.0 (2011), https://tools.ietf.org/html/rfc6101
18. Goodin, D.: Web Authentication Authority Suffers Security Breach (2011), http://www.theregister.co.uk/2011/06/21/startssl_security_breach/
19. Gutman, P.: PKI: It's Not Dead, Just Resting. Computer 35(8), 41–49 (2002)
20. Hoffman, P., Schlyter, J.: IETF Internet-Draft: Using Secure DNS to Associate Certificates with Domain Names For TLS (draft-ietf-dane-protocol-06) (2011), http://tools.ietf.org/html/draft-ietf-dane-protocol-06

21. International Telecommunication Union: ITU-T Recommendation X.1035: Password-Authenticated Key Exchange (PAK) Protocol (2007), http://www.itu.int/rec/T-REC-X.1035/en
22. Keizer, G.: Hackers May Have Stolen Over 200 SSL Certificates (2011), https://www.computerworld.com/s/article/9219663/Hackers_may_have_stolen_over_200_SSL_certificates
23. Kirk, J.: KPN Stops Issuing SSL Certificates After Possible Breach (2011), https://www.pcworld.com/businesscenter/article/243275/kpn_stops_issuing_ssl_certificates_after_possible_breach.html
24. Langley, A.: Revocation Doesn't Work (2011), http://www.imperialviolet.org/2011/03/18/revocation.html
25. Laurie, B., Langley, A.: Certificate Authority Transparency and Auditability (2011), http://www.links.org/files/CertificateAuthorityTransparencyandAuditability.pdf
26. Leyden, J.: Inside 'Operation Black Tulip': DigiNotar Hack Analysed (2011), http://www.theregister.co.uk/2011/09/06/diginotar_audit_damning_fail/
27. Leyden, J.: Trustwave Admits Crafting SSL Snooping Certificate (2012), http://www.theregister.co.uk/2012/02/09/tustwave_disavows_mitm_digital_cert/
28. MacKenzie, P.: The PAK suite: Protocols for Password-Authenticated Key Exchange. In: IEEE P1363.2: Password-Based Public-Key Cryptography (2002)
29. MacKenzie, P.D., Patel, S.: Hard Bits of the Discrete Log with Applications to Password Authentication. In: Menezes, A. (ed.) CT-RSA 2005. LNCS, vol. 3376, pp. 209–226. Springer, Heidelberg (2005)
30. Marlinspike, M.: Convergence (2011), http://convergence.io/
31. Oiwa, Y., Takagi, H., Watanabe, H., Suzuki, H.: PAKE-based Mutual HTTP Authentication for Preventing Phishing Attacks (Poster). In: Proceedings of the International Conference on World Wide Web, WWW (2009)
32. Oppliger, R., Hauser, R., Basin, D.: SSL/TLS Session-Aware User Authentication. Computer 41(3), 59–65 (2008)
33. Parno, B., Kuo, C., Perrig, A.: Phoolproof Phishing Prevention. In: Di Crescenzo, G., Rubin, A. (eds.) FC 2006. LNCS, vol. 4107, pp. 1–19. Springer, Heidelberg (2006)
34. Richmond, R.: An Attack Sheds Light on Internet Security Holes (2011), http://www.nytimes.com/2011/04/07/technology/07hack.html
35. Singel, R.: Law Enforcement Appliance Subverts SSL (2010), http://www.wired.com/threatlevel/2010/03/packet-forensics/
36. Soghoian, C., Stamm, S.: Certified Lies: Detecting and Defeating Government Interception Attacks against SSL (Short Paper). In: Danezis, G. (ed.) FC 2011. LNCS, vol. 7035, pp. 250–259. Springer, Heidelberg (2012)
37. Taylor, D., Wu, T., Mavrogiannopoulos, N., Perrin, T.: RFC 5054 - Using the Secure Remote Password (SRP) Protocol for TLS Authentication (2007), http://tools.ietf.org/html/rfc5054
38. Wendlandt, D., Andersen, D.G., Perrig, A.: Perspectives: Improving SSH-style Host Authentication with Multi-path Probing. In: Proceedings of the USENIX Annual Technical Conference, ATC (2008)
39. Williams, N.: RFC 5056 - On the Use of Channel Bindings to Secure Channels (2007), http://tools.ietf.org/html/rfc5056
40. Wu, T.: The Secure Remote Password Protocol. In: Proceedings of the Network and Distributed System Security Symposium (1998)

X.509 Forensics: Detecting and Localising the SSL/TLS Men-in-the-Middle

Ralph Holz, Thomas Riedmaier, Nils Kammenhuber, and Georg Carle

Network Architectures and Services
Fakultät für Informatik
Technische Universität München
{holz,riedmaie,kammenhuber,carle}@net.in.tum.de

Abstract. Although recent compromises and admissions have given new credibility to claimed encounters of Man-in-the-middle (MitM) attacks on SSL/TLS, very little proof exists in the public realm. In this paper, we report on the development and deployment of Crossbear, a tool to detect MitM attacks on SSL/TLS and localise their position in the network with a fair degree of confidence. MitM attacks are detected using a notary approach. For the localisation, we use a large number of traceroutes, conducted from so-called hunters from many positions on the Internet. Crossbear collects this data, orchestrates the hunting from a central point and provides the data for analysis. We outline the design of Crossbear and analyse the degree of effectivity that Crossbear achieves against attackers of different kinds and strengths. We also explain how analysis can make use of out-of-band sources like lookups of Autonomous Systems and geo-IP-mapping. Crossbear is already available, and 150 hunters have been deployed on the global PlanetLab testbed.

Keywords: Man-in-the-middle attack, detection, localisation, X.509, SSL/TLS.

1 Introduction

The Secure Socket Layer/Transport Layer Security protocol suite (SSL/TLS) is commonly used on the Internet, and especially the WWW, to provide confidentiality, authentication and data integrity. A key feature is its use of the X.509 PKI to address the key distribution problem. In X.509, Certification Authorities (CAs) issue certificates to entities, with each certificate asserting a binding of entity name (e.g., a WWW domain) and the corresponding public key. The X.509 PKI forms a hierarchy where CAs at the root may issue certificates directly to an entity or delegate this process to (one or more) subordinate CAs. The result is a chain of certificates. Verifiers must trust the CAs at the root and, transitively, the subordinate CAs along the chain to verify a end-host certificate. Thus, Web browsers commonly ship with a list of root CAs deemed trustworthy (the 'root store'). A remarkable property of X.509 implementations in browsers is that all CAs in the root store *and* thus also all subordinate CAs are equally

S. Foresti, M. Yung, and F. Martinelli (Eds.): ESORICS 2012, LNCS 7459, pp. 217–234, 2012.

capable of issuing certificates to *any* domain. This was always perceived to be problematic as it reduces the strength of the whole PKI to the weakest CA. An attacker with control over just one CA is able to stage MitM attacks against any domain. This happened to the DigiNotar CA in 2011 when an attacker was able to issue more than 500 forged certificates [1]. As the revocation infrastructure was also deemed compromised, all major browsers reacted by blacklisting forged certificates directly in the browser. The forged certificates were allegedly used in a Man-in-the-middle attack (MitM) staged against citizens of Iran.

It is this latter kind of attack that this paper is concerned with. While we may suspect from [1] that a MitM attack happened, and may speculate who the victims were, it remains curiously unknown how many MitM attacks really happen in the wild. Most reports seem to exist only in the form of blog posts or forum entries, e.g., [2,3,4], with claims ranging from attackers in hotel networks to state-level attacks against citizens of a country. In these cases, all attacks were actually easily detectable because the MitM did not bother to forge certificates but used invalid certificates and relied on users to ignore browser warnings. Unfortunately, affected users seem unlikely to store the MitM's certificate; nor do they record how they have connected to the Internet or to which WWW server (only [3] provides a copy of the fake certificate). Without proper evidence, however, we as a security community cannot know how pressing the problem of MitM attackers really is.

Our tool, Crossbear, has been developed as a response to this lack of hard data. It aims to make a first step towards gathering data and providing proof of the existence of MitM attacks. With the on-going deployment of Crossbear, we invite the interested community in our quest to give answers to questions like how many SSL/TLS MitM attackers exist on the Internet, which certificates do they use, and where are they located in the network. We are fully aware that, in particular, localisation is difficult to perform in the face of an adaptive attacker attempting to counter our methods; however, we are certainly going to raise the bars for evil-doers and hard evidence will likely help to increase public awareness. We also emphasise that Crossbear is intended as a tool for the savvy user or travelling hacktivist who wishes to contribute in the investigation of this important attack on one of the backbone protocols of the Internet, and not as a reinforcement or replacement for the current PKI (like, e.g., Perspectives and Convergence, see Section 2).

Crossbear builds on the well-understood notary concept, but with a twist: it employs a large number of so-called *hunters* distributed over the Internet that compare certificates they receive in a SSL/TLS handshake and record the IP route they have to that SSL/TLS server. This is reported to a central server where certificates and routes are analysed and further hunting initiated, i.e., more hunters asked to connect to the potential victim server and to report certificates and IP routes. A comparison of the IP routes from hunters that are affected by the MitM and by those who are not yields an approximation of the MitM's location in the network. The accuracy increases with the number of hunters.

Contributions and organisation. The remainder of this paper is organised as follows. Section 2 presents related work and positions Crossbear as a tool to combine detection, localisation, and reporting. Section 3 outlines the design of the Crossbear ecosystem and highlights relevant design decisions. Section 4 analyses to which degree Crossbear can be an effective tool against different kinds of attackers of varying strength. It also gives an estimate of the needed numbers of hunters and shows how out-of-band information can help where pure tracerouting will fail. We conclude with a summary and invitation to participate.

2   Background and Related Work

The weaknesses of the X.509 PKI for SSL/TLS have been described in several research papers as well as at hacking symposia. Vratonjic et al. presented a study of the Alexa Top 1 Million list [5]. Holz et al. presented an extensive study [6] that covers 1.5 years and includes observation points from around the globe, as well as data from traffic monitoring. Eckersley and Burns presented a survey based on scans of the IPv4 space [7]. These efforts showed that certification practices are not very stringent at best, and authentication errors common. As Sunshine et al. [8] found that users are likely unable to decide whether a browser warning indicates a threat or can be safely ignored, this constitutes a serious weakness. Regardless of user abilities, Soghoian and Stamm warned that governments can compel CAs to issue forged certificates for state-level MitM attacks [9]. In such a case, browsers would not even show a warning.

The number of proposals to strengthen or replace the X.509 PKI suggests how little confidence is placed in it. Two replacements, EFF's Sovereign Keys [10] and Google's Certificate Transparency [11], are based on public logs, i.e., public append-only timelines with certificate information. Both are still in the design phase. It is unclear if they will be successful. A different idea is to employ a notary approach, which is also a key idea in Crossbear. This concept is based on the observation that a MitM is unlikely to control all network paths between a server and its clients. Thus, SSL/TLS clients can ask third-party observers (the notaries) whether they observe the same certificate from a given server. As long as the route to at least one notary remains outside of the attacker's control, this results in a mismatch between the certificates reported by the notaries and the one observed by the client.

To our knowledge, Perspectives [12] was the first notary-based project. The idea is to make initial contact to an unknown server robust against a MitM. The project periodically scans WWW hosts to generate a database of public keys. Browsers with the Perspectives add-on can compare keys from the database with those they are observing. Since 2011, Convergence [13] provides a similar service on the basis of observed certificates. The Convergence notaries do not conduct pro-active scanning and connect to a WWW server only when a client reports a yet unknown certificate. The browser-side add-on relies entirely on the notaries and essentially disables the use of the normal X.509 PKI. Convergence emphasises so-called 'trust-agility': users can choose to use different notaries when their current ones have been compromised. This, however, requires that users understand the involved technologies and consequences.

All notary concepts share the problem of lack of privacy: notary operators know which sites users access. Convergence employs a kind of onion-routing to mediate this. Crossbear does not address privacy issues: as its purpose is to collect and report data about real attacks, privacy could not be a design goal.

3   Crossbear Design and Ecosystem

Crossbear's purpose is the collection of data that is likely to contain proof of a MitM attack. One particular working hypothesis that we would like to see either verified or falsified is that there are primarily two kinds of attackers. The first kind consists of MitM attacks close to the victim client, e.g., on wireless access points. The other kind are 'state-level' attackers, i.e., such attackers that can control whole ISPs and plant the MitM software on network border routers with the goal of monitoring all SSL/TLS traffic from within their country to one or several external services (e.g., Web mailers or social networks).

3.1   Principle of Operation

Key idea. Crossbear deploys a large number of so-called hunters on the Internet, distributed over as many Autonomous Systems and networks as possible. We implemented two kinds of hunters. The first is an add-on for the Mozilla Firefox Web browser; the other is a stand-alone application. The add-on is used for both detection and localisation, the stand-alone applications only for localisation.

The Crossbear server holds a list of servers that are reportedly attacked by a MitM. This list is pulled at regular intervals by the hunters, which will then connect via SSL/TLS to the reportedly attacked servers. They extract the certificate chain the server sends and record the IP route to the server by doing a traceroute. This information is then sent to back to the central server, where it can be analysed.

Detection. Possibly attacked servers are reported automatically with the help of the Firefox add-on. We elaborate on this in Section 3.2. Naturally, a user of the browser add-on is warned if an ongoing MitM is detected.

Localisation. The position of the attacker can be approximated by *cross-bearing*, i.e., comparing the routes that hunters recorded and determining the intersection points for routes that have been found to be poisoned and those that have been found to be clean. This is illustrated in Fig. 1, where the Crossbear server receives different certificates and traceroutes from the victim Alice and from the hunters Bob, Charlie, and Dave. This allows it to guess that the attacker is located in the vicinity of Alice because the intersection between her traceroute and Bob's traceroute is already at router R4, and Bob reports a clean connection. We discuss the effectivity of cross-bearing against attackers of various strengths and positions in Section 4.

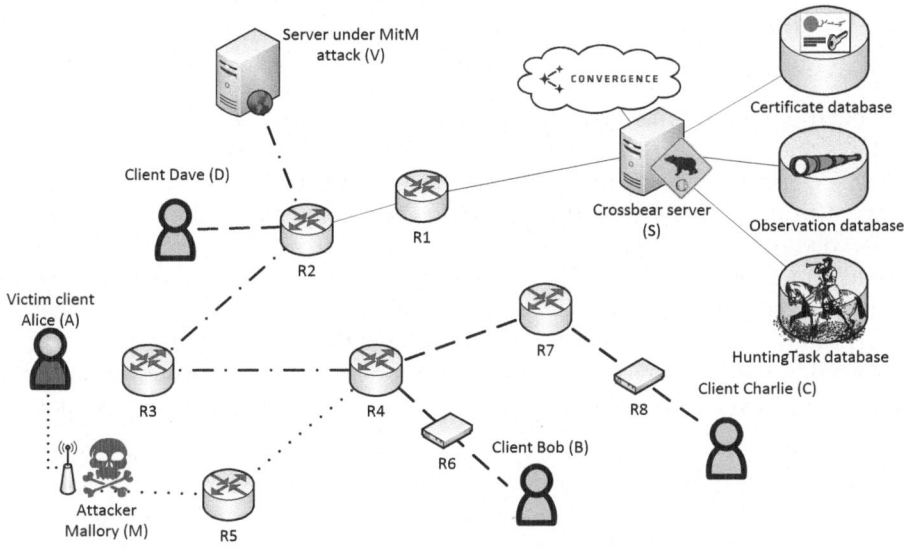

Fig. 1. Components of the Crossbear system

Further vantage points. The Crossbear server uses Convergence [13] as a source of independent observations from other vantage points on the Internet. It queries Convergence notaries and stores certificate information plus additional independent temporal information, e.g., for how long a given certificate has been observed.

Out-of-band information sources. We also store additional information we obtain from sources other than hunters.

- CAs used: We store which CAs a domain uses. Domains like, e.g., Google have always remained customers of the same CAs for longer periods of time[1].
- WHOIS information: We retrieve the AS number of all hosts in a traceroute. For a reported MitM attack, we also take into account how many reports from the ASes in the country in question have reached us, and whether the reported forged certificates share properties. The latter is motivated by the observation that an attacker is less likely to compel or compromise more than one CA.
- Geo-IP-mapping: Hosts in a traceroute are also looked up in geo-IP databases. Although imperfect, this allows to guess which countries SSL/TLS traffic has traversed.

We elaborate on the use of this information in Section 4.

---

[1] For Google, this has been confirmed to the authors in private e-mail.

3.2 Details of the Detection Process

MitM attacks are detected with the add-on for the Web browser.

Protecting the Communication with the Server. All Crossbear clients
(add-ons and hunters) communicate with the Crossbear server via TLS. To protect this channel against MitM attacks, the server certificate is hard-coded into
clients. If a client finds that the received server certificate does not match the
hard-coded one, its current behaviour is to refuse to operate and offer the user
to send an automatic mail or fax to the Crossbear team that contains all details
about the incident (including the forged certificate). While not yet implemented,
the next major version of Crossbear may support the server signing its messages.
This would allow to bypass the attacker even over a poisoned connection. Note
that clients never sign messages: they do not have IDs and can thus not be
authenticated.

Certificate Verification. Fig. 2 shows how certificate verification works. If
user Alice (A) connects to a Web server V via SSL/TLS and the connection
is under attack by a MitM, she will receive a forged certificate. A thus always
sends a `CertVerifyRequest` to the Crossbear server S. The message includes
the observed certificate chain, V's domain name and A's IP address. S stores
this together with a timestamp. It then connects to V itself and stores the corresponding data. S also queries Convergence notaries for known certificates for
V and stores the results with the observation period that Convergence reports.
This result is sent to A (`CertVerifyResult` message). There are three optional
messages. If the certificate comparison suggests a MitM, S includes a hunting
task for A, i.e., a request to conduct a traceroute to V. S also includes a reference
timestamp and a `PublicIPNotification`. We explain the latter in Section 3.3.

Score over Certificate Properties. The Crossbear server also computes a
score that is reported to client add-ons. The score is a weighted sum over a
number of properties. The motivation here is to reduce the number of false
positive warnings for human users of the add-on, i.e., occasions where S detects
a certificate mismatch, but V's certificate is actually valid. This can occur for
server farms with multiple different certificates deployed, or for sites that change
their certificates very frequently.

    The primary criterion in the score is the comparison of the certificates that
client and S have encountered. However, S also takes the *last continuous observation period* (LCOP) into account, which expresses for how long *only* the
certificate in question has been observed. Further criteria are the number of previous observations and the certificates that Convergence reports (together with
their LCOP). Our weights are chosen thus that 'critical' combinations of properties yield a score of less than 100. When a score is below this (user-adjustable)
threshold, our add-on displays a warning. Where several factors (completely
or almost) counter-balance a certificate mismatch, the warning will either be
suppressed or a user is at least given the server's score indicating the factors
that make the certificate likely valid (recall that Crossbear is intended for savvy
users). We list the most relevant factors in Table 1.

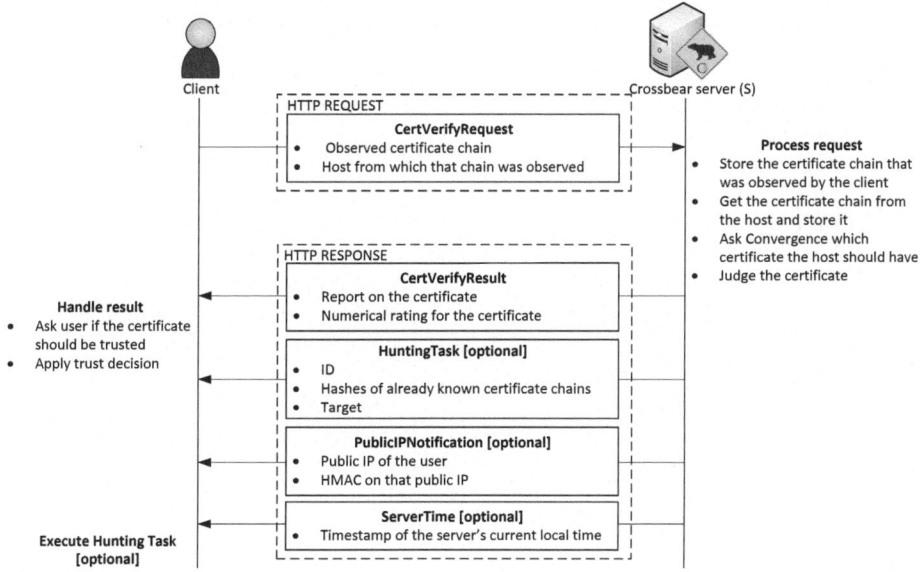

Fig. 2. Protocol flow including the certificate verification request and hunting tasks

When the certificate score is above the threshold, the browser add-on caches the observed (host, certificate) combinations. When the threshold is not reached and a warning is displayed, the user is asked if the combination should be exempted and cached. We have experimented with the default settings over the course of several months and found that false positives occur only rarely. For popular sites that use several certificates (like Facebook), they have become rare (due to the server observations) and are not annoying due to the caching. They can still happen in the small time window when a site that frequently changes its certificates (like Google) does so and neither hunters nor Convergence have yet observed this. The more popular a site is, the less frequently this happens.

3.3 Details of the Hunting Process

Hunting is the process of determining a suspected attacker's network location, i.e., his position in an AS, sub-network or (with the help of Geo-IP databases) approximate geographic position.

Every hunter pulls the list of active hunting tasks from the Crossbear server at regular intervals. A hunting task can also be sent to a client together with a certificate judgement indicating a possible MitM attack. A `ServerTime` message is used to give a reference time to use when results are reported back to the Crossbear server. The hunter then starts to execute the tasks (see Fig. 3). The hunting starts with conducting a full SSL/TLS handshake and extracting the certificate chain. The next step is to record the route that IP packets take towards

Table 1. Parameters used in computing a score for a reported certificate. C_c is the certificate observed by the client, C_s the certificate observed by the Crossbear server (S). V is the victim server.

Property and score	Rationale
Certificate comparison:	
80 if $C_c = C_s$	S observes same certificate
0 if $C_c \neq C_s$	Potential MitM
-100 if S cannot get certificate from V	S likely blocked
LCOP:	
$\frac{days \cdot 2}{3}$ if LCOP ongoing	C_c still observed
$\frac{days}{3}$ if LCOP ended in the past	C_c observed in the past only
Observations: $\frac{count}{30}$	Number of observations
Convergence:	
$\frac{days \cdot 2}{3}$ if certificates match	Confirmation
$\frac{days}{3}$ matched in past, but not now	Outdated confirmation
-20 if never observed	Weak indication of MitM
0 if no reply from Convergence	Inconclusive

the destination. This is done with a standard ICMP traceroute. Certificate chain and route are sent to the Crossbear server.

We require hunters to send a `PublicIPNotification` request to the Crossbear server before they can conduct a traceroute and submit results. The reply to a `PublicIPNotification` contains the public IP address *that the Crossbear server observes* plus a HMAC of it, keyed with a secret key that only the Crossbear server knows and that is replaced every 30 minutes. Hunters must prepend their thus determined public IP address to the traceroute and include the HMAC. This serves several purposes. First, it is necessary to inform hunters with multiple IP addresses (e.g., IPv4 and IPv6), or which are located behind a NAT, of the IP address to conduct the traceroute from. Second, it acts as a protection against completely deliberate forgery of traceroute results: it forces a hunter to be reachable from the IP address it claims to have. While a powerful attacker is still able to spoof IP addresses of the system it controls, or of attached systems, this prevents him from submitting results allegedly from networks that are not under his control. Finally, knowledge of the claimed source of the traceroute enables us to draw on publicly available BGP dumps (e.g., Route Views [14]). This can aid in testing the plausibility of a route during the analysis process. We discuss this in Section 4.

3.4   Status of Deployment

Crossbear is available in version 1.5 [15]. Stand-alone hunters have been implemented and are already deployed on the PlanetLab testbed in 150 different locations on the globe. The Crossbear server is hosted at Technische Universität München. At the time of writing, Crossbear has just finished its beta phase; our database contains about 4,000 certificate observations conducted by our server

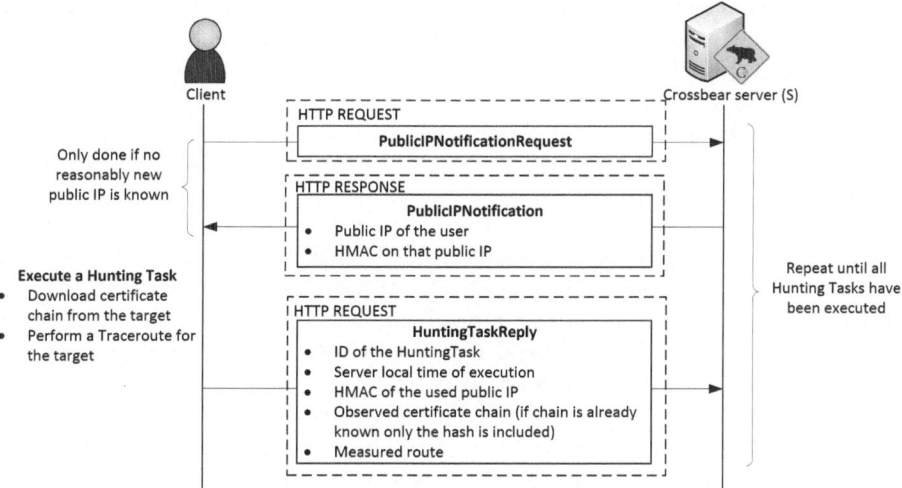

Fig. 3. Crossbear's protocol for the execution of Hunting Tasks

plus another 2,000 retrieved from Convergence notaries. Results have been reported from more than 150 unique IP or /24-sub-networks. We have not found indications of MitM attacks so far, however. Current work includes providing the hunting functionality as a module for OONI, a distributed framework to monitor network interferences on the Internet [16].

4   Analysis and Discussion of Effectivity

We analyse the degree to which Crossbear can be an effective tool. We also discuss counter-attacks against Crossbear.

4.1   Attacker Model

The attacker is assumed to have the full control over a 'system' on the path from the client to the victim server. A system can be either a router or an entire Autonomous System (AS) through which traffic is forwarded. The attacker does not control any other path in the network. In particular, he can only 'impersonate' IP addresses (i.e., spoof them *and* intercept replies addressed to them) from the system he controls or systems that are attached to it, and whose upstream and downstream traffic is routed through it. An attacker controlling several systems can be modelled as separate attacks, with the addition that the attacker can use impersonated IP addresses from the other attacking systems as well.

We structure our discussion along two dimensions. Firstly, we distinguish attacker types by their selectivity against clients:

Non-selective attacker: The non-selective attacker stages his MitM attack against all clients attached to his system. There are two sub-types: attackers that MitM only the connections to some SSL/TLS server(s) and attackers that MitM every SSL/TLS connection.

Selective attacker: The selective attacker stages his MitM attack against a *sub-set* of clients attached to the system he controls. The same two sub-types as above exist.

Secondly, we distinguish by the position of the attacker in the network. We give special focus to locations that give an attacker most impact: towards the periphery of the Internet and close to the client; towards the periphery and close to the victim server; and in a central location of the network topology (i.e., an important router or well-connected transit AS).

This is motivated by the suspected kinds of attacks in the MitM reports like [2,3,4], which Crossbear was designed to address primarily. These attackers are depicted in Fig. 4a and 4b. The first kind is a non-selective attacker who operates close to the client, e.g., a poisoned wireless access point. The second kind is a much more powerful but also non-selective attacker who controls an entire system to which several sub-systems are attached. An example is a state-level attacker who stages a MitM attack against the population of his own country by controlling traffic passing his border system(s).

Fig. 4c and 4d show attackers that Crossbear (and indeed any tracing system) is less effective against. Fig. 4c is a selective attacker that is located close to the client but acts only against a sub-set of the clients attached to the system he controls. Fig. 4d is the most powerful and cunning attacker we consider: He is in control of an important system in the Internet core (e.g., an important transit AS) and stages his attack against just a sub-set of client systems at the periphery. A possible example is state-condoned industrial espionage where a government agency stages a MitM attack on traffic passing through their AS. Note that MitM attacks become more difficult the more the attacker moves towards the core of the network: the attacker needs to modify both directions of the traffic; but phenomena such as hot-potato routing [17] and BGP peering policies like valley-free routing [18] often cause IP packets to take different return paths.

We discuss now how effective Crossbear is for each scenario and which additional steps can be taken to aid detection and localisation.

4.2   Detection

In general, ongoing MitM attacks can be reliably detected by a Crossbear client/hunter because the queried Crossbear server observes a different certificate for the victim server. This is true for all attacker types in Fig. 4. Note that if the attacker chooses to MitM the connection to the Crossbear server, this is detected and the add-on will react to it (see Section 3.2).

The only attack that cannot be reliably detected by certificate comparison is when the attacker is on all paths from the vantage points to the victim server. This is a weakness all notary systems share. Such an attacker would either have

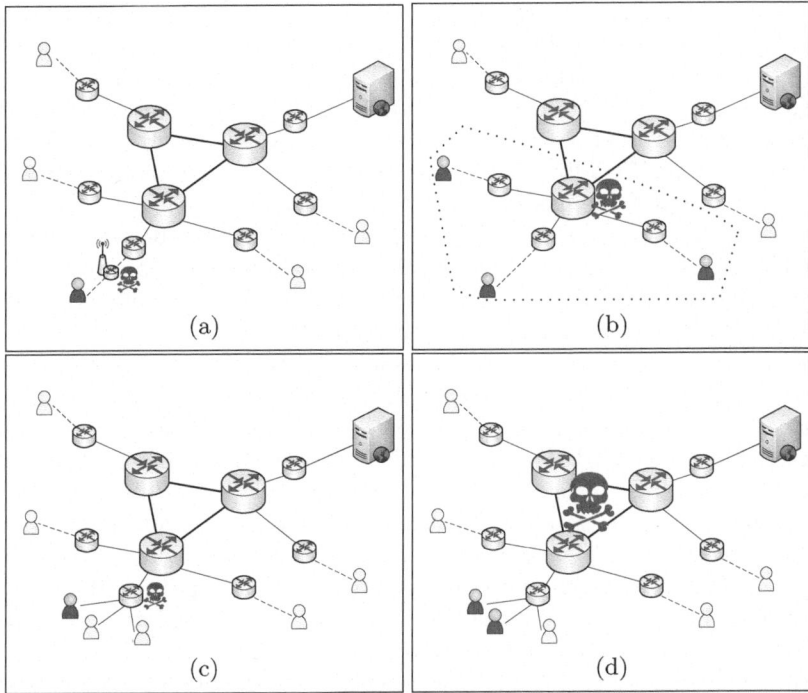

Fig. 4. (a) Non-selective attacker in vicinity of client. (b) Non-selective state-level attacker. (c) Selective attacker in vicinity of client. (d) Selective (super-) attacker in core of network.

to hijack BGP routes (as proposed in [19]) or position himself on a point in the network where all paths to the destination have already converged, i.e., close to the victim server. If the victim server has been observed previously, however, Crossbear can still profit from information available at the server. For example, when important certificate properties like the issuing CA change, this will flag a client report for manual verification. However, if the victim server has never been observed before, the attack is not detectable by any notary system.

4.3 Localisation

The ability to accurately trace the attacker's position in the network depends entirely on the attacker acting selectively or non-selectively.

The Non-Selective Attacker. The non-selective attacker lends itself well to localisation. In order for this to work, Crossbear needs a traceroute from the victim client and from at least one hunter that is attached to an upstream system (from the attacker's point of view) and which reports a clean connection. The accuracy increases the closer that upstream system is towards the attacker's own position and if that view is corroborated by other hunters either downstream (reporting poisoned connections) or upstream (reporting clean connections).

We present a rough estimate of how many hunters are required in order to locate a non-selective MitM attacker. To this end, we derive a closed-form model to estimate the average number of hunters needed to detect a MitM with a certain probability. We fully acknowledge that we require a number of simplifying assumptions to make the model suitable for analysis.

Our model only requires the distribution of path lengths between victim client and victim server and the distribution of node degrees as input. We have derived such topological data from publicly available router-level maps and from measurements from our own university network.

Our analysis is based on an observation that holds for most Internet traffic: Once two traffic flows with the same destination converge at a point in the network, they will not separate again until they reach their target. This is a characteristic of standard IP routing which is based on the destination but not on the source address. Exceptions exist (e.g., ECMP, CoS differentiation) but are rare; thus our model will hold for most cases. Given a path from victim client to victim server via an attacker, traceroutes from hunters will join the path at some point. Due to the genericity of our model, we can apply it at router level (i.e., to find the router conducting the MitM attack) as well as at an AS level (i.e., to find the AS conducting the attack).

In the following, we use the generic term *node* to denote a router or an AS.

Closed-form model for estimating the number of hunters. We assume that initially there is only one victim client C and one victim server V. Let the path $C \leftrightsquigarrow V$ consist of intermediate nodes X_j, where X_2 is connected to $X_1 = V$ and X_ℓ is connected to C. Traffic $C \leftrightsquigarrow V$ is subject to a MitM attack at $M =: X_m$. After C suspects that its traffic exchanged with V is being attacked, hunters $H_1, \ldots, H_n$ conduct SSL/TLS handshakes and traceroutes to V.

In order to accurately locate the attacker at $X_m := M$, we require that traffic from some hunter H_1 joins the path $C \rightsquigarrow V$ exactly at X_m, and we need another hunter H_2 whose traffic joins the path on the last undisturbed hop X_{m-1}. See Fig. 5 for a graphical explanation. Calculating the probability for these placements yields the probability for attack localisation.

Our model makes the following assumptions: (1) The attacker intercepts the traffic exchanged between C and V at a single node M. (2) The MitM attacker M is not selective, i.e., all traffic for V passing through M is attacked. (3) For simplicity, we assume that the traffic path $V \leftrightsquigarrow C$ is symmetric, as well as any section $V \leftrightsquigarrow X_j$ of any path $V \leftrightsquigarrow X_k \leftrightsquigarrow H_i$. Note that real-word routing often results in asymmetric paths. However, our model remains usable as long as the path lengths do not differ significantly. (4) In all nodes along the path $C \leftrightsquigarrow V$, traffic is routed purely according to the destination address (an exception is M, who may choose to divert the attacked traffic). This means that any traffic sent to V follows a tree with root V: once two traffic flows $H_1 \rightsquigarrow V, H_2 \rightsquigarrow V$ have converged at some intermediate node X, they will not separate until they reach V. The same considerations apply for the opposite traffic originated by V: once

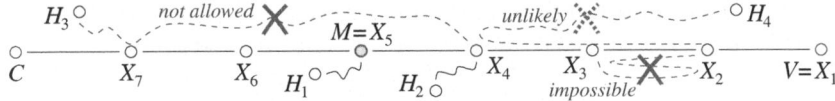

Fig. 5. Notation for the model

its flows separate, they cannot converge again. However, note that due to hot potato routing, assumption 4 may not hold on an AS level if the node under consideration is a large-scale AS and the ingress points of H_1's and H_2's traffic are very different, e.g., on different continents. (5) The probability for a node to be selected as the location for a hunter H_i is the same across all nodes.

Probability that a hunter covers a node. We estimate the probability that traffic from a randomly placed hunter H_1 traverses a given intermediate node X_j. For simplicity, we only analyse the traffic direction $\{C, H_i\} \rightsquigarrow V$. Call X_{j-1} the *successor* of X_j. Assume we already know the probability $\Pr[X_{j-1}]$ that H_1's traffic passes successor X_{j-1}. We now make the further assumption that (6) the probability that traffic is forwarded to a specific neighbour of X_j (e.g., X_{j-1}) is evenly distributed among all neighbours of X_j. The only exception is its successor X_{j-2}, which cannot be chosen: any path $H_1 \rightsquigarrow X_{j-2} \rightarrow X_{j-1} \rightarrow X_{j-2}$ implies a routing loop (Fig. 5, line labelled 'impossible'). If X_j has d_j neighbours (i.e., has degree d_j), then the probability that H_1's traffic comes from X_j is $1/(d_j - 1)$. Hence the overall probability that H_1's traffic passes X_j is $\Pr[X_j] = \prod_{k=1}^{j} 1/(d_k - 1)$. Note that this assumption is actually overly conservative: In reality, certain neighbours can be ruled out due to hot potato routing, valley-free routing, topological position etc.; e.g., in Fig. 5 a direct path $X_2 \rightsquigarrow H_4$ is much more likely than the dotted path labelled 'unlikely'. Hence d_j is effectively reduced and the probability that H_1's traffic crosses X_j is thus higher than our estimate.

Probability for correct placement. To locate the attacker at X_m, we need (*requirement I*) one hunter H_1 who also experiences the attack and whose traffic separates right at X_m, and (*requirement II*) another hunter H_2 whose traffic separates nearer to V at X_{m-1}, i.e., it just escapes the MitM attack. To meet requirement I, the traffic must not come via the predecessor X_{m+1}. Neither can it come from the successor X_{m-1} (routing loop argument). Under assumption (6), the probability that a hunter H_1 meets our requirement I is thus $\Pr[\text{req I}] := (d_m - 2)/(d_m - 1) \cdot \Pr[X_m]$. Similarly, the probability that a hunter H_2 meets our requirement II is $\Pr[\text{req II}] := (d_{m-1} - 2)/(d_{m-1} - 1) \cdot \Pr[X_{m-1}]$.

As the placement of n hunters can be viewed as a Bernoulli trial, the probability that the traffic of at least one of n hunters satisfies requirement II is $1 - (1 - \Pr[\text{req II}])^n$, and the probability that at least one of the remaining $(n-1)$ hunters satisfies requirement I is $1 - (1 - \Pr[\text{req I}])^{n-1}$. Hence the probability that both requirements are satisfied and that the attacker can be located at node X_m is $\Pr[\text{locate}(X_m)] := 1 - (1 - \Pr[\text{req II}])^n \cdot 1 - (1 - \Pr[\text{req I}])^n$. If we allow a defined uncertainty of M's position, we have to consider cases where H_1's and H_2's traffic flows separate one or two hops further towards C or V.

Arbitrary positions of C, V and M. In reality, the hop distance ℓ between C and V is not fixed but can be seen as a discrete random variable that, on a realistic router-level graph, can assume integer values between 2 and about 30 (for AS graphs, this number is naturally smaller). Note that ℓ has not played a role in our calculations so far, as our probability is only affected by m, i.e., the number of hops between attacker and victim server. We can calculate an aggregate detection probability for the attacker by summing over all possible values of ℓ, and summing over all possible locations m of the attacker. Our final closed-form model is thus:

$$\Pr[\text{locate}] := \sum_{k=1}^{max\ path\ length} \left(\Pr[\ell = k] \cdot \sum_{m=1}^{k} \Pr[\text{locate}(X_m)] \right) \qquad (1)$$

Topological data for the closed-form model. To fill in the necessary distributions for the number of hops ℓ and the node degrees d_j, we collected data on both IP router as well as AS topologies. Rocketfuel [20] provides router-level maps gained from sophisticated measurements. As networks mainly change in size but not significantly in fundamental structure, we conjecture that these somewhat dated maps are still usable for our application. Since they do not reveal the positions of clients or servers, we only calculated an average degree $\bar{d}$ and use $d_j = \bar{d}$ in our model. Across all Rocketfuel topologies, the average degree is 3.98. We obtained the typical number of IP hops by issuing traceroutes from our university network to about 30,000 randomly chosen hosts from the Alexa list [21] of the top 1 million most popular Web sites. The distribution of the path lengths (range 5–28, mean 15.28, median 15 hops) loosely resembles a bell curve, suggesting that data collected from other vantage points will not be fundamentally different.

For constructing a (partial) AS graph, we used the RouteViews archive [14] and combined the 07/07/2011, 12:00h MRT-formatted full-table RIBs from Oregon IX, Equinix Ashburn, ISC/PAIX, KIXP, LINX, DIXIE/WIDE, RouteViews-4, Sydney, and São Paulo. From this graph, we determined an average degree of 3.51, as well as the distribution of path lengths (range 1–17, mean 3.25, median 3 hops). Again, the data does not reveal locations of clients and servers, so these calculations have to be taken with a grain of salt.

Results using the model. Fig. 6 summarises the information we can gain from our model. The model suggests that we only need a very small number of hunters to localise the AS in which an attacker resides (dash-dotted line). With as little as 100 hunters randomly distributed across the Internet, chances to pinpoint the attacker to an AS approach 100 %. At the router level, however, the picture looks different. The model suggests that just 10 hunters are needed to pinpoint the attacker to a single router (solid line) or to a set of two (dashed line) or

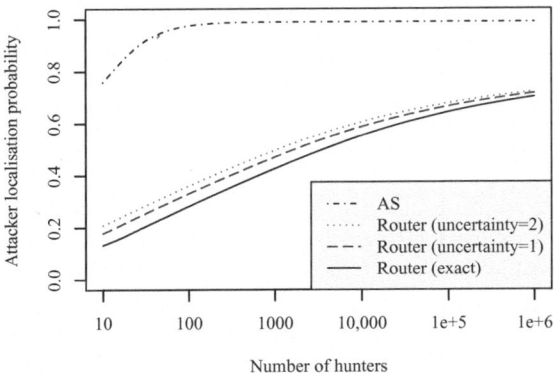

Fig. 6. Estimating the number of hunters required to pinpoint an attacker

three routers (dotted line) on the path to the attacked server with a probability between 10 % and 20 %. This probability rises to roughly 50 % if about 5,000 hunters can be employed. However, even with one million hunters, we only have about a 70 % chance to pinpoint a malicious router. Our conclusion here is that Crossbear works well in tracing an attacking AS, but much less so in tracing the exact router. However, this is quite acceptable: Crossbear works well against our state-level attacker from Fig. 4b. As for the attacker on the wireless access point (Fig. 4a), successful localisation needs exact placement of hunters in the same ISP network anyway, rather than a large global number of hunters.

The Challenge of Selective Attackers. Selective attackers can neither be localised directly nor on-the-fly. Indeed, the possibility of selective attackers requires that every reported attack is carefully analysed manually.

Consider Fig. 4c and 4d: no hunter, not even downstream, experiences the attack. As far as tracerouting is concerned, these attackers become indistinguishable from the one in Fig. 4a. A major challenge thus lies in telling them apart. However, the attacker may still leave clues that, using the out-of-band information described in Section 3.1, point to the nature of the attack.

Assume that we are in possession of traceroutes from all clients that are affected by the MitM. Ideally, we also have traceroutes from seemingly non-affected hunters in the same AS, and ASes in the same country, and ASes that are attached to an AS that is further upstream. Recall that the attacker cannot deliberately forge traceroutes as the PublicIPNotification mechanism forces him to be able to intercept replies to his IP address. Thus, he can only choose his source IP from the system he controls or one that is attached to it. Also recall that a traceroute can be tested for plausibility to some degree with available BGP data (e.g., [14]). The hints we are looking for are poisoned routes from different stub ASes, i.e., ASes on the network periphery. If we find such routes in our data, we can conjecture that the MitM is located either where traffic from these AS converges (the earliest possible location), or further upstream. The only plausible alternative would be to assume simultaneous attackers against multiple AS. This is possible, but one way to tell them apart is to investigate if the forged certificates share properties (like issuer, key lengths, X.509v3 extensions). If they do, this points to a common rule set for creation, thus two separate MitM attacks are less likely. The next step to execute is now to look up the AS and countries of all hops in the traceroutes. A hint that a selective state-level attacker is indeed at work is then if we find that the source IPs in the traceroutes belong to an AS/country which we associate with radical monitoring of their own population. If the earliest possible location is in that country, that is another hint.

If we do not find anything of the kind, however, our chances become slimmer. One pattern that is still worthwhile to look for is the one that the selective super-attacker in the core of the network (Fig. 4d) should show. If the purpose of the attacker is indeed industrial espionage, one may expect that the MitM reports and traceroutes are primarily from companies within a select few countries.

Naturally, all of the above is a mere test of plausibility, and we acknowledge that the proposed methods require (comparatively) intensive manual labour. However, we wish to point out that until now the research community has practically no data at all about MitM attacks occuring in the wild. Any report providing such data will advance current research. The MitM attack in [3], for example, became known thanks to external reports and because someone made the effort to try and inform the outside world. Receiving automated reports is thus useful even where automatic localisation is not possible. This is why we advertise Crossbear as a tool to record as much data as possible about attacks, but not as a silver bullet in exposing attackers.

4.4   Attacks against Crossbear

Due to Crossbear's open nature, there are several options for particularly aggressive attackers. Many of these cannot be entirely avoided and have to be dealt with in a reactive way.

Hunters do not need to register nor do they have IDs. This was a conscious choice to encourage user participation. As is true for all such systems, however, one consequence is that attackers can freely send forged data to the Crossbear server. Such injections are particularly hard to detect if the attacker employs 'malicious hunters'. Here, the attacker first drops the connections of all honest hunters in the system he controls or that are attached to it (note that this may lead to out-of-band reports). Then, his malicious hunters send forged reports stating that the connection via the attacker is fine and no MitM is detected. The Crossbear server will thus have received only one report of a possible MitM (from the client victim) and a large number of forged reports. The only defence that Crossbear has here is that the attacker's source IP is ascertained. As long as the attacker is not in the core of the network, this will result in a suspicious cluster of reports from the same AS or country. The attacker can again offset this by renting and using other computers, e.g., in the cloud. This might be revealed by implausible traceroutes, but blacklisting such attackers becomes much harder (and effectively an arms race).

The Crossbear server is a single point of failure. The usual (pro-active and reactive) DoS defences on the IP level can be taken. However, attackers can inflict more serious damage with the above attack or by, e.g., flooding the server with alleged MitM reports (which lead to hunting processes being initiated). These attacks can only be detected by continuously monitoring requests and reports, with special focus on reports from recurring systems or countries.

5 Conclusion

We have described how our tool, Crossbear, can be employed to detect and localise MitM attacks on SSL/TLS, and we have analysed against which attacker types it is particularly effective.

Crossbear can reliably detect and report MitM attacks by most attacker types. Crossbear's effectivity in localising the attacker's position in the network depends strongly on the kind of attacker it faces. Best results can be expected against an attacker who stages a non-selective MitM attack, like attackers close to the victim client or state-level attackers monitoring all SSL/TLS traffic to some WWW servers. Selective attackers cannot be accurately localised. However, they do leave hints in the reported data that a careful analysis can use to reveal or assess the nature of the attack. We have also analysed active measures that an attacker can take against Crossbear. Like all open systems, Crossbear shows a certain vulnerability here. However, such counter attacks leave hints, too.

We thus advertise Crossbear as a tool to make a step forward in the reporting and possibly also in the localisation of MitM attacks in the wild, but we expressively do not market it as a silver bullet to expose all kinds of attackers. We wish to invite the research community to participate. Naturally, our data will be shared.

Acknowledgments. We wish to thank Christian Grothoff and Johann Schlamp for their valuable input. We also wish to thank OONI, and in particular Jacob Appelbaum, for their offer to accept Crossbear as a module.

References

1. Mozilla Security Blog: DigiNotar removal follow up (2011), `https://blog.mozilla.com/security/2011/09/02/diginotar-removal-follow-up/` (last retrieved in April 2012)
2. Engert, K.: Man-In-The-Middle experience in Warsaw. Blog entry (June 2011), `https://kuix.de/blog/comments.php?y=11&m=06&entry=entry110616-171707` (last retrieved in April 2012)
3. Eckersley, P.: A Syrian man-in-the-middle attack against Facebook (May 2011), `https://www.eff.org/deeplinks/2011/05/syrian-man-middle-against-facebook` (last retrieved in April 2012)
4. Borhani, A.: Is This MITM Attack to Gmail's SSL? Forum post (August 2011), `https://www.google.com/support/forum/p/gmail/thread?tid=2da6158b094b225a&hl=en` (last retrieved in April 2012)

5. Vratonjic, N., Freudiger, J., Bindschaedler, V., Hubaux, J.P.: The inconvenient truth about Web certificates. In: 10th Workshop on Economics of Information Security, WEIS 2011 (June 2011)
6. Holz, R., Braun, L., Kammenhuber, N., Carle, G.: The SSL landscape – a thorough analysis of the X.509 PKI using active and passive measurements. In: Proc. 11th Annual Internet Measurement Conference (IMC 2011), Berlin, Germany. ACM, Sheridan (2011)
7. Eckersley, P., Burns, J.: Burns: Is the SSLiverse a safe place? Talk at 27C3 (2010), https://www.eff.org/files/ccc2010.pdf (last retrieved in April 2012)
8. Sunshine, J., Egelman, S., Almuhimedi, H., Atri, N., Cranor, L.F.: Crying wolf: an empirical study of SSL warning effectiveness. In: Proc. 18th USENIX Security Symposium, pp. 399–416 (2009)
9. Soghoian, C., Stamm, S.: Certified Lies: Detecting and Defeating Government Interception Attacks against SSL (Short Paper). In: Danezis, G. (ed.) FC 2011. LNCS, vol. 7035, pp. 250–259. Springer, Heidelberg (2012)
10. Electronic Frontier Foundation: The Sovereign Keys project (2011), https://www.eff.org/sovereign-keys (last retrieved in April 2012)
11. Laurie, B., Langley, A.: Certificate transparency (2012), http://www.certificate-transparency.org/ (last retrieved in April 2012)
12. Wendlandt, D., Andersen, D.G., Perrig, A.: Perspectives: Improving SSH-style host authentication with multi-path probing. In: Proc. USENIX 2008 Ann. Techn. Conf. (ATC) (2008)
13. Thoughtcrime Labs/IDS: Convergence (2011), http://convergence.io (last retrieved in April 2012)
14. Advanced Network Technology Center, University of Oregon: Route views project (2012), http://www.routeviews.org/ (last retrieved in April 2012)
15. Riedmaier, T., Holz, R.: Crossbear repository, https://github.com/crossbear/Crossbear (last retrieved in April 2012)
16. Filastò, A., Appelbaum, J.: OONI: Open observatory of network interference. In: Proc. 2nd USENIX Workshop on Free and Open Communications on the Internet (FOCI 2012) (August 2012)
17. Teixeira, R., Shaikh, A., Griffin, T., Rexford, J.: Dynamics of hot-potato routing in IP networks. In: Proc. Joint Int. Conf. on Measurement and Modeling of Computer Systems (SIGMETRICS), pp. 307–319. ACM, New York (2004)
18. Qiu, S., McDaniel, P., Monrose, F.: Toward valley-free inter-domain routing. In: Proc. IEEE Int. Conf. on Communications (ICC), pp. 2009–2016 (June 2007)
19. Hepner, C., Zmijewski, E.: Defending against BGP man-in-the-middle attacks. Talk at BlackHat (2009), https://www.renesys.com/tech/presentations/pdf/blackhat-09.pdf (last retrieved in April 2012)
20. Spring, N., Mahajan, R., Wetherall, D.: Measuring ISP topologies with Rocketfuel. In: Proc. ACM SIGCOMM, pp. 133–145. ACM, Pittsburgh (2002)
21. Alexa Internet Inc.: Top 1,000,000 sites (updated daily) (2009-2011), http://s3.amazonaws.com/alexa-static/top-1m.csv.zip (last retrieved in April 2012)

A Practical Man-In-The-Middle Attack on Signal-Based Key Generation Protocols

Simon Eberz[1], Martin Strohmeier[2], Matthias Wilhelm[1], and Ivan Martinovic[2]

[1] University of Kaiserslautern, Germany
[2] University of Oxford, UK

Abstract. Generating secret keys using physical properties of the wireless channel has recently become a popular research area. The main security assumption of these protocols is that a sufficiently distant adversary is unable to guess a generated secret due to the unpredictable behavior of multipath signal propagation. In this paper, we introduce a practical and efficient man-in-the-middle attack against such protocols. Using this attack, we demonstrate: (i) intentional sabotaging of key generation schemes, which leads to a high key disagreement rate, and (ii) a key recovery that reveals up to 47 % of the generated secret bits. We analyze statistical countermeasures (often proposed in related work) and show that attempting to detect such attacks results in a high false positive rate, questioning the overall benefit of such schemes. We implement and experimentally validate the attacks using off-the-shelf hardware, without assuming any technological advantage for the adversary.

1 Introduction

Communications over the wireless channel are affected by physical wave phenomena such as reflection, diffraction, or scattering, which contribute to a complex multipath behavior of transmitted signals. The measured channel response at the receiver is therefore considered a frequency- and position-dependent random variable that carries a certain amount of information entropy and can serve as a source of randomness. An additional physical property exploited in key generation protocols is channel reciprocity. If the channel response between the two transmitters, Alice and Bob, is sampled over a short time interval (depending on mobility patterns and the transmission frequency), both transmitters generate highly correlated estimates. Since sampling the wireless channel response is inherently given during any wireless message exchange, this approach offers an interesting alternative method to generate symmetric secret keys without relying on asymmetric cryptography. One of the main assumptions is that an eavesdropper (Eve) is unable to guess the generated bits because her view of the channel between Alice and Bob de-correlates rapidly with distance and thus results in inaccurate estimates. Concretely, it is assumed that if Eve is positioned at least half a wavelength λ away from Alice and Bob, then her estimates are de-correlated from those computed by Alice and Bob (for more information, see, e.g. [1]). Similarly, if an active attacker (Mallory) attempts to inject packets into

S. Foresti, M. Yung, and F. Martinelli (Eds.): ESORICS 2012, LNCS 7459, pp. 235–252, 2012.

the channel during key generation, he is unable to control how his signal is received at both sides, which results in a key disagreement. In case of the 2.4 GHz ISM frequency band, $\lambda/2$ is approximately 6.25 cm, which makes physical key generation attractive for WLAN and wireless sensor network applications.

The variety of existing protocols signify the importance of understanding the overall security of signal-based key generation schemes under a realistic adversarial setting. In this work, we assume an active attacker without additional knowledge or technological advantage. His only "toolbox" is the broadcast nature of the wireless channel that allows him to eavesdrop and inject packets at will. The main goal of a MITM attacker is to reveal the secret key generated by Alice and Bob. This is done by injecting his own information during the channel response estimation, which is subsequently used by Alice and Bob as part of their secret key. To avoid key disagreements that may lead to attack detection, he waits for *injection opportunities* that help him to keep the key generation protocol intact and still succeed. We also show that the attacker has an efficient way of forcing Alice and Bob to re-run the key generation protocol in case the number of opportunities for key recovery is too small, or simply to launch a DoS attack (we refer to this as *sabotaging attack*). To quantify the impact of these opportunities, we introduce the *attack efficiency* and *key recovery rate* metrics. As the goal of this work is to offer practical insights, we implement the key generation protocol by Mathur et al. [1] and evaluate our attack against it. Finally, we discuss countermeasures and show that an attempt to statistically detect our attack results in a high false positive rate, i.e., it leads to the rejection of a large number of legitimate packets required by the key generation protocol. Since Alice and Bob cannot be sure how many of Mallory's bits were successfully injected (in our experiments we were successful in revealing up to 47.4 % of the key) and this may be improved further by using better radio hardware, they are left without any reliable method on estimating the correct length of the secret, which questions the general applicability of such protocols.

1.1   Signal-Based Key Generation Protocols

In this subsection, we provide a bird's-eye view on physical key generation schemes (see [2,3] for detailed overviews). The three general phases that are shared by most signal-based key generation protocols are (see Fig. 1a):

Quantization Phase: Alice and Bob create a time series of the wireless channel response by exchanging packets and measuring channel properties. Examples for such properties are the received signal strength indicator (RSSI) and the channel impulse response (CIR). RSSI is often preferred because of its simplicity (it can easily be measured on a per-packet basis with off-the-shelf hardware). To create the initial secret bitstream, the series needs to be quantized by both nodes, i.e., the measurements need to be mapped to symbols. This requires calculating thresholds using a single threshold/multi-threshold approach or dynamic threshold schemes (for more details, see Section 6). Fig. 1b shows how measurements can be converted into bits by using two thresholds.

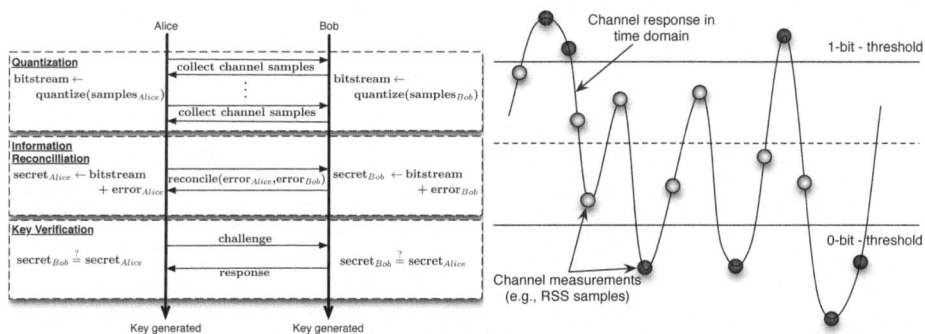

(a) Timing diagram, illustrating the commu-(b) A sample quantizer. All measure-
nication between Alice and Bob, and process-ments above the 1-bit threshold and being steps during the protocol phases.   low the 0-bit threshold are converted into
bits, resulting in a 1100100 bit sequence.

Fig. 1. A general overview of the signal-based key generation

Information Reconciliation Phase: After quantization, the generated sequences at Alice's and Bob's side are likely to disagree because of noise and
radio hardware artifacts. Both then apply information reconciliation methods
to identify and correct such errors. Error correcting codes are one possibility to
achieve this [4]; alternatively, many protocols use an interactive approach and
reveal some information about their errors to reconcile their shared secret. If
both nodes fail to agree on a common key, the samples are discarded and the
protocol needs to be re-run. Some protocols also try to de-correlate their bitstream by using hash functions to extract randomness from the given imperfect
input sequence [5], the so-called privacy amplification [6].

Key Verification Phase: Finally, both parties need to cryptographically verify
the mutual secret. Usually this is done using a simple challenge-response protocol. An unsuccessful response constitutes a key disagreement and the process
starts from the beginning. If protocols use dynamic thresholds, the quantization phase can be adapted by decreasing the number of possible thresholds,
i.e., adapting a tradeoff between secrecy (the key length) and a successful key
agreement rate.

2   General Idea of the Man-In-The-Middle Attack

The general idea of our attack is to "poison" the quantization phase between Alice
and Bob. An active attacker attempts to impersonate both participants and to
inject spoofed packets during the quantization phase, which are subsequently
used in the key generation. In the best case, Alice and Bob agree on a common
key of that Mallory knows a (preferably large) part.

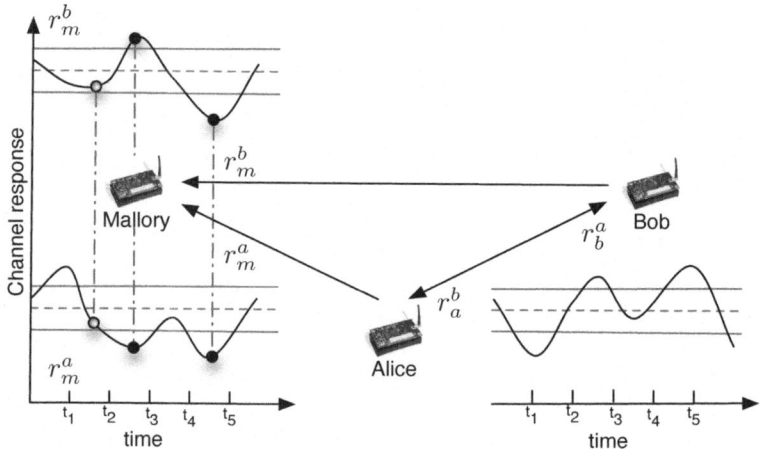

Fig. 2. Overview of the attack principle. Three different cases are depicted from Mallory's view of r_m^a and r_m^b: Case 1 in interval $[t_1 - t_2]$ is discarded as it lies within the thresholds. Case 2 in interval $[t_2 - t_3]$ is a sabotaging opportunity. Case 3 in interval $[t_4 - t_5]$ provides a key recovery opportunity.

2.1 Assumptions

We make the following assumptions about the attacker and the environment:

- The attacker adheres to all given security constraints and assumptions of physical key generation schemes. Specifically, he is not violating any constraints on the physical distance, such as being near legitimate transmitters.
- The attacker is always in transmission range of both Alice and Bob.
- The attacker is able to freely control his own transmission power up to a given (common) hardware limitation.
- The attacker is able to destroy legitimate packets sent by Alice and Bob when required, e.g., by employing reactive jamming as described in [7].

2.2 Injection Opportunities for Sabotage and Key Recovery Attacks

There is a number of challenges when injecting packets during the quantization phase. A naive attacker may send spoofed packets purely at random; however, he would not know how they are received. In consequence, this attack is futile and likely leads to a key disagreement because Alice's estimate of the injected packets differs greatly from Bob's. On the other hand, if the attacker constantly sends with a strong signal to superimpose Alice's and Bob's communication, he might be able to inject some packets but risks easy detection by statistical countermeasures. This means that we need a more sensitive approach to enable efficient control over the outcomes of our injected packets. The key idea of our attack is to find *opportunities* where we exploit the reciprocity of the channel in the same way as Alice and Bob use it to generate the correlated estimates.

We use a notation similar to [1]: r_x^y denotes the channel response received by node x from a probe signal sent by node y. The channel responses of two subsequent probes between Alice and Bob are thus defined as

$$r_a^b = s \cdot h + n_a$$
$$r_b^a = s \cdot h + n_b \tag{1}$$

with s being the probe signal, n_x the independent noise process at node x and h a stochastic process describing the wireless channel between Alice and Bob. Furthermore, Mallory's overheard signals are

$$r_m^b = s \cdot h_{bm} + n_m$$
$$r_m^a = s \cdot h_{am} + n_m \tag{2}$$

with h_{xm} denoting the channel between node x and Mallory. If Mallory is more than $\lambda/2$ away from Alice and Bob, h_{am} and h_{bm} are assumed to be uncorrelated with h.

However, while Mallory does not know *how* exactly his packet is received by Alice or Bob, he does know that the differential in the channel response is correlated. Hence, injected packets received by Alice or Bob preserve this differential. Assuming that n_m is similar and thus negligible at two subsequent measurements, the scenario in Fig. 2 shows two useful cases for Mallory's injections:

1. $r_m^b \ggg r_m^a$ (or vice versa): Mallory measures a large differential as seen in interval $[t_2 - t_3]$. Due to the channel reciprocity, it follows that for a spoofed answer by Mallory the responses are $r_b^m \ggg r_a^m$. Knowing that an injected packet will cause a highly differential channel response at both Alice and Bob, this constitutes an opportunity to produce highly differential estimates for Alice and Bob in the quantization phase ($\rightarrow$ sabotage attack).
2. $r_m^b \approx r_m^a$: Mallory measures a small differential as seen in interval $[t_4 - t_5]$. Here, it follows that for a spoofed answer by Mallory the responses are $r_b^m \approx r_a^m$. Knowing that an injected packet causes a similar channel response at both Alice and Bob, this constitutes an opportunity to generate similar values for Alice and Bob in the quantization phase ($\rightarrow$ key recovery attack).

2.3   Measuring the Success of MITM Attacks

We define several metrics for the two attacks to quantify the success of this approach in attacking physical key-generation protocols:

Sabotage Attack

1. *Attack interval*: Defines how many probes made by Alice and Bob are sampled on average until a single disagreement bit can be injected. The ratio reflects the time to find opportunities and have a successful spoof showing up in the quantized bits. Obviously, the faster the attack is done, the better.
2. *Required spoof attempts*: This ratio measures how many spoof attempts are necessary to cause a single disagreement bit. Fewer attempts mean a reduced chance of detection for the attacker, thus it should be as low as possible.

Table 1. A summary of the notation used

Symbol	Meaning
$d/d_{\max}$	(Max.) Perceived RSSI difference by the attacker
q_+/q_-	High/low threshold for excursions
$L/\tilde{L}$	Messages exchanged for information reconciliation
α	Parameter needed for threshold calculation
m	Number of packets above/below threshold needed for excursion
h_u	Vector of channel estimates of node u
σ	Standard deviation of RSSI

Key Recovery Attack

1. *Key recovery rate*: The success of the key recovery attack is measured by the number of bits of a secret key that are guessed by Mallory. Importantly, this measure is sensitive to wrong guesses as they rapidly increase the search space (i.e. the duration of the brute-force attacks)[1].
2. *Key recovery efficiency*: Defined as the percentage of spoofing attempts that are successfully injected and form a bit in the key. As the detection probability increases with the attacker's activity, a high efficiency is preferable.

3 Attacking a Concrete Key Generation Protocol

To illustrate the effectiveness of our attack concept in the real world, we apply it in a practical scenario. We consider the protocol described by Mathur et al. [1], the best representative, and implement it on standard off-the-shelf MicaZ hardware.

The measured wireless channel characteristic r of this protocol is the received signal strength indicator (RSSI), taken on a per-packet basis. The quantization phase consists of three separate steps: probing, quantization, and subsequent bit conversion. First, Alice sends a probe to Bob, who then responds with a probe of his own. These exchanges use a pre-defined frequency of 20 Hz (i.e., a 50 ms gap between probes). Both parties save the (highly correlated) received signal strength of the packets. This process is repeated n times, depending on the desired key length. When the probing completes, both Alice and Bob have obtained n estimates of the channel, which are saved as vectors h_a and h_b, respectively. They now independently calculate the thresholds $q_+^u = \text{mean}(h_u) + \alpha \cdot \sigma(h_u)$ and $q_-^u = \text{mean}(h_u) - \alpha \cdot \sigma(h_u)$, where α is a protocol parameter (0.5 in this case) and $\sigma(h_u)$ denotes the standard deviation of h_u. The results are quantized as follows:

$$Q(x) = \begin{cases} 0 & \text{if } x < q_- \\ 1 & \text{if } x > q_+ \end{cases}$$

---

[1] A bit-string of length ℓ with i errors results in an additional brute-force factor of $\sum_{i=1}^{\ell} \binom{\ell}{i}$.

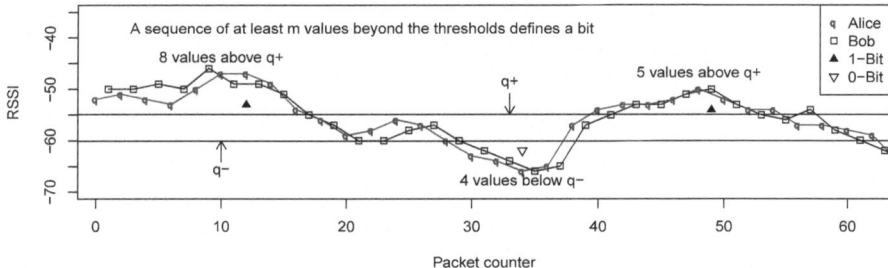

Fig. 3. Illustration of the bit generation process in our implementation of [1], with an excursion being quantized with 4 or more subsequent packets over threshold q_+ or below threshold q_-

Alice and Bob then parse their measurements to find so-called *excursions*, i.e., m or more consecutive values in h_u that lie above q_+ or below q_- (where $m = 4$ is again a protocol parameter). An excursion above q_+ is converted to a 1-bit, while an excursion below q_- denotes a 0-bit. To reconcile the information, Alice sends a list of k excursions in the form of array indexes $L = \ell_1, \ell_2, \ldots, \ell_k$ to Bob. Bob checks if his measurements h_b contain excursions of length $\geq m-1$ at the locations specified in L. Subsequently, he sends back a list $\widetilde{L}$ that contains the indexes matching with excursions on his side. Excursions in L but not in $\widetilde{L}$ are dropped by both parties. After exchanging the L-messages, the quantizer function is applied to all elements defined by the indexes in $\widetilde{L}$ to form the bit string. Fig. 3 illustrates the process for our choice of $m = 4$. Alice and Bob should now have agreed on an identical key. A disagreement can only occur if m consecutive values lie above q_+ in h_a and below q_- at the same index in h_b or vice-versa. When this is noticed during key verification, the batch of bits is discarded and the protocol is restarted.

3.1   Implementation of the MITM Attacks

The experimental setup consists of two mobile motes (Alice and Bob) and one stationary attacker, Mallory. In our scenario, the two legitimate nodes and the attacker are in the same room. The distance between Alice/Bob and Mallory is always greater than 15 cm, as required by the security assumptions. Alice and Bob are moved independently within the room to create the necessary uncorrelated measurements. While this scenario does not make unreasonable assumptions, the attacker might not be able to be in the same room. Thus, in a second scenario with Mallory in a different room, we analyze whether the attack still yields satisfying results under these more difficult circumstances.

Detecting Attack Opportunities. The key parameter defining opportunities is the maximum RSSI difference $d_{\max}$ between probes. It is intuitive that the number of spoofing attempts increases when $d_{\max}$ is increased. After the probing phase, Mallory creates two arrays h_a and h_b, containing his own view of the two

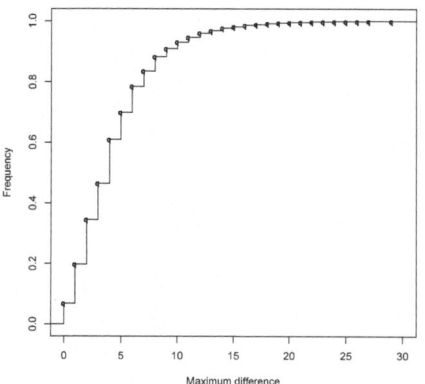
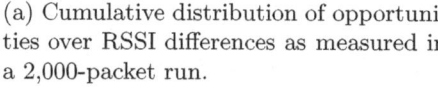
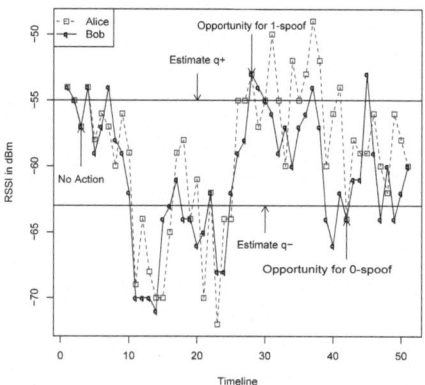

(a) Cumulative distribution of opportunities over RSSI differences as measured in a 2,000-packet run.

(b) Examples of key recovery opportunities as seen by the attacker. An opportunity is found when Alice and Bob's RSSI values are similar and exceed a threshold.

Fig. 4. Injection opportunities

independent channels between him and Alice/Bob, as illustrated in Fig. 4b. The difference d_i at packet counter i is computed as $d_i = |h_a[i] - h_b[i]|$. The optimal opportunity is at $d_i = 0$, but larger values of d are also suitable for the attack because only differences $d \geq \sigma(h_u)$ typically lead to a key disagreement. The results are summarized in Table 2 and Fig. 4a, showing that opportunities occur reasonably often. The number of excursions for the attack is sufficiently high as well, even if there are only a few of length $m \geq 4$ with $d = 0$. This does not constitute a problem, although it might reduce the attack's effectiveness.

Thresholds and Their Estimation. Besides finding the perfect attack timing, one needs to estimate values for q_+ and q_-. Exact knowledge of both thresholds is not necessary; if a packet is part of an excursion, the attacker knows that it lies either above q_+ or below q_-. Fig. 5 illustrates this: an estimated threshold only causes a wrong guess if the assumed value of q_+ lies below the actual value of q_- (or vice-versa). With $\alpha = 0.5$, the difference between q_+ and q_- equals the standard deviation σ. Accordingly, any mistake in deriving both thresholds smaller than this standard deviation might result in fewer recovered bits, but does not lead to bit errors. To reduce the probability of a bit error and to increase the attack's robustness, a security margin is added to the estimated thresholds.

One method to estimate thresholds is scenario-based guessing, relying on the fact that average RSSI and standard deviation change only slightly between independent protocol runs. Such data can be collected for several scenarios and used as reference for an attack. While this method has proven useful in our experiments, it may not be possible to find thresholds suitable for any setup,

Table 2. Number of opportunities in 8,000 packets and resulting excursions in our implementation of [1] (left). Real (q_+^A) and derived (q_+^M) thresholds (right).

d	Opportunities	Excursions	Run Nr.	q_+^A	q_+^M	$\left| q_+^A - q_+^M \right|$	σ
0	542 (6.8%)	15	1	−52.7	−51	1.7	7.4
1	1030 (12.9%)	77	2	−49.5	−49	0.5	6.5
2	1187 (14.8%)	132	3	−51.3	−50	1.3	8.2
3	955 (11.9%)	182	4	−53.1	−52	1.1	7.7

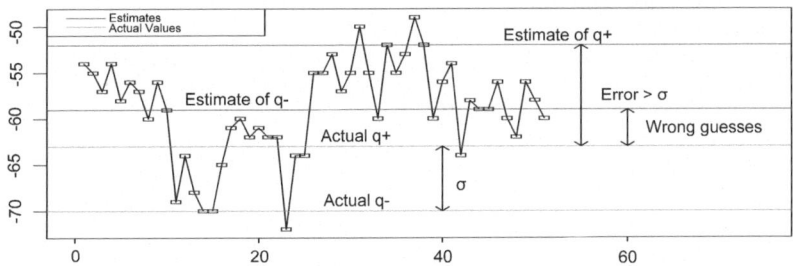

Fig. 5. Effects of inaccurate thresholds. Only the area between the actual q_+ threshold and the estimated q_- threshold is susceptible to wrong bit guesses.

rendering it unpractical. Another possibility is to manipulate the setup phase of a protocol run. Algorithm 1 exploits the information about excursions that an attacker gains from the L-messages. Mallory waits for opportunities and sends spoofed messages without taking the thresholds into consideration. Afterwards, he checks the L-messages to find his own probes. If the number of spoof attempts was statistically significant then the thresholds should be well reflected in the attacker's spoof trace.

Table 2 shows that this approach yields very accurate approximations of q_+, the error $\left| q_+^A - q_+^M \right|$ being considerably lower than σ. However, deriving q_- failed, as too few successful spoofs were detected in the lower RSSI-spectrum. One possibility to deal with this is to ignore the negative threshold and to only use q_+ to detect 1-bits, which slightly reduces the overall key recovery rate. Another method is to simply define a sufficiently large distance x between q_+ and q_- and setting $q_- = q_+ - x$. As explained above, if this distance is greater than the standard deviation σ, this does not lead to bit errors. Considering the values of σ, $x = 10$ is a conservative assumption.

3.2   Sabotaging Attack

In the protocol of Mathur et al., a key disagreement occurs only if m or more packets are received with a difference in signal strength greater than the standard deviation σ. Thus, to deliberately cause a bit error, an attacker sends packets when the difference between the RSSI of the last packets *exceeds* a pre-defined

Algorithm 1. Estimation of thresholds in the setup phase

1: **Input** : $d_{\max}$
2: **Output** : Estimates of q_+ and q_-
3: **while** $i < n$ **do**
4:     Receive packets i_{Alice}, i_{Bob}
5:     **if** ($|\text{RSSI}_{\text{Alice}} - \text{RSSI}_{\text{Bob}}| \leq d_{\max}$ **then**
6:         Send $m + 2$ spoofed probes to Alice and Bob
7:         $spoofs$.add(i, $\text{RSSI}_{\text{Alice}}$)
8:     **end if**
9: **end while**
10: Receive $\widetilde{L}$ from Bob
11: Sort $spoofs$ descending by RSSI
12: $l := spoofs$.length
13: Check for longest sequence S in $spoofs[0, \ldots, \ell/2]$ with $a \in \widetilde{L} \; \forall a \in S$
14: $q_+ = \min(S)$
15: Check for longest sequence S in $spoofs[\ell/2 + 1, \ldots, \ell]$ with $a \in \widetilde{L} \; \forall a \in S$ and $|S| > 3$
16: $q_- = \max(S)$
17: **if** $q_- = $ null **then**
18:     $q_- := q_+ - x$
19: **end if**
20: **Return** q_+, q_-

threshold $d_{\max}$. As no quantization is needed on the attacker's side, knowing the values for q_+ and q_- is not crucial, although they can help making the attack more precise by reducing the number of necessary packets. In our first implementation, the attacker simply waits until he receives two consecutive packets with a greatly differing RSSI and starts injecting packets. A single bit error is generally enough to force a complete restart of the protocol because no additional error correction schemes are implemented and the location of the error is unknown. In a further refined version, we altered the attacker's own sending strength to make the attack more efficient: every packet sent to the node with the higher RSSI uses the maximum sending strength; packets to the other node are sent with a significantly lower power while still allowing for the correct reception of the packet. This power adaptation ensures a greater difference in the reception of the packets and is more likely to create a disagreement excursion.

3.3   Key Recovery Attack

The attacker monitors the wireless channel and scans the received data for key recovery opportunities. If one is found, he starts to inject messages. To ensure an excursion, Mallory sends $m + 2$ unicast probes to both Alice and Bob. At the same time, Mallory stores whether the opportunity was triggered by a high or low RSSI value to determine the bit afterwards. Algorithm 2 describes this in more detail.

In addition to sending spoofed messages, the attack requires to destroy the legitimate packets sent by Alice and Bob. To simulate such a jamming effect, upon receiving a spoofed probe, the motes voluntarily cease their transmission

Algorithm 2. Key recovery attack

1: **Input** : Estimates of q_+ and q_- from Algorithm 1, d_{max}
2: **Output** : Known part of secret key
3: **while** $i < n$ **do**
4:     Receive packets i_{Alice}, i_{Bob}
5:     **if** $(|RSSI_{Alice} - RSSI_{Bob}| \leq d_{max})$ & $(RSSI_{Alice} > q_+ \,|\, RSSI_{Alice} < q_-)$ **then**
6:         Send $m + 2$ spoofed probes to Alice and Bob
7:         $spoofs$.add$(i, RSSI_{Alice})$
8:     **end if**
9: **end while**
10: Receive $\widetilde{L}$ from Bob
11: **for all** j in $\widetilde{L}$ **do**
12:     **if** $\widetilde{L}[j] \in spoofs$ **then**
13:         $key[j] := $ quantize$(spoofs[j].rssi)$
14:     **end if**
15: **end for**
16: **Return** key

until the attack is over.[2] If the index of a spoofed packet appears in $\widetilde{L}$, the attacker can derive the RSSI of the packet from his own saved measurement and infer the resulting bit.

4 Results

4.1 Sabotaging Attack

For the sabotaging attack, we conducted 9 identical runs comprising 5,000 probes overall. The results in Table 3a show the efficiency of using a fixed transmission strength. While the success depends on the nodes' movement and the erratic nature of the wireless channel, we can assume with 95 % confidence that 142.37 probes are enough to cause one successful disagreement. Likewise, 7.17 spoofing attempts result in one disagreement. Assuming 2,000 probe messages are necessary to generate a key with reasonable length, this leaves roughly 93 % of the setup phase to recover the key while still ensuring a key disagreement with very high probability once the protocol run finishes.

Table 3b reflects the gain in efficiency when employing the adaptive sending power approach. In the previous version, 100 packets are not enough to achieve a reliable key disagreement; however, adjusting the sending strength raises the efficiency significantly. On average, the number of disagreements almost doubles for the same amount of probes or spoofing attempts. Again assuming a 2,000 packets run, the attacker now requires less than 4 % of the protocol's duration to sabotage the complete run with 95 % confidence. This comparatively small number of packets ensures that the distortion effect is kept minimal, preventing detection. In combination with the key recovery attack, the increasing efficiency enables the attacker to start sabotaging at a later point in the setup phase, thus generating more accurate thresholds.

[2] Recent work [7] shows that reactive jamming is successful at rates $> 99.9\%$.

246   S. Eberz et al.

Table 3. Results of the sabotaging attack with 95 % confidence intervals. Both metrics improve significantly when adjusting the attacker's sending strength.

(a) Constant sending strength.   (b) Adjusted sending strength.

	Attack interval	Required spoof attempts	Attack interval	Required spoof attempts
Mean	113.58	6.01	62.41	3.30
Variance	1403.25	2.30	333.25	0.61
Error	12.49	0.50	6.09	0.26
Upper limit	84.79	4.84	48.38	2.70
Lower limit	142.37	7.17	76.45	3.90

4.2 Key Recovery Attack

The results of the first scenario with all motes in the same room are documented in Table 4. Note that the threshold estimates are close to the actual values, which helps to mitigate bit errors. The most conservative setting $d = 0$ results in about 40 % of the key being revealed (assuming a length of 64 bit, this would speed up a brute force attack by factor 2^{23}) and indeed the highest key recovery efficiency. More than half of the sequences sent by the attacker cause an excursion with both Alice and Bob. Increasing the maximum difference to 1 reduced the efficiency below 50 %, but greatly increased the key recovery rate. Further increase of the tolerance level decreases the efficiency with no benefits to the percentage of the key known to the attacker. Another insight gained from the results is that the revealed bits are almost exclusively 1-bits. This can be explained by the fact that the difference in the reception of spoofed packets at Alice and Bob increases with the distance between Alice/Bob and the attacker. However, this is not a real issue if the overall number of bits is sufficient because the attacker is not interested in specific random keys.

The results of the second scenario with Mallory in a different room show that the attack performs better if the attacker is physically close to the conversation partners. Both key recovery rate and efficiency are about halved. The number of successfully created excursions above q_+ has decreased to near zero and most of the retrieved bits are 0-bits. This is intuitive because the attacker does not increase his sending strength enough to match the weakening caused by the wall. On the other hand, due to the weakened signal strength, the condition of receiving signals below q_- is fulfilled most of the time. This results in a rather poor key recovery efficiency. Yet, the attack is successful independent of the physical proximity of the attacker. The efficiency can easily be improved if the attacker is able to use superior antennas as well as to increase the sending strength without being limited by regulations or power consumption.

Table 4. Key recovery attack results for two scenarios and different d_{max}

	Same room			Different rooms		
d_{max}	0	1	2	0	1	2
q_+ (actual/assumed)	-57.4/-55	-54.2/-55	-53/-55	-53.8/-52	-53.2/-52	-53/-55
q_- (actual/assumed)	-65/-65	-62/-65	-62/-65	-61/-62	-61.3/-62	-62/-65
Spoof attempts	76	91	130	55	78	130
Bits recovered (0/1)	10/32	12/33	5/27	11/3	14/2	14/4
Resulting key length	108	95	84	64	69	71
Key rec. efficiency [%]	**55.3**	**49.5**	**24.6**	**25.5**	**20.5**	**13.8**
Key rec. rate [%]	**38.9**	**47.4**	**38.1**	**21.9**	**23.1**	**25.3**

5   Possible Countermeasures

There is one obvious countermeasure to spoofing attacks: Alice could recognize that Mallory is impersonating her when he is sending a packet that carries her own MAC address. Yet, the standard setting in most commercial wireless adapters is to discard such packets, not to forward them above the MAC layer. Furthermore, wireless network interfaces are typically not able to send while in monitor mode, rendering this approach impractical for most applications. The authors of [1] propose a scheme that generates radio fingerprints, which are then used to distinguish legitimate from spoofed packets [8]. Obviously, the attacker must not be present at this point of time, which is a strong assumption. Additionally, the fingerprint is bound to the receiver/transmitter pair as well as the environment where it was generated. This makes it impossible to pre-generate fingerprints in a safe environment. In this section, we look at defensive schemes that would allow Alice and Bob to generate identical keys despite Mallory's presence, while ensuring a high level of uncertainty for the attacker. To achieve this, they have to selectively remove a high percentage of Mallory's packets and keep the false positive rate as low as possible. In any case, such an approach would limit the secret key rate because the original messages cannot be recovered. Other countermeasures include the introduction of time into the given protocols. This opens additional statistical detection vectors but is likely to introduce new difficulties on its own and is not currently present in the discussed protocols.

Table 5. Effects of packet-based filtering for three selected thresholds

(a) Attacker involvement.

Threshold [dB]	Discarded spoofs	Discarded legit
10	216 (61.0 %)	522 (31.7 %)
15	126 (35.6 %)	216 (13.1 %)
20	54 (15.25 %)	78 (4.74 %)

(b) Standard run.

Threshold [dB]	Discards
10	564 (28.2 %)
15	150 (7.5 %)
20	36 (1.8 %)

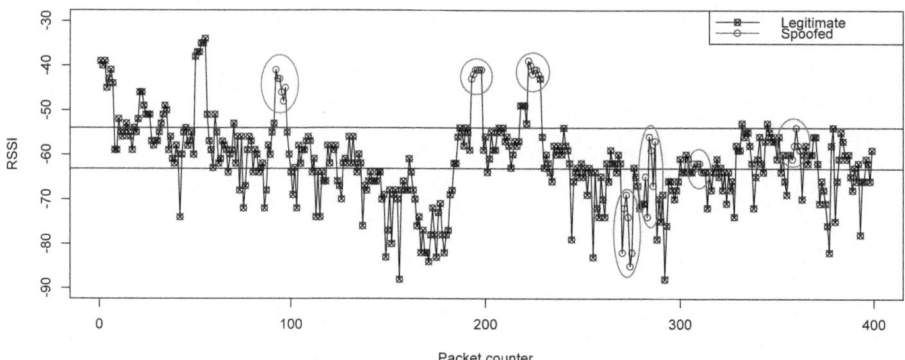

Fig. 6. Packet trace with spoofed and legitimate packets. While there are spoofs that seem like outliers at first, overall they are difficult to distinguish from a large number of legitimate packets with similar or even more extreme values.

5.1   Packet-Based Detection

One approach is to discard a packet when the RSSI value differs from the previous packet by more than a threshold t. However, the signal strength of the following packets in the spoof sequence is relatively consistent. So, when an attack is detected, Alice and Bob must not only discard the packet that caused the detection but also the following $m - 1$ packets (where m is the unknown number of packets sent per spoof attempt). Fig. 6 shows a pattern generated by the attacker's activity, illustrating how some of the spoofed packets might look suspicious. Yet, legitimate packets often follow similar patterns, making false positives likely. Table 5 lists the results of the filtering mechanism in a 2,000 packet run. With a strict threshold of 10 dB, the majority of spoofed packets (61 %) is rejected. However, a large part of the legitimate ones is filtered as well, leaving only 63 % of all packets for quantization. Raising the threshold to 15 dB, only one third of the injected packets is removed and the key length is reduced by 17 %. A threshold higher than 15 dB has negligible effects on both spoofed and legitimate packets. If the same filtering mechanism is used without the presence of an active attacker, the impact is smaller but a threshold of 10 dB still removes more than a quarter of legitimate packets in every run. Thus, to generate the same key length the number of packets must be increased by one third. That is, packet-based detection requires to prolong the run if suspicious packets were discarded. And because attacks are rare events it is not desirable to severely limit the average performance of the system.

5.2   Run-Based Detection

Another approach, conceptually close to [8], is to determine whether an attack occurred after a complete protocol run to potentially discard the run. There are several statistics that could be altered predictably by an attack, such as the variance of RSSI values. We also tested this method against our implementation.

Table 6. Percentage of packets over given distance from median RSSI

Min. difference from median	Standard [%]	Spoofed [%]	Standard (LOS Break) [%]
10	22.75	25.2	27.4
15	11.6	16.7	14.3
20	3.5	5.2	5.4
25	1.2	1.1	1.1

Table 6 summarizes the results for different scenarios and shows that reliably accepting the legitimate run also means not to detecting an attacker. Normal occurrences, such as breaks in the line-of-sight between Alice and Bob, render at least this simple implementation of the run-based detection unsuccessful. Even an imperfect reference value, causing few false positives, would require a large amount of training data because its variance strongly depends on the scenario.

6   Related Work

In 1993, Maurer introduced a concept that describes an abstract broadcast channel accessible to three parties. This channel provides strongly correlated information to two parties and weaker correlated information to the third party [9]. Consequently, even if an adversary is able to sample the same channel, secure keys can still be generated by the two legitimate participants.

With the widespread deployment of wireless networks, this idea was recently used to generate secret keys between two parties over a wireless channel by exploiting channel reciprocity (see Table 7 for an overview). In these protocols, several different sources of information are used; the most common one is the received signal strength indicator (RSSI) because it can be easily measured on a per-packet basis on off-the-shelf hardware. The RSSI method is used in several works [10,2,11,1]. While RSSI provides a convenient channel property, there are several others that were proposed as information sources, e.g., the channel impulse response (CIR) [12,1,13,14] that allows fine-grained measurements but requires specialized hardware, or the carrier phase [15]. Most of these protocols generate entropy by random device movements, although frequency-selective fading experienced through frequency hopping can also be used to generate secret keys in stationary scenarios [16].

While most protocols assume a passive attacker, the authors of [1,13] propose countermeasures against active attacks by employing radio fingerprinting [8]. However, despite the tremendous number of different protocols, there is little research on the attacker's side. A side-channel attack on signal-based key generation schemes by exploiting re-radiation is proposed in [20], which requires precise knowledge of the participants' positions. As this information is often hard to obtain and generally not considered public, the practical applicability can be difficult. Edman et al. [21] present a passive attack that puts the practical applicability of the theoretical foundations of signal-based key generation protocols in doubt, i.e., the assumption that the RSSI is uncorrelated at distances

Table 7. Overview of recent physical key generation schemes

Channel property[a]	RSSI [17,18,10,19,1,16,13]	CIR [12,1,13,14]	Phase [15]
Entropy source	Movement [17,10,19,12,11,1,13,14]	Channel-selective fading [16]	Angle of arrival [18]
Hardware	802.15.4 [17,18,19,11,16]	UWB [10,12]	802.11a [1,13]
Quantization	1-threshold [18,10]	2-thresholds [17,12,1,13]	Dynamic multi-threshold [19,11,15,16,14]
Error correction	Block-based parity [17]	Quantization-dependent [18,10,19,12,1,16]	Error correction codes [13,14]
Attacker model	Passive [17,18,10,19,12,15,16,14]	Active [11,1,13]	—

[a] Some protocols use multiple channel properties.

greater than $\lambda/2$. According to the authors, a relatively high cross-correlation exists even at larger distances (up to 90 cm), enabling passive attackers to guess 50 % of the key or more by pure eavesdropping. Our contribution consists of a flexible active attack in a realistic scenario, requiring only publicly available information and off-the-shelf hardware, and is entirely independent of physical proximity. In order to demonstrate our attack's practicality, we successfully apply it to the protocol described in [1] without violating any security assumptions. In summary, we believe that the attack described in this work is applicable to all protocols that use RSSI-based quantization of the wireless channel.

7   Conclusion

In this paper, we introduced a novel idea for a man-in-the-middle attack based on *injection opportunities* against signal-based key generation schemes. Using this idea, without assuming any advantage for the adversary, we implemented an attack that exploits imperfect error correction and allows to disrupt a protocol run by deliberately forcing a key disagreement. Following the same idea, we designed a more severe *key recovery* attack that is able to reveal large parts of the secret key generated between two legitimate transmitters. We demonstrated its performance by attacking a concrete protocol in different scenarios using off-the-shelf hardware. Typically, between 40 % and 50 % of the secret key were revealed to the attacker. This success rate decreases with larger distances between the attacker and the legitimate nodes. However, this mitigating factor could easily be improved by using superior hardware or increased sending power. In the worst case, we still recovered around 25 % of the key correctly.

Besides evaluating the attack itself, we analyzed potential countermeasures. We examined statistical mechanisms to detect an attacker and filter spoofs on a per-packet basis or to reject compromised runs entirely (as oftentimes mentioned in related work). However, without a significant amount of training data the approach was shown to cause a prohibitively large number of false positives. Given these practical problems, simply generating longer keys to impede brute-force attacks could be superior. Yet, such a high price to pay might undermine the advantages of current key generation protocols.

References

1. Mathur, S., Trappe, W., Mandayam, N., Ye, C., Reznik, A.: Radio-telepathy: extracting a secret key from an unauthenticated wireless channel. In: Garcia-Luna-Aceves, J.J., Sivakumar, R., Steenkiste, P. (eds.) Proceedings of the 14th ACM International Conference on Mobile Computing and Networking (MOBICOM 2008), pp. 128–139. ACM (September 2008)
2. Jana, S., Premnath, S.N., Clark, M., Kasera, S.K., Patwari, N., Krishnamurthy, S.V.: On the effectiveness of secret key extraction from wireless signal strength in real environments. In: Shin, K.G., Zhang, Y., Bagrodia, R., Govindan, R. (eds.) Proceedings of the 15th International Conference on Mobile Computing and Networking (MOBICOM 2009), pp. 321–332. ACM (September 2009)
3. Li, Z., Xu, W., Miller, R., Trappe, W.: Securing wireless systems via lower layer enforcements. In: Poovendran, R., Juels, A. (eds.) Proceedings of the 5th ACM Workshop on Wireless Security (WiSe 2006), pp. 33–42. ACM (September 2006)
4. Dodis, Y., Reyzin, L., Smith, A.: Fuzzy Extractors: How to Generate Strong Keys from Biometrics and Other Noisy Data. In: Cachin, C., Camenisch, J.L. (eds.) EUROCRYPT 2004. LNCS, vol. 3027, pp. 523–540. Springer, Heidelberg (2004)
5. Impagliazzo, R., Levin, L.A., Luby, M.: Pseudo-random generation from one-way functions. In: Proceedings of the 21st Annual ACM Symposium on Theory of Computing (STOC 1989), pp. 12–24. ACM (May 1989)
6. Cachin, C., Maurer, U.: Linking information reconciliation and privacy amplification. Journal of Cryptology 10(2), 97–110 (1997)
7. Wilhelm, M., Martinovic, I., Schmitt, J.B., Lenders, V.: Reactive jamming in wireless networks: How realistic is the threat? In: Proceedings of the 4th ACM Conference on Wireless Network Security (WiSec 2011), pp. 47–52. ACM, New York (2011)
8. Xiao, L., Greenstein, L., Mandayam, N., Trappe, W.: Fingerprints in the ether: Using the physical layer for wireless authentication. In: Proceedings of the IEEE International Conference on Communications 2007 (ICC 2007), pp. 4646–4651. IEEE (June 2007)
9. Maurer, U.M.: Protocols for Secret Key Agreement by Public Discussion Based on Common Information. In: Brickell, E.F. (ed.) CRYPTO 1992. LNCS, vol. 740, pp. 461–470. Springer, Heidelberg (1993)
10. Azimi-Sadjadi, B., Kiayias, A., Mercado, A., Yener, B.: Robust key generation from signal envelopes in wireless networks. In: Ning, P., De Capitani di Vimercati, S., Syverson, P.F. (eds.) Proceedings of the 14th ACM Conference on Computer and Communications Security (CCS 2007), pp. 401–410. ACM (October 2007)
11. Liu, H., Yang, J., Wang, Y., Chen, Y.: Collaborative secret key extraction leveraging received signal strength in mobile wireless networks. In: Greenberg, A.G., Sohraby, K. (eds.) Proceedings of the 31st IEEE International Conference on Computer Communications (INFOCOM 2012), pp. 927–935. ACM (March 2012)

12. Hamida, S.B., Pierrot, J.B., Castelluccia, C.: An adaptive quantization algorithm for secret key generation using radio channel measurements. In: Al Agha, K., Badra, M., Newby, G.B. (eds.) Proceedings of the 3rd International Conference on New Technologies, Mobility and Security (NTMS 2009), pp. 1–5 (December 2009)

13. Ye, C., Mathur, S., Reznik, A., Shah, Y., Trappe, W., Mandayam, N.B.: Information-theoretically secret key generation for fading wireless channels. IEEE Transactions on Information Forensics and Security 5(2), 240–254 (2010)

14. Zhang, J., Kasera, S.K., Patwari, N.: Mobility assisted secret key generation using wireless link signatures. In: Proceedings of the 29th IEEE International Conference on Computer Communications (INFOCOM 2010), pp. 1–5. IEEE (March 2010)

15. Wang, Q., Su, H., Ren, K., Kim, K.: Fast and scalable secret key generation exploiting channel phase randomness in wireless networks. In: Proceedings of the 30th IEEE International Conference on Computer Communications (INFOCOM 2011), pp. 1422–1430. IEEE (April 2011)

16. Wilhelm, M., Martinovic, I., Schmitt, J.B.: Secret keys from entangled sensor motes: Implementation and analysis. In: Proceedings of the 3rd ACM Conference on Wireless Network Security (WiSec 2010), pp. 139–144. ACM (March 2010)

17. Ali, S.T., Sivaraman, V., Ostry, D.: Secret key generation rate vs. reconciliation cost using wireless channel characteristics in body area networks. In: Proceedings of the IEEE/IFIP 8th International Conference on Embedded and Ubiquitous Computing (EUC 2010), pp. 644–650. IEEE (December 2010)

18. Aono, T., Higuchi, K., Ohira, T., Komiyama, B., Sasaoka, H.: Wireless secret key generation exploiting reactance-domain scalar response of multipath fading channels. IEEE Transactions on Antennas and Propagation 53(11), 3776–3784 (2005)

19. Croft, J., Patwari, N., Kasera, S.K.: Robust uncorrelated bit extraction methodologies for wireless sensors. In: Abdelzaher, T.F., Voigt, T., Wolisz, A. (eds.) Proceedings of the 9th ACM/IEEE International Conference on Information Processing in Sensor Networks (IPSN 2010), pp. 70–81. ACM (April 2010)

20. Döttling, N., Lazich, D., Müller-Quade, J., de Almeida, A.S.: Vulnerabilities of Wireless Key Exchange Based on Channel Reciprocity. In: Chung, Y., Yung, M. (eds.) WISA 2010. LNCS, vol. 6513, pp. 206–220. Springer, Heidelberg (2011)

21. Edman, M., Kiayias, A., Yener, B.: On passive inference attacks against physical-layer key extraction. In: Proceedings of the 4th European Workshop on System Security (Eurosec 2011), pp. 8–13. ACM (April 2011)

The Silence of the LANs:
Efficient Leakage Resilience for IPsec VPNs

Ahmad-Reza Sadeghi[1,2,3], Steffen Schulz[1,2,4], and Vijay Varadharajan[4]

[1] System Security Lab, Technische Universität Darmstadt
[2] System Security Lab, Ruhr-University Bochum
[3] Fraunhofer SIT, Darmstadt
[4] Information and Network Security Research Lab, Macquarie University

Abstract. Virtual Private Networks (VPNs) are increasingly used to build logically isolated networks. However, existing VPN designs and deployments neglect the problem of traffic analysis and covert channels. Hence, there are many ways to infer information from VPN traffic without decrypting it. Many proposals were made to mitigate network covert channels, but previous works remained largely theoretical or resulted in prohibitively high padding overhead and performance penalties.

In this work, we (1) analyse the impact of covert channels in IPsec, (2) present several improved and novel approaches for covert channel mitigation in IPsec, (3) propose and implement a system for dynamic performance trade-offs, and (4) implement our design in the Linux IPsec stack and evaluate its performance for different types of traffic and mitigation policies. At only 24% overhead, our prototype enforces tight information-theoretic bounds on all information leakage.

Keywords: IPsec, VPNs, covert channels, performance trade-offs.

1 Introduction

Virtual Private Networks (VPNs) are popular means for enterprises and organizations to securely connect their network sites over the Internet. Their security is implemented and enforced by VPN gateways that tunnel the transferred data in secure channels, thus logically connecting the remote sites in an isolated network. Abstracted this way, VPNs are increasingly used in scenarios that secure channels were not designed for: to logically isolate networks, providing "networks as a service" in virtualized environments like Clouds, Trusted Virtual Domains, or the Future Internet [1–3]. What is not considered in these scenarios is the long known problem of covert channels.

Covert channels violate the system security policy by using channels "*not intended for information transfer at all*" [4, 5]. While there is a large body of research on covert channels, few works have considered the practical implementation and performance impact of comprehensive covert channel mitigation in modern networks. We believe such work is important for a number of reasons, especially regarding VPNs and network virtualization:

S. Foresti, M. Yung, and F. Martinelli (Eds.): ESORICS 2012, LNCS 7459, pp. 253–270, 2012.
© Springer-Verlag Berlin Heidelberg 2012

(1) Insider Threat: In contrast to end-to-end secure channels, where the end-points are implicitly trusted, VPNs are also used for logical network isolation and perimeter security enforcement. In this context, the members of a VPN are often not fully trusted, but instead the trust is reduced to central policy enforcement points, the VPN gateways, which should prevent undesired information flows. However, malicious insiders in the LAN may leak information through the VPN gateways using covert channels, thus circumventing the security policy. Examples of such insiders can be actual humans or stealth malware, engaging in industrial espionage, leaking realtime financial transaction data, or disclosing large amounts of data from physically secured institutions (e.g., to Wikileaks).

(2) Traffic Analysis: By analysing traffic patterns and meta-data, it is also possible to infer information about transferred data without assuming a malicious insider [6, 7]. Such "passive" Man-in-the-Middle (MITM) scenarios are becoming more prevalent with network virtualization, allowing co-located, supposedly isolated systems to analyse each other [8]. To mitigate such attacks, a common approach is to consider the maximum possible information leakage by a colluding malicious insider. In limiting this maximum information leakage, covert channel analysis and mitigation thus also affects traffic analysis [9].

(3) Combination with Detection: Although application-layer firewalls and intrusion detection systems are widely deployed, carefully designed covert channels remain hard to detect [10, 11]. In these systems, the adversary chooses a weaker signal and mimics the patterns of regular channel usage. Covert channel mitigation can be useful here to induce noise, forcing the adversary to use a stronger signal and thus facilitate detection. We expect the combination of covert channel mitigation and detection to significantly reduce the performance penalty of covert channel mitigation by allowing less intrusive pattern enforcement.

Contributions. This paper provides for the first time an explicit analysis of covert channels in IPSec based VPNs and a comprehensive set of techniques and mechanisms to mitigate them. We identify and categorize the different types of covert channels and determine their capacity. We develop a framework for mitigation of these covert channels and describe mechanisms and techniques for high-performance covert channel mitigation. In particular, we propose an algorithm for on-demand adjustment of traffic pattern enforcement that increases peak network performance while also reducing overhead during reduced usage. We present a practical instantiation of this framework for the Linux IPSec stack and analyse its performance for different kinds of traffic. In contrast to previous works, which achieve throughput rates in the range of modem speed [9, 12] and taunt the performance impact of proposed mitigation mechanisms [13], our prototype achieves 169 Mbit/s in a 200 Mbit/s VPN link at only 24% overhead.

Outline. After defining the problem of VPN covert channels in Section 2, we discuss efficient covert channel mitigation and performance trade-offs in Section 3. An implementation for the Linux IPsec stack is presented and evaluated in Section 4. We discuss related work in Section 5 and conclude in Section 6.

2   Problem Setting and Adversary Model

In the following we define the problem of covert channels in VPNs. Note that our definition differs from previous, less explicit considerations, which consider communication between legitimate VPN participants and are better described as steganographic channels [14–16]. Although we limit ourselves to VPNs in state-of-the-art IPsec configuration [17], most of our results can be generalized.

2.1   System Model and Terminology

As illustrated in Figure 1(a), we consider a VPN comprised of two or more Local Area Networks (LANs) that are inter-connected over an insecure Wide Area Network (WAN). In our scenario, the security goal of the VPN is not only to provide a secure channel (confidentiality, authenticity, integrity) but also to *confine* communication of LAN hosts to the VPN, i.e., to isolate the *protected* from the *unprotected* domain. VPNs are increasingly used for such logical isolation, to create secure virtualized or overlay networks, or simply enforce perimeter security in large companies [1–3]. This de-facto security goal of isolating the protected from the unprotected domain, and its efficient implementation, is the main focus of this work.

For this purpose, we distinguish *legitimate* channels that transfer and protect user data according to the VPN security policy from *covert* channels that can be used to circumvent this policy. Covert channels exist because the legitimate channel acts as a shared resource between the protected and unprotected domain, exhibiting certain *characteristics* that can be manipulated and measured by different parties. We denote channels from the protected to unprotected domain and vice versa as *outbound* and *inbound* covert channels, respectively.

We measure the security of our system using the Shannon capacity of the covert channels, i.e., the information theoretic limit on the amount of information that can be transferred through them [6]. The covert channel capacity is given in bits per legitimate channel packet (bpp) or, where applicable, in bits per second (bps). The capacity of each covert channel *type* is denoted as C^{type}. The capacities are classified as maximum (m) vs. remaining (r) covert channel rate for inbound (in) vs. outbound (out) covert channels. For example, the maximum capacity of the outbound covert channel based on packet size is denoted as $C^{\text{PktSize}}_{m,out}$, or as $C^{\text{PktSize}}_{r,out}$ after countermeasures have been applied. The remaining *aggregated* inbound and outbound covert channel rates are denoted as $\hat{C}_{r,in}$ and $\hat{C}_{r,out}$, respectively.

2.2   Adversary Model

The adversary controls one or more compromised hosts in the LAN sites as well as an active MITM in the WAN. We refer to the LAN hosts controlled by the adversary as (malicious) *insiders*, regardless of whether they are controlled by actual humans or stealth malware. The adversary's goal is to establish a

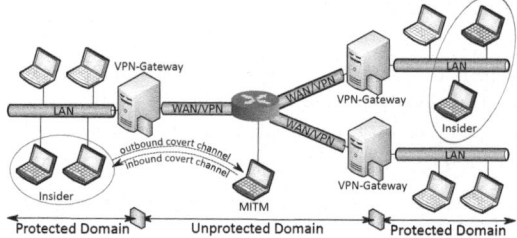

Class	Type	Capacity C_m in bpp	
		Outbound	Inbound
storage	ECN	2	1
	DS	6	6
	Flags	1	-
timing/ channel- logic	PktSize	8.4	-
	IPD	≥ 1	≥ 1
	PktOrd	-	> 6.58
	PktDrop	-	1
	PMTUD	-	0.13
amplify	DestIP	$\log_2(N)$	-

(a) A VPN with three LAN sites. The adversary aims to exchange information between the MITM and malicious insiders using covert channels.

(b) Inbound and outbound covert channels capacities for an IPsec VPN with $N + 1$ endpoints.

Fig. 1. Problem scenario: A complex VPN with multiple identified covert channels

communication channel between the MITM and one or more possibly colluding malicious insiders, as illustrated in Figure 1(a). This would allow the adversary to send instructions to the insiders or to leak information from the protected to the unprotected domain, breaching the perimeter security of the VPN. For this purpose, we assume a state-of-the-art IPsec configuration with authenticated encryption using ESP in tunnel mode [17], and the cryptographic primitives and keys of the VPN are securely enforced by the VPN gateways. However, the legitimate VPN traffic can be manipulated by malicious parties in the protected and unprotected domains to exchange information that "survives" these packet transformation enforced by the VPN gateways.

Unfortunately, no systematic approach is known for identifying network covert channels apart from exhaustive search, and the categorization as storage or timing channels can be ambiguous [5]. We used a comprehensive analysis on the IPsec specification and related work on covert channels in network protocols (cf. Section 5), as well as source code analysis and testing[1] to identify potential covert channels in IPsec VPNs. IP-Tunneling and authenticated encryption by the IPsec gateways greatly simplified this problem, as none of the protocol headers that the MITM can read or modify (i.e., the outer IP and Encapsulated Security Payload (ESP) header) are directly available to the LAN hosts.

In total, we have identified only eight covert channels. As shown in Figure 1(b), the available covert channels comprise three storage-based channels based on fields in the outer IP header (ECN, DS, Flags) and five timing-based covert channels that manipulate Inter-Packet Delay (IPD), packet order (PktOrd), WAN capacity (PktDrop), and Path MTU Discovery (PMTUD). The remaining characteristic of the respective destination LAN of a packet (DestIP) does not constitute a covert channel in its own right but can act as amplification of other covert channels. A detailed discussion of the covert channels we identified in IPsec VPNs is available in the full version [18].

---

[1] Specifically, we examined the IPsec implementations of the current Linux 2.6.32 to 2.6.38 and OpenBSD 4.7 to 4.8 releases.

We emphasize that some of these channels are implementation dependant, e.g., the treatment of ECN header flags or PMTUD at the VPN gateway, while others (IPD, PktSize, PktOrd) are generic problems faced by all packet-oriented channels. While we are confident to have identified all covert channels, we cannot account for all possible implementations and interpretations of IPsec. Hence in this paper we limit our considerations to the identified attack vectors.

3   Covert Channel-Resilient IPsec

In this section we present the design of a high-performance covert channel-resilient IPsec, i.e., a system with low, known covert channel capacity and high throughput. We present novel or improved techniques for efficient covert channel mitigation in Section 3.1. Section 3.2 considers the performance of different mitigation strategies, introducing on-demand performance trade-offs. Finally, we derive the remaining aggregated inbound and outbound covert channel capacities of the system in Section 3.3.

3.1   Covert Channel Mitigation

In the following we present and improve efficient mitigation mechanisms for each of the covert channels identified in Section 2.2.

Packet Size (PktSize). The packet size characteristic is usually addressed by padding packets to maximum size or assuming them to be of constant size [6]. However, as the product throughput = $\text{pkt\_size} \cdot \text{pkt\_rate}$ is constant for a given link, enforcement of small packet sizes can reduce the load per packet significantly, allowing higher packet rates and more simultaneous connections.

It was previously proposed to allow multiple alternate packet sizes [19], but then the ratio between packets of different sizes creates another covert channel. Mode Security [20] was proposed to manage the switching between different enforcement modes and audit such a remaining covert channel. However, real network traffic is often mixed, i.e., packet streams using different packet sizes are often transmitted at the same time. Moreover, the enforcement of small packet sizes is problematic for IP protocols: With Path MTU Discovery (PMTUD), the connection endpoints quickly detect and adapt to the maximum allowed packet size of an IP route, but only slowly recover to a larger MTU using a conservative trial-and-error approach. This active adaption also makes it harder for the VPN gateways to estimate the actual demand for larger packets.

We address these problems by combining packet padding with transparent fragmentation and multiplexing, mechanisms that were previously only considered for traffic obfuscation [21]. Packet fragmentation *within* IPsec allows us to efficiently and transparently enforce various packet sizes at the gateway without influencing the channel's Path MTU (PMTU). This is different from regular IP fragmentation before or after IPsec processing, which results in visible fragments either on the LAN or WAN sides that could again be used as covert channels.

On the other hand, packet multiplexing can be used to reduce packet padding overhead, and in general to reduce the IPsec encapsulation overhead (ESP, IP).

When working with mixed traffic, the sender gateway first fragments large packets and then attempts to multiplex small packets or fragments into the padding area of previously processed packets that are still in the packet buffer. At the receiving gateway, packets are first de-multiplexed and then defragmented.

Inter-Packet Delay (IPD). The covert channel based on IPDs and its mitigation were subject of several previous works (e.g., [6, 10, 22–24]). In theory, it is easily eliminated by enforcing a fixed IPD at the VPN gateway, inserting dummy packets when no real packets are available [24]. However, due to the very high packet rates in modern networks, even short periods of non-optimal enforcement of IPDs (and thus packet rate) at the VPN gateway quickly result in packet loss due to packet buffer overflows or network congestion. This is particularly critical for Internet protocols, where packet loss triggers congestion avoidance, degrading overall throughput independently of the packet rate enforced by the VPN gateways. The effect can be partly mitigated with large packet buffers; however, large buffers can also create high packet delays, degrading network responsiveness [26]. Also, the optimal enforced packet rate can be very large in modern networks, creating a high computational overhead for the time-synchronous packet processing. For example, to saturate a 100 Mbit/s link with 200 byte packets, an average IPD of $\frac{500 \; byte}{100 \cdot 10^6 \; byte/s} = 2\mu s$ should be enforced. Finally, one must consider inaccuracies in the timing enforcement that appear at high system loads [23, 25]: Since high activity on the LAN interface can influence the system load of the gateway, a LAN host may induce inaccuracies in the IPD enforcement of the gateway that can again be measured by the Man-in-the-Middle (MITM), yielding $C_r^{\text{IPD}'} = 0.16$ bps [9].

We have implemented the traffic reshaping inside the Linux kernel, using the modern High-Precision Event Timer (HPET) infrastructure for packet scheduling with nanosecond resolution. This substantially reduces the overhead of context switching and buffering, allowing an IPDs in the range of microseconds rather than several milliseconds (e.g., [9, 12]) and noticeably improves throughput and responsiveness. To maintain good system performance at even higher packet rates we use packet bursts, i.e., we translate very low IPDs into bursts of multiple packets at correspondingly larger delays. For optimal packet buffering our system adjusts the buffer size depending on the currently enforced IPD. This prevents long delays at low rates while allowing generous buffering at high rates.

To address the problem of timing inaccuracies, we use the high resolution of the HPET timers to monitor and actively *compensate* for timing inaccuracies in randomized IPD enforcement. Specifically, we exploit the fact that determining timing inaccuracies during randomized IPD enforcement is harder for the remote MITM than for the local system. The adversary always requires significantly more measurements to first detect the variance of the random IPD enforcement and then the inaccuracy in the enforced variance [23], while the VPN gateway itself can directly compare the intended versus actual packet sending time. Hence, the gateway can approximate the current inaccuracy faster, requiring less measurement samples. Given this knowledge of unintended change in IPD variance, we let the VPN gateways compensate for the enforcement inaccuracy by dynamically compensating the variance of the IPD enforcement. This prevents the adversary from ever measuring the actual inaccuracy, eliminating the timing channel ($C_r^{\text{IPD}} = 0$). However, further evaluation with specialized network hardware is needed to confirm (the non-existance of) this effect.

Packet Order (PktOrd). Sequence numbers in protocol headers have been used before to create a covert or steganographic channel based on packet reordering [16, 27]. However, in contrast to previous works we can eliminate this channel in the VPN scenario using the IPsec anti-replay window and secure sequence numbers in Encapsulated Security Payload (ESP).

IPsec implementations maintain a bitmap of the last r seen and unseen sequence numbers so that replay attacks within the window size can be detected and older packets discarded. To eliminate communication through packet reordering, we propose to implement this window as a packet buffer, where new packets are inserted *sorted* by their ESP sequence number and leave the buffer as the window advances. As a result, all packets forwarded from the VPN gateway into the LAN are ordered and the covert channel is eliminated: $C_{r,in}^{\text{PktOrd}} = 0$.

Unfortunately, the approach is problematic for low packet rates, since the window may advance slowly and individual packets are not forwarded fast enough. We solve this issue by establishing a certain maximum IPD (e.g., 50ms) at the sender and assure that at least r dummy packets are sent by a gateway before a connection is stopped. These constraints are necessary in any case to assure network responsiveness and hide short periods of inactivity.

Packet Drops (PktDrop). In general, it appears impossible to eliminate covert channels based on packet dropping in the WAN. Mitigation with error correction codes is expensive and easily defeated by dropping even more packets. Instead, we propose to mitigate the channel by injecting noise, by *increasing* packet loss proportionally to the actual packet loss.

Specifically, the gateways maintain a buffer p of size d. At the sender gateway, packets are buffered in p and their order is randomized before encapsulation. At the receiver gateway, the packets are again collected in p and the number of dropped packets i is determined based on their ESP sequence number. If $i > 0$, the gateway drops another j packets from the current buffer, such that $i + j = 2^x$, where $1 < x \leq \log_2(d)$, and forwards the remaining packets after randomizing their order once again. As a result, the MITM can choose the overall number of packets to be dropped but cannot select which packets to drop, resulting in a symbol space of $\log_2(d) + 1$ packets per window d. The remaining covert channel capacity is then $C_{r,in}^{\text{PktDrop}} = \frac{1}{d} \cdot \log_2(\log_2(d) + 1)$ bpp.

Similar to the above packet re-ordering mitigation, the inbound packet buffer at the receiving gateway is problematic for very low traffic rates and requires similar restrictions to assure a steady stream of (dummy) packets. The implementation can be simplified at the cost of a slightly higher covert channel rate

by removing the randomization buffer at the sending gateway and re-using the
anti-replay window for dropping the additional j packets.

Path MTU Discovery (PMTUD). To our knowledge, no previous work
considered the possibility of covert channels based on PMTUD, in particular
with respect to VPNs. Since PMTUD is critical for good network performance,
we do not disable it but instead mitigate the channel by enforcing limits on the
rate and values that are propagated by the VPN gateways into the LAN.

In particular, we limit the possible PMTU values by maintaining a list of
common PMTU values and only propagate the respective next lower PMTU to
the LAN. Such common PMTUs values can be established on site or can be
derived from previously proposed performance optimizations for PMTUD [28].
The rate limitation of PMTU propagation is problematic in general, as a lack of
MTU adaption will lead to packet loss. However, in our case the current PMTU is
always known to the trusted VPN gateways, which can then use the transparent
fragmentation feature from PktSize enforcement to translate between LAN and
WAN packet sizes. Considering the 10 most common PMTUs and an average
interval of, e.g., 2 minutes [28] between propagation of PMTU changes, our
measures reduce the covert channel rate to less than $C_{r,in}^{\mathrm{PMTUD}} = 0.02$ bps.

Storage-Based Channels (ECN, DS, Flags). The storage-based covert
channels exploiting the Explicit Congestion Notification (ECN), Differentiated
Services (DS) and IPv4 Flags handling of IP/IPsec are easily eliminated by resetting the respective fields of the outer IP header at encapsulation and ignoring
them during decapsulation. Normalizing the IPv4 Flags field is unproblematic
as en-route fragmentation is deprecated in IP. However, eliminating the ECN
and DS covert channels disables these performance optimizations in the WAN.

3.2   Mitigation Policies and Performance

In this section, we discuss different covert channel mitigation policies that can
be enforced using the techniques described in Section 3.1. We start by discussing
the problems of previously proposed Fully Padded Channel and Mode Security
approaches, and then propose a new system for on-demand, dynamic adaption
of the enforced channel characteristics. We focus on the IPD and PktSize enforcement mechanisms, since they have by far the highest performance impact.

Fully Padded Channel. When applied without any performance trade-offs,
the mitigation mechanisms described in Section 3.1 result in a *fully padded
channel*: The WAN packet stream is constantly padded to the maximum desired throughput rate and packet size. However, this mitigation policy has several disadvantages: (1) The system must compromise between high throughput
and responsiveness, likely opting to enforce maximum packet sizes to reduce
fragmentation overhead; (2) the maximum (desired) network load is constantly
enforced in both directions, reducing overall performance due to network congestion; (3) TCP/IP congestion avoidance algorithms do not work, since any rate

throttling is compensated by additional channel padding. In case of temporary reductions in WAN capacity, this leads to repeated packet loss and throttling, until the network is not usable anymore. Hence, the fully padded channel policy is unfit for practical use, except in private/dedicated physical infrastructures.

Mode Security. Mode Security is a generic scheme for trading covert channel-resilience against system performance. This is done by organizing system operation in a set of alternative *operation modes* that can be switched at a certain rate [20]. The current operation mode is then selected such that performance penalty and/or overhead produced by the covert channel mitigation is minimized. Since the operation mode is typically adapted depending on the actually required usage, the adaption itself may be exploited as a covert channel. In this case, the covert channel capacity can be given as $C_{out}^{\text{ModeSec}} = R \cdot \log_2(M)$, where M is the number of operation modes and R is the maximum rate at which the operation mode can be changed (transition rate).

Mode Security was used to estimate the theoretic network overhead and covert channel capacity [6]. However, this assumes an algorithm that can determine the optimal operation mode to switch to. To the best of our knowledge, no practical implementation and evaluation of this mechanism exists; in particular, no strategies have been proposed to automatically determine and apply the optimal operation mode in the face of often unpredictable traffic, with exponential rate increases and congestion avoidance algorithms. In fact, our attempts to directly apply Mode Security to on-demand covert channel mitigation resulted in poor performance, with TCP throughput benchmarks becoming stuck at very low packet rates or completely losing the connection.

On-Demand Mode Security Management. An algorithm for on-demand adaptation in network covert channel mitigation must accommodate multiple conflicting constraints. It must quickly react to changes in channel usage to elude congestion avoidance algorithms, yet the amount of possible mode changes should be minimal. Moreover, the employed packet queue should buffer packet bursts at various average packet rates, yet react quickly when the current average rate is overused by dropping individual packets. We address these conflicts using the following regulation mechanisms:

Token Bucket Filter. We generalize the transition rate R of the Mode Security paradigm to a token bucket filter [29]. Tokens are generated at a fixed rate R and each mode transition consumes a token from the token bucket. This allows us to "save up" unused mode transitions in form of tokens and consume them on demand, at temporarily higher rates than R. The amount of cached tokens is limited by the token bucket size and the *average transition rate* $\bar{R}$ is bound by the rate R at which new tokens are generated. Thus, the token bucket filter allows us to immediately react to changes in network usage, before connection throttling kicks in or network delays become noticeable. Further, the token bucket status may influence and optimize decisions on the operation mode to be enforced.

```
1  while true do
2  │   (r_LAN, r_frag, r_mplex) ← get-stats()
3  │   r_opt ← r_LAN + r_frag − r_mplex
4  │   r_avg ← 0.1 · r_opt + 0.9 · r_avg
5  │   case r_opt > 0.9 · r_now
6  │   │   r_amp ← (r_max − r_opt)/t_num
7  │   │   r_new ← r_opt + ½ r_quant + r_amp
8  │   case r_now > 1.1 · r_avg ∧ t_num > t_dec
9  │   │   r_new ← r_avg
10 │   r_new ← quantatize(r_new, r_quant)
11 │   sleep(ival)
```

Type	Max. Capacity C_m in bpp		Rem. Capacity C_r in bps	
	Outbound	Inbound	Outbound	Inbound
ECN	2	1	0	0
DS	6	6	0	0
Flags	1	-	0	-
PktSize	8.4	-	0	-
IPD	≥ 1	≥ 1	0	0
PktOrd	-	> 6.58	-	0
PktDrop	-	1	-	≤ 5
PMTUD	-	0.13	-	0.02
DestIP	$\log_2(N)$	-	$\log_2(N)$	-
Overall	> 18.4	> 15.64	0	≤ 5.02

(a) Simplified pseudo-code for dynamic (b) Maximum and remaining covert channel packet rate adjustment in steps of capacities for VPNs with $N+1$ endpoints. r_{quant}.

Fig. 2. Design of high-performance covert channel mitigation

Aggressive Increase. Network throughput is scaled mainly based on its packet rate r, with typically exponential rate increase until the first network bottleneck is detected. While the optimum WAN packet rate r_{opt} is easily calculated based on the currently observed LAN rate r_{LAN}, fragmented and multiplexed packets (r_{frag}, r_{mplex}), the derivation of the next enforced packet rate r_{new} is more involved, as shown in Figure 2(a).

To adequately consider exponential rate increases without requiring too frequent changes to r_{now}, our rate increase phase is designed to constantly *overestimate* the current optimal packet rate r_{opt}, by increasing r_{now} as soon as it is approached by r_{opt} (cf. Figure 2(a), Line 5). Combined with buffering and short monitoring intervals $ival \approx 200$ms, this approach successfully eludes congestion avoidance algorithms and prevents undesired throughput throttling. However, the overestimation should also not be too large, as it directly affects the padding overhead and can also reduce the inbound traffic rate due to the imposed network load. Moreover, all stored tokens may be used up before a reasonably high packet rate $r_{\text{now}} \approx r_{\text{max}}$ is reached, resulting in bad performance until new tokens are generated. Hence we also include an amplification mechanism that increases the rate r_{opt} in larger steps r_{amp}, depending on the currently available amount of tokens r_{num} (Line 6f.). This prevents the system from becoming "stuck" at low packet rates, at the cost of potentially high padding overhead in cases where such amplification was not required.

Conservative Slowdown. When putting the WAN channel in a state of decreased performance, we must take care that sufficient transition tokens are available to adequately adapt to a possible subsequent usage increase as outlined above. In contrast to the aggressive rate increase policy, any reduction in the enforced traffic rate is therefore delayed until a certain amount of tokens t_{dec} have been collected in the token bucket. Moreover, to reduce the impact of short-term fluctuations in the packet rate, the rate is only reduced based on the longer-time average traffic rate r_{avg}, as shown in Figure 2(a) Line 8f. Overall, the described approach saves up tokens in the "slowdown" phases while aggressively spending them in the "increase" phase, creating an equilibrium around t_{dec} and r_{avg}.

Dynamic Queue Size with RED. When dynamically adjusting the overall throughput of the WAN channel, we must also adjust the size of the packet queue accordingly. At small rates, a lot of packets may build up in a large queue, leading to large delays and timeouts. Similarly, a small queue is not effective at supporting a channel with high packet rates. Hence, we dynamically adapt the queue size based on the desired maximum buffering delay and the currently enforced packet rate. Eventually, the WAN channel or its enforcement policy may also reach a point where further rate increases are not possible. In this case, the endpoints should be notified of the current throughput limit as quickly as possible, without dropping several packets at once due to full buffers. We achieve this by deploying Random Early Detection (RED) [30] as the packet queue's dropping policy, so that packets are randomly dropped with increasing queue usage.

We implemented several variations of this approach and evaluated the effect of different parameters on the short-term and long-term usage adaption. The achieved performance and adaptation behavior is presented in Section 4.3.

3.3 Remaining Covert Channel Capacity

In the following we summarize the identified covert channels and derive the aggregated remaining covert channel capacity of our covert channel-resilient VPN.

Unfortunately, it is not possible to give all the covert channel rates in a closed form and with comparable units. Several covert channels also depend on additional parameters like network PMTU or minimum WAN packet rate. To provide a reasonable overview of the overall effectiveness of the covert channel mitigation, we have used the capacity estimations derived in the examples of Section 3.1, assuming a state-of-the-art IPsec VPN configuration (cf. Section 2).

Figure 2(b) lists the individual covert channel capacities for the unmitigated (C_m) and mitigated (C_r) case. Considering that today's networks easily transmit several thousand packets per second, i.e., 1 bpp $\gg$ 1 bps, our system results in significant improvements over standard IPsec. In fact, all outbound covert channels are completely eliminated, except for the DestIP channel. However, as explained in Section 2.2, the DestIP characteristic does not by itself constitute a covert channel but can only be used to amplify other channels. Hence, the overall remaining covert channel capacity is given by $\hat{C}_{r,out} = C_{out}^{\text{ModeSec}} \cdot C_{out}^{\text{DestIP}}$.

For the less critical inbound covert channels (e.g., control channels for stealth malware), only the channels based on PMTUD and PktDrop remain. The Pkt-Drop covert channel has the highest impact with $C_{r,in}^{PktDrop} \leq 5$ bps and is easy to exploit. Since the PMTUD channel could be exploited at the same time, their capacities must be added up: $\hat{C}_{r,in} = C_{r,in}^{\text{PktDrop}} + C_{r,in}^{\text{PMTUD}} = 5.02$ bps.

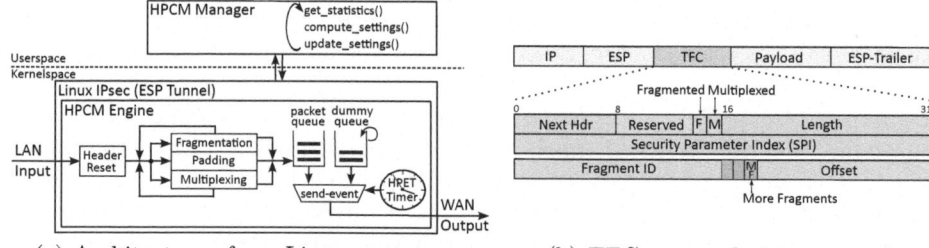

(a) Architecture of our Linux prototype.   (b) TFC encapsulation protocol.

Fig. 3. Implementation architecture and encapsulation protocol

4   Practical Covert Channel Mitigation with Linux

In this section we describe the instantiation of our system based on the Linux IPsec stack and analyse the achieved network performance and behavior.

In our prototype implementation and evaluation we only consider the mitigation of *outbound* covert channels, since information leakage from the protected to the unprotected domain is usually considered more critical (e.g., consider Bell-LaPadula [31]). Moreover, from our discussions in Section 3 it is clear that outbound covert channel mitigation is more efficient, as it requires less buffering and processing but is more effective in reducing the covert channel capacity.

4.1   Architecture and Implementation Details

We have implemented a High-Performance Covert Channel Mitigation (HPCM) system inside the IPsec stack of the Linux kernel. The architecture and encapsulation protocol are based on the Traffic Flow Confidentiality (TFC) project, a system for probabilistic traffic flow obfuscation and re-routing in IPsec [21]. We revised and extended TFC to support High-Precision Event Timers (HPETs), fragmentation, multiplexing and dummy packet generation that is indistinguishable from real traffic payloads, elimination of storage-based covert channels in the encapsulation headers and, most importantly, a interface for packet processing statistics and flexible policy enforcement in userspace. The resulting architecture is illustrated in Figure 3(a). In kernelspace, the HPCM Engine processes packets as part of the IPsec subsystem, rewriting problematic header fields and enforcing the currently desired size and IPD constraints as described in Section 3.1. In userspace, the HPCM Manager collects processing statistics from the enforcement engine and combines them with the observed inbound LAN traffic to determine the optimal enforcement parameters, as presented in Section 3.2.

For flexible packet padding and rerouting, TFC deploys its own encapsulation protocol with explicit signalling flags and length header [21]. To also support transparent fragmentation and multiplexing within our system, we extend the TFC protocol with an optional 32 bit fragmentation extension header as illustrated in Figure 3(b). The employed header format is compatible with the IPv4

Table 1. Throughput and transaction rate for regular and modified IPsec VPN

Benchmarks	No Padding			Fully Padded		On-Demand
	IP	ESP	TFC	1422	800	$\bar{R} = 10^{-1}$s
LAN Throughput (Mbit/s)	570	201	175	58	75	169
TCP Transaction Rate (Hz)	1756	1462	1364	611	740	532
LAN/WAN Overhead (%)	0	10	13	(73)	(61)	≈24
Relative Throughput (%)	283	100	87	28	37	84

header format, allowing us to reuse the existing IP defragmentation framework of Linux for defragmenting TFC payloads. Also note that the additional Security Parameter Index (SPI) field is only required due to restrictions of the Linux IPsec framework, and could be removed to reduce the TFC protocol overhead.

4.2 Testbed and Raw Performance

In this section we describe the performance achieved by our prototype in terms of network throughout, transaction rate (i.e., roundtrip time) and protocol overhead. Our testbed corresponds to the VPN scenario in Figure 1(a), except that we use only two LAN sites with one physical host per LAN. The Man-in-the-Middle (MITM) is implemented as an Ethernet bridge between the two VPN gateways, allowing reliable observation of all transmitted packets. For our evaluation, the MITM is completely passive and only used to provide independent performance measurements of the WAN. All hosts are 3.2 Ghz Intel Core i5-650 machines, equipped with two Intel PCIe GBit network cards and 4GB system memory. All network links are established at full-duplex GBit/s speed.

We have used the Netperf[2] benchmarks TCP_STREAM and TCP_RR to measure the maximum TCP throughput and transaction rate between the LAN sites. By comparing LAN and WAN throughput, we can determine the protocol overhead of the covert channel mitigation, including dummy packets and packet padding.

We list the overall performance results in Table 1. The first two columns show the testbed performance for raw IP (plain-text) transmission and IPsec ESP tunneling. With 570 Mbit/s, the raw transmission does not reach the expected GBit throughput, likely due to deficient hardware or drivers. As the LAN hosts and the MITM measure the same IP payloads, there is no LAN/WAN overhead. With 201 Mbit/s, the throughput of a standard IPsec ESP tunnel is already notably slower due to 10% protocol overhead but mainly computational constraints of the VPN gateways. As our covert channel mitigation is an extension of this ESP tunnel configuration, we normalize the relative throughput to 100%.

For reference and confirmation of the expected implementation overhead of our prototype, we next evaluated the raw performance of our HPCM Engine compared to the standard IPsec ESP tunnel. The third column "TFC" of Table 1 lists the achieved network performance when tunneling TFC inside ESP with with all covert channel mitigation techniques *disabled*. The overall LAN/WAN overhead of 13% (or 3% when compared with the ESP tunnel) is the result of the 8 to 12 byte TFC protocol encapsulation plus some computational overhead.

---

[2] http://www.netperf.org

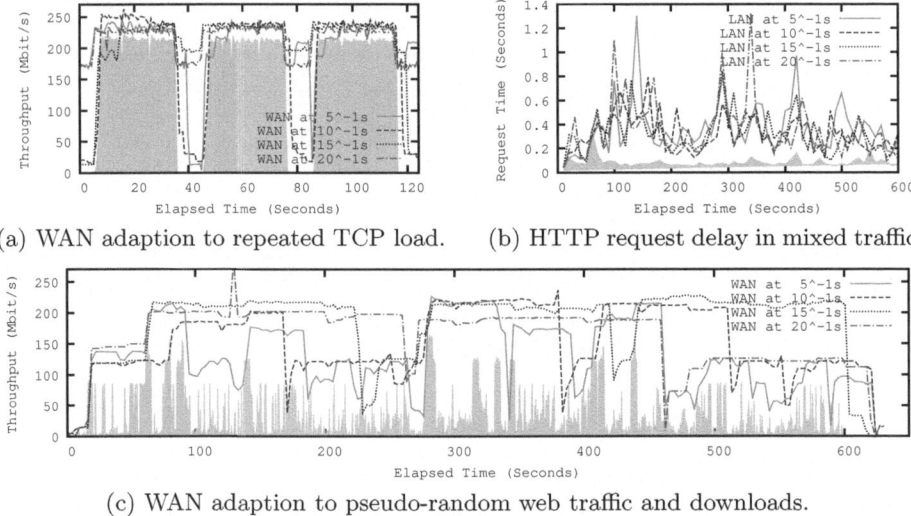

(a) WAN adaption to repeated TCP load.   (b) HTTP request delay in mixed traffic.

(c) WAN adaption to pseudo-random web traffic and downloads.

Fig. 4. Behavior of mode adaptation for different token generation rates R. For reference, the grey filled graph shows LAN performance without time/size padding.

4.3   Covert Channel Mitigation Performance

We now describe the behavior and performance of different mitigation policies.

The fourth and fifth column of Table 1 show the performance of a "fully padded channel", enforcing packet sizes of 1422 and 800 bytes at the maximum possible packet rate. For this purpose, we first measured the maximum bi-directional throughput of the VPN channel (201 Mbit/s per direction) and then selected the desired packet rate (inverse IPD) such that the bidirectional channel capacity is almost[3] saturated. We then again measured the maximum (uni-directional) throughput and roundtrip time. As shown in Table 1, the fully padded channel configuration achieves rather poor performance in both configurations, reaching only 37% and 28% of the ESP tunnel throughput. Observe that the enforcement of 800 byte packet size achieves higher transaction rate as well as higher throughput. We believe this is due to the overhead of padding TCP acknowledgements to maximum packet size.

We have also implemented and tested an instantiation of our on-demand mode security management scheme presented in Section 3.2. As shown in the last column of Table 1, the employed mode adaption heuristics reach almost the same maximum throughput as the raw TFC encapsulation without time/size padding (169 Mbit/s vs. 175 Mbit/s). The LAN/WAN overhead is slightly higher (24% vs. 13%) and the transaction rate rather low. The high throughput despite relatively high overhead is explained by the mode adaption behavior: As shown in Figure 4(a), the WAN channel adapts to the maximum possible

---

[3] As explained in Section 3.2, it is critical that the link is not fully saturated since congestion leads to packet loss and congestion avoidance does not work.

throughput, but suffers overhead in the rate increase and especially rate decrease phases. As desired by our design in Section 3.2, the main impact of reduced token regeneration rates $\bar{R} \leq 15^{-1}s$ in Figure 4(a) is the increased overhead in the intervals *between* TCP loads, when the rate is not decreased to save tokens.

Finally, we have investigated the ability of our on-demand mode security management to adapt to random, highly heterogeneous traffic patterns one would expect from a VPN with many users. We used Tsung, a traffic load testing tool[4], to record several HTTP sessions in our network, partly also including larger ($\approx$ 60 MB) HTTP downloads. We then configured one of our testbed LANs to act as Internet gateway for the other LAN and used Tsung to replay the recorded HTTP sessions in a pseudo-random fashion with 60 to 80 simultaneous users. Figure 4(c) shows how the WAN traffic enforcement for four different token regeneration rates $\bar{R}$ dynamically adapts to the LAN usage (grey filled). For $\bar{R} \leq 15^{-1}s$, only the larger peaks in LAN usage influence the WAN traffic enforcement, reducing information leakage at the cost of padding overhead. As shown in Figure 4(b), the mean duration of responding to individual HTTP requests is kept within reasonable limits. However, in contrast to unpadded traffic (grey filled) the accumulated request delays become noticeable to the user.

In the presented configuration, our mode adaption algorithm switches packet sizes in steps of 100 bytes and packet rates in steps of 1000 packets per second. Considering the maximum WAN packet rate of about 250.000 packets/s, we can derive $C_{r,out}^{\mathrm{ModeSec}} = \bar{R} \cdot \log_2(\frac{1500}{100} \cdot \frac{250000}{1000}) = \bar{R} \cdot 11.87$ and an overall outbound covert channel capacity of, e.g., $\hat{C}_{r,out} = 0.6$ bps for $\bar{R} = 20^{-1}s$ and $N = 1$.

5   Related Work

Several works consider the problem of covert channels and covert channel mitigation in Internet protocols [32, 33], yet we know of no works that specially discuss the problem of covert channels in IPsec. The covert channels we identify in IPsec are generally known, but we found no previous discussion of the PMTUD channel. Additionally, the PktSize [19], PktSort [11, 27] and DestIP [19] characteristics have different impact in IPsec, and the discussion of storage-based covert channels in the IPsec specification [14] proved to be inaccurate.

Although the IPD-based covert channel is generally well-known [6, 10, 19, 22, 34], the problem of inaccuracies in timing enforcement during increased system load remained unsolved [9, 23]. We consider this complication in our design in Section 3.1 and present a compensation mechanism that detects and compensates unintended timing inaccuracies. Also, while most works simply assume that packets are of constant size [24] or padded to the maximum desired size [19, 33], our adoption of multiplexing and fragmentation enables flexible packet size enforcement. The combination of different mitigation techniques makes our implementation the first prototype for comprehensive covert channel mitigation.

---

[4] http://tsung.erlang-projects.org

Regarding performance trade-offs, Mode Security was proposed as a general approach to adapt to resource usage by switching between different operation modes [20]. A similar approach called Traffic Stereotyping was proposed for networks [19]. To our knowledge, there is only one system that uses Mode Security to optimize covert channel mitigation, which aims to provide sender anonymity based on dynamic re-routing and IPD enforcement [6,24]. They assume a trusted network stack on each network endpoint and a periodic global negotiation to achieve an equalized traffic matrix [24]. A performance analysis was done based on statistics collected from a medium-sized network [12]; however, no actual performance measurements of their system have been provided and the problem of determining the optimal enforcement mode was left unsolved. Alternatively, Net-Camo [34] requires its endpoints to explicitly request their delay and throughput demands beforehand. We extend on these works by proposing a practical algorithm to determine the optimal operation mode on-demand. As we do not aim for sender-anonymity, we do not require mix-networks and various attacks on mixes do not apply to our approach (e.g., [35, 36]).

In contrast to probabilistic traffic obfuscation schemes such as HTTPOS [37] or Traffic Morphing [38], our framework enforces an information-theoretic boundary for the maximum information leakage. As argued in Section 1, covert channel detection schemes such as [39, 40] are complementary to our work and should be used where mitigation is costly, e.g., for the PktSort and PktDrop characteristics.

While we know of no practical performance measurements for comprehensive covert channel elimination, an overhead of 45%-56% was reported solely for obfuscating the packet size in website traffic [7, 38].

6 Conclusion and Future Work

We have motivated the problem of covert channels in Virtual Private Networks (VPNs) and presented the design, implementation, and performance of a covert channel-resilient VPN. We identified several covert channels and presented new countermeasures. We have investigated the problem of on-demand adaption of operation modes and presented an implementation for comprehensive, high-performance covert channel mitigation in the Linux IPsec stack. Our evaluation shows that on-demand rate adaption is feasible and practical even for highly unpredictive traffic. In more predictable throughput benchmarks, our system achieves remarkable 169 Mbit/s in a 201 Mbit/s VPN connection (84%).

As part of our future work, we will consider the effectiveness of alternative trade-off and normalization strategies. Furthermore, we aim to investigate the impact of inaccuracies in IPD enforcement.

Acknowledgments. We thank Amir Herzberg, Haya Shulmann and Thomas Schneider for their insightful comments and review of earlier versions of this work.

References

1. Cohesive Flexible Technologies: VPN-Cubed (2012), http://cohesiveft.com
2. Catuogno, L., Dmitrienko, A., Eriksson, K., Kuhlmann, D., Ramunno, G., Sadeghi, A.-R., Schulz, S., Schunter, M., Winandy, M., Zhan, J.: Trusted Virtual Domains – Design, Implementation and Lessons Learned. In: Chen, L., Yung, M. (eds.) INTRUST 2009. LNCS, vol. 6163, pp. 156–179. Springer, Heidelberg (2010)
3. Carapinha, J., Feil, P., Weissmann, P., Thorsteinsson, S.E., Etemoğlu, Ç., In-gthórsson, Ó., Çiftçi, S., Melo, M.: Network Virtualization - Opportunities and Challenges for Operators. In: Berre, A.J., Gómez-Pérez, A., Tutschku, K., Fensel, D. (eds.) FIS 2010. LNCS, vol. 6369, pp. 138–147. Springer, Heidelberg (2010)
4. Lampson, B.W.: A note on the confinement problem. Communications of the ACM 16(10) (1973)
5. National Computer Security Center: A Guide to Understanding Covert Channel Analysis of Trusted System (1993)
6. Venkatraman, B.R., Newman-Wolfe, R.E.: Capacity estimation and auditability of network covert channels. In: Research in Security and Privacy (S&P), Oakland, CA. IEEE (1995)
7. Liberatore, M., Levine, B.N.: Inferring the source of encrypted HTTP connections. In: Computer and Communications Security (CCS). ACM (2006)
8. Ristenpart, T., Tromer, E., Shacham, H., Savage, S.: Hey, you, get off of my cloud: exploring information leakage in third-party compute clouds. In: Computer and Communications Security (CCS). ACM (2009)
9. Graham, B., Zhu, Y., Fu, X., Bettati, R.: Using covert channels to evaluate the effectiveness of flow confidentiality measures. In: Parallel and Distributed Systems (ICPADS). IEEE (2005)
10. Liu, Y., Ghosal, D., Armknecht, F., Sadeghi, A.-R., Schulz, S., Katzenbeisser, S.: Hide and Seek in Time — Robust Covert Timing Channels. In: Backes, M., Ning, P. (eds.) ESORICS 2009. LNCS, vol. 5789, pp. 120–135. Springer, Heidelberg (2009)
11. Murdoch, S.J., Lewis, S.: Embedding Covert Channels into TCP/IP. In: Barni, M., Herrera-Joancomartí, J., Katzenbeisser, S., Pérez-González, F. (eds.) IH 2005. LNCS, vol. 3727, pp. 247–261. Springer, Heidelberg (2005)
12. Venkatraman, B.R., Newman-Wolfe, R.E.: Performance analysis of a method for high level prevention of traffic analysis using measurements from a campus network. In: Computer Security Applications Conference (ACSAC). IEEE (1994)
13. Millen, J.: 20 years of covert channel modeling and analysis. In: Research in Security and Privacy (S&P), Oakland, CA. IEEE (1999)
14. Kent, S., Seo, K.: Security Architecture for the Internet Protocol. RFC 4301 (2005)
15. Ahsan, K.: Covert channel analysis and data hiding in TCP/IP. Master's thesis, Department of Electrical and Computer Engineering, University of Toronto (2002)
16. Kundur, D., Ahsan, K.: Practical internet steganography: Data hiding in IP. In: Texas Workshop on Security of Information Systems (2003)
17. Degabriele, J.P., Paterson, K.G.: On the (in)security of IPsec in MAC-then-encrypt configurations. In: Computer and Communications Security (CCS). ACM (2010)
18. Sadeghi, A.R., Schulz, S., Varadharajan, V.: The silence of the LANs: Efficient leakage resilience for IPsec VPNs (full version). Technical report (2012)
19. Girling, C.G.: Covert channels in LAN's. IEEE Transactions on Software Engineering 13(2) (1987)
20. Browne, R.: Mode security: An infrastructure for covert channel suppression. In: Research in Security and Privacy (S&P), Oakland, CA. IEEE (1994)

21. Kiraly, C., Teofili, S., Lo Cigno, R., Nardelli, M., Delzeri, E.: Traffic Flow Confidentiality in IPsec: Protocol and Implementation. In: Fischer-Hübner, S., Duquenoy, P., Zuccato, A., Martucci, L. (eds.) The Future of Identity in the Information Society. IFIP, vol. 262, pp. 311–324. Springer, Boston (2008)
22. Moskowitz, I.S., Miller, A.R.: Simple timing channels. In: Research in Security and Privacy (S&P), Oakland, CA. IEEE (1994)
23. Fu, X.: On Traffic Analysis Attacks and Countermeasures. PhD thesis, Texas A&M University (2005)
24. Venkatraman, B.R., Newman-Wolfe, R.E.: Transmission schedules to prevent traffic analysis. In: Computer Security Applications Conference (ACSAC). IEEE (1994)
25. Fu, X., Graham, B., Bettati, R., Zhao, W.: On effectiveness of link padding for statistical traffic analysis attacks. In: International Conference on Distributed Computing Systems (ICDCS). IEEE, Washington, DC (2003)
26. Gettys, J.: Bufferbloat: Dark buffers in the Internet. IEEE Internet Computing 15(3) (2011)
27. El-Atawy, A., Al-Shaer, E.: Building covert channels over the packet reordering phenomenon. In: International Conference on Computer Communications (INFOCOM). IEEE (2009)
28. Mogul, J., Deering, S.: Path MTU discovery. RFC 1191 (1990)
29. Zhao, W., Olshefski, D., Schulzrinne, H.: Internet quality of service: An overview. Technical report, Columbia University (2000)
30. Braden, B., Clark, D., Crowcroft, J., Davie, B., Deering, S., Estrin, D., Floyd, S., Jacobson, V., Minshall, G., Partridge, C., Peterson, L., Ramakrishnan, K., Shenker, S., Wroclawski, J., Zhang, L.: Recommendations on Queue Management and Congestion Avoidance in the Internet. RFC 2309 (1998)
31. Bell, D.E.: Looking back on the Bell-LaPadula model. In: Computer Security Applications Conference (ACSAC). IEEE (2005)
32. Llamas, D., Allison, C., Miller, A.: Covert channels in internet protocols: A survey (2006)
33. Zander, S., Armitage, G., Branch, P.: A survey of covert channels and countermeasures in computer network protocols. Comm. Surveys & Tutorials 9(3) (2007)
34. Guan, Y., Fu, X., Xuan, D., Shenoy, P.U., Bettati, R., Zhao, W.: NetCamo: Camouflaging network traffic for QoS-guaranteed mission critical applications. Trans. on Systems, Man, and Cybernetics - Systems and Humans 31(4) (2001)
35. Shmatikov, V., Wang, M.H.: Timing Analysis in Low-Latency Mix Networks: Attacks and Defenses. In: Gollmann, D., Meier, J., Sabelfeld, A. (eds.) ESORICS 2006. LNCS, vol. 4189, pp. 18–33. Springer, Heidelberg (2006)
36. Abraham, T., Wright, M.: Selective cross correlation in passive timing analysis attacks against Low-Latency mixes. In: Global Communications Conference (GLOBECOM). IEEE (2010)
37. Luo, X., Zhou, P., Chan, E.W.W., Lee, W., Chang, R.K.C., Perdisci, R.: HTTPOS: Sealing information leaks with browser-side obfuscation of encrypted flows. In: Network and Distributed Systems Security (NDSS). Internet Society (2011)
38. Wright, C.V., Coull, S.E., Monrose, F.: Traffic morphing: An efficient defense against statistical traffic analysis. In: Network and Distributed Systems Security (NDSS). Internet Society (2009)
39. Berk, V., Giani, A., Cybenko, G.: Detection of covert channel encoding in network packet delays. Technical Report TR536, Dartmouth College (2005)
40. Gilbert, P.A., Bhattacharya, P.: An approach towards anomaly based detection and profiling covert TCP/IP channels. In: Information, Communications and Signal Processing (ICICS). IEEE (2009)

Security of Patched DNS

Amir Herzberg and Haya Shulman

Computer Science Department,
Bar Ilan University,
Ramat Gan, Israel
{amir.herzberg,haya.shulman}@gmail.com

Abstract. Most caching DNS resolvers still rely for their security, against poisoning, on validating that the DNS responses contain some 'unpredictable' values, copied from the request. These values include the 16 bit identifier field, and other fields, randomised and validated by different 'patches' to DNS. We investigate the prominent patches, and show how attackers can circumvent all of them, namely:

- We show how attackers can circumvent source port randomisation, in the (common) case where the resolver connects to the Internet via different NAT devices.
- We show how attackers can circumvent IP address randomisation, using some (standard-conforming) resolvers.
- We show how attackers can circumvent query randomisation, including both randomisation by prepending a random nonce and case randomisation (0x20 encoding).

We present countermeasures preventing our attacks; however, we believe that our attacks provide additional motivation for adoption of DNSSEC (or other MitM-secure defenses).

Keywords: DNS security, DNS poisoning, Kamisky attack, Network Address Translator, NAT, DNS server selection, Internet security.

1 Introduction

Correct and efficient operation of the Domain Name System (DNS) is essential for the operation of the Internet. However, there is a long history of vulnerabilities and exploits related to DNS, mostly focusing on *DNS poisoning*. In a poisoning attempt the attacker causes recursive DNS servers (resolvers) to cache an incorrect, fake DNS record, e.g., mapping VIC-Bank.com to an IP address controlled by the attacker. DNS poisoning can facilitate many other attacks, such as injection of malware, phishing, website hijacking/defacing and denial of service.

The main technique for DNS poisoning is by sending forged responses to DNS requests which were sent by resolvers; to foil this, resolvers validate responses using different mechanisms. Currently, most resolvers rely only on non-cryptographic validation, mainly, confirming that the response echoes some unpredictable (random) values sent with the request, such as in the DNS transaction ID field, the source port selected by the resolver, or within the resource

S. Foresti, M. Yung, and F. Martinelli (Eds.): ESORICS 2012, LNCS 7459, pp. 271–288, 2012.

(domain) name; e.g., see RFC 5452 [1] for more details. Obviously, such mechanisms are insecure against a Man-in-the-Middle (MitM) attacker, who can read the randomness from the request and send a fake response with the valid identifiers.

Furthermore, even a weaker - and more common - *off-path, spoofing attackers*, may be able to send valid DNS responses and cause DNS poisoning, when the validated values are predictable or limited. For example, some DNS implementations use predictable identifiers (sequential, or using a weak pseudorandom generator); e.g., in [2], Klein shows how to predict the identifier for the then-current version of Bind 9, a widely-used DNS server, and how this can be exploited for highly-efficient DNS poisoning by a spoofing attacker. Indeed, as pointed out already in 1995 by Vixie [3], the identifier field alone is simply too short (16 bits) to provide sufficient defense against a determined spoofing attacker, who can foil it by sending many (but not too many) fake responses.

To improve DNS security, the IETF published DNSSEC [4,6,5], an extension to DNS, using cryptography (signatures and hashing) to ensure security (even) against MitM attackers. However, in spite of the publication of DNSSEC already in 1997 [7], and the wide awareness to its existence, deployment is still limited - e.g., less than 2% as reported in [8] for April, 2012. There are also many caching DNS resolvers that still do not support, or do not perform validation of, DNSSEC [9]; see discussion of the deployment status of DNSSEC in [10]. Furthermore, due to implementation errors DNSSEC protection may fail, even when both the resolver and zone deploy it: validation of signatures of important top level domains, e.g., mil, fails since the root does not delegate the public signature key of mil but instead provides an incorrect indication that mil does not support DNSSEC. This results in resolvers falling back to a non-validating mode.

Indeed the deployment of DNSSEC is progressing slowly, due to challenges (see [10]), and possibly due to the recent improvements ('patches') to non-cryptographic defenses, causing 'if it ain't broke, don't fix it' response. These patches are mainly by deploying new sources of 'unpredictability' in DNS requests and responses, such as use of random source ports [11,12], random DNS server selection [1] and random capitalisation of the domain name [13].

This manuscript focuses on relying on such non-cryptographic 'patches' to defend against DNS poisoning. This has two goals: to help improve these patches, since evidently they will remain widely used for years; and to further motivate adoption of more secure solutions such as DNSSEC, by pointing out weaknesses in the patches. While these specific weaknesses can be fixed (and we show how - often, easily), their existence should motivate the adoption of better security measures such as DNSSEC, providing security against MitM attacker and allowing for better validation of security, e.g., see [14].

1.1   Patching Caching DNS Resolvers against Poisoning

Many researchers have identified vulnerabilities and improvements in the approach of relying on an 'unpredictability' of some fields in a DNS request and proposed patches; we next review some of the main results. Bernstein, [15], suggested to improve DNS's defense against spoofed responses by sending the request from a *random port*, which can add a significant amount of entropy[1]. To prevent *birthday attack*, where attacker causes resolver to issue multiple queries for same domain in order to increase the probability of a match with one of multiple fake responses, Bernstein [15] and others suggest to limit the maximal number of concurrent requests for the same resource record (to one or to some small number); this technique is usually referred to as the *birthday protection*.

Many implementations did not implement these suggestions till the recent Kaminsky attack, [11,12], which introduced two critical improvements, allowing devastating attacks on many Internet applications. The first improvement was to control the time at which the resolver sends queries (to which the attacker wishes to respond), by sending to the resolver queries for a non-existing host name, e.g., with a random or sequential prefix of the domain name. The second improvement was to add, in the spoofed responses sent to the resolver, a type NS DNS record (specifying a new name for the domain name server) and/or a type A 'glue' DNS record (specifying the IP address of that domain's name server). These records poison the resolver's entries for the victim name server. Hence, if the attack succeeds once (for one record), the adversary controls the entire name space of the victim.

As a result of Kaminsky's attack, it became obvious that changes were needed to prevent DNS poisoning. Indeed, major DNS resolvers were quickly patched. The most basic patches were known measures - source port randomisation and birthday protection (see above). These and other additional patches were summarised in RFC 5452 [1], including the use of random (valid) IP addresses for the name server. Additional patches, implemented by some resolvers, are to randomise DNS queries by randomly 'case toggling' the domain name (0x20 encoding [13]), or by adding a random prefix to the domain name [16].

It is tempting to interpret the analysis in [13,17,1,16] as indication that the 'patches' may suffice to make poisoning impractical, reducing the motivation for deployment of more systematic improvements. However, we caution against this conclusion. This work shows that in common scenarios, attackers can often circumvent some or all of the 'patches', making it still feasible to poison resolvers that rely on validation of 'unpredictable' values copied from requests to responses (rather than relying on cryptographic security, as in DNSSEC).

Some concerns with 'patches' were presented in earlier works. In particular, the most widely and easily deployed 'patch' is clearly source port randomisation. However, security experts, e.g., [18,12], noted that DNS resolvers located behind firewall/NAT devices, that use sequential assignment of external ports, were still vulnerable to the poisoning attack. On the other hand, it was widely believed that 'port-randomising' NAT devices, that sufficiently randomise the external ports, could retain or even improve the defense against DNS cache poisoning, e.g., see [12]. In addition, it was believed that 'port-preserving' NAT devices, that leave the source port intact (if it were not already allocated to another

---

[1] The exact amount of entropy added depends on the number of available ports, which may be below 2^{16}.

host), can be safely used with port-randomising resolvers, e.g., see [19]. Our results show otherwise, i.e., some of our attacks show how to circumvent port randomisation, in the resolver-behind-NAT scenario, even for port-randomising and port-preserving NATs.

Note that the resolver-behind-NAT scenario is common [20,21]. A recent study, [9], of DNSSEC deployment by recursive resolvers observed that a large number of recursive DNS resolvers is located behind NAT devices, and often many resolvers are even behind the same NAT device. Furthermore, [22] found that 90% out of 20,000 DSL lines (from a major European ISP) were located behind a NAT device.

1.2   Attacker Model

In our attacks, we assume an off-path, spoofing adversary connected to the Internet and a compromised (by the adversary) host, running malware, on the local network; the attacker model is depicted in Figure 1. Depending on the attack, we assume different capabilities on the malware running on the internal host. The attacks in Section 2 assume a non-spoofing (user-mode) compromised host (zombie) on the local network (zombies exist in many networks, e.g., see [23]); the zombie can open user mode sockets and can send arbitrary (non-spoofed) pack-

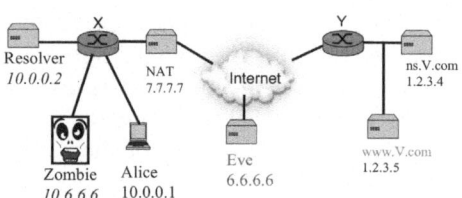

Fig. 1. Attack scenario and network configuration: in attacks in Section 2 we assume that the DNS resolver is located behind a NAT device, along with a benign client and a zombie; In Sections 3 and 4 we assume a puppet and do not require a NAT. The off-path spoofer Eve is located on the Internet.

ets, [24]. In these attacks we also assume that the resolver is located behind a NAT device. The attacks in Sections 3 and 4 use a puppet (a script confined by a browser), and do not require the network to be connected to the Internet via a NAT.

1.3   Contributions

The security of patched DNS resolvers relies on the randomness provided by the validation fields. We show that it is possible to reduce and often to nullify the randomness, thereby exposing the resolvers to Kaminsky-style poisoning attacks. Our attacks apply to all widely-deployed 'patches':

Source-port randomisation. In Section 2 we expose vulnerabilities in common source port allocation algorithms used by popular NAT devices. The vulnerabilities allow to circumvent source port randomisation, thus enabling prediction of the source port allocated to the queries of the resolver. We tested our attacks in a lab setting against several NAT devices, see Table 1. The type of the NAT that the resolver resides behind is important in deciding which attack to launch.

DNS server IP randomisation. We present techniques to predict (or force) the IP address of the name server to which the resolver will send its DNS request (Section 3). Our techniques rely on fragmented DNS responses.

Domain name randomisation. We show (Section 4) that randomisation of DNS queries via 0x20, or by prepending a random string, is not always effective and does not introduce protection against poisoning attacks.

In addition to exposing the vulnerabilities, we also propose countermeasures. However, our most important contribution may be in motivating the adoption of systematic, secure defenses against poisoning, such as DNSSEC.

2   Source Port (de)Randomisation

In this section we present techniques to trap/predict the external port that will be allocated by the NAT device to the DNS request, of the DNS resolver, which the attacker wishes to poison. This phase allows to reduce (in some cases even nullify) the randomness added by source port randomisation (SPR). We tested our trap/predict attacks against patched DNS resolvers (supporting SPR and random transaction ID selection) and popular NAT devices, that implement different mechanisms for randomisation of source ports, allocated by the NAT to outbound packets; see Table 1.

We identified the following common (random) ports allocation algorithms: (1) *random* allocation (Section 2.1) where NAT selects ports at random from a pool of available ports until all ports are exhausted; (2) *per-destination sequential* allocation (Section 2.2) where the NAT selects the first port to each destination at random, and subsequent packets to that destination are allocated consecutive mappings; (3) *port preserving*[2] allocation, where the NAT preserves the original port in the outgoing packets, and allocates sequentially upon collision; (4) *restricted random* allocation, where the NAT maintains a mapping table that is smaller than the pool of available ports.

We also checked the source port allocation process of the NAT devices, which we tested in this work, via the DNS-OARC online `porttest` tool, [25]. The tool assigns one of the possible three scores: GREAT, GOOD and POOR, rating the 'unpredictability' of the ports allocation process. The tool reported a GREAT score for all the NAT devices tested in this work. Yet we present techniques that allow the attacker to trap/predict the ports assigned to resolvers' DNS requests. The conclusion is that ports that 'appear' to be random should not be taken as indication of security. Indeed, as we show in this work, there are ways to circumvent this line of defense. In what follows we show trap-then-poison (Section 2.1) and predict-then-poison (Section 2.2) attacks for selected NAT devices; attacks for other NAT devices, in Table 1, apply with slight variations and can be found in the extended version of this work [10].

Our descriptions and figures use illustrative choices of IP addresses, e.g., 10.6.6.6 (for zombie), 6.6.6.6 (for spoofing adversary Eve), 1.2.3.4 (for the authoritative name server of the 'victim' domain, V.com), and so on.

---

[2] We present the attack against port preserving NAT in the full version of the paper [10].

Table 1. Summary of the source port derandomisation attacks presented in this work, against different types of NAT devices that were tested

Vendor	Port Allocation	Porttest Rating [25]	Vulnerability [Section]
Checkpoint (R70/FW-1)	restricted random (cannot be trapped)	great	Resistant to attacks
Linux Netfilter Iptables (kernel 2.6) with '–random'	per-dest first random then sequential	great	Predict attack [Section 2.2]
Linux Netfilter Iptables (kernel 2.6)	preserving (sequential if collide)	great	Predict attack [10]
Windows XP ICS (Service Pack 3)	first random then sequential	great	Predict attack [Section 2.2]
Windows XP WinGate (Release 2.6.4)	preserving (random if collide)	great	Trap attack [Section 2.1]
CISCO IOS (release 15)	preserving (random if collide)	great	Trap attack [Section 2.1]
CISCO ASA (release 5500)	random (can be trapped)	great	Trap attack [Section 2.1]

The NAT allocates mappings (permutations) between the addressing used by the internal host, identified by the tuple $(S_{IP}{:}S_{Port}, D_{IP}{:}D_{Port})$, and the addressing used by the external host, identified by the tuple $(NAT_{IP}{:}NAT_{Port}, D_{IP}{:}D_{Port})$, with the same values of $D_{IP}{:}D_{Port}$ in both tuples. We denote such mappings (permutations) by function $f(\cdot)$.

Our attacks begin with a phase which allows the spoofer, Eve, to learn the port that will be allocated by the NAT to the DNS request of the DNS resolver. The port learning phase is performed with the help of a non-spoofing zombie, running with user-mode privileges.

2.1   Trap-Then-Poison for Random Ports Allocation

The attack in this section relies on the fact that the NAT implements *outbound refresh mapping* for UDP connections, as specified in requirement 6 of RFC 4787 [26] (and implemented in most NATs). Namely, the NAT maintains the mappings from an internal (source) $S_{IP} : S_{port}$ pair to an external port NAT_{port}, for T seconds since a packet was last sent from $S_{IP}{:}S_{port}$ (on the internal side of the NAT) to the external network, using this mapping. We further assume that the NAT device selects an external port at random for each outgoing packet, e.g., CISCO ASA. The NAT device silently drops outgoing packets, sent from $S_{IP}{:}S_{port}$ to $D_{IP}{:}D_{port}$, when all external ports for $D_{IP}{:}D_{port}$ are currently mapped to other sources; this is the typical expected NAT behaviour, see [26].

The attack begins when the zombie contacts the attacker's command-and-control center, identifies its location, and receives a signal to initiate the attack. We next describe the steps of the attack; also illustrated with simplifications in Figure 2.

1. The zombie, at address 10.6.6.6, sends UDP packets to 1.2.3.4:53, i.e., to the DNS port (53) of the name server of the 'victim' domain, whose fully

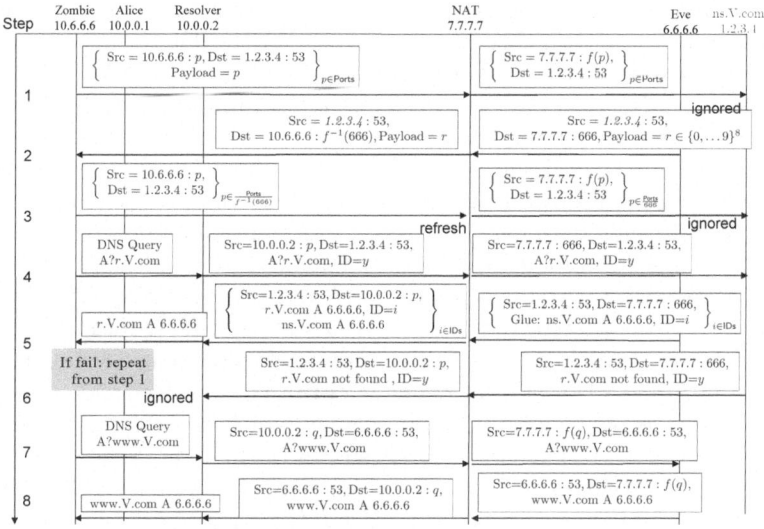

Fig. 2. DNS trap-then-poison attack with random ports allocation, for configuration in Figure 1

qualified domain name (FQDN) is **ns.V.com**, from each port p in the set of available ports Ports. To handle faults, the payload of each packet contains the sending port $p \in$ Ports. The NAT allocates to each packet it forwards to **ns.V.com** a 'random' permutation f over Ports; the allocation of each external port $f(p)$ to a specific internal port p is held for T seconds, unless refreshed. Since none of these packets is a legitimate DNS packet, the authoritative name server ns.V.com ignores all of them, and does not send back any response.

2. After step 1 completed[3], Eve sends a packet with a spoofed source address 1.2.3.4:53, to external port 666 of the NAT (i.e., to 7.7.7.7:666). Since 7.7.7.7:666 is currently mapped to the internal IP address 10.6.6.6 and some port $f^{-1}(666)$, the NAT relays the packet to this IP and port. Thereby, the zombie learns the mapping of external port 666 to the internal port $f^{-1}(666)$; this will be crucial in the continuation of the attack, where we 'force' the query of the resolver to be sent using external port 666 (the 'trap'). This packet contains as a payload a random string of 8, or so, digits to be used as the prefix of the FQDN in the query sent in the attack (in step 4).

3. After receipt of the packet on port $f^{-1}(666)$ in step 2, the zombie waits until the mappings established in step 1 are about to expire, i.e., until $t_3 = t_1 + T$ (where t_1 is the time of step 1). At t_3, the zombie sends additional empty UDP packets, to all ports in Ports, *except* port $f^{-1}(666)$. As a result, the NAT refreshes the mappings on all of these ports; only the mapping for port 666 times out, and hence this becomes the *trap*: i.e., the only available external port of the NAT, which can be allocated for UDP packets whose destination is 1.2.3.4:53.

---

[3] Eve can learn it is time to send the packet at the beginning of step 2, e.g., by an appropriate packet from the zombie to Eve upon completion of step 1.

4. Following to step 3, the attacker knows that the external port 666 of the NAT is the only port which can be allocated to the UDP packets sent from the internal network to the authoritative name server, at 1.2.3.4:53. The zombie sends a single DNS query to the resolver, for a random FQDN r.V.com; the use of a random 'subdomain' r allows to evade the caching of the resolver and ensures that the resolver issues a DNS query for this FQDN. The resolver then sends a query to **ns.V.com**, from some 'random' (more precisely, unpredictable to attacker) port which we denote p, and using some random identifier i.

5. Next, Eve sends a forged response per each $i \in 2^{16}$ values of the ID field. If one of these responses matches all of the validation fields in the query, the resolver accepts the poisoned records [r.V.com A 6.6.6.6] and [V.com NS r.V.com]. Namely, from this point on, the resolver considers 6.6.6.6 as a valid IP address for the authoritative DNS server of **ns.V.com**. The resolver also forwards the response [r.V.com A 6.6.6.6] to the zombie, which detects the successful attack, and informs Eve (this phase is not shown in the figure).

6. The resolver receives a legitimate 'non-existing domain' (NXDOMAIN) response from the 'real' name server, at 1.2.3.4. If the attack succeeded this response is ignored, since the query is not pending any more. Otherwise, the resolver forwards the NXDOMAIN response to the zombie, who will inform Eve; they will repeat the attack from step 1 (as soon as the ports expire on the NAT).

7. Finally, steps 7 and 8 illustrate subsequent poisoning of 'real' FQDN within the **V.com** domain. Since, following step 5, the resolver uses the 'poisoned' mappings [ns.V.com A 6.6.6.6], all subsequent requests for this domain are sent to 6.6.6.6.

2.2 Predict-Then-Poison for Per-destination Sequential Ports

In practice, due to efficiency considerations, NAT devices often do not select a random external port for *every* outgoing packet, but, depending on the NAT device, select the first port (for a tuple defined by $< S_{IP} : S_{Port}, D_{IP} : D_{Port}, protocol >$) at random, and subsequent ports are increased sequentially (for that tuple), until NAT refreshes its mapping for that tuple (if no packets arrived, e.g., after 30 seconds). For a different tuple, e.g., different destination IP, a new random port is selected for first packet, while subsequent packets are assigned sequentially increasing port numbers. When the NAT refreshes the mapping, i.e., by default 30 seconds, the port for outgoing packets with destination IP and port tuple is selected at random again. This behaviour is consistent with prominent NAT devices, e.g., Iptables NAT, Carrier Grade NAT [27].

In this section we present predict-then-poison attack on a *per-destination port randomising* NAT. A variation of the attack, which applies to *port preserving* NAT, is presented in full version of this work, [10]. In contrast to 'trap' attacks, the 'predict' attacks exploit an insufficient source port randomisation mechanism of the NAT, which allows to produce much more efficient attacks by predicting the source port allocated for the DNS requests by the NAT. In particular, the zombie is only required to generate and send three packets during the attack: first packet creates a mapping in the NAT table (so that packets from Eve can

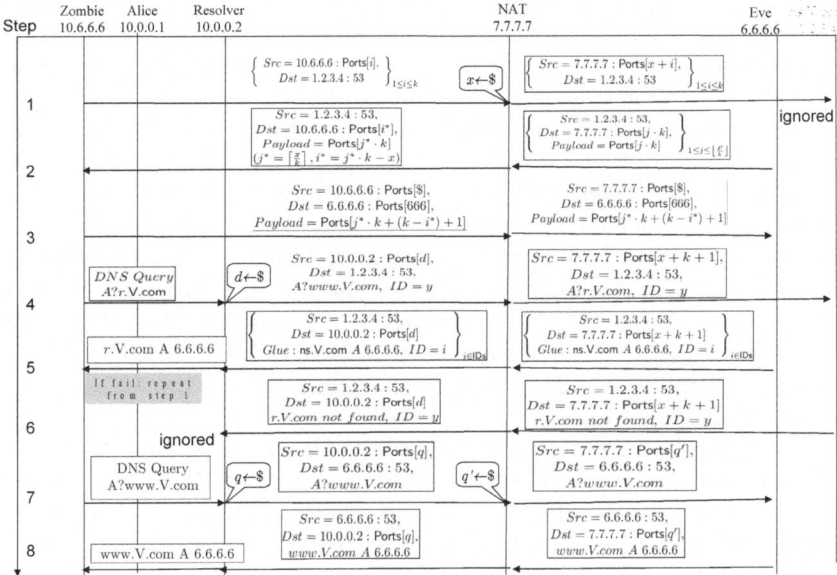

Fig. 3. Predict-then-poison DNS attack, for configuration in Figure 1, assuming per-destination port sequential NAT

come through), subsequent packet lets Eve know which external port was used by the NAT, and the third packet is a DNS query which the zombie sends to local resolver for some random name in the victim domain $r.$**V.com**. The attack can be optimised by having the zombie transmit k packets[4] ($1 \leq k \leq 2^{16}$) from consecutive ports; Eve then sends $\lfloor \frac{P}{k} \rfloor$ packets ($P \equiv |\mathsf{Ports}|$), such that j-th packet is sent to port $\mathsf{Ports}[j \cdot k]$. The steps of the attack (in Figure 3) follow.

1. Zombie opens the ports (to the destination IP address of the authoritative DNS), i.e., sends k UDP packets from sequentially increasing ports $\mathsf{Ports}[1],...,\mathsf{Ports}[k]$. All k packets have 1.2.3.4:53 as the destination IP address and UDP port respectively (i.e., the name server of the victim domain, whose FQDN is **ns.V.com**). The NAT assigns a randomly selected port $\mathsf{Ports}[x]$ to the first packet (in the sequence of k packets) that it receives, the rest $k-1$ packets are assigned consecutive (sequentially increasing) external ports.

2. Eve sends $\lfloor \frac{P}{k} \rfloor$ UDP packets, to sequentially increasing (by a factor of k) external ports of the NAT, with spoofed source IP 1.2.3.4:53. The payload of each packet contains the destination port number. The zombie receives exactly one packet from Eve, w.l.o.g. on port $\mathsf{Ports}[i^*]$, and with payload containing $j^* \cdot k$ (i.e., packet that was sent to port with index $\mathsf{Ports}[j^* \cdot k]$ of the NAT).

3. Next the zombie calculates the port that will be assigned by the NAT to the DNS query of the local resolver: $\mathsf{Ports}[j^* \cdot k + (k - i^*) + 1]$, and sends it to

---

[4] Typically, it may be preferable for zombie to issue less packets (i.e., to use smaller k) to evade detection.

Eve in the payload (from some (random) source port Ports[$] to a destination port 666, on which Eve is configured to be listening). Since the destination IP address of the packet sent to Eve is different from that of the authoritative name server, NAT will select an external port at random, and not consecutively, i.e., some Ports[$] s.t., with high probability Ports[$] $\neq$ Ports[$x + k + 1$].

4. The zombie then issues a DNS query to the local resolver, asking for a random FQDN r.**V.com**. Since this domain name most likely does not exist in the cache, the resolver sends a DNS query from some (random) port Ports[d] containing a random identifier, to the authoritative name server **ns.V.com**. Note that the destination in the query of the local resolver is the same as the one that was used in the UDP packets of the zombie (i.e., the authoritative name server), the NAT will allocate the next available (consecutive) port to the query of the resolver, i.e., Ports[$x + k + 1$], following the sequence of ports assigned to the packets of zombie.

5. As soon as Eve receives the packet containing the external port of the NAT that is mapped to the internal port of the resolver, she will generate and transmit P packets with different values in the ID field, with spoofed source IP address (ostensibly originating from **ns.V.com**). The destination port in all the packets is Ports[$j^* \cdot k + (k - i^*) + 1$], and the response contains: [r.V.com A 6.6.6.6] and [V.com NS r.V.com]. Since this port was allocated by the NAT to the query sent by the resolver, the NAT will forward all these DNS responses to the resolver.

6. Eventually when the authentic response 'non-existing domain' (NXDO-MAIN) of the real name server at 1.2.3.4 arrives, the resolver will ignore it if one of the maliciously crafted packets (sent by Eve) matched and gets accepted. The remaining steps are identical to steps (7) and (8), presented in Section 2.1, Figure 2.

2.3   Experimental Evaluation

We next describe the setting that we used for validation of the attacks in this section. We also summarise our results for each NAT device, against which we tested the attacks, in Table 1; the NAT devices were selected from different categories, i.e., proprietary NAT devices, e.g., Checkpoint, SOHO NAT devices, e.g., windows XP ICS, and other prominent NAT devices. This list of NAT devices that we tested is of course not exhaustive, but since we found that almost all of them, except one, allowed the attacker to reduce source port randomisation of the resolver, it is very likely that many more may be vulnerable to our (or other) attacks, e.g., Carrier Grade NAT of Juniper Networks (based on the technical report, [27], published in 2011).

Testbed Setup. Figure 1 illustrates the testbed used for the experimental evaluation of our attacks. The testbed consists of a NAT enabled gateway, which has two network cards. One card is connected via an ethernet cable to a switch, connecting a benign client, a compromised host, and a DNS resolver. The other is connected to Eve (also via a switch). The DNS resolver is running Unbound 1.4.1 software. The tests were run concurrently with other benign uses of the network. We report on the results of the success of the DNS cache poisoning, by running trap and predict attacks against popular NAT devices, in Table 1, and in more detail in the technical report [10].

2.4 Improved Port Allocation Mechanism

The recommendations, [28], for NAT behaviour do not specify the implementation of port allocation mechanism. As a result, the developers and designers of NAT devices follow different approaches which may seem secure. Based on our findings we identify two design factors in ports allocation mechanism of the NAT: (1) the process via which the ports are selected (i.e., random, preserving, sequential); (2) the mapping table which maintains the allocated ports.

Randomise Ports Selection. Use port randomisation, but either with separate, random external port for each internal port, or at least with pseudo-random (but not sequential) increments between external port numbers[5]. Random ports assignment prevents the 'predict' attacks.

Restricted Mapping Table. The mapping table of allocated ports, maintained by the NAT, should be smaller than the pool of all the ports[6], e.g., half or less of the total of number of ports; a smaller mapping table prevents the attacker from trapping the port. For each arriving packet NAT should randomly select and assign a port from the pool of ports. Each time an entry is removed from the table when the external port is freed, e.g., the entry is refreshed after a timeout, NAT should select a new random port from the pool of ports.

3   IP Addresses (de)Randomisation

DNS resolvers can increase the entropy in DNS requests by randomising the IP addresses, i.e., selecting the source/destination IP addresses in the DNS request at random, and then validating the same addresses in the DNS response. Selecting random source IP address is rare, the resolvers are typically allocated one (or few) IP address as IPv4 addresses are a scarce resource. Furthermore, resolvers behind NAT devices use the IP of the NAT for their requests, and the address of the resolver is generally known [1].

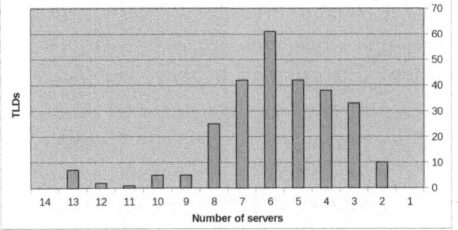

Fig. 4. The number of IP addresses in use by Top Level Domains (TLDs)

In contrast, most operators of DNS zones use a number of authoritative name servers for performance, robustness, and enhanced resilience to cache poisoning

---

[5] A pseudo-random permutation will provide as efficient data structure and lookup, as when using sequential allocation.

[6] This approach was supported only by the Checkpoint NAT which allowed it to evade our trap attacks.

attacks. We found that the majority of top level domains (TLDs) use 5 to 7 authority name servers, and important domains, e.g., COM, use 13 authority servers[7]; see Figure 4.

When zone operators employ multiple authority servers, the resolver should send the query to the one with the shortest response time, and avoid querying non-responsive name servers, see [30,31]. However, there are no instructions on how to implement the server selection algorithm; as a result different resolvers, and even different versions thereof, implement different server selection algorithms, often resulting in inefficient implementations, [32].

Indeed, the selection of the authority server by the caching resolver can often be predicted, e.g., if the attacker can measure the latency from the resolver to the authority name servers for a sufficient amount of time. However, this requires a significant effort from the attacker, and may not always result in precise prediction.

We focus on a weaker attacker which does not keep track of the latency to all the servers. However, our technique enables the attacker to predict the target name server's IP, for resolvers which avoid querying unresponsive name servers, as per the recommendations in [32,31]. We exploit the fact that when the target name server is not responsive, i.e., queries time-out, the resolver does not send subsequent queries to it, but only periodically, probes the target server until it becomes responsive. The (standard-conforming) Unbound (1.4.1) resolver sets this probing interval to 15 minutes. A similar behaviour was observed by [32] in PowerDNS, with the exception that PowerDNS sets the interval to 3 minutes. It appears that relying on the DNS server IP address randomisation for additional entropy requires careful study of particular resolver in question.

3.1 Predicting the Destination IP Address

The idea of destination IP prediction phase, in Figure 5, is to exploit large DNS responses which result in fragmentation; fragmented IP traffic has been exploited for denial of service attacks in the past, e.g., [33,34,35]. We performed the attack against a 404.GOV domain[8], whose *non-existing domain* responses exceed 1500 bytes and thus get fragmented en-route.

This phase, of forcing the resolver to use a specific IP, requires a puppet, i.e., a script confined in a browser, which issues DNS requests via the local caching DNS resolver, at IP 1.2.3.4 in Figure 5.

In steps 1 and 2 the puppet coordinates with the spoofer and issues a DNS request for \$123.404.GOV (where \$123 is a random prefix). In steps 3 and 4, the spoofer sends a forged second fragment, for all the possible name servers (i.e., a total of 2 spoofed fragments) except one which the attacker wants the resolver to use for its queries during the poisoning phase; the 404.GOV domain has three name servers. This ensures that only one IP address results in a valid response, and the other two result in malformed DNS packets. The spoofed

---

[7] The list of TLDs is taken from the list published by IANA [29].

[8] Many other zones return responses which get fragmented, e.g., MIL TLD; we focused on 404.GOV since it has only three name servers, which simplifies the presentation.

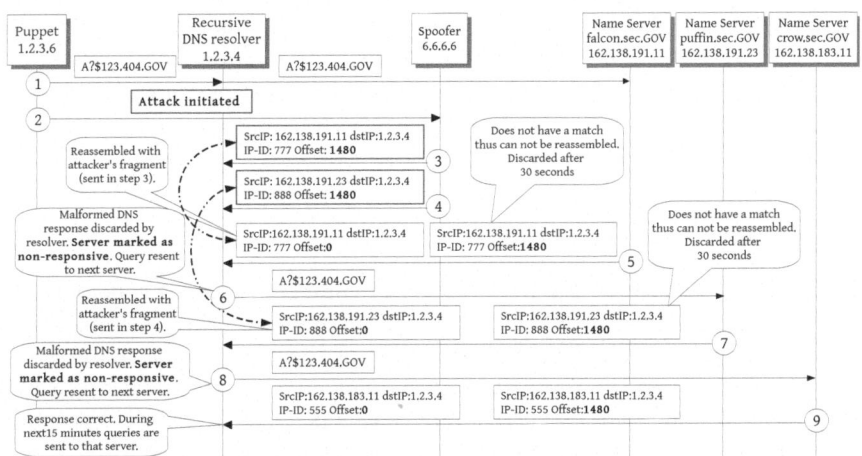

Fig. 5. The destination IP address prediction attacks: spoofing attacker crafts a forged second fragment that gets reassembled with the authentic first fragment and results in a malformed packet, which is discarded by the resolver

second fragment is incorrect, and contains a single arbitrary byte (in addition to headers). In step 5, the spoofed second fragment is reconstructed with the authentic first fragment resulting in a malformed DNS packet which leaves the fragments reassembly buffer. This malformed DNS response is then discarded by the resolver, and the IP of the name server is marked[9] as 'non-responsive'. When the authentic second fragment arrives, it does not have a match and is discarded after a timeout. As a result the resolver does not receive the response, and after a timeout it resends the DNS request to the next DNS server, step 6. The same procedure applies here, and the response is discarded. In step 9 a valid response arrives from IP 162.138.183.11. Note that the resolver sends two queries to each server and marks the name server as non-responsive when *two* queries to that server result in a timeout; for simplicity in Figure 5 we present the process for one query to each server. As a result of 'wrecking' the responses from all name servers except one, we forced the resolver to direct all its queries for 404.GOV domain to one name server at IP 162.138.183.11.

Note that crafting a forged second fragment that would get matched with the authentic first fragment requires a match with the identification field (IP-ID) in the IP header. According to [36,34] the fragments of a datagram are associated with each other by their protocol number, the value in their IP-ID field, and by the source/destination address pair. Therefore the attacker is required to hit the correct IP-ID value, which is used by the name server in its DNS response. Many domains, as well as 404.gov, use per-destination sequential incrementing IP-ID values (or even globally sequential incrementing IP-ID, e.g., Windows OS). Other domains (mainly top level domains and the root servers) increment the IP-ID value in randomised quotas; we provide more details on this in [10].

---

[9] In reality the resolver marks the server as 'non-responsive' after two unsuccessful respopnses, and this is easily handled by the attacker by sending two spoofed fragments with consecutive IP-ID in each IP header.

The IP-ID allocation algorithm does not have a significant impact[10] on our attacks against Unbound (and alike) resolvers, as the number of 'misses', i.e., valid responses arriving to the resolver from some IP, does not prevent the attack since two failed (timed-out) queries suffice for Unbound to mark the server as non-responsive for 15 minute interval.

3.2   Experimental Evaluation

The Wireshark capture, in Figure 6, that was run on the resolver, demonstrates the experimental evalutation, i.e., the DNS packets entering/leaving the network card of the resolver. During the course of the experiment the puppet issued 6000 queries[11] to the resolver. The spoofer initiates the attack by sending three spoofed fragments to each IP address except 162.138.183.11. For simplicity, the capture presents only the packets exchanged between the resolver and the name server of 404.gov at 162.138.191.23 (by adjusting a corresponding filter in wireshark); the complete capture contains queries/responses from other name servers too. Packets numbered 18-20 are the forged fragments sent by the spoofer, with sequentially incrementing IP-IDs. Then zombie triggers a DNS request (packet 29). The response from the name server contains two fragments, packets 33 and 34. The first fragment is reassembled with a spoofed fragment (packet 18), resulting in a malformed packet which is discarded by the resolver.

The second fragment is discarded after a timeout. In packet 48 the resolver requests a public verification key of the 404.gov zone. The response contains three fragments 49-51; the first fragment is reconstructed with the spoofed fragment in packet 20, which also results in a malformed DNS response and is discarded. Note that this request, in packet 48, was sent at 19:28. Based on our tests it can be seen that when Unbound encounters a timeout twice for the same destination

No.	Time	Source	Destination	Protocol	Info
18	19:28:47.243364	162.138.191.23	132.70.6.119	IP	Fragmented IP protocol (proto=UDP 0x11, off=1480, ID=2cc8) [Reassembled in #33]
19	19:28:47.243393	162.138.191.23	132.70.6.119	IP	Fragmented IP protocol (proto=UDP 0x11, off=1480, ID=2cc9)
20	19:28:47.243402	162.138.191.23	132.70.6.119	IP	Fragmented IP protocol (proto=UDP 0x11, off=1480, ID=2cca) [Reassembled in #49]
29	19:28:49.334286	132.70.6.119	162.138.191.23	DNS	Standard query A 1123456789000987654321.404.gov
33	19:28:49.488072	162.138.191.23	132.70.6.119	DNS	Standard query response, No such name[Malformed Packet]
34	19:28:49.488117	162.138.191.23	132.70.6.119	IP	Fragmented IP protocol (proto=UDP 0x11, off=1480, ID=2cc8)
40	19:28:49.497916	132.70.6.119	162.138.191.23	DNS	Standard query AAAA crow.sec.gov
44	19:28:49.650954	162.138.191.23	132.70.6.119	DNS	Standard query response
48	19:28:49.864784	132.70.6.119	162.138.191.23	DNS	Standard query DNSKEY 404.gov
49	19:28:50.018788	162.138.191.23	132.70.6.119	DNS	Standard query response DNSKEY DNSKEY DNSKEY DNSKEY DNSKEY DNSKEY[Malformed Packet]
50	19:28:50.018836	162.138.191.23	132.70.6.119	IP	Fragmented IP protocol (proto=UDP 0x11, off=1480, ID=2cca)
51	19:28:50.018850	162.138.191.23	132.70.6.119	IP	Fragmented IP protocol (proto=UDP 0x11, off=2960, ID=2cca)
6840	19:43:52.478800	132.70.6.119	162.138.191.23	DNS	Standard query A 8441234567890098765432.404.gov

Fig. 6. The wireshark capture of the attack, presenting only the packets exchanged between the name server 162.183.191.23 and the resolver. As can be observed, after two malformed responses the resolver refrains from sending further queries to that name server for 15 minutes. Fragmented packets are coloured in white, DNS requests in black, and reassembled DNS fragments in blue.

---

[10] Windows OS allows for a more efficient attack requiring less DNS queries.

[11] Note that our goal was to test the behaviour of the resolver, and to check the frequency of the queries to non-responsive servers; in real attack, once the IP-ID is known, it suffices to issue two queries to mark the server as non-responsive.

IP, it stops sending further packets to that destination for 15 minutes. Indeed, the next packet that is sent to that IP is packet number 6848, at time 19:43. The same scenario was observed with IP 162.138.191.11. The queries between 19:28 and 19:43 were sent only to 162.138.183.11, avoiding 162.138.191.11 and 162.183.191.23. Note that even if some of the responses (between packets 33 and 49) were valid and accepted by resolver, e.g., if they were not fragmented, it did not make a difference, and two timed-out responses in a 15 minute interval were sufficient for Unbound to stop querying those IP addresses; this also implies that the success probability of the attack does not depend on the IP-ID selection mechanism.

3.3   Improved IP Address Randomisation

The attack we presented holds against a specific DNS resolver software, however we caution that variations of our ideas may apply to other server selection algorithms, and we believe that in the long term best answer to our derandomisation attacks is to deploy DNSSEC.

In the meanwhile we suggest (1) increasing the number of IP addresses, both of the name server and of the DNS resolver, e.g., an approach recently proposed by [37] is to superficially increase the number of IP addresses of the resolver for its DNS requests by *reusing* the available IP addresses allocated to the network. Derandomising the IP addresses of the resolver seems to be a challenging task for the attacker; and (2) improving name server selection mechanisms, in particular, it seems that further investigation of server selection mechanism is required to adjust the recommendations in [32,31] to enhance the robustness of resolvers against such (or similar) attacks.

4   DNS Query (de)Randomisation

In this section we describe two prominent defenses, 'case toggling' and random prefix, which are known to add significant extra entropy to DNS requests and show simple ways to circumvent them.

'cASe toGgLiNg'. Dagon et al. [13] present *0x20 encoding* for prevention of DNS poisoning. The technique is to randomly toggle the case of letters of which the domain name consists, and validate them in response. However, we believe that the distribution of domain queries with sufficient 0x20 characters, as reported by Dagon et al., is not indicative of the number of characters in queries that attackers will try to poison, and hence the impact of 0x20 encoding can be easily circumvented. In fact, in Kaminsky-style attacks, the query is intentionally for a non-existing domain name chosen by the attacker, e.g., .com and .uk; indeed the attackers prefer to poison a response to com rather than to www.google.com. Also note that poisoning com allows the attacker a control over all subdomains of com (including www.google.com).

RANDOM PREFIX. Prepending a random prefix to a DNS query[12] can ensure that a sufficiently large DNS query is sent, allowing to apply the 0x20 encoding on more letters and also making it more difficult for the attacker to guess the query (and the case of each letter).

The DNS query is composed of subdomains, at most 63 bytes each, separated by dots, s.t., the total number of characters cannot exceed 255 bytes. So, prepending a random string $1 to query abc.tld, results in $1.abc.tld and increases the query by the size of $1.

A naive implementation of this protection mechanism can be foiled by the attacker. The attacker that wishes to poison an entry for some top level domain, e.g., com, can issue a maximal size DNS query, i.e., 255 bytes, consisting of numbers, that will not allow prepending any more characters: 1-36.1-36.1-36.1-33.com (the '1-36' denotes a string containing all numbers between 1 and 36). As a result, the attacker circumvents the 0x20 protection (which does not apply to numbers) and further avoids the addition of a random prefix to DNS request (since the query is already of maximal size). A slight variation of this attack, see [38], also foils protection offered by WSEC DNS [16].

The size of queries to top level domains should be restricted, to prevent circumventing the query randomisation defenses by attackers.

5   Conclusions

Currently, the popular protection used by most DNS resolvers against poisoning relies on echoing the validation fields in DNS response. Such mechanisms are clearly insufficient to prevent poisoning by MitM attackers. A secure standard alternative exists: DNSSEC, which uses cryptography to achieve verifiable security. However, the deployment of DNSSEC is quite slow. One reason are significant interoperability and performance concerns; another reason may be the existence of several 'patches', adding more 'unpredictable' identifiers. Such 'patches' are trivial to deploy and involve no or negligible overhead, hence, administrators may prefer to deploy them instead of deploying DNSSEC.

We study the major proposed 'patches', and find vulnerabilities in all of them. Our 'trap' and 'predict' attacks show that source ports may be disclosed or impacted by network devices such as NAT gateways. We show that the attacker can also nullify IP address randomisation of standard-conforming resolvers such as Unbound, forcing the resolver to query a specific name server. We also describe simple techniques to circumvent the DNS query randomisation via a random prefix and 0x20 encoding. We validated our attacks against popular NAT devices and standard DNS resolver software. Our derandomisation attacks are deployed 'sequentially' in phases, removing the randomisation of each identifier independently, and eventually strip the DNS request of the entropy offered by those 'unpredictability' fields, exposing the caching DNS resolvers to efficient poisoning attacks by off-path spoofing adversaries.

---

[12] A random prefix is a variation of the defense proposed in [16].

We show simple and effective countermeasures to our attacks. However, while using such 'patched patches' is tempting and easy, we believe that our work shows the importance of basing security on solid, strong foundations, as provided by DNSSEC, i.e., cryptographic protocols designed and analysed to ensure security even against MitM attackers.

References

1. Hubert, A., van Mook, R.: Measures for Making DNS More Resilient against Forged Answers. RFC 5452 (Proposed Standard) (January 2009)
2. Klein, A.: BIND 9 DNS cache poisoning. Report, Trusteer, Ltd., 3 Hayetzira Street, Ramat Gan 52521, Israel (2007)
3. Vixie, P.: DNS and BIND security issues. In: Proceedings of the 5th Symposium on UNIX Security, pp. 209–216. USENIX Association, Berkeley (1995)
4. Arends, R., Austein, R., Larson, M., Massey, D., Rose, S.: DNS Security Introduction and Requirements. RFC 4033 (Proposed Standard) (March 2005); Updated by RFC 6014
5. Arends, R., Austein, R., Larson, M., Massey, D., Rose, S.: Protocol Modifications for the DNS Security Extensions. RFC 4035 (Proposed Standard) (March 2005); Updated by RFCs 4470, 6014
6. Arends, R., Austein, R., Larson, M., Massey, D., Rose, S.: Resource Records for the DNS Security Extensions. RFC 4034 (Proposed Standard) (March 2005); Updated by RFCs 4470, 6014
7. Eastlake 3rd, D., Kaufman, C.: Domain Name System Security Extensions. RFC 2065 (Proposed Standard) (January 1997); Obsoleted by RFC 2535
8. Eggert, L.: DNSSEC deployment trends, http://eggert.org/meter/dnssec
9. Gudmundsson, O., Crocker, S.D.: Observing DNSSEC Validation in the Wild. In: SATIN (March 2011)
10. Herzberg, A., Shulman, H.: Security of Patched DNS, technical report 12-04 (April 2012), http://u.cs.biu.ac.il/~herzbea/security/12-04-derandomisation.pdf
11. Kaminsky, D.: It's the End of the Cache As We Know It. Presentation at Blackhat Briefings (2008)
12. CERT: Multiple DNS implementations vulnerable to cache poisoning. Technical Report Vulnerability Note 800113, CERT (2008)
13. Dagon, D., Antonakakis, M., Vixie, P., Jinmei, T., Lee, W.: Increased DNS forgery resistance through 0x20-bit encoding: security via leet queries. In: Ning, P., Syverson, P.F., Jha, S. (eds.) ACM Conference on Computer and Communications Security, pp. 211–222. ACM (2008)
14. Bau, J., Mitchell, J.C.: A security evaluation of DNSSEC with NSEC3. In: Network and Distributed Systems Security (NDSS) Symposium. The Internet Society (2010)
15. Bernstein, D.J.: DNS Forgery (November 2002) Internet publication at, http://cr.yp.to/djbdns/forgery.html
16. Perdisci, R., Antonakakis, M., Luo, X., Lee, W.: WSEC DNS: Protecting recursive DNS resolvers from poisoning attacks. In: DSN, pp. 3–12. IEEE (2009)
17. Dagon, D., Antonakakis, M., Day, K., Luo, X., Lee, C.P., Lee, W.: Recursive DNS architectures and vulnerability implications. In: Sixteenth Network and Distributed Systems Security (NDSS) Symposium. The Internet Society (2009)
18. Cross, T. (updated) DNS cache poisoning and network address translation. Post at IBM's Frequency X blog (July 2008), http://blogs.iss.net/archive/dnsnat.html

19. Wikipedia: Network address translation (September 2010)
20. Ford, B., Srisuresh, P., Kegel, D.: Peer-to-peer communication across network address translators. In: USENIX Annual Technical Conference, General Track, USENIX, pp. 179–192 (2005)
21. Rosenberg, J., Weinberger, J., Huitema, C., Mahy, R.: STUN - Simple Traversal of User Datagram Protocol (UDP) Through Network Address Translators (NATs). RFC 3489 (Proposed Standard) (March 2003); Obsoleted by RFC 5389
22. Maier, G., Schneider, F., Feldmann, A.: NAT Usage in Residential Broadband Networks. In: Spring, N., Riley, G.F. (eds.) PAM 2011. LNCS, vol. 6579, pp. 32–41. Springer, Heidelberg (2011)
23. Dan Tynan, P.: Your PC may be a haven for spies (2004)
24. Arbor Networks: Worldwide infrastructure security report (2010), http://dns.measurement-factory.com/surveys/201010/
25. DNS-OARC: Domain Name System Operations Analysis and Research Center (2008), https://www.dns-oarc.net/oarc/services/porttest
26. Audet, F., Jennings, C.: Network Address Translation (NAT) Behavioral Requirements for Unicast UDP. RFC 4787 (Best Current Practice) (January 2007)
27. Juniper Networks: Carrier Grade NAT Implementation Guide (2011)
28. Bradner, S.: RFC 3978 Update to Recognize the IETF Trust. RFC 4748 (Best Current Practice) (October 2006); Obsoleted by RFC 5378
29. Internet Corporation for Assigned Names, Numbers: Top Level Domains List (April 2012), http://www.iana.org
30. Mockapetris, P.: Domain names - concepts and facilities. RFC 1034 (Standard) (November 1987); Updated by RFCs 1101, 1183, 1348, 1876, 1982, 2065, 2181, 2308, 2535, 4033, 4034, 4035, 4343, 4035, 4592, 5936
31. Larson, M., Barber, P.: Observed DNS Resolution Misbehavior. RFC 4697 (Best Current Practice) (October 2006)
32. Yu, Y., Wessels, D., Larson, M., Zhang, L.: Authority server selection of dns caching resolvers. ACM SIGCOMM Computer Communication Reviews (April 2012)
33. Kaufman, C., Perlman, R., Sommerfeld, B.: DoS Protection for UDP-Based Protocols. In: Atluri, V., Liu, P. (eds.) Proceedings of the 10th ACM Conference on Computer and Communication Security (CCS 2003). ACM Press, New York (2003)
34. Heffner, J., Mathis, M., Chandler, B.: IPv4 Reassembly Errors at High Data Rates. RFC 4963 (Informational) (July 2007)
35. Gilad, Y., Herzberg, A.: Fragmentation Considered Vulnerable: Blindly Intercepting and Discarding Fragments. In: Proc. USENIX Workshop on Offensive Technologies (August 2011)
36. Postel, J.: Internet Protocol. RFC 791 (Standard) (September 1981); Updated by RFC 1349
37. Herzberg, A., Shulman, H.: Unilateral Antidotes to DNS Poisoning. In: Security and Privacy in Communication Networks - 7th International ICST Conference. Proceedings, SecureComm 2011. LNICST. Springer, London (2011)
38. Herzberg, A., Shulman, H.: Antidotes for DNS Poisoning by Off-Path Adversaries. In: ARES (2012)

Revealing Abuses of Channel Assignment Protocols in Multi-channel Wireless Networks: An Investigation Logic Approach

Qijun Gu[1], Kyle Jones[1], Wanyu Zang[2], Meng Yu[2], and Peng Liu[3]

[1] Texas State University, San Marcos, TX 78666, USA
[2] Virginia Commonwealth University, Richmond, VA 23284, USA
[3] Pennsylvania State University, University Park, PA 16802, USA

Abstract. This paper presents a novel specification-based investigation logic and applies it to tackle abuse of channel assignment protocols in multi-channel wireless networks. The investigation logic looks into malicious operations that violate the specification of channel assignment protocols. With logged operations, it reconstructs the process of channel assignment as an information flow that captures essential dependency relations among protocol-specific channel assignment operations. Then, it derives and applies reasoning rules to conduct consistency check over the logged operations and identify the source of abuse where the logged operations are inconsistent. Through simulation, the proposed investigation logic presents desired quality with zero false negative rate and very low false positive rate.

1 Introduction

Recent studies [5,15] have shown that using multiple non-interfering channels appropriately can significantly reduce interference among neighboring nodes and improve the overall capacity of a wireless network. Various channel assignment (CA) protocols have been developed for multi-channel wireless networks [16,2,28,8]. However, CA protocols are vulnerable to various new attacks [6,21,11,30], in addition to existing security threats in single channel wireless networks. These *new* threats can effectively ruin the "good will" of the CA protocols, reduce the network throughput, and downgrade the quality of network access. Examining these attacks, we found that it is very easy for attackers to abuse CA protocols to cause channel conflicts in multi-channel networks. Attackers can claim wrong, no-existing or incomplete channel information. Attackers can conduct mis-operations to provide different channel information to different nodes. All such abuses of CA protocols force or misguide the victims to change channels so that the network capacity is worse utilized or even the network access is disabled.

Unfortunately, securing multi-channel wireless networks is not as simple as adapting the existing defenses in single channel wireless networks. Authentication-based defense approaches [31,18] have been studied in multi-channel networks.

S. Foresti, M. Yung, and F. Martinelli (Eds.): ESORICS 2012, LNCS 7459, pp. 289–306, 2012.
© Springer-Verlag Berlin Heidelberg 2012

They ensure the integrity of the node identity and the information carried in channel assignment packets. But, their defense capacity is limited to non-authentic information. For example, they cannot stop compromised nodes from providing authentic information with compromised credentials, or stop attackers from providing in-consistent yet authentic information to victims. Intrusion detection frameworks [25,9] have also been proposed in multi-channel networks. These frameworks still have their stands on the assumption that intrusive actions can be observed as in single channel wireless networks. Nevertheless, CA protocols intend to have nodes work on different channels and thus channel assignment operations (including attackers') on a particular channel may not be observed at all when intrusion detection agents are "cruising" on other channels.

Knowing the difficulties of securing multi-channel wireless networks, we explore new means of investigating abuses of CA protocols based on *evidence* (i.e. logged channel assignment operations). We propose a specification-based investigation logic to reveal abuses of CA protocols. Our proposal is built upon the fact that all good nodes will follow CA protocols in channel assignment. Any abuse of CA protocols must inherently have some operations or information that are either contradictory to the protocols or inconsistent inside the abuse itself. A key difference between the abuse investigation and existing intrusion detection in wireless networks is that it exploits the dependency among evidence. The investigation gathers both true and phony evidence in network, builds dependency among evidence using a generalized model of protocol specifications, and locates the inconsistency among evidence. The investigation helps the network administrators to track down the sources of abuse that inevitably results in contradictory evidence.

The investigation is challenging in several aspects though. First, CA protocols vary in their specifications. The operations and the causal relations among operations are specified by protocols, while the operations performed by nodes are stochastic and determined by the channel condition at the time being. Hence, it is neither simple to reconstruct the possible attack scenes nor straightforward to identify the relations among evidence. Second, nodes have only localized views on their channels, and may miss information due to packet loss. The evidence they can provide is always limited to what they can observe on their channels and in their neighborhood. The evidence provided by nodes may not directly include the information about attackers. The limited information is also an obstacle to justifying the operations of good nodes. Third, attackers can compromise deployed nodes to obtain credentials and provide seemingly authentic channel information. Evidence built upon such authentic but wrong information may deceive investigators. Attackers can "lie" in investigation by providing phony evidence that are not generated from their attack operations. Meanwhile, it is hard to identify phony evidence as attackers can claim that the phony evidence is established on information and operations missed by other nodes.

The proposed investigation logic contributes to the security of multi-channel wireless networks in the following aspects: **(1) An investigation model that captures essential dependency relations among protocol-specific**

channel assignment operations. CA protocols are complex in nature for managing multiple channels and multiple radio interfaces. We identify three types of dependency among operations. We show that such relations would enable one to link together channel assignment operations among nodes and rebuild the channel assignment process with the use of standard operation logs. Unlike static logic-based approaches that analyze security protocols or security configurations, the investigation is adapted to the dynamic evidence derived from channel assignment traffic and operations. **(2) Investigation reasoning rules that identify the source of abuse where the evidence is inconsistent.** Based on stochastic profiles of channel assignment operations, we identify two types of inconsistency that need different investigation mechanisms. Various investigation logic rules are derived to detect possible abuses with each category of evidence, and algorithms are developed to apply the investigation rules to locate inconsistency among evidence and identify the suspects involved with the suspicious evidence. Although the investigation does not directly locate the exact attacker, it enables the investigator to quickly narrow down the investigation onto a small range of suspicious operations and reduce investigation efforts and costs in orders of magnitude.

The rest of the paper is organized as follows. Section 2 states the assumptions, the threat model, and the investigation goal. Then, we propose the investigation model in Section 3, and the investigation reasoning in Section 4. Evaluation is given in Section 5. Related work is discussed in Section 6. Finally, we summarize our work in Section 7.

2   Preliminary

2.1   Network Model and Assumptions

Similar to many studies for multi-channel wireless networks, we assume a wireless network has multiple *non-interfering communication channels* (channels for short thereafter). The number of channels is specified by communication protocols. For example, IEEE802.11A has 13 channels, and IEEE802.11B has 3. To communicate with neighbors on different channels, a node is equipped with multiple *radio interfaces*. A node obtains its channels through the interaction with their neighbors following a CA protocol. Then, the node switches its radio interfaces onto the obtained channels. The gateway nodes of a network are the nodes statically connected to the wired network. They have pre-assigned channels. All other nodes obtain their channels after joining the network. We also assume good nodes in the network do not have the knowledge of the whole network. Each node can only observe network traffic on its working channels in its vicinity. If an attacker is communicating with a victim on the victim's channel while no other nodes are working on the victim's channel, no nodes other than the victim and the attacker can know the attacker's action.

2.2   Threat Model and Assumptions

For security, we assume proper authentication schemes have been applied. Meanwhile, we assume attackers can disseminate wrong but authentic channel information. For example, attackers can capture and compromise some deployed nodes to obtain credentials. We also assume attackers can lie during investigation. They can create phony evidence from wrong or non-existing operations, as long as they can authenticate the evidence. The only trusted nodes in network are the gateways, which are usually better secured than other nodes.

Multi-channel wireless networks are vulnerable to various attacks. Based on the common characteristics of attacks, we define two types of attacks that perform malicious actions in channel assignment to deceive the perception of good nodes on channels and make good nodes to switch to channels that are only "perceived" better. The formulation and implication of the two types of attacks will be discussed in detail in Section 3.4.

Definition 1. Type-I attack: *a malicious operation that violates the specification of a protocol and a good node does not perform.*

Definition 2. Type-II attack: *a malicious operation that follows the specification of a protocol but a good node may only perform with a low probability.*

2.3   Investigation Goal

Based on the above observations of the known threats, we define *good operations* as the operations that follow the specification of CA protocols, including using verifiable channel information, taking specified actions, and transmitting specified packets. Correspondingly, *malicious operations* do not use verifiable channel information, do not take specified actions, or do not transmit specified packets.

The objective of our investigation is not to identify which node or which operation triggers other nodes to change channels. Rather, *our investigation goal is to identify the malicious operations that violate the specification of CA protocols*. Because such malicious operations lead to the aforementioned attacks, our investigation can deter attackers from launching such attacks.

As malicious operations violate the specification of CA protocols, they must leave traces that in fact mismatch the actual status and audit data in good nodes and are not justifiable by attacker-provided information. Hence, if we could detect the mismatch in the traces that are supposed to hold consistent information, we could identify the malicious actions. Based on this rationale, we propose an investigation logic that can effectively investigate a possible attack.

3   Investigation Model

The foundation of our investigation is built upon the specification of CA protocols and the operations of nodes in channel assignment. This section presents the notations and the modeling used in the investigation logic.

3.1   Notations

To investigate the past operations of nodes, we first model the logged operations with a triple $\langle \mathbb{A}, \mathbb{M}, \mathbb{K} \rangle$ based on an earlier audit model in [13]. In this model, $\mathbb{A}$ is a set of nodes, $\mathbb{M}$ is a set of messages, and $\mathbb{K}$ is a set of actions. The investigation model captures the relation among the operations of nodes in channel with the three components:

Nodes could be honest (good) or dishonest (malicious). Gateways of a multi-channel network are assumed to be honest nodes in this paper, as they are usually better protected physically and logically than other nodes.

Messages include internally maintained information, externally transmitted packets, and so on. They are the information used in channel assignment, and are recorded for investigation. Fields of a message m is protocol-specific, and could include identities, assigned channels, traffic quality metrics, paths, sequence numbers (or time marks), neighbors' channel and traffic information, and so on.

Actions are operations performed by nodes in $\mathbb{A}$ over messages in $\mathbb{M}$. An action k is thus defined as $k = \{m \overset{a:\rho}{\to} r\}$, where $a \in \mathbb{A}$ is the acting node, $m \in \mathbb{M}$ is the input message, $r \in \mathbb{M}$ is the result message, and ρ is the operation. The action k means that a performs ρ on the input m and gets the result r. k is a *fixed* action if r is fixed given m. Otherwise, if r is random given m, k is a *random* action.

Actions can be *concatenated or combined*. Given two actions $k_1 = \{m_1 \overset{a:A}{\to} r_1\}$ and $k_2 = \{m_2 \overset{b:B}{\to} r_2\}$, the two actions are *concatenated* as $k_1 \| k_2$, if the result of k_1 is an input of k_2, i.e. $r_1 \subseteq m_2$. The two actions are *combined* as $k_1 \cup k_2$, if the results of k_1 and k_2 are the input of another action $k_3 = \{m_3 \overset{c:C}{\to} r_3\}$, i.e. $r_1 \cup r_2 \subseteq m_3$.

Actions are also categorized as external and internal. An action is *external* if either the input or the result of the action is a transmitted packet. For example, two external actions are involved when a sends m_a to b: $k_a = \{m_a \overset{a:S}{\to} p_{ab}\}$ and $k_b = \{p_{ab} \overset{b:R}{\to} m_a\}$, where p_{ab} is a transmitted packet containing m_a, S means sending, and R means receiving. The two external actions are concatenated as $k_a \| k_b$, and simplified as $k_{ab} = k_a \| k_b = \{m_a \overset{a:S}{\to} p_{ab}\} \| \{p_{ab} \overset{b:R}{\to} m_a\} = \{m_a \overset{ab:SR}{\to} m_a\}$. An action is *internal* if both the input and the result of the action are ϕ or internally kept information by the node. For example, the internal action for a's periodic timer is $k_a = \{m_a \overset{a:\sigma}{\to} m_a\}$, where σ is timer and m_a is the information kept in a. The timer action is simplified as σ. Another example of internal action is that a updates its neighbor information m_a with a received update m_b from its neighbor b. The internal action is $\{(m_b \cup m_a) \overset{a:U}{\to} m_a'\}$, where U means updating and m_a' is the neighbor information after update.

3.2   Dependency among Actions

In a sequence of actions, we observe that the input of an action is usually the output of an earlier action. Thereby, we can concatenate an action with an earlier action. The concatenation of the two actions represents the dependency between the two actions as defined below. We show three types of dependent actions that capture all possible dependency among actions in processes.

Definition 3. *Action x depends on an earlier action y if they can be concatenated as $y\|x$. x is called a* dependent action *and y is the* dependency *of x.*

-   **Dependent Internal Actions.** After a node obtains a channel, it needs to conduct periodic operations to keep update with its neighbors and select better channels. These operations form a sequence of internal actions inside each individual node. Three types of internal actions are involved: periodic timer action, update action, and channel selection action. The three types of internal actions are dependent internal actions and are concatenated with earlier internal or external actions.
-   **Dependent External Actions.** The operations of individual nodes are not isolated. A node needs to send its latest channel to other nodes so that they can keep up-to-date information with each other. The sending and receiving actions involved in the information exchange are concatenated as dependent external actions. This type of dependent actions establish the connections between the operations of different nodes when they communicate to exchange information.
-   **Leaf Actions.** CA protocols require nodes to conduct the channel assessment operation to assess the traffic condition of their channels. The assessment actions do not take any results from other actions as input. Hence, although they are internal actions, they do not depend on any earlier actions. The leaf actions cannot be concatenated to any earlier actions, but are always concatenated to later dependent internal actions.

3.3   Process Model

Although CA protocols vary, the operations of good nodes can always be represented as a process. A **process** is a triple $\langle \mathbb{S}, s_0, \Rightarrow \rangle$, where $\mathbb{S}$ is a set of states, s_0 is the starting state, and $\Rightarrow$ is a sequence of concatenated actions. In channel assignment, states are aligned with the assigned channels. For example, s_ϕ is the state without assigned channel and s_c is the state with an assigned channel c. If a node changes from s_1 to s_2 after action k, the process is $s_1 \overset{k}{\Rightarrow} s_2$.

As each node maintains the information of its neighbors and channel conditions, dependent internal actions in $\Rightarrow$ are concatenated to form an information flow of the process as illustrated in Figure 1(a). Let m_t be the information a node maintains and ρ_t be the internal operation at time t. The dependent internal actions are concatenated in the order of updating m_t.

The information flow of a node's process starts with $m_{t_0} = \phi$ in state s_{t_0} at t_0. Over a sequence of time points $t_0, t_1, t_2, ...$, the node conducts a sequence of operations $\rho_{t_1}, \rho_{t_2}, ...$ Each operation ρ_{t_j} takes $m_{t_{j-1}}$ as input and outputs m_{t_j} to operation $\rho_{t_{j+1}}$. The information flow is segmented with different states. The last operation in each state segment is what the node performs to select new channels.

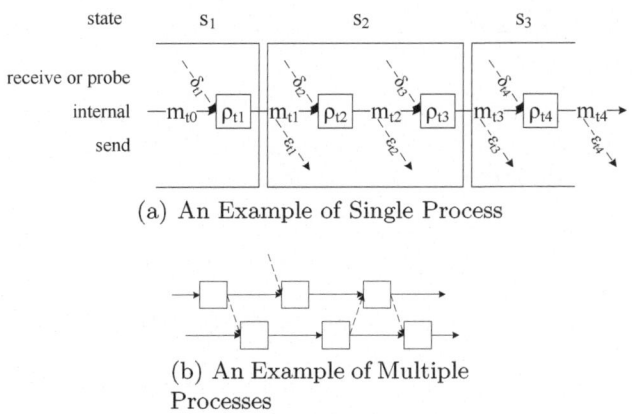

(a) An Example of Single Process

(b) An Example of Multiple Processes

Fig. 1. Process Model

ρ_{t_j} also take δ_{t_j} as input, which is a union of new information of channels received between t_{j-1} and t_j. $\delta_{t_j} = \phi$ indicates that the node didn't perceive any change in channels. Otherwise, $\delta_{t_j} = \cup m_{*a} \cup q_c \cup f_l$, which includes the messages received from neighbors and the results of channel and link assessments. Hence, δ_{t_j} is the results of combined dependent external actions and leaf actions. The output m_{t_j} of operation ρ_{t_j} may also be sent out as $\epsilon_{t_j} \subseteq m_{t_j}$ to neighbors through the sending action.

Processes of multiple nodes are further modeled as interconnected chains via δ_t and ϵ_t. Figure 1(b) shows two processes of two neighbor nodes. As they exchange information, their processes are interconnected. The connections of chains represent the dependency of dependent external actions.

The process model captures the dependency among actions of good nodes and represents the protocol specification as an information flow of processing m_t. Hence, abuse of CA protocols is in fact an attempt to change or break the information flow. The hypothesis of our investigation is that no attack presents to affect the channel assignment if the information flow can be verified.

3.4   Statistic Profile of Actions

As outlined in [12], the actions in the process are stochastic. $\mathbb{K}$ (the set of actions as discussed in the above investigation model) is a mixture of a good action set $\mathbb{G}$ and a malicious action set $\mathbb{B}$, i.e. $\mathbb{K} = \mathbb{G} \cup \mathbb{B}$. Following Definitions 1 and 2, the set of type-I attacks is $\mathbb{B}_{\mathbb{I}} = \overline{\mathbb{G}} \cap \mathbb{B}$ and the set of type-II attacks is $\mathbb{B}_{\mathbb{II}} = \mathbb{G} \cap \mathbb{B}$.

Let $G(t) \in \mathbb{G}$ be a possible good action at t, and let $B(t) \in \mathbb{B}$ be a possible malicious action at t. Let $k(t)$ be the logged action at time t. Then, $k(t) \in \mathbb{K}$ is either $G(t)$ or $B(t)$. Following the notations of [12], we define the following probabilities for good actions and malicious actions.

– $g(k(t)) = Pr\{G(t) = k(t)\}$ is the probability that the good action at t is $k(t)$.

– $b(k(t)) = Pr\{B(t) = k(t)\}$ is the probability that the malicious action at t is $k(t)$.

Let $k_g(t) \in \mathbb{G}$ be the logged good action at t, $k_I(t) \in \mathbb{B}_\mathrm{I}$ be the logged type-I attack action at t, $k_{II}(t) \in \mathbb{B}_\mathrm{II}$ be the logged type-II attack action at t. We have the following statistic profiles of good actions and malicious actions.

1. Statistic profile of good actions:
   – $g(k_g(t)) = 1$ for fixed good actions, because a fixed action always has only one specific result at t.
   – $0 < g(k_g(t)) < 1$ for random good actions, because a random action may end with different results at t.
   – $g(k_I(t)) = 0$ for good actions, because $k_I(t) \notin \mathbb{G}$ due to $\mathbb{B}_\mathrm{I} \cap \mathbb{G} = \phi$.
   – $0 < g(k_{II}(t)) < 1$ for random good actions, because $k_{II}(t) \in \mathbb{B}_\mathrm{II}$ and $\mathbb{B}_\mathrm{II} \subset \mathbb{G}$.
2. Statistic profile of malicious actions:
   – $b(k_g(t)) = 0$ for type-I attack actions, because $k_g(t) \notin \mathbb{B}_\mathrm{I}$ due to $\mathbb{B}_\mathrm{I} \cap \mathbb{G} = \phi$.
   – $0 < b(k_I(t)) \leq 1$ for type-I attack actions.
   – $0 < b(k_{II}(t)) \leq 1$ for type-II attack actions.

As discussed in the investigation models, actions can be classified as fixed and random. The dependent external actions and the dependent internal actions (excluding the last internal action at the end of each state in a process) are usually fixed actions, because their results are fixed given their inputs. The dependent internal action at the end of each state in a process is the channel selection action. It is fixed if the CA algorithm of the protocol is deterministic, e.g. the algorithm always selects the least used channel. Otherwise, it is random if the CA algorithm is non-deterministic. The leaf actions are usually random actions, because their results are the assessment of channel condition that always includes noise and errors.

4   Investigation Reasoning

For investigation, the actions are recorded by nodes and later retrieved to reconstruct the processes by investigators. A log entry includes the input, the result, the operation, and the sequence number of the action. Because the abuse actions violate the protocol specification, the log entries corresponding to the abuse will not fit into the information flow. The key of investigation is to locate such problematic log entries by conducting consistency checks on $\mathbb{M}$ and $\mathbb{K}$ following the information flow.

4.1   Consistency

As discussed in [12], the effectiveness of investigation is limited by the disparity of $b(k(t))$ and $g(k(t))$ for $k(t) \in \mathbb{B}_\mathrm{I} \cup \mathbb{B}_\mathrm{II}$. When the two probabilities are very different, the investigation can detect malicious actions with high confidence. When the two probabilities are highly similar, the investigation cannot distinguish between good and malicious actions. In other words, when malicious actions follow the same statistic profile of good actions, attackers in fact behave as good nodes and thus do not threat channel assignment.

The investigation measures the disparity of the two probabilities as $d(k(t)) = |\log b(k(t)) - \log g(k(t))|$. Then, the overall disparity of all past actions is given in Eq.(1), where D_I is the disparity between type-I attack actions and good actions and D_{II} is the disparity between type-II attack actions and good actions. Note that actions in $\mathbb{G} \cap \overline{\mathbb{B}_{II}}$ will not be performed by attackers, and thus $D_{\mathbb{G} \cap \overline{\mathbb{B}_{II}}} = 0$.

$$D = \sum_t d(k(t)) = \sum_t |\log b(k(t)) - \log g(k(t))| = D_I + D_{II} \qquad (1)$$

$D_I = \sum_t d(k_I(t))$. Because $g(k_I(t)) = 0$, $D_I = \sum_t |\log b(k_I(t)) - \log 0|$.
$D_{II} = \sum_t d(k_{II}(t)) = \sum_t |\log b(k_{II}(t)) - \log g(k_{II}(t))|$. Because the goal of a good random action is to improve the channel usage, a good node will less likely to perform a type-II attack action that results in worse channel usage, and thus $b(k_{II}(t)) \geq g(k_{II}(t))$. Thereby, $D_{II} = \sum_t (\log b(k_{II}(t)) - \log g(k_{II}(t))) > 0$, and $\sum_t \log b(k_{II}(t)) > \sum_t \log g(k_{II}(t))$.

The above disparity analysis shows quantitatively and theoretically how attack actions are inconsistent with good actions. However, in practice, we do not know exactly $\mathbb{B}_I$ and $\mathbb{B}_{II}$, and their statistic profiles $b(k_I(t))$ and $b(k_{II}(t))$. Therefore, in the following, we propose reasoning rules to conduct consistency checks for investigating the two types of attacks based on the analysis of D_I and D_{II}.

4.2   Consistency Check on Type-I Attack

The disparity D_I shows that the inconsistency of a type-I attack action can be detected when a logged action should not occur but present in log. Hence, the consistency check on type-I attack is equivalent to the check on whether or not a logged action can fit into the processes built upon the log. The consistency check on type-I attack includes two steps: (i) rebuild processes from log and (ii) check dependency among actions.

Rebuild Processes. As discussed in Section 3.3, the process of a node is made of dependent and leaf actions that form an information flow. Upon investigation, the procedure in Algorithm 1 is executed to rebuild the processes for all nodes. If the information flow is not complete due to a missing earlier dependency action, inconsistency is detected. Lemma 1 states that such an inconsistent situation is caused by a type-I attack or a lie.

Lemma 1. *For a dependent action, if the search of an earlier dependency action in Algorithm 1 fails, (i) at least one of the two actions is a type-I attack action, or (ii) at least one of the owners of the two actions lies.*

Algorithm 1. Procedure of rebuilding processes

1: Collect log entries over an investigation period
2: **for** each node **do**
3:     Sort log entries according to their sequence numbers
4:     **for** each log entry **do**
5:         **if** the action is a dependent internal action **then**
6:             Search earlier dependent internal actions following its inputs
7:             Report inconsistency on the current action if search fails
8:             Add edges with the earlier actions that can be concatenated
9:         **end if**
10:        **if** the action is a sending action **then**
11:            Search earlier dependent internal action
12:            Report inconsistency on the current action if search fails
13:            Add an edge from the earlier internal action to the current action
14:        **end if**
15:        **if** the action is a receiving action **then**
16:            Search the sending action from the sending node
17:            Report inconsistency on the current action if search fails
18:            Add an edge from the sending action to the current action.
19:        **end if**
20:    **end for**
21: **end for**

Dependency Check on Dependent Actions. Although the information flow presents the dependency relations among logged actions, the actions may contain false information. For example, attackers provide bogus log entries in order to form a complete information flow in a rebuilt process. The bogus log entries will then cause inconsistency on the dependency among actions. To inspect dependent actions, investigation needs to check the *operation consistency* and the *dependency consistency* of the actions.

Definition 4. Operation consistency*: A logged action is operation consistent if the logged result matches the result of the action given the logged input.*

Definition 5. Dependency consistency*: Assume in the information flow of a process, a logged dependent action has edges with some earlier dependency actions. The dependent action is dependency consistent if the logged input of the action is the union of the logged results of the earlier dependency actions.*

To evade investigation, attacking nodes must lie to ensure that the logged actions can pass the two dependency checks. Because attacking nodes can only provide bogus actions in their own processes, they must provide actions with self-sustained operation consistency and dependency consistency in the processes that can prove each other. Lemma 2 and Lemma 3 can be established to ensure that no type-I attack can enable attackers to evade the investigation by lying on dependencies.

Lemma 2. *An attacking node cannot lie with a set of bogus type-I attack actions with self-sustained consistency to evade investigation.*

Lemma 3. *A set of colluding attacking nodes cannot lie with a set of bogus type-I attack actions with self-sustained consistency to evade investigation.*

Theorem 1. *A type-I attack is detectable with 100% guarantee.*

4.3   Consistency Check on Type-II Attack

The disparity D_{II} shows that the inconsistency of a type-II attack action can be detected when a logged action should occur less but present too often in log. Although we do not know the exact statistic profile of type-II attack $b(k_{II}(t))$, we can establish Lemma 4 stating that $\sum_t \log b(k_{II}(t))$ is an approximate of the entropy of type-II attack actions. Then, we can further establish Theorem 2 that type-II attack actions are detectable.

Lemma 4. *Let* T *be the number of type-II attack actions in log.* $\lim_{T \to \infty} -\sum_t \log b(k_{II}(t)) = H_T(\mathbb{B}_{II})$, *where* $H_T(\mathbb{B}_{II})$ *is the entropy of the* T *type-II attack actions.*

Theorem 2. *Given* $H_T(\mathbb{B}_{II})$, *type-II attack actions are detectable with their cumulative information content as good random actions, i.e.* $-\lim_{T \to \infty} \sum_t \log g(k_{II}(t)) > H_T(\mathbb{B}_{II})$.

Accordingly, the consistency check on a type-II attack action is to compare the information content of a logged action as a random good action with the entropy of the action. Since we do not have $H_T(\mathbb{B}_{II})$, the detectability only works in theory. In practice, we develop heuristic consistency check on two types of random good actions: (i) leaf actions and (ii) channel selection actions.

Cross-Verification on Leaf Actions. Leaf actions are stochastic in that they are used to sample time-variant channel conditions. In particular, we see two types of leaf actions for all the protocols we have studied. Our investigation logic cross-verifies them with other log entries based on some heuristics.

- The *link failure action* occurs when a node changes its channel or leaves the network which results in the link failure. An attacking node may exploit this action to claim the change in its channel usage. The heuristic of our investigation is to compare the channel of the link before and after the failure. A logged link failure action is determined as a type-II attack action, if the channel of the link is not changed.
- The *channel assessment action* measures the channel usage condition. To verify a logged channel assessment action, our investigation compares the assessed channel condition with the channel usage information in the log entries of its neighbor nodes. A logged channel assessment action is

---

Algorithm 2. Procedure of Consistency Check

1: Start from a logged channel selection action.
2: Initiate an empty set INV
3: Add the starting action to INV
4: **repeat**
5:     Follow the information flow edges of the logged actions.
6:     Add the dependency actions and the edges to INV
7: **until** no more dependency actions in the investigation window
8: **for** each dependent action in INV **do**
9:     Check the operation consistency of the action
10:    Check the dependency consistency of the action with its dependency actions
11:    **if** the action does not satisfy the consistency **then**
12:        Report the action, its dependency action, and the owners of these logged
    actions
13:    **end if**
14: **end for**
15: **for** each leaf action and channel selection action in INV **do**
16:    Verify the action according to its type
17:    **if** the log entry does not satisfy the consistency **then**
18:        Report the log entry, the log entries used for verification, and the owners of
    these log entries as suspicious
19:    **end if**
20: **end for**

---

determined as a type-II attack action if the difference of the channel usage falls outside a reasonable statistical range.

Entropy Check on Channel Selection Actions. In most CA protocols, the channel selection action is a random action. When a node finds a set of better channels, the node can select a new channel or stay at its current channel with some probabilities. Following Theorem 2, we substitute $H_T(\mathbb{B}_{\text{II}})$ with $H_T(\mathbb{G})$. This heuristic is based on (i) the simplification that $g(k_g(t))$ and $b(k_{II}(t))$ are symmetrically skewed, because a less performed good action will be more performed by attackers and vise verse; (ii) the information content of a less performed good action is larger than the entropy.

4.4   Procedure of Consistency Check

Algorithm 2 shows the procedure of applying the two consistency checks after the processes are rebuilt. It first identifies the log entries needed for investigation and extracts them out to form a reasoning graph for investigation. Then, it verifies the consistency among these log entries. It reports both the inconsistent log entries that cannot be justified and the supporting log entries that are directly involved in the verification of the inconsistent log entry.

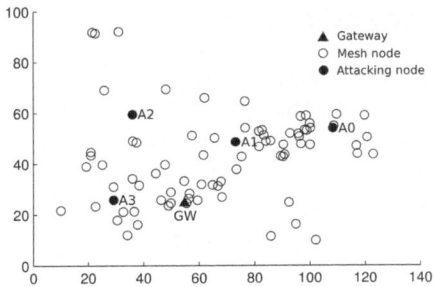

Fig. 2. Topology of Roofnet

5   Evaluation

5.1   Simulation Settings

The investigation logic has been implemented in the multi-channel wireless network simulation framework [14] in OMNET++/INET [1]. The investigation logic has been tested with two CA protocols MCR [15] and ROMA [8]. We use the topology of Roofnet to build the network for simulation. Roofnet is a testbed of wireless mesh network [3]. The coordinates of the mesh nodes in Roofnet are published online.

Figure 2 shows the reconstruction of the topology with 90 deployed good nodes in simulation. Each node is equipped with two radio interfaces. According to the specifications, 13 channels are used for IEEE802.11A and 3 channels for IEEE802.11B. The channel capacity is set to $2Mbps$ per channel. Good nodes are given random starting time points within the first 30 seconds, from which they start searching channels to join the network. Once they get channels, they broadcast their channel and load information every 10 seconds following the CA protocols, and send traffic to the gateway.

We also deploy 4 attacking nodes to inject false CA packets following the known attack techniques [21,11,30]. For type-I attack, the attacking nodes inject non-existing channel usage packets, and send different channel usage packets to different nodes. For type-II attack, the attacking nodes notify other nodes of newly assigned channels, which are less possibly selected by good nodes.

In simulation, we vary the traffic volume of good nodes so that the load of aggregated traffic at the gateway ranges from 10% to 80% of channel capacity at the gateway, i.e. $200Kbps$ to $1600Kbps$. We fixed the communication range of each router but adjusted the distance among routers proportionally to control the node degree, i.e. the number of neighbors per router. The average node degrees are set to 9, 14, and 27 for simulation with different network density. Each experiment ran 200 seconds and all data points are the averages over 10 repeats.

5.2 Quality of Investigation

The quality of investigation logic is measured by the false positive (*FP*) rate (the percentage of good actions that are determined as malicious) and the false negative (*FN*) rate (the percentage of attack actions that are determined as good). Note that the two rates do not indicate the quality of final judgment on good and malicious nodes. Our investigation goal is to mark suspicious attack actions so that the intrusion detection can zero onto the nodes involved with the marked actions.

In simulation, the FN rates achieved by the investigation logic are 0 for two reasons. First, the type-I attack actions do not follow the specification. They cannot evade detection following Theorem 1. Second, the type-II attack actions in simulation always have lower probabilities than the good actions performed by good nodes. They can thus be detected using Theorem 2. This result indicates that the investigation logic will not miss any attack actions.

Figures 3(a) and 4(a) show the overall FP rates with MCR and ROMA. The overall FP rates are below 2% for MCR and below 1% for ROMA. With further examination, we find that the FP rate of type-I attack (i.e. a good action is determined as a type-I attack) is zero. Hence, the FP actions are in fact determined as type-II attack. We calculated the FP rates of type-II attack with only the good actions, which could be mis-classified, as illustrated in Figures 3(b) and 4(b). Because the number of such good actions is only a small portion (4% to 10%) of all good actions, the overall FP rates are low even though the FP rates of type-II attack could be as high as 30%.

With further examination of the FPs of type-II attack, we find the actions and the reasons that lead to the FPs. First, the leaf actions of channel assessment and link failure could be determined as type-II attack. The leaf action of channel assessment reports the channel condition perceived by nodes. Such perception can hardly be accurate and uniform among different nodes. A good node may perceive a channel condition that appears abnormal to other nodes and thus the leaf action of this channel assessment will be determined as a type-II attack action. Similar reason applies to the leaf action of link failure when a link fails due to temporary communication problems.

The other action that could be determined as type-II attack is the channel selection action. For MCR, when a node finds a better channel, it may switch to that channel at a probability of 60%. In contrast, for ROMA, the node will switch to the better channel. Hence, for MCR, when the node stays on its current channel, the channel selection action is more likely determined as type-II attack. It is also the reason that MCR's FP rate of type-II attack is significantly larger than ROMA's.

Another observation of Figures 3 and 4 is that the traffic load may influence the FP rate only when the network is dense. When the node degree is 27 (i.e. a node has 27 neighbors in average), the FP rates grow as the traffic load increases. This is because the network is less stable with the growing traffic load in a dense network. The instability of network contributes more into the uncertainty

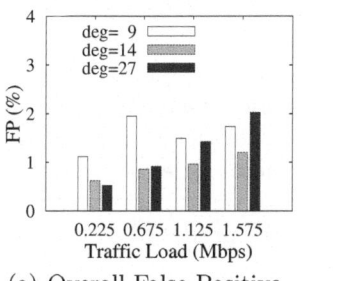
(a) Overall False Positive

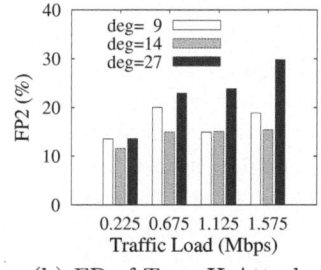
(b) FP of Type-II Attack

Fig. 3. False Positive with MCR

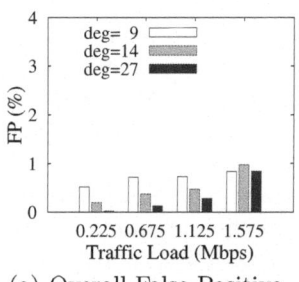
(a) Overall False Positive

(b) FP of Type-II Attack

Fig. 4. False Positive with ROMA

in channel assessment and link failure, which results in more wrong perceptions of channel and link conditions in good nodes.

6   Related Works

6.1   Logic Methodology

The taxonomy of secure protocol analysis methods includes two methodologies to handle not-so-sophisticated attacks, which are Protocol Logic and Model Checking [7,20,19], and two methodologies to handle sophisticated attacks, which are Poly-ti e calculus [17] and Symbolic methods (MSR) [4]. We choose to adopt the logic methodology due to its simplicity and efficiency.

BAN logic has been used for describing security protocols. It formulates the security protocol analysis problem as feeding "formal protocol" and "intruder model" as two inputs into an analysis tool, which finds errors. Compared with this problem formulation, a major difference is that our investigation logic does not require an explicit intruder model. Instead, our investigation logic is *specification-based*, that is, it is based on specification of expected protocol behavior. In this way, our investigation logic has the potential capability to identify unknown attacks.

Datalog is another logic-based approach used in security systems. The Mul-VAL [23,22] analyzes the vulnerabilities of a system. It adopts Datalog as the modeling language for system elements, which are configuration, privilege, reasoning rules, and so on, in analysis. The Datalog-based logic approaches are different from our investigation logic in that our objective is to track down the sources of protocol abuses instead of finding vulnerabilities in protocols or system configurations. In addition, they build reasoning graphs based on static information, while our reasoning graph adapts to evidence produced by dynamic channel assignment traffic and operations.

6.2   Node Compromise Detection

A number of node compromise detection schemes have been studied in wireless sensor and ad hoc network [29,24,27,26]. A compromised node may behave less trustable after compromise as it will conduct malicious operations to serve attackers. Hence, researchers proposed reputation-based trust management schemes [10,27], in which the reputation of each node is evaluated by other nodes or the system in accordance with its activities. A node with low reputation will be considered as untrustable. Various approaches can be used to evaluate the trust of a node, such as Bayesian-based [10] and entropy-based [27].

Attackers may insert malicious code into compromised nodes to conduct attack operations. Remote software-attestation schemes [29,24] were proposed with which the base station or the neighbors of a suspect node can detect the compromise via checking the change of the code image inside the node. In our study, attackers do not need to run extra malicious code in compromised node. They mainly need the credentials from the compromised nodes to abuse CA protocols in an authentic manner.

Our work is different from all the above works in that we look into the inherent properties of attacks rather than detecting if a node has been changed by attackers. We base our investigation logic on the fact that abusing CA protocols will violate the specification of the protocols, whether or not the attacking nodes are made from compromised nodes. The investigation logic tracks down to the attack activities directly without inspecting if the attack activities are caused by the change of nodes.

7   Conclusions

In this paper, we presented a specification-based investigation logic for revealing abuse of CA protocols in multi-channel wireless networks. We identified the key dependency relations among channel assignment operations and modeled the process of channel assignment as information flows with logged actions that are collected from nodes. We showed the fundamental differences among good actions and malicious actions based on their statistic profiles. We developed investigation reasoning approaches that inspect consistency among actions to locate the sources of abuse. We implemented the investigation logic and conducted simulation with two CA protocols. The simulation shows that the investigation logic can achieve decent quality of zero false negative rate and low false positive rate.

Acknowledgments. This work was supported by the National Science Foundation under Grant No. 0915318, 1048339, and 0916469.

References

1. INET, http://inet.omnetpp.org/
2. Alicherry, M., Bhatia, R., Li, L.E.: Joint channel assignment and routing for throughput optimization in multi-radio wireless mesh networks. In: Proc. of ACM MobiCom, pp. 58–72 (2005)
3. Bicket, J., Aguayo, D., Biswas, S., Morris, R.: Architecture and evaluation of an unplanned 802.11b mesh network. In: Proc. of ACM Mobicom, pp. 31–42 (2005)
4. Boreale, M., Buscemi, M.G.: A method for symbolic analysis of security protocols. Theor. Comput. Sci. 338(1-3), 393–425 (2005)
5. Chereddi, C., Kyasanur, P., Vaidya, N.H.: Design and implementation of a multi-channel multi-interface network. In: Proc. of International Workshop on Multi-Hop Ad Hoc Networks: from Theory to Reality, pp. 23–30 (2006)
6. Clark, S., Goodspeed, T., Metzger, P., Wasserman, Z., Xu, K., BBlaze, M.: Why (special agent) Johnny (still) can't encrypt: a security analysis of the APCO project 25 two-way radio system. In: Proc. of USENIX Security (2011)
7. Datta, A., Derek, A., Mitchell, J.C., Roy, A.: Protocol composition logic (pcl). Electr. Notes Theor. Comput. Sci. 172, 311–358 (2007)
8. Dhananjay, A., Zhang, H., Li, J., Subramanian, L.: Practical, distributed channel assignment and routing in dual-radio mesh networks. In: Proc. of ACM SIGCOMM, vol. 39, pp. 99–110 (2009)
9. Ferreira, E.W.T., de Oliveira, R., Carrijo, G.A., Bhargava, B.: Intrusion Detection in Wireless Mesh Networks Using a Hybrid Approach. In: Proc. of IEEE International Conference on Distributed Computing Systems Workshops, pp. 451–454 (2009)
10. Ganeriwal, S., Srivastava, M.B.: Reputation-based framework for high integrity sensor networks. In: SASN, pp. 66–77 (2004)
11. Gu, Q., Yu, M., Zang, W., Liu, P.: Lightweight Attacks against Channel Assignment Protocols in MIMC Wireless Networks. In: Proc. of IEEE ICC (2011)
12. Helman, P., Liepins, G.: Statistical Foundations of Audit Trail Analysis for the Detection of Computer Misuse. IEEE Transaction on Software Engeering 19(9), 886–901 (1993)
13. Jagadeesan, R., Jeffrey, A., Pitcher, C., Riely, J.: Towards a Theory of Accountability and Audit. In: Backes, M., Ning, P. (eds.) ESORICS 2009. LNCS, vol. 5789, pp. 152–167. Springer, Heidelberg (2009)
14. Kim, H., Gu, Q., Yu, M., Zang, W., Liu, P.: A Simulation Framework for Performance Analysis of Multi-Interface and Multi-Channel Wireless Networks in INET/OMNET++. In: Proc. of Communications and Networking Simulation Symposium (2010)
15. Kyasanur, P., Vaidya, N.H.: Routing and link-layer protocols for multi-channel multi-interface ad hoc wireless networks. SIGMOBILE Mob. Comput. Commun. Rev. 10(1), 31–43 (2006)

16. Lin, X., Rasool, S.: A Distributed Joint Channel-Assignment, Scheduling and Routing Algorithm for Multi-Channel Ad Hoc Wireless Networks. In: Proc. of IEEE INFOCOM, pp. 1118–1126 (2007)
17. Lincoln, P., Mitchell, J.C., Mitchell, M., Scedrov, A.: A probabilistic poly-time framework for protocol analysis. In: ACM Conference on Computer and Communications Security, pp. 112–121 (1998)
18. Martignon, F., Paris, S., Capone, A.: Design and implementation of MobiSEC: A complete security architecture for wireless mesh networks. Computer Networks 53(12), 2192–2207 (2009)
19. Mitchell, J.C.: Finite-State Analysis of Security Protocols. In: Vardi, M.Y. (ed.) CAV 1998. LNCS, vol. 1427, pp. 71–76. Springer, Heidelberg (1998)
20. Mitchell, J.C.: Security analysis of network protocols: logical and computational methods. In: PPDP, pp. 151–152 (2005)
21. Naveed, A., Kanhere, S.S.: Security Vulnerabilities in Channel Assignment of Multi-Radio Multi-Channel Wireless Mesh Networks. In: Proc. of IEEE GLOBECOM, pp. 1–5 (2006)
22. Ou, X., Boyer, W.F., McQueen, M.A.: A scalable approach to attack graph generation. In: ACM Conference on Computer and Communications Security, pp. 336–345 (2006)
23. Ou, X., Govindavajhala, S., Appel, A.W.: Mulval: A logic-based network security analyzer. In: 14th USENIX Security Symposium (2005)
24. Seshadri, A., Perrig, A., van Doorn, L., Khosla, P.: SWATT: SoftWare-based AT-Testation for Embedded Devices. In: Proc. of IEEE Symposium on Security and Privacy, pp. 272–284 (2004)
25. Shin, D.-H., Bagchi, S.: Optimal monitoring in multi-channel multi-radio wireless mesh networks. In: Proc. of ACM MobiHoc, pp. 229–238 (2009)
26. Song, H., Xie, L., Zhu, S., Cao, G.: Sensor node compromise detection: the location perspective. In: IWCMC, pp. 242–247 (2007)
27. Sun, Y.L., Han, Z., Yu, W., Liu, K.J.R.: A trust evaluation framework in distributed networks: Vulnerability analysis and defense against attacks. In: INFOCOM (2006)
28. Xing, K., Cheng, X., Ma, L., Liang, Q.: Superimposed code based channel assignment in multi-radio multi-channel wireless mesh networks. In: Proc. of ACM MobiCom, pp. 15–26 (2007)
29. Yang, Y., Wang, X., Zhu, S., Cao, G.: Distributed software-based attestation for node compromise detection in sensor networks. In: SRDS, pp. 219–230 (2007)
30. Zang, W., Gu, Q., Yu, M., Liu, P.: An attack-resilient channel assignment mac protocol. In: NBiS, pp. 246–253 (2009)
31. Zhu, H., Lin, X., Lu, R., Ho, P.-H., Shen, X.: SLAB: A secure localized authentication and billing scheme for wireless mesh networks. IEEE Transactions on Wireless Communications 7(10), 3858–3868 (2008)

Exploring Linkability of User Reviews

Mishari Almishari and Gene Tsudik

Computer Science Department, University of California, Irvine
{malmisha,gts}@ics.uci.edu

Abstract. Large numbers of people all over the world read and contribute to various review sites. Many contributors are understandably concerned about privacy in general and, specifically, about linkability of their reviews (and accounts) across multiple review sites. In this paper, we study linkability of community-based reviewing and try to answer the question: *to what extent are "anonymous" reviews linkable, i.e., highly likely authored by the same contributor?* Based on a very large set of reviews from one very popular site (Yelp), we show that a high percentage of ostensibly anonymous reviews can be accurately linked to their authors. This is despite the fact that we use very simple models and equally simple features set. Our study suggests that contributors reliably expose their identities in reviews. This has important implications for cross-referencing accounts between different review sites. Also, techniques used in our study could be adopted by review sites to give contributors feedback about linkability of their reviews.

1   Introduction

In recent years, popularity of various types of review and community-knowledge sites has substantially increased. Prominent examples include Yelp, Tripadvisor, Epinions, Wikipedia, Expedia and Netflix. They attract multitudes of readers and contributors. While the former usually greatly outnumber the latter, contributors can still number in hundreds of thousands for large sites, such as Yelp or Wikipedia. For example, Yelp had more than 39 million visitors and reached 15 million reviews in late 2010 [1]. To motivate contributors to provide more (and more useful/informative) reviews, certain sites even offer rewards [2].

With the surge in popularity of community-based reviewing, more and more people contribute to review sites. At the same time, there has been an increased awareness with regard to personal privacy. Internet and Web privacy is a broad notion with numerous aspects, many of which have been explored by the research community. However, privacy in the context of review sites has not been adequately studied. Although there has been a lot of recent research related to reviewing, its focus has been mainly on extracting and summarizing opinions from reviews [5, 6, 15] as well as determining authenticity of reviews [8, 9, 11].

In the context of community-based reviewing, contributor privacy has several aspects: (1) some review sites do not require accounts (i.e., allow ad hoc reviews) and contributors might be concerned about linkability of their reviews, and (2)

S. Foresti, M. Yung, and F. Martinelli (Eds.): ESORICS 2012, LNCS 7459, pp. 307–324, 2012.
© Springer-Verlag Berlin Heidelberg 2012

many active contributors have accounts on multiple review sites and prefer these accounts not be linkable. The flip side of the privacy problem is faced by review sites themselves: how to address spam-reviews and sybil-accounts?

The goal of this paper is to explore and measure linkability of reviews by investigating how close and related are a person's reviews. That is, how accurately we can link a set of anonymous reviews to their original author. Our study is based on over $1,000,000$ reviews and $\simeq 2,000$ contributors from Yelp. This paper makes the following contributions:

1. We provide a privacy measurement study where we extensively assess and measure reviews' linkability and show that anonymous reviews are accurately de-anonymized in the presence of very simple features. For example, using only alphabetical letter distributions, we can link up to 83% (and 96% with few additional features) of the anonymous reviews to their real authors. We believe that the findings in this study are very important and alarming for reviewers who are concerned about their privacy.
2. We propose several models and improvements that quite accurately link "anonymous" reviews.

Our results have several implications. One of them is the ability to cross-reference contributor accounts between multiple (and similar) review sites. If a person regularly contributes to two similar review sites under different accounts, anyone can easily link them, since many people tend to consistently maintain their traits in writing reviews. This is possibly quite detrimental to personal privacy. Another implication is the ability to correlate reviews ostensibly emanating from different accounts that are produced by the same author. Our approach can thus be very useful in detecting self-reviewing and, more generally, review spam [8] whereby one person contributes from multiple accounts to artificially promote or criticize products or services.

One envisaged application of our technique is to have it integrated into review site software. This way, review authors could obtain feedback indicating the degree of linkability of their reviews. It would then be up to each author to adjust (or not) the writing style and other characteristics.

2   Background

This section provides some background about statistical tools used in our study. We use two well-known approaches based on: (1) Naïve Bayes Model [10], (2) Kullback-Leibler Divergence Metric [4]. We briefly describe them below.

2.1   Naïve Bayes Model

Naïve Bayes Model (NB) is a probabilistic model based on the eponymous assumption stating that all features/tokens are conditionally independent given the class. Given tokens: $T_1, T_2, ..., T_n$ in document D, we classify D by returning the class value with maximum probability:

$$Class = argmax_C P(C|D) = argmax_C P(C|T_1, T_2, ..., T_n) \tag{1}$$

Since $P(T_1, T_2, ..., T_n)$ is the same for all C values, and assuming $P(C)$ is the same for all class values, the above equation is reduced to:

$$Class = argmax_C P(T_1|C)P(T_2|C).....P(T_n|C)$$

Probabilities are estimated, from all class C documents (D_C), using the Maximum-Likelihood estimator [4] along with Laplace smoothing [12] as follows:

$$P(T_i|C) =$$
$$\frac{Num\ of\ Occurrences\ of\ T_i\ in\ D_C\ +\ 1}{Num\ of\ Occurrences\ of\ Tokens\ in\ D_C\ +\ Num\ of\ Possible\ Tokens}$$

2.2 Kullback-Leibler Divergence Metric

Kullback-Leibler Divergence (KLD) metric measures the distance between two distributions. For any two distributions P and Q, it is defined as:

$$D_{kl}(P\|Q) = \sum_i P(i)log(\frac{P(i)}{Q(i)})$$

KLD is always positive: the closer to zero, the closer Q is to P. It is an asymmetrical metric, i.e., $D_{kl}(P\|Q) \neq D_{kl}(Q\|P)$. To transform it into a symmetrical metric, we use the following formula (that has been used in [17]):

$$SymD_{kl}(P,Q) = 0.5 \times (D_{kl}(P\|Q) + D_{kl}(Q\|P)) \tag{2}$$

Basically, $SymD_{kl}$ is a symmetrical version of D_{kl} that measures the distance between two distributions. As discussed below, it is used heavily in our study. In the rest of the paper, the term "KLD" stands for $SymD_{kl}$[1].

3 Data Set and Study Settings

Data Set. Clearly, a very large set of reviews authored by a large number of contributors is necessary in order to perform a meaningful study. To this end, we collected $1,076,850$ reviews for $1,997$ contributors from yelp.com, a very popular site with many prolific contributors. The minimum number of reviews per contributor is 330, the maximum – $3,387$ and the average – 539 reviews,

---

[1] Note that, under certain conditions, NB and asymmetrical KLD models could be equivalent. That is, $argmax_{Class}P(Class|T_1, T_2, ..., T_n)$ is equivalent to $argmin_{Class}D_{kl}(Token\_distribution\|Class\_distribution)$, where $T_1, T_2, ...T_n$ are the tokens of a document D and $Token\_distribution$ is their derived distribution. The proof for this equivalency is in [17]. However, this equivalence does not hold when we use the symmetrical version $SymD_{kl}$.

with a standard deviation of 354. For the purpose of this study, we limited authorship to prolific contributors, since this provides more useful information for the purpose of review linkage. Note that 50% of the contributors authored fewer than 500 reviews and 76% authored fewer than 600. Only 6% of the contributors exceed 1,000 reviews. Additionally, 50% of the contributors write reviews shorter than 140 words (on average) and 75% – have average review size smaller than 185. Also, 97% of contributors write reviews shorter than 300 words. The overall average review size is relatively small – 149 words.

Study Settings. Our central goal is to study linkability of relatively prolific reviewers. Specifically, we want to understand – for a given prolific author – to what extent some of his/her reviews relate to, or resemble, others. To achieve that, we first randomly order the reviews of each contributor. Then, for each contributor U with N_U reviews, we split the randomly ordered reviews into two sets:

1. First $N_U - X$ reviews: We refer to this as the **identified record** (IR) of U.
2. Last X reviews: These reviews represent the full set of anonymous reviews of U from which we derive several subsets of various sizes. We refer to each of these subset as an **anonymous record** (AR) of U. An AR of size i consists of the first i reviews of the full set of anonymous reviews of U. We vary the AR size for the purpose of studying the user reviews linkability under different numbers of anonymous reviews.

Since we want to restrict the AR size to a small portion of the complete user reviews set, we restrict X to 60 as this represents less than 20% of the minimum number of reviews for authors in our set (330 total). We use the **identified records** (IRs) of all contributors as the training set upon which we build models for linking anonymous reviews. (Note that the IR size is not the same for all contributors, while the AR size is uniform.) Thus, our problem is reduced to matching an anonymous record to its corresponding IR. Specifically, one anonymous record serves as an input to a matching/linking model and the output is a sorted list of all possible account-ids (i.e., IRs) listed in a descending order of probability, i.e., the top-ranked account-id corresponds to the contributor whose IR represents the most probable match for the input anonymous record. Then, if the correct account-id of the actual author is among top T entries, the matching/linking model has a hit; otherwise, it is a miss. We refer to the ratio of the users anonymous records (of a specific size) whose corresponding identified record is among the most probable top T entries as Top-T linkability(or hit) ratio.

Consequently, our study boils down to exploring matching/linking models that maximize the linkability(hit) ratio of the anonymous records for varying values of both T and AR sizes. We consider two values of T: 1 (perfect hit) and 10 (near-hit). Whereas, for the AR size, we experiment with a wider range of values which includes: 1, 5, 10, 20, 30, 40, 50 and 60.

Even though our focus is on the linkability of prolific users, we also attempt to assess performance of our models for non-prolific users. For that, we slightly

Table 1. Notation and abbreviations

NB	Naïve Bayes Model
KLD	Symmetrical Kullback-Leibler Divergence Model
R	Token Type: rating, unigram or digram
LR	Linkability Ratio
AR	Anonymous Record
IR	Identified Record (corresponding to a certain reviewer)
$SymD_{KLD}(IR, AR)$	symmetric KLD distance between IR and AR

change the problem setting by making the IR size smaller; this is discussed in Section 4.4.

4   Analysis

As mentioned in Section 2, we use Naïve Bayes (NB) and Kullback-Leibler Divergence (KLD) models. Before analyzing the collected data, we tokenize all reviews and extract four types of tokens:

1. **Unigrams:** set of all single letters. We discard all non-alphabetical characters.
2. **Digrams:** set of all consecutive letter-pairs. We discard all non-alphabetical characters.
3. **Rating:** rating associated with the review. (In Yelp, this ranges between 1 and 5).
4. **Category:** category associated with the place/service being reviewed. There are 28 categories in our dataset,

Note that we experimented our models on larger token sets, namely trigram and stemmed-word sets. Surprisingly, they mostly perform worse(in terms of linkability) than unigrams or digrams. Before proceeding, we re-cap abbreviations and notation in Table 1.

4.1   Methodology

We begin with the brief description of the methodology for the two models.

Naïve Bayes (NB) Model. For each account IR, we built an NB model, $P(token_i|IR)$, from its identified record. Probabilities are estimated using the Maximum-Likelihood estimator [4] and Laplace smoothing [12] as shown in 2. We then construct four models corresponding to the four aforementioned token types. That is, for each IR, we have $P_{unigram}$, P_{digram}, $P_{category}$ and P_{rating}.

To link an anonymous record AR to an account IR with respect to token type R, we first extract all R-type tokens from AR, $T_{R_1}, T_{R_2}, ... T_{R_n}$ (Where T_{R_i} is the i-th R token in AR). Then, for each IR, we compute the probability $P_R(IR|T_{R_1}, T_{R_2}, ... T_{R_n})$. Finally, we return a list of accounts sorted in decreasing order of probabilities. The top entry represents the most probable match.

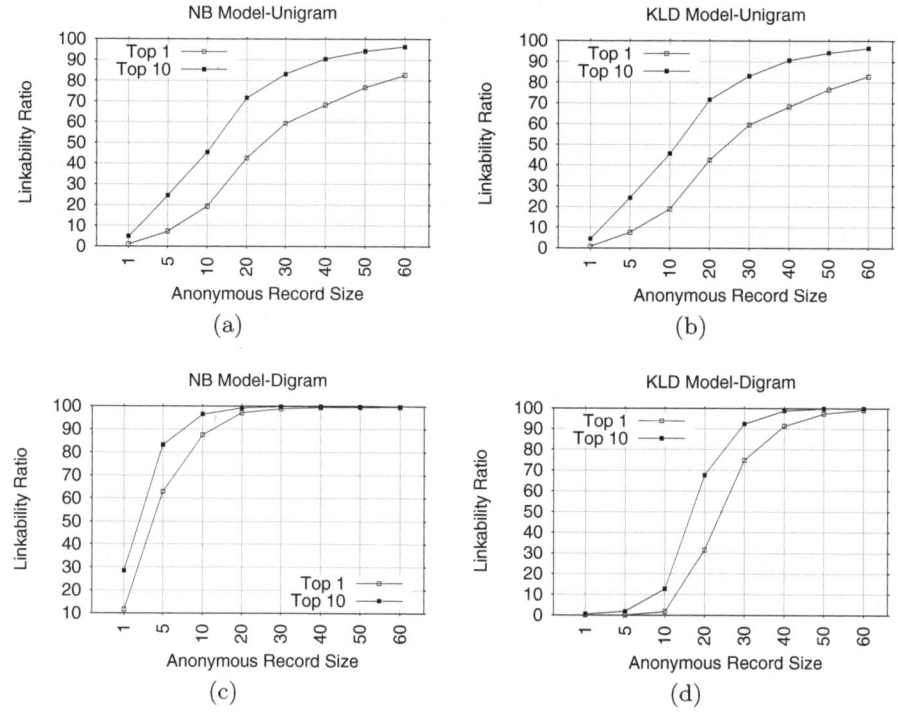

Fig. 1. LRs of NB and KLD models for unigrams and digrams

Kullback-Leibler Divergence (KLD) Model. We use symmetric KLD (see Section 2) to compute the distance between anonymous and identified records. To do so, we first compute distributions of all records and then we smooth the distributions via Laplace smoothing [12](same as the probability estimation in explained in Naive Bayesian in Section 2). As before, we compute four distributions. To link AR with respect to token type R, we compute $SymD_{kl}$ between the distribution of R for AR and the distribution of R for each IR. Then, we return a list sorted in ascending order of $SymD_{KLD}(IR, AR)$ values. The first entry represents the account with the most likely match.

4.2   Study Results

We now present the results corresponding to the lexical tokens. Then, in the next section, we experiment with some combinations of lexical and non-lexical ones.

Lexical – Results. Figures 1(a) and 1(b) depict LRs (Top-1 and Top-10) for NB and KLD with the unigram token. As expected, with the increase in the anonymous record size, the LR grows: it is high in both Top-1 and Top-10 plots.

For example, in Top-1 of both figures, the LRs are around: 19%, 59% and 83% for anonymous record sizes of 10, 30 and 60, respectively. Whereas, in Top-10 of both figures, the LRs are around: 45.5%, 83% and 96% for same record sizes. This suggests that reviews are highly linkable based on trivial single-letter distributions. Note that the two models exhibit similar performance.

Figures 1(c) and 1(d) consider the digram token. In both models, the LR is impressively high: it gets as high as 99.6%/99.2% in Top-1 for NB/KLD for an AR size of 60. For example, the Top-1 LRs in NB are: 11.7%, 62.9%, 87.5% and 97.1%, for respective AR sizes of 1, 5, 10 and 20. Whereas, in KLD, the Top-1 LRs for record sizes of 10, 30 and 60 are: 1.9%,74.9% and 99.2%, respectively.

Unlike unigrams – where LRs in both models are comparable – KLD in digram starts with LRs considerably lower than those of NB. However, the situation changes when the record size reaches 50, with KLD performing comparable to NB. One reason for that could be that KLD improves when the distribution of ARs is more similar to that of corresponding identified records; this usually occurs for large record sizes, as there are more tokens.

Not surprisingly larger AR sizes entail higher LRs. With NB, a larger record size implies that, a given AR has more tokens in common with the corresponding IR. Thus, an increase in the prediction probability $P(IR|T_1, T_2, ...T_n)$. For KLD, a larger record size causes the distribution derived from the AR to be more similar to the one derived from the corresponding IR.

4.3   Improvement I: Combining Lexical with Non-lexical Tokens

In an attempt to improve the LR, we now combine the lexical tokens with the non-lexical ones.

Combining Tokens Methodology. This is straightforward in the NB. We simply increase the list of tokens in the unigram- or digram-based NB by adding the non-lexical tokens. Thus, for every IR, we have the following: $P(lexical\_token_i|IR)$, $P(category\_token_i|IR)$ and $P(rate\_token_i|IR)$.

Combining non-lexical with lexical tokens in KLD is less clear. One way is to simply average $SymD_{KLD}$ values for both token types. However, this might degrade the performance, since lexical distributions may convey much more information than their non-lexical counterparts. Thus, giving them the same weight would not yield better results. Instead, we combine them using a weighted average. First, we compute the weighted average of rating and category $SymD_{KLD}$:

$$SymD_{KLD\_r\_c}(P,Q) =$$
$$\beta \times SymD_{KLD\_r}(P,Q) + (1 - \beta) \times SymD_{KLD\_c}(P,Q)$$

Then, we combine the above with $SymD_{KLD}$ of the lexical tokens to compute the final weighted average:

$$SymD_{KLD\_l\_r\_c}(P,Q) =$$
$$\alpha \times SymD_{KLD\_l}(P,Q) + (1 - \alpha) \times SymD_{KLD\_r\_c}(P,Q)$$

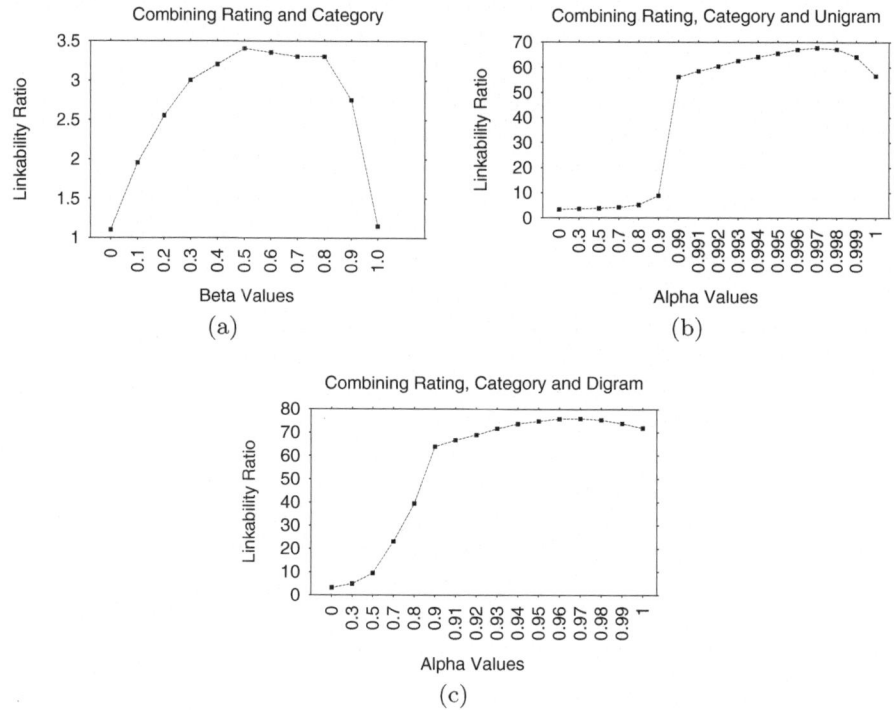

Fig. 2. Results of combining different tokens using different β and α values

Thus, our goal is to get the right β and α values. Intuitively, lexical $SymD_{KLD}$ should have more weight as it carries more information. Since there is no clear way of assigning weight values, we experiment with several choices and pick the one with the best performance; we discuss the selection process below. We experiment only within the IR set and then verify the results generalize to the AR. This is done as follows:

First, for every IR, we allocate the last 30 reviews as a testing record and the remainder – as a training record. Then, we experiment with $SymD_{KLD\_r\_c}$ using several β values and set β to the value that yields the highest LR based on the testing records. Then, we experiment with $SymD_{KLD\_l\_r\_c}$ using several α values and, similarly, pick the one with the highest LR.

Since β or α could assume any values, we need to restrict their choices. For β, we experiment with a range of values, from 0 to 1.00 in 0.1 increments. For α, we expect the optimal value to exceed 0.9, since the LR for lexical tokens is probably higher than non-lexical ones. Therefore, we experiment with the weighted average by varying α between 0.9 and 0.99 in 0.01 increments.

If the values exhibit an increasing trend (i.e., $SymD_{KLD\_l\_r\_c}$ at α of 0.99 is the largest in this range) we continue experimenting in the $0.99--1.00$ range in 0.001 increments. Otherwise, we stop. For further verification, we also experiment

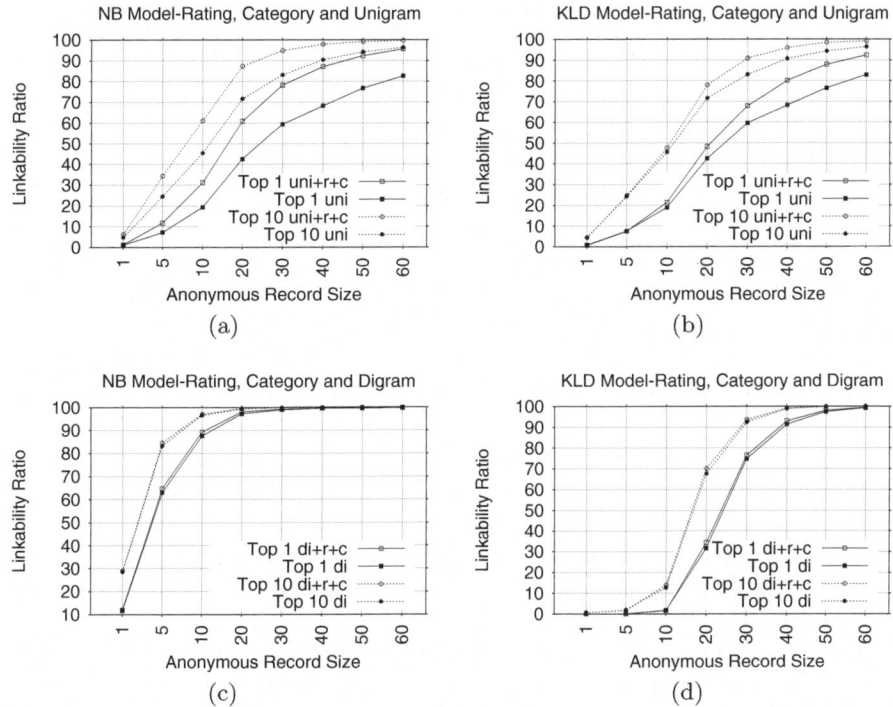

Fig. 3. LRs for NB and KLD for combining ratings and categories with unigrams or digrams

with smaller α values: $0.0, 0.3, 0.5, 0.7$, and 0.8, all of which yield LRs significantly lower than 0.9 for both the unigram and digram. We acknowledge that we may be missing α or β values that could further optimize $SymD_{KLD\_r\_c}$. However, results in the following section show that our selection yields good results.

Figure 2(a) shows LRs (Top-1) for β values. The LR gradually increases until it tops off at 3.4% with $\beta = 0.5$ and then it gradually decreases. Figure 2(b) shows LRs (Top-1) for α values in the unigram case. The LR has an increasing trend until it reaches 67.8% with $\alpha = 0.997$ and then it decreases. Figure 2(c) shows LRs (Top-1) for α values in the diagram case where it tops off at 75.9% with $\alpha = 0.97$. Thus, the final values are 0.5 for β and $0.997/0.97$ for *alpha* in the unigram/digram case. Even though we extract α and β values by testing on a record size of 30, the results in following sections show that the derived weights are effective when tested on ARs of other sizes.

Combining Lexical with Non-Lexical Tokens – Results. Figures 3(a) and 3(b) show Top-1 and Top-10 plots in NB and KLD models of unigram tokens before and after combining them with rating and category tokens. Adding non-lexical tokens to unigrams substantially increases LRs in several record sizes.

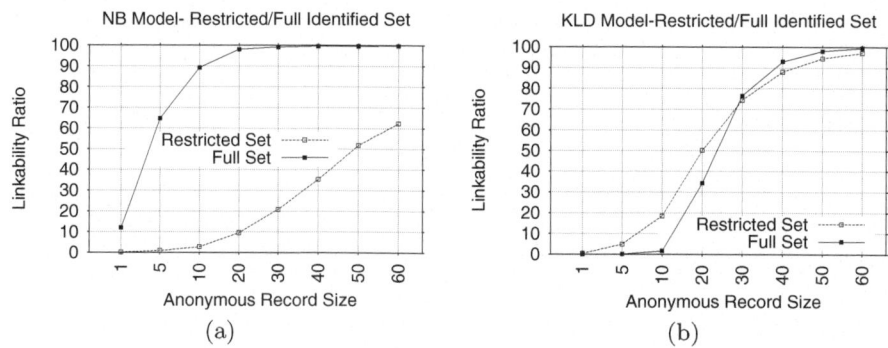

Fig. 4. LRs for NB and KLD in full and restricted identified set

In NB, the gain in Top-1 LRs ranges from 0.25-18.9% (1.4 - 15.7% for Top-10 LRs). In KLD, the gain in Top-1 LRs ranges from 2.5-11.9 (2-7.8% in Top-10 LRs) for most record sizes. These findings shows how effective is combining the non-lexical tokens with the unigrams. In fact, we can accurately identify almost all ARs.

Figures 3(c) and 3(d) show the effect of adding ratings and categories to digrams. The overall effect is less: in NB (KLD) model, the increase in Top-1 LRs ranges from 0.3-1.8% (0.2-2.7%) for most record sizes. The increase is very similar in Top-10 plots.

4.4   Restricting Identified Record Size

In previous sections, our analysis was based on using the full data set. That is, except for the anonymous part of the data set, we use all of the user reviews as part of our identified set. Although the LR is high in many cases, it is not clear how the models will perform when we restrict the IR size. To this end, we re-evaluate the models with the same problem settings, however, with a restricted IR size. We restrict the IR size to the AR size; both randomly selected without replacement.

Figures 4(a) and 4(b) show two Top-1 plots in NB and KLD models: one plot corresponds to the restricted identified set and the other − to the full set. Tokens used in the models consist of digrams, ratings and categories (since this combination gives the highest LR). Unlike the previous sections, where NB and KLD behaved similarly, the two models now behave differently when restricting the identified set. While NB performs better than KLD on the full set, the latter performs much better than NB when the identified set is restricted. In fact, in some cases, KLD performs better when the set is restricted.

The reason for this improved KLD performance might be the following: in the symmetric KLD distance function, the distributions of both the IR and AR have to be very close in order to match regardless of the size of the IR; unlike the NB, where larger training sets would lead to better estimates of the token probabilities and thus more accurate predictions.

In KLD, we achieve high LRs for many record sizes. For example, Top-1 LRs in the restricted set are 74.5%, 88% and 97.1% when the anonymous (and identified) record sizes are 30, 40 and 60, respectively. Whereas, the LRs in the full set for the same AR sizes are: 76.5% , 93% and 99.4%. When the record size is less than 30, KLD performs better in the restricted set than the full one. For example, when the AR size is 20, the LR in the restricted set is 50.1% and 34.3% in the full set. In NB, Top-1 LR in the restricted set is lower than the full set. For instance, it is 20.8%, 35.3% and 62.4% for AR sizes of: 30, 40 and 60, respectively. Whereas, for the same sizes, the LR is more than 99% in the full set.

This result has one very important implication: even with very small IR sizes, many anonymous users can be identified. For example, with only IR and AR sizes of only 30, most users can be accurately linked (75% in Top-1 and 90% in Top-10). This situation is very common since many real-world users generate 30 or more reviews over multiple sites. Therefore, even reviews from less prolific accounts can be accurately linked.

4.5   Improvement II: Matching All ARs at Once

We now experiment with another natural strategy of attempting to match all ARs at once.

Methodology. In previous sections, we focus on independently linking one AR at a time. That is, the input to our matching/linking model is one AR and the output is the user of the closest IR. If we change the problem settings and make the input a set of ARs(instead of one) where each AR belongs to a different user, we may be able to improve the linkabilty knowing that an AR cannot be mapped to more than one user. To this end, we construct algorithm $Match\_All()$ in Figure 5 as an add-on to the KLD models suggested in previous sections where the input is a set of ARs, each of which belongs to a different user. The number of ARs in the input is equal to the number of users in our dataset.

$SymD_{KLD}(IR_j, AR_i)$ symmetrically measures the distance between their (IR_j's and AR_i's) distributions. Since every AR maps to a distinct IR (AR_i maps to IR_i), it would seem that lower $SymD_{KLD}$ would lead to a better match. We use this intuition to design $Match\_All()$. As shown in the figure, $Match\_All()$ picks the smallest $SymD_{KLD}(IR_j, AR_i)$ as the map between IR_j and AR_i and then deletes the pair (IR_j, V_{kj}) from all remaining lists in S_L. The process continues until we compute all matches. Note that, for any $List_{AR_k}$, (IR_j, V_{kj}) is deleted from the list only when there is another pair (IR_j, V_{lj}) in $List_{AR_l}$, such that $SymD_{KLD}(IR_j, AR_l) \leq SymD_{KLD}(IR_j, AR_k)$, and IR_j has been selected as the match for AR_l.The output of the algorithm is a match-list: $S_M = \{(IR_{i_1}, AR_{j_1}), ..., (IR_{i_n}, AR_{j_n})\}$.

We now consider how $Match\_All()$ could improve the LR. Suppose that we have two ARs: AR_i and AR_j along with corresponding sorted lists L_i and

---

Algorithm *Match_All*: Pseudo Code

Input: (1) Set of ARs: $S_{AR} = \{AR_1, AR_2, ..., AR_n\}$
    (2) Set of reviewer-ids / identified records:
    $S_{IR} = \{IR_1, IR_2, ..., IR_n\}$
    (3) Set of matching lists for each AR:
    $S_L = \{List_{AR_1}, .., List_{AR_n}\}$
Output: Matching list: $S_M = \{(IR_{i_1}, AR_{j_1}), ..., (IR_{i_n}, AR_{j_n})\}$
  1: set $S_M = \emptyset$
  2: While $|S_{AR}| \neq 0$:
  3:    Find AR_i with smallest $SymD_{KLD}$ in all lists in S_L
  4:    Get corresponding reviewer-id IR_j
  5:    Add (IR_j, AR_i) to S_M
  6:    Delete AR_i from S_{AR}
  7:    Delete $List_{AR_i}$ from S_L
  8:    For each $List_t$ in S_L,
  9:      Delete tuple containing IR_j from $List_t$
  10:   End For
  11: End While

NOTE 1: $List_{AR_i}$ in S_L is a list of pairs (IR_j, V_{ij}) where $V_{ij} = SymD_{KLD}(IR_j, AR_i)$, for all j
NOTE 2: $List_{AR_i}$ is sorted in increasing order of V_{ij}, i.e., IR_j with lowest $SymD_{KLD}(IR_j, AR_i)$ at the top.

Fig. 5. Pseudo-Code for matching all ARs at once

L_j and assume that IR_i is at the top of each list. Using only KLD (as in previous sections), we would return IR_i for both ARs and thus miss one of the two. Whereas, *Match_All*, would assign IR_i to **only** one AR – the one with the smaller $SymD_{KLD}(IR_i, ...)$ value. We would intuitively suspect that $SymD_{KLD}(IR_i, AR_i) < SymD_{KLD}(IR_i, AR_j)$ since IR_i is the right match for AR_i and thus their distributions would probably be very close. If this is the case, *Match_All* would delete IR_i (erroneous match) from the top of L_j which could help clearing up the way for IR_j (correct match) to the top of L_j.

We note that there is no guarantee that *Match_All*() will always work: one mistake in early rounds would lead to others in later rounds. We believe that *Match_All*() works better if $SymD_{KLD}(IR_i, AR_i) < SymD_{KLD}(IR_j, AR_i)$ $(j \neq i)$ holds most of the time.

In the next section, we show the results of *Match_All*() when we experiment with the KLD model with digram, rating and category tokens.[2]

Results. Figures 6(a) and 6(b) show the effect of *Match_All*() on Top-1 LRs in both the restricted identified set and the full identified set, respectively. The combination of diagram, rating and category tokens are used. Each figure shows two Top-1 plots: one for the LR after using *Match_All* and the other – for the LR

---

[2] We also tried *Match_All*() with the NB model and it did not improve the LR.

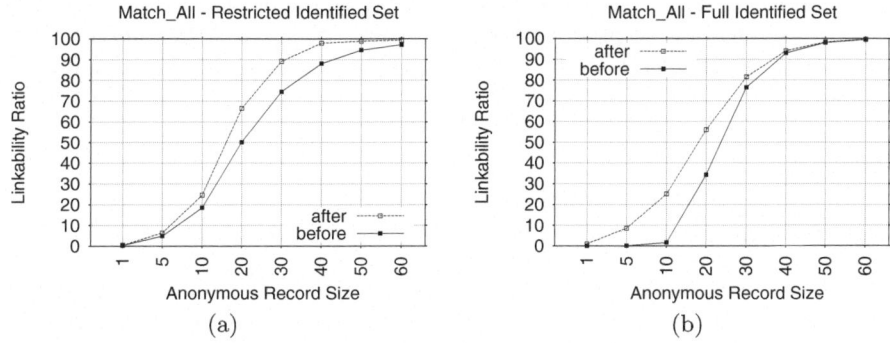

Fig. 6. Effects of $Match\_All()$ on LRs in full and restricted identified set: before and after plots

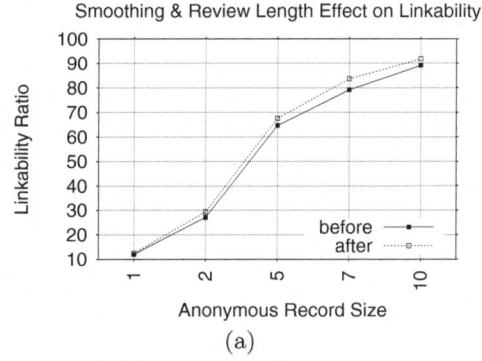

Fig. 7. Effects of smoothing and review length on LRs: before and after plots

before using it. Clearly, $Match\_All$ is effective in improving the LR for almost all record sizes. For the restricted set, the gain in the LR ranges from 1.6-16.4% for nearly all AR sizes. A Similar increase is observed in the full set that ranges from 1-23.4% for most record sizes. This shows that the $Match\_All$ is very effective when used with diagram, rating and category tokens. The privacy implication of $Match\_All$ is important as it significantly increases the LR for small ARs in the restricted set. This shows that privacy of less prolific users is exposed even more with $Match\_All$.

4.6 Improvement III: Improving Linkability for Small Anonymous Records

Although most of the proposed exhibits high LR's when the AR size is large, the linkability is not as high for small record sizes. For improving the LR for small AR (in the full identified set), we consider the NB model that uses diagrams, ratings and categories as its tokens (see Section 4.3) as a base for our improvement. We use this model as it performs the best for small ARs comparable to other models. To that end, we first change the way we smooth the probabilities as follows:

$$P(token_i|IR) =$$
$$\frac{Num\ of\ Occurrences\ of\ Token_i\ in\ IR\ +\ \eta}{Num\ of\ Occurrences\ of\ all\ Tokens\ in\ IR + \eta \times Num\ of\ Possible\ Tokens}$$

Unlike the models in the previous sections, η could take values other than 1. In fact, we experiment with several different values and we find that η value of 0.5 gives the best performance[3]. The intuition is that setting η to a value less than 1 may help downscale the effect of noisy digrams that the user rarely use. Additionally, we leverage the length of the reviews, the number of the alphabetical letters, as an additional feature to the model. We consider the length of the reviews as we intuitively believe that different users tend to write longer/shorter reviews than others. We model the length as a normal distribution and we use the maximum likelihood estimate to set the distribution parameters [4, 12].

Figure 7 shows the effect of this improvement. For clarity, we only show the improvement resulting from combining the two aforementioned steps. As shown, the Top-1 LRs gain roughly ranges from 0.5%-5%. For example, for AR size of 5, 7 and 10, the Top-1 LR approximately increases from 65%, 79% and 89% to 68%, 84% and 92%, respectively. Similar increases are observed in the Top-10 LR which reach 88%/98% for AR size of 5/10 (and up to 30%/54% for AR size of 1/2).

4.7   Study Summary

We now summarize the main findings and conclusions of our study.

1. The LR becomes very high – reaching up to $\sim 99.5\%$ in both KLD and NB when using only digram tokens. (See Section 4.2).
2. Surprisingly, using only unigrams, we can link up to 83% in both NB and KLD models, with 96% in Top-10. (See Section 4.2). This suggests that reviewers expose a great deal merely from their single letter distributions.
3. Non-lexical tokens are very useful in tandem with lexical tokens, especially, the unigram: we observe a $\sim 19\%/12\%$ Top-1 LR increase in NB/KLD for some cases. (See Section 4.3).
4. Relying only on unigram, rating and category tokens, we can accurately link 96%/92% of the ARs (size 60) in NB/KLD. (See Section 4.3).
5. Restricting the IR size does not always degrade linkability. In KLD, we can link as many as 97% ARs when the IR size is small. (See Section 4.4).
6. Linking all ARs at once (instead of each independently) helps improve accuracy. The gain is up to 16/23% in restricted/full set. (See Section 4.5).

---

[3] Note that we experiment η on only the training set and pick the best value.

7. Generally, NB performs better than KLD when we use the full identified set and KLD performs better when we use the restricted identified set.
8. Combining review length with different smoothing techniques is helpful in increasing the linkability for small AR and the Top-1/Top-10 LR reach 92%/98% for AR size of 10(See Section 4.6).

5   Discussion

Implications. We believe that the results of, and techniques used in, this study have several implications. One implication is the possibility to cross-reference accounts (and reviews) among multiple (similar)review sites. If a person contributes to two similar review sites under two identities, it is likely that sets of reviews from these sites can be linked. This could be quite detrimental to contributors' privacy. Another implication is the ability to correlate – on the same review site – multiple accounts that are in fact manipulated by the same person. This could make our techniques very useful in detecting review spam [8], whereby a contributor authors reviews under different accounts to tout (also self-promote) or criticize a product or a service. One concrete application of our techniques is via integration with the review site's front-end software in order to provide feedback to authors indicating the degree of linkability of their reviews. For example, when the reviewer logs in, a linkability nominal/categorical value (e.g. high, medium, and low) could be shown indicating how some of his/her reviews (selected randomly) are linkable to the rest. It would then be up to to the individual to maintain or modify their reviewing patterns to be less linkable.

Prolific Users. While there are clearly many more occasional (non-prolific) reviewers than prolific ones, we believe that our study of prolific reviewers is important, for two reasons. First, the number of prolific contributors is still quite large. For example, from only one review site – Yelp – we identified $\sim$ 2,000 such reviewers. Second, given the spike of popularity of review sites [1], we believe that, in the near future, the number of such prolific contributors will grow substantially. Also, even many occasional reviewers, with the passage of time, will enter the ranks of "prolific" ones, i.e., by slowly accumulating a sufficient corpus of reviews over the years. Nevertheless, our study suggests that privacy is not high even for non-prolific users, as discussed in Section 4.5. For example, when both IR and AR sizes are only 20 (i.e., total per user contribution is 40 reviews), we can accurately link around 70% of anonymous records to their reviewers.

Anonymous Record Size. Our models perform best when the AR size is 60. However, for every reviewer in our dataset, 60 represents less than 20% of that person's total number of reviews. Also, using NB coupled with digram, rating, category and length features, we can accurately link most anonymous records when AR size is small (see Section 4.6).

Unigram Tokens. While our best-performing models are based on digram tokens, we also obtain high linkability results from unigram tokens that reach up to

83% (96% in the Top 10) in NB or KLD. The results improve to 96/92% when we combine unigrams with rating and category tokens. Note that the number of tokens in unigram-based models is 59 (26) tokens with (without) combining them with rating and category tokens. Whereas, the number of tokens in diagram-based models is 676 (709 when combined with rating and category tokens). This makes linkability accuracy based on unigram models very comparable to its diagram counterpart, while the number of tokens is significantly fewer. This implies a substantial reduction in resources and processing power in unigram-based models which would make them scale better. For example, if we assume that the attacker wants to link a set of anonymous reviews to *many* large review datasets, unigram-based models would scale better, while maintaining similar level of accuracy.

6   Related Work

Many authorship analysis studies are in the literature. Among the most related recent studies are [3,13,14]. In [14], a large scale author identification techniques (based on linguistic stylometry) are evaluated on blog de-anonymization. While the problem formulation is similar to ours, there are notable differences. First, we study the linkability in a different context; i.e., user reviews. User reviews have ratings and categories, which prove useful in some scenarios, while blogs(used in [14]) do not. Additionally, user reviews are shorter while blogs could be as long as an article. Moreover, user reviews are mainly about user evaluations of a specific service/product while blogs could be very random, such as news reporting or literature-related work. Second, our study points to high linkability ratios in user reviews, nearly 100% Top-1 linkability ratio, where as in [14], the Top-1 linkability ratio is around 20% [4]. Third, our study shows high linkability ratios in the presence of very simple features.

A related problem is explored in [13]. It focuses on identifying authors based on reviews in both single- and double-blinded academic peer-reviewing processes of scientific journals and conferences. Naïve Bayes classifier is used – along with word-based tokens – to identify authors and the best result is around 90%. This work is different from ours in several aspects. First, it explores the author identification in a very restricted domain; i.e., academic paper reviews. Second, the number of candidate authors is around 20 which is less than ours($\sim$ 2000). Third, the number of features used in [13] is large where unigram, bigram, and trigrams based on words(a sequence of one, two and three words) are used. In ours, we only use unigrams and bigrams that are based on letters (in addition to the ratings and categories). The work in [3] also considered author identification and similarity detection by incorporating a rich set of stylistic features along with a novel technique(based on Karhunen-Loeve-transforms) to extract write-prints. An identification performance of 91% is achieved. The same approach is

---

[4] Note in [14], the identification accuracy is increased to 80% by not making a guess when there is not enough confidence; however, this does not increase the linkability ratio (recall is low).

tested on a large set of Buyer/Seller Ebay feedback comments collected from Ebay. Such comments typically reflect one's experience when dealing with a buyer or a seller. Unlike our general-purpose reviews, these comments do not review products, services or places of different categories. Additionally, the scale of the problem is different and the analysis is performed for only 100 authors. An author identification technique based on frequent pattern write prints is shown in [7] and author identification techniques based on extracting lexical, syntactic, structural and content-specific features and then feeding them to some classifiers are shown in [18]. For a comprehensive overview of authorship analysis studies, we refer to [16].

While many of the author identification studies are somewhat similar to our present work, there are some notable differences. First, we perform authorship identification analysis in a context that has not been extensively explored – generic user reviews. User reviews are generally are less formal and less restricting in the choice of words. In a review, the author generally assesses something and thus the text conveys some evaluation and personal opinions. In addition, reviews contain other non-textual information, such as the ratings and categories of things being reviewed. These types of extra information provide added leverage(shown in 4.3). Second, our problem formulation is different. We study linkability of reviews in the presence of a large number of prolific contributors where the number of anonymous reviews could be more than one (up to 60 reviews). Whereas, most prior work attempts to identify authors from a small set of authors, each with small sets of texts. Third, we show high linkability ratios in the presence of very simple features. For example, reviewers can be accurately identified from their letter distributions. These measurement results are very alarming for users concerned about their privacy.

7   Conclusion

Large numbers of Internet users are becoming frequent visitors and contributors to various review sites. At the same time, they are concerned about their privacy. In this paper, we study linkability of reviews. Based on a large set of reviews, we show that a high percentage (99% in some cases) are linkable, even though we use very simple models and very simple features set. Our study suggests that users reliably expose their identities in reviews. This has certain important implications for cross-referencing accounts among different review sites and detecting people who write reviews under different identities. Additionally, techniques used in this study could be adopted by review sites to give contributors feedback about linkability of their reviews.

Acknowledgement. The authors are very thankful to Paolo Gasti, Claude Castelluccia and Alexander Ihler for their useful insights. We also thank the anonymous reviewers for their helpful feedback. This work was partially supported by the Ministry of Higher Education, Saudi Arabia.

324   M. Almishari and G. Tsudik

References

1. Yelp By The Numbers,
   http://officialblog.yelp.com/2010/12/2010-yelp-by-the-numbers.html
2. Yelp Elite Squad, http://www.yelp.com/faq#what_is_elite_squad
3. Abbasi, A., Chen, H.: Writeprints: A Stylometric Approach to Identity-Level Identification and Similarity Detection in Cyberspace. ACM Transactions on Information Systems (2008)
4. Bishop, C.M.: Pattern Recognition and Machine Learning. Springer (2006)
5. Dave, K., Lawrence, S., Pennock, D.M.: Mining the Peanut Gallery: Opinion Extraction and Semantic Classification of Product Reviews. In: International Conference on World Wide Web (2003)
6. Hu, M., Liu, B.: Mining and Summarizing Customer Reviews. In: ACM SIGKDD International Conference on Knowledge Discovery and Data Mining (2004)
7. Iqbal, F., Binsalleeh, H., Fung, B., Debbabi, M.: A unified data mining solution for authorship analysis in anonymous textual communications. Information Sciences (INS): Special Issue on Data Mining for Information Security (2011)
8. Jindal, N., Liu, B.: Opinion Spam and Analysis. In: ACM International Conference on Web Search and Data Mining (2008)
9. Jindal, N., Liu, B., Lim, E.-P.: Finding Unusual Review Patterns Using Unexpected Rules. In: Proceedings of the 19th ACM International Conference on Information and Knowledge Management (2010)
10. Lewis, D.: Naive(bayes) at forty:the independence assumption in information retrieval. In: Proceedings of the 10th European Conference on Machine Learning (1998)
11. Lim, E.-P., Nguyen, V.-A., Jindal, N., Liu, B., Lauw, H.: Detecting Product Review Spammers using Rating Behaviors. In: Proceedings of the 19th ACM International Conference on Information and Knowledge Management (2010)
12. Mitchell, T.: Machine Learning. McGraw Hill (1997)
13. Nanavati, M., Taylor, N., Aiello, W., Warfield, A.: Herbert West – Deanonymizer. In: 6th USENIX Workshop on Hot Topics in Security (2011)
14. Narayanan, A., Paskov, H., Gong, N.Z., Bethencourt, J., Stefanov, E., Shin, E.C.R., Song, D.: On the Feasibility of Internet-Scale Author Identification. In: IEEE Symposium on Security and Privacy (2012)
15. Pang, B., Lee, L., Vaithyanathan, S.: Thumbs up? Sentiment Classification using Machine Learning Techniques. In: Empirical Methods on Natural Language Processing Conference (2002)
16. Stamatatos, E.: A Survey of Modern Authorship Attribution Methods. Journal of the American Society for Information Science and Technology (2009)
17. Yadav, S., Reddy, A.K., Reddy, A.N., Ranjan, S.: Detecting Algorithmically Generated Malicious Domain Names. In: Internet Measurement Conference (2010)
18. Zheng, R., Li, J., Chen, H., Huang, Z.: A Framework for Authorship Identification of Online Messages: Writing Style Features and Classification Techniques. Journal of the American Society for Information Science and Technology (2006)

Formal Analysis of Privacy
in an eHealth Protocol

Naipeng Dong*, Hugo Jonker, and Jun Pang

Faculty of Sciences, Technology and Communication, University of Luxembourg

Abstract. Given the nature of health data, privacy of eHealth systems is of prime importance. An eHealth system must enforce that users remain private, even if they are bribed or coerced to reveal themselves or others. Consider e.g. a pharmaceutical company that bribes a pharmacist to reveal information which breaks a doctor's privacy. In this paper, we identify and formalise several new but important privacy notions on enforcing doctor privacy. Then we analyse privacy of a complicated and practical eHealth protocol. Our analysis shows to what extent these properties as well as properties such as anonymity and untraceability are satisfied by the protocol. Finally, we address the found ambiguities resulting in privacy flaws, and propose suggestions for fixing them.

1   Introduction

Traditionally, data in health care (e.g., patient records) was stored on paper files. Given the sensitive nature of health data, handling this data must meet strict security and privacy requirements. This was relatively easily satisfied by controlling access to the physical documents. Those who had access could be considered trusted not to violate security nor privacy of the data. With the advent of eHealth systems – systems that digitally store and exchange health data – security and particularly privacy requirements were often achieved using access control (e.g., see [1, 2]).

However, the introduction of eHealth systems has changed the setting. The main benefit of eHealth systems is that they facilitate the digital exchange of information amongst various roles in health care. This has two major consequences: the health care data is shared digitally with more parties, such as pharmacists and insurance companies; and, this data can be easily shared by any party with an outsider. Clearly, the assumption of a trusted network can no longer hold in such a setting. Given that it is trivial for a malicious entity to intercept or even alter digital data in transit, access control approaches to privacy and security are no longer sufficient. In this paper, we consider security and privacy of the involved parties with respect to an outsider, the Dolev-Yao adversary [3], who controls the communication network (i.e. the adversary can observe, block, create and alter information). In this setting, communication security and privacy are mainly achieved by employing cryptographic communication protocols. It is

---

* Supported by the National Research Fund, Luxembourg, project PHD-09-027.

S. Foresti, M. Yung, and F. Martinelli (Eds.): ESORICS 2012, LNCS 7459, pp. 325–342, 2012.
© Springer-Verlag Berlin Heidelberg 2012

well known that designing such protocols is error-prone: time and again, flaws
have been found in protocols that claimed to be secure (e.g., electronic voting
systems [4, 5] have been broken [6, 7]). Therefore, we believe that the claims
of an eHealth protocol must be verified before the protocol is used in practice.
Without verifying that a protocol satisfies its security claims, subtle flaws may
go undiscovered.

In order to verify whether a protocol satisfies security and privacy requirements, each property must be formally defined. Various security and privacy
properties have already been defined in the literature, such as secrecy, authentication, anonymity and untraceability. We refer to these properties as regular
security and privacy properties. While they are necessary to ensure security and
privacy, by themselves these regular properties are not sufficient. Benaloh and
Tuinstra pointed out the risk of subverting a voter [4] to sell her vote. This
idea, of coercing or bribing a party into nullfying their privacy, is hardly considered in the literature of eHealth systems (notable exceptions include [8, 9]).
However, this notion is important for health care – e.g., a pharmaceutical company may bribe doctors to prescribe only their medicine. Therefore, we consider
not only privacy with respect to a Dolev-Yao adversary, but also privacy in the
presence of an active coercer – someone who is bribing or threatening parties
to reveal their privacy. We refer to these properties as enforced privacy properties. In particular, we identify the following notions of privacy [10] to counter
doctor bribery: *prescribing-privacy*: a doctor cannot be linked to his prescriptions; *enforced prescribing-privacy*: preventing doctor bribes; *independency of
prescribing-privacy*: preventing others to reduce a doctor's prescribing-privacy;
and *independency of enforced prescribing-privacy*: preventing anyone from affecting a doctor's enforced prescribing-privacy.

Contributions. We identify three notions of enforced privacy in eHealth systems and are the first to provide formal definitions for them. In addition, we
develop an in-depth applied pi model of the DLVV08 eHealth protocol [9] which
is rather complicated and aims for practical usage in Belgium. Furthermore, we
formally analyse privacy and enforced privacy properties of the protocol, as well
as regular security and privacy properties. We find ambiguities in the protocol
which lead to flaws on privacy, and propose suggestions for fixing them. The
modelling and full analysis of the DLVV08 protocol can be found in [11].

2   The Applied Pi Calculus

The applied pi calculus is a language designed for modelling and analysing security protocols [12]. It assumes an infinite set of names (modelling channels and
data), an infinite set of variables and a set of functions (to model cryptographic
primitives). A *term* is a name or variable, or a function applied to other terms.
Terms are used to model messages. An equational theory E defines equivalences
between terms. A protocol is modelled as a set of roles running in parallel. The
behaviour of each role is modelled as a process, defined as follows.

$P, Q ::= 0 \mid P \mid Q \mid !P \mid \nu n.P \mid \text{in}(u, x).P \mid \text{out}(u, M).P \mid \text{if } M =_E N \text{ then } P \text{ else } Q$

$A, B ::= P \mid A \mid B \mid \nu n.A \mid \nu x.A \mid \{M/x\}$

A plain process P, Q can be the empty process 0, two sub-processes running in parallel $P \mid Q$, a replication $!P$, a name restriction on a process $\nu n.P$, an input or output action followed by a process ($\text{in}(u, x).P$ and $\text{out}(u, M).P$, respectively), or a conditional choice based on the equational theory (if... then... else). To this, extended processes add variable restrictions and active substitution.

The semantics of applied pi consists of three parts: *structural equivalence*, which defines equivalence relations between two processes which only differ in structure; *internal reduction* which defines sub-process communication rules and *if-then-else* evaluation rules; and *labelled reduction* which defines reduction rules to model the communication between the adversary and the protocol. We use "$P\{M/x\}$" (equivalently: "let $x = M$ in P") to denote syntactical replacement of x with M in process P. Names and variables are *free* if they are not delimited by restriction and by inputs. A process is *closed* if it does not contain free variables. Several equivalence relations on processes are defined in applied pi. We use labelled bisimilarity ($\approx_\ell$), which is based on static equivalence of processes. Labelled bisimilarity compares the dynamic behaviour of processes, while static equivalence compares the static states of processes. For more details, see [12].

Applied pi assumes the Dolev-Yao adversary [3], which controls the network and can eavesdrop, block, create, and inject messages, as well as applying cryptographic primitives (e.g., decrypting eavesdropped messages). Normally, dishonest users are considered as part of the adversary. However, coerced/bribed users are not modelled as part of the adversary, as the adversary does not fully trust them.

3   Formalising Privacy Properties

In order to formally verify privacy properties of a protocol, the first step is to give precise definitions of privacy properties. Properties such as anonymity and untraceability have been formally studied in the literature (e.g., [13–18]), which can be lifted to the eHealth domain. In eHealth it is important to protect doctor's prescription behaviour against bribery. Such kinds of privacy properties have not been studied formally so far.

In this section, we first define prescribing-privacy to model protecting a doctor's prescription behaviour without considering bribery. Next, we formally define three new privacy properties to protect a doctor's prescribing-privacy against bribery: *enforced prescribing-privacy*, *independency of prescribing-privacy*, and *independency of enforced prescribing-privacy*. In the end, we briefly show the definitions of anonymity, strong anonymity, untraceability and strong untraceability for eHealth protocols.

In the following discussions, we model an eHealth protocol EHP as a n-role well-formed [17] protocol of the form: $EHP = \nu \tilde{m}.init.(!R_1 \mid \ldots \mid !R_n)$. In particular, we have a doctor role R_{dr} of the form: $R_{dr} = \nu \text{Id}_{dr}.init_{dr}.!P_{dr}$, where

$P_{dr} = \nu \texttt{presc}.main_{dr}$. Essentiality, this formalisation allows us to model an unbounded number of users and represent each user as an instance of a role. We focus on the behaviour of a doctor. Each doctor is associated with an identify and can execute an infinite number of sessions. Within each session, the doctor will create a prescription. Processes $init$ and $init_{dr}$ model the initialisation of the protocol and the doctor role. Process P_{dr} models a session of the doctor role. Furthermore, we use $\mathcal{C}$ to denote a context (a process with a hole) consisting of honest users; Id_{dr} and $presc$ are free variables; A and B are free names, representing doctor identities known to the adversary; and a and b are two free names, representing two different prescriptions.

3.1 Prescribing-Privacy

Prescribing-privacy aims to protect doctors' prescription behaviour, which can be captured by the unlinkability of a doctor and his prescriptions. Unlinkability is normally modelled as indistinguishability when two honest users swap their actions (or items), e.g., see the formalisation of vote privacy [19]. Thus, prescribing-privacy is modelled as the equivalence of two doctor processes: in the first process, an honest doctor A prescribes a in one of his sessions and another honest doctor B prescribes b in one of his sessions; in the second one, A prescribes b and B prescribes a.

Definition 1 (Prescribing-privacy). *A well-formed eHealth protocol EHP satisfies prescribing-privacy if*

$$
\begin{aligned}
\mathcal{C}[&\big(init_{dr}\{\texttt{A}/Id_{dr}\}.(!P_{dr}\{\texttt{A}/Id_{dr}\} \mid main_{dr}\{\texttt{A}/Id_{dr}, \texttt{a}/presc\})) \mid \\
&\big(init_{dr}\{\texttt{B}/Id_{dr}\}.(!P_{dr}\{\texttt{B}/Id_{dr}\} \mid main_{dr}\{\texttt{B}/Id_{dr}, \texttt{b}/presc\}))] \\
\approx_{\ell} \mathcal{C}[&\big(init_{dr}\{\texttt{A}/Id_{dr}\}.(!P_{dr}\{\texttt{A}/Id_{dr}\} \mid main_{dr}\{\texttt{A}/Id_{dr}, \texttt{b}/presc\})) \mid \\
&\big(init_{dr}\{\texttt{B}/Id_{dr}\}.(!P_{dr}\{\texttt{B}/Id_{dr}\} \mid main_{dr}\{\texttt{B}/Id_{dr}, \texttt{a}/presc\}))].
\end{aligned}
$$

3.2 Enforced Prescribing-Privacy

Enforced privacy properties have been proposed and formally studied in different domains to prevent bribery and coercion, for instance, receipt-freeness and coercion-resistance in voting [19, 20], receipt-freeness in online auction [21]. In eHealth, De Decker et al. [9] identify the need to prevent a pharmaceutical company from bribing a doctor to favour their medicine. Hence, doctor's prescribing-privacy should be enforced by protocols to prevent doctor bribery.

This means that intuitively, even if a doctor collaborates, the adversary cannot be certain that the doctor has followed his instructions. Bribed users cannot be modelled as part of the adversary, as they are not trusted by the adversary. In addition, we need to model how bribed users share information obtained from channels hidden from the adversary. Inspired by Delaune et al.'s formalisation of receipt-freeness in electronic voting [19], we define enforced prescribing-privacy to be satisfied if there exists a process where the bribed doctor does not follow the adversary's instruction (e.g., prescribing a particular medicine), which is indistinguishable from a process where she does.

Modelling this property necessitates modelling a doctor who genuinely reveals all her private information to the adversary. In [19], this is achieved by process transformation P^{chc}, which transforms a plain process P into one which shares all private information over the channel chc with the adversary. In addition, we also use their other transformation $P^{\setminus \text{out(chc,·)}}$. This [19] models a process P which erases all outputs on channel chc. Formally, $P^{\setminus \text{out(chc,·)}} := \nu \text{chc}.(P \mid !\text{in(chc}, x))$.

Definition 2 (Enforced prescribing-privacy). *A well-formed eHealth protocol EHP satisfies enforced prescribing-privacy, if there exist processes $init'_{dr}$ and P'_{dr}, such that:*

1)
$$\mathcal{C}\big[\big(init'_{dr}\{A/Id_{dr}\}.(!P_{dr}\{A/Id_{dr}\} \mid P'_{dr}\{A/Id_{dr}\})\big) \mid$$
$$\big(init_{dr}\{B/Id_{dr}\}.(!P_{dr}\{B/Id_{dr}\} \mid main_{dr}\{B/Id_{dr}, a/presc\})\big)\big]$$
$$\approx_{\ell} \mathcal{C}\big[\big((init_{dr}\{A/Id_{dr}\})^{\text{chc}}.(!P_{dr}\{A/Id_{dr}\} \mid (main_{dr}\{A/Id_{dr}, a/presc\})^{\text{chc}})\big) \mid$$
$$\big(init_{dr}\{B/Id_{dr}\}.(!P_{dr}\{B/Id_{dr}\} \mid main_{dr}\{B/Id_{dr}, b/presc\})\big)\big];$$

2)
$$init'_{dr}\{A/Id_{dr}\}^{\setminus \text{out(chc,·)}}.(P'_{dr}\{A/Id_{dr}\}^{\setminus \text{out(chc,·)}})$$
$$\approx_{\ell} init_{dr}\{A/Id_{dr}\}.(main_{dr}\{A/Id_{dr}, b/presc\}),$$

where $init'_{dr}\{A/Id_{dr}\}.(!P_{dr}\{A/Id_{dr}\} \mid P'_{dr}\{A/Id_{dr}\})$ is a closed plain process, and chc is a fresh channel name.

3.3   Independency of Prescribing-Privacy

Usually, eHealth systems have to deal with a complex constellation of roles: doctors, patients, pharmacists, insurance companies, medical administration, etc. Each of these roles has access to different private information and has different privacy concerns. An untrusted role may be bribed to reveal private information to the adversary such that the adversary can break another roles' privacy. De Decker et al. [9] also note that preserving doctor privacy is not sufficient to prevent bribery: pharmacists could act as *go-betweens*. For instance, pharmacists may have sensitive data which can be revealed to the adversary to break a doctor's prescribing-privacy. To prevent a party (not a doctor) to do this, eHealth protocols are required to satisfy *independency of prescribing-privacy*, meaning that even if another party R_i reveals their information (i.e., R_i^{chc}), the adversary should not be able to break a doctor's prescribing-privacy.

Definition 3 (Independency of prescribing-privacy). *A well-formed eHealth protocol EHP satisfies* prescribing-privacy independent of role R_i *if*

$$\mathcal{C}\big[!R_i^{\text{chc}} \mid \big(init_{dr}\{A/Id_{dr}\}.(!P_{dr}\{A/Id_{dr}\} \mid main_{dr}\{A/Id_{dr}, a/presc\})\big) \mid$$
$$\big(init_{dr}\{B/Id_{dr}\}.(!P_{dr}\{B/Id_{dr}\} \mid main_{dr}\{B/Id_{dr}, b/presc\})\big)\big]$$
$$\approx_{\ell} \mathcal{C}\big[!R_i^{\text{chc}} \mid \big(init_{dr}\{A/Id_{dr}\}.(!P_{dr}\{A/Id_{dr}\} \mid main_{dr}\{A/Id_{dr}, b/presc\})\big) \mid$$
$$\big(init_{dr}\{B/Id_{dr}\}.(!P_{dr}\{B/Id_{dr}\} \mid main_{dr}\{B/Id_{dr}, a/presc\})\big)\big].$$

where R_i is a non-doctor role.

Note that we assume a worst situation in which a pharmacist genuinely cooperates with the adversary. For example, the pharmacist forwards all information obtained from channels hidden from the adversary.

3.4 Independency of Enforced Prescribing-Privacy

We have discussed two situations where a doctor prescription behaviour can be revealed when either the doctor or another different party cooperates with the adversary. It is natural to consider the conjunction of these two, i.e., a situation in which the adversary coerces both a doctor and another party (not a doctor). Since the adversary obtains more information, this constitutes a stronger attack on doctor's prescribing-privacy. To address this problem, we define *independency of enforced prescribing-privacy*, which is satisfied when a doctor's prescribing-privacyis preserved even if both the doctor and another party reveal their private information to the adversary.

Definition 4 (Independency of enforced prescribing-privacy). *A well-formed eHealth protocol EHP satisfies* enforced prescribing-privacy independent *of role* R_i, *if there exist processes* $init'_{dr}$ *and* P'_{dr}, *such that:*

$$
\begin{aligned}
1) \quad & \mathcal{C}[!R_i^{\mathrm{chc}} \mid (init'_{dr}\{A/Id_{dr}\}.(!P_{dr}\{A/Id_{dr}\} \mid P'_{dr}\{A/Id_{dr}\})) \mid \\
& \qquad (init_{dr}\{B/Id_{dr}\}.(!P_{dr}\{B/Id_{dr}\} \mid main_{dr}\{B/Id_{dr}, a/presc\}))] \\
\approx_\ell \; & \mathcal{C}[!R_i^{\mathrm{chc}} \mid ((init_{dr}\{A/Id_{dr}\})^{\mathrm{chc}}.(!P_{dr}\{A/Id_{dr}\} \mid (main_{dr}\{A/Id_{dr}, a/presc\})^{\mathrm{chc}})) \mid \\
& \qquad (init_{dr}\{B/Id_{dr}\}.(!P_{dr}\{B/Id_{dr}\} \mid main_{dr}\{B/Id_{dr}, b/presc\}))];
\end{aligned}
$$

$$
\begin{aligned}
2) \quad & init'_{dr}\{A/Id_{dr}\}^{\setminus \mathrm{out}(\mathrm{chc},\cdot)}.(P'_{dr}\{A/Id_{dr}\}^{\setminus \mathrm{out}(\mathrm{chc},\cdot)}) \\
\approx_\ell \; & init_{dr}\{A/Id_{dr}\}.(main_{dr}\{A/Id_{dr}, b/presc\}),
\end{aligned}
$$

where $init'_{dr}\{A/Id_{dr}\}.(!P_{dr}\{A/Id_{dr}\} \mid P'_{dr}\{A/Id_{dr}\})$ *is a closed plain process,* R_i *is a non-doctor role, and* chc *is a fresh channel name.*

We conjecture that independency of enforced prescribing-privacy implies independency of prescribing-privacy and enforced prescribing-privacy, each of which also implies prescribing-privacy.

3.5 Anonymity and Strong Anonymity

Anonymity is a property that protect users' identities. We model anonymity as indistinguishability of processes initiated by two different users.

Definition 5 (Doctor anonymity). *A well-formed eHealth protocol EHP satisfies doctor anonymity for a doctor* A *if there exists another doctor* B, *such that*

$$
\mathcal{C}[init_{dr}\{A/Id_{dr}\}.!P_{dr}\{A/Id_{dr}\}] \approx_\ell \mathcal{C}[init_{dr}\{B/Id_{dr}\}.!P_{dr}\{B/Id_{dr}\}].
$$

A stronger notion of anonymity is defined in [17], capturing the situation that the adversary cannot even find out whether a user (with identity A) has participated in a session of the protocol or not.

Definition 6 (Strong doctor anonymity [17]). *A well-formed eHealth protocol EHP satisfies strong doctor anonymity, if*

$$
EHP \approx_\ell \nu\tilde{m}.init.(!R_1 \mid \ldots \mid !R_n \mid (init_{dr}\{A/Id_{dr}\}.!P_{dr}\{A/Id_{dr}\})).
$$

Similarly, we can define anonymity and strong anonymity for patient and other roles in an eHealth protocol, by replacing the doctor role with a different role.

3.6 Untraceability and Strong Untraceability

Untraceability is a property preventing the adversary from tracing a user, meaning that he cannot tell whether two executions are initiated by the same user.

Definition 7 (Doctor untraceability). *A well-formed eHealth protocol EHP satisfies doctor untraceability if, for any two doctors* A *and* B ≠ A,

$$C[init_{dr}\{A/Id_{dr}\}.(P_{dr}\{A/Id_{dr}\} \mid P_{dr}\{A/Id_{dr}\})]$$
$$\approx_\ell C[(init_{dr}\{A/Id_{dr}\}.P_{dr}\{A/Id_{dr}\}) \mid (init_{dr}\{B/Id_{dr}\}.P_{dr}\{B/Id_{dr}\})].$$

A stronger notion of untraceability is proposed in [17] that captures the adversary's inability to distinguish the situation where one user executes the protocol multiple times from no user executing the protocol more than once.

Definition 8 (Strong doctor untraceability [17]). *A well-formed eHealth protocol EHP satisfies strong doctor untraceability, if*

$$EHP \approx_\ell \nu\tilde{m}.init.\big(!R_1 \mid \ldots \mid !R_{i-1} \mid !R_{i+1} \mid !R_n \mid !(\nu Id_{dr}.init_{dr}.P_{dr})\big).$$

Similarly, we can define untraceability and strong untraceability for patient and other roles in a protocol, by replacing the doctor role with a different role.

4 Description and Modelling of the DLVV08 Protocol

De Decker. et al develop a complex healthcare protocol for the Belgium situation [9], which captures most aspects of the current Belgian healthcare practice and aims to provide a strong guarantee of privacy for patients and doctors.

To ensure security and privacy properties, the DLVV08 protocol employs cryptographic primitives such as privacy-preserving credential systems and verifiable public key cryptography. We briefly describe the used primitives and explain how to model them in applied pi. Then we briefly discuss the DLVV08 protocol and focus on the modelling of two sub-protocols in details.

4.1 Cryptographic Primitives

Zero-Knowledge Proofs. A zero-knowledge proof (ZKP) is a cryptographic scheme in which one party (the prover) proves to another party (the verifier) that a statement is true, without leaking any information on the statement. A ZKP scheme can be either interactive or non-interactive. We model non-interactive ZKPs as zk($secrets, pub\_info$), where $secrets$ models private information and pub_info models public information [22, 23]. Verification of a ZKP is modelled as Vfy-zk(zk($secrets, pub\_info$), $verif\_info$), with a proof zk($secrets, pub\_info$) to be verified, and some verification information $verif\_info$. Since the private information in a ZKP is known only by the prover, only he can construct a correct ZKP. To verify a ZKP is to check whether a specific relation between the secret information and the verification formation is satisfied. Since pub_info and *verif_info* happen to be the same in all ZK proof verifications in this paper, the generic structure of a verification is $\mathsf{Vfy\text{-}zk}(\mathsf{zk}(x, \mathsf{f}(x, y)), \mathsf{f}(x, y)) = \mathsf{true}$, where x denotes private information and y denotes public information.

In DLVV08, both anonymous authentication and verifiable encryption are essentially ZKPs. Anonymous authentication is modelled as a ZKP with a credential as public information, while verifiable encryption is modelled as a ZKP with the encrypted message as part of the public information. The specific function to check a ZKP of type x is denoted as $\mathsf{Vfy\text{-}zk}_x$, e.g., verification of a patient's anonymous authentication is modelles by function $\mathsf{Vfy\text{-}zk}_{\mathsf{Auth}_{pt}}$.

Signed Proofs of Knowledge. Signed proofs of knowledge uses proofs of knowledge as a digital signature scheme (for details see [24]). Intuitively, a prover signs a message using some private information, which can be considered as a secret signing key. The prover uses a proof of knowledge to convince the verifier that he possesses the private signing "key". We denote a signed proof of knowledge as $\mathsf{spk}(secrets, pub\_info, msg)$, which models a message msg and public verification information pub_info signed with signing key $secrets$ [25]. What knowledge is proven depends on the instance of the proof and is captured by the verification functions for the specific proofs. These proofs are verified by checking that the signature is correct given the signed message and the verification information, generically: $\mathsf{Vfy\text{-}spk}\left(\mathsf{spk}\left(x, \mathsf{f}(x, y), m\right), \mathsf{f}(x, y), m\right) = \mathsf{true}$. Note that specific verification functions depend on the proof to be verified.

Further Cryptographic Primitives Used. A *digital credential* proves that the owner possesses some specific properties. We model a doctor credential as a private function drcred with the doctor's private information as parameter. Similarly, a patient's credential is modelled as a private function ptcred. Functions $\mathsf{getpublic}$, $\mathsf{getSpkVinfo}$ and $\mathsf{getSpkMsg}$ model retrieving public information from a ZKP, from a signed proof of knowledge, and obtaining the message from a signed proof of knowledge, respectively. Bit-commitments, hash functions, encryptions and signing messages are modelled by functions commit, hash, enc, and sign, respectively. Opening a commitment, decryption and retrieving the message from a signature are modelled as functions open, dec and $\mathsf{getsignmsg}$.

4.2 Description of the DLVV08 Protocol

The protocol involves five roles: doctor, patient, pharmacist, medicine prescription administrator (MPA) and health insurance institute (HII).

- A doctor has an identity ($\mathtt{Id}_{dr}$), a pseudonym (Pnym_{dr}), and an anonymous doctor credential ($Cred_{dr}$) issued by trusted authorities.
- A patient has an identity ($\mathtt{Id}_{pt}$), a pseudonym (Pnym_{pt}), an HII ($\mathtt{Hii}$), a social security status ($\mathtt{Sss}$), a health expense account ($\mathtt{Acc}$) and an anonymous patient credential ($Cred_{pt}$) issued by trusted authorities.
- Pharmacists, MPA, and HII are public entities, each of which has an identity ($\mathtt{Id}_{ph}$, Id_{mpa}, $\mathtt{Id}_{hii}$), a secret key (sk_{ph}, sk_{mpa}, sk_{hii}) and an authorised public key certificate (pk_{ph}, pk_{mpa}, pk_{hii}) issued by trusted authorities.

The DLVV08 protocol works as follows: a doctor prescribes medicines to a patient; next the patient obtains medicine from a pharmacist according to the prescription; following that, the pharmacist forwards the prescription to his MPA, the MPA checks the prescription and refunds the pharmacist; finally, the MPA sends invoices to the patient's HII and is refunded.[1] Each step is described as a sub-protocol in [9]. Due to space limitations and the fact that the studied privacy properties mainly involve doctors, patients and pharmacists, we focus on the first two sub-protocols: the doctor-patient sub-protocol and the patient-pharmacist sub-protocol.

4.3   Underspecification of the DLVV08 Protocol

The DLVV08 protocol leaves the following issues unspecified:

a1 whether a zero-knowledge proof is transferable;
a2 whether an encryption is probabilistic;
a3 whether a patient/doctor uses a fresh identity/pseudonym for each session;
a4 whether credentials are freshly generated in each session;
a5 what a patient's social security status is and how it can be modified;
a6 how many HIIs exist and whether a patient can change his HII;
a7 whether a patient/doctor can obtain a credential by requesting one;
a8 what type of communication channels are used (public or untappable).

To be able to discover potential flaws on privacy, we make the following (weakest) assumptions in our modelling of the DLVV08 protocol:

s1 the zero-knowledge proofs used are non-interactive and transferable;
s2 encryptions are not probabilistic;
s3 a patient/doctor uses the same identity and pseudonym in every session;
s4 a patient/doctor has the same credential in every session;
s5 a patient's social security status is the same in every session;
s6 there are many HIIs, different patients may have different HIIs, and a patient's HII is fixed and cannot be changed;
s7 a patient/doctor's credential can be obtained by requesting one;
s8 the communication channels are public.

4.4   Modelling the Doctor-Patient Sub-protocol

This sub-protocol is used for a doctor, whose steps are labelled $\mathbf{d}i$ in Fig. 1, to prescribe medicine for a patient, whose steps are labelled $\mathbf{t}i$ in Fig. 2.

First, the doctor anonymously authenticates to the patient using credential $Cred_{dr}$ (**d1**). The patient reads in the doctor authentication (**t1**), obtains the doctor credential (**t2**), and verifies the authentication (**t3**). If the verification in

---

[1] As we do not focus on properties such as revocability and reimbursement, we do not consider the other two roles: public safety organisation (PSO) and social security organisation (SSO).

```
let  P_dr =
  d1.     out(ch, zk((Pnym_dr, Id_dr), drcred(Pnym_dr, Id_dr)));
  d2.     in(ch, (rcv_Auth_pt, rcv_PtProof));
  d3.     let c_Cred_pt = getpublic(rcv_Auth_pt) in
  d4.     let (c_Comt_pt, = c_Cred_pt) = getpublic(rcv_PtProof) in
  d5.     if Vfy-zk_Auth_pt(rcv_Auth_pt, c_Cred_pt) = true then
  d6.     if Vfy-zk_PtProof(rcv_PtProof, (c_Comt_pt, c_Cred_pt)) = true then
  d7.     νpresc;
  d8.     νr_dr;
  d9.     let PrescriptID = hash(presc, c_Comt_pt, commit(Pnym_dr, r_dr)) in
  d10.    out(ch, (spk((Pnym_dr, r_dr, Id_dr), (commit(Pnym_dr, r_dr), drcred(Pnym_dr, Id_dr)),
                  (presc, PrescriptID, commit(Pnym_dr, r_dr), c_Comt_pt)), r_dr)).
```

Fig. 1. The doctor process P_{dr}

(**t3**) succeeds, the patient anonymously authenticates himself to the doctor using his credential (**t5**, the first zk function), generates a nonce r_{pt} (**t4**), computes a commitment with the nonce as opening information, and proves that the patient identity used in the patient credential is the same as in the commitment, thus linking the patient commitment and the patient credential (**t5**, the second zk).

The doctor reads in the patient authentication as rcv_Auth_{pt} and the patient proof as $rcv\_PtProof$ (**d2**), obtains the patient credential from the patient authentication (**d3**), obtains the patient commitment c_Comt_{pt} and the patient credential from the patient proof, tests whether the credential matches the one embedded in the patient authentication (**d4**), then verifies the authentication (**d5**) and the patient proof (**d6**). If the verification in the previous item succeeds, the doctor generates a prescription presc (**d7**), generates a nonce r_{dr} (**d8**), computes a prescription identity $PrescriptID$ (**d9**), and computes a commitment $Comt_{dr}$ using the nonce as opening information (**d10**). Next, the doctor signs the message (presc, $PrescriptID$, $Comt_{dr}$, c_Comt_{pt}) using a signed proof of knowledge. This proves the pseudonym used in the credential $Cred_{dr}$ is the same as in the commitment $Comt_{dr}$, thus linking the prescription to the credential. The doctor sends the signed proof of knowledge together with the open information of the doctor commitment r_{dr} (**d10**).

The patient reads in the prescription as $rcv\_PrescProof$ and the opening information of the doctor commitment (**t6**), obtains the prescription c_presc, prescription identity $c\_PrescriptID$, doctor commitment c_Comt_{dr}, and tests the patient commitment signed in the receiving message (**t7**). Then the patient verifies the signed proof of prescription (**t8**). If this succeeds, the patient obtains the doctor's pseudonym c_Pnym_{dr} by opening the doctor commitment (**t9**).

4.5   Modelling the Patient-Pharmacist Sub-protocol

This sub-protocol is used for a patient, whose steps are labelled ti in Fig. 3, to obtain medicine from a pharmacist, whose steps are labelled hi in Fig. 4.

```
let  P_pt-p1 =
  t1.        in(ch, rcv_Auth_dr);
  t2.        let c_Cred_dr = getpublic(rcv_Auth_dr) in
  t3.        if Vfy-zk_Auth_dr (rcv_Auth_dr, c_Cred_dr) = true then
  t4.        νr_pt;
  t5.        out(ch, (zk((Id_pt, Pnym_pt, Hii, Sss, Acc), ptcred(Id_pt, Pnym_pt, Hii, Sss, Acc)),
                      zk((Id_pt, Pnym_pt, Hii, Sss, Acc),
                         (commit(Id_pt, r_pt), ptcred(Id_pt, Pnym_pt, Hii, Sss, Acc)))));
  t6.        in(ch, (rcv_PrescProof, rcv_r_dr));
  t7.        let (c_presc, c_PrescriptID, c_Comt_dr, = commit(Id_pt, r_pt))
                = getSpkMsg(rcv_PrescProof) in
  t8.        if Vfy-spk_PrescProof (rcv_PrescProof, (c_Cred_dr, c_presc, c_PrescriptID,
                         c_Comt_dr, commit(Id_pt, r_pt))) = true then
  t9.        let c_Pnym_dr = open(c_Comt_dr, rcv_r_dr) in 0.
```

Fig. 2. The patient process P_{pt} in doctor-patient sub-protocol

First, the pharmacist authenticates to the patient using a public key authentication (**h1**). Note that the pharmacist does not authenticate anonymously, and that the pharmacists's MPA identity is embedded. The patient reads in the pharmacist authentication rcv_Auth_{ph} (**t10**) and verifies the authentication (**t11**). If the verification succeeds, the pharmacist obtains the pharmacist's MPA identity from the authentication (**t12**), thus obtains the public key of MPA (**t13**). Then the patient anonymously authenticates himself to the pharmacist, and proves his social security status using the proof $PtAuthSss$ (**t14**). The patient generates a nonce which will be used in a signed proof of knowledge (**t15**), and computes verifiable encryptions vc_1, vc_2, vc_3, vc'_3, vc_4 and vc_5 (**t16-t21**). These divulge the patient's HII, the doctor's pseudonym, and the patient's pseudonym to the MPA, the patient's pseudonym to the HII, and the patient pseudonym and HII to the social safety organisation, respectively. The patient encrypts vc_5 with MPA's public key as c_5 (**t22**). The patient computes a signed proof of knowledge $PtSpk$ which proves that the patient identity embedded in the prescription is the same as in his credential[2]. The patient sends the prescription $rcv\_PrescProof$, the signed proof $PtSpk$, and vc_1, vc_2, vc_3, vc'_3, vc_4, c_5 to the pharmacist (**t23**). The pharmacist reads in the authentication $rcv\_PtAuthSss$ (**h2**), obtains the patient credential and his social security status (**h3**), verifies the authentication (**h4**). If the verification succeeds, the pharmacist reads in the patient's prescription $rcv_{ph}\_PrescProof$, the signed proof of knowledge rcv_{ph}_PtSpk, the verifiable encryptions rcv_vc_1, rcv_vc_2, rcv_vc_3, $rcv\_vc'_3$, rcv_vc_4, and cipher text rcv_c_5 (**h5**); and verifies $rcv_{ph}\_PrescProof$ (**h6-h8**), rcv_{ph}_PtSpk (**h9-h10**), and rcv_vc_1, rcv_vc_2, rcv_vc_3, $rcv\_vc'_3$, rcv_vc_4 (**h11-h20**). If all the verifications succeed, the pharmacist charges the patient, and delivers the medicine (neither are

---

[2] In the prescription, this identity is contained in a commitment. For simplicity, we model the proof using the commitment instead of the prescription. The link between commitment and prescription is ensured when the proof is verified (**h10**).

```
let  P_pt-p2 =
t10.        in(ch, rcv_Auth_ph);
t11.        if Vfy-sign(rcv_Auth_ph, rcv_pt-pk_ph) = true then
t12.        let (= c_pt_Id_ph, c_pt_Id_mpa) = getsignmsg(rcv_Auth_ph, rcv_pt-pk_ph) in
t13.        let c_pt-pk_mpa = key(c_pt_Id_mpa) in
t14.        out(ch, zk((Id_pt, Pnym_pt, Hii, Sss, Acc),
                       (ptcred(Id_pt, Pnym_pt, Hii, Sss, Acc), Sss)));
t15.        νnonce;
t16.        let vc_1 = zk((Id_pt, Pnym_pt, Hii, Sss, Acc),
                       (ptcred(Id_pt, Pnym_pt, Hii, Sss, Acc), enc(Hii, c_pt-pk_mpa))) in
t17.        let vc_2 = zk((c_Pnym_dr, rcv_r_dr),
                       (rcv_PrescProof, enc(c_Pnym_dr, c_pt-pk_mpa))) in
t18.        let vc_3 = zk((Id_pt, Pnym_pt, Hii, Sss, Acc),
                       (ptcred(Id_pt, Pnym_pt, Hii, Sss, Acc), enc(Pnym_pt, pk_sso))) in
t19.        let vc'_3 = zk((Id_pt, Pnym_pt, Hii, Sss, Acc),
                       (ptcred(Id_pt, Pnym_pt, Hii, Sss, Acc), enc(Hii, pk_sso))) in
t20.        let vc_4 = zk((Id_pt, Pnym_pt, Hii, Sss, Acc),
                       (ptcred(Id_pt, Pnym_pt, Hii, Sss, Acc), enc(Pnym_pt, c_pt-pk_mpa))) in
t21.        let vc_5 = zk((Id_pt, Pnym_pt, Hii, Sss, Acc),
                       (ptcred(Id_pt, Pnym_pt, Hii, Sss, Acc), enc(Pnym_pt, c_pt-pk_hii))) in
t22.        let c_5 = enc(vc_5, c_pt-pk_mpa) in
t23.        out(ch, (rcv_PrescProof,
                     spk((Id_pt, Pnym_pt, Hii, Sss, Acc),
                       (ptcred(Id_pt, Pnym_pt, Hii, Sss, Acc), commit(Id_pt, r_pt)), nonce),
                     vc_1, vc_2, vc_3, vc'_3, vc_4, c_5));
t24.        in(ch, rcv_invoice);
t25.        let ReceiptAck = spk((Id_pt, Pnym_pt, Hii, Sss, Acc),
                       ptcred(Id_pt, Pnym_pt, Hii, Sss, Acc),
                       (c_PrescriptID, c_pt_Id_ph, vc_1, vc_2, vc_3, vc'_3, vc_4, c_5)) in
t26.        out(ch, ReceiptAck).
```

Fig. 3. The patient process P_{pt} in patient-pharmacist sub-protocol

modelled as they are out of DLVV08's scope). Then the pharmacist generates an invoice with the prescription identity embedded in it and sends the invoice to the patient (**h21**).

The patient reads in the invoice (**t24**), computes a receipt: a signed proof of knowledge *ReceiptAck* which proves that he receives the medicine (**t25**); and sends the signed proof of knowledge to the patient (**t26**). The pharmacist reads in the receipt *rcv_ReceiptAck* (**h22**) and verifies its correctness (**h23**).

4.6 Claimed Privacy Properties

The DLVV08 protocol claims to satisfy the following privacy properties:

- Prescribing-privacy: the protocol protects a doctor's prescription behaviour.
- Enforced prescribing-privacy: the protocol prevents pharmaceutical companies from rewarding doctors for prescribing their medicine.

```
let   P_ph =
h1.       out(ch, sign((Id_ph, c_ph_Id_mpa), sk_ph));
h2.       in(ch, rcv_PtAuthSss);
h3.       let (c_ph_Cred_pt, c_ph_Sss) = getpublic(rcv_PtAuthSss) in
h4.       if Vfy-zk_PtAuthSss(rcv_PtAuthSss, (c_ph_Cred_pt, c_ph_Sss)) = true then
h5.       in(ch, (rcv_ph_PrescProof, rcv_ph_PtSpk,
                    rcv_vc_1, rcv_vc_2, rcv_vc_3, rcv_vc'_3, rcv_vc_4, rcv_c_5));
h6.       let (c_ph_Comt_dr, c_ph_Cred_dr) = getSpkVinfo(rcv_ph_PrescProof) in
h7.       let (c_ph_presc, c_ph_PrescriptID, = c_ph_Comt_dr, c_ph_Comt_pt)
              = getSpkMsg(rcv_ph_PrescProof) in
h8.       if Vfy-spk_PrescProof(rcv_ph_PrescProof, (c_ph_Cred_dr, c_ph_presc,
                                 c_ph_PrescriptID, c_ph_Comt_dr, c_ph_Comt_pt)) = true then
h9.       let c_msg = getSpkMsg(rcv_ph_PtSpk) in
h10.      if Vfy-spk_PtSpk(rcv_ph_PtSpk, (c_ph_Cred_pt, c_ph_Comt_pt, c_msg)) = true then
h11.      let (= c_ph_Cred_pt, c_Enc_1) = getpublic(rcv_vc_1) in
h12.      if Vfy-zk_VEncHii(rcv_vc_1, (c_ph_Cred_pt, c_Enc_1, rcv_ph_pk_mpa)) = true then
h13.      let (= rcv_ph_PrescProof, c_Enc_2) = getpublic(rcv_vc_2) in
h14.      if Vfy-zk_VEncDrnymMpa(rcv_vc_2, (rcv_ph_PrescProof,
                                 c_Enc_2, rcv_ph_pk_mpa)) = true then
h15.      let (= c_ph_Cred_pt, c_Enc_3) = getpublic(rcv_vc_3) in
h16.      if Vfy-zk_VEncPtnym(rcv_vc_3, (c_ph_Cred_pt, c_Enc_3, pk_sso)) = true then
h17.      let (= c_ph_Cred_pt, c_Enc'_3) = getpublic(rcv_vc'_3) in
h18.      if Vfy-zk_VEncHii(rcv_vc'_3, (c_ph_Cred_pt, c_Enc'_3, pk_sso)) = true then
h19.      let (= c_ph_Cred_pt, c_Enc_4) = getpublic(rcv_vc_4) in
h20.      if Vfy-zk_VEncPtnym(rcv_vc_4, (c_ph_Cred_pt, c_Enc_4, rcv_ph_pk_mpa)) = true then
h21.      out(ch, invoice(c_ph_PrescriptID));
h22.      in(ch, rcv_ReceiptAck);
h23.      if Vfy-spk_ReceiptAck(rcv_ReceiptAck, (c_ph_Cred_pt, c_ph_PrescriptID,
              Id_ph, rcv_vc_1, rcv_vc_2, rcv_vc_3, rcv_vc'_3, rcv_vc_4, rcv_c_5)) = true then 0.
```

Fig. 4. The pharmacist process P_{ph} in Patient-Pharmacist sub-protocol

- Independency of prescribing-privacy: pharmacists are not able to provide evidence to pharmaceutical companies about doctors' prescription.
- Patient anonymity: no party should be able to determine a patient's identity.
- Patient untraceability: prescriptions issued to the same patient should not be linkable to each other.

5   Analysis

We analyse (enforced) prescribing-privacy, independence of (enforced) prescribing-privacy, (strong) patient and doctor anonymity, (strong) patient and doctor untraceability of the DLVV08 protocol, under the assumptions stated in Sect. 4.3. Doctor anonymity and untraceability are not required by the protocol but are still interesting to analyse. The verification results are summarised in Tab. 1.

The above privacy properties are modelled using equivalences in the applied pi calculus (see Sect. 3). To verify them is to check the satisfiability of the corresponding equivalence between processes, which can be captured by a bi-process

Table 1. Verification of the DLVV08 protocol with original/revised assumptions

checked privacy property	initial model	cause(s)	improvement	revised
prescribing-privacy	×	s4	s4'	√
enforced presc.-priv.	× (with s4')		s8'	√
independency of presc.-priv.	√ (with s4')			√
independ. of enf. presc.-priv.	× (with s4')		s8'	×
patient anonymity	√			√
strong patient anonymity	√			√
doctor anonymity	×	s4	s4'	√
strong doctor anonymity	×	s4	s4'	√
patient untraceability	×	s2, s4, s5, s6	s2', s4", s5', s6'	√
strong patient untraceability	×	s2, s4, s5, s6	s2', s4", s5', s6'	√
doctor untraceability	×	s3	s3'	√
strong doctor untraceability	×	s3	s3'	√

and automatically checked in the tool ProVerif [26]. A bi-process models two processes sharing the same structure and differing only in terms or destructors. The two processes are written as one process with choice-constructors which tells ProVerif the spots where the two processes differ. For example, choice$[x, y]$ means that the first process uses x to replace choice$[x, y]$ while the second process uses y. The context C in the DLVV08 protocol for the analysis of privacy properties is defined as $C = \nu\tilde{m}.init.(!R_{pt} \,|!R_{dr} \,|!R_{ph} \,| \_)$.

5.1 Prescribing-Privacy

The verification shows that the DLVV08 protocol does not satisfy prescribing-privacy, i.e., the adversary can distinguish whether a prescription is prescribed by doctor A or doctor B. In the prescription proof, a prescription is linked to a doctor credential. And a doctor credential is linked to a doctor identity. Thus, the adversary can link a doctor to his prescription. To break the link, one way is to make sure that the adversary cannot link a doctor credential to a doctor identity. This can be achieved by adding randomness to the credential (s4').

5.2 Enforced Prescribing-Privacy

The definition of enforced prescribing-privacy is modelled as the existence of a process P'_{dr}, such that the two equivalences in Def. 2 are satisfied. Due to the existence quantification, we cannot verify the property directly using ProVerif.

Examining the DLVV08 protocol, we find an attack on enforced prescribing-privacy, even after fixing prescribing privacy (with assumption s4'). A bribed doctor is able to prove to the adversary of his prescription as follows:

1. A doctor communicates with the adversary to agree on a bit-commitment that he will use, which links the doctor to the commitment.
2. The doctor uses the agreed bit-commitment in the communication with his patient. This links the bit-commitment to a prescription.

3. Later, when the patient uses this prescription to get medicine from a pharmacist, the adversary can observe the prescription being used. This proves that the doctor has really prescribed the medicine.

Formally, using ProVerif, we can show that if a doctor reveals all his information to the adversary, the doctor's prescribing-privacy is broken. To prove that there exist no alternative precesses for a doctor to cheat the adversary, we assume that there exists a process P'_{dr} which satisfies the definition of enforced prescribing-privacy, and then derive some contradiction. A bribed doctor reveals the nonces used in the commitment and the credential to the adversary. Thus, the adversary links a bribed doctor to his commitment and credential. In the prescription proof, a prescription is linked to a doctor's commitment and credential. Suppose there exists a process P'_{dr} in which the doctor lies to the adversary that he prescribed a, while the adversary observes that the commitment or the credential is linked to b. The adversary can detect that the doctor has lied.

5.3 Doctor's (Enforced) Prescribing-Privacy

The doctor's prescribing-privacy independent of the pharmacist is modelled by replacing R_i with R_{ph} in Def. 3. The verification shows that the protocol (after fixing the flaw on prescribing-privacy with assumption s4') satisfies this property.

Similarly, the doctor's enforced prescribing-privacy independent of pharmacist is defined as replacing R_i with R_{ph} in Def. 4. The flaw described in Sect. 5.2 is also applied here. Intuitively, when a doctor can prove his prescription without the pharmacist sharing information with the adversary, the doctor can prove it when the pharmacist genuinely cooperates with the adversary.

5.4 (Strong) Patient and Doctor Anonymity

Our verification show that the protocol satisfies patient anonymity and strong patient anonymity but not doctor anonymity, nor strong doctor anonymity.

For strong doctor anonymity, the adversary can distinguish a process initiated by an unknown doctor and a known doctor. Given a doctor process, where the doctor has identity A, pseudonym $Pnym_{dr}$, and credential $drcred(Pnym_{dr}, A)$. $Pnym_{dr}$ and $drcred(Pnym_{dr}, A)$ are revealed. We assume that the adversary knows another doctor identity B. The adversary can fake an anonymous authentication by faking the zero-knowledge proof as $zk((Pnym_{dr}, B), drcred(Pnym_{dr}, A))$. If the zero-knowledge proof passes the corresponding verification $Vfy\text{-}zk_{Auth_{dr}}$ by the patient, then the adversary knows that the doctor process is executed by the doctor B. Otherwise, not.

For the same reason, doctor anonymity fails the verification. Both flaws can be fixed by requiring a doctor to generate a new credential in each session (s4').

5.5 (Strong) Patient and Doctor Untraceability

The DLVV08 protocol does not satisfy patient/doctor untraceability (see Def. 7), nor strong untraceability (see Def. 8).

The adversary can distinguish sessions initiated by one doctor and by different doctors. The doctor's pseudonym is revealed and a doctor uses the same pseudonym in all sessions. Sessions with the same doctor pseudonyms are initiated by the same doctor. For the same reason, doctor untraceability also fails. Both of them can be fixed by requiring a doctor to freshly generate his pseudonym in each session (s3').

For strong patient untraceability, the adversary can distinguish sessions initiated by one patient (with identical social security statuses) and initiated by different patients (with different social security statuses). Second, the adversary can distinguish sessions initiated by one patient (with identical cipher texts $\mathsf{enc}(\mathtt{Pnym}_{pt}, \mathtt{pk}_{sso})$ and identical cipher texts $\mathsf{enc}(\mathtt{Hii}, \mathtt{pk}_{sso})$) and initiated by different patients (with different cipher texts $\mathsf{enc}(\mathtt{Pnym}_{pt}, \mathtt{pk}_{sso})$ and different cipher texts $\mathsf{enc}(\mathtt{Hii}, \mathtt{pk}_{sso})$). Third, since the patient credential is the same in all sessions and is revealed, the adversary can also trace a patient by the patient's credential. Fourth, the adversary can distinguish sessions using the same HII and sessions using different HIIs. For the same reasons, patient untraceability fails. Both flaws can be fixed by revising the assumptions (s5', s2', s4" and s6').

5.6 Addressing the Flaws of the DLVV08 Protocol

We modify assumptions in Sect. 4.3 to fix the flaws found in our analysis.

s2' The encryptions are probabilistic.

s3' A doctor's pseudonym is freshly generated in every session.

s4' A doctor freshly generates an unpredictable credential in each session. We model this with another parameter (a random number) of the credential. Following this, anonymous authentication using these credentials proves knowledge of the used randomness.

s4" A patient freshly generates a credential in each session.

s5' A patient's social security status is different in each session.

s6' All patients share the same HII.

The modified protocol is verified again using ProVerif. The verification results show that the protocol with revised assumptions satisfies prescribing-privacy, doctor anonymity and strong anonymity, patient and doctor untraceability and strong untraceability.

To make the protocol satisfy enforced prescribing-privacy, we apply the following assumption on communication channels.

s8' The communication channels are untappable, except that communication channels for authentications remain public.

Our model of the protocol is accordingly modified as follows: replacing channel ch in lines **d10**, **t6** with an untappable channel ch_{dp}, replacing channel ch in lines **t23**, **t26**, **h5**, **h22** with an untappable channel ch_{ptph}, and replacing channel ch in lines **t24**, **h21** with an untappable channel ch_{phpt}. We prove that the protocol (with **s4'** and **s8'**) satisfies enforced prescribing-privacy by showing the existence of a process P'_{dr} such that the equivalences in Def. 2 are satisfied.

However, with the above assumptions the DLVV08 protocol does not satisfy independency of enforced prescribing-privacy. We first show that P'_{dr} is not sufficient for proving this with ProVerif. Then we prove (analogous to the proof in Sect. 5.2) that there is no alternative process P'_{dr} which satisfies Def. 4. Intuitively, all information sent over untappable channels are received by pharmacists and can be genuinely revealed to the adversary by the pharmacists (do not lie by assumption). Hence, there still exist links between a doctor, his nonces, his commitment, his credential and his prescription, when the doctor is bribed/coerced to reveal the nonces used in the commitment and the credential to the adversary.

6   Conclusion

In this paper, we have identified new privacy requirements for eHealth systems and formalised them in the applied pi calculus. Then we took the DLVV08 protocol as a case study. We have found ambiguities in the protocol and privacy flaws as consequence, and proposed possible solutions for fixing them. We hope that our findings can help to clarify and improve the design of the DLVV08 protocol, satisfying a number of necessary privacy requirements.

References

1. Reid, J., Cheong, I., Henricksen, M., Smith, J.: A Novel Use of rBAC to Protect Privacy in Distributed Health Care Information Systems. In: Safavi-Naini, R., Seberry, J. (eds.) ACISP 2003. LNCS, vol. 2727, pp. 403–415. Springer, Heidelberg (2003)
2. Currim, F., Jung, E., Xiao, X., Jo, I.: Privacy policy enforcement for health information data access. In: Proc. 1st ACM Workshop on Medical-grade Wireless Networks, pp. 39–44. ACM (2009)
3. Dolev, D., Yao, A.C.C.: On the security of public key protocols. IEEE Transactions on Information Theory 29(2), 198–207 (1983)
4. Benaloh, J., Tuinstra, D.: Receipt-free secret-ballot elections (extended abstract). In: Proc. 26th Symposium on Theory of Computing, pp. 544–553. ACM (1994)
5. Lee, B., Kim, K.: Receipt-free electronic voting through collaboration of voter and honest verifier. In: Proc. Japan-Korea Joint Workshop on Information Security and Cryptology, pp. 101–108 (2000)
6. Hirt, M., Sako, K.: Efficient Receipt-Free Voting Based on Homomorphic Encryption. In: Preneel, B. (ed.) EUROCRYPT 2000. LNCS, vol. 1807, pp. 539–556. Springer, Heidelberg (2000)
7. Lee, B., Kim, K.: Receipt-Free Electronic Voting with a Tamper-Resistant Randomizer. In: Deng, R.H., Qing, S., Bao, F., Zhou, J. (eds.) ICICS 2002. LNCS, vol. 2513, pp. 389–406. Springer, Heidelberg (2002)
8. Matyáš, V.: Protecting doctors' identity in drug prescription analysis. Health Informatics Journal (3-4), 205–209 (1998)
9. De Decker, B., Layouni, M., Vangheluwe, H., Verslype, K.: A Privacy-Preserving eHealth Protocol Compliant with the Belgian Healthcare System. In: Mjølsnes, S.F., Mauw, S., Katsikas, S.K. (eds.) EuroPKI 2008. LNCS, vol. 5057, pp. 118–133. Springer, Heidelberg (2008)

10. Dong, N., Jonker, H.L., Pang, J.: Challenges in eHealth: From Enabling to Enforcing Privacy. In: Liu, Z., Wassyng, A. (eds.) FHIES 2011. LNCS, vol. 7151, pp. 195–206. Springer, Heidelberg (2012)

11. Dong, N., Jonker, H.L., Pang, J.: Formal analysis of an eHealth protocol. Technical report, University of Luxembourg (2012) Report and ProVerif code are available at, http://satoss.uni.lu/naipeng/publication.php

12. Abadi, M., Fournet, C.: Mobile values, new names, and secure communication. In: Proc. 28th ACM Symposium on Principles of Programming Languages, pp. 104–115. ACM (2001)

13. Schneider, S., Sidiropoulos, A.: CSP and Anonymity. In: Martella, G., Kurth, H., Montolivo, E., Bertino, E. (eds.) ESORICS 1996. LNCS, vol. 1146, pp. 198–218. Springer, Heidelberg (1996)

14. van Deursen, T., Mauw, S., Radomirović, S.: Untraceability of RFID Protocols. In: Onieva, J.A., Sauveron, D., Chaumette, S., Gollmann, D., Markantonakis, K. (eds.) WISTP 2008. LNCS, vol. 5019, pp. 1–15. Springer, Heidelberg (2008)

15. Backes, M., Hriţcu, C., Maffei, M.: Automated verification of remote electronic voting protocols in the applied pi-calculus. In: Proc. 21st IEEE Computer Security Foundations Symposium, pp. 195–209. IEEE CS (2008)

16. Küsters, R., Truderung, T.: An epistemic approach to coercion-resistance for electronic voting protocols. In: Proc. 30th IEEE Symposium on Security and Privacy, pp. 251–266. IEEE CS (2009)

17. Arapinis, M., Chothia, T., Ritter, E., Ryan, M.: Analysing unlinkability and anonymity using the applied pi calculus. In: Proc. 23rd IEEE Computer Security Foundations Symposium, pp. 107–121. IEEE CS (2010)

18. Küsters, R., Truderung, T., Vogt, A.: A game-based definition of coercion-resistance and its applications. In: Proc. 23rd IEEE Computer Security Foundations Symposium, pp. 122–136. IEEE CS (2010)

19. Delaune, S., Kremer, S., Ryan, M.D.: Verifying privacy-type properties of electronic voting protocols. Journal of Computer Security 17(4), 435–487 (2009)

20. Jonker, H.L., Mauw, S., Pang, J.: A formal framework for quantifying voter-controlled privacy. Journal of Algorithms in Cognition, Informatics and Logic 64(2-3), 89–105 (2009)

21. Dong, N., Jonker, H.L., Pang, J.: Analysis of a Receipt-Free Auction Protocol in the Applied Pi Calculus. In: Degano, P., Etalle, S., Guttman, J. (eds.) FAST 2010. LNCS, vol. 6561, pp. 223–238. Springer, Heidelberg (2011)

22. Backes, M., Maffei, M., Unruh, D.: Zero-knowledge in the applied pi-calculus and automated verification of the direct anonymous attestation protocol. In: Proc. IEEE Symposium on Security and Privacy, pp. 202–215. IEEE CS (2008)

23. Li, X., Zhang, Y., Deng, Y.: Verifying Anonymous Credential Systems in Applied Pi Calculus. In: Garay, J.A., Miyaji, A., Otsuka, A. (eds.) CANS 2009. LNCS, vol. 5888, pp. 209–225. Springer, Heidelberg (2009)

24. Brands, S.A.: Rethinking Public Key Infrastructures and Digital Certificates: Building in Privacy. MIT Press (2000)

25. Delaune, S., Ryan, M., Smyth, B.: Automatic Verification of Privacy Properties in the Applied Pi-Calculus. In: Proc. 2nd Joint iTrust and PST Conferences on Privacy, Trust Management and Security. IFIP Conference Proceedings, vol. 263, pp. 263–278. Springer (2008)

26. Blanchet, B.: An efficient cryptographic protocol verifier based on prolog rules. In: Proc. 14th IEEE Computer Security Foundations Workshop, pp. 82–96. IEEE CS (2001)

PRIVATUS: Wallet-Friendly Privacy Protection for Smart Meters

Jinkyu Koo, Xiaojun Lin, and Saurabh Bagchi

Purdue University, West Lafayette, IN 47907, USA
{kooj,linx,sbagchi}@purdue.edu

Abstract. In smart power grids, a smart meter placed at a consumer-end point reports fine-grained usage information to utility providers. Based on this information, the providers can perform demand prediction and set on-demand pricing. However, this also threatens user privacy, since users' specific activity or behavior patterns can be deduced from the finely granular meter readings. To resolve this issue, we design PRIVATUS, a privacy-protection mechanism that uses a rechargeable battery. In PRIVATUS, the meter reading reported to the utility is probabilistically independent of the actual usage at any given time instant. PRIVATUS also considerably reduces the correlation between the meter readings and the actual usage pattern over time windows. Further, using stochastic dynamic programming, PRIVATUS charges/discharges the battery in the optimal way to maximize savings in the energy cost, given prior knowledge of time periods for the various price zones.

Keywords: smart grid, smart meter, privacy, cost saving, dynamic programming, battery.

1 Introduction

A smart grid is a type of the electrical grid in which electricity delivery systems are equipped with computer-based remote control and automation, which can revolutionize the way that energy is generated and consumed. A key component of the smart grid is the use of the smart meters, which measure energy usage at a fine granularity (e.g., once in a few minutes). However, by gathering hundreds of data points even in a day via the smart meter, the utility companies and third parties may learn a lot about our daily lives, *e.g.*, when we wake up, when we go out for work, and when we come back after work. In an industrial setting, this may be used to reveal details of the industrial process being used, or when a new process is adopted (which is achievable if the new machinery has electricity usage very distinct from prior machinery). Because of this privacy concern, there have been lawsuits to stop the installation of smart meters [1]. As a result, such privacy concerns have delayed the wide and quick deployment of smart grids.

There are a number of possible threat models for the above privacy risks. Given that we do need to report our energy usage profile to the utility company, the most important threat is that the metering data may be unwittingly disclosed from the utility company to third-party vendors. This problem is well illustrated

S. Foresti, M. Yung, and F. Martinelli (Eds.): ESORICS 2012, LNCS 7459, pp. 343–360, 2012.
© Springer-Verlag Berlin Heidelberg 2012

in an article in MSNBC RedTape [2]. This article introduces a possible scenario with the smart grid that you get a discount with your power company at the cost that your auto insurance company may learn when you are home from the utility company. Additionally, due to possibly poor implementation of cryptography mechanisms, an eavesdropper on the wireless channel between the consumer's premises and the wireless network collection point may also determine the usage.

To resolve this issue, *the first objective of this paper is to make it difficult for an adversary to infer, based on the energy usage profile reported to the utilities, what is going on inside the house.* We achieve this objective by putting a rechargeable battery at the user-end point (*e.g.*, a home). The rechargeable battery acts like a buffer between the power grid and the end user in such a way that the actual energy usage pattern looks different from the energy usage pattern reported to the utility.

Additionally, the rechargeable battery provides us with an opportunity to lower the energy bill, by exploiting the time-of-use (TOU) pricing feature of smart grid, whereby electricity price varies according to pre-established time zones during a day. Basically, the cost-saving will be accomplished by charging the battery when the price is low and using the saved energy from the battery when the price is high. However, the two goals of privacy protection and cost saving are not always compatible with each other. *Our goal is therefore to achieve as much energy cost savings as possible, subject to privacy protection constraints.* To the best of our knowledge, we are the first to propose a mechanism that considers both privacy protection and cost saving simultaneously.

In this paper, we present PRIVATUS, our solution that *guarantees* that instantaneous values of the actual usage and the energy draw visible outside the home are independent in an information-theoretic sense. Further, the patterns of both of these variables are also designed to look dissimilar. We set up a dynamic programming problem that minimizes the energy cost while preserving the privacy guarantee mentioned above.

We evaluate our solution in terms of both the privacy information leakage and the cost saving, and compare it to a previous solution that masked high frequency variation in energy usage [3]. In our simulation environment, PRIVATUS can preserve at least 83% of the uncertainty of the actual usage sequences. In addition, PRIVATUS can achieve 72% of the theoretically-possible maximum cost saving with a 6.43kWh battery. This translates to a saving of $16 per month in a typical residential pricing plan [4], assuming the average daily usage of 30kWh. We believe that this saving could provide an extra and significant incentive for users to invest in our solution in addition to privacy protection. The interested reader is referred to Appendix A for further discussion about this incentive.

2   Related Work

There has been extensive research about privacy protection in the area of database systems, where the goal is to provide statistical information (such as sum, average, or maximum) without revealing sensitive information about

individuals. The common approach to achieve this goal is data perturbation
[5, 6]. However, none of methods in this area is directly applicable to hide
the privacy information in the meter readings from the smart meters, because
the utility companies do have to know precise meter reading records for billing
purpose.

Recently, many studies raised the privacy concern in the smart grid both from
a technical perspective and from a legal perspective [7–9]. However, only a few
works have been proposed so far on the design of technical solutions to handle the
privacy issue in the smart grid. Rial *et. al.* [10] proposed a privacy-preserving metering system, where the energy bill for a specific period is calculated by the user
and then sent to the utility company. This system allows the user not to report
the fine-granularity meter readings. However, it limits the power grid operator's
capability such as demand prediction. Kalogridis *et. al.* [3] used a rechargeable
battery to perform low-pass filtering over the load profile. Their algorithm forces
the battery to charge (or discharge) a certain amount of energy if possible, when
the required load is smaller (or larger) than the previously metered load. Thus,
the high-frequency variation on energy usage profile is not visible to the smart
meter. This approach can help eliminate load signatures that indicate which appliance is being used. However, the low-frequency components of a load profile
are still revealed without any protection. Further, the proposed solution did not
consider the cost-saving opportunity of using the rechargeable battery. Another
work using the rechargeable battery is proposed by Varodayan *et. al.* [11]. They
considered a simple binary-state battery model, where the battery is probabilistically charged by drawing the energy from the grid and discharged to feed the
appliances. However, in their model, the charging and discharging processes at a
given time instant are not independent of each other. This leads to a high level
of information leakage (at least 0.5 bit for one-bit information). The authors
also failed to consider the possible saving in the electricity cost by using the
rechargeable battery.

Our work also adopts the rechargeable battery to protect the user privacy,
but we design a mechanism by which the charging and discharging processes are
guaranteed to be independent of each other at a given time instant. Further,
our design also considers to reduce the correlation between the sequences of
the charging and discharging processes over multiple time instants (instead of
just for a single time instant). This makes it difficult for the adversary to make
a meaningful guess on the user behavior by observing the sequence of meter
readings. In addition, our design ensures that the way of charging the battery is
optimal in the sense that we can maximize the average saving in the energy cost.
This is achieved by controlling the charging process by dynamic programming.

3   System Model

Suppose that the smart meter measures the energy consumption once in every
fixed interval (*e.g.*, 15 minutes), which we call the *measurement interval*. We
denote by $X(n)$ the amount of energy consumed in the n-th measurement interval. We call $X(n)$ the *use process*. Denote the amount of energy that we draw

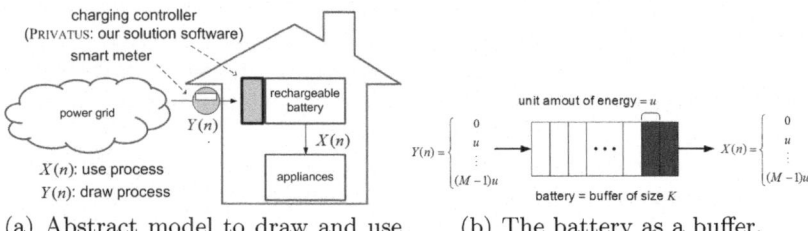

(a) Abstract model to draw and use energy.   (b) The battery as a buffer.

Fig. 1. System model

from the power grid in the n-th measurement interval by $Y(n)$, which we call the *draw process*. The smart meter measures $Y(n)$ and reports it to the utility. Without any special technique, *i.e.*, as it happens today, the draw process $Y(n)$ is the same as the use process $X(n)$. What we want to achieve in this paper is to de-correlate $X(n)$ and $Y(n)$ so that even if an adversary can observe $Y(n)$, no information is leaked about the use process $X(n)$. Toward this end, we put a rechargeable battery at the user-end as shown in Figure 1(a). The rechargeable battery acts as a buffer between $X(n)$ and $Y(n)$: instead of directly feeding $X(n)$ by $Y(n)$, we charge the battery by $Y(n)$, and use the saved energy in the battery to supply $X(n)$. We will design an algorithm in the charging controller, which will choose the value of $Y(n)$ carefully to ensure that the battery always has the appropriate level of energy (*i.e.*, no shortage to feed $X(n)$ or no overflow), and that $X(n)$ looks independent of $Y(n)$.

We assume that the values of $X(n)$ and $Y(n)$ may take any of the M different levels $\{0, u, 2u, \ldots, (M-1)u\}$, where u represents a unit amount of energy. We denote by $B(n)$ the energy level remaining in the battery at the *end* of the n-th measurement interval. Assuming for simplicity that there is no energy loss when charging and discharging the battery (for extension to the case with energy loss, see Appendix A), the value of $B(n)$ can be expressed as

$$B(n) = B(0) + \sum_{m=1}^{n} D(m),\tag{1}$$

where $D(m) = Y(m) - X(m)$ and $B(0)$ is the initial energy level of the battery that is also a multiple of u. Note that $D(n)$ also takes its value as a multiple of u, which is over the range $[-(M-1)u, (M-1)u]$. We model the battery as a buffer of size K as illustrated in Figure 1(b), which implies that the battery capacity is Ku, *i.e.*, the range of $B(n)$ is $0 \le B(n) \le Ku$.

The probability distributions of $X(n)$ and $Y(n)$ are described by $p_X(i;n)$ and $p_Y(i;n)$, respectively, where $p_X(i;n) = P(X(n) = iu)$ and $p_Y(i;n) = P(Y(n) = iu)$. Define the distribution vectors of $X(n)$ and $Y(n)$ as $P_X(n) = [p_X(0;n), p_X(1;n), \ldots, p_X(M-1;n)]$ and $P_Y(n) = [p_Y(0;n), p_Y(1;n), \ldots, p_Y(M-1;n)]$, respectively. We assume that $P_X(n)$ is known to the user (*i.e.*, the home owner). We also assume that $X(n)$ is independent, but does not need to be identically distributed across the measurement interval index n. This means that for instance,

$X(5)$ is independent of $X(11)$, but $P_X(5)$ can be different from $P_X(11)$. As we will see later, $P_Y(n)$ is our control parameter.

We are interested in the case where the electricity price per unit amount of energy varies from time to time. More specifically, we first focus on the case where there exist two time zones within a day, one of which has a low rate R_L (dollars/u) and the other has a high rate R_H (dollars/u). The zone with a low rate is called the *low-price zone* and the other is called the *high-price zone*. For ease of exposition, we assume that the measurement intervals from $n = 1$ to $n = n_L$ fall into the low-price zone, and the measurement intervals from $n = n_L + 1$ to $n = n_H$ correspond to the high-price zone. We treat the initial point $n = 0$ as the beginning of a day and the end of the measurement interval of $n = n_H$ as the end of the day. In Appendix A, we will discuss how we can generalize the solution to handle the case with more than two price zones in a day, and the case when the low-price and high-price zones are interleaved.

Because of the page limit, this paper assumes that the total amount of energy usage per day is the same over days on average. Appendix A introduces a way to release this assumption and generalize our solution.

4   Solution Approach I: Basic Formulation

4.1   Mapping between $X(n)$ and $Y(n)$

In order to hide $X(n)$ from an external adversary (*i.e.*, an adversary outside the home), we make $Y(n)$ be independent of $X(n)$. This implies that observing $Y(n)$ gives no meaningful information about $X(n)$. This is achieved when we map $X(n)$ to $Y(n)$ in such a way that $p_Y(i; n) \equiv P(Y(n) = iu) = P(Y(n) = iu | X(n) = ju)$ for any possible i and j. Practically, we achieve this by probabilistically choosing the value of $Y(n)$ according to $P_Y(n)$, which is decided before the n-th measurement interval starts, *without considering what the value of $X(n)$ will be*.

However, selecting $Y(n)$ randomly without being aware of $X(n)$ may cause energy shortage or overflow in the battery. For example, when $B(n-1) = 0$ (*i.e.*, there is no energy remaining in the battery before the n-th measurement interval starts), if $Y(n)$ is chosen to be zero, we cannot feed any non-zero value of $X(n)$. This means that sometimes we cannot use the appliances when we want. Similarly, when $B(n-1) = Ku$ (*i.e.*, the battery is full), a non-zero value of $Y(n)$ does not make sense if $X(n) = 0$, since we cannot draw the energy from the power grid unless we throw it away.

To handle this issue, we put a restriction on $P_Y(n)$ when the energy left in the battery is smaller than $(M-1)u$ (near-empty) or larger than $(K - (M-1))u$ (near-full), which we call the *corner cases*. More specifically, when $B(n-1) = ju$ for $j < (M-1)$, we choose $P_Y(n)$ such that $p_Y(i; n) = 0$ for $i < (M-1) - j$. Similarly, when $B(n-1) = (K - j)u$ for $j < (M-1)$, we choose $P_Y(n)$ such that $p_Y(i; n) = 0$ for $i > j$. We refer the readers to [12] for more detailed explanation of what this restriction means. The rationale behind this restriction on $P_Y(n)$

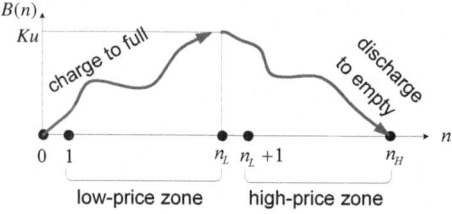

Fig. 2. Desired battery state profile

is that the battery must always have enough amount of energy to feed $X(n)$ even at the near-empty case, and that we never charge the battery more than its capacity whatever $X(n)$ is.

4.2 Strategy for Charging/Discharging the Battery

The only way to achieve cost saving by exploiting the time-of-use pricing policy is to charge the battery in the low-price zone and use the stored energy in the high-price zone. If we charge iu amount of energy in the low-price zone and use it in the high price zone, we can save $(R_H - R_L)i$ (dollars). For this reason, the maximum possible cost saving is $(R_H - R_L)K$ (dollars) per day, which is obtained when we charge the battery from empty to full in the low-price zone and discharge the battery to zero by feeding $X(n)$ in the high-price zone. Note that the maximum cost saving is proportional to the battery capacity Ku.

Therefore, our strategy to achieve the saving in the energy bill is to force the battery state to follow the trend shown in Figure 2. We achieve this by changing $P_Y(n)$ for every n, which is discussed in detail in the following subsection.

4.3 Basic Approach

We first define the distribution vector space $\mathcal{P}$ as follows.

$$\mathcal{P} = \left\{ [p_0, p_1, \ldots, p_{(M-1)}] : \sum_{i=0}^{M-1} p_i = 1, 0 \leq p_i \leq 1 \right\}, \qquad (2)$$

where we limit the value of p_i to be a multiple of a constant c $(0 < c < 1)$, in order to make $\mathcal{P}$ be a finite set. For example, when $c = 0.1$ and $M = 4$, the distribution vector space $\mathcal{P}$ contains $[0.1, 0.2, 0.3, 0.4]$ and $[0.5, 0.5, 0, 0]$ as two of its elements. Then, $P_Y(n)$ is assigned one element in $\mathcal{P}$ in the n-th measurement interval. Recall that we force some elements of $P_Y(n)$ to be zero, depending on the battery level (Section 4.1). Therefore, the possible choice set in the n-th measurement interval is dependent on $B(n-1)$ and we denote it by $\mathcal{P}_{B(n-1)}$. Now, the key question for us is *"what would be the best choice for $P_Y(n) \in \mathcal{P}_{B(n-1)}$ for each n to maximize the cost saving?"* This question is answered by solving the following stochastic optimal control problems:

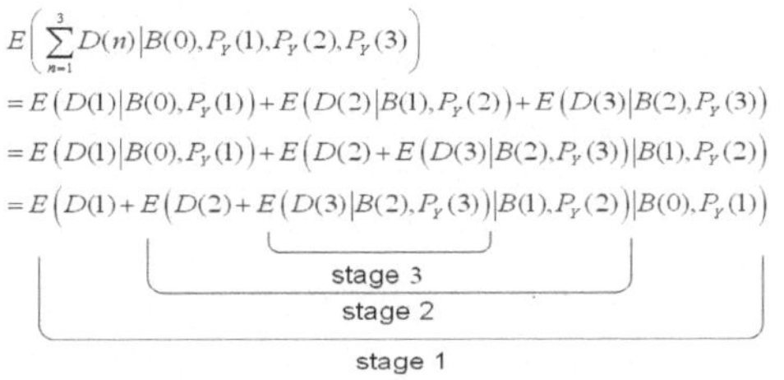

$$E\left(\sum_{n=1}^{3} D(n)|B(0), P_Y(1), P_Y(2), P_Y(3)\right)$$

$$= E\left(D(1)|B(0), P_Y(1)\right) + E\left(D(2)|B(1), P_Y(2)\right) + E\left(D(3)|B(2), P_Y(3)\right)$$

$$= E\left(D(1)|B(0), P_Y(1)\right) + E\left(D(2) + E\left(D(3)|B(2), P_Y(3)\right)|B(1), P_Y(2)\right)$$

$$= E\left(D(1) + E\left(D(2) + E\left(D(3)|B(2), P_Y(3)\right)|B(1), P_Y(2)\right)|B(0), P_Y(1)\right)$$

stage 3

stage 2

stage 1

Fig. 3. An example to derive the dynamic programming framework

$$\max_{\substack{P_Y(n)\in\mathcal{P}_{B(n-1)} \\ 0<n\leq n_L}} E\left(B(n_L)|B(0), P_Y(1), P_Y(2), \ldots, P_Y(n_L)\right) \tag{3}$$

in the low-price zone, and

$$\min_{\substack{P_Y(n)\in\mathcal{P}_{B(n-1)} \\ n_L<n\leq n_H}} E\left(B(n_H)|B(n_L), P_Y(n_L+1), P_Y(n_L+2), \ldots, P_Y(n_H)\right) \tag{4}$$

in the high-price zone. Namely, we maximize (or minimize) the expected amount of the energy in the battery when each zone ends, given the battery level at the beginning of the zone and the distribution vectors $P_Y(1)$ through $P_Y(n_L)$ (or $P_Y(n_L + 1)$ through $P_Y(n_H)$). We solve these optimization problems using dynamic programming [13].

To see how we use dynamic programming, let us first consider the following simple example in the low-price zone, where $n_L = 3$. Then, the optimization objective is to maximize $E\left(B(3)|B(0), P_Y(1), P_Y(2), P_Y(3)\right)$, which is equal to $B(0) + E\left(\sum_{n=1}^{3} D(n)|B(0), P_Y(1), P_Y(2), P_Y(3)\right)$, where $D(n) = Y(n) - X(n)$ as introduced earlier. Since $B(0)$ is given, we only need to focus on maximizing $E\left(\sum_{n=1}^{3} D(n)|B(0), P_Y(1), P_Y(2), P_Y(3)\right)$, which can be re-written as shown in Figure 3. Note in the figure that the calculations can be done recursively. Stage 2 calculations are based on stage 3, stage 1 only on stage 2. Thus, the optimal solution can be performed by maximizing the stage 3, stage 2, and stage 1 in this order. In this manner, we first compute the optimal value of $P_Y(3)$ given $B(2)$, then we compute the optimal value of $P_Y(2)$ given $B(1)$ until we reach and compute the optimal value of $P_Y(1)$. In the general case, $P_Y(n_L)$ is computed first and then other $P_Y(n)$'s are computed in a backward direction (time-wise) till $P_Y(1)$ is computed.

Namely, the optimal solution for (3) is obtained by a backward-directional computation procedure. In general, this procedure can be described by the following recursive equation, called the Bellman equation:

$$J(n_L + 1, B(n_L)) = 0,$$

$$J(n, B(n-1)) = \max_{P_Y(n)\in\mathcal{P}_{B(n-1)}} E\left(D(n) + J(n+1, B(n))|B(n-1), P_Y(n)\right),$$

$$\tag{5}$$

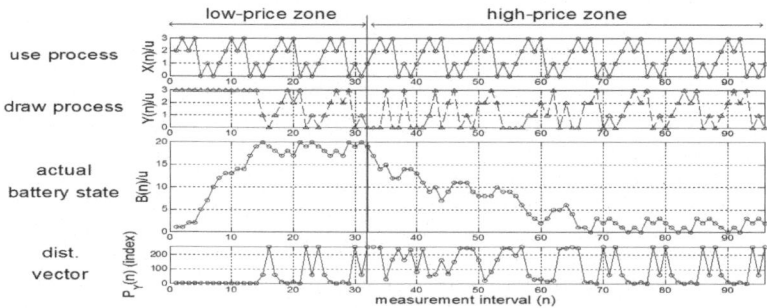

Fig. 4. Simulation results for the basic approach

for $n = n_L, (n_L - 1), \ldots, 1$. Solving (5) results in the optimal decision for $P_Y(n)$ when the value of $B(n - 1)$ is given, in the sense that $P_Y(n)$ will maximize $E(B(n_L))$. Refer to [12] for further detail to solve (5). The optimal solution for (4) can also be obtained in a similar way.

In summary, what we have done is to calculate a decision table. Each entry in the decision table maps the given values of n and $B(n-1)$ to the optimal vector $P_Y(n)$ at the state. Note that the decision table can be pre-calculated before the run-time. During the run-time, we just look up the decision table for a given state, *i.e.*, n and $B(n - 1)$, and probabilistically choose the value of $Y(n)$ via the distribution specified by the decision table entry. The size of this table can be large in practice if K and n_H are large. Thus, calculating the decision table can be computationally expensive. However, note that the table can be reused from one day to another till the distribution of the use process $X(n)$ changes significantly. Discussion about table complexity can be found at [12].

4.4 Simulation Study for the Basic Approach

We now present simulation results for our basic solution approach. By this simulation study, we will identify the issues with the basic approach, which will motivate us to improve our solution in Section 5.1 and propose PRIVATUS.

In the simulation, we choose $M = 4$, $K = 20$, and $c = 0.1$. We fix each measurement interval to be 15 minutes and thus we have 96 measurement intervals a day. Thus, the value of n_H becomes $n_H = 96$ and we set $n_L = 32$. In order to see more clearly what $Y(n)$ looks like compared to $X(n)$, we make $X(n)$ as a known repeated pattern, instead of generating it randomly (Figure 4).

A sample result of the simulation is shown in Figure 4, where "$P_Y(n)$ (index)" in the bottom graph means the index number of the element in $\mathcal{P}$ selected as $P_Y(n)$. We can see that at each measurement interval, the values of $X(n)$ and $Y(n)$ are mapped to each other in a random fashion. Further, the battery level indeed moves according to the trend that it is charged to the full level in the low-price zone and fully discharged in the high-price zone. However, we also observe that there exist similar patterns for the sequences of $X(n)$ and $Y(n)$ for

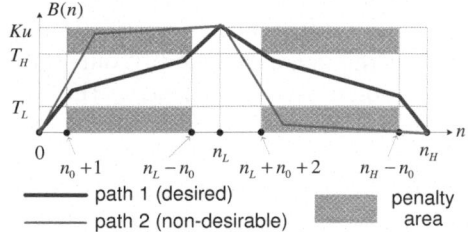

Fig. 5. Penalty areas

the measurement intervals of $16 \leq n \leq 32$ and $70 \leq n \leq 96$. More precisely, we see that the value of $X(n)$ highly likely reappears as the value of $Y(n+1)$ when the battery is at the corner cases. This is an undesirable behavior because if the adversary learns this characteristic, he or she may infer the original values of $X(n)$ with high accuracy by observing the values of $Y(n+1)$. Through this, we realize that our point-by-point de-correlation between $X(n)$ and $Y(n)$ leaves an obvious vulnerability in practice.

After more careful study, we find that this issue occurs because of two reasons: **(R1)** The first reason is that we charge/discharge the battery too fast. In the low-price zone, the battery reaches the full state much earlier than the end of the zone. Once at the full state, the battery stays close to the near-full states, since there is no benefit to bring the energy level down to a lower one according to our optimization objective in (3). The near-constant energy level of the battery implies that whatever the value of $X(n)$ is, the draw process $Y(n)$ should somehow compensate for it. Since the value of $Y(n)$ is chosen before the value of $X(n)$, we see this compensation effect in $Y(n+1)$. Similar logic applies to the high-price zone; **(R2)** The second reason is that we have too much freedom when choosing $P_Y(n)$. As a result, the draw process can take a specific symbol with a very high probability to compensate the use process. For example, if $X(n) = 3u$ and the draw process needs to compensate it (due to the first reason), the basic approach will likely choose $P_Y(n+1) = [0, 0, 0, 1]$. This implies that we will charge with the current value of $3u$ with probability 1 at the $(n+1)$-th measurement interval. In other words, due to the high degree of freedom to choose $P_Y(n)$, $Y(n)$ is chosen to be very similar to $X(n-1)$ in the corner cases.

In the next section, we will propose PRIVATUS that suppresses these undesirable effects **(R1)** and **(R2)**.

5 Solution Approach II: Advanced Formulation

5.1 Advanced Approach: PRIVATUS

In order to fix **(R1)**, we introduce penalty areas for when the battery level gets too close to empty or too close to full as shown in Figure 5. The penalty areas correspond to the battery states higher than the upper threshold T_H or lower than the lower threshold T_L. In each zone (low-priced or high-priced), the penalty areas begin after n_0 measurement intervals, and end n_0 measurement intervals before the end of the zone. We modify our optimization objective in such a way that we incur some penalty, whenever the battery state $B(n)$ falls into the penalty areas. Hence, the optimal decision for $P_Y(n)$ would be changed to the one that still charges or discharges the battery according to the trend in Figure 2, but does not hit the penalty areas in the middle of the zones. In this sense, the modified optimization objective would result in "path 1"-like battery profile rather than "path 2"-like one in Figure 5. The "path 2"-like battery profile is what we have seen in the basic approach.

We consider the *effective battery state* $B_e(n)$ in the optimization objective function, instead of the actual battery state $B(n)$. The effective battery state $B_e(n)$ is designed to increase as the actual battery state $B(n)$ increases in the low-price zone (or $B(n)$ decreases in the high-price zone). However, every time $B(n)$ goes into a penalty area, $B_e(n)$ is deducted by some penalty amount. Denote by $[x]^+$ the projection of x to non-negative values, *i.e.*, $[x]^+ = x$ if $x > 0$, and $[x]^+ = 0$ if $x \leq 0$. Then, the effective battery state $B_e(n)$ in the low-price zone is defined as $B_e(n) = B_e(0) + \sum_{m=1}^{n} D_e(m)$. Here, $B_e(0) = \alpha B(0)$ and $D_e(m)$ is given as, if $m \leq n_0$ or $m > n_L - n_0$ (*i.e.*, in near-beginning or near-end of the low-price zone), $D_e(m) = \alpha D(m)$, and if $m > n_0$ and $m \leq n_L - n_0$,

$$D_e(m) = \alpha D(m) - \beta \left([B(m) - T_H]^+ + [T_L - B(m)]^+\right), \qquad (6)$$

where α and β are positive integers, $T_L = (M-1)u$, and $T_H = (K - (M-1))u$. In the high-price zone, we define $B_e(n)$ as $B_e(n) = B_e(n_L) + \sum_{m=n_L+1}^{n} D_e(m)$, where $B_e(n_L) = \alpha(Ku - B(n_L))$, and further, if $m \leq n_L + n_0$ or $m > n_H - n_0$, $D_e(m) = -\alpha D(m)$, and if $m > n_L + n_0$ and $m \leq n_H - n_0$,

$$D_e(m) = -\alpha D(m) - \beta \left([B(m) - T_H]^+ + [T_L - B(m)]^+\right). \qquad (7)$$

Note that if we ignore the second terms in (6) and (7), we simply have $B_e(n) = \alpha B(n)$ in the low-price zone, and $B_e(n) = \alpha(Ku - B(n))$ in the high-price zone. That is, $B_e(n)$ increases from zero to the maximum αKu in both zones as $B(n)$ moves like in Figure 2. Thus, our optimization objective for achieving the maximal cost saving is to maximize $E(B_e(n_L))$ in the low-price zone and $E(B_e(n_H))$ in the high-price zone, given initial conditions. On the other hands, the terms leading by β in (6) and (7) take into account the penalty. Whenever $D(n)$ causes $B(n)$ to fall into a penalty area, we subtract $\beta[B(n) - T_H]^+$ or $\beta[T_L - B(n)]^+$ from $B_e(n)$. Hence, we will expect that in the optimal decision for $P_Y(n)$, $B(n)$ would avoid hitting the penalty area, or $B(n)$ would attempt to get out of a penalty area if $B(n-1)$ was already in the penalty area. The relative magnitudes of α and β determines how sensitive we are to the penalty. If β is very large compared to α, $B(n)$ may not even go close to the penalty area to avoid any chance of incurring a high penalty score. Refer to [12] to see more detail about the choices for α and β.

On the other hand, to address (**R2**), we adopt two strategies. *First*, we put the restriction on $\mathcal{P}_{B(n-1)}$ that it only contains the vectors $v \in \mathcal{P}$ such that

$\|v - V_k\| < T_k$. Here, T_k is a threshold at $B(n-1) = ku$, and V_k is the distribution vector of $Y(n)$ for which the possible values of $Y(n)$ at $B(n-1) = ku$ are selected equi-probably. For instance, when $M = 4$ and $K = 10$, we have $V_5 = [0.25, 0.25, 0.25, 0.25]$ when $B(n-1) = 5u$, and $V_1 = [0.5, 0.5, 0, 0]$ when $B(n-1) = u$. With this strategy, we are forcing the different elements of $P_Y(n)$ to be more or less equal, thus eliminating the possibility that $Y(n)$ is chosen deterministically (or with a high probability). By controlling the threshold T_k, we can control how close to equal probability we want. If T_k is low, then the choices are close to equally probable, but we also lose controllability in forcing $B(n)$ to the desired state according to the trend in Figure 2.

Second, we add one more restriction on $P_Y(n)$ in non-corner cases (*i.e.*, battery neither empty nor full) such that it does not differ significantly from $P_Y(n-1)$. If the two differ significantly, then $Y(n)$ may try compensating for the use value in the previous measurement interval and will hence track $X(n-1)$. Therefore, our strategy is that $\|P_Y(n) - P_Y(n-1)\| < T_D$, where T_D is called the distance threshold. We enforce this restriction to be applied only when the actual battery state stays in non-corner cases for two consecutive measurement intervals, *i.e.*, $T_L \leq B(n-2) \leq T_H$ and $T_L \leq B(n-1) \leq T_H$. Our intention behind this is to quickly get out of the corner cases (which hits the penalty areas). In the extreme case, with this strategy, $P_Y(n-1) = P_Y(n)$ implying that $Y(n)$ is independent of $X(n-1)$.

Reflecting all the changes, the optimal choice for $P_Y(n)$ in the low-price zone is obtained by solving the following Bellman equation.

$$J(S(n_L + 1)) = 0,$$
$$J(S(n)) = \max_{P_Y(n) \in \mathcal{P}^*_{B(n-1)}} E\left(D_e(n) + J(S(n+1))|S(n)\right), \qquad (8)$$

for $n = n_L, (n_L - 1), \ldots, 1$. Here, $S(n)$ represents the state vector defined as $S(n) = [n, B(n-1), B_e(n-1), P_Y(n-1)]$. $\mathcal{P}^*_{B(n-1)}$ is defined as a subset of $\mathcal{P}$ whose element v is such that the two restrictions described above are satisfied, *i.e.*, $v \in \mathcal{P}_{B(n-1)}$, and if $T_L \leq B(n-2) \leq T_H$ and $T_L \leq B(n-1) \leq T_H$, $\|v - P_Y(n-1)\| < T_D$. The optimal choice for $P_Y(n)$ in the high-price zone can also be decided in a similar way.

5.2   Simulation Study for PRIVATUS

Now, we conduct a simulation test for PRIVATUS. In order to see the difference from the basic approach, we use the same simulation environment as in Section 4.4. We choose $T_k = 0.3$ for $k = 3, 4, \ldots, 17$; $T_k = 0.25$ for $k = 2, 18$; $T_k = 0.2$ for $k = 1, 19$; $T_k = 0.1$ for $k = 0, 20$. With these threshold values, $\mathcal{P}_k$ only contains $[0, 0, 0.4, 0.6]$, $[0, 0, 0.5, 0.5]$, and $[0, 0, 0.6, 0.4]$ for $k = 1, 19$, for instance. For the remaining parameters, we set $\alpha = 2$, $\beta = 1$, $n_0 = 3$, and $T_D = 0.2$.

Figure 6 shows a sample result for the simulation, where the solid red lines in the "$B(n)/u$" graph indicate the energy levels corresponding to the penalty area thresholds T_H and T_L. First, we can see that $B(n)$ follows the trend in

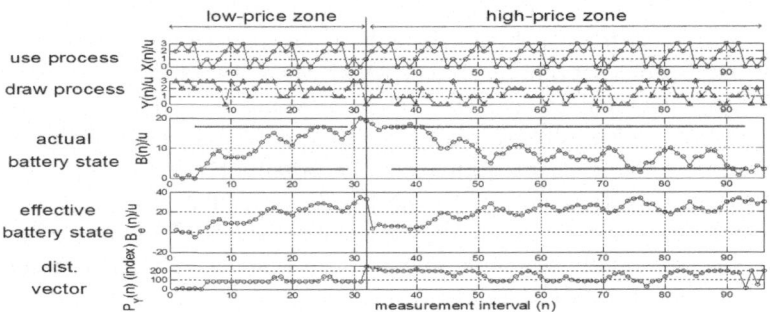

Fig. 6. Simulation results for PRIVATUS

Figure 2, and it seldom hits the penalty area as we desired. Although $B(n)$ enters the penalty area at around $n = 39, 76, 92$, we can also see that $B(n)$ tries to get out of penalty area quickly. As a result, the battery neither goes to the full-state too quickly in the low-price zone, nor goes to the empty-state too quickly in the high-price zone. Second, in the "$P_Y(n)$(index)" graph, we observe that for many times, the decision for $P_Y(n)$ remains the same, or the speed of changing a decision becomes much slower (compared to the result in Figure 4). By these two fixes, we see that the correlation between the use process and the draw process is significantly reduced. We can no longer find similar patterns between the two. The point-by-point comparison of $X(n)$ and $Y(n)$ still gives no meaningful clue from $Y(n)$ to $X(n)$, as this is by design that is maintained in the basic approach and PRIVATUS. Of course, this might be seen as a subjective interpretation of the result. Thus, in the experiment section, we will consider a metric to quantitatively measure how well we are protecting the privacy and re-visit these results.

6   Experiment

6.1   Metrics and Simulation Parameters

First, we define the metric of information leakage from the use process to the draw process as follows: for a positive integer m,

$$L^s_{(n,m)} = I(\bar{X}_{(n,m)}; \bar{Y}^s_{(n,m)})/H(\bar{X}_{(n,m)}), \tag{9}$$

where $\bar{X}_{(n,m)}=[X(n-m+1),X(n-m),...,X(n)]$, and $\bar{Y}^s_{(n,m)}=[Y(n-m+1+s),Y(n-m+s),...,Y(n+s)]$, and s is a non-negative integer called the timeshift offset. Here, $H(\mathcal{X})$ denotes the *uncertainty* of $\mathcal{X}$, and $I(\mathcal{X};\mathcal{Y})$ is the mutual information between $\mathcal{X}$ and $\mathcal{Y}$. Namely, $H(\mathcal{X}) = -\sum_i P(\mathcal{X} = i) \log P(\mathcal{X} = i)$ and

$$I(\mathcal{X};\mathcal{Y})=\sum_i \sum_j P(\mathcal{X}=i,\mathcal{Y}=j) \log \frac{P(\mathcal{X}=i,\mathcal{Y}=j)}{P(\mathcal{X}=i)P(\mathcal{Y}=j)} \tag{10}$$

Note that $\bar{X}_{(n,m)}$ and $\bar{Y}^s_{(n,m)}$ represent sequences of length m in the use process and the draw process, respectively, with the draw process being time delayed by s

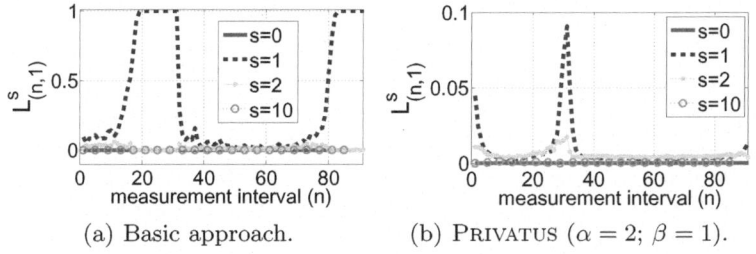

(a) Basic approach.   (b) PRIVATUS ($\alpha = 2$; $\beta = 1$).

Fig. 7. Information leakage when $K = 20$ and $m = 1$

measurement intervals. Since $I(\bar{X}_{(n,m)}; \bar{Y}^s_{(n,m)}) = H(\bar{X}_{(n,m)}) - H(\bar{X}_{(n,m)})|\bar{Y}^s_{(n,m)})$, the metric $L^s_{(n,m)}$ can be interpreted as a measure of the *uncertainty reduction* in $\bar{X}_{(n,m)}$ by observing $\bar{Y}^s_{(n,m)}$, normalized to the uncertainty of $\bar{X}_{(n,m)}$. Thus, by this metric, we can quantify *how uncertain the adversary is when he attempts to guess the sequence $\bar{X}_{(n,m)}$ of the use process, based on the observed sequence $\bar{Y}^s_{(n,m)}$ of the draw process.* For example, the adversary knows that $\bar{X}_{(n,m)}$ is surely the same as $\bar{Y}^s_{(n,m)}$, when $L^s_{(n,m)} = 1$. In contrast, $L^s_{(n,m)} = 0$ means that $\bar{Y}^s_{(n,m)}$ gives no clue about $\bar{X}_{(n,m)}$ at all.

Second, given that the battery capacity is Ku, we define the metric for the cost saving for a day as

$$S_{(r,K)} = E\left(-\sum_{m=1}^{n_L} rR_H D(m) - \sum_{m=n_L+1}^{n_H} R_H D(m)\right), \qquad (11)$$

where r denotes the ratio of R_L to R_H. The term $S_{(r,K)}$ is *the expected difference between the original cost for what the user actually consumes* $(\sum_{m=1}^{n_L} rR_H X(m) + \sum_{m=n_L+1}^{n_H} R_H X(m))$, *and the money that a user pays to the utility company* $(\sum_{m=1}^{n_L} rR_H Y(m) + \sum_{m=n_L+1}^{n_H} R_H Y(m))$. A positive value of $S_{(r,K)}$ means that we achieve cost saving. If $S_{(r,K)}$ is negative, it means that we have to pay more compared to the baseline no-privacy-protection scheme.

To be consistent with the previous simulations (in Figures 4 and 6), we use the same parameters as before (*i.e.*, $M = 4$; $K = 20$; $n_L = 32$; $n_H = 96$; $\alpha = 2$; $\beta = 1$; $n_0 = 3$; $c = 0.1$) throughout the whole experiments, unless otherwise stated. However, we randomly generate $X(n)$ through $P_X(n) = [0.5, 0.2, 0.2, 0.1]$ in the low-price zone and $P_X(n) = [0.1, 0.3, 0.4, 0.2]$ in the high-price zone. This setting results in about $138u$ for the expected daily usage $E(\sum_{n=1}^{n_H} X(n))$. To get the results, we run 100,000 days in such a way that the remaining energy in the battery at the end of a day becomes the initial energy level of the battery in the next day.

6.2   Information Leakage and Cost Saving

General Performance Trend: Figure 7 shows the general performance trend of our solution approaches (for $m = 1$). We can see that when $s = 0$, $X(n)$

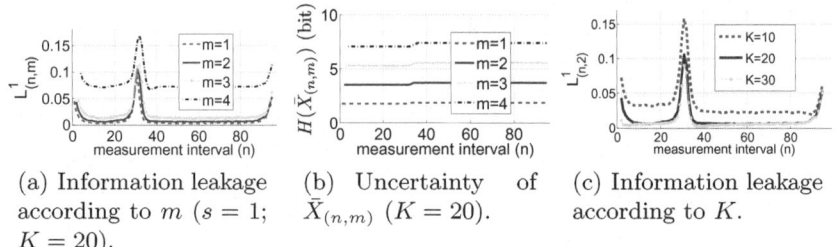

(a) Information leakage according to m ($s = 1$; $K = 20$).

(b) Uncertainty of $\bar{X}_{(n,m)}$ ($K = 20$).

(c) Information leakage according to K.

Fig. 8. Effects of sequence length m and capacity K in PRIVATUS ($\alpha = 2$; $\beta = 1$)

and $Y(n)$ are indeed independent in both the basic approach and PRIVATUS. We can also see that information leakage is the highest when $s = 1$, *i.e.*, $X(n)$ and $Y(n + 1)$ has the highest dependency in our solution approaches. This is due to our solution's inherent nature that $Y(n)$ is chosen to change the current battery state resulting from $X(n - 1)$ and the previous battery state. Figure 7(a) confirms again that in the basic approach, this issue can be quite significant because $Y(n)$ perfectly compensates $X(n - 1)$ and reveals all information about $X(n - 1)$ (*i.e.*, $L^1_{(n,1)} = 1$) when the battery is in the corner cases. However, we see in Figure 7(b) that this compensation effect is greatly reduced. That is, in PRIVATUS, $Y(n)$ results in mostly near-zero uncertainty reduction about $X(n - 1)$. In even the worst case (for some measurement intervals, with delay of 1 measurement interval), the uncertainty reduction is less than 10%. We see that the worst-case information leakage in the advanced approach occurs around the price zone boundaries. We suspect that this is because around the price zone boundaries, there is no penalty defined and thus the battery state has a relatively higher chance to remain costant, which again makes it more likely that $Y(n)$ tries to compensate for $X(n - 1)$. On the other hand, we can see from the case when $s = 10$ that, with higher delays (*i.e.*, larger values of s), the sequences of the use process and the draw process become independent.

Effect of Sequence Length: In Figure 8(a), we see that in PRIVATUS, the information leakage increases as the sequence length m increases. This seems to imply that the adversary gains more information when he observes longer sequences. However, note from Figure 8(b) that the uncertainty of the use-process sequence $H(\bar{X}_{(n,m)})$ also grows as m increases. In Figure 8(b), x-bit uncertainty can be understood in such a way that approximately the use-process sequence has 2^x possible realizations with equal probability $1/2^x$. Since $M = 4$, the uncertainty of the use-process sequence becomes larger by a factor close to $\log_2 4$ (more precisely, $\log_2 2^{1.7}$ in our simulation setting) as m increases by 1. Thus, the minor increment in percentage-wise uncertainty reduction does not make it easier for the adversary to make guesses about the use-process sequence. For example, when $m = 3$ and $n = 32$, the uncertainty of the use-process sequence is 5.3 bits and uncertainty reduction is 11%. This implies that the remaining uncertainty of the use-process sequence after observing the draw-process sequence is $5.3(1 - 0.11) = 4.72$ bits, *i.e.*, the adversary faces the uncertainty to pick one out

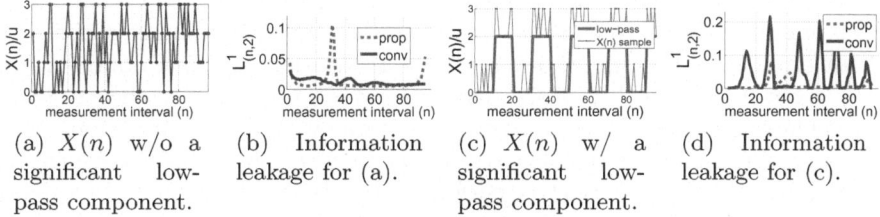

(a) $X(n)$ w/o a significant low-pass component.

(b) Information leakage for (a).

(c) $X(n)$ w/ a significant low-pass component.

(d) Information leakage for (c).

Fig. 9. Information leakage comparison between PRIVATUS with $\alpha = 2$ and $\beta = 1$ (legend: 'prop') and an existing scheme [3] (legend: 'conv'), when $K = 20$ and $m = 2$. The higher is $L^1_{(n,2)}$, the worse is the information leakage.

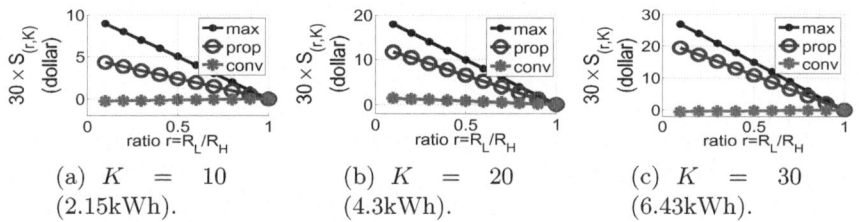

(a) $K = 10$ (2.15kWh).

(b) $K = 20$ (4.3kWh).

(c) $K = 30$ (6.43kWh).

Fig. 10. Cost saving comparison between PRIVATUS and an existing scheme [3]. Here, we set $u = 0.2143$kWh and $R_H = \$0.033/u = \$0.155/$kWh. This results in the average daily usage (*i.e.*, $E(\sum_{n=1}^{n_H} X(n))$) equal to 30kWh.

of $2^{5.3(1-0.11)} = 26.3$ possible sequences, in order to make a guess about the use-process sequence. On the other hand, when $m = 4$ and $n = 32$, the uncertainty is 7.0 bits and the uncertainty reduction is 17%. This results in $2^{7.0(1-0.17)} = 56.1$ possible sequences as candidates for the use-process sequence. Therefore, we conclude that the adversary has no advantage in observing a longer sequence in the draw process.

Effect of Battery Capacity: Figure 8(c) shows how PRIVATUS acts when the battery capacity varies. We can infer from the figure that when the battery capacity is too small, information leakage may be significant. This can be explained again by the compensation effect of our solution. If the battery capacity is too small, there is not much room for the battery state to fluctuate between the two penalty area thresholds T_L and T_H (see Figure 6). This means that the battery state remains relatively constant, which makes the compensation effect prominent. On the other hand, once the battery capacity is above a threshold, further increasing the battery capacity leads to little benefit in terms of further reducing the information leakage.

Comparison to Prior Work: In Figures 9 and 10, we compare PRIVATUS ('prop' in the figures) with an existing scheme ('conv' in the figures) proposed by Kalogridis *et. al.* [3]. Kalogridis' scheme performs a simple low-pass filtering over the use process in a best-effort manner without considering the energy cost factor. Thus, it reduces the high frequency variations in the resulting draw process. Kalogridis' scheme needs to estimate the value of $X(n)$ beforehand (refer to [3] for detail). We assume in the simulation that the estimation is perfect (*i.e.*, without errors). Figure 9(a) shows a sample realization of $X(n)$, obtained from $P_X(n)$ given in Section 6.1. Note that since $X(n)$ is randomly chosen among M possible values from $P_X(n)$, which is the same within each price-zone, there is not a significant low-frequency component in $X(n)$. In this case, we can see from Figure 9(b) that PRIVATUS performs slightly better than Kalogridis' to keep the privacy information, except at the price zone boundaries. However, if there is a significant low-pass component in $X(n)$, PRIVATUS will provide much better privacy protection than Kalogridis'. This is because Kalogridis' scheme still allows the low-pass component of load profile to be revealed. To see this, we generate $X(n)$ by adding a random value 0 or u to a rectangular pulse whose period is 20 measurement intervals, as shown in Figure 9(c). Comparison result in such a case is given in Figure 9(d). Indeed, PRIVATUS results in better lower information leakage than Kalogridis' when there exists a considerable low-frequency component in $X(n)$. Meanwhile, Figure 10 shows that from the cost saving point of view, PRIVATUS has a huge advantage against Kalogridis'. In all of the cases studied, Kalogridis' scheme does not achieve a significant cost saving. On the other hand, compared to the maximum possible cost saving, computed according to Section 4.2 ('max' in the figures), PRIVATUS achieves the saving of 48% of the maximum when $K = 10$, 66% of the maximum when $K = 20$, and 72% of the maximum when $K = 30$. Thus, PRIVATUS strikes a desirable balance between privacy and cost saving. Considering that the average electricity consumption for a U.S. residential customer was 30kWh per day [14], Figure 10(c) shows that a typical home can achieve about \$16 saving for a month with a 6.43kWh battery, based on the following tariff example: $R_L = 0.04/\text{kWh}$ and $R_H = 0.15/\text{kWh}$ [4].

7   Conclusion and Future Work

In order to resolve the privacy issue in smart grid, we proposed PRIVATUS to de-correlate the meter reading information from user behavior. PRIVATUS uses a rechargeable battery to make the meter reading reported to the utilities look independent of the actual usage at any given measurement interval. The correlation between the meter readings and the actual usage pattern over multiple measurement intervals is also reduced by changing the probability distribution of charging the battery in each interval through careful design. PRIVATUS is also geared to the future of time-of-use pricing of electricity and it ensures that the battery is charged to achieve the maximal savings in the energy cost. We formulate the problem rigorously and use stochastic dynamic programming to devise our solution. The experiment results show that PRIVATUS is successfully able to hide the actual usage from what is drawn from the grid, and achieves considerable amount of saving in the energy cost, subject to the availability of a reasonable-sized battery. Compared to prior work, we achieve much better privacy when there is a conspicuous low-frequency component in load profile, and significantly higher cost savings.

Our future work will focus on generalizing PRIVATUS under more dynamic scenarios, *e.g.*, where the price zones are dynamically changed from one day to the next, or the price varies over time in a demand-driven and adaptive manner.

Acknowledgments. This work has been partially supported by the National Science Foundation through award CNS-0831999. Any opinions, findings, and conclusions or recommendations expressed in this material are those of the author(s) and do not necessarily reflect the views of the National Science Foundation.

References

1. Beckman, H.: Lawsuit filed to stop installaton of smart meters, http://napervillesun.suntimes.com/news/9723766-418/lawsuit-filed-to-stop-smart-meter-installation.html
2. Sullivan, B.: What will talking power meters say about you?, http://redtape.msnbc.msn.com
3. Kalogridis, G., Efthymiou, C., Denic, S.Z., Lewis, T.A., Cepeda, R.: Privacy for smart meters: Towards undetectable appliance load signatures. In: 2010 First IEEE International Conference on Smart Grid Communications (2010)
4. Tucson electric power: Residential time-of-use pricing plan, https://www.tep.com/doc/customer/rates/R-21F.pdf
5. Agrawal, D., Aggarwal, C.C.: On the design and quantification of privacy preserving data mining algorithms. In: PODS 2001, pp. 247–255. ACM, New York (2001)
6. Sweeney, L.: k-anonymity: a model for protecting privacy. Int. J. Uncertain. Fuzziness Knowl.-Based Syst. 10, 557–570 (2002)
7. Stallman, R.: Is digital inclusion a good thing? How can we make sure it is? Comm. Mag. 48, 112–118 (2010)
8. Khurana, H., Hadley, M., Lu, N., Frincke, D.A.: Smart-grid security issues. IEEE Security and Privacy 8, 81–85 (2010)
9. Quinn, E.L.: Privacy and the new energy infrastructure. In: SSRN (2009)
10. Rial, A., Danezis, G.: Privacy-preserving smart metering. In: Proceedings of the 10th Annual ACM Workshop on Privacy in the Electronic Society, WPES 2011. ACM (2011)
11. Varodayan, D.P., Khisti, A.: Smart meter privacy using a rechargeable battery: Minimizing the rate of information leakage. In: ICASSP (2011)
12. Koo, J., Lin, X., Bagchi, S.: Technical Report: Wallet-Friendly Privacy Protection for Smart Meters, https://engineering.purdue.edu/~linx/papers.html
13. Bertsekas, D.P., Shreve, S.E.: Stochastic Optimal Control: The Discrete-Time Case. Athena Scientific (2007)
14. Administration, U.E.I.: Average electricity consumption for a us residential customer, http://www.eia.gov/tools/faqs/faq.cfm?id=97&t=3
15. U.S. Department of Energy: Battery power for your residentialsolar electric system, http://www.nrel.gov/docs/fy02osti/31689.pdf

A   Discussion

Battery Cost: In Section 6, we showed that a 6.43kWh battery can achieve $16 saving per month, assuming 30kWh use in a day. People may argue that this is the relatively small savings compared to the high battery cost. Indeed, initial costs for residential batteries range from $80 to $200 per kWh [15], and thus the battery cost of 6.43kWh may range from $514 to $1,280. However, note that people buy a hybrid car to save the fuel-cost and the environment, although it requires a considerable initial cost due to the battery. Even though the fuel saving of the hybrid cars does not completely offset its high cost, the fuel saving serves as a significant incentive for consumers (who may only be mildly environment-conscious) to buy hybrid cars. Similarly, in our case, the cost savings will encourage privacy-conscious customers to buy our solution. In addition, given a 6.43kWh battery and $16 saving per month, the battery cost may be balanced out by the saving in 2.6 to 6.6 years. We think that this is similar to the period to recover the additional cost of a hybrid car compared to a normal car.

Energy Loss in a Battery: By multiplying coefficients (< 1) by $X(n)$ and $Y(n)$ in (1), our model can be easily extended to include the energy loss in the battery that occurs when charging and discharging.

More Than Two Price Zones: Once we know the rates of energy usage and the boundaries of each price zone, we can calculate the desired pattern of battery charge and discharge—akin to that in Figure 2. Namely, what we need to do is to calculate to what level the battery can be charged or discharged in each zone. Then, the solution approach outlined earlier applies directly to the case with more than two price zones.

Interleaved Low-Price and High-Price Zones: This situation is equivalent to the case where there are multiple price zones, one group of which have a low price, and the other group have a high price. Thus, this case can be treated in the same way as the above.

The Amount of Energy Usage Per Day Varying Over Days: This paper focuses on hiding the energy consumption pattern within a day. Across days, the total usage per day can still be revealed to the adversary (by which the adversary may know whether you are home or not for a given day). The other part of PRIVATUS, which is not presented in this paper due to the page limit, handles this issue. At the high level, the solution is to flatten the energy use across days, by charging more in days with less usage and by using the saved energy in days with more usage. The solution does not affect the current randomization framework within each day; it only modifies the total use in each day.

SHARP: Private Proximity Test and Secure Handshake with Cheat-Proof Location Tags

Yao Zheng[1], Ming Li[2], Wenjing Lou[1], and Y. Thomas Hou[1]

[1] Virginia Polytechnic Institute and State University
{zhengyao,wjlou,thou}@vt.edu
[2] Utah State University
ming.li@usu.edu

Abstract. A location proximity test service allows mobile users to determine whether they are in close proximity to each other, and has found numerous applications in mobile social networks. Unfortunately, existing solutions usually reveal much of users' private location information during proximity test. They are also vulnerable to location cheating where an attacker reports false locations to gain advantage. Moreover, the initial trust establishment among unfamiliar users in large scale mobile social networks has been a challenging task. In this paper, we propose a novel scheme that enables a user to perform (1) privacy-preserving proximity test without revealing her actual location to the server or other users not within the proximity, and (2) secure handshake that establishes secure communications among stranger users within the proximity who do not have pre-shared secret. The proposed scheme is based on a novel concept, i.e. location tags, and we put forward a location tag construction method using environmental signals that provides location unforgeability. Bloom filters are used to represent the location tags efficiently and a fuzzy extractor is exploited to extract shared secrets between matching location tags. Our solution also allows users to tune their desired location privacy level and range of proximity. We conduct extensive analysis and real experiments to demonstrate the feasibility, security, and efficiency of our scheme.

1 Introduction

The proliferation of smartphones has given rise to location-based service (LBS), which has drawn considerable research attention in recent years. The key enabler of LBS is the availability of user locations, which can be easily measured and reported by a smartphone today. With LBS, users report their locations in real-time to a location server, which allows users to ubiquitously query places of interest around them, or test if their friends are within certain physical proximity. Especially, the latter is called "proximity test" [1] and has found numerous mobile applications, for example, to locate nearby friends (e.g., in a mobile social network [2]), or in an emergency situation to find nearby medical personnel (e.g., in mobile healthcare [3, 4]), only to name a few. The former is representative for

S. Foresti, M. Yung, and F. Martinelli (Eds.): ESORICS 2012, LNCS 7459, pp. 361–378, 2012.
© Springer-Verlag Berlin Heidelberg 2012

proximity test between friends, while the latter is an example of proximity test between strangers, who may not share any secret a prior.

Similar to many LBS services, there are many security and privacy concerns associated with proximity test that may prevent its widespread adoption. One of the major security concerns is that the reported locations could be easily forged by malicious users in order to exploit the benefits of proximity test service. There are many incentives for users to not report their locations truthfully. For example, in [5], a location cheating attack has been discovered in which the attacker reports false locations to gain revenue by acquiring shopping coupons. In addition, a curious user may try to profile other users' locations by setting hers to any desired place. Thus, it is essential to provide *location unforgeability* in proximity match, so as to ensure the social welfare of LBS. On the other hand, the *location privacy* is also an important concern for common users. The primary reason is that the location servers are often operated by third-party service provider such as a cloud platform, which tends to be not fully trusted by people since the location data could be leaked to the server or outsider attackers [6]. Meanwhile, users also do not want to simply let all her friends or even strangers in the system know about her location and track her down.

To design a *privacy-preserving* proximity test scheme that is also *cheat-proof* involves several challenges. First and foremost, given the mobile and distributed nature of LBS users, how can we make sure that a user's reported location is truthful without involving a trusted authority? Some researchers suggest a distributed proof approach using presence evidences from peer devices [7]. However, the proof generation involves the use of digital signature which further requires a public-key infrastructure (PKI). This would require significant modifications to the existing security architecture. In addition, the traditional cryptography-based methods do not guard against stolen/compromised keys or credentials. Ideally, each device should extract unforgeable location tags relying on its own. Second, shared keys are usually required for preserving privacy during proximity test and secure communications between matched users. However, the initial trust establishment among users in a large-scale mobile social network remains a difficult task, simply because managing shared keys with everyone else is not scalable without a trusted authority. Most existing solutions to date have relied on a-priori shared secrets between each pair of users [1, 8], which severely limits their applicability and scalability. Finally, efficiency and usability need to be achieved simultaneously. To achieve strong privacy guarantee, previous protocols either rely on computational intensive cryptographic primitives, or do so at a cost of high communication overhead.

In this paper, we propose a novel proximity test scheme that is secure against location cheating, and also performs secure handshakes between matched users to secure their subsequent communication without relying on pre-shared secrets. We focus on a general one-to-many proximity match setting, that is, user Alice can find out from a group of users the one(s) that are within certain proximity to her with the help of a semi-trusted server. In order to defeat location cheating, we propose a novel form of location representation – *spatial-temporal location tag* that is constructed from wireless signals captured in a device's surrounding environment, such as WiFi and cell tower signals. An attacker cannot forge a location tag if she is not at the corresponding location and time, due to the high freshness (entropy) and spatial variety of environmental signals. Our proposed privacy-preserving proximity test protocol is then based on the location tags. We exploit *fuzzy extractor* [9], a lightweight crypto primitive, to extract secret keys automatically between users within certain proximity, while ensuring that a user's location is revealed to neither the server nor users not within proximity. We also make use of *bloom filter* to efficiently represent users' location tags.

1.1 Our Contributions

The main contributions of this paper are as follows.

(1) We propose a novel form of user location representation – spatial-temporal location tag, to defeat location cheating attacks in LBS. We demonstrate our concept using collected real-world WiFi and cellular signal traces, and employ entropy analysis to show the feasibility of generating unforgeable location tags in practice.

(2) We propose a novel private proximity test scheme based on spatial-temporal location tags, which performs proximity test and establishes secure handshake between one user and many others at the same time. We uniquely combine bloom filter and fuzzy extractor to meet the stringent privacy and efficiency requirements. Our scheme also supports user-defined privacy level, and avoids the complexity of key management among users as it does not rely on prior-shared secrets.

(3) We carry out both thorough security analysis and performance evaluation. We first quantitatively characterize the security level of our protocol using entropy analysis. Then, using a proof-of-concept implementation, we study the system functionality and overhead, and show its superiority over existing protocols in efficiency. To the best of our knowledge, this is the first work that systematically studies unforgeable location tag and its use in location-based services.

1.2 Related Work

For privacy in location-based services, most previous works have been focusing on privacy in location queries, i.e., a model in which users report their "encrypted" location data to a central database server to perform range or k-nearest-neighbor (kNN)) queries [10–13]. Note that in this model the database stored in the server is assumed to be public. In contrast, the recently emerged *proximity test* is a different model where location-based matching is done only between users, while the users' locations are private information. In this paper we focus on proximity test.

Proximity Test: Proximity test is a special form of location sharing [6], where the information being shared is whether or not two users are within a certain range or in the same geographic region. The main privacy concern in proximity test is that user's actual location may be involuntarily revealed to either the server or other users. To this end, a privacy-preserving proximity test solution is proposed in [8], using a grid-based encryption algorithm. In [14], Mascetti et. al. proposed proximity detection schemes based on service provider (SP) filtering, in which privacy protection is achieved by user-chosen location representation that controls its granularity. However, their protocol leaks coarse-grained location information to the server. In [1], Narayanan et. al. proposed a suite of private proximity test protocols. The possibility of constructing location tags from environmental signals was noted; however, their protocols either require pre-shared secret key between users, or is not scalable and efficient enough to handle one-to-many proximity test as studied in our paper. Another proximity test scheme was proposed in [15], where users can also control their privacy levels via leveled publishing. The protocol is based on keyed hashing which suffers from dictionary attack. In [16], Lin et. al. proposed a proximity test scheme by applying shingling technique [17] on GSM cellular message. However, they did not thoroughly analyze its security. In this paper, we carry out a systematic study of unforgeable location tags and its use in proximity test, and formally analyze the security using entropy theory.

Private Matching: Our proposed scheme constructs location tags and takes the location tags as the inputs to private matching scheme to realize proximity test. Different location tag construction methods will yield different types of location tags with different data structure representation, which in turn demand different secure matching algorithms. Secure inner product computation has been proposed to compute the number of matching keywords between two binary-valued vector inputs, where each bit in the vector represents the presence or absence of a keyword [18]. Secure multi-party computation (SMC) techniques have also been used in private matching. For example, in [19], Freeman et. al. proposed a private set intersection protocol using homomorphic encryption, where the inputs to be matched are two sets of elements. In this paper, we are matching two location tags, which are environmental signals represented using bloom filter and further coded using BCH coding. The method used to realize the private matching is also very different from previous known private matching methods. Essentially our matching method is based on polynomial reconstruction. Compared to previous private matching algorithm, our scheme is more efficient because it does not involve any public key cryptography operations.

2   System Model and Design Challenges

2.1   System Overview

Our system model consists of two types of entities: a *server* and a large number of *users*. Users are subscribers of the proximity test service provided by the server. For convenience, we use *Alice* to refer to the user who initiates the proximity test, and *Bob/Charlie/David et al* to refer to the testees upon Alice's request. The centralized online server that provides the service is only responsible for assisting participants relay messages. The selection of the testee group is based on certain criteria specified in each test request. At the end of the proximity test, the testee(s) that are within the proximity of Alice will establish a secret key with Alice, while the testees faraway will learn nothing about Alice's location. The server also remains oblivious to the result of the proximity test.

Our security goal is to prevent location forgery from all users and the privacy goal is to prevent unnecessary leakage of users' location information against both other users and the server.

2.2 Design Challenges and Goals

We noticed that proximity test between strangers is usually one-to-many. Consider the following example. A patient in an emergency situation may only wish to grant nearby emergency medical technicians (EMT) access to her personal health data on her phone. Since the patient can not specify which EMT she wants to test, she can only select a group of EMTs based on certain searching criteria, e.g. EMTs from organization A. Previous client-server based solution [1] becomes inefficient in such circumstances because the test has to be done one-to-one. To cope with this problem, we choose a broadcast system model since it allows non-interactive proximity testing [1] while using less bandwidth than client-server model. Some particular challenges and our design goals based on the broadcast system model are as follows.

Distance-Bounded Key Establishment: The main motivation of our study is to address the situation when Alice wishes to test the proximity with a group of users she has not met. Hence, if a proximity test yields a positive result (i.e., two users are close by), a secure handshake protocol shall follow, allowing Alice and Bob to establish a secure channel to communicate subsequently. If the proximity test needs to be carried out between each pair of users, it will be more communication-efficient if the handshake can be performed in non-interactive fashion.

Tunable Granularity Level: One main drawback of broadcast model is users' loss of granularity control of proximity testing, since Alice can not implement different granularities for different users in the broadcast messages. In order to achieve fine-grained privacy control, our design should allow users to negotiate a mutually agreed granularity level before proximity test.

Security: The main security goal for proximity test is to design *unforgeable location tags* so that the protocol is robust against *location cheating*. A location cheating happens when one party is able to convince the other party with an untruthful location. In our case, if Bob can trick Alice into believing that he is within her proximity while he actually is not, he has successfully launched a location cheating attack. Unforgeable location is extremely important for location based services. To the best of our knowledge, we are among the first to address the location unforgeability in proximity test.

Privacy: From the server perspective, the privacy goal of the protocol is to conceal users' location information from the server. Specifically, after the proximity test, the server can not infer users' locations. From the users' perspective, users should have location privacy against each other when they are far away. When they are nearby, user should learn nothing except the fact that they are close.

Efficiency: Existing private proximity test protocols [1, 8] operate on pairs of users. If Alice wants to test a group of n users, she has to run the protocol n times with each and every user in the group. This results in a bandwidth complexity of $O(n)$ and a computation complexity of $O(n)$ at Alice side. Our goal is to design an efficient protocol where Alice and each participant only submit their location tags once to the server. This leads to a communication complexity of $O(1)$ at user's side. This represents significant efficiency improvement comparing to the existing schemes.

3   Location Tags from Environmental Signals

Introduced in [1], a *location tag* can be regarded as a token of proof associated with a point in space and time. It is a collection of signals presented at a certain location at a certain time. From the functionality point of view, a good location tag should at least have the *reproducibility* property: If two measurements at the same space and time yield tags T_1 and T_2, then T_1 and T_2 match with high probability. On the other hand, from the security point of view, in order to be cheat-proof, a good location tag must have *unpredictability* property: An adversary not at a specific place and time is unable to produce a tag that matches the tag constructed at that location at that time. Note that this feature basically requires a location tag carries high entropy.

3.1   Sources of Location Tags

In our study, we have explored two possible sources of location tags: (1) using 802.11 frames in WiFi network. (2) using control messages in 4G LTE network. We consider 802.11 frame headers as a perfect location tag source with appropriate length and sufficient entropy. In our early design, we also tried using frame bodies as location tag sources. Though the resulting location tags pass the entropy and unpredictability evaluation, the low reproducibility quality rendered the location tag unusable. The shortcoming of WiFi-based location tag is its limited range. To provide wider coverage, we also study the possibility of generating location tags through cellular network traffic. The control messages, such as the temporary cell radio-network temporary identifier (TC-RNTI), are messages sent between LTE eNodeB (i.e., base station) and users' terminals for identification and resource allocation. They are usually locally assigned by the eNodeB

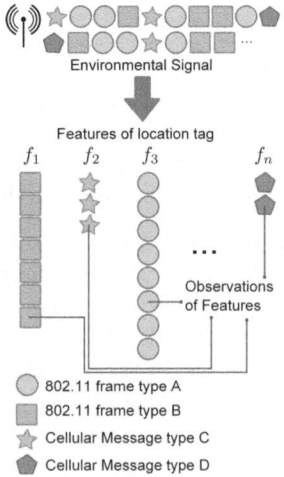

Fig. 1. Features, observations of location tag

and can be captured by all terminals. For example, the TC-RNTI is a 16-bit random number assigned to mobile terminal. Therefore, users who observe similar set of TC-RNTIs are likely under the same region.

For each location tag source, the amount of traffic necessary to generate a distinct and secure location tag is significant. Consequently, it consumes storage space and computing power of mobile devices to store and process the data. To cope with this problem, we propose to divide the traffic into different groups based on the types of frames and store them using a space-efficient data structure. As shown in figure 1, each type of 802.11 frames or cellular messages forms a *feature* of the signal source. A location tag, therefore, can be represented by a collection of features $\{f_1, f_2, ..., f_z\}$ of the signal source. Each feature consists of many elements, or *observations*, which corresponding to data capture from one 802.11 frame or cellular message. For storage efficiency, we utilize a bloom filter to represent the many observations for each feature, which we will discuss in detail in section 4.

3.2   Entropy and Unpredictability

A good location tag should be time-variant and have sufficiently high entropy in order to satisfy the unpredictability requirement. The most straight forward way to measure the entropy of location tags is by measuring the length of the random values contained in the location tag. However, it is not difficult to see that not all sources we used are truly random. Hence, the traditional method tends to overestimate the entropy amount. In order to estimate the entropy more accurately, we use techniques from statistical language processing [20], namely n-gram Markov model, to evaluate the entropy contained in location tags.

The idea is that, if a feature of a location tag is a sequence of observations, the randomness of the feature can be interpreted as the probability that an adversary successfully predicts the next observation based on previous n observations. This probability can be modeled using an n-gram Markov model. For a feature consists of N observations $w_1, ..., w_N$, the probability that the adversary successfully predicts the entire sequence is

$$P(w_1, ..., w_N) = \prod_{i=1}^{N} P(w_i | w_{i-n+1}, ..., w_{i-1}) \tag{1}$$

where the conditional probabilities can be computed from the following formula

$$P(w_i | w_{i-n+1}, ..., w_{i-1}) = \frac{C(w_{i-n+1}, ..., w_{i-1}, w_i)}{\sum_{x \in V} C(w_{i-n+1}, ..., w_{i-1}, x)} \tag{2}$$

where $C(w_1, ..., w_n)$ represents the frequency of n-gram $w_1, ..., w_n$ in the initial sequence. In our experiment, the size of the captured observations for each feature is between 2000 to 5000 depending on the type of features. Due to the computation capability of our workstation, we use a trigram model to estimate the entropy of the sequence. According to the definition of *Shannon entropy*, the entropy of the feature is calculated as

$$\mathbf{H}(w_1, ..., w_N) = P(w_1, ..., w_N) \log P(w_1, ..., w_N) \tag{3}$$

We show the entropy of 802.11 frame headers in figure 2. The beacon frames contain the least amount of entropy since they are transmitted at a regular 1,024 microseconds (μs) intervals with consecutive sequence numbers. The probing request frames, on the other hand, contain the most amount of entropy since the algorithm used to scan for access points is not explicitly defined in 802.11 standard. The interval and format of probing frames are different depending on the device drivers and user's access pattern [21]. In figure 3, we show the entropy of LTE control messages. Among them, the TC-RNTI and UL-Grant messages contain the highest entropy since the eNodeB issues different TC-RNTI and UL-Grant for the same terminal during each random access session. Compared to that, the entropy in random access preamble and C-RNTI is significantly lower due to limited formats or timing variations. Heuristic results show that location tags with entropy higher than 64 *bits* is considered "unpredictable" [1]. Therefore, only by including multiple features we can construct location tags that are unpredictable to adversaries.

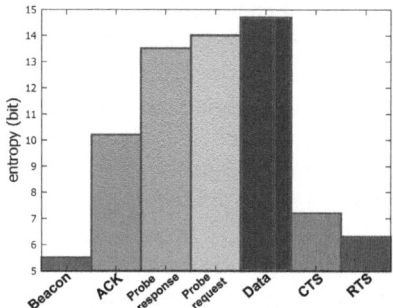

Fig. 2. 802.11 frame headers entropy

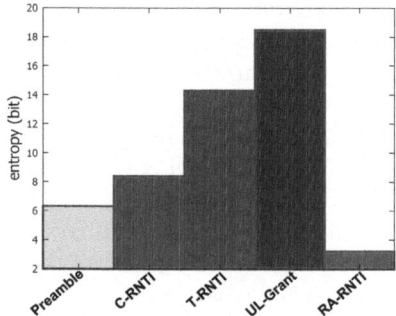

Fig. 3. LTE control messages entropy

4   SHARP: Private Proximity Test and Secure Handshake Protocol

Our private proximity test and secure handshake protocol, **SHARP**, is a two-step protocol designed for one-to-many proximity test between users that share no prior-secrets. During the first step, upon receiving the request from Alice, the server identifies a group of users designated by Alice and notifies users to construct their location tags simultaneously. Alice embeds a temporary session key K in her location tag and sends it to the group. During the second step, users in the group first try to extract K. Only those within a coarse-grained proximity of Alice can succeed, who then return a keyed hash of their current locations using grid map representation to Alice for fine-grained matching. We exploit bloom filter, a space-efficient randomized data structure, to compactly represent everyone's location tag while using fuzzy extractor technique to accomplish secure handshake. The protocol has the following main advantages: (1) it is far more scalable in that it effectively filters out users who are far away during key establishment without letting Alice interact with each and every one of them. (2) it allows users to control granularity by negotiating the size of cells on the grid map.

4.1   Bloom Filter and Fuzzy Extractor

A Bloom filter is a space-efficient probabilistic data structure that is used to succinctly represent a set in order to support membership queries [22]. A bloom filter is a bit array of length m, and k independent hash functions $H_1(), H_2(), ..., H_k()$: $\{0,1\}^* \to \{0,1\}^{\log m}$ are used to insert and query the original data elements in the array by their hashed locations. In a bloom filter based membership test, false positives are possible, but false negatives are not. In our case, we represent each feature of a location tag with a bloom filter by adding all the observations into the bloom filter.

A fuzzy extractor [9] is a pair of randomized procedures, *generate* and *reproduce*, that allow one to extract some randomness value from an input and then successfully reproduce it from any inputs that is similar to the original input. In our case, the randomness value represents the temporary session key K, whereas the input represents the location tag. In other words, only a user with a similar location tag can reproduce K. In [9], Dodis et. al. proposed using *error correcting code* as a building block of fuzzy extractor. Particularly, we use the BCH error correcting code in our implementation. It has been shown that BCH code can be decoded in polynomial time w.r.t. the *weight* of the received corrupted codeword using syndrome decoding. The details of syndrome decoding can be found in [9, 23].

4.2   System Setup

As shown in figure 4, the system adopts a *grid reference* to represent locations, where grid indices represent areas covered by grid cells. Users share a list of coordinate-axis aligned grid system $G = \{g_0, ..., g_l\}$ of different levels. At each level l, the grid cell size, i.e., width and height, is fixed and equal to $L(l)$. Let $L(0) > L(1) > ... > L(l)$. Additionally, the system defines a security parameter κ, a cryptographic hash function $\mathcal{H}(\cdot) : \{0,1\}^* \to \{0,1\}^s$, and a keyed cryptographic hash function $\mathcal{H}'(\cdot, \cdot) : \{0,1\}^s \times \{0,1\}^* \to \{0,1\}^s$ (can be an HMAC instantiated by SHA-256). Note that, $\mathcal{H}$, $\mathcal{H}'$ and G are known by all users and the server.

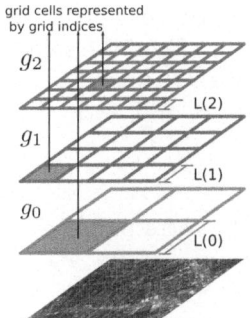

grid cells represented by grid indices

g_2

g_1

g_0

L(2)

L(1)

L(0)

Fig. 4. Grid reference system

4.3   Proximity-Based Filtering

The protocol starts by Alice sending her test request to the server, declaring the user group she wants to test. Upon receiving the request, the server broadcasts a synchronization signal to Alice and her intended testing group, and all users construct their location tags by collecting observations from a set of features $\{f_1, f_2, ..., f_z\}$. For each f, Alice constructs a bloom filter bit array B_f with a given false positive rate p.

Alice adds each observation w of f into B_f by hashing it to k positions in the bit array using $H_1(), H_2(), ..., H_k()$. Alice then computes t "syndromes"[1] using the following equation, where t is the number of errors that the BCH code can correct:

$$S_i = \sum_{x \in B_f} x^i \quad i \in \{1, 3, ..., 2t-1\} \tag{4}$$

where x represents the index of those positions in B_f that are set to 1. The computations are done within a Galois Field. Assume the resulting syndrome set for each B_f is $\mathsf{syn}(B_f) = (S_1, S_3, ..., S_{2t-1})$. Alice generates a location tag T that can tolerate up to t errors in each feature:

$$T = \{\mathsf{syn}(B_{f_1}), ..., \mathsf{syn}(B_{f_z})\} \tag{5}$$

Next, in order to embed a secret session key in the location tag, Alice creates a fuzzy extractor by hashing all the location features by computing $B_0 = \mathcal{H}(B_{f_1} \| B_{f_2} \| \cdots \| B_{f_z})$. Alice then generates a κ-bit random number (helper string) y, and computes $K = \mathcal{H}'(B_0, y)$ as the temporary session key. Alice can control testing granularity by choosing a subset $G_{Alice} \subset G$. Let $|B| = \{|B_{f_1}|, ..., |B_{f_z}|\}$, representing the length of all bloom filters. Together, Alice sends a message $m_a = \{\text{"Alice"}, T, |B|, y, G_{Alice}\}$ to the server. The server broadcasts m_a to the testing user group.

4.4   Fine-Grained Proximity Test

Upon receiving m_a, Bob tries to extract Alice's temporary session key using his observations of the features set. For each feature, Bob creates a bloom filter bit array B'_f of the same length as B_f and uses $\mathsf{syn}(B_f)$ to correct the difference between B_f and B'_f. Assume the syndromes of B'_f is $\mathsf{syn}(B'_f) = (S'_1, S'_3, ..., S'_{2t-1})$, Let $\sigma_i = S'_i - S_i$. The *error detecting vector* [9] of B'_f is:

$$\mathsf{syn}(B'_f) = (\sigma_1, \sigma_3, ..., \sigma_{2t-1}) \tag{6}$$

The corresponding *error correcting vector* $\mathsf{supp}(B'_f)$, which represents the difference of B_f and B'_f, can only be computed correctly from $\mathsf{syn}(B'_f)$ when $\mathsf{supp}(B'_f) < t$ [9].

$$\mathsf{supp}(B'_f) = B_f \; \Delta \; B'_f \triangleq \{x \in B_f \cup B'_f | x \notin B_f \cap B'_f\} \tag{7}$$

---

[1] Intuitively, a syndrome is an error checking value of a codeword (here, B_f is considered as a codeword).

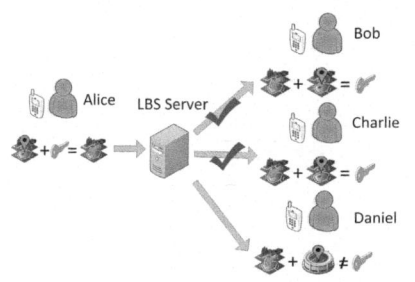

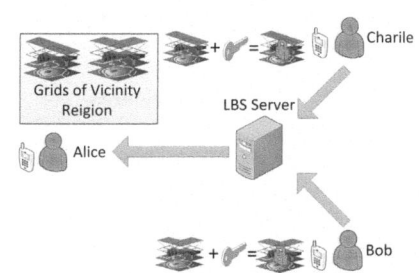

(a) Initial Proximity-based Filtering: Alice embeds a secret key in her location tag

(b) Fine-Grained Proximity Test: Alice learns users' locations by evaluating the grid indices

Fig. 5. Two steps of SHARP

When Bob and Alice are nearby, the difference between B_f and B'_f is smaller than t. Bob succeeds in computing $\mathrm{syn}(B'_f)$ and obtains the original B_f through

$$B_f = B'_f \ \Delta \ \mathrm{supp}(B'_f) \tag{8}$$

Once Bob reconstructed all the B_fs, he can derive the original B_0 and recover $K = \mathcal{H}'(B_0, y)$. Bob can control the testing granularity by searching through G_{Alice} to find a reasonable granularity level and blind his grid index b with K, by computing $B = \mathcal{H}'(K, b||\text{"Bob"})$. If Bob does not agree on any of the granularity levels, he has two choices: (1) submit nothing indicating he does not allow Alice to carry out fine-grained proximity test. (2) submit multiple location index numbers to mask his actual location. Finally, Bob sends the message $m_b = \{\text{"Bob"}, B\}$ back to server.

The server forwards m_b to Alice. Alice can then searches through all the grid cells that she regarded as in her proximity; if she can find one b that is within one of her nearby cells and satisfies $\mathcal{H}'(K, b||\text{"Bob"}) = B$, then Alice learns that Bob is located in b. After that, Alice knows a list of users within her proximity range, and she can choose to securely communicate with one (or more) of them using the session key K.

Note that, an attacker may try to send back multiple malformed responses to Alice to exhaust her resources. However, dealing with denial-of-service attack is out of the scope of this paper. We can use existing methods, for example, IPSec or TLS where the server can authenticate the users.

5   Security and Privacy Analysis

5.1   Entropy Loss and Location Unforgeability

SHARP provides unforgeable (unpredictable) location tags. In section 3 we evaluated the entropy contained in location tag sources. However, best practices mandate that we also consider the entropy loss during data processing. In this

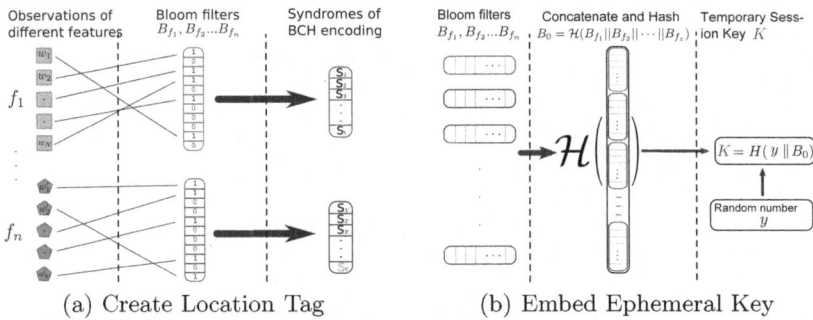

(a) Create Location Tag   (b) Embed Ephemeral Key

Fig. 6. Construct location tag using fuzzy extractor and bloom filter

section, we derive the total entropy loss in our design. Consequently, we show that total amount of entropy loss is limited and the remaining guessing entropy of location tag remains high.

Assuming the location source contains h_0 bits of entropy. In our protocol, the entropy loss happens in two places: (1) when we pack the location tag sources into bloom filters. (2) when we generate the fuzzy extractor from bloom filters. Note that when packing a set of elements into a bloom filter, the entropy loss is related to the probability rate of false positive [22]. Consider a bloom filter of length m is used to represent a set of n_b elements. From [22], the probability of a false positive is

$$p = (1 - (1 - \frac{1}{m})^{kn_b})^k \approx (1 - e^{-kn_b/m})^k = (1 - v)^k \qquad (9)$$

where $v = 1 - p^{1/k}$ is probability of a bit being set to 1 in the bloom filter. Hence the entropy loss during bloom filter construction is

$$h_1 = (1 + v \log v + (1 - v) \log(1 - v))h_0 \qquad (10)$$

By taking the derivative of the formula, p has a global minimum value $(1/2)^k = (0.6185)^{m/n}$ when $k = (\ln 2) \cdot (m/n)$. However, we shall explicitly note that in our design, balancing among m, n, k to achieve minimum p is not our main focus.

The second entropy loss happens during fuzzy extractor construction. In general, [24] shows that the entropy loss of a fuzzy extractor is upper-bounded by its entropy loss on the uniform distribution of inputs. In particular, the input of the fuzzy extractor in our design is the bloom filter bit array of length m. Assuming we apply BCH code with code length n_B to the bit array. Since the BCH code family is optimal for $t \ll n_B$ by the Hamming bound [23]. the entropy loss of syndrome fuzzy extractor with a BCH code is

$$h_2 = \frac{t(h_0 - h_1)}{n_B} \log(n_B + 1) \qquad (11)$$

The overall entropy loss of our design is thus

$$h = h_1 + h_2 \tag{12}$$

Particularly, in Table 1, we show the entropy loss using a location tag source of entropy equal to 64 bits. In our evaluation, the average length of the bloom filter is $m = 2^{10} = 1024(bits)$. The total entropy loss is around 7.8 bits. Therefore, the remaining guessing entropy remains high to secure the protocol against location cheating attack.

Table 1. Entropy Loss

false positive rate	error tolerance	entropy loss
0.01	10/1024	3.7 *bits*
0.01	30/1024	7.1 *bits*
0.1	10/1024	4.3 *bits*
0.1	30/1024	8.7 *bits*

5.2 Location Privacy

When Alice and Bob are far apart, the set difference between their location tags, A and B, will be greater than t. This means Bob can not correct all the errors using BCH syndrome, and therefore his view of Alice's location tag is indistinguishable from random. Next, when multiple users $b_1, ..., b_n$ outside of Alice's proximity range collude, denoting their location tags by $B_1, ...B_n$, we have

$$A \; \Delta \; B_i > t \quad 1 \leq i \leq n \tag{13}$$

Assuming B_is are pairwise disjoint. It is easy to see that the symmetric difference between the joint location tags $B = B_1 \bigcup B_2, ..., \bigcup B_n$ and A is still greater than t. Hence, Alice has privacy when multiple unmatched users collude. The server can not learn Alice's location or secret session key, since it is infeasible to record the environmental signal of all locations at all times.

We should note that unlike previous work [1] in our protocol, when Alice and Bob are nearby, Alice still has location privacy against Bob. The reasons is: Bob only gains knowledge of Alice's rough whereabouts during the key establishment step. In the second step, Bob does not receive any message from Alice, therefore can not know Alice's exact location even if the matching result is positive. Bob, too, can protect his location privacy against Alice by hiding his actual location within multiple grid indices. Compared with protocol using expensive PTSI operation, we achieve the same privacy level with less computational cost.

6 Experimental Evaluation

6.1 Experiment Setup

To test our design, we carry out a proof-of-concept experiment on the 802.11g WLAN network on campus. We use Dell inspiron 5100 with a 32-bit, 533MHz

Pentium 4 CPU to log the WLAN traffic at varying distances. Using the logged data, we evaluate the performance of **SHARP** from the following aspects: (1) we measured the success probability of extracting temporary key using location tags. (2) we evaluated how the success rate is affected by the size of the bloom filter, clock synchronization error, and user mobility. (3) we measured the CPU time required to generate the location tag and to extract the temporary key. The detailed experiment configuration is as follows.

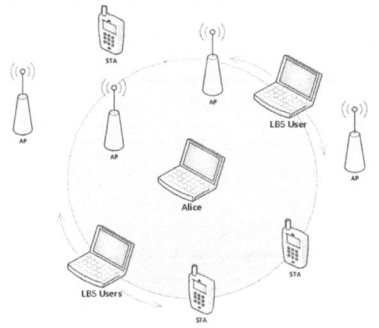
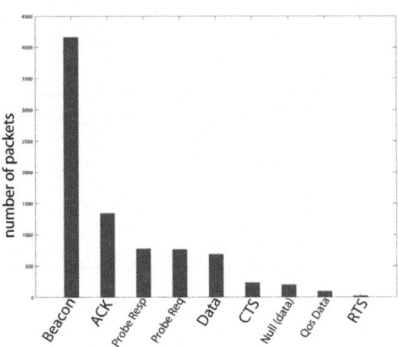

Fig. 7. Experiment configuration   **Fig. 8.** Traffic Summary

1. We deployed three client laptops at different locations running Wireshark in the promiscuous mode. All three laptops are loosely synchronized before the test.

2. We configured one of the laptop to act as Alice. Before each capture, Alice sends out the synchronization signal to state the starting time of next capture. The other two laptops were configured as testees who participate in the proximity test. They receive the synchronization signal and schedule the next capture. Each capture is carried out for ten seconds. Captures are repeated for multiple times at the radius of $0meter$, $5meter$, $10meter$, $15meter$, $20meter$, $25meter$, $30meter$ and $35meter$.

3. After each capture, the program running on Alice reads frames from the capture ($.pcap$) file and sorts them according to the frame type of the packets. It generates the location tags based on captured packets and sends the size of the bloom filters to the other two laptops. Upon receiving these parameters, the other two laptops generate their location tags.

In figure 8, we show the histogram of various frame types from traffic analysis. During the test, we saw an average of 8432 packets on channel one. Half of them are 802.11 beacon packets. The rest of the packets are ACK, Probe response, Probe request, etc. In table 2, we show that an average of 105 different MAC addresses was detected during the test. 95 of them are 802.11 client stations whereas 10 of them are 802.11 access points. According to [25], our testing environment can be considered as a typical WLAN networks scenario in metropolitan areas.

Table 2. Number of 802.11 station and access points detected during the test

Wireless Stations			Access Points		
avg	max	min	avg	max	min
95	121	73	10	13	9

6.2 Location Tag Reproducibility

Figure 9(a) shows users' success probability of extracting Alice's temporary session key at various distances. Interestingly, there is a clear cut-off distance in the graph. Within 30 meters, the difference between location tags is fairly small which indicates Bob can successfully reproduce Alice's location tag. Beyond 30 meters, with quickly increased probability Bob won't be able to reproduce Alice's location tag due to the larger difference between location tags. In other words, the location tags we tested are either nearly disjoint or nearly identical. Thus, an efficient test that can accept near-identical sets and reject near-disjoint set is sufficient for our purpose. In [16], Lin *et al.* showed similar result using paging channel messages in GSM cellular networks. Hence, with all these findings, we argue that BCH error correcting coding approach with small t is superior to private cardinality threshold set matching approach [19] for our purpose in term of practicality and usability.

Bloom Filter and Reproducibility. In figure 9(b), we show how the size of the bloom filter affects location tag reproducibility. It appears that when we increase the false positive rate of the bloom filter, the success probability at the far side increases. The reason is that increasing the false positive rate f is equivalent to reducing the length of the bit array. When the length of a bloom filter is small, the probability that each bit in the bit array being set to 1 increases. If the probability increases to 100%, the bloom filter contains no information entropy. The corresponding location tag becomes independent of location. Hence the difference between location tags is always 0 regardless of the distance. Clearly, there is a balance between the entropy loss versus the location tag reproducibility. When bloom filter is large, the entropy loss is small, yet it requires Bob to have stronger error correcting capability to reproduce the location tag. When the bloom filter is small, the location tag reproducibility is high, yet, the location tag itself become less distinct.

Clock Synchronization Error and Reproducibility. We tested the protocol's performance against clock synchronization error. As shown in figure 9(c), when users did not start the location feature extraction process simultaneously, the average difference between location tags increased. Yet, the cut-off distance stays the same. Hence, our protocol only requires very loose time synchronization between users.

Mobility and Reproducibility. We evaluated how the users' mobility affects the performance of the protocol. In the experiment, we let Bob randomly move slowly around Alice. Compared with the stationary case, Bob's chance of successfully extracting Alice's secret key slightly increases. The reason is when Bob is moving, he is able to see more access points and wireless stations compare to a stationary testee. However, the advantage Bob gains by moving is minimal since each capture window is only 10 seconds.

6.3   Storage and Communication Efficiency

The use of the bloom filter and BCH encoding during location feature extraction reduces the communication cost of the protocol. In this section, we show the location tag size and location generation time of our protocol.

Location Tag Size. We compared the size of the location tag of our design and the location tag generated through other polynomial based reconstruction [1]. We defined the fuzzy match threshold as follows. Assume a total number of n packets are captured. For our protocol, in order to generate a total of (n, t) fuzzy match, the number of t is distributed into each location tag source according to the total number of observations from that source. For example, if a location feature contains m packets, we create a $(m, \frac{tm}{n})$ fuzzy match. In [1], the location tag is generated by create a $n - t$ degree polynomial.

As shown in figure 9(e), if the size of each packet's hash value is k bit, the size of the location tag generated in [1] is approximately $2(n - t)k$, whereas the location tag generated with SHARP is approximately $t \ln(\frac{n \ln(p)}{m})$. SHARP clearly shows superior performance to polynomial based location tag construction. This is due to the usage of bloom filter and the fact that the location tag in SHARP only consists of the syndromes of the BCH code.

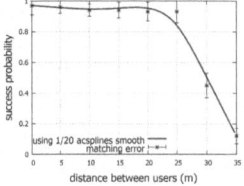 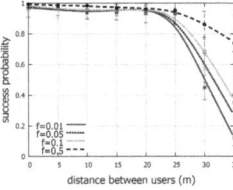 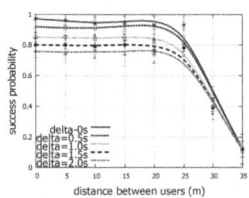

(a) Probability of successful key establishment versus distance

(b) Probability of successful key establishment versus false positive rate of bloom filters

(c) Probability of successful key establishment versus clock synchronization error

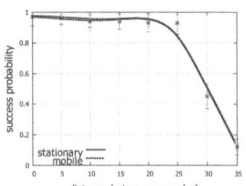 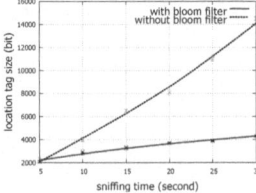 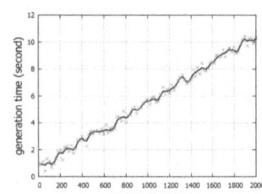

(d) Probability of successful key establishment versus mobility

(e) Location tag size versus sniffing time

(f) Location tag generation time versus number of observations

Location Tag Generation Time. In Figure 9(f), we show the location tag generation time of our design. The main part of the generation time is contributed by: (1) Adding element to the bloom filter, and (2) calculating BCH syndromes. In (1), in order to add one element to the bloom filter, k hash functions are used. In our implementation, we use a 160 bit SHA-1 hash function which costs around $0.5ms$ to finish on the laptop. The total time of part (1) will grow linearly with the number of observations. In (2) the time consumption of BCH encoding is polynomial in $\log n$, where n is the size of the bloom filter [9]. Therefore, the time consumption of (1) dominates the overall location tag generation time.

7   Conclusion

In this paper, we address the privacy and security issues of proximity test in location based services. We aim at letting users to find others who are within a certain geographical region or range with a help of a oblivious server, without pre-established secret keys while hiding user location information from the server. In order to prevent location cheating, we propose to use multiple types of real-time and location-dependent environmental signals to construct location tag. The location tag is the key to proximity matching, where fuzzy extractor is exploited to extract a secret key from two matching users. In addition, the location tag is organized in a bloom filter, such that users can choose their own matching sensitivity at ease via tuning the parameter of the bloom filter. Furthermore, we also improve the accuracy and fine-grainedness of the proximity test using geographical grid and keyed hashing. We allow user to control granularity by negotiating between different grid cell sizes. Through both theoretical analysis and experimental evaluation, we show that our location tag has enough freshness and entropy to defend against location cheating. Our scheme is mostly non-interactive, does not require strict synchronization, and enjoys high scalability and efficiency.

Acknowledgments. This work was partially supported by US National Science Foundation under grants CNS-1155988, CNS-1156318, and CNS-0910531.

References

1. Narayanan, A., Thiagarajan, N., Lakhani, M., Hamburg, M., Boneh, D.: Location privacy via private proximity testing. In: Proc. 18th Annual Network & Distributed System Security Symposium (2011)
2. Li, M., Cao, N., Yu, S., Lou, W.: Findu: Privacy-preserving personal profile matching in mobile social networks. In: Proc. 30th IEEE International Conference on Computer Communications (2011)
3. Li, M., Lou, W., Ren, K.: Data security and privacy in wireless body area networks. Journal of Wireless Communications 17(1) (2010)
4. Liang, X., Lu, R., Chen, L., Lin, X., Shen, X.: Pec: A privacy-preserving emergency call scheme for mobile healthcare social networks. Journal of Communications and Networks 13(2) (2011)
5. He, W., Liu, X., Ren, M.: Location cheating: A security challenge to location-based social network services. In: Proc. 31st IEEE International Conference on Distributed Computing Systems (2011)

6. Tsai, J.Y., Kelley, P.G., Cranor, L.F., Sadeh, N.: Location-sharing technologies: Privacy risks and controls. I/S: A Journal of Law & Policy for the Information Society 6, 119–317 (2010)
7. Zhu, Z., Cao, G.: Applaus: A privacy-preserving location proof updating system for location-based services. In: Proc. 30th IEEE International Conference on Computer Communications (2011)
8. Šikšnys, L., Thomsen, J.R., Šaltenis, S., Yiu, M.L., Andersen, O.: A Location Privacy Aware Friend Locator. In: Mamoulis, N., Seidl, T., Pedersen, T.B., Torp, K., Assent, I. (eds.) SSTD 2009. LNCS, vol. 5644, pp. 405–410. Springer, Heidelberg (2009)
9. Dodis, Y., Ostrovsky, R., Reyzin, L., Smith, A.: Fuzzy Extractors: How to Generate Strong Keys from Biometrics and Other Noisy Data. In: Cachin, C., Camenisch, J.L. (eds.) EUROCRYPT 2004. LNCS, vol. 3027, pp. 523–540. Springer, Heidelberg (2004)
10. Meyerowitz, J., Choudhury, R.R.: Hiding stars with fireworks: Location privacy through camouflage. In: Proc. 15th ACM Annual International Conference on Mobile Computing and Networking (2009)
11. Talukder, N., Ahamed, S.I.: Preventing multi-query attack in location-based services. In: Proc. 3rd ACM Conference on Wireless Network Security (2010)
12. Ghinita, G., Kalnis, P., Khoshgozaran, A., Shahabi, C., Tan, K.L.: Private queries in location based services: Anonymizers are not necessary. In: Proc. ACM SIGMOD International Conference on Management of Data (2008)
13. Chang, W., Wu, J., Tan, C.C.: Enhancing mobile social network privacy. In: Proc. IEEE Global Communications Conference (2011)
14. Mascetti, S., Bettini, C., Freni, D., Wang, X.S., Jajodia, S.: Privacy-aware proximity based services. In: Proc. 10th IEEE International Conference on Mobile Data Management: Systems, Services and Middleware (2009)
15. Šikšnys, L., Thomsen, J.R., Šaltenis, S., Yiu, M.L.: Private and flexible proximity detection in mobile social networks. In: Proc. 11th IEEE International Conference on Mobile Data Management (2010)
16. Lin, Z., Kune, D.F., Hoppe, N.: Efficient private proximity testing with gsm location sketches. In: Proc. 32nd International Cryptology Conference (2012)
17. Broder, A.Z., Glassman, S.C., Manasse, M.S., Zweig, G.: Syntactic clustering of the web. Computer Networks and ISDN Systems 29(8-13), 1157–1166 (1997)
18. Wong, W.K., Cheung, D.W., Kao, B., Mamoulis, N.: Secure knn computation on encrypted databases. In: Proc. 35th ACM SIGMOD International Conference on Management of Data (2009)
19. Freedman, M.J., Nissim, K., Pinkas, B.: Efficient Private Matching and Set Intersection. In: Cachin, C., Camenisch, J.L. (eds.) EUROCRYPT 2004. LNCS, vol. 3027, pp. 1–19. Springer, Heidelberg (2004)
20. Manning, C.D., Schütze, H.: Foundations of Statistical Natural Language Processing. MIT Press (1999)
21. Franklin, J., McCoy, D., Tabriz, P., Neagoe, V., Randwyk, J.V., Sicker, D.: Passive data link layer 802.11 wireless device driver fingerprinting. In: Proc. 15th USENIX Security Symposium (2006)
22. Mitzenmacher, M.: Compressed bloom filters. IEEE/ACM Transactions on Networking (TON) 10(5), 604–612 (2002)
23. Lint, J.H.V.: Introduction to Coding Theory, vol. 86. Springer (1999)
24. Reyzin, L.: Entropy loss is maximal for uniform inputs. Technical report, Boston University Computer Science Department (2007)
25. Shrikhande, K.V., White, I.M., Rudee Wonglumsom, D., Gemelos, S.M., Rogge, M.S., Fukashiro, Y., Avenarius, M., Kazovsky, L.G.: Hornet: A packet-over-wdm multiple access metropolitan area ring network. Journal on Selected Areas in Communications 18(10), 2004–2016 (2000)

Secure Proximity Detection for NFC Devices Based on Ambient Sensor Data

Tzipora Halevi[1], Di Ma[3], Nitesh Saxena[2], and Tuo Xiang[3]

[1] Polytechnic Institute of New York University
[2] University of Alabama at Birmingham
[3] University of Michigan-Dearborn

Abstract. In certain applications, it is important for a remote server to securely determine whether or not two mobile devices are in close physical proximity. In particular, in the context of an NFC transaction, the bank server can validate the transaction if both the NFC phone and reader are precisely at the same location thereby preventing a form of a devastating relay attack against such systems.

In this paper, we develop secure proximity detection techniques based on the information collected by ambient sensors available on NFC mobile phones, such as audio and light data. These techniques can work under the current payment infrastructure, and offer many advantages. First, they do not require the users to perform explicit actions, or make security decisions, during the transaction – just bringing the devices close to each other is sufficient. Second, being based on environmental attributes, they make it very hard, if not impossible, for the adversary to undermine the security of the system. Third, they provide a natural protection to users' location privacy as the explicit location information is never transmitted to the server. Our experiments with the proposed techniques developed on off-the-shelf mobile phones indicate them to be quite effective in significantly raising the bar against known attacks, without affecting the NFC usage model. Although the focus of this work is on NFC phones, our approach will also be broadly applicable to RFID tags or related payment cards equipped with on-board audio or light sensors.

Keywords: NFC, RFID, relay attacks, context awareness, sensors.

1 Introduction

Radio Frequency Identification (RFID) systems are becoming increasingly ubiquitous in both public and private domains enabling computerized identification of objects and individuals. An RFID system usually consists of RFID tags and readers. Tags are miniaturized wireless radio devices that store information, such as a unique identification number, about their corresponding subject. Readers broadcast queries to tags in their radio transmission ranges for information contained in tags and tags reply with such information. Some of the prominent RFID applications include supply chain management (inventory control) [1],

S. Foresti, M. Yung, and F. Martinelli (Eds.): ESORICS 2012, LNCS 7459, pp. 379–396, 2012.

e-passports [2], credit cards [3], driver's licenses [4, 5], vehicle systems (toll collection or car key) [6, 7, 8], access cards (building, parking or public transport) [9], and medical implants [10].

NFC, or Near Field Communication [11], is an upcoming RFID technology which allows devices, such as smartphones, to have both RFID tag and reader functionality. In particular, the use of NFC-equipped mobile devices as payment tokens (such as the Google Wallet app) is considered to be the next generation of payment system and the latest buzz in the US financial industry. Technological companies, such as Google and Apple, financial institutions, such as JPM, Visa, Mastercard and Citi, and telecommunication providers, such as Verizon and T-Mobile, have worked together and started launching test programs of NFC based payment system in the US [12]. It is predicted that mobile payments using NFC will reach $670 billion by 2015 [13].

Due to the inherent weaknesses of underlying wireless radio communication, NFC systems are plagued with a wide variety of security and privacy threats similar to the RFID systems [14]. In particular, the threat of *relay attacks* on such devices is real. One class of these attacks is referred to as "ghost-and-leech" [15]. In this attack, an adversary, called a "leech," relays the information surreptitiously read from a legitimate RFID tag to a colluding entity known as a "ghost." The ghost can then relay the received information to a corresponding legitimate reader and vice versa in the other direction. This way a ghost and leech pair can succeed in impersonating a legitimate RFID tag without actually possessing the device.

The focus of this paper is on a more severe form of relay attacks, called "reader-and-ghost". It involves a malicious reader and an unsuspecting owner intending to make a transaction [16][1]. In this attack, the malicious reader, serving the role of a leech and colluding with the ghost, can fool the owner of the card into approving a transaction which she did not intend to make (e.g., paying for a diamond purchase made by the adversary while the owner only intends to pay for food). We note that addressing this problem requires *transaction verification*, i.e., validation that the tag is indeed authorizing the intended payment amount. The feasibility of executing reader-and-ghost attacks has already been demonstrated on the Chip-and-PIN credit card system [16].

With an expected ubiquitous deployment of NFC systems, there is a pressing need for the development of security primitives to defeat the relay attacks. Doing so, however, presents a unique and formidable set of challenges. Although the NFC devices are not as constrained as the stand-alone RFID tags, the inherent difficulty stems from the unusual usability requirements imposed by NFC applications (originally geared for automation). Consequently, solutions designed for NFC systems need to satisfy the requirements of the underlying applications in terms of not only *efficiency* and *security*, but also *usability*.

---

[1] In contrast to the "ghost-and-leech" attack, the owner in the "reader-and-ghost" attack is aware of the interrogation from the (malicious) reader.

1.1 Sensing-Enabled Automated Defense

Although a variety of solutions to address the reader-and-leech attacks exist, many of them do not fully meet the requirements of the underlying NFC applications in terms of (one or more of): efficiency, security and usability. We discuss prior work in Section 2.

In an attempt to resolve this situation, this paper proposes the use of sensing technologies for preventing reader-and-ghost relay attacks without necessitating any changes to the traditional NFC phone usage model, i.e., without incorporating any explicit user involvement beyond what is practiced today.

The premise of our work is a current technological advancement that enables many NFC phones with low-cost sensing capabilities. Various types of sensors have been incorporated on many NFC phones, including accelerometers, microphones, and light sensors. This new generation of NFC phones can facilitate numerous promising applications for ubiquitous sensing and computation. They also suggest new ways of providing security and privacy services by leveraging the unique properties of the physical environment or physical status of the phone (or its owner).

The physical environment measured by these sensors offers a rich set of attributes that are unique in space, time, and to individual objects. These attributes – such as sound and light – reflect either the current condition of a phone's surrounding environment or the condition of the phone (or its owner) itself. An NFC phone can therefore acquire useful *contextual information*, and this information can be utilized for enhanced security.

1.2 Our Contributions

In this paper, we show that the contextual information can be effectively leveraged to defend against the reader-and-ghost attacks on NFC devices.

Specifically, we develop a new transaction verification mechanism that can determine the proximity (or lack thereof) between a valid server and a valid phone by *correlating certain sensor data* extracted from the two devices. This is based on the assumption that certain ambient information, extracted by the NFC device and reader at the same time (transaction time), will be highly correlated if the two devices are in close physical proximity. Said differently, if a certain sensor attached to the server and the same type of sensor attached to the phone report mismatching ambient information, this will indicate that the server and phone are (most likely) not at the same location or close to each other. In particular, we demonstrate that *audio sensors* (microphones) and *ambient light sensors* can be effectively used for such transaction verification. We present several techniques that can be used for determining similarity between two short audio signals as well as between the light data extracted by the valid NFC phone and valid reader, and show that these techniques are quite useful in significantly raising the bar against the reader-and-ghost attacks.

Our approach can be seamlessly deployed on the current payment infrastructure, and offers many advantages. First, it does not require the users to perform explicit actions, or make security decisions, during the transaction – just bringing the devices close to each other is sufficient. Second, being based on environmental attributes, the approach makes it very hard, if not impossible, for the adversary to undermine the security of the system. Third, it provides a natural protection to users' location privacy as the explicit location information is never transmitted to the server. Our experiments with the proposed techniques developed on popular mobile platforms (Java ME and Android) indicate them to be fairly robust to errors and effective for off-the-shelf mobile phones.

1.3   Scope of Our Work

Errors are inherent to any context recognition approach. Our approach is no different in this regard in that it would yield non-zero, although quite low, false positive and false negative rates in practice. Thus, the proposed approaches can not guarantee absolute security and usability. However, our technique significantly raises the bar even for sophisticated adversaries without affecting the NFC phones usage model. Moreover, although the proposed technique can work in a stand-alone fashion, it can also be used in conjunction with other security mechanisms, such as cryptographic distance bounding protocols [16], to provide stronger cross-layer security protection. In addition, our proximity detection approach is broadly applicable in the realm of other wireless (or wired) devices equipped with sensors.

1.4   Paper Outline

The rest of the paper is organized as follows. We review related work in Section 2. We present, in Section 3, the current payment system and our threat model, and provide a higher level overview of our proximity detection approach. Next, we elaborate on our proximity detection techniques based on audio and light sensor data in Section 4. Finally, we report on our experimentation and associated results in Section 5, followed by a discussion in Section 6. Section 7 provides concluding remarks.

2   Related Prior Work

In this section, we discuss prior work that is applicable to address the problem of reader-and-ghost attacks.

The distance bounding protocols have been explicitly proposed for preventing reader-and-ghost relay attacks [16, 6]. A distance bounding protocol is a cryptographic challenge-response authentication protocol which allows the verifier to measure an upper-bound of its distance from the prover [17]. (We stress that traditional "non-distance-bounding" cryptographic authentication protocols are completely ineffective in defending against relay attacks). Using this protocol, a valid RFID reader can verify whether the valid tag is within a close proximity thereby detecting both ghost-and-leech and reader-and-ghost relay attacks

[16, 6]. However, these protocols may not be currently feasible on commodity devices (such as NFC phones) due to their high sensitivity to time delay or need for special-purpose hardware.

A straight-forward solution to the reader-and-ghost attacks is to show the transaction details (e.g., the amount of transaction) on the NFC device itself [18], and have the user validate the details. This approach, however, is problematic because it requires explicit user involvement that may lead to the success of an attack. In particular, users will need to compare the amount/currency displayed on the reader's screen and that on their NFC phone's screen. If they make an error in the comparison, they may still be susceptible to the attack. Human users are known to make such mistakes (as demonstrated in [19]).

As suggested in [16], and demonstrated in [20], GPS data can be used in a straight-forward manner to determine whether the NFC phone and the reader are in close proximity. As opposed to our sensor-centric approach, however, the use of GPS data relies on an additional infrastructure (GPS). GPS is also known to not work well in an indoor environment (which is where the payment transactions take place commonly). Moreover, since GPS information is directly sent to the payment server, this approach raises location privacy concerns – users' location during the transaction is revealed to a potentially untrusted third party.

Our idea of secure proximity detection based on sensor information is related to the Bump application [21]. This application associates two phones based on a mutually shared "bump" event. However, there are significant differences between the two approaches. First, we work with audio/light data, while Bump uses accelerometer as well as GPS data. Second, we do not require users to explicitly Bump their devices; rather only bringing the phone close to the reader is sufficient (a gesture that already needs to be performed as part of the payment process). Third, we develop open-source sensor data correlation and similarity detection techniques, whereas the techniques employed by the Bump server are not transparent.

3 Background and Overview

3.1 Payment Infrastructure, and Threat Model

EMV, named after its creators, Europay, Mastercard and Visa, is a global standard for debit and credit card payments. Payment systems based on EMV have been introduced across the world, known by a variety of different names such as "Chip and PIN" [16]. Mastercards PayPass is another EMV compatible "contactless" payment protocol. Figure 1 presents a simplified version of the EMV-based mobile payment system which consists of three entities of interest: the cardholder, the merchant and the issuer bank which issues the card. The payment application (such as Google Wallet) on the NFC-enabled phone of a cardholder stores the details such as the credit card number, name of the owner, and expiration date. It also stores a symmetric key shared with its issuer bank. The Point-of-Sale (PoS) terminal at the merchant side is equipped with NFC Contactless Readers (such as MasterCard PayPass). A transaction starts with the merchant issuing a challenge to the payment app. The app calculates a cryptographic response based on the challenge and other information using the key shared with the issuer bank. It then transfers the response to the merchant terminal using the NFC chip on the mobile device. The response is next forwarded by the terminal to the issuer bank which verifies the response and approves the transaction, if authentication is successful.

In the rest of this paper, we use the terms card, card holder and (NFC) phone interchangeably, all depicting the valid user's device involved in a transaction.

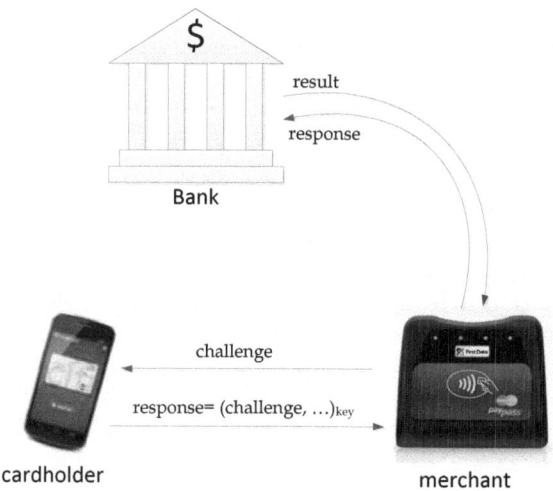

Fig. 1. Online authorization in a mobile payment system

Our proposed approach can work under the current payment infrastructure. It is meant to defend specifically against the reader-and-ghost attacks which NFC payment systems are susceptible to. We call the NFC card (reader) under attack a valid card (reader), and call the tag (reader) controlled by the adversary as malicious card (reader).

Under the threat model of the reader-and-ghost attack, originally called the "mafia fraud" attack [22, 16], the adversary controls a malicious reader and card pair, just like in the ghost-and-leech attack. However, the malicious reader controlled by the reader-and-ghost adversary is a legitimate reader or believed by the valid card to be a legitimate reader. Hence, the valid card (or its owner) is aware of and agrees to communicate with the malicious reader. That is, interrogations from the malicious reader to the valid card are not surreptitious as in the ghost-and-leech attacks. The goal of the adversary is still to impersonate the valid card.

We assume that the adversary does not have direct access to the valid card. So tampering or corrupting the card physically is not possible, or can be easily detected. The adversary is also unable to tamper the card remotely through injected malicious code. We further assume that the adversary is unable to spoof the ambient sensor signals, such as by changing the environmental conditions. We also do not consider loss or theft of card.

In addition to security, our threat model also considers the privacy of the card owners. In particular, a (malicious) bank server may be interested in determining the location of a card owner at the time of transaction, and track the whereabouts of the owner. Thus, transmitting explicit location information to the bank server, such as when using the GPS sensors, would be prone to location privacy attacks.

3.2   Overview of Our Approach

As mentioned above, our approach can work under the current mobile payment infrastructure. The card (NFC phone) already shares a symmetric key with its issuer bank. We only require that both the card and terminal measure certain location-dependent information using on-board sensors (such as audio and ambient light). Location-dependent data captured by both sensors are then forwarded to the bank. The bank server decides whether to approve the transaction after "comparing" the data received from the two ends. Figure 2 provides an overview of our approach. The user-side sensor generates its location-dependent information loc_{card} while the merchant-side sensor generates its version of location-dependent information $loc_{merchant}$. loc_{card} is protected (e.g., via MAC) with the key shared with the issuer bank before it is sent to the merchant's terminal which then forwards its own location information $loc_{merchant}$ along with the (phone's) card credentials to the bank for transaction verification and authorization. Since the integrity of loc_{card} is protected by the shared key between the card and bank, a malicious reader would be unable to change this value.

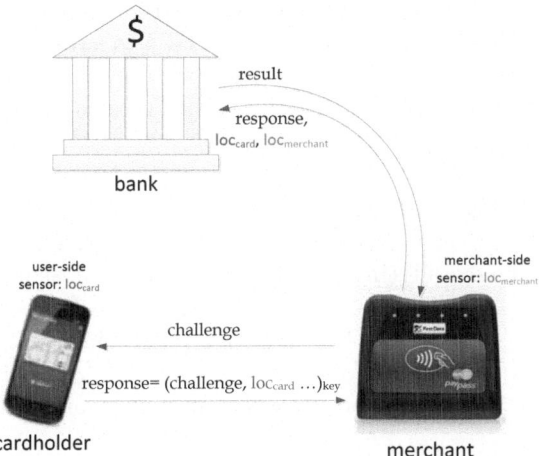

Fig. 2. Online authorization in a mobile payment system enhanced with our proximity detection approach

4 Proximity Detection Techniques

4.1 Correlation Using Audio

We explore the use of audio sensors (microphones) for accomplishing the afore-mentioned approach to proximity detection. This choice is motivated by the intuition that the audio data captured at two different locations at a given time is different to some extent.

We first need to determine if the audio recordings captured from the same location have higher similarity than recordings taken at different locations. To this end, we investigate a few methods to detect such similarity including: time-based methods, frequency-based methods as well as a combined time-frequency method.

Time-Based Similarity Detection: To detect the similarity between the time-based signals X_i and X_j, we propose using two methods: *correlation* and *difference*. The signals will first be normalized according to their energy (so that each signal had a total energy equal to 1). Then, in the first method, the correlation between each two signals will be calculated and the maximum correlation will be used. Therefore, the correlation based similarity between two signals X_i and X_j can be measured by:

$$S_c(i,j) = \max(Cross\text{-}Corr(X_i, X_j)) \text{ and } D_c(i,j) = 1 - S_c(i,j) \qquad (1)$$

In the second method, the distance between each bit of the signals is calculated and the overall Euclidean norm of the distance is used as below:

$$D_d(i,j) = \|X_i - X_j\| \text{ and } S_d(i,j) = 1 - D_d(i,j) \qquad (2)$$

Frequency-Based Similarity Detection: In the frequency-based detection approach, we use Fast Fourier Transform (FFT) to create the frequency co-efficients for each recorded signal. We then use both the correlation and the difference between the FFT coefficients in order to evaluate the similarity between different segments taken at the same place (in consecutive time periods) vs. recordings taken at different locations.

Time-Frequency Based Similarity Detection: This novel method combines both the time and frequency based measurements to create a point in 2-D space. In this technique, the overall time-frequency similarity measure is calculated by:

$$D(i,j) = \sqrt{(D_{c,time}(i,j))^2 + (D_{d,frequency}(i,j))^2} \text{ and } S(i,j) = 1 - D(i,j) \quad (3)$$

This implies that the similarity measurement will be higher for closer signals.

4.2 Correlation Using Ambient Light

We also explore the use of light sensors for the purpose of proximity detection. This choice is inspired by an observation that different types of places may have different lighting conditions. For example, fast food restaurants usually use bright lights to attract customers and to signify a place bustling with activity and very fast service, while fine dinning restaurants typically use low-intensity of light to create an intimate and leisurely atmosphere. As lighting conditions are location dependent, the ambient light can be used as the contextual information to determine the proximity between two devices (or a lack thereof).

Unlike ambient audio which can be heavily affected by surrounding human/ non-human activity, indoor ambient light (without natural light) is intuitively quite steady over time as the lighting infrastructure usually remains untapped – this intuition is later validated through the experiments as illustrated in Section 5.1. Hence, in this case, we use a simple strategy that involves just comparing the mean value of the illuminance data to determine whether ambient light readings captured from the same location have higher similarity than recordings taken at different locations.

Let L_i and L_j be the mean value of illuminance data captured in a short time interval by two devices at location i and j. The difference of mean value is calculated as:

$$D(i,j) = |L_i - L_j| \qquad (4)$$

As long as $D(i,j)$ is below a threshold, we consider the two readings to be similar enough and believe that they are captured from the same location. Otherwise, the two readings are believed to be captured from different locations. We will discuss how to establish the threshold via experiments in Section 5.1.

5 Experiments and Results

To evaluate our Near Field Communication (NFC) phone sensor data correlation techniques, we develop a proof-of-concept prototype on mobile phones, which allows us to collect data from different locations, and demonstrate the feasibility of our proximity detection approach.

5.1 Audio Data Experiments

In this section, we present our evaluation of the techniques for transaction verification based on audio data correlation.

Data Collection: The goal of sensor data correlation is to detect whether the valid card (phone) and valid reader are at the same or different locations. Therefore, we needed to collect the sensor data when the two devices are located in close physical proximity as well as when they are at two different locations. We work with two mobile phones (two Nokia N97s), simulating a valid NFC device and a valid RFID reader.

To enable recording of background sounds using the phones, we developed a program that captures audio from the phone's built-in microphone and installed it on two mobile phones. The program was designed to record up to 30 seconds of continuous audio data. The audio-capturing programs were launched on both phones and activated at about the same time to record the samples (the phones were synchronized by means of a wireless signal). We recorded, with the microphones, a few audio samples at different locations. We needed to determine if it was possible to distinguish between recordings taken at the same location versus at different locations.

We first examined the likelihood that different techniques can be used to find similarities between recordings taken at the same location and differentiate between recordings taken at separate locations. To determine the performance of the different techniques and find the optimal one, we initially created our "first dataset". For this, we used 7 groups of 20 1-sec recordings (for a total of 140 distinctive 1-sec audio recordings). Each group of recordings was captured at a separate location at consecutive time periods. The recordings were taken from 5 different locations, including a few retail stores and fast food restaurants. Specifically, we recorded surrounding noise at: McDonald's and Target (samples captured at two different occasions in each of the two), Wendy's, and our university cafeteria and library. We explored a few signal processing methods to detect the similarities between the different recordings taken at the same location at consecutive time periods vs. the similarities between recordings taken at different locations. The dataset was used to test the different techniques and find the optimal detection method.

To test the performance of the detection method in both a normal usage scenario (i.e., when no attacks occur) as well as in attack scenario, we created a "second dataset". For this dataset, we again took recordings at different locations with two phones simultaneously, separated by a distance of 3-12 inches. In this case, we collected the data from 5 different locations, including a concert hall, library (at two different locations), Mcdonalds and a coffee shop. We recorded at each location 20 1-sec segments from the two sensors simultaneously (located a few inches apart), capturing a total of 200 separate (100 pairs) 1-sec audio recordings.

All recorded audio files were then converted from the 3GPP format to the WAV format to be fed into our matlab algorithms for signal correlation (discussed in Section 4.1). Conversion from 3GPP to WAV, unlike the inverse, is considered lossless, since there is no compression used in WAV format. Thus, no important information was lost during this conversion.

Performance of Similarity Detection Techniques: We test the performance of various techniques, outlined in Section 4, to identify which one can most accurately detect the similarity between recordings taken at the same location. Specifically, in every test group, we use 5 pairs of 1-sec recording segments. The two samples in each pair were taken by two different sensors at the same location simultaneously (each pair was recorded at a separate location). For all the techniques, we calculated the probability that the recording, identified as the most similar one to a given recording, was the recording taken at the same location.

We ran the test for the dataset collected previously. Our results showed that the time-based "correlation" (Equation 1) gave better result (38% detection rate) compared to the "distance" (Equation 2) between the signals (which resulted in detection rate of 14%). Also, our tests showed that frequency-coefficients based distance yielded better results (50% detection rate) compared to time-based methods and to frequency-based distance methods (which resulted in 39% detection rate). Finally, our tests also demonstrated that the result corresponding to time-frequency classification is superior to all other methods, with a successful detection rate of 53%. In the rest of our analysis, therefore, we use the time-frequency based technique.

Performance of Audio-Based Proximity Detection: We next used the test dataset to determine the performance of our time-frequency detection on data taken under normal usage as well as attack scenario. We calculated the time-frequency distance measure between each two different samples. We found the square distance $D(i,j)^2$ (Section 4.1) and used it as our data features. For each pair of locations, we calculate the mean of the square distance. We generated a confusion matrix for our dataset as shown in Table 1.

Table 1. Confusion Matrix of Square Time-Frequency Distance

	Concert Hall	Library	McDonalds	Library (2)	Cafe
Concert Hall	0.4678	1.7889	1.8645	1.7556	1.8412
Library	1.7889	0.8539	1.7878	1.6753	1.7545
McDonalds	1.8645	1.7878	0.6018	1.7962	1.7241
Library (2)	1.7556	1.6753	1.7962	0.8213	1.8140
Cafe	1.8412	1.7545	1.7241	1.8140	0.5289

To distinguish between recordings taken at the same approximate location we compare the time-frequency square distance between each recorded signal and the one taken by the second microphone at the same location as well as with all the recordings taken at different locations. We construct the similarity matrix s using the similarity measurements and use it as our feature data. We use the input data to train the classifier to find the similarity threshold for each couple of samples. We use the *SimpleLogistics classifier* from the WEKA package to classify the samples. We run a 10-fold classification, which partitions the data into 10 partitions, trains the classifier over 9 of the partitions (which act as the training set) and classify the remaining samples (the testing set). This is repeated for each partition and training set in the dataset.

We note that the classifier arrived at a simple classification formula: if $y = 11.49 \times Corr - 8.69 < 0$, then both samples will be considered to be taken at the same place. Otherwise, they will be considered to be taken at different locations. This is a simple calculation (one multiplication and one addition) and will take the server a negligible amount of time to validate whether both samples were captured at the same location.

Using the classifier results, we find the detection rate for each pair of locations
in which the samples were taken (where one sample is captured in each location).
The detection rate is calculated over all the pairs of samples which were taken at
the two locations, by dividing the number of pairs of samples that were correctly
classified by the number of total pairs of samples (taken at those locations).
The result of the correct recognition rates can be found in Table 2. As can be
seen from the table, our audio signal based correlation technique yields 100%
detection rate.

Table 2. Experimental result of "positives" using WEKA SimpleLogistics classifier

	Concert Hall	Library	McDonalds	Library (2)	Cafe
Concert Hall	100%	100%	100%	100%	100%
Library	N/A	100%	100%	100%	100%
McDonalds	N/A	N/A	100%	100%	100%
Library (2)	N/A	N/A	N/A	100%	100%
Cafe	N/A	N/A	N/A	N/A	100%

False Accept Rate vs. False Reject Rate: We next determined the probabilities of incorrectly approving the transaction with an unauthorized phone
and rejecting the transaction with an authorized phone, by calculating the False
Accept Rate (FAR) vs. the False Reject Rate (FRR). FAR is the sum of false
positives, which occur when the audio signal captured by a valid reader matches
the audio signal captured by a phone, even when the two devices are at different
locations. FRR, on the other hand, is the sum of false negatives, and denotes
the probability that the transaction is rejected even when the valid phone and
valid reader are in close physical proximity.

Using the classifier results, since our detection rates are 100%, our FAR and
FRR are both clearly equal to 0%. This indicates that our audio-based proximity
detection technique is very robust.

5.2   Light Data Experiments

In this section, we present our evaluation of the techniques for transaction verification based on light data correlation.

Data Collection: We conducted this set of experiment with two mobile phones
(Google Nexus S) which are equipped with ambient light sensors. The light sensor
on the phone is generally utilized for the purpose of auto-adjustment of screen
brightness. We develop a simple Android application to capture data readings
from the light sensor. The sampling rate is set to be 25 Hz which records 50 data
points every 2 seconds.

As in the audio test, to simulate a normal usage, we used two phones representing the valid NFC phone making the transaction and the valid reader. They
are separated by a distance of 3-12 inches and hand-held during the transaction.

To simulate attack scenarios, we recorded light data at five different locations with different business types: two different types of restaurants (fast food restaurant vs. fine dining restaurant), two different types of retailer stores (supermarket vs. department store) and a car dealership. Our purpose is to find (dis)similarity in term of lighting conditions at locations of different business types.

Threshold Establishment: Figures 3 and 4 prove our intuition that lighting conditions are location-dependent. Curves in Figure 3 illustrates that lighting data collected from the aforementioned five different locations. Although light readings at a specific location fluctuate around a baseline, these curves are parallel to one other and clearly disparate which means the mean value can be used to distinguish different locations. Illuminance readings can be affected by several factors. The first is that the user cannot hold the phone firmly static. So the orientation of the phone and its relative position to the surrounding light sources can change which can affect the light sensor readings. Also, at different types of locations, surrounding human movements such as hand waving, may induce shadowing effect on the sensor causing changes to the data readings. Figure 4 shows the mean value of the data we collected from various locations and it gives us a more direct view of how the mean values of illuminance differ at different locations.

As described in Section 4.2, the transaction should be approved when the difference of mean values captured by two sensors is below a threshold, which indicates that the phone and the reader are at the same place. The transaction should be terminated otherwise, i.e., if the difference of mean values is above the threshold. To establish the threshold, we recorded 10 samples of light data, each consisting of 50 data points over a period of 2 seconds, on both devices at each location selected. From the captured data, we generate a confusion matrix as shown in Table 3. Values across the diagonal represent the average mean difference when phone and reader are at the same location while the others represent the average mean difference when the two devices are at different locations. From the table, we can observe that the threshold could be chosen in the range between 20.6 and 55.3 (lux) if we want to distinguish between these locations. The lower bound (20.6) is the maximum difference when the two phones are placed at the same location while the upper bound (55.3) is the minimum difference when phones are put at two different locations.

We picked 38 lux as the threshold value, and measure the performance of light-based proximity detection as discussed in the next section. We note that an interesting observation from the table is that the brighter the place, the higher is difference of readings captured by two devices at the said location.

Performance of Light-Based Proximity Detection: We further collected 40 samples of light data on both phones at each location. We then calculate their mean difference according to Equation 4 and compare the result using the threshold value 38. Similar to the audio tests, we next find the detection rate for each pair of locations in which the samples were taken (where one sample is

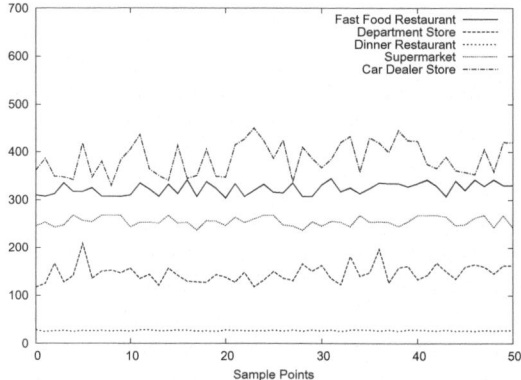

Fig. 3. Illuminance data over time at different locations

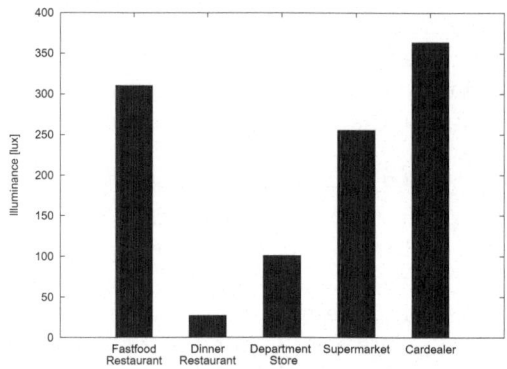

Fig. 4. Mean illuminance at different locations

captured in each location). The detection rate is calculated over all the pairs of samples which were taken at the two locations, by dividing the number of pairs of samples that were correctly classified by the number of total pairs of samples (taken at those locations). Our experimental results of the light-based detection rate is shown in Table 4.

False Accept Rate vs. False Reject Rate: We next determined the FAR and FRR for the light-based detection method, similar to the case of our audio data tests. We found that our FAR is equal to 6.5% while the FRR is equal to 5%. This means that the light-based detection is likely to fail, both under normal scenario and attack scenario, although on only on a small fraction of times.

Although these error rates are non-zero and higher than that produced by our audio-based correlation technique, these results generally demonstrate good recognition rates, especially for locations with smaller mean difference such as fine dining and department store.

Table 3. Confusion Matrix of Mean Difference (lux)

	Fine Dining	Department Store	Supermarket	Fast Food	Car Dealer
Fine Dining	1.1	71.0	283.5	291.9	347.1
DepartmentStore	71.0	6.4	163.6	220.9	276.1
Supermarket	283.5	163.6	9.9	58.3	113.5
Fast Food	291.9	220.9	58.3	17.0	55.3
Car Dealer	347.1	276.1	113.5	55.3	20.6

Table 4. Experimental results of "positives" based on mean differences (threshold 38 lux)

	Fine Dining	Department Store	Supermarket	Fast Food	Car Dealer
Fine Dining	100%	97.5%	100%	100%	100%
DepartmentStore	N/A	100%	100%	100%	100%
Supermarket	N/A	N/A	95%	82.5%	95%
Fast Food	N/A	N/A	N/A	92.5%	60%
Car Dealer	N/A	N/A	N/A	N/A	87.5%

6   Discussion

6.1   Audio vs. Light Data Proximity Detection

Our results show that audio and ambient light can serve as two different means of detecting proximity between two NFC devices involved in a transaction. Both result in quite low error rates, FAR as well as FRR, demonstrating the effectiveness of our approach. In fact, our experiments with the audio-based proximity detection approach yields no errors at all.

This suggests that audio is a potentially stronger signal for detecting the proximity of two devices when compared to light. The robustness of audio in this regard could be attributed to the fact that audio at two distinct locations is highly distinct in nature. On the other hand, the use of light is likely to result in a few false accepts in scenarios where the lighting conditions of two distinct locations is similar enough, and in a few false rejects in scenarios where the orientation of two close by phones affects their recorded light readings.

These results imply that when using our audio-based approach, it will be very difficult, if not impossible, for the attacker to succeed in launching the reader-and-ghost relay attack. When using the light sensor, in contrast, the adversary will need to choose a remote location having very similar lighting conditions as the one where a valid card is located at the time of transaction. This restriction, however, still significantly complicates the task of the attacker. Nevertheless, the specific attack demonstrated in [16] where the valid card is at a restaurant and the valid reader is at a jewellery store can be easily prevented when using our light based approach.

We note that our data was taken at locations typical to financial transactions. These are likely to be commercial environments, such as restaurants, shops and department stores. Since these are environments with customers, there will likely always be some background noise (e.g., due to people talking) which will be captured by the sensors. Therefore, this demonstrates a promising feasibility of our approach. While we can not completely rule out the probability of a false accept, our results show that it is unlikely that the attacker can capture similar enough audio data at a far-off location.

6.2   Location Privacy of Card Owners

As discussed in Section 3, our threat model covers the privacy of the card owners when making transactions. In particular, we are interested in protecting the location privacy of the card owners from a malicious bank server during the transaction process. Our sensor-centric proximity detection approach indeed provides a natural protection in this regard. In fact, we do not even need to use private proximity testing protocols proposed in the literature [23]. This is due to the fact that our approach does not require the card or the reader to transmit their explicit location information (unlike the GPS-based approach of [20]). Rather, only the captured audio or light readings are sent to the server. Although these readings possess some correlation with the exact location, it seems very difficult to infer this location just by analyzing these readings. This is especially true for the audio readings since they fluctuate over time drastically. The only possibility for the attacker to learn the location of the owner in this case is to be physically present at the said location at the time of transaction.

6.3   Manipulating Physical Environment

If the adversary can tamper with the physical environment, at the side of the valid card (NFC phone) and/or valid reader, it can enforce the two devices to capture similar enough data even from different locations. For example, if the adversary can induce similar lighting or acoustic conditions at two different locations at the time of the transaction, then it may succeed in launching the reader-and-leech attack. However, tampering with such environmental attributes (light or audio) looks like a daunting task. It may require sophisticated equipment as well as close proximity to the devices and will likely be easily detected. We believe this characteristic to be an inherent strength of our proximity detection approach.

6.4   Other Sensors

It is a natural question as to what other sensors are suitable for the purpose of proximity detection.

Temperature sensors are likely not going to be useful because indoor temperatures at different locations do not vary significantly. We also tried to use magnetic field data in this context, given that most modern phones come equipped with magnetometers. However, we could not find any method to detect the similarity between measurements taken at the same location (at consecutive time periods) vs. measurements taken at different locations. Therefore, we conclude that a magnetometer does not provide data which can be used reliably to derive a location-specific information. This is because the magnetic sensor readings are dominated by the Earth's background magnetic field, which do not change significantly across different locations. Odor sensors might be more promising for our application. However, we are not aware of any commercial phones that possess odor sensors as yet.

7   Conclusions

In this paper, we developed a secure proximity detection approach based on the information collected by audio and ambient light sensors available on NFC mobile phones. This approach is geared for preventing reader-and-ghost attacks, and offer many advantages. First, it does not require the users to perform explicit actions during the underlying operation – just bringing the devices close to each other is sufficient. Second, being based on environmental attributes, our approach makes it very hard, if not impossible, for the adversary to undermine the security of the system. Third, it provides a natural protection to users' location privacy as the explicit location information is never transmitted to the server.

Our evaluation of the proposed mechanism on common mobile platforms demonstrate its feasibility in effectively and significantly raising the bar against the reader-and-ghost attacks without negatively affecting the currently employed usage model of the underlying NFC applications. In particular, we found the audio-based detection to be quite powerful. In the future, we plan on identifying other sensors (besides microphones and light sensors), and combinations thereof, that can be used for the purpose of proximity detection.

Acknowledgments. We thank Moti Yung and ESORICS'12 anonymous reviewers for their valuable feedback. We also thank Sam Cleaveland, Justin Lin and Chatchai Satienpattanakul for their help with audio data collection.

References

1. epic.org: Wal-Mart begins tagging and tracking merchandise with RFID (July 2010), http://epic.org/2010/07/wal-mart-begins-tagging-and-tr.html
2. U.S. Department of State: The U.S. electronic passport, http://travel.state.gov/passport/passport_2498.html
3. EMVCo: About EMV (November 2009), http://www.emvco.com/about_emv.aspx
4. Washington State Department of Licensing: Enhanced driver license/ID card, http://www.dol.wa.gov/about/news/priorities/edl.html
5. NYS DMV: Enhanced driver licenses and non-driver identification cards (July 2010), http://www.nydmv.state.ny.us/broch/C158.pdf

6. Francillon, A., Danev, B., Capkun, S.: Relay attacks on passive keyless entry and start systems in modern cars. Cryptology ePrint Archive, Report 2010/332 (2010), http://eprint.iacr.org/

7. ITGlobal Consulting LTD: RFID toll road payment, http://www.itglobalconsulting.com/rfidtollroadpayment.asp

8. Infowars.com: Texas Department of Transportation to instate RFID TxTag (September 2005), http://www.infowars.com/articles/bb/toll_roads_tx_tag.htm

9. RFID Asia: New Ez-Link contactless smart cards converge transit and payment applications (December 2008), http://journal.rfid-asia.info/2008/12/new-ez-link-contactless-smart-cards.htm

10. Medical News Today: VeriChip corporation announces phase II development of in vivo glucose-sensing RFID microchip with RECEPTORS LLC (October 2009), http://www.medicalnewstoday.com/articles/165894.php

11. ISO: Near field communication interface and protocol (nfcip-1)——iso/iec 18092:2004 (2004), http://www.iso.org/iso/catalogue_detail.htm?csnumber=38578

12. Gilman, J.: Next-gen payments. Technical report, Tuck School of Business at Dartmouth (2011)

13. Calamia, M.: Mobile payments to surge to $670 billion by 2015 (July 2011), http://www.mobiledia.com/news/96900.html

14. Juels, A.: RFID security and privacy: A research survey. IEEE Journal on Selected Areas in Communications 24(2), 381–394 (2006)

15. Kfir, Z., Wool, A.: Picking virtual pockets using relay attacks on contactless smartcard. In: Security and Privacy for Emerging Areas in Communications Networks (Securecomm) (2005)

16. Drimer, S., Murdoch, S.J.: Keep your enemies close:Distance bounding against smartcard relay attacks. In: 16th USENIX Security Symposium (August 2007)

17. Brands, S., Chaum, D.: Distance Bounding Protocols. In: Helleseth, T. (ed.) EUROCRYPT 1993. LNCS, vol. 765, pp. 344–359. Springer, Heidelberg (1994)

18. Nithyanand, R., Tsudik, G., Uzun, E.: Readers Behaving Badly: Reader Revocation in PKI-Based RFID Systems. In: Gritzalis, D., Preneel, B., Theoharidou, M. (eds.) ESORICS 2010. LNCS, vol. 6345, pp. 19–36. Springer, Heidelberg (2010)

19. Kobsa, A., Nithyanand, R., Tsudik, G., Uzun, E.: Usability of Display-Equipped RFID Tags for Security Purposes. In: Atluri, V., Diaz, C. (eds.) ESORICS 2011. LNCS, vol. 6879, pp. 434–451. Springer, Heidelberg (2011)

20. Ma, D., Prasad, A.K., Saxena, N., Xiang, T.: Location-aware and safer cards: Enhancing rfid security and privacy via location sensing. In: ACM Conference on Wireless Network Security (WiSec) (to appear, April 2012)

21. technologies Inc, B.: Bump Application

22. Desmedt, Y.G., Goutier, C., Bengio, S.: Special Uses and Abuses of the Fiat Shamir Passport Protocol. In: Pomerance, C. (ed.) CRYPTO 1987. LNCS, vol. 293, pp. 21–39. Springer, Heidelberg (1988)

23. Narayanan, A., Thiagarajan, N., Lakhani, M., Hamburg, M., Boneh, D.: Location privacy via private proximity testing. In: Network and Distributed System Security Symposium (NDSS) (2011)

Enhancing Location Privacy for Electric Vehicles (at the *Right* time)

Joseph K. Liu[1], Man Ho Au[2], Willy Susilo[2], and Jianying Zhou[1,*]

[1] Cryptography and Security Department
Institute for Infocomm Research, Singapore
{ksliu,jyzhou}@i2r.a-star.edu.sg
[2] School of Computer Science and Software Engineering
University of Wollongong, Australia
{aau,wsusilo}@uow.edu.au

Abstract. An electric vehicle is a promising and futuristic automobile propelled by electric motor(s), using electrical energy stored in batteries or another energy storage device. Due to the need of battery recharging, the cars will be required to visit recharging infrastructure very frequently. This may disclose the users' private information, such as their location, which may expose users' privacy. In this paper, we provide mechanisms to enhance location privacy of electric vehicles at the right time, by proposing an anonymous payment system with privacy protection support. Our technique further allows traceability in the case where the cars are stolen.

1 Introduction

An electric vehicle (also known as EV) is powered by an electric motor instead of a gasoline engine. The electric motor obtains energy from a controller, which regulates the amount of power based on the driver's use of an accelerator pedal. The electric vehicle uses energy stored in its rechargeable batteries, which can be recharged by the common household electricity for normal charging (slow charging). Electric vehicles have several potential benefits compared to conventional internal combustion automobiles that include a significant reduction of urban air pollution as they do not emit harmful tailpipe pollutants from the onboard source of power at the point of operation (zero tail pipe emissions); reduced greenhouse gas emissions from the onboard source of power depending on the fuel and technology used for electricity generation to charge the batteries; and less dependence on foreign oil, which for many developed and emerging countries is a cause of concern due to its vulnerability to price shocks and supply disruption.

Future electric vehicles may even support Vehicle-to-grid (V2G). The concept allows V2G cars to provide power to help balance loads by "valley filling"

---

* The first and fourth authors are supported by the EMA project SecSG-EPD090005RFP(D). The third author is supported by ARC Future Fellowship FT0991397.

S. Foresti, M. Yung, and F. Martinelli (Eds.): ESORICS 2012, LNCS 7459, pp. 397–414, 2012.

(charging at night when the demand is low) and "peak shaving" (sending power back to the grid when the demand is high). It can enable utilizing new ways to provide regulation services (keeping voltage and frequency stable) and provide spinning reserves (meet sudden demands for power). In future development, it has been proposed that such use of electric vehicles could buffer renewable power sources such as wind power, for example, by storing excess energy produced during windy periods and providing it back to the grid during high load periods, thus effectively stabilizing the intermittency of wind power. If the car has installed solar panel, it may further generate additional electricity and sell it back to utilities when it is parked outside under a sunshine. One may also regard this application of vehicle-to-grid technology as a renewable energy approach that can penetrate the baseline electric market.

Despite their potential benefits, widespread adoption of electric vehicles faces several hurdles and limitations. One of the major problems is the driving range. Most electric vehicles can only go about 100 to 150 km before recharging, while gasoline vehicles can go over 500 km before refueling. This may be sufficient for city trips or other short hauls. Nevertheless, people can be concerned that they would run out of energy from their battery before reaching their destination, a worry known as the range anxiety.

One of the solutions is to install more fast charging stations with high-speed charging capability so that consumers could recharge the 100 km battery of their electric vehicle to 80 percent in about 30 minutes. Electric vehicle drivers may then charge their vehicles at their homes, offices, shopping malls or car parks outside restaurants when they are having dinner.

LOCATION PRIVACY CONCERN. Paying for recharging in those infrastructures may disclose the users private information such as their location privacies [1]. Those location privacies include the drivers' living places, working companies, the amusement places they usually go, etc. [2–4]. Privacy is regarded as a fundamental human right and leaking them is possible to identify at many negative effects [5–7]. The first one is Location-based "spam", which means that the location information could be used by malicious businesses to bombard an individual with unsolicited marketing for products or services related to that individuals location. Another negative effect is that the location can be used to infer an individual's political views, state of health, or personal preferences. Furthermore, the disclosure of location privacy may also result in safety problems. For example, it may be used by unscrupulous persons such as the robbers for stalking or physical attacks.

The location privacy problem does not exist in gasoline cars. There are two main reasons for that. First, when the car is running out of gasoline, drivers may choose to pay cash instead of credit card when they pay for the gasoline in the gas station. Cash is a form of anonymous payment that cannot be traced. Second, gasoline vehicles do not need to be re-filled within a short distance. Even for daily drivers they may only re-fill the gasoline once a week. Activities within that week will be unknown even if they choose to pay by credit card at the gas station. Another reason is that EV can support V2G charging which is not existed in gasoline cars.

We will examine other payment systems and their impact on location privacy in Section 1.2.

REVOCATION OF LOCATION PRIVACY AT THE "RIGHT" TIME. Yet providing unconditional location privacy is not always good. In the case that when a car is stolen, the car owner definitely wants to know the location of his stolen car. Currently some anti-theft or thief-tracing devices can be installed in the car (e.g. GPS with GSM communication device) so that if the car is stolen, the device will send a signal to the car owner telling about the current location of the stolen car. Although these kind of devices can be used to trace any stolen car, the installation and running cost are very high. It is fine for a luxury car as the cost of the anti-theft device compared to the cost of the car itself is just negligible. However, for some lower-end used cars, it is impractical to install such devices where the price is comparable to the value of the used car.

The short driving range is one of the disadvantages of electric vehicles. Yet on the other side, it provides a cheap solution to trace a stolen vehicle. As the vehicle is required to be re-charged very frequently, charging stations can be used to trace any stolen vehicle. If a stolen car is being re-charged at a charging station, the charging station can report to the police or the car owner about the location of this stolen car. It may also refuse to provide charging service to any stolen cars.

1.1   Contributions

In this paper, we enhance the location privacy of electric vehicles at the right time, by proposing a new payment system that provides the following privacy related features:

TWO-WAY ANONYMOUS PAYMENT: It supports anonymous payment *in both directions*. First, the electric vehicle remains anonymous when it re-charges at any charging station. It further supports V2G system. That is, if the car wants to sell back its stored or solar generated electricity to the grid through the charging station, it will receive its credit anonymously. The location privacy of the car is protected *in normal operations*.

TRACEABILITY OF STOLEN CAR: If the electric vehicle is stolen, the owner may provide some secret information to charging stations so that next time when the stolen car is being re-charged at any charging station, its location will be revealed.

We argue that our system is practical, as it also provides some additional features that can be favoured by users or supplier:

1. **Prevention of Cheating User:** Different from e-cash which cannot prevent users from cheating or double-spending (it can only *detect* such behaviour),

our payment system supports prevention of any cheating behaviour. If any party does not follow the algorithms, the other party can stop providing service immediately. This protects the supplier from being cheated. (The difference between prevention and detection of cheating user will be further explained in Section 1.2.)

2. **Support Judging Authority (JA):** In case there are some disputes between two parties (maybe due to some physical factors such as sudden breakdown of electricity supply), the affected party may submit all transactions to a Judging Authority. The authority can reveal the identity and investigate the situation.

3. **Low Implementation Cost:** Our system does not require any special security device (e.g. different from ATM). Our security comes from cryptographic algorithms. Our system is also efficient enough to be implemented into mobile device (e.g. smart phone) for the user side.
   Also different from some of the current theft-tracing anti-stolen devices, we do not require any GPS or GSM communication. Thus the cost is much cheaper than those devices.

4. **Lost Protection of Prepaid Credit:** Since our system is account based, we support lost protection. That is, even if the user has lost his mobile device (used for charging), the credit stored in his account cannot be used by any party. He can regain his credit by providing some authenticated information.

We further analyze our system in security, efficiency and cost to prove that it is practical to be used.

1.2   Existing Payment Systems

There are many different forms of existing payment systems. We examine some of the most practical ones and explain why they are not suitable for electric vehicles.

- **Paper cash:** Different from gas stations, charging stations for electric vehicles are all machine operated. If they allow cash payment, the installation costs will be very large due to high security requirement of cash machine (similar to those for ATM). Note that currently there are many ticketing machine installed in car parks or automatic selling machines (e.g. selling softdrink) which can accept paper cash or coins. However, as the cost for car park or softdrink is far less than charging electric vehicles, the physical security requirement can be much lower. Thus although paper cash can provide anonymity, the high installation and running cost are the main obstacles that are disfavoured by supplier to adopt paper cash as a kind of payment system in the charging station.

- **E-cash:** Alternatively, e-cash is the electronic form of paper cash which also provides anonymity. However, e-cash is mainly used in small amount transaction (e.g. a few dollars) instead of large amount transaction (e.g. a few hundred dollars) due to security and efficiency concerns. In order to support

two-way payments, transferrable e-cash is needed and it has been shown complexity of transferrable e-cash grows linearly in the number of transfer supported [8][1]. Apart from that, off-line e-cash cannot provide double-spending *prevention*. It can only *detect* double-spending and *reveal* the identity of the double-spender when the electronic coins are deposited back to the bank. If a cheating user double-spends many times before going bankrupt, the deceived shops cannot get back the money that they deserved to have. Furthermore, different from credit card, e-cash does not provide lost protection. No one will put a few thousand or even a few hundred dollars in the e-wallet. Thus e-cash is only suitable for small amount transaction. Charging for an electric vehicle definitely does not belong to the small amount transaction category.
– **Prepaid cash card or cash coupon:** Prepaid cash card or cash coupon is another common way of anonymous e-payment. However, similar to e-cash, it does not support lost protection. Executing large amount transaction may bring inconvenience to user: They may neither want to bring many coupons together, nor buy the coupons or topup everyday. In addition, it also does not fully support 2-ways transactions, which is a necessary requirement for the future Vehicle-to-grid system.
– **Paypal:** Paypal is a kind of most commonly used electronic prepaid system. However, it requires a third party (PayPal company). If the authority colludes with the PayPal company (e.g. by telling the PayPal company the exact time and location of a particular transaction), the user can be traced. Thus we regard PayPal providing *partial location privacy* only.
– **Credit card:** Credit card is a widely adopted payment system for large amount transaction instead. It also supports 2-ways transaction. Nevertheless, credit card is not anonymous. Due to the frequent charging requirement for electric vehicles, location privacy will be lost by tracing the credit card payment easily.

Note that none of the existing payment systems can support traceability of stolen cars. We summarize the comparison of our system with some existing payment systems in Table 1.

2   System Architecture

2.1   Entities

We consider a system which is composed of the following entities:

1. **User:** A user refers to an electric vehicle or driver, which depends on the mode of operation (will be defined in next Section).
2. **Supplier:** It refers to the power grid company. It supplies (sells) electricity to the cars, and also collects (buy) electricity back from the cars. It is responsible for account opening. Every user needs to obtain an account from it and deposits some money into this account.

---

[1] A recent approach achieve constant size transferrable e-cash, at the expense that the user storage is linear to the number of his spent coins[9].

Table 1. Comparison of existing payment systems

Scheme	Location privacy	Prevent. of cheating	Support JA	Low implement cost	Lost protect.	2-ways transac.	Stolen car trace.
Paper cash	✓	✓	×	×	×	✓	×
Prepaid cashcard /Cash coupon	✓	✓	×	✓	×	✗	×
Transferrable e-cash	✓	×	✗ [a]	✓	×	✓	×
Credit card	×	✓	✓	✓	✓	✓	×
PayPal	✗	✓	✓	✓	✓	✓	×
Our system	✓	✓	✓	✓	✓	✓	✓

[a] Most of the existing e-cash systems do not support judge, though some of them (e.g. [10–13]) do support judge.

3. **Judging Authority (JA):** It is responsible to investigate into some disputed transactions between user and power company. It has the power to *open* any transaction in case of any dispute. It maybe the government authority or the court.

2.2 Overall Structure

We briefly describe the overall structure of our system. It can be implemented in two different modes:

1. **Portable Mode:** In the portable mode, the account unit for user is per person. That is, if a person has more than one electric vehicles, he can use one single account to manage all cars. The hardware device for the user interface will be a portable device (e.g. smart phone). Note that data connectivity is *not* required.
   When the user is driving his car to the charging station, his portable device will communicate with the charging station. Thus traceability of stolen car cannot be operated under this mode. This mode maybe suitable for those users who want to manage more than one car in a single account; or if the car is driven by different persons everyday (e.g. taxi).
2. **Embedded Mode:** In the embedded mode, the account unit for user is per car. That is, one single car has an unique account. The hardware device for the user interface will be an In-Car-Unit.
   Traceability of stolen car is supported under this mode. This maybe suitable for those users whose car is used by themselves or their family only. Similar to portable mode, data connectivity is not required. However, a USB storage device (e.g. USB thumb drive) is needed in order to support traceability of stolen car.

Our system contains the following processes regardless of the running mode:

- Registration: The user contacts the supplier for registration and account opening. He needs to pay a deposit for his account so that the balance should have at least D dollars. The supplier returns a token to the user which stores the current value of this account. The user may store this token into his smart phone or In-Car-Unit. (The supplier may develop a new app, or a new physical device for this.) The token is valid for a period of time (e.g. a month). The user needs to update the token before the expiration date.
- Charging: The user presents his token (from his smart phone) and carries an interactive protocol with the charging station, which first checks with the grid management server to confirm the grid capacity is fine. If the price is dynamic (if it is within peak period the price maybe set higher) it further checks with the grid management server for the updated price. Other than that, *the charging station works as a front-end terminal and the major (cryptographic) computation (e.g. those involving secret key) is done in the supplier's billing server.* It communicates with the billing server to make sure the token is valid. If it is valid and the balance of the user account is larger than the price of the requested service, the charging station starts to charge the car. The user obtains an updated token with decremented balance and stores it into the his portable device (e.g. smartphone).

The process is described in Figure 1.

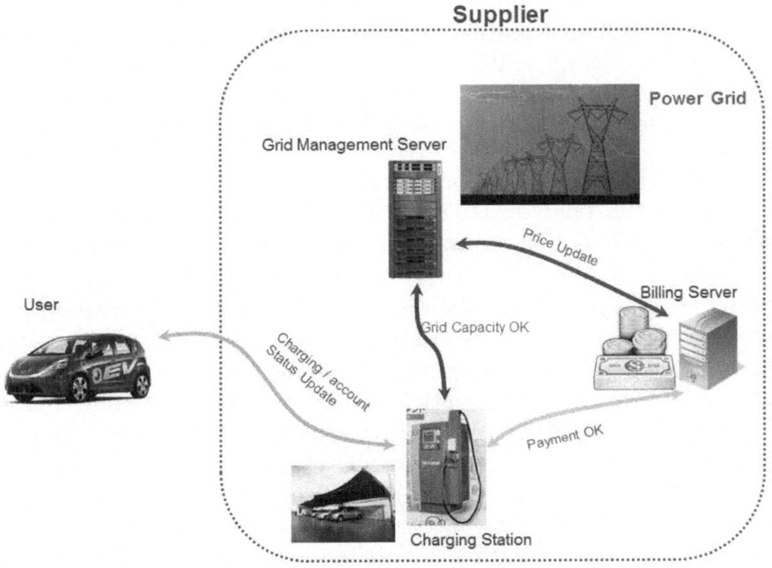

Fig. 1. Charging/Topup Scenario

- **Discharging or Topup**: The process is similar to charging. The only difference is that upon completion of the protocol, the user's updated token contains an incremented balance.
- **Statement**: Every statement period, the user goes to the supplier to topup the balance in the account if it is less than D dollars and update his token.
- **Tracing Stolen Car** (Embedded mode): If the user's car has been stolen, he needs to retrieve from his backup token and sends the backup token to the supplier. It checks whether this information is correct. If yes, in case a vehicle using this token is being charged in any charging station, it will report to the user and the police about the location.
- **Report of Lost Token** (Optional): If the user has backuped every newly generated token, in case he has lost his token (e.g. if his smart phone is stolen), he needs to retrieve from his backup and sends the backup token to the supplier. It checks whether this information is correct. If yes, it will block any party from using his lost token. The process is similar to the report of lost credit card.
- **Open** (Optional): If the user has some disputes with the supplier, he may reveal his identity together with the corresponding transaction information (e.g. location, time) to the JA. It may also request the supplier to provide related information and investigate this particular transaction.

3   Primitives

In this section we first review some cryptographic primitives that will be used.

Bilinear Pairing. Bilinear pairing (or bilinear map) is a popular building block in public key cryptography. We briefly review its property here. Let $\mathbb{G}, \mathbb{G}_T$ be two cyclic groups of prime order p where p is of λ-bit for some security parameter λ. A function $\hat{e} : \mathbb{G} \times \mathbb{G} \rightarrow \mathbb{G}_T$ is called a bilinear pairing if the following holds:

1. *Bilinearity*: For all $g, h \in \mathbb{G}$, and $a, b \in \mathbb{Z}_p$, $\hat{e}(g^a, h^b) = \hat{e}(g, h)^{ab}$.
2. *Non-degeneracy*: There exists $g \in \mathbb{G}$ such that $\hat{e}(g, g)$ has order p in $\mathbb{G}_T$.
3. *Computability*: It is efficient to compute $\hat{e}(g, h)$ for all $g, h \in \mathbb{G}$.

Commitment. Our system uses the well known commitment scheme due to Pedersen [14]. Let $\mathbb{G}$ be a cyclic group of prime order p and g, h be generators of $\mathbb{G}$. On input a value $x \in \mathbb{Z}_p$, the committer randomly chooses $r \in \mathbb{Z}_p$, computes and outputs $C = g^x h^r$ as a commitment of value x. To reveal the value committed in C, the committer outputs (x, r). Everyone can test if $C = g^x h^r$. Sometimes we say r is the opening of C with respect to x. One could extend the commitment scheme to allow committing a tuple of elements $(x_1, \ldots, x_n)$ at the same time by setting $C = g_1^{x_1} \cdots g_n^{x_n} h^r$, where g_i are independent generators of $\mathbb{G}$.

We use $\mathsf{CMT}(x)$ (resp. $\mathsf{CMT}(x_1, \ldots, x_n)$) to denote a Pedersen Commitment of a value x (resp. $(x_1, \ldots, x_n)$). Note that this commitment scheme is homomorphic: $\mathsf{CMT}(a) * \mathsf{CMT}(b)$ gives $\mathsf{CMT}(a + b)$ and the opening of the later is the sum of that of the formers.

BBS+ Signature. We employ the signature scheme proposed by Au et al. [15], which is based on the schemes of Camenisch and Lysyanskaya [16] and of Boneh et al. [17]. Their scheme is called BBS+ signature. Due to space limitation, full description of BBS+ signature will be given in the full version of this paper [18].

Zero-knowledge Proof. A zero-knowledge proof [19] is an interactive protocol for one party, the prover, to prove to another party, the verifier, that some statement is true, without revealing anything other than the veracity of the statement. We follow the notation introduced by Camenisch and Stadler [20]. For example, $\mathcal{PK}\{(x) : y = g^x\}$ denotes a zero-knowledge proof that the prover knows an integer x such that the statement $y = g^x$ holds. For the details, reader may refer to the full version of this paper [18].

4 Our Proposed System

4.1 Assumptions

As discussed, our system is constructed using cryptographic techniques and hence, it does not depend on any proprietary hardware. Nonetheless, we would like to re-state that security of any cryptographic algorithms depends on the confidentiality of the secret key. Implicitly, when we state some values are to be kept secret, we assume they are stored privately inside the user's device. For example, the secret value stored inside the user's device (e.g. the smartphone) should be kept away from the adversary. This is assumed to be achieved by external means, such as keeping the device to be always in possession or set it to be password-protected.

Our system can only protect location privacy of the payment system and when considering its physical security, it is out of the scope of this paper. For instance, suppose a physical camera is installed in each charging station and it records the physical identifier of the vehicle (e.g. registration plate number), and therefore, it is obvious that location privacy cannot be maintained. This is analogous to the use of physical money. Suppose the cash register records the image of the payer, then it is always possible to link the payment from the user across different locations, and therefore anonymity is no longer preserved.

We further assume that all communication channels are encrypted and authenticated. When considering some attacks such as IP hijacking, distributed denial-of-service attack, man-in-the-middle attack etc., it is out of the scope of this paper.

4.2 High Level Description

Our construction is motivated from the reputation-based blacklistable anonymous authentication system [21]. Authentication in their system results in an increase or decrease in the user reputation, which is stored at the user side. We adapt their idea and view the reputation as the user's balance. A top-up transaction is an authentication that leads to an increase in reputation. Likewise, a charging transaction is an authentication that leads to a decrease in reputation.

- **Registration:** User pays a deposit D for registration. The balance B of the user is the value D. Supplier assigns a unique identifier I to the user. User chooses a random number s. User sends $\mathsf{CMT}(I, B, s)$ to the supplier and obtains σ_s which is a BBS+ signature on (I, B, s). Due to the property of the commitment scheme, the value s remains hidden to the supplier. User stores (σ_s, I, B, s) as his secret.
- **Charging:** The user charges his vehicle with fee v as follow. User is in possession of (σ_s, I, B, s). He/she first checks if the balance $B > v$. If yes, the user randomly chooses a number s' and sends $\mathsf{CMT}(I)$, $\mathsf{CMT}(B)$, $\mathsf{CMT}(B - v)$, $\mathsf{CMT}(s')$, s to the supplier. The user proves to the supplier, in zero-knowledge, that he/she knows four values (σ_s, I, B, s) such that the following statements are true:

  1. σ_s is a valid signature on (I, B, s)
  2. $\mathsf{CMT}(I)$, $\mathsf{CMT}(B)$, $\mathsf{CMT}(B - v)$, $\mathsf{CMT}(s')$ are formed correctly
  3. $B - v > 0$

  The supplier further checks that s has never been shown by anybody. Note that this check is necessary as it ensures the user cannot use his previous balance after making a payment. After that, the supplier creates a new signature $\sigma_{s'}$ on the tuple (I, B', s') where $B' = B - v$ for the user.

  We stress again that in the process, all that the supplier can infer are the commitments, but not the actual values, of I, B, $B - v$, s', and thus the user's identity remains hidden.
- **Discharging or Topup:** Discharging or topup the balance is similar to the Charging process. User is in possession of (σ_s, I, B, s). Let say the topup amount is v. The user chooses a new random number s' and sends $\mathsf{CMT}(I)$, $\mathsf{CMT}(B)$, $\mathsf{CMT}(s')$, s to the supplier. The user proves to the supplier, in zero-knowledge, that he/she knows four values (σ_s, I, B, s) such that the following statements are true:

  1. σ_s is a valid signature on (I, B, s)
  2. $\mathsf{CMT}(I)$, $\mathsf{CMT}(B)$, $\mathsf{CMT}(s')$ are formed correctly

  The supplier further checks that s has never been shown by anybody. After that, the supplier creates $\mathsf{CMT}(B + v)$ from $\mathsf{CMT}(B)$ and v and issues a new signature $\sigma_{s'}$ on the tuple (I, B', s') where $B' = B + v$ for the user.
- **Statement:** Every statement period, the user sends (I, B, s) to the supplier, along with a proof that he has a signature σ_s on the tuple (I, B, s). The supplier further checks s has never been shown by anybody. The user pays the amount d such that $D = B + d$. The user then sends $\mathsf{CMT}(s')$ to the supplier and obtains a new signature $\sigma_{s'}$ from the supplier which is a signature on (I, D, s').
- **Tracing Stolen Car:** (Embedded mode) Assume the user has done a backup for every newly generated token. In case of his car being stolen, the user could report to the supplier immediately and present the value s so that the use of the stolen device could be identified. Any charging station receiving this s in the future will terminate the service and report to the user and the police.

- **Report of Lost Token:** (Optional) Assume the user has done a backup for every newly generated token. In case of losing the token (e.g. iPod has been lost or stolen), the user could report to the supplier immediately and present the value s so that the use of the stolen device could be identified. Then, a new token containing the same balance could be issued to the user easily. Further details are discussed in Section 5.
- **Open:** (Optional) Observe that the user secret after each operations contains the same identifier I and that I is either sent in plain (in the statement protocol) or in the commitment $\mathsf{CMT}(I)$ (in all other protocols). Suppose we replace the function $\mathsf{CMT}(I)$ with an encryption of I under the public key of a trusted party called judge, that party would be capable of revealing the identifier of the user in any transactions. Further details are discussed in Section 5.

4.3   Detailed Description

We first describe our system under the portable mode. Later we will show how to modify it into the embedded mode.

Portable Mode

- **System Setup:** Let $\hat{e} : \mathbb{G} \times \mathbb{G} \to \mathbb{G}_T$ be a bilinear map as discussed. In practice, we could use asymmetric pairing (such as type D pairing) for better space efficiency. $\mathbb{G}$ will be chosen so that it is of prime order p where p is of length λ, the security parameter. Let $g, g_0, g_1, g_2, g_3 \in_R \mathbb{G}$. The supplier randomly picks $\gamma \in_R \mathbb{Z}_p$ and computes $w = g^\gamma$. The system parameter is $\mathsf{param} = (\mathbb{G}, \mathbb{G}_T, \hat{e}, g, g_0, g_1, g_2, g_3, w)$ and the secret key of the supplier is γ.
- **Registration:** Each user is assigned a unique identity I in the system. In practice, this could be his driver license number. Let D be the deposit. The user engages the supplier and enrolls into the system as follow.
  1. The user randomly picks $y', s \in_R \mathbb{Z}_p$, computes and sends $C = g_0^{y'} g_3^s$ to the supplier, along with the following proof: $\mathcal{PK}_1\{(y', s) : C = g_0^{y'} g_3^s\}$. $\mathcal{PK}_1$ assures the supplier that the value C is computed correctly. Precise description of the proof (and subsequent proofs) will be given in the full version of this paper [18].
  2. The supplier randomly picks $y'', e \in_R \mathbb{Z}_p$, computes $A = (Cgg_0^{y''} g_1^I g_2^D)^{\frac{1}{e+\gamma}}$ and returns (A, y'', e) to the user.
  3. The user computes $y = y' + y''$ and checks if $\hat{e}(A, wg^e) \stackrel{?}{=} \hat{e}(gg_0^y g_1^I g_2^D g_3^s, g)$. User parses $\sigma_s = (A, e, y)$ and stores a four tuple (σ_s, I, D, s). Note that σ_s is a BBS+ signature on the tuple (I, D, s).

  The registration protocol is shown in figure 2.
- **Charging:** Let v be the value of the transaction. The user parses his storage as $\left(\tilde{\sigma}_s := (\tilde{A}, \tilde{e}, \tilde{y}), I, \tilde{B}, \tilde{s}\right)$ and checks if $\tilde{B} - v \geq 0$. Next, they engages in the following protocol.

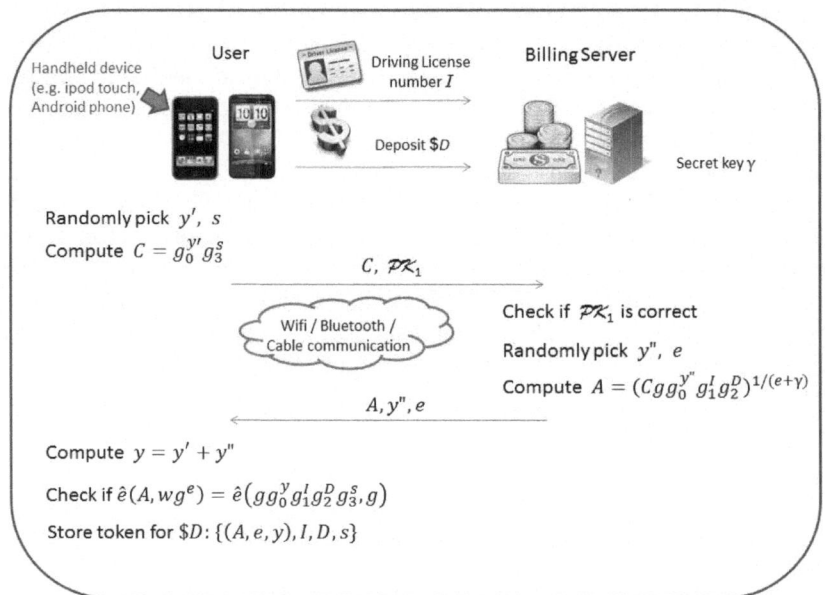

Fig. 2. Registration

1. The user randomly picks $y', s \in_R \mathbb{Z}_p$, computes and sends $C = g_0^{y'} g_1^I g_2^{\tilde{B}} g_3^s$ as well as $\tilde{s}$ to the supplier, along with the following proof: $\mathcal{PK}_2\{(\tilde{A}, \tilde{e}, \tilde{y}, I, \tilde{B}, y', s) : C = g_0^{y'} g_1^I g_2^{\tilde{B}} g_3^s \wedge \hat{e}(\tilde{A}, wg^{\tilde{e}}) = \hat{e}(gg_0^{\tilde{y}} g_1^I g_2^{\tilde{B}} g_3^{\tilde{s}}, g) \wedge D \geq \tilde{B} - v \geq 0\}$.

2. The supplier checks that $\tilde{s}$ has never been used[2] and randomly picks $y'', e \in_R \mathbb{Z}_p$, computes $A = (Cgg_0^{y''} g_2^{-v})^{\frac{1}{e+\gamma}}$ and returns (A, y'', e) to the user.

3. The user computes $y = y' + y''$, $B = \tilde{B} - v$ and checks if $\hat{e}(A, wg^e) \overset{?}{=} \hat{e}(gg_0^y g_1^I g_2^B g_3^s, g)$. User parses $\sigma_s = (A, e, y)$ and stores a four tuple (σ_s, I, B, s). Note that σ_s is a BBS+ signature on the tuple (I, B, s).

The charging protocol is shown in figure 3.

- **Topup:** Let v be the topup value. The user parses his storage as $(\tilde{\sigma}_s := (\tilde{A}, \tilde{e}, \tilde{y}), I, \tilde{B}, \tilde{s})$ and checks if $\tilde{B} + v \leq D$. We assume D is the maximum account balance. Next, they engages in the following protocol.

   1. The user randomly picks $y', s \in_R \mathbb{Z}_p$, computes and sends $C = g_0^{y'} g_1^I g_2^{\tilde{B}} g_3^s$ as well as $\tilde{s}$ to the supplier, along with the following proof: $\mathcal{PK}_3\{(\tilde{A}, \tilde{e}, \tilde{y}, I, \tilde{B}, y', s) : C = g_0^{y'} g_1^I g_2^{\tilde{B}} g_3^s \wedge \hat{e}(\tilde{A}, wg^{\tilde{e}}) = \hat{e}(gg_0^{\tilde{y}} g_1^I g_2^{\tilde{B}} g_3^{\tilde{s}}, g) \wedge D \geq \tilde{B} + v \geq 0\}$.

   2. The supplier checks that $\tilde{s}$ has never been used and randomly picks $y'', e \in_R \mathbb{Z}_p$, computes $A = (Cgg_0^{y''} g_2^v)^{\frac{1}{e+\gamma}}$ and returns (A, y'', e) to the user.

---

[2] The practical issue of the checking process will be described in the full version of this paper [18].

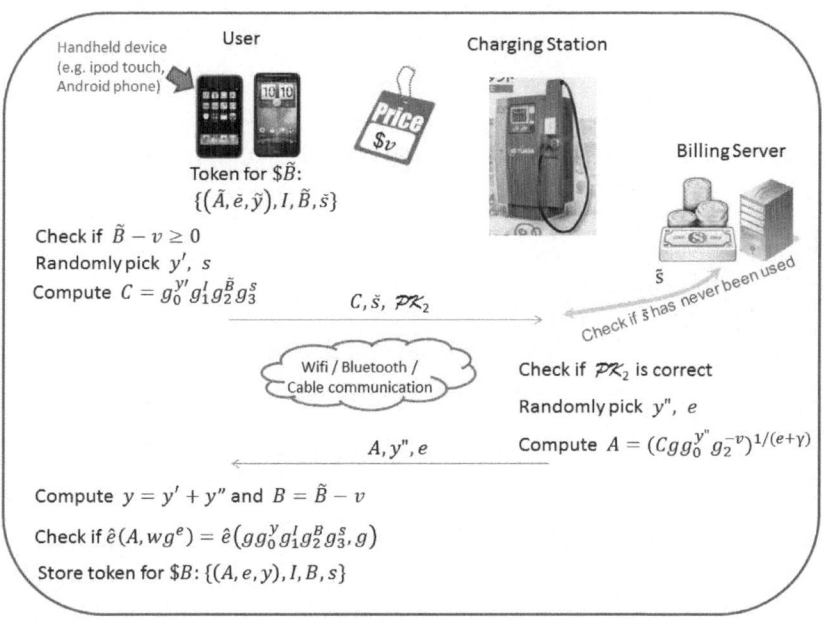

Fig. 3. Charging

3. The user computes $y = y' + y''$, $B = \tilde{B} + v$ and checks if $\hat{e}(A, wg^e) \stackrel{?}{=} \hat{e}(gg_0^y g_1^I g_2^B g_3^s, g)$. User parses $\sigma_s = (A, e, y)$ and stores a four tuple (σ_s, I, B, s). Note that σ_s is a BBS+ signature on the tuple (I, B, s).

- **Statement:** The user parses his storage as $\left(\tilde{\sigma}_s := (\tilde{A}, \tilde{e}, \tilde{y}), I, \tilde{B}, \tilde{s}\right)$ and pays $v = D - \tilde{B}$ to settle his account. Next, they engages in the following protocol.

 1. The user randomly picks $y', s \in_R \mathbb{Z}_p$, computes and sends $C = g_0^{y'} g_3^s$ as well as $\tilde{s}, I, \tilde{B}$ to the supplier, along with the following proof: $\mathcal{PK}_4\{(\tilde{A}, \tilde{e}, \tilde{y}, y', s) : C = g_0^{y'} g_3^s \wedge \hat{e}(\tilde{A}, wg^{\tilde{e}}) = \hat{e}(gg_0^{\tilde{y}} g_1^I g_2^{\tilde{B}} g_3^{\tilde{s}}, g)\}$.

 2. The supplier checks that $\tilde{s}$ has never been used and randomly picks $y'', e \in_R \mathbb{Z}_p$, computes $A = (Cgg_0^{y''} g_1^I g_2^D)^{\frac{1}{e+\gamma}}$ and returns (A, y'', e) to the user.

 3. The user computes $y = y' + y''$ and checks if $\hat{e}(A, wg^e) \stackrel{?}{=} \hat{e}(gg_0^y g_1^I g_2^D g_3^s, g)$. User parses $\sigma_s = (A, e, y)$ and stores a four tuple (σ_s, I, D, s). Note that σ_s is a BBS+ signature on the tuple (I, D, s).

The statement protocol is shown in figure 4.

Embedded Mode: In embedded mode, all operations are the same, except that on the user side operations are run in the In-Car-Unit instead of the portable device. We assume this In-Car-Unit is tamper resistance in order to support tracing of stolen car.

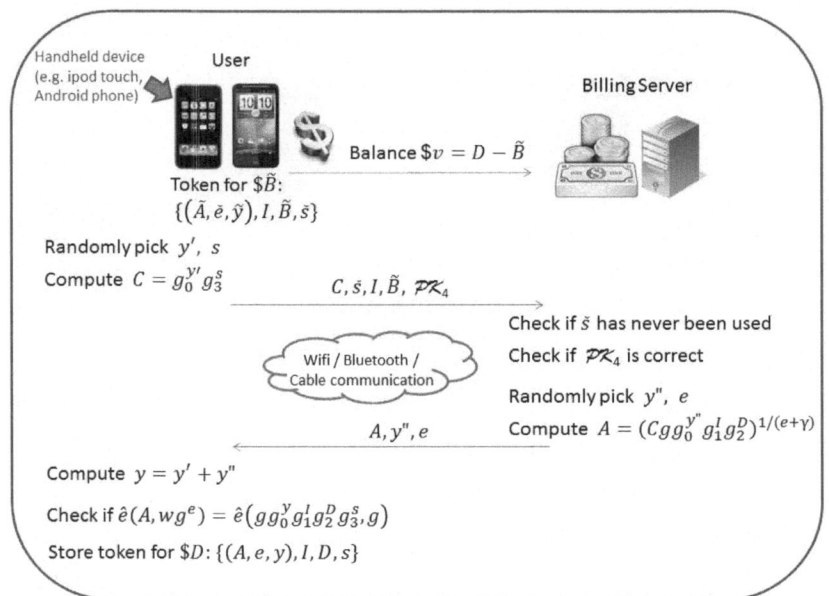

Fig. 4. Statement

In order to support traceability of stolen car, the user needs to backup the newly generated token after each operation (including Registration, Charging, Topup, Statement) into his backup device (e.g. USB thumb drive).

Tracing Stolen Car: In case the car is stolen and the user wants to trace his stolen car, he can reveal his token $\{(A,e,y),I,D,s\}$ to the supplier (and all charging stations). Any charging station receiving the token containing s in the future will refuse to provide service and report to the user and the police immediately since that means the stolen car is at that charging station requesting a service.

Note that this requires the user to report the lost before the thief makes a recharge. In this aspect it is similar to credit card. In our extension described in Section 5.3, we discuss how the thief can be traced even if he/she makes a recharge before the user's report.

5 Extensions

5.1 Incorporating Token Expiry

In our basic construction, token never expires and the supplier needs to store all the s forever. An expiration mechanism can be incorporated easily. Let $H : \{0,1\}^* \to \mathbb{G}$ be a collision-resistant hash function. Let $T \in \{0,1\}^*$ be the identifier of current time period. In practice, T could be the bit string Jan2012,

Feb2012, etc. The public parameter g_1, g_2, g_3 in param is replaced with the hash function H.

Let T_j be the current period and T_{j+1} be the next period. For example, $T_j =$ Jan2012 and $T_{j+1} =$ Feb2012. In the protocols, the value g_i will be replaced with $H(T,i)$ for $i = 1$ to 3. At the end of period T_j, all users will contact the supplier in the statement protocol. During the execution of the protocol, $g_i = H(T_{j+1}, i)$ will be used in the computation of the value A. Thus, in period T_{j+1}, the user will be using $g_i = H(T_{j+1}, i)$ for charging and topup and the previous token will not be usable.

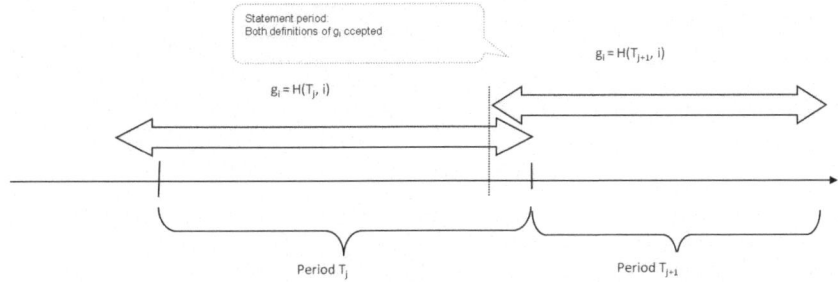

Fig. 5. Timeline demonstrating the expiration mechanism

Of course, to accommodate the user who executes the statement protocol before the end of T_j, both $g_i = H(T_j, i)$ and $g_i = H(T_{j+1}, i)$ will be accepted at the end of period T_j. Fig.5 illustrates our idea. This extension does not alter the efficiency of our system.

5.2 Incorporating Judge (<u>Open</u> Operation)

Sometimes giving user too much privacy is not preferable. Thus, it is natural to introduce an external entity to the system, called judge, which is capable of identifying the user in all transactions. The judge would be trusted to exhibit its power in appropriate situation only, for example, under the court order. To introduce this additional feature, we review another cryptographic tool called verifiable encryption.

Verifiable Encryption. A verifiable encryption scheme is a public key encryption scheme with an additional feature. In its basic form, it allows a prover to prove to a verifier that the plaintext PT encrypted in a known ciphertext CT under the public key of a third party PKE satisfies some binary relation R. The concept of verifiable encryption was introduce in [22]. In [23], it has been shown that any public key encryption scheme can be turned into a verifiable encryption scheme for all relation having a 3-move proof-of-knowledge protocol (as known as honest verifier zero-knowledge protocol). An efficient construction of such primitive has been proposed in [24].

Introducing Judge in Our System. Let PKE be the public key of the judge. Recall that in all our protocols, user is required to send $C = g_0^{y'} g_1^I g_2^{\tilde{B}} g_3^s$ (or $C = g_0^{y'} g_3^s$ in case $\tilde{B}$ and I are sent in plain in registration and statement). In our extension, a user is required to produce a ciphertext CT which is the encryption of $(y', I, \tilde{B}, s)$ under the public key PKE, and produces a proof that CT is the encryption of the correct values with respect to C. In this case, the judge can always decrypt CT and obtains the values $(y', I, \tilde{B}, s)$ and traces the action of the user.

The most efficient verifiable encryption due to [24] has a message space of $\mathbb{Z}_n$, where n is the product of two primes. One subtlety arises since the values $(y', I, \tilde{B}, s)$ in our basic construction are treated as elements of $\mathbb{Z}_p$. Direct combination of the two would not be secure since a cheating user can encrypt his identity as $I + kp$ for some integer k and produce a proof that he has encrypted his identity. The decrypted value from the Judge would be $I + kp \bmod n$, which may not be $I \bmod p$. To make it compatible with our system, we can change our groups of prime order p to groups of composite number n. This change, however, would make the pairing operation rather inefficient. The reason is that $|p| = 170$ would offer a similar security compared with $|n| = 1024$.

A more effective alternative is to employ the signature scheme [25] instead of BBS+ if judge is introduced in our system[3], which works in a cyclic group of unknown order. In that case, $(y', I, \tilde{B}, s)$ are all treated as integers within a specific range and the above attack is not possible.

5.3   Report of Lost Token/ Tracing Stolen Car

The user token is completely software-based. The user should backup his secret (σ_s, I, B, s) in another USB storage device after each recharge or topup. He sends the token to the supplier to report his lost. The supplier checks whether it is a valid one. If yes, it extracts the value s and blocks any future transaction involving s. The supplier also issues a new token to the user using **Statement** operation associated with his remaining balance. This process is similar to the traceability of stolen car described in the Section 4.3.

In the case of the lost token (or the lost car in the embedded mode) that has been used by the thief already for recharge, it still could be located. In this situation, the judge will open all transactions within the range of the electric vehicle and look for the identity of the lost token/vehicle. Hence, the lost token can still be traced.

6   Practicality Analysis

Due to space limitaion, efficiency, cost and security analysis data of our scheme will be given in the full version of this paper [18].

---

[3] In other words, BBS+ is more efficient in systems without the need of a Judge. With judge, [25] will be more efficient.

7   Concluding Remarks

In this paper, we presented a mechanism to enhance location privacy for electric vehicles. Our proposed solution provides an anonymous payment system with privacy protection support. In the case where traceability is required, such as when the electric vehicle is stolen, this feature can also be provided. Hence, our solution provides location privacy enhancement at the right time, which will make the adoption of electric vehicles practical.

Our system provides an option to incorporate a judge who can open all transactions in case of any dispute. Currently the judge cannot selectively open a particular user but to open every user's transactions. We leave it as an open problem to allow the judge *selectively* open a particular user while keeping others unopened.

We also note that the scheme described in this paper is specifically designed for electric vehicles. However, we do not eliminate the possibility to apply our scheme (or modified version) in other environments if they find it suitable.

References

1. Chia, M., Krishnan, S., Zhou, J.: Challenges and Opportunities in Infrastructure Support for Electric Vehicles and Smart Grid in a Dense Urban Environment. To Appear in IEEE International Electric Vehicle Conference 2012 (2012)
2. Hoh, B., Gruteser, M., Xiong, H., Alrabady, A.: Enhancing security and privacy in traffic-monitoring systems. IEEE Pervasive Computing 5(4), 38–46 (2006)
3. Liao, L., Patterson, D.J., Fox, D., Kautz, H.A.: Learning and inferring transportation routines. Artif. Intell. 171(5-6), 311–331 (2007)
4. Golle, P., Partridge, K.: On the Anonymity of Home/Work Location Pairs. In: Tokuda, H., Beigl, M., Friday, A., Brush, A.J.B., Tobe, Y. (eds.) Pervasive 2009. LNCS, vol. 5538, pp. 390–397. Springer, Heidelberg (2009)
5. Duckham, M.: Moving forward: location privacy and location awareness. In: SPRINGL, pp. 1–3. ACM (2010)
6. Bilogrevic, I., Jadliwala, M., Kalkan, K., Hubaux, J.P., Aad, I.: Privacy in Mobile Computing for Location-Sharing-Based Services. In: Fischer-Hübner, S., Hopper, N. (eds.) PETS 2011. LNCS, vol. 6794, pp. 77–96. Springer, Heidelberg (2011)
7. Freudiger, J., Shokri, R., Hubaux, J.P.: Evaluating the Privacy Risk of Location-Based Services. In: Danezis, G. (ed.) FC 2011. LNCS, vol. 7035, pp. 31–46. Springer, Heidelberg (2012)
8. Chaum, D., Pedersen, T.P.: Transferred Cash Grows in Size. In: Rueppel, R.A. (ed.) EUROCRYPT 1992. LNCS, vol. 658, pp. 390–407. Springer, Heidelberg (1993)
9. Fuchsbauer, G., Pointcheval, D., Vergnaud, D.: Transferable Constant-Size Fair E-Cash. In: Garay, J.A., Miyaji, A., Otsuka, A. (eds.) CANS 2009. LNCS, vol. 5888, pp. 226–247. Springer, Heidelberg (2009)
10. Brickell, E.F., Gemmell, P., Kravitz, D.W.: Trustee-based tracing extensions to anonymous cash and the making of anonymous change. In: SODA, pp. 457–466. ACM/SIAM (1995)
11. Camenisch, J., Piveteau, J.M., Stadler, M.: An efficient fair payment system. In: ACM Conference on Computer and Communications Security, pp. 88–94. ACM (1996)

12. Blazy, O., Canard, S., Fuchsbauer, G., Gouget, A., Sibert, H., Traoré, J.: Achieving Optimal Anonymity in Transferable E-Cash with a Judge. In: Nitaj, A., Pointcheval, D. (eds.) AFRICACRYPT 2011. LNCS, vol. 6737, pp. 206–223. Springer, Heidelberg (2011)
13. Carbunar, B., Shi, W., Sion, R.: Conditional e-payments with transferability. J. Parallel Distrib. Comput. 71(1), 16–26 (2011)
14. Pedersen, T.P.: Non-interactive and Information-Theoretic Secure Verifiable Secret Sharing. In: Feigenbaum, J. (ed.) CRYPTO 1991. LNCS, vol. 576, pp. 129–140. Springer, Heidelberg (1992)
15. Au, M.H., Susilo, W., Mu, Y.: Constant-Size Dynamic k-TAA. In: De Prisco, R., Yung, M. (eds.) SCN 2006. LNCS, vol. 4116, pp. 111–125. Springer, Heidelberg (2006)
16. Camenisch, J., Lysyanskaya, A.: Signature Schemes and Anonymous Credentials from Bilinear Maps. In: Franklin, M. (ed.) CRYPTO 2004. LNCS, vol. 3152, pp. 56–72. Springer, Heidelberg (2004)
17. Boneh, D., Boyen, X., Shacham, H.: Short Group Signatures. In: Franklin, M. (ed.) CRYPTO 2004. LNCS, vol. 3152, pp. 41–55. Springer, Heidelberg (2004)
18. Liu, J.K., Au, M.H., Susilo, W., Zhou, J.: Enhancing location privacy for electric vehicles (at the right time). Cryptology ePrint Archive, Report 2012 (2012), http://eprint.iacr.org/
19. Goldwasser, S., Micali, S., Rackoff, C.: The Knowledge Complexity of Interactive Proof Systems. SIAM J. Comput. 18(1), 186–208 (1989)
20. Camenisch, J., Stadler, M.: Efficient Group Signature Schemes for Large Groups (Extended Abstract). In: Kaliski Jr., B.S. (ed.) CRYPTO 1997. LNCS, vol. 1294, pp. 410–424. Springer, Heidelberg (1997)
21. Au, M.H., Kapadia, A., Susilo, W.: BLACR: TTP-Free Blacklistable Anonymous Credentials with Reputation. In: NDSS. The Internet Society (2012)
22. Stadler, M.: Publicly Verifiable Secret Sharing. In: Maurer, U.M. (ed.) EUROCRYPT 1996. LNCS, vol. 1070, pp. 190–199. Springer, Heidelberg (1996)
23. Camenisch, J., Damgård, I.: Verifiable Encryption, Group Encryption, and Their Applications to Separable Group Signatures and Signature Sharing Schemes. In: Okamoto, T. (ed.) ASIACRYPT 2000. LNCS, vol. 1976, pp. 331–345. Springer, Heidelberg (2000)
24. Camenisch, J., Shoup, V.: Practical Verifiable Encryption and Decryption of Discrete Logarithms. In: Boneh, D. (ed.) CRYPTO 2003. LNCS, vol. 2729, pp. 126–144. Springer, Heidelberg (2003)
25. Camenisch, J., Lysyanskaya, A.: A Signature Scheme with Efficient Protocols. In: Cimato, S., Galdi, C., Persiano, G. (eds.) SCN 2002. LNCS, vol. 2576, pp. 268–289. Springer, Heidelberg (2003)

Design and Implementation of a Terrorist Fraud Resilient Distance Bounding System

Aanjhan Ranganathan[1], Nils Ole Tippenhauer[1], Boris Škorić[2],
Dave Singelée[3], and Srdjan Čapkun[1]

[1] ETH Zurich, 8092 Zurich, Switzerland
{Aanjhan.Ranganathan,Nils.Tippenhauer,Srdjan.Čapkun}@inf.ethz.ch
[2] TU Eindhoven, Eindhoven, Netherlands
b.skoric@tue.nl
[3] K.U. Leuven ESAT/SCD-COSIC, Leuven, Belgium
Dave.Singelee@esat.kuleuven.be

Abstract. Given the requirements of fast processing and the complexity of RF ranging systems, distance bounding protocols have been challenging to implement so far; only few designs have been proposed and implemented. Currently, the most efficient implementation of distance bounding protocols uses analog processing and enables the prover to receive a message, process it and transmit the reply within 1 ns, two orders of magnitude faster than the most efficient digital implementation. However, even if implementing distance bounding using analog processing clearly provides tighter security guarantees than digital implementations, existing analog implementations do not support resilience against *Terrorist Fraud* attacks; they protect only against *Distance Fraud* and *Mafia Fraud* attacks. We address this problem and propose a new, hybrid digital-analog design that enables the implementation of Terrorist Fraud resilient distance bounding protocols. We introduce a novel attack, which we refer to as the "double read-out" attack and show that our proposed system is also secure against this attack. Our system consists of a prototype prover that provides strong security guarantees: if a dishonest prover performs the Terrorist Fraud attack, it can cheat on its distance bound to the verifier only up to 4.5 m and if it performs Distance Fraud or Mafia Fraud attacks up to 0.41 m. Finally, we show that our system can be used to implement existing (Terrorist Fraud resilient) distance bounding protocols (e.g., the Swiss Knife and Hancke-Kuhn protocol) without requiring protocol modifications.

Keywords: Secure Ranging, Distance Bounding, Terrorist Fraud.

1 Introduction

Wireless localization solutions that emerged in the last decade [19] promise to support a broad set of security- and safety-critical applications, including people and asset tracking, emergency and rescue support [9], secure routing [16] and access control [12,24]. Given the sensitivity of location information in those applications, this information needs to be obtained and/or verified securely.

S. Foresti, M. Yung, and F. Martinelli (Eds.): ESORICS 2012, LNCS 7459, pp. 415–432, 2012.

One of the most prominent problems in the field of secure localization is that of proximity verification: how can one device (the verifier) establish its distance, either exact or as an upper bound to another device (the prover). This problem was first introduced in [4] and prompted a design of a set of distance bounding protocols [29,30,14,25,20,26,5,6,21,22,27]. Broader deployment of wireless networks and the attacks on proximity-based access control systems (e.g., in cars [10]), routing [15] and payment systems [11] led to an increased interest in the design and implementation of distance bounding protocols [18,29,25,13]. The security of these protocols was mainly analyzed against three types of attacks: Distance Fraud attacks, Mafia Fraud attacks and Terrorist Fraud. Distance bounding protocols were further formally analyzed in a number of works [2,5,3].

Distance bounding protocols rely on the exchange of timed challenges and responses between the verifier and the prover. However, given that the prover is not trusted by the verifier and no assumptions can be made about its processing capabilities, the time that the prover spends in processing the verifier's challenge should be negligible compared to the measured round-trip time, which depends on the speed of light. If the verifier would overestimate the prover's processing time (i.e., the prover is able to process signals in a shorter time than expected), the prover would be able to pretend to be closer to the verifier. The challenge in implementing distance bounding protocols is therefore first to implement a prover that is able to receive, process and transmit signals in negligible time.

Although a number of protocols have been proposed, it is not clear if the proposed distance bounding protocols can be implemented with the required tight processing (and therefore security) guarantees or can be integrated within the existing RF ranging systems. For example, almost all distance bounding protocols assume that a prover will be able to receive a single bit of the challenge, XOR it or compare it with some locally stored value, and transmit the response; all within negligible time. XORs and comparisons require digital processing and the most efficient implementation in the open literature that can realize such distance bounding protocols requires 170 ns [28] and thus enables the attacker to cheat on its distance by at most 27 m. An alternative implementation of distance bounding protocols, using analog processing was proposed in [25] enabling signal reception/processing/transmission within 1 ns and thus provided a tight security guarantee of 15 cm. Instead of using XOR or comparison, this design relied on a processing function called Challenge Reflection with Channel Selection (CRCS), which can be implemented using only analog processing techniques. In [13], a design for implementing a secure distance bounding channel for the rapid bit-exchange in a near-field environment was presented. The experimental implementation used improvised wideband pulses and achieved a distance bound of 1 m in the case of Mafia Fraud attacks and 11 m for Distance Frauds.

However, even if implementing distance bounding using analog processing techniques clearly provides tighter security guarantees than digital implementations, existing analog implementations do not support resilience against *Terrorist Fraud* attacks; they are only suited for the prevention of *Distance Fraud* and *Mafia Fraud* attacks. We address this problem and propose a new, hybrid digital-analog design of a distance bounding system called *Switched Challenge Reflector with Carrier Switching* that enables the implementation of Terrorist Fraud resilient distance bounding protocols such as the Swiss Knife Protocol [17]. Our system does not introduce new processing functions at the prover (such as CRCS); instead, it uses the "bit comparison" function that is commonly used in a number of distance bounding protocols including the Hancke-Kuhn protocol [14].

In our proposed design, the verifier transmits challenges on two different carrier frequencies; the switching time synchronized with the prover. Four possible reply channels are created before activating the appropriate reflected carrier frequency. Based on the credentials held by the prover and the carrier frequency of the received challenge, an activation circuity inside the system appropriately enables the reply channel. Analysis of our prototype shows that the verifier can be cheated only up to 4.5 m in the scenario of a Terrorist Fraud attack and further only up to 0.41 m under a Distance or Mafia Fraud attacker model. Given its design, our system can be used to implement existing Terrorist Fraud resilient distance bounding protocols (e.g., the Swiss Knife protocol). Furthermore, it can be used to implement all distance bounding protocols that follow the Hancke-Kuhn construction without requiring any modifications of the protocol.

2   Background

The goal of a distance bounding protocol is that a verifier establishes an upper bound on its distance to a prover. Although many distance bounding protocols were proposed so far [4,23,29,20,14,30,17], they all follow a similar pattern. The protocols consist of either two or three phases. In the first phase, the verifier and the prover agree or commit to the nonces that will be used in the rest of the protocol. In the second phase, also called the rapid bit exchange, the verifier challenges the prover with a number of single-bit challenges to which the prover replies with single-bit replies. The verifier measures the round-trip times of these challenge-reply pairs, based on which the verifier estimates its upper distance bound to the prover. The distance D between the verifier and the prover is calculated using the equation $D = \frac{c \cdot (t_{RTOF} - t_p)}{2}$, where c is the speed of light ($3 \cdot 10^8$ m/s), t_{RTOF} is the round-trip time elapsed and t_p is the processing delay at the prover before responding to the challenge. The final phase of the protocol is used for confirmation and authentication; note that in a number of protocols this last phase is not present.

Traditionally, the security of distance bounding protocols was evaluated by analyzing their resilience against three types of attacks: *Distance Fraud, Mafia Fraud* and *Terrorist Fraud* attacks. In a Distance Fraud attack a dishonest prover tries to shorten the distance measured by the verifier (e.g., by sending its replies before receiving the challenges). This type of attack is executed by the dishonest prover alone, without collusion with other (external) parties.

Mafia Fraud attacks, also called relay attacks, were first described by Desmedt [8]. In this type of attack, both the prover and verifier are honest. The external attacker attempts to shorten the distance measured between the honest prover and the verifier by relaying the communications between the entities.

Finally, in the Terrorist Fraud attacks, a dishonest prover collaborates with an external attacker to convince the verifier that he is closer than he really is. All countermeasures to Terrorist Fraud make the assumption that the dishonest prover is unwilling to reveal his long-term (private or secret) key to the attacker that he collaborates with. Possible grounds for this unwillingness are impersonation, i. e., the external attacker can later use the key to impersonate the dishonest prover, and traceability, i. e., the key may later be used to implicate the dishonest prover in performing a Terrorist Fraud attack. Furthermore, from the perspective of the verifier, it is impossible to distinguish between the external attacker and the prover if the attacker knows the long term key of the prover. Recently, another type of an attack, called the Distance Hijacking attack was introduced [7]. In this attack a dishonest prover convinces the verifier that it is at a distance at which some other honest prover resides, which differs from the actual physical distance of the dishonest prover to the verifier.

2.1   Terrorist Fraud Resilient Protocols

Terrorist Fraud resilient protocols preserve the basic structure of distance bounding protocols, but bind the prover's long term secret to the nonces that are exchanged in the protocol. This prevents the prover from simply handing over the nonces to the external attacker without disclosing its long term secret.

We illustrate the operation of these protocols through an example: the *Swiss Knife* protocol. This protocol was proposed by Kim *et al.* in 2009 [17] (see Fig. 1). The protocol assumes that the verifier has a database containing prover identities (ID) and their symmetric keys (x) and that each prover possesses his own identifier and key. The protocol is executed in three phases.

Preparation phase: From its locally generated nonce N^B, a shared secret x and a constant C^B, the prover creates two m-bit strings (R^0 and R^1) using a keyed pseudorandom function f. Disclosing both R^0 and R^1 would immediately reveal m bits of x.

Rapid-bit-exchange phase: In each round i of the rapid-bit-exchange phase, the verifier sends a random single-bit challenge c_i. Upon reception of c_i', the prover replies with the value taken from R_i^0, if $c_i' = 0$ and from R_i^1, if $c_i' = 1$. c_i' denotes the modification of c_i over the channel either due to an attack or due to transmission errors.

Concluding phase: The prover sends a Message Authentication Code (MAC) computed over the nonces and received challenges. The verifier then makes a number of checks: he tries to find an entry x in his database for which the MAC is valid; he checks if the number of transmission errors in the challenges are not too high; if the number of incorrect responses to correctly received challenges is not too high; and if the responses were sent in time. If all these checks pass, the verifier authenticates itself to the prover by computing a MAC on the prover's nonce N^B.

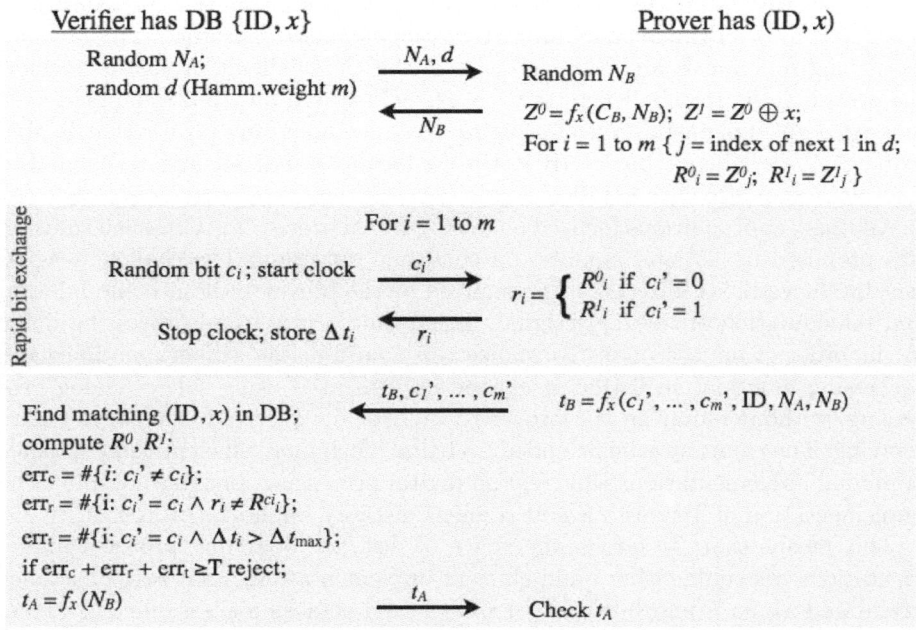

Fig. 1. The Swiss Knife protocol. Picture adapted from [17]

In this protocol, the values of the registers R^0 and R^1 are bound to the prover's long term secret x. If the prover would like to perform a terrorist attack, it would need to give R^0 and R^1 to the external attacker, thus disclosing x.

2.2 Implementations of Distance Bounding Protocols

The security of distance bounding protocols largely depends on the assumption that the prover's processing time is negligible compared to the measured challenge-response round-trip times. Given that the verifier does not trust the prover and cannot estimate the prover's hardware and processing capabilities, the safest assumption that the verifier can make is that the prover is able to process the challenges and transmit the replies in negligible time. If the verifier overestimates the prover's processing time (i.e., the prover is able to process signals in a shorter time than expected), the prover would be able to pretend to be closer, thus violating the distance bound. The challenge in implementing distance bounding protocols is therefore first to implement a prover that is able to receive, process and transmit signals in negligible time.

Implementations of distance bounding protocols took two distinct directions. One set of solutions focused on digital signal processing, that would enable the implementation of arbitrary processing functions at the prover. In the case of the Swiss Knife protocols, the prover's processing function is the bit comparison (interpretation of the verifier's challenge bit) and the read-out of the register value. This processing function was initially proposed in the Hancke-Kuhn protocol [14]. In the Brands and Chaum's distance bounding protocol, the prover's processing function is an XOR; upon receiving the challenge from the verifier, the prover XORs the challenge bit with a locally stored bit. In [28] Tippenhauer presented an implementation of a digital distance bounding prover that is able to receiver a challenge bit, XOR it with a locally stored bit and transmit the computed response within 170ns.

Another set of solutions focused on analog signal processing. One such solution was proposed in [25] and is based on challenge reflection. The challenge signal sent by the verifier is directly retransmitted by the prover without demodulation and remodulation of the reply signal. This resulted in a small processing delay in the order of nanoseconds. To realize this solution, the authors modified the processing function, such that it can be implemented using solely analog processing, without requiring the prover to digitize the received challenges before replying. The resulting scheme ended up being much more efficient than distance bounding implementations that rely on digital processing, but did not allow the implementation of Terrorist Fraud resilient distance bounding protocols.

This means that, so far, in the space of distance bounding protocol implementations, we could either build efficient implementations, that resist Distance Fraud and Mafia Fraud but not Terrorist Fraud attacks, or less efficient implementations that resist all three types of attacks.

3   Switched Challenge Reflector with Carrier Shifting

As discussed in Section 2, one of the open problems in distance bounding protocol design space is the realization of Terrorist Fraud resilient distance bounding with low processing delay at the prover. Prover designs based on digital signal processing techniques allow implementation of processing functions such as XOR or register read-out based on challenge bits. However, the process of demodulating the received challenge, computing the response (e.g., XOR with a shared secret), modulating and transmitting back the response incurs significant processing delay. This delay allows attackers executing Distance and Mafia Frauds to gain distance in the order of several tens of meters. Although solutions using only analog processing techniques achieved low processing delay, implementing processing functions such as register selections (critical for Terrorist Fraud resilience) gives rise to new attack scenarios. Due to the nature of analog signals and components, such solutions based on register selection are vulnerable to a new attack that we call the "double read-out" attack (detailed in Section 4) which could potentially leak the long-term shared secret. Here we present a hybrid digital-analog solution to this problem, which we call Switched Challenge Reflector with Carrier Shifting (SCRCS). We show that a prover implementing SCRCS has low processing delay and resists not only Mafia and Distance Frauds but also Terrorist Fraud attacks without allowing any possible "double read-out" attacks.

3.1   Design Overview

In Terrorist Fraud resilient protocols [26,17,30], the verifier challenges the prover with randomly selected bits; in each of the m rounds, based on the received challenge bit the prover replies with a bit from one of the two local registers. The prover's processing therefore consists of receiving the challenge bit and then transmitting a bit from one of the registers, selected based on the received challenge bit. We design SCRCS to implement this functionality.

In our system the verifier challenges the prover with a challenge signal $c(t)$; if the verifier wants the prover to respond with a value from register R^0, it transmits a signal on a predefined carrier frequency ω_0 (encoding the challenge bit "0") and if it wants to query R^1, it transmits on the carrier frequency ω_1 (thus encoding the challenge bit "1").

The prover implements switched challenge reflection with carrier shifting. Figure 2 shows the two main building blocks of the prover: (i) Channel Shifter and (ii) Switched Channel Activator. The prover takes as input the challenge signal $c(t)$, which will be at the carrier frequency ω_0 or ω_1; its Channel Shifter component (details in Section 3.2) creates two copies of the received signal: at $\omega_0 + \omega_\Delta$ and $\omega_0 - \omega_\Delta$ or at $\omega_1 + \omega_\Delta$ and $\omega_1 - \omega_\Delta$ where $\omega_\Delta < (\omega_1 - \omega_0)/2$. The two created signals (e.g., the signals at $\omega_0 \pm \omega_\Delta$) are then fed into the Switched Channel Activator circuit which then, depending on the current value of the queried register, outputs $(r(t))$ only one of the two signals (e.g., the signal at $\omega_0 + \omega_\Delta$). The Switched Channel Activator circuit is constructed such that it only allows either the signals at $\omega_0 \pm \omega_\Delta$ or signals at $\omega_1 \pm \omega_\Delta$ but not both simultaneously.

The start of each rapid bit exchange round i.e., the times at which the verifier switches its challenge carrier frequency is synchronized with the prover. This is achieved by the verifier sending an initial preamble defining the exact starting time of the rounds in the rapid-bit exchange phase. This allows the prover to provide an accurate clock to the switched channel activator block (details in Section 3.3) that is responsible for enabling the appropriate reply channel.

Below we discuss our prover design in more detail.

3.2   Channel Shifter

The channel shifter receives the incoming challenge signal $c'(t)$ and applies filters creating four possible reply channels. Figure 3 illustrates in detail the operation of channel shifter module. The received challenges are mixed with an offset frequency ω_Δ ($\omega_\Delta < (\omega_1 - \omega_0)/2$). Based on the carrier frequency on which the challenge is transmitted, the mixer output signal consists of two out of four possible frequency components ($\omega_0 \pm \omega_\Delta$ or $\omega_1 \pm \omega_\Delta$). A set of low-pass and high-pass filters separate the frequency components resulting in four possible reply channels. These are then fed into the switched channel activator block.

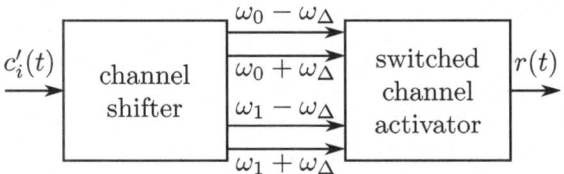

Fig. 2. Overview of the switched challenge reflector with carrier shifting

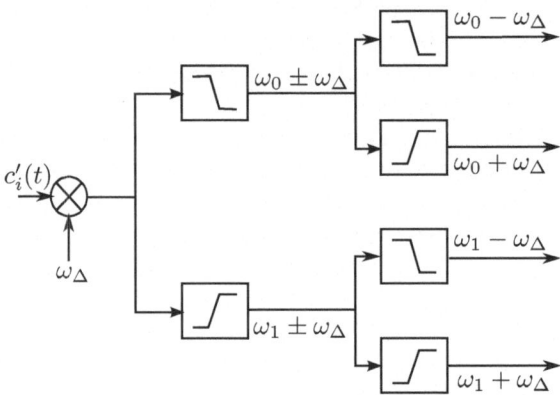

Fig. 3. The channel shifter. The incoming signal $c(t)$ contains the challenges on either carrier frequency ω_0 or ω_1. After mixing $c(t)$ with ω_Δ, the signal is filtered appropriately to generate the four possible response channels: $\omega_0 - \omega_\Delta, \omega_0 + \omega_\Delta, \omega_1 - \omega_\Delta, \omega_1 + \omega_\Delta$.

3.3   Switched Channel Activator

The switched channel activator module enables the appropriate reply channel based on amount of energy detected in each of the four signals output by the channel shifter. The module consists of two clocked registers R^0 and R^1, a channel activation circuitry and a memory element to store which channel was activated every round as shown in Figure 4. Both the memory and registers R^0 and R^1 are clocked with the signal CLK, which signals the start of each round in the rapid bit-exchange phase of the protocol. The output $r(t)$ depends on the carrier frequency of $c'(t)$ and the content of R^0 and R^1 during the current round. For example, if the challenge is sent on ω_i, the output is on the channel $\omega_i + (2R^i - 1)\omega_\Delta$. The channel activation circuitry detects the carrier frequency of the challenge signal based on energy detection. Once a channel is activated, it will disable the other channel's activation circuit (i.e. $O_1 = \overline{EN_0}$).

Channel Activation: Figure 5 shows the internals of the channel activation circuitry. The channel activation mechanism ensures that only one of the output channels is activated in each round of the rapid-bit exchange. After this initial activation, the channel then stays active for the remainder of the current round, reflecting all challenges on this frequency. This selection requires an initial energy and carrier detection, which takes δ_a time in each round of the rapid bit exchange.

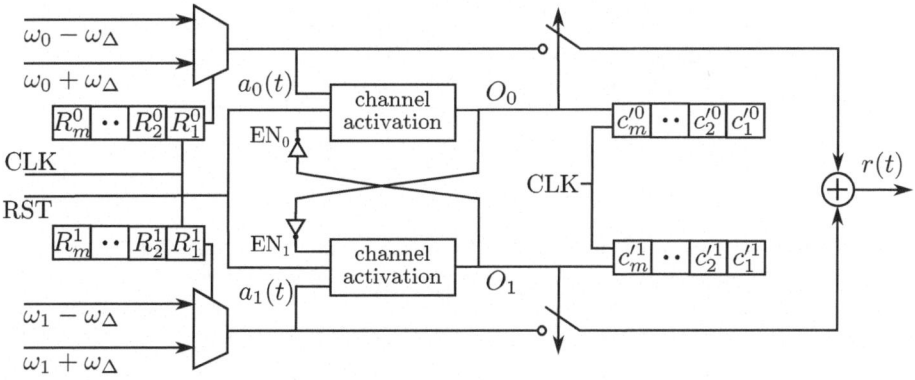

Fig. 4. Switched channel activator. The registers R^0 and R^1 select which two of the four reply channels are used in this round. The channel in which sufficient energy is encountered first gets enabled. After a channel is activated, it stays active until the end of this rapid bit-exchange round while the other channels remain de-activated until the end of this round.

After δ_a, the correct reply channel is activated and reflects $c'(t)$ with very low delay (incurred by mixing and filtering). The selection of the reply channel is based on the first carrier frequency which contained energy above the threshold T^E. After each round in the rapid bit exchange, all reply channels are deactivated by asserting the RST signal until energy is encountered again in the next round.

Security of Terrorist Fraud resilient protocols relies on the fact that extracting the contents of both the registers R^0 and R^1 compromises the long term shared secret. In fully digital implementation of provers it is not possible to read-out both the register contents simultaneously. However, in our design due to the nature of analog signals and components, there is a possibility of extracting both register contents. We explain this in detail in Section 4. The important role of the channel activation module is to prevent an attacker from executing such *double read-out* attacks by ensuring only one reply channel is active at any given point in time of a particular round.

Synchronization between the Verifier and Prover: Synchronization between the verifier and the prover is essential for easy verification of the reflected signal later in the concluding phase of the protocol. As discussed in Section 3.1, a preamble sequence transmitted by the verifier is used to establish this synchronization and to generate the switched channel activator's CLK signal. Using this clock, channels are reset at the start of each round of the rapid bit-exchange. It is important to note that the processing time of the preamble does not have strict limitations or security implications. The prover can take some deterministic time δ_p to process the preamble, as long as the challenge data sequence starts at a time greater than δ_p after the preamble.

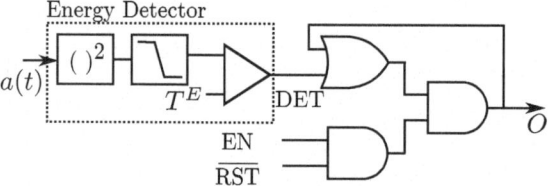

Fig. 5. Internals of channel activation. We obtain a DC component of the squared signal to detect energy in the channel and store the value for this round in a latch-like circuit. The channel activation can be disabled by pulling EN (enable signal) low and is automatically reset at the beginning of each round of the rapid-bit exchange (RST).

4   Security Analysis

We investigate the security impact of our proposed distance bounding system with respect to each of the three attack scenarios. In addition, we consider a fourth attack: *double read-out attacks* on Terrorist and Mafia Fraud resilient systems with multiple registers at the prover side.

4.1   Resilience against Distance Fraud Attacks

In Distance Fraud attacks, the malicious prover is further than D away from the verifier. In order to shorten the measured distance, he will have to send the reply signal $r(t)$ earlier than an honest prover. To achieve this goal, the prover has two options: (a) predict the challenge signal $c(t)$, including the carrier frequency used for each round, or (b) reflect $c(t)$ in with less delay than expected.

The probability to correctly predict the challenge signal $c(t)$ for m rounds of rapid bit exchange depends on the nature of the baseband data signal modulated on the challenge carrier. In the worst case, a constant data signal is modulated on the carrier, which enables the malicious prover to predict it. In this case, our system matches the security analysis of the distance bounding protocol it is used in, as the malicious prover only has to predict which of the registers R^0 and R^1 gets queried in each round. If the baseband signal in $c(t)$ contains data which is unpredictable for the prover, the chance to send a early correct $r(t)$ is strictly smaller than predicted by the overlying protocol. An exact specification depends on the nature of the baseband data signal.

In the following, we analyze the security impact of timing parameters (see Figure 6).

Reflection Delay (δ_r): Even if the malicious prover can reflect the challenge with less delay than expected, this will only yield an improvement in the order of nanoseconds. In our implementation, the reflection delay δ_r once the channel is activated is around 3 ns. This means the attacker can only gain a distance advantage of 50 cm by reducing δ_r to 0.

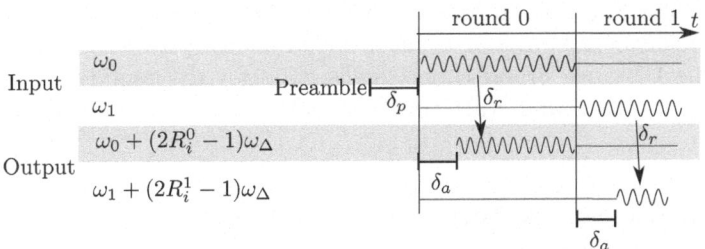

Fig. 6. Timing related variables for challenge reflection : In each round, channel activation adds an initial delay δ_a. After channel activation, the challenges are reflected with a very small delay δ_r. The start time of each round depends on the initial preamble synchronization by the prover.

Activation Delay (δ_a)**:** If the prover is able to shorten δ_a, the correct channel can be activated sooner. Nevertheless, this will not shorten the reflection delay δ_r, and therefore not influence the measured distance for this attack case.

Round start time (δ_p)**:** In our design, we assume that the prover was able to establish the exact start time for each round due to a synchronization preamble sent earlier. This time is required to successfully run the protocol—if the timing is changed, the protocol will most likely fail, instead of returning a wrong distance measure.

If the malicious prover (or external attacker) advances the local round start time of the prover, the channel might be activated by the previous round's carrier frequency. This leads to incorrect reflection of the challenge in 50% of the rounds. If the round start time at the prover is delayed, the prover will not switch to the correct reply channel early enough. Since we have a strict requirement for δ_a, the channel activation delay, this will also cause the protocol to fail. Therefore, changing the round start time does not give an advantage to either malicious prover or external attacker.

4.2   Resilience against Mafia Fraud Attacks

In the Mafia Fraud, an external attacker close to the verifier tries to impersonate the prover. To successfully impersonate the prover, the attacker can either (a) guess the content of the registers R^0 and R^1 in advance (with probability as predicted in the original protocols), or (b) try to send *early challenges* to the honest prover, to obtain the actual content of registers in advance. Since our system allows the prover to record the received challenges, these can be sent to the verifier in the concluding phase of the protocol later. If the protocol performs this reconciliation on the received challenges, the attacker will have to correctly predict the challenge carrier frequencies used in each round of the rapid-bit-exchange to avoid detection. If no reconciliation phase is supported by the protocol (as in [14]), the attacker's chances are better as discussed in the original protocol.

As the Mafia Fraud is an external attack, the attacker cannot influence the processing delays δ_p, δ_a and δ_r of an involved honest prover. The same reasoning as in the Distance Fraud attack holds good for the round start time. Any modification to the round start time will only result in failure of the protocol execution.

4.3   Resilience against Terrorist Fraud Attacks

In a Terrorist Fraud attack, an attacker close to the verifier tries to impersonate the prover. The prover will support the attacker, if this does not compromise his long-term secret. In our rapid-bit-exchange scheme, the content of both registers R^0 and R^1 is needed by the attacker to successfully impersonate the prover. But as both register values combined allow the attacker to derive the long-term secret, the prover will not be able to provide these.

Another possibility is for the attacker to early detect the current round's challenge carrier frequency, forward it to the malicious prover and obtain that round's register value. In this case, the long term secret of the malicious prover would not be revealed. To estimate the impact of this attack, we consider a strong attacker and prover with both zero processing time for incoming challenges and messages. In this setting, the attacker could use the channel activation time at the start of each round to forward the current round's challenge carrier frequency. In this setting, the attacker could shorten the measured distance by up to $\delta_a/2$. As this delay is typically short ($< 30\,\mathrm{ns}$ in our implementation), the maximal gain is only in the range of few meters ($\approx 2.5\,\mathrm{m}$ for $30\,\mathrm{ns}$ and instantaneous processing).

Reducing the preamble processing delay δ_p will not yield an advantage to the attacker, while a reduction of the reflection delay can reduce the measured distance as discussed above.

4.4   Double Read-Out Attacks

The double read-out attack targets a potential implementation weakness of analog provers with multiple registers. If the attacker manages to simultaneously query (read-out) the values from both registers of the prover, he would be able to reconstruct the prover's long term secret in Terrorist Fraud resilient protocols. In the case of Mafia Fraud resilient protocols, this would allow the attacker to mount a Mafia Fraud attack instead.

Analog implementations e.g., those that would build on CRCS [25] would typically allow a double read-out attack, since they would not prevent the verifier (and the attacker) to transmit the challenge signals on both carrier frequencies simultaneously. To prevent this attack, a digital component is needed (e.g., a channel activation component) that prevents that both register values are transmitted by the prover simultaneously.

More precisely, consider our SCRCS scheme without the channel activation part, i.e. we assume that only the challenge signal and the values of R^0 or R^1 are used to determine the reply channel. In this setting, the attacker could craft a challenge signal which alternates between two challenge carrier frequencies within each round of the rapid bit-exchange and obtain the content of both registers, allowing him to derive the prover's long term secret. Although this attack will most likely be detected by challenge reconciliation in the concluding phase (the MAC'ed c' sent by the prover), the long term secret would still be revealed to the attacker.

In our system, this attack is prevented by the channel activation circuit—this circuit will only allow one register to be read in each round (see Figure 4 and Figure 5). To show that both registers can never be read at the same round, we first show that signal O_i, once activated, can only be deactivated by $\overline{RST}$. In Boolean logic, we can write $O_i = (DET_i \vee O_i) \wedge \overline{RST} \wedge EN_i$, with $\vee$ as boolean OR and $\wedge$ as AND. Therefore, once O_i is high, it only transitions to false (low) if either $\overline{RST}$ or EN_i are low. Using $j = |i-1|$ we can write $\neg EN_i = O_j$. Therefore, once O_i is true (high) and assuming that $\overline{RST}$ is high, O_i can only turn false if O_j is also true. Using the equation above, one can write $EN_i = \neg[(DET_j \vee O_j) \wedge \overline{RST} \wedge EN_j]$. Since O_i is true and $EN_j = \neg O_i$, O_j will always return false. Summarizing, this result shows that a channel can only be deactivated if both channels are true, which cannot happen once one channel is activated. Therefore, both registers cannot be read in the same round.

In addition, our design also prevents unintentional double read-out by the verifier, which might occur if the round start timing of the prover is not aligned well with the verifier. As discussed above, our channel activation will cause the protocol to fail in this case, instead of unintentionally revealing the long-term secret of the prover.

5   Implementation and Analysis

In this section we describe our prototype implementation of the prover and the results of our experiments. We implement our design using commercially available RF modules [1]. The analog components of the prover implementing the switched challenge reflection with carrier shifting is shown in Figure 7. The two carrier frequencies $\omega_0 = 3.5\,\text{GHz}$ and $\omega_1 = 5\,\text{GHz}$ used for transmitting the challenge signal $c(t)$ are generated using function generators and given as input to the prover.

5.1   Channel Shifter

As described in Section 3.2 the channel shifter is implemented using a mixer and six filters (3 low-pass and 3 high-pass). In Figure 7, components 1–4d constitute the channel shifter module. The received signal is amplified and mixed (2) with an intermediate frequency $\omega_\Delta = 500\,\text{MHz}$ generated by a voltage controlled oscillator (1).

Depending on the received carrier frequency (ω_0 or ω_1), the mixer output contains either the frequency components $\omega_0 \pm \omega_\Delta$ or $\omega_1 \pm \omega_\Delta$. This signal now passes through the combination of low-pass and high-pass filters separating the

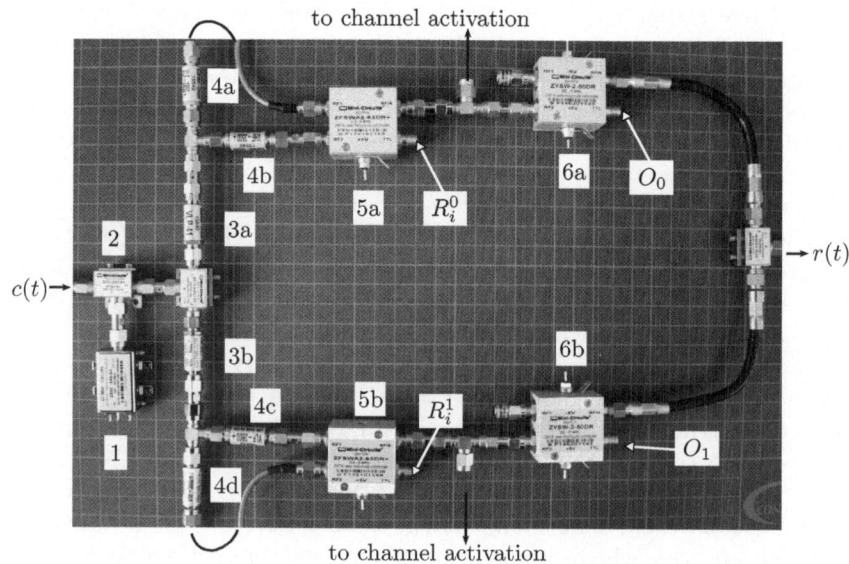

Fig. 7. Experimental Setup: 1: voltage controlled oscillator; 2: mixer; 3a,3b, 4a, 4b, 4c, 4d: filters that constitutes the channel shifter module; 5a, 5b: switches whose output depends on the contents of registers R_i^0 and R_i^1; 6a, 6b: switches that activate the reply channel based on the channel activation circuit outputs (O_0, O_1).

signal into four possible reply channels. For example, if $c(t)$ was transmitted on ω_0, the filters 3a, 4a and 4b (see Figure 7) create the signals with frequency components $\omega_0 + \omega_\Delta$ and $\omega_0 - \omega_\Delta$. Similarly for ω_1, filters 3b, 4c and 4d output $\omega_1 + \omega_\Delta$ and $\omega_1 - \omega_\Delta$. These shifted signals are then fed to the switched channel activator block.

5.2   Channel Activation

The channel activation circuitry constitutes an important part of the prover design to prevent double read-out attacks, as explained in Section 4. The circuit is implemented using a mixer squaring the signal followed by a low-pass filter and a switch. The output of the low-pass filter is the control voltage for the switch. The switch, with one input connected to 5 V and the other grounded acts as a threshold detector whose output is a logic high when its control voltage is above T^E.

We measured the time delay of the channel activation circuitry from the moment the signal is available for energy detection (output of switches 5a, 5b) until the channel is actually activated or deactivated (depends on control signals O_0, O_1 to switches 6a, 6b). Figure 8 shows the control voltage V_{ctrl} and the

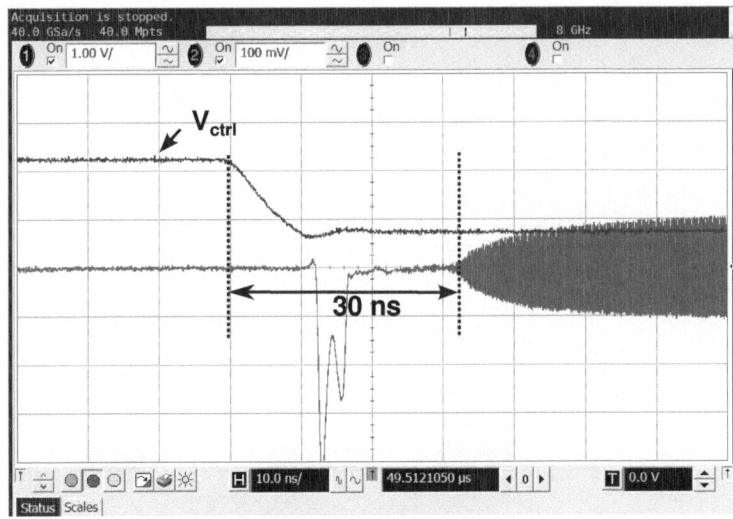

Fig. 8. Delay in switching channels

channel signal. We can see that the switching delay δ_a is approximately 30 ns. As discussed in Section 4 the delay δ_a does not have any security implications in the scenarios of Distance and Mafia Frauds. In the case of Terrorist Fraud an attacker can shorten the distance only up to 4.5 m for $\delta_a = 30$ ns.

5.3   Challenge Reflection Delay

The time taken by the prover to process and reflect back the challenge (δ_r) directly impacts the maximum distance advantage an attacker gains as discussed in Section 4. The challenge signal $c(t)$ is pulse modulated using a $2\,\mu s$ pulse in order to capture and estimate the delay more accurately. The challenge is processed by the prover circuit, and the delay is estimated by tapping into the signal at the circuit's input and output. An oscilloscope with high sampling rate of 40 GSa/s is used to visualize the delay of the signals. Figure 9 shows both input challenge signal and the prover output with a delay of approximately 2.75 ns. This implies that a dishonest prover can gain a maximum distance of 0.41 m by implementing SCRCS with 0 ns delay. The measured delay is independent of the carrier frequency on which the challenge is transmitted and same for both the carrier frequencies (ω_0 and ω_1).

Table 1 summarizes all the delays and the attack scenarios in which they are applicable. It is important to note that these delays would be further reduced by implementing the system as an integrated circuit.

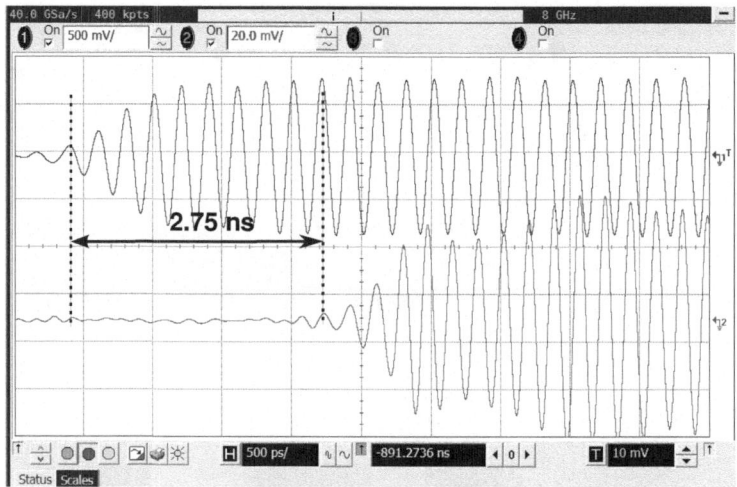

Fig. 9. Prover path delay: The total delay incurred due to mixing, filtering and channel activation switch is estimated to be 2.75ns

Table 1. Summary of prover delays and the attack scenarios under which they are applicable. Reducing or enlarging round start time δ_p would only cause the protocol to fail.

Delay	Max. distance gained	Attack Scenario
$\delta_r = 2.75 \, \text{ns}$	0.41 m	DF, MF and TF
$\delta_a = 30 \, \text{ns}$	4.5 m	TF
δ_p	-NA-	-NA-

6   Summary

In this paper, we designed and implemented a distance bounding system that is resilient to the three well-known distance modification attacks: Distance, Mafia and Terrorist Frauds. Our mixed digital-analog realization allows challenge processing delays of the order of few nanoseconds, thereby limiting the maximum distance an attacker can cheat on. To the best of our knowledge, this is the first implementation of a distance bounding system that is secure against all the three forms of attacks, while having a low processing delay. We introduced a new attack called the "double read-out" attack and showed how our proposed system is secure against it.

With the example of the Swiss Knife protocol, we illustrated how our system design allows implementation of existing Terrorist Fraud resilient protocols and also other distance bounding protocols that are based on the Hancke-Kuhn construction model. We conclude from the delay measurements of our prover prototype that the attacker will be able to decrease distance by not more than

4.5 m in the Terrorist Fraud scenario. This was derived from the processing delay of 2.75 ns and delay incurred during channel activation. This bound further reduced to 0.41 m for the Distance and Mafia Fraud cases. We plan to explore realizing a complete prototype system including the verifier and analyze its security and performance under different real-world environments and applications.

Acknowledgments. This work was funded by the Swiss National Science Foundation (SNSF) under the grant 200020_129605 and NCCR-MICS. The work of Dave Singelée is supported in part by the IAP Programme P6/26 BCRYPT of the Belgian State, by the European Commission under contract number ICT-2007-216676 ECRYPT NoE phase II, by the Flemish IWT SBO project MobCom, and by the Research Council K.U.Leuven: GOA TENSE.

References

1. Mini-Circuits, http://www.minicircuits.com
2. Avoine, G., Bingöl, M.A., Kardaş, S., Lauradoux, C., Martin, B.: A framework for analyzing RFID distance bounding protocols. J. Comput. Secur. 19(2), 289–317 (2011)
3. Basin, D., Capkun, S., Schaller, P., Schmidt, B.: Let's Get Physical: Models and Methods for Real-World Security Protocols. In: Berghofer, S., Nipkow, T., Urban, C., Wenzel, M. (eds.) TPHOLs 2009. LNCS, vol. 5674, pp. 1–22. Springer, Heidelberg (2009)
4. Brands, S., Chaum, D.: Distance Bounding Protocols. In: Helleseth, T. (ed.) EUROCRYPT 1993. LNCS, vol. 765, pp. 344–359. Springer, Heidelberg (1994)
5. Bussard, L., Bagga, W.: Distance-Bounding Proof of Knowledge to Avoid Real-Time Attacks. In: Proceedings of 20th International Conference on Security and Privacy in the Age of Ubiquitous Computing, pp. 223–238 (May 2005)
6. Capkun, S., Buttyn, L., Hubaux, J.P.: Sector: secure tracking of node encounters in multi-hop wireless networks. In: Workshop on Security of Ad Hoc and Sensor Networks (SASN), pp. 21–32. ACM (October 2003)
7. Cremers, C., Rasmussen, K.B., Schmidt, B., Capkun, S.: Distance Hijacking Attacks on Distance Bounding Protocols. In: Proceedings of the 33rd IEEE Symposium on Security and Privacy (May 2012)
8. Desmedt, Y., Goutier, C., Bengio, S.: Special Uses and Abuses of the Fiat Shamir Passport Protocol. In: Pomerance, C. (ed.) CRYPTO 1987. LNCS, vol. 293, pp. 21–39. Springer, Heidelberg (1988)
9. Fischer, C., Gellersen, H.: Location and Navigation Support for Emergency Responders: A Survey. IEEE Pervasive Computing 9, 38–47 (2010)
10. Francillon, A., Danev, B., Čapkun, S.: Relay Attacks on Passive Keyless Entry and Start Systems in Modern Cars. In: Proceedings of the 18th Annual Network and Distributed System Security Symposium. The Internet Society (February 2011)
11. Francis, L., Hancke, G., Mayes, K., Markantonakis, K.: On the security issues of NFC enabled mobile phones. International Journal of Internet Technology and Secured Transactions 2 (December 2010)
12. Gupta, S.K.S., Mukherjee, T., Venkatasubramanian, K., Taylor, T.B.: Proximity Based Access Control in Smart-Emergency Departments. In: Proceedings of the 4th Annual IEEE International Conference on Pervasive Computing and Communications Workshops, pp. 512–516 (March 2006)

13. Hancke, G.P.: Design of a secure distance-bounding channel for RFID. J. Netw. Comput. Appl. 34(3), 877–887 (2011)
14. Hancke, G.P., Kuhn, M.G.: An RFID distance bounding protocol. In: Proceedings of the 1st International Conference on Security and Privacy for Emerging Areas in Communication Networks, pp. 67–73 (September 2005)
15. Hu, Y.C., Perrig, A., Johnson, D.B.: Packet leashes: A defense against wormhole attacks in wireless networks. In: INFOCOM (2003)
16. Hu, Y.C., Perrig, A., Johnson, D.B.: Ariadne: A Secure On-Demand Routing Protocol for Ad Hoc Networks. Wireless Networks 11(1-2), 21–38 (2005)
17. Kim, C.H., Avoine, G., Koeune, F., Standaert, F.-X., Pereira, O.: The Swiss-Knife RFID Distance Bounding Protocol. In: Lee, P.J., Cheon, J.H. (eds.) ICISC 2008. LNCS, vol. 5461, pp. 98–115. Springer, Heidelberg (2009)
18. Kuhn, M., Luecken, H., Tippenhauer, N.O.: UWB Impulse Radio Based Distance Bounding. In: Proceedings of the 7th Workshop on Positioning, Navigation and Communication, pp. 28–37 (March 2010)
19. Liu, H., Darabi, H., Banerjee, P., Liu, J.: Survey of Wireless Indoor Positioning Techniques and Systems. IEEE Transactions on Systems, Man, and Cybernetics 37(6), 1067–1080 (2007)
20. Munilla, J., Ortiz, A., Peinado, A.: Distance bounding protocols with void-challenges for RFID. Printed handout at the Workshop on RFID Security, RFIDSec (2006)
21. Peris-Lopez, P., Castro, J.C.H., Estévez-Tapiador, J.M., van der Lubbe, J.C.A.: Shedding Some Light on RFID Distance Bounding Protocols and Terrorist Attacks. CoRR abs/0906.4618 (2009)
22. Peris-Lopez, P., Castro, J.C.H., Estévez-Tapiador, J.M., Palomar, E., van der Lubbe, J.C.A.: Cryptographic puzzles and distance-bounding protocols: Practical tools for RFID security. In: IEEE International Conference on RFID, pp. 45–52 (April 2010)
23. Poturalski, M., Flury, M., Papadimitratos, P., Hubaux, J.P., Boudec, J.Y.L.: Distance Bounding with IEEE 802.15.4a: Attacks and Countermeasures. IEEE Transactions on Wireless Communications 10(4), 1334–1344 (2011)
24. Rasmussen, K.B., Castelluccia, C., Heydt-Benjamin, T.S., Čapkun, S.: Proximity-based Access Control for Implantable Medical Devices. In: Proceedings of the 16th ACM conference on Computer and Communications Security, pp. 410–419. ACM (November 2009)
25. Rasmussen, K.B., Čapkun, S.: Realization of RF Distance Bounding. In: Proceedings of the 19th USENIX Security Symposium, pp. 389–402 (August 2010)
26. Reid, J., Nieto, J.M.G., Tang, T., Senadji, B.: Detecting relay attacks with timing-based protocols. In: Proceedings of the 2nd ACM Symposium on Information, Computer and Communications Security, pp. 204–213 (March 2007)
27. Singelée, D., Preneel, B.: Distance Bounding in Noisy Environments. In: Stajano, F., Meadows, C., Capkun, S., Moore, T. (eds.) ESAS 2007. LNCS, vol. 4572, pp. 101–115. Springer, Heidelberg (2007)
28. Tippenhauer, N.O.: Physical-Layer Security Aspects of Wireless Localization. Ph.D. thesis, ETH Zurich, Switzerland (2012), draft version
29. Tippenhauer, N.O., Čapkun, S.: ID-Based Secure Distance Bounding and Localization. In: Backes, M., Ning, P. (eds.) ESORICS 2009. LNCS, vol. 5789, pp. 621–636. Springer, Heidelberg (2009)
30. Tu, Y.J., Piramuthu, S.: RFID Distance Bounding Protocols. In: First International EURASIP Workshop on RFID Technology, Vienna, Austria (September 2007)

Applying Divertibility to Blind Ballot Copying in the Helios Internet Voting System

Yvo Desmedt and Pyrros Chaidos*

University College London, UK

Abstract. Cortier & Smyth have explored ballot copying in the Helios e-voting platform as an attack against privacy. They also pointed out that their approach to ballot copying could be detected by a modified Helios. We revisit ballot copying from a different viewpoint: as a tool to prevent vote diffusion (the division of votes among multiple weak candidates) and to lessen the effect of established voting blocs. Our approach is based on *blinding* the ballot casting protocol to create an undetectable copy. A willing voter can cooperate with a prospective copier, helping the copier produce a blinded copy of his ballot without revealing his vote. We prove that Helios is unable to detect the copying. The possibility of such cooperation between voters is manifested only in internet voting and as such is a fundamental difference between internet and booth voting.

1 Introduction

Electronic voting, suggested by Chaum in [12] is one of the more important areas of computer security. It is identified as such in the "Four Grand Challenges in Trustworthy Computing" report [14]:

> There are many new systems planned or currently under design that have significant societal impact, and there is a high probability that we will come to rely on these systems immediately upon their deployment. Among these systems are electronic voting systems, ... A grand research challenge is to ensure that these systems are highly trustworthy despite being attractive targets for attackers.

The move towards electronic voting is justified by factors such as convenience, accessibility and ease of use but more importantly by the existence of provable security properties unavailable to conventional systems, for example *universal verifiability* [39,17] which satisfies the need for transparent elections by enabling election participants as well as outsiders to effectively audit an election. However, even as internet voting systems have been deployed alongside paper ballots in local as well as parliamentary elections [25,29,30], the security of electronic voting systems in general has been often found lacking [4,34].

---

* Pyrros Chaidos was supported by an EPSRC scholarship (EP/G037264/1 – Security Science DTC). A preliminary version of this work was presented at the CRYPTO 2011 rump session.

S. Foresti, M. Yung, and F. Martinelli (Eds.): ESORICS 2012, LNCS 7459, pp. 433–450, 2012.

Helios [1] is a state of the art web-based, universally verifiable Internet voting system. To facilitate universal verifiability, Helios ballots are encrypted and public. Ballots are cast over the Internet via a web browser. Since users have full control over the ballots they submit, Helios is susceptible to coercion, and is thus best suited for use in low-coercion environments. This might appear to limit its use to "low-stakes" elections but may not necessarily be the case. In Estonian parliamentary elections [25] for example, the ability of overwriting a vote with a later one is used in place of coercion resistance. As such, it is conceivable that a system like Helios might be used in a high profile election.

Even though Helios has been based on 30 years of sound cryptographic primitives, previous works have described attacks against Helios compromising both secrecy [15] and correctness [24]. The former, presented by Cortier & Smythe in the 2011 Computer Security Foundations Symposium exploits the lax checking of Helios against duplicate votes. In light of these attacks, security using an add-on approach may be unavoidable even for systems designed with security built-in. Our work has a different goal though: blinded ballot copying. A *blinded* copy of a ballot is a copy that cannot be detected as such. Instead of a forced relationship between coerced and coercer, this form of ballot copying relies on the cooperation of both parties, and is based on trust rather than threats or bribes. This demonstrates how an unspecified property of Helios (the ability to create blinded copies of votes) can be expanded upon to build a secondary system on top of it. The potential for this was also mentioned in [7], independently of [21].

Assume that Alice, Bob, Carol and Dianne are coworkers. Carol and Dianne are candidates for the "employee of the year award". Bob has recently returned from a project abroad and is unsure about the candidates. He would like to ask Alice whom he trusts. Alice does not want to reveal her choice so as not to upset the other candidate. Our goal is to provide a system where Alice (the voter) can assist Bob (the copier) in producing a copy of her ballot whilst ensuring that:

- Bob will not learn anything about Alice's vote that is not also revealed by the tally, but will know that the ballot produced by the copying system contains the same vote as Alice's.
- Alice cannot distinguish the ballot that is produced by the system from a random valid ballot. Therefore, the copier is explicitly given the option of backing out (by using his own choice instead of the copied one) undetected.
- Helios (or any observer) cannot recognise the ballot produced by the system as a copy.

Such a system would allow groups of voters to organise around a trusted figure, partly avoiding the spoiler effect [3] prevalent in plurality elections, thus increasing the weight of their vote and the possibility of obtaining a desired result (to the degree where trust in the original voter is well-deserved).

Using non-malleable encryption (instead of Elgamal) will only make our collaboration between a voter and copiers more complex, but cannot avoid it (due to secure multi-party computation). In fact the only solution seems to necessitate the use of private-key encryption (for example by using code voting) so that a potential copier is able to decrypt a copied vote, making blinded copying impossible.

Even with this caveat, this demonstrates internet voting introduces new features not foreseen by 30 years of research.

2   Background

Our work is based on modifying the protocols used by Helios so that they involve three parties (voter, copier, Helios) instead of just two. As such, we need to explain the design and operation of Helios before describing the modifications.

Helios 3.0 [1,2] is a state of the art web-based voting system, based on decades of cryptographic research. An important feature implemented by Helios is universal verifiability [39,17] : any party, even one uninvolved in the election can opt to verify the integrity of an election that uses Helios. This is achieved by making the ballots cast by each voter public, albeit encrypted with the ElGamal [23] cryptosystem.

Each ballot also contains a proof of its validity which can be verified without requiring specific knowledge or access and without revealing the contents of the ballot. The proofs of validity are based on a disjunctive version of the Chaum-Pedersen protocol [16,11] previously used in [17]. This ensures that no invalid ballots have been accepted and that no ballot tampering has taken place. The public list of ballots also guards against the election officials injecting votes from unregistered voters if the registration list is public. As the encryption scheme used is additively homomorphic, the product of all encrypted votes is an encryption of the sum of all votes. Since the encrypted ballots are all public, there is no way for a corrupt server to tamper with the product in an undetected way. The vote sum is obtained by the election trustees using threshold decryption. Each trustee is able to provide a partial decryption factor along with a proof of correctness for his individual calculations. The partial decryption factors are then combined to arrive at the decrypted result. Again, once the partial decryption factors have been made public there is no opportunity for foul play.

In this section we will analyze the parts of Helios that are relevant to this work. We will start by briefly mentioning the relevant parts of the Helios Implementation before moving to the cryptographic design. The design of Helios 3.0 is based on the ElGamal cryptosystem [23], used for encrypting votes and homomorphic tallying. It also uses disjunctive zero-knowledge proofs of equality to ensure ballot validity.

2.1   Current Helios Implementation

As mentioned in [33] Helios has 4 main components: an election builder, a voting booth, a ballot casting server and an audit server. From the perspective of implementing ballot copying, we are mostly concerned with the inner workings of the voting booth since we need to be able to extract data in order to capture the encryption randomness and also inject it to allow the copied and blinded ballot to be actually submitted. The ballot casting server concerns us only with respect to the tests performed against incoming ballots, according to the Helios specifications [33]. The workings of the other two components are not relevant.

Voting Booth. The Helios voting booth is a web application that reads the parameters of an election, presents the user with the questions he can vote on, encrypts his choices and calculates the appropriate proofs to construct a valid ballot and then allows the user to either audit *or* submit it. The randomness used in the encryption is only revealed if the user chooses to audit his ballot in which case he will need to create a new one before voting. This is implemented as a weak form of coercion resistance, but is easily bypassed[1] if the voter executes a JavaScript command during the preparation of the ballot.

Ballot Casting Server. After the ballot is constructed and saved as a JSON (JavaScript Object Notation) [18] object, the voting booth submits it to the ballot casting server using the HTTP POST method. The ballot casting server then checks the ballot for validity and compares it against already cast ballots and rejects is if it is identical to one.

2.2   Additive Homomorphic ElGamal

The ElGamal [23] cryptosystem is a public-key encryption system based on the Diffie–Hellman [22] key exchange protocol. ElGamal is also homomorphic and can be used with threshold decryption, both desirable properties for e-voting. Helios relies on both of these properties. The operations of ElGamal are as follows:

- **Key Generation**: Choose a large prime[2] $p = bq + 1$ such that q is also prime and $b \geq 2$. Choose an element g of Z_p^* with order q. Choose a secret key $x < q$ and let $h = g^x \bmod p$. The public key is then (p, q, g, h) and the private key (p, q, g, h, x).
- **Encryption**: Given a public key (p, q, g, h), encrypt a message $m < q$ as such: Choose a random blind $0 \leq r < q$. Let $\alpha = g^r$ and $\beta = m \cdot h^r$. The ciphertext c is then $c = (\alpha, \beta)$.
- **Decryption**: Given a private key (p, q, g, h, x) and a ciphertext $c = (\alpha, \beta)$, the decrypted message is $\mu = \alpha^{-x} \cdot \beta$

Homomorphic Property. An important property of ElGamal is that it is homomorphic: the product of two ciphertexts is a cipher text which corresponds to the product of the messages in the original ciphertexts. Let two ciphertexts c_1, c_2 be the encryptions of m_i with blind r_i for $i = 1, 2$. Then $c_1 \cdot c_2 = (\alpha_1 \cdot \alpha_2, \beta_1 \cdot \beta_2) = (g^{r_1 + r_2}, m_1 \cdot m_2 \cdot h^{r_1 + r_2})$ i.e. $c_1 \cdot c_2$ is the encryption of $m_1 \cdot m_2$ with blind $r_1 + r_2$.

A special case of homomorphic operation is when c_2 corresponds to the message $m_2 = 1$ in which case the resulting ciphertext is a re-encryption of m_1 with a different blind.

---

[1] In fact, early versions of Helios included a "Coerce Me!" button which revealed the encryption randomness without invalidating the ballot.

[2] In the case of Helios b is fixed to 2.

Votes. In the context of Helios, the homomorphic property is used in order to calculate an encrypted *sum* of votes from individual encrypted ballots without the need to decrypt them individualy. However, as described above, ElGamal is multiplicatively homomorphic, whereas vote tallies are sums. In order to bridge this gap, in Helios a variant of the encoding used in [17]. Cramer et al. encode votes of "no" as 1 and votes of "yes" as g. In this way, the product of n votes v_i of which m are "yes" will be $\prod_{i=1}^{n} v_i = g^m$ i.e. the log of the product will be the sum of the votes i.e. the scheme is additively homomorphic. Most elections have more options than "yes" and "no", so Helios models them as a series of "yes-no" questions about each option, with a limit on the number of "yes" answers equal to the number of selections allowed in the original question. For example, given a question with 3 choices, from which exactly one may be selected, a vote would be of the form:

$$V = (\alpha_0, \beta_0), (\alpha_1, \beta_1), (\alpha_2, \beta_2) \tag{1}$$
$$= (g^{r_0}, g^{m_0} \cdot h^{r_0}), (g^{r_1}, g^{m_1} \cdot h^{r_1}), (g^{r_2}, g^{m_2} \cdot h^{r_2}) \tag{2}$$

In the above vote, r_i represents the randomness used in the encryption and m_i the answers of the voter to each of the 3 options. We note that a vote of the above form might be *invalid*, for example if $m_i > 1$ for some i, or if every m_i is 1, even though the election parameters only allow the voter to choose one option. A particularly insidious voter might even have $m_0 = -100$, making his vote cancel out 100 honest votes for the first option. Helios guards against this by requiring the voter to provide a *zero-knowledge* proof of his ballot's validity. *Note:* Helios supports a threshold variant of ElGamal, but this is not relevant to this work.

2.3   Proofs of Knowledge

As seen in the above example, a voter must provide a proof that the value of his vote falls into the range permitted by the election parameters. As such, he must prove that the individual vote for each option is either a "yes" or a "no" and furthermore that the total number of "yes" votes is within the range of the allowed number of selections. In more concrete terms, the voter is asked to prove that each m_i is either 0 or 1 (an *individual proof* in Helios terminology), and that the sum $\sum_{i=0}^{n-1} m_i$ is inside the range of allowed selections as specified in the election's definition (a *total proof*).

The proofs of validity used by Helios are offline disjunctive zero knowledge proofs of equality between discrete logs. In the rest of this section, we will offer a brief overview of the underlying concepts as well as their use in Helios.

Proofs of Knowledge. *Zero knowledge proofs of knowledge* [26] are a concept related to *zero knowledge interactive proofs* [32], the difference being that in proofs of knowledge the prover is supplied with an auxiliary input called a *witness* which enables it to convince the verifier. An algorithm called a *witness extractor* can then output that witness if given oracle access to the prover. Intuitively, in a proof of knowledge we want three things to hold: first, an honest prover given a correct witness almost always convinces the verifier. Second, if a witness extractor is allowed to "interrogate" a successful prover, he will in most cases be able to extract the witness. Third, even if the verifier behaves in a dishonest way, he learns nothing useful.

Computational Assumptions. The prover and verifier in our setting are polynomially bounded. Furthermore, we assume the the Decisional Diffie Hellman assumption [6,22] holds. This is also a requirement for the semantic security of the ElGamal scheme.

Definition 1 (Decisional Diffie Helman assumption). *Let G be a cyclic group and g a generator with prime order q. Then, given $a, b, c \in_R Z_q$ the following tuples cannot be distinguished by a polynomially bounded turing machine: $(g^a, g^b, g^c), (g^a, g^b, g^{ab})$. The bound is on $|q| = \lceil \log_2 q \rceil$.*

Disjunctive Proofs of Equality between Discrete Logarithms. To prove that an encrypted individual vote (α, β) is valid one must prove that either the corresponding plaintext is either $g^0 = 1$, in which case $\log_g \alpha = \log_h \beta$, or g^1 in which case $\log_g \alpha = \log_h \beta/g$. As the prover needs to prove the *disjunction* of the two statements we have a *disjunctive proof of knowledge*.

Total proofs can be carried out in the same way, the difference being that for individual proofs the range of exponents is always $[0, 1]$ whereas for total votes it ranges from the minimum number of selections to the maximum. For total proofs the ciphertext used is the homomorphic product of the individual ciphertexts.

Therefore, the main component of the proofs of knowledge used in Helios is a protocol to prove equality between discrete logs [11] along with a construction that enables the prover to prove the disjunction of many statements without revealing which one is in fact true [16].

The Chaum-Pedersen protocol [11] for discrete log equality is essentially a parallel version of the Schnorr protocol [40]. We note that the Chaum-Pedersen protocol (as well as the underlying Schnorr protocol) is only provably zero knowledge against adversaries who behave honestly. There is no known simulator for dishonest adversaries [11].

Cramer et al. provide a construction for disjunctive proofs [16,27] where the prover can prove one statement from a set and simulate proofs for the other ones, without the verifier knowing which of the subproofs are simulated. In the context of Helios, this allows the voter to indicate that the plaintext of his ballot is one out of a number of allowed values without revealing which one.

We explain the details of the construction of Cramer et al. [16] as applied to the Chaum-Pedersen protocol [11]. We take advantage of the fact that since the Chaum-Pedersen protocol is honest-verifier zero knowledge, if the voter can choose the challenge c, he can simulate the proofs as follows:

Protocol 1. Simulated Chaum-Pedersen Protocol.

Step 1 Simulated Proof: Choose random challenge c and response s. Let the
commitments be $a = g^s/\alpha^c$ and $b = h^s/(\beta/g^v)$.
Step 2 Partial Verification: Check that $g^s = a \cdot \alpha^c$ and that $h^s = b \cdot (\beta/g^v)^c$.

*In order to force the voter to provide at least one honest proof, he is not given
complete choice of the challenges.* The Verifier is allowed to specify the sum of
the challenges used in the subproofs. This allows the voter to simulate all but
one of the Chaum-Pedersen proofs and let the challenge of the real subproof be
as a balancing factor in the sum. Suppose the voter needs to prove that the value
v encoded by $(\alpha, \beta) = (g^r, h^r g^v)$ is in [min, max]. He will simulate the proofs for
$i \in [\text{min}, \text{max}] \setminus \{v\}$ and produce a real proof for $i = v$.

Protocol 2. Disjunctive Chaum-Pedersen Protocol.

Step 1 Prover (Voter): For $i \in [\text{min}, \text{max}] \setminus \{v\}$: Choose random challenge
c_i and response s_i. Let the commitments be $a_i := g^{s_i}/\alpha^{c_i}$ and $b_i :=$
$h^{s_i}/(\beta/g^i)^{c_i}$. Choose commitment (a_v, b_v) such that $(a_v, b_v) = (g^w, h^w)$
for some w.
Step 2 Verifier (Helios): Choose $T \in_R Z_q$.
Step 3 Prover (Voter): Let $c_v := T - \sum_{i \neq v} c_i$ and $s_v := rc_v + w$.
Step 4 Verifier (Helios): Check if $g^{s_i} \stackrel{?}{=} a \cdot \alpha^{c_i}$ and that $h^{s_i} \stackrel{?}{=} b \cdot (\beta/g^i)^{c_i}$ for
$i \in [\text{min}, \text{max}]$. Check if $T \stackrel{?}{=} \sum_{i=min}^{max} c_i$.

Non-Interactive Proofs. For practical reasons, Helios implements the above
protocol offline rather than online. This requires less communication with the
Helios server and does not require the Helios server to hold the state of proof
protocols in progress. This is done by way of the Fiat-Shamir heuristic [28]
which replaces the random challenge issued by the verifier with a hash of the
commitments. This also facilitates universal verifiability since the generation of
the challenge is beyond the control of the (potentially dishonest) Helios server.
The result of this modification is that the protocol can be performed entirely by
the voter with the final ballot submitted to Helios for verification.

The offline version of the protocol is zero knowledge in the *random oracle
model*. For zero knowledge proofs under the random oracle model, the hash
function used in the protocol is assumed to be an oracle under the control of
the simulator. As such, the simulator can choose the value returned by the hash
function on any input with the only limitation being consistency (i.e. after setting
$H(x) = y$, the simulator is not allowed to set $H(x) = y' \neq y$. The random oracle
model has been criticised as [31,9] have shown that it is possible to construct
protocols that are secure under the random oracle model but provably insecure
in general. Nonetheless, these results have not led to a vulnerability being found
in a currently used protocol.

For example, suppose we have an election with 3 options of which exactly one
may be selected (as in the vote example). We follow the notation of protocol 2

in that a_i, b_i represent the commitments of a proof, s_i the solution and c_i the challenge. The individual proofs would then be of the form:

$$P_i = ((a_{i,0}, b_{i,0}, a_{i,1}, b_{i,1}), (c_{i,0}, s_{i,0}, , c_{i,1}, s_{i,1})), \text{ for } i \in \{0, 1, 2\} \qquad (3)$$

And the total proof would be of the form:

$$P_\Sigma = ((a_{\Sigma,1}, b_{\Sigma,1}), (c_{\Sigma,1}, s_{\Sigma,1}))$$

To check if one of the above proofs is valid, Helios would set $T := H(a_{\min}, b_{\min}, \cdots, a_{\max}, b_{\max})$ and run the last step of protocol 2.

Note: w.l.o.g. and in the interest of readability we will limit ourselves to ballots consisting of a single encrypted "yes"-"no" vote and it's corresponding proof of validity.

Blind Signatures and Diverted Proofs. Blind signatures [10,11], involve signing a document through an intermediary (in our case, the copier) without the original signer (the voter) being able to trace the end product. Blind signatures have been suggested by Chaum [10] for use with anonymous electronic cash, where banks sign "coins" proving their authenticity but are unable to trace their use, and voting where authorities can supply signed blank ballots to authenticated voters but are then unable to track them once filled.

Divertible proofs [37,19] are a similar notion to blind signatures, but in an on-line setting. An intermediate party is introduced between the prover and verifier, playing the role of the verifier against the prover and that of the prover against the verifier. The intermediate is called a *warden* in some cases (for example, if he is introduced to enforce to ensure honest behaviour) or a man in the middle in others.

2.4   Related Work

Even though we do not regard our work as an actual attack against Helios, previous attacks highlight some of the techniques used as well as some of the assumptions in Helios' specification that enable data extraction and injection.

A Ballot Replay Attack. Cortier & Smyth [15] attack a voter's privacy by means of a replay attack. In the base version of their attack, a ballot is recast either verbatim or with minor differences in the representation of the signatures by a number of parties under the control of the attackers. The existing checks performed by the Hellios ballot casting server were somewhat lax. In some scenarios the additional votes for the original voter's chosen party or candidate will significantly bias the election result, thus violating privacy. The authors offer the French legislative elections as an example of such a scenario. A more complex version of their attack involves a permutation of the voter's choices making the malicious ballots slightly harder to detect. Our work is similar in that it also involves effectively replaying a vote but different in that the original voter consents to that. Also, the replayed vote *cannot* be detected as such.

An Attack against the Voter's Web-Browser. Esteghari & Desmedt [24] describe an attack which essentially installs a rootkit in the user's web-browser by exploiting a vulnerability in Adobe Reader. The rootkit then secretly changes the user's vote to a different one, and also hides any evidence of foul play. Helios, operating under the assumption that the user's browser is trustworthy, accepts the changed vote instead of the intended one.

While our work also affects the voting booth running at the user's browser, an important difference is that participation from both parties is *consensual* and not based on deception or exploits.

3   A Ballot-Blinding Protocol

We will split the description of our ballot-blinding protocol in two parts. We will first describe how a copier can re-encrypt an encrypted vote (making it indistinguishable to a random one assuming the DDH problem is hard) along with the appropriate modifications to keep the corresponding proof valid.

Note that since the randomness used in the ElGamal encryption is required to construct the real subproof it is impossible to simply copy and blind a cast ballot without extra information. On the other hand, if a voter were to publish the randomness used in his ballot to enable blinded copying he would be sacrificing his privacy! For that reason, we will describe an online protocol between a willing voter (who has already cast a ballot) and a copier. The protocol allows the copier to produce a "new" proof of knowledge for the encrypted vote.

The copier can combine the two parts: first he obtains a new (indistinguishable) proof of validity of the voter's encrypted vote and then he re-encrypts the encrypted vote making it indistinguishable as well. The result is a ballot that is equivalent to the original in that it contains the same vote but indistinguishable from it. Moreover, it does not leak the original vote.

3.1   Vote Blinding

We describe a transformation that a copier can perform to an already cast ballot that is based on re-encrypting the vote contained in the ballot. Because of the re-encryption, the proof contained in the ballot must also be modified to stay valid.

Given a vote $(\alpha, \beta) = (g^r, h^r g^v), v \in 0, 1$, a copier is able to re-encrypt it as $(\alpha', \beta') = (g^{r+z}, h^{r+z} g^v), v \in 0, 1$. To do that, he does not need knowledge of r as he can simply calculate $(\alpha', \beta') = (g^z \alpha, h^z \beta)$.

Lemma 1. *If z is chosen to be uniformly random in Z_q then (α', β') is indistinguishable from a random vote by adversaries who cannot solve the DDH problem, regardless of them knowing r or v.*

Proof. Since z is uniformly random in Z_q, it follows that $g^z \alpha$ is uniformly random in $\langle g \rangle$. Since α' is g^s for some s, $\beta'/g^v = h^s$ and $s, x = \log_g h$ are independently chosen, then $(h, g^s, \beta'/g^v)$ is a DDH problem instance which the adversary could solve if he was able to distinguish (α', β') from a random encrypted vote.   □

Furthermore, if the copier has access to a valid proof for (α, β) he can transform it to a valid proof for (α', β').

Lemma 2. *If (V, P) is a valid ballot, with $V = (\alpha, \beta)$ as in (1) and $P = ((a_0, b_0, a_1, b_1), (c_0, s_0, c_1, s_1))$ as in Protocol 2, then $((g^z \alpha, h^z \beta), (a_0, b_0, a_1, b_1),$ $(c_0, s_0 + c_0 z, c_1, s_1 + c_1 z))$ is also a valid ballot and vice versa.*

Proof. If $a_i = g^{s_i}/\alpha^{c_i}$ holds then $a_i = g^{s_i + c_i z}/(g^z \alpha)^{c_i}$ also holds. Similarly, if $b_i = h^{s_i}/(\beta/g^i)^{c_i}$ holds then $b_i = h^{s_i + c_i z}/(h^z \beta/g^i)^{c_i}$ also holds. For the opposite direction we note that re-applying the transformation for $-z$ produces the original ballot. □

The above transformation can be used as a variant of the attack described in [15] since it provides another way of replaying ballots without copying them verbatim. Nonetheless, the attack variant can be stopped in a similar way to the one suggested by Cortier and Smyth. Since the commitments a_i, b_i and challenges c_i of the proof are unchanged, a future version of Helios could defend against the attack by modifying the ballot casting server to reject votes which reuse past commitment values.

It is clear from the above discussion that blinding the entire ballot is necessary. Towards that, we describe a protocol that blinds the proofs of a ballot. The proof blinding protocol requires two assumptions: First, that original voter cooperates with the the copier and second, that the voter has access to the randomness used in encrypting his ballot. Fortunately, the second assumption can be fulfilled in the current Helios implementation.

3.2   Proof Blinding

Blinding the proof of a ballot is more involved: on one hand, creating a valid proof requires access to the randomness used in the encryption but on the other, revealing that *witness* would compromise a voter's privacy. Our solution is based on the concepts of *divertible protocols* [37,19] and *blind signatures* [10,11].

Suppose the voter has cast an encrypted vote $(\alpha, \beta) = (g^r, h^r g^v), v \in 0, 1$ with an appropriate proof, and the copier is requesting a different proof in order to copy it. Note that (α, β) is public but (r, v) is private to the voter. Since the hash function H() is public, Helios does not take part in the protocol. The notation used for the commitments is the same as in Protocol 2, but the roles of the parties are different. The voter still takes the role of the prover, but the copier takes the role of an intermediate verifier who ultimately submits the resulting ballot to Helios.

Protocol 3. Proof Blinding Protocol

Step 1 Voter: Choose $w \in_R Z_q$ and let $a_v := g^w, b_v := h^w$. Let $\lambda := 1 - v$ and choose $c_\lambda, s_\lambda \in_R Z_q$ and let $a_\lambda := g^{s_\lambda}/\alpha^{c_\lambda}$ and $b_\lambda := h^{s_\lambda}/(\beta/g^\lambda)^{c_\lambda}$. Send (a_0, b_0, a_1, b_1) as a commitment to the copier.

Step 2 Copier: Choose $\Delta_0, \Delta_1, k_0, k_1 \in_R Z_q$. Let $A_i := a_i g^{k_i}/\alpha^{\Delta_i}$, $B_i := b_i h^{k_i}/(\beta/g^i)^{\Delta_i}$ for $i = 0, 1$. Let $c := H(A_0, B_0, A_1, B_1)$ be the challenge that Helios would issue. Let $C := c - \Delta_0 - \Delta_1$, send C to voter as a challenge.

Step 3 Voter: Let $c_v := C - c_\lambda$ and let $s_v := w + rc_v$, send (c_0, s_0, c_1, s_1) to copier as a reply.

Step 4 Copier: Check that $C \overset{?}{=} c_0 + c_1$, $a_i \overset{?}{=} g^{s_i}/\alpha^{c_i}$ and $b_i \overset{?}{=} h^{s_i}/(\beta/g^i)^{c_i}$ for $i = 0, 1$. If yes, accept and let $C_i := c_i + \Delta_i$ and $S_i := s_i + k_i$. Let $V := ((\alpha, \beta), (A_0, B_0, A_1, B_1), (C_0, S_0, C_1, S_1))$ and send V to Helios. Otherwise, reject.

We will now examine Protocol 3 with regard to correctness, indistinguishability and security.

Correctness. We will first prove that our protocol satisfies *completeness* and (special) *soundness*.

Lemma 3. *The proof blinding protocol is complete and furthermore if an honest copier accepts then the resulting ballot V will be accepted by Helios.*

Proof. Completeness holds trivially. Indeed, we have:

- *$C = c_0 + c_1$ since the voter calculates $c_v := C - c_\lambda$ in Step 3.*
- *For $i = \lambda$, we have $a_\lambda = g^{s_\lambda}/\alpha^{c_\lambda}$ and $b_\lambda = h^{s_\lambda}/(\beta/g^\lambda)^{c_\lambda}$ from Step 1.*
- *For $i = v$, we must check if $a_v \overset{?}{=} g^{s_v}/\alpha^{c_v} = g^{w+rc_v}/\alpha^{c_v}$ which holds since $a_v = g^w$ (from Step 1) and $\alpha^{c_v} = g^{rc_v}$. Similarly: $b_v \overset{?}{=} h^{s_v}/(\beta/g^v)^{c_v} = h^{w+rc_v}/(\beta/g^v)^{c_v}$ holds since $b_v = h^w$ and $\beta/g^v = h^r$.*

For the second property, we need to show that $C_0 + C_1 = H(A_0, B_0, A_1, B_1)$ and that given that $a_i = g^{s_i}/\alpha^{c_i}$ and $b_i = h^{s_i}/(\beta/g^i)^{c_i}$ hold (since the copier has access to a valid vote) it also holds that: $A_i = g^{S_i}/\alpha^{C_i}$ and $B_i = h^{S_i}/(\beta/g^i)^{C_i}$. This is straightforward by substituting the blinded variables A_i, B_i, C_i, S_i with their definitions. □

Lemma 4. *Protocol 3 has the special soundness property.*

Proof. Suppose a voter can (given the same commitments (a_0, b_0, a_1, b_1)) provide answers to two different challenges C, C'. This means that for the two answers (c_0, s_0, c_1, s_1) and (c_0', s_0', c_1', s_1'), we must have $c_i \neq c_i'$ for at least one $i \in \{0, 1\}$. We will now show that such a voter can calculate a witness for the vote's validity (i.e. the encryption randomness used in encrypting the vote).:

$$a_i = g^{s_i}/\alpha_i^c \text{ and } a_i = g^{s_i'}/\alpha_i^{c_i'} \text{ we have:}$$

$$g^{s_i}/\alpha^{c_i} = g^{s_i'}/\alpha^{c_i'}$$

$$g^{s_i - s_i'} = \alpha^{c_i - c_i'} \text{ thus:}$$

$$\log_g \alpha = \frac{c_i - c_i'}{s_i - s_i'}.$$

□

Indistinguishability

Lemma 5. *Given the view of the original voter, the blinded proof of knowledge $((A_0, B_0, A_1, B_1), (C_0, S_0, C_1, S_1))$ is unconditionally indistinguishable from a valid proof produced independently.*

Proof. We observe that $C_i = c_i + \Delta_i$ and $S_i = s_i + k_i$ with Δ_i and k_i being uniformly random in Z_q. Thus, the challenges and responses are independent of the ones used in the original proof. For the commitments, we note that given (C_0, S_0, C_1, S_1), the values of (A_0, B_0, A_1, B_1) are uniquely determined (because for any valid proof: $A_i = g^{S_i}/\alpha^{C_i}$ and $B_i = h^{S_i}/(\beta/g^i)^{C_i}$), so if a voter is able to distinguish $(A_0, B_0, A_1, B_1), (C_0, S_0, C_1, S_1)$ from an independent proof he would also be able to distinguish (C_0, S_0, C_1, S_1). □

Security. Our goal is to ensure that the blinded protocol does not leak the value of the voter's vote to one of the other parties. The proof of knowledge protocol used by Helios is based on applying the construction of Cramer et al. [16] to the Chaum-Pedersen protocol [11] for proving the equivalence of discrete logs.

Lemma 6. *Under the random oracle model, the voter-copier interaction is zero-knowledge for a copier who follows the protocol.*

Proof. Under the random oracle model, and assuming that the DDH problem is hard, we will describe a simulator for Voter-Copier interactions when the voter is honest. We note that even an honest prover needs to simulate the proof corresponding to $i = \lambda$. The main difference is that the simulator will simulate both proofs and rely on its control of the hash function via the random oracle model to match the challenge. The simulator proceeds as follows:

1. For $i \in 0, 1$ choose $c_i, s_i \in_R Z_q$ and let $a_i := g^{s_i}/\alpha^{c_i}$ and $b_i := h^{s_i}/(\beta/g^i)^{c_i}$.
2. Choose $\Delta_0, \Delta_1, k_0, k_1 \in_R Z_q$. Let $A_i := a_i g^{k_i}/\alpha^{\Delta_i}$, $B_i := b_i h^{k_i}/(\beta/g^i)^{\Delta_i}$ for $i = 0, 1$. Set $H(A_0, B_0, A_1, B_1) := c_0 + c_1 + \Delta_0 + \Delta_1$. And let $c := H(A_0, B_0, A_1, B_1)$ Let $C := c - \Delta_0 - \Delta_1$
3. $C_i := c_i + \Delta_i$ and $S_i := s_i + k_i$.

The communication transcript between the simulated voter and copier is then $((a_0, b_0, a_1, b_1), c, (c_0, s_0, c_1, s_1))$ and the simulated output of the copier to Helios is $((\alpha, \beta), (A_0, B_0, A_1, B_1), (C_0, S_0, C_1, S_1))$. Against adversaries who cannot solve the DDH problem (and thus distinguish $(a_i, b_i) = (g^{s_i}/\alpha^{c_i}, h^{s_i}/(\beta/g^i)^{c_i})$ from $(a_i, b_i) = (g^w, h^w)$) the output of the simulator is indistinguishable to genuine transcripts and outputs, since after the commitments are issued the simulator follows the same steps as the ones taken by the copier. □

We can also use the above simulator to prove that the protocol is also zero-knowledge with respect to the copier "interacting" with Helios. Since the Fiat-Shamir heuristic [28] is used to replace the verifier's challenge with a hash of the the prover's commitments, Helios is unable to deviate from honest behaviour.

We also note that the simulator's control of the output of the hash function is explicitly allowed under the random oracle model (see [5, Sect. 5.1]).

The copier however has the option to ignore the protocol and issue arbitrary challenges to the voter. On the other hand, achieving indistinguishability requires that the copier keeps his coin rolls private. As such, it is conceivable that a dishonest voter can craft challenges in a way that compromises the voter's privacy. Given any limited-size subset of the challenge space (the limit being polynomial in the bit-length of q) we can achieve zero-knowledge even against cheating copiers (we explore this option in the next section). As such, we follow [11] in conjecturing that even in the unrestricted case, a cheating copier gains no useful information. This conjecture is also supported by the fact that the copier's control is weakened compared to the Chaum-Pedersen protocol, since he cannot control the individual challenged but only dictate their sum.

Note: The disjunctive proof construction in [16] can provide *witness indistinguishability* [27], but in the case of the Helios disjunctive proofs there is a unique valid witness $w = (r, v)$ for every encrypted vote $(\alpha, \beta) = (g^r, h^r g^v)$. As such the witness indistinguishability property is inconsequential.

3.3   A Combined Protocol for Blinded Copying

The vote blinding transformation of Sect. 3.1 and the proof blinding protocol (Protocol 3) can each partially blind a ballot (the vote and the proof respectively). They can be easily combined to completely blind a ballot as follows: The copier executes the proof blinding protocol with the cooperation of the voter but does not submit the resulting ballot V. Instead, he proceeds to apply the vote blinding transformation to V, producing V' which he then submits to Helios.

Theorem 1. *The combined ballot copying protocol is complete, sound and zero-knowledge for honest-verifiers under the random oracle model. Furthermore, assuming the DDH assumption holds, the ballots produced are accepted by Helios and indistinguishable from random valid ballots, even for the voter.*

Proof. Completeness, soundness and honest-verifier zero-knowledge under the random oracle model are satisfied by the proof copying protocol and are not impacted by the transformation (Lemma 2). Indistinguishability holds because of Lemmas 1 and 5.   □

4   A Multi-round Variant with Short Challenges

Since blinding the offline protocol does not achieve zero-knowledge, we explore a variant that can guarantee it. Furthermore, we avoid the use of the random oracle model in order to achieve a stronger proof.

The main obstruction to achieving zero-knowledge lies with the use of the Schnorr [40] protocol as the basis of the proof construction (since the Chaum-Pedersen protocol is a parallel version of Schnorr's). Our approach to guaranteeing the voter's privacy with regard to a dishonest copier is to adapt ideas

446   Y. Desmedt and P. Chaidos

from [8] while keeping the rest of the proof construction. For this we reduce the challenge space so that $c < \log q$. Since the challenge space is now polynomial in size compared to the security factor (the bit-size of q), the protocol can be simulated thus making it zero-knowledge.

We first present the modified protocol used by a voter for submitting a vote to Helios. It is repeated t times, and a dishonest voter cannot succeed with probability greater that $\log q^{-t}$. Compared to the original, offline protocol the only difference is the challenge generation: instead of using a hash function, a (short) challenge is selected randomly.

We then *divert* the online protocol in order to achieve an equivalent result to blinding. We follow the notation used in Protocol 2 for the proof commitments and (1) for the vote.

Protocol 4. Online Ballot Verification.

Step 1. Voter: Choose $w \in_R Z_q$ and let $a_v := g^w, b_v := h^w$. Let $\lambda := 1 - v$, choose $c_\lambda, s_\lambda \in_R Z_q$ and let $a_\lambda := g^{s_\lambda}/\alpha_\lambda^c$ and $b_\lambda := h^{s_\lambda}/(\beta/g^\lambda)^{c_\lambda}$. Send (a_0, b_0, a_1, b_1) as a commitment to Helios.

Step 2. Helios: Choose $c \in_R Z_{\lceil \log q \rceil}$, send c to the voter as a challenge.

Step 3. Voter: Let $c_v := c - c_\lambda$ and let $s_v := w + rc_v$, send (c_0, s_0, c_1, s_1) to copier as reply.

Step 4. Helios: Check if $c \stackrel{?}{=} c_0 + c_1$, $a_i \stackrel{?}{=} g^{s_i}/\alpha^{c_i}$ and $b_i \stackrel{?}{=} h^{s_i}/(\beta/g^i)^{c_i}$ for $i = 0, 1$. If yes, accept, otherwise, reject.

Protocol 4 is *complete, sound* and *zero-knowledge*. Completeness is maintained from the original Helios protocol as only the challenge generation is different. Thus an honest voter will always be able to convince Helios. We will now prove that the protocol satisfies the special soundness property and is zero-knowledge.

Lemma 7. *Protocol 4 satisfies special soundness.*

Proof. We repeat the argument of Lemma 4: suppose a (potentially dishonest) voter can, given one set of commitments, answer two different challenges. Then he would be able to calculate $\log_g \alpha$. Thus no dishonest verifier who does not know $\log_g \alpha$ has a better than $1/\log q$ chance to complete a round successfully. □

Lemma 8. *Protocol 4 is zero-knowledge under the DDH assumption.*

Proof. We will describe a simulator for the online protocol.

1. *For $i \in 0, 1$ choose $c_i, s_i \in_R Z_q$ and let $a_i := g^{s_i}/\alpha^{c_i}$ and $b_i := h^{s_i}/(\beta/g^i)^{c_i}$. Send the commitments to the Verifier.*
2. *If the Verifier replies with $c = c_0 + c_1$, output the transcript (a_0, b_0, a_1, b_1), $c, (c_0, s_0, c_1, s_1)$. Otherwise, reset the Verifier and return to Step 1.*

Against verifiers who cannot solve the DDH problem, a set of simulated commitments is indistinguishable to a set of random elements, so the verifier's reply, $V(a_0, b_0, a_1, b_1)$ will be independent of $c = c_0 + c_1$. As such, the simulator has *a* $1/\lceil \log q \rceil$ *chance to guess the challenge correctly in one try and thus runs in expected polynomial time. Again, under the DDH assumption the simulated transcripts are indistinguishable from normal ones.* □

We now present a way to divert the above protocol such that blinded ballot copying can take place, while achieving zero-knowledge even against dishonest copiers. As in the offline case, suppose the voter has cast an encrypted vote $(\alpha, \beta) = (g^r, h^r g^v), v \in 0, 1$ with appropriate proof, and the copier is requesting a different proof in order to copy it. We also assume that the copier has blinded the vote by re-encrypting it as $(\alpha', \beta') = (g^z \alpha, h^z \beta)$ and has presented the blinded rather than the original vote to Helios. Again, we follow the notation used in Protocol 2 for the proof commitments.

Protocol 5. Diverted Ballot Verification.

Step 1. Voter: Choose $w \in_R Z_q$ and let $a_v := g^w, b_v := h^w$. Let $\lambda := 1 - v$ and choose $c_\lambda, s_\lambda \in_R Z_q$ and let $a_\lambda := g^{s_\lambda}/\alpha_\lambda^c$ and $b_\lambda := h^{s_\lambda}/(\beta/g^\lambda)^{c_\lambda}$. Send (a_0, b_0, a_1, b_1) as a commitment to the copier.

Step 2. Copier: Choose $\Delta_0, \Delta_1, k_0, k_1 \in_R Z_q$. Let $A_i := a_i g_i^k/\alpha^{\Delta_i}$, $B_i := b_i h_i^k /(\beta/g^i)^{\Delta_i}$ for $i = 0, 1$. Send (A_0, B_0, A_1, B_1) to Helios as a commitment.

Step 3. Helios: Choose $c \in_R Z_{\lceil \log q \rceil}$, send c to copier as a challenge.

Step 4. Copier: Let $C := c - \Delta_0 - \Delta_1$, send C to voter as a challenge.

Step 5. Voter: Let $c_v := C - c_\lambda$ and let $s_v := w + rc_v$, send (c_0, s_0, c_1, s_1) to copier as a reply.

Step 6. Copier: Check if $C \stackrel{?}{=} c_0 + c_1$, $a_i \stackrel{?}{=} g^{s_i}/\alpha_i^c$ and $b_i \stackrel{?}{=} h^{s_i}/(\beta/g^i)^{c_i}$ for $i = 0, 1$. If yes, accept and let $C_i := c_i + \Delta_i$ and $S_i := s_i + k_i$. Let $S_i' := S_i + zC_i$ Send (C_0, S_0', C_1, S_1') to Helios. Otherwise, reject.

Theorem 2. *The diverted ballot verification protocol is a divertible interactive zero knowledge proof of validity for helios ballots.*

Proof. (sketch) First we prove that both interactions are zero-knowledge. Completeness transfers over from the offline blinded copying protocol since the only difference from the offline protocol is the challenge generation and vote blinding (point to Lemma for VB). Special soundness holds for both interactions (see Lemma 7). Furthermore, the simulator of Lemma 8 can be used to prove that both interactions are zero knowledge.

It is easy to see that neither the copier or Helios can calculate a witness directly as that would solve the discrete logarithm problem.

Finally, indistinguishability transfers over from the offline version. □

As the diverted ballot verification protocol is provably zero-knowledge, the transcripts cannot be used as signatures: they might be signatures for invalid ballots produced by a simulator operated by a dishonest voter and a dishonest Helios. As such, the universal verifiability property of Helios no longer holds. Such a modification would thus require trust to be placed on the bulletin board administrator, something that diverges significantly from the original design of Helios but is necessary if we want to achieve zero-knowledge and avoid using the random oracle model.

5   Conclusion and Further Work

We have described a protocol which enables voters to allow people who trust them to copy their vote without revealing it in the process. This can be used as an alternative to public endorsements. In settings where one person's expertise or judgement is well regarded our protocol offers the ability for others to trust his judgement without forcing him to reveal his opinion –this can be especially important in small, local elections where revealing one's vote can lead to rivalries (of course in a small or close election the tally [20] or even the result might reveal information). We also include an online variant of the protocol which offers greater security to the voter but requires a trusted server to accept ballots.

Blinded vote copying would also reduce the power of traditional voting blocs. A voting bloc is a club or special interest group that coordinates its voting. They achieve stronger [38] representation compared to individual voters by not diffusing their votes. The trust requirements for blinded vote copying are more relaxed than in a typical voting bloc since the "leader" does not need to make his vote public. By making the creation of voting blocs easier we thus create a more even voting field without needing to change the electoral system.

Since our main contribution is honest-verifier zero-knowledge a natural continuation would be implementing a trusted warden that facilitates the copying.

It would also be interesting to replace the original voter with a coalition of voters, essentially providing a framework (thus avoiding the complexity of secure multi-party computation) for holding a primary election amongst the members of the coalition. This can lower the barrier for creating a voting bloc further since there is no need for a single person to be singled out as the decision maker.

Another avenue for future research would be using a witness-hiding protocol such as Schnorr-Okamoto [36] instead of Schnorr as a proof of knowledge for discrete logs and integrating it with a homomorphic encryption scheme. The result would then be witness-hiding (which is adequate for security since the witness in our case includes the vote) rather than honest-verifier zero-knowledge.

In the context of internet voting, the issues of untrusted platforms and the lack of a private voting booth (generalised under "physical assumptions") have been known and well described (see eg. [35,13]). We argue that the potential for voter cooperation is a third characteristic, unique to internet voting. It is therefore natural to state a more general open problem: What other differences exist between e-booth and internet voting?

Acknowledgments. The authors would like to thank Dr. Niel Ferguson for suggesting the topic of encrypted copying during CRYPTO 2007. We also thank the referees for suggesting that code-voting prohibits blinded copying and for pointing out [7].

References

1. Adida, B.: Helios: Web-based Open-Audit Voting. In: USENIX Security Symposium, pp. 335–348 (2008)

2. Adida, B., de Marneffe, O., Pereira, O., Quisquater, J.J.: Electing a University President using Open-Audit Voting: Analysis of real-world use of Helios. In: 2009 Electronic Voting Technology Workshop/Workshop on Trustworthy Elections (EVT/WOTE 2009) (Online proceedings) (2009)
3. Arrow, K.J.: Social Choice and Individual Values, 2nd edn. Yale University Press, New Haven (1963)
4. Balzarotti, D., Banks, G., Cova, M., Felmetsger, V., Kemmerer, R., Robertson, W., Valeur, F., Vigna, G.: Are your votes really counted?: testing the security of real-world electronic voting systems. In: Proceedings of the 2008 International Symposium on Software Testing and Analysis, pp. 237–248. ACM (2008)
5. Bellare, M., Rogaway, P.: Random oracles are practical: A paradigm for designing efficient protocols. In: Proceedings of the 1st ACM Conference on Computer and Communications Security, pp. 62–73. ACM (1993)
6. Boneh, D.: The Decision Diffie-Hellman Problem. In: Buhler, J.P. (ed.) ANTS 1998. LNCS, vol. 1423, pp. 48–63. Springer, Heidelberg (1998)
7. Bulens, P., Giry, D., Pereira, O.: Running mixnet-based elections with Helios. In: Electronic Voting Technology Workshop/Workshop on Trustworthy Elections. Usenix (2011)
8. Burmester, M., Desmedt, Y., Beth, T.: Efficient zero-knowledge identification schemes for smart cards. The Computer Journal 35(1), 21 (1992)
9. Canetti, R., Goldreich, O., Halevi, S.: The random oracle methodology, revisited. Journal of the ACM (JACM) 51(4), 557–594 (2004)
10. Chaum, D.: Blind signatures for untraceable payments. In: Advances in Cryptology: Proceedings of Crypto., vol. 82, pp. 199–203 (1983)
11. Chaum, D., Pedersen, T.: Wallet Databases with Observers. In: Brickell, E.F. (ed.) CRYPTO 1992. LNCS, vol. 740, pp. 89–105. Springer, Heidelberg (1993)
12. Chaum, D.L.: Untraceable electronic mail, return addresses, and digital pseudonyms. Commun. ACM 24(2), 84–90 (1981)
13. Clark, J., Hengartner, U.: Selections: Internet Voting with Over-the-Shoulder Coercion-Resistance. In: Danezis, G. (ed.) FC 2011. LNCS, vol. 7035, pp. 47–61. Springer, Heidelberg (2012)
14. Computing Research Association: Four grand challenges in trustworthy computing (2003)
15. Cortier, V., Smyth, B.: Attacking and fixing Helios: An analysis of ballot secrecy. In: Proceedings of the 24th Computer Security Foundations Symposium, CSF 2011 (2011)
16. Cramer, R., Damgård, I., Schoenmakers, B.: Proof of Partial Knowledge and Simplified Design of Witness Hiding Protocols. In: Desmedt, Y.G. (ed.) CRYPTO 1994. LNCS, vol. 839, pp. 174–187. Springer, Heidelberg (1994)
17. Cramer, R., Gennaro, R., Schoenmakers, B.: A secure and optimally efficient multi-authority election scheme. European Transactions on Telecommunications 8(5), 481–490 (1997)
18. Crockford, D.: Javascript object notation (July 2006), http://www.ietf.org/rfc/rfc4627.txt
19. Desmedt, Y.G., Goutier, C., Bengio, S.: Special Uses and Abuses of the Fiat Shamir Passport Protocol. In: Pomerance, C. (ed.) CRYPTO 1987. LNCS, vol. 293, pp. 21–39. Springer, Heidelberg (1988)
20. Desmedt, Y., Kurosawa, K.: Electronic voting: Starting over? In: Zhou, J., López, J., Deng, R.H., Bao, F. (eds.) ISC 2005. LNCS, vol. 3650, pp. 329–343. Springer, Heidelberg (2005)

21. Desmedt, Y., Chaidos, P.: Blinding ballot copying in Helios: from Condorcet to IACR. In: CRYPTO 2011 Rump Session (2011), http://rump2011.cr.yp.to/
22. Diffie, W., Hellman, M.: New directions in cryptography. IEEE Transactions on Information Theory 22(6), 644–654 (1976)
23. Elgamal, T.: A public key cryptosystem and a signature scheme based on discrete logarithms. IEEE Transactions on Information Theory 31(4), 469–472 (1985)
24. Estehghari, S., Desmedt, Y.: Exploiting the client vulnerabilities in internet e-voting systems: hacking Helios 2.0 as an example. In: Proceedings of the 2010 International Conference on Electronic Voting Technology/Workshop on Trustworthy Elections. EVT/WOTE 2010, pp. 1–9. USENIX Association, Berkeley (2010)
25. Estonian National Electoral Committee: E-voting system -general overview (2010), http://www.vvk.ee/public/dok/General_Description_E-Voting_2010.pdf
26. Feige, U., Fiat, A., Shamir, A.: Zero-knowledge proofs of identity. Journal of Cryptology 1(2), 77–94 (1988)
27. Feige, U., Shamir, A.: Witness indistinguishable and witness hiding protocols. In: Proceedings of the Twenty-Second Annual ACM Symposium on Theory of Computing, pp. 416–426. ACM (1990)
28. Fiat, A., Shamir, A.: How to Prove Yourself: Practical Solutions to Identification and Signature Problems. In: Odlyzko, A.M. (ed.) CRYPTO 1986. LNCS, vol. 263, pp. 186–194. Springer, Heidelberg (1987)
29. Gerlach, J., Gasser, U.: Three case studies from switzerland: E-voting. Berkman Center Research Publication No. 3 (2009)
30. Gjøsteen, K.: Analysis of an internet voting protocol. Cryptology ePrint Archive, Report 2010/380 (2010)
31. Goldwasser, S., Kalai, Y.: On the (in) security of the Fiat-Shamir paradigm. In: Proceedings of 44th Annual IEEE Symposium on Foundations of Computer Science, pp. 102–113. IEEE (2003)
32. Goldwasser, S., Micali, S., Rackoff, C.: The knowledge complexity of interactive proof-systems. In: Proceedings of the Seventeenth Annual ACM Symposium on Theory of Computing, pp. 291–304. ACM (1985)
33. Helios Voting: Helios v3 verification specs (August 2011), http://documentation.heliosvoting.org/verification-specs/helios-v3-verification-specs
34. Jacobs, B., Pieters, W.: Electronic voting in the Netherlands: from early adoption to early abolishment. In: Foundations of Security Analysis and Design V, pp. 121–144 (2009)
35. Mote Jr., C.: Report of the national workshop on internet voting: issues and research agenda. In: Proceedings of the 2000 Annual National Conference on Digital Government Research, pp. 1–59. Digital Government Society of North America (2000)
36. Okamoto, T.: Provably Secure and Practical Identification Schemes and Corresponding Signature Schemes. In: Brickell, E.F. (ed.) CRYPTO 1992. LNCS, vol. 740, pp. 31–53. Springer, Heidelberg (1993)
37. Okamoto, T., Ohta, K.: Divertible Zero Knowledge Interactive Proofs and Commutative Random Self-reducibility. In: Quisquater, J.-J., Vandewalle, J. (eds.) EUROCRYPT 1989. LNCS, vol. 434, pp. 134–149. Springer, Heidelberg (1990)
38. Penrose, L.: The elementary statistics of majority voting. Journal of the Royal Statistical Society 109(1), 53–57 (1946)
39. Sako, K., Kilian, J.: Receipt-Free Mix-Type Voting Scheme. In: Guillou, L.C., Quisquater, J.-J. (eds.) EUROCRYPT 1995. LNCS, vol. 921, pp. 393–403. Springer, Heidelberg (1995)
40. Schnorr, C.: Efficient signature generation by smart cards. Journal of Cryptology 4(3), 161–174 (1991)

Defining Privacy for Weighted Votes, Single and Multi-voter Coercion

Jannik Dreier, Pascal Lafourcade, and Yassine Lakhnech

Université Grenoble 1, CNRS, Verimag, France
{Jannik.Dreier,Pascal.Lafourcade,Yassine.Lakhnech}@imag.fr

Abstract. Most existing formal privacy definitions for voting protocols are based on observational equivalence between two situations where two voters swap their votes. These definitions are unsuitable for cases where votes are weighted. In such a case swapping two votes can result in a different outcome and both situations become trivially distinguishable. We present a definition for privacy in voting protocols in the Applied π-Calculus that addresses this problem. Using our model, we are also able to define multi-voter coercion, i.e. situations where several voters are attacked at the same time. Then we prove that under certain realistic assumptions a protocol secure against coercion of a single voter is also secure against coercion of multiple voters. This applies for Receipt-Freeness as well as Coercion-Resistance.

1 Introduction

Privacy is a key requirement in elections as voters can otherwise be blackmailed, coerced or may be susceptible to vote-buying. Typically privacy is split into three different properties:

- *Vote-Privacy*: The votes are kept private.
- *Receipt-Freeness*: A voter cannot construct a receipt which allows him to prove to a third party that he voted for a certain candidate. This is to prevent vote-buying.
- *Coercion-Resistance*: Even when a voter interacts with a coercer during the entire voting process, the coercer cannot be sure whether the voter followed his instructions or actually voted for another candidate.

The design of complex protocols such as voting protocols is known to be error-prone. This is why formal verification is an ideal tool to ensure the correctness and security of voting protocols. It has already been used to analyze properties such as Verifiability, Privacy, Receipt-Freeness and Coercion-Resistance [1–12].

However, most existing symbolic definitions of Privacy are based on the idea of swapping votes. If the votes are private, a case where Alice votes "yes" and Bob votes "no" should be indistinguishable from a case where Alice votes "no" and Bob votes "yes". Yet this definition is unsuitable for some situations, for example in companies where votes are weighted according to the proportion of

S. Foresti, M. Yung, and F. Martinelli (Eds.): ESORICS 2012, LNCS 7459, pp. 451–468, 2012.
© Springer-Verlag Berlin Heidelberg 2012

shares held by each shareholder. Consider the following example: Alice owns 50% of the stocks, and Bob and Carol each hold 25%. The cases where Alice and Bob swap votes are now easily distinguishable if Carol votes "yes" all the time, as the result of the vote is different: 75% vs. 50% vote for "yes". Note that there are still situations where privacy is ensured in the sense that different situations give the same result. The last outcome (50% yes, 50% no) could - for example - also be announced if Alice votes "yes" and Bob and Carol vote "no". Protocols supporting vote weights have been proposed, for example Eliasson and Zúquete [13] developed a voting system supporting vote weights based on REVS [14], which itself is based on the protocol by Fujioka et al. [15].

Our Contributions: To address this issue, we define a symbolic privacy notion in the Applied π-Calculus [16] that takes weighted votes into account. Instead of requiring two executions where voters swap votes to be bisimilar, we require two executions to be bisimilar if they publish the same result, independent of the mapping between voters and votes. We analyze the relationship of our notion to the existing swap-based ones and give precise conditions for formally proving the equivalence between them. Then, we generalize our notion to Receipt-Freeness and Coercion-Resistance for weighted votes. We use a variant of the protocol by Eliasson and Zúquete [13] as a case study for our definition, and provide a partially automated proof using ProVerif [17].

In the cases of coercion most existing definitions only consider one attacked voter. Our model also allows to define a case with multiple coerced voters, and we analyze the relationship between this and the single-voter case. In particular, we give a formal proof that single- and multi-voter coercion are equivalent for a given protocol if it satisfies some modularity and de-composability properties. Using two existing protocols, we show that theses properties are realistic.

Related Work: Previous research on formal verification of voting protocols concerned privacy properties (privacy, receipt-freeness and coercion-resistance) [1–8], election verifiability [9, 10], or both [11, 12].

In the symbolic model, privacy is usually defined as observational equivalence of two cases where a pair of voters swap their votes [1–5, 8, 12]. The definitions mainly differ in the way they model voting processes and deal with specifics of protocols. Some of them can be verified automatically using standard tools (e.g. ProVerif [17] and ProSwapper [18]). This swap-based approach was not designed for weighted votes and, as explained above, may lead to unexpected results in this case.

The other main approach roots in the computational model. In this case the real-world protocol is compared to an ideal situation and the attacker's advantage is analyzed [7, 11]. Our symbolic definition is somewhat related to this computational approach, as we also consider some information – the result – to be leaked even in an ideal situation, and only forbid further leakage. Another possibility is to consider the overall advantage of the attacker without comparing it to an ideal situation [19]. This advantage is always non-negligible as in certain situations the votes are always revealed, e.g. in the case of an unanimous vote.

A third approach was proposed by Langer et al. [20]. The authors developed verifiability and privacy notions based on (un-)linkability between a voter and his vote. Their definitions have to be instantiated with a concrete formal process and attacker model. To define unlinkability, they rely on indistinguishability of runs where votes are swaped, with the same issues as described above.

Küsters and Truderung [6] were the first to explicitly consider multi-voter coercion. In their abstract model, Single-Voter Coercion and Multi-Voter Coercion turned out to be different in general. Subsequently they proposed a modified definition of Coercion-Resistance that implies both Single- and Multi-Voter Coercion-Resistance. In our model Single- and Multi-Voter Coercion are equivalent under certain assumptions on the protocol, hence we do not need to change the initial definition. Additionally, the conditions allow us to precisely characterize the difference between both notions.

Outline: In the next section, we present the Applied π-Calculus and recall the privacy definitions given by Delaune et al. [2]. In Section 3, we introduce our privacy definition and show under which condition it is equivalent to the existing ones. Then, in Section 4, we define Single- and Multi-Voter Receipt-Freeness, analyze their relationship and prove their equivalence under certain assumptions. In Section 5 we define Single- and Multi-Voter Coercion-Resistance and again prove their equivalence under the same hypotheses, before concluding in Section 6.

2 Preliminaries

In this section we recall the Applied π-Calculus, introduce our model of voting protocols and present existing privacy definitions.

2.1 Applied π-Calculus

The Applied π-Calculus [16] is a formal language to describe concurrent processes. The calculus consists of *names* (which typically correspond to data or channels), *variables*, and a *signature* Σ of *function symbols* which can be used to build *terms*. Functions typically include encryption and decryption – for example enc(*message*, *key*), dec(*message*, *key*) – hashing, signing etc. Terms are correct (i.e. respecting arity and sorts) combinations of names and functions. We distinguish the type "channel" from other *base* types. To model equalities we use an equational theory E which defines a relation $=_E$. A classical example which describes the correctness of symmetric encryption is dec(enc(*message*, *key*), *key*) $=_E$ *message*. Processes are constructed using the grammars detailed in Figure 1.

The substitution $\{M/x\}$ replaces the variable x with term M. We denote by $fv(A)$, $bv(A)$, $fn(A)$, $bn(A)$ the free variables, bound variables, free names or bound names respectively. A process is *closed* if all variables are bound or defined by an active substitution. The *frame* $\Phi(A)$ of an active process A is obtained by replacing all plain processes in A by 0. This frame can be seen as a representation

$P, Q, R :=$		plain processes
0		null process
$P|Q$		parallel composition
$!P$		replication
$\nu n.P$		name restriction ("new")
if $M = N$ then P		conditional
else Q		
$in(u, x).P$		message input
$out(u, x).P$		message output

(a) Plain process

$A, B, C :=$	active processes
P	plain process
$A|B$	parallel composition
$\nu n.A$	name restriction
$\nu x.A$	variable restriction
$\{M/x\}$	active substitution

(b) Extended process

Fig. 1. Grammars for *plain* and *extended* or *active* processes

of what is statically known to the exterior about a process. The domain $dom(\Phi)$ of a frame Φ is the set of variables for which Φ defines a substitution. An evaluation context $C[\_]$ denotes an active process with a hole for an active process that is not under replication, a conditional, an input or an output. In the rest of the paper we use the following usual notions of equivalence and bisimilarity based on the original semantics [16] given in our technical report [21].

Definition 1 (Equivalence in a Frame [16]). *Two terms M and N are equal in the frame ϕ, written $(M = N)\phi$, if and only if $\phi \equiv \nu\tilde{n}.\sigma$, $M\sigma = N\sigma$, and $\{\tilde{n}\} \cap (fn(M) \cup fn(N)) = \emptyset$ for some names $\tilde{n}$ and some substitution σ.*

Definition 2 (Static Equivalence ($\approx_s$) [16]). *Two closed frames ϕ and ψ are statically equivalent, written $\phi \approx_s \psi$, when $dom(\phi) = dom(\psi)$ and when for all terms M and N we have $(M = N)\phi$ if and only if $(M = N)\psi$. Two extended processes A and B are statically equivalent ($A \approx_s B$) if their frames are statically equivalent.*

The intuition behind this definition is that two processes are statically equivalent if the messages exchanged with the environment cannot be distinguished by an attacker (i.e. all operations on both sides give the same results). This idea can be extended to *labeled bisimilarity*.

Definition 3 (Labeled Bisimilarity ($\approx_l$) [16]). *Labeled bisimilarity is the largest symmetric relation $\mathcal{R}$ on closed active processes, such that $A \mathcal{R} B$ implies:*

1. $A \approx_s B$,
2. *if $A \to A'$, then $B \to^* B'$ and $A' \mathcal{R} B'$ for some B',*
3. *if $A \xrightarrow{\alpha} A'$ and $fv(\alpha) \subseteq dom(A)$ and $bn(\alpha) \cap fn(B) = \emptyset$, then $B \to^* \xrightarrow{\alpha} \to^* B'$ and $A' \mathcal{R} B'$ for some B'.*

In this case each interaction on one side can be simulated by the other side, and the processes are statically equivalent at each step during the execution, thus an attacker cannot distinguish both sides.

2.2 Modeling Voting Protocols

We model voting protocols in the Applied π-Calculus as follows.

Definition 4 (Voting Protocol). *A voting protocol is a tuple $(V, A_1, \ldots, A_m, \tilde{n})$ where V is the process that is executed by the voter, the A_j's are the processes executed by the election authorities, and $\tilde{n}$ is a set of private channels. We also assume the existence of a particular public channel res that is only used to publish the result of the election.*

Note that we have only one process for the voters. This means that different voters will execute the same process, but with different variable values (e.g. the keys, the vote etc.). To reason about privacy, we talk about instances of a voting protocol, which we call *voting processes*.

Definition 5 (Voting Process). *A voting process of a voting protocol $(V, A_1, \ldots, A_m, \tilde{n})$ is a closed process*

$$\nu\tilde{n}'.(V\sigma_{id_1}\sigma_{v_1}|\ldots|V\sigma_{id_n}\sigma_{v_n}|A_1|\ldots|A_l),$$

where $l \leq m$, $\tilde{n}'$ includes the secret channel names $\tilde{n}$, $V\sigma_{id_i}\sigma_{v_i}$ are the processes executed by the voters, σ_{id_i} is a substitution assigning the identity to a process (this determines for example the secret keys), σ_{v_i} specifies the vote and A_j's are the election authorities which are required to be honest.

The restricted channel names model private channels. Note that we only model the honest authorities as unspecified parties are subsumed by the attacker.

2.3 Existing Privacy Definitions

Before we can formally define privacy, we need the following two transformations. The first one turns a process P into another process P^{ch} that reveals all its inputs and secret data on the channel ch.

Definition 6 (Process P^{ch} [2]). *Let P be a plain process and ch be a channel name. P^{ch} is defined as follows:*

- $0^{ch} \hat{=} 0$,
- $(P|Q)^{ch} \hat{=} P^{ch}|Q^{ch}$,
- $(\nu n.P)^{ch} \hat{=} \nu n.\mathsf{out}(ch, n).P^{ch}$ *if n is a name of base type,* $(\nu n.P)^{ch} \hat{=} \nu n.P^{ch}$ *otherwise,*
- $(\mathsf{in}(u, x).P)^{ch} \hat{=} \mathsf{in}(u, x).\mathsf{out}(ch, x).P^{ch}$ *if x is a variable of base type,* $(\mathsf{in}(u, x).P)^{ch} \hat{=} \mathsf{in}(u, x).P^{ch}$ *otherwise,*
- $(\mathsf{out}(u, M).P)^{ch} \hat{=} \mathsf{out}(u, M).P^{ch}$,
- $(!P)^{ch} \hat{=} !P^{ch}$,
- $(\text{if } M = N \text{ then } P \text{ else } Q)^{ch} \hat{=} \text{if } M = N \text{ then } P^{ch} \text{ else } Q^{ch}$.

In the remainder we assume that $ch \notin fn(P) \cup bn(P)$ before applying the transformation. The second transformation does not only reveal the secret data, but also takes orders from an outsider before sending a message or branching.

Definition 7 (Process P^{c_1, c_2} [2]). *Let P be a plain process and c_1, c_2 be channel names. P^{c_1, c_2} is defined as follows:*

- $0^{c_1,c_2} \triangleq 0$,
- $(P|Q)^{c_1,c_2} \triangleq P^{c_1,c_2}|Q^{c_1,c_2}$,
- $(\nu n.P)^{c_1,c_2} \triangleq \nu n.\mathrm{out}(c_1,n).P^{c_1,c_2}$ *if* n *is a name of base type,* $(\nu n.P)^{c_1,c_2} \triangleq \nu n.P^{c_1,c_2}$ *otherwise,*
- $(\mathrm{in}(u,x).P)^{c_1,c_2} \triangleq \mathrm{in}(u,x).\mathrm{out}(c_1,x).P^{c_1,c_2}$ *if* x *is a variable of base type,* $(\mathrm{in}(u,x).P)^{c_1,c_2} \triangleq \mathrm{in}(u,x).P^{c_1,c_2}$ *otherwise,*
- $(\mathrm{out}(u,M).P)^{c_1,c_2} \triangleq \mathrm{in}(c_2,x).\mathrm{out}(u,x).P^{c_1,c_2}$ *where* x *is a fresh variable,*
- $(!P)^{c_1,c_2} \triangleq !P^{c_1,c_2}$,
- $(\text{if } M = N \text{ then } P \text{ else } Q)^{c_1,c_2} \triangleq \mathrm{in}(c_2,x).\text{if } x = true \text{ then } P^{c_1,c_2} \text{ else } Q^{c_1,c_2}$ *where* x *is a fresh variable and true is a constant.*

To hide the output of a process, we use the following definition.

Definition 8 (Process $A^{\backslash out(ch,\cdot)}$ [2]). *Let A be an extended process. We define the process $A^{\backslash out(ch,\cdot)}$ as* $\nu ch.(A|!in(ch,x))$.

We now recall the privacy definitions given by Delaune et al. [2], which are the bases for many other definitions [1, 3–5, 8, 12]. Their main idea for defining privacy is simple: A protocol respects privacy if any two instances where two voters swap votes are bisimilar.

Definition 9 (Swap-Privacy (SwP) [2]). *A protocol satisfies* Swap-Privacy (SwP) *if for any context S corresponding to a voting process with a hole for two voters and for all votes σ_{v_A} and σ_{v_B} we have*

$$S\left[V\sigma_{id_A}\sigma_{v_A}|V\sigma_{id_B}\sigma_{v_B}\right] \approx_l S\left[V\sigma_{id_A}\sigma_{v_B}|V\sigma_{id_B}\sigma_{v_A}\right].$$

In the literature S may sometimes contain corrupted or coerced voters (e.g. in [8]), here we will suppose that it contains only honest voters and authorities to be able to clearly distinguish single- and multi-voter coercion.

Defining Receipt-Freeness is a bit more complicated as the voter will execute some counter strategy, i.e. a different process, to fake the receipt, but it can still be expressed as a bisimilarity between two situations. In the first situation, the targeted voter votes a and reveals his secret data. In the second situation, he executes another process – the counter-strategy – which allows him to vote b and fake the secret data in a way that both instances are bisimilar. A protocol is receipt-free if such a process – a counter-strategy – exists.

Definition 10 (Swap-Receipt-Freeness (SwRF) [2]). *A protocol satisfies* Swap-Receipt-Freeness (SwRF) *if for any context S corresponding to a voting process with a hole for two voters and for all votes σ_{v_A} and σ_{v_B} there exists a process V' such that $V'^{\backslash out(chc,\cdot)} \approx_l V\sigma_{id_A}\sigma_{v_B}$ and*

$$S\left[(V\sigma_{id_A}\sigma_{v_A})^{chc}|V\sigma_{id_B}\sigma_{v_B}\right] \approx_l S\left[V'|V\sigma_{id_B}\sigma_{v_A}\right].$$

One could define Coercion-Resistance in the same way, but in that case the attacker could force the targeted voter to vote d (and not a) in the situation where he complies with the instructions. This would make both situations trivially distinguishable by just looking at the result. To prevent this, Delaune et al. [2] use a context C that is required to force the voter to vote a, but can otherwise interact in any way with the voter.

Definition 11 (Swap-Coercion-Resistance (SwCR) [2]). *A protocol satisfies* Swap-Coercion-Resistance (SwCR) *if for any context S corresponding to a voting process with a hole for two voters and for all votes σ_{v_A} and σ_{v_B} there exists a process V' such that for any context C with $C = \nu c_1.\nu c_2.(\_|P)$ and $\tilde{n} \cap fn(C) = \emptyset$, $S\left[C\left[(V\sigma_{id_A}\sigma_{v_A})^{c_1,c_2}\right]|V\sigma_{id_B}\sigma_{v_B}\right] \approx_l VP'_A\left[(V\sigma_{id_A}\sigma_{v_A})^{chc}|V\sigma_{id_B}\sigma_{v_B}\right]$ we have $C\left[V'\right]^{\backslash out(chc,\cdot)} \approx_l V\sigma_{id_A}\sigma_{v_B}$ and*

$$S\left[C\left[(V\sigma_{id_A}\sigma_{v_A})^{c_1,c_2}\right]|V\sigma_{id_B}\sigma_{v_B}\right] \approx_l S\left[C\left[V'\right]|V\sigma_{id_B}\sigma_{v_A}\right].$$

Delaune et al. [2] showed that any protocol ensuring (SwCR) ensures (SwRF), and any protocol ensuring (SwRF) ensures (SwP).

3 Defining Privacy

Our privacy definition is based on the observation that - as the result of the vote is always published - some knowledge about the voter's choices can always be inferred from the outcome. The classical example is the case of a unanimous vote where the contents of all votes are revealed just by the result. Yet - as already discussed in the introduction - there can also be other cases where some of the votes can be inferred from the result, in particular in the case of weighted votes. If for example Alice holds 66% of the shares and Bob 34%, both votes are always revealed when announcing the result: If one option gets 66% and the other 34%, it is clear which one was chosen by Alice or Bob. However, if we have a different distribution of the shares (e.g. 50%, 25% and 25%), some privacy is still possible as there several situations with the same result. Thus our main idea: If two instances of a protocol give the same result, an attacker should not be able to distinguish them. Note that this includes the classic definition where votes are swapped, if this give the same result.

3.1 Formal Definition

To express this formally, we need to define the result of an election. As defined above, we suppose that the result is always published on a special channel *res*. The following definition allows us to hide all channels except for a specified channel c, which we can use for example to reason about the result on channel *res*.

Definition 12 ($P|_c$). *Let $P|_c = \nu\tilde{ch}.P$ where $\tilde{ch}$ are all channels except for c, i.e. we hide all channels except for c.*

Now we can formally define our privacy notion: If two instances of a protocol give the same result, they should be bisimilar.

Definition 13 (Vote-Privacy (VP)). *A voting protocol ensures* Vote-Privacy (VP) *if for any two instances $VP_A = \nu\tilde{n}.(V\sigma_{id_1}\sigma_{v_1^A} \mid \ldots \mid V\sigma_{id_n}\sigma_{v_n^A} \mid A_1 \mid \ldots \mid A_l)$ and $VP_B = \nu\tilde{n}.(V\sigma_{id_1}\sigma_{v_1^B} \mid \ldots \mid V\sigma_{id_n}\sigma_{v_n^B} \mid A_1 \mid \ldots \mid A_l)$ we have*

$$VP_A|_{res} \approx_l VP_B|_{res} \Rightarrow VP_A \approx_l VP_B.$$

A simple interpretation of this definition is that everything apart from the result on channel *res* has to remain private. This obviously relies heavily on the notion of "result" and the modeling of the protocol. Typically the result will only contain only the sum of all votes, which corresponds to a simple and intuitive understanding of privacy.

Some protocols may leak some additional information, for example the number of ballots on the bulletin board. For instance in the protocol by Juels et al. [11] voters can post fake ballots. In this case, the above definition of the result may lead to a too restrictive privacy notion, since two situations with the same votes but a different number of fakes are required to be bisimilar. To address this issue, we can include the number of ballots in the result if we want to accept the additional leakage. This gives very fine-grained control about the level of privacy we want to model.

Note that if the link between a voter and his vote is also published as part of the result on channel *res*, our definition of privacy may be true although this probably does not correspond to the intuitive understanding of privacy. This is however coherent within the model since everything apart from the result is private; simply the result itself leaks too much information.

3.2 Link to Existing Definitions

To establish the relationship of our definition and the existing ones, we need to formally characterize their difference. Intuitively the swap-based definition assumes that swapping two votes will not change the result. This can be formalized as follows: If two instances of the protocol with the same voters give the same result, then the votes are a permutation of each other, and vice versa. This precludes weighted votes, thus the name "Equality of Votes".

Definition 14 (Equality of Votes (EQ)). *A voting protocol respects* Equality of Votes (EQ) *if for any* $VP_A = \nu \tilde{n}.(V\sigma_{id_1}\sigma_{v_1^A} | \ldots | V\sigma_{id_n}\sigma_{v_n^A} | A_1 | \ldots | A_l)$ *and* $VP_B = \nu \tilde{n}.(V\sigma_{id_1}\sigma_{v_1^B} | \ldots | V\sigma_{id_n}\sigma_{v_n^B} | A_1 | \ldots | A_l)$ *we have*

$$VP_A|_{res} \approx_l VP_B|_{res} \Leftrightarrow \exists \pi : \forall i : \sigma_{v_i^B} = \sigma_{v_{\pi(i)}^A},$$

where π is a permutation.

This allows us to formally prove that our definition is equivalent to the existing ones if (EQ) holds.

Theorem 1 (Equivalence of Privacy Definitions). *If a protocol respects (EQ), then (VP) and (SwP) are equivalent.*

The full formal proof can be found in our technical report [21]. Intuitively, because of (EQ), two instances of a protocol can only have the same result if the votes are a permutation of each other. As any permutation can be written as a sequence of simple permutations (swaps), (SwP) is enough to generate any possible permutation, which gives (VP). Conversely, the definition of (SwP) becomes just a particular case of (VP).

It is easy to see that this condition (EQ) is necessary: If a protocol uses weighted votes (e.g. Alice 66%, Bob 34%), it may satisfy (VP), but not (SwP).

Similarly, consider the following example: In the official result announced on channel res, a pre-selected candidate always wins - this could be the case if the authorities are dishonest and want to manipulate the election outcome. If however at the same time the ballots on the bulletin board allow to calculate the result, such a protocol may ensure (SwP) – if the ballots cannot be linked to the voters –, but not (VP) because two instances with a different outcome based on the ballots will have the same "result" on res. Note that such a protocol would contradict (EQ) because we have instances where the votes are not a permutation of each other, but still give the same result.

3.3   Example: A Variant of FOO

Eliasson and Zúquete [13] propose an implementation of a voting system supporting vote weights based on REVS [14], which itself is based on the protocol by Fujioka et al. [15], often referred to as "FOO".

Informal Description: The protocol by Fujioka et al. [15]. is split into three phases. In the first phase, the voter obtains the administrator's signature on a commitment to his vote:

- Voter V_i chooses his vote v_i and computes a commitment $x_i = \xi(v_i, k_i)$ for a random key k_i.
- He blinds the commitment using a blinding function χ, a random value r_i and obtains $e_i = \chi(x_i, r_i)$.
- He signs e_i and sends the signature $s_i = \sigma_{V_i}(e_i)$ together with e_i and his identity to the administrator A.
- The administrator checks if V_i has the right to vote, has not yet voted, and if the signature s_i is correct. If all tests succeed, he signs $d_i = \sigma_A(e_i)$ and sends it back to V_i.
- V_i unblinds the signature and obtains $y_i = \delta(d_i, r_i)$. He checks the signature.

In the second phase, the actual voting takes place:

- Voter V_i sends (x_i, y_i) to the collector C through an anonymous channel.
- C checks the administrator's signature and enters (x_i, y_i) into a list.

When all ballots are cast or when the deadline is over, the counting phase begins:

- The collector publishes the list of correct ballots.
- V_i verifies that his commitment appears on the list and sends r_i together with the commitment's index l on the list to C using an anonymous channel.
- The collector C opens the l-th ballot using r_i and publishes the vote.

Adding Vote Weights: In [13] Eliasson and Zúquete discuss several possibilities on how to implement weights in this protocol:

- including the weight in the vote (which requires trusting the voter for correctness or zero-knowledge proofs to verify the weight)
- using different keys when the vote is signed by the administrator, where each key corresponds to a different weight
- using multiple ballots per voter, i.e. if for example voter A holds 70% and voter B 30% of the shares, voter A sends 7 and voter B 3 ballots.

We implemented the latter variant in the Applied π-Calculus. Using a manual proof (see [21] for details) we can show that

$$VP_A|_{res} \approx_l VP_B|_{res} \Rightarrow \sum_{i=1}^{n} v_i^A * w_i = \sum_{i=1}^{n} v_i^B * w_i. \tag{1}$$

Using a python script available on our website [22] that generates all cases to check based on the number of voters and the discrete weight distribution, we can use Proverif to then establish (2) which gives that this variant ensures (VP).

$$\sum_{i=1}^{n} v_i^A * w_i = \sum_{i=1}^{n} v_i^B * w_i \Rightarrow VP_A \approx_l VP_B \tag{2}$$

4 Receipt-Freeness

In this section we define receipt-freeness for weighted votes. We first consider the case where only one voter is attacked, then we define multi-voter attacks.

4.1 Single-Voter Receipt-Freeness (SRF)

We combine the idea by Delaune et al. (Def. 10) with our definition of Privacy: If two instances of a voting protocol give the same result, they should be bisimilar even if one voter reveals his secret data in one case or fakes it in the other.

Definition 15 (Single-Voter Receipt Freeness (SRF)). *A voting protocol ensures* Single-Voter Receipt Freeness (SRF) *if for any voting processes* $VP_A = \nu\tilde{n}.(V\sigma_{id_1}\sigma_{v_1^A} \mid \ldots \mid V\sigma_{id_n}\sigma_{v_n^A} \mid A_1 \mid \ldots \mid A_l)$, $VP_B = \nu\tilde{n}.(V\sigma_{id_1}\sigma_{v_1^B} \mid \ldots \mid V\sigma_{id_n}\sigma_{v_n^B} \mid A_1 \mid \ldots \mid A_l)$ *and any number* $i \in \{1, \ldots, n\}$ *there exists a process* V_i' *such that we have* $V_i'^{\backslash out(chc_i, \cdot)} \approx_l V\sigma_{id_i}\sigma_{v_i^B}$ *and*

$$VP_A|_{res} \approx_l VP_B|_{res} \Rightarrow VP_A' \left[(V\sigma_{id_i}\sigma_{v_i^A})^{chc_i} \right] \approx_l VP_B' [V_i'],$$

where VP_A' *and* VP_B' *are like* VP_A *and* VP_B, *but with holes for the voter* $V\sigma_{id_i}$.

As for (VP), our definition is equivalent to the existing one based on swapping if the protocol ensures (EQ), which is the case if it does not use weighted votes. Similarly to swap-based definitions, (SRF) is stronger than (VP). The proof is analogous to the proof in the swap-based model (see [21] for details).

4.2   Multi-voter Receipt-Freeness (MRF)

We now generalize the idea of Receipt-Freeness to the case where multiple voters are attacked. Instead of only considering one attacked voter i, we consider a set I of attacked voters. To be receipt-free, it should be possible for all attacked voters to fake the receipt. Note that we assume that there is always at least one honest voter, except for the case with only one voter.

Definition 16 (Multi-Voter Receipt Freeness (MRF)). *A voting protocol ensures* Multi-Voter Receipt Freeness (MRF) *if for any voting processes* $VP_A = \nu\tilde{n}.(V\sigma_{id_1}\sigma_{v_1^A} \mid \dots \mid V\sigma_{id_n}\sigma_{v_n^A} \mid A_1 \mid \dots \mid A_l)$, $VP_B = \nu\tilde{n}.(V\sigma_{id_1}\sigma_{v_1^B} \mid \dots \mid V\sigma_{id_n}\sigma_{v_n^B} \mid A_1 \mid \dots \mid A_l)$ *and any subset* $I \subset \{1,\dots,n\}$, $I \neq \{1,\dots,n\}$ *if* $n > 1$, *then there exists processes* V_i' *such that we have* $\forall i \in I : V_i'^{\backslash out(chc,\cdot)} \approx_l V\sigma_{id_i}\sigma_{v_i^B}$ *and*

$$VP_A|_{res} \approx_l VP_B|_{res} \Rightarrow VP_A' \left[\big|_{i \in I} (V\sigma_{id_i}\sigma_{v_i^A})^{chc_i} \right] \approx_l VP_B' \left[\big|_{i \in I} V_i' \right],$$

where VP_A' *and* VP_B' *are like* VP_A *and* VP_B, *but with holes for all voters* $V\sigma_{id_i}, i \in I$.

By choosing $I = \{i\}$ we obtain that (MRF) implies (SRF). Under certain conditions the converse is also true. To prove this, we define a "generalized voting process" which is like a voting process, but some voters might be under attack.

Definition 17 (Generalized Voting Process). *A* Generalized Voting Process *is a voting process* VP *with variables for the voter's processes that can either be a "normal" voter or a voter communicating with the intruder, i.e.* $VP = \nu\tilde{n}.(V_1|\dots|V_n|A_1|\dots|A_l)$ *where* $V_i \approx_l V\sigma_{id_i}\sigma_{v_i}$ *or* $V_i^{\backslash out(chc_i,\cdot)} \approx_l V\sigma_{id_i}\sigma_{v_i}$.

The next definition captures the key properties required for our proof. It expresses two modularity conditions of a voting protocol.

Definition 18 (Modularity (Mod)). *A voting protocol is* modular (Mod) *if it is* composable *and* decomposable. *A voting protocol is* composable *if for any generalized voting processes* VP_A *and* VP_B *there exists a generalized voting process* VP *such that* $VP \approx_l VP_A|VP_B$. *A voting protocol is* decomposable *if any generalized voting process* $VP = \nu\tilde{n}.(V_1|\dots|V_n|A_1|\dots|A_l)$ *can be decomposed into processes* $VP_i = \nu\tilde{n}_i.(V_i|A_1^i|\dots|A_l^i)$ *where*

$$VP \approx_l VP_1|\dots|VP_n. \tag{3}$$

Imagine a protocol where in order to escape coercion the voters can claim that a certain ballot on the bulletin board is their ballot, but it was actually prepared by some honest authority to allow the voters to create a fake receipt. If we suppose that this ballot exists only once no matter how many voters are attacked, it would be enough for a single voter to fake his receipt. However we cannot compose two instances with one attacked voter each, as they would use the same fake ballot which would be noticeable for the attacker. Hence the above definition also captures the fact that faking the receipt to escape coercion can be done by each voter independently.

Another property we need for our proof is *Correctness*, i.e. the fact that if in two instances the voters' choices are the same, they give the same result[1].

Definition 19 (Correctness (Cor)). *A voting protocol is* correct *if for any generalized voting processes* $VP_A = \nu \tilde{n}_A.(V_{1,A}|\dots|V_{n,A}|A_1|\dots|A_l)$ *and* $VP_B = \nu \tilde{n}_B.(V_{1,B}|\dots|V_{n,B}|A_1|\dots|A_l)$ *with for any* i *and* $X \in \{A,B\}$: $V_{i,X}^{\backslash out(chc_i,\cdot)} \approx_l V\sigma_{id_i}\sigma_{v_i}$, *we have*

$$VP_A|_{res} \approx_l VP_B|_{res} \tag{4}$$

It is easy to see that Correctness is implied by Equality of Votes as the identity is a permutation, hence any protocol ensuring (EQ) ensures (Cor) [21]. Putting everything together, we are able to prove the equivalence of (SRF) and (MRF).

Theorem 2. *If a protocol is modular, correct and ensures Single-Voter Receipt Freeness, it also ensures Multi-Voter Receipt Freeness.*

The full proof is given in our technical report [21]. The main idea is that we can decompose an instance with multiple attacked voters into instances with at most one attacked voter, where we can apply the single-voter assumption, and recompose the result. Note that the assumptions (Mod), (EQ) are satisfied by many well-known protocols (e.g. [15, 23, 24]), we illustrate this on an example.

Remark. We have to be careful when modeling protocols using a full PKI. If we model the PKI inside the voting process, decomposing a protocol would result in two instances using different keys, which will most probably be visible to an attacker and the bisimilarity (3) will not hold. A possible solution could be to externalize the PKI into a context K such that $K[VP] \approx_l K[VP_1|VP_2]$, which ensures that VP_1 and VP_2 use the same keys. This would allow us to obtain the same result for protocols such as [25, 26].

4.3   Example: Protocol by Okamoto

The protocol by Okamoto [24] uses trapdoor commitments to achieve (SwRF), but it is not (SwCR) [2].

Informal Description: The protocol is split in 3 phases. In the first phase the voter obtains a signature on a commitment to his vote from the administrator:

- Each voter V_i chooses his vote v_i and computes a trapdoor commitment $x_i = \xi(v_i, k_i, td_i)$ for a random key k_i and a trapdoor td_i.
- V_i blinds the commitment using a blinding function χ, a random value r_i and obtains $e_i = \chi(x_i, r_i)$.

---

[1] This does not entirely cover intuitive correctness as it will be fulfilled by protocols always giving the same result independently from the votes, but it will fail for a protocol announcing a random result.

- V_i signs e_i and sends the signature $s_i = \sigma_{V_i}(e_i)$ together with e_i and his identity to the administrator A.
- The administrator checks if V_i has the right to vote, has not yet voted, and if the signature s_i is correct. If all tests succeed, he signs $d_i = \sigma_A(e_i)$ and sends it back to V_i.
- V_i checks the signature, unblinds d_i using δ and obtains $y_i = \delta(d_i, r_i)$.

In the second phase the actual voting takes place:

- V_i sends the signed trapdoor commitment y_i to the collector C through an anonymous channel.
- C checks the administrator's signature.
- V_i sends (v_i, r_i, x_i) to the *timeliness* member T through an untappable anonymous channel.

When all ballots are cast or when the deadline is over, the counting phase begins:

- C publishes the list of correct ballots (x_i, y_i).
- T publishes a randomly shuffled list of votes v_i and a zero-knowledge proof that he knows a permutation π for which $x_{\pi(i)} = \xi(v_i, r_i)$.

Analysis: The protocol is receipt-free because the trapdoor allows a voter to open the commitment in any way to fake a receipt for any candidate as formally shown by Delaune et al. [2]. Here we use a slightly modified version of their model to show that it also respects $(\mathrm{MRF})^2$, see technical report [21] for details.

It is also easy to see that the protocol ensures (EQ) as votes are not weighted and the honest timeliness members will publish the correct result. We can also find that it is *modular* by analyzing the structure of the voting processes. In the case of n voters, we have the form

$$\nu \mathrm{chT}.(V_1| \ldots |V_n \underset{i=1,\ldots,n}{\quad|\quad} \mathrm{processT}),$$

where processT is the process executed by the timeliness member and chT is the private channel between voters and the timeliness member. For $k \in \{1, \ldots, n-1\}$, a possible decomposition would be

$$\nu \mathrm{chT}.(V_1| \ldots |V_k \underset{i=1,\ldots,k}{\quad|\quad} \mathrm{processT})|\nu \mathrm{chT}.(V_{k+1}| \ldots |V_n \underset{i=k+1,\ldots,n}{\quad|\quad} \mathrm{processT}),$$

which is obviously bisimilar. It is easy to see that this also works for composing processes. This is because each instance contains the same private channel and as many processT as voters. Thus the protocol is modular, and using Theorem 2 we have that the protocol by Okamoto ensures (MRF).

Note that this would also hold for a variant of the protocol with weighted votes. Similarly to the first example we could implement this using multiple ballots, and the resulting protocol ensures (SRF), (MRF), (Cor) and (Mod), but neither (EQ) nor (SwRF).

---

[2] Essentially we do not use the key distribution process as no keys are required to be secret. We model them as free variables instead.

5   Coercion-Resistance

After discussing Receipt-Freeness, we now define Coercion-Resistance. As before, we start with Single-Voter Coercion-Resistance.

5.1   Single-Voter Coercion (SCR)

In this case, we combine (VP) with (SwCR): If two instances of a voting protocol give the same result, they should be bisimilar even if one voter interacts with the attacker in one case or only pretends to do so in the other case. The coercion is modeled by the context C that interacts with the voter and tries to force him to vote for a certain candidate.

Definition 20 (Single-Voter Coercion-Resistance (SCR)). *A voting protocol ensures* Single-Voter Coercion-Resistance (SCR) *if for any voting processes* $VP_A = \nu\tilde{n}.(V\sigma_{id_1}\sigma_{v_1^A} \mid \ldots \mid V\sigma_{id_n}\sigma_{v_n^A} \mid A_1 \mid \ldots \mid A_l)$, $VP_B = \nu\tilde{n}.(V\sigma_{id_1}\sigma_{v_1^B} \mid \ldots \mid V\sigma_{id_n}\sigma_{v_n^B} \mid A_1 \mid \ldots \mid A_l)$ *and any number* $i \in \{1,\ldots,n\}$ *there exists a process* V_i' *such that for any context* C_i *with* $C_i = \nu c_1.\nu c_2.(\_|P_i)$ *and* $\tilde{n} \cap fn(C) = \emptyset$, $VP_A'\left[C_i\left[(V\sigma_{id_i}\sigma_{v_i^A})^{c_1,c_2}\right]\right] \approx_l VP_A'\left[(V\sigma_{id_i}\sigma_{v_i^A})^{chc_i}\right]$ *we have* $C_i[V_i']^{\backslash out(chc,\cdot)} \approx_l V\sigma_{id_i}\sigma_{v_i^B}$ *and*

$$VP_A|_{res} \approx_l VP_B|_{res} \Rightarrow VP_A'\left[C_i\left[(V\sigma_{id_i}\sigma_{v_i^A})^{c_1,c_2}\right]\right] \approx_l VP_B'\left[C_i[V_i']\right],$$

where VP_A' *and* VP_B' *are like* VP_A *and* VP_B, *but with a holes for the voter* $V\sigma_{id_i}$.

As above, we can easily link this definition to the existing swap-based definition using (EQ): If a protocol respects (EQ), (SCR) and (SwCR) are equivalent. The proof given in [21] is similar to the (SRF) case.

5.2   Multi-voter Coercion (MCR)

We now discuss Multi-Voter Coercion-Resistance. To model the case where multiple voters are attacked, we consider the set I of attacked voters.

Definition 21 (Multi-Voter Coercion-Resistance (MCR)). *A voting protocol ensures* Multi-Voter Coercion-Resistance (MCR) *if for any voting processes* $VP_A = \nu\tilde{n}.(V\sigma_{id_1}\sigma_{v_1^A} \mid \ldots \mid V\sigma_{id_n}\sigma_{v_n^A} \mid A_1 \mid \ldots \mid A_l)$, $VP_B = \nu\tilde{n}.(V\sigma_{id_1}\sigma_{v_1^B} \mid \ldots \mid V\sigma_{id_n}\sigma_{v_n^B} \mid A_1 \mid \ldots \mid A_l)$ *and any subset* $I \subset \{1,\ldots,n\}$, $I \neq \{1,\ldots,n\}$ *if* $n > 1$, *there exists processes* V_i' *such that for any contexts* $C_i, i \in I$ *with* $C_i = \nu c_1.\nu c_2.(\_|P_i)$ *and* $\tilde{n} \cap fn(C) = \emptyset$, $VP_A'\left[\underset{i \in I}{|}C_i\left[(V\sigma_{id_i}\sigma_{v_i^A})^{c_1,c_2}\right]\right] \approx_l$ $VP_A'\left[\underset{i \in I}{|}(V\sigma_{id_i}\sigma_{v_i^A})^{chc_i}\right]$ *we have* $\forall i \in I : C_i[V_i']^{\backslash out(chc,\cdot)} \approx_l V\sigma_{id_i}\sigma_{v_i^B}$ *and*

$$VP_A|_{res} \approx_l VP_B|_{res} \Rightarrow VP_A'\left[\underset{i \in I}{|}C_i\left[(V\sigma_{id_i}\sigma_{v_i^A})^{c_1,c_2}\right]\right] \approx_l VP_B'\left[\underset{i \in I}{|}C_i[V_i']\right],$$

where VP'_A and VP'_B are like VP_A and VP_B, but with holes for all voters $V\sigma_{id_i}, i \in I$.

As for (MRF), (MCR) implies (SCR), and (MCR) resp. (SCR) is stronger than (MRF) resp. (SRF) (for the proofs, see the technical report [21]). We also have equivalence between (SCR) and (MCR) under the same assumptions as in the case of Receipt-Freeness using a similar proof.

5.3   Example: Bingo Voting

Bingo Voting was developed by Bohli et al. [23] to achieve coercion-resistance as well as individual and universal verifiability by using a trusted random number generator (RNG) and a voting booth.

Informal Description: We consider an election with k voters and l candidates. The protocol is split into three phases: The pre-voting phase, the voting phase and the post-voting phase. In the pre-voting phase, the voting machine generates k random values $n_{i,j}$ for every candidate p_j. It commits to the $k \cdot l$ pairs $(n_{i,j}, p_j)$ and publishes the shuffled commitments.

In the voting phase, the voter enters the voting booth and selects the candidate he wants to vote for on the voting machine. The RNG generates a random number r which is transmitted to the voting machine and displayed to the voter. The voting machine chooses for each candidate a dummy vote except for the voter's choice. For this candidate the random value from the RNG is used and the receipt (a list of all candidates and the corresponding dummy or real votes) is created. Finally the voter checks that the number displayed on the RNG corresponds to the entry of his candidate on the receipt.

In the post-voting phase the voting machine announces the result, publishes all receipts and opens the commitments of all unused dummy votes. The machine also generates non-interactive zero-knowledge proofs that each unopened commitment was actually used as a dummy vote in one of the receipts.

Analysis: The protocol satisfies (SwRF) as the receipt contains only random numbers, and it is impossible for the attacker to know which entry corresponds to the random value generated by the RNG [4]. It also ensures (SwCR) as voting takes places inside a secured voting booth. This was formally proven in the DKR-model [4], and we use the same model to show that it satisfies (MCR). As before, it is easy to see that the protocol ensures Equality of Votes and hence Correctness as votes are not weighted. By analyzing the structure of the voting process, we can see that the protocol also is *modular*. In the case of n voters, we have the following voting process

$$\nu\text{privChM}_1 \ldots \nu\text{privChM}_n.\nu\text{privChRM}_1 \ldots \nu\text{privChRM}_n.$$
$$\nu\text{privChR}_1 \ldots \nu\text{privChR}_n.(V_1 | \ldots | V_n | M_{1,\ldots,n;l} | R_1 | \ldots | R_n)$$

where R_i are the trusted random number generators, $M_{1,\ldots,n;l}$ is the voting machine process for n voters from 1 to n and l candidates, and privChM_i,

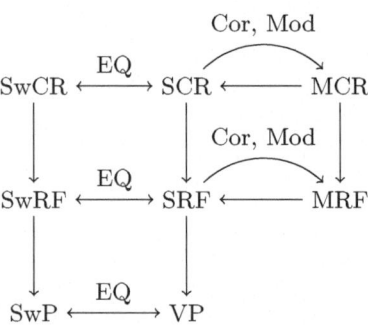

Fig. 2. Relations among the notions. A $\xrightarrow{C}$ B means that under the assumption C a protocol ensuring A also ensures B.

privChRM$_i$ and privChR$_i$ are the private channels between the voter and the voting machine, the RNG and the voting machine, and the RNG and the voter respectively. For $k \in \{1, \ldots, n-1\}$, this can be rewritten as

$$\nu\mathrm{privChM}_1 \ldots \nu\mathrm{privChM}_k.\nu\mathrm{privChRM}_1 \ldots \nu\mathrm{privChRM}_k.$$
$$\nu\mathrm{privChR}_1 \ldots \nu\mathrm{privChR}_k.(V_1| \ldots |V_k|M_{1,\ldots,k;l}|R_1| \ldots |R_k)|$$
$$\nu\mathrm{privChM}_{k+1} \ldots \nu\mathrm{privChM}_n.\nu\mathrm{privChRM}_{k+1} \ldots \nu\mathrm{privChRM}_n.$$
$$\nu\mathrm{privChR}_{k+1} \ldots \nu\mathrm{privChR}_n.(V_{k+1}| \ldots |V_n|M_{k+1,\ldots,n;l}|R_{k+1}| \ldots |R_n)$$

as $M_{1,\ldots,n;l} \approx_l M_{1,\ldots,k;l}|M_{k+1,\ldots,n;l}$. This can be easily seen from the applied π-code [21]. It is easy to see that this also works for composing processes. Hence we have all necessary conditions and obtain that Bingo Voting ensures (MCR).

6   Conclusion

We presented an intuitive definition of privacy for voting protocols that generalizes to situations with weighted votes. We extended the definition to include Receipt-Freeness and Coercion-Resistance as well. We considered situations where only one voter is under attack, and others where multiple voters are attacked. We were able to show that - under the assumptions that votes are not weighted and correctly counted - the single voter case is equivalent to (SwP), (SwRF), (SwCR) as defined by Delaune et al. [2]. Moreover, we proved that the multi-voter case is equivalent to the single-voter case if the protocol is correct (Cor) and respects a modularity condition (Mod). This condition allows us to compose and decompose protocols, which expresses the fact the different parts of the protocol are independent. Figure 2 summarizes our results. Finally, we illustrated our work by analyzing two existing protocols. As future work, we would like to translate these symbolic definitions to the computational setting.

Acknowledgments. This work was partly supported by the ANR project ProSe (decision ANR 2010-VERS-004).

References

1. Backes, M., Hritcu, C., Maffei, M.: Automated verification of remote electronic voting protocols in the applied pi-calculus. In: IEEE Computer Security Foundations Symposium, pp. 195–209 (2008)
2. Delaune, S., Kremer, S., Ryan, M.: Verifying privacy-type properties of electronic voting protocols. Journal of Computer Security 17, 435–487 (2009)
3. Delaune, S., Kremer, S., Ryan, M.D.: Verifying Privacy-Type Properties of Electronic Voting Protocols: A Taster. In: Chaum, D., Jakobsson, M., Rivest, R.L., Ryan, P.Y.A., Benaloh, J., Kutylowski, M., Adida, B. (eds.) Towards Trustworthy Elections. LNCS, vol. 6000, pp. 289–309. Springer, Heidelberg (2010)
4. Dreier, J., Lafourcade, P., Lakhnech, Y.: Vote-Independence: A Powerful Privacy Notion for Voting Protocols. In: Garcia-Alfaro, J., Lafourcade, P. (eds.) FPS 2011. LNCS, vol. 6888, pp. 164–180. Springer, Heidelberg (2012)
5. Dreier, J., Lafourcade, P., Lakhnech, Y.: A formal taxonomy of privacy in voting protocols. In: First IEEE International Workshop on Security and Forensics in Communication Systems (ICC 2012 WS - SFCS) (2012)
6. Küsters, R., Truderung, T.: An Epistemic Approach to Coercion-Resistance for Electronic Voting Protocols. In: 2009 IEEE Symposium on Security and Privacy (S&P 2009), pp. 251–266. IEEE Computer Society (2009)
7. Moran, T., Naor, M.: Receipt-Free Universally-Verifiable Voting with Everlasting Privacy. In: Dwork, C. (ed.) CRYPTO 2006. LNCS, vol. 4117, pp. 373–392. Springer, Heidelberg (2006)
8. Smyth, B., Cortier, V.: Attacking and fixing helios: An analysis of ballot secrecy. In: Proceedings of the 24th IEEE Computer Security Foundations Symposium (CSF 2011), pp. 297–311. IEEE (2011)
9. Kremer, S., Ryan, M., Smyth, B.: Election Verifiability in Electronic Voting Protocols. In: Gritzalis, D., Preneel, B., Theoharidou, M. (eds.) ESORICS 2010. LNCS, vol. 6345, pp. 389–404. Springer, Heidelberg (2010)
10. Smyth, B., Ryan, M.D., Kremer, S., Kourjieh, M.: Towards Automatic Analysis of Election Verifiability Properties. In: Armando, A., Lowe, G. (eds.) ARSPA-WITS 2010. LNCS, vol. 6186, pp. 146–163. Springer, Heidelberg (2010)
11. Juels, A., Catalano, D., Jakobsson, M.: Coercion-resistant electronic elections. In: Proceedings of the 2005 ACM Workshop on Privacy in the Electronic Society. WPES 2005, pp. 61–70. ACM (2005)
12. Kremer, S., Ryan, M.: Analysis of an Electronic Voting Protocol in the Applied Pi Calculus. In: Sagiv, M. (ed.) ESOP 2005. LNCS, vol. 3444, pp. 186–200. Springer, Heidelberg (2005)
13. Eliasson, C., Zúquete, A.: An electronic voting system supporting vote weights. Internet Research 16(5), 507–518 (2006)
14. Joaquim, R., Zúquete, A., Ferreira, P.: Revs - a robust electronic voting system. In: IADIS International Conference e-Society 2003, Lisboa, Portugal, June 3-6 (2003)
15. Fujioka, A., Okamoto, T., Ohta, K.: A Practical Secret Voting Scheme for Large Scale Elections. In: Zheng, Y., Seberry, J. (eds.) AUSCRYPT 1992. LNCS, vol. 718, pp. 244–251. Springer, Heidelberg (1993)
16. Abadi, M., Fournet, C.: Mobile values, new names, and secure communication. In: Proceedings of the 28th ACM SIGPLAN-SIGACT Symposium on Principles of Programming Languages, POPL 2001, pp. 104–115. ACM, New York (2001)
17. Blanchet, B., Abadi, M., Fournet, C.: Automated verification of selected equivalences for security protocols. Journal of Logic and Algebraic Programming 75(1), 3–51 (2008)

18. Klus, P., Smyth, B., Ryan, M.D.: Proswapper: Improved equivalence verifier for proverif (2010), http://www.bensmyth.com/proswapper.php
19. Küsters, R., Truderung, T., Vogt, A.: A game-based definition of coercion-resistance and its applications. In: Proceedings of the 2010 23rd IEEE Computer Security Foundations Symposium. CSF 2010, pp. 122–136. IEEE Computer Society, Washington, DC (2010)
20. Langer, L., Jonker, H., Pieters, W.: Anonymity and Verifiability in Voting: Understanding (Un)Linkability. In: Soriano, M., Qing, S., López, J. (eds.) ICICS 2010. LNCS, vol. 6476, pp. 296–310. Springer, Heidelberg (2010)
21. Dreier, J., Lafourcade, P., Lakhnech, Y.: On defining privacy in the presence of weighted votes and the equivalence of single and multi-voter coercion. Technical Report TR-2012-2, Verimag Research Report (March 2012), http://www-verimag.imag.fr/TR/TR-2012-2.pdf
22. Dreier, J.: The code and scripts used to automatically verify the examples (2011), http://www-verimag.imag.fr/~dreier/papers/foo-weighted-code.zip
23. Bohli, J.M., Müller-Quade, J., Röhrich, S.: Bingo Voting: Secure and Coercion-Free Voting Using a Trusted Random Number Generator. In: Alkassar, A., Volkamer, M. (eds.) VOTE-ID 2007. LNCS, vol. 4896, pp. 111–124. Springer, Heidelberg (2007)
24. Okamoto, T.: An electronic voting scheme. In: Proceedings of the IFIP World Conference on IT Tools, pp. 21–30 (1996)
25. Lee, B., Boyd, C., Dawson, E., Kim, K., Yang, J., Yoo, S.: Providing Receipt-Freeness in Mixnet-Based Voting Protocols. In: Lim, J.-I., Lee, D.-H. (eds.) ICISC 2003. LNCS, vol. 2971, pp. 245–258. Springer, Heidelberg (2004)
26. Wen, R., Buckland, R.: Masked Ballot Voting for Receipt-Free Online Elections. In: Ryan, P.Y.A., Schoenmakers, B. (eds.) VOTE-ID 2009. LNCS, vol. 5767, pp. 18–36. Springer, Heidelberg (2009)

TorScan: Tracing Long-Lived Connections and Differential Scanning Attacks*

Alex Biryukov, Ivan Pustogarov, and Ralf-Philipp Weinmann

University of Luxembourg

Abstract. Tor is a widely used anonymity network providing low-latency communication capabilities. The anonymity provided by Tor heavily relies on the hardness of linking a user's entry and exit nodes. If an attacker gains access to the topological information about the Tor network instead of having to consider the network as a fully connected graph, this anonymity may be reduced. In fact, we have found ways to probe the connectivity of a Tor relay. We demonstrate how the resulting leakage of the Tor network topology can be used in attacks which trace back a user from an exit relay to a small set of potential entry nodes.

1 Introduction

Anonymity clearly was not a concern when the Internet Protocol was designed. Hence it comes as no surprise that internet communications are traceable. Today, the consequences of linking your traffic profile to your persona vary: they range from ISPs selling your aggregated web browsing history to marketers in democratic countries to being imprisoned for criticizing the government online in countries with repressive regimes. For many people, the first approach to hiding their identity is a public proxy server. This however is no panacea: the owner of the proxy can be forced to reveal any logs potentially stored – or even worse, the server may turn out to be a honeypot of the organization the party is trying to hide from. A better solution is to forward traffic through a chain of network nodes, so-called *relays*.

In 1996, Goldschlag, Reed and Syverson [1] presented *Onion Routing*, a design limiting traffic analysis on low-latency communication that was inspired by Chaum's mix networks [2]. Tor is the refined successor of the original Onion Routing Project. The Tor network is a low-latency anonymity network which at the time this of writing comprised of 2500-3000 relays with an estimated number of daily users (unique IPs) exceeding 400,000. In comparison to single-hop proxies, forwarding TCP streams through multiple relays increases the anonymity of the users significantly: each hop along the route only knows its successor and predecessor. Tor tries hard to achieve low traffic latency to provide a good user experience, thus sacrificing some anonymity for performance. To keep latency low and network throughput high, Tor relays do not delay incoming messages and do not use padding.

---

* The full version of this paper will appear on *eprint.iacr.org*

S. Foresti, M. Yung, and F. Martinelli (Eds.): ESORICS 2012, LNCS 7459, pp. 469–486, 2012.

One way to undermine the anonymity of a Tor user is to reveal the pair of the corresponding entry and exit nodes; this is supposed to be hard. Once the correspondence between the entry and exit nodes is known, the anonymity of the observed connection is reduced to the case of two known sequentially connected proxies, or to the case of a single proxy if the attacker controls the exit node. Though this will not allow us to immediately determine the actual originator of the connection, this is already a significant information leak because triplets of guard nodes can serve as unique user identifiers within the Tor network, and also because knowing the entry node tells the attacker where to target next. Namely, other attacks may be launched to compromise the entry node, or the entry node's operator/ISP could be presented with legal demands to reveal the network logs. Given that the exit node is known, the probability of correctly guessing the entry node is $\frac{1}{n}$, where n is the number of guards in the Tor network. For an adversary with less visibility than a global passive adversary and a fully connected network, increasing this probability is far from straightforward. Still in reality, not all entry and exit nodes are connected via three hop paths (which is default for Tor) at a given point of time. This observation can become the basis of several novel attacks on Tor, as will be shown in the paper. The main contributions of this paper are:

(i) We present two ways to reveal the connectivity of nodes in the Tor network: one using canonical connections which are a part of the Tor specification; the other is a more generic technique, namely a timing attack on the connection establishment between two relays.

(ii) We present novel attacks which are based on the *connectivity scanning* approach. The first attack allows to identify the guard node which was used in a circuit carrying a long-lived connection – such as an SSH session or a large file download. The second attack, which we have chosen to call *differential scan attack*, uses recurrent connections to reveal all guard nodes of a user.

(iii) We give some guidance on countermeasures that can be implemented to make the Tor network more resilient to leakage of topology information.

The rest of the paper is organized as follows: in the next section, we summarize aspects of the Tor specification which are relevant for the connectivity scanning techniques and for the description of our attacks. Thereafter we give a short overview of previous attacks on Tor. We describe our techniques for revealing the connectivity of Tor relays in Section 3. In Section 4.1, we describe our attack on long-lived streams. The differential scan attack is described in Section 4.2. An analysis of our attacks is performed in Section 5. We discuss the potential countermeasures in Section 6 and conclude in Section 7.

2   Background

Tor is a popular volunteer-based overlay network used to conceal user's location or behavior from adversaries conducting network surveillance or traffic analysis. Using Tor makes it more difficult to trace Internet activity for TCP applications.

To connect to a server through Tor, a client first chooses a path (i.e. a sequence of Tor relays: *guard*, *middle*, and *exit*) which will then carry data back and forth between the client and the server. To choose a path, the client obtains the list of available Tor routers and their parameters from a document called *Network Consensus*. Each Tor router in the list is uniquely identified by the SHA-1 message digest of its RSA public key. To prevent sampled profiling attacks each user has a fixed triplet of guard nodes which does not change for approximately one month. Each time the user needs to choose a guard node, he chooses it uniformly from this triplet.

After the sequence of relays is chosen, the client starts to build a circuit, one hop at a time. First, the user sets up a TLS connection with the guard node and uses COMMAND_CREATE and COMMAND_CREATED cells[1] to negotiate a Diffie-Hellman (DH) key. This creates a one-hop circuit. The client extends the circuit to the middle node through the guard node: he sends a RELAY COMMAND_EXTEND cell to the guard in which he specifies the address, the digest of the middle router, and the first step of DH key exchange encrypted by the middle node's public key. Once the guard node receives the cell, it establishes a TLS connection with the middle node and sends it the encrypted portion of the DH handshake. The middle node decrypts it and replies with the second step of DH exchange which is forwarded to the client within a RELAY COMMAND_EXTENDED cell. In this way the second hop of the circuit is established.

If during the circuit construction process the middle node rejects the connection, the guard node sends a COMMAND_DESTROY cell, specifying the error code, so that the client is forced to choose another sequence of relay nodes and try to construct a new circuit. If the circuit is extended successfully up to the middle node, the rest of the circuit is established in the same way. After the circuit has been built, the client can start transmitting and receiving data over this circuit. All TCP connections of the user's application are translated into Tor streams which are multiplexed over the circuit. Using the initially chosen circuit for a long time makes profiling attacks easier: the longer the duration of the circuit, the more time the attacker has to reveal it. For this reason, circuits older than 10 minutes are not allowed to carry new streams (for new streams a new circuit should be constructed.) After 10 minutes a circuit dies unless it carries a long-lived stream. In the latter case, the lifetime of the circuit equals the lifetime of the long-lived stream. In other words, a circuit is not destroyed until at least one stream is attached to it. In a similar way, a TLS connection between two Tor relays is not closed if it carries at least one circuit. A TLS connection without circuits between two Tor routers lives for three minutes. There is one exception to the rule. A circuit which has never carried a stream (a *clean* circuit[2]) lives for 1 hour.

When a pair of Tor routers or a Tor router and a client have several circuits between them, they try to tunnel them over a single TLS connection. In Figure 1 communication between two Tor routers is shown. The routers use a single

---

[1] Tor protocol messages are called "cells".

[2] Once a new stream is attached to the circuit, it is marked as "dirty".

TLS connection (which is also called Onion Routing connection) which carries a number of circuits, two in this picture (which may belong to different end users). Multiple streams of one user may be multiplexed over a single circuit.

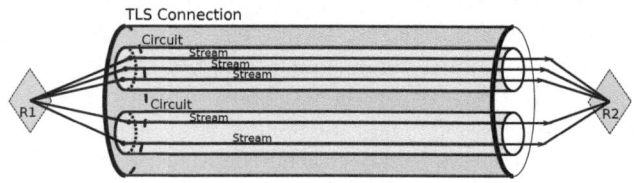

Fig. 1. Circuits and streams multiplexing

2.1 Related Papers

Many different attacks on low-latency anonymity networks in general and on the Tor network in particular are described in the literature. The most successful attacks can be categorized into passive traffic analysis attacks, active traffic analysis attacks, and attacks based on information leakage from specific applications. Passive traffic analysis attacks assume that an attacker passively observes a number of connections in an anonymity network and tries to correlate these connections either between themselves [3–8] or with a predefined traffic pattern [9]. Active traffic analysis attacks assume that an attacker can inject traffic or delay traffic passing through the Tor network, thus modifying traffic and/or timing patterns of a targeted flow [10–13]. Application specific attacks use the fact that applications may establish TCP connections directly (including connections to malicious servers) ignoring Tor and may establish UDP connections which are not supported by Tor [14]. Also, some applications may leak IP addresses in protocol messages.

The attacks presented in this paper do not require monitoring nor sending significant amounts of traffic (only a limited number of Tor protocol management cells) which makes these attacks relatively cheap. They also do not require the attacker to have the global view of the network needed by a number of passive traffic analysis attacks. In addition, the attacks presented in this paper are orthogonal to the previous attacks and thus can be used to improve some existing attacks making them more practical by reducing the traffic costs, or the number of monitored nodes (for ex. Murdoch's attack [10]). Finally, the attacks presented here do not rely on the details of a particular user application or protocol.

3   Revealing Tor Connectivity Dynamics

Consider an attacker who wants to link the exit and the guard node of a circuit and thus decrease the anonymity of the user. Given the Tor network connectivity information, she can determine possible 3-hop paths from the exit node to the set of guard nodes and eliminate those which are impossible, thus already decreasing the claimed anonymity of Tor network to some extent. However, the decrease of anonymity depends on the connectivity of the exit router as well as on the connectivity of its adjacent routers. Even for low bandwidth routers[3], connectivity at a given point in time can be as high as 120-300. For routers from the set of 10% fastest routers, the connectivity may be higher than 1500. Thus, exploiting Tor topology at just one point in time may not be sufficient. A much more efficient way would be to observe Tor connectivity changes over time. Indeed, an application that requires a persistent connection, will force the routers in the circuit to maintain a connection between them for the application's lifetime at least. An attacker who wants to trace such a communication needs to observe the exit node for a while and eliminate routers which it looses connections to. On the other hand, if user's application drops a connection, an attacker may observe a new defect in the topology and link this defect with the user's application (note that if the attacker controls the exit node, she can cause the connection to drop.) In this way, we come to a simple but powerful idea: observation of local Tor network connectivity dynamics gives us a way to decrease the anonymity provided by Tor. More specifically, to trace long-lived (or persistent) connections and to reveal short-lived connections.

3.1   Canonical Connectivity Scanning

We will now show how an attacker can scan a Tor relay to find out what TLS connections are established with other relays. To explain how this works, we first have to delve into details of the Tor specification. In order to prevent an attacker from forcing a relay to open a new TLS connection for each extend request, a Tor relay uses an existing connection (if any) corresponding to the fingerprint specified in the extend request no matter what IP address was indicated. This could potentially allow a malicious party to perform a man-in-the-middle attack. For the two relays R_1, R_2, the attacker would send an extend request with a forged IP address X to R_1 before other circuits (and hence a connection) are established between R_1 and R_2. If the machine at IP address X was then to connect to R_2 and forward all of the traffic it received from R_1 to R_2 and vice versa, it could perform a byte-counting attack. To prevent this from happening, Tor uses a countermeasure called *"canonical connections"*. Briefly, a connection to a router is canonical if the destination IP address of this connection corresponds to the one in the consensus. If a Tor relay gets an extend request with a fingerprint, it should use an existing canonical connection corresponding to this fingerprint.

We noticed that Canonical connections give an attacker a convenient way to determine how routers in the Tor network are connected to each other. When sending a RELAY EXTEND cell, the circuit originator specifies both the identity fingerprint and the IP address of the router he wants to extend the circuit to.

---

[3] Everywhere in the paper, when speaking of bandwidth we mean not the advertised bandwidth but actual figures from the *Consensus* measured by Tor authorities and used by the Tor client to choose routers for the circuits.

Assume that the attacker wants to figure out whether a router A is connected to a router B. In order to do this, the attacker forges a Tor `RELAY EXTEND` cell with the fingerprint of router B and `127.0.0.1` with an unreachable port (port 1 for example) and sends it to router A. When the cell is received, the reaction of router A depends on whether it has a connection to router B:

- If A has a canonical connection to B (it should be noted that if a connection exists it is almost always canonical), router A ignores the IP address from the forged `RELAY_EXTEND` cell and uses the already established TLS connection, extends the circuit and sends back `RELAY_EXTENDED` cell.
- If A does not have a connection to B then it tries to make a new TLS connection using the address from the received cell. Obviously, the connection attempt is refused which causes router A to send a `DESTROY` cell to the attacker.

By inspecting the cell the attacker receives back from router A, she can determine whether router A is connected to router B. Evidently, the attacker can probe router A for connection with any router contained in the consensus[4].

3.2   Connectivity Probing via Timing Attacks

We now consider a second, somewhat less powerful approach for determining whether two relays are already connected. When a client extends a circuit from relay R_1 to relay R_2, the time until he received the `RELAY EXTENDED` reply from R_2 depends on whether a TLS connection between R_1 and R_2 is already set up or whether it needs to be established first. In the later case, both the additional network and the cryptographic latency are considerable. A TLS connection setup between Tor relays can cause huge delays, especially if version 2 or above of the handshake protocol is used. This delay is caused by network latency and the large number of protocol steps until the `CREATE` cell can be sent (see Figure 2 for details). If a TLS connection needs to be set up to create a circuit, a delay on the order of 7.5 round-trip times is added to the circuit creation until the `CREATE` cell is received by R_1. Approximately 6.5 round trips are required for the TLS connection setup alone, another round-trip for the v2 handshake. By sending multiple `RELAY EXTEND` requests and comparing the time it takes for the first one to arrive versus subsequent ones, we can determine whether a relay is connected to another relay. This has been confirmed with experiments. The disadvantage of this method is that network jitter as well as cell forwarding delays by the relay scanned can add significant amounts of noise which makes the method less reliable. Moreover, in contrast to the method described in the previous subsection, this method will really establish TLS connections to all routers that are scanned and not just prolong the lifetimes of the connections that are already open.

---

[4] By coincidence, this scanning technique can not only be used to scan the connectivity of a Tor router, but also to scan for open ports on random IP addresses from a relay that has an all-reject exit-policy.

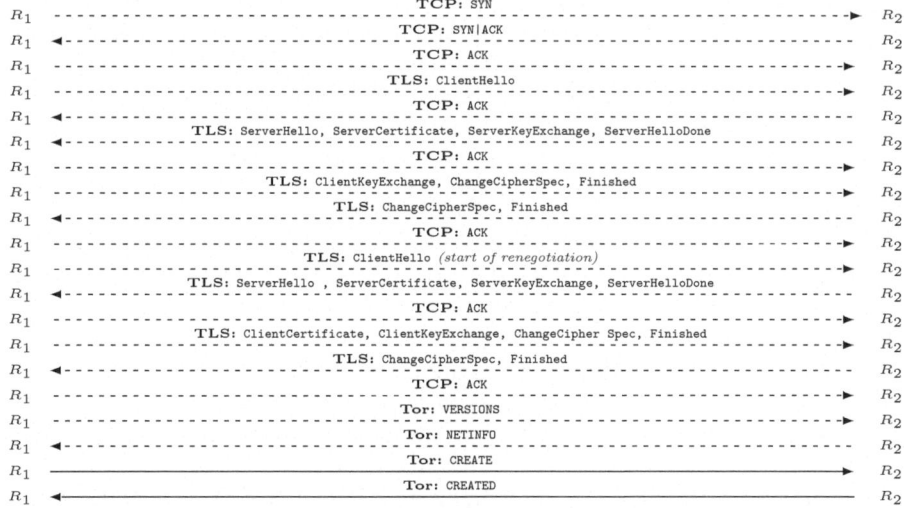

Fig. 2. Tor circuit setup. The last two steps are performed always. Steps marked with dashed lines are performed only when there is no TLS-connection between R_1 and R_2.

4   Attacking Tor Using Connectivity Dynamics

4.1   Tracing Long-Lived Streams

Tor is used by many people to establish long-lived SSH sessions, download very large files (sometimes using file-sharing applications, even though this is frowned upon) and to communicate over instant messaging networks. The latter usage of Tor is particularly important for countries with repressive regimes such as China, Iran, or Syria: people are regularly sent to prison or worse for statements critical of their government. The use-cases described above imply long-lived TCP-streams which necessarily create long-lived TLS-connections between Tor routers which are used to carry the stream. Thus, we show how an attacker knowing the exit node of a long-lived TCP-stream can link it with the guard node using our scanning techniques[5].

One-Hop Attack. In this attack, we assume that the attacker controls one or more fast exit routers which see a significant fraction of the traffic exiting the Tor network, thus she gets access to pseudonyms of the users (ex. cookies, logins). This is not an unrealistic scenario; some organizations have control over sizable portions of the total exit traffic: according to the consensus current at the time

---

[5] One important note is that in the current Tor protocol, the connections between two routers which last more than 7 days are marked as "bad" for new circuits and no new circuits can be added to such connections. However persistent circuits inside these connections are not closed and will continue running. We cannot see these persistent OR connections using our probing techniques after 7 days have elapsed.

of writing this paper, 7.2% of total exit capacity were provided by the Chaos Computer Club, 5.9% by Torservers.net and 5.4% by Formless Networking LLC. The attacker is curious to connect the pseudonyms with the guard triplets for the users that pass through her Exit relays. Assume that one of the attackers' nodes E (see Figure 3) is selected as the exit node of a circuit. By looking at the traffic pattern, the attacker will be able to infer that the connection to the exit node is likely to be of long-lived type. The attacker then starts the attack:

1. The attacker starts scanning the middle node M for connectivity using either of the techniques described in the previous section. The set of connected nodes necessarily includes the guard node G in question and makes up its initial anonymity set.
2. Next, the attacker continues with the connectivity scanning of the middle node for several hour or even days in hope that the majority of the nodes of the initial anonymity set will disconnect (nodes with dash lines on Figure 3.)
3. The attack stops when the anonymity set of the guard node is considerably reduced or when the user closes the long-lived TCP-stream.

Fig. 3. Long-lived connections attack   **Fig. 4.** Differential scanning attack

When the attack is finished, the user's guard node will be contained in the resulting anonymity set (node G and another node with the solid line on Figure 3) along with some number of other connections that can be considered as "noise". The attacker may also infer extra information from the speed of the connection, which will indicate whether the middle or the guard node are the bottleneck for the traffic of the long-lived circuit; this helps her to further shrink the set of candidates for the guard node since it allows to discard very active routers from the list of candidate guard nodes.

Two-Hop Attack. This attack does not require the attacker to control any relays in the Tor network and can be performed by a server (or an attacker close to the server) who tries to reveal the guard nodes of pseudonymous users connecting to the server. The attack starts from connectivity scanning of the exit node (similar to one-hop attack) in order to reduce the anonymity set of the middle node. After having narrowed down the set sufficiently, the candidate middle nodes are scanned resulting in the anonymity set of the guard node.

The attack might be successful if either middle or guard nodes are low-bandwidth which might be inferred from the connection latency by the attacker. We also assume that exit node is medium or low-bandwidth. The difficulty in the two-hop attack comes from the fact that many middle nodes reachable from the exit node would come from a set of active routers with many connections. This will result in hundreds of candidate guard nodes even after several days of scanning. This effect happens due to "immortal"connections formed between active routers, which we will describe in Section 5. In spite of its simplicity, the described attack is quite powerful since:

(i)   it does not require control over any relays in the Tor network. The attacker merely probes relays (probing could be also done from a distributed set of addresses);

(ii) it is cheap in terms of bandwidth: in order to scan one router the aggregated amount of traffic that needs to be sent and received is less than 5 MBytes (for the current size of 3000 routers in Tor network);

(iii) it is fast: the average time of scanning one router is 20 seconds and scanning of different routers can be easily parallelized.

Experimental Results. In order to estimate how efficient the attacks can be in the wild, we used Python to implement a rudimentary Tor client which provides basic functionality. The client can establish a TLS connection to an arbitrary Tor router, complete Diffie-Hellman key establishment and send and receive Tor relay cells. In other words, the client is able to create and extend arbitrary chosen circuits. Using canonical connectivity scanning, our client is able to check a Tor router for connectivity with 99% of other routers in the Tor network in less than 30 seconds.

In order to check the correctness of the proposed canonical connectivity scanning, we scanned two routers under our control omicron and Layercake for five days from February 11th until February 16th, 2012. During the experiment the routers had bandwidth weights in the range [500 - 1500] for omicron and in the range [15000-55000] for layercake which means that the later was in the top 10% set of fastest and thus most frequently chosen routers. Both relays had Guard flags and did not have Exit flags. Since the routers were operated by us, we could gather the real time statistics directly from them using the Tor control port. We then compared the results from the canonical connectivity scan and from the control port. Figure 5 shows the number of persistently connected Tor routers over time, i.e. those routers which were connected to our routers at the start of the experiment and never disconnected during the experiment. The close match of the results as shown on Figure 5 demonstrates that canonical connections scanning provides reliable results. The slight difference in the results is explained by the difference of scanning frequency: for canonical connection scanning, each sample cannot be taken faster than every three minutes (i.e. the lifetime of an idle Tor TLS connection); the data from the routers control port however was fetched every ten seconds. According to Figure 5, for the router with bandwidth weight 1500 (omicron), the number of persistently connected routers decayed from 303 to 20 in just 12 hours. This matches with our prediction from Section 5.1. It then took 4 days for another 18 routers to disconnect. Our target connection was among the remaining ones. The decay rate of persistent connections of the high-bandwidth router (layercake) looks similar: the number of persistent connections drops sharply from 1116 to 300 in 12 hours and then decays slowly. We tested canonical connection scanning against several Tor routers not under our control. The result for one such router with bandwidth weight in range [2040-2190] is shown on Figure 6. We observed a very similar behaviour: a big chunk of connections drop quickly, and then it decays slowly. After two days of scanning, we found 12 persistent connections.

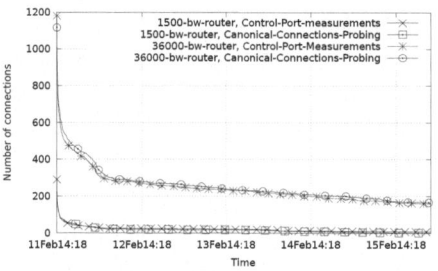 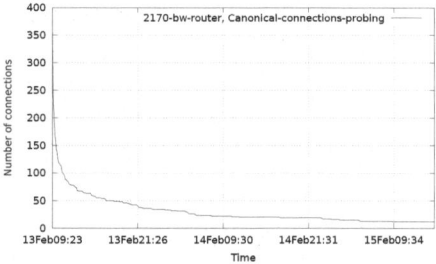

Fig. 5. Decay rate of persistent connections: Canonical vs control port scan

Fig. 6. Persistent connections decay rate for a random router

4.2 Differential Scan Attack

Attack Description. Consider user which periodically checks some Web server or a web service that instructs the user's browser to periodically re-establish streams. Google Mail for instance builds a series of short-lived (around 2 minutes) TCP sessions. Another example are news web sites with auto-refresh contents. In this section, we describe an attack on such recurrent connections. The aim of the attacker is to find at least one of the guard nodes of a pseudonymous user (identified by a cookie or a login credential) that uses such a service for several days. Note that this attack does not require a single long-lived circuit or session. It just requires that a Tor client is connected to the Tor network for non-negligible amount of time within the span of a month (i.e. as long as the guards are still valid).

Similar to Section 4.1, in this attack, the attacker has control over a significant fraction of the exit capacity of the Tor network. Assume that a user visits a Web server S (see Figure 4) that causes recurrent connections to occur. Ten minutes after the first connection, his initial circuit should expire and the user's Tor client will try to build a new circuit. Given a sufficient number of exit nodes controlled by the attacker, the circuit will include one of the attacker's exit nodes E. Once the exit node receives incoming traffic destined to the web server it executes the following sequence of steps:

1. The exit node E observing the stream to the web server determines the middle node M of the circuit that caused the stream to be established and transmits it to the attacker.
2. The attacker probes the connectivity of M and remembers the list of routers connected to it (nodes connected to M both with dash and solid lines on Figure 4).
3. E sends a DESTROY cell[6] down the circuit which leads to the circuit termination. The circuit termination may lead to the connection termination between the middle node and the user's guard node with some probability which can be estimated using expressions from Section 5.2.
4. The attacker waits for three minutes and starts the scan of M again.
5. The attacker computes the difference between the sets obtained via the first and the second scans, i.e. he determines connections which were present in the first list but absent in the second (node G and another node with dash line.) We say that we have a differential with node G and M if G is in the difference.
6. The attacker then repeats steps 1-3 each time one of her exit nodes is chosen for the recurrent connection.
7. Once an attacker has performed the above steps often enough, and given that the circuit closure event caused the connections closure frequently, she can derive the user's three guard nodes: the probability of having the guard node in the difference should converge to $1/3$.

This attack can be further enhanced by scanning the full network at regular and frequent intervals. Then if the connection to the malicious Exit arrives shortly after the full network scan, the attacker will have additional differential connectivity information in order to filter the noise. Our experiments have shown that the full network scan can be done in 3 minutes using 20 hosts (using Amazon EC2 service, a day of full network scans with 3 minutes between scans costs around 80 USD).

A similar but less stealthy approach can be used to track any users connection. Assume that a user connecting to a server chose one of the attacker's exit nodes. This allows the attacker to inject a small piece of code in each HTML document requested by the user, which artificially creates recurrent connections. Specifically the user can be redirected to an arbitrary address and port. Note that in the current Tor network, aggregated exit bandwidth for different port is different, thus by choosing the appropriate port range, the attacker can increase the probability that her exit node is chosen: at the time of the experiment total exit capacity was approximately $5 \cdot 10^6$ Kbytes/s, the bandwidth capacity of scarce ports[7] was about $1.2 \cdot 10^6$ Kbytes/s.

Experimental Results. We have implemented a proof of concept version of our differential scanning technique and have tested it using sets of paths generated by a modified version of the Tor client – this client does not create any circuits

[6] If the attacker wants to be more stealthy she can just wait until the circuit expires.
[7] There are several scarce ports still usable by Web browsers.

but simply outputs randomly generated paths with user-specified constraints. These paths are then used to build circuits through the control port of the Tor daemon. After a circuit has been built, a scan is conducted, then the circuit is torn down, the program waits for 200 seconds and scans again. To perform experiments more quickly we have implemented this in a parallelized manner on Amazon's EC2 platform so that many (non-interfering) experiments can be conducted in parallel. As a first experiment, we used only one guard node with capacity of 36500 and allowed for middle nodes with capacity of 1600 or lower in the consensus[8]. For 150 paths, 125 successful differential scans were performed. The target guard node has appeared 58 times in the difference sets topping the list of potential guards.

1. C37B234FAD013453B90375EB55864FEBC876104A: 58 (PPrivCom052) bw=36500
2. CA1CF70F4E6AF9172E6E743AC5F1E918FFE2B476: 35 (spfTOR3) bw=29800
3. 0B7ED44C67DBE50313F0B32BD335D093D0474CE8: 33 (bauruine2) bw=117000
4. 847B1F850344D7876491A54892F904934E4EB85D: 31 (tor26) bw=20
5. DB8C6D8E0D51A42BDDA81A9B8A735B41B2CF95D1: 30 (rainbowwarrior) bw=81300
6. 173B220F9F32F39086D5661274A47485EDA26131: 29 (TorExitProgressbar9) bw=650
7. 1603DFE9FC373ECDA39046FADB5A76B87A4BA36B: 27 (StickItToTheMan) bw=46800
8. 1F52D692FA2C21B23FAD4D711A7BF17BAE2673DF: 26 (alice) bw=7170
9. 47916CAB5878C810E7EF71A316D37FC823CC7F52: 26 (CCN) bw=53100
10. 95A0D58710EA9B61DAD3A01CAD3BE77DACA76BEF: 25 (OccupyMyPants) bw=30300

This shows that differential probing works in practice: there's a drastic reduction in the anonymity set of the guard nodes, even for high capacity guard nodes. Below is the concrete data of one of the experiments in which we had chosen guards of capacity 300, 412, and 501, constrained the capacity of the middle nodes to 30,000 and scanned different middle nodes in 134 trials[9]:

1. A58E0F05C1939725D7247BA60BA3135DB88209BC: 43 (jef0lewkia), bw = 501
2. D3378ABA009078158DB59E8B36B8EBB88B309BA7: 40 (torn0t), bw = 412
3. 2629979FD21BF3B522E818B73F6F8D0B5D8A5CF0: 40 (tapir), bw = 300
4. A9C039A5FD02FCA06303DCFAABE25C5912C63B26: 29 (chaoscomputerclub5), bw = 173000
5. FA486415B86D28CD047D10F76768E4E88A182F71: 28 (ZhangPoland1), bw = 56400
6. 131B60B9AFE6AEA60042132D648798534ABEA07E: 28 (wagtail), bw = 24400
7. 4536ED68D9DB4B2FF532AD43A632AAF600B798CC: 27 (Unnamed), bw = 116
8. 1D8625690AB9729FB2040D8194EC0D6789A4D092: 25 (TOR1CINIPAC), bw = 43900
9. FC35DE87F6E4022693323275F6B8EEE5F72FD21B5: 24 (Unzane), bw = 3160
10. CA1CF70F4E6AF9172E6E743AC5F1E918FFE2B476: 23 (spfTOR3), bw = 28700

Again, although we have some spurious low-bandwidth routers in the top ten, these results show that the attack described above works well in practice. In real life, the attacker will perform scans for any circuit which has been detected to be established by a unique pseudonym of a user and for which the middle node is below a certain threshold bandwidth.

We now try to estimate how many measurements the attacker should make when low capacity guards are being used. There are 1,440 minutes in a day; this means that if the attacker is unlucky (i.e. his exit is not selected and then she

---

[8] See Section 5 for justification of the choice of the bandwidths. In brief: (1) the product of bandwidths of the guard node and middle node should not exceed 300 million to avoid "immortal connections ; (2) the attack works best when either the guard or the middle node are not high-bandwidth.

[9] jef0lewkia was involved in 43 circuits, torn0t in 45 and tapir in 46 out of 134.

needs to wait for 10 minutes until the circuit expires in order to get another chance) there are 144 measurement chances per day. The fact that an attacker controlling a fraction f of the exit bandwidth tears down circuits to which she gets access, increases the number of measurement slots available to the attacker by $\frac{1}{1-f}$, which for $f = 1/3$ results in $144\frac{f}{1-f} = 72$ slots. If the upper bound for the capacity of the middle node is set to 30000 then (according to Figure 9) there is about 40% chance for a circuit to go through such middle node. This reduces the amount of measurements to 29 per day. The attacker will continue the attack until he obtains about 40 measurements, which means the attack will run for about 1 day. Note that the attack is very successful if the bandwidth of one of the user guard nodes is below 500. There is about 3% chance that a user's client has chosen a guard node with low capacity, i.e. $G_{min} < 500$, into his triplet of guard nodes. Thus this attack could affect more than 10,000 daily users of the Tor network. If the attacker performs the attack for 7 days, it suffices for her to control only 5% of the exit bandwidth.

5 Analysis of the Attacks

5.1 Long-Lived Connections

In Section 4.1, one could notice that after a relatively short period of scanning time, when the number of connections drops to some value, the reduction rate of the anonymity set of the guard node becomes negligible. This value can be considered as a threshold for this attack which we try to estimate in this section.

We measured circuit duration distributions over a two high bandwidth routers connection (layercake bw=35300, and bouazizi bw=69700 for 13 of Feb 2012, see Figure 7) and a connection between a high bandwidth router and a non-high bandwidth router (omicron bw=491 and for 13 of Feb 2012, and layercake). Circuits with lifetime longer than 2 hours constitute less than 1.5% of the total number of circuits. From this we can assume that the majority of long-lived connections in Tor are not because of long-lived circuits but because the short-lived circuit creation rate over this connection is high and there is always at least one circuit inside this connection which prevents it from closing. Such *immortal* connections form if the product of bandwidths of the two routers exceeds a certain threshold as will be shown below.

Figure 8 shows the number of new circuits per ten seconds gathered during two days on one of our active routers. We observed that: (1) circuits arrive according to the non-homogeneous Poisson process; (2) assuming that client circuit arrival rate is proportional to the guard router's bandwidth, we estimate an average circuit arrival rate R in the whole Tor network to be about 900 circuits per second (not at peak times). In the expressions below one can also use the value of circuit arrival rate for the specific time of the day instead of the average value; (3) the average circuit duration time t_{avg} is about 200 seconds which varies only slightly for routers with different bandwidth weights. We now estimate the probability that a pair of routers A and B is connected with almost immortal

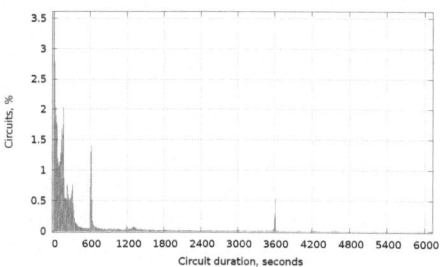

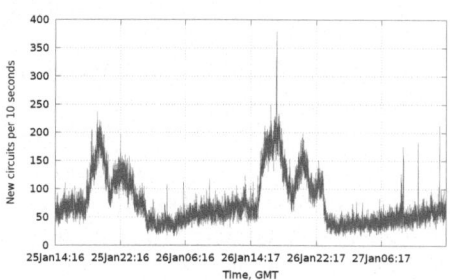

Fig. 7. Circuit duration distribution between two high-bandwidth routers

Fig. 8. Circuit arrival rate for an active high bandwidth router

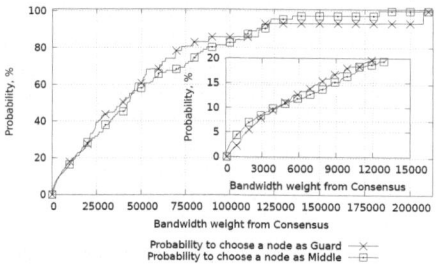

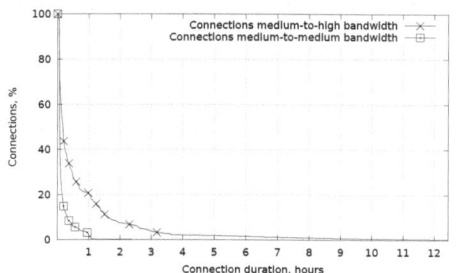

Fig. 9. Probability for a node to be chosen as a guard and a middle node

Fig. 10. Connection duration distribution

connection. Note that a TLS-connection between Tor relays is closed only if no circuits were carried over this connection for three minutes. In other words, for a connection to stay open, the time between arrivals of two consecutive circuits should not exceed the average circuit duration plus 3 minutes. Denote by Δt the time of the attack. Then during this time, $\Delta t \cdot R \cdot p_{a,b}$ new circuits will arrive. Here $p_{a,b}$ is the probability of routers A and B to form an edge in a new circuit: $p_{a,b} = 2 \cdot \frac{bw_a bw_b}{bw_{total}} \left(\frac{1}{bw_{guards}} + \frac{1}{bw_{exit}} \right)$, where bw_{guards} is the total bandwidth of guard nodes, bw_{exit} is the total bandwidth of exit nodes, bw_{total} is the total bandwidth of the whole Tor network, bw_a and bw_b are bandwidths of routers A and B respectively[10]. Taking into account that circuits arrive according to the Poisson distribution, the probability to have an "immortal connection" can be computed using the following expression:

---

[10] This expression for $p_{a,b}$ is an approximation since it does not take into account all peculiarities of the Tor path selection algorithm, in particular, the expression ignores weights which are assigned to a relay based on its position in the circuit and its flags. We compared our approximation with the precise calculation and found that simpler approximation is sufficient for our purposes and makes the analysis easier to understand.

$$P_{immortal}(A, B) = (1 - e^{-R \cdot (t_{avg} + t_{idle}) \cdot p_{a,b}})^{\Delta t \cdot R \cdot p_{a,b}},$$

where $t_{idle} = 180$ seconds. A connection between A and B almost never closes if $P_{immortal}(A, B)$ is close to 1. Using this expression we find that immortal connections are formed between routers of bandwidth $> 17,500$ (or routers with product of bandwidths above 300 million). Given the bandwidth of a router, an attacker can estimate the number of immortal connections that it has and decide whether it is worthwhile to perform the attack. Figure 11 shows complementary cumulative bandwidth distribution of Tor relays along with the share (i.e. the percentage of total number of Tor relays) of persistent connections for each bandwidth[11]. For example, if an attacker decides to scan a Tor relay with bandwidth weight of 5000, she can expect that this relay has about 1% of "immortal" connections. Given 3000 Tor relays, this yields the anonymity set of 30 relays. If $bw < 1300$, the attack is expected to give the unique solution[12]. Note that although only few routers have large percentage of immortal connections, these routers are high-bandwidth and and are selected more frequently.

In order to give a first order approximation of how long we should wait until a persistent connection is detectable among other "non-immortal" connections, we collected connection duration statistics from Tor routers operated by us for 7 days. Figure 10 shows the connection duration distribution for two pairs of routers: medium-to-medium bandwidth, medium-to-high bandwidth. In ten hours, 99% of all non-immortal connections should disconnect for both cases. Thus, we expect that if a persistent connection under observation has a duration of more then 10 hours, the probability of its successful identification depends mostly on the number of immortal connections.

5.2   Differential Scanning Attack

In this section, we explore the limits of the differential scan attack. Assume that an attacker tries to reveal a guard node g by observing circuits $\{c_1, ..., c_k\}$ which leads to scanning of a set of middle nodes $M = \{m_{c_1}, m_{c_2}, ..., m_{c_k}\}$. Let T denote the set of all Tor relays and $|T| = n$. Then we define $d : M \times T \longrightarrow \{0, 1\}$ in the following way:

$$d(m_{c_i}, r) = \begin{cases} 1 & \text{if observed a differential between } m_{c_i} \text{ and } r \text{ for circuit } c_i \\ 0 & \text{otherwise.} \end{cases}$$

The success of the attack depends on: (1) $Signal = \sum_{i=1}^{k} d(m_{c_i}, g)$, i.e. number of differentials with guard node g, and (2) $Noise_{r_j} = \sum_{i=1}^{k} d(m_{c_i}, r_j)$, number of differentials with some other Tor relay r_j, $j = 1, ..., n$. We then use signal-to-noise ratio $SNR = \frac{Signal}{\max_j \{Noise_{r_j}\}}$ as a measure of the success of the attack.

---

[11] Note that bandwidth distribution can be approximated by the Pareto distribution with minimal value $x_m = 350$ and exponent $\alpha = 0.85$.

[12] For 11th of February 17:00, 2012, there were 2388 nodes out of 2897 with bandwidth less than 1300. Their aggregated capacity was 371,159 out of 9,458,556 total capacity of the whole Tor network.

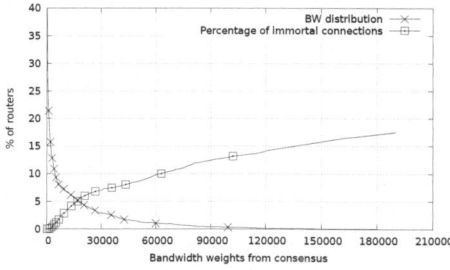
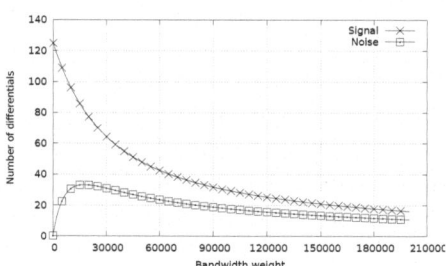

Fig. 11. Tor bandwidth distribution and share of immortal connections

Fig. 12. Signal and Noise for differential scan

We first estimate the Signal and $\text{Prob}[d(m_{c_i}, g) = 1]$. Denote by t_0 the time when c_i was destroyed. $d(m_{c_i}, g_1) = 1$ iff the connection which carried c_i closes 3 minutes after c_i is destroyed. This happens if no new circuit with duration t arrives during $[t_0 - t; t_0]$ and no circuits arrive during $[t_0; t_0 + t_{idle}]$. Let $f(t)$ be the probability density distribution of the circuit duration. Then given that the circuits arrive according Poisson distribution, we have:

$$\text{Prob}[d(m_{c_i}, g_1) = 1] = e^{- \int_0^\infty R \cdot p_{a,b} \cdot t \cdot f(t) dt} \cdot e^{-R \cdot p_{a,b} \cdot t_{idle}} = e^{-R \cdot p_{a,b} \cdot (t_{avg} + t_{idle})},$$

where R is the current circuit arrival rate of the whole Tor network, and $p_{a,b}$ is the probability of router A and B to form an edge in a circuit (see Section 5.1). To estimate the *Noise* and $\text{Prob}[d(m_{c_i}, r) = 1]$ for some Tor relay $r \neq g$ we use the following approach: $d(m_{c_i}, r) = 1$ if: (a) at the time of the first scan, there is a connection between m_{c_i} and r; (b) there is no connection at the time of the second scan. Then we can derive (details are in the full paper):

$$\text{Prob}[d(m, r) = 1] = \left(1 - \frac{e^{-\lambda_{a,b} \cdot (t_{avg} + t_{idle})}}{\lambda_{a,b}(t_{avg} + t_{idle}) + 1} \right) \cdot e^{-\lambda_{a,b} \cdot (t_{avg} + t_{idle})},$$

where $\lambda_{a,b} = R \cdot p_{a,b}$.

To demonstrate how the above expressions work, we used the set of 125 middle nodes from the experiment described in Section 4.2 with bandwidth weights equal or less then 1600. Figure 12 shows: (a) the Signal of the guard node against its bandwidth. (b) the Noise of a Tor relay against its bandwidth. As can be seen from the figure, for low-bandwidth nodes the signal is close to its maximum value. This happens since for this type of node, the probability that the connection between it and a middle node carries just one circuit is very high. Low circuit arrival rate of a low-bandwidth relay also implies the low value of noise since the probability to have a connection between it and a middle node is low.

6   Discussion and Potential Countermeasures

In this paper, we have shown two ways to extract topology information of the Tor network. One way to determine the real connectivity of Tor relays is to exploit a Tor countermeasure against man-in-the-middle attacks called canonical connections. This method is cheap but can be eliminated in future versions of Tor by changing the specification. A potential countermeasure would be to abolish canonical connections. Of course this must be done while preserving the circuit multiplexing feature. An obvious approach is to identify connections not only by the fingerprint but by both the fingerprint and the IP address of the relay. This prevents our attack, but needs to be weighed against a possibility to perform denial-of-service by resource exhaustion against Tor relays.

A different approach for measuring relay connectivity is to use timing information of the connection establishment as a side channel: circuit extension by one hop takes much less time if the link on this hop already exists. This method is less robust then the one exploiting canonical connections, but at the same time the countermeasures are not straightforward; experiences in side-channel cryptanalysis have shown that simple countermeasures like adding randomized delays can often be defeated. At the same time, a fully connected graph for the Tor network – i.e. having each relay connected to all the other relays at all times – probably is too expensive from a performance standpoint. The balance to strike here is to add sufficient noise to make timing attacks unreliable to attackers.

Finally we note that since our connectivity revealing techniques are orthogonal to the existing attacks described in the literature, they can be used to improve many of them substantially. Indeed, during the times when the number of Tor routers was small, several attacks were available to adversaries. These attacks allowed to link the exit and entry nodes of a user's circuit. However, once the number of Tor routers grew, those attacks became too expensive in terms of required bandwidth and time. This is because for those attacks to be successful, exhaustive probing of each link in the Tor network was required. Given a way to determine the real connectivity of Tor network, these attacks can become practical again since the amount of links to be probed is significantly reduced.

7   Conclusion

All prior research on Tor assumed opacity of the Tor network topology – meaning that the attacker had to assume a fully connected graph. In practice, the real degree of a node in this graph is substantially smaller than its maximum at any given point in time. For the first time, we have shown methods to determine the real connectivity of relays in the Tor network and the dynamics of the topology of the whole Tor network. Based on this, we described several novel attacks that use this information to deanonymize the entry points of the users into the Tor network.

Acknowledgments. We would like to thank anonymous reviewers for numerous useful comments.

References

1. Goldschlag, D.M., Reed, M.G., Syverson, P.F.: Hiding Routing Information. In: Anderson, R. (ed.) IH 1996. LNCS, vol. 1174, pp. 137–150. Springer, Heidelberg (1996)
2. Chaum, D.: Untraceable electronic mail, return addresses, and digital pseudonyms. Communications of the ACM 24(2), 84–88 (1981)
3. Danezis, G.: The Traffic Analysis of Continuous-Time Mixes. In: Martin, D., Serjantov, A. (eds.) PET 2004. LNCS, vol. 3424, pp. 35–50. Springer, Heidelberg (2005)
4. Serjantov, A., Sewell, P.: Passive Attack Analysis for Connection-Based Anonymity Systems. In: Snekkenes, E., Gollmann, D. (eds.) ESORICS 2003. LNCS, vol. 2808, pp. 116–131. Springer, Heidelberg (2003)
5. Back, A., Möller, U., Stiglic, A.: Traffic Analysis Attacks and Trade-Offs in Anonymity Providing Systems. In: Moskowitz, I.S. (ed.) IH 2001. LNCS, vol. 2137, pp. 245–257. Springer, Heidelberg (2001)
6. Levine, B.N., Reiter, M.K., Wang, C., Wright, M.: Timing Attacks in Low-Latency Mix Systems. In: Juels, A. (ed.) FC 2004. LNCS, vol. 3110, pp. 251–265. Springer, Heidelberg (2004)
7. Bissias, G.D., Liberatore, M., Jensen, D., Levine, B.N.: Privacy Vulnerabilities in Encrypted HTTP Streams. In: Danezis, G., Martin, D. (eds.) PET 2005. LNCS, vol. 3856, pp. 1–11. Springer, Heidelberg (2006)
8. Zhu, Y., Fu, X., Graham, B., Bettati, R., Zhao, W.: On Flow Correlation Attacks and Countermeasures in Mix Networks. In: Martin, D., Serjantov, A. (eds.) PET 2004. LNCS, vol. 3424, pp. 207–225. Springer, Heidelberg (2005)
9. Panchenko, A., Niessen, L., Zinnen, A.: Website fingerprinting in onion routing based anonymization networks, pp. 1–10. ACM (2011)
10. Murdoch, S.J., Danezis, G.: Low-cost traffic analysis of Tor. In: Proceedings of the 2005 IEEE Symposium on Security and Privacy, pp. 183–195. IEEE CS (2005)
11. Yu, W., Fu, X., Graham, S., Xuan, D., Zhao, W.: Dsss-based flow marking technique for invisible traceback. In: Proceedings of the 2007 IEEE Symposium on Security and Privacy, SP 2007, pp. 18–32. IEEE Computer Society, Washington, DC (2007)
12. Wang, X., Reeves, D.S.: Robust correlation of encrypted attack traffic through stepping stones by manipulation of interpacket delays. In: Proceedings of the 10th ACM Conference on Computer and Communications Security, CCS 2003, pp. 20–29. ACM, New York (2003)
13. Wang, X., Chen, S., Jajodia, S.: Network flow watermarking attack on low-latency anonymous communication systems. In: Proceedings of the 2007 IEEE Symposium on Security and Privacy, SP 2007, pp. 116–130. IEEE Computer Society, Washington, DC (2007)
14. Manils, P., Chaabane, A., le Blond, S., Kaafar, M., Castelluccia, C., Legout, A., Dabbous, W.: Compromising tor anonymity exploiting p2p information leakage. Technical Report 00471556, INRIA (April 2010),
http://arxiv.org/abs/1004.1461

Introducing the gMix Open Source Framework for Mix Implementations

Karl-Peter Fuchs, Dominik Herrmann, and Hannes Federrath

University of Hamburg, Computer Science Department, Germany

Abstract. In this paper we introduce the open source software framework gMix which aims to simplify the implementation and evaluation of mix-based systems. gMix is targeted at researchers who want to evaluate new ideas and developers interested in building practical mix systems. The framework consists of a generic architecture structured in logical layers with a clear separation of concerns. Implementations of mix variants and supportive components are organized as plug-ins that can easily be exchanged and extended. We provide reference implementations for several well-known mix concepts.

1 Introduction

Mix networks are well-known privacy-enhancing technologies that provide anonymous communication. The basic principle of *mixes* was suggested by David Chaum in 1981 [5]. Since then, a large number of concepts and strategies has been proposed. Application areas include e-mail [5,6], voting [5,28,31], location-based services [19] as well as low-latency communication (e. g., for TCP, HTTP [2,16], DNS [18] and ISDN [29]). So far, the only practically deployed systems are Mixmaster [6] and Mixminion [9] (anonymous transport of electronic mails) and the general-purpose anonymization services Tor [16], JAP (JonDonym) [2] and I2P.[1] The source code of these systems has reached a rather high complexity due to continuous security and performance optimizations, though: for instance, Tor consists of more than 63,000 lines of ANSI-C code. Therefore, it becomes increasingly difficult to understand these systems or to extend them with novel proposals from the research community. Moreover, there is a large body of scientific work without a publicly available or practically usable implementation, e. g., [8,11,13,14,22,23,29,32,33,37].

This situation has three undesirable consequences. First of all, there are considerable efforts involved in implementing a newly proposed scheme for evaluation or production purposes, because most of the time researchers will have to re-invent the wheel, i. e., find solutions for common challenges typically encountered in mix-based systems. Secondly, without an easily accessible implementation it is impossible to repeat and reproduce previous experiments. Thirdly, even if implementations *are* available, it is still difficult to compare the results from

---

[1] Downloads at `sourceforge.net/projects/mixmaster`, `mixminion.net`, `www.torproject.org`, `anon.inf.tu-dresden.de` and `www.i2p2.de`.

S. Foresti, M. Yung, and F. Martinelli (Eds.): ESORICS 2012, LNCS 7459, pp. 487–504, 2012.

one's own experiments with previous work, because of different implementations, runtime environments or missing details regarding the experimental setup. Repeatability, reproducibility and rigor in experimental research are critical for quality research, though.

With the *gMix* project we want to improve the current situation. We believe that the availability of a software framework can serve as an *enabler* here. In fields like cryptography or machine learning, frameworks such as *BouncyCastle* and *Weka* have greatly simplified access to a wide selection of implementations and led to widespread adoption.[2] To the best of our knowledge, in the domain of privacy-enhancing technologies such a software framework does not exist so far. The goals of the *gMix* project are as follows:

1. to provide a repository with compatible, adaptable mix implementations,
2. to simplify development of novel, practically usable mix-based systems and
3. to simplify evaluation of mix systems in a controlled and realistic setting.

Our Contribution. To address the aforementioned objectives we have designed an open and generic architecture for existing and future mixing schemes and built a Java framework with a plug-in mechanism. Our solution embraces the *separation of concerns* paradigm and allows a developer to build a concrete mix from the existing implementations of individual software components with no or only little changes to the code. We have already built reference implementations for various existing mixing schemes to provide a working foundation. At the time of this writing there are implementations for over ten output strategies, four recoding schemes and several auxiliary components (cf. Sect. 5). Furthermore, *gMix* includes a load generator and tools for recording results to simplify experimental evaluation. All components use configuration files, which may improve repeatability of experiments, if these files are published together with a paper. The *gMix* project is hosted at https://www.informatik.uni-hamburg.de/SVS/gmix/. Source code is released under GPLv3.

This paper is structured as follows: In Sect. 2 we start out with a high-level overview of the framework. We proceed by discussing its layered architecture (Sect. 3), the overall communication model within the architecture (Sect. 4), and by providing an overview of the currently available implementations (Sect. 5). Notes regarding plug-in compatibility are provided in Sect. 6. In Sect. 7 we present experimental tools which are used in Sect. 8 for a performance evaluation. We conclude the paper in Sect. 9.

2   Framework Overview

The fundamental design of the gMix Framework *(generic mix framework)* is inspired by the layer architecture of the *TCP/IP Model*. The main idea is to extend the *TCP/IP Model* with mix-specific layers, while preserving simple, *standard*

---

[2] Downloads at www.bouncycastle.org and www.cs.waikato.ac.nz/ml/weka

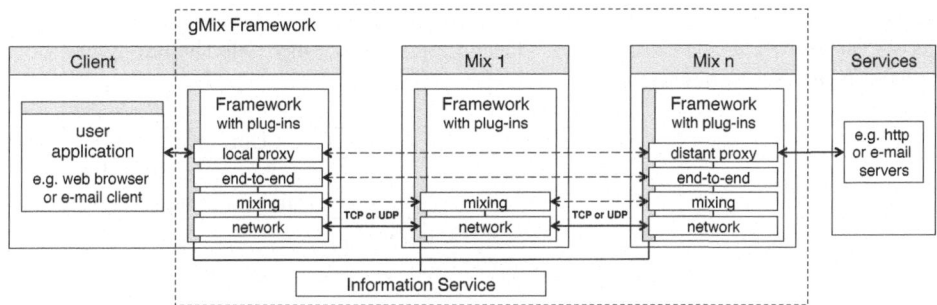

Fig. 1. Overview of the gMix architecture

access to anonymous channels through interfaces almost equal to those of *normal* TCP or UDP sockets. The concrete realization of the anonymous channels (e. g., the *output strategy* and *recoding scheme*) is highly customizable. Layers are implemented as plug-ins and can thus be easily exchanged or composed to a specific mix via configuration files. Additional *low-level* components generally needed for realizing a distributed system are provided as well.

The framework consists of components for clients, mix nodes and an *Information Service*. The *Information Service* can be used for discovery, grouping mixes into cascades and as a public board for information exchange. Clients and mixes form an *overlay network* via *normal* TCP or UDP sockets (cf. Fig. 1). Client and mix plug-ins can be run on a single host to allow peer-to-peer networks.

Anonymous channels can be established between clients and exit nodes (*Mix n* in Fig. 1) and are routed via intermediate mixes through the *overlay network* (*Mix 1* in Fig. 1). For compatibility with standard software and *normal* Internet services, proxy servers can be used as end points of the anonymous channels on both clients and exit nodes. For end-to-end anonymity, public services (e. g., a web server) may be run directly on mix nodes and privacy-preserving user applications, such as a web browser that suppresses identifying pieces of information [20], can be implemented.

The framework can be configured to provide the socket types shown in Table 1. We distinguish between *Stream* and *Datagram Sockets*. *Stream Sockets* are almost equal to *normal* TCP sockets. They feature *connect* and *disconnect* methods as well as *Input* and *Output Streams* with standard *read, write* and *flush* methods. *Datagram Sockets* are more flexible. A developer can configure several options. Choosing *duplex = true, connection-based = false, reliable = false* and *order-preserving = false* would result in a UDP/IP-like socket. Choosing *reliable = true* might be a good choice for e-mail mixes. Setting *connection-based = true* and *reliable = false* would be favorable for anonymizing VoIP traffic. *Connection-based* means that all messages sent through the socket will be tagged with the same random identifier (*Channel ID*). The exit node will use this identifier to map messages to the respective socket end point.

Table 1. Socket types available in the gMix architecture. The sockets are used to access the *mixing layers* from the *end-to-end layers*, i. e., they hide the anonymization process from user applications.

	StreamSocket	DatagramSocket
options	duplex	duplex, connection-based, reliable, order-preserving
implicit properties	connection-based, reliable, order-preserving	–

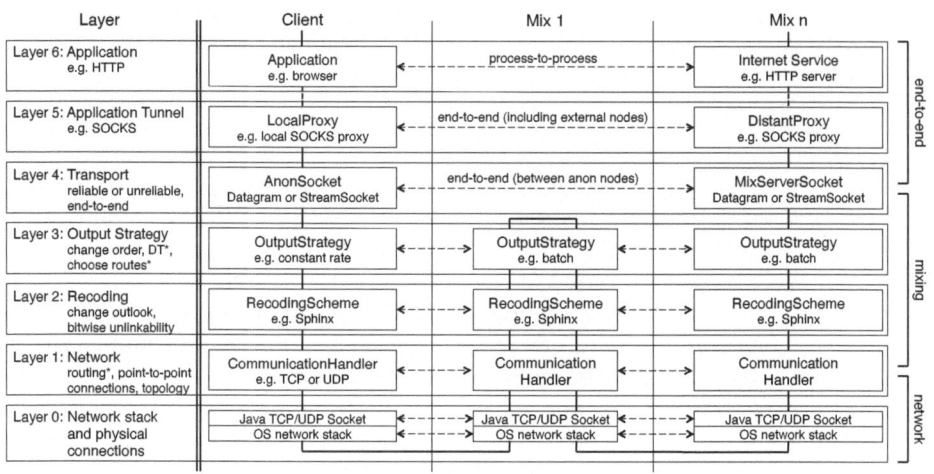

Fig. 2. Abstraction layers of the gMix framework

3 Communication Model and Layered Architecture

The abstraction layers of the gMix architecture are shown in Fig. 2 for the case of communication between a client and a server via two mixes.

Layer 0 represents the physical or logical connections between the nodes of the anonymization network (i. e., hosts running the client and mix components of the framework, *anon nodes*). In most cases, communication will be realized via TCP or UDP sockets opened by the Java Virtual Machine the framework is executed in. As the higher layers of our architecture do not require direct interaction with Layer 0 sockets, various transport protocols (e. g., streaming protocols like SCTP), Internet layer protocols (e. g., IPv6 or IPsec) and application layer protocols (e. g., TLS or DTLS) qualify for implementation.

Instead of using protocol-specific addresses directly, every mix chooses a random number (*Global Identifier*) during its initialization and publishes it via the *Information Service* along with its actual address information that may vary among plug-ins (e. g., IPv4 or IPv6 addresses and port numbers). Translating between *Global Identifiers* and actual addresses is a *Layer 1* task. Higher-order layers use the *Global Identifiers* only.

Layer 1 provides point-to-point connections between *anon nodes*. Its purpose is to hide the details of the underlying (*Layer 0*) communication channels by providing primitives to exchange messages between *anon nodes* (*hop-to-hop*). Its functionality is closely related to the *Internet Layer* of the *TCP/IP Model*, except that (end-to-end) source and destination addresses must be excluded for anonymity reasons, of course. As a result, each mix will get to know only the *next hop* of a message (addresses of further hops are hidden due to encryption).

Choosing the actual message routes is a *Layer 3* task. *Layer 1* will just forward messages *to the next hop* and is thus the *lowest* layer of our *overlay network*. We distinguish between two well-known [4,7,17] types of **routing** for mix messages: *free routes* and *fixed routes*. With *free routes*, the client chooses a series of mixes (e. g., from a list obtained from the *Information Service*) and adds their addresses to the respective header fields of the layered encryption for each mix. With *fixed routes*, mixes can be organized as cascades: All messages belonging to a *fixed route* will travel along the same path. No address information is stored in the mix messages. *Layer 3* plug-ins may choose one of the fixed routes, but not define their own. The *Information Service* can be used to establish and organize cascades.

The general purpose of **Layer 2** is to make it cryptographically difficult to link messages entering and leaving mixes, i. e., to provide bitwise unlinkability of mix messages and to pad them to equal length. This is typically realized by *recoding* (i. e., encrypting or decrypting) messages. As some recoding schemes are deterministic and are thus prone to replay attacks, while others are not, we chose to make *Layer 2* responsible for detecting replays of messages as well. If a deterministic scheme is employed, a replay detection as used in JonDonym [24] can be implemented here. The plug-ins are also responsible for publishing and retrieving information needed for recoding messages (e. g., public keys or initialization vectors) via the *Information Service*.

Layer 3 realizes another core function of a mix, the *output strategy* or *flushing algorithm*. Its purpose is to hide the true sender of a message among other senders, thus building an anonymity set. This is achieved by delaying and re-ordering messages. In his initial work [5], Chaum suggested to collect (or *batch*) messages until a certain threshold is reached, then putting out all messages together in lexicographic order. Since then, numerous output strategies have been proposed (e. g., [3,5,6,11,13,14,23,29,32,33,36,37]). While these output strategies are highly different in terms of delay and anonymity characteristics, from an architectural point of view, they are fairly equal as already shown in [14]. As some output strategies require clients to send in a specific fashion, not necessarily dependent on the flow characteristics of the user traffic (e. g., at constant rate), we chose to make Layer 3 responsible for initiating the creation and dropping of **dummy messages**: dummy messages contain random data instead of *normal* payload. They are put into the stream of *normal* messages to hamper traffic analysis. While dummy messages may reduce the available bandwidth, they can also reduce latency, e. g., if the output strategy requires a certain number of messages to flush. If all users send messages constantly, the sending of real messages becomes *unobservable* [8,29]. We discuss arising dependencies between Layer 2 and 3 in Sect. 6.1.

Layer 4 is the interface between the *mixing layers* (1–3) and the *end-to-end layers* 5 and 6. It can be used to establish end-to-end anonymous channels between anon nodes with the socket primitives of Table 1. For *free routes*, a *Global Identifier* can be specified as destination address. The aforementioned *Channel IDs* are used to map different messages of a *connection-based* anonymous channel to the respective sockets. Different *Layer 5* services running on a single node are distinguished by *service port numbers* that work like *normal* port numbers in the *TCP/IP Model*.

In **Layer 5**, application-level proxies (e. g., SOCKS, HTTP, DNS, FTP, SMTP, or VoIP proxies) can be implemented to enable end-to-end communication with hosts not part of the overlay network. *Layer 5* client plug-ins will open a local proxy on the client (i. e., in the area of protection of the client) and tunnel the application level connections (e. g., SOCKS connections established by a web browser) through *Layers 4 to 0* to an exit node running a *distant proxy* (the corresponding *Layer 5* mix plug-in). The *distant proxy* will forward the data of the tunnelled connections to their respective destinations (e. g., *normal* web servers). A plug-in developer can choose whether an anonymous tunnel shall be established for each application level connection or all connections shall be multiplexed through a single anonymous tunnel.

With the socket interfaces of *Layer 4* being very equal to *normal* sockets, we expect easy adaptation of existing proxy software. Since *Layer 5* is the first layer not required to be written completely in Java, proxy services written in different languages should be integrable by implementing an adapter class in Java.

Layer 6 is the layer closest to the user and equivalent to the *application layer* of the *TCP/IP Model*. It refers to higher-level application protocols and end-to-end connections between application programs. The concrete realization of these programs and protocols is out of the scope of our model, though.

4   Inter-layer Communication

To support different implementations (i. e., plug-ins) of the abstraction layers, standard interfaces between the framework and plug-ins are needed. As a result, we had to choose a common model for communication between layers and define a uniform internal message format. We considered two common architectural designs: (1) using a single loop to iterate over all layers or (2) to use a **thread-based approach with asynchronous I/O between layers**. We chose the latter as this in our view

- simplifies the implementation of multiple threads on one layer to speed up operation (e. g., for the recoding scheme),
- allows parallel operation on different layers (e. g., decrypting messages on *Layer 2* while new messages are received via *Layer 1*),
- allows to run several distinct instances on a single layer concurrently (e. g., communication handlers for client and mix connections on *Layer 1*) and

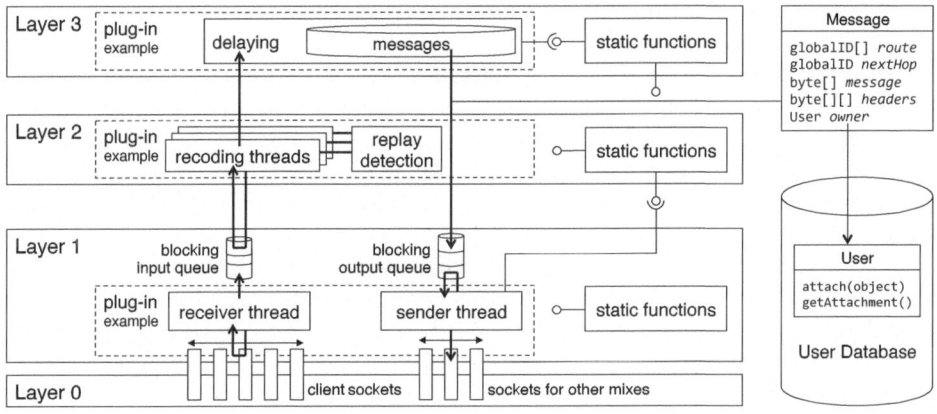

Fig. 3. Inter-layer communication patterns and separation of plug-in and framework concerns. Example of a simplex mix handling client connections.

– leads to more understandable implementations because of loose coupling and a clear separation of concerns.

For process synchronization, we use blocking queues with a wait-notify mechanism (cf. Fig. 3) between *Layer 1* and *Layer 2* (blocking conditions are *empty* and *full* for *getMessage* and *addMessage* operations, respectively). The queues are part of the framework, not the plug-ins. As a result, plug-in developers will not have to implement synchronization mechanisms themselves, unless they decide to have different threads (requiring shared resources) within their plug-ins.

For the **internal message format**, i.e., the Java objects exchanged between layers, we chose a generic solution, defining only the general purpose of a field rather than its actual content. As a result, individual contents and headers may be defined by plug-in developers for each layer. While this allows for tailored solutions, it also requires that plug-ins are developed pair-wise for clients and mixes, unless another plug-in speaking the same protocol is already implemented (we discuss dependencies between plug-ins in Sect. 6.1). In the remainder of this section we will focus on the details of the internal message format and further mechanisms included with the framework to keep state across multiple layers and assure compatibility between (plug-ins of) different layers.

As illustrated in Fig. 3, the Java objects exchanged between layers contain a byte array with the actual bit representation of the message to be eventually transmitted via *Layer 0*. Each layer is allowed to add additional headers. End-to-end headers (*Layer 4* and above) can be added directly to the *message* field. Headers that are required at each hop (i.e., in *Layer 3*) must be stored in the data structure *headers*. *Layer 2* implementations (recoding schemes) must indicate, whether they are capable of adding additional header fields for each mix (cf. Sect. 6.1). Currently, the only implementation requiring additional headers is the stop-and-go output strategy [23].

End-to-end destination addresses of *messages* are chosen on *Layer 4* and stored in the data structure *route*. In *free route* setups, *Layer 3* may add the addresses of further hops. The *route* information is stored in the layered encryption by the recoding scheme (*Layer 2*). Due to the encryption of the *message* on *Layer 2*, the cleartext field *nextHop* is needed for routing purposes on *Layer 1*. This field can also be re-set at each hop to allow for adaptive or random routing.

For keeping state, the component *User Database* is available. It stores a data structure (*user*) for each connected *client*. For each message, a reference to the respective user object is set on *Layer 1*, which allows for immediate access without look-up delays on all layers. Plug-ins can *attach* individual objects to each *user*. The *Java generics* mechanism is used to assure compile-time type safety.

Layers may offer *static functions* to adjacent layers. For example *recoding scheme* plug-ins may offer an interface to create dummy messages for *output strategy* plug-ins. Classes of general use for different plug-ins of the same layer can be offered as *static functions* as well, e.g., a class for *replay detection*.

5   Status of Development and Available Implementations

Started in 2011, the gMix project is still under heavy development. While individual implementations are quite basic, others have already reached practicable quality. The framework can load individual plug-in combinations specified in a config file. The *Information Service* can be used to organize mixes in cascades via network (for real deployment) or on a single workstation (for testing, measurement and teaching) without having to deal with individual IP addresses or port numbers. A load generator can be used to evaluate components and test implementations (cf. Sect. 7). A PKI is not included yet, but will be added soon. Framework and plug-ins currently consist of more than 16,000 SLOC in total. At present, the mix plug-ins listed in Table 2 are available.

On *Layer 3*, we have implemented the output strategies described in [5,6,14,23,33] and [37]. On the client side (not included in Table 2), we offer implementations to send at *constant rate*, send requests and receive replies *alternately* and to send data *immediately* on request of *Layer 4* (e.g., for datagram services). Another implementation mimics the general behavior of TCP/IP sockets by waiting a configurable amount of time for packets to be filled before forwarding them.

Currently we offer four *Layer 2* implementations: Two plug-ins (*RSA_AES_Channel* and *RSA_AES_LossTolerantChannel*) are supposed to be used for low-latency mix systems and streaming data. Both use RSA (in OAEP mode with configurable key size) to establish anonymous channels. Data is sent in cells of configurable size, each layer encrypted with AES. The *RSA_AES_Channel* scheme uses OFB and is *order-preserving* (cf. [38]). The *RSA_AES_LossTolerantChannel* employs AES in CBC mode with explicit initialization vectors (IV). With this mode and IVs prepended to each encryption layer, each cell can be decrypted separately, i.e., lost cells can be tolerated (the same mechanism is used in DTLS). We use HMAC-SHA256 for

Table 2. Currently available plug-ins and their *general* capabilities (**D**uplex, **R**eliable, Connection-**B**ased and **O**rder-**P**reserving, cf. Table 1 and Sect. 6.1). *True, false* and *any* values should be seen as properties of our implementations, not as general properties of the concepts as some may be implemented differently.

MIX PLUG-INS	D	R	CB	OP
Layer 3				
BinomialPool [14,32], BasicBatch [5], BasicPool [6], ThresholdPool [33], TimedBatch [33], CottrellPool [6], ThresholdAndTimedBatch [33], ThresholdOrTimedBatch [33], BatchWithTimeout [33], TimedDynamicPool [6], CottrellRandomDelay [6], CottrellTimedPool [6]	any	true	false	false
StopAndGo [23]	any	false	false	false
SynchronousBatch (simplified version of [29]), DLPA [37]	any	true	true	true
NoDelay (will forward data immediately as in [2,16])	any	true	any	true
Layer 2				
Sphinx [10] (*SPHINX* in Sect. 8)	false	true	false	false
RSA_OAEP_AES_OFB (*RSA-OFB* in Sect. 8)	false	true	false	false
RSA_AES_Channel (*SYM-CH* in Sect. 8)	any	true	true	true
RSA_AES_LossTolerantChannel (*LT-CH* in Sect. 8)	false	true	true	false
Layer 1				
Mix-Client TCP FCFS Sync. I/O, Mix-Client TCP Round-robin Sync. I/O, Mix-Client TCP FCFS Async. I/O, Mix-Mix TCP Multiplexed Sync. I/O	any	true	any	true
Mix-Client UDP FCFS Async. I/O, Mix-Mix UDP Async. I/O	false	false	any	false

message integrity in both cases. The two remaining plug-ins are *Sphinx* and *RSA_OAEP_AES_OFB*. The very compact *Sphinx* scheme [10] is optimized for services with typically short messages (e. g., electronic mail or micro-blogging).[3] The *RSA_OAEP_AES_OFB* plug-in is pretty close to the original suggestion of David Chaum [5], except that we use a hybrid scheme with RSA in OAEP and AES in OFB mode.

On *Layer 1*, we have implemented several mix plug-ins to handle client connections via different protocols (TCP, UDP), with varying scheduling mechanism (first-come first-served, round-robin) and with diverse I/O models (asynchronous and synchronous I/O). For connections between mixes, a plug-in capable of multiplexing messages of different clients through a single TCP connection is available (*Mix-Mix TCP Multiplexed Sync. I/O*). Using UDP between mixes is possible as well (*Mix-Mix UDP Async. I/O*).

6   Mix Composition and Compatibility

The layer concept of the *gMix* architecture provides a highly structured and in our opinion easily comprehensible view of a mix. Nevertheless, it also introduces

---

[3] Our implementation is a Java port of the Python implementation provided at `crysp.uwaterloo.ca/software/` using Curve25519 ECDH.

additional complexity, because the developer is faced with the decision to select adequate implementations on each layer.

Currently, we require the developer to choose a reasonable plug-in composition, or use predefined configurations included with the framework. As we expect the target audience of *gMix* to consist of researchers and developers familiar with mix systems, we do not consider this to be an issue for now. Nevertheless, simplifying the composition of plug-ins and investigating and documenting the dependencies between different mix concepts is certainly a desirable goal.

In Sect. 6.1 we discuss some important dependencies and their implications for plug-in development. Afterwards we present a rather basic, but extendable matching mechanism for capabilities and requirements that we plan to include in a future version of the framework in Sect. 6.2.

6.1   Dependencies and Implications for Plug-in Development

During plug-in development we found that most dependencies between implementations are closely related to the socket options of Layer 4 (cf. Table 1). Given the strict interfaces between the framework layers and taking those dependencies into account, many plug-ins of different layers are compatible without further efforts. We will therefore illustrate these dependencies along with the basic **capabilities** of our current plug-ins first, before we discuss **dummy traffic** and highlight **design choices for plug-in development**.

The **capabilities** of the current plug-ins for Layer 4 socket options are displayed in Table 2 (*Duplex*, *Connection-Based*, *Reliable* and *Order-Preserving*). While **true** and **false** indicate whether a plug-in has a certain capability or not, **any** means that a plug-in is *adaptive*, i.e., it can be configured to offer the respective capability (for example, a Layer 1 plug-in using UDP can introduce sequence numbers for packets in order to support *order-preserving* transfer).

The **duplex** capability specifies whether or not a plug-in distinguishes between request and reply messages. On Layer 1, *duplex* simply means that plug-ins can receive as well as send messages. The Layer 2 plug-in *Sphinx* does not make a difference between requests and replies, i.e., this protocol does not exhibit the duplex property according to our definition. On Layer 3, plug-ins that collect both requests and replies within a joint message pool (i.e., they are part of a common anonymity set) are defined to be simplex. To support duplex sockets on Layer 4, all lower-layer plug-ins must support *duplex* as well. If that is not the case, two simplex sockets can be established on Layer 4 to offer end-to-end duplex connections (and more secure simplex plug-ins like *Sphinx* can be used).

As stated before, the **connection-based** attribute is used to describe plug-ins that allow the linking of packets that belong to the same anonymous channel. For instance, the Layer 3 plug-in *SynchronousBatch* will collect a message for each channel before output and must therefore know which messages belong to which channel. The same applies for the Layer 2 plug-in *RSA_AES_Channel*, as it is required to use the same cipher instance for each message of a channel. To support *connection-based* Layer 2 and Layer 3 plug-ins, Layer 1 plug-ins are required to *tag* individual packets of one connection with the same random identifier. The identifier must of course be changed from mix to mix and be deactivated for non-connection-based sockets for security reasons.

The attribute **order-preserving** is only of relevance for *connection-based* sockets. For instance, using the *RSA_AES_Channel* plug-in will require that Layer 3 and Layer 1 plug-ins do not change the order of messages belonging to one channel as ciphers on client and mixes must stay in sync.

Dummy Traffic. In addition to the dependencies discussed above and described in Sect. 4 (concerning the routing mechanisms *free* and *fixed routes*), another dependency arises when combining *connection-based* sockets with non-end-to-end **dummy traffic**, i. e., when mixes are supposed to generate dummy messages for a certain channel (as for example with the *DLPA* plug-in [37]). In case of *stateful* recoding schemes (the decryption of subsequent messages depends on the decryption results of previous messages), the recoding component of a mix will not be able to generate an indistinguishable dummy for successive mixes due to the state of the client cipher being secret.

End-to-end dummy traffic (Layer 4) does not introduce additional dependencies, as Layer 2 plug-ins will have to add and remove padding for payloads smaller than designated anyway. An end-to-end dummy message can be considered a normal mix message with a payload field containing padding only. Dummy traffic introduced by mixes in case of *stateless* recoding schemes is straightforward as well since mixes can use client-side plug-ins to generate messages, too.

Design Choices for Plug-in Development. Whether plug-ins are compatible or not is not always an inherent property of the mix concept implemented, but often a design choice of the developer. It is an important decision, whether to strive for adaptivity (plug-ins will be more complex and difficult to understand and modify) or simplicity (individual plug-ins will be less complex, but the number of plug-ins will increase and code redundancy across plug-ins may become an issue). While the final choice will always be made by the implementer of a plug-in, we suggest to strive for simple plug-ins. So far we chose to implement adaptive plug-ins in two cases only: When a plug-in is expected to need a certain requirement for most use cases and *making it adaptive* basically means that some part of its functionality can be *turned off* (e. g., a Layer 1 TCP connection handler that can be configured to only read but not write data), or when making a plug-in adaptive can be achieved by adding only a few lines of code.

6.2   Matching Mechanism for Capabilities and Requirements

To simplify the composition of compatible plug-ins to individual mixes and to document the capabilities, requirements and dependencies of plug-ins, we plan to include a rather simple but extendable *matching mechanism* in the future. The basic idea of our proposal is inspired by the capability mechanism used in *Weka*, a framework for machine learning algorithms. In our case, requirements arising from rather *general* design choices (e. g., which topology shall be used or which

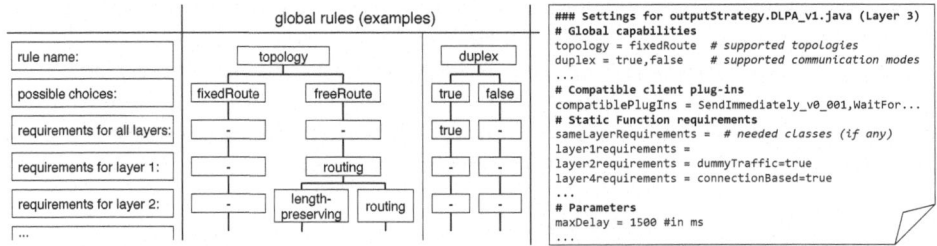

Fig. 4. Modeling dependencies as *global rules*, *requirements* and *capabilities*

socket type shall be available on Layer 4) could be stored as a set of *global rules*, i. e., *requirements* could be specified for each layer (cf. left side of Fig. 4: choosing the *free route topology* would for example require a *length-preserving* recoding scheme on Layer 2 that is able to include *routing* information within the message headers). If developers specify the *global capabilities* (cf. right side of Fig. 4) of their plug-ins, i. e., which of the *requirements* defined in the *global rules* they fulfill, an automated matching is possible. As a result, invalid compositions can be detected, or suitable plug-ins suggested. Adding further security or quality of service attributes to plug-in descriptions might be an option as well.

As described before, plug-ins must be implemented pair-wise for clients and mixes, as compatibility cannot be assumed. Nevertheless, some plug-ins may *be* compatible. For those, we suggest a *white list* (parameter *compatiblePlugIns* in Fig. 4): If a compatible plug-in is specified, the requirement to implement mix or client counterparts can be relaxed. Requirements for classes of general use for different plug-ins (the *static functions* described in Sect. 4) should be specified by plug-in developers as well (parameters *sameLayerRequirements* and *layerXrequirements* for *static functions* required on the same or on another layer).

We believe that the *matching mechanism* outlined above can serve as a useful tool for modeling and verifying dependencies and will help developers to get a better understanding of design options for individual plug-ins.

7   Experimentation Tools

Evaluating mix systems in terms of performance is a challenging task. Common methods include *manual mathematical analysis* (e. g., based on queueing theory), *discrete-event network simulation* (a simulation program is used to model the behavior of network nodes and communication lines on a single workstation), *network emulation* (a *real* local area network is used; traffic is routed through an emulation workstation that alters packet flow according to the characteristics of the network situation of interest) and *evaluation in real world settings* (like the Internet) or within *global research networks* (e. g., PlanetLab).

While each evaluation method has advantages and drawbacks, in our view *network emulation* fits best with our goal of *evaluating existing and new mix techniques in a controlled and realistic setting* (cf. Sect. 1). It allows to use physical network nodes running a *full* mix implementation instead of relying on simplified models of mix node behavior. An experimenter can specify various network attributes (e. g., bandwidth, round-trip-time, jitter, packet loss, packet duplication or packet reordering) and evaluate their influence on the overall performance without the need to distribute network nodes across the Internet.

The need for empirical evaluation tools is increasingly recognized in the privacy community. Recently, two promising approaches have been suggested for Tor: ExperimenTor [1] and Shadow [21]. Both of them address deployment and automated testing. On the other hand, they are tightly integrated with Tor and therefore difficult to extend or adapt to other applications and mixing concepts. The main advantage of our framework in this respect is the high number of different plug-ins available for comparison and the possibility of extension with new proposals. Reproducibility of results is simplified as the source code of *gMix* has been published and configuration files of individual experiments (containing plug-in names, version numbers and parameters) can be released together with a scientific publication (e. g., in the appendix or on a website).

To simplify testing we have included a *load generator* that automatically instantiates several clients on a single workstation and makes them send messages according to commonly used statistical models (e. g., according to a poisson process or at a uniform rate). To support more realistic evaluations we plan to add more advanced statistical traffic models as well as extend the *load generator* to replay traffic according to log files recorded in real-world settings.

8   Performance Evaluation

Given the limited space and the high number of possible plug-in-combinations, parameters and test scenarios, we have to focus on a small subset of evaluations for this publication. The basic goal of this section is to assess the performance of the framework and to demonstrate that Java and our architectural design offer adequate performance to build practical mix systems rather than evaluating the effects of different output or dummy policies. To this end, we focus on an evaluation of the recoding scheme plug-ins (which introduce the highest computational cost of all mix components) and evaluate the influence of parallelization, as the framework is optimized to take advantage of multi core systems. To determine the throughput limits we performed several tests in a controlled lab environment with 1 Gbit/s Ethernet (*Setup 1: Lab Environment*). In a second test scenario (*Setup 2: Emulated Environment*), we add a network emulator to reproduce one of the findings of [30], i. e., the negative influence of packet loss when messages of different users are multiplexed over a single TCP connection. Configuration files used for the experiments can be downloaded from the project website (https://www.informatik.uni-hamburg.de/SVS/gmix/).

8.1   Test Parameters

All experiments have been carried out using multiple, identically configured off-the-shelf desktop machines (Intel i5-2400 3.1GHz quad core CPUs, 8 GB RAM).

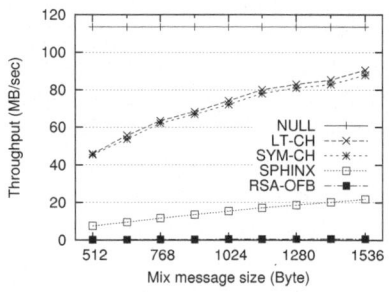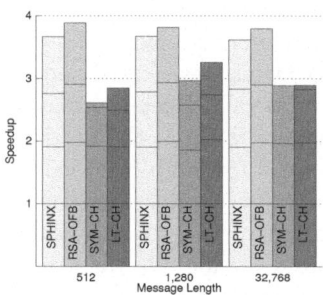

Fig. 5. Throughput for various message sizes and recoding schemes

Fig. 6. Speedup gained by using up to 4 recoding threads

The software environment consisted of CentOS 6 Linux running the OpenJDK v1.6.0_22 64 bit ServerVM and Linux Kernel v2.6.32. The MTU value (maximum transmission unit) within the network was 1500 bytes. Motivated by practical anonymity systems, we use 128 bit AES keys (Tor and JonDonym) and 2048 bit RSA keys. For *Sphinx* we use Dan Bernstein's Curve25519 as suggested in [10].

8.2 Lab Environment

We start out by comparing the achievable throughput for all recoding schemes of Table 2. The throughput refers to the payload only (excluding the overhead for mix message headers). We deploy load generators on 4 workstations to simulate a total of 32 clients that send mix packets at maximum rate to a single mix via the Layer 1 plug-in *Mix-Client TCP Round-robin Sync. I/O* in simplex mode.

Figure 5 shows the throughput for various mix message lengths below the MTU (1500 byte). Without cryptographic operations the mix achieves a throughput of 116.1 MB/s (*NULL cipher*). The two *channel schemes SYM-CH* and *LT-CH* (cells sent through anonymous channels are encrypted symmetrically only) allow for up to 93 MB/s, the two schemes using a hybrid cryptosystem for each message (*SPHINX* and *RSA-OFB*) for up to 22.3 MB/s and 0.7 MB/s, respectively. Sphinx seems to be fast enough to saturate a 100 Mbit/s communication line despite its hybrid cryptosystem. As expected, the aggregated throughput increases with the message size for all plug-ins, as the constant overhead per message for headers and switching between ciphers becomes less relevant.

Message dwell times, i. e., the time messages are delayed in the mix (measured on Layer 1 with 512 byte message size) are below 1.2 ms (*SYM-CH*), 0.7 ms (*LT-CH*), 1.2 ms (*SPHINX*) and 44.7 ms (*RSA-OFB*) for 95 % of messages.

Figure 6 shows the *speedup*, i. e., to what extent the recoding scheme plug-ins benefit from the availability of multiple CPU cores. For instance, for a message length of 512 bytes the throughput for Sphinx increases from 2.1 MB/s (which is equivalent to a speedup of 1 for this scheme) to 4 MB/s (which is 1.9×2.1 MB/s) if two threads are used. The two schemes using a hybrid cryptosystem benefit most from multi-threading and scale almost linearly. On the other hand the

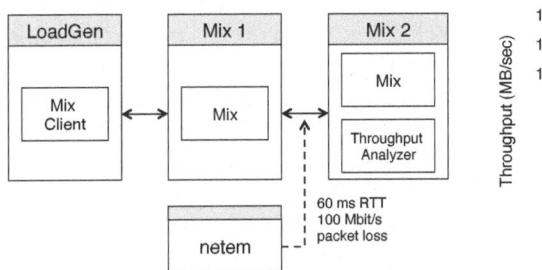 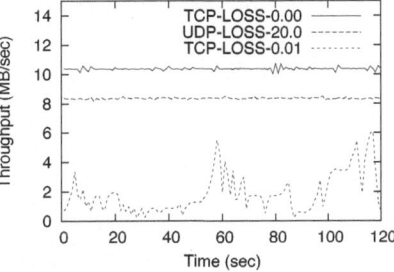

Fig. 7. Setup for emulated environment (cf. Sect. 8.3)

Fig. 8. Effect of packet loss on multi-plexed TCP connections

channel schemes profit less, as (depending on message size) two threads can be enough to saturate the network.

We repeated our experiments using a single CPU core (with the Linux kernel directive *maxcpus=1*) and found that the resulting throughput is still and constantly well above 14 MB/s (*SYM-CH*), i. e., switching between Layer 1 and Layer 2 threads (which is under control of the JVM) does not lead to fluctuating throughput for communication links slower than 100 Mbit/s in our setup.

As a reference point for the perceived results, we measured throughput for a Tor node (v0.2.2.35) in our test setting as well (using *netio* via *tsocks*). With mix packets sized 512 byte (equal to Tor's cell size), a maximum throughput of 46 MB/s is possible with the *SYM-CH* plug-in (quad core), while we measured 37 MB/s for the Tor node. The comparable performance is interesting as on the one hand Tor is written in C, but on the other hand it does not support multi-threading for message recoding. In this experiment our framework manages to compensate for the slower performance of Java by a better utilization of the available hardware. In the end it achieves a similar throughput as an implementation in C, at the cost of a higher number of instruction cycles (cf. the throughput of only 14 MB/s in case of *maxcpus=1*). We conclude that – despite the use of Java and its generic architecture – our framework offers adequate crypto performance for practical scenarios with up to 100 Mbit/s links. Real-world performance, i. e., when mixes are distributed over the Internet, cannot be deduced from these results, though, due to network congestion, differing bandwidth of anon nodes and predefined routes once packets have been sent (source routing) [12].

8.3   Emulated Environment

In the following experiment, we use a cascade of two mixes and shape traffic using the freely available network link emulator *Netem* [25][4] to show one of the findings of [30]: the negative influence of packet loss when messages of different

---

[4] A comparative study of network link emulators can be found in [27]. For even more sophisticated evaluations, virtual network emulators (e. g., Emulab [39] or Modelnet [35], like in [1]) can be employed.

users are multiplexed over a single TCP connection. RTT between mixes was set to 60 ms. Bandwidth was limited to 100 Mbit/s to assure crypto overhead is not the limiting factor. The experimental setup is shown in Fig. 7.

We use the *Mix-Mix TCP Multiplexed Sync. I/O* plug-in between mixes and configure the emulator to drop messages between the two mixes to show the effect. For comparison, we provide results for the UDP Layer 1 plug-ins as well. Figure 8 shows that even for *low* packet loss of 0.01 %, TCP throughput is highly unstable as the messages of all users are blocked by a dropped message of a single user, i. e., the operating system TCP buffer will not forward any data (possibly packets of other users) until the lost packet is retransmitted. While this effect was already shown in [30], we want to stress that we were able to reproduce this finding simply by combining existing plug-ins and without writing a single line of code.

9   Conclusion

In this paper we proposed a generic architecture for mixes and our open source implementation, the *gMix framework*. First and foremost, the gMix framework aims to provide easy access to the central components of a mix, which are structured into distinct logical layers. Secondly, we strive for easily understandable implementations to allow developers to build a fully functional mix from a set of rather simple components (plug-ins). Thirdly, the *gMix* framework aims to improve the process of the evaluation of mixes. At the moment, this objective is addressed with a load generator. Tools for test automation will be included in the future. Moreover, the consequent use of configuration files ensures repeatability of experiments and reproducibility of results.

We see our work as a first step towards the standardization of mix systems which can help lower the bar for research of mixes as well as their deployment in practice. In the long run we hope that the availability of a comprehensive software framework will serve as an enabler for mixes and will lead to the increased dissemination of privacy-enhancing technologies in existing and new application areas as well as to new proposals that can be integrated into deployed systems like Tor or JonDonym.

References

1. Bauer, K., Sherr, M., McCoy, D., Grunwald, D.: ExperimenTor: A Testbed for Safe Realistic Tor Experimentation. In: Workshop on Cyber Security Experimentation and Test (2011)
2. Berthold, O., Federrath, H., Köpsell, S.: Web MIXes: A System for Anonymous and Unobservable Internet Access. In: Federrath, H. (ed.) Anonymity 2000. LNCS, vol. 2009, pp. 115–129. Springer, Heidelberg (2001)
3. Berthold, O., Langos, H.: Dummy Traffic against Long Term Intersection Attacks. In: Dingledine, R., Syverson, P.F. (eds.) PET 2002. LNCS, vol. 2482, pp. 110–128. Springer, Heidelberg (2003)

4. Böhme, R., Danezis, G., Díaz, C., Köpsell, S., Pfitzmann, A.: On the PET Workshop Panel "Mix Cascades Versus Peer-to-Peer: Is One Concept Superior?". In: Martin, Serjantov [26], pp. 243–255
5. Chaum, D.: Untraceable Electronic Mail, Return Addresses, and Digital Pseudonyms. Communications of the ACM 24(2), 84–90 (1981)
6. Cottrell, L.: Mixmaster and Remailer Attacks (1995), http://www.obscura.com/~loki/remailer-essay.html
7. Danezis, G.: Mix-Networks with Restricted Routes. In: Dingledine [15], pp. 1–17
8. Danezis, G., Diaz, C., Troncoso, C., Laurie, B.: Drac: An Architecture for Anonymous Low-Volume Communications. In: Atallah, M.J., Hopper, N.J. (eds.) PETS 2010. LNCS, vol. 6205, pp. 202–219. Springer, Heidelberg (2010)
9. Danezis, G., Dingledine, R., Mathewson, N.: Mixminion: Design of a Type III Anonymous Remailer Protocol. In: IEEE Symposium on Security and Privacy, pp. 2–15. IEEE Computer Society (2003)
10. Danezis, G., Goldberg, I.: Sphinx: A Compact and Provably Secure Mix Format. In: IEEE Symposium on Security and Privacy, pp. 269–282. IEEE Computer Society (2009)
11. Danezis, G., Sassaman, L.: Heartbeat Traffic to Counter (n-1) Attacks: Red-Green-Black Mixes. In: Jajodia, S., Samarati, P., Syverson, P.F. (eds.) WPES, pp. 89–93. ACM (2003)
12. Dhungel, P., Steiner, M., Rimac, I., Hilt, V., Ross, K.W.: Waiting for Anonymity: Understanding Delays in the Tor Overlay. In: Peer-to-Peer Computing, pp. 1–4. IEEE (2010)
13. Díaz, C., Preneel, B.: Taxonomy of Mixes and Dummy Traffic. In: Deswarte, Y., Cuppens, F., Jajodia, S., Wang, L. (eds.) International Information Security Workshops, pp. 215–230. Kluwer (2004)
14. Díaz, C., Serjantov, A.: Generalising Mixes. In: Dingledine [15], pp. 18–31
15. Dingledine, R. (ed.): PET 2003. LNCS, vol. 2760. Springer, Heidelberg (2003)
16. Dingledine, R., Mathewson, N., Syverson, P.: Tor: The Second-Generation Onion Router. In: 13th USENIX Security Symposium, pp. 303–320 (2004)
17. Dingledine, R., Shmatikov, V., Syverson, P.F.: Synchronous Batching: From Cascades to Free Routes. In: Martin, Serjantov [26], pp. 186–206
18. Federrath, H., Fuchs, K.P., Herrmann, D., Piosecny, C.: Privacy-Preserving DNS: Analysis of Broadcast, Range Queries and Mix-Based Protection Methods. In: Atluri, V., Diaz, C. (eds.) ESORICS 2011. LNCS, vol. 6879, pp. 665–683. Springer, Heidelberg (2011)
19. Federrath, H., Jerichow, A., Pfitzmann, A.: MIXes in Mobile Communication Systems: Location Management with Privacy. In: Anderson, R.J. (ed.) IH 1996. LNCS, vol. 1174, pp. 121–135. Springer, Heidelberg (1996)
20. Huber, M., Mulazzani, M., Weippl, E.: Tor HTTP Usage and Information Leakage. In: De Decker, B., Schaumüller-Bichl, I. (eds.) CMS 2010. LNCS, vol. 6109, pp. 245–255. Springer, Heidelberg (2010)
21. Jansen, R., Hopper, N.: Shadow: Running Tor in a Box for Accurate and Efficient Experimentation. In: Proceedings of the Network and Distributed System Security Symposium. Internet Society (2012)
22. Kate, A., Goldberg, I.: Using Sphinx to Improve Onion Routing Circuit Construction. In: Sion [34], pp. 359–366.
23. Kesdogan, D., Egner, J., Büschkes, R.: Stop-and-Go-MIXes Providing Probabilistic Anonymity in an Open System. In: Aucsmith, D. (ed.) IH 1998. LNCS, vol. 1525, pp. 83–98. Springer, Heidelberg (1998)

24. Köpsell, S.: Vergleich der Verfahren zur Verhinderung von Replay-Angriffen der Anonymisierungsdienste AN.ON und Tor. In: Dittmann, J. (ed.) Sicherheit 2006. LNI, vol. 77, pp. 183–187. GI (2006)
25. Linux Foundation: Netem (2009), http://www.linuxfoundation.org/collaborate/workgroups/networking/netem
26. Martin, D., Serjantov, A. (eds.): PET 2004. LNCS, vol. 3424. Springer, Heidelberg (2005)
27. Nussbaum, L., Richard, O.: A Comparative Study of Network Link Emulators. In: Wainer, G.A., Shaffer, C.A., McGraw, R.M., Chinni, M.J. (eds.) SpringSim. SCS/ACM (2009)
28. Park, C., Itoh, K., Kurosawa, K.: Efficient Anonymous Channel and All/Nothing Election Scheme. In: Helleseth, T. (ed.) EUROCRYPT 1993. LNCS, vol. 765, pp. 248–259. Springer, Heidelberg (1994)
29. Pfitzmann, A., Pfitzmann, B., Waidner, M.: ISDN-MIXes: Untraceable Communication with Small Bandwidth Overhead. In: Effelsberg, W., Meuer, H.W., Müller, G. (eds.) Kommunikation in Verteilten Systemen. Informatik-Fachberichte, vol. 267, pp. 451–463. Springer, Heidelberg (1991)
30. Reardon, J., Goldberg, I.: Improving Tor using a TCP-over-DTLS Tunnel. In: USENIX Security Symposium, pp. 119–134. USENIX Association (2009)
31. Sako, K., Kilian, J.: Receipt-Free Mix-Type Voting Scheme. In: Guillou, L.C., Quisquater, J.-J. (eds.) EUROCRYPT 1995. LNCS, vol. 921, pp. 393–403. Springer, Heidelberg (1995)
32. Serjantov, A.: A Fresh Look at the Generalised Mix Framework. In: Borisov, N., Golle, P. (eds.) PET 2007. LNCS, vol. 4776, pp. 17–29. Springer, Heidelberg (2007)
33. Serjantov, A., Dingledine, R., Syverson, P.F.: From a Trickle to a Flood: Active Attacks on Several Mix Types. In: Petitcolas, F.A.P. (ed.) IH 2002. LNCS, vol. 2578, pp. 36–52. Springer, Heidelberg (2003)
34. Sion, R. (ed.): FC 2010. LNCS, vol. 6052. Springer, Heidelberg (2010)
35. Vahdat, A., Yocum, K., Walsh, K., Mahadevan, P., Kostic, D., Chase, J.S., Becker, D.: Scalability and Accuracy in a Large-Scale Network Emulator. In: OSDI (2002)
36. Venkitasubramaniam, P., Tong, L.: Anonymous Networking with Minimum Latency in Multihop Networks. In: IEEE Symposium on Security and Privacy, pp. 18–32. IEEE Computer Society (2008)
37. Wang, W., Motani, M., Srinivasan, V.: Dependent Link Padding Algorithms for Low Latency Anonymity Systems. In: Ning, P., Syverson, P.F., Jha, S. (eds.) ACM Conference on Computer and Communications Security, pp. 323–332. ACM (2008)
38. Westermann, B., Wendolsky, R., Pimenidis, L., Kesdogan, D.: Cryptographic Protocol Analysis of AN.ON. In: Sion [34], pp. 114–128.
39. White, B., Lepreau, J., Stoller, L., Ricci, R., Guruprasad, S., Newbold, M., Hibler, M., Barb, C., Joglekar, A.: An Integrated Experimental Environment for Distributed Systems and Networks. In: OSDI (2002)

Secure and Efficient Outsourcing of Sequence Comparisons[*]

Marina Blanton[1], Mikhail J. Atallah[2],
Keith B. Frikken[3], and Qutaibah Malluhi[4]

[1] Department of Computer Science and Engineering, University of Notre Dame
[2] Department of Computer Science, Purdue University
[3] Computer Science and Software Engineering, Miami University
[4] Computer Science and Engineering Department, Qatar University

Abstract. We treat the problem of secure outsourcing of sequence comparisons by a client to remote servers, which given two strings λ and μ of respective lengths n and m, consists of finding a minimum-cost sequence of insertions, deletions, and substitutions (also called an *edit script*) that transform λ into μ. In our setting a client owns λ and μ and outsources the computation to two servers without revealing to them information about either the input strings or the output sequence. Our solution is non-interactive for the client (who only sends information about the inputs and receives the output) and the client's work is linear in its input/output. The servers' performance is $O(\sigma mn)$ computation (which is optimal) and communication, where σ is the alphabet size, and the solution is designed to work when the servers have only $O(\sigma(m+n))$ memory. By utilizing garbled circuit evaluation in a novel way, we completely avoid public-key cryptography, which makes our solution particularly efficient.

1 Introduction

Design and development of secure outsourcing techniques of various functionalities to untrusted servers are getting growing attention in the research community. The rapid growth in availability of cloud services makes such services attractive for clients with limited computing or storage resources who are unable to procure and maintain their own computing infrastructure. Security and privacy considerations, however, stand on the way of harnessing the full benefits of cloud computing and prevent clients from placing their sensitive data on the cloud. This is the problem that secure outsourcing techniques aim to address.

This work develops efficient techniques for secure outsourcing of a specific type of computation, namely sequence comparisons. Secure computation and outsourcing of sequence comparisons, in particular for genomic sequences, has been a subject of prior research. The results include [1–10], which securely implement computation of the edit distance, finite automata evaluation, the Smith-Waterman and other algorithms. Because individual DNA and protein sequences

---

[*] Portions of this work were supported by NSF Grants CNS-0915436, CNS-0913875, CNS-0915843, and CCF-0939370; an NPRP grant from the Qatar National Research Fund; AFOSR Grant FA9550-09-1-0223; and sponsors of the CERIAS center.

S. Foresti, M. Yung, and F. Martinelli (Eds.): ESORICS 2012, LNCS 7459, pp. 505–522, 2012.

commonly used in such comparisons are highly sensitive and vulnerable to re-identification even when anonymized, the need for techniques that allow such sequences to be privately processed has been recognized and is reflected by the list of available publications above. Furthermore, given the large lengths of such sequences, it is not surprising that there is an increasing need for such computation to be outsourced by resource limited clients. These outsourcing techniques should enable the desired computation without revealing any information about the sequences to the parties performing the computation.

Techniques for securely computing the edit distance based on dynamic programming have been studied in [1, 6, 9]. The work [2, 3] is the only one we are aware of that treats the problem of secure outsourcing of the edit distance and [3] is the only work that treats the computation of the edit script (defined as a minimum-cost sequence of insertions, deletions, and substitutions that transform one input string λ into the other input string μ). An edit script contains important information about the types of differences that cannot always be deduced from the edit distance alone. For that reason, we revisit the problem of secure outsourcing of the edit distance and the corresponding edit script computation and improve the performance of known results.

It is well known that computing the edit distance (or the edit script) of two strings λ and μ of size n and m, respectively, requires $O(mn)$ work. Because n and m are often large in genomic computations, the need to reduce the memory footprint of secure sequence comparisons was recognized in prior literature. This applies to our setting of securely outsourcing a task to resourceful servers as well, as the memory requirement of $O(mn)$, or more generally $O(\sigma mn)$, where σ is the alphabet size, will prevent them from processing strings longer than a few thousand characters. The edit distance can be computed one row or one column of the $m \times n$ matrix at a time, which uses only $O(m + n)$ memory. This is the approach taken in [3] based on homomorphic encryption, and the publications that use garbled circuit evaluation [6, 9] also partition the circuit into sub-circuits, so that the memory requirement of $O(m + n)$ can be achieved.

The above partitioning approach does not work when the computation consists of producing an edit script (rather than just the edit distance) while keeping the memory requirement at $O(m + n)$. Furthermore, the only known result for securely computing an edit script with the linear memory requirement for the servers carrying out the computation requires them to perform $O(mn \min(m, n))$ work with the same amount of communication [3]. We substantially improve the performance of the existing secure edit script outsourcing techniques to require the servers to perform only $O(mn)$ work with the same $O(m + n)$ memory requirement for the servers. This also implies that when the servers have $O(m+n)$ memory, the round complexity of the solution improves from $O((\min(m, n)^2)$ in [3] to $O(\min(m, n))$ in this work (we note that the number of rounds in this work is primarily bounded by the ratio of the overall amount of communication and the amount of available memory, while it is fixed at $O((\min(m, n)^2)$ in [3]).

Besides the obvious complexity improvements, our solution has additional advantages. Similar to [3], we assume that a client outsources its computation to two non-colluding computation servers, but unlike [3], no homomorphic encryption is used. In fact, our solution completely avoids public-key cryptography by utilizing garbled circuit techniques in a novel way. To the best of our knowledge, this is the first time secure two-party computation or outsourcing techniques are realized without reliance on any public-key operations (e.g., the solutions in [6, 9] have to invoke Oblivious Transfer (OT) protocols). This gives us fast general secure outsourcing techniques, which are of independent interest.

Our solution is non-interactive for the client, who only sends information about its inputs to the servers and receives the computation outcome from which it reconstructs the output. Its communication and computation is thus $O(m+n)$.

Lastly, our solution works for any alphabet Σ of size σ, from which λ and μ are drawn. Because σ may not be treated as constant, we include it in our analysis. In particular, the servers' space requirements are $O(\sigma(m+n))$, their computation and communication are $O(\sigma mn)$, and the client's work and communication are $O(\sigma(m + n))$ (prior results have the same factor σ in their complexities).

As noted above, we make the same assumption of non-colluding servers as the prior work that improve upon. A natural question that one might ask is how viable such an assumption is. The practical viability of using non-colluding servers has been well demonstrated, for instance, by the Sharemind system [11] and the company that develops it, where three non-colluding servers are used (we only use two). One possible instantiation of our solution would be to use two servers, each from a different service provider. Collusion of both servers would require corruption of both service providers, which is unlikely in practice.

2   Preliminaries

Problem Statement. We treat the problem of secure outsourcing of the edit distance and the corresponding edit script computation by a client C for any strings $\lambda = \lambda_1 \ldots \lambda_n$ and $\mu = \mu_1 \ldots \mu_m$ over alphabet $\Sigma = \{1, \ldots, \sigma\}$ to two computational servers S_1 and S_2. In its general form considered here, the sequence comparisons problem requires quadratic work [12].

In our outsourcing context, C must perform only work linear in the size of its inputs, with the super-linear work done by the remote servers. Furthermore, the security requirement is such that neither S_1 nor S_2 learns anything about the client's inputs or output other than the lengths of the input strings and the alphabet size (i.e., the servers learn only the problem size).

More formally, we assume that S_1 and S_2 do not collude and if they are semi-honest, they follow the computation as prescribed but might attempt to learn additional information from the messages that they observe. Security in this case is guaranteed if both S_1's and S_2's views can be simulated by a simulator with no access to either C's inputs or output other than the parameters n, m, and σ and such simulation is indistinguishable from the real protocol execution. This is a standard definition that can be found, e.g., in [13].

Generic techniques for modifying the garbled circuit techniques to enable security against covert or fully malicious participants are known (see, e.g., [14–16]).

Furthermore, the standard garbled circuit techniques, as used in this work, already offer protection against one party, namely, malicious circuit evaluator. The specifics of our setting, however, enable us to design an effective mechanism for detecting and eliminating malicious behavior at low cost. Because the techniques we use are resilient to misbehavior of one of the parties, we can run the solution twice, with the roles of S_1 and S_2 swapped on the second run. When the client obtains two results that disagree, it will know that one of the servers did not comply with its prescribed behavior. As in our protocols neither server learns any outputs, creation and evaluation of an incorrect circuit does not pose security risks to the client. This means that the cost of the solution in the malicious model is twice the cost of the solution in the semi-honest model.

Review of Edit Distance via Dynamic Programming. We briefly review the standard dynamic programming algorithm for the edit distance, using the same notation and terminology as in [3]. Let $M(i,j)$, for $0 \leq i \leq m$ and $0 \leq j \leq n$, be the minimum cost of transforming the prefix of λ of length j into the prefix of μ of length i, i.e., the cost of transforming $\lambda_1 \ldots \lambda_j$ into $\mu_1 \ldots \mu_i$. Then $M(0,0) = 0$, $M(0,j) = \sum_{k=1}^{j} D(\lambda_k)$ for $1 \leq j \leq n$ and $M(i,0) = \sum_{k=1}^{i} I(\mu_k)$ for $1 \leq i \leq m$. Furthermore, for all $1 \leq i \leq m$ and $1 \leq j \leq n$ we have that

$$M(i,j) = \min \begin{cases} M(i-1, j-1) + S(\lambda_j, \mu_i) \\ M(i-1, j) + I(\mu_i) \\ M(i, j-1) + D(\lambda_j) \end{cases}$$

where $S(\lambda_j, \mu_i)$ is the cost of substituting character λ_j with character μ_i, $D(\lambda_j)$ is the cost of deleting λ_j, and $I(\mu_i)$ is the cost of inserting μ_i. Hence $M(i,j)$ can be evaluated row-by-row or column-by-column in $\Theta(mn)$ time [17]. Observe that, of all entries of the M-matrix, only three $M(i-1, j-1)$, $M(i-1, j)$, and $M(i, j-1)$ are involved in the computation of the final value of $M(i,j)$.

Our solution works even when $S : \Sigma \times \Sigma \to \mathbb{N}$, $I : \Sigma \to \mathbb{N}$, and $D : \Sigma \to \mathbb{N}$ are arbitrary functions that are implemented using table lookups.

Grid Graph View of the Problem. The interdependencies among the entries of the M-matrix induce an $(m+1) \times (n+1)$ *grid* directed acyclic graph (DAG) associated with the string editing problem. It is easy to see (and well-known) that the string editing problem can be viewed as a shortest-path problem on a grid DAG, which is *implicitly* described by the two input strings and the cost tables (otherwise there is no hope of achieving the linear-space performance we seek). We say that an $\ell_1 \times \ell_2$ grid DAG is a directed acyclic graph whose vertices are the $\ell_1 \ell_2$ points of an $\ell_1 \times \ell_2$ grid, and such that the only edges from grid point (i,j) are to grid points $(i, j+1)$, $(i+1, j)$, and $(i+1, j+1)$. Figure 1 shows an example of a grid DAG and our convention of drawing the points such that point (i,j) is at the ith row from the top and the jth column from the left. Note that the top-left point is $(0,0)$ and has no edge entering it (i.e., is a *source*), and that the bottom-right point is (m,n) and has no edge leaving it (i.e., is a *sink*).

An $(m+1) \times (n+1)$ grid DAG G is associated with the string editing problem in the natural way: The vertices of G are in one-to-one correspondence with the entries of the M-matrix, and the *cost* of an edge from vertex (k, ℓ) to (i,j) is

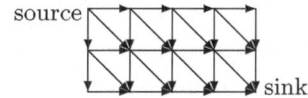

Fig. 1. Example of a 2×4 grid DAG

equal to $D(\lambda_j)$ if $k = i$ and $\ell = j - 1$, to $I(\mu_i)$ if $k = i - 1$ and $\ell = j$, and to $S(\lambda_j, \mu_i)$ if $k = i - 1$ and $\ell = j - 1$. We restrict our attention to edit paths which do no obviously inefficient moves (such as inserting then deleting the same symbol) and thus only consider edit scripts that apply at most one edit operation to a given symbol. Such edit scripts that transform λ into μ or vice versa are in one-to-one correspondence to the weighted paths of G that originate at the source (i.e., $M(0,0)$) and end at the sink (i.e., $M(m,n)$).

Garbled Circuit Evaluation. Our solution uses techniques based on Yao's two-party garbled circuit evaluation originated in [18]. Garbled circuit evaluation allows two parties to securely evaluate any function represented as a Boolean circuit. The basic idea is that, given a circuit composed of gates, one party P_1 creates a garbled circuit by assigning to each wire i two randomly chosen labels or keys $\ell_0^{(i)}$ and $\ell_1^{(i)}$, where $\ell_b^{(i)}$ encodes bit b. P_1 also encodes gate information in a way that given keys corresponding to the input wires (encoding specific inputs), the key corresponding to the output of the gate on those inputs can be recovered. This is often achieved by representing each gate as a table of encrypted values, where, e.g., for a binary gate g with input wires i, j and output wire k, the table consists of four values of the form $\mathsf{Enc}_{\ell_{b_i}^{(i)}, \ell_{b_j}^{(j)}}(\ell_{g(b_i, b_j)}^{(k)})$.

The second party, P_2, evaluates the circuit using keys corresponding to inputs of both P_1 and P_2 (without learning anything in the process). That is, P_2 directly obtains keys corresponding to P_1's input bits from P_1 and engages in the OT protocol to obtain keys corresponding to P_2's input bits. Garbled circuit evaluation consists of processing the gates in topological order, during which one entry of each gate's table is decrypted allowing P_2 to learn the output wire's key. Security relies on the fact that P_2 does not have a correspondence between the labels it decrypts and the bits that they represent. At the end, the result of the computation can be recovered by linking the output labels to the bits which they encode (e.g., by having P_1 send all output wire labels and their meaning to P_2). Recent literature [19–21] provides optimizations that significantly reduce computation and communication overhead associated with garbled circuits.

Prior Results. Using the fact that computing a row of the matrix depends only on entries from its current and previous rows, computing the edit distance (not path) is done with S_1 and S_2 in [2, 3] using $O(\sigma(m+n))$ space and $O(\sigma m n)$ time in $O(\min(m, n))$ rounds. Similarly, securely computing the edit distance in the two-party setting using garbled circuit evaluation is done in [6, 9] by partitioning the overall computation into multiple sub-circuits or rounds to achieve the same result. Computing the path itself took in [3] an extra factor of $\min(m, n)$ work and rounds. One of our main goals is therefore removing that extra factor for the path (as opposed to the distance) computation. Our solution is also more flexible in terms of its round complexity even for the distance computation. In addition to asymptotic complexity savings, the fact that our solution does not use expensive public-key operation makes it significantly more efficient (even for the distance computation) than [2, 3] which made an extensive use of homomorphic encryption. Furthermore, our technique for removing the need for public-key operations is of independent interest for secure computation outsourcing.

Lastly, [9] that implements the idea of partitioning a circuit into sub-circuits (which we use as well) and provides circuit optimizations for a special case of edit distance computation is complementary to our work. Because a distance protocol is used as a subroutine in our solution, some of these circuit optimization techniques can be applied to and integrated in our solution.

3   Overview of the Solution

Before describing our solution in detail, we provide an intuition behind it. First, notice that if the amount of available memory is $O(mn)$, it is easy to compute the edit script. That is, first compute all elements of the matrix M. Then, starting from $M(m, n)$, follow the link to either $M(i-1, j)$, $M(i-1, j-1)$, or $M(i, j-1)$ that produced the current value of $M(i, j)$ (breaking ties arbitrarily), until the process terminates at $M(0, 0)$. The produced path corresponds to the desired edit script that the client would like to learn. This approach, however, does not work if the amount of available memory is $o(mn)$ because the value stored at any given $M(i, j)$ might be necessary for reconstructing the path.

To address this problem without increasing the cost of the overall computation beyond $O(\sigma mn)$, we can use a recursive solution, which works as follows: in the first round, instead of computing all elements of M as described earlier, we compute the elements in the "top half" of the matrix as before and also compute the elements of the "bottom half" of the matrix in the reverse direction starting from $M(m, n)$ (see section 4 for detail). Then for each element $M(m/2, j)$ of the middle row we add the distances computed from the top and from the bottom and determine the position of the element with the minimum sum. In section 4 we denote this element by $M(m/2, \theta(m/2))$. Because we know that the computed element has to lie on a path that results in the minimum edit distance, to determine other parts of this path, we can safely disregard all cells from the top half that lie to the right of $M(m/2, \theta(m/2))$ and all cells from the bottom half that lie to the left of $M(m/2, \theta(m/2))$. We then recursively apply this algorithm to the remaining portions of the matrix (which together contain only a half of the elements of M) which allows us to reconstruct all points of the path. While this approach doubles the amount of computation (i.e., the work is $\leq 2mn$ compared to the original mn), it is suitable for our situation when the amount of available space is only linear in m and n.

Now notice that this solution works in a traditional setting, but in our case revealing the position of the minimum element $M(m/2, \theta(m/2))$ (which is necessary for determining what parts of the matrix should be discarded for the next round), leaks important information about the edit path to the computational servers and violates security requirements. Our solution is to recurse on sub-problems of slightly larger size without revealing information about the value of $\theta(m/2)$. In particular, we form two sub-problems of size $1/2$ and $1/4$ of the original, where the $1/2$ sub-problem consists of the top (resp. bottom) half and the $1/4$ sub-problem consists of the right bottom (resp. top left) quadrant when $\theta(m/2) \geq n/2$ (resp. $\theta(m/2) < n/2$). This ensures that the asymptotic complexity of the solution does not change (the work is $\leq 4mn$), while hiding information about the path. This process, however, requires care because the strings that form the sub-problems of fixed size must be padded based on the value of $\theta(m/2)$. That is, we need to ensure that the way the strings are padded (as a prefix or suffix of an existing string) should not affect the overall result. We achieve this by extending the alphabet with a new character with carefully chosen insertion, substitution, and deletion costs so as to take a certain path within the matrix and not alter the edit distance.

The last remaining bit that we want the computational servers to prevent from learning is whether the subtask of size $1/2$ corresponds to the top or bottom portion of the problem (which, once again, leaks information about the edit path). This is achieved by always having the sub-tasks of different sizes in a fixed order and obliviously assigning the correct portion of the grid to a sub-task. This allows us to obtain a solution that can be safely outsourced to the computational servers and meets their space requirements.

Having arrived at the oblivious algorithm for computing an edit script with $O(\sigma(m + n))$ memory and $O(mn)$ overall work, we now need to see how this computation can be securely outsourced. Recall that our solution relies on garbled circuit evaluation which we use in a new way. The first idea that we employ is for the client to produce garbled circuit's random labels corresponding to the wires of its inputs only (two labels per input bit). The client sends the labels for all wires to S_1, who forms the rest of the circuit for the computation. The client also sends to S_2 one label per wire that corresponds to its input value. Once the circuit is formed, S_2 will be able to evaluate it using the labels. In this case, no OT protocols (or any other public-key operations) are necessary.

Note that this approach is general and by itself would be sufficient to result in a secure outsourcing solution for most types of functions with no public-key cryptography involved at any point in the protocol. For our problem, however, it does not lead to a non-interactive (for the client) solution because after the first round of the computation, the servers will need to contact the client again to obtain the labels for the next round of the computation (since they are not allowed to know what input values or labels are to be reused in the consecutive round). Because the depth of the recursion in our algorithm is $O(\log(\min(m, n)))$, the client has to participate in $O(\log(\min(m, n)))$ interactions with the servers. This forms our preliminary solution in section 5.

To eliminate the client's involvement, we employ the second idea, which consists of the servers using the output wire labels from the current round of the computation as the input wire labels for the sub-problems in the next round. This solution requires a great care to ensure that all input labels for the next round are formed correctly and computed obliviously (inside a garbled circuit) and is described in section 6. We thus obtain our target result in which the solution is non-interactive for the client, the client's work is $O(\sigma(n+m))$, the servers' work is $O(\sigma mn)$, the entire computation can be carried out within $O(\sigma(m+n))$ space, and no public-key operations are used at any point.

4   Enabling the Computation to be Performed Obliviously

As a first step toward building our result, we design an algorithm that allows the computation to be performed in $O(\sigma mn)$ time using $O(\sigma(m+n))$ space. To be suitable for secure outsourcing, the algorithm must be oblivious or data-independent (i.e., it always performs the same sequence of steps regardless of the inputs). This will ensure that no information about the inputs is leaked based on the algorithm itself. We therefore first describe a procedure for such computation and later refine and instantiate it with secure building blocks to obtain the overall solution with the desired performance.

To build our solution, we first need to extend the distance-computation to the computation of an optimal *edit path* (i.e., a minimum-cost sequence of operations on λ that turn it into μ). We adapt the approach of [3] that combines the distance computation algorithm with a backward version of it which we review next.

The Backward Version of the Distance Computation. The algorithm mentioned in section 2 is a distance rather than path algorithm. It computes the length of a shortest path from vertex $(0,0)$ to any vertex (i,j) in the grid graph G. We call this the *forward* algorithm and denote its M matrix as M_F where F is a mnemonic for "forward." Let G^R denote the *reverse* of G, i.e., the graph obtained from G by reversing the direction of every edge. Clearly, in G^R vertex (m,n) is the source and vertex $(0,0)$ is the sink, and every v-to-w shortest path in G^R corresponds to a similar shortest path in G *but in the backwards direction* (i.e., w-to-v). We thus use M_B to denote the matrix that is to G^R what matrix M_F was to graph G (B is a mnemonic for "backward"). Then $M_B(i,j)$ denotes the length of a shortest path in G^R from the source of G^R (vertex (m,n)) to vertex (i,j), which is equal to the length of a shortest path in G from (i,j) to (m,n). The edit distance we seek is therefore $M_B(0,0)$ (which is the same as $M_F(m,n)$). Defined in terms of the two input strings, $M_B(i,j)$ is the edit distance from the suffix of λ of length $n-j$, to the suffix of μ of length $m-i$. Therefore computing M_B in an analogous manner to the computation of M_F involves filling in its entries by *decreasing* (rather than increasing) row and column order. An algorithm for M_B follows from any algorithm for M_F, which we thus assume and use in the subsequent description.

Note that $M_F(i,j) + M_B(i,j)$ is the length of a shortest source-to-sink path *constrained to go through vertex* (i,j) and hence might not be the shortest possible source-to-sink path. However, if the shortest source-to-sink path goes though vertex (i,j), then $M_F(i,j) + M_B(i,j)$ is equal to the length of the shortest path. We use M_C to denote $M_F + M_B$ (where C stands for "constrained").

Oblivious Edit Path Computation. We can now describe our oblivious edit path algorithm with the desired bounds. Similar to the structure of computation in [3], we find for each row i of M_C the column $\theta(i)$ of the minimum entry of that row, with ties broken in favor of the rightmost such entry. Note that $M_C(i, \theta(i))$ is the edit distance $M_F(m, n)$. Computing the θ function provides an implicit description of the edit path because:

- If $\theta(i+1) = \theta(i) = j$, then the edit path "leaves" row i through the vertical edge from vertex (i, j) to vertex $(i+1, j)$. The cost of that edge is that of inserting μ_{i+1}.
- If $\theta(i+1) = \theta(i) + \delta$, where $\delta > 0$, then the client can "fill in" the portion of the edit path from vertex $(i, \theta(i))$ to vertex $(i+1, \theta(i) + \delta)$ in $O(\delta)$ time (such a "thin" problem on a $2 \times \delta$ subgrid is trivially solvable in $O(\delta)$ time). The cumulative cost of all such "thin problem solutions" is $O(n)$ because the sum of all such δ's is $\leq n$.

Without loss of generality, let $m \leq n$. For reasons that will become apparent, similar to [3] we introduce a new symbol ϵ that does not occur in Σ and denote $\Sigma_\epsilon = \Sigma \cup \epsilon$. We assign to ϵ an insertion cost of 0, a deletion cost of ∞, and an ∞ cost for any substitution in which it is involved. In practice, ∞ can be set to be $(m + n)$ times the largest cost appearing in the cost tables for Σ (whether it is insertion, deletion, or substitution).

Because given $\theta(0), \ldots, \theta(m)$, C can compute the edit path in linear additional time, we give an algorithm for computing the θ function. It proceeds in $\log m$ rounds, the kth of which consists of 2^{k-1} grid graphs (each described implicitly by two substrings of μ and λ) of respective dimensions $(m/2^{k-1}) \times n_1, \ldots,$ $(m/2^{k-1}) \times n_{2^{k-1}}$, where $\sum_{t=1}^{2^{k-1}} n_t = (3/4)^{k-1} n$ as explained below. The first round proceeds as follows:

1. Run the forward edit distance algorithm to compute row $m/2$ of M_F.
2. Run the backward edit distance algorithm to compute row $m/2$ of M_B.
3. Compute $\theta(m/2)$ as the minimum of $M_C(m/2, j)$ across all $0 \leq j \leq n$.

The two subproblems of round 2 could, *if one were not concerned about information leakage*, be defined by the following two sub-grids: (i) the $(m/2) \times \theta(m/2)$ one that lies to the left and above vertex $(m/2, \theta(m/2))$ and is described implicitly by the strings $\mu_1, \ldots, \mu_{m/2}$ and $\lambda_1, \ldots, \lambda_{\theta(m/2)}$; and (ii) the $m/2 \times (n - \theta(m/2))$ one that lies to the right and below vertex $(m/2, \theta(m/2))$ and is described implicitly by the strings $\mu_{(m/2)+1}, \ldots, \mu_m$ and $\lambda_{\theta(m/2)+1}, \ldots, \lambda_n$. The area of those two subgrids is half the original, but their size would leak the value $\theta(m/2)$ during outsourced computation. We fix this by using, for round 2, subgrids whose size does not depend on $\theta(m/2)$ and yet their combined area is $3/4$ of the original, as described below. In what follows, we assume without loss of generality that $\theta(m/2) \geq n/2$. While in this description it appears that the fact that $\theta(m/2) \geq n/2$ is leaked, in our actual protocol described later this information is not revealed and the execution is fully oblivious.

- The first subgrid is of size $(m/2) \times n$ and is defined by the strings $\mu_1, \ldots, \mu_{m/2}$ and $\lambda_1, \ldots, \lambda_{\theta(m/2)}, \epsilon, \ldots, \epsilon$. The appending of the $n - \theta(m/2)$ symbols of type ϵ at the end of the second string hides $\theta(m/2)$ without changing the answer because the edit path for that subproblem has to use the $n - \theta(m/2)$ horizontal edges of 0 cost that link vertex $(m/2, \theta(m/2))$ to the vertex $(m/2, n)$.

Table 1. Matrices for edit distance between strings AACG and AGAC

(a) M_F	(b) M_B	(c) M_C	(d) θ

0	1	2	3	4
1	0	1	2	3
2	1	2	3	2
3	2	1	2	3
4	3	2	1	2

2	3	4	5	4
3	2	3	4	3
2	1	2	3	2
3	2	1	2	1
4	3	2	1	0

2	4	6	8	8
4	2	4	6	6
4	2	4	6	4
6	4	2	4	4
8	6	4	2	2

$\theta(0) = 0$
$\theta(1) = 1$
$\theta(2) = 1$
$\theta(3) = 2$
$\theta(4) = 4$

Fig. 2. Illustration of θ function computation

- The second subgrid is of size $(m/2) \times (n/2)$ and is defined by the strings $\mu_{(m/2)+1}, \ldots, \mu_m$ and $\epsilon, \ldots, \epsilon, \lambda_{\theta(m/2)+1}, \ldots, \lambda_n$. The pre-pending of the $(n/2) - \theta(m/2)$ ϵ symbols at the beginning of the second string hides $\theta(m/2)$ without changing the answer because the edit path for that subproblem has to use the $(n/2) - \theta(m/2)$ horizontal edges of 0 cost that link vertex $(m/2, n/2)$ to the vertex $(m/2, \theta(m/2))$.

A pair of 3rd-round sub-problems is derived from each 2nd-round subgrid in the same way as above, thus the third round consists of 4 subgrids whose total (combined) number of columns is $9n/16$ (namely, $n/4$, $n/8$, $n/8$, and $n/16$) and the total number of rows is m ($m/4$ rows for each).

Because the total (combined) problem size decreases by a factor of $3/4$ from one round to the next, the overall work of the above algorithm is as claimed: $O(\sigma mn)$. More precisely, the recurrence is $T(m, n) = T(\frac{m}{2}, n) + T(\frac{m}{2}, \frac{n}{2}) + \alpha\sigma mn$, and by easy induction it can be shown that $T(m, n) \leq 4\alpha\sigma mn$. Space is linear because each invocation of the edit-distance protocol uses linear space.

To clarify the above notions, we give a small example using strings AACG and AGAC with insertion and deletion costs of 1, and substitution cost of 0 for equal characters and 2 for non-equal characters. The 5×5 DAG for this example is like the one in Figure 1. Table 1 provides matrices M_F, M_B, M_C and the values for θ. Notice that $M_B(0, 0) = M_F(4, 4) = 2$ is the edit distance between these strings. Also, the shortest path goes through $M(i, \theta(i))$ for any row i.

Figure 2 also demonstrates our algorithm for edit path computation, where at each iteration a given (sub-)grid is partitioned into two subgrids of $1/2$ and $1/4$ of its original size and the remaining $1/4$ is removed. In the figure, shaded areas correspond to string padding with character ϵ. In the figure, because $\theta(m/2) < n/2$, the top subgrid has size $1/4$ and the bottom subgrid has size $1/2$. In the second round, $\theta(m/4) > n/4$ and therefore the top subgrid is further partitioned into subgrids of size $1/8$ and $1/16$, resp.; also, $\theta(3m/4) > n/2$ and therefore the bottom grid is partitioned into subgrids of size $1/4$ and $1/8$, resp.

5   Preliminary Protocol for Secure Edit Path Outsourcing

The above algorithm can be executed in the secure outsourcing setting using the round complexity of $O(\log m)$ – or, more generally, $O(\log(\min(m, n)))$ – if the servers can afford $O(\sigma mn)$ space. If, however, the servers have only linear space $O(\sigma(m + n))$, their round complexity increases to $O(\min(m, n))$ because the computation uses the total of $O(\sigma mn)$ space. This does not affect the client's round complexity, which in our preliminary solution described next is $O(\log(\min(m, n)))$. We subsequently improve it in section 6 to make it non-interactive for the client at no extra (for the client) cost.

Having described the structure of the computation, we now proceed with the description of the secure outsourcing protocol for the edit path. Recall that the client's work should be $O(\sigma(m + n))$, while the servers perform $O(\sigma mn)$ work. The protocol consists of executing the same procedure for each sub-problem in each round (starting with the problem of size $m \times n$ in round 1), at the end of which the client learns the value of the θ function at a single point. That is, for a subgrid defined by strings $\hat{\mu}_{k+1}, \ldots, \hat{\mu}_{k+a}$ and $\hat{\lambda}_{\ell+1}, \ldots, \hat{\lambda}_{\ell+b}$, the client learns $\theta(k + a/2)$ and the servers learn nothing. Here $\hat{\mu}_i$ and $\hat{\lambda}_j$ are from Σ_ϵ since after the first round each subgrid is formed by prepending or appending a number of ϵ characters to portions of the original strings.

In this protocol the client performs $O(\sigma(a+b))$ work for a subgrid of size $a \times b$, and the servers perform $O(\sigma ab)$ work. The client's work is thus characterized by recurrence $T(m, n) = T(\frac{m}{2}, n) + T(\frac{m}{2}, \frac{n}{2}) + \beta\sigma(m + n)$ and can be shown to be $\leq 4\beta\sigma(m + n)$ using the total of $O(\log m)$ rounds. In what follows, we describe a protocol for a subgrid defined by strings $\hat{\mu}_{k+1}, \ldots, \hat{\mu}_{k+a}$ and $\hat{\lambda}_{\ell+1}, \ldots, \hat{\lambda}_{\ell+b}$, in which the client learns the θ value and prepares two subgrids for the next round.

For the sake of the current description, suppose that S_1 has access to $\hat{\mu}_{k+1}, \ldots,$ $\hat{\mu}_{k+a}$, but wants to keep the string private from S_2, and S_2 has access to $\hat{\lambda}_{\ell+1}, \ldots,$ $\hat{\lambda}_{\ell+b}$, but likewise wants to keep its string private from S_1. S_1 and S_2 can engage in secure two-party computation, where S_1 inputs each $\hat{\mu}_i$ and the corresponding $I(\hat{\mu}_i)$, and S_2 inputs each $\hat{\lambda}_j$, the corresponding $D(\hat{\lambda}_j)$, and a vector $S(\hat{\lambda}_j, \cdot)$ that defines the cost of substituting $\hat{\lambda}_j$ with every character in Σ_ϵ. Then to be able to proceed with each step of the dynamic programming problem, they compute each $M(i, j)$ as specified, where the computation proceeds in an oblivious way as follows:

1. for $t = 1$ to $\sigma + 1$ do
2. $c = (\hat{\mu}_i \overset{?}{=} t)$;
3. $s_t = c \cdot S(\hat{\lambda}_j, t)$;
4. $s = \sum_{t=1}^{\sigma+1} s_t$;
5. $M(i, j) = \min(M(i-1, j-1) + s, M(i-1, j) + I(\hat{\mu}_i), M(i, j-1) + D(\hat{\lambda}_j))$.

Here $(x \overset{?}{=} y)$ denotes an equality test that outputs a bit which is 1 iff $x = y$. The procedure obliviously chooses the correct substitution cost from vector $S(\hat{\lambda}_j, \cdot)$ and uses it to compute $M(i, j)$. The cost of computing $M(i, j)$ is thus $O(\sigma)$.

To take this to the outsourcing context in which neither S_1 nor S_2 have access to the input strings or the output, we will now have the client C provide all of the inputs that S_1 and S_2 will use without learning any information about them (other than the lengths m, n, and σ). In particular, one server, say S_1, will be responsible for garbled circuit construction for a subgrid problem using oblivious execution described above, while the second server, S_2, will evaluate it on the client's inputs without knowing the meaning of the random labels that it handles. In a traditional implementation, we would have S_1 build a garbled circuit and send it to S_2, after which the client and S_1 engage in OT so that the client learns the (random) labels of the input wires corresponding to all of its inputs (namely, $\hat{\mu}_{k+1}, \ldots, \hat{\mu}_{k+a}$, $\hat{\lambda}_{\ell+1}, \ldots, \hat{\lambda}_{\ell+b}$, $I(\hat{\mu}_i)$ for each $k < i \leq k + a$, and $D(\hat{\lambda}_j)$ and $S(\hat{\lambda}_j, \cdot)$ for each $\ell < j \leq \ell + b$). The client then would send the labels it received from S_1 to S_2, S_2 would evaluate the garbled circuit on the client-supplied input wire labels and send the labels corresponding to the output wires to C. S_1 then would send to C the meaning of all output wire labels and C learns the result. We, however, propose a more efficient solution in which the need for computationally-intensive OTs is entirely eliminated. In detail, we have the client generate all input wire labels that it consequently sends to S_1. S_1 uses these labels to produce a garbled circuit that it sends to S_2. S_1 also sends all output wires and their meaning to C. C then sends the labels corresponding to its private input to S_2, who evaluates the circuit as before and sends the labels corresponding to the output to C.

Input: C has private strings $\hat{\mu}_{k+1}, \ldots, \hat{\mu}_{k+a}$ and $\hat{\lambda}_{\ell+1}, \ldots, \hat{\lambda}_{\ell+b}$ and the corresponding insertion, deletion, and substitution costs, namely, $I(\hat{\mu}_i)$ for $k < i \leq k + a$ and $D(\hat{\lambda}_j)$ and $S(\hat{\lambda}_j, \cdot)$ for $\ell < j \leq \ell + b$. S_1 and S_2 contribute no input.

Output: C obtains $\theta(k + a/2)$ and new pairs of strings $\hat{\mu}'_{k'+1}, \ldots, \hat{\mu}'_{k'+a/2}$, $\hat{\lambda}'_{\ell'+1}, \ldots, \hat{\lambda}'_{\ell'+b}$ and $\hat{\mu}''_{k''+1}, \ldots, \hat{\mu}''_{k''+a/2}$, $\hat{\lambda}''_{\ell''+1}, \ldots, \hat{\lambda}''_{\ell''+b/2}$ that define subgrids for the next round. S_1 and S_2 learn nothing.

Protocol 1

1. C generates $a(s_\Sigma + s_C) + b(s_\Sigma + s_C + s_C |\Sigma_\epsilon|)$ pairs of random labels $(\ell_0^{(t)}, \ell_1^{(t)})$, where $s_\Sigma = \lceil \log(|\Sigma_\epsilon|) \rceil = \lceil \log(\sigma + 1) \rceil$ is the size of binary representation of an alphabet character, s_C is the size of binary representation of costs[1] in tables $I(\cdot)$, $D(\cdot)$, and $S(\cdot, \cdot)$, and $t \in [1, s_\Sigma(a + b) + s_C(a + 2b + \sigma b)]$.

2. C sends all $(\ell_0^{(t)}, \ell_1^{(t)})$ to S_1 who uses them as the input wire labels in constructing a garbled circuit.

3. C sends a single label $\ell_{b_t}^{(t)}$ for each t to S_2, where b_t is 0 or 1 depending on the corresponding bit of C's input.

4. S_1 sends the garbled circuit to S_2 and all output wire labels to C, which we denote by $(\hat{\ell}_0^{(t)}, \hat{\ell}_1^{(t)})$ for $t = [1, s_b]$, where $s_b = \lceil \log b \rceil$ is the size of the binary representation of the output $\theta(k + a/2)$ which takes on b possible values.

5. S_2 evaluates the garbled circuit using the input labels received from C and sends labels $\hat{\ell}_{b_t}^{(t)}$ that correspond to the computed output for $t \in [1, s_b]$ to C.

6. C recovers the meaning of the output (i.e., the bit b_t) for each $\hat{\ell}_{b_t}^{(t)}$ using previously received labels $(\hat{\ell}_0^{(t)}, \hat{\ell}_1^{(t)})$. Let b' denote the output $\theta(k + a/2)$.

---

[1] For simplicity of presentation we use fixed length s_C for costs in all tables, but this does not need to be the case. Also, because ϵ character is not present in the original strings, the values of s_Σ and s_C can be adjusted accordingly in the first round.

7. C forms two new sub-problems based on the value of b'. If $b' \geq b/2$, C sets:
   - $\hat{\mu}'_{k'+1}, \ldots, \hat{\mu}'_{k'+a/2} = \hat{\mu}_{k+1}, \ldots, \hat{\mu}_{k+a/2}$,
   - $\hat{\lambda}'_{\ell'+1}, \ldots, \hat{\lambda}'_{\ell'+b} = \hat{\lambda}_{\ell+1}, \ldots, \hat{\lambda}_{\ell+b'}, \epsilon, \ldots \epsilon$,
   - $\hat{\mu}''_{k''+1}, \ldots, \hat{\mu}''_{k''+a/2} = \hat{\mu}_{k+(a/2)+1}, \ldots, \hat{\mu}_{k+a}$,
   - $\hat{\lambda}''_{\ell''+1}, \ldots, \hat{\lambda}''_{\ell''+b/2} = \epsilon, \ldots, \epsilon, \hat{\lambda}_{\ell+b'+1}, \ldots, \hat{\lambda}_{\ell+b}$.

   Otherwise, C sets:
   - $\hat{\mu}'_{k'+1}, \ldots, \hat{\mu}'_{k'+a/2} = \hat{\mu}_{k+(a/2)+1}, \ldots, \hat{\mu}_{k+a}$,
   - $\hat{\lambda}'_{\ell'+1}, \ldots, \hat{\lambda}'_{\ell'+b} = \epsilon, \ldots, \epsilon, \hat{\lambda}_{\ell+b'+1}, \ldots, \hat{\lambda}_{\ell+b}$,
   - $\hat{\mu}''_{k''+1}, \ldots, \hat{\mu}''_{k''+a/2} = \hat{\mu}_{k+1}, \ldots, \hat{\mu}_{k+a/2}$,
   - $\hat{\lambda}''_{\ell''+1}, \ldots, \hat{\lambda}''_{\ell''+b/2} = \hat{\lambda}_{\ell+1}, \ldots, \hat{\lambda}_{\ell+b'}, \epsilon, \ldots, \epsilon$.

C, S_1 and S_2 can now engage in the next round of computation using two newly determined subgrids. Note that the solution works even when the insertion, deletion, and substitution cost tables are private and known only to C.

6   Reducing Client's Involvement

While the solution above already significantly outperforms prior work, in this section we further improve it by making the protocol non-interactive for the client. Now the client initially sends data to S_1 and S_2 and at the end of the computation receives the result from S_1 and S_2 and recovers the edit path.

Our idea in eliminating the client's interaction such that no oblivious transfer for garbled circuit evaluation has to be introduced consists of using output wires of a garbled circuit as input wires for the garbled circuits used in the next round. To be able to do so, the server needs to obliviously compute the input strings for the next round of computation, the wires of which will then be reused in subsequent garbled circuits. Let S_1 and S_2 compute $\theta(m/2)$ in the first round of the computation, where C provides inputs $\mu_1, \ldots, \mu_m$, $\lambda_1, \ldots, \lambda_n$, $I(\mu_i)$ for $i = 1, \ldots, m$, and $D(\lambda_j)$ and $S(\lambda_j, \cdot)$ for $j = 1, \ldots, n$ in the manner described above. After determining the value of $\theta(m/2)$, S_1 and S_2 can proceed with obliviously computing strings $\mu'_1, \ldots, \mu'_{m/2}$, $\lambda'_1, \ldots, \lambda'_n$ and $\mu''_1, \ldots, \mu''_{m/2}$, $\lambda''_1, \ldots, \lambda''_{n/2}$ (with the corresponding insertion, deletion, and substitution costs) which will become inputs for the next round as follows:

1. $c = (\theta(m/2) \overset{?}{<} n/2)$;
2. for $i = 1$ to $m/2$ do
3. $\quad \mu'_i = (1 - c)\mu_i + c\mu_{(m/2)+i}$;
4. $\quad \mu''_i = c\mu_i + (1 - c)\mu_{(m/2)+i}$;
5. for $j = 1$ to n do
6. $\quad c_j = (\theta(m/2) \overset{?}{\leq} j)$; $\quad$ // can always set $c_n = 1$
7. $\quad \lambda'_j = (1 - c \oplus c_j)\lambda_j + (c \oplus c_j)\epsilon$;
8. for $j = 1$ to $n/2$ do
9. $\quad \lambda''_j = c(c_j\epsilon + (1 - c_j)\lambda_j) + (1 - c)(c_{(n/2)+j}\lambda_{(n/2)+j} + (1 - c_{(n/2)+j})\epsilon)$;

The computation of the μ'_i's and μ''_i's above is rather straightforward. To compute λ'_j's (for the larger $1/2$ part), when c is set, the larger area corresponds to the bottom rows and the beginning needs to be populated with ϵ characters. So we keep λ_j if c_j is set and replace it with ϵ otherwise. When c is not set, the larger area comes from the top rows and erasing happens at the end. In this case, we keep λ_j if c_j is not set and replace it with ϵ otherwise. The expression for λ_j' above corresponds to this logic in a more compact form. To compute λ_j'''s (for the $1/4$ part), when c is set, the top left quadrant is used and padding happens at the end. Thus, if c_j is set, use ϵ, and use λ_j otherwise. When c is not set, we are using the bottom right quadrant with padding in the beginning. So if $c_{(n/2)+j}$ is set, use $\lambda_{(n/2)+j}$ and use ϵ otherwise.

Referring back to the example in Figure 2, the value of c determines whether the size of the top or bottom subgrid should be reduced and the values of c_j determine what portions of the strings should be replaced with ϵ. As part of the computation, the servers always process the $1/2$-sized and $1/4$-sized grids in the same way, regardless of from what portion of the original grid they come. This means that a subgrid processing purely depends on its size, while the origin of a subgrid of any given size is protected (i.e., unlike this computation, the positioning of subgrids in Figure 2 is not oblivious).

The above allows the servers to compute the strings themselves for the next round of the computation, but we also want to ensure that they are able to compute the rest of the input which consists of insertion, deletion, and substitution costs. Here we demonstrate oblivious computation of such values on the example of strings $\mu_1', \ldots, \mu_{m/2}'$, $\lambda_1', \ldots, \lambda_n'$. The costs for strings $\mu_1'', \ldots, \mu_{m/2}''$, $\lambda_1'', \ldots, \lambda_{n/2}''$ can be computed analogously. From the privacy point of view, we distinguish between two cases: (i) the insertion, deletion, and substitution cost tables are public (i.e., known to the servers) and (ii) the cost tables are private (i.e., known only to the client). Whether the cost tables are public or not will affect how a garbled circuit is constructed, but the computation built into the circuit must proceed obliviously regardless of that fact. In particular, when the cost tables are public, their values will be input into circuits as constants (in which case two inputs wires – one encoding a 0 and another encoding a 1 – can be used to encode all constants), while when they are private, the client will need to additionally produce input wires for all constant values that comprise the cost tables and communicate their values to S_1 and S_2 in the same manner as for all other private inputs. What follows describes oblivious computation of $I(\mu_i')$, $D(\lambda_j')$, and $S(\lambda_j', \cdot)$ for the next round.

1. for $i = 1$ to $m/2$ do
2. $I(\mu_i') = 0$;
3.   for $t = 1$ to $\sigma + 1$ do
4. $c = (\mu_i' \stackrel{?}{=} t)$;
5. $I(\mu_i') = I(\mu_i') + c \cdot I(t)$;
6. for $j = 1$ to n do
7. $D(\lambda_j') = 0$; $S(\lambda_j', \cdot) = \langle 0, \ldots, 0 \rangle$;
8.   for $t = 1$ to $\sigma + 1$ do
9. $c = (\lambda_j' \stackrel{?}{=} t)$;
10. $D(\lambda_j') = D(\lambda_j') + c \cdot D(t)$;
11. $S(\lambda_j', \cdot) = S(\lambda_j', \cdot) + c \cdot S(t, \cdot)$;

For compactness of presentation, we define operations on vectors $S(\lambda'_i, \cdot)$ and $S(t, \cdot)$ in a single step, but it should be understood that all addition, multiplication, and assignment operations in this case are performed element-wise.

The above allows S_1 and S_2 to produce all inputs for the next round of the computation. Because the cost tables for insertion, deletion, and substitution are needed for each subgrid computation, when their values are public, S_1 will as before encode the constants into each circuit it forms. When, on the other hand, such values are private and should not be revealed to S_1 or S_2, S_1 will use the same wire labels for the constants as the ones provided by the client in the first round, and S_2 will also reuse the labels that it received from the client for these constants in the first round of the computation. We note that while in general reuse of garbled circuits or their parts is not safe from the privacy point of view, in this case the servers can use the same wires in multiple circuits because the labels (or inputs) on which S_2 evaluates the circuits are always the same. This means that the labels themselves do not change and do not allow S_2 to learn any information contained in the cost tables. All other labels in garbled circuits are chosen anew and therefore S_2 cannot deduce any information as a result of gate evaluation. This allows us to obtain the overall protocol as follows:

Input: C has private strings $\mu_1, \ldots, \mu_m$ and $\lambda_1, \ldots, \lambda_n$. The insertion, deletion, and substitution cost tables can be C's additional private input or known to all parties. S_1 and S_2 do not contribute any input.

Output: C obtains the edit path. S_1 and S_2 learn nothing.

Protocol 2

1. C generates two random labels $(\ell_0^{(t)}, \ell_1^{(t)})$ for each bit of its input $\mu_1, \ldots, \mu_m$, $\lambda_1, \ldots, \lambda_n$, $I(\mu_i)$ for each $i \in [1, m]$, $D(\lambda_j)$ and $S(\lambda_j, \cdot)$ for each $j \in [1, n]$, $I(\cdot)$, $D(\cdot)$, and $S(\cdot, \cdot)$ resulting in $t \in [1, s_\Sigma(m+n) + s_C(m+n+3\sigma+\sigma^2))]$.

2. C sends all $(\ell_0^{(t)}, \ell_1^{(t)})$ to S_1, and it sends a single label $\ell_{b_t}^{(t)}$ for each t to S_2, where b_t is 0 or 1 depending on the corresponding bit of C's input.

3. S_1 uses the pairs of labels it received from C as the input wire labels in constructing a garbled circuit that produces $\theta(m/2)$, strings $\mu'_1, \ldots, \mu'_{m/2}$, $\lambda'_1, \ldots, \lambda'_n$ and the corresponding $I(\mu'_i)$, $D(\lambda'_j)$, and $S(\lambda'_j, \cdot)$, as well as strings $\mu''_1, \ldots, \mu''_{m/2}$, $\lambda''_1, \ldots, \lambda''_{n/2}$ and the corresponding $I(\mu''_i)$, $D(\lambda''_j)$, and $S(\lambda''_j, \cdot)$. Let the pairs of the output wire labels that correspond to $\theta(m/2)$ be denoted by $(\hat{\ell}_0^{(t)}, \hat{\ell}_1^{(t)})$, where $t \in [1, \lceil \log(n) \rceil]$, the labels corresponding to the output labels for the first sub-problem be denoted by $(\ell_0'^{(t)}, \ell_1'^{(t)})$, where $t \in [1, s_\Sigma(m/2+n) + s_C(m/2+n+\sigma n)]$, and the labels corresponding to the output labels for the second sub-problem be denoted by $(\ell_0''^{(t)}, \ell_1''^{(t)})$, where $t \in [1, s_\Sigma(m+n)/2 + s_C(m+n+\sigma n)/2]$.

4. S_1 sends its garbled circuit to S_2, which S_2 evaluates using the input labels received from C. S_1 stores for later reference pairs of labels $(\hat{\ell}_0^{(t)}, \hat{\ell}_1^{(t)})$ and S_2 stores the labels for the same wires $\hat{\ell}_{b_t}^{(t)}$ that it computed.

5. S_1 and S_2 now engage in the second round of the computation, where for the first circuit S_1 uses pairs $(\ell_0'^{(t)}, \ell_1'^{(t)})$ as the input wire labels as well as the pairs of the input wire labels from C that correspond to cost tables $I(\cdot)$,

$D(\cdot)$, and $S(\cdot, \cdot)$. After the circuit is formed S_1 sends it to S_2 who uses the labels $\ell_{b_t}^{\prime(t)}$ it computed in the first round as well as the labels for the cost tables supplied by C in the first round to evaluate this circuit.

6. S_1 forms and S_2 evaluates the second circuit of the second round and all circuits in consecutive rounds analogously. As before, for each circuit they store the labels of the output wires that correspond to evaluation of $\theta(\cdot)$ on a specific point (i.e., S_1 stores a pair of labels for each ouput bit and S_2 stores a label per output bit that it obtained as a result of circuit evaluation).

7. When S_1 and S_2 reach the bottom of recursion, S_1 sends pairs $(\hat{\ell}_0^{(t)}, \hat{\ell}_1^{(t)})$ and S_2 sends values $\hat{\ell}_{b_t}^{(t)}$ from each circuit to C. C uses the labels to reconstruct the values of the θ function on all evaluated points, from which it reconstructs the edit path as described in section 4.

We obtain the final result in which the servers' communication and computation is $O(\sigma mn)$ and the work is dominated by the same number of symmetric key or hash function operations for garbled circuit generation and evaluation. The solution works when the servers have only $O(\sigma(m + n))$ space. The client's communication and computation is $O(\sigma(m + n))$, where work is dominated by generation of the same number of random labels. The round complexity for the client is $O(1)$ and for the servers it can be expressed as a function of their space: when the space is $O(\sigma mn)$, the round complexity is $O(\log(\min(m, n)))$; when the space is lower, the round complexity increases as below. Security analysis is omitted due to space considerations and can be found in the full version.

Achieving Linear Space at the Servers. As previously mentioned, our solution was designed to ensure that the servers can carry out the computation using only $O(\sigma(m + n))$ space as m and n can be large. Because the circuit size starts from $O(\sigma mn)$ (before it exponentially reduces in each round), S_1 will generate and send to S_2 a part of the overall circuit before the next portion can be produced. Similarly, S_2 will receive and evaluate a part of a circuit at a time. Because the entries of the M-matrix can be computed row by row (or column by column), when the servers' space is constrained, the part of the circuit generated and evaluated in each round will follow the same structure of the computation (i.e., a circuit corresponding to the computation of one or more rows is produced and evaluated at a time). This causes the number of times S_1 and S_2 interact to increase from the minimum $O(\log \min(m, n))$. As the size of each circuit reduces in consecutive rounds, S_1 and S_2 will be able to process a larger portion of a circuit and then multiple circuits per interaction. Thus, the number of interactions for the servers is $O(\min(m, n))$ when they only have $O(\sigma(m + n))$ space available. In other words, for servers with memory constraints of $o(\sigma mn)$, there is a tradeoff between their space capacity and the number of interactions. This obviously does not affect the client who only sends and later receives its data.

Performance. To gain insights into performance of our solution, we compute the size of garbled circuits as a function of parameters m, n, and σ and approximate the protocol's runtime. For concreteness, we set the cost of insertion and

Table 2. Servers' combined computation and communication

Value of $n = m$	Number of gates	Computation	Communication
250	50×10^6	8.3 min	1.4 GB
500	221×10^6	36.6 min	6.2 GB
1000	966×10^6	161 min	27.0 GB

deletion to be 1, and the cost of substitution with a different character to be 2 and with the same character to be 0.

In the circuit, we want to use the smallest possible number of bits to represent values and store intermediate results. This in particular means that the size of representation of input characters, substitution costs, and intermediate matrix values will differ. Also, with the free XOR gates technique of [19], we can implement equality testing of two ℓ-bit values using $\ell - 1$ non-free gates (i.e., XOR the inputs and compute OR of the resulting bits), multiplication of an ℓ-bit value by a bit using ℓ AND gates, addition of k ℓ-bit values from which at most one is non-zero (as on line 4 of matrix cell computation in section 5) using $k\ell$ OR gates, and regular addition and minimum as in [21]. All constants are encoded using the total of two input wires. For an $m \times n$ matrix with $\sigma = 4$, this gives us $< (n-1)(m-1)(7\log(n+m)+18)$ non-XOR gates for the first round (without using ϵ) and $< (n-1)(m-1)(25\log(n+m)+16)$ for all consecutive rounds. Thus, implementing the preliminary protocol in section 5 involves $< (n-1)(m-1)(82\log(n+m)+64)$ non-XOR gates. $O(\log(n+m))$ bits are used to represent matrix elements $M(i,j)$. Removing client's involvement in the protocol introduces additional $\approx 84m + 3n(54\log(n+m)+\log n+29)$ non-XOR gates. We note that the number of gates in our edit distance computation is larger than, e.g., in [9] for computing the Levenshtein's distance due to the generality of the edit distance problem we are solving. Some of the circuit optimizations from [9] can be applied to special cases of our problem to result in smaller circuits and faster performance.

Table 2 provides estimated number of gates and runtime of our solution assuming processing 100 non-free gates per msec (based on evaluation results in [9, 22]) on single-threaded commodity hardware. Communication is computed using 25% savings per gate [20]. The client's work is only to generate $9n + m$ pairs of short random labels and communicate them to the servers ($180n + 20m$ bytes). This is computed assuming that the costs of insertion and deletion are known and fixed and the servers can add costs for ϵ to the circuits. We conclude that our techniques can be applied even to problems of large size.

References

1. Atallah, M., Kerschbaum, F., Du, W.: Secure and private sequence comparisons. In: ACM Workshop on the Privacy in Electronic Society (WPES) (2003)
2. Atallah, M.J., Li, J.: Secure Outsourcing of Sequence Comparisons. In: Martin, D., Serjantov, A. (eds.) PET 2004. LNCS, vol. 3424, pp. 63–78. Springer, Heidelberg (2005)
3. Atallah, M., Li, J.: Secure outsourcing of sequence comparisons. International Journal of Information Security 4(4), 277–287 (2005)

4. Szajda, D., Pohl, M., Owen, J., Lawson, B.: Toward a practical data privacy scheme for a distributed implementation of the Smith-Waterman genome sequence comparison algorithm. In: NDSS (2006)
5. Troncoso-Pastoriza, J., Katzenbeisser, S., Celik, M.: Privacy preserving error resilient DNA searching through oblivious automata. In: CCS, pp. 519–528 (2007)
6. Jha, S., Kruger, L., Shmatikov, V.: Toward practical privacy for genomic computation. In: IEEE Symposium on Security and Privacy, pp. 216–230 (2008)
7. Frikken, K.: Practical Private DNA String Searching and Matching through Efficient Oblivious Automata Evaluation. In: Gudes, E., Vaidya, J. (eds.) Data and Applications Security XXIII. LNCS, vol. 5645, pp. 81–94. Springer, Heidelberg (2009)
8. Blanton, M., Aliasgari, M.: Secure Outsourcing of DNA Searching via Finite Automata. In: Foresti, S., Jajodia, S. (eds.) Data and Applications Security and Privacy XXIV. LNCS, vol. 6166, pp. 49–64. Springer, Heidelberg (2010)
9. Huang, Y., Evans, D., Katz, J., Malka, L.: Faster secure two-party computation using garbled circuits. In: USENIX Security Symposium (2011)
10. Baldi, P., Baronio, R., De Cristofaro, E., Gasti, P., Tsudik, G.: Countering GATTACA: Efficient and secure testing of fully-sequenced human genomes. In: CCS, pp. 691–702 (2011)
11. Bogdanov, D., Laur, S., Willemson, J.: Sharemind: A Framework for Fast Privacy-Preserving Computations. In: Jajodia, S., Lopez, J. (eds.) ESORICS 2008. LNCS, vol. 5283, pp. 192–206. Springer, Heidelberg (2008)
12. Wong, C., Chandra, A.: Bounds for the string editing problem. Journal of the ACM 23(1), 13–16 (1976)
13. Goldreich, O.: Foundations of Cryptography: Volume 2, Basic Applications. Cambridge University Press (2004)
14. Aumann, Y., Lindell, Y.: Security Against Covert Adversaries: Efficient Protocols for Realistic Adversaries. In: Vadhan, S.P. (ed.) TCC 2007. LNCS, vol. 4392, pp. 137–156. Springer, Heidelberg (2007)
15. Lindell, Y., Pinkas, B.: An Efficient Protocol for Secure Two-Party Computation in the Presence of Malicious Adversaries. In: Naor, M. (ed.) EUROCRYPT 2007. LNCS, vol. 4515, pp. 52–78. Springer, Heidelberg (2007)
16. Lindell, Y., Pinkas, B.: Secure Two-Party Computation via Cut-and-Choose Oblivious Transfer. In: Ishai, Y. (ed.) TCC 2011. LNCS, vol. 6597, pp. 329–346. Springer, Heidelberg (2011)
17. Wagner, R., Fischer, M.: The string to string correction problem. Journal of the ACM 21(1), 168–173 (1974)
18. Yao, A.: How to generate and exchange secrets. In: FOCS, pp. 162–167 (1986)
19. Kolesnikov, V., Schneider, T.: Improved Garbled Circuit: Free XOR Gates and Applications. In: Aceto, L., Damgård, I., Goldberg, L.A., Halldórsson, M.M., Ingólfsdóttir, A., Walukiewicz, I. (eds.) ICALP 2008, Part II. LNCS, vol. 5126, pp. 486–498. Springer, Heidelberg (2008)
20. Pinkas, B., Schneider, T., Smart, N., Williams, S.: Secure Two-Party Computation Is Practical. In: Matsui, M. (ed.) ASIACRYPT 2009. LNCS, vol. 5912, pp. 250–267. Springer, Heidelberg (2009)
21. Kolesnikov, V., Sadeghi, A.R., Schneider, T.: Improved Garbled Circuit Building Blocks and Applications to Auctions and Computing Minima. In: Garay, J.A., Miyaji, A., Otsuka, A. (eds.) CANS 2009. LNCS, vol. 5888, pp. 1–20. Springer, Heidelberg (2009)
22. Blanton, M., Gasti, P.: Secure and Efficient Protocols for Iris and Fingerprint Identification. In: Atluri, V., Diaz, C. (eds.) ESORICS 2011. LNCS, vol. 6879, pp. 190–209. Springer, Heidelberg (2011)

Third-Party Private DFA Evaluation on Encrypted Files in the Cloud

Lei Wei and Michael K. Reiter

Department of Computer Science, University of North Carolina at Chapel Hill
{lwei,reiter}@cs.unc.edu

Abstract. Motivated by the need to outsource file storage to untrusted clouds while still permitting limited use of that data by third parties, we present practical protocols by which a client (the third-party) can evaluate a deterministic finite automaton (DFA) on an encrypted file stored at a server (the cloud), once authorized to do so by the file owner. Our protocols provably protect the privacy of the DFA and the file contents from a malicious server and the privacy of the file contents (except for the result of the evaluation) from an honest-but-curious client (and, heuristically, from a malicious client). We further present simple techniques to detect client or server misbehavior.

1 Introduction

Outsourcing file storage to storage service providers (SSPs) and "clouds" can provide significant savings to file owners in terms of management costs and capital investments. However, because cloud storage can heighten the risk of file disclosure, prudent file owners encrypt their cloud-resident files to protect their confidentiality. This encryption introduces difficulties in managing access to these files by partially trusted third parties, however. Third-party service providers who are contracted to analyze files stored in the cloud generally cannot do so if the files are encrypted. For example, periodically "scanning" files to detect new malware, as is common today for PC platforms, cannot presently be performed on encrypted files by a third party. Moreover, with some exceptions (see §2), third-party customers generally cannot search the files if they are encrypted. Searches on genome datasets, pharmaceutical databases, document corpora, or network logs are critical for research in various fields, but the privacy constraints of these datasets may mandate their encryption, particularly when stored in the cloud.

These difficulties are compounded when the third party views its queries on the files to be sensitive, as well. New malware signatures may be sensitive since releasing them enables attackers to design malware to evade them (e.g., [37]). Customers of datasets in numerous domains (e.g., pharmaceutical research) may view their research interests, and hence their queries, as private.

As a step toward resolving this tension among file protection, search access by authorized third parties, and privacy for third-party queries, in this paper

S. Foresti, M. Yung, and F. Martinelli (Eds.): ESORICS 2012, LNCS 7459, pp. 523–540, 2012.

we introduce protocols by which a third-party (called the "client") can perform private searches on encrypted files (stored at the "server"), once it is authorized to do so by the file owner. The type of searches that our protocols enable is motivated by the scenarios above, which in many cases involve pattern matching a file against one or more regular expressions. Multi-pattern string matching is especially common in analysis of content for malware (e.g., [31,24]) and also is commonplace in searches on genome data, for example. In fact, there are now a number of available genome databases (e.g., [1,2]) and accompanying tools for multi-pattern matching against them (e.g., [6]). With the goal of improving privacy in such applications, we develop protocols to evaluate a deterministic finite automaton (DFA) of the client's choice on the plaintext of the encrypted file and to return the final state to the client to indicate which, if any, of the patterns encoded in the DFA were matched. We stress that while there is much work on secure two-party computation including the specific case of private DFA evaluation on a private file (see §2), few works have anticipated the possibility that the file is available only in encrypted form. This setting will become more common as data-storage outsourcing grows.

The security properties we prove for our protocols include privacy of the DFA and file contents against arbitrary server adversaries, and privacy of the file (except what is revealed by the evaluation result) against honest-but-curious client adversaries. Though our proofs are limited to only honest-but-curious client adversaries, we also provide heuristic justification for the security of our protocols against arbitrary client adversaries. Our protocols appear to be extensible with standard techniques to provably protect file privacy against arbitrary client adversaries, but we stop short of doing so in light of the substantially greater cost it would impose and our motivating scenarios involving third parties that the file owner must authorize and so presumably trusts to some extent. We do, however, discuss efficient heuristics to detect a misbehaving client or server that highlight new opportunities in the cloud storage setting.

A central observation that facilitates our protocols is that a DFA transition function can be encoded as a bivariate polynomial over the ring of an additively homomorphic encryption scheme with which the file characters are encrypted. In our protocols, the client, who has this polynomial as input, and the server, who has the encrypted file as input, obliviously perform DFA state transitions by jointly evaluating this polynomial. Neither party learns the current state at any point of the protocol execution; instead, they share the current state at each step, requiring that the polynomial be adapted in each round to accommodate this sharing.

We believe our protocols will be efficient enough for many practical scenarios. They support evaluation of any DFA over an alphabet Σ on any file consisting of ℓ symbols drawn from Σ, and require the file to be stored using ℓm ciphertexts where $m = |\Sigma|$. Since m is a multiplicative factor in the storage cost, our protocols are best suited to small alphabets Σ, e.g., bits ($m = 2$), bytes ($m = 256$), alphanumeric characters ($m = 36$), or DNA nucleotides ($m = 4$ for "A", "C", "G", and "T"). Specifically, in §4, we present a protocol that leverages additively homomorphic encryption (e.g., [28]) and transmits $O(\kappa \ell nm)$ bits, for κ a security parameter, to evaluate a DFA of n states. In §5, we leverage additively homomorphic encryption that also supports *one* homomorphic multiplication of ciphertexts (e.g., [8]) to construct a protocol that transmits only $O(\kappa \ell(n + m))$ bits. Our techniques could also be utilized with fully homomorphic encryption to produce a noninteractive protocol with a communication cost of $O(nm)$ fully homomorphic ciphertexts and, in particular, that is independent of the file length ℓ. Before describing our protocols, we discuss related work in §2 and clarify our goals in §3.

2   Related Work

The functionality offered by our protocols could be implemented with general "computing on encrypted data" [30] or two-party secure computation [36,18]. These techniques tend to yield less efficient protocols than one designed for a specific purpose, and our case will be no exception. The former achieves computations non-interactively using fully homomorphic encryption, for which existing implementations [14,11,32,33] are much more costly than the techniques we use [15]. The latter utilizes a "garbled circuit" construction that is of size linear in the circuit representation of the function to be computed. Despite progress on practical implementations of this technique [26,5,29], this limitation renders it much more communication-intensive for the problem we consider.

Two-party private DFA evaluation, in which a server has a file and a client has a DFA to evaluate on that file, has been a topic of recent focus. Troncoso-Pastoriza et al. [34] presented the first such protocol, which they proved secure in the honest-but-curious setting. Frikken [12] presented a protocol for the same setting that improved on the round complexity and computational costs. Gennaro et al. [13] developed a protocol that they proved secure against arbitrary adversaries, and Mohassel et al. [27] presented a protocol for arbitrary adversaries that significantly reduces the number of asymmetric operations. Our work differs from these in that in our protocols, the file is available to the parties only in ciphertext form. In this respect, the protocol of Blanton and Aliasgari [7] is relevant; they proposed a protocol for an "outsourcing" model, in which the DFA owner and file owner secret-share the DFA and file, respectively, between two other hosts, who then interactively evaluate the DFA on the file without reconstructing either one. While our protocol utilizes secret sharing, as well — in our case, of the file owner's file-decryption key — it shares much less data and does not share the client's DFA (or thus require two parties between which to share it) at all.

By two-party sharing the file-decryption key and using this to compute on encrypted data, our protocols are related to Choi et al.'s [9]. This work developed a protocol based on garbled circuits by which two parties can evaluate a general function after a private decryption key has been shared between them. This protocol can be used to solve the problem we propose, but inherits the aforementioned limitations of garbled circuits.

Two-party pattern-matching and search problems other than DFA evaluation have also been studied, e.g., by Jha et al. [22], Hazay and Lindell [19], Katz and Malka [23], and Hazay and Toft [20]. Again, these works input the plaintext file to one party and so do not directly apply to our setting. Of particular note, though, is a protocol due to Ishai and Paskin [21] to evaluate a branching program (which can be used to encode a DFA) on encrypted data. Translated to our context, their scheme enables a client holding a branching program P and provided the ciphertext c_1 for plaintext data $\sigma \in \Sigma^\ell$ to compute a ciphertext c_2 of $P(\sigma)$. Conceivably if the data owner shared the decryption key between the client and the server who provided c_1 (as in our protocol), the client could then recover $P(\sigma)$ by jointly decrypting c_2 with the server, without involvement from the data owner. However, when this protocol is applied to DFAs, c_1 could be of length quadratic in ℓ and, because c_2 is encrypted in a nested fashion, its joint decryption would seem to require ℓ rounds of interaction, each round with messages of length $O(\ell)$.

Additional related work is discussed in our accompanying technical report [35].

3   Problem Description

A deterministic finite automaton M is a tuple $\langle Q, \Sigma, \delta, q_{\text{init}} \rangle$ where Q is a set of $|Q| = n$ states; Σ is a set (*alphabet*) of $|\Sigma| = m$ symbols; $\delta : Q \times \Sigma \to Q$ is a transition function; and q_{init} is the initial state. (A DFA can also specify a set $F \subseteq Q$ of accepting states. We will discuss extensions of our protocols to this case.)

Our goal is to enable a client holding a DFA M to interact with a server holding the ciphertext of a file to evaluate M on the file plaintext. More specifically, the client should output the final state to which the file plaintext drives the DFA; i.e., if the plaintext file is a sequence $\langle \sigma_k \rangle_{k \in [\ell]}$ where $[\ell]$ denotes the set $\{0, 1, \ldots, \ell - 1\}$ and where each $\sigma_k \in \Sigma$, then the client should output $\delta(\ldots \delta(\delta(q_{\text{init}}, \sigma_0), \sigma_1), \ldots, \sigma_{\ell-1})$. We also permit the client to learn the file length ℓ and the server to learn both ℓ and the number of states n in the client's DFA.[1] The client should learn nothing else about the file, however, and the server should learn nothing else about the file or the client's DFA.

Because the file exists in the system only in encrypted form, some private-key information must be injected into the protocol to enable a DFA to be evaluated on the file plaintext. Since (only) the data owner holds the private key, one approach would be to involve the data owner in the protocol. However, in keeping with the goals of cloud outsourcing, our protocols require the data owner only to authorize the client to perform DFA evaluations with the server — but not to participate in those evaluations herself. In our protocols, this authorization

---

[1] Since exposing the final state reduces file entropy by $\log_2 n$ bits, presumably the server should learn n so as to monitor for excessive exposure or to charge for the information learned by the client. Moreover, the client can arbitrarily inflate n by adding unreachable states. As such, we consider disclosing n to the server to be practically necessary but of little threat to the client.

occurs by the data owner sharing the private file-decryption key between the client and server. As a result, a client and server that collude could pool their information to decrypt the file. Here we assume no such collusion, however, for two reasons. First, we are primarily motivated by scenarios in which the client represents a partially trusted service provider or customer, and so even if the cloud server were to be compromised, we presume this party would not be the cause. So, we prove security against only a client or server acting in isolation and with primary attention to only an honest-but-curious client (though we also heuristically justify the security of our protocol against an arbitrary client). Second, even without sharing the file decryption key between the client and server, the functionality offered by our protocol (i.e., evaluating a DFA on the file) would enable a colluding client and server to evaluate arbitrary (and arbitrarily many) DFAs on the file, eventually permitting its decryption anyway. The only defense against collusion that we see would be to involve the data owner in the protocol; again, we do not explore this possibility here.

Our protocols do not retrieve the file based on the DFA evaluation results, e.g., in a way that hides from the server what file is being retrieved. However, once the client learns the final state of the DFA evaluation, it can employ various techniques to retrieve the file privately (e.g., [17]). Moreover, some of our motivating scenarios in §1, e.g., malware scans of cloud-resident files by a third party, may not require file retrieval but only that matches be reported to the file owner.

4 A Secure DFA Evaluation Protocol

In this section we present a protocol that meets the goals described in §3. We give the construction in §4.1, and then we define and prove security against server and client adversaries in §4.2 and §4.3, respectively.

4.1 Construction

Let "$\leftarrow$" denote assignment and "$s \stackrel{\$}{\leftarrow} S$" denote the assignment to s of a randomly chosen element of set S. Let κ denote a security parameter.

Encryption Scheme.   Our scheme is built using an additively homomorphic encryption scheme with plaintext space $\mathbb{R}$ where $\langle \mathbb{R}, +_{\mathbb{R}}, \cdot_{\mathbb{R}} \rangle$ denotes a commutative ring. Specifically, an encryption scheme $\mathcal{E}$ includes algorithms Gen, Enc, and Dec where: Gen is a randomized algorithm that on input 1^{κ} outputs a public-key/private-key pair $(pk, sk) \leftarrow \mathsf{Gen}(1^{\kappa})$; Enc is a randomized algorithm that on input public key pk and plaintext $m \in \mathbb{R}$ (where $\mathbb{R}$ can be determined as a function of pk) produces a ciphertext $c \leftarrow \mathsf{Enc}_{pk}(m)$, where $c \in C_{pk}$ and C_{pk} is the ciphertext space determined by pk; and Dec is a deterministic algorithm that on input a private key sk and ciphertext $c \in C_{pk}$ produces a plaintext $m \leftarrow \mathsf{Dec}_{sk}(c)$ where $m \in \mathbb{R}$. In addition, $\mathcal{E}$ supports an operation $+_{pk}$ on ciphertexts such that for any public-key/private-key pair (pk, sk),

$\text{Dec}_{sk}(\text{Enc}_{pk}(m_1) +_{pk} \text{Enc}_{pk}(m_2)) = m_1 +_{\mathbb{R}} m_2$. Using $+_{pk}$, it is possible to implement $\cdot_{pk}$ for which $\text{Dec}_{sk}(m_2 \cdot_{pk} \text{Enc}_{pk}(m_1)) = m_1 \cdot_{\mathbb{R}} m_2$.

We also require $\mathcal{E}$ to support two-party decryption. Specifically, we assume there is an efficient randomized algorithm Share that on input a private key sk outputs shares $(sk_1, sk_2) \leftarrow \text{Share}(sk)$, and that there are efficient deterministic algorithms Dec^1 and Dec^2 such that $\text{Dec}_{sk}(c) = \text{Dec}^2_{sk_2}(c, \text{Dec}^1_{sk_1}(c))$.

An example of an encryption scheme $\mathcal{E}$ that meets the above requirements is due to Paillier [28] with modifications by Damgård and Jurik [10]; we henceforth refer to this scheme as "Pai". In this scheme, the ring $\mathbb{R}$ is $\mathbb{Z}_N$ where $N = pp'$ and p, p' are primes, and the ciphertext space C_{pk} is $\mathbb{Z}^*_{N^2}$.

We use $\sum_{pk}$ to denote summation using $+_{pk}$; $\sum_{\mathbb{R}}$ to denote summation using $+_{\mathbb{R}}$; and $\prod_{\mathbb{R}}$ to denote the product using $\cdot_{\mathbb{R}}$ of a sequence. For any operation op, we use t_{op} to denote the time required to perform op; e.g., t_{Dec} is the time to perform a Dec operation.

Encoding δ in a Bivariate Polynomial over $\mathbb{R}$. A second ingredient for our protocol is a method for encoding a DFA $\langle Q, \Sigma, \delta, q_{\text{init}} \rangle$, and specifically the transition function δ, as a bivariate polynomial $f(x, y)$ over $\mathbb{R}$ where x is the variable representing a DFA state and y is the variable representing an input symbol. That is, if we treat each state $q \in Q$ and each $\sigma \in \Sigma$ as distinct elements of $\mathbb{R}$, then we would like $f(q, \sigma) = \delta(q, \sigma)$. We can achieve this by choosing f to be the interpolation polynomial

$$f(x, y) = \sum_{\sigma \in \Sigma} \left(f_\sigma(x) \cdot_{\mathbb{R}} \Lambda_\sigma(y) \right) \quad \text{where} \quad \Lambda_\sigma(y) = \prod_{\substack{\sigma' \in \Sigma \\ \sigma' \neq \sigma}} \frac{y -_{\mathbb{R}} \sigma'}{\sigma -_{\mathbb{R}} \sigma'} \quad (1)$$

is a Lagrange basis polynomial and $f_\sigma(q) = \delta(q, \sigma)$ for each $q \in Q$. Note that $\Lambda_\sigma(\sigma) = 1$ and $\Lambda_\sigma(\sigma') = 0$ for any $\sigma' \in \Sigma \setminus \{\sigma\}$.

Calculating (1) requires taking multiplicative inverses in $\mathbb{R}$. While not every element of a ring has a multiplicative inverse in the ring, fortunately the ring $\mathbb{Z}_N$ used in Paillier encryption, for example, has negligibly few elements with no inverses, and so there is little risk of encountering an element with no inverse. Using (1), we can calculate coefficients $\langle \lambda_{\sigma j} \rangle_{j \in [m]}$ so that $\Lambda_\sigma(y) = \sum_{j=0}^{m-1} \lambda_{\sigma j} \cdot_{\mathbb{R}} y^j$. For our algorithm descriptions, we encapsulate this calculation in the procedure $\langle \lambda_{\sigma j} \rangle_{\sigma \in \Sigma, j \in [m]} \leftarrow \text{Lagrange}(\Sigma)$.

Each f_σ needed to compute $f(x, y)$ can again be determined as a Lagrange interpolating polynomial and then expressed as $f_\sigma(x) = \sum_{i=0}^{n-1} a_{\sigma i} \cdot_{\mathbb{R}} x^i$. In our pseudocode, we encapsulate this calculation as $\langle a_{\sigma i} \rangle_{\sigma \in \Sigma, i \in [n]} \leftarrow \text{ToPoly}(Q, \Sigma, \delta)$.

Protocol Steps. Our protocol, denoted $\Pi_1(\mathcal{E})$, is shown in Fig. 1. Pseudocode for the client is aligned on the left of the figure and labeled c101–c116; the server pseudocode is on the right of the figure and labeled s101–s112; and messages exchanged between them are aligned in the center and labeled m101–m106. The client receives as input a public key pk under which the file (at the server) is encrypted; a share sk_1 of the private key sk corresponding to pk; another public key pk'; and the DFA $\langle Q, \Sigma, \delta, q_{\text{init}} \rangle$. The server receives as input the public key pk; a share sk_2 of the private key sk; the alphabet Σ; and ciphertexts $c_{kj} \leftarrow \mathsf{Enc}_{pk}((\sigma_k)^j)$ of the k-th file symbol σ_k, for each $j \in [m]$ and for each $k \in [\ell]$ where ℓ denotes the file length in symbols. We assume that sk_1 and sk_2 were generated as $(sk_1, sk_2) \leftarrow \mathsf{Share}(sk)$. Note that no information about sk' (the private key corresponding to pk') is given to either party, and so pk' ciphertexts (ρ created in c107 and c115 and sent in m103 and m105, respectively) are indecipherable and ignored in the protocol. These ciphertexts are included to simplify the proof of privacy against **client** adversaries (§4.3) and can be elided in practice. We do not discuss these values further in this section.

The protocol is structured as matching **for** loops executed by the client (c105–c113) and server (s103–s111). The client begins the k-th loop iteration with an encryption α of the current DFA state after being blinded by a random injection $\pi_1 : Q \to \mathbb{R}$ it chose in the $(k-1)$-th loop at line c109 (or, if $k = 0$, then in line c103), where $\mathsf{Injs}(Q \to \mathbb{R})$ denotes the set of injections from Q to $\mathbb{R}$. The client uses its share sk_1 of sk to create the "partial decryption" β of α (c106) and sends α, β to the server (m103). The server uses its share sk_2 to complete the decryption of α to obtain the blinded state γ (s104). We stress that because γ is blinded by π_1, γ reveals no information about the current DFA state to the **server**. The server then computes, for

```
client(pk, sk_1, pk',                          server(pk, sk_2, Σ,
      ⟨Q, Σ, δ, q_init⟩)                             ⟨c_kj⟩_{k∈[ℓ],j∈[m]})

c101. n ← |Q|, m ← |Σ|            s101. m ← |Σ|
c102. π_0 ← I                     s102. ⟨λ_σj⟩_{σ∈Σ,j∈[m]}
c103. π_1 ←$ Injs(Q → ℝ)                ← Lagrange(Σ)
c104. α ← Enc_pk(π_1(q_init))
                          ⟶  n  ⟶
        m101.
                          ⟵  ℓ  ⟵
        m102.
c105. for k ← 0...ℓ − 1            s103. for k ← 0...ℓ − 1
c106.   β ← Dec^1_{sk_1}(α)
c107.   ρ ← Enc_pk'(π_1)
                        ⟶ α,β,ρ ⟶
        m103.
                                  s104.   γ ← Dec^2_{sk_2}(α, β)
c108.   π_0 ← π_1                  s105.   for σ ∈ Σ
                                                      m−1
c109.   π_1 ←$ Injs(Q → ℝ)        s106.     Ψ_σ ← Σ^pk λ_σj ·_pk c_kj
                                                      j=0
c110.   δ' ← Blind(δ, π_0, π_1)   s107.     for i ∈ [n]
c111.   ⟨a_σi⟩_{σ∈Σ,i∈[n]}        s108.       μ_σi ← γ^i ·_pk Ψ_σ
          ← ToPoly(Q, Σ, δ')      s109.     endfor
                                  s110.   endfor
                    ⟵ ⟨μ_σi⟩_{σ∈Σ,i∈[n]} ⟵
        m104.
                          n−1
c112.   α ← Σ^pk Σ^pk a_σi ·_pk μ_σi
                   σ∈Σ  i=0
c113. endfor                      s111. endfor
c114. β ← Dec^1_{sk_1}(α)
c115. ρ ← Enc_pk'(π_1)
                        ⟶ α,β,ρ ⟶
        m105.
                                  s112. γ* ← Dec^2_{sk_2}(α, β)
                          ⟵ γ* ⟵
        m106.
c116. return π_1^{-1}(γ*)
```

Fig. 1. Protocol $\Pi_1(\mathcal{E})$, described in §4

each $\sigma \in \Sigma$ (s105), a value Ψ_σ such that $\Lambda_\sigma(\sigma_k) = \mathsf{Dec}_{sk}(\Psi_\sigma)$ (s106) by utilizing coefficients $\langle \lambda_{\sigma j} \rangle_{\sigma \in \Sigma, j \in [m]}$ output from Lagrange (s102). The server then returns (in m104) values $\langle \mu_{\sigma i} \rangle_{\sigma \in \Sigma, i \in [n]}$ created so that $\mathsf{Dec}_{sk}(\mu_{\sigma i}) = \gamma^i \cdot_{\mathbb{R}} \Lambda_\sigma(\sigma_k)$ (s108).

Meanwhile, the client selects a new random injection $\pi_1 \xleftarrow{\$} \mathsf{Injs}(Q \to \mathbb{R})$ (c109). The client then constructs a new DFA transition function δ' reflecting the injection it chose in the last round (now denoted π_0, see line c108) and the new injection π_1 it chose for this round. Specifically, it creates a new DFA state transition function δ' defined as $\delta'(q, \sigma) = \pi_1(\delta(\pi_0^{-1}(q), \sigma))$ for all $\sigma \in \Sigma$ and $q \in \pi_0(Q)$ where $\pi_0(Q) = \{\pi_0(q)\}_{q \in Q}$; we denote this step as $\delta' \leftarrow \mathsf{Blind}(\delta, \pi_0, \pi_1)$ in line c110. That is, δ' "undoes" the previous injection π_0, applies δ, and then applies the new injection π_1. The client then interpolates a bivariate polynomial $f(x, y)$ such that $f(q, \sigma) = \delta'(q, \sigma)$ in line c111, using the algorithm described previously. The client then uses these coefficients and $\langle \mu_{\sigma i} \rangle_{\sigma \in \Sigma, i \in [n]}$ sent from the server (message m103) to assemble a ciphertext α of the new DFA state under the injection π_1 (c112).

After ℓ loop iterations, the client interacts with the server once more to decrypt the final state. It sends α and its partial decryption β to the server (m105), for which the server completes the decryption (s112) and returns the result (m106).

Protocol $\Pi_1(\mathcal{E})$ can be modified to return only a binary indication of whether the DFA's final state is an accepting one, if the DFA specifies a set F of accepting states. Specifically, the client can construct a polynomial $\hat{f}(x)$ that evaluates to 1 on states in F and 0 on other states. Then, rather than interacting with the server to decrypt the final state, the client can interact with the server once to evaluate $\hat{f}(x)$ on the (unknown) final state and again to decrypt this result. We omit details here due to space limitations.

For brevity, Fig. 1 omits numerous checks that the client and server should perform to confirm that the values each receives are well-formed. For example, the client should confirm that $\mu_{\sigma i} \in C_{pk}$ for each $\sigma \in \Sigma$ and $i \in [n]$, upon receiving these in m104. The server should similarly confirm the well-formedness of the values it receives.

An Alternative Using Fully Homomorphic Encryption. Our technique of encoding the DFA transition function δ using a bivariate polynomial $f(x, y)$ over $\mathbb{R}$ could also be used with fully homomorphic encryption [14,11] to create a noninteractive protocol. The client could encrypt each coefficient $a_{\sigma i}$ of f under the public key pk and send these ciphertexts to the server, enabling the server to perform computations c112 by itself. At the end, the server could send a half decrypted final state back to the client, who would complete the decryption to obtain the result. This protocol achieves communication costs of $O(nm)$, which is independent of the file length. That said, existing fully homomorphic schemes are far less efficient than additively homomorphic schemes, and so the resulting protocol will be less communication-efficient than $\Pi_1(\mathcal{E})$ for many practical file lengths and DFA sizes.

4.2   Security against Server Attacks

In this section we show that the server, by executing this protocol (even arbitrarily maliciously), gains no advantage in either determining the DFA the client is evaluating or the plaintext of the file in its possession. That is, we show only the *privacy* of the file and DFA inputs against server adversaries. In this section, we are not concerned with showing that a client can detect server misbehavior,

Experiment $\mathbf{Expt}^{\text{s-dfa}}_{\Pi_1(\mathcal{E})}(S_1, S_2)$
  $(pk, sk) \leftarrow \mathsf{Gen}(1^\kappa)$
  $(sk_1, sk_2) \leftarrow \mathsf{Share}(sk)$
  $(pk', sk') \leftarrow \mathsf{Gen}(1^\kappa)$
  $(\ell, \langle \sigma_k \rangle_{k \in [\ell]}, M_0, M_1, \phi) \leftarrow S_1(pk, sk_2)$
  if $M_0.Q \neq M_1.Q$ **or** $M_0.\Sigma \neq M_1.\Sigma$
    then return 0
  $b \xleftarrow{\$} \{0, 1\}$
  $m \leftarrow |M_b.\Sigma|$
  for $k \in [\ell], j \in [m]$
    $c_{kj} \leftarrow \mathsf{Enc}_{pk}((\sigma_k)^j)$
  $b' \leftarrow S_2^{\mathsf{clientOr}(pk, sk_1, pk', M_b)}(\phi, \langle c_{kj} \rangle_{k \in [\ell], j \in [m]})$
  if $b' = b$
    then return 1
    else return 0

Experiment $\mathbf{Expt}^{\text{s-file}}_{\Pi_1(\mathcal{E})}(S_1, S_2)$
  $(pk, sk) \leftarrow \mathsf{Gen}(1^\kappa)$
  $(sk_1, sk_2) \leftarrow \mathsf{Share}(sk)$
  $(pk', sk') \leftarrow \mathsf{Gen}(1^\kappa)$
  $(\ell, \langle \sigma_{0k} \rangle_{k \in [\ell]}, \langle \sigma_{1k} \rangle_{k \in [\ell]}, M, \phi) \leftarrow S_1(pk, sk_2)$

  $b \xleftarrow{\$} \{0, 1\}$
  $m \leftarrow |M.\Sigma|$
  for $k \in [\ell], j \in [m]$
    $c_{kj} \leftarrow \mathsf{Enc}_{pk}((\sigma_{bk})^j)$
  $b' \leftarrow S_2^{\mathsf{clientOr}(pk, sk_1, pk', M)}(\phi, \langle c_{kj} \rangle_{k \in [\ell], j \in [m]})$
  if $b' = b$
    then return 1
    else return 0

(a) Experiment $\mathbf{Expt}^{\text{s-dfa}}_{\Pi_1(\mathcal{E})}$

(b) Experiment $\mathbf{Expt}^{\text{s-file}}_{\Pi_1(\mathcal{E})}$

Fig. 2. Experiments for proving security of $\Pi_1(\mathcal{E})$ against server adversaries

a property often called *correctness*. $\Pi_1(\mathcal{E})$ could be augmented using standard tools to enforce correctness, with an impact on performance; we do not explore this here. Instead, in §6 we describe novel extensions to $\Pi_1(\mathcal{E})$ that could be used to detect server misbehavior.

We formalize our claims against server compromise by defining two separate server adversaries. The first server adversary $S = (S_1, S_2)$ attacks the DFA $M = \langle Q, \Sigma, \delta, q_{\text{init}} \rangle$ held by the client, as described in experiment $\mathbf{Expt}^{\text{s-dfa}}_{\Pi_1(\mathcal{E})}$ in Fig. 2(a). S_1 first generates a file $\langle \sigma_k \rangle_{k \in [\ell]}$ and two DFAs M_0, M_1. (Note that we use, e.g., "$M_0.Q$" and "$M_1.Q$" to disambiguate their state sets.) S_2 then receives the ciphertexts $\langle c_{kj} \rangle_{k \in [\ell], j \in [m]}$ of its file, information ϕ created for it by S_1, and oracle access to $\mathsf{clientOr}(pk, sk_1, pk', M_b)$ for b chosen randomly.

$\mathsf{clientOr}$ responds to queries from S_2 as follows, ignoring malformed queries. The first query (say, consisting of simply "start") causes $\mathsf{clientOr}$ to begin the protocol; $\mathsf{clientOr}$ responds with a message of the form n (i.e., of the form of m101). The second invocation by S_2 must include a single integer ℓ (i.e., of the form of m102); $\mathsf{clientOr}$ responds with a message of the form α, β, ρ, i.e., three values as in m103. The next $\ell - 1$ queries by S_2 must contain nm elements of C_{pk}, i.e., $\langle \mu_{\sigma i} \rangle_{\sigma \in \Sigma, i \in [n]}$ as in m104, to which $\mathsf{clientOr}$ responds with three values as in message m103. The next query to $\mathsf{clientOr}$ again must contain nm elements of C_{pk} as in m104, to which $\mathsf{clientOr}$ responds with three values as in m105. The next (and last) query by S_2 can consist simply of a value in $\mathbb{R}$, as in message m106.

Eventually S_2 outputs a bit b', and $\mathbf{Expt}^{\text{s-dfa}}_{\Pi_1(\mathcal{E})}(S) = 1$ only if $b' = b$. We say the *advantage* of S is $\mathbf{Adv}^{\text{s-dfa}}_{\Pi_1(\mathcal{E})}(S) = 2 \cdot \mathbb{P}\left(\mathbf{Expt}^{\text{s-dfa}}_{\Pi_1(\mathcal{E})}(S) = 1\right) - 1$ and define $\mathbf{Adv}^{\text{s-dfa}}_{\Pi_1(\mathcal{E})}(t, \ell, n, m) = \max_S \mathbf{Adv}^{\text{s-dfa}}_{\Pi_1(\mathcal{E})}(S)$ where the maximum is taken over all adversaries S taking time t and selecting a file of length ℓ and DFAs containing n states and an alphabet of m symbols.

We reduce DFA privacy against server attacks to the IND-CPA [4] security of the encryption scheme. IND-CPA security is defined using the experiment in Fig. 3, in which an adversary U is provided a public key $\hat{pk}$ and access to an oracle $\mathsf{Enc}^{\hat{b}}_{\hat{pk}}(\cdot,\cdot)$ that consistently encrypts either the first of its two inputs (if $\hat{b} = 0$) or the second of those inputs (if $\hat{b} = 1$). Eventually U outputs a guess $\hat{b}'$ at $\hat{b}$, and $\mathbf{Expt}^{\text{ind-cpa}}_{\mathcal{E}}(U) = 1$ only if $\hat{b}' = \hat{b}$. The IND-CPA advantage of U is defined as $\mathbf{Adv}^{\text{ind-cpa}}_{\mathcal{E}}(U) = 2 \cdot \mathbb{P}\left(\mathbf{Expt}^{\text{ind-cpa}}_{\mathcal{E}}(U) = 1\right) - 1$. Then, $\mathbf{Adv}^{\text{ind-cpa}}_{\mathcal{E}}(t, w) = \max_U \mathbf{Adv}^{\text{ind-cpa}}_{\mathcal{E}}(U)$ where the maximum is taken over all adversaries U executing in time t and making w queries to $\mathsf{Enc}^{\hat{b}}_{\hat{pk}}(\cdot,\cdot)$.

Our theorem statements throughout this paper omit terms that are negligible as a function of the security parameter κ. The following theorem is proved in our accompanying technical report [35].

Theorem 1. $\mathbf{Adv}^{\text{s-dfa}}_{\Pi_1(\mathcal{E})}(t, \ell, n, m) \leq 2\mathbf{Adv}^{\text{ind-cpa}}_{\mathcal{E}}(t', \ell+1)$ *for* $t' = t + t_{\mathsf{Gen}} + t_{\mathsf{Share}}$.

The second **server** adversary $S = (S_1, S_2)$ attacks the file ciphertexts $\langle c_{kj}\rangle_{k\in[\ell], j\in[m]}$ as in experiment $\mathbf{Expt}^{\text{s-file}}_{\Pi_1(\mathcal{E})}$ shown in Fig. 2(b). S_1 produces two equal-length plaintext files $\langle \sigma_{0k}\rangle_{k\in[\ell]}$, $\langle \sigma_{1k}\rangle_{k\in[\ell]}$ and a DFA M. S_2 receives the ciphertexts $\langle c_{kj}\rangle_{k\in[\ell], j\in[m]}$ for file $\langle \sigma_{bk}\rangle_{k\in[\ell]}$ where b is chosen randomly. S_2 is also given oracle access to $\mathsf{clientOr}(pk, sk_1, pk', M)$. Eventually S_2 outputs a bit b', and $\mathbf{Expt}^{\text{s-file}}_{\Pi_1(\mathcal{E})}(S) = 1$ iff $b' = b$. We say the *advantage* of S is $\mathbf{Adv}^{\text{s-file}}_{\Pi_1(\mathcal{E})}(S) = 2 \cdot$

Experiment $\mathbf{Expt}^{\text{ind-cpa}}_{\mathcal{E}}(U)$
$(\hat{pk}, \hat{sk}) \leftarrow \mathsf{Gen}(1^{\kappa})$
$\hat{b} \xleftarrow{\$} \{0, 1\}$
$\hat{b}' \leftarrow U^{\mathsf{Enc}^{\hat{b}}_{\hat{pk}}(\cdot,\cdot)}(\hat{pk})$
if $\hat{b}' = \hat{b}$
  then return 1
  else return 0

Fig. 3. $\mathbf{Expt}^{\text{ind-cpa}}_{\mathcal{E}}(U)$

$\mathbb{P}\left(\mathbf{Expt}^{\text{s-file}}_{\Pi_1(\mathcal{E})}(S) = 1\right) - 1$ and then $\mathbf{Adv}^{\text{s-file}}_{\Pi_1(\mathcal{E})}(t, \ell, n, m) = \max_S \mathbf{Adv}^{\text{s-file}}_{\Pi_1(\mathcal{E})}(S)$ where the maximum is taken over all adversaries $S = (S_1, S_2)$ taking time t and producing (from S_1) files of ℓ symbols and a DFA of n states and alphabet of size m. The following theorem is proved in our technical report [35].

Theorem 2. $\mathbf{Adv}^{\text{s-file}}_{\Pi_1(\mathsf{Pai})}(t, \ell, n, m) \leq 2\mathbf{Adv}^{\text{ind-cpa}}_{\mathsf{Pai}}(t', \ell+1) + \mathbf{Adv}^{\text{ind-cpa}}_{\mathsf{Pai}}(t', \ell m)$ *for* $t' = t + t_{\mathsf{Gen}} + t_{\mathsf{Share}}$.

4.3 Security against Client Attacks

In this section we show security of $\Pi_1(\mathcal{E})$ against honest-but-curious **client** adversaries and heuristically justify its security against malicious ones. (We also introduce novel extensions to detect a misbehaving **client** in §6.) Since the **client** has the DFA in its possession, privacy of the DFA against a **client** adversary is not a concern. The proof of security against the **client** therefore is concerned with the privacy of only the file. However, by the nature of what the protocol computes for the **client** — i.e., the final state of a DFA match on the file — the **client** can easily distinguish two files of its choosing simply by running the protocol correctly using a DFA that distinguishes between the two files it chose.

For this reason, we adapt the notion of indistinguishability to apply only to files that produce the same final state for the **client**'s DFA. So, in the experiment

$\mathbf{Expt}^{\texttt{c-file}}_{\Pi_1(\mathcal{E})}$ (Fig. 4) that we use to define file security against client adversaries, the adversary $C = (C_1, C_2)$ succeeds (i.e., $\mathbf{Expt}^{\texttt{c-file}}_{\Pi_1(\mathcal{E})}(C)$ returns 1) only if the two files $\langle \sigma_{0k} \rangle_{k \in [\ell]}$ and $\langle \sigma_{1k} \rangle_{k \in [\ell]}$ output by C_1 both drive the DFA M, also output by C_1, to the same final state (denoted $M(\langle \sigma_{0k} \rangle_{k \in [\ell]}) = M(\langle \sigma_{1k} \rangle_{k \in [\ell]})$).

This caveat aside, the experiment is straightforward: C_1 receives public key pk, private-key share sk_1, and another public key pk', and returns the two ℓ-symbol files (for ℓ of its choosing) $\langle \sigma_{0k} \rangle_{k \in [\ell]}$ and $\langle \sigma_{1k} \rangle_{k \in [\ell]}$ and a DFA M. Depending on how b is then chosen, one of these files is encrypted using pk and then provided to the server, to which C_2 is given oracle access (denoted $\mathsf{serverOr}(pk, sk_2, M.\Sigma, \langle c_{kj} \rangle_{k \in [\ell], j \in [m]}))$.

Adversary C_2 can invoke $\mathsf{serverOr}$ first with a message containing an integer n (i.e., with a message of the form m101), to which $\mathsf{serverOr}$ returns ℓ (m102). C_2 can then invoke $\mathsf{serverOr}$

Experiment $\mathbf{Expt}^{\texttt{c-file}}_{\Pi_1(\mathcal{E})}(C_1, C_2)$
$(pk, sk) \leftarrow \mathsf{Gen}(1^\kappa)$
$(sk_1, sk_2) \leftarrow \mathsf{Share}(sk)$
$(pk', sk') \leftarrow \mathsf{Gen}(1^\kappa)$
$(\ell, \langle \sigma_{0k} \rangle_{k \in [\ell]}, \langle \sigma_{1k} \rangle_{k \in [\ell]}, M, \phi)$
$\qquad\qquad\qquad \leftarrow C_1(pk, sk_1, pk')$
if $M(\langle \sigma_{0k} \rangle_{k \in [\ell]}) \neq M(\langle \sigma_{1k} \rangle_{k \in [\ell]})$
$\quad$ then return 0
$b \xleftarrow{\$} \{0, 1\}$
$m \leftarrow |M.\Sigma|$
for $k \in [\ell], j \in [m]$
$\quad c_{kj} \leftarrow \mathsf{Enc}_{pk}((\sigma_{bk})^j)$
$b' \leftarrow C_2^{\mathsf{serverOr}(pk, sk_2, M.\Sigma, \langle c_{kj} \rangle_{k \in [\ell], j \in [m]})}(\phi)$
if $b' = b$
$\quad$ then return 1
$\quad$ else return 0

Fig. 4. Experiment $\mathbf{Expt}^{\texttt{c-file}}_{\Pi_1(\mathcal{E})}$

up to $\ell + 1$ times. The first ℓ such invocations take the form α, β, ρ and correspond to messages of the form m103. Each such invocation elicits a response $\langle \mu_{\sigma i} \rangle_{\sigma \in \Sigma, i \in [n]}$ (i.e., of the form m104). The last client invocation is of the form α, β, ρ and corresponds to m105. This invocation elicits a response γ^* (i.e., m106). Malformed or extra queries are rejected by $\mathsf{serverOr}$.

As discussed in §1, we show file privacy against *honest-but-curious* client adversaries $C = (C_1, C_2)$, i.e., C_2 invokes $\mathsf{serverOr}$ exactly as $\Pi_1(\mathcal{E})$ prescribes, using DFA M output by C_1. We define the advantage of C to be $\mathbf{hbcAdv}^{\texttt{c-file}}_{\Pi_1(\mathcal{E})}(C) = 2 \cdot \mathbb{P}\left(\mathbf{Expt}^{\texttt{c-file}}_{\Pi_1(\mathcal{E})}(C) = 1\right) - 1$ and $\mathbf{hbcAdv}^{\texttt{c-file}}_{\Pi_1(\mathcal{E})}(t, \ell, n, m) = \max_C \mathbf{Adv}^{\texttt{c-file}}_{\Pi_1(\mathcal{E})}(C)$ where the maximum is taken over honest-but-curious client adversaries C running in total time t and producing files of length ℓ and a DFA of n states over an alphabet of m symbols. Our technical report [35] proves:

Theorem 3. $\mathbf{hbcAdv}^{\texttt{c-file}}_{\Pi_1(\mathsf{Pai})}(t, \ell, n, m) \leq \mathbf{Adv}^{\texttt{ind-cpa}}_{\mathsf{Pai}}(t', \ell m(1 + n))$ *for* $t' = t + t_{\mathsf{Gen}} + (\ell + 1) \cdot t_{\mathsf{Dec}}$.

We have found extending this result to fully malicious client adversaries to be difficult for two reasons. First, $\mathbf{Expt}^{\texttt{c-file}}_{\Pi_1(\mathcal{E})}$ does not make sense for a malicious client, since C_2 is not bound to use the DFA M output by C_1. As such, C_2 can use a different DFA — in particular, one that enables it to distinguish between the files output by C_1. Second, even ignoring the final state γ^* sent back to the client, we have been unable to reduce the ability of the client adversary to distinguish between two files on the basis of m104 messages to breaking the IND-CPA security of $\mathcal{E}$; intuitively, the difficulty derives from the simulator's inability to decrypt α values provided by C_2. (The ciphertext ρ enables the simulator to "track" the plaintext of α in the honest-but-curious case — see the proof of Theorem 3 in our technical report [35] — but ρ might contain useless information in the malicious case.)

Nevertheless, since *only* ciphertexts for which the client does not hold the decryption key are sent to the client in those messages, we are confident in conjecturing that our protocol leaks no information to even a malicious client about the file, beyond what it gains from the protocol output γ^*, assuming $\mathcal{E}$ is IND-CPA secure. Of course, the above proof difficulties for a malicious client could be ameliorated by introducing zero-knowledge proofs to the protocol to enforce correct behavior, but with considerable added expense to the protocol. Instead, in §6 we introduce more novel (albeit still heuristic) approaches to detecting client (or server) misbehavior in our setting.

```
client(pk, sk_1, pk',                    server(pk, sk_2, Σ,
       ⟨Q, Σ, δ, q_init⟩)                        ⟨c_kj⟩_{k∈[ℓ],j∈[m]})

c201. n ← |Q|, m ← |Σ|              s201. m ← |Σ|
c202. π_0 ← I                        s202. ⟨λ_σj⟩_{σ∈Σ,j∈[m]}
c203. π_1 ←$ Injs(Q → ℝ)                   ← Lagrange(Σ)
c204. α ← Enc_pk(π_1(q_init))
                          n
        m201. ─────────────────────────→
                          ℓ
        m202. ←─────────────────────────
c205. for k ← 0...ℓ−1                s203. for k ← 0...ℓ−1
c206.   β ← Dec¹_{sk_1}(α)
c207.   ρ ← Enc_{pk'}(π_1)
                       α,β,ρ
        m203. ─────────────────────────→
                                     s204. γ ← Dec²_{sk_2}(α, β)
c208.   π_0 ← π_1                     s205. for σ ∈ Σ
                                                        m−1
c209.   π_1 ←$ Injs(Q → ℝ)           s206.   Ψ_σ ← Σ^{pk}_{j=0} λ_σj ·_pk c_kj
c210.   δ' ← Blind(δ, π_0, π_1)      s207. endfor
c211.   ⟨a_{σi}⟩_{σ∈Σ,i∈[n]}          s208. r ←$ ℝ
          ← ToPoly(Q, Σ, δ')          s209. γ ← γ +_ℝ r
                                     s210. for i ∈ [n]
                                     s211.   ν_i ← Enc_pk(r^i)
                                     s212. endfor
                   γ,⟨Ψ_σ⟩_{σ∈Σ},⟨ν_i⟩_{i∈[n]}
        m204. ←─────────────────────────────
c212.   for σ ∈ Σ, i ∈ [n]
c213.     μ_{σi} ← γ^i ·_pk Ψ_σ
c214.   endfor
c215.   ⟨â'_{σi}⟩_{σ∈Σ,i∈[n]}
          ← Shift(⟨ν_i⟩_{i∈[n]},
                  ⟨a_{σi}⟩_{σ∈Σ,i∈[n]})
                              n−1
c216.   α ← Σ^{pk}_{σ∈Σ} Σ^{pk}_{i=0} â'_{σi} ⊙_pk μ_{σi}
c217. endfor                         s213. endfor
c218. β ← Dec¹_{sk_1}(α)
c219. ρ ← Enc_{pk'}(π_1)
                       α,β,ρ
        m205. ─────────────────────────→
                                     s214. γ* ← Dec²_{sk_2}(α, β)
                          γ*
        m206. ←─────────────────────────
c220. return π_1^{-1}(γ*)
```

Fig. 5. Protocol $\Pi_2(\mathcal{E})$, described in §5

5   An Alternative Protocol

The second protocol we present has the same goals as $\Pi_1(\mathcal{E})$ but incurs less communication costs. Specifically, whereas the communication cost of $\Pi_1(\mathcal{E})$ is $O(\kappa \ell n m)$ bits, the protocol we present in this section, called $\Pi_2(\mathcal{E})$, sends only $O(\kappa \ell (n+m))$ bits. $\Pi_2(\mathcal{E})$ accomplishes this in part by exploiting a cryptosystem that is additively homomorphic and that offers the ability to homomorphically "multiply" ciphertexts once. That is, the cryptosystem supports a new operator $\odot_{pk}$ that satisfies $\mathsf{Dec}_{sk}(\mathsf{Enc}_{pk}(m_1) \odot_{pk} \mathsf{Enc}_{pk}(m_2)) = m_1 \cdot_{\mathbb{R}} m_2$, but the result of a $\odot_{pk}$ operation (or any other ciphertext resulting from $+_{pk}$ or $\cdot_{pk}$ operations in which it is used) cannot be used in a $\odot_{pk}$ operation. After we present our protocol, we will discuss various options for instantiating this encryption scheme within it.

Protocol $\Pi_2(\mathcal{E})$ is shown in Fig. 5. Note that the input arguments to both the client and the server are identical to those in $\Pi_1(\mathcal{E})$. The structure of the protocol is also very similar to $\Pi_1(\mathcal{E})$, with the only differences being in how the server performs each loop iteration (s204–s212) and how the client forms the new encrypted DFA state α (c212–c216). We now summarize the primary innovations represented by these differences.

After the k-th m203 message, the server constructs an encryption Ψ_σ of $\Lambda_\sigma(\sigma_k)$ (s206). Rather than computing $\mu_{\sigma i} \leftarrow \gamma^i \cdot_{pk} \Psi_\sigma$, however, the server sends $\langle \Psi_\sigma \rangle_{\sigma \in \Sigma}$ to the client in m204. Each $\mu_{\sigma i}$ is then built at the client, instead (c212–c214), which is the main reason we get better communication efficiency.

Since each $\mu_{\sigma i}$ is built at the client, the server must send γ in m204. To hide the current DFA state from the client, the server blinds γ with a random $r \in \mathbb{R}$ (s208–s209) before returning it. So, the client needs to accommodate r without knowing it when performing the DFA state transition. The client cannot perform the polynomial evaluation using the $f(x, y)$ it constructed (c211) on the $\langle \mu_{\sigma i} \rangle_{\sigma \in \Sigma, i \in [n]}$ as in $\Pi_1(\mathcal{E})$ since $f(x, y)$ is designed for an input $q \in \pi_0(Q)$, not $q + r$. To overcome this, the client constructs a shifted polynomial $f'(x, y)$ such that $f'(q + r, \sigma) \doteq f(q, \sigma)$ for all $q \in \pi_0(Q)$, and so $f'(x, y)$ will correctly translate the blinded input to the next DFA state. What is left to describe is how to construct $f'(x, y)$.

If we set $f'(x, y) = \sum_{\sigma \in \Sigma}^{\mathbb{R}} (f'_\sigma(x) \cdot_{\mathbb{R}} \Lambda_\sigma(y))$ where $f'_\sigma(x) = \sum_{i=0}^{n-1} a'_{\sigma i} \cdot_{\mathbb{R}} x^i$, then it suffices if $f'_\sigma(x +_{\mathbb{R}} r) = f_\sigma(x)$ for all $\sigma \in \Sigma$. Note that

$$f_\sigma(x -_{\mathbb{R}} r) = \sum_{i=0}^{n-1}{}^{\mathbb{R}} a_{\sigma i} \cdot_{\mathbb{R}} (x -_{\mathbb{R}} r)^i = \sum_{i=0}^{n-1}{}^{\mathbb{R}} a_{\sigma i} \cdot_{\mathbb{R}} \sum_{i'=0}^{i}{}^{\mathbb{R}} \binom{i}{i'} \cdot_{\mathbb{R}} x^{i-i'} \cdot_{\mathbb{R}} (-_{\mathbb{R}} r)^{i'} \quad (2)$$

$$= \sum_{i=0}^{n-1}{}^{\mathbb{R}} \left(\sum_{i'=0}^{n-1-i}{}^{\mathbb{R}} a_{\sigma(i+i')} \cdot_{\mathbb{R}} \binom{i+i'}{i'} \cdot_{\mathbb{R}} (-_{\mathbb{R}} r)^{i'} \right) \cdot_{\mathbb{R}} x^i$$

where (2) follows from the binomial theorem. Therefore, setting

$$a'_{\sigma i} \leftarrow \sum_{i'=0}^{n-1-i}{}^{\mathbb{R}} a_{\sigma(i+i')} \cdot_{\mathbb{R}} \binom{i+i'}{i'} \cdot_{\mathbb{R}} (-_{\mathbb{R}} 1)^{i'} \cdot_{\mathbb{R}} r^{i'} \quad (3)$$

ensures $f'_\sigma(x +_{\mathbb{R}} r) = f_\sigma(x)$ and so $f'(x +_{\mathbb{R}} r, \sigma) = f(x, \sigma)$.

The client knows all the terms in (3) except r^i. That is exactly the reason the server sends in m204 the ciphertext ν_i of r^i, for each $i \in [n]$ (see s211). The client can then calculate a ciphertext $\hat{a}'_{\sigma i}$ of the coefficient of x^i in f'_σ by using the additive homomorphic property of the encryption scheme:

$$\hat{a}'_{\sigma i} \leftarrow \sum_{i'=0}^{n-1-i}{}^{pk} \left(a_{\sigma(i+i')} \cdot_{\mathbb{R}} \binom{i+i'}{i'} \cdot_{\mathbb{R}} (-_{\mathbb{R}} 1)^{i'} \right) \cdot_{pk} \nu_{i'} \quad (4)$$

In our pseudocode, the calculations (4) are encapsulated within the operation $\langle \hat{a}'_{\sigma i} \rangle_{\sigma \in \Sigma, i \in [n]} \leftarrow \mathsf{Shift}(\langle \nu_i \rangle_{i \in [n]}, \langle a_{\sigma i} \rangle_{\sigma \in \Sigma, i \in [n]})$ on line c215.

After the client obtains $\langle \hat{a}'_{\sigma i} \rangle_{\sigma \in \Sigma, i \in [n]}$ and $\langle \mu_{\sigma i} \rangle_{\sigma \in \Sigma, i \in [n]}$, it performs polynomial evaluation at step c216 to assemble the ciphertext of the next DFA state by taking advantage of the one multiplication homomorphism of the cryptosystem. This is where the additional homomorphism helps to achieve much better communication complexity.

The privacy of the file and DFA from server adversaries and the privacy of the file from client adversaries can be proved for $\Pi_2(\mathcal{E})$ very similarly to how they are proved for $\Pi_1(\mathcal{E})$. In fact, Theorems 1–3 hold for $\Pi_2(\mathcal{E})$ unchanged, once instantiated with a suitable encryption scheme $\mathcal{E}$. That said, certain choices of $\mathcal{E}$ can require that the protocol be adapted, as discussed below.

Instantiating $\mathcal{E}$. Protocol $\Pi_2(\mathcal{E})$ requires an additively homomorphic encryption scheme $\mathcal{E}$ that also supports the "one time" homomorphic multiplication operator $\odot_{pk}$. Perhaps the most well-known such cryptosystem is due to Boneh, Goh and Nissim [8], and moreover, this cryptosystem also supports two-party decryption with a cost comparable to regular decryption [8]. The primary difficulty in instantiating $\mathcal{E}$ with this cryptosystem, however, is that decryption — and specifically in $\Pi_2(\mathcal{E})$, the operation $\mathsf{Dec}^2_{sk_2}$ — requires computing a discrete logarithm in a large group, which is generally intractable. That said, if the ciphertext is known to encode one of a small number of possible plaintexts, then $\mathsf{Dec}^2_{sk_2}$ can be adapted to test the ciphertext for each of these plaintexts efficiently. As such, to adapt $\Pi_2(\mathcal{E})$ to employ this cryptosystem, we can augment messages m203 and m205 with $\pi_1(Q)$ (listed in random order), for the injection π_1 at the time the message is sent. This would permit the server to perform $\mathsf{Dec}^2_{sk_2}(\alpha, \beta)$ in lines s204, s214 by testing for these n possible plaintexts. It does, however, have the unfortunate side effect of enabling our proofs for the analogs of Theorems 1 and 2 for $\Pi_2(\mathcal{E})$ to go through only for honest-but-curious server adversaries. $\Pi_2(\mathcal{E})$ instantiated in this way still appears to be secure even against malicious server adversaries, though at this point we can claim this only heuristically.

Two other possibilities for instantiating $\mathcal{E}$ in $\Pi_2(\mathcal{E})$ are due to Gentry, Halevi and Vaikuntanathan [16][2] and Lauter, Naehrig, and Vaikuntanathan [25]. The primary challenge posed by these cryptosystems is that two-party decryption algorithms for them have not been investigated. Each of these schemes is amenable to sharing its private key securely, after which decryption can be performed using generic two-party computation [36,3]. These instantiations retain $\Pi_2(\mathcal{E})$'s provable security against malicious server adversaries (i.e., the analogs of Theorems 1 and 2), but $\Pi_2(\mathcal{E})$ instantiated this way may be less cost-efficient than $\Pi_1(\mathsf{Pai})$ for many values of n and m.[3] Of course, customized two-party decryption algo-

---

[2] Because we require the plaintext ring to be commutative, we would restrict the plaintext space of the Gentry et al. cryptosystem to diagonal square matrices, versus the arbitrary square matrices over which it is defined.

[3] For example, for the Gentry et al. scheme, a "garbled" arithmetic circuit [3] for secure two-party decryption using additively shared keys would be of size $O(\kappa^6 \log^5(n+m))$ bits.

rithms for these cryptosystems could restore the efficiency of $\Pi_2(\mathcal{E})$, suggesting a useful open problem for the community.

6   Heuristics to Detect Misbehavior

In this section we describe simple extensions to our protocols to detect client or server misbehavior. The detection ability offered by these techniques is only heuristic, but they provide a practical deterrent to misbehavior and, at least as importantly, highlight possibilities outside standard techniques (zero-knowledge proofs) that might be brought to bear to detect misbehavior in data outsourcing situations.

Detecting server Misbehavior.   We showed in §4.2 that both the file privacy and the client's DFA privacy are protected against an arbitrarily malicious server. That said, a malicious server could cause the protocol to return an incorrect result by undetectably executing the protocol incorrectly. Here we describe a defense that, while offering weak guarantees, gives insight into new opportunities provided in the cloud outsourcing setting studied in this paper.

The central idea is that in addition to the authentic encrypted file, the data owner also stores at the server (i) another "decoy" encrypted file of the same length as the authentic file and (ii) the plaintext of the decoy file, digitally signed by the data owner. However, the server is not told which one of the two encrypted files is the decoy. When a client wants to evaluate a DFA M on the (authentic) file, it executes two instances of the protocol in parallel with the server on each of the two encrypted files, while also retrieving (and authenticating, by its digital signature) the plaintext of the decoy file. If the client's DFA when applied to the plaintext of the decoy file evaluates to state q, then the client checks that at least one of the two protocol executions results in q. If neither outcome is q, then it detects that the server has behaved incorrectly. (Of course, if the client divulges when it has detected the server misbehaving, then this might enable the server to infer which of the encrypted files is the decoy, though the client could nevertheless report the misbehavior to the data owner outside the view of the server.)

A malicious server could try to guess which file is the decoy and execute the protocol faithfully on that file, while misbehaving on the other one to alter the result. Obviously the chance it guesses correctly is $\frac{1}{2}$. A server could also misbehave for both files, hoping that one of the protocol executions results in the correct final state for the decoy file. The probability of succeeding in this attack is a function of the decoy file and of the specific DFA that the client is evaluating. To improve the probability of detecting a misbehaving server, the client could also create more DFA queries to evaluate on both files. Moreover, additional decoy files could be stored at the server to increase the chance that a misbehaving server is detected.

Detecting client Misbehavior.   A similar but slightly more involved technique could be used to heuristically detect client misbehavior in our protocols. In this technique, at the beginning of the protocol in which the client will use DFA $\langle Q,\ \Sigma,\ \delta,\ q_{\text{init}} \rangle$, the server creates and sends to the client another DFA $\langle Q,\ \Sigma',$

δ', $q_{\text{init}}\rangle$ where $\Sigma' \cap \Sigma = \emptyset$, i.e., another DFA with the same states and the same initial state but a different (and nonoverlapping) alphabet. Note that to create this DFA, the server need only know Q and q_{init}, which in the absence of δ reveal nothing about the pattern for which the client is searching (aside from the number n, which is conveyed to the server in the protocol already). The client then executes the protocol using the combined DFA $\langle Q, \Sigma \cup \Sigma', \delta \cup \delta', q_{\text{init}}\rangle$.[4] As above, the client runs two instances of the protocol in parallel: the server uses the authentic file in one instance; in the other, it creates and uses another file of the same length but consisting of characters in Σ'. After the protocol completes, the client sends the final states back to the server, which checks to be sure that the pair of final states include the result of applying $\langle Q, \Sigma', \delta', q_{\text{init}}\rangle$ to the file it created before telling the client which of the pair of states is the correct result.[5]

This technique for detecting client misbehavior relies on the inability of the client to detect which of the two files consists of elements of Σ and which consists of elements of Σ'— a property that we argued heuristically in §4.3 holds against a malicious client. It also depends on the file and DFA created by the server; as in the defense against server misbehavior above, this can be strengthened with multiple DFAs and files.

7   Conclusion

With the growth of cloud storage, it is imperative to develop efficient techniques for enabling the same sorts of third-party access to cloud-resident files that is commonplace today for privately stored files — e.g., malware scans or searches by authorized partners. Encryption of cloud-resident files, however, hinders these sorts of third-party access.

In this paper, we have developed protocols for enabling DFA evaluation on encrypted files by third parties authorized by the file owner. Our protocols provably protect the privacy of the DFA from an arbitrarily malicious server holding the ciphertext file, as well as the privacy of the file from the server and from an honest-but-curious client performing the DFA evaluation (and even from an arbitrarily malicious client, heuristically). Our protocols employ additively homomorphic cryptosystems or small extensions thereof, for which practical implementations exist. The costs of our protocols in terms of storage, communication and computation suggest that they are practical for many domains, particularly ones where files consist of symbols from a limited alphabet, and are more practical than protocols that would result from applying general private two-party computation or fully homomorphic encryption to this problem.

---

[4] Because doing so requires the server to hold ciphertexts $\langle c_{kj}\rangle_{k\in[\ell], j\in[|\Sigma|+|\Sigma'|]\setminus[|\Sigma|]}$, the data owner must additionally provide these ciphertexts when it stores the file.

[5] Divulging the final states to the server reveals minimal information about the pattern for which the client was searching (assuming the elements of Q are encoded as random elements of $\mathbb{R}$), specifically whether the final state was q_{init}. Even this leakage can be avoided by designing the DFA so it never returns to q_{init}.

Acknowledgments. We are grateful to Dan Boneh for helpful clarifications about the Boneh-Goh-Nissim cryptosystem [8]. This research was supported in part by NSF award 0910483 and by a gift from NEC.

References

1. GenBank, http://www.ncbi.nlm.nih.gov/genbank/
2. United Kingdom National DNA Database,
   http://www.npia.police.uk/en/8934.htm
3. Applebaum, B., Ishai, Y., Kushilevitz, E.: How to garble arithmetic circuits. In: 52nd IEEE Symposium on Foundations of Computer Science (2011)
4. Bellare, M., Desai, A., Pointcheval, D., Rogaway, P.: Relations among Notions of Security for Public-Key Encryption Schemes. In: Krawczyk, H. (ed.) CRYPTO 1998. LNCS, vol. 1462, p. 26. Springer, Heidelberg (1998)
5. Ben-David, A., Nisan, N., Pinkas, B.: FairplayMP: A system for secure multi-party computation. In: 15th ACM Conference on Computer and Communications Security (2008)
6. Betel, D., Hogue, C.: Kangaroo – a pattern-matching program for biological sequences. BMC Bioinformatics 3 (2002)
7. Blanton, M., Aliasgari, M.: Secure Outsourcing of DNA Searching via Finite Automata. In: Foresti, S., Jajodia, S. (eds.) Data and Applications Security and Privacy XXIV. LNCS, vol. 6166, pp. 49–64. Springer, Heidelberg (2010)
8. Boneh, D., Goh, E.J., Nissim, K.: Evaluating 2-DNF formulas on ciphertexts. In: Kilian, J. (ed.) TCC 2005. LNCS, vol. 3378, pp. 325–341. Springer, Heidelberg (2005)
9. Choi, S.G., Elbaz, A., Juels, A., Malkin, T., Yung, M.: Two-Party Computing with Encrypted Data. In: Kurosawa, K. (ed.) ASIACRYPT 2007. LNCS, vol. 4833, pp. 298–314. Springer, Heidelberg (2007)
10. Damgård, I., Jurik, M.: A Generalisation, a Simplification and Some Applications of Paillier's Probabilistic Public-Key System. In: Kim, K.-c. (ed.) PKC 2001. LNCS, vol. 1992. Springer, Heidelberg (2001)
11. van Dijk, M., Gentry, C., Halevi, S., Vaikuntanathan, V.: Fully Homomorphic Encryption over the Integers. In: Gilbert, H. (ed.) EUROCRYPT 2010. LNCS, vol. 6110, pp. 24–43. Springer, Heidelberg (2010)
12. Frikken, K.B.: Practical Private DNA String Searching and Matching through Efficient Oblivious Automata Evaluation. In: Gudes, E., Vaidya, J. (eds.) Data and Applications Security XXIII. LNCS, vol. 5645, pp. 81–94. Springer, Heidelberg (2009)
13. Gennaro, R., Hazay, C., Sorensen, J.S.: Text Search Protocols with Simulation Based Security. In: Nguyen, P.Q., Pointcheval, D. (eds.) PKC 2010. LNCS, vol. 6056, pp. 332–350. Springer, Heidelberg (2010)
14. Gentry, C.: Fully homomorphic encryption using ideal lattices. In: 41st ACM Symposium on Theory of Computing (2009)
15. Gentry, C., Halevi, S.: Implementing Gentry's Fully-Homomorphic Encryption Scheme. In: Paterson, K.G. (ed.) EUROCRYPT 2011. LNCS, vol. 6632, pp. 129–148. Springer, Heidelberg (2011)
16. Gentry, C., Halevi, S., Vaikuntanathan, V.: A Simple BGN-Type Cryptosystem from LWE. In: Gilbert, H. (ed.) EUROCRYPT 2010. LNCS, vol. 6110, pp. 506–522. Springer, Heidelberg (2010)
17. Gentry, C., Ramzan, Z.: Single-Database Private Information Retrieval with Constant Communication Rate. In: Caires, L., Italiano, G.F., Monteiro, L., Palamidessi, C., Yung, M. (eds.) ICALP 2005. LNCS, vol. 3580, pp. 803–815. Springer, Heidelberg (2005)

18. Goldreich, O., Micali, S., Wigderson, A.: How to play any mental game. In: 19th ACM Symposium on Theory of Computing (1987)
19. Hazay, C., Lindell, Y.: Efficient protocols for set intersection and pattern matching with security against malicious and covert adversaries. Journal of Cryptology 23(3) (2010)
20. Hazay, C., Toft, T.: Computationally Secure Pattern Matching in the Presence of Malicious Adversaries. In: Abe, M. (ed.) ASIACRYPT 2010. LNCS, vol. 6477, pp. 195–212. Springer, Heidelberg (2010)
21. Ishai, Y., Paskin, A.: Evaluating Branching Programs on Encrypted Data. In: Vadhan, S.P. (ed.) TCC 2007. LNCS, vol. 4392, pp. 575–594. Springer, Heidelberg (2007)
22. Jha, S., Kruger, L., Shmatikov, V.: Towards practical privacy for genomic computation. In: 29th IEEE Symposium on Security and Privacy (2008)
23. Katz, J., Malka, L.: Secure text processing with applications to private DNA matching. In: 17th ACM Conference on Computer and Communications Security (2010)
24. Kojm, T.: ClamAV, http://www.clamav.net
25. Lauter, K., Naehrig, M., Vaikuntanathan, V.: Can homomorphic encryption be practical? In: 3rd ACM Workshop on Cloud Computing Security (October 2011)
26. Malkhi, D., Nisan, N., Pinkas, B., Sella, Y.: Fairplay – a secure two-party computation system. In: 13th USENIX Security Symposium (August 2004)
27. Mohassel, P., Niksefat, S., Sadeghian, S., Sadeghiyan, B.: An Efficient Protocol for Oblivious DFA Evaluation and Applications. In: Dunkelman, O. (ed.) CT-RSA 2012. LNCS, vol. 7178, pp. 398–415. Springer, Heidelberg (2012)
28. Paillier, P.: Public-Key Cryptosystems Based on Composite Degree Residuosity Classes. In: Stern, J. (ed.) EUROCRYPT 1999. LNCS, vol. 1592, p. 223. Springer, Heidelberg (1999)
29. Pinkas, B., Schneider, T., Smart, N., Williams, S.: Secure Two-Party Computation Is Practical. In: Matsui, M. (ed.) ASIACRYPT 2009. LNCS, vol. 5912, pp. 250–267. Springer, Heidelberg (2009)
30. Rivest, R., Adleman, L., Dertouzos, M.: On data banks and privacy homomorphisms. Foundations of Secure Computation (1978)
31. Roesch, M.: Snort – lightweight intrusion detection for networks. In: 13th USENIX Conference on System Administration (1999)
32. Smart, N.P., Vercauteren, F.: Fully Homomorphic Encryption with Relatively Small Key and Ciphertext Sizes. In: Nguyen, P.Q., Pointcheval, D. (eds.) PKC 2010. LNCS, vol. 6056, pp. 420–443. Springer, Heidelberg (2010)
33. Stehlé, D., Steinfeld, R.: Faster Fully Homomorphic Encryption. In: Abe, M. (ed.) ASIACRYPT 2010. LNCS, vol. 6477, pp. 377–394. Springer, Heidelberg (2010)
34. Troncoso-Pastoriza, J.R., Katzenbeisser, S., Celik, M.: Privacy preserving error resilient DNA searching through oblivious automata. In: 14th ACM Conference on Computer and Communications Security (2007)
35. Wei, L., Reiter, M.K.: Third-party DFA evaluation on encrypted files. Tech. Rep. TR11-005, Department of Computer Science, University of North Carolina at Chapel Hill (2011)
36. Yao, A.C.: Protocols for secure computations. In: 23rd IEEE Symposium on Foundations of Computer Science (1982)
37. Zhuge, J., Holz, T., Song, C., Guo, J., Han, X., Zou, W.: Studying malicious websites and the underground economy on the Chinese web. In: Workshop on the Economics of Information Security (June 2008)

New Algorithms for Secure Outsourcing of Modular Exponentiations

Xiaofeng Chen[1], Jin Li[2], Jianfeng Ma[3], Qiang Tang[4], and Wenjing Lou[5]

[1] State Key Laboratory of Integrated Service Networks (ISN),
Xidian University, Xi'an 710071, P.R. China
xfchen@xidian.edu.cn
[2] School of Computer Science and Educational Software,
Guangzhou University, Guangzhou 510006, P.R. China
jinli71@gmail.com
[3] School of Computer Science and Technology,
Xidian University, Xi'an 710071, P.R. China
jfma@mail.xidian.edu.cn
[4] APSIA Group, SnT, University of Luxembourg,
6, rue Richard Coudenhove-Kalergi, L-1359 Luxembourg
tonyrhul@gmail.com
[5] Department of Computer Science,
Virginia Polytechnic Institute and State University, USA
wjlou@vt.edu

Abstract. Modular exponentiations have been considered the most expensive operation in discrete-logarithm based cryptographic protocols. In this paper, we propose a new secure outsourcing algorithm for exponentiation modular a prime in the one-malicious model. Compared with the state-of-the-art algorithm [33], the proposed algorithm is superior in both efficiency and checkability. We then utilize this algorithm as a subroutine to achieve outsource-secure Cramer-Shoup encryptions and Schnorr signatures. Besides, we propose the first outsource-secure and efficient algorithm for simultaneous modular exponentiations. Moreover, we prove that both the algorithms can achieve the desired security notions.

Keywords: Cloud computing, Outsource-secure algorithms, Modular exponentiation.

1 Introduction

Cloud computing, the long-standing vision of computing as a utility, enables convenient and on-demand network access to a centralized pool of configurable computing resources. One of the most attractive benefits of the cloud computing is the so-called outsourcing paradigm, where the resource-constraint devices can outsource their large computation workloads to the cloud servers in a pay-per-use manner. As a result, the enterprises can avoid large capital outlays in hardware/software deployment and maintenance.

S. Foresti, M. Yung, and F. Martinelli (Eds.): ESORICS 2012, LNCS 7459, pp. 541–556, 2012.
© Springer-Verlag Berlin Heidelberg 2012

Despite the tremendous benefits, outsourcing computation also inevitably involves in some new security concerns and challenges. Firstly, the cloud servers are not (fully) trusted. Actually, it is impossible to find a trusted server for all outsourcers in cloud paradigm. On the other hand, the computation tasks often contain some sensitive information that should not be exposed to the cloud servers. Therefore, the first security challenge is the *secrecy* of the outsourcing computation: the cloud servers should not learn anything about what it is actually computing (including the *secret* inputs and the outputs). We argue that the encryption can only provide a partial solution to this problem since it is very difficult to perform meaningful computations over the encrypted data. Secondly, the semi-trusted cloud servers may return an invalid result. For example, the servers might contain a software bug that will fail on a constant number of invocation. Moreover, the servers might decrease the amount of the computation due to financial incentives and then return a computationally indistinguishable (invalid) result. Therefore, the second security challenge is the *checkability* of the outsourcing computation: the outsourcer should have the ability to detect any failures if the cloud servers misbehave. Trivially, the test procedure should never be involved in some other complicated computations since the computationally limited devices such as RFID tags or smartcard may be incapable to accomplish the test. At the very least, it must be *far more* efficient than accomplishing the computation task itself (recall the motivation for outsourcing computations).

The problem of secure outsourcing expensive computations has been well studied in the cryptography community. Chaum and Pedersen [17] firstly introduced the idea of "wallets with observers" that allows a piece of hardware installed on the client's device to carry out some computations for each transaction. Golle and Mironov [31] first introduced the concept of ringers to elegantly solve the problem of verifying computation completion for the "inversion of one-way function" class of outsourcing computations. Hohenberger and Lysyanskaya [33] presented the security model for outsourcing cryptographic computations, and proposed the first outsource-secure algorithm for modular exponentiations.

Our Contribution. In this paper, we propose a new secure outsourcing algorithm of modular exponentiation in the one-malicious model. To the best of our knowledge, it seems that the proposed algorithm is the second one for exponentiation modular a prime. Compared with the state-of-the-art algorithm [33], the proposed algorithm is superior in both efficiency and checkability. Similar to [33], we also utilize this algorithm as a subroutine to achieve outsource-secure Cramer-Shoup encryptions and Schnorr signatures. Another main contribution of this paper is the first outsource-secure and efficient algorithm for *simultaneous* modular exponentiations, which efficiency is (surprisingly) comparable to that of outsourcing only *one* modular exponentiation in [33].

1.1   Related Work

Abadi et al. [2] proved the impossibility of secure outsourcing an exponential computation while locally doing only polynomial time work. Therefore, it is meaningful only to consider outsourcing expensive polynomial time computations. The theoretical computer science community has devoted considerable attention to the problem of how to securely outsource different kinds of expensive computations. Atallah et al. [3] presented a framework for secure outsourcing of scientific computations such as matrix multiplications and quadrature. However, the solution used the disguise technique and thus allowed leakage of private information. Atallah and Li [4] investigated the problem of computing the edit distance between two sequences and presented an efficient protocol to securely outsource sequence comparisons to two servers. Benjamin and Atallah [8] addressed the problem of secure outsourcing for widely applicable linear algebra computations. However, the proposed protocols required the expensive operations of homomorphic encryptions. Atallah and Frikken [1] further studied this problem and gave improved protocols based on the so-called weak secret hiding assumption. Recently, Wang et al. [45] presented efficient mechanisms for secure outsourcing of linear programming computations.

In the cryptographic community, there are also plenty of research work on the securely outsourcing computations. In 1992, Chaum and Pedersen [17] firstly introduced the notion of wallets with observers, a piece of secure hardware installed on the client's computer to perform some expensive computations. Hohenberger and Lysyanskaya [33] proposed the first outsource-secure algorithm for modular exponentiations based on the two previous approaches of precomputation [15,24,40,42] and server-aided computation [10,29,39,46].

Since the servers (or workers) are not trusted by the outsourcers, Golle and Mironov [31] first introduced the concept of ringers to solve the trust problem of verifying computation completion. The following researchers focused on the other trust problem of retrieving payments [7,19,20,43]. Besides, Gennaro et al. [27] first formalized the notion of verifiable computation to solve the problem of verifiably outsourcing the computation of an arbitrary functions, which has attracted the attention of plenty of researchers [11,13,14,28,30,34,35,38]. Gennaro et al. [27] also proposed a protocol that allowed the outsourcer to efficiently verify the outputs of the computations with a computationally sound, *non-interactive* proof (instead of interactive ones). Benabbas et al. [12] presented the first practical verifiable computation scheme for high degree polynomial functions based on the approach of [27]. In 2011, Green et al. [26] proposed new methods for efficiently and securely outsourcing decryption of attribute-based encryption (ABE) ciphertexts. Based on this work, Parno et al. [41] showed a construction of a multi-function verifiable computation scheme.

1.2 Organization

The rest of the paper is organized as follows: Some security definitions for outsourcing computation are given in Section 2. The proposed new outsource-secure modular exponentiations algorithm and its security analysis are given in Section 3. The proposed outsource-secure Cramer-Shoup encryptions and Schnorr signatures are given in Section 4. The secure and efficient outsourcing algorithm for simultaneous modular exponentiations is given in Section 5. Finally, conclusions will be made in Section 6.

2   Definition of Security

Informally, we say that T securely outsources some work to U, and (T, U) is an *outsource-secure* implementation of a cryptographic algorithm Alg if (1) T and U implement Alg, i.e., Alg $= T^U$ and (2) suppose that T is given oracle access to an adversary U' (instead of U) that records all of its computation over time and tries to act maliciously, U' cannot learn anything interesting about the input and output of $T^{U'}$. In the following, we introduce the formal definitions for secure outsourcing of a cryptographic algorithm [33].

Definition 1. *(Algorithm with outsource-I/O) An algorithm Alg obeys the outsource input/output specification if it takes five inputs, and produces three outputs. The first three inputs are generated by an honest party, and are classified by how much the adversary $A = (E, U')$ knows about them, where E is the adversarial environment that submits adversarially chosen inputs to Alg, and U' is the adversarial software operating in place of oracle U. The first input is call the honest, secret input, which is unknown to both E and U'; the second is called the honest, protected input, which may be known by E, but is protected from U'; and the third is called the honest, unprotected input, which may be known by both E and U. In addition, there are two adversarially-chosen inputs generated by the environment E: the adversarial, protected input, which is known to E, but protected from U'; and the adversarial, unprotected input, which may be known by E and U. Similarly, the first output called secret is unknown to both E and U'; the second is protected, which may be known to E, but not U'; and the third is unprotected, which may be known by both parties of A.*

The following definition of outsource-security ensures that the malicious environment E cannot gain any knowledge of the secret inputs and outputs of T^U, even if T uses the malicious software U' written by E.

Definition 2. *(Outsource-security) Let Alg be an algorithm with outsource I/O. A pair of algorithms (T, U) is said to be an outsource-secure implementation of Alg if:*

1. *Correctness: T^U is a correct implementation of Alg.*
2. *Security: For all probabilistic polynomial-time adversaries $A = (E, U')$, there exist probabilistic expected polynomial-time simulators (S_1, S_2) such that the following pairs of random variables are computationally indistinguishable.*
   - *Pair One.* $\text{EVIEW}_{\text{real}} \sim \text{EVIEW}_{\text{ideal}}$:
     - *The view that the the adversarial environment E obtains by participating in the following* real *process:*

$$\mathrm{EVIEW}^i_{\mathrm{real}} = \{(\mathrm{istate}^i, x^i_{hs}, x^i_{hp}, x^i_{hu}) \leftarrow I(1^k, \mathrm{istate}^{i-1});$$
$$(\mathrm{estate}^i, j^i, x^i_{ap}, x^i_{au}, \mathrm{stop}^i) \leftarrow E(1^k, \mathrm{EVIEW}^{i-1}_{\mathrm{real}}, x^i_{hp}, x^i_{hu});$$
$$(\mathrm{tstate}^i, \mathrm{ustate}^i, y^i_s, y^i_p, y^i_u) \leftarrow$$
$$T^{U'(\mathrm{ustate}^{i-1})}(\mathrm{tstate}^{i-1}, x^{j^i}_{hs}, x^{j^i}_{hp}, x^{j^i}_{hu}, x^i_{ap}, x^i_{au}):$$
$$(\mathrm{estate}^i, y^i_p, y^i_u)\}$$

$\mathrm{EVIEW}_{\mathrm{real}} = \mathrm{EVIEW}^i_{\mathrm{real}}$ *if* $\mathrm{stop}^i = \mathrm{TRUE}$.

The real process proceeds in rounds. In round i, the honest (secret, protected, and unprotected) inputs $(x^i_{hs}, x^i_{hp}, x^i_{hu})$ are picked using an honest, stateful process I to which the environment E does not have access. Then E, based on its view from the last round, chooses (0) the value of its estate_i variable as a way of remembering what it did next time it is invoked; (1) which previously generated honest inputs $(x^i_{hs}, x^i_{hp}, x^i_{hu})$ to give to $T^{U'}$ (note that E can specify the index j^i of these inputs, but not their values); (2) the adversarial, protected input x^i_{ap}; (3) the adversarial, unprotected input x^i_{au}; (4) the Boolean variable stop^i that determines whether round i is the last round in this process. Next, the algorithm $T^{U'}$ is run on the inputs $(\mathrm{tstate}^{i-1}, x^{j^i}_{hs}, x^{j^i}_{hp}, x^{j^i}_{hu}, x^i_{ap}, x^i_{au})$, where tstate^{i-1} is T's previously saved state, and produces a new state tstate^i for T, as well as the secret y^i_s, protected y^i_p and unprotected y^i_u outputs. The oracle U' is given its previously saved state, ustate^{i-1}, as input, and the current state of U' is saved in the variable ustate^i. The view of the real process in round i consists of estate^i, and the values y^i_p and y^i_u. The overall view of E in the real process is just its view in the last round (i.e., i for which $\mathrm{stop}^i = \mathrm{TRUE}$.).

- *The* ideal *process:*

$$\mathrm{EVIEW}^i_{\mathrm{ideal}} = \{(\mathrm{istate}^i, x^i_{hs}, x^i_{hp}, x^i_{hu}) \leftarrow I(1^k, \mathrm{istate}^{i-1});$$
$$(\mathrm{estate}^i, j^i, x^i_{ap}, x^i_{au}, \mathrm{stop}^i) \leftarrow E(1^k, \mathrm{EVIEW}^{i-1}_{\mathrm{ideal}}, x^i_{hp}, x^i_{hu});$$
$$(\mathrm{astate}^i, y^i_s, y^i_p, y^i_u) \leftarrow \mathsf{Alg}(\mathrm{astate}^{i-1}, x^{j^i}_{hs}, x^{j^i}_{hp}, x^{j^i}_{hu}, x^i_{ap}, x^i_{au});$$
$$(\mathrm{sstate}^i, \mathrm{ustate}^i, Y^i_p, Y^i_u, \mathrm{rep}^i) \leftarrow S_1^{U'(\mathrm{ustate}^{i-1})}$$
$$(\mathrm{sstate}^{i-1}, \cdots, x^{j^i}_{hp}, x^{j^i}_{hu}, x^i_{ap}, x^i_{au}, y^i_p, y^i_u);$$
$$(z^i_p, z^i_u) = \mathrm{rep}^i(Y^i_p, Y^i_u) + (1 - \mathrm{rep}^i)(y^i_p, y^i_u):$$
$$(\mathrm{estate}^i, z^i_p, z^i_u)\}$$

$\mathrm{EVIEW}_{\mathrm{ideal}} = \mathrm{EVIEW}^i_{\mathrm{ideal}}$ *if* $\mathrm{stop}^i = \mathrm{TRUE}$.

The ideal process also proceeds in rounds. In the ideal process, we have a stateful simulator S_1 who, shielded from the secret input x^i_{hs}, but given the non-secret outputs that Alg produces when run all the inputs for round i, decides to either output the values (y^i_p, y^i_u) generated by Alg, or replace them with some other values (Y^i_p, Y^i_u). Note that this is captured by having the indicator variable rep^i be a bit that determines whether y^i_p will be replaced with Y^i_p. In doing so, it is allowed to query oracle U'; moreover, U' saves its state as in the real experiment.

- *Pair Two.* UVIEW$_{\text{real}} \sim$ UVIEW$_{\text{ideal}}$:
  - *The view that the untrusted software U' obtains by participating in the* real *process described in Pair One.* UVIEW$_{\text{real}} =$ ustate^i *if* stop$^i =$ TRUE.
  - *The* ideal *process:*

$$\text{UVIEW}^i_{\text{ideal}} = \{(\text{istate}^i, x^i_{hs}, x^i_{hp}, x^i_{hu}) \leftarrow I(1^k, \text{istate}^{i-1});$$
$$(\text{estate}^i, j^i, x^i_{ap}, x^i_{au}, \text{stop}^i) \leftarrow E(1^k, \text{estate}^{i-1}, x^i_{hp}, x^i_{hu}, y^{i-1}_p, y^{i-1}_u);$$
$$(\text{astate}^i, y^i_s, y^i_p, y^i_u) \leftarrow Alg(\text{astate}^{i-1}, x^{j^i}_{hs}, x^{j^i}_{hp}, x^{j^i}_{hu}, x^i_{ap}, x^i_{au});$$
$$(\text{sstate}^i, \text{ustate}^i) \leftarrow S_2^{U'(\text{ustate}^{i-1})} (\text{sstate}^{i-1}, x^{j^i}_{hu}, x^i_{au}):$$
$$(\text{ustate}^i)\}$$

UVIEW$_{\text{ideal}} =$ UVIEW$^i_{\text{ideal}}$ *if* stop$^i =$ TRUE.

In the ideal process, we have a stateful simulator S_2 who, equipped with only the unprotected inputs (x^i_{hu}, x^i_{au}), queries U'. As before, U' may maintain state.

Definition 3. *(α-efficient, secure outsourcing) A pair of algorithms (T, U) is said to be an α-efficient implementation of Alg if (1) T^U is a correct implementation of Alg and (2) $\forall$ inputs x, the running time of T is no more than an α-multiplicative factor of the running time of Alg.*

Definition 4. *(β-checkable, secure outsourcing) A pair of algorithms (T, U) is said to be an β-checkable implementation of Alg if (1) T^U is a correct implementation of Alg and (2) $\forall$ inputs x, if U' deviates from its advertised functionality during the execution of $T^{U'}(x)$, T will detect the error with probability no less than β.*

Definition 5. *((α, β)-outsource-security) A pair of algorithms (T, U) is said to be an (α, β)-outsource-secure implementation of Alg if it is both α-efficient and β-checkable.*

3 New and Secure Outsourcing Algorithm of Modular Exponentiations

3.1 Security Model

Hohenberger and Lysyanskaya [33] first presented the so-called *two untrusted program model* for outsourcing exponentiations modulo a prime. In the two untrusted program model, the adversarial environment E writes the code for two (potentially different) programs $U' = (U'_1, U'_2)$. E then gives this software to T, advertising a functionality that U'_1 and U'_2 may or may not accurately compute, and T installs this software in a manner such that all subsequent communication between any two of E, U'_1 and U'_2 must pass through T. The new adversary attacking T is $\mathcal{A} = (E, U'_1, U'_2)$. Moreover, we assume that at most one of the programs U'_1 and U'_2 deviates from its advertised functionality on a non-negligible fraction of the inputs, while we cannot know which one and security means that there is a simulator $\mathcal{S}$ for both. This is named as the one-malicious version of two untrusted program model (i.e., "one-malicious model" for the simplicity). In the real-world applications, it is equivalent to buy the two copies of the advertised software from two different vendors and achieve the security as long as one of them is honest.

In the security model [33], a subroutine named *Rand* is used in order to speed up the computations. The inputs for *Rand* are a prime p, a base $g \in \mathbb{Z}_p^*$, and possibly some other values, and the outputs for each invocation are a random, independent pair of the form $(b, g^b \mod p)$, where $b \in \mathbb{Z}_q$. There are two approaches to implement this functionality. One is for a trusted server to compute a table of random, independent pairs in advance and then load it into the memory of T. For each invocation of *Rand*, T just retrieves a new pair in the table (the table-lookup method).[1] The other is to apply the well-known preprocessing techniques. By far, the most promising preprocessing algorithm is the EBPV generator [40], which is secure against adaptive adversaries and runs in time $O(\log^2 n)$ for an n-bit exponent. On input a sufficiently large subset of truly random (k, g^k) pairs, EBPV generator outputs a pair (l, g^l) that is statistically close to the uniform distribution. Therefore, we argue that T can never control the output of the subroutine *Rand*, especially the value of l for both of the approaches.

3.2 Outsourcing Algorithm

In this section, we propose a new secure outsourcing algorithm **Exp** for exponentiation modulo a prime in the one-malicious model. In **Exp**, T outsources its modular exponentiation computations to U_1 and U_2 by invoking the subroutine *Rand*. A requirement for **Exp** is that the adversary $\mathcal{A}$ cannot know any useful information about the inputs and outputs of **Exp**. Similar to [33], $U_i(x, y) \to y^x$ also denotes that U_i takes as inputs (x, y) and outputs $y^x \mod p$, where $i = 1, 2$.

Let p, q be two large primes and $q | p - 1$. The input of **Exp** is $a \in \mathbb{Z}_q^*$, and $u \in \mathbb{Z}_p^*$ such that $u^q = 1 \mod p$ (for an arbitrary base u and an arbitrary power a). The output of **Exp** is $u^a \mod p$. Note that a may be secret or (honest/adversarial) protected and u may be (honest/adversarial) protected. Both of a and u are computationally blinded to U_1 and U_2.

To implement this functionality using U_1 and U_2, T firstly runs *Rand* twice to create two blinding pairs (α, g^α) and (β, g^β). We denote $v = g^\alpha \mod p$ and $\mu = g^\beta \mod p$.

Our trick is a more efficient solution to logically split u and a into random looking pieces that can be computed by U_1 and U_2. The first logical divisions are

$$u^a = (vw)^a = g^{a\alpha} w^a = g^\beta g^\gamma w^a,$$

where $w = u/v$ and $\gamma = a\alpha - \beta$.

---

[1] In most applications, the pair cannot be reused. For example, reusing such a pair in Schnorr signature will result in the secret key exposure of the signer.

The second logical divisions are

$$u^a = g^\beta g^\gamma w^a = g^\beta g^\gamma w^{k+l} = g^\beta g^\gamma w^k w^l,$$

where $l = a - k$.

Next, T runs *Rand* to obtain three pairs (t_1, g^{t_1}), (t_2, g^{t_2}), and (t_3, g^{t_3}).

T queries U_1 in random order as
$U_1(t_2/t_1, g^{t_1}) \to g^{t_2}$;
$U_1(\gamma/t_3, g^{t_3}) \to g^\gamma$;
$U_1(l, w) \to w^l$.

Similarly, T queries U_2 in random order as
$U_2(t_2/t_1, g^{t_1}) \to g^{t_2}$;
$U_2(\gamma/t_3, g^{t_3}) \to g^\gamma$;
$U_2(k, w) \to w^k$.

Finally, T checks that both U_1 and U_2 produce the correct outputs, i.e., $g^{t_2} = U_1(t_2/t_1, g^{t_1}) = U_2(t_2/t_1, g^{t_1})$ and $U_1(\gamma/t_3, g^{t_3}) = U_2(\gamma/t_3, g^{t_3})$. If not, T outputs "error"; otherwise, T can compute $u^a = \mu g^\gamma w^k w^l$.

Remark 1. In the one-malicious model, the equation $U_1(\gamma/t_3, g^{t_3}) = U_2(\gamma/t_3, g^{t_3})$ implies both U_1 and U_2 produce the correct g^γ. Therefore, the partial computation result g^γ also plays the role of a test query. This is slightly different from the technique in [33] while it indeed improves the efficiency and checkability of the computations.

Remark 2. Trivially, the proposed algorithm **Exp** can be extend to the outsource-secure scalar multiplications on elliptic curves, i.e., aU for any $a \in \mathbb{Z}_q^*$.

3.3 Security Analysis

Theorem 1. *In the one-malicious model, the algorithms $(T, (U_1, U_2))$ are an outsource-secure implementation of **Exp**, where the input (a, u) may be honest, secret; or honest, protected; or adversarial, protected.*

Proof. The proof is similar to [33]. The correctness is trivial and we only focus on security. Let $\mathcal{A} = (E, U_1', U_2')$ be a PPT adversary that interacts with a PPT algorithm T in the one-malicious model.

Firstly, we prove Pair One $EVIEW_{real} \sim EVIEW_{ideal}$:

If the input (a, u) is anything other than honest, secret, then the simulator S_1 behaves the same way as in the real execution. If (a, u) is an honest, secret input, then the simulator S_1 behaves as follows: On receiving the input on round i, S_1 ignores it and instead makes three random queries of the form (α_j, β_j) to both U_1' and U_2'. S_1 randomly tests two outputs (i.e., $\beta_j^{\alpha_j}$) from each program. If an error is detected, S_1 saves all states and outputs $Y_p^i=$"error", $Y_u^i=\varnothing$, $rep^i=1$ (i.e., the output for ideal process is $(estate^i, \text{"error"}, \varnothing)$). If no error is detected, S_1 checks the remaining two outputs. If all checks pass, S_1 outputs $Y_p^i=\varnothing$, $Y_u^i=\varnothing$, $rep^i=0$ (i.e., the output for ideal process is $(estate^i, y_p^i, y_u^i)$); otherwise, S_1 selects a random element r and outputs $Y_p^i=r$, $Y_u^i=\varnothing$, $rep^i=1$ (i.e., the output for ideal process is $(estate^i, r, \varnothing)$). In either case, S_1 saves the appropriate states. The input distributions to (U_1', U_2') in the real and ideal experiments are computationally indistinguishable. In the ideal experiment, the inputs are chosen uniformly at random. In the real experiment, each part of all three queries that T makes to any one program is independently re-randomized and thus computationally indistinguishable from random. If (U_1', U_2') behave honest in the round i, then $EVIEW_{real}^i \sim EVIEW_{ideal}^i$ (this is because $T^{(U_1', U_2')}$ perfectly executes **Exp** in the real experiment and S_1 simulates with the same outputs in the ideal experiment, i.e., $rep^i=0$). If one of (U_1', U_2') is dishonest in the round i, then it will be detected by both T and S_1 with probability $\frac{2}{3}$, resulting in an output of "error"; otherwise, the output of **Exp** is corrupted (with probability $\frac{1}{3}$). In the real experiment, the three outputs generated by (U_1', U_2') are multiplied together along with a random value. In the ideal experiment, S_1 also simulates with a random value r. Thus, $EVIEW_{real}^i \sim EVIEW_{ideal}^i$ even when one of (U_1', U_2') is dishonest. By the hybrid argument, we conclude that $EVIEW_{real} \sim EVIEW_{ideal}$.

Secondly, we prove Pair Two $UVIEW_{real} \sim UVIEW_{ideal}$:

The simulator S_2 always behaves as follows: On receiving the input on round i, S_2 ignores it and instead makes three random queries of the form (α_j, β_j) to both U_1' and U_2'. Then S_2 saves its states and the states of (U_1', U_2'). E can easily distinguish between these real and ideal experiments (note that the output in the ideal experiment is never corrupted). However, E cannot communicate this information to (U_1', U_2'). This is because in the round i of the real experiment, T always re-randomizes its inputs to (U_1', U_2'). In the ideal experiment, S_2 always generates random, independent queries for (U_1', U_2'). Thus, for each round i we have $UVIEW_{real}^i \sim UVIEW_{ideal}^i$. By the hybrid argument, we conclude that $UVIEW_{real} \sim UVIEW_{ideal}$. $\square$

Theorem 2. *In the one-malicious model, the algorithms $(T, (U_1, U_2))$ are an $(O(\frac{\log^2 n}{n}), \frac{2}{3})$-outsource-secure implementation of **Exp**.*

Proof. The proposed algorithm **Exp** makes 5 calls to *Rand* plus 7 modular multiplication (MM) and 3 modular inverse (MInv) in order to compute $u^a \mod p$ (we omit other operations such as modular additions). Also, **Exp** takes $O(\log^2 n)$ or $O(1)$ MM using the EBPV generator or table-lookup method, respectively, where n is the bit of the a. On the other hand, it takes roughly $1.5n$ MM to compute $u^a \mod p$ by the square-and-multiply method. Thus, the algorithms $(T, (U_1, U_2))$ are an $O(\frac{\log^2 n}{n})$-efficient implementation of **Exp**.

On the other hand, U_1 (resp. U_2) cannot distinguish the two test queries from all of the three queries that T makes. If U_1 (resp. U_2) fails during any execution of **Exp**, it will be detected with probability $\frac{2}{3}$. $\square$

3.4   Comparison

We compare the proposed algorithm with Hohenberger-Lysyanskaya's algorithm in [33]. We denote by MM a modular multiplication, by MInv a modular inverse, and by $\mathrm{Rand}^{\mathrm{Invoke}}$ an invocation of the subroutine *Rand*. We omit other operations such as modular additions in both algorithms. Table 1 presents the comparison of the efficiency and the checkability between Hohenberger-Lysyanskaya's algorithm and our proposed algorithm **Exp**.

Table 1. Comparison of the two algorithms

	Algorithm [33]	Algorithm **Exp**
MM	9	7
MInv	5	3
Invoke(*Rand*)	6	5
Invoke(U_1)	4	3
Invoke(U_2)	4	3
Checkability	$\frac{1}{2}$	$\frac{2}{3}$

Compared with Hohenberger-Lysyanskaya's algorithm, the proposed algorithm **Exp** is superior in both efficiency and checkability. More precisely, **Exp** requires only 7 MM, 3 MInv, 5 invocation of *Rand*, and 3 invocation of U_1 and U_2 for each modular exponentiation. Note that the modular exponentiation is the most basic operation in discrete-logarithm based cryptographic protocols, and millions of such computations may be outsourced to the server every day. Thus, our proposed algorithm can save huge of computational resources for both the outsourcer T and the servers U_1 and U_2.

4   Secure Outsourcing Algorithms for Encryption and Signatures

In this section, we propose two secure outsourcing algorithms for Cramer-Shoup encryption scheme [18] and Schnorr signature scheme [42].

4.1   Outsource-Secure Cramer-Shoup Encryptions

The proposed outsource-secure Cramer-Shoup encryption scheme consists of the following efficient algorithms:

- **System Parameters Generation:** Let $\mathbb{G}$ be an abelian group of a large prime order q. Let g be a generator of $\mathbb{G}$. Define a cryptographic secure hash function $H : \mathbb{G}^3 \to \mathbb{Z}_q$. The system parameters are $SP = \{\mathbb{G}, q, g, H\}$.
- **Key Generation:** On input 1^l, run the key generation algorithm to obtain the secret/public key pair (SK, PK), here $SK = (w, x, y, z) \in_R \mathbb{Z}_q^* \times \mathbb{Z}_q^3$, $PK = (W, X, Y, Z) = (g^w, g^x, g^y, g^z)$.
- **Encryption:** On input the public key PK and a message $m \in \mathbb{G}$, the outsourcer T runs the subroutine *Rand* and generates the ciphertext C as follows:

1. T runs *Rand* to obtain a pair $(k, r = g^k \mod p)$.
2. T firstly runs **Exp** to obtain $\mathbf{Exp}(k, W) \to s$, $\mathbf{Exp}(k, Z) \to t$ and then computes $e = mt$, and $h = H(r, s, e)$.
3. T runs **Exp** to obtain $\mathbf{Exp}(k, X) \to \alpha$, $\mathbf{Exp}(kh, Y) \to \beta$ and then computes $\gamma = \alpha\beta$.
4. T outputs the ciphertext $C = (r, s, e, \gamma)$.

- **Decryption:** On input the verification key y, the message m, and the signature $\sigma = (e, s)$, the outsourcer T runs the subroutine **Exp** and verifies the signature σ as follows:
  1. T computes $h = H(r, s, e)$.
  2. T runs **Exp** to obtain $\mathbf{Exp}(w, r) \to \psi_1$ and $\mathbf{Exp}(x + yh, r) \to \psi_2$.
  3. If and only if $s = \psi_1$ and $\gamma = \psi_2$, T runs **Exp** to obtain $\mathbf{Exp}(z, r) \to t$ computes $m = et^{-1}$.
  4. T outputs m.

Remark 3. We present a secure outsourcing algorithm for Cramer-Shoup encryption scheme CS1b. Compared with [33], we do not use a new subroutine *Rand'* that produces a triple $(b, g^b \mod p, g'^b \mod p)$, while our algorithm requires one more invocation of **Exp** (only) for encryption. Trivially, we could present outsouce-secure Cramer-Shoup encryption scheme CS1a (running either *Rand* or *Rand'*).

4.2   Outsource-Secure Schnorr Signatures

The proposed outsource-secure Schnorr signature scheme consists of the following efficient algorithms:

- **System Parameters Generation:** Let p and q be two large primes that satisfy $q|p - 1$. Let g be an element in $\mathbb{Z}_p^*$ such that $g^q = 1 \mod p$. Define a cryptographic secure hash function $H : \{0, 1\}^* \to \mathbb{Z}_p$. The system parameters are $SP = \{p, q, g, H\}$.
- **Key Generation:** On input 1^l, run the key generation algorithm to obtain the signing/verification key pair (x, y), here $y = g^{-x} \mod p$.
- **Signature Generation:** On input the singing key x and a message m, the outsourcer T runs the subroutine *Rand* and generates the signature σ as follows:
  1. T runs *Rand* to obtain a pair $(k, r = g^k \mod p)$.
  2. T computes $e = H(m\|r)$ and $s = k + xe \mod q$.
  3. T outputs the signature $\sigma = (e, s)$.
- **Signature Verification:** On input the verification key y, the message m, and the signature $\sigma = (e, s)$, the outsourcer T runs the subroutine **Exp** and verifies the signature σ as follows:
  1. T runs **Exp** to obtain $\mathbf{Exp}(s, g) \to \psi_1$ and $\mathbf{Exp}(e, y) \to \psi_2$.
  2. T computes $r' = \psi_1\psi_2 \mod p$ and $e' = H(m\|r')$.
  3. T outputs 1 if and only if $e' = e$.

Remark 4. The proposed outsource-secure Schnorr signature scheme is basically same as that in [33]. Note that the subroutine **Exp** is only used for the signature verification.

5   Outsource-Secure Algorithm of Simultaneous Modular Exponentiations

In this section, we focus on simultaneous modular exponentiations $u_1^a u_2^b \mod p$, which play an important role in many cryptographic primitives such as chameleon hashing [5,6,21,22,36,44] and trapdoor commitment [9,16,23,25,32]. Trivially, a simultaneous modular exponentiation can be carried out by invoking 2 modular exponentiations. This requires roughly $3n$ MM, where n is the bit of a and b. However, the computation cost is only $1.75n$ MM (i.e., roughly 1.17 modular exponentiation) if we use the Algorithm 14.88 of [37].

In the following, we propose an efficient outsource-secure algorithm of simultaneous modular exponentiations **SExp** in the one-malicious model.

Let p, q be two large primes and $q|p-1$. Given two arbitrary bases $u_1, u_2 \in \mathbb{Z}_p^*$ and two arbitrary powers $a, b \in \mathbb{Z}_q^*$ such that the order of u_1 and u_2 is q. The output of **SExp** is $u_1^a u_2^b \mod p$.

Similarly, T firstly runs $Rand$ twice to create two blinding pairs (α, g^α) and (β, g^β). We denote $v = g^\alpha \mod p$ and $\mu = g^\beta \mod p$.

The first logical divisions are

$$u_1^a u_2^b = (vw_1)^a (vw_2)^b = g^\beta g^\gamma w_1^a w_2^b,$$

where $w_1 = u_1/v$, $w_2 = u_2/v$, and $\gamma = (a+b)\alpha - \beta$.

The second logical divisions are

$$u_1^a u_2^b = g^\beta g^\gamma w_1^a w_2^b = g^\beta g^\gamma w_1^k w_1^l w_2^t w_2^s,$$

where $l = a - k$ and $s = b - t$.

Next, T runs $Rand$ to obtain three pairs (t_1, g^{t_1}), (t_2, g^{t_2}), and (t_3, g^{t_3}).

T queries U_1 in random order as
$U_1(t_2/t_1, g^{t_1}) \rightarrow g^{t_2}$;
$U_1(\gamma/t_3, g^{t_3}) \rightarrow g^\gamma$;
$U_1(k, w_1) \rightarrow w_1^k$;
$U_1(t, w_2) \rightarrow w_2^t$.

Similarly, T queries U_2 in random order as
$U_2(t_2/t_1, g^{t_1}) \rightarrow g^{t_2}$;
$U_2(\gamma/t_3, g^{t_3}) \rightarrow g^\gamma$;
$U_2(l, w_1) \rightarrow w_1^l$;
$U_2(s, w_2) \rightarrow w_2^s$.

Finally, T checks that both U_1 and U_2 produce the correct outputs, i.e., $g^{t_2} = U_1(t_2/t_1, g^{t_1}) = U_2(t_2/t_1, g^{t_1})$ and $U_1(\gamma/t_3, g^{t_3}) = U_2(\gamma/t_3, g^{t_3})$. If not, T outputs "error"; otherwise, T can compute $u_1^a u_2^b = \mu g^\gamma w_1^k w_1^l w_2^t w_2^s$.

Note that **SExp** requires only 10 MM, 4 MInv, 5 invocation of $Rand$, and 4 invocation of U_1 and U_2 for each modular exponentiation. Therefore, the computation cost of **SExp** is much less than that of double running **Exp**. Moreover, it is even comparable to that of outsourcing *one* modular exponentiation [33].

Table 2. Efficiency comparison for two algorithms

	Algorithm [33]	Algorithm **SExp**
MM	9	10
MInv	5	4
Invoke($Rand$)	6	5
Invoke(U_1)	4	4
Invoke(U_2)	4	4
Checkability	$\frac{1}{2}$	$\frac{1}{2}$

Table 2 presents the comparison of the efficiency and the checkability between Hohenberger-Lysyanskaya's *Exp* algorithm and our proposed algorithm **SExp**.

Similar to theorem 3.2, we can easily prove the following theorem:

Theorem 3. *In the one-malicious model, the algorithms* $(T, (U_1, U_2))$ *are an* $(O(\frac{\log^2 n}{n}), \frac{1}{2})$-*outsource-secure implementation of* ***SExp***.

6   Conclusions

In this paper, we propose two outsource-secure and efficient algorithms for modular exponentiations and simultaneous modular exponentiations, which are the most basic and expensive operations in many discrete-logarithm cryptosystems. Compared with the algorithm [33], the proposed algorithm is superior in both efficiency and checkability.

The security model of our outsourcing algorithms requires the outsourcer to interact with two non-colluding cloud servers (the same as [33]). Therefore, an interesting open problem is whether there is an efficient algorithm for secure outsourcing modular exponentiation using only one untrusted cloud sever.

Acknowledgments. We are grateful to the anonymous referees for their invaluable suggestions. This work is supported by the National Natural Science Foundation of China (Nos. 60970144 and 61100224), and China 111 Project (No. B08038). Besides, Lou's work was supported by US National Science Foundation under grant CNS-1155988.

References

1. Atallah, M.J., Frikken, K.B.: Securely outsourcing linear algebra computations. In: Proceedings of the 5th ACM Symposium on Information, Computer and Communications Security (CCS), pp. 48–59 (2010)
2. Abadi, M., Feigenbaum, J., Kilian, J.: On hiding information from an oracle. In: Proceedings of the 19th Annual ACM Symposium on Theory of Computing (STOC), pp. 195–203 (1987)

3. Atallah, M.J., Pantazopoulos, K.N., Rice, J.R., Spafford, E.H.: Secure outsourcing of scientific computations. Advances in Computers 54, 216–272 (2001)
4. Atallah, M.J., Li, J.: Secure outsourcing of sequence comparisons, International Journal of Information Security, 277–287 (2005)
5. Ateniese, G., de Medeiros, B.: Identity-Based Chameleon Hash and Applications. In: Juels, A. (ed.) FC 2004. LNCS, vol. 3110, pp. 164–180. Springer, Heidelberg (2004)
6. Ateniese, G., de Medeiros, B.: On the Key Exposure Problem in Chameleon Hashes. In: Blundo, C., Cimato, S. (eds.) SCN 2004. LNCS, vol. 3352, pp. 165–179. Springer, Heidelberg (2005)
7. Blanton, M.: Improved Conditional E-Payments. In: Bellovin, S.M., Gennaro, R., Keromytis, A.D., Yung, M. (eds.) ACNS 2008. LNCS, vol. 5037, pp. 188–206. Springer, Heidelberg (2008)
8. Benjamin, D., Atallah, M.J.: Private and cheating-free outsourcing of algebraic computations. In: Proceeding of the 6th Annual Conference on Privacy, Security and Trust (PST), pp. 240–245 (2008)
9. Brassard, G., Chaum, D., Crepeau, C.: Minimum disclosure proofs of knowledge. Journal of Computer and System Sciences 37(2), 156–189 (1988)
10. Beaver, D., Feigenbaum, J., Kilian, J., Rogaway, P.: Locally random reductions: Improvements and applications. Journal of Cryptology 10(1), 17–36 (1997)
11. Ben-Or, M., Goldwasser, S., Kilian, J., Wigderson, A.: Multi-prover interactive proofs: How to remove intractability assumptions. In: Proceedings of the ACM Symposium on Theory of Computing (STOC), pp. 113–131 (1988)
12. Benabbas, S., Gennaro, R., Vahlis, Y.: Verifiable Delegation of Computation over Large Datasets. In: Rogaway, P. (ed.) CRYPTO 2011. LNCS, vol. 6841, pp. 111–131. Springer, Heidelberg (2011)
13. Blum, M., Luby, M., Rubinfeld, R.: Program result checking against adaptive programs and in cryptographic settings. DIMACS Series in Discrete Mathematics and Theoretical Computer Science, pp. 107–118 (1991)
14. Blum, M., Luby, M., Rubinfeld, R.: Self-testing/correcting with applications to numerical problems. Journal of Computer and System Science, 549–595 (1993)
15. Boyko, V., Peinado, M., Venkatesan, R.: Speeding up Discrete Log and Factoring Based Schemes via Precomputations. In: Nyberg, K. (ed.) EUROCRYPT 1998. LNCS, vol. 1403, pp. 221–235. Springer, Heidelberg (1998)
16. Di Crescenzo, G., Ostrovsky, R.: On Concurrent Zero-Knowledge with Preprocessing (Extended Abstract). In: Wiener, M. (ed.) CRYPTO 1999. LNCS, vol. 1666, pp. 485–502. Springer, Heidelberg (1999)
17. Chaum, D., Pedersen, T.P.: Wallet Databases with Observers. In: Brickell, E.F. (ed.) CRYPTO 1992. LNCS, vol. 740, pp. 89–105. Springer, Heidelberg (1993)
18. Cramer, R., Shoup, V.: Design and analysis of practical public-key encryption schemes secure against adaptive chosen ciphertext attack. SIAM Journal of Computing 33, 167–226 (2003)
19. Carbunar, B., Tripunitara, M.: Conditional Payments for Computing Markets. In: Franklin, M.K., Hui, L.C.K., Wong, D.S. (eds.) CANS 2008. LNCS, vol. 5339, pp. 317–331. Springer, Heidelberg (2008)
20. Carbunar, B., Tripunitara, M.: Fair payments for outsourced computations. In: Proceedings of the 7th Annual IEEE Communications Society Conference on Sensor, Mesh and Ad Hoc Communications and Networks (SECON), pp. 529–537. IEEE (2010)

21. Chen, X., Zhang, F., Kim, K.: Chameleon Hashing Without Key Exposure. In: Zhang, K., Zheng, Y. (eds.) ISC 2004. LNCS, vol. 3225, pp. 87–98. Springer, Heidelberg (2004)
22. Chen, X., Zhang, F., Susilo, W., Mu, Y.: Efficient Generic On-Line/Off-Line Signatures Without Key Exposure. In: Katz, J., Yung, M. (eds.) ACNS 2007. LNCS, vol. 4521, pp. 18–30. Springer, Heidelberg (2007)
23. Fischlin, M., Fischlin, R.: Efficient Non-malleable Commitment Schemes. In: Bellare, M. (ed.) CRYPTO 2000. LNCS, vol. 1880, pp. 413–431. Springer, Heidelberg (2000)
24. Even, S., Goldreich, O., Micali, S.: On-line/Off-line digital signatures. Journal of Cryptology 9(1), 35–67 (1996)
25. Gennaro, R.: Multi-trapdoor Commitments and Their Applications to Proofs of Knowledge Secure Under Concurrent Man-in-the-Middle Attacks. In: Franklin, M. (ed.) CRYPTO 2004. LNCS, vol. 3152, pp. 220–236. Springer, Heidelberg (2004)
26. Green, M., Hohenberger, S., Waters, B.: Outsourcing the Decryption of ABE Ciphertexts. In: Proceedings of the 20th USENIX Conference on Security (2011), http://static.usenix.org/events/sec11/tech/full-papers/Green.pdf
27. Gennaro, R., Gentry, C., Parno, B.: Non-interactive Verifiable Computing: Outsourcing Computation to Untrusted Workers. In: Rabin, T. (ed.) CRYPTO 2010. LNCS, vol. 6223, pp. 465–482. Springer, Heidelberg (2010)
28. Goldwasser, S., Kalai, Y.T., Rothblum, G.N.: Delegating computation: interactive proofs for muggles. In: Proceedings of the ACM Symposium on the Theory of Computing (STOC), pp. 113–122 (2008)
29. Girault, M., Lefranc, D.: Server-Aided Verification: Theory and Practice. In: Roy, B. (ed.) ASIACRYPT 2005. LNCS, vol. 3788, pp. 605–623. Springer, Heidelberg (2005)
30. Goldwasser, S., Micali, S., Rackoff, C.: The knowledge complexity of interactive proof-systems. SIAM Journal on Computing 18(1), 186–208 (1989)
31. Golle, P., Mironov, I.: Uncheatable Distributed Computations. In: Naccache, D. (ed.) CT-RSA 2001. LNCS, vol. 2020, pp. 425–440. Springer, Heidelberg (2001)
32. Garay, J., MacKenzie, P., Yang, K.: Strengthening Zero-knowledge Protocols Using Signatures. In: Biham, E. (ed.) EUROCRYPT 2003. LNCS, vol. 2656, pp. 177–194. Springer, Heidelberg (2003)
33. Hohenberger, S., Lysyanskaya, A.: How to Securely Outsource Cryptographic Computations. In: Kilian, J. (ed.) TCC 2005. LNCS, vol. 3378, pp. 264–282. Springer, Heidelberg (2005), http://www.cs.jhu.edu/
34. Kilian, J.: A note on efficient zero-knowledge proofs and arguments. In: Proceedings of the ACM Symposium on Theory of Computing (STOC), pp. 723–732 (1992)
35. Kilian, J.: Improved Efficient Arguments. In: Coppersmith, D. (ed.) CRYPTO 1995. LNCS, vol. 963, pp. 311–324. Springer, Heidelberg (1995)
36. Krawczyk, H., Rabin, T.: Chameleon hashing and signatures. In: Proceeding of the 7th Annual Network and Distributed System Security Symposium (NDSS), pp. 143–154 (2000)
37. Menezes, A., van Oorschot, P., Vanstone, S.: Handbook of Applied Cryptography. CRC Press (1996)
38. Micali, S.: CS proofs. In: Proceedings of the 35th Annual Symposium on Foundations of Computer Science (FOCS), pp. 436–453 (1994)
39. Matsumoto, T., Kato, K., Imai, H.: Speeding up Secret Computations with Insecure Auxiliary Devices. In: Goldwasser, S. (ed.) CRYPTO 1988. LNCS, vol. 403, pp. 497–506. Springer, Heidelberg (1990)

40. Nguyen, P.Q., Shparlinski, I.E., Stern, J.: Distribution of modular sums and the security of server aided exponentiation. In: Proceedings of the Workshop on Comp. Number Theory and Crypt., pp. 1–16 (1999)

41. Parno, B., Raykova, M., Vaikuntanathan, V.: How to Delegate and Verify in Public: Verifiable Computation from Attribute-Based Encryption. In: Cramer, R. (ed.) TCC 2012. LNCS, vol. 7194, pp. 422–439. Springer, Heidelberg (2012)

42. Schnorr, C.P.: Efficient signature generation for smart cards. Journal of Cryptology 4(3), 239–252 (1991)

43. Shi, L., Carbunar, B., Sion, R.: Conditional E-Cash. In: Dietrich, S., Dhamija, R. (eds.) FC 2007 and USEC 2007. LNCS, vol. 4886, pp. 15–28. Springer, Heidelberg (2007)

44. Shamir, A., Tauman, Y.: Improved Online/Offline Signature Schemes. In: Kilian, J. (ed.) CRYPTO 2001. LNCS, vol. 2139, pp. 355–367. Springer, Heidelberg (2001)

45. Wang, C., Ren, K., Wang, J.: Secure and practical outsourcing of linear programming in cloud computing. In: Proceedings of the 30th IEEE International Conference on Computer Communications (INFOCOM), pp. 820–828 (2011)

46. Wu, W., Mu, Y., Susilo, W., Huang, X.: Server-Aided Verification Signatures: Definitions and New Constructions. In: Baek, J., Bao, F., Chen, K., Lai, X. (eds.) ProvSec 2008. LNCS, vol. 5324, pp. 141–155. Springer, Heidelberg (2008)

Towards Symbolic Encryption Schemes

Naveed Ahmed[1], Christian D. Jensen[1], and Erik Zenner[2]

[1] DTU Informatics, Denmark
{Naah,Christian.Jensen}@imm.dtu.dk
[2] University of Applied Sciences Offenburg, Germany
erik.zenner@hs-offenburg.de

Abstract. Symbolic encryption, in the style of Dolev-Yao models, is ubiquitous in formal security models. In its common use, encryption on a whole message is specified as a single monolithic block. From a cryptographic perspective, however, this may require a resource-intensive cryptographic algorithm, namely an authenticated encryption scheme that is secure under chosen ciphertext attack. Therefore, many reasonable encryption schemes, such as AES in the CBC or CFB mode[1], are not among the implementation options.

In this paper, we report new attacks on CBC and CFB based implementations of the well-known Needham-Schroeder and Denning-Sacco protocols. To avoid such problems, we advocate the use of refined notions of symbolic encryption that have natural correspondence to standard cryptographic encryption schemes.

Keywords: Encryption, Assumptions, Implementation.

1 Introduction

A private-key encryption scheme enables two honest parties that share a key to privately communicate over a network, in such a way that a dishonest man-in-middle, the adversary, is unable to gain any non-trivial information about the communication. The requirements of cryptographic encryption may include left-right indistinguishability (IND) and non-malleability (NM), which can be characterized in different attack settings [2].

Over the years, many abstractions of cryptographic encryption have been proposed. The most popular abstraction is the Dolev-Yao model [3]. In this symbolic model, two types of simplifications are introduced. Firstly, binary strings and functions are replaced by symbolic terms and derivation rules. In particular, this results in idealized encryption functions—either an adversary can decrypt a symbolic ciphertext (e.g., if he can derive the key) or the adversary gets absolutely no information about the plaintext. The second simplification is related to the capabilities of an adversary, namely the adversary is modelled as a non-deterministic strategy that is limited to selecting its actions from a small set of

---

[1] i.e., cipher block chaining (CBC) and cipher feedback mode of encryption (CFB) [1].

S. Foresti, M. Yung, and F. Martinelli (Eds.): ESORICS 2012, LNCS 7459, pp. 557–572, 2012.

(pre-defined) logic rules. The security models that use these two abstractions are commonly referred to as symbolic/formal security models.

A symbolic model is simpler than its cryptographic counterpart, and therefore one can avoid relatively complicated and long proofs of traditional cryptography. More importantly, computers can do the tedious job of proving (and similarly verifying) the proofs of security.

Unfortunately, any security assurance in a symbolic model does not automatically translate to the underlying computational cryptography and, therefore, to its hardware/software implementation. In any implementation of symbolic encryption, a system designer has to make certain security critical decisions, related to, e.g., mode of encryption, block alignment, and message authentication code. Many attacks targeting the implementation of encryption are known [4, 5].

One approach to address such issues is to always rely on the most stringent interpretation of encryption [2], i.e., an encryption scheme that is private and non-malleable against an adversary that has adaptive access to encryption and decryption oracles. Such strong requirements, however, often implies a resource-intensive implementation.

We note that encryption or decryption oracles are not present in many protocols. Moreover, the security of a protocol does not always depend on non-malleability or privacy of the encryption. Therefore, in our view, one should use symbolic encryption in such a way that it closely mimics an actual cryptographic encryption scheme. In this way, not only one can avoid many implementation related ambiguities but also a level of safe optimization can be achieved, e.g., if a protocol is secure with ECB based encryption.

Our contributions in this paper are summarized in the following.

We present new attacks on the CBC and CFB based implementations of the Needham-Schroeder symmetric-key (NSSK) protocol [6], without exploiting the previously known vulnerability [7]. These attacks also work with the seven-round version of the NSSK protocol [8], which is an improved version of the original NSSK protocol after the flaw [7] was discovered. Further, we report new attacks on CBC and CFB based implementations of the Denning-Sacco symmetric-key (DSSK) protocol [7], which is another improved version of the NSSK protocol, and which does not suffer any attacks to the best of our knowledge.

It is worth mentioning that the CBC mode is semantically secure in traditional CPA (chosen plaintext attack) model [9], and the CFB mode is secure against an even more powerful adversary who has an access to block-wise online encryption oracle [10]. Our attacks, although are CPAs, are against the protocol security and not against the CBC/CFB security, which indicates that these protocols entail more stringent requirements on encryption, such as non-malleability.

Further, we advocate a few refined ways of using symbolic encryption that have natural correspondence to standard cryptographic constructions. The refined notions require different implementation resources and, therefore, a level of safe optimization can be achieved while still relying on symbolic encryption.

The rest of the paper is arranged as follows. In Sect. 2, we briefly examine the prior art. Next, in Sect. 3 and Sect. 4, we present the new attacks. In Sect. 5, we list down a few symbolic encryption schemes and show that these schemes provide different levels of security in a symbolic model. In Sect. 7, we discuss our contribution in a broader perspective, and in Sect. 8 we conclude our work. In the paper, exclusive-or ($\oplus$) is abbreviated as Xor and a distinction should be observed between *symbolic encryption* [11, 12] and *cryptographic encryption* [2, 13].

2 Related Work

Meadows [14] presents an extensive survey of the works that rely on symbolic encryption. We here do not discuss formal security analysis as such and only focus on the implementation perspective of symbolic encryption.

Moore [15] was probably the first to highlight the security problems that may occur in implementing symbolic encryption. Boyd [16] describes a few possible attacks on the NSSK protocol based on some strong assumptions such as the use of a stream cipher for encryption, however, the presentation does not come close to that of ours. Mao and Boyd [17] discuss some general vulnerabilities that may occur when using cipher-block-chaining mode for implementing encryption. Bellovin [4] reported vulnerabilities in the earlier versions of IPsec by exploiting CBC-mode encryption.

Stubblebine et al. [18] investigates modes of encryption for discovering *known pairs* and *chosen texts*, using the NRL Protocol Analyzer. Our attack makes use of chosen texts, in which a party can be used as an encryption oracle; this is then exploited by an adversary who obtains the ciphertext against a plaintext. In the same line of work, Kremer and Ryan [19] model ECB and CBC mode using Blanchet's protocol verifier. Interestingly, they use the NSSK protocol as a case study but stop after indicating the existence of chosen texts in the protocol. Nevertheless, the existence of chosen texts is quite common in cryptographic protocols and often does not lead to insecure encryption.

An interesting case is that of encryption-only-mode of IPsec, for which Paterson and Yau [5] exploited CBC mode of encryption. Their attacks work if an implementation does not follow the standard strictly. Later, Degabriele and Paterson [20] published another attack that works only if an implementation strictly follows the standard.

Chevalier et al. [21] extend the Dolev-Yao intruder with the capability to exploit Xor operator, as used in CBC, and they show that the protocol insecurity problem is NP-complete. Küsters and Truderung developed a verification method that can reduce the protocol models that are *Xor-linear* to Xor free models, which then can be analysed using existing tools [22]; however, the CBC based NSSK protocol is not Xor-linear due to the nested encryption.

In our view, the multiplicity error of DSSK protocol [23] is not a valid attack because it does not violate the claimed goals [7], namely neither confidentiality of the session key nor the entity authentication of participants is violated. Similarly, a reported type flaw [24] is based on a somewhat dubious assumption: if $\{T\} \equiv \{T, \{B, K_{AB}, T\}_{SA}\}$. Even if this assumption holds, the session key remains confidential and there is no violation of authentication.

In a slightly bigger picture, an impressive amount of research has been done for establishing a theoretically sound link between symbolic cryptography and complexity-theoretic cryptography [25–27]. In the line of universal composability, Ran Canetti and Herzog [28] show that the Dolev-Yao model can be layered on top of the traditional universal composability framework. Currently, this approach is limited to so-called simple protocols: the protocols that use only those cryptographic schemes that have some standard symbolic counterparts.

Another related line of work is on the security of online ciphers started by Bellare et al. [29]. In an online cipher, encryption of a plaintext block only depends on the current block and the previous blocks of the plaintext. Note that the requirements of a cipher are more stringent than an encryption scheme, because one is not allowed to use random initializing vectors (iv) in the construction of a cipher. Without a random iv, CBC and CFB modes are the candidates of online cipher, for which Fouque et al. [10] show that the CFB mode is provably secure and the CBC mode is not secure. The CBC mode is provably secure with a randomly chosen iv [9].

The attacks presented in this paper are based on the actual construction of CBC and CFB modes (using random IVs), but we still use symbolic abstraction to model the underlying cipher. We believe this level of abstraction is a good compromise between computational cryptography (where a cipher is modelled as a pseudorandom permutation) and symbolic cryptography (where the whole encryption scheme is modelled as a perfect cipher). At this abstraction level, which probably has not been explored in the prior art, we present a few symbolic encryption schemes.

3   NSSK Protocol

The NSSK protocol [6] is a key establishment protocol, based on symmetric encryption and the notion of a trusted third-party (TTP). In this paper, we assume that when a session expires then the session key is safely discarded, because this assumption prohibits the previously known flaw [7] resulting in a "secure" NSSK protocol. The protocol narrations are listed in the following.

$$(1)\ A \longrightarrow S : A, B, N_A$$
$$(2)\ S \longrightarrow A : \{N_A, B, K_{AB}, \{K_{AB}, A\}_{SB}\}_{SA}$$
$$(3)\ A \longrightarrow B : \{K_{AB}, A\}_{SB}$$
$$(4)\ B \longrightarrow A : \{N_B\}_{AB}$$
$$(5)\ A \longrightarrow B : \{N_B - 1\}_{AB}$$

Here A and B represent the initiator and responder roles that parties can take during an execution of the protocol; S is the role of a trusted third-party (TTP). It is assumed that S knows the identities of all legitimate entities (principals), and shares a long-term secret key with each of them, namely, S shares K_{SA} and K_{SB} with A and B respectively. The term K_{AB} denotes a session key. The notation $\{\ldots\}_{AB}$ stands for a ciphertext computed using a key K_{AB}.

The first message is a request from A to the TTP that A wishes to establish a key with B, by sending its identity, the identity of the peer entity and a nonce. On receiving the request the TTP generates a random session key K_{AB}. The TTP replies with a message encrypted with A's long-term key, K_{SA}. This message includes a session key K_{AB}, and another encrypted message containing the same session key but encrypted with B's long term key, which A sends to B in the next step.

When B receives the message, it decrypts it using K_{SB}, then verifies that it contains B's identity, and if successful, then B considers K_{AB} as a valid session key. To verify the freshness of the session key, B sends a nonce, N_B, to A encrypted using the session key. On receiving the message in Step 4, A decrypts it and sends $N_B - 1$ to B encrypted using the same session key. This completes the protocol. If both parties terminate without generating any error then A and B assume that K_{AB} is a valid session key for the subsequent communication.

As per the standard cryptographic assumption, the initializing vectors (iv) in CBC and CFB modes are public values. We assume that the attacker is an insider, i.e., $\mathcal{I}$ is a legitimate network entity and shared $K_{S\mathcal{I}}$ with the TTP. An attacker $\mathcal{I}$ in the role of A is denoted by $\mathcal{I}(A)$.

For the simplicity of exposition, we assume that each term of the protocol is encoded in a separate block, e.g., the implementation of $\{N_1, N_2\}_{AB}$ using CBC mode of encryption results in the following ciphertext: $iv, c_1 = \{N_1 \oplus iv\}_{AB}, \{N_2 \oplus c_1\}_{AB}$. If blocks are not encoded with this perfect alignment then less efficient versions of the reported attacks may exist that require more computation and communication on the part of the adversary[2]. Nevertheless, the cryptographic security guarantees [9, 10] are valid independent of the block alignments in a plaintext.

In the following we describe the attacks against CBC and CFB based implementations. These attacks are also applicable on the seven-round version of the NSSK protocol [8], which does not suffer from the old-session-key attack [7].

NSSK with CBC Mode of Encryption

The attack is shown in Fig. 1, which consists of three setup phases followed by the main attack phase. The superscripts in iv^a, iv^b and iv^c are labels used to easily distinguish between initialization vectors in Setup-(a), Setup-(b) and Setup-(c) respectively; a subscript, such as '1' in iv_1, is used to distinguish different values of initialization vectors. The notation '=' is used to introduce intermediate terms to simplify the description of the attack.

In Setup-(a), $\mathcal{I}$ obtains the term $\{iv_2^a \oplus K_1\}_{SB}$, which he sends as a nonce in Setup-(b) to obtain c_1^b. In Setup-(c), $\mathcal{I}$ obtains the term c_1^c by sending K_1 as a nonce; K_1 can be computed by $\mathcal{I}$ in Setup-(a).

---

[2] For instance, in an attack on IPsec [5] that is based on address rewriting, the first phase of the attack succeeds with a probability of 2^{-17}, due to a specific block alignment of IPsec. This means that an attacker may have to repeat the first phase 2^{17} times in order to succeed.

Messages
Setup-(a)

(1) $\mathcal{I} \longrightarrow S : \mathcal{I}, B, N_{\mathcal{I}}$
(2) $S \longrightarrow \mathcal{I} : iv_1^a, iv_2^a, c_1^a = \{iv_1^a \oplus N_{\mathcal{I}}\}_{S\mathcal{I}}, c_2^a = \{c_1^a \oplus B\}_{S\mathcal{I}}, c_3^a = \{c_2^a \oplus K_1\}_{S\mathcal{I}}, c_4^a = \{c_3^a \oplus \{iv_2^a \oplus K_1\}_{SB}\}_{S\mathcal{I}}, c_5^a = \{c_4^a \oplus \{\{iv_2^a \oplus K_1\}_{SB} \oplus \mathcal{I}\}_{SB}\}_{S\mathcal{I}}$

Setup-(b)

(1) $\mathcal{I}(A) \longrightarrow S : A, B, \{iv_2^a \oplus K_1\}_{SB}$
(2) $S \longrightarrow \mathcal{I}(A) : iv_1^b, iv_2^b, c_1^b = \{iv_1^b \oplus \{iv_2^a \oplus K_1\}_{SB}\}_{SA}, c_2^b = \{c_1^b \oplus B\}_{SA}, c_3^b = \{c_2^b \oplus K_2\}_{SA}, c_4^b = \{c_3^b \oplus \{iv_2^b \oplus K_2\}_{SB}\}_{SA}, c_5^b = \{c_4^b \oplus \{\{iv_2^b \oplus K_2\}_{SB} \oplus A\}_{SB}\}_{SA}$

Setup-(c)

(1) $\mathcal{I}(A) \longrightarrow S : A, B, K_1$
(2) $S \longrightarrow A : iv_1^c, iv_2^c, c_1^c = \{iv_1^c \oplus K_1\}_{SA}, c_2^c = \{c_1^c \oplus B\}_{SA}, c_3^c = \{c_2^c \oplus K_3\}_{SA}, c_4^c = \{c_3^c \oplus \{iv_2^c \oplus K_3\}_{SB}\}_{SA}, c_5^c = \{c_4^c \oplus \{\{iv_2^c \oplus K_3\}_{SB} \oplus A\}_{SB}\}_{SA}$

Attack

(1) $A \longrightarrow S : A, B, N_A$
(2a) $S \longrightarrow \mathcal{I}(A) : iv_1, iv_2, c_1 = \{iv_1 \oplus N_A\}_{SA}, c_2 = \{c_1 \oplus B\}_{SA}, c_3 = \{c_2 \oplus K_4\}_{SA}, c_4 = \{c_3 \oplus \{iv_2 \oplus K_4\}_{SB}\}_{SA}, c_5 = \{c_4 \oplus \{\{iv_2 \oplus K_4\}_{SB} \oplus A\}_{SB}\}_{SA}$

(2b) $\mathcal{I}(S) \longrightarrow A : iv_1, iv_2, c_1 = \{iv_1 \oplus N_A\}_{SA}, c_2 = \{c_1 \oplus B\}_{SA}, c_1^c = \{iv_1^c \oplus K_1\}_{SA}, c_1^b = \{iv_1^b \oplus \{iv_2^a \oplus K_1\}_{SB}\}_{SA}, c_1^b = \{iv_1^b \oplus \{iv_2^a \oplus K_1\}_{SB}\}_{SB}$

(3a) $A \longrightarrow \mathcal{I}(B) : c_1^c \oplus iv_1^b \oplus \{iv_2^a \oplus K_1\}_{SB}, c_1^b \oplus iv_1^b \oplus \{iv_2^a \oplus K_1\}_{SB}$
(3b) $\mathcal{I}(A' = c_6 \oplus iv_2^a \oplus K_1) \longrightarrow B : iv_2^a, c_6 = \{iv_2^a \oplus K_1\}_{SB}, \{iv_2^a \oplus K_1\}_{SB}$
(4a) $B \longrightarrow \mathcal{I}(A') : \{N_B\}_{K_1}$
(4b) $\mathcal{I}(B) \longrightarrow A : \{N_B\}_{c_2 \oplus iv_1^c \oplus K_1}$
(5a) $A \longrightarrow \mathcal{I}(B) : \{N_B - 1\}_{c_2 \oplus iv_1^c \oplus K_1}$
(5b) $\mathcal{I}(A') \longrightarrow B : \{N_B - 1\}_{K_1}$

Fig. 1. Attack on CBC-version of NSSK Protocol

Messages
Attack

(1) $A \longrightarrow S : A, B, N_A$
(2a) $S \longrightarrow \mathcal{I}(A) : iv_1, iv_2, c_1 = \{iv_1\}_{SA} \oplus N_A, c_2 = \{c_1\}_{SA} \oplus B, c_3 = \{c_2\}_{SA} \oplus K_4, c_4 = \{c_3\}_{SA} \oplus \{iv_2\}_{SB} \oplus K_4, c_5 = \{c_4\}_{SA} \oplus \{\{iv_2\}_{SB} \oplus K_4\}_{SB} \oplus A$

(2b) $\mathcal{I}(S) \longrightarrow A : iv_1, iv_2, c_1 = \{iv_1\}_{SA} \oplus N_A, c_2 = \{c_1\}_{SA} \oplus B, R_1, c_2 = \{c_1\}_{SA} \oplus B, R_2$

(3) $A \longrightarrow \mathcal{I}(B) : iv_2, \{R_1\}_{SA} \oplus c_2, \{c_2\}_{SA} \oplus R_2$
(4) $\mathcal{I}(B) \longrightarrow A : iv_4, \{iv_4\}_{K_1'} \oplus N_{\mathcal{I}}, \quad \text{where } K_1' = \{c_2\}_{SA} \oplus R_1$
(5) $A \longrightarrow \mathcal{I}(B) : iv_5, \{iv_5\}_{K_1'} \oplus (N_{\mathcal{I}} - 1)$

Fig. 2. Attack on CFB-version of NSSK Protocol

In the main phase of the attack, $\mathcal{I}$ replays the two terms, c_1^b and c_1^c, in place of c_3 and c_4 in the step (2b). This completes the attack on A, i.e., $\mathcal{I}$ can know impersonate as B to A with a known session key $c_2 \oplus iv_1^c \oplus K_1$.

The attack can be further extended to B if $c_6 \oplus iv_2^a \oplus K_1$ represents some valid identity. If this is the case then, in the step (3b), $\mathcal{I}$ replays $iv_2^a, \{iv_2^a \oplus K_1\}_{SB}$, which he obtains in Setup-(a). In this way B believes in K_1 as a new session key shared with a party whose identity is $c_6 \oplus iv_2^a \oplus K_1$. At this stage, $\mathcal{I}$ has successfully deceived both A and B into accepting the session keys that he knows. There are two different session keys, namely, A's session key is $c_2 \oplus iv_1^c \oplus K_1$ and B's session key is K_1. Now, $\mathcal{I}$ can play a man-in-middle role in any subsequent communication.

NSSK with CFB Mode of Encryption

In the attack on CFB version of the protocol, $\mathcal{I}$ is able to impersonate as B to A. In the step (2a), an adversary $\mathcal{I}$ intercepts the server's reply to A. The adversary replaces the terms c_3, c_4, and c_5 of the step (2a) with R_1, c_2, and R_2 and sends the resultant message to A in the step (2b); here R_1 and R_2 are any adversary's generated values.

When A receives the message in the step (2b), it decrypts R_1 to obtain a session key, which results in the value $K_1' = \{c_2\}_{SA} \oplus R_1$. Although the term $\{c_2\}_{SA}$ is not known to $\mathcal{I}$ at this stage, $\mathcal{I}$ can obtain $\{c_2\}_{SA}$ in the step 3, in which the term $\{c_2\}_{SA} \oplus R_2$ occurs in its second half. As R_2 is known to $\mathcal{I}$, the session key K_1' can be derived.

4   DSSK Protocol

Denning and Sacco [7] improves the NSSK protocol using time-stamps. The modified protocol is as follows:

$$(1)\ A \longrightarrow S : A, B$$
$$(2)\ S \longrightarrow A : \{B, K_{AB}, T, \{A, K_{AB}, T\}_{SB}\}_{SA}$$
$$(3)\ A \longrightarrow B : \{A, K_{AB}, T\}_{SB}$$

The protocols works essentially in the same way as the NSSK protocol. The new term T represents a time-stamp, and it is assumed that the local clocks of all network parties are loosely synchronized.

DSSK with CBC Mode of Encryption

This attack is listed in Fig 3, in which the adversary succeeds in impersonating B to A, i.e, at the end of the attack $\mathcal{I}$ in the role of B has a shared key with A. In the setup phase, $\mathcal{I}$ sends a request to S for establishing a connection with A, and as a result, $\mathcal{I}$ receives the terms $\bar{c}_5^a$ and $\bar{c}_6^a$, which are later used in the main phase of the attack.

In the main phase of the attack, $\mathcal{I}$ intercepts the reply from S and replace c_2 and c_3 with $\bar{c}_5^a$ and $\bar{c}_6^a$ respectively. Consequently, the last three messages will decrypt to some random data when A later sends them to B, however, $\mathcal{I}$ can pretend to be B. The session key for A and $\mathcal{I}(B)$ is $K_1 \oplus \bar{c}_4^a \oplus c_1$. Clearly, this term is computable by $\mathcal{I}$ because K_1, $\bar{c}_4^a$ and c_1 are known to $\mathcal{I}$.

The term $\bar{c}_6^a$ is decrypted to T_1. The Setup phase of the attack needs to be in real-time (in a loose sense) so that the difference between T_1 and T_2 is tolerable. As per the authors of the protocol, the definition of real-time is quite relaxed, namely a delay up to $\triangle t_1 + \triangle t_2$ is tolerable, where $\triangle t_1$ is the interval representing normal time-shift between A's local clock and the server clock, and $\triangle t_2$ is the expected network delay. This value is typically equal to a few seconds for most of the networks, such as the Internet.

Messages
Setup
(1) $\mathcal{I} \longrightarrow S : \mathcal{I}, A$
(2) $S \longrightarrow \mathcal{I} : iv_1^a, iv_2^a, c_1^a = \{A \oplus iv_1^a\}_{S\mathcal{I}}, c_2^a = \{K_1 \oplus c_1^a\}_{S\mathcal{I}}, c_3^a = \{T_1 \oplus c_2^a\}_{S\mathcal{I}}, c_4^a = \{(\bar{c}_4^a = \{\mathcal{I} \oplus iv_2^a\}_{SA}) \oplus c_3^a\}_{S\mathcal{I}}, c_5^a = \{(\bar{c}_5^a = \{K_1 \oplus \bar{c}_4^a\}_{SA}) \oplus c_4^a\}_{S\mathcal{I}}, c_6^a = \{(\bar{c}_6^a = \{T_1 \oplus \bar{c}_5^a\}_{SA}) \oplus c_5^a\}_{S\mathcal{I}}$
Attack
(1) $A \longrightarrow S : A, B$
(2a) $S \longrightarrow \mathcal{I}(A) : iv_1, iv_2, c_1 = \{B \oplus iv_1\}_{SA}, c_2 = \{K_2 \oplus c_1\}_{SA}, c_3 = \{T_2 \oplus c_2\}_{SA}, c_4 = \{\{A \oplus iv_2\}_{SB} \oplus c_3\}_{SA}, c_5 = \{\{K_2 \oplus \{A \oplus iv_2\}_{SB}\}_{SB} \oplus c_4\}_{SA}, c_6 = \{\{T_2 \oplus \{K_2 \oplus \{A \oplus iv_2\}_{SB}\}_{SB}\}_{SB} \oplus c_5\}_{SA}$
(2b) $\mathcal{I}(S) \longrightarrow A : iv_1, iv_2, c_1 = \{B \oplus iv_1\}_{SA}, \bar{c}_5^a, \bar{c}_6^a, c_4, c_5, c_6$
(3) $A \longrightarrow \mathcal{I}(B) : $ random data

Fig. 3. Attack on CBC-version of DSSK Protocol

Messages
Setup
(1) $\mathcal{I} \longrightarrow S : \mathcal{I}, A$
(2) $S \longrightarrow \mathcal{I} : iv_1^a, iv_2^a, c_1^a = \{iv_1^a\}_{S\mathcal{I}} \oplus A, c_2^a = \{c_1^a\}_{S\mathcal{I}} \oplus K_1, c_3^a = \{c_2^a\}_{S\mathcal{I}} \oplus T_1, c_4^a = \{c_3^a\}_{S\mathcal{I}} \oplus (\bar{c}_4^a = \{iv_2^a\}_{SA} \oplus \mathcal{I}), c_5^a = \{c_4^a\}_{S\mathcal{I}} \oplus (\bar{c}_5^a = \{\bar{c}_4^a\}_{SA} \oplus K_1), c_6^a = \{c_5^a\}_{S\mathcal{I}} \oplus (\bar{c}_6^a = \{\bar{c}_5^a\}_{SA} \oplus T_1)$
Attack
(1) $A \longrightarrow S : A, B$
(2a) $S \longrightarrow \mathcal{I}(A) : iv_1, iv_2, c_1 = \{iv_1\}_{SA} \oplus B, c_2 = \{c_1\}_{SA} \oplus K_2, c_3 = \{c_2\}_{SA} \oplus T_2, c_4 = \{c_3\}_{SA} \oplus \{iv_2\}_{SB} \oplus A, c_5 = \{c_4\}_{SA} \oplus \{\{iv_2\}_{SB} \oplus A\}_{SB} \oplus K_2, c_6 = \{c_5\}_{SA} \oplus \{\{\{iv_2\}_{SB} \oplus A\}_{SB} \oplus K_2\}_{SB} \oplus T_2$
(2b) $\mathcal{I}(S) \longrightarrow A : iv_1, iv_2, c_1 = \{iv_1\}_{SA} \oplus B, \bar{c}_5^a, \bar{c}_6^a, c_1, R_1, R_2$
(3) $A \longrightarrow \mathcal{I}(B) : iv_2, \{\bar{c}_6^a\}_{SA} \oplus c_1, \{c_1\}_{SA} \oplus R_1, \{R_1\}_{SA} \oplus R_2$

Fig. 4. Attack on CFB-version of DSSK Protocol

DSSK with CFB Mode of Encryption

This attack is similar to the attack on the CBC version. The adversary $\mathcal{I}$ obtains the terms $\bar{c}_5^a$ and $\bar{c}_6^a$ in the setup phase. In the main phase, $\mathcal{I}$ intercepts the reply from the server in the step (2a) and replaces the terms c_2, c_3, c_4, c_5, and c_6 with $\bar{c}_5^a$, $\bar{c}_6^a$, c_1, R_1, and R_2 respectively; here, R_1 and R_2 are any values known to $\mathcal{I}$.

When A receives the modified message in the step (2b), the session key is computed to be $\{c_1\}_{SA} \oplus \bar{c}_5^a$. The term $\{c_1\}_{SA}$ is not known to $\mathcal{I}$; that is why c_4 and c_5 of the step (2a) were replaced by c_1 and R_1. The decryption of c_1 and R_1 results in $\{\bar{c}_6^a\}_{SA} \oplus c_1$ and $\{c_1\}_{SA} \oplus R_1$, which A sends supposedly to B in the step (3). In this way, $\mathcal{I}$ can derive the term $\{c_1\}_{SA}$. The decryption of $\bar{c}_6^a$ results in T_1, which is a valid time-stamp based on the same arguments presented for the CBC version.

5   Private-Key Symbolic Encryption Schemes

The reported attacks cannot be produced in a security model in which encryption is specified as one monolithic ciphertext, which hides the structure of a ciphertext. On the other hand, a ciphertext resulting from a block-cipher based encryption scheme always has a semantic structure.

We propose that symbolic encryption should be specified using the abstraction of a block-cipher, because the output of a block cipher can be safely assumed as a monolithic ciphertext. Further, a block cipher is the most natural abstraction of actual implementation and can be instantiated, e.g., with an appropriate algorithm from Advance Encryption Standard (AES).

In a formal security model that supports the Xor operator, it is quite straight forward to specify commonly used cryptographic encryption schemes, such as CBC and CFB. In our proposal, however, we do not assume that the support for the Xor operator is available. The motivation of this exclusion is contemporary and based on the observation that properly incorporating the Xor operator in formal security models is a long-standing open problem [21, 22]. The Xor operator is not supported by most of the verification tools, e.g., OFMC [11], LySa [12], and Spi-calculus [30]. On the other hand, the proposed Xor-free encryption schemes can be seamlessly used in existing formal security models.

Our assumptions are as follows. We consider a block-cipher as a family of pseudo random permutations (PRP) [31]. We consider three types of adversaries that are computationally bounded in a sense that their attacks strategies terminate in a polynomial time. The three types are passive adversary, CPA-adversary (i.e, an adversary who can access an encryption oracle), and CPA/CCA-adversary (i.e., an adversary who can access both encryption and decryption oracles.)

A few notations used in the following sections are as follows. An *overline* on a variable name, such as $\overline{M}_1$, indicates that the variable is on binary strings. We use the the notation $\mathcal{U}_s$ to represent the uniform distribution on strings of size s. The notation $\overline{U}_s$ is used to represent a random variable on the uniform distribution: $\overline{U}_s \leftarrow \mathcal{U}_s$. The concatenation of random variables $\overline{U}_s^1, \ldots, \overline{U}_s^n$ is just another random variable $\overline{U}_{ns}$, where $\overline{U}_{ns} \leftarrow \mathcal{U}_{ns}$. The notation $dist[.]$ represents the probability distribution of its argument, e.g., $dist[\overline{U}_s^1]$ is $\mathcal{U}_s$.

In the following, we define a minimal symbolic encryption system.

Definition 1 (Symbolic Encryption System). *On the set of all base terms* $\mathcal{V}$*, with a security parameter* $s = log_2(|\mathcal{V}|)$*, we define a private-key symbolic encryption system as follows.*

- $M ::= M, M \mid V \mid \{M\}_K \mid \{C\}_K^{-1}$
- $V ::= x \in \mathcal{V}$
- $K ::= M$ *(Syntactic sugar to indicate that the term* K *is being used as a key)*
- $C ::= \{M\}_K$ *(Syntactic sugar to indicate that the term is a ciphertext)*
- *Cancellation Rule :* $M = \{\{M\}_K\}_K^{-1} = \{\{M\}_K^{-1}\}_K$
- *Encryption Rule : Given* K *and* M*,* $\{M\}_K$ *can be derived.*
- *Decryption Rule : Given* K *and* C*,* $\{C\}_K^{-1}$ *can be derived.*

Here M*,* K*,* C *and* V *are the formal expression; while* M*,* K *and* C *are the corresponding meta-variables.*

To define the semantics of the symbolic encryption system, we use the notion of variadic ciphers [32], which can take binary strings of different lengths as inputs. The reason for employing a variadic cipher is based on the fact that M in Def. 1 consists of a variable number of base terms. To model the arbitrary size of a key

(K in Def. 1), we extend the notion of a variadic cipher to an idealized variadic cipher (IVC), namely a family of functions that contains an infinite number of variadic functions. We represent the i-th idealized variadic cipher as $\Pi_i(.)$.

The notion of an IVC can be compared to a traditional cipher, which is modelled as a family containing a fixed number of PRPs (pseudo random permutations) and all of the PRPs are of the same size, e.g., AES with 256 bit key is a family containing 2^{256} PRPs of size 128 bit. Note, however, that the use of IVCs is just for a simpler exposition. Later, we define our symbolic schemes in such a way that only the restricted forms of IVCs occur that can be instantiated with traditional ciphers.

Definition 2 (Cryptographic Semantics). *The cryptographic semantics of the symbolic encryption system in Def. 1 are as follows.*

- $V \stackrel{def}{=} \overline{V} \in \{0,1\}^s$ *(Each base term is encoded as a bit string of a fixed length s, such that $s = log_2(|\mathcal{V}|)$)*
- $M_1, M_2 \stackrel{def}{=} \overline{M_1, M_2}$ *(Concatenation of two bit strings)*
- $\{M\}_K \stackrel{def}{=} \overline{\{M\}_K} = \Pi_{\overline{K}}(\overline{M})$,
  where $\Pi_{\overline{K}}(\overline{M})$ is the $\overline{K}$th cipher in a family of IVCs.
- $\{C\}_K^{-1} \stackrel{def}{=} \overline{\{C\}_K^{-1}}$, *such that $\overline{C} = \Pi_{\overline{K}}(\overline{\{C\}_K^{-1}})$.*

Definition 3 (Security). *We define the following three security properties, assuming that K is not known to the adversary.*

WP-security *(Weak Privacy Against Passive Attack)* $\stackrel{def}{=}$ *It is infeasible for a passive adversary $\mathcal{I}$ to compute $\overline{C}$ for a known $\overline{M}$, s.t., $C = \{M\}_K$. Further, it is also infeasible for $\mathcal{I}$ to compute $\overline{M}$ for a known $\overline{C}$, s.t., $M = \{C\}_K^{-1}$.*

NM-security *(Non-malleability Against CPA/CCA)* $\stackrel{def}{=}$ *It is infeasible for a CPA/CCA-adversary to compute $\overline{C'}$ for a known $\overline{C}$, s.t., a pre-specified relation $\mathcal{R}(\overline{M}, \overline{M'})$ holds[3], where $M = \{C\}_K^{-1}$ and $M' = \{C'\}_K^{-1}$.*

IND-security *(Indistinguishability Against CPA)* $\stackrel{def}{=}$ *It is infeasible for a CPA-adversary to distinguish between the probability distributions $dist[\overline{\{M\}_K}]$ and $\mathcal{U}_l$, for all values of M, where $l = |\overline{\{M\}_K}|$. [4]*

Clearly, WP-security is implied by IND-security, because if an adversary can recover the plaintext from a ciphertext then he can always distinguish between the ciphertext and a random bit string. In our proofs, we also use the fact that if an encryption function is deterministic then it cannot be IND-secure [13]. Note that IND-security and NM-security are not comparable in our model, because we use the abstraction of a cipher, which is a deterministic encryption algorithm for a fixed key. As shown by Katz and Yung [2], for probabilistic encryption, there are well-defined relations between NM-security and IND-security under different attack models.

---

[3] E.g., $\overline{M} = \overline{M_1}, \overline{M_2}$ and $\overline{M'} = \overline{M_2}, \overline{M_1}$

[4] Equivalently, $\mathcal{I}$ can only succeeds in the indistinguishability experiment (IND-P2-C0) [2] with a negligible probability.

Claim 1 (Soundness of Symbolic Encryption System). *The symbolic encryption function* $\{M\}_K$ *is WP,NM-secure if a CPA/CCA-adversary cannot derive K.*

Proof (Sketch). As per the semantics, $\{M\}_K$ is a PRP corresponding to $\Pi_{\overline{K}}(\overline{M})$. For a secret K, mapping from $\overline{M}$ to $\Pi_{\overline{K}}(\overline{M})$ is secret, which implies weak privacy for a polynomial-time adversary. The mapping from an input to the output is random, which implies non-malleability. The formal proof is trivial (but tedious) and is left out.   □

In the following, we introduce four symbolic encryption schemes. The direct implementations of these schemes, as per the semantics, assume the existence of one of the two ciphers corresponding to the key size s and $2s$, e.g., AES-128 and AES-256.

Definition 4 (Symbolic Encryption Schemes). *Let M and K be the two variable of symbolic encryption system with semantics $\overline{M}$ and $\overline{K}$, such that $|\overline{M}| \leq s^c$ and $|\overline{K}| = s$, for a constant c. Let $\overline{M}_1, \ldots, \overline{M}_N$ be the parsing of $\overline{M}$, such that $|\overline{M}_i| = s$, for $1 \leq i \leq N$. ECB symbolic encryption (ECB-SE), bulk symbolic encryption (BLK-SE), randomized symbolic encryption (RND-SE), and randomized-bulk symbolic encryption (RNB-SE), are defined by the ECB-rule, BLK-rule, RND-rule, and RNB-rule respectively.*

$$ECB\text{-}rule\text{:} \quad \frac{\{M\}_K}{\{M_1\}_K, \ldots, \{M_i\}_K, \ldots, \{M_N\}_K}$$

$$BLK\text{-}rule\text{:} \quad \frac{\{M\}_K}{\{M_1, \ldots, M_i, \ldots, M_N\}_K}$$

$$RND\text{-}rule\text{:} \quad \frac{\{M\}_K}{V_1, \{M_1\}_{K,V_1}, \ldots, V_i, \{M_i\}_{K,V_i}, \ldots, V_N, \{M_N\}_{K,V_N}}$$

$$RNB\text{-}rule\text{:} \quad \frac{\{M\}_K}{V_1, \{M_1, \ldots, M_i, \ldots, M_N\}_{K,V_1}}$$

In the above definition, s^c stands for a polynomial in s; without a polynomial length restriction, none of the existing cryptographic encryption schemes is secure. In the above rules, the base terms $V_1, \ldots, V_N$ appear as free variables, therefore these variables are assumed to be instantiated with unique values in each instance of a protocol. Also note that, e.g., the key used to create ciphertext $\{M_1, \ldots, M_i, \ldots, M_N\}_{K,V_1}$ is K, V_1, which semantically corresponds to the concatenation of $\overline{K}$ and $\overline{V}_1$. The main motivation for the above division is their correspondence to some of the existing cryptographic schemes, as described in the following sections.

6   Security Analysis

In the following, we analyse these schemes for the security properties in Def. 3.

Claim 2. *The ECB-SE is WP-secure, but it is neither NM-secure nor IND-secure.*

Proof. Each encrypted term $\{M_i\}_K$ in the ECB scheme is a PRP and is WP,NM-secure (Claim 1). From WP,NM-security of the terms, we derive the security properties of the whole scheme.

It is clear that the WP-security of the scheme can be reduced to the WP-security of its terms, because if a passive adversary can recover the plaintext $\overline{M_1}, \ldots, \overline{M_N}$ then he can invert a PRP on N different values. The same observation holds for deriving ciphertexts from plaintexts.

The scheme is not IND-secure because it is a deterministic function [13]. The ECB scheme is not NM-secure due to a simple attack. In the attack, an adversary permutes the individual encrypted terms. For example, given a ciphertext $\{M_1\}_K, \{M_2\}_K$, the adversary can produce another valid ciphertext $\{M_2\}_K, \{M_1\}_K$ that has a related plaintext to the plaintext of the first ciphertext. This completes the proof.   □

Claim 3. *The output distribution of RND-SE is $\mathcal{U}_{Ns}$.*

Proof. The size of each i-th term in a ciphertext of RND-SE is $|\overline{\{M_i\}_{K,V_i}}| = s$, as per Def. 4. Therefore, the number of plausible ciphertexts for the i-th term is 2^s. In each term, V_i is used as part of the key. Being V_i a free variable, each application of RND-rule uses a new value. With a secret $\overline{K}$, there are 2^s equally probable values for the key $\overline{K}, \overline{V}_i$, in every application of the RNB-rule. Consequently, the output of $\Pi_{\overline{K}, \overline{V}_i}(\overline{M})$ is evenly distributed on 2^s plausible ciphertexts for a known value of $\overline{M}$.

Therefore, we have $\overline{U_s^i} = \overline{\{M_i\}_{K,V_i}}$ where $dist[\overline{U_s^i}] = \mathcal{U}_s$, for $1 \le i \le N$. The distribution of complete ciphertext is $dist[\overline{U_s^1}, \ldots, \overline{U_s^N}] = \mathcal{U}_{Ns}$.   □

Claim 4. *The RND-SE is WP,IND-secure, but it is not NM-secure.*

Proof. The RND-SE is clearly not NM-secure, because the same permutation attack of Claim 2 also works for the RND-SE. Since WP-security is implied by IND-security, we only need to prove that RND-SE is IND-secure. For IND-security, a CPA-adversary cannot distinguish between a ciphertext corresponding to the adversary's plaintext and a random string $\overline{U_{Ns}}$, where $\overline{U_{Ns}} \leftarrow \mathcal{U}_{Ns}$. From Claim 3, the output distribution of RND-SE is $\mathcal{U}_{Ns}$, which is same as that of the random bit string. Hence, RND-SE is WP,IND-secure but is not NM-secure.   □

Claim 5. *The BLK-SE is WP,NM-secure, but it is not IND-secure.*

Proof. This scheme represents one variadic PRP and is therefore WP,NM-secure (Claim 1). The scheme is deterministic, therefore it cannot be IND-secure [13].
                                               □

Claim 6. *The scheme RNB-SE is WP,IND,NM-secure.*

The ciphertext of the scheme is also a single variadic PRP and is therefore WP,NM-secure. To show that it is IND-secure, similar to Claim 4, the probability distribution of a ciphertext corresponding to a known plaintext must be computationally indistinguishable from a random bit string for a CPA-adversary.

The size of the ciphertext in RNB-SE is Ns, therefore the domain corresponding to plausible ciphertexts is of size 2^{Ns}. Since the term $\overline{V}$ is assigned a new value on each application of RNB-rule, there are 2^s uniformly distributed values for the key $\overline{K}, \overline{V}$. Consequently, there are 2^s uniformly distributed values for the ciphertext.

To violate IND-security, a CPA-adversary is required to distinguish between the following two distributions: the uniform distribution on 2^s strings each of size Ns (corresponding to the ciphertext); and the uniform distribution $\mathcal{U}_{Ns}$ (corresponding to a random string.) The most efficient known technique to distinguish between two uniform distributions is to compare the number of collisions in the lists of values drawn from the respective distributions.

From the birthday problem, we know that in a list of q ciphertexts computed from the same plaintext, an upper bound on the probability of any collision is $0.5q(q-1)2^{-s}$, and for random strings drawn from $\mathcal{U}_{Ns}$ a lower bound on the probability of any collision is $0.3q(q-1)2^{-Ns}$. Although the maximum difference between the probabilities of collisions, namely $0.5q(q-1)2^{-s} - 0.3q(q-1)2^{-Ns}$, is relatively large, but the difference is only noticeable if an adversary is able to generate at least one collision.

Since $0.5q(q-1)2^{-s} > 0.3q(q-1)2^{-Ns}$ and $0.5q(q-1)2^{-s}$ is negligible in s assuming q is polynomial in s, the probability of occurrence of a collision is negligible. For a polynomial-time adversary, q must be a polynomial in s. Therefore, we conclude that adversary cannot distinguish between the two distributions. Hence, RNB-SE is IND,NM,WP-secure.   □

The results presented in this section are listed in Table 1. In all of the encryption schemes in Def. 4 the key size is fixed: it is s for ECB-SE and BLK-SE, and it is $2s$ for RND-SE and RNB-SE. Further, for ECB-SE and RND-SE, the block size is also fixed. This means that ECB-SE and RND-SE can be implemented with traditional block ciphers, and BLK-SE and RNB-SE schemes can be implemented with variadic ciphers [32]. Besides such semantic-oriented implementations, other cryptographic algorithms can be chosen for an implementation using the security properties (Claim 2-6) of each scheme.

We know that a cryptographic message authentication code (MAC) can be used to provide the non-malleability of a plaintext under encrypt-then-MAC method (i.e., MAC of ciphertext) [33]. Further note that CBC/CFB mode of encryption provide IND-security under CPA [9, 10].

Therefore, e.g., ECB-SE can be implemented using AES in ECB mode of encryption; RND-SE can be implemented using AES in CBC mode of encryption; BLK-SE can be implemented using AES in ECB mode along with a message authentication code (MAC); and RNB-SE can be implemented using AES in CBC mode along with a MAC. It is certainly possible (perhaps after extending the system of Def. 1) to define symbolic schemes that correspond to other forms of cryptographic encryption, such as the counter mode of encryption.

7   Discussion

In practice, it is nonetheless dangerous to assume that a system developer will actually discover and use the correct cryptographic scheme that meets the security requirements of a particular use of symbolic encryption. System developers often use an implementation instance that seems appropriate, e.g., in this paper, the CBC implementations of encryption in NSSK and DSKK protocols indeed guarantee privacy in a strong sense [13]; however, non-malleability of the cipher-texts, an implicit assumption, is also required for the security of these protocols.

One may always choose to employ a strong encryption scheme meeting the requirements of RNB-SE however, the cost associated with such an overly cautious approach cannot be ignored in practice. For example, if the symbolic model of a protocol that uses ECB-SE is secure then this means that the protocol can be implemented in a relatively efficient manner: a random number generator is not required; the algorithm for message authentication code (MAC, used to guarantee non-malleability) is not required; and communication bandwidth is reduced because we do not need to transmit initialization vectors and MAC codes. Moreover, parallelisation of the encryption process is straight forward.

In many applications, such optimizations can make a huge difference, e.g., for a hypervisor which has to process millions of requests per second, and a sensor node in which memory, computational power and energy are scarce resources. Many symbolic protocols remain secure when encryption requirements are met by a weaker symbolic encryption scheme, such as ECB-SE and CBC mode of encryption; in this way a level of safe optimization can be achieved.

It is important to remember that safely instantiating a symbolic encryption scheme with a cryptographic encryption scheme does not mean that the resultant protocol will be secure, because there are many attacks that do not rely on encryption, e.g., Lowe's attack [34] on public-key version of Needham-Schroeder protocol relies on the assumption of a corrupt insider, Denning-Sacco's attack [7] relies on the availability of a compromised old session key. Moreover, there are many security vulnerabilities that are outside the realm of (mathematical) cryptography, e.g., buffer-overflow.

Table 1. Summary of Results

Scheme	WP	IND	NM	Instantiation Examples
ECB-SE	√	×	×	AES-128 in ECB mode of encryption
BLK-SE	√	×	√	(1) AES-128 in ECB mode of encryption with SHA-256 as MAC (2) Variadic cipher
RND-SE	√	√	×	(1,2) AES-128 in CBC/CFB mode of encryption
RNB-SE	√	√	√	(1,2) AES-128 in CBC/CFB mode of encryption with SHA-256 as MAC (3) Variadic cipher with a randomized key

8   Conclusion

In this paper, we reported new attacks on reasonable implementations of well-known protocols. It appears that there is no inherent limitation in symbolic models which may have prevented detecting these attacks. We notice that encryption on multiple terms is traditionally specified as one big monolithic encrypted block, which, however, is not a good way of specifying it for practice-oriented security analysis. We presented four refined ways in which encryption can be specified in a symbolic model. The proposed specifications not only help to avoid many implementation vulnerabilities similar to the reported attacks, but they also provide a degree of safe optimization. We hope that our work will bring symbolic encryption closer to the secure implementation of encryption.

References

1. Dworkin, M.: Recommendation for block cipher modes of operation. methods and techniques. Technical report, DTIC Document (2001)
2. Katz, J., Yung, M.: Complete characterization of security notions for probabilistic private-key encryption. In: Theory of Computing. ACM (2000)
3. Dolev, D., Yao, A.: On the security of public key protocols. IEEE Trans. on Information Theory (1983)
4. Bellovin, S.: Problem areas for the IP security protocols. In: USENIX UNIX Security Symp. (1996)
5. Paterson, K.G., Yau, A.K.L.: Cryptography in Theory and Practice: The Case of Encryption in IPsec. In: Vaudenay, S. (ed.) EUROCRYPT 2006. LNCS, vol. 4004, pp. 12–29. Springer, Heidelberg (2006)
6. Needham, R., Schroeder, M.: Using encryption for authentication in large networks of computers. Communications of the ACM 21(12), 993–999 (1978)
7. Denning, D., Sacco, G.: Timestamps in key distribution protocols. Communications of the ACM 24(8), 533–536 (1981)
8. Needham, R., Schroeder, M.: Authentication revisited. Operating Systems Review 21(1) (1987)
9. Goldwasser, S., Bellare, M.: Lecture notes on cryptography. Course "Cryptography and computer security" at MIT 1999 (1996) 1999
10. Fouque, P.-A., Martinet, G., Poupard, G.: Practical Symmetric On-Line Encryption. In: Johansson, T. (ed.) FSE 2003. LNCS, vol. 2887, pp. 362–375. Springer, Heidelberg (2003)
11. Basin, D., Mödersheim, S., Vigano, L.: Ofmc: A symbolic model checker for security protocols. International Journal of Information Security 4(3), 181–208 (2005)
12. Bodei, C., Buchholtz, M., Degano, P., Nielson, F., Nielson, H.: Static validation of security protocols. Journal of Computer Security 13(3), 347–390 (2005)
13. Goldwasser, S., Micali, S.: Probabilistic encryption. J. of Computer and System Sciences 28(2) (1984)
14. Meadows, C.: Formal methods for cryptographic protocol analysis: Emerging issues and trends. Selected Areas in Communications 21(1), 44–54 (2003)
15. Moore, J.: Protocol failures in cryptosystems. Proc. of the IEEE 76(5), 594–602 (1988)
16. Boyd, C.: Hidden assumptions in cryptographic protocols. In: Proc. of Computers and Digital Techniques, vol. 137, pp. 433–436. IET (1990)

17. Mao, W., Boyd, C.: On the use of encryption in cryptographic protocols. In: Codes and Cyphers (1995)
18. Stubblebine, S., Meadows, C.: Formal characterization and automated analysis of known-pair and chosen-text attacks. IEEE J. on Selected Areas in Communications 18(4), 571–581 (2000)
19. Kremer, S., Ryan, M.: Analysing the vulnerability of protocols to produce known-pair and chosen-text attacks. Electronic Notes in Theoretical Computer Science 128(5), 87–104 (2005)
20. Degabriele, J., Paterson, K.: Attacking the IPsec standards in encryption-only configurations. In: IEEE Symp. S&P, pp. 335–349. IEEE (2007)
21. Chevalier, Y., Kusters, R., Rusinowitch, M., Turuani, M.: An NP decision procedure for protocol insecurity with XOR. In: Logic in CS. IEEE (2003)
22. Küsters, R., Truderung, T.: Reducing protocol analysis with xor to the xor-free case in the horn theory based approach. In: Proc. of CCS. ACM (2008)
23. Lowe, G.: A family of attacks upon authentication protocols. Technical Report 1997/5, University of Leicester (1997)
24. Chevalier, Y., Vigneron, L.: Automated Unbounded Verification of Security Protocols. In: Brinksma, E., Larsen, K.G. (eds.) CAV 2002. LNCS, vol. 2404, pp. 125–171. Springer, Heidelberg (2002)
25. Abadi, M., Rogaway, P.: Reconciling two views of cryptography. In: TCS: Exploring New Frontiers of Theoretical Informatics, pp. 3–22 (2000)
26. Herzog, J.C., Liskov, M., Micali, S.: Plaintext Awareness via Key Registration. In: Boneh, D. (ed.) CRYPTO 2003. LNCS, vol. 2729, pp. 548–564. Springer, Heidelberg (2003)
27. Micciancio, D., Warinschi, B.: Soundness of Formal Encryption in the Presence of Active Adversaries. In: Naor, M. (ed.) TCC 2004. LNCS, vol. 2951, pp. 133–151. Springer, Heidelberg (2004)
28. Canetti, R., Herzog, J.: Universally composable symbolic security analysis. J. of Cryptology (2011)
29. Bellare, M., Boldyreva, A., Knudsen, L.R., Namprempre, C.: Online Ciphers and the Hash-CBC Construction. In: Kilian, J. (ed.) CRYPTO 2001. LNCS, vol. 2139, pp. 292–309. Springer, Heidelberg (2001)
30. Abadi, M., Gordon, A.D.: Reasoning About Cryptographic Protocols in the Spi Calculus. In: Mazurkiewicz, A., Winkowski, J. (eds.) CONCUR 1997. LNCS, vol. 1243, pp. 59–73. Springer, Heidelberg (1997)
31. Luby, M., Rackoff, C.: How to Construct Pseudo-random Permutations from Pseudo-random Functions. In: Williams, H.C. (ed.) CRYPTO 1985. LNCS, vol. 218, pp. 447–447. Springer, Heidelberg (1986)
32. Bellare, M., Rogaway, P.: On the Construction of Variable-Input-Length Ciphers. In: Knudsen, L.R. (ed.) FSE 1999. LNCS, vol. 1636, pp. 231–244. Springer, Heidelberg (1999)
33. Bellare, M., Namprempre, C.: Authenticated Encryption: Relations among Notions and Analysis of the Generic Composition Paradigm. In: Okamoto, T. (ed.) ASIACRYPT 2000. LNCS, vol. 1976, pp. 531–545. Springer, Heidelberg (2000)
34. Lowe, G.: Breaking and fixing the Needham-Schroeder public-key protocol using FDR. Tools and Algos. for the Construction and Analysis of Systems (1996)

Decision Procedures for Simulatability[*]

Charanjit S. Jutla[1] and Arnab Roy[2]

[1] IBM T.J. Watson Research Center,
Yorktown Heights, NY 10598, USA
[2] Fujitsu Laboratories of America,
Sunnyvale, CA 94058, USA

Abstract. We address the question of automatically proving security theorems in the universally composable (UC) model for ideal and real functionalities composed of if-then-else programs with uniform random number generation and data objects from the additive group of $\mathbb{F}_{2^m}$. We prove that for this restricted yet powerful language framework, there is an effective procedure to decide if a real functionality realizes an ideal functionality, and this procedure is in computational time independent of m, which is essentially the security parameter.

To this end, we consider multivariate *pseudo-linear* functions, which are functions computed by branching programs over data objects from the additive group of $\mathbb{F}_{2^m}$. The conditionals in such programs are built from equality constraints over linear expressions, closed under negation and conjunction.

Let $f_1, f_2, ..., f_k$ be k pseudo-linear functions in n variables, and let f be another pseudo-linear function in the same n variables. We show that if f is a function of the given k functions, then it must be a *pseudo-linear* function of the given k functions. This generalizes the straightforward claim for just linear functions. Proceeding further, we generalize the theorem to randomized pseudo-linear functions. We also prove a more general theorem where the k functions can in addition take further arguments, and prove that if f can be represented as an iterated composition of these k functions, then it can be represented as a probabilistic pseudo-linear iterated composition of these functions. Additionally, we allow f itself to be a randomized function, i.e. we give a procedure for deciding if f is a probabilistic sub-exponential (in m) time iterated function of the given k randomized functions. The decision procedure runs in computational time independent of m.

1 Introduction

Security primitives and protocols are deceptively concise. While they may have a short description, a very specialized level of expertise is required for developing these protocols and reasoning as to why they meet a specific security goal. In the last few decades, the field of cryptography has come a long way in understanding

[*] Authors were supported in part by the Department of Homeland Security under grant FA8750-08-2-0091.

S. Foresti, M. Yung, and F. Martinelli (Eds.): ESORICS 2012, LNCS 7459, pp. 573–590, 2012.

fundamental principles and laying down the framework of specifying security goals and proof methods on a firm formal footing.

Concomitant to the maturity of this field, a substantial research community has grown around attempting to consolidate and automate these reasoning principles so that that the manual need to provide tedious and cumbersome proofs is removed. Importantly, automation provides greater assurance since all possible corner cases are also considered, eliminating subtle errors.

Related Work. Majority of previous work in formal methods [1–4] has focused on abstracting some of the fundamental primitives of cryptography, *viz.*, encryption, signatures, hashes and so on, as part of the language of specifying the protocols. Though some of these methodologies have even led to automation of the verification procedure [5], all these systems have only been proven sound, and there has been very limited work on completeness of these logics (cf. [6]). Another drawback has been the coarseness of specification required by these lines of work. The work by [7] is a promising approach to reason about fine-grained primitives by leveraging axiomatization of bounded arithmetic [8], but because of its still rather general number-theoretic approach, it may still be incomplete (see [9]). Similarly, newer works like CertiCrypt [10] and EasyCrypt [11] show sequence of human-generated games to be indistinguishable by employing general purpose theorem-provers, which clearly do not possess a completeness property. Important works [12, 13] have also tried to leverage the UC paradigm (also see [14] for decision procedures for equality of probabilistic terms), but still the simulators in these works have to be human-generated. In particular, these approaches focus on proving indistinguishability of games/processes, but if there is a simulator required to act as a wrapper around the ideal functionality, then the simulator is built by humans.

Our Contributions. In this paper, we take a purely algebraic approach to the problem and focus on using the UC paradigm to build an appropriate specification and definition language which is fairly general and yet complete (and even efficiently decidable; specifically with complexity independent of the security parameter). In particular, we seek an automated procedure which finds a simulator if it exists and returns failure if the protocol is not simulatable in the ideal world. To start with, in this work we focus on specification and definition languages which are general enough to capture a rich class of high level protocols that use cryptographic primitives as ideal functionalities.

In the UC framework [15], which builds on the ideal process emulation paradigm of [16], the specification of the target (multi-party) protocol is given by an *ideal functionality* which is handed all the inputs, and which computes the respective outputs all the while interacting with an adversary in a specified way. Thus, the *specification language* is just the language in which the ideal functionality can be defined. The actual protocol is a set of definitions, one for each of the parties for their internal computation and interaction with other parties and/or the adversary. Thus the *definition language* is a language in which the code of each party in the real protocol can be defined. A protocol is (informally) considered *secure* if for every adversary in the real protocol, there is an adversary interacting with the ideal functionality, such that it is impossible to efficiently distinguish between the two[1]. Most such proofs of security are obtained by a black box simulation paradigm, i.e. by obtaining a Simulator that simulates the "view" of the real world adversary, while accessing the latter only in a black-box manner. In such a black box paradigm (which in the case of UC security is known to be sufficient (see [15] Sec. 4.3.2)), the question of security of the real protocol boils down to deciding if the view of the adversary (and/or the Environment) in the real protocol can be efficiently simulated by accessing the ideal functionality's interface.

For our base language, both the specification language and the definition language are just if-then-else or **branching programs** involving data objects from the additive group of fields of characteristic two. The conditionals are built from equality constraints of linear expressions, closed under negation and conjunction. The multivariate functions computed by such programs are called *pseudo-linear* functions, because they are piece-wise linear over different linear subspaces. Before we define these functions more formally, we state the completeness theorem for such pseudo-linear functions, which allows us to claim efficient decidability of simulatability.

While for linear multivariate functions a *completeness theorem* which states that if a linear function f of n variables is a function of k other linear functions (in the same n variables), then f must be a *linear function* of the k linear functions, is well known and rather easy to prove, a similar completeness result for pseudo-linear functions is novel and not so easy to prove.

Thus, one of the main results of this paper is a theorem which states that if a pseudo-linear multivariate function f of n variables is a *function* of k pseudo-linear functions $f_1, f_1, ..., f_k$ (in the same n variables), then f must be a *pseudo-linear* function (say, g) of $f_1, f_2, ..., f_k$. Note that it is given that f itself is a pseudo-linear function in the original n variables. Thus in this context, if a simulator must simulate a real-world pseudo-linear function f using pseudo-linear ideal functionality subroutines, then we can restrict the search for simulators to the space of pseudo-linear functions. Since the size of this space is independent of the security parameter[2], this search can be efficient.

Proceeding further, we include random number generation as an additional primitive in both the specification and the definition language, and *extend* the procedures to decide if a *probabilistic poly time* simulator exists for the given set of *randomized* ideal functionalities and *randomized* target function. To this end, we first establish that any randomized pseudo-linear function is statistically equivalent to a randomized pseudo-linear function that generates a *single*

---

[1] Technically, in the UC framework, the distinguisher is just the Environment, which also gets to control and see the inputs and outputs of the honest parties and can control the Adversary as well.

[2] This space can be of size exponential or more in the size of the function descriptions, but since the functions in cryptographic applications tend to be simple and small, we focus on the security parameter as the real complexity parameter.

random number. We call the later class of functions, Simplified Randomized Pseudo-Linear (SRPL) functions.

To model the fact that a simulator can iteratively compose various calls to the different functions in the ideal functionality, we *prove a more general theorem* involving arbitrary iterations of k randomized pseudo-linear functions $f_1(z, y), f_2(z, y), ..., f_k(z, y)$, where y are arguments which the simulator can supply. We construct iterated compositions of these functions and establish that they are bounded in number. The completeness theorem in this setting shows that if there is no simulator which is an iterated composition of these functions, then all probabilistic poly-time simulators are distinguishable from the target function on more than a certain non-negligible fraction of the probability space for any input. This is a much harder theorem to prove because (i) the compositions are distributions rather than fixed quantities and (ii) we are ruling out all simulators which are "close enough" to the target function rather than being exactly same.

For cryptographic applications, this means that an algorithmic search for a simulator in proving that a protocol in this language realizes an ideal functionality (also in this language) is *independent* of the security parameter, as the bounds in the completeness theorem are independent of the field size (the security parameter is usually related to the field size). Since the program sizes in cryptographic protocols are usually small, this can lead to efficient theorem proving.

Open Problems and Scope. We note here that if the real protocol is given in the hybrid model, i.e. by making calls to some other ideal functionalities (to avoid confusion, we will call them hybrid functionalities), our decision procedure still works as long as these hybrid functionalities are also in the same language. To address the situation that the adversary, which may have access to these hybrid functionalities, may call these functionalities an indefinite number of times, we do need to prove a (meta-) theorem which essentially says that it suffices to prove simulatability for adversaries restricted to making a constant number of calls to each of these hybrid functionalities. Such theorems may be easy to prove on a protocol basis, but there is also scope for general theorems based on the structure of these functionalities. This also implies that hybrid functionalities (e.g. Random Oracle or public key encryption (PKE)) that can have indefinitely many table entries, need only be in-lined in the target function with the tables restricted to constant number of entries. Additionally, some hybrid functionalities (e.g. PKE) may require function symbols in their specification – in case of PKE these are the encryption and decryption functions e and d. However, because these function symbols are uninterpreted, i.e. have no constraints on them, an easy extension of our theorems handles such function symbols.

In the future, similar extension to realization of ideal functionalities (i.e. instead of just hybrid functionalities) which support simple tables and uninterpreted functions can be envisioned. Since, most such functionalities, e.g. PKE, are realized using specific algebraic structures, this would require appropriate axiomatization of their underlying operations and computational assumptions (see e.g. [17]). While most cryptographic functionalities which support tables with the size of the entries fixed and with operations limited to keyword search (e.g. PKE, Random Oracle, Ideal Cipher etc.) lead to, or are expected to lead to decidable simulatability, if we allow arbitrary sized entries in tables, and further allow some non-trivial operations on the entries, the question of simulatability becomes *undecidable* [18]. Finally, we remark that our completeness results require sufficiently large fields (as a function of the number of variables in the functionalities), but given that most UC proofs only seek proofs of simulatability which do not depend on the security parameters, our completeness theorem covers all such UC proofs.

While the decision procedures in this work can be exponential or even double-exponential time in the program sizes, the exact complexity of these problems remains open. Further, for cryptographic protocols one does not expect the worst case exponential blowup in state-space (space of pseudo-linear functions) and further work is required in this direction. Finally, there is a tantalizing possibility of extending our work to synthesis (human-assisted or otherwise) of real protocols given an ideal functionality as specification.

The inability to handle arbitrary sequence of adversary calls in the real world limits the applicability of our current results to practical cryptographic protocols. However, we believe that our results open up a new and exciting line of research in this area with promising directions to explore. We believe this is the first work that seeks complete decision procedures for the problem of statistical simulatability.

Organization. The next section formally defines pseudo-linear functions, and proves a basis, an interpolation theorem and the Completeness theorem for pseudo-linear functions. Section 3 extends the set of primitives to include random number generation and proves a completeness theorem for deciding simulatability. Section 4 considers iterated composition of randomized pseudo-linear functions and proves a completeness theorem. Section 5 relates the results in this paper to proof automation in the UC model. Finally, Section 6 concludes with a discussion on work in progress and open problems.

Due to space constraints, most of the proofs are deferred to the full version of the paper [18].

2   Pseudo-Linear Functions

In this section we introduce and formally define pseudo-linear functions. We begin with examples of how pseudo-linear polynomials relate to branching programs with bit-wise exclusive-or operations (which is just addition in fields of characteristic two). So, consider a finite field $\mathbb{F}_q$, where $q = 2^m$. We adopt the convention that $l_*(\boldsymbol{x})$ denote linear polynomials over the components of $\boldsymbol{x}$ which are elements of $\mathbb{F}_{2^m}$. To start with, an equality constraint of the form $l_1(\boldsymbol{x}) = l_2(\boldsymbol{x})$ can then be written as

$$1 + (l_1(\boldsymbol{x}) + l_2(\boldsymbol{x}))^{q-1}$$

which evaluates to 1 if $l_1(\boldsymbol{x}) = l_2(\boldsymbol{x})$, and evaluates to zero otherwise. Similarly, $l_1(\boldsymbol{x}) = 0$ *and* $l_2(\boldsymbol{x}) = 0$ can be written as

$$(1 + l_1(\boldsymbol{x})^{q-1}) \cdot (1 + l_2(\boldsymbol{x})^{q-1})$$

As a final example, an expression "if $(l_1(\boldsymbol{x}) = 0$ *and* $l_2(\boldsymbol{x}) = 0)$ then $l_3(\boldsymbol{x})$ else $l_4(\boldsymbol{x})$" can be written as

$$(1 + l_1(\boldsymbol{x})^{q-1}) \cdot (1 + l_2(\boldsymbol{x})^{q-1}) \cdot (l_3(\boldsymbol{x}) + l_4(\boldsymbol{x})) \ + \ l_4(\boldsymbol{x})$$

Formally, a **pseudo-linear** multivariate polynomial defined over sub-field $\mathbb{F}_2$ is then a polynomial which is a sum of guarded linear-terms; a *guarded linear-term* is a polynomial which is the product of a linear (over $\mathbb{F}_2$) polynomial[3] and zero or more linear-guards; a *linear-guard* is a linear (over $\mathbb{F}_2$) polynomial raised to the power $(q - 1)$. Since, in this paper we will only be dealing with pseudo-linear polynomials defined over $\mathbb{F}_2$, from now on we will implicitly assume that. A pseudo-linear polynomial in n variables and defined over $\mathbb{F}_2$, however does yield a function from $(\mathbb{F}_q)^n$ to $\mathbb{F}_q$, which we call a **pseudo-linear function**. Thus, even though the polynomial is defined over $\mathbb{F}_2$, the underlying field will be $\mathbb{F}_q$, and hence the algebra of the polynomials is modulo $(x_i^q = x_i)$ (for i ranging from 1 to n). They are also further restricted by the fact that all expressions in the guards are linear instead of affine, but we can also introduce constant additive terms from $\mathbb{F}_q$ [18].

We observe that pseudo-linear polynomials are closed under pseudo-linear transformations, i.e. given a pseudo-linear polynomial, raising it to the power $(q-1)$, and multiplying it by another pseudo-linear polynomial yields just another pseudo-linear polynomial. More importantly, the branching programs mentioned in the introduction compute exactly the pseudo-linear functions. We make this connection more formal in Section 5.

2.1   A Basis for Pseudo-linear Functions

Let X denote a set of n variables $\{x_1, x_2, \cdots, x_n\}$ from $\mathbb{F}_q$. Let $\mathcal{L}$ stand for the set of all linear expessions, including zero, over elements of X. We define the set of **elementary pseudo-linear** (EPSELIN) polynomials to be all polynomials of the form

$$\prod_{l \in J}(1 + l(\boldsymbol{x})^{q-1}) \cdot \prod_{l \in \mathcal{L} \backslash J} l(\boldsymbol{x})^{q-1} \cdot p(\boldsymbol{x})$$

where $p(\boldsymbol{x})$ is in $\mathcal{L}$, and J is any subset of $\mathcal{L}$ which is closed under addition, i.e. J is a subspace of $\mathcal{L}$. We also include the zero polynomial amongst the elementary pseudo-linear polynomials. Note that if $\mathcal{L} \backslash J$ included a linearly-dependent term of J, then the above polynomial reduces to zero in $\mathbb{F}_q$.

Related to the earlier definition of a linear-guard, we will refer to expressions of the form

$$\prod_{l \in J}(1 + l(\boldsymbol{x})^{q-1}) \cdot \prod_{l \in \mathcal{L} \backslash J} l(\boldsymbol{x})^{q-1}$$

---

[3] Which is just a sum of variables for a field of characteristic 2.

as just **guards**. We will mainly be focusing on guards corresponding to J which are linear subspaces.

For the next definition, we will require that the n variables be ordered by their indices. Thus x_1 is considered to be of lesser index than x_2, and so on. This also induces a lexicographic ordering on all equal-sized subsets of the n variables X. An elementary pseudo-linear polynomial with the above notation will be called a **reduced elementary pseudo-linear** (REPSELIN) polynomial if it satisfies the following:

1. Let r be the rank of J ($r \leq \min(n, |J|)$).
2. Let R be the lexicographically greatest set of r variables occuring in J which can be expressed in terms of smaller indexed variables (or just zero) when the elements of J are set to zero. This for example, can be accomplished by considering a row-echelon normal form of J. As a simple instance, if $J = \{x_1 + x_2, x_2 + x_3, x_3 + x_1\}$, then $R = \{x_2, x_3\}$, since setting the elements of J to 0 will imply $x_3 = x_2 = x_1$.
3. None of the variables in R occur in $p(\boldsymbol{x})$.

To justify this definition, we note that if an elementary pseudo-linear polynomial is not reduced, then it is equivalent to a reduced one. One implication of the above definition is that if $p(\boldsymbol{x})$ is non-zero then it itself cannot be in J. Recall, J is closed under addition, by definition of EPSELIN-polynomials. Let r be the rank of J. Let $\bar{J}$ be the r sized subset of J which forms a basis of J, and which define the variables R by the row-echelon normal form of J. Thus, all $l(\boldsymbol{x})$ in J *must have at least one variable from* R. Thus, $p(\boldsymbol{x})$ cannot be in J.

Finally, we define a REPSELIN-polynomial to be a **basic pseudo-linear** polynomial if the linear term $p(\boldsymbol{x})$ is just a variable from X. Note that since the basic polynomial is REPSELIN, from item (3) above it follows that this variable is not from R.

Lemma 1. *Every pseudo-linear polynomial can be expressed as a sum of basic pseudo-linear polynomials.*

We will now show that the basic pseudo-linear polynomials actually form a *basis* for pseudo-linear polynomials. Before that we need some more notation. Let $\mathcal{Q}(X)$ be the set of all basic pseudo-linear polynomials in variables X. Further, let $\mathcal{G}(X)$ be the set of all guards *which form a part of these polynomials* $\mathcal{Q}(X)$. Let $|\mathcal{G}(X)| = t$. The guards can then be named w.l.o.g. g_1, g_2, ...,g_t. Recall, for each guard g_i, there is associated a subset of variables X, namely R, that do not occur in any linear terms $p(\boldsymbol{x})$. We refer to all linear combinations of $X \backslash R$ as $\mathcal{P}_i(X)$, including the linear term zero. Let $|\mathcal{P}_i(X)| = s_i + 1$. Note that $(s_i + 1)$ is two to the power of the size of the subset of variables associated with g_i. The linear terms in $\mathcal{P}_i(X)$ can be named $p_i^j(\boldsymbol{x})$, j ranging from 0 to s_i (not to be confused with exponent). W.l.o.g., zero will always be $p_i^0(\boldsymbol{x})$.

Thus, any pseudo-linear function $\phi(\boldsymbol{x})$ can be represented as a sum (over $\mathbb{F}_2$) of polynomials from $\mathcal{Q}(X)$, i.e.,

$$\phi(\boldsymbol{x}) = \sum_{i \in T} g_i(\boldsymbol{x}) \cdot p_i^{j(\phi,i)}(\boldsymbol{x})$$

where T is a subset of $[1..t]$, and each $p_i^{j(\phi,i)}(\boldsymbol{x}) \in \mathcal{P}_i(X)$. In fact, we do not even need to take a subset T of $[1..t]$; all zero terms just imply that $j(\phi, i) = 0$, by our notation above that $p_i^0(\boldsymbol{x})$ is always taken to be zero. Thus the above representation of $\phi(\boldsymbol{x})$ is totally defined by the map $j(\phi, \cdot)$.

While we state and prove the following theorem only for large fields, as only for such fields do the basic pseudo-linear polynomials form a basis, a slightly more complicated characterization can be given for smaller fields.

Lemma 2 (Basis). *For fields of size $q > 2^n$, the basic pseudo-linear polynomials in n variables form a basis for pseudo-linear polynomials in n variables.*

Detailed proofs can be found in the full version of the paper [18].

Lemma 3 (Homomorphism). *For any pseudo-linear functions $\phi_1(\boldsymbol{x})$ and $\phi_2(\boldsymbol{x})$, and for all $i \in [1..t]$,*

$$p_i^{j(\phi_1+\phi_2,i)} = p_i^{j(\phi_1,i)} + p_i^{j(\phi_2,i)}$$

Proof. Follows from the fact that the basic pseudo-linear polynomials form a basis for pseudo-linear polynomials.

2.2   Interpolation Property and the Completeness Theorem

Before we prove the main theorem, we need a few more definitions and related lemmas. Let $f_1, f_2, ..., f_k$ be k pseudo-linear functions in n variables X, over a field $\mathbb{F}_q$ $(q = 2^m)$. Collectively, we will refer to these polynomials as F. For any pseudo-linear polynomial $f(\boldsymbol{x})$ in X, let its representation in terms of the basis be given by $j(f, \cdot)$. Since each of the polynomials from F, i.e. $f_1(\boldsymbol{x}), f_2(\boldsymbol{x}), ..., f_k(\boldsymbol{x})$ is pseudo-linear, it can be represented by $j(f_s, \cdot)$ $(s \in [1..k])$. Further, each linear combination of F is represented similarly.

We say that two guards $g_a(\boldsymbol{x})$ and $g_b(\boldsymbol{x})$ are F-**equivalent** if for every linear combination ϕ of functions from F, it is the case that $j(\phi, a) = 0$ iff $j(\phi, b) = 0$. In this case, we write $a \cong_F b$, which is an equivalence relation.

Lemma 4. *If a and b are F-equivalent then if for some subset $S \subseteq [1..k]$, the linear combination $\sum_{s \in S} p_a^{j(f_s,a)}$ is identically zero , then so is $\sum_{s \in S} p_b^{j(f_s,b)}$.*

The lemma follows by Lemma 3. Thus, if k' is the rank of $p_a^{j(f_s,a)}$ $(s \in [1..k])$, then it is also the rank of $p_b^{j(f_s,b)}$. In fact, we can take the exact same k' indices from $(s \in [1..k])$, w.l.o.g. $[1..k']$, to represent the basis for the k linear expressions, for both a and b.

Let $\mathcal{L}(F)$ denote the set of all linear combinations of functions in F. For any pseudo-linear function $f(\boldsymbol{x})$, and any set F of pseudo-linear functions in X, we say that $f(\boldsymbol{x})$ has the F-**interpolatable** property if it satisfies the following two conditions:

(i) $\forall i \in [1..t] : \exists \phi_\star \in \mathcal{L}(F) : j(f, i) = j(\phi_\star, i)$, and

(ii) For every $a, b \in [1..t]$ such that a and b are F-equivalent, w.l.o.g. by Lemma 4, let the first k' functions out of (k functions) $p_a^{j(f_s,a)}$ (out of $p_b^{j(f_s,b)}$), represent their basis (resp. for b). Then, if the $\phi_\star$ in (i) is given by $\sum c_s^a p_a^{j(f_s,a)}$ and $\sum c_s^b p_b^{j(f_s,b)}$, respectively for a and b, then for all $s \in [1..k']$, $c_s^a = c_s^b$.

Lemma 5. *If f is a pseudo-linear function in X, and f satisfies the F-interpolatable property for some set F of pseudo-linear polynomials in X, then f is a pseudo-linear function of F.*

While the main completeness theorem below is stated for only large finite fields, it holds for all finite fields of characteristic two.

Theorem 1. *Let $f_1, f_2, ..., f_k$ be k pseudo-linear functions in n variables X, over a field $\mathbb{F}_q$ ($q = 2^m$), such that $q > 2^n$. Collectively, we will refer to these polynomials as F. Let f be another pseudo-linear function in X. Then, if f is a function of F, then f is a pseudo-linear function of F.*

3   Randomized Pseudo-linear Functions

In this section we consider randomized pseudo-linear functions, or distributions over pseudo-linear families of pseudo-linear functions. A pseudo-linear family of pseudo-linear functions is given by a pseudo-linear function f' in variables $\boldsymbol{x}$ and $\boldsymbol{r}$, where the variables $\boldsymbol{r}$ parametrize the family. Given such an f', a randomized pseudo-linear function f (in $\boldsymbol{x}$) is given by choosing $\boldsymbol{r}$ uniformly and randomly. The simulation question then becomes whether one can generate the target function distribution by sampling the input function distributions.

When we regard the $\boldsymbol{r}$ as formal variables, we can apply Lemma 2 to deduce that f' is expressible in terms of the basic pseudo-linear polynomials in $(\boldsymbol{x}, \boldsymbol{r})$. In particular,

$$f'(\boldsymbol{x}, \boldsymbol{r}) = \sum_{i \in T} g_i(\boldsymbol{x}, \boldsymbol{r}) \cdot p_i^{j(f',i)}(\boldsymbol{x}, \boldsymbol{r})$$

where T is the set of indices of all the guards over $(\boldsymbol{x}, \boldsymbol{r})$.

Consider a guard g_i in just the space of the input variables $\boldsymbol{x}$, with associated set J, i.e. $g_i = \prod_{l \in \mathcal{L} \setminus J} l(\boldsymbol{x})^{q-1} \cdot \prod_{l \in J}(1 + l(\boldsymbol{x})^{q-1})$. Consider the set of super-guards $\mathbb{I}_i$ which extend J to $\mathcal{L} \cup \mathcal{L}(\boldsymbol{r})$ and each super-guard $I \in \mathbb{I}_i$ corresponds to a different subspace $J_r \subseteq \mathcal{L}(\boldsymbol{r})$ added to the subspace J (and then taking closure). Thus, we get a set of guards g_I ($I \in \mathbb{I}_i$) corresponding to each guard g_i. From now on, when clear from context, we will refer to the randomized function as $f(\boldsymbol{x}, \boldsymbol{r})$, to signify the random variables over which the distribution is defined.

We now show that given any randomized pseudo-linear function $f(\boldsymbol{x}, \boldsymbol{r})$, there is a randomized pseudo-linear function in just one random variable $\hat{r}$, such that it is statistically indistinguishable from f. The *new* randomized pseudo-linear function $\hat{f}$ in just one random variable $\hat{r}$ and the same input variable set $\boldsymbol{x}$, is defined in the following way:

- The function $\hat{f}$ will have the same p as f for guards involving only $\boldsymbol{x}$. For guards involving $\hat{r}$, p will be set to zero.
- For each guard g_i (with associated J), consider its extension super-guard $I_0 \in \mathbb{I}_i$ corresponding to $J_r = \{0\}$, In this case, J_{I_0} is just J. Suppose $p_{I_0}^{j(f,I_0)}(\boldsymbol{x}, \boldsymbol{r}) = l_1(\boldsymbol{x}) + l_2(\boldsymbol{r})$. If l_2 is not identically 0, then set $p_i^{j(\hat{f},i)}(\boldsymbol{x}) = \hat{r}$, otherwise set $p_i^{j(\hat{f},i)}(\boldsymbol{x}) = l_1(\boldsymbol{x})$.

Lemma 6. *Let* $\log q > 2(\rho + \chi)$, *where* ρ *is the number of random variables and* χ *is the number of input variables in* f. *The distribution* $f(\boldsymbol{x})$ *is statistically indistinguishable from* $\hat{f}(\boldsymbol{x})$ *with advantage* $< 1/\sqrt{q}$.

We will refer to the functions of the form of $\hat{f}$ as *Simplified Randomized Pseudo-Linear* functions (SRPL). These are functions which can be expressed with guards from $\boldsymbol{x}$ only and just one random variable. Lemma 6 indicates that we can just focus on SRPL functions since any randomized pseudo-linear function is statistically close to an SRPL function.

Lemma 7 (Homomorphism). *For any SRPL functions* $\phi_1(\boldsymbol{x})$ *and* $\phi_2(\boldsymbol{x})$, *and for all* $i \in [1..t]$,
$$p_i^{j(\phi_1 + \phi_2, i)} = p_i^{j(\phi_1, i)} + p_i^{j(\phi_2, i)}$$
with the rule that $\hat{r} + \cdot$ *is re-written as* $\hat{r}$.

Proof. Follows from the fact that for a fixed $\boldsymbol{x}$, exactly one of the guards evaluates to 1 and the rest evaluate to 0. Also, adding a uniformly distributed random number to any quantity yields a uniformly distributed random number.

Theorem 2. *Let* $f_1, f_2, ..., f_k$ *be* k *SRPL functions in* n *variables* X, *over a field* $\mathbb{F}_q$ *(*$q = 2^m$*), such that* $q > 2^n$. *Collectively, we will refer to these polynomials as* F. *Let* f *be another SRPL function in* X. *Then if there exists a probabilistic poly-time (in* $\lg q$*) algorithm* S^F *which makes oracle calls to* F, *such that the distribution* $f(X)$ *is statistically indistinguishable from the distribution* $S^F(X)$, *then* f *is an SRPL function of the set of functions* F.

4   Completeness Theorem for Randomized Simulators and Iterated Composition of SRPL Functions

In this section, we consider SRPL functions which can take arguments, modeling oracles which are SRPL functions of secret values and arguments. Thus, for instance it may be required to find if there exists a *randomized simulator* which given access to functionalities which are SRPL functions of secret parameters X and arguments supplied by simulator/adversary, can compute a given SRPL function.

This generalizes the problem from the previous sections, where the simulator could not pass any arguments to the given functions. For simplicity, we will deal here with functions which only take a single argument, and thus all the functions can be written as $f_i(\boldsymbol{x}, y)$, each SRPL in $\boldsymbol{x}$ and y.

So, given a collection of k SRPL functions $F(X, y)$, we now define an **iterated composition of** F. Let $\mathbb{F}_q$ be the underlying field as before. An iterated composition σ of F is a length t sequence of pairs (t an arbitrary number), the first component of the s-th ($s \in [1..t]$) pair of σ being a function ϕ_s from F, and the second component an arbitrary *randomized* function γ_s of $s - 1$ arguments (over $\mathbb{F}_q$).

Given an iterated composition σ of F, one can associate a function f^σ of X with it as follows by induction. For σ of length one, f^σ is just $\phi_1(\boldsymbol{x}, \gamma_1())$, recalling that $\phi_1 \in F$. For σ of length t,

$$f^\sigma(\boldsymbol{x}) = \phi_t(\boldsymbol{x}, \gamma_t(f^{\sigma_{|1}}(\boldsymbol{x}), f^{\sigma_{|2}}(\boldsymbol{x}), ..., f^{\sigma_{|t-1}}(\boldsymbol{x})))$$

where $\sigma_{|j}$ is the prefix of σ of length j.

Since, SRPL functions in n variables over $\mathbb{F}_q$ are just polynomials in n variables, there is a finite bound on t, after which no iterated composition of F can produce a new SRPL function of the n variables. The collection of all functions that can be obtained by iterated composition of F will be referred to as **terms**(F). The expression **terms**$_T(F)$ will stand for the collection of functions obtained by iterated compositions of F of length less than T. In particular we will be interested in T which is bounded by polynomials in $\log q$ and/or n, the number of variables in X.

Recall the functions in F now have an additional argument y. As before, $\mathcal{L}(G)$, for any set of functions G will denote the set of all linear combinations (over $\mathbb{F}_2$) of functions from G. Below we define the class $\mathcal{I}^i(F)$ of SRPL functions in X, for i an arbitrary natural number. In fact, since the inductive definition will sometimes use functions in both X and y, we will just define this class as SRPL functions in X and y, though for different y, they would evaluate to the same value. In other words, for an arbitrary guard $g_a(\boldsymbol{x})$, which corresponds to a subset $J \subseteq \mathcal{L}(X)$ (J is closed under addition), there are many **super-guards** when viewed as a function of X and y, namely with subsets $J' \subseteq \mathcal{L}(X, y)$ (J' closed under addition) such that $J \subseteq J'$ and $(\mathcal{L}(X) \backslash J) \subseteq (\mathcal{L}(X, y) \backslash J')$. Thus, for all these super-guards, a SRPL function $\phi(X)$ will have the same $j(\phi, \cdot)$ value (see Section 2).

However, and more importantly, with y set to some linear expression $l(\boldsymbol{x}) \in \mathcal{P}_a(X)$ (including zero), *exactly one* of these (super-)guards has the property that $J'_{y|l(\boldsymbol{x})} = J$ (Note the subscript $y|l(\boldsymbol{x})$ means $l(\boldsymbol{x})$ is substituted for every occurrence of y in J'). This particular J' is given by

$$J' = \mathcal{L}(J, \{y + l(\boldsymbol{x})\})$$

In this case we say that this super-guard of g_s is consistent with $y + l(\boldsymbol{x}) = 0$. The super-guard corresponding to $J' = J$ will be called the **degenerate super-guard** of $g_a(\boldsymbol{x})$.

Now we define the SRPL function which is the composition of f_s and h, i.e. $f_s \circ h$, where f_s is a SRPL function in X and y, and h is a SRPL function in X, by defining its components in the basis for SRPL functions. For any guard $g_i(\boldsymbol{x})$ (of functions in X), let $g_I(\boldsymbol{x}, y)$ be the unique (super-) guard, mentioned in the previous paragraph, which is consistent with y set to $p_i^{j(h,i)}$ (note the map j here is for guards corresponding to X, and in general it will be clear from context whether we are referring to map j for guards corresponding to X or X, y). Then, define

$$p_I^{j(f_s \circ h, I)}(\boldsymbol{x}, y) = p_I^{j(f_s, I)}(\boldsymbol{x}, p_i^{j(h,i)}(\boldsymbol{x}, y))$$

Further, for all I' which are super-guards of i, we set $p_{I'}^{j(f_s \circ h, I')}$ to be the same value (as $f_s \circ h$ is only a function of X). Note that since each p is just a linear function, this implies that each component of $f_s \circ h$ is a linear function of X (and hence X, y). In particular, $(f_s \circ h)(\boldsymbol{x}) = f_s(\boldsymbol{x}, h(\boldsymbol{x}))$.

Define **Compose**$(F(X, y), H(X))$, where $F(X, y)$ are a set of SRPL functions in X, y and $H(X)$ is a set of SRPL functions in X, to be the set of all functions $f_s \circ h$, where $f_s \in F(X, y)$ and $h \in H(X)$.

For each SRPL function f_s of X and y, we also need to define a SRPL function (in X called **degenerate**(f_s)), which for each guard $g_a(\boldsymbol{x})$, defines the corresponding p function using its degenerate super-guard. Thus,

$$p_a^{j(\text{degenerate}(f_s), a)}(\boldsymbol{x}) = p_I^{j(f_s, I)}(\boldsymbol{x}, 0),$$

where I is the degenerate super-guard of g_a.

Now, we are ready to define the iterated SRPL functions. Define

$$\mathcal{I}^0(F) = \mathcal{L}(\text{Compose}(F, \text{degenerate}(F)))$$
$$\mathcal{I}^{i+1}(F) = \mathcal{L}(\mathcal{I}^i(F) \cup \text{Compose}(F, \mathcal{I}^i(F))), \text{ for } i \geq 0.$$

Since, these functions are just polynomials over finite fields (in fact defined over $\mathbb{F}_2$), the above iteration reaches a fixed-point at an i bounded by a function only of n. We will denote the fixed-point by just $\mathcal{I}(F)$. Now, we generalize the definitions of F-equivalence and F-interpolatable from Section 2.2. Two guards $g_a(\boldsymbol{x})$ and $g_b(\boldsymbol{x})$ are said to be F^*-equivalent if for every $\phi(\boldsymbol{x})$ in $\mathcal{I}(F)$, it is the case that $j(\phi, a) = 0$ iff $j(\phi, b) = 0$ and $j(\phi, a) = \$$ iff $j(\phi, b) = \$$, where $j(\phi, \cdot) = \$$ indicates the special index for the single random variable. The definition of F^*-**interpolatable** property is same as the F-interpolatable property except that $\mathcal{L}(F)$ is replaced by $\mathcal{I}(F)$ and the random variable is accounted for.

Lemma 8. *If f is an SRPL function of n variables X over a field $\mathbb{F}_q$, and f satisfies the F^*-interpolatable property, for some set F of SRPL polynomials in X, y, then there exists a probabilistic poly-time (in $\lg q$) algorithm S^F, such that the distribution $f(X)$ is statistically indistinguishable from the distribution $S^F(X)$, with error at most $2^n/q$.*

Theorem 3. *Let $f_1, f_2, ..., f_k$ be k SRPL functions in n variables X and an additional variable y, over a field $\mathbb{F}_q$ such that $q > 2^{4n}$. Collectively, we will refer to these polynomials as $F(X, y)$. Let T be a positive integer less than $2^n (< q^{1/4})$. Let f be another SRPL function in X. Then if there exists a probabilistic* *poly-time (in* $\lg q$*) algorithm* $S^{terms_T(F(X,y))}$*, such that the distribution* $f(X)$ *is statistically indistinguishable from the distribution* $S^{terms_T(F(X,y))}(X)$*, then* f *is* F^**-interpolatable.*

5   Proof Automation in the Universally Composable Model

A proof of security in the Universally Composable (UC) model boils down to the following: as input, we are given two sets of algorithms: one called an *Ideal Functionality* which is a set of algorithms $F = \{F_1, F_2, \cdots\}$, and another *Real Protocol* which is a set of algorithms $P = \{P_1, P_2, \cdots\}$. We say that P realizes F if it is possible to construct an algorithm S, called ideal world adversary (usually built as a simulator), that invokes the functions in F, such that the following holds: *For any PPT algorithm A, there exists a PPT algorithm S, such that for any PPT environment Z, the execution of A with calls to P is indistinguishable from the execution of S with calls to F.*

We now formally describe the language $L^{\$,\oplus,\text{if}}$ in Table 1 which corresponds to the branching programs over data objects from fields of characteristic two as mentioned in the introduction.

Table 1. Grammar for the Language $L^{\$,\oplus,\text{if}}$

(expressions)	AE	::=	$x_1 \mid x_2 \mid \cdots$	variables
	XE	::=	$AE \mid AE \oplus XE$	bitwise xor expression
	BE	::=	$\text{true} \mid (XE == XE) \mid BE \wedge BE \mid \neg BE$	boolean expression
(assignments)	a	::=	$x \leftarrow \$$	assign new random no.
			$x := XE$	assign xor expression
(program)	π	::=	$a;$	single action
			$\pi a;$	sequence of actions
			$\text{if } BE \text{ then } \pi \text{ else } \pi$	conditional

Definition 1 ($L^{\$,\oplus,\text{if}}$). *An Ideal Functionality* F *and a real protocol* P *are in the language* $L^{\$,\oplus,\text{if}}$ *if*

- *F is a set of programs* $\{f_1(\boldsymbol{x}, \boldsymbol{y}), f_2(\boldsymbol{x}, \boldsymbol{y}), \cdots\}$.
- *P is a single program* $\{f(\boldsymbol{x})\}$.

such that $f_1(\boldsymbol{x}, \boldsymbol{y}), f_2(\boldsymbol{x}, \boldsymbol{y}), \cdots$ *and* $f(\boldsymbol{x})$ *are all described as* $L^{\$,\oplus,\text{if}}$ *programs, as defined in Table 1.*

The **semantics** of this language is that $\boldsymbol{x}$ is a set of inputs passed by the environment at the outset of execution and $\boldsymbol{y}$ is a set of parameters that the simulator is allowed to pass to the functionalities. All the parameters and random numbers are represented as $\lg q$-bit strings, corresponding to elements in $\mathbb{F}_q$. The programs in F can be called *in any order* and an *arbitrary number of times*, whereas P is called *only once*. This means that the real world adversary A does not send any message to the protocol - however, the environment Z initializes the arguments x as per its choice. At the end, the protocol sends a value $f(x)$ to the adversary A. The challenge for the simulator S is to generate a statistically indistinguishable value using the functions in the ideal functionality F. It can call these functions in any order and an arbitrary number of times with arguments of its choice. It doesn't know the values x, but observes the results of the ideal functionality calls. The simulatability question is then whether a probabilistic poly-time simulator exists which can produce an acceptable result for any choice of the environment supplied arguments.

The following lemma connects the language $L^{\$,\oplus,\text{if}}$ to our results in the previous sections.

Lemma 9. *All the variables in an $L^{\$,\oplus,\text{if}}$ program $f(z)$ are randomized pseudolinear in z.*

We now proceed to the main theorem.

Theorem 4 (Completeness of $L^{\$,\oplus,\text{if}}$). *There is a decision procedure, which given an Ideal Functionality F and a Real Protocol P described in the language $L^{\$,\oplus,\text{if}}$, decides if P realizes F in the Universally Composable model.*

Proof (Theorem 4). By Lemma 9, all the functions in P and F compute randomized pseudo-linear functions in the inputs. By Lemma 6, with negligible error, we can assume that these are given as SRPL functions. Observe that a simulator employing T calls to the ideal functionality computes over values in $\mathbf{terms}_T(F(X, y))$.

Now, by Theorem 3, if f is simulatable using $\mathbf{terms}_T(F(X, y))$, with $T < q^{1/4}$, then f is F^*-interpolatable. F^*-interpolatability can be decided by computing $\mathcal{I}(F)$, which can be computed in time independent of $\lg q$. Further, by Lemma 8, if f is F^*-interpolatable, then there exists a probabilistic polynomial time (in $\lg q$) simulator.

6   Work in Progress and Open Problems

Consider an extension of the language $L^{\$,\oplus,\text{if}}$, where we add a fixed number of variables to the Ideal world that are persistent across subroutine calls. Let us call this language $L^{\$,\oplus,\text{if},\text{state}}$. We describe the key ideas for developing a decision procedure for $L^{\$,\oplus,\text{if},\text{state}}$, which is a work in progress.

We first construct stateful iterated compositions of $L^{\$,\oplus,\text{if},\text{state}}$ subroutines. We construct a tree where each node is such a composition and its subtrees denote further compositions extending its own computation. The key observation is that there is only a finite number of such nodes which are distinct modulo renaming of uniformly random quantities. In other words, the nodes fall into a finite number of equivalence classes modulo permutation of uniformly random quantities and hence represent the *same randomized algorithm*. An important property of these equivalence classes is that two members of a class lead to subtrees which are equivalent as sets.

This leads to the conclusion that there is a finite set of stateful iterated compositions. A considerably harder theorem is to prove completeness: if there is a probabilistic poly-time simulator, then there is a simulator which is a stateful iterated composition of the subroutines. Based on our work so far this result seems plausible, and we pose a formal proof of such to be an *open problem*.

Key Ideas for Encryption and Signatures. The UC formulation of the encryption and signature primitives makes them expressible in very abstract terms. We leverage the fact that standard notions of security of these primitives have been shown to be equivalent to the UC formulation. Specifically, we express protocols in the *hybrid model*, where the concrete operations for encryptions and signatures are replaced by their ideal counterpart. The proofs of security translate due to the *Composition Theorem* supported by the UC framework.

Signatures. The UC formulation of signatures can be found in [15]. In addition to the operations in $L^{\$,\oplus,\mathsf{if}}$, we need function variables (*viz.*, s and v) and storage (for the records). For a single session of a protocol, the honest protocol participants only do a bounded number of signatures. However, the adversary may make an unbounded number of calls to the verification function - but this does not create any requirement for more storage. Hence the language $L^{\$,\oplus,\mathsf{if},\mathsf{state}}$ suffices for the storage part.

As regards the function variables s, v, v', observe that they do not have to satisfy any equation. Hence they can be treated as *uninterpreted* function symbols. For example $s(m)$ can be represented as the tuple $\langle "s", m \rangle$, where $"s"$ is a constant string. To support these entities, we only need to define tuples, constants and equality of tuples.

Public-Key Encryption. The UC formulation of PKE can be found in [15]. The discussion on signatures carries over to PKE. In addition, we need to distinguish the ciphertexts being output on separate invocations of the Encryption subroutine. This can be done by tagging the ciphertexts with a uniformly random quantity generated at each invocation: $[r \leftarrow \$; \ c := \langle e', \mathbf{0}, r \rangle\,;]$.

However, in contrast to the signature functionality, the adversary can induce a requirement for unbounded storage by calling the Encryption subroutine multiple times. The language $L^{\$,\oplus,\mathsf{if},\mathsf{state}}$ is only able to support a bounded number of such calls - hence we only have a conditional security proof. While for individual protocols it can be rather simple to prove that it suffices to show realizability for an adversary which makes only a bounded (or even single) number of calls to the hybrid encryption functionality, it is an interesting open problem to prove a structural meta-theorem which establishes the sufficiency of a bounded number of calls for a general class of protocols.

6.1   Password-Based Key Exchange

Password-based key exchange is an important security problem which has been studied extensively in cryptographic research [19], and which brings out the power of the UC framework particularly well. Canetti et al [20] proposed an Ideal Functionality for password-based key exchange. (See [20] for a formal description of this ideal functionality $\mathcal{F}_{\mathrm{PWKE}}$).

Consider two parties P_i and P_j that wish to come up with a common cryptographically strong key based on the fact that they share the same password. The idea is to capture the fact that modulo the adversary outright guessing the password exactly during an active session between the parties, it has no control (or information) on the key being generated. It is allowed to interrupt sessions by tampering with the messages being exchanged, but doing so only results in the parties ending up with different uniformly randomly distributed keys. If, however, the session is not interrupted, the parties end up with the same key which is distributed uniformly and randomly and is not controlled by the adversary.

We describe a protocol Π_{ICPwKE} in the ideal cipher model (Figure 1), which is a candidate to realize $\mathcal{F}_{\mathrm{PWKE}}$. In the ideal cipher model, the results of two decryptions are the same if the key is identical. Otherwise, the results are uniformly and independently random. The protocol is symmetric from the perspective of both the participants - so we describe the actions of just one party P_i. Both parties get a password from the environment $\mathcal{E}$. Party P_i generates a random number r_1, encrypts it and sends the ciphertext c_1 to the peer. When it receives a response c_2', it first checks whether its own message was reflected. If so, it outputs a random key to the environment. Otherwise, it decrypts the response using its password pw_1 and xors the plaintext with r_1. The resulting quantity is output as its key to the environment.

Party P_i	Adv	Party P_j
$\mathcal{E}$		$\mathcal{E}$
$\downarrow pw_1$		$\downarrow pw_2$
$r_1 \leftarrow \$$		$r_2 \leftarrow \$$
$c_1 \leftarrow enc_{pw_1}(r_1)$		$c_2 \leftarrow enc_{pw_2}(r_2)$
	$\xrightarrow{c_1} \quad \xleftarrow{c_2}$	
	$\xleftarrow{c_2'} \quad \xrightarrow{c_1'}$	
if ($c_2' == c_1$) then $sk_1 \leftarrow \$$		if ($c_1' == c_2$) then $sk_2 \leftarrow \$$
else		else
$\quad d_1 \leftarrow dec_{pw_1}(c_2')$		$\quad d_2 \leftarrow dec_{pw_2}(c_1')$
$\quad sk_1 \leftarrow r_1 \oplus d_1$		$\quad sk_2 \leftarrow r_2 \oplus d_2$
$\downarrow sk_1$		$\downarrow sk_2$
$\mathcal{E}$		$\mathcal{E}$

Fig. 1. Protocol for Password-based Key Exchange using Ideal Cipher

Consider the following *ideal functionality for the ideal cipher* primitive. The functionality takes two arguments: a key and a plaintext. It has a table where each entry is a triplet (key, plaintext, ciphertext). The table is initially empty. It supports two subroutines: encrypt(key, plaintext) and decrypt(key, ciphertext). The **encrypt** subroutine, given input $(key, plaintext)$, generates a random number r, stores $(key, plaintext, r)$ in the table and outputs r. The **decrypt** subroutine, given input $(key, ciphertext)$, looks up if there is an entry $(key, p, ciphertext)$ in the table. If so, it outputs p. Otherwise, it generates a random number r, stores $(key, r, ciphertext)$ in the table and outputs r.

Now consider the real-world scenario where the adversary intercepts the first message c_1 and changes it to c_1' before transmitting to P_j. The adversary's action may involve querying the ideal cipher in the hybrid model. More importantly, if the password is weak, the adversary maybe able to guess the password, and hence a proper simulation would require the simulator to extract this password guess from the call to the ideal cipher, and use that in the TestPwd subroutine of $\mathcal{F}_{\text{PWKE}}$.

We now describe how an extension of our decision procedure might automatically figure out such a simulator, as the languages for the real protocol (in the ideal cipher hybrid model) and for the ideal functionality $\mathcal{F}_{\text{PWKE}}$ are covered by the language $L^{\$,\oplus,\text{if},\text{state}}$. First, however we need a theorem which states that it suffices to consider an adversary which makes only a single call to the hybrid ideal cipher functionality. It is plausible that such meta-theorems can be proven as general structural theorems and that is an interesting open problem. We can then in-line a single ideal cipher call in a serialization of the protocol (the variables input by the adversary can be named, say kk and rr). Observe that the following operations are sufficient to describe the ideal cipher functionality: equality testing, conditional branches, random number generation and table storage and lookups. When we consider a constant number of calls to the ideal cipher, the table operations reduce to assignment statements and equality testing. The ideal functionality $\mathcal{F}_{\text{PWKE}}$ is clearly supported by the language $L^{\$,\oplus,\text{if},\text{state}}$. Finally, notice that the variables c_1' and c_2' are also available to the simulator. Thus the decision problem is whether the serialization of the protocol (with a single inlined ideal cipher call) can be obtained as a randomized iterated composition of $\mathcal{F}_{\text{PWKE}}$, where the simulator also has access to variables kk, rr, c_1' and c_2'.

Acknowledgements. The authors would like to thank Daniele Micciancio, Russell Impagliazzo and referees for helpful comments.

References

1. Abadi, M., Rogaway, P.: Reconciling Two Views of Cryptography. In: Watanabe, O., Hagiya, M., Ito, T., van Leeuwen, J., Mosses, P.D. (eds.) TCS 2000. LNCS, vol. 1872, pp. 3–22. Springer, Heidelberg (2000)

2. Cortier, V., Warinschi, B.: Computationally Sound, Automated Proofs for Security Protocols. In: Sagiv, M. (ed.) ESOP 2005. LNCS, vol. 3444, pp. 157–171. Springer, Heidelberg (2005)
3. Canetti, R., Herzog, J.C.: Universally Composable Symbolic Analysis of Mutual Authentication and Key-Exchange Protocols. In: Halevi, S., Rabin, T. (eds.) TCC 2006. LNCS, vol. 3876, pp. 380–403. Springer, Heidelberg (2006)
4. Datta, A., Derek, A., Mitchell, J.C., Roy, A.: Protocol composition logic (pcl). Electr. Notes Theor. Comput. Sci. 172, 311–358 (2007)
5. Blanchet, B.: A computationally sound mechanized prover for security protocols. In: IEEE Symposium on Security and Privacy, pp. 140–154. IEEE Computer Society (2006)
6. Micciancio, D., Warinschi, B.: Completeness theorems for the abadi-rogaway language of encrypted expressions. Journal of Computer Security 12(1), 99–130 (2004)
7. Impagliazzo, R., Kapron, B.M.: Logics for reasoning about cryptographic constructions. In: FOCS, pp. 372–383. IEEE Computer Society (2003)
8. Parikh, R.: Existence and feasibility in arithmetic. J. Symb. Log. 36(3), 494–508 (1971)
9. Buss, S.R.: Bounded arithmetic, proof complexity and two papers of parikh. Ann. Pure Appl. Logic 96(1-3), 43–55 (1999)
10. Barthe, G., Grégoire, B., Béguelin, S.Z.: Formal certification of code-based cryptographic proofs. In: POPL, pp. 90–101 (2009)
11. Barthe, G., Grégoire, B., Heraud, S., Béguelin, S.Z.: Computer-Aided Security Proofs for the Working Cryptographer. In: Rogaway, P. (ed.) CRYPTO 2011. LNCS, vol. 6841, pp. 71–90. Springer, Heidelberg (2011)
12. Pereira, O., Lynch, N., Liskov, M., Kaynar, D., Cheung, L., Segala, R., Canetti, R.: Analyzing Security Protocols Using Time-Bounded Task-PIOAs. Discrete Event Dynamic Systems 18, 111–159 (2008)
13. Ramanathan, A., Mitchell, J., Scedrov, A., Teague, V.: Probabilistic Bisimulation and Equivalence for Security Analysis of Network Protocols. In: Walukiewicz, I. (ed.) FOSSACS 2004. LNCS, vol. 2987, pp. 468–483. Springer, Heidelberg (2004)
14. Barthe, G., Daubignard, M., Kapron, B., Lakhnech, Y., Laporte, V.: On the Equality of Probabilistic Terms. In: Clarke, E.M., Voronkov, A. (eds.) LPAR-16 2010. LNCS, vol. 6355, pp. 46–63. Springer, Heidelberg (2010)
15. Canetti, R.: Universally composable security: A new paradigm for cryptographic protocols. In: FOCS, pp. 136–145 (2001)
16. Goldreich, O., Micali, S., Wigderson, A.: How to play any mental game or a completeness theorem for protocols with honest majority. In: STOC, pp. 218–229. ACM (1987)
17. Canetti, R., Gajek, S.: Universally composable symbolic analysis of diffie-hellman based key exchange. Cryptology ePrint Archive, Report 2010/303 (2010), http://eprint.iacr.org/
18. Jutla, C.S., Roy, A.: A completeness theorem for pseudo-linear functions with applications to UC security. In: Electronic Colloquium on Computational Complexity (ECCC), vol. 17, p. 92 (2010)
19. Bellovin, S.M., Merritt, M.: Augmented encrypted key exchange: A password-based protocol secure against dictionary attacks and password file compromise. In: ACM Conference on Computer and Communications Security, pp. 244–250 (1993)
20. Canetti, R., Halevi, S., Katz, J., Lindell, Y., MacKenzie, P.: Universally Composable Password-Based Key Exchange. In: Cramer, R. (ed.) EUROCRYPT 2005. LNCS, vol. 3494, pp. 404–421. Springer, Heidelberg (2005)

Model-Checking Bisimulation-Based Information Flow Properties for Infinite State Systems

Deepak D'Souza and K.R. Raghavendra

Department of Computer Sc. & Automation, Indian Institute of Science, India
{deepakd,raghavendrakr}@csa.iisc.ernet.in

Abstract. Bisimulation-based information flow properties were introduced by Focardi and Gorrieri [1] as a way of specifying security properties for transition system models. These properties were shown to be decidable for finite-state systems. In this paper, we study the problem of verifying these properties for some well-known classes of infinite state systems. We show that all the properties are undecidable for each of these classes of systems.

Keywords: model-checking, pushdown system, petri net, process algebra, bisimulation, information flow.

1 Introduction

Information flow properties are a way of specifying security properties of systems, dating back to the work of Goguen and Meseguer [2] in the eighties. In this framework, a system is modelled as having high-level (or confidential) events as well as low-level (or public) events, and a typical property requires that the high-level events should not *influence* the outcome of low-level events. In other words, the sequence of low-level events observed from a system execution, should not reveal "too much" information about the high-level events that may have taken place during the execution.

There is a great variety of information flow properties proposed in the literature and can be broadly classified into the following categories. The original formulation of *non-interference* by Goguen and Meseguer was *state-based* in the sense that it spoke about the state of the system after a sequence of events: the state reached by the system after executing a sequence of low and high-level events, must be the same (from the low-level observer's point of view) as the state reached after executing only the low-level events in the sequence. As non-interference is often too strong a requirement (for example a typical password checking program is interfering), many relaxations to non-interference have been proposed in the literature. Some information flow properties are *trace-based* in that they specify information flow security as a property of the set of traces or executions produced by the system and its variants. For example, the *strong non-deterministic non-interference* (SNNI) property [1] states that the set of traces after hiding high-level events (replacing them with ϵ-transitions) should be the

S. Foresti, M. Yung, and F. Martinelli (Eds.): ESORICS 2012, LNCS 7459, pp. 591–608, 2012.

same as the set of traces with high-level events deleted. This corresponds to non-inference of the occurrence of high-level events, as every low-level observation of a trace is itself a possible trace in the system. Finally there are properties based on the *structure* of the system model. For example, the property *Bisimulation-based Strong Non-deterministic Non-interference (BSNNI)* is the same as SNNI except that the check is on bisimulation equivalence rather than trace equivalence. These properties are termed bisimulation based information flow properties and are studied by Focardi and Gorrieri in [1].

We motivate bisimulation-based information flow properties with an example adapted from Focardi and Gorrieri [1]. Consider the component of an access-control system implementing the *no read up* policy as described by the state transition system in Fig. 1. The transition lRl represents a low user requesting to read a low object. Similarly lRh, hRl and hRh represent low reading high, high reading low and high reading high requests respectively. The acc_grant_l and acc_grant_h transitions grant the read access request originating from low and high users respectively. The acc_deny_l transition denies the read access request from a low user on a high object. Here the events lRl, lRh, acc_grant_l and acc_deny_l are low events and hRl, hRh and acc_grant_h are high events. The attacker observes only the low-level events in any execution of the system. We want the semantic property of *non-inference*: the attacker should not be able to infer the occurrence or non-occurrence of high-level events in any system execution.

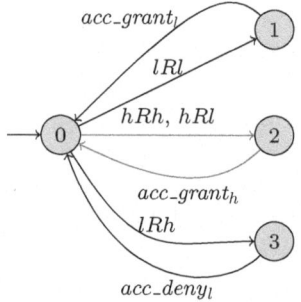

Fig. 1. Implementation of *no read up* without high interrupts

It is easy to see that the system satisfies the property of non-inference. This system satisfies both SNNI and BSNNI.

Consider a slight modification of the example with high-level interrupts as shown in Fig. 2. High-level interrupts h_stop_1, h_stop_2, h_stop_3 and h_stop_4 when fired halts the system by taking it to a trap-state. This system satisfies SNNI but not non-inference. A low user can never conclude that a high-level interrupt has been executed; however when he asks to read a low object and if he sees acc_grant_l then he knows that the h_stop_1 event did not happen. This subtle information flow can be exploited in order to construct an information channel

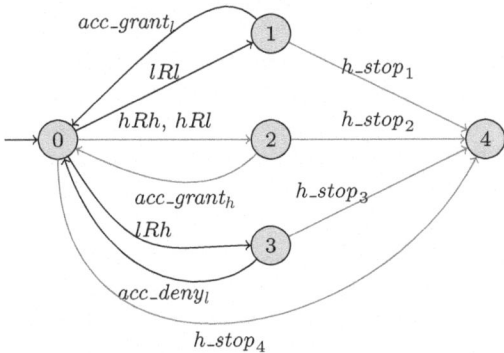

Fig. 2. Implementation of *no read up* with high interrupts

from high level to low level. In order to detect these kind of flows, bisimulation-based information flow properties are used. As we show in Section 2, the system in Fig. 2 does not satisfy BSNNI.

In general bisimulation-based equivalence is a finer equivalence than trace-based equivalence and detects possible high level deadlocks that can compromise the security of the system [1]. The problem of checking bisimulation-based properties has been shown to be decidable for finite-state systems and has been implemented in a tool called *CoSec* [3,4].

The problem of model-checking most of the known trace-based information flow properties is shown to be decidable [5]. However the problem of model-checking these trace-based properties for pushdown systems is shown to be undecidable [6].

A natural question that arises is whether the bisimulation-based properties continue to be decidable for well-known classes of infinite state systems like pushdown systems, Petri nets and process algebras [7]. We show in this paper that the problem of checking any of these bisimulation properties is undecidable for each of these classes of systems. To show these, we adapt the proofs by

- Srba [8] showing the undecidability of checking weak bisimilarity for pushdown systems.
- Jancar [9] showing the undecidability of checking strong bisimilarity for Petri nets.
- Srba [10] showing the undecidability of checking weak bisimilarity for process algebras.

We note that the problem of checking bisimulation-based properties appears to be weaker than the problem of checking bisimilarity for given classes of systems, in the sense that the former reduces to the latter in the case when the class is closed under the hiding and deletion of transitions. However, our results nonetheless show that the problem of checking these bisimulation-based properties continues to be undecidable for the classes mentioned above.

2   Bisimulation Relations and Games

We begin by defining the basic system model of labelled transition systems. For binary relations R and S, we denote relational composition and reflexive transitive closure by $R \cdot S$ and R^* respectively. For an alphabet Σ, we use Σ^* to denote the set of all finite words on Σ. The concatenation of two words u and v will be denoted by $u \cdot v$ or simply uv.

A *labelled transition system (LTS)* M is a tuple $(Q, \Sigma, \to, s_0)$ where Q is a set of states, Σ is a set of labels, $\to \subseteq Q \times (\Sigma \cup \{\epsilon\}) \times Q$ is a set of labelled transitions and $s_0 \in Q$ is the initial state. We sometimes write $s \xrightarrow{a} t$ instead of $(s, a, t) \in \to$. For $q \in Q$, we write M_q to denote the LTS $(Q, \Sigma, \to, q)$. For $c \in \Sigma \cup \{\epsilon\}$, we define $\xrightarrow{c} = \{(s, t) \mid s \xrightarrow{c} t\}$. The *weak transition relation* $(\Rightarrow)$ induced by M is defined as follows. Let $c \in \Sigma \cup \{\epsilon\}$:

$$\xRightarrow{c} = \begin{cases} \xrightarrow{\epsilon}^* \cdot \xrightarrow{c} \cdot \xrightarrow{\epsilon}^* & \text{if } c \in \Sigma \\ \xrightarrow{\epsilon}^* & \text{if } c = \epsilon. \end{cases}$$

The language generated by M, denoted by $L(M)$, is the set $\{a_1 a_2 \cdots a_n \in \Sigma^* \mid \exists s_1, s_2, \ldots, s_n, s \xRightarrow{a_1} s_1 \xRightarrow{a_2} \cdots \xRightarrow{a_n} s_n \}$.

Let $M_1 = (Q_1, \Sigma, \to_1, s_1)$ and $M_2 = (Q_2, \Sigma, \to_2, s_2)$ be two LTS's. A relation $R \subseteq Q_1 \times Q_2$ is a *weak bisimulation* between M_1 and M_2 if and only if whenever $(s, t) \in R$ and $s \xrightarrow{c}_1 s'$ with $c \in \Sigma \cup \{\epsilon\}$ then there exists $t' \in Q_2$ such that $t \xRightarrow{c}_2 t'$ and $(s', t') \in R$ and conversely, whenever $t \xrightarrow{c}_2 t'$ with $c \in \Sigma \cup \{\epsilon\}$ then there exists $s' \in Q_1$ such that $s \xRightarrow{c}_1 s'$ and $(s', t') \in R$. For $p_1 \in Q_1, p_2 \in Q_2$, we write $p_1 \approx p_2$ if and only if there exists a weak bisimulation containing (p_1, p_2). M_1 is said to be weakly bisimilar to M_2, written $M_1 \approx M_2$, if and only if $s_1 \approx s_2$. It is easy to see that the union R_{max} of all weak bisimulations between M_1 and M_2 is also a weak bisimulation. Two states p and q of an LTS M are said to be weakly bisimilar, written $p \approx q$, if and only if there is a weak bisimulation between two copies of M containing (p, q).

Weak bisimilarity has an elegant characterisation in terms of *bisimulation games*. Though the results in the section are folklore in the literature, the details are not readily availabile in our experience. Hence we include the proofs of these results.

Definition 1. *Let p_1 and p_2 be two states in LTS M_1 and M_2 respectively. A bisimulation game starting from p_1 and p_2 is a game between two players: an attacker and a defender. The game is played in rounds. In each round the players change the current states q_1 and q_2 (initially p_1 and p_2) according to the following rule.*

1. *The attacker chooses an $i \in \{1, 2\}, c \in \Sigma \cup \{\epsilon\}$ and $q_i' \in Q_i$ such that $q_i \xrightarrow{c}_i q_i'$.*
2. *The defender responds by choosing a $q_{3-i}' \in Q_{3-i}$ such that $q_{3-i} \xRightarrow{c}_{3-i} q_{3-i}'$.*
3. *The states q_1' and q_2' become the current states.*

Let $K = (\{1, 2\} \times \Sigma \times Q_1 \times Q_2) \cdot (Q_1 \times Q_2)$. A finite play is a string in the language $(Q_1 \times Q_2) \cdot K^*$. An infinite play is a string in $(Q_1 \times Q_2) \cdot K^\omega$. The *positions $1 + 2i$, $i \geq 0$, in a play, are the positions of the attacker (where it is his turn to make a move). A valid move by the attacker extends this string with an element from $(\{1, 2\} \times \Sigma \times Q_1 \times Q_2)$ representing his selection of the component and the transition. The positions $2i$, $i \geq 0$, in a play, are the positions of the defender. A valid move by the defender extends this string with an element from $(Q_1 \times Q_2)$ representing his selection of the transition obeying the above rule. A play is valid if and only if it is formed by the alternate sequence of valid moves from the attacker and the defender. Let the set of valid plays be denoted by Plays. Let $Plays_A$ and $Plays_D$ denote the set of valid plays ending with the attacker's position and the defender's position respectively. Then $Plays = Plays_A \uplus Plays_D$. A partial map associating valid moves to plays in $Plays_P$, is a strategy for the player P. A play α is according to a strategy π of a player P if and only if at every position of the player P in α, the move prescribed by π is taken. A strategy π is valid for a player P if and only if for every play in $Plays_P$ according to π, π is defined. A valid strategy for the defender is also a winning strategy for her. A valid strategy $f\pi$ for the attacker is winning if and only if there is no infinite play according to π.*

The following result is well known [11,12]. See also [13] for a detailed proof.

Lemma 1. *Let M_1 and M_2 be two LTS's with countable number of states. Let p and q be states in M_1 and M_2 respectively. Then*

1. *$p \approx q$ iff the defender has a winning strategy starting from p and q.*
2. *$p \not\approx q$ iff the attacker has a winning strategy starting from p and q.*   □

3 Bisimulation-Based Information Flow Properties

We recall different bisimulation-based information flow properties defined in the literature.

Let $M = (Q, \Sigma, \rightarrow, s)$ be an LTS and $X \subseteq \Sigma$. Then $M \setminus X$ denotes the LTS obtained from M by deleting all transitions labelled by elements in X. M/X denotes the LTS obtained from M by replacing all transitions labelled by elements in X with ϵ (silencing).

Let the set of events Σ (or synonymously actions) be partitioned into inputs (I) and outputs (O). Let Σ again be partitioned into high (H) and low (L) events. Each event a in Σ has a complementary action which we denote by $\bar{a}$ in Σ. We assume the sets H and L are closed under complementation i.e, $\bar{\mathsf{H}} = \{\bar{a} \mid a \in \mathsf{H}\} = \mathsf{H}$ and $\bar{\mathsf{L}} = \{\bar{a} \mid a \in \mathsf{L}\} = \mathsf{L}$. Let $\mathcal{E}_{\mathsf{H}}$ denote the set of all systems whose language over Σ is a subset of H^*.

Given $M_1 = (Q_1, \Sigma, \rightarrow_1, s_1)$, $M_2 = (Q_2, \Sigma, \rightarrow_2, s_2)$, the composition of M_1 and M_2 denoted by $M_1|M_2$ is defined to be $(Q_1 \times Q_2, \Sigma, \rightarrow, (s_1, s_2))$ where $(p, q) \xrightarrow{c} (p', q')$ if $p \xrightarrow{c}_1 p'$ or $q \xrightarrow{c}_2 q'$ and $(p, q) \xrightarrow{\epsilon} (p', q')$ if $p \xrightarrow{a}_1 p'$ and $q \xrightarrow{\bar{a}}_2 q'$.

The bisimulation-based information flow properties [1] are variants of the trace-based non-deterministic non-interference (NNI), a natural generalization of non-interference [2] to non-deterministic systems. The basic idea is that an

LTS satisfies NNI when nothing about the execution of high input events leaks to the observation of a low-user. More precisely, an LTS M satisfies NNI if and only if $L((M \setminus (\mathsf{H} \cap \mathsf{I}))/\mathsf{H}) = L(M/\mathsf{H})$. The following defintions are taken from [1]. In the definition below we fix an LTS $M = (Q, \Sigma, \rightarrow, s)$ over Σ partitioned into I, O and H, L.

Definition 2. *a. **Bisimulation-based Non-deterministic Noninterference (BNNI)**. M satisfies BNNI iff $M/\mathsf{H} \approx (M \setminus (\mathsf{I} \cap \mathsf{H}))/\mathsf{H}$.*

  *b. **Bisimulation-based Strong Non-deterministic Non-interference (BSNNI)**. M satisfies BSNNI iff $M/\mathsf{H} \approx M \setminus \mathsf{H}$.*

  *c. **Bisimulation-based Non Deducibility on Compositions (BNDC)**. M satisfies BNDC iff $\forall M' \in \mathcal{E}_\mathsf{H}$, $M/\mathsf{H} \approx (M|M') \setminus \mathsf{H}$.*

  *d. **Strong BNNI (SBNNI)**. M satisfies SBNNI iff for all reachable states q in M, M_q satisfies BNNI.*

  *e. **Strong BSNNI (SBSNNI)**. M satisfies SBSNNI iff for all reachable states q in M, M_q satisfies BSNNI.*

  *f. **Strong BNDC (SBNDC)**. M satisfies SBNDC iff for all reachable states q, r and for all $h \in \mathsf{H}$, such that $q \xrightarrow{h} r$ in M, $M_q \setminus \mathsf{H} \approx M_r \setminus \mathsf{H}$.*

There are other bisimulation-based properties proposed in [14] – persistent BNDC and dynamic BNDC. They are both shown to be equivalent to SBSNNI [14]. Hence we focus on the properties listed in Definition 2.

Consider the example LTS M in Fig. 2. We show that M does not satisfy BSNNI by describing the winning strategy for the attacker in the bisimulation game on $M \setminus \mathsf{H}$ and M/H. The attacker chooses the transition $0 \xrightarrow{\epsilon} 2$ in M/H. There are no ϵ-transitions from state 0 in $M \setminus \mathsf{H}$. Hence the defender is forced to stay at state 0. The attacker chooses the transition $2 \xrightarrow{\epsilon} 4$ in M/H. Again the defender is forced to stay at state 0. Now the attacker chooses the transition $0 \xrightarrow{lRl} 1$ in $M \setminus \mathsf{H}$. The defender is required to make a coresponding move from state 4 in M/H on lRl. As there is no such move, the attacker wins. Thus the attacker has a winning strategy and hence $M \setminus \mathsf{H} \not\approx M/\mathsf{H}$. Thus M does not satisfy BSNNI.

4 Model-Checking Pushdown Systems

We now consider the problem of model-checking pushdown systems for bisimulation-based information flow properties. We first define some required notions.

Definition 3. *A pushdown system (PDS) is of the form $P = (Q, \Sigma, \Gamma, \rightarrow, s_0, S)$, where Q is a finite set of control states, Σ is a finite input alphabet, Γ is a finite stack alphabet, $\rightarrow \subseteq ((Q \times (\Sigma \cup \{\epsilon\}) \times \Gamma) \times (Q \times \Gamma^*))$ is the transition relation, $s_0 \in Q$ is the starting state, and $S \in \Gamma$ is the initial stack symbol. If $((p, a, A), (q, B_1 B_2 \cdots B_k)) \in \rightarrow$, this means that whenever the machine is in state p with A on top of the stack, it can do an a-labelled transition to pop A off* the stack, push $B_1 B_2 \cdots B_k$ onto the stack (such that B_1 becomes the new top of the stack symbol), and enter state q. If $((p, \epsilon, A), (q, B_1 B_2 \cdots B_k)) \in \rightarrow$, this means that whenever the machine is in state p with A on top of the stack, it can do an ϵ-labelled transition to pop A off the stack, push $B_1 B_2 \cdots B_k$ onto the stack and enter state q.

A PDS $P = (Q, \Sigma, \Gamma, \longrightarrow, s_0, S)$ induces an LTS $M_P = (Q \times \Gamma^*, \Sigma, \rightarrow, (s_0, S))$. The *configurations* of P form the states of M_P. A configuration of P describes the current state and the current stack contents. Given a configuration $(p, A\beta)$ for some $A \in \Gamma$ and $\beta \in \Gamma^*$, the next configuration relation $\rightarrow$ on any $c \in \Sigma \cup \{\epsilon\}$ gives $(q, \gamma\beta)$ if $((p, c, A), (q, \gamma)) \in \longrightarrow$. This is written $(p, A\beta) \xrightarrow{c} (q, \gamma\beta)$. We will write a configuration of the form (p, α) as simply $p\alpha$ in the sequel.

The problem of model checking a bisimulation-based information flow property θ for PDS's is – given a PDS P, does M_P satisfy θ? We show that this problem is undecidable for each of the properties in Definition 2.

Srba in [8] shows that the problem of checking weak bisimilarity between two pushdown systems is undecidable. The idea is to reduce the halting problem of Minsky machines with two counters to the problem of checking weak bisimilarity between two pushdown systems.

Definition 4. *A Minsky machine R with two counters c_1 and c_2 is a finite sequence $R = (L_1 : I_1, L_2 : I_2, \ldots, L_{n-1} : I_{n-1}, L_n : halt)$, where $n \geq 1, L_1, \ldots, L_n$ are pairwise different labels, and $I_1, \ldots, I_{n-1}$ are instructions of the following two types– **increment:** $c_r := c_r + 1$; goto L_j, **test and decrement:** if $c_r = 0$ then goto L_j else $c_r := c_r - 1$; goto L_k, where $1 \leq r \leq 2$ and $1 \leq j, k \leq n$. A configuration of a Minsky machine R is a triple (L_i, v_1, v_2) where L_i is the instruction label $(1 \leq i \leq n)$, and v_1, v_2 are nonnegative integers representing the values of counters c_1 and c_2 respectively. The transition relation on configurations is defined in a natural way.*

The problem of deciding whether a Minsky machine R halts with an initial counter values set ot zero is undecidable [15].

Given a Minsky machine R with two counters c_1, c_2, Srba constructs a pushdown system P_R on a stack alphabet $\{C_1, C_2, S\}$ and two configurations of P_R: $p_1 S$ and $p'_1 S$ such that R halts if and only if $p_1 S \approx p'_1 S$. The proof idea is as follows. A configuration of R, (L_i, v_1, v_2), is represented by a pair of processes $p_i \gamma S$ and $p'_i \gamma' S$ where $\gamma, \gamma' \in \{C_1, C_2\}^*$ such that the number of occurrences of C_1 and C_2 in γ (and also in γ') is equal to v_1 and v_2 respectively. The instruction of the type $L_i : c_r := c_r + 1$; goto L_j, where $1 \leq j \leq n$ and $1 \leq r \leq 2$, is simulated by $p_i X \xrightarrow{a} p_j C_r X$ and $p'_i X \xrightarrow{a} p'_j C_r X$. To simulate a test and decrement instruction, say L_i : if $c_r = 0$ then goto L_j else $c_r := c_r - 1$; goto L_k, where $1 \leq j, k \leq n$ and $1 \leq r \leq 2$, consider the bisimulation game at $(p_i \gamma S, p'_i \gamma' S)$. The attacker forces the defender to rearrange the stack contents at γ and γ' such that C_r's are brought on top. Then C_r is popped if there is one at both γ and γ'. The crucial transition distinguishing p_n and p'_n is: $p_n X \xrightarrow{halt} p_n X$. When R halts, the attacker's aim is to reach p_n by faithfully simulating R's halting computation. Then he chooses $halt$ transition for which the defender cannot match.

Hence the attacker wins and $p_1 S \not\approx p_1' S$. When R diverges, the defender forces the attacker to correctly simulate the moves of R. The attacker never reaches p_n, hence inducing an infinite game. Thus the defender wins and $p_1 S \approx p_1' S$. The reader is referred to [8] for the detailed proof.

Theorem 1 ([8]). *R halts iff $p_1 S \not\approx p_1' S$ in M_{P_R}.*   □

From Srba's construction, we observe that:

1. $p_1 S$ has no ϵ-transitions
2. if there is a winning strategy for the attacker from $(p_1 S, p_1' S)$ then there is one from $(p_1 S, p_1' S)$ beginning with a transition from $p_1 S$.

In general, let P be a PDS and $p_1 \alpha$, $p_2 \beta$ its configurations satisfying the conditions:

1. $p_1 \alpha$ has no ϵ-transitions
2. if there is a winning strategy for the attacker from $(p_1 \alpha, p_2 \beta)$ then there is one from $(p_1 \alpha, p_1 \beta)$ beginning with a transition from $p_1 \alpha$.

Then we call the problem of checking whether $p_1 \alpha \approx p_2 \beta$ the *restricted PDS bisimulation problem*. It follows then from the construction in [8] that:

Theorem 2. *The restricted PDS bisimulation problem is undecidable.*   □

We now reduce the restricted PDS bisimulation problem to the problem of checking each of the bisimulation-based information flow properties for PDS's. Let the PDS $P = (Q, \Sigma, \Gamma, \longrightarrow, s_0, S)$ and its configurations $p_1 \alpha$, $p_2 \beta$ be an instance of the restricted PDS bisimulation problem. We construct P' from P such that $P' = (Q \cup \{s\}, \Sigma \cup \{k, \bar{k}\}, \Gamma, \longrightarrow', s, S)$ such that $s \notin Q$ and $\longrightarrow' = \longrightarrow \cup \{((s, k, S), (p_1, \alpha)), ((s, \epsilon, S), (p_2, \beta))\}$ where $k, \bar{k}$ are the only high (and input) events. That is $\mathsf{H} = \mathsf{I} = \{k, \bar{k}\}$. Informally, the induced LTS $M_{P'}$ of P' has a new start state sS with a high-event k edge – $sS \xrightarrow{k} p_1 \alpha$ and an ϵ-edge – $sS \xrightarrow{\epsilon} p_2 \beta$. The initial part of the induced LTS $M_{P'}$ is shown in Fig. 3. We fix the PDS P, its configurations $p_1 \alpha$, $p_2 \beta$ and the PDS P' constructed from P as described above for the rest of the section.

Lemma 2. *The configurations $p_1 \alpha$ and $p_2 \beta$ are weakly bisimilar i.e., $p_1 \alpha \approx p_2 \beta$ in M_P iff $M_{P'}$ satisfies BSNNI.*

Proof. ($\Leftarrow$:) Suppose $p_1 \alpha \not\approx p_2 \beta$ in M_P. Then we have a winning strategy π for the attacker from $p_1 \alpha$ and $p_2 \beta$ in M_P beginning with a move from $p_1 \alpha$. We claim that the attacker has a winning strategy in the game starting at sS (of $M_{P'} \setminus \mathsf{H}$) and sS (of $M_{P'}/\mathsf{H}$). We now describe that strategy. The attacker chooses sS of $M_{P'}/\mathsf{H}$ and takes the edge ϵ to $p_1 \alpha$ (Fig. 4). The defender now has to make a move from sS of $M_{P'} \setminus \mathsf{H}$ (Fig. 5) and has many choices.

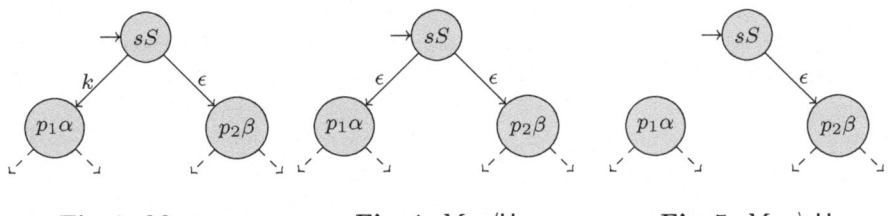

Fig. 3. $M_{P'}$ **Fig. 4.** $M_{P'}/\mathsf{H}$ **Fig. 5.** $M_{P'} \setminus \mathsf{H}$

- **Defender makes an ϵ-move to $p_2\beta$.** The attacker plays π and wins.
- **Defender stays at sS.** The attacker makes the first move according to π. From the definition of the restricted PDS bisimulation problem, the first move of π is a non-ϵ edge from $p_1\alpha$, say $p_1\alpha \overset{a}{\to} r$, for some state r in $M_{P'}/\mathsf{H}$. The defender is forced to respond with the same non-ϵ move from $p_2\beta$, say $sS \overset{\epsilon}{\Rightarrow} p_2\beta \overset{a}{\Rightarrow} r'$ for some state r' in $M_{P'} \setminus \mathsf{H}$. Now the attacker can play according to π and win, since π also serves as the winning strategy for the attacker from (r, r').
- **Defender takes $sS \overset{\epsilon}{\to} p_2\beta \overset{\epsilon}{\Rightarrow} q$.** Note that the non-$\epsilon$ responses enabled at q are also enabled at $p_2\beta$. Hence the attacker can play according to π and win.

Thus the attacker has a winning strategy and hence sS (of $M_{P'} \setminus \mathsf{H}$) and sS (of $M_{P'}/\mathsf{H}$) are not weakly bisimilar. Thus $M_{P'}$ does not satisfy BSNNI.

($\Rightarrow$:) Suppose $p_1\alpha \approx p_2\beta$ in M_P. Then we have a winning strategy π for the defender from $p_1\alpha$ and $p_2\beta$ in M_P. We now describe the winning strategy for the defender from sS (of $M_{P'} \setminus \mathsf{H}$) and sS (of $M_{P'}/\mathsf{H}$). There are three cases:

- **Attacker chooses the transition $sS \overset{\epsilon}{\to} p_1\alpha$ in $M_{P'}/\mathsf{H}$.** The defender chooses $sS \overset{\epsilon}{\to} p_2\beta$ of $M_{P'} \setminus \mathsf{H}$ and thereafter plays π to win.
- **Attacker chooses the transition $sS \overset{\epsilon}{\to} p_2\beta$ in $M_{P'}/\mathsf{H}$.** The defender chooses $sS \overset{\epsilon}{\to} p_2\beta$ of $M_{P'} \setminus \mathsf{H}$ and imitates the attacker from here on. Either the attacker gets stuck or goes on to play the infinite bisimulation game. In both cases, the defender wins.
- **Attacker chooses $sS \overset{\epsilon}{\to} p_2\beta$ in $M_{P'} \setminus \mathsf{H}$.** The defender chooses $sS \overset{\epsilon}{\to} p_2\beta$ of $M_{P'}/\mathsf{H}$ and and imitates the attacker from here on. Either the attacker gets stuck or goes on to play the infinite bisimulation game. In both cases, the defender wins.

Thus the defender has a winning strategy and hence $M_{P'} \setminus \mathsf{H} \approx M_{P'}/\mathsf{H}$. Thus $M_{P'}$ satisfies BSNNI. $\qquad\square$

Lemma 3. *$M_{P'}$ satisfies BSNNI iff $M_{P'}$ satisfies BNNI.*

Proof. As $\mathsf{H} = \mathsf{I} = \{k, \bar{k}\}$, we have $\mathsf{H} \cap \mathsf{I} = \mathsf{H}$. Hence $M_{P'} \setminus (\mathsf{H} \cap \mathsf{I}) = M_{P'} \setminus \mathsf{H}$. Hence $M_{P'}$ satisfies BNNI iff $M_{P'}$ satisfies BSNNI. $\qquad\square$

We now consider the problem of checking BNDC for pushdown systems. Let $M = (Q_M, \mathsf{H}, \to_M, m_0)$ be any LTS in $\mathcal{E}_\mathsf{H}$. We define an equivalence relation $\equiv$ on the states of $(M_{P'}|M) \setminus \mathsf{H}$ as $(q\gamma, m) \equiv (q'\gamma', m')$ if and only if $q\gamma = q'\gamma'$. For every state $(q\gamma, m)$ of $(M_{P'}|M) \setminus \mathsf{H}$, let $[q\gamma] = \{(q'\gamma', m') \mid (q'\gamma', m') \equiv (q\gamma, m)\}$ denote its equivalence class. Let $N = (Q_N, \Sigma, \to_N, [sS])$ denote the quotient LTS $((M_{P'}|M) \setminus \mathsf{H})/\equiv$, where $Q_N = \{[q\gamma] \mid q\gamma \text{ is a state in } M_{P'}\}$, $[q\gamma] \xrightarrow{c}_N [q'\gamma']$, $c \in \Sigma \cup \{\epsilon\}$, if and only if there exist states m, m' in M such that $(q\gamma, m) \xrightarrow{c} (q'\gamma', m')$ in $(M_{P'}|M) \setminus \mathsf{H}$. Let N' be the LTS same as N with all the ϵ self loops deleted. The Fig. 6 shows a part of the LTS N'. The transition $[sS] \xrightarrow{\epsilon}_N [p_1\alpha]$ is represented using dotted arrow indicating that the transition may or may not be present. This transition is present if and only if there is a transition of the form $m_0 \xRightarrow{\bar{k}}_M m$ for some state m. We note that M can have only transitions with labels $k, \bar{k}$ or ϵ. Thus the ϵ-transitions from M and the ϵ-transitions due to synchronization between M and $M_{P'}$ on $k, \bar{k}$, are the only possible contributions from M to N.

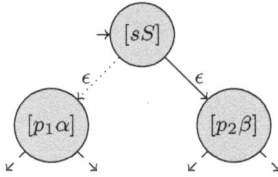

Fig. 6. N'

Let R and S be two LTS's. Let R^ϵ be any LTS constructed from R by adding ϵ self loops arbitrarily. Then it is easy to see that:

Lemma 4. $R \approx S$ iff $R^\epsilon \approx S$.

Lemma 5. $(M_{P'}|M) \setminus \mathsf{H} \approx N'$.

Proof. We construct the winning strategy for the defender. The strategy is essentially to mimic the moves of the attacker. The defender chooses to maintain the game at same positions (with respect to $M_{P'}$). That is, at any point the attacker starts from $((q\gamma, m)$ and $[q\gamma])$ where $q\gamma$ and m are states of $M_{P'}$ and M respectively. Consider the case when the attacker chooses the transition $[sS] \xrightarrow{\epsilon}_N [p_1\alpha]$ in N'. We observe that this happens only when M has a transition of the form $m_0 \xRightarrow{\bar{k}}_M m$ for some state m. The defender chooses the transition $(sS, m_0) \xRightarrow{\epsilon} (p_1\alpha, m)$ in $(M_{P'}|M) \setminus \mathsf{H}$, leaving the attacker to play from $[p_1\alpha]$ of N' and $(p_1\alpha, m)$ of $(M_{P'}|M) \setminus \mathsf{H}$. All the other cases are easy to see. Eventually either the attacker gets stuck or goes on to play the infinite bisimulation game. In both cases, the defender wins. Hence $(M_{P'}|M) \setminus \mathsf{H} \approx N'$. for the attacker's initial choices.   □

Lemma 6. *The configurations $p_1\alpha$ and $p_2\beta$ are weakly bisimilar i.e., $p_1\alpha \approx p_2\beta$ in M_P iff $M_{P'}$ satisfies BNDC.*

Proof. ($\Leftarrow$:) Suppose $p_1\alpha \not\approx p_2\beta$ in M_P. From Lemma 2, we know that $M_{P'}$ does not satisfy BSNNI. That is, $M_{P'} \setminus H \not\approx M_{P'}/H$. Consider the LTS $M = (\{m\}, H, \emptyset, m)$. We note that $M \in \mathcal{E}_H$. It is easy to see that $M_{P'}|M$ is isomorphic to $M_{P'}$. This implies that $(M_{P'}|M) \setminus H \not\approx M_{P'}/H$. Hence $M_{P'}$ does not satisfy BNDC.

($\Rightarrow$:) Suppose $p_1\alpha \approx p_2\beta$ in M_P. Then we have a winning strategy π for the defender from $p_1\alpha$ and $p_2\beta$ in M_P. Let $M = (Q_M, H, \rightarrow_M, m)$ be any LTS in $\mathcal{E}_H$. From Lemma 5, we know that $(M_{P'}|M) \setminus H \approx N'$. It is easy to see that the subtrees of $[p_1\alpha]$ and $[p_2\beta]$ in N' are isomorphic to the subtrees of $p_1\alpha$ and $p_2\beta$ in $M_{P'}$ respectively. We now show that $N' \approx M_{P'}/H$. We construct a winning strategy for the defender. Consider the different cases for the attacker's choices.

- **Attacker chooses the transition** $[sS] \xrightarrow{\epsilon}_N [p_2\beta]$ **in** N'. The defender chooses $sS \xrightarrow{\epsilon} p_2\beta$ of $M_{P'}/H$. The defender imitates the attacker choices (with respect to the states from $M_{P'}$) from here on. Either the attacker gets stuck or goes on to play the infinite bisimulation game. In both cases, the defender wins.
- **Attacker chooses the transition** $[sS] \xrightarrow{\epsilon}_N [p_1\alpha]$ **in** N'. The defender chooses $sS \xrightarrow{\epsilon} p_1\alpha$ from $M_{P'}/H$. The defender imitates the attacker choices (with respect to the states of $M_{P'}$) from here on. Either the attacker gets stuck or goes on to play the infinite bisimulation game. In both cases, the defender wins.
- **Attacker chooses the transition** $sS \xrightarrow{\epsilon} p_2\beta$ **in** $M_{P'}/H$. The defender chooses $[sS] \xrightarrow{\epsilon} [p_2\beta]$. The defender imitates the attacker choices (with respect to the states of $M_{P'}$) from here on. Either the attacker gets stuck or goes on to play the infinite bisimulation game. In both cases, the defender wins.
- **Attacker chooses the transition** $sS \xrightarrow{\epsilon} p_1\alpha$ **in** $M_{P'}/H$. Note that there may not be a transition of the form $[sS] \xrightarrow{\epsilon}_N [p_1\alpha]$ as shown in Fig. 6. The defender chooses $[sS] \xrightarrow{\epsilon} [p_2\beta]$. The defender plays π from here on and wins.

Hence the defender has a winning strategy and thus $N' \approx M_{P'}/H$. From Lemma 5 and the transitive property of $\approx$, we have $(M_{P'}|M)\setminus H \approx M_{P'}/H$ for any $M \in \mathcal{E}_H$. Thus $M_{P'}$ satisfies BNDC. □

It follows from Lemmas 2, 3 and 6 that the problem of checking BNNI, BSNNI and BNDC for pushdown systems is undecidable. Now we consider the properties SBNNI, SBSNNI and SBNDC.

Lemma 7. *The configurations $p_1\alpha$ and $p_2\beta$ are weakly bisimilar i.e., $p_1\alpha \approx p_2\beta$ in M_P iff $M_{P'}$ satisfies SBSNNI.*

Proof. ($\Leftarrow$:) Suppose $p_1\alpha \not\approx p_2\beta$ in M_P. Then from Lemma 2, $M_{P'}$ does not satisfy BSNNI. Hence $M_{P'}$ does not satisfy SBSNNI.

($\Rightarrow$:) Suppose $M_{P'}$ does not satisfy SBSNNI. Then there exists some state m in $M_{P'}$ such that m of $M_{P'} \setminus H$ and m of $M_{P'}/H$ are not weakly bisimilar. Then there exists a winning strategy π for the attacker from m of $M_{P'}/H$ and m of $M_{P'} \setminus H$. Note that there are no H-edges in $M_{P'}$ except for $sS \xrightarrow{k} p_1\alpha$. Hence for all states m other than sS, m of $M_{P'}/\mathsf{H}$ and m of $M_{P'} \setminus \mathsf{H}$ are weakly bisimilar. This implies that sS of $M_{P'}/\mathsf{H}$ and sS of $M_{P'} \setminus \mathsf{H}$ are not weakly bisimilar. Then $M_{P'}$ does not satisfy BSNNI. From Lemma 2, we have $p_1\alpha \not\approx p_2\beta$ in M_P.   □

Lemma 8. *$M_{P'}$ satisfies SBSNNI iff $M_{P'}$ satisfies SBNNI.*

Proof. From Lemma 3, $M_{P'}$ satisfies BSNNI if and only if $M_{P'}$ satisfies BNNI. Hence $M_{P'}$ satisfies SBSNNI if and only if $M_{P'}$ satisfies SBNNI.   □

Lemma 9. *The configurations $p_1\alpha$ and $p_2\beta$ are weakly bisimilar i.e., $p_1\alpha \approx p_2\beta$ in M_P iff $M_{P'}$ satisfies SBNDC.*

Proof. ($\Leftarrow$:) Suppose $p_1\alpha \not\approx p_2\beta$ in M_P. Then there is a winning strategy π for the attacker from $p_1\alpha$ and $p_2\beta$ in M_P begining with $p_1\alpha$. We show that the strategy π serves as the winning strategy for the attacker from sS and $p_1\alpha$ of $M_{P'} \setminus \mathsf{H}$ as well. From the definition of the restricted PDS bisimulation problem, the attacker chooses a non-ϵ transition from $p_1\alpha$ in π as the first move, say $p_1\alpha \xrightarrow{a} q$ for some $a \in \Sigma$ and $q \in Q \times \Gamma^*$. The defender is forced to choose $sS \xrightarrow{\epsilon} p_2\beta \xrightarrow{a} q'$ for some $q' \in Q \times \Gamma^*$. For any choice of q' from the defender, π serves as the winning strategy for the attacker from sS and $p_1\alpha$ of $M_{P'} \setminus \mathsf{H}$ as well. Thus sS of $M_{P'} \setminus \mathsf{H}$ and $p_1\alpha$ of $M_{P'} \setminus \mathsf{H}$ are not weakly bisimilar. Hence $M_{P'}$ does not satisfy SBNDC.

($\Rightarrow$:) Suppose $p_1\alpha \approx p_2\beta$. Then there is a winning strategy π for the defender from $p_1\alpha$ and $p_2\beta$ in M_P. We now describe the winning strategy for the defender from sS and $p_1\alpha$ of $M_{P'}\setminus\mathsf{H}$. Consider the different cases for the attacker's choices.

- **Attacker chooses $sS \xrightarrow{\epsilon} p_2\beta$.** The defender stays at $p_1\alpha$ itself. From the next round, the defender plays according to π and wins.
- **Atacker chooses some transition from $p_1\alpha$.** The defender chooses the transition from $p_2\beta$ according to π after $sS \xrightarrow{\epsilon} p_2\beta$.

Thus defender has a winning strategy and hence $sS \approx p_1\alpha$ in $M_{P'} \setminus \mathsf{H}$. Hence $M_{P'}$ satisfies SBNDC.   □

Finally from Lemmas 2, 3, 6, 7, 8 and 9 we have:

Theorem 3. *The problem of model-checking pushdown systems for any of the bisimulation-based properties - BNNI, BSNNI, BNDC, SBNNI, SBSNNI and SBNDC is undecidable.*   □

5   Model Checking Petri Nets

We study the problem of model checking each of the bisimulation-based information flow properties in Definition 2 for Petri nets. We begin by defining a Petri net. Let $\mathbb{N}$ denote the set of nonnegative integers.

Definition 5. *A Petri net (PN) is a tuple $N = (P, T, \Sigma, F, L, M_0)$, where P and T are finite disjoint sets of places and transitions respectively, Σ is a finite set of actions, $F : (P \times T) \cup (T \times P) \mapsto \mathbb{N}$ is a flow function, $L : T \mapsto \Sigma \cup \{\epsilon\}$ is a labelling and M_0 is an initial marking (a marking is a function $M : P \mapsto \mathbb{N}$ that gives the number of tokens for each place).*

A PN $N = (P, T, \Sigma, F, L, M_0)$ naturally induces an LTS $M_N = (Q, \Sigma, \rightarrow, M_0)$ where Q is the set of markings and $\rightarrow$ is the set of transitions. A transition t is enabled at a marking M, denoted by $M \xrightarrow{t}$, if $M(p) \geq F(p, t)$, for every $p \in P$. A transition t enabled at a marking M may fire yielding the marking M', denoted by $M \xrightarrow{t} M'$, where $M'(p) = M(p) - F(p, t) + F(t, p)$, for all $p \in P$. For any $c \in \Sigma \cup \{\epsilon\}$, by $M \xrightarrow{c} M'$ we mean that $M \xrightarrow{t} M'$ for some t with $L(t) = c$.

The problem of model checking a bisimulation-based information flow property θ for PN's is – given a PN N, does M_N satisfy θ? We show that this problem is undecidable for each of the properties in Definition 2.

Jancar [9] shows that the problem of checking strong bisimilarity for PN's is undecidable by a reduction from the halting problem of Minsky machines. Given a Minsky machine R with two counters c_1 and c_2 (cf. Definition 4), he constructs PN's $N_1 = (P_1, T_1, F_1, L_1, M_1)$ and $N_2 = (P_2, T_2, F_2, L_2, M_2)$ such that R halts if and only if $M_1 \not\approx M_2$. For every instruction label L_i, $1 \leq i \leq n$, of R, the places s_i^1 and s_i^2 are created in N_1 and N_2 respectively. The places c_1^1, c_2^1 and c_1^2, c_2^2 are created corresponding to the counters c_1 and c_2 of R in N_1 and N_2 respectively. The PN's N_1 and N_2 simulate the moves of R. At s_n^1 the transition t_F^1 is enabled only when s_n^1 has at least one token. The transition t_F^2 is not enabled even when s_n^2 has tokens. So, when R halts, the attacker simulates R's halting computation in N_1 forcing the defender to simulate R's moves in N_2. The attacker reaches the marking with s_n^1 having at least one token. He wins by making a t_F^1 move for which the defender does not have a matching response. Hence the attacker wins and $M_1 \not\approx M_2$. When R diverges, the defender forces the attacker to simulate R moves either in N_1 or N_2. This induces an infinite game and the defender wins. Thus $M_1 \approx M_2$.

As in the case of Srba's pushdown system construction, here also we observe that if there is a winning strategy for the attacker from (M_1, M_2), there is one beginning with M_1. There are no ϵ-transitions in N_1 and N_2. Hence in general, let M_1 and M_2 be markings in N_1 and N_2 respectively such that M_1 does not have any ϵ-transitions and if there is a winning strategy for the attacker from (M_1, M_2), then there is one beginning with M_1. Then we call the problem of checking whether $M_1 \approx M_2$, the restricted PN bisimulation problem. It follows then from Jancar's construction that:

Theorem 4. *The restricted PN bisimulation problem is undecidable.*   □

We reduce the restricted PN bisimulation problem to the problem of checking each of the bisimulation-based information flow properties for PN's. Let the PN's

$N_1 = (P_1, T_1, F_1, L_1, M_1)$ and $N_2 = (P_2, T_2, F_2, L_2, M_2)$ be an instance of the restricted PN bisimulation problem. We assume that the sets P_1, P_2 and T_1, T_2 are disjoint. We construct a PN N from N_1 and N_2 such that $N = (P_1 \cup P_2 \cup \{s\}, T_1 \cup T_2 \cup \{t_k, t_\epsilon\}, \Sigma \cup \{k, \bar{k}\}, F, L, M)$ where $k, \bar{k}$ are the only high (and input) events. That is $\mathsf{H} = \mathsf{I} = \{k, \bar{k}\}$. The initial marking M has one token at s and no tokens at all other places i.e., $M(s) = 1$ and $M(p) = 0$, $p \neq s$. The components F and L are described in Fig. 7.

$$F(x,y) = \begin{cases} F_1(x,y) & \text{if both } x \text{ and } y \text{ are in } N_1 \\ F_2(x,y) & \text{if both } x \text{ and } y \text{ are in } N_2 \\ 1 & \text{if } (x,y) = (s, t_k) \\ 1 & \text{if } (x,y) = (s, t_\epsilon) \\ M_1(y) & \text{if } x = t_k \text{ and } y \text{ in } N_1 \\ M_2(y) & \text{if } x = t_\epsilon \text{ and } y \text{ in } N_2 \end{cases} \qquad L(t) = \begin{cases} L_1(t) & \text{if } t \in T_1 \\ L_2(t) & \text{if } t \in T_2 \\ k & \text{if } t = t_k \\ \epsilon & \text{if } t = t_\epsilon \end{cases}$$

Fig. 7. Description of PN N

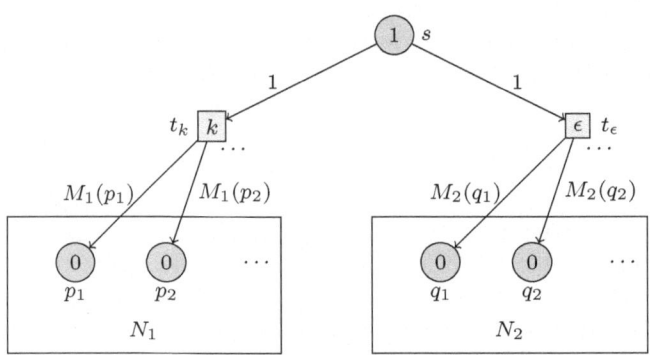

Fig. 8. Constructed Petri net N

The PN N is shown in Fig. 8. Informally, the induced LTS M_N of N has the initial marking M with a high-event k edge – $M \overset{k}{\to} M'$ where $M'(s) = 0$, $M'(p) = M_1(p)$ when $p \in P_1$, $M'(p) = 0$ when $p \in P_2$, and an ϵ-edge – $M \overset{\epsilon}{\to} M''$ where $M''(s) = 0$, $M''(p) = 0$ when $p \in P_1$, $M''(p) = M_2(p)$ when $p \in P_2$. The initial part of the induced LTS M_N is shown in Fig. 9. We fix the PN's N_1, N_2, its markings M_1, M_2 respectively and the PN N constructed from N_1, N_2 as described above for the rest of the section.

Lemma 10. *The markings M_1 and M_2 are weakly bisimilar i.e., $M_1 \approx M_2$ iff M_N satisfies BSNNI.*

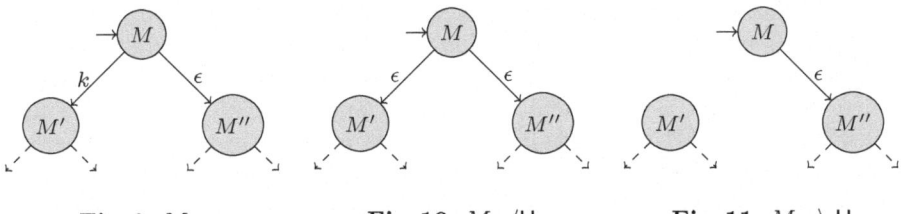

Fig. 9. M_N **Fig. 10.** M_N/H **Fig. 11.** $M_N \setminus H$

Proof. From Definition 2, we need to show that $M_1 \approx M_2$ if and only if M of M_N/H (cf. Fig. 10) and M of $M_N \setminus H$ (cf. Fig. 11) are weakly bisimilar. It is easy to prove this from the arguments similar to the arguments in the proof of Lemma 2.   □

Likewise from the similar arguments as in Section 4, we have:

Theorem 5. *The problem of model-checking Petri nets for any of the bisimulation-based properties - BNNI, BSNNI, BNDC, SBNNI, SBSNNI and SBNDC is undecidable.*   □

6   Model Checking Process Algebras

We now study the problem of model checking each of the bisimulation-based information flow properties in Definition 2 for process algebras. We begin by defining a process algebra.

Definition 6. *Let Const be a set of process constants. The class of process expressions over Const is given by $E ::= \epsilon \mid X \mid E.E \mid E\|E$ where 'ϵ' is the empty process, X ranges over Const, '.' is the operator of sequential composition, and $\|$ stands for parallel composition.*

A process algebra (PA) N is a tuple (P, Σ, Δ) where P is the initial process expression, Σ is an alphabet and Δ is a finite set of rules of the form $X \xrightarrow{c} E$ where $X \in Const$, $c \in \Sigma \cup \{\epsilon\}$ and E is a process expression.

A PA $N = (P, \Sigma, \Delta)$ determines an LTS $M_N = (Q, \Sigma, \rightarrow, P)$ where the states in Q are process expressions and the transition $\rightarrow$ is the least relation satisfying the following rules. Let $c \in \Sigma \cup \{\epsilon\}$.

$$\frac{(X \xrightarrow{c} E) \in \Delta}{X \xrightarrow{c} E} \qquad \frac{E \xrightarrow{c} E'}{E.F \xrightarrow{c} E'.F} \qquad \frac{E \xrightarrow{c} E'}{E\|F \xrightarrow{c} E'\|F} \qquad \frac{F \xrightarrow{c} F'}{E\|F \xrightarrow{c} E\|F'}$$

The problem of model checking a bisimulation-based information flow property θ for PA's is – given a PA N, does M_N satisfy θ? We show that this problem is undecidable for each of the properties in Definition 2.

Srba [10] has shown that the problem of checking weak bisimilarity for process algebras is undecidable by a reduction from Post's correspondence problem. The Post's correspondence problem (PCP) is defined as – given a nonempty alphabet Σ and two lists $A = [u_1, u_2, \ldots, u_n]$ and $B = [v_1, v_2 \ldots, v_n]$ where $n > 0$ and $u_k, v_k \in \Sigma^+$ for all $k, 1 \le k \le n$, the question is to decide whether the (A, B)-instance has a solution, i.e., whether there is an integer $m \ge 1$ and a sequence of indices $i_1, i_2, \ldots, i_m \in \{1, 2, \ldots, n\}$ such that $u_{i_1} u_{i_2} \cdots u_{i_m} = v_{i_1} v_{i_2} \cdots v_{i_m}$. According to the classical result due to Post, this problem is undecidable [16].

Given a (A, B)-instance of PCP, Srba constructs a PA N and two process expressions $X \| C$ and $X' \| C$ such that (A, B)-instance has a solution if and only if $X \| C \approx X' \| C$. As in the case of Srba's pushdown system construction, here also we observe that if there is a winning strategy for the attacker from $(X \| C, X' \| C)$, there is one beginning with $X \| C$. There are no ϵ-transitions at $X \| C$. Hence in general, let E and F be two process expressions of a PA N such that E does not have any ϵ-transitions and if there is a winning strategy for the attacker from (E, F), then there is one beginning with E. Then we call the problem of checking whether $E \approx F$, the restricted PA bisimulation problem. It follows then from Srba's construction that:

Theorem 6. *The restricted PA bisimulation problem is undecidable.*   □

We reduce the restricted PA bisimulation problem to the problem of checking each of the bisimulation-based information flow properties for PA's. Let the PA $N = (P, \Sigma, \Delta)$ and its process expressions E, F be an instance of the restricted PA bisimulation problem. Then we construct N' from N such that $N' = (S, \Sigma \cup \{k, \bar{k}\}, \Delta \cup \{S \xrightarrow{k} E, S \xrightarrow{\epsilon} F\})$ where $S \notin Consts$ of N, $k, \bar{k}$ are the only high (and input) events. That is $\mathsf{H} = \mathsf{I} = \{k, \bar{k}\}$.

From the similar arguments as in Section 4 and using the construction of N' as described above, we have:

Theorem 7. *The problem of model-checking process algebras for any of the bisimulation-based properties - BNNI, BSNNI, BNDC, SBNNI, SBSNNI and SBNDC is undecidable.*   □

7   Conclusions

We have shown that model-checking bisimulation-based information flow properties, proposed in the literature, for some well-known classes of infinite state systems is undecidable.

The problem of checking when two deterministic pushdown systems are weakly bisimilar has been shown to be decidable in [17]. This does not imply directly the decidability of checking bisimulation-based properties for deterministic pushdown systems. This is because the *hiding* operation may make the system non-deterministic.

Basic process algebras (BPAs) and Basic parallel processes (BPPs) are subclasses of pushdown systems. The decision problem of checking two BPAs or two BPPs for weak bisimilarity is still open. However it is decidable to check whether two totally normed BPAs or two totally normed BPPs are weakly bisimilar [18]. It will be interesting to explore the model-checking problem for these classes.

Acknowledgements. We thank Jiri Srba, Colin Stirling and Faron Moller for insightful email discussions.

References

1. Focardi, R., Gorrieri, R.: A classification of security properties for process algebras. Journal of Computer Security 3(1), 5–33 (1995)
2. Goguen, J.A., Meseguer, J.: Security policies and security models. In: Proceedings of IEEE Symposium on Security and Privacy, pp. 11–20 (April 1982)
3. Focardi, R., Gorrieri, R.: The compositional security checker: A tool for the verification of information flow security properties. Software Engineering 23(9), 550–571 (1997)
4. Bossi, A., Focardi, R., Piazza, C., Rossi, S.: A proof system for information flow security. In: Logic Based Program Synthesis and Transformation, pp. 956–956 (2003)
5. D'Souza, D., Raghavendra, K.R., Sprick, B.: An automata based approach for verifying information flow properties. In: Proceedings of the Second Workshop on Automated Reasoning for Security Protocol Analysis (ARSPA) (2005); Electronic Notes in Theoretical Computer Science 135(1), 39–58 (2005)
6. D'Souza, D., Holla, R., Raghavendra, K.R., Sprick, B.: Model-checking trace-based information flow properties. Journal of Computer Security 19(1), 101–138 (2011)
7. Srba, J.: Roadmap of infinite results. Current Trends In Theoretical Computer Science, The Challenge of the New Century 2, 337–350 (2004)
8. Srba, J.: Undecidability of Weak Bisimilarity for Pushdown Processes. In: Brim, L., Jančar, P., Křetínský, M., Kučera, A. (eds.) CONCUR 2002. LNCS, vol. 2421, pp. 579–593. Springer, Heidelberg (2002)
9. Jancar, P.: Decidability Questions for Bismilarity of Petri Nets and Some Related Problems. In: Enjalbert, P., Mayr, E.W., Wagner, K.W. (eds.) STACS 1994. LNCS, vol. 775, pp. 581–592. Springer, Heidelberg (1994)
10. Srba, J.: Undecidability of Weak Bisimilarity for PA-Processes. In: Ito, M., Toyama, M. (eds.) DLT 2002. LNCS, vol. 2450, pp. 197–209. Springer, Heidelberg (2003)
11. Harwood, W.T., Moller, F., Setzer, A.: Weak Bisimulation Approximants. In: Ésik, Z. (ed.) CSL 2006. LNCS, vol. 4207, pp. 365–379. Springer, Heidelberg (2006)
12. Stirling, C.: Local Model Checking Games (Extended Abstract). In: Lee, I., Smolka, S.A. (eds.) CONCUR 1995. LNCS, vol. 962, pp. 1–11. Springer, Heidelberg (1995)
13. D'Souza, D., Raghavendra, K.R.: Model-checking bisimulation-based information-flow properties for infinite state systems. Technical report, Department of Computer Science and Automation, Indian Institute of Science (2012)

14. Focardi, R., Rossi, S.: Information flow security in dynamic contexts. In: Proc. of the IEEE Computer Security Foundations Workshop (CSFW 2002), Citeseer, pp. 307–319 (2002)
15. Minsky, M.L.: Computation: finite and infinite machines. Prentice-Hall, Inc., Upper Saddle River (1967)
16. Post, E.: A variant of a recursively unsolvable problem. Bulletin of the American Mathematical Society 52(4), 264–268 (1946)
17. Stirling, C.: Decidability of bisimulation equivalence for pushdown processes. Technical report (2000)
18. Hirshfeld, Y.: Bisimulation trees and the decidability of weak bisimulations. Electronic Notes in Theoretical Computer Science 5, 2–13 (1997)

Identity-Based Traitor Tracing with Short Private Key and Short Ciphertext

Fuchun Guo, Yi Mu, and Willy Susilo

Centre for Computer and Information Security Research
School of Computer Science and Software Engineering
University of Wollongong, Wollongong, Australia
{fuchun,ymu,wsusilo}@uow.edu.au

Abstract. Identity-based traitor tracing (IBTT) scheme can be utilized to identify a private (decryption) key of any identity that is illegally used in an identity-based broadcast encryption scheme. In *PKC'07*, Abdalla *et al.* proposed the first IBTT construction with short private key. In *CCS'08*, Boneh and Naor proposed a public-key traitor tracing, which can be extended to IBTT with short ciphertext. With a further exploration, in this paper, we propose the first IBTT with short private key *and* short ciphertext. Private key and ciphertext are both order of $O(l_1 + l_2)$, where l_1 is the bit length of codeword of fingerprint codes and l_2 is the bit length of group element. To present our IBTT scheme, we introduce a new primitive called *identity-based set encryption* (IBSE), and then describe our IBTT scheme from IBSE and fingerprint codes based on the Boneh-Naor paradigm. Our IBSE scheme is provably secure in the random oracle model under the variant of q-BDHE assumption.

Keywords: Traitor tracing, identity-based, private key, ciphertext.

1 Introduction

1.1 Traitor Tracing

The concept of traitor tracing was introduced by Chor, Fiat, and Naor in [13]. One of the applicable scenarios of traitor tracing is to provide copyright protection in a Pay-TV setting. A copyrighted TV program is encrypted using a secure encryption scheme, where only legitimate subscribers are assigned with a decryption key for decrypting the program. An obvious problem in this scenario is that a Pay-TV subscriber could sell its decryption key to non-subscribers so that they can receive the program illegally and can even produce pirate decoders. Traitor tracing was proposed to identify the traitors who violate the copyright restrictions. A traitor tracing scheme comprises an encryption key, a tracing key and n decryption keys, where n is the number of users. Each legitimate user (subscriber) is given a unique decryption key, and any of the decryption keys can decrypt the encrypted item. More importantly, the tracing key can trace at least one decryption key used to create pirate decoders. A traitor tracing is

S. Foresti, M. Yung, and F. Martinelli (Eds.): ESORICS 2012, LNCS 7459, pp. 609–626, 2012.
© Springer-Verlag Berlin Heidelberg 2012

said to be t-collusion resistant if the tracing is still successful against t colluded users (traitors).

The concept of identity-based traitor tracing (IBTT) was introduced by Abdalla *et al.* [2]. IBTT provides the tracing capability for identity-based encryption, where the private key of each identity is possessed by a group user. The ID-based traitor tracing exhibits broader applications. To motivate this, let us consider a more complex Pay-TV scheme. Subscribers could subscribe to multiple channels, which are sold separately. Hence, if each channel requires a distinct encryption key, many keys will be required. There is also an implication of key expiry. If a decryption key is expired, the entire scheme must be reset and re-encryptions are required. The non-ID-based schemes are inapplicable to this scenario, while the IBTT scheme is desirable. In an IBTT scheme, the encryption key can be the channel name along with an expiry date. The Pay-TV dealer only needs to manage the master secret key of the IBTT scheme and can easily handle the key management and revocation.

1.2 State of the Art

IBTT constructions are built from identity-based encryptions and fingerprint codes. The first approach proposed by Abdalla *et al.* [2] is based on the identity-based encryption with wildcards (WIBE) [1] and fingerprint codes. This IBTT construction provides a short private key, consisting of one codeword and three group elements. The ciphertext has to be sufficiently long and it consists of $O(l_1)$ number of group elements, where l_1 is the bit length of codeword. The second approach introduced by Boneh and Naor [8] enables IBTT construction from any IBE and fingerprint codes. This generic construction is short in ciphertext consisting of one index and two constant-size ciphertexts of IBE. The private key has to be sufficiently long and consists of one l_1-bit codeword and $O(l_1)$ number of private keys of IBE.

The existing IBTT schemes can only offer *either* a short private key *or* a short ciphertext, *but not both*. Since long private key increases the hardware cost of secure storage and long ciphertext requires a big bandwidth in communication, our goal is to achieve both short private key and short ciphertext. In this paper, we propose an IBTT scheme based on a new encryption primitive and fingerprint codes. Our IBTT construction captures both features of short private key and short ciphertext. The comparison is given in Table 1.

Table 1. Comparison of identity-based traitor tracing. Here, l_1 denotes the bit length of codeword and l_2 denotes the bit length of group element.

IBTT Schemes	Private Key Size	Ciphertext Size
[2]	$O(l_1 + l_2)$	$O(l_1 l_2)$
[8]	$O(l_1 l_2)$	$O(l_1 + l_2)$
Ours	$O(l_1 + l_2)$	$O(l_1 + l_2)$

1.3   Our Contributions

We propose the first IBTT with short private key and short ciphertext. Intuitively, our IBTT scheme can be outlined as follows. Let n be the number bound of users for each identity, t be the collusion bound, and l_1 be the corresponding codeword length of fingerprint codes [30,10]. Our t-collusion resistant IBTT scheme generates both private key and ciphertext of size $O(l_1 + l_2)$, where l_2 denotes the length of group element. Precisely, our private key consists of one codeword and two group elements; our ciphertext is composed of one index and two constant-size ciphertexts. Our IBTT scheme utilizes the fingerprint codes and it gives the black-box tracing capability [23]. It provides the same properties as other code-based traitor tracing schemes, where it is applicable for stateless pirate decoders and the tracing key is secret.

We construct our IBTT from fingerprint codes and a new cryptographic primitive: *identity-based set encryption* (IBSE). Roughly speaking, in an IBSE scheme, an aggregated private key of identities $\mathbb{ID} = \{ID_1, ID_2, \cdots, ID_L\}$ can decrypt all ciphertexts for any identity $ID \in \mathbb{ID}$ as long as the encryption for identity ID takes input an additional identity set $\mathbb{S}_{ID}$ satisfying $\mathbb{ID} \subseteq \mathbb{S}_{ID}$. For example, let $\mathbb{ID} = \{ID_1, ID_2\}$ and $\mathbb{S}_{ID} = \{ID_1, ID_2, ID_3, ID_4\}$. If a message is encrypted using ID_1 (or ID_2) and $\mathbb{S}_{ID}$, the private key of $\mathbb{ID}$ enables to decrypt the message. Our generic IBTT construction shows that the private key of IBTT is composed of one codeword of fingerprint codes and two private keys of IBSE. The ciphertext of IBTT consists of an index and two ciphertexts of IBSE. Therefore, the private key size and the ciphertext size of IBTT are heavily dependent on its original IBSE scheme. In the remainder of this paper, we focus on constructing a secure IBSE scheme with a short private key and a short ciphertext, where both sizes are constant independent of the cardinality of $\mathbb{ID}$ and $\mathbb{S}_{ID}$. The proposed IBSE scheme in this paper is provably secure in random oracles based on the variant of q-BDHE assumption [5,7].

1.4   Related Work

Since its seminal introduction in [13], many schemes in developing traitor tracing have been produced. A summary of traitor tracing categories can be found in [9,8,3]. Notably, Kiayias and Yung [23] and other researchers (e.g. [12,15,8,3] introduced a black-box tracing scheme, where the tracing procedure is only allowed to have black-box access to pirate decoders. Naor and Pinkas [24] and others (e.g. [11,17]) proposed a trace-and-revoke scheme, where decryption keys in pirate decoders can be traced and then revoked without affecting any other legitimate decoders. Pfitzmann [25] and other researchers [22,12] achieved public traceability in which the tracing key can be public. Kiayias and Yung [21] and others [26,29] explored stateful pirate decoders, which can keep the state between decryptions.

Since the seminal work of fingerprint codes introduced by Boneh and Shaw [10], many code-based traitor tracing schemes have been proposed [23,27,26,29,15,8,3]. These schemes exhibit black-box tracing capability, and the schemes in [8,3] even offer constant-size ciphertext. The main drawback of code-based traitor tracing schemes is the large private key size, which is significantly dependent on the length of codewords. The imperfect decoders further increase the private key length. We refer the readers to [8,3] for further discussions.

Traitor tracing schemes associated with short ciphertext have been studied in [23,15,9,8,3]. Some of them [23,15] achieved a constant rate for long messages but not a constant size. Boneh, Sahai and Waters [9] proposed a scheme with a ciphertext size $O(\sqrt{n})$ and a constant-size private key, where n is the number of users. Using fingerprint codes, it is able to achieve constant-size ciphertext [8,3], but the private-key size is large. To the best of our knowledge, there exists *no* traitor tracing schemes where both ciphertext and private key are short or have a constant size.

Identity-based traitor tracing was first introduced by Abdalla *et al.* [2]. They managed to achieve a short private key from the IBE scheme with wildcards [1,31], where the private key is composed of one codeword and three group elements. However, the ciphertext is not constant and composed of $O(l_1)$ number of group elements for an l_1-bit codeword.

It seems not hard to construct identity-based traitor tracing schemes with short ciphertext by extending the code-based traitor tracing scheme [8,3,4] into code-based identity-based traitor tracing using an identity-based encryption. This type of construction, however, is not more efficient than code-based public key traitor tracing in terms of private-key size, which requires $O(l_1)$ number of group elements for an l_1-bit codeword.

A potential approach for reducing the private-key size of code-based IBTT could be by building the traitor tracing scheme from another variant of identity-based encryption scheme. For example, we can replace an IBE scheme with a multi-identity and a single-key decryption scheme (MISKD) [19,20], where many private keys of distinct identities can be aggregated into a single one. This single private key decrypts all ciphertexts for any identity mapped to this key. Unfortunately, the current MISKD schemes are accompanied with a linear-size ciphertext, which is determined by the aggregated number of private keys. It is a tradeoff between utilizing IBE scheme and MISKD scheme for IBTT construction. The IBE-based IBTT gives a long private key, while the MISKD-based IBTT gives a long ciphertext. We will present a detailed comparison of IBE, MISKD and our IBSE schemes in later sections.

2   Identity-Based Set Encryption and Identity-Based Traitor Tracing

In Appendix A, we review the definition of fingerprint codes [30,10] and identity-based traitor tracing (IBTT) [2]. Instead of directly proposing our IBTT, we first define the new primitive of identity-based set encryption (IBSE) and give a generic construction of IBTT from IBSE and fingerprint codes. Then in the rest of this paper we propose a concrete IBSE that enables the IBTT construction with short private key and short ciphertext.

2.1   Definition of Identity-Based Set Encryption

In identity-based set encryption (IBSE), messages are encrypted to a single recipient identity. This is the common feature among the encryption notions of IBE, MISKD [19,20] and our IBSE. In comparison with IBE, IBSE produces three differences as follows.

- The key generation algorithm of IBSE enables to compute a single private key for multi-identity $\mathbb{ID} = \{ID_1, ID_2, \cdots, ID_L\}$. Normally, this private key $d_\mathbb{ID}$ is shorter in length than the sum of all separated private keys from a traditional IBE.
- The encryption algorithm of IBSE requires the recipient's identity ID along with an identity set $\mathbb{S}_{ID}$, if the private key of recipient is $d_\mathbb{ID}$ for multi-identity $\mathbb{ID}$ including ID. The encryption algorithm allows to pick any identity set $\mathbb{S}_{ID}$ satisfying $\mathbb{ID} \subseteq \mathbb{S}_{ID}$.
- The decryption algorithm of IBSE requires the private key $d_\mathbb{ID}$ of $\mathbb{ID}$ along with the recipient's identity ID, the multi-identity $\mathbb{ID}$ and the identity set $\mathbb{S}_{ID}$. Decryption on a ciphertext for ID requires $ID \in \mathbb{ID}$ and $\mathbb{ID} \subseteq \mathbb{S}_{ID}$.

In comparison with MISKD, IBSE requires an identity set $\mathbb{S}_{ID}$ satisfying $\mathbb{ID} \subseteq \mathbb{S}_{ID}$ in both encryption and decryption. IBSE can be seemed as a variant of MISKD by setting $\mathbb{S}_{ID}$ as the universe. We compare IBSE to IBE and MISKD in Table 2.

Table 2. Comparison of IBE, MISKD and IBSE

Schemes	Key Generation	Encryption	Decryption	Decryption Condition
IBE	ID	ID	d_{ID}	−
MISKD	$\mathbb{ID}$	ID	$d_\mathbb{ID}, ID, \mathbb{ID}$	$ID \in \mathbb{ID}$
IBSE	$\mathbb{ID}$	$ID, \mathbb{S}_{ID}$	$d_\mathbb{ID}, ID, \mathbb{ID}, \mathbb{S}_{ID}$	$ID \in \mathbb{ID}$ & $\mathbb{ID} \subseteq \mathbb{S}_{ID}$

An IBSE scheme consists of four algorithms as follows.

Setup$_S(N, \lambda)$. The setup algorithm takes as input N, the cardinality of identity set (i.e., $|\mathbb{S}_{ID}| = N$), and a security parameter λ, and returns a master public key MPK and a master secret key MSK.

KGen$_S(\mathbb{ID}, MSK)$. The key generation algorithm takes as input identities $\mathbb{ID} = \{ID_1, ID_2, \cdots, ID_L\}$ with $L \leq N$ and the master secret key MSK, and returns a private key $d_\mathbb{ID}$ for $\{ID_1, ID_2, \cdots, ID_L\}$.

Enc$_S(ID, \mathbb{S}_{ID}, M, MPK)$. The encryption algorithm takes as input an identity ID, the identity set $\mathbb{S}_{ID}$ containing N distinct identities (including ID) and the message M, and returns a ciphertext $C \leftarrow \mathsf{Enc}_S(ID, \mathbb{S}_{ID}, M, MPK)$.

Dec$_S(C, d_\mathbb{ID}, ID, \mathbb{ID}, \mathbb{S}_{ID})$. The decryption algorithm takes as input the ciphertext C, the private key $d_\mathbb{ID}$, identity ID, identities $\mathbb{ID}$ and the identity set $\mathbb{S}_{ID}$. The algorithm returns a message M or $\perp$.

The correctness requires that for all (MPK, MSK), $ID, \mathbb{ID}, \mathbb{S}_{ID}$, and $d_{\mathbb{ID}}$ if $ID \in \mathbb{ID}$ and $\mathbb{ID} \subseteq \mathbb{S}_{ID}$, we have

$$\mathsf{Dec}_S\big(\mathsf{Enc}_S(ID, \mathbb{S}_{ID}, M, MPK), d_{\mathbb{ID}}, ID, \mathbb{ID}, \mathbb{S}_{ID}\big) = M.$$

Security. The full security notion for IBSE scheme is similar to the IND-ID-CCA notion for IBE scheme. We name it IND-ID-Set-CCA, which is secure against chosen-ciphertext attack. It is stated as follows:

Setup. The challenger runs the $\mathsf{Setup}_S(N, \lambda)$ algorithm to generate (MPK, MSK) and gives the adversary MPK.

Phase 1. The adversary makes private key queries and decryption queries.

- For a private key query on $\mathbb{ID}$ ($|\mathbb{ID}| \leq N$) from the adversary, the challenger runs the $\mathsf{KGen}_S(\mathbb{ID}, MSK)$ algorithm, and returns the private key $d_{\mathbb{ID}}$ to the adversary.
- For a decryption query on $(ID, \mathbb{S}_{ID}, \mathbb{ID}, C)$ from the adversary, the challenger runs the $\mathsf{KGen}_S(\mathbb{ID}, MSK)$ algorithm to compute $d_{\mathbb{ID}}$, runs the decryption algorithm $\mathsf{Dec}_S(C, d_{\mathbb{ID}}, ID, \mathbb{ID}, \mathbb{S}_{ID})$, and returns the decryption result to the adversary.

Challenge. The adversary outputs $(ID^*, \mathbb{S}_{ID^*}, M_0, M_1)$ to be challenged, where $ID^* \in \mathbb{S}_{ID^*}$. This challenge identity must be different from other identities for private key query. The challenger responds by flipping a coin $c \in \{0, 1\}$, running the $\mathsf{Enc}_S(ID^*, \mathbb{S}_{ID^*}, M_c)$ algorithm, and returning the challenge ciphertext C^* to the adversary.

Phase 2. The adversary can make further private key queries and decryption queries in this phase, except a private key query on any $\mathbb{ID}$ satisfying $ID^* \in \mathbb{ID}$ and all decryption queries on C^* for ID^*.

Guess. The adversary returns a guess $c' \in \{0, 1\}$ and wins the game if $c' = c$.

Remark 1. In this security model, the adversary submits both ID^* and $\mathbb{S}_{ID}^*$ for challenge. Let $\mathbb{ID}$ be the identities queried in the security model. There are two different definitions on $\mathbb{ID}$ with regard to $(ID^*, \mathbb{S}_{ID^*})$.

- ID^* cannot be one of identities in $\mathbb{ID}$.
- ID^* can be one of identities in $\mathbb{ID}$, but $\mathbb{ID} \not\subseteq \mathbb{S}_{ID}^*$.

We adopt the first definition for our IBSE scheme. Notice that the second definition is more stronger but it does not fit for those schemes with dynamic key aggregation. For example, let $d_{\mathbb{ID}_1}$ be the private key of $\mathbb{ID}_1 = \{ID_1, ID_2, ID_3, ID_4\}$, and $d_{\mathbb{ID}_2}$ be the private key of $\mathbb{ID}_2 = \{ID_1, ID_2\}$. If the private key $d_{\mathbb{ID}_3}$ of $\mathbb{ID}_3 = \{ID_3, ID_4\}$ is computable from $d_{\mathbb{ID}_1}$ and $d_{\mathbb{ID}_2}$, it is easy to verify the stronger definition does not work when $ID^* = ID_3$, $\mathbb{S}_{ID^*} = \mathbb{ID}_3$, and the private key query on $\mathbb{ID}_1$ is allowed.

We let the number of private key query be q_1 and let the number of decryption query be q_2. We define the advantage of the adversary in the above game as $\mathsf{Adv}_S = \big| \Pr[c' = c] - \frac{1}{2} \big|$.

Definition 1. *An IBSE scheme is (T, q_1, q_2, ϵ)-secure against IND-ID-Set-CCA attacks if for all T-polynomial time adversaries who make q_1 private key queries at most and q_2 decryption queries at most, we have $\epsilon = \mathsf{Adv}_S$ is a negligible function of λ.*

Definition 2. *An IBSE scheme is $(T, q_1, 0, \epsilon)$-secure against IND-ID-Set-CPA attacks if for all T-polynomial time adversaries who make q_1 private key queries at most and 0 decryption queries at most, we have $\epsilon = \mathsf{Adv}_S$ is a negligible function of λ. In this case, we write (T, q_1, ϵ) the shorthand of $(T, q_1, 0, \epsilon)$.*

2.2 Generic Construction of IBTT

Let $(\mathsf{Setup}_S, \mathsf{KGen}_S, \mathsf{Enc}_S, \mathsf{Dec}_S)$ be an identity-based set encryption scheme and $(\mathsf{Gen}_{FC}, \mathsf{Tra}_{FC})$ be a fingerprint code. Our identity-based traitor tracing scheme is described as follows:

Setup$_T(\lambda)$. Let $l_1 = l_1(\lambda)$ be the length of codeword in the fingerprint codes. The setup algorithm of IBTT scheme sets $N = l_1$, and runs the Setup_S algorithm two times to generate two key pairs (MPK_{S_0}, MSK_{S_0}) and (MPK_{S_1}, MSK_{S_1}). The master public key MPK and the master secret key MSK are

$$MPK = (MPK_{S_0}, MPK_{S_1}), \quad MSK = (MSK_{S_0}, MSK_{S_1}).$$

KGen$_T(ID, MSK)$. The algorithm works as follows:

- Run the Gen_{FC} algorithm to generate (Γ_{ID}, tk_{ID}) for ID, where $\Gamma_{ID} = \{\overline{w}^{(1)}, \overline{w}^{(2)}, \cdots, \overline{w}^{(n)}\}$ and tk_{ID} is the tracing key. We require that the Gen_{FC} algorithm always computes the same (Γ_{ID}, tk_{ID}) for ID. This can be accomplished, for example, using a pseudo-random function.
- Let $\mathbb{ID}_{ID,i,0}$ and $\mathbb{ID}_{ID,i,1}$ be two identity sets defined as

$$\mathbb{ID}_{ID,i,0} = \{ID|k|0 : \ k = 1, 2, \cdots, l_1, \ s.t. \ w_k^{(i)} = 0\}$$
$$\mathbb{ID}_{ID,i,1} = \{ID|k|1 : \ k = 1, 2, \cdots, l_1, \ s.t. \ w_k^{(i)} = 1\}.$$

Compute the private keys

$$d_{\mathbb{ID}_{ID,i,0}} \leftarrow \mathsf{KGen}_S(\mathbb{ID}_{ID,i,0}, MSK_{S_0}), d_{\mathbb{ID}_{ID,i,1}} \leftarrow \mathsf{KGen}_S(\mathbb{ID}_{ID,i,1}, MSK_{S_1}).$$

The private key of ID for the ith user is $d_{ID,i} = (\overline{w}^{(i)}, d_{\mathbb{ID}_{ID,i,0}}, d_{\mathbb{ID}_{ID,i,1}})$.

Enc$_T(ID, M, MPK)$. The algorithm works as follows:

- Let $\mathbb{S}_{ID,0}$ and $\mathbb{S}_{ID,1}$ be two identity sets defined as

$$\mathbb{S}_{ID,0} = \{ID|k|0 : \ k = 1, 2, \cdots, l_1\}, \ \mathbb{S}_{ID,1} = \{ID|k|1 : \ k = 1, 2, \cdots, l_1\}.$$

- Choose $j \in \{1, 2, \cdots, l_1\}$ at random and compute

$$C_{ID,0} \leftarrow \mathsf{Enc}_S(ID|j|0, \ \mathbb{S}_{ID,0}, \ M, \ MPK_{S_0})$$
$$C_{ID,1} \leftarrow \mathsf{Enc}_S(ID|j|1, \ \mathbb{S}_{ID,1}, \ M, \ MPK_{S_1}).$$

The ciphertext is $C = (j, C_{ID,0}, C_{ID,1})$.

$\mathbf{Dec}_T(C, d_{ID,i})$. For the ith user with the private key $d_{ID,i}$, if $w_j^{(i)} = 0$, compute $\mathbb{ID}_{ID,i,0}$ and $\mathbb{S}_{ID,0}$ from ID and $\overline{w}^{(i)}$, and output

$$\mathsf{Dec}_S\big(C_{ID,0},\ d_{\mathbb{ID}_{ID,i,0}},\ ID|j|0,\ \mathbb{ID}_{ID,i,0},\ \mathbb{S}_{ID,0}\big).$$

Otherwise, compute $\mathbb{ID}_{ID,i,1}$ and $\mathbb{S}_{ID,1}$ from ID and $\overline{w}^{(i)}$, and output

$$\mathsf{Dec}_S\big(C_{ID,1},\ d_{\mathbb{ID}_{ID,i,1}},\ ID|j|1,\ \mathbb{ID}_{ID,i,1},\ \mathbb{S}_{ID,1}\big).$$

$\mathbf{Trace}_T(\mathcal{PD}_{ID}, ID, MSK)$. The tracing algorithm works as follows:

- For $j = 1, 2, \cdots, l_1$, randomly choose a message $M_j \neq 0$ and does as follows:
  - Compute the ciphertexts

$$C_{ID,0} \leftarrow \mathsf{Enc}_S\big(ID|j|0, \mathbb{S}_{ID,0}, M_j, MPK_{S_0}\big)$$
$$C'_{ID,1} \leftarrow \mathsf{Enc}_S\big(ID|j|1, \mathbb{S}_{ID,1},\ 0\ , MPK_{S_1}\big).$$

  - Send $C_j = (j, C_{ID,0}, C'_{ID,1})$ to the pirate decryption box $\mathcal{PD}_{ID}$.
  - Let the return from $\mathcal{PD}_{ID}$ be M'_j. Define the bit $w_j = 0$ if $M'_j = M_j$ or $w_j = 1$ otherwise.

  Output the l_1-bit codeword $\overline{w}^* = w_1 w_2 \cdots w_{l_1}$.
- Compute the tracing key tk_{ID} for ID from Gen_{FC}. Run the $\mathsf{Tra}_{FC}(\overline{w}^*, tk_{ID})$ algorithm to output the set of traitors $\mathbb{T}_{ID} \subseteq \{1, 2, \cdots, n\}$.

Our IBTT scheme above is extended from the Boneh-Naor public-key traitor tracing scheme [8]. We do not change their paradigm, but replace the public-key encryption scheme with the IBSE scheme. The following theorem shows that our IBTT scheme is t-collusion resistant. Due to the page limit, we defer the proof in the full version of this paper.

Theorem 1. *Given an identity-based set encryption scheme* ($\mathsf{Setup}_S, \mathsf{KGen}_S, \mathsf{Enc}_S,$ Dec_S), *which is IND-ID-Set-CPA secure and fingerprint codes* ($\mathsf{Gen}_{FC}, \mathsf{Tra}_{FC}$), *which is t-collusion resistant, our IBTT scheme is a t-collusion resistant identity-based traitor tracing scheme.*

Particularly, using the notation of appendix A, for all $t > 0, n > t$, and all polynomial time adversaries attacking IBTT, there exist polynomial time adversaries attacking IBSE such that

$$\mathsf{Adv}_T^s \leq (2l_1) \cdot \mathsf{Adv}_S, \quad \mathsf{Adv}_T^c \leq l_1 \cdot \mathsf{Adv}_S + \mathsf{Adv}_{FC} + \frac{l_1}{|\mathcal{M}|},$$

where l_1 denotes the bit length of codeword and $\mathcal{M}$ denotes the message space.

2.3   Comparison of IBTT Constructions

We give an IBTT construction from IBSE scheme in subsection 2.2 by following the Boneh-Naor paradigm. Notice that the IBSE scheme used to construct the IBTT scheme can be replaced with IBE scheme (e.g. [6,31,18]) or MISKD scheme (e.g.[19,20]). The difference is the representation of private key and ciphertext. In our generic IBTT scheme, each private key is associated with one codeword $\overline{w}^{(i)}$ and l_1 distinct identities $\{ID|k|w_k^{(i)} : k = 1, 2, \cdots, l_1\}$. And each ciphertext is composed of one index j and two ciphertexts of its original encryption scheme. If the encryption scheme is the MISKD or IBSE, according to our above construction, the private keys associated with l_1 identities can be aggregated into two private keys. Otherwise, it will produce l_1 private keys using the IBE scheme.

Let K_X be the private key and C_X be the ciphertext of X encryption scheme. Let X$\rightarrow$ IBTT be the IBTT construction from X encryption scheme. We give a summary of private key length and ciphertext length in Table 3.

Table 3. Comparison of IBTT constructions

Constructions	Private Key Size	Ciphertext Size
IBE$\rightarrow$ IBTT	$|\overline{w}|+l_1 \cdot |K_{IBE}|$	$|j| + 2 \cdot |C_{IBE}|$
MISKD$\rightarrow$ IBTT	$|\overline{w}|+2 \cdot |K_{MISKD}|$	$|j| + 2 \cdot |C_{MISKD}|$
IBSE$\rightarrow$ IBTT	$|\overline{w}|+2 \cdot |K_{IBSE}|$	$|j| + 2 \cdot |C_{IBSE}|$

The table exhibits that only MISKD$\rightarrow$ IBTT or IBSE$\rightarrow$ IBTT could capture both short private key and short ciphertext. However, the ciphertext of current MISKD schemes [19,20] has a linear size, and we cannot achieve IBTT scheme with short private key and short ciphertext from the existing MISKD schemes. The remaining candidate is IBSE$\rightarrow$ IBTT. In the next section, we show how to construct an IBSE scheme with short private key and short ciphertext, where both size are constant independent of $\mathbb{ID}$ and $\mathbb{S}_{ID}$. It will enable an IBTT construction with short private key and short ciphertext.

3   IBSE with Short Private key and Short Ciphertext

3.1   Definitions

Let $\mathcal{G}_B$ be a generator of bilinear groups. Taking as input a security parameter λ, it outputs bilinear groups $(g, p, \mathbb{G}, \mathbb{G}_T, e)$. Here, $\mathbb{G}, \mathbb{G}_T$ are two (multiplicative) cyclic groups of prime order p, g is a generator of $\mathbb{G}$ and $e : \mathbb{G} \times \mathbb{G} \rightarrow \mathbb{G}_T$ is the bilinear map. The bilinear map e is a map with the following three properties:

- For all $u, v \in \mathbb{G}, a, b \in \mathbb{Z}_p, e(u^a, v^b) = e(u, v)^{ab}$.
- $e(g, g)$ is a generator of $\mathbb{G}_T$.
- It is efficient to compute the bilinear map e.

The security of our scheme is based on the variant of q-bilinear Diffie-Hellman exponent assumption (q-BDHE), which has been used in [5,7,18]. We modify the BDHE assumption by using one group generator instead of two. The modified q-BDHE assumption is defined as follows, which can be justified in the generic group model by the result proved in [5].

Modified q-Bilinear Diffie-Hellman Exponent Problem:

Input: $g,\ g^{(a)},\ g^{(a^2)},\ \cdots,\ g^{(a^q)},\ g^{(a^{2q+2})},\ g^{(a^{2q+3})},\cdots,\ g^{(a^{3q+1})} \in \mathbb{G}^{2q+1}$.

Output: $e(g,g)^{(a^{2q+1})}$.

Definition 3. *The (T, q, ϵ)-BDHE assumption holds in $\mathbb{G}$ if for all T-polynomial time adversaries, the advantage of solving the modified q-BDHE problem is ϵ at most, which is a negligible function of λ.*

3.2 Our Construction

In our IBSE construction, the private key structure for an individual identity is similar to the identity-based broadcast encryption in [28], and the encryption structure is modified from the identity-based broadcast encryption in [14] to achieve constant-size ciphertext. Our IBSE scheme is IND-ID-Set-CPA secure in the random oracles under the modified q-BDHE assumption. We can naturally extend it to CCA security using the technique due to Fujisaki-Okamoto [16] in the random oracle model.

Setup$_S(N, \lambda)$. The setup algorithm takes as input N and a security parameter λ. It first generates the bilinear groups $(g, p, \mathbb{G}, \mathbb{G}_T, e)$ by running $\mathcal{G}_B(\lambda)$. The algorithm randomly chooses $h \in \mathbb{G}$ and $\alpha \in \mathbb{Z}_p$. It picks two collision-resistant hash functions at random $H_1 : \{0,1\}^* \to \mathbb{Z}_p$ and $H_2 : \{0,1\}^* \to \{0,1\}^{l_m}$. Here, l_m denotes the length of messages to be encrypted. The algorithm computes $h_1 = h^\alpha$ and $g_i = g^{(\alpha^i)}$ for $i = 1, 2, \cdots, N$. The master secret key MSK is α and the master public key MPK is

$$MPK = \big(h, h_1, g, g_1, g_2, \cdots, g_N, p, \mathbb{G}, \mathbb{G}_T, e, H_1, H_2\big).$$

KGen$_S(\mathbb{ID}, MSK)$. The key generation algorithm takes as input identities $\mathbb{ID} = \{ID_1, ID_2, \cdots, ID_L\}$ with $L \leq N$ and the master secret key α. It computes the private key $d_{\mathbb{ID}}$ as

$$d_{\mathbb{ID}} = h^{\frac{1}{\alpha - H_1(ID_1)} + \frac{1}{\alpha - H_1(ID_2)} + \cdots + \frac{1}{\alpha - H_1(ID_L)}} \in \mathbb{G}.$$

Enc$_S(ID, \mathbb{S}_{ID}, M, MPK)$. The encryption algorithm takes as input an identity ID, an identity set $\mathbb{S}_{ID} = \{ID_1', ID_2', \cdots, ID_N'\}$ ($ID \in \mathbb{S}_{ID}$), a message $M \in \{0,1\}^{l_m}$ and the master public key MPK. Let

$$(\alpha - \mathbb{S}_{ID}) = \prod_{i=1}^{N} \big(\alpha - H_1(ID_i')\big).$$

The algorithm picks a random $r \in \mathbb{Z}_p$ and outputs the ciphertext $C = (c_1, c_2, c_3)$ $\in \mathbb{G}^2 \times \{0,1\}^{lm}$ as

$$c_1 = \left(g^{(\alpha - \mathbb{S}_{ID})}\right)^r, \quad c_2 = \left(h^{\alpha - H_1(ID)}\right)^r, \quad c_3 = H_2\left(e\left(g^{\frac{(\alpha - \mathbb{S}_{ID})}{\alpha - H_1(ID)}}, h\right)^r\right) \oplus M.$$

$\mathbf{Dec}_S(C, d_{\mathbb{ID}}, ID, \mathbb{ID}, \mathbb{S}_{ID})$. The decryption algorithm takes as input the cipher-text C, the private key $d_{\mathbb{ID}}$, the identity ID, the identities $\mathbb{ID}$ and the identity set $\mathbb{S}_{ID}$. If $ID \in \mathbb{ID}$ and $\mathbb{ID} \subseteq \mathbb{S}_{ID}$, we let the polynomial function $f(x)$ be

$$f(x) = \left(x - \mathbb{S}_{ID}\right) \cdot \left(\sum_{i=1}^{L} \frac{1}{x - H_1(ID_i)}\right)$$

$$= \frac{(x - \mathbb{S}_{ID})}{x - H_1(ID)} + \left(x - H_1(ID)\right) \cdot \left(\sum_{i=0}^{N-2} f_i x^i\right),$$

where f_i is the coefficient of x^i. The algorithm computes the message M by

$$c_3 \oplus H_2\left(e(c_1, d_{\mathbb{ID}}) \cdot e\left(c_2, \prod_{i=1}^{N-2} g_i^{f_i} \cdot g^{f_0}\right)^{-1}\right).$$

3.3   Correctness

In the encryption algorithm, $(\alpha - \mathbb{S}_{ID})$ and $\frac{(\alpha - \mathbb{S}_{ID})}{\alpha - H_1(ID)}$ are two polynomial func-tions in α, $g^{(\alpha - \mathbb{S}_{ID})}$ and $g^{\frac{(\alpha - \mathbb{S}_{ID})}{\alpha - H_1(ID)}}$ can be computed from the coefficients of polynomial functions and $r, g, g_1, g_2, \cdots, g_N$.

In the decryption algorithm, we have

$$e(c_1, d_{\mathbb{ID}}) = e\left(\left(g^{(\alpha - \mathbb{S}_{ID})}\right)^r, h^{\sum_{i=1}^{L} \frac{1}{\alpha - H_1(ID_i)}}\right) = e\left(g^{f(\alpha)}, h\right)^r$$

$$e\left(c_2, \prod_{i=1}^{N-2} g_i^{f_i} \cdot g^{f_0}\right)^{-1} = e\left(\left(h^{\alpha - H_1(ID)}\right)^r, g^{\sum_{i=0}^{N-2} f_i \alpha^i}\right)^{-1}$$

$$= e\left(g^{-\left(\alpha - H_1(ID)\right) \cdot \left(\sum_{i=0}^{N-2} f_i \alpha^i\right)}, h\right)^r$$

$$e(c_1, d_{\mathbb{ID}}) \cdot e\left(c_2, \prod_{i=1}^{N-2} g_i^{f_i} \cdot g^{f_0}\right)^{-1} = e\left(g^{\frac{(\alpha - \mathbb{S}_{ID})}{\alpha - H_1(ID)}}, h\right)^r.$$

3.4   Comparison of IBE, MISKD and IBSE

We provide the comparison of IBE, MISKD and IBSE in Table 4 under the assumption that a user has to manage L distinct identities. The IBE scheme (e.g. [6,31,18]) has a very simple structure in encryption and decryption, but it cannot aggregate private keys into a short one. The MISKD scheme (e.g. [19,20]) enables private key aggregation into a single one but the ciphertext size is not constant. In comparison with the MISKD, IBSE is able to aggregate private keys without expanding ciphertext size for decryption. Our IBSE scheme is short in both private key and ciphertext.

We realize the short private key and short ciphertext, at the price of complex encryption and decryption. An identity set $\mathbb{S}_{ID}$ such that $\mathbb{ID} \subseteq \mathbb{S}_{ID}$ must be known by the encryptor and the decryptor; otherwise, a ciphertext cannot be decrypted using the aggregated private key $d_{\mathbb{ID}}$. However, this provides a negligible implication on our IBTT construction since $\mathbb{S}_{ID}$ is computable from ID. Other applications using the IBSE primitive should be carefully checked.

Table 4. Comparison of IBE, MISKD and IBSE with L identities

Schemes	Private Key Size	Ciphertext Size
IBE	$O(L)$	$O(1)$
MISKD	$O(1)$	$O(L)$
IBSE	$O(1)$	$O(1)$

3.5   Security Proof

Theorem 2. *Suppose the hash functions H_1, H_2 are two random oracles. Let q_{H_1} and q_{H_2} be the query number to the oracles H_1 and H_2 respectively. Let $q = \{q_{H_1}, N\}_{max}$. Assuming the modified q-BDHE assumption is (T', ϵ')-hard, our IBSE scheme is (T, q_1, ϵ)-secure under IND-ID-Set-CPA attacks.*

$$T = T' - O(q_{H_1} t_e), \quad q_1 \le q_{H_1}, \quad \epsilon = q_{H_1} q_{H_2} \epsilon',$$

where t_e denotes the average time of an exponentiation in $\mathbb{G}$.

Proof. Suppose there exists an adversary who can break the IBSE scheme with advantage (t, q_1, ϵ). We construct an algorithm $\mathcal{B}$ that solves the modified q-BDHE assumption with advantage (t', ϵ') at least. The algorithm $\mathcal{B}$ is given

$$\left(g, g^{(a)}, g^{(a^2)}, \cdots, g^{(a^q)}, g^{(a^{2q+2})}, g^{(a^{2q+3})}, \cdots, g^{(a^{3q+1})}\right),$$

and the aim of $\mathcal{B}$ is to output $e(g,g)^{(a^{2q+1})} \in \mathbb{G}_T$. The algorithm $\mathcal{B}$ interacts with the adversary $\mathcal{A}$ as below.

Setup. The algorithm $\mathcal{B}$ randomly chooses $\{I_1, I_2, \cdots, I_{q_{H_1}}, b\}$ from $\mathbb{Z}_p$, and picks a random $i^* \in \{1, 2, \cdots, q_{H_1}\}$. Let $F(x) \in \mathbb{Z}_p[x]$ be a $(q_{H_1} - 1)$-degree polynomial function as

$$F(x) = b \prod_{i=1, i \neq i^*}^{q_{H_1}} (x - I_i) = F_{q_{H_1}-1} x^{q_{H_1}-1} + \cdots + F_2 x^2 + F_1 x + F_0.$$

It sets $g_i = g^{(a^i)}$ for all $i = 1, 2, \cdots, N$ and computes $h = g^{F(a)}, h_1 = g^{aF(a)}$ from the challenge input and $F(x)$. The algorithm $\mathcal{B}$ forwards $MPK = (h, h_1, g, g_1, g_2,$

$\cdots, g_N, p, \mathbb{G}, \mathbb{G}_T, e)$ except the two hash functions to the adversary and sets H_1, H_2 as random oracles.

Hash Queries. At any time, the adversary can query H_1, H_2.

- For an identity query on ID to the random oracle H_1, the algorithm $\mathcal{B}$ maintains a list $\mathcal{L}_{H_1}$ and responds as follows. If there has been already a tuple (ID, I) in the list $\mathcal{L}_{H_1}$, the algorithm responds with $H_1(ID) = I$. Otherwise, let ID be the ith distinct query to H_1. The algorithm $\mathcal{B}$ responds by returning $H_1(ID) = I_i$ to the adversary, and adding (ID, I_i) to $\mathcal{L}_{H_1}$.
- For a random query on R to the random oracle H_2, the algorithm $\mathcal{B}$ maintains a list $\mathcal{L}_{H_2}$ and responds as follows. If R is not in the list, the algorithm responds by randomly choosing a different $Y \in \mathbb{Z}_p$, returning $H_2(R) = Y$ to the adversary, and adding (R, Y) to $\mathcal{L}_{H_2}$. Otherwise, there has been already a tuple (R, Y) in the list and the algorithm responds with $H_2(R) = Y$.

Phase 1. For a key query on $\mathbb{ID} = \{ID_1, ID_2, \cdots, ID_L\}$ from the adversary, the challenger responds as follows.

- Let the response for ID_i in the list $\mathcal{L}_{H_1}$ be (ID_i, I_i) for all $i = 1, 2, \cdots, L$. If $I_i = I_{i^*}$ holds for any $i \in \{1, 2, \cdots, L\}$, the algorithm aborts the simulation.
- When $I_i \neq I_{i^*}$ holds for all $i = 1, 2, \cdots, L$, we have that $H_1(ID_1), H_1(ID_2)$, $\cdots, H_1(ID_L)$ are all the roots of $F(x)$. Then, we deduce that

$$F_{\mathbb{ID}}(x) = F(x) \cdot \left(\frac{1}{x - H_1(ID_1)} + \frac{1}{x - H_1(ID_2)} + \cdots + \frac{1}{x - H_1(ID_L)} \right)$$

is a $(q_{H_1} - 2)$-degree at most polynomial function. $\mathcal{B}$ can compute

$$d_{\mathbb{ID}} = h^{\frac{1}{\alpha - H_1(ID_1)} + \frac{1}{\alpha - H_1(ID_2)} + \cdots + \frac{1}{\alpha - H_1(ID_L)}}$$

$$= g^{F(\alpha) \cdot \left(\frac{1}{\alpha - H_1(ID_1)} + \frac{1}{\alpha - H_1(ID_2)} + \cdots + \frac{1}{\alpha - H_1(ID_L)} \right)} = g^{F_{\mathbb{ID}}(a)}$$

from $F_{\mathbb{ID}}(x)$ and $g, g^{(a)}, \cdots, g^{(a^q)}$, and $d_{\mathbb{ID}}$ is a valid private key of $\mathbb{ID}$.

Challenge. The adversary outputs $(ID^*, \mathbb{S}_{ID^*}, M_0, M_1)$ to be challenged. If the tuple (ID^*, I^*) in the list $\mathcal{L}_{H_1}$ satisfies $I^* \neq I_{i^*}$, abort; otherwise, the algorithm randomly chooses $c_3^* \in \{0, 1\}^{l_m}$. Since $ID^* \in \mathbb{S}_{ID^*}$, we let $F'(x) = \frac{(x - \mathbb{S}_{ID^*})}{x - I^*}$ be an $(N-1)$-degree polynomial function. The algorithm randomly chooses $r' \in \mathbb{Z}_p$ and computes the challenge ciphertext (c_1, c_2, c_3) by

$$c_1 = g^{r'\left(a^{2q+2} - I^{*2q+2}\right)F'(a)}, \quad c_2 = g^{r'\left(a^{2q+2} - I^{*2q+2}\right)F(a)}, \quad c_3 = c_3',$$

where both c_1 and c_2 are computable from $F'(x), F(x)$ and the challenge input.

Let the randomness r be $r = r' \cdot \frac{a^{2q+2} - I^{*2q+2}}{a - I^*}$, which is also universally random in $\mathbb{Z}_p$. We have

$$g^{r'\left(a^{2q+2} - I^{*2q+2}\right)F'(a)} = g^{r' \cdot \frac{\left(a^{2q+2} - I^{*2q+2}\right)}{\left(a - I^*\right)} \cdot \left(a - \mathbb{S}_{ID^*}\right)} = \left(g^{(\alpha - \mathbb{S}_{ID^*})}\right)^r,$$

$$g^{r'\left(a^{2q+2} - I^{*2q+2}\right)F(a)} = g^{r' \cdot \frac{\left(a^{2q+2} - I^{*2q+2}\right)}{\left(a - I^*\right)} \cdot F(a)(a - I^*)} = \left(h^{\alpha - H_1(ID^*)}\right)^r,$$

and the challenge ciphertext is equivalent to

$$\left(\left(g^{(\alpha - \mathbb{S}_{ID^*})} \right)^r, \ \left(h^{\alpha - H_1(ID^*)} \right)^r, \ c_3^* \right).$$

According to our setting, there must exist a hash query on $e\left(g^{\frac{(\alpha - \mathbb{S}_{ID^*})}{\alpha - H_1(ID^*)}}, h \right)^r$ to H_2 in order to decrypt the message in the challenge ciphertext.

$$M = H_2\left(e\left(g^{\frac{(\alpha - \mathbb{S}_{ID^*})}{\alpha - H_1(ID^*)}}, h \right)^r \right) \oplus c_3^*.$$

Guess. The adversary returns a guess $c' \in \{0,1\}$ of c. Let $F''(x)$ be the $(2q + N + q_{H_1} - 1)$-degree polynomial function

$$F''(x) = r' \cdot \frac{x^{2q+2} - I^{*2q+2}}{x - I^*} \cdot F'(x) \cdot F(x),$$

and F_i'' be the coefficient of x^i in $F''(x)$. We have that

$$e\left(g^{\frac{(\alpha - \mathbb{S}_{ID^*})}{\alpha - H_1(ID^*)}}, h \right)^r = e(g,g)^{F''(a)}.$$

It is easy to verify that F_{2q+1}'' is equal to $r'F'(I^*)F(I^*)$ which is nonzero, and that $e(g,g)^{F_i'' \cdot a^i}$ for all $i \neq 2q+1$ are computable from the challenge input. The algorithm $\mathcal{B}$ picks a random tuple (R, Y) from the list $\mathcal{L}_{H_2}$ and computes

$$\left(R \cdot \prod_{i=1, i \neq 2q+1}^{2q+N+q_{H_1}-1} e(g,g)^{-F_i'' \cdot a^i} \right)^{\frac{1}{r'F'(I^*)F(I^*)}} = e(g,g)^{a^{2q+1}}$$

as the solution to the q-BDHE assumption.

We have completed the simulation proof of our IBSE scheme. To complete the proof, it remains to analyze the probability of successful simulation. We define the three types of events A_i, A^*, A_s:

- A_i is the event that the algorithm $\mathcal{B}$ can generate the ith private key query on ID_i. Let (ID_i, I_i) be the response for ID_i in the list $\mathcal{L}_{H_1}$. This indicates that $I_i \neq I_{i^*}$ holds for ID_i.
- A^* is the event that the algorithm $\mathcal{B}$ does not abort in the challenge phase. Let (ID^*, I^*) be the response for ID^* in the list $\mathcal{L}_{H_1}$. This indicates $I^* = I_{i^*}$.
- A_s is the event that what the algorithm $\mathcal{B}$ randomly picks from the list $\mathcal{L}_{H_2}$ is equal to $e\left(g^{\frac{(\alpha - \mathbb{S}_{ID^*})}{\alpha - H_1(ID^*)}}, h \right)^r$. Let q_{H_2} be the number of queries to the random oracle H_2. If the adversary ever made a query on $e\left(g^{\frac{(\alpha - \mathbb{S}_{ID^*})}{\alpha - H_1(ID^*)}}, h \right)^r$ to the random oracle, the probability of choosing a correct R_i is $1/q_{H_2}$.

According to the definition of security model, the adversary cannot query the private key of the challenge identity. With $1/q_{H_1}$ probability, the simulation does not abort till the guess phase. Therefore, if the adversary can break the IBSE scheme, the probability of successfully reducing the attack to solving the modified q-BDHE assumption is $\Pr\left[\bigwedge_{i=1}^{q_1} A_i \bigwedge A^* \bigwedge A_s\right] = \frac{1}{q_{H_1} q_{H_2}}$. Hence, if the adversary can break the scheme with probability ϵ, we can reduce the proof to solve the modified q-BDHE assumption with probability $\epsilon/(q_{H_1} q_{H_2})$.

The time complexity of our simulation is mainly dominated by the private key generation, where each private key computation takes $O(q_{H_1})$ exponentiations. The above analysis yields the theorem and we complete the proof.   □

4 IBTT with Short Private Key and Short Ciphertext

In Section 2, we gave a generic IBTT construction from IBSE and fingerprint codes. In Section 3, we presented our IBSE scheme with short private key and short ciphertext. Putting our concrete IBSE scheme into the generic IBTT construction, we yield an identity-based traitor tracing with short private key and short ciphertext.

The private key of our IBTT scheme is $d_{ID,i} = \left(\overline{w}^{(i)}, d_{\mathbb{ID}_{ID,i,0}}, d_{\mathbb{ID}_{ID,i,1}}\right)$, where $\overline{w}^{(i)}$ is the l-bit length of codeword, and $d_{\mathbb{ID}_{ID,i,0}}, d_{\mathbb{ID}_{ID,i,1}}$ are private keys of an IBSE scheme. We have $d_{\mathbb{ID}_{ID,i,0}}, d_{\mathbb{ID}_{ID,i,1}} \in \mathbb{G}$ from our IBSE scheme, and therefore our private key is short and composed of one codeword and two group elements.

The ciphertext of our IBTT scheme is denoted by $C = \left(j, C_{ID,0}, C_{ID,1}\right)$, where j is the index from $[1, l_1]$, and $C_{ID,0}, C_{ID,1}$ are ciphertexts of an IBSE scheme. We have $C_{ID,0}, C_{ID,1} \in \mathbb{G}^2 \times \{0,1\}^{l_m}$ from our IBSE scheme, and therefore our ciphertext is short composed of one index, four group elements and two encrypted messages. The hybrid encryption technique will further reduce the two encrypted long messages into two encrypted short-random keys and one long message encrypted with the short-random key.

Computational Efficiency. We note that our IBTT scheme gives a tradeoff in private key size and computational efficiency. Our encryption/decryption requires to perform linear number of exponentiations, while the generic construction [8] only fulfils constant-number exponentiations for the same task. This tradeoff seems hard to be solved especially for decryption. This is because the decryption on a ciphertext for an identity with a private key of multi-identity must produce redundancy. It requires additional computations to remove them for decryption. Nevertheless, it is still interesting to explore more efficient IBTT schemes with short private key and short ciphertext.

Imperfect Decoders. The above traitor tracing assumes that the adversary produces a perfect pirate decoder that is able to decrypt all well-formed ciphertexts. Boneh and Naor also considered imperfect pirate decoders in their work. The countermeasure is by utilizing a powerful fingerprint code, which has to increase the length of codewords. Fortunately, we are able to use their fingerprint codes to construct our IBTT scheme against imperfect decoders. As the private key of IBSE is constant, the private key of our IBTT scheme only increases the length of codeword. The private key is still short. We observe that another solution for imperfect decoders is given in [3]. It requires a shorter codeword but a longer ciphertext compared to [8]. We refer the reader to [3] for the detail.

5   Conclusion

We introduced the first identity-based traitor tracing with short private key and short ciphertext. The private key consists of one codeword and two group elements; the ciphertext is composed of one index and two constant-size ciphertexts. It saves both secure storage and bandwidth for IBTT applications. We also introduced the new primitive of identity-based set encryption for multi-identity scenarios. Our proposed IBSE scheme is short in both private key and ciphertext, and is provably secure in the random oracles under the modified q-BSDH assumption.

Acknowledgement. We would like to thank the anonymous reviewers for their helpful comments and suggestions. This work has been supported by ARC Discovery Grant DP110101951.

References

1. Abdalla, M., Catalano, D., Dent, A.W., Malone-Lee, J., Neven, G., Smart, N.P.: Identity-Based Encryption Gone Wild. In: Bugliesi, M., Preneel, B., Sassone, V., Wegener, I. (eds.) ICALP 2006. LNCS, vol. 4052, pp. 300–311. Springer, Heidelberg (2006)
2. Abdalla, M., Dent, A.W., Malone-Lee, J., Neven, G., Phan, D.H., Smart, N.P.: Identity-Based Traitor Tracing. In: Okamoto, T., Wang, X. (eds.) PKC 2007. LNCS, vol. 4450, pp. 361–376. Springer, Heidelberg (2007)
3. Billet, O., Phan, D.H.: Efficient Traitor Tracing from Collusion Secure Codes. In: Safavi-Naini, R. (ed.) ICITS 2008. LNCS, vol. 5155, pp. 171–182. Springer, Heidelberg (2008)
4. Billet, O., Phan, D.H.: Traitors Collaborating in Public: Pirates 2.0. In: Joux, A. (ed.) EUROCRYPT 2009. LNCS, vol. 5479, pp. 189–205. Springer, Heidelberg (2009)
5. Boneh, D., Boyen, X., Goh, E.-J.: Hierarchical Identity Based Encryption with Constant Size Ciphertext. In: Cramer, R. (ed.) EUROCRYPT 2005. LNCS, vol. 3494, pp. 440–456. Springer, Heidelberg (2005)
6. Boneh, D., Franklin, M.: Identity-Based Encryption from the Weil Pairing. In: Kilian, J. (ed.) CRYPTO 2001. LNCS, vol. 2139, pp. 213–229. Springer, Heidelberg (2001)
7. Boneh, D., Gentry, C., Waters, B.: Collusion Resistant Broadcast Encryption with Short Ciphertexts and Private Keys. In: Shoup, V. (ed.) CRYPTO 2005. LNCS, vol. 3621, pp. 258–275. Springer, Heidelberg (2005)
8. Boneh, D., Naor, M.: Traitor tracing with constant size ciphertext. In: Ning, P., Syverson, P.F., Jha, S. (eds.) ACM CCS 2008, pp. 501–510. ACM (2008)
9. Boneh, D., Sahai, A., Waters, B.: Fully Collusion Resistant Traitor Tracing with Short Ciphertexts and Private Keys. In: Vaudenay, S. (ed.) EUROCRYPT 2006. LNCS, vol. 4004, pp. 573–592. Springer, Heidelberg (2006)

10. Boneh, D., Shaw, J.: Collusion-secure fingerprinting for digital data. IEEE Transactions on Information Theory 44(5), 1897–1905 (1998)
11. Boneh, D., Waters, B.: A fully collusion resistant broadcast, trace, and revoke system. In: Juels, A., Wright, R.N., di Vimercati, S.D.C. (eds.) ACM CCS 2006, pp. 211–220. ACM (2006)
12. Chabanne, H., Phan, D.H., Pointcheval, D.: Public Traceability in Traitor Tracing Schemes. In: Cramer, R. (ed.) EUROCRYPT 2005. LNCS, vol. 3494, pp. 542–558. Springer, Heidelberg (2005)
13. Chor, B., Fiat, A., Naor, M.: Tracing Traitors. In: Desmedt, Y.G. (ed.) CRYPTO 1994. LNCS, vol. 839, pp. 257–270. Springer, Heidelberg (1994)
14. Delerablée, C.: Identity-Based Broadcast Encryption with Constant Size Ciphertexts and Private Keys. In: Kurosawa, K. (ed.) ASIACRYPT 2007. LNCS, vol. 4833, pp. 200–215. Springer, Heidelberg (2007)
15. Fazio, N., Nicolosi, A., Phan, D.H.: Traitor Tracing with Optimal Transmission Rate. In: Garay, J.A., Lenstra, A.K., Mambo, M., Peralta, R. (eds.) ISC 2007. LNCS, vol. 4779, pp. 71–88. Springer, Heidelberg (2007)
16. Fujisaki, E., Okamoto, T.: Secure Integration of Asymmetric and Symmetric Encryption Schemes. In: Wiener, M. (ed.) CRYPTO 1999. LNCS, vol. 1666, pp. 537–554. Springer, Heidelberg (1999)
17. Garg, S., Kumarasubramanian, A., Sahai, A., Waters, B.: Building efficient fully collusion-resilient traitor tracing and revocation schemes. In: Al-Shaer, E., Keromytis, A.D., Shmatikov, V. (eds.) ACM CCS 2010, pp. 121–130. ACM (2010)
18. Gentry, C.: Practical Identity-Based Encryption Without Random Oracles. In: Vaudenay, S. (ed.) EUROCRYPT 2006. LNCS, vol. 4004, pp. 445–464. Springer, Heidelberg (2006)
19. Guo, F., Mu, Y., Chen, Z.: Identity-Based Encryption: How to Decrypt Multiple Ciphertexts Using a Single Decryption Key. In: Takagi, T., Okamoto, T., Okamoto, E., Okamoto, T. (eds.) Pairing 2007. LNCS, vol. 4575, pp. 392–406. Springer, Heidelberg (2007)
20. Guo, F., Mu, Y., Chen, Z., Xu, L.: Multi-Identity Single-Key Decryption without Random Oracles. In: Pei, D., Yung, M., Lin, D., Wu, C. (eds.) Inscrypt 2007. LNCS, vol. 4990, pp. 384–398. Springer, Heidelberg (2008)
21. Kiayias, A., Yung, M.: On Crafty Pirates and Foxy Tracers. In: Sander, T. (ed.) DRM 2001. LNCS, vol. 2320, pp. 22–39. Springer, Heidelberg (2002)
22. Kiayias, A., Yung, M.: Breaking and Repairing Asymmetric Public-Key Traitor Tracing. In: Feigenbaum, J. (ed.) DRM 2002. LNCS, vol. 2696, pp. 32–50. Springer, Heidelberg (2003)
23. Kiayias, A., Yung, M.: Traitor Tracing with Constant Transmission Rate. In: Knudsen, L.R. (ed.) EUROCRYPT 2002. LNCS, vol. 2332, pp. 450–465. Springer, Heidelberg (2002)
24. Naor, M., Pinkas, B.: Efficient Trace and Revoke Schemes. In: Frankel, Y. (ed.) FC 2000. LNCS, vol. 1962, pp. 1–20. Springer, Heidelberg (2001)
25. Pfitzmann, B.: Trials of Traced Traitors. In: Anderson, R. (ed.) IH 1996. LNCS, vol. 1174, pp. 49–64. Springer, Heidelberg (1996)
26. Phan, D.H.: Traitor Tracing for Stateful Pirate Decoders with Constant Ciphertext Rate. In: Nguyên, P.Q. (ed.) VIETCRYPT 2006. LNCS, vol. 4341, pp. 354–365. Springer, Heidelberg (2006)
27. Phan, D.H., Safavi-Naini, R., Tonien, D.: Generic Construction of Hybrid Public Key Traitor Tracing with Full-Public-Traceability. In: Bugliesi, M., Preneel, B., Sassone, V., Wegener, I. (eds.) ICALP 2006. LNCS, vol. 4052, pp. 264–275. Springer, Heidelberg (2006)

28. Sakai, R., Furukawa, J.: Identity-based broadcast encryption. IACR Cryptology ePrint Archive 2007, 217 (2007)
29. Sirvent, T.: Traitor tracing scheme with constant ciphertext rate against powerful pirates. Tech. rep. (2006), http://eprint.iacr.org/2006/383.pdf
30. Tardos, G.: Optimal probabilistic fingerprint codes. In: STOC 2003, pp. 116–125. ACM (2003)
31. Waters, B.: Efficient Identity-Based Encryption Without Random Oracles. In: Cramer, R. (ed.) EUROCRYPT 2005. LNCS, vol. 3494, pp. 114–127. Springer, Heidelberg (2005)

A   Fingerprint Codes and Identity-Based Traitor Tracing

The fingerprint codes [8] are defined as follows with two algorithms.

- Let $\overline{w} \in \{0,1\}^{l_1}$ be an l_1-bit codeword. We write $\overline{w} = w_1 w_2 \cdots w_{l_1}$ and assume w_i is the ith bit of $\overline{w}$.
- Let $\mathbb{W} = \{\overline{w}^{(1)}, \overline{w}^{(2)}, \cdots, \overline{w}^{(t)}\}$ be a set containing t codewords in $\{0,1\}^{l_1}$. We say that a codeword $\overline{w} = w_1 w_2 \cdots w_{l_1}$ is feasible for the set $\mathbb{W}$, if for all $i = 1, 2, \cdots, l_1$ there exists a $j \in \{1, 2 \cdots, t\}$ such that the ith bit of $\overline{w}^{(j)}$, denoted by $w_i^{(j)}$, is equal to w_i.
- Let $F(\mathbb{W})$ be a feasible set of $\mathbb{W}$, if it includes all codewords feasible for $\mathbb{W}$.

Gen$_{FC}(n, t, \lambda)$. On input the number of codewords n, the collusion bound t and a security parameter λ, the generation algorithm outputs a set Γ containing n codewords $\{\overline{w}^{(1)}, \overline{w}^{(2)}, \cdots, \overline{w}^{(n)}\}$ in $\{0,1\}^{l_1}$ with length $l_1 = l_1(n, t, \lambda)$ and a tracing key tk.

Tra$_{FC}(\overline{w}^*, tk)$. On input a codeword $\overline{w}^* \in \{0,1\}^{l_1}$ and the tracing key tk, the tracing algorithm outputs a subset of $\{1, 2, \cdots, n\}$. Informally, let $\mathbb{W}$ be a subset of Γ, if $\overline{w}^* \in F(\mathbb{W})$, we have that the output is a subset of $\mathbb{W}$.

An IBTT scheme consists of the following five algorithms.

Setup$_T(\lambda)$. The setup algorithm takes as input a security parameter λ and returns a key pair (MPK, MSK), where MPK denotes master public key and MSK denotes master secret key.

KGen$_T(ID, n, t, MSK)$. The key generation algorithm takes as input an identity ID, the number bound of users n, the collusion bound of traitors t, and the master secret key MSK. The algorithm returns n private keys $\{d_{ID,1}, d_{ID,2}, \cdots, d_{ID,n}\}$, where $d_{ID,i}$ is given to the ith user.

Enc$_T(ID, M, MPK)$. The encryption algorithm takes as input an identity ID, a message M and the master public key MPK and returns a ciphertext C denoted by $C = \mathsf{Enc}_T(ID, M, MPK)$.

Dec$_T(C, d_{ID,i})$. The decryption algorithm takes as input the ciphertext C and a private key $d_{ID,i}$ and outputs $\mathsf{Dec}_T(C, d_{ID,i}) \in \{M, \bot\}$.

Trace$_T(\mathcal{PD}_{ID}, ID, MSK)$. The tracing algorithm takes as input $\mathcal{PD}_{ID}$, a pirate decryption box for ID, the identity ID and the master secret key MSK and returns a set of traitors $\mathbb{T} \subseteq \{1, 2, \cdots, n\}$.

Identity-Based Encryption with Master Key-Dependent Message Security and Leakage-Resilience[*]

David Galindo[1], Javier Herranz[2], and Jorge Villar[2]

[1] University of Luxembourg
david.galindo@uni.lu
[2] Universitat Politècnica de Catalunya, Dept. Matemàtica Aplicada IV
{jherranz,jvillar}@ma4.upc.edu

Abstract. We introduce the concept of identity-based encryption (IBE) with master key-dependent chosen-plaintext (mKDM-sID-CPA) security. These are IBE schemes that remain secure even after the adversary sees encryptions, under some initially selected identities, of functions of the master secret keys. We then show that the Canetti, Halevi and Katz (Eurocrypt 2004) transformation delivers chosen-ciphertext secure key-dependent encryption (KDM-CCA) schemes when applied to mKDM-sID-CPA secure IBE schemes. Previously only one generic construction of KDM-CCA secure public key schemes was known, due to Camenisch, Chandran and Shoup (Eurocrypt 2009), and it required non-interactive zero knowledge proofs (NIZKs). Thus we show that NIZKs are not intrinsic to KDM-CCA public key encryption. As a proof of concept, we are able to instantiate our new concept under the Rank assumption on pairing groups and for affine functions of the secret keys. The scheme is inspired by the work by Boneh, Halevi, Hamburg and Ostrovsky (Crypto 2008). Our instantiation is only able to provide security against single encryption queries, or alternatively, against a *bounded* number of encryption queries. Secondly, we show that a special parameters setting of our main scheme provides master-key leakage-resilient identity-based encryption against chosen-plaintext attacks. This recently proposed security notion aims at taking into account security against side-channel attacks that only decrease the entropy of the master-key up to a certain threshold. Thirdly, we give new and better reductions between the Rank problem (previously named as Matrix-DDH or Matrix d-Linear problem) and the Decisional Linear problem.

1 Introduction

Master-Key Dependent Encryption. Until recently public key encryption (PKE) schemes were only required to provide confidentiality against adversaries

[*] Supported by the National Research Fund, Luxembourg C09/IS/04. Partially supported by the Spanish research project MTM2009-07694, and the European Commission through the ICT programme under contract ICT-2007-216676 ECRYPT II.

S. Foresti, M. Yung, and F. Martinelli (Eds.): ESORICS 2012, LNCS 7459, pp. 627–642, 2012.
© Springer-Verlag Berlin Heidelberg 2012

that see encryptions of plaintexts that depend solely on public information. That is, it was assumed (and even advocated) that an encryption scheme would never be used to encrypt its own decryption key. This requirement is certainly reasonable for many applications, but it has been challenged both by practical and foundational reasons [1,2]. The paradigmatic case is the scenario of *circular encryptions*, where for $n \geq 2$ public/secret key pairs $(pk_1, sk_1), \ldots, (pk_n, sk_n)$, the adversary is given the ciphertexts $Enc_{pk_1}(sk_2), Enc_{pk_2}(sk_3), \ldots, Enc_{pk_n}(sk_1)$, and still semantic security shall hold. Thus, a dedicated stronger security notion called *key-dependent message* security has emerged in the last few years [3]. Roughly speaking, it is required that semantic security holds even if the adversary sees encryptions of plaintexts that depend on the decryption keys. Such a scenario arises in systems that require hard-disk encryption, in computational soundness results in the area of formal methods, or in specific cryptographic protocols for anonymous credentials or fully homomorphic encryption. For the motivation, applications and history of key-dependent message security we refer to the excellent survey by Malkin, Teranishi and Yung [4].

The first breakthrough was due to Boneh, Halevi, Hamburg and Ostrovsky (BHHO) [5], who proposed a public key encryption scheme with indistinguishability against key-dependent chosen-plaintext attacks (KDM-CPA) in the standard model under the Decisional Diffie-Hellman assumption for affine functions of the secret key. Shortly after Applebaum, Cash, Peikert, and Sahai [6] proposed an efficient KDM-CPA secure scheme for affine functions under the Learning Parity with Noise assumption. Brakerski and Goldwasser [7] extended the BHHO scheme to a suite of KDM-CPA schemes secure under subgroup indistinguishability assumptions.

Camenisch, Chandran and Shoup [8] proposed a generic construction of chosen-ciphertext secure key-dependent encryption (KDM-CCA) schemes in the public key setting, that requires in particular a KDM-CPA secure scheme and specialized non-interactive zero knowledge proofs (NIZKs). By applying their transformation to (a variation of) the BHHO scheme, they obtained a KDM-CCA secure scheme under the Decision Linear assumption on pairing groups.

Master-Key Leakage-Resilient Identity-Based Encryption. Side channel attacks are often effective in recovering the secret key of cryptosystems that are provably secure otherwise [9,10]. On the other hand, it is desirable to extend the traditional provable security methodology to also include side channel attacks. This area of contemporary cryptography is usually referred to as *leakage-resilient cryptography* and it has been an increasingly active arena in recent years. Current security models assume an upper bound on the type or amount of information about the secret key that an adversary might learn from side-channel data. Here we allow the adversary to mount master-key leakage attacks, by allowing it to obtain the result of efficiently computable functions of the master-key. These functions might be asked adaptively, subject to the restriction that after all the queries the master-key has enough entropy left and that no master-key leakage queries are allowed after the adversary receives the challenge ciphertext. For the definitions of master-key leakage resilience we refer the reader to [11]. We stress that in our case the adversary mounts a selective-identity chosen-plaintext attack with master-key leakage, that we denote as mIND-sID-LCPA. Let λ be the bit-length sum of the outputs obtained by the adversary via master-key leakage queries. λ is called the leakage parameter and it is assumed that $\lambda < L$, where L is the master-key length. The relative leakage (or leakage ratio) of the system is defined as λ/L.

Our Contribution. We initiate here the study of identity-based encryption (IBE) schemes secure against key dependent messages. This has a double interest, since IBE is relevant by itself [12] and by its numerous applications [13]. In IBE there are two types of secret keys, on the one hand a master secret key SK_i corresponding to the master public key PK_i; on the other hand the secret keys $sk[id]$ belonging to individual users id. This gives rise to two levels of key-dependent message security, depending on whether the adversary is allowed to ask for encryptions of functions of the master-keys or the user-keys. We choose here to deal only with master key-dependent messages (mKDM security). The first reason is that this allows us to update mKDM-sID-CPA to KDM-CCA. Secondly, in some cases master-key dependent security implies a restricted form of user-key dependent security "for free" (see Section 4.2 for the case of our scheme).

Informally, we say that an IBE scheme has master key-dependent indistinguishability against selective-identity and chosen plaintext attacks (mKDM-sID-CPA security for short) if no adversary is able to distinguish between encryptions of a particular message $\mathfrak{m}$ and encryptions of some functions of a set of master secret keys, under a certain set of identities chosen by the adversary ahead of time. We are able to give an instantiation of a mKDM-sID-CPA secure IBE in the standard model, under the Rank assumption over bilinear groups. The Rank assumption states that it is difficult to distinguish whether an $n \times n$ matrix has rank r_1 or r_2, where $2 \le r_1 < r_2 \le n$. As an additional contribution, which may be of independent interest, we give a new reduction between the Rank problem and the Decisional Linear problem. Our new reduction improves that of [14] from a linear to a logarithmic factor and can be used to improve the reduction from the Rank assumption to the Decisional Diffie-Hellman problem given in [5] in a similar fashion.

We also show that a slight modification of the new mKDM-sID-CPA secure IBE scheme maintains its security properties in the presence of leakage of parts of the master secret key. This implies, in particular, new chosen ciphertext secure public key encryption secure in the presence of leakage [14] which compare favourably with previous related work.

One of the most well-known applications of IBE in the theory of cryptography is the CHK generic construction of chosen-ciphertext secure public key encryption out of chosen-plaintext secure identity-based encryption. We show that the same transformation can be applied to the KDM setting, resulting in KDM-CCA secure public key encryption out of mKDM-sID-CPA secure identity-based encryption. Thus we show a practical generic construction for key-dependent chosen-ciphertext security that dispenses with the need of NIZKs from [8].

Plugging our concrete IBE scheme into the Canetti-Halevi-Katz transformation gives rise to a KDM-CCA secure encryption scheme under the Decisional Linear assumption. One drawback of our chosen-ciphertext secure schemes is that the public key size depends on the number of encryption queries per public key (but importantly ciphertext-size does not); in other words, we were only able to prove security against a *bounded* number of encryption queries per public key.

Concurrent and Independent Related Work. Concurrent work by Alperin-Sheriff and Peikert [15] deals with the related notion of user key-dependent message security. We stress that their IBE construction has a drawback similar to ours: therein, the size of the master public key, the user secret keys and the ciphertext depend on the parameter n, which is the maximum number of user secret keys involved in an encryption query. Also concurrently to this work, Hofheinz [16] has proposed a PKE scheme with KDM-CCA security in the standard model with compact ciphertexts. His construction is direct and does not use key-dependent IBE.

Organization. In Section 2 we recall previous KDM security notions for public key encryption. In Section 3 we define master key-dependent indistinguishability against selective-identity and chosen-plaintext attacks for identity-based encryption. We show then that the celebrated CHK transformation from passively-secure IBE to chosen-ciphertext PKE also holds in the KDM setting. Section 4 contains an instantiation of identity-based encryption with master key-dependent security in the standard model under the Decisional Linear assumption. Although we refer to the full version of this work [17] for the complete security proof, we include in this Section 4 a key part of it which may be of independent interest: a new and better relation between the Decisional Linear problem and the Rank problem. In Section 5 we discuss the leakage-resilience properties of (a slight variation of) our new IBE scheme. We end in Section 6 by outlining future research directions.

2   Preliminaries: KDM Secure Public Key Encryption

A public key encryption scheme Π supporting ciphertexts consists of four probabilistic polynomial algorithms, $\Pi = (\Pi.\mathsf{Stp}, \Pi.\mathsf{KG}, \Pi.\mathsf{Enc}, \Pi.\mathsf{Dec})$. The setup protocol $\Pi.\mathsf{Stp}$ takes as input a security parameter λ and outputs some public information pms, including plaintext space $\mathcal{M}$ and secret key space $\mathcal{S}$. The security parameter λ is included in the string pms, which is implicitly an input to the remaining algorithms. The key generation protocol $\Pi.\mathsf{KG}_{\mathsf{pms}}$ on input the empty string ε outputs a pair of secret and public keys, (sk, pk), where the secret key sk belongs to the set $\mathcal{S}$ of possible secret keys. The encryption protocol takes as input a public key pk and a message $m \in \mathcal{M}$ and outputs a ciphertext $C = \Pi.\mathsf{Enc}_{\mathsf{pms}}(pk, m)$. Finally, the decryption protocol takes as input secret key sk and a ciphertext C, and outputs $\tilde{m} = \Pi.\mathsf{Dec}_{\mathsf{pms}}(sk, C)$, where $\tilde{m} \in \mathcal{M} \cup \{\bot\}$. The correctness property requires that $\Pi.\mathsf{Dec}_{\mathsf{pms}}(sk, \Pi.\mathsf{Enc}_{\mathsf{pms}}(pk, m)) = m$, for any message $m \in \mathcal{M}$ and parameters pms generated by $\Pi.\mathsf{Stp}$ and any pair (sk, pk) generated by $\Pi.\mathsf{KG}_{\mathsf{pms}}$.

Informally, security with respect to key dependent messages under chosen plaintext attacks (KDM-CPA) requires that an adversary is not able to distinguish between encryptions of a particular message $\mathfrak{m}$ and encryptions of some functions (chosen by the adversary from a specific set of functions $\mathcal{F}$) of a set of secret keys. In the case of security with respect to key dependent messages under chosen ciphertext attacks (KDM-CCA), the adversary is given additional access to a decryption oracle that he can query for ciphertexts of his choice, as long as these ciphertexts are different to those the adversary has to distinghish.

For concrete security concerns, in the following definitions two integer parameters $n, q_e \geq 1$ are given as input to the security game, representing respectively the number of users in the system and the maximum number of encryption queries per user allowed to the adversary. To formalize this notion, we follow the definitions in [8,4]. Let $n, q_e \geq 1$ be integers and let $\mathcal{F} = \{f : \mathcal{S}^n \to \mathcal{M}\}$ be a finite set of efficiently computable functions. KDM-CPA security of a public key encryption scheme Π is defined with respect to the set of functions $\mathcal{F}$ through the following two experiments between a challenger and an adversary $\mathcal{A}_\Pi$. Let $\mathfrak{m} \in \mathcal{M}$ be a fixed message.

Experiment $\mathbf{ExpKDM\text{-}CCA}_{\mathcal{A}_\Pi}^{b,\Pi}(\lambda, n, q_e)$ is defined as follows, for $b = 0, 1$.

1. **Initialization.** The challenger runs $\mathsf{pms} \leftarrow \Pi.\mathsf{Stp}(\lambda)$ and then runs n times $(sk_i, pk_i) \leftarrow \Pi.\mathsf{KG}_{\mathsf{pms}}$ to produce n pairs $(sk_1, pk_1), \ldots, (sk_n, pk_n)$. The public keys $(pk_1, \ldots, pk_n)$ and pms are sent to $\mathcal{A}_\Pi$. A list L_{quer} is initially set to empty.

2. **Queries.** The adversary $\mathcal{A}_\Pi$ can adaptively make two types of queries to the challenger.
   (a) **Encryption queries.** For each $1 \leq i \leq n$ the adversary $\mathcal{A}_\Pi$ can make up to q_e encryption queries of the form (i, f) with $f \in \mathcal{F}$. The challenger computes $m = f(sk_1, \ldots, sk_n) \in \mathcal{M}$, and then sets $C = \Pi.\mathsf{Enc}_{\mathsf{pms}}(pk_i, m)$ in Experiment $b = 0$, and sets $C = \Pi.\mathsf{Enc}_{\mathsf{pms}}(pk_i, \mathfrak{m})$ in Experiment $b = 1$. The resulting ciphertext C is sent to $\mathcal{A}_\Pi$ and the tuple (i, C) is added to the list L_{quer}.
   (b) **Decryption queries.** $\mathcal{A}_\Pi$ can make a decryption query of the form (i, C), as long as $(i, C) \notin L_{\mathsf{quer}}$. The challenger sends back to $\mathcal{A}_\Pi$ the output $\Pi.\mathsf{Dec}_{\mathsf{pms}}(sk_i, C)$.

3. **Final guess.** The adversary $\mathcal{A}_\Pi$ outputs a bit $b' \in \{0, 1\}$.

Let us denote as Ω_b the event that $\mathcal{A}_\Pi$ outputs $b' = 1$ in Experiment $\mathbf{ExpKDM\text{-}CCA}_{\mathcal{A}_\Pi}^{b,\Pi}(\lambda, n, q_e)$. For any adversary $\mathcal{A}_\Pi$ as above let

$$\mathbf{AdvKDM\text{-}CCA}_{\mathcal{A}_\Pi}^{\Pi}(\lambda, n, q_e) = |\Pr[\Omega_0] - \Pr[\Omega_1]|$$

For any t, n, q_e we define the advantage function of the scheme Π for key-dependent message security against chosen-ciphertext attacks (KDM-CCA) as

$$\mathbf{AdvKDM\text{-}CCA}(\Pi, \lambda, n, q_e; t) = \max_{\mathcal{A}_\Pi} \left\{ \mathbf{AdvKDM\text{-}CCA}_{\mathcal{A}_\Pi}^{\Pi}(\lambda, n, q_e) \right\},$$

where the maximum is over adversaries $\mathcal{A}_\Pi$ with time-complexity t and making no more than q_e encryption queries for each $1 \leq i \leq n$.

Definition 1. *A public key encryption scheme Π is polynomially-secure against key dependent chosen-ciphertext attacks with respect to the set of functions $\mathcal{F}$ if $\mathbf{AdvKDM\text{-}CCA}(\Pi, \lambda, n, q_e; t)$ is negligible in λ for all polynomial values of t, n, q_e.*

We refer to *security against single encryption queries* when $q_e = 1$, which means that the adversary can make several encryption queries but each one for a different public key. In this work we consider $\mathcal{F}$ to be the set of *affine functions*. This contains as particular cases constant functions (which lead to the notion of IND-CCA security in the multi-user setting [18]) and projections $f_i(sk_1, \ldots, sk_n) = sk_i$, for $1 \leq i \leq n$. An encryption scheme which is KDM-CCA-secure with respect to a set of functions containing projections achieves *clique security*, which in particular captures circular security.

3   From mKDM-sID-CPA Secure IBE to KDM-CCA Secure PKE

In this section we recall the Canetti-Halevi-Katz transformation [19] and show that it can be used to build IND-CCA encryption with key-dependent message security.

One-Time Signatures. We start by recalling the syntactic definition and security properties of one-time signatures. A (one-time) signature scheme $\Theta = (\Theta.\mathsf{Stp}, \Theta.\mathsf{KG}, \Theta.\mathsf{Sign}, \Theta.\mathsf{Vfy})$ consists of four probabilistic polynomial time algorithms. $\mathsf{pms}_\Theta \leftarrow \Theta.\mathsf{Stp}(1^\lambda)$ is the setup protocol, which produces some common public parameters (that will be an implicit input for the rest of protocols) for a given security parameter. $(sk_\Theta, vk_\Theta) \leftarrow \Theta.\mathsf{KG}()$ is the key generation protocol, which outputs a secret signing key sk_Θ and a public verification key vk_Θ. The signing protocol $\theta \leftarrow \Theta.\mathsf{Sign}(sk_\Theta, m)$ takes as input the signing key and a message m, and outputs a signature θ. Finally, the verification protocol $\{1, 0\} \leftarrow \Theta.\mathsf{Vfy}(vk_\Theta, m, \theta)$ takes as input the verification key, a message and a signature, and outputs 1 if the signature is valid, or 0 otherwise.

Regarding security, we consider an adversary $\mathcal{F}_\Theta$ in the multi-user setting, with N users. $\mathcal{F}_\Theta$ first receives N verification keys $\{vk_\Theta^{(i)}\}_{1 \leq i \leq N}$ obtained from running $\Theta.\mathsf{Stp}(1^\lambda) \to \mathsf{pms}_\Theta$ once and then running N times the protocol $\Theta.\mathsf{KG}() \to (sk_\Theta^{(i)}, vk_\Theta^{(i)})$, for $i = 1, \ldots, N$. The adversary can make at most one signature query of the form (i, m_i), for each $i = 1, \ldots, N$, for messages m_i of his choice, obtaining as answer valid signatures $\Theta.\mathsf{Sign}(sk_\Theta^{(i)}, m_i) \to \theta_i$. Finally $\mathcal{F}_\Theta$ outputs a tuple $(i^\star, m^\star, \theta^\star)$. We say that the adversary $\mathcal{F}_\Theta$ succeeds if $\Theta.\mathsf{Vfy}(vk_\Theta^{(i^\star)}, m^\star, \theta^\star) \to 1$ and $(m^\star, \theta^\star) \neq (m_{i^\star}, \theta_{i^\star})$.

We denote $\mathcal{F}_\Theta$'s success probability in the above game as $\mathbf{AdvOTS}_{\mathcal{F}_\Theta}^\Theta(\lambda, N)$. The signature scheme Θ is *one-time strongly unforgeable* if $\mathbf{AdvOTS}_{\mathcal{F}_\Theta}^\Theta(\lambda, N)$ is a negligible function of the security parameter $\lambda \in \mathbb{N}$, for any polynomial-time attacker $\mathcal{F}_\Theta$ against Θ and any polynomial value of N.

mKDM-sID-CPA Identity-Based Encryption. An identity-based encryption scheme Γ consists of five probabilistic polynomial algorithms,

$\Gamma = (\Gamma.\text{Stp}, \Gamma.\text{Mkg}, \Gamma.\text{Ukg}, \Gamma.\text{Enc}, \Gamma.\text{Dec})$. The setup protocol, $\Gamma.\text{Stp}$ takes as input a security parameter λ and outputs some system-wide parameters ibp to be shared by all the master authorities in the system. In particular, ibp includes the description of the sets of admissible identities, plaintexts and ciphertexts, $\mathcal{I}, \mathcal{M}, \mathcal{C}$ respectively. The string ibp is an implicit input to the remaining algorithms. $\Gamma.\text{Mkg}_{\text{ibp}}$ on input the empty string outputs (PK, SK), where PK is the master public key and SK is the master secret key. The user's key generation protocol, $\Gamma.\text{Ukg}_{\text{ibp}}$, on input the master secret key SK and an identity id, outputs the user's decryption key $sk[id]$. The encryption algorithm $\Gamma.\text{Enc}_{\text{ibp}}$ takes as input PK, an admissible identity id and a plaintext m and outputs a ciphertext $c = \Gamma.\text{Enc}_{\text{ibp}}(PK, id, m)$. Finally, the decryption protocol takes as input a decryption key $sk[id]$ and an admissible ciphertext c and outputs $\tilde{m}$, where $\tilde{m}$ is an admissible plaintext or the reject symbol $\bot$. The correctness property requires that $\Gamma.\text{Dec}_{\text{ibp}}(\Gamma.\text{Ukg}(SK, id), \Gamma.\text{Enc}_{\text{ibp}}(PK, id, m)) = m$, for any identity $id \in \mathcal{I}$, message $m \in \mathcal{M}$, parameters ibp generated by $\Gamma.\text{Stp}(1^k)$ and any pair (PK, SK) generated by $\Gamma.\text{Mkg}_{\text{ibp}}()$.

Informally, we say that an IBE scheme has master key-dependent indistinguishability against selective-identity and chosen plaintext attacks (mKDM-sID-CPA security, for short) if no adversary is able to distinguish between encryptions of a particular message $\mathfrak{m}$ and encryptions of some functions (chosen by the adversary from a specific set of functions $\mathcal{F}$) of a set of master secret keys.

We formalize next this notion. Let $n, q_e \geq 1$ be integers and let $\mathcal{F} = \{f : \mathcal{T}^n \to \mathcal{M}\}$ be a finite set of efficiently computable functions, where $\mathcal{T}$ is the set of master secret keys and $\mathcal{M}$ the set of admissible plaintexts. mKDM-sID-CPA security is defined with respect to the set of functions $\mathcal{F}$ through the following two experiments between a challenger and an adversary $\mathcal{A}_\Gamma$. Let $\mathfrak{m} \in \mathcal{M}$ be a fixed message.

Experiment $\mathbf{ExpKDM\text{-}sID\text{-}CPA}_{\mathcal{A}_\Gamma}^{b,\Gamma}(\lambda, n, q_e)$ is defined as follows, for $b = 0, 1$.

1. **Setup.** The challenger runs ibp $\leftarrow \Gamma.\text{Stp}(\lambda)$. The adversary $\mathcal{A}_\Gamma$ on input ibp outputs a tuple $\mathcal{I}^\star$ of $n \cdot q_e$ identities $\mathcal{I}^\star = (id_1^1, \ldots, id_1^{q_e}, \ldots, id_n^1, \ldots, id_n^{q_e})$.

2. **Initialization.** The challenger runs n times $\Gamma.\text{Mkg}_{\text{ibp}}$ to obtain n pairs $(PK_1, SK_1), \ldots, (PK_n, SK_n)$. The master public keys $(PK_1, \ldots, PK_n)$ are sent to $\mathcal{A}_\Gamma$.

3. **Queries.** The adversary $\mathcal{A}_\Gamma$ can adaptively make two types of queries to the challenger:

   (a) **Encryption Queries.** For every index i such that $1 \leq i \leq n$, a counter j is kept, with initial value $j = 1$. $\mathcal{A}_\Gamma$ can make encryption queries of the form (i, f), where $f \in \mathcal{F}$. The challenger computes $m = f(SK_1, \ldots, SK_n) \in \mathcal{M}$, and then sets $c = \Gamma.\text{Enc}_{\text{ibp}}(PK_i, id_i^j, m)$ when $b = 0$, and sets $c = \Gamma.\text{Enc}_{\text{ibp}}(PK_i, id_i^j, \mathfrak{m})$ if $b = 1$, where j is the current counter value. After the ciphertext c is sent to $\mathcal{A}_\Gamma$, the counter is updated as $j \leftarrow j + 1$. $\mathcal{A}_\Gamma$ can make up to q_e encryption queries per index i.

(b) **Private key Queries.** $\mathcal{A}_{\Gamma}$ can make users' private key queries of the form (i, id), where $1 \leq i \leq n$ and $id \neq id_i^j$ for all $j \in \{1, \ldots, q_e\}$. The challenger computes $sk_i[id] = \Gamma.\mathsf{Ukg}_{\mathsf{ibp}}(SK_i, id)$ and gives it back to $\mathcal{A}_{\Gamma}$.

4. **Final guess.** The adversary $\mathcal{A}_{\Gamma}$ outputs a bit $b' \in \{0, 1\}$.

Let us denote as Ω_b the event that $\mathcal{A}_{\Gamma}$ outputs $b' = 1$ in the above experiment. For any adversary $\mathcal{A}_{\Gamma}$ let $\mathbf{Adv\text{-}mKDM\text{-}sID\text{-}CPA}_{\mathcal{A}_{\Gamma}}^{\Gamma}(\lambda, n, q_e) = |\Pr[\Omega_0] - \Pr[\Omega_1]|$. For any t, n, q_e we define $\mathbf{Adv\text{-}mKDM\text{-}sID\text{-}CPA}(\Gamma, \lambda, n, q_e; t)$ as the quantity $\max_{\mathcal{A}_{\Gamma}} \left\{ \mathbf{Adv\text{-}mKDM\text{-}sID\text{-}CPA}_{\mathcal{A}_{\Gamma}}^{\Gamma}(\lambda, n, q_e) \right\}$, where the maximum is taken over adversaries $\mathcal{A}_{\Gamma}$ with time-complexity t.

Definition 2. *An identity-based encryption scheme Γ is secure against selective-identity and master key-dependent chosen plaintext attacks (mKDM-sID-CPA) with respect to the set of functions $\mathcal{F}$ if $\mathbf{Adv\text{-}mKDM\text{-}sID\text{-}CPA}(\Gamma, \lambda, n, q_e; t)$ is negligible in λ for polynomial values of n, t, q_e.*

Canetti-Halevi-Katz Transformation in the KDM Setting. Let $\Gamma = (\Gamma.\mathsf{Stp}, \Gamma.\mathsf{Mkg}, \Gamma.\mathsf{Ukg}, \Gamma.\mathsf{Enc}, \Gamma.\mathsf{Dec})$ be an IBE scheme and let $\Theta = (\Theta.\mathsf{KG}, \Theta.\mathsf{Sign}, \Theta.\mathsf{Vfy})$ be a one-time signature scheme. We use the well-known Canetti-Halevi-Katz transformation [19] to construct from these two primitives a public-key encryption scheme $\Pi = (\Pi.\mathsf{Stp}, \Pi.\mathsf{KG}, \Pi.\mathsf{Enc}, \Pi.\mathsf{Dec})$, as follows:

$\Pi.\mathsf{Stp}(1^{\lambda})$: run $\mathsf{ibp} \leftarrow \Gamma.\mathsf{Stp}(1^{\lambda})$ and $\mathsf{pms}_{\Theta} \leftarrow \Theta.\mathsf{Stp}(1^{\lambda})$. We assume that verification keys output by Θ lie in the identities space of Γ. Define the output of the setup protocol as $\mathsf{pms} = (\mathsf{ibp}, \mathsf{pms}_{\Theta})$.

$\Pi.\mathsf{KG}_{\mathsf{pms}}()$: parse $\mathsf{pms} = (\mathsf{ibp}, \mathsf{pms}_{\Theta})$, run $(PK, SK) \leftarrow \Gamma.\mathsf{Mkg}_{\mathsf{ibp}}()$ and define the secret key as $sk = SK$ and the public key as $pk = PK$.

$\Pi.\mathsf{Enc}_{\mathsf{pms}}(pk, m)$: to encrypt a plaintext $m \in \mathcal{M}$ for a receiver with public key pk, parse $\mathsf{pms} = (\mathsf{ibp}, \mathsf{pms}_{\Theta})$ and proceed as follows. Run $(sk_{\Theta}, vk_{\Theta}) \leftarrow \Theta.\mathsf{KG}()$ and set $id = vk_{\Theta}$; run $c \leftarrow \Gamma.\mathsf{Enc}_{\mathsf{ibp}}(pk, id, m)$; run $\theta \leftarrow \Theta.\mathsf{Sign}(sk_{\Theta}, c)$. The final ciphertext output by the algorithm is $C = (vk_{\Theta}, c, \theta)$.

$\Pi.\mathsf{Dec}_{\mathsf{pms}}(sk, C)$: parse $\mathsf{pms} = (\mathsf{ibp}, \Theta)$ and $C = (vk_{\Theta}, c, \theta)$. First of all, run $\Theta.\mathsf{Vfy}(vk_{\Theta}, c, \theta)$. If the output bit is 0, then stop and output $\perp$. Otherwise, set $id = vk_{\Theta}$ and run $sk[id] \leftarrow \Gamma.\mathsf{Ukg}_{\mathsf{ibp}}(sk, id)$ and output the result of running $\Gamma.\mathsf{Dec}_{\mathsf{ibp}}(sk[id], c)$.

Theorem 1. *If Γ enjoys mKDM-sID-CPA security with respect to a set of functions $\mathcal{F}$ and the signature scheme Θ is one-time strongly unforgeable, then the constructed public-key encryption scheme Π enjoys KDM-CCA security with respect to the same set of functions $\mathcal{F}$.*

The proof of this theorem, which is similar to that in [19], can be found in [17].

4 A New mKDM-sID-CPA Secure IBE Scheme for $q_e = 1$

In this section we propose an identity-based encryption scheme enjoying mKDM-sID-CPA security for $q_e = 1$. The new scheme upgrades the KDM-CPA techniques in [5] to the IBE setting.

4.1 Bilinear Pairings, Matrices and Hardness Assumptions

Let $\mathcal{G}$ be a group of prime order q admitting a bilinear pairing. That is, let $\mathcal{G}_T$ be a multiplicative group of prime order q and let $e(\cdot,\cdot) : \mathcal{G} \times \mathcal{G} \to \mathcal{G}_T$ an efficiently computable bilinear map. We will denote as $g_T = e(g,g)$ the generator of $\mathcal{G}_T$ induced by g a given generator of $\mathcal{G}$. Note that, due to the bilinear properties of the pairing, for any two integers $a, b \in \mathbb{Z}_q$ we have $g_T^{ab} = e(g^a, g^b) = e(g^a, g)^b = e(g^b, g)^a$.

These operations extend to vectors and matrices in a natural way. Let $\mathbb{Z}_q^{\ell_1 \times \ell_2}$ denote the set of all $\ell_1 \times \ell_2$ matrices and $\mathbb{Z}_q^{\ell_1 \times \ell_2 ; r}$ the matrices with rank r. In the special case of invertible matrices we will write $\mathrm{GL}_\ell(\mathbb{Z}_q) = \mathbb{Z}_q^{\ell \times \ell ; \ell}$. Let $\mathcal{G}^{\ell_1 \times \ell_2}$ and $\mathcal{G}_T^{\ell_1 \times \ell_2}$ denote the set of all $\ell_1 \times \ell_2$ matrices over $\mathcal{G}$ and $\mathcal{G}_T$ respectively. Therefore, for any two matrices $\mathbf{A} \in \mathbb{Z}_q^{\ell_1 \times \ell_2}$ and $\mathbf{B} \in \mathbb{Z}_q^{\ell_2 \times \ell_3}$, we have $g^{\mathbf{AB}} = (g^{\mathbf{A}})^{\mathbf{B}} \in \mathcal{G}^{\ell_1 \times \ell_3}$. Again, we can naturally extend these definitions to matrices and bilinear pairings: if $\mathbf{A} \in \mathbb{Z}_q^{\ell_1 \times \ell_2}$ and $\mathbf{B} \in \mathbb{Z}_q^{\ell_2 \times \ell_3}$, then $e(g^{\mathbf{A}}, g^{\mathbf{B}}) = g_T^{\mathbf{AB}}$. Furthermore, if $\mathbf{C} \in \mathbb{Z}_q^{\ell_3 \times \ell_4}$, then it holds $g_T^{\mathbf{ABC}} = e(g^{\mathbf{AB}}, g^{\mathbf{C}}) = e(g^{\mathbf{A}}, g^{\mathbf{BC}}) \in \mathcal{G}_T^{\ell_1 \times \ell_4}$.

The security of our scheme will be reduced to the hardness of the Decisional Linear (DLin) problem [20]. The DLin problem consists in distinguishing between the distributions $(g, g^x, g^y, g^z, g^t, g^{(x^{-1}z + y^{-1}t)}) \in \mathcal{G}^6$ and $(g, g^x, g^y, g^z, g^t, g^u) \in \mathcal{G}^6$, where g is a generator of $\mathcal{G}$ and $x, y, z, t, u \in_R \mathbb{Z}_q$ are chosen independently and at random. The problem is formally defined through the following two experiments between a challenger and a solver $\mathcal{A}_{\mathbf{DLin}}$. Experiment $\mathbf{ExpDLin}^b_{\mathcal{A}_{\mathbf{DLin}}}(\mathcal{G})$ is defined as follows, for $b = 0, 1$.

1. The challenger chooses a generator g of $\mathcal{G}$ and random $x, y, z, t, u \in_R \mathbb{Z}_q$ independently and uniformly distributed.
   In Experiment $b = 0$, the challenger sends $(g, g^x, g^y, g^z, g^t, g^{(x^{-1}z + y^{-1}t)}) \in \mathcal{G}^6$ to $\mathcal{A}_{\mathbf{DLin}}$.
   In Experiment $b = 1$, it sends $(g, g^x, g^y, g^z, g^t, g^u) \in \mathcal{G}^6$ to $\mathcal{A}_{\mathbf{DLin}}$.
2. The solver $\mathcal{A}_{\mathbf{DLin}}$ outputs a bit $b' \in \{0, 1\}$.

Let us denote as Ω_b the event that $\mathcal{A}_{\mathbf{DLin}}$ outputs $b' = 1$ in Experiment $\mathbf{ExpDLin}^b_{\mathcal{A}_{\mathbf{DLin}}}(\mathcal{G})$. Let $\mathbf{AdvDLin}_{\mathcal{A}_{\mathbf{DLin}}}(\mathcal{G}) = |\Pr[\Omega_0] - \Pr[\Omega_1]|$. We can then define $\mathbf{AdvDLin}(\mathcal{G}; t) = \max_{\mathcal{A}_{\mathbf{DLin}}} \{\mathbf{AdvDLin}_{\mathcal{A}_{\mathbf{DLin}}}(\mathcal{G})\}$, where the maximum is taken over adversaries $\mathcal{A}_{\mathbf{DLin}}$ running in time at most t.

Definition 3. *The* Decisional Linear assumption *in* $\mathcal{G}$ *states that* $\mathbf{AdvDLin}(\mathcal{G}; t)$ *is negligible in* $\lambda = \log |\mathcal{G}|$ *for any value of* t *that is polynomial in* λ.

4.2 A mKDM-sID-CPA Secure Scheme

Let us consider the IBE scheme $\Gamma = (\Gamma.\mathsf{Stp}, \Gamma.\mathsf{Mkg}, \Gamma.\mathsf{Ukg}, \Gamma.\mathsf{Enc}, \Gamma.\mathsf{Dec})$ defined as follows:

$\Gamma.\mathsf{Stp}(1^\lambda)$: a pairing group $(\mathcal{G}, \mathcal{G}_T, e(\cdot, \cdot))$ of prime order q, where q is λ-bits long, and generators $g \in \mathcal{G}, g_T = e(g, g) \in \mathcal{G}_T$ are chosen. A second security parameter $\ell > 4\lambda$ is also considered. Therefore, we define $\mathsf{ibp} = (\lambda, \ell, q, \mathcal{G}, g, \mathcal{G}_T, g_T, e(\cdot, \cdot))$.

$\Gamma.\mathsf{Mkg}_{\mathsf{ibp}}()$: firstly, take $\mathbf{S} \in_R \mathbb{Z}_q^{2 \times \ell;2}$, $\widetilde{\mathbf{S}} \in_R \mathbb{Z}_q^{\ell \times 2;2}$ and a binary vector $\boldsymbol{x} \in_R$ $\{0,1\}^{\ell \times 1}$, and compute $g_T^{\boldsymbol{y}} = g_T^{-\mathbf{S}\boldsymbol{x}} \in \mathcal{G}_T^{2 \times 1}$. Then define the matrices $\mathbf{F}_{id}$ and $\widetilde{\mathbf{F}}_{id}$ for $id \in \mathbb{Z}_q$ as $\mathbf{F}_{id} = \mathbf{S}\mathbf{T}_{id} \in \mathbb{Z}_q^{2 \times \ell}$ and $\widetilde{\mathbf{F}}_{id} = \mathbf{T}_{id}\widetilde{\mathbf{S}} \in \mathbb{Z}_q^{\ell \times 2}$, where $\mathbf{T}_{id} = \mathbf{T_0}+id\mathbf{T_1} \in \mathbb{Z}_q^{\ell \times \ell}$ is a random (matrix) polynomial of degree 1, with $\mathbf{T_0} \in_R \mathbb{Z}_q^{\ell \times \ell}$ and $\mathbf{T_1} \in \mathrm{GL}_\ell(\mathbb{Z}_q)$. Note that it holds $\mathbf{F}_{id}\widetilde{\mathbf{S}} = \mathbf{S}\widetilde{\mathbf{F}}_{id}$ for any $id \in \mathbb{Z}_q$. The public and master secret keys are then $PK = (g^{\mathbf{S}}, g^{\widetilde{\mathbf{S}}}, g^{\mathbf{S}\mathbf{T_0}}, g^{\mathbf{S}\mathbf{T_1}}, g^{\mathbf{T_0}\widetilde{\mathbf{S}}}, g^{\mathbf{T_1}\widetilde{\mathbf{S}}}, g_T^{-\mathbf{S}\boldsymbol{x}})$ and $SK = g_T^{\boldsymbol{x}} \in \mathcal{G}_T^{\ell \times 1}$.

$\Gamma.\mathsf{Ukg}_{\mathsf{ibp}}(SK, id)$: for an identity $id \in \mathbb{Z}_q$ the secret key $sk[id] = (g^{\boldsymbol{d}_1}, g^{\boldsymbol{d}_2}) \in \mathcal{G}^{\ell \times 1} \times \mathcal{G}^{\ell \times 1}$ is generated as $g^{\boldsymbol{d}_1} = g^{\boldsymbol{x}} \cdot g^{\widetilde{\mathbf{F}}_{id}\boldsymbol{t}}$ and $g^{\boldsymbol{d}_2} = g^{\widetilde{\mathbf{S}}\boldsymbol{t}}$, where $\boldsymbol{t} \in_R \mathbb{Z}_q^{2 \times 1}$ and $g^{\boldsymbol{x}}$ is computed component-wise from $SK = g_T^{\boldsymbol{x}}$ (remember $\boldsymbol{x}$ is a binary vector). The user can verify the validity of $sk[id]$ by checking the equation $g_T^{-\mathbf{S}\boldsymbol{x}} \cdot e(g^{\mathbf{S}}, g^{\boldsymbol{d}_1}) = e(g^{\mathbf{F}_{id}}, g^{\boldsymbol{d}_2})$.

$\Gamma.\mathsf{Enc}_{\mathsf{ibp}}(PK, id, m)$: to encrypt a message $m \in \mathcal{G}_T$ for an identity id and master public key PK, a row vector $\boldsymbol{r} \in_R \mathbb{Z}_q^{1 \times 2}$ is chosen and the ciphertext $(g^{\boldsymbol{c}_1}, g^{\boldsymbol{c}_2}, c) \in \mathcal{G}^{1 \times \ell} \times \mathcal{G}^{1 \times \ell} \times \mathcal{G}_T$ is computed as $g^{\boldsymbol{c}_1} = g^{\boldsymbol{r}\mathbf{S}}$, $g^{\boldsymbol{c}_2} = g^{\boldsymbol{r}\mathbf{F}_{id}}$ and $c = g_T^{-\boldsymbol{r}\mathbf{S}\boldsymbol{x}} \cdot m$. The ciphertext fulfils the equation $e(g^{\boldsymbol{c}_1}, g^{\widetilde{\mathbf{F}}_{id}}) = e(g^{\boldsymbol{c}_2}, g^{\widetilde{\mathbf{S}}})$.

$\Gamma.\mathsf{Dec}_{\mathsf{ibp}}(sk[id], C)$: let $(g^{\boldsymbol{c}_1}, g^{\boldsymbol{c}_2}, c)$ be a ciphertext for an identity id. The user who owns $sk[id] = (g^{\boldsymbol{d}_1}, g^{\boldsymbol{d}_2})$ recovers $m = c \cdot e(g^{\boldsymbol{c}_1}, g^{\boldsymbol{d}_1})/e(g^{\boldsymbol{c}_2}, g^{\boldsymbol{d}_2})$.

A Simpler but Insecure Scheme. Notice that an extension of the Boneh *et al.* KDM-CPA scheme [5] *à la* Boneh and Boyen [21] leads to an insecure scheme, in the following sense. Let us consider the case where user-keys would have been of the form $sk[id] = (g^{\boldsymbol{d}_1}, g^{\boldsymbol{d}_2})$ with $g^{\boldsymbol{d}_1} = g^{\boldsymbol{x}} F_{id}^{\boldsymbol{t}}$ and $g^{\boldsymbol{d}_2} = g^{\boldsymbol{t}}$, where $\boldsymbol{t} \in_R \mathbb{Z}_q^\ell$ and $F_{id} \in \mathcal{G}$ is defined as $F_{id} = T_0 T_1^{id}$ for $T_0, T_1 \in_R \mathcal{G}$ (ciphertexts would be changed accordingly). In such a case, an adversary that obtains a single user-key $sk[id]$ can compute $e(g^{\boldsymbol{d}_1}, g) = g_T^{\boldsymbol{x}} \cdot e(F_{id}, g^{\boldsymbol{t}})$ on the one hand, and $e(F_{id}, g^{\boldsymbol{d}_2}) = e(F_{id}, g^{\boldsymbol{t}})$ on the other hand. The adversary thus recovers $g_T^{\boldsymbol{x}}$, which leads to the recovery of master secret key, since $\boldsymbol{x} \in \{0,1\}^\ell$. For this reason we are forced to "hide" $\boldsymbol{t}$ even more, by multiplying it with the matrix $\widetilde{\mathbf{S}} \in \mathrm{GL}_\ell(\mathbb{Z}_q)$. This makes scheme description and security proofs more intricate, for example because some care must be taken regarding the invertibility and the probability distribution of such matrices $\widetilde{\mathbf{S}} \in \mathrm{GL}_\ell(\mathbb{Z}_q)$, when master public keys are rerandomized.

Affine Functions. Let us define the set of affine functions $\mathcal{F} = \{f : \mathcal{T}^n \to \mathcal{G}_T\}$, where $\mathcal{T}$ is the set of master secret keys. Let $SK_1, \ldots, SK_n \in \mathcal{G}_T^\ell$ be n secret keys generated by $\Gamma.\mathsf{Ukg}_{\mathsf{ibp}}()$. Following the notation in [5], for every $n\ell$-vector $\boldsymbol{u} = (u_i)$ over $\mathbb{Z}_q$, every $n\ell$-vector $\boldsymbol{s} \in \mathcal{G}_T^{n\ell}$ and every scalar $H \in \mathcal{G}_T$, let $f_{\boldsymbol{u},H}(\boldsymbol{s}) = \prod_{i=1,\ldots,n\ell} g_T^{u_i} \cdot s_i + H \in \mathcal{G}_T$. Then, $\mathcal{F} = \{f_{\boldsymbol{u},H} : \mathcal{G}_T^{n\ell} \to \mathcal{G}\}_{\boldsymbol{u} \in \mathbb{Z}_q^{n\ell}, H \in \mathcal{G}_T}$.

Additionally, since the algorithm $\Gamma_0.\mathsf{Ukg}_{\mathsf{ibp}}(SK, id)$ can be seen as an affine function from $\mathcal{G}^\ell$ to $\mathcal{G}^{2\ell}$, we obtain uKDM-sID-CPA security [15] with respect to the set of affine functions from $\mathcal{G}^{2n\ell}$ to $\mathcal{G}_T$. Alas, this is is only a restricted form of uKDM-sID-CPA security, since in particular we can not encrypt the j-th selection function $(sk[id_1], \ldots, sk[id_n]) \mapsto sk[id_j]$, as $sk[id_j] \in \mathcal{G}^{2\ell}$.

4.3   mKDM-sID-CPA Security of Γ and KDM-CCA Secure Public Key Encryption

The scheme Γ is mKDM-sID-CPA secure with respect to the set of affine functions $\mathcal{F}$ and for $q_e = 1$ encryption queries per master public key, assuming the hardness of the Decisional Linear problem in the group $\mathcal{G}$. The proof of the following theorem, which is technically quite involved, can be found in [17]. In the latter reference it is also discussed how to extend this scheme to another IBE scheme that allows a predefined number of encryption queries $q_e >> 1$, with the downside that the master public key has length linear in q_e. A similar problem is encountered in the uKDM-sID-CPA IBE scheme from [15], where the efficiency of the scheme depends linearly in n, the number of participants involved in the security game.

Theorem 2. **Adv-mKDM-sID-CPA**$(\Gamma, \lambda, \ell, n, 1; t) \leq$
$$2(3n+4)2^{-\lambda} + 8\left(\lceil 1.71 \log_2 \ell \rceil + 1\right) \mathbf{AdvDLin}(\mathcal{G}; t').$$

Note that in our case the loss factor in the reduction is constant with respect to the number n of master keys. The factor only grows logarithmically on the security parameter ℓ. When the CHK transformation is applied to our IBE scheme together with Mohassel's one-time signature scheme [22], the resulting public key scheme achieves KDM-CCA security for $q_e = 1$, with a reduction loss factor that does not depend on n.

Although the result stated in Theorem 2 relates the KDM security of our scheme with the hardness of the Decisional Linear problem, the actual proof relates the security of the scheme with the hardness of a different problem, the Rank problem. The final result is obtained by applying a new and better relation between the Rank problem and the Decisional Linear problem, which may be of independent interest. The details are given in the following section.

4.4   The Rank Problem

We consider an assumption related to matrices. Given a (multiplicative) cyclic group $\mathcal{G}$ of prime order q, the **Rank**$(\mathcal{G}, \ell_1, \ell_2, r, s)$ problem informally consists of distinguishing if a given matrix in $\mathbb{Z}_q^{\ell_1 \times \ell_2}$ has rank r or has rank s for given integers $r \neq s$, when the matrix is hidden in the exponent of a generator g of $\mathcal{G}$. The problem is formally defined through the following two experiments between a challenger and a distinguisher $\mathcal{A}_{\mathbf{Rank}}$. For $b = 0, 1$, experiment **ExpRank**$_{\mathcal{A}_{\mathbf{Rank}}}^b(\mathcal{G}, \ell_1, \ell_2, r, s)$ is defined as follows.

1. In Experiment $b = 0$, the challenger chooses $\mathbf{M} \in_R \mathbb{Z}_q^{\ell_1 \times \ell_2; r}$ and sends $g^{\mathbf{M}}$ to $\mathcal{A}_{\mathbf{Rank}}$.
   In Experiment $b = 1$, it chooses $\mathbf{M} \in_R \mathbb{Z}_q^{\ell_1 \times \ell_2; s}$ and sends $g^{\mathbf{M}}$ to $\mathcal{A}_{\mathbf{Rank}}$.
2. The solver $\mathcal{A}_{\mathbf{Rank}}$ outputs a bit $b' \in \{0, 1\}$.

Let us denote as Ω_b the event that $\mathcal{A}_{\mathbf{Rank}}$ outputs $b' = 1$ in Experiment **ExpRank**$_{\mathcal{A}_{\mathbf{Rank}}}^b(\mathcal{G}, \ell_1, \ell_2, r, s)$. For any such adversary $\mathcal{A}_{\mathbf{Rank}}$ let

$$\mathbf{AdvRank}_{\mathcal{A}_{\mathbf{Rank}}}(\mathcal{G}, \ell_1, \ell_2, r, s) = |\Pr[\Omega_0] - \Pr[\Omega_1]|$$

We can then define

$$\mathbf{AdvRank}(\mathcal{G}, \ell_1, \ell_2, r, s; t) = \max_{\mathcal{A}_{\mathbf{Rank}}} \{\mathbf{AdvRank}_{\mathcal{A}_{\mathbf{Rank}}}(\mathcal{G}, \ell_1, \ell_2, r, s)\},$$

where the maximum is taken over adversaries $\mathcal{A}_{\mathbf{Rank}}$ running in time at most t.

Definition 4. *The* $\mathbf{Rank}(\mathcal{G}, \ell_1, \ell_2, r, s)$ *assumption in a group* $\mathcal{G}$ *states that* $\mathbf{AdvRank}(\mathcal{G}, \ell_1, \ell_2, r, s; t)$ *is negligible in* $\lambda = \log |\mathcal{G}|$ *for any value of* t *that is polynomial in* λ.

The Rank assumption appeared in recent papers under the names Matrix-DDH [5] and Matrix d-Linear [14]. Therein, it was already proved that the Rank problem is harder than the Decisional Linear problem. However, the reduction given in the next proposition substantially improves the reductions previously given. Namely, the loss factor is no longer linear but logarithmic in the rank.

Proposition 1. *For any* ℓ_1, ℓ_2, r, s *such that* $2 \le s < r \le \min(\ell_1, \ell_2)$ *we have*

$$\mathbf{AdvRank}(\mathcal{G}, \ell_1, \ell_2, r, s; t) \le \left\lceil \frac{\log(3r) - \log(3s - 2)}{\log 3 - \log 2} \right\rceil \mathbf{AdvDLin}(\mathcal{G}; t')$$
$$\le \lceil 1.71(\log_2 r - \log_2(s - 1)) \rceil \mathbf{AdvDLin}(\mathcal{G}; t'),$$

where $t' = t + \mathcal{O}(\ell_1 \ell_2 (\ell_1 + \ell_2))$, *taking the cost of an exponentiation in* $\mathcal{G}$ *as one time unit.*

Before proving the proposition, we note that the $\mathbf{Rank}(\mathcal{G}, \ell_1, \ell_2, r, s)$ problem is random self-reducible, because given $\mathbf{M}_0 \in \mathbb{Z}_q^{\ell_1 \times \ell_2; k}$, for random $\mathbf{L} \in_{\mathbf{R}} \mathrm{GL}_{\ell_1}(\mathbb{Z}_q)$ and $\mathbf{R} \in_{\mathbf{R}} \mathrm{GL}_{\ell_2}(\mathbb{Z}_q)$ the product $\mathbf{LM}_0\mathbf{R}$ is uniformly distributed in $\mathbb{Z}_q^{\ell_1 \times \ell_2; k}$. For the actual proof of Proposition 1, we use the following result.

Lemma 1. *Any distinguisher for* $\mathbf{Rank}(\mathcal{G}, \ell_1, \ell_2, k - \delta, k)$, $\ell_1, \ell_2 \ge 3$, $k \ge 3$, $1 \le \delta \le \lfloor \frac{k}{3} \rfloor$ *can be converted into a distinguisher for the Decisional Linear* (DLin) *problem, with the same advantage and running essentially within the same time.*

Proof. We will use the notation $\mathbf{A} \oplus \mathbf{B}$ for block matrix concatenation:

$$\mathbf{A} \oplus \mathbf{B} = \left(\begin{array}{c|c} \mathbf{A} & 0 \\ \hline 0 & \mathbf{B} \end{array} \right)$$

In addition, we will denote I_ℓ and $0_{\ell_1 \times \ell_2}$ for the neutral element in $\mathrm{GL}_\ell(\mathbb{Z}_q)$ and the null matrix in $\mathbb{Z}_q^{\ell_1 \times \ell_2}$, respectively. Given the DLin instance $(g, g^x, g^y, g^z, g^t, g^u)$ the DLin distinguisher builds the $\ell_1 \times \ell_2$ matrix

$$\mathbf{M} = \underbrace{\begin{pmatrix} x & 0 & 1 \\ 0 & y & t \\ z & 1 & u \end{pmatrix} \oplus \cdots \oplus \begin{pmatrix} x & 0 & 1 \\ 0 & y & t \\ z & 1 & u \end{pmatrix}}_{\delta \text{ times}} \oplus I_{k-3\delta} \oplus 0_{(\ell_1 - k) \times (\ell_2 - k)}$$

and submits the randomized matrix $g^{\mathbf{LMR}}$ to the $\mathbf{Rank}(\mathcal{G}, \ell_1, \ell_2, k - \delta, k)$ distinguisher, where $\mathbf{L} \in_{\mathbf{R}} \mathrm{GL}_{\ell_1}(\mathbb{Z}_q)$ and $\mathbf{R} \in_{\mathbf{R}} \mathrm{GL}_{\ell_2}(\mathbb{Z}_q)$. Notice that if $u = x^{-1}z + y^{-1}t \mod q$ then the resulting matrix is a random matrix in $\mathcal{G}^{\ell_1 \times \ell_2; k - \delta}$. Otherwise, it is a random matrix in $\mathcal{G}^{\ell_1 \times \ell_2; k}$. $\square$

We can now apply a hybrid argument to prove Proposition 1. Let us consider the sequence of integers $\{r_i\}$ defined by the recurrence $r_0 = s$ and $r_{i+1} = \lfloor \frac{3r_i}{2} \rfloor$, and let k be the smallest index such that $r_k \geq r$. Then define a sequence of random matrices $\{\mathbf{M}_i\}$, where $\mathbf{M}_i \in_R \mathbb{Z}_q^{\ell_1 \times \ell_2; r_i}$ for $i = 0, \ldots, k-1$, and $\mathbf{M}_k \in_R \mathbb{Z}_q^{\ell_1 \times \ell_2; r}$. For any distinguisher $\mathcal{A}_{\mathbf{Rank}}$ with running time upper bounded by t, let $p_i = \Pr[1 \leftarrow \mathcal{A}_{\mathbf{Rank}}(g^{\mathbf{M}_i})]$. By Lemma 1, we have that for $i = 0, \ldots, k-2$

$$|p_{i+1} - p_i| = \mathbf{AdvRank}_{\mathcal{A}_{\mathbf{Rank}}}(\mathcal{G}, \ell_1, \ell_2, r_{i+1}, r_i) \leq \mathbf{AdvDLin}(\mathcal{G}; t'),$$
$$|p_k - p_{k-1}| = \mathbf{AdvRank}_{\mathcal{A}_{\mathbf{Rank}}}(\mathcal{G}, \ell_1, \ell_2, r, r_{k-1}) \leq \mathbf{AdvDLin}(\mathcal{G}; t')$$

Therefore, $\mathbf{AdvRank}_{\mathcal{A}_{\mathbf{Rank}}}(\mathcal{G}, \ell_1, \ell_2, r, s) = |p_k - p_0| \leq$
$$|p_1 - p_0| + \ldots + |p_k - p_{k-1}| \leq k \cdot \mathbf{AdvDLin}(\mathcal{G}; t').$$
On the other hand, since $\lfloor \frac{3x}{2} \rfloor \geq \frac{3x-1}{2}$ then $r_k \geq \left(\frac{3}{2}\right)^k \left(s - \frac{2}{3}\right)$, which implies that $k \leq \frac{\log(3r) - \log(3s-2)}{\log 3 - \log 2}$. □

In [17] we prove this same relation between the Rank problem and another computational problem, the Decisional 3-Party Diffie-Hellman (D3DH) problem [23,24,25]. As a consequence, the mKDM-CPA security of our scheme may rely on either the Decisional Linear assumption or the Decisional 3-Party Diffie-Hellman assumption.

5 Leakage-Resilient Identity-Based Encryption and Applications

The Boneh *et al.* KDM-CPA secure PKE scheme [5] was shown to be resilient against a leakage of up to $L(1 - o(1))$ bits of the secret key under a suitable parameters selection by Naor and Segev [14]. Similar results have been proven for other extensions of Boneh *et al.* scheme, notably in [6,7]. We show that this is also the case for our scheme by slightly changing the parameters. More precisely, an improved parameters setting of our mKDM-sID-CPA scheme provides master-key leakage resilience in the relative leakage model [11], with leakage ratio $1 - o(1)$, under the Decisional Linear assumption. Such a property is particularly useful, since IBE schemes that are secure against master-key leakage resilient and selective-identity chosen-plaintext attacks imply chosen ciphertext secure public key encryption secure in the presence of leakage [14].

Some Technical Tools. To give an intuition on why our scheme is leakage-resilient we need to recall some technical tools.

Definition 5 (Min-entropy). *The min-entropy of a random variable X is defined as $\mathcal{H}_\infty(X) = -\log(\max_x \Pr[X = x])$.*

Intuitively, the min-entropy of a random variable measures the difficulty of any adversary, even unbounded, to predict the value of the variable. The notion that measures how hard is predicting X given knowledge of another random variable Y is that of average min-entropy.

Definition 6 (Average min-entropy). *The average min-entropy of X given Y is defined as $\mathcal{H}_\infty(X|Y) = -\log\left(\mathbb{E}_{y \leftarrow Y}\left[\max_x \Pr[X = x|Y = y]\right]\right)$.*

Definition 7 (Statistical distance). *The statistical distance between two random variables X, Y over a finite set Ω is defined as*

$$\mathcal{D}(X, Y) = \frac{1}{2} \sum_{\omega \in \Omega} |\Pr[X = \omega] - \Pr[Y = \omega]|$$

Lemma 2 ([26] adapted). *Let A, B be random variables such that $\mathcal{H}_\infty(A|B) \geq h$. Let $\mathcal{H} = \{H_{\boldsymbol{v}} : \mathbb{Z}_q^\ell \to \mathbb{Z}_q\}_{\boldsymbol{v} \in \mathbb{Z}_q^\ell}$ be the family of universal hash functions $\boldsymbol{x} \mapsto \boldsymbol{vx}$. Let V be the uniform distribution in $\mathbb{Z}_q^\ell$. If $\log q \leq h - 2t$ holds, then $\mathcal{D}\left((H_V(A), V, B), (U_{\mathbb{Z}_q}, V, B)\right) \leq 2^{-t}$.*

For the definitions of master-key leakage resilience we refer the reader to [11]. For our current exposition it suffices to say that we are considering an standard IND-sID-CPA adversary which is allowed to decrease the min-entropy of the master-key by a given number of bits *before the challenge ciphertext is known*. We refer to our leakage security notion as IND-sID-LCPA (where L stands for leakage attacks).

Scheme and Master-Leakage Resilience. The modified IBE scheme $\varGamma' = (\mathsf{Stp}, \mathsf{Mkg}, \mathsf{Ukg}, \mathsf{Enc}, \mathsf{Dec})$ is obtained by only changing the set from which the master secret key SK is chosen. Instead of choosing $\boldsymbol{x} \in_R \mathbb{Z}_2^\ell$ in $\varGamma.\mathsf{Mkg}$ from Section 4.2, the scheme $\varGamma'$ chooses $\boldsymbol{x} \in_R \mathbb{Z}_q^\ell$.

Note that the average min-entropy of the master secret key $\boldsymbol{x}$ given the public key and λ bits of leakage is $h = \ell \log q - 2 \log q - \lambda$. Let us set $\ell = 3 + \frac{\lambda + 2t}{\log q}$. Then Lemma 2 guarantees that $g_T^{-\boldsymbol{vx}} \in \mathcal{G}_T$ is $\frac{1}{2^t}$-statistically close to the uniform distribution in $\mathcal{G}_T$. This turns out to be enough for proving mIND-sID-LCPA security, since in the simulation the legitimate ciphertext $(g^{r\mathbf{S}}, g^{r\mathbf{F}_{id}}, g_T^{-r\mathbf{S}\boldsymbol{x}} \cdot m_\beta)$ is replaced by the illegitimate ciphertext $(g^{\boldsymbol{v}}, g^{\boldsymbol{v}\mathbf{T}_{id}}, g_T^{-\boldsymbol{vx}} \cdot m_\beta)$ with $\boldsymbol{v} \in_R \mathbb{Z}_q^\ell$, and the adversary can not tell the difference thanks to the Decision Linear assumption. Finally, the adversary will not be able to tell the difference (information-theoretically) between an encryption of m_0 or m_1 because thanks to Lemma 2 $g_T^{-\boldsymbol{vx}} \in \mathcal{G}_T$ is statistically close to uniform.

We briefly comment on efficiency. For instance, for $\ell = 6$ our IBE scheme offers master-key leakage-resilience against $\frac{1}{2} - o(1)$ leakage ratio. In this case the ciphertext consists of 12 elements in $\mathcal{G}$ and 1 element in $\mathcal{G}_T$. By using the CHK transformation we obtain chosen-ciphertext leakage security under DLIN with leakage ratio $\frac{1}{2} - o(1)$ and ciphertext consisting of 18 elements in $\mathcal{G}$ and 1 element in $\mathcal{G}_T$. This compares favourably with existing schemes in the relative-leakage model.

Let us point out that via the IBE-to-signatures transformation, where messages to be signed play the role of identities, existentially unforgeable signature schemes can be obtained. Thus we only need to provide a full-identity secure variant of our master-leakage resilient scheme to obtain existentially unforgeable signature schemes secure against $1 - o(1)$ leakage-ratio under the Decisional Linear assumption. One possibility is to use a random oracle H to construct the elements $\mathbf{F}_{H(m)}$ and $\widetilde{\mathbf{F}}_{H(m)}$. Alternatively, we can use a matrix-based analogue of Waters' hash function [27] to implement $H(m)$; in this way, and at the cost of increasing the size of the public key of the signer, we obtain existentially unforgeable signature schemes secure against $1 - o(1)$ leakage-ratio in the standard model under the Decisional Linear assumption.

6   Open Problems

Given the current state of the art ([15] and this work), the most prominent open problem is to build mKDM-sID-CPA secure IBE schemes for $q_e, n \geq 1$ where the master public key and ciphertext sizes do not depend on the number of challenge queries q_e nor on the number of users n. Another interesting research direction is to build efficient mKDM-sID-CPA secure IBE schemes from lattices, which would lead to the first lattice-based KDM-CCA secure public key encryption schemes.

References

1. Abadi, M., Rogaway, P.: Reconciling two views of cryptography (the computational soundness of formal encryption). J. Cryptology 15(2), 103–127 (2002)
2. Camenisch, J.L., Lysyanskaya, A.: An Efficient System for Non-transferable Anonymous Credentials with Optional Anonymity Revocation. In: Pfitzmann, B. (ed.) EUROCRYPT 2001. LNCS, vol. 2045, pp. 93–118. Springer, Heidelberg (2001)
3. Black, J., Rogaway, P., Shrimpton, T.: Encryption-Scheme Security in the Presence of Key-Dependent Messages. In: Nyberg, K., Heys, H.M. (eds.) SAC 2002. LNCS, vol. 2595, pp. 62–75. Springer, Heidelberg (2003)
4. Malkin, T., Teranishi, I., Yung, M.: Efficient Circuit-Size Independent Public Key Encryption with KDM Security. In: Paterson, K.G. (ed.) EUROCRYPT 2011. LNCS, vol. 6632, pp. 507–526. Springer, Heidelberg (2011)
5. Boneh, D., Halevi, S., Hamburg, M., Ostrovsky, R.: Circular-Secure Encryption from Decision Diffie-Hellman. In: Wagner, D. (ed.) CRYPTO 2008. LNCS, vol. 5157, pp. 108–125. Springer, Heidelberg (2008)
6. Applebaum, B., Cash, D., Peikert, C., Sahai, A.: Fast Cryptographic Primitives and Circular-Secure Encryption Based on Hard Learning Problems. In: Halevi, S. (ed.) CRYPTO 2009. LNCS, vol. 5677, pp. 595–618. Springer, Heidelberg (2009)
7. Brakerski, Z., Goldwasser, S.: Circular and Leakage Resilient Public-Key Encryption under Subgroup Indistinguishability. In: Rabin, T. (ed.) CRYPTO 2010. LNCS, vol. 6223, pp. 1–20. Springer, Heidelberg (2010)
8. Camenisch, J., Chandran, N., Shoup, V.: A Public Key Encryption Scheme Secure against Key Dependent Chosen Plaintext and Adaptive Chosen Ciphertext Attacks. In: Joux, A. (ed.) EUROCRYPT 2009. LNCS, vol. 5479, pp. 351–368. Springer, Heidelberg (2009)
9. Kocher, P.C.: Timing Attacks on Implementations of Diffie-Hellman, RSA, DSS, and Other Systems. In: Koblitz, N. (ed.) CRYPTO 1996. LNCS, vol. 1109, pp. 104–113. Springer, Heidelberg (1996)

10. Kocher, P.C., Jaffe, J., Jun, B.: Differential Power Analysis. In: Wiener, M. (ed.) CRYPTO 1999. LNCS, vol. 1666, pp. 388–397. Springer, Heidelberg (1999)
11. Lewko, A., Rouselakis, Y., Waters, B.: Achieving Leakage Resilience through Dual System Encryption. In: Ishai, Y. (ed.) TCC 2011. LNCS, vol. 6597, pp. 70–88. Springer, Heidelberg (2011)
12. Shamir, A.: Identity-Based Cryptosystems and Signature Schemes. In: Blakely, G.R., Chaum, D. (eds.) CRYPTO 1984. LNCS, vol. 196, pp. 47–53. Springer, Heidelberg (1985)
13. Boneh, D., Franklin, M.: Identity-Based Encryption from the Weil Pairing. In: Kilian, J. (ed.) CRYPTO 2001. LNCS, vol. 2139, pp. 213–229. Springer, Heidelberg (2001)
14. Naor, M., Segev, G.: Public-Key Cryptosystems Resilient to Key Leakage. In: Halevi, S. (ed.) CRYPTO 2009. LNCS, vol. 5677, pp. 18–35. Springer, Heidelberg (2009)
15. Alperin-Sheriff, J., Peikert, C.: Circular and KDM Security for Identity-Based Encryption. In: Fischlin, M., Buchmann, J., Manulis, M. (eds.) PKC 2012. LNCS, vol. 7293, pp. 334–352. Springer, Heidelberg (2012)
16. Hofheinz, D.: Circular chosen-ciphertext security with compact ciphertexts. Cryptology ePrint Archive, Report 2012/150 (2012), http://eprint.iacr.org/
17. Galindo, D., Herranz, J., Villar, J.: Identity-based encryption with master key-dependent message security and applications. Cryptology ePrint Archive, Report 2012/142 (2012), http://eprint.iacr.org/
18. Bellare, M., Boldyreva, A., Micali, S.: Public-Key Encryption in a Multi-user Setting: Security Proofs and Improvements. In: Preneel, B. (ed.) EUROCRYPT 2000. LNCS, vol. 1807, pp. 259–274. Springer, Heidelberg (2000)
19. Canetti, R., Halevi, S., Katz, J.: Chosen-ciphertext security from identity-based encryption. In: [28], pp. 207–222
20. Boneh, D., Boyen, X., Shacham, H.: Short Group Signatures. In: Franklin, M. (ed.) CRYPTO 2004. LNCS, vol. 3152, pp. 41–55. Springer, Heidelberg (2004)
21. Boneh, D., Boyen, X.: Efficient selective-id secure identity-based encryption without random oracles. In: [28], pp. 223–238
22. Mohassel, P.: One-Time Signatures and Chameleon Hash Functions. In: Biryukov, A., Gong, G., Stinson, D.R. (eds.) SAC 2010. LNCS, vol. 6544, pp. 302–319. Springer, Heidelberg (2011)
23. Laguillaumie, F., Paillier, P., Vergnaud, D.: Universally Convertible Directed Signatures. In: Roy, B. (ed.) ASIACRYPT 2005. LNCS, vol. 3788, pp. 682–701. Springer, Heidelberg (2005)
24. Boneh, D., Sahai, A., Waters, B.: Fully Collusion Resistant Traitor Tracing with Short Ciphertexts and Private Keys. In: Vaudenay, S. (ed.) EUROCRYPT 2006. LNCS, vol. 4004, pp. 573–592. Springer, Heidelberg (2006)
25. Green, M., Hohenberger, S.: Practical Adaptive Oblivious Transfer from Simple Assumptions. In: Ishai, Y. (ed.) TCC 2011. LNCS, vol. 6597, pp. 347–363. Springer, Heidelberg (2011)
26. Dodis, Y., Ostrovsky, R., Reyzin, L., Smith, A.: Fuzzy extractors: How to generate strong keys from biometrics and other noisy data. SIAM J. Comput. 38(1), 97–139 (2008)
27. Waters, B.: Efficient Identity-Based Encryption Without Random Oracles. In: Cramer, R. (ed.) EUROCRYPT 2005. LNCS, vol. 3494, pp. 114–127. Springer, Heidelberg (2005)
28. Cachin, C., Camenisch, J.L. (eds.): EUROCRYPT 2004. LNCS, vol. 3027. Springer, Heidelberg (2004)

Unique Group Signatures

Matthew Franklin and Haibin Zhang

Dept. of Computer Science, University of California, Davis, California 95616, USA
{franklin,hbzhang}@cs.ucdavis.edu

Abstract. We initiate the study of *unique group signature* such that
signatures of the same message by the same user will always have a
large common component (i.e., unique identifier). It enables an efficient
detection algorithm, revealing the identities of illegal users, which is fundamentally different from previous primitives. We present a number of
unique group signature schemes (without random oracles) under a variety of security models that extend the standard security models of
ordinary group signatures. Our work is a beneficial step towards mitigating the well-known group signature paradox, and it also has many
other interesting applications and efficiency implications.

Keywords: Anonymity, anonymous authentication, detection algorithm,
group signature, unique signature, verifiable random function.

1   Introduction

Group signatures, introduced by Chaum and van Heyst [11], are very useful
tools in applications where the signer's privacy should be protected and in case
of abuse some authorities can identify the misbehaving user. However, a well-
known group signature "paradox" is that it is difficult for the group manager
to identify a "misbehaving" user since all of signatures are anonymous. The
group manager obviously cannot afford to open *all* of group signatures signed,
for this is inefficient, and more importantly, it would compromise the privacy
of every signer. Typically, the group manager identifies possible misbehaving
users by observing whether some surprising documents are signed, or a huge
amount of documents are signed within a short period, or some other "rules"
are broken. These empirical test methods only provide the group manager with
rough estimation about what signatures are suspicious. Trying to open and reveal
the identities of suspicious signatures has a risk of jeopardizing legal users, while
the illegal users may still be well-hidden.

Let us consider the motivating example of group signature due to Chaum and
van Heyst [11]: "A company has several computers, each connected to the local
network. Each department of that company has its own printer (also connected
to the network) and only persons of that department are allowed to use their
department's printer. Before printing, therefore, the printer must be convinced
that the user is working in that department. At the same time, the company

S. Foresti, M. Yung, and F. Martinelli (Eds.): ESORICS 2012, LNCS 7459, pp. 643–660, 2012.

wants privacy: the user's name may not be revealed. If, however, someone discovers at the end of the day that a printer has been used too often, the director must be able to discover who misused that printer, to send him a bill."

The above opening policy, in practice, is problematic: it is not fair to reveal all identities of the persons who use the printer that is "used too much", since the identities of legal users might as well be revealed. It does not even make sense to say what is "used too much", as a dedicated adversary might use the same printer every day such that the times of uses are always slightly below the daily threshold, while the others would not dare to use the printer.

In this case, the rule that this company would like to enforce is to limit the number of times within some period that group members can use the service. If anyone who accessed the service beyond the allowed quota then its identity should be revealed by the group authority. At the same time, it is equally desirable for this company to detect *other* malicious printing any time—for instance, one printing process that uses up all the paper—which is prohibitive. In other words, once a user signs a message more than a predetermined value then it shall be almost always (efficiently) detected, but the group manager can always open signatures any time in case of other misbehavior.

We define *unique group signature* as a first step towards mitigating this paradox. We may say that a group signature scheme is "unique" if it is computationally infeasible for a signer to produce two different group signatures of the same message, such that both will pass the verification procedure (by analogy with the well-studied notion of uniqueness for ordinary signature schemes). We adopt a less stringent but more general definition such that if a signer produces two different group signatures of the same message, then both signatures will always have a large common component (hereinafter *unique identifier*) which is otherwise highly unlikely to occur. Ideally, if one user indeed signs two different signatures on one message then there should be an (efficient) *detection algorithm* that can reveal the identity of this user. With carefully defined other security notions, this primitive (still called unique group signature) serves as a perfect solution of dealing with the above problem.

A closely related question was first asked by Damgård, Dupont, and Pedersen [12] in their paper on *unclonable group identification scheme*. An unclonable group identification scheme enables a user to authenticate to a server with complete anonymity provided that no other users try to use the first user's secret key to authenticate to the server within the same time period ("cloning attack"), while allowing the user's identity to be traced if they do misbehave in this way. They point out the inadequacy of existing group signature schemes for this purpose: "...This achieves anonymity but does not protect against cloning." Indeed, "This...is actually false for known schemes, since these are probabilistic and produce randomly varying signature even if the message is fixed." Our unique group signature can be deemed as important progress on this interesting open question, and it also has many applications beyond unclonable group identification.

Informally speaking, unique group signatures (suitably defined) are adequate for unclonable group identification. For example, the user might send

identification requests that include a signed message of the form "service_name ||
date" where || denotes concatenation. The server accepts if the signature is valid,
and if it doesn't have the same large common component as another identification request received earlier in the day. For this application (and many others),
we further need a *non-colliding* property for a unique group signature. A unique
group signature is non-colliding if two different signers almost never produce the
same unique identifier of the same message.

In another application, the user might send authentication requests that in-
clude a signed message of the form "service_name || date || j", where j is any
integer between 1 and the (daily) authentication bound k. The server accepts if
the signature is valid, and if it doesn't have the same large common component
as another authentication request from earlier in the day. This yields a variant of
periodic k-times anonymous authentication scheme [23,22,24,8]. Of course, many
variations are possible by varying the space of messages to be signed.

Notice that for both of these applications, the server can choose whether or
not to ask the group manager to reveal the identities of misbehaving users. For
minor misbehavior (such as an attempt to authenticate to a service a few more
times than the allowed bound, which might be due to innocent human or software
or network error) the extra attempts could be detected and ignored. This lets
the service provider reserve the relatively harsh penalty of anonymity revocation
for more significant (sustained and persistent) misbehavior.

Also note that the deterministic and uniqueness property of our unique signature can lead to very fast processing of data. For example, a service provider
carrying out a "first come, first kept" policy on a stream of ℓ requests would need
only $\mathcal{O}(\ell \log \ell)$ operations (via appropriate tree structures), or $\mathcal{O}(\ell)$ expected operations (via hash tables). This is particularly useful when there are many users
to be processed.

Though it can also deal with some applications that k-times anonymous authentication and more generalized e-token system [8] can, our primitive (even
in this respect) is in essence a different one with distinct features and benefits
(further discussion and comparison coming shortly).

TWO MODELS. This paper studies both the static group signature setting due
to Bellare, Micciancio, and Warinschi (BMW) [4] and the dynamic group signature setting due to Bellare, Shi, and Zhang (BSZ) [5]. Intuitively, the static
setting has a single authority (called the group manager), which the dynamic
setting splits into two: an issuer for enrolling members, and an opener for tracing
identities. One might feel that studying static setting is not quite necessary as
one could focus on the more involved and generalized dynamic group signature
setting. First, this does not make sense *syntactically*, since a dynamic group
model is not simply an extension of a static group model. Static group signature models realistic scenarios that the group manager takes full control of the
group user generation, and the secret signing key is distributed to each member,
preferably, *without* interaction. (Otherwise, the members have to be supported
by a trusted PKI, which usually is not the case in such a setting.) Instead, in
the dynamic group setting, PKI support and interactive Join/Issue between the

group issuer and group users are both *inevitable*. Second, this does not make sense *technically*, as we shall see, asking for non-interaction raises a few subtle issues in the static setting, making constructing an efficient scheme equally difficult. Third, we believe that static group signature is still *conceptually* more simple and starting from such a non-trivial point will make our presentation much clearer. Last, *constructionally*, our results for static unique group signature are both general and more efficient, while for the dynamic group setting our results are only semi-modular and a little less efficient.

HOW TO MODEL UNIQUE GROUP SIGNATURE? We offer the "strongest" achievable definitions of security for both settings, but here we only highlight the case of dynamic model. On the one hand, the security requirements of dynamic unique group signatures are all simple and clear. Three of them (i.e., CCA-anonymity, traceability, and non-frameability) are based on previous security definitions of ordinary group signatures, while the uniqueness requirement is a quite natural and intuitive one. This is good, whether for understanding the definitions, or for designing the constructions. The uniqueness security notion formalizes the intuition that one signer can only sign one message once. Jumping ahead, we argue that defining uniqueness in the group signature setting raises subtle issues that must be carefully treated.

On the other hand, they are in fact very carefully defined *on the whole*. Recall that our goal is to present a group signature system where each group member can only sign any message once, equipped with an (efficient) detection algorithm such that the identities of ones who disobey such a rule can be revealed and should otherwise be never leaked. All definitions of security are designed to this end. A few seemingly reasonable variants of definitions turn out to be inadequate.

The detection algorithm of our dynamic CCA-anonymous unique group signature is as simple as one could imagine: if the detection authority (i.e., the opener) ever found two different valid group signatures on the same message with the same unique identifier, then it runs the opening algorithm Open to extract their identities i and j (possibly i equals j), and adds them (it) to the misbehaving user set. However, all of these on detection algorithm have to be formally defined, otherwise it leaves one without any notion for what it means to have a *good* detection algorithm. Also note that our defined security properties do *not* even involve any properties of detection algorithms. Instead, we show that once the group system satisfies the four basic security requirements, it gives rise to a good (*complete* and *sound*) detection algorithm.

CONSTRUCTIONS. In this paper, we present both the general constructions and efficient instantiations for both static and dynamic group models without relying on random oracles. In the static setting, our general scheme follows the BMW two-level signature construction but uses a *verifiable random function* (VRF) [21] as the second-level signature. We also give a simpler construction for a unique group signature that is secure in a relaxed yet reasonable model. They *together* lead to our final efficient instantiation using Groth-Sahai proof system [19]. All of our constructions (either general or specific) are constant-size, and the instantiation is as efficient as the-state-of-the-art. Our construction for the unique group signatures in the dynamic setting is semi-modular, and can be instantiated efficiently. The construction can even admit efficient *concurrent-join* which allows many entities concurrently engage in the Join/Issue protocol with the issuer. In building the schemes, we identify new and useful techniques that we believe can be used in other privacy-preserving primitives. We highlight two of them. The first one is a PRF with NIZK proof that can degenerate into a unique signature. In many signature-related primitives, one not only need prove a deterministic function in a zero-knowledge sense but also prove knowledge of input to the function. There are many existing techniques, but ours gives the constructions that can be more efficient and rely on weaker assumptions. The other technique is what we call *"double-chaining certification"*, which is used to achieve our unique group signature in the dynamic setting. In essence, this allows us to separate the unique identifier generation process from tracing process, thereby resulting in efficient and intuitive constructions.

APPLICATIONS AND COMPARISON BETWEEN OTHER PRIMITIVES. Our primitive is designed to mitigate the group signature paradox and also motivated by other privacy-preserving constructions, such as k-times anonymous authentication, unclonable group identification protocol, and more generalized e-token systems (periodic k-times anonymous authentication) [8]. The latter primitives are closely related to group signatures, but do *not* have an opening authority that can *always* de-anonymize signed messages.

On the other hand, our primitive can be as well used in applications where (periodic) k-times anonymous authentication is needed as illustrated earlier. Indeed, one can simply use a range proof to extend unique group signature to handle cases for $k > 1$, or one can easily achieve constant-size scheme by registering k public keys for one user at a time. (Note one of our instantiations supports efficient concurrent-join.) However, our primitive, in this respect, has distinct features.

First, the detection algorithms for other primitives are made *public*, meaning that if the a user signs more than the authentication bound k then its identity can be publicly known. This can be both *good* and *bad*: if an honest user accidentally signs slightly more than what is required because of hardware breakdown or clock desynchronization, then the public identity disclosure might not be the most reasonable choice. In fact, we are not aware of any implementations with such stringent mechanisms in *real* applications. Our unique group signature in the dynamic group setting supports in essence a different identity disclosure strategy where the detection authority (other than the group provider) is responsible to detect and reveal disobeyers by the detection algorithm Det. Anyone including the group provider and group members can find publicly misbehaving signatures and report to the detection authority. In our setting, this algorithm is even coupled with a detection proving algorithm DetProve that ensures the detection authority to behave correctly with a proof that the revealed identities are ones of the disobeyers. The opener reserves the right to open persistent misbehaving users to the public, or contact and warn them privately, or send the identity and the corresponding proof into court as it sees fit. As far as we are concerned, two flavors of revelation are both interesting and should be used depending on specific applications.

Second, it was argued in [23], for their applications only, of course, that it is preferable that the users (who honestly follow the protocol specification) should enjoy anonymity even from the group provider. For the traditional group signature schemes, this requirement is not satisfied. But in the dynamic group model, the group provider might be a distinct entity from the opener who acts as the detection authority. Indeed, the reliance on some other party is inevitable if we do not want to enforce public identity discovery.

Third, in the context of k-times anonymous authentication, to the best of our knowledge, all previous constructions (e.g., [8,22,24,23]) uses an idea originally from e-cash system. The detection algorithm of our primitive is fundamentally different from those. It turns out, perhaps somewhat counter-intuitive, that modeling and achieving "right" detection without using public discovery is actually more challenging.

Last, as mentioned earlier, our primitives can be used in a more efficient way such that no detection algorithm is involved. Namely, the deterministic and unique property of our unique signature lead to very fast processing of data. We are not aware of other primitives admitting such efficient detection.

2   Preliminaries

NOTATIONS. If x is a string then $|x|$ denotes its length. The empty string is denoted ε. If S is a set then $|S|$ denotes its size and $s \xleftarrow{\$} S$ denotes the operation of selecting an element s of S uniformly at random. $\emptyset$ denotes the empty set, while $\varnothing$ denotes a vector of empty sets. If n is an integer $[n]$ denotes the set $\{1, 2, \cdots, n\}$. If $\mathcal{A}$ is a randomized algorithm then we write $z \xleftarrow{\$} \mathcal{A}(x, y, \cdots)$ to indicate the operation that runs $\mathcal{A}$ on inputs $x, y, \cdots$ and a uniformly selected r from an appropriately required domain and outputs z. A function $\epsilon(\lambda) \colon \mathbb{N} \rightarrow \mathbb{R}$ is *negligible* if, for any positive number d, there exists some constant $\lambda_0 \in \mathbb{N}$ such that $\epsilon(\lambda) < (1/\lambda)^d$ for any $\lambda > \lambda_0$. For definitions of primitives and cryptographic assumptions, please refer the full version [15, Section 2].

3   Unique Group Signature Models

In this section we present models of unique group signatures in the static setting (following BMW [4]) and in the dynamic setting (following BSZ [5]).

3.1   Static Setting Model

Following [4], a *static group signature scheme* $\mathcal{SGS}$ consists of four algorithms (GK, GS, GV, Open). There is only one group authority which we call the *group manager*. The *group key generation* algorithm GK takes as input the security parameter λ to form a fixed-size group with n members where n may be related to λ, returning a tuple $(gpk, gmsk, \boldsymbol{gsk})$, where gpk is the *group public key*, $gmsk$ is the *group manager secret key*, and $\boldsymbol{gsk}$ is an n-vector of *secret signing keys* with $gsk[i]$ for each user i. The secret keys are usually distributed to members without interaction. The *group signing* algorithm GS takes as input $gsk[i]$ and a message m to return a signature σ under $gsk[i]$. The *group verification* algorithm GV takes as input the group public key gpk, a message m, and a signature σ for m to return a single bit b. We say that σ is a *valid* signature of m if $\mathsf{GV}(gpk, m, \sigma) = 1$. The *opening* algorithm Open takes the group public key gpk, group manager secret key $gmsk$, a message m, and a signature σ to return an identity i or $\perp$ (indicating failure). Basic *correctness* property is required: for all security parameter λ and integer n, all $(gpk, gmsk, \boldsymbol{gsk}) \xleftarrow{\$} \mathsf{GK}(1^\lambda)$, all $i \in [n]$, and all message $m \in \{0,1\}^*$, it holds that $\mathsf{GV}(gpk, m, \mathsf{GS}(gsk[i], m)) = 1$ and $\mathsf{Open}(gpk, gmsk, m, \mathsf{GS}(gsk[i], m)) = i$.

For our purposes, we consider *static unique group signatures* where the signatures should have the form of $(m, \sigma) = (m, \tau, \psi)$ where τ is the *unique identifier* for the message m and some group member i, and ψ is the rest of the signature. (One can view the unique identifier as a special *tag*.) We define for static unique group signature three security requirements: uniqueness, anonymity, and traceability. The uniqueness requirement formalizes the intuition that one user can only sign one message once, while the last two requirements are adapted from ones for the regular static group signatures with the restraints of being unique.

Uniqueness. Unlike defining uniqueness for a stand-alone signature (i.e., unique signature), it is "tricky" to do so in the context of group signature that involves multiple users. Intuitively, any single group member should not generate more than one valid signatures for any message m. However, it is not quite adequate, for, an adversary may (adaptively) corrupt multiple group members to gain an additional advantage. (In the full version [15, Appendix B], we give a separation result, showing that there exist schemes satisfying a weakened uniqueness definition where the adversary can only corrupt one user but not the standard uniqueness that we define shortly.) We thus give adversary access to a *user secret oracle*, $\mathsf{USK}(\cdot)$, which, when queried with an identity $i \in [n]$, answers with the secret signing key $gsk[i]$ for user i. In the static group signature setting, once the secret key of a user is revealed then it is said to be *corrupted*. Let CU denote a set of corrupted users. Since the group has a fixed-size n, a set of uncorrupted (i.e., honest) users is $[n]/\mathrm{CU}$. The adversary is also given access to a *user signing oracle*, $\mathsf{GS}(\cdot, \cdot)$, which when queried with an identity i of a user and a message m, returns $\mathsf{GS}(gsk[i], m)$. Note that we do not require that adversary only ask uncorrupted users for this oracle. Let GS denote a set of message-signature pairs queried via the $\mathsf{GS}(\cdot, \cdot)$ oracle. We write GS_m to denote a set of users with which adversary calls $\mathsf{GS}(\cdot, m)$. We write $\mathrm{GS}_\mathbf{M}$ where $\mathbf{M}$ is a set of the messages queried to denote a vector of sets with GS_m for each $m \in \mathbf{M}$. For maximal security, we also provide adversary with the secret of the group manager $gmsk$. Formally, given a static signature scheme $\mathcal{SGS}$ of a fixed-size n, we associate to an adversary $\mathcal{A}$ the following experiment:

Experiment Exp$_{\mathcal{SGS},n}^{\text{unique}}(\mathcal{A})$

$(gpk, gmsk, \boldsymbol{gsk}) \xleftarrow{\$} \mathcal{SGS}.\text{Gen}(1^\lambda); \ \text{CU} \leftarrow \emptyset; \ \text{GS} \leftarrow \emptyset$

$(m, \sigma_1, \cdots, \sigma_{|\text{CU}|+1}) \xleftarrow{\$} \mathcal{A}^{\text{USK}(\cdot), \text{GS}(\cdot, \cdot)}(gpk, gmsk)$

for $i \leftarrow 1$ **to** $|\text{CU}| + 1$ **do**

    if $\text{GV}(gpk, m, \sigma_i) = 0$ **or** $(m, \sigma_i) \in \text{GS}$ **then return** 0

for $i, j \leftarrow 1$ **to** $|\text{CU}| + 1$ **do**

    if $i \neq j$ **and** $\tau_i = \tau_j$ **then return** 0

return 1

where, above, each σ_i is of the form (τ_i, ψ_i). We define the advantage of $\mathcal{A}$ in the above experiment as

$$\mathbf{Adv}_{\mathcal{SGS},n}^{\text{unique}}(\mathcal{A}) = \Pr[\mathbf{Exp}_{\mathcal{SGS},n}^{\text{unique}}(\mathcal{A}) = 1].$$

In the above experiment, adversary is expected to output *exactly* $|\text{CU}|+1$ *new* and *valid* signatures which have *distinct* unique identifiers w.r.t. the *same* message.

A CAVEAT. We first emphasize that the above notion is the one that we shall use in this paper. However, we do point out some "inadequacies" by considering the following scenario: it is entirely possible that some of keys correspond to one same unique identifier (i.e., they "collide"), while some other keys might generate more unique identifiers than *required*. To put it differently, it might be the case that a set of users of size k who do not collude ought to create $k - 1$ unique identifiers as two of them collide, but when they collude they can create k unique identifiers. This does not contract our uniqueness security, but such a collusion clearly makes them sign messages beyond their own.

NON-COLLIDING PROPERTY. In light of this (and as required by some applications mentioned in the introduction), we impose a restriction on our static unique group signature. We say that a group signature is *non-colliding* if any of two different (honest) signers (who follow the scheme specification) almost never produce the same *unique identifier* of the same message. More formally, for all security parameter λ and integer n, all $(gpk, gmsk, \boldsymbol{gsk}) \xleftarrow{\$} \text{GK}(1^\lambda)$, all $i, j \in [n]$ and $i \neq j$, and all message $m \in \{0, 1\}^*$, it holds that

$$\Pr[(\tau_i, \psi_i) \xleftarrow{\$} \text{GS}(gsk[i], m); (\tau_j, \psi_j) \xleftarrow{\$} \text{GS}(gsk[j], m) : \ \tau_i = \tau_j] \leq \epsilon(\lambda).$$

Above, the probability is taken over the coins of the group key generation algorithm and group signing algorithm.

The above requirement can resolve the "issue" above. Indeed, if the above-mentioned circumstance happens then an adversary who corrupted a set of group members can always "honestly" generate signatures *again* and pick "enough" signatures with different unique identifiers to attack the uniqueness property. It also makes our primitive justifiable in a few applications—only via this property one can safely achieve the functionality of restricted anonymous authentication (as mentioned in the introduction). Jumping ahead, we claim that the non-colliding property is needed as well in justifying the security of the detection algorithm of unique group signature. We refer to the full version [15] for further discussion on definitional choices and issues on uniqueness.

Anonymity. Due to the uniqueness property, we cannot achieve the strongest anonymity definition of security as defined in BMW [4]. (The group signature signed by each member i is a partly deterministic function of the gpk, $gsk[i]$, and the message m. If the adversary is given all of the secret keys $\boldsymbol{gsk}$ then it can attack the full-anonymity game simply by re-computing.) Thus a slightly weaker yet still very strong anonymity security notion is used: the adversary can adaptively corrupt the users of the group; for uncorrupted users, adversary is given a signing oracle; in the challenge stage, adversary is not allowed to submit challenge queries with identities of corrupted users, and not allowed to submit challenge queries with at least one of the identities and the message being the same as ones queried before. We write $\mathsf{Open}(\cdot, \cdot)$ to denote the *opening oracle*, which when queried with a message m and a candidate signature σ, answers with $\mathsf{Open}(gpk, gmsk, m, \sigma)$. Specifically, given a static group signature scheme $\mathcal{SGS}$ of a fixed-size n, we associate to an adversary $\mathcal{A}$ the following experiment:

> **Experiment $\mathbf{Exp}^{\mathrm{anon}}_{\mathcal{SGS},n}(\mathcal{A})$**
> $(gpk, gmsk, \boldsymbol{gsk}) \xleftarrow{\$} \mathcal{SGS}.\mathsf{Gen}(1^\lambda)$; $\mathrm{CU} \leftarrow \emptyset$; $\mathrm{GS_M} \leftarrow \varnothing$
> $(i_0, i_1, m, \mathsf{s}) \xleftarrow{\$} \mathcal{A}^{\mathsf{USK}(\cdot),\mathsf{GS}(\cdot,\cdot),\mathsf{Open}(\cdot,\cdot)}(\mathsf{find}, gpk)$
> $b \xleftarrow{\$} \{0,1\}$; $\sigma \xleftarrow{\$} \mathsf{GS}(gsk[i_b], m)$
> $b' \xleftarrow{\$} \mathcal{A}^{\mathsf{USK}(\cdot),\mathsf{GS}(\cdot,\cdot),\mathsf{Open}(\cdot,\cdot)}(\mathsf{guess}, \sigma, \mathsf{s})$
> **if** $b' \neq b$ **then return** 0
> **return** 1

where it is mandated that for each $d \in \{0,1\}$ we have $i_d \notin \mathrm{CU}$ and $i_d \notin \mathrm{GS}_m$, and in the guess phase the adversary $\mathcal{A}$ did not query $\mathsf{Open}(\cdot, \cdot)$ with m and σ. We define the advantage of $\mathcal{A}$ in the above experiment as

$$\mathbf{Adv}^{\mathrm{anon}}_{\mathcal{SGS},n}(\mathcal{A}) = \Pr[\mathbf{Exp}^{\mathrm{anon}}_{\mathcal{SGS},n}(\mathcal{A}) = 1] - 1/2.$$

We use the term "CPA-anonymity" to denote the following weakening of the security definition for anonymity [7]: The adversary is never given access to the opening oracle.

Traceability. The traceability security definition is the same as one in BMW [4]. We recall it by considering the experiment that associated to an adversary $\mathcal{A}$:

> **Experiment $\mathbf{Exp}^{\mathrm{trace}}_{\mathcal{SGS},n}(\mathcal{A})$**
> $(gpk, gmsk, \boldsymbol{gsk}) \xleftarrow{\$} \mathcal{SGS}.\mathsf{Gen}(1^\lambda)$; $\mathrm{CU} \leftarrow \emptyset$; $\mathrm{GS_M} \leftarrow \varnothing$
> $(m, \sigma) \xleftarrow{\$} \mathcal{A}^{\mathsf{USK}(\cdot),\mathsf{GS}(\cdot,\cdot)}(gpk, gmsk)$
> **if** $\mathsf{GV}(gpk, m, \sigma) = 0$ **then return** 0
> **if** $\mathsf{Open}(m, \sigma) = \bot$ **then return** 1
> **if** $\mathsf{Open}(m, \sigma) = i$ **and** $i \notin \mathrm{CU}$ **and** $i \notin \mathrm{GS}_m$ **then return** 1
> **return** 0

The advantage of $\mathcal{A}$ in the above experiment is defined as

$$\mathbf{Adv}^{\mathrm{trace}}_{\mathcal{SGS},n}(\mathcal{A}) = \Pr[\mathbf{Exp}^{\mathrm{trace}}_{\mathcal{SGS},n}(\mathcal{A}) = 1].$$

3.2   Dynamic Setting Model

In the dynamic group setting, there are two more features: it allows one to add members to the group; the authority is separated into the *opener* and the *issuer*. An issuer is responsible to enroll members, while an opener traces the identities of signatures signed by the users enrolled. A *dynamic group signature scheme* $\mathcal{DGS}$ consists of six algorithms (GK, Join/Issue, GS, GV, Open, Judge). We consider *dynamic unique group signatures* having the form of (m, τ, ψ) where τ is the *unique identifier*. A secure unique group signature in the dynamic setting should satisfy correctness and non-colliding property and four security notions: uniqueness, anonymity, traceability and non-frameability. Overall, the definitions in dynamic setting are more *involved* and refer the full version [15] for details.

3.3   Detection Algorithms

We show how our security definitions in *both* settings imply efficient *detection algorithms* that can find who do not follow the algorithm specification *and* disobey the rule that one group member can only sign any message once. Here we only focus on the more involved dynamic setting, and one can easily get similar (but weak) results for the static group setting.

The detection algorithm Det takes as input two different group signatures σ_1 and σ_2 for the same message m and outputs $\bot$ or $\mathcal{I}$ or (b, i, j, θ) for $b \in \{0, 1\}$. The algorithm returns $\bot$ if at least for one of σ_1 and σ_2 it holds that $\mathsf{GV}(gpk, m, \sigma_t) = 0$ $(t \in \{0, 1\})$. If $b = \mathcal{I}$ then the detection algorithm is claiming that at least one of the two signatures was not generated by the group members registered in the **reg**. (Note that group *issuer* can always generate group signatures on his own by adding dummy users.) In this case, it might have an additional output μ that is a proof that at least one of the signatures was generated by the group issuer. If $b = 0$ then it is claiming that two signatures were generated by two different signers—a rule that the system would like to enforce. In this case, it does not need a proof of the claim. (But one could ask a proof if desired.) In case $b = 1$, it is claiming that two signatures were generated by rule disobeyers i and j, where $i, j \geq 1$, i could be equal to j, and θ is a proof of this claim that is verified by the DetProve algorithm.

The *detection proving* algorithm DetProve takes as input the group public key gpk, two valid signatures σ_1 and σ_2 of m, and a vector (b, i, j, θ) output from Det (m, σ_1, σ_2) where $b = 1$, $i, j \geq 1$, and θ is a non-empty string to output a single bit d indicating whether θ is a correct proof that both of i and j disobey the rule.

The detection algorithm should satisfy *completeness* and *soundness* properties described below.

Completeness. The set LU of legal users (who follow the rule that one signer can only sign one message once) will almost never be wrongly detected by the detection algorithm.

Soundness. If $\mathsf{Det}(m, \sigma_1, \sigma_2) = (1, i, j, \theta)$ and $\mathsf{DetProve}(gpk, m, \sigma_1, \sigma_2, \mathsf{Det}(m, \sigma_1, \sigma_2)) = 1$ then *both* i and j are illegal users (who did not follow the specification of the protocol or the rule).

Alg $\mathsf{Det}(m, \sigma_1 = (\tau_1, \psi_1), \sigma_2 = (\tau_2, \psi_2))$
  if $\mathsf{GV}(m, \sigma_1) = 0$ **or** $\mathsf{GV}(m, \sigma_1) = 0$ **then**
    return $\perp$
  $(i, \omega_i) \leftarrow \mathsf{Open}(m, \sigma_1)$
  $(j, \omega_j) \leftarrow \mathsf{Open}(m, \sigma_2)$
  if $i = 0$ **or** $j = 0$ **then**
    return $(\mathcal{I}, \mu)$
  if $\tau_1 = \tau_2$ **then**
    return $(1, i, j, (\omega_i, \omega_j))$
  return $(0, \varepsilon)$

Alg $\mathsf{DetProve}(m, \sigma_1, \sigma_2)$
  if $\mathsf{Det}(m, \sigma_1, \sigma_2) \neq (1, i, j, (\omega_i, \omega_j))$ **then**
    return 0
  if $\mathsf{Judge}(gpk, (i, \omega_i), m, \sigma_1, \boldsymbol{reg}) = 1$ **and**
    $\mathsf{Judge}(gpk, (j, \omega_j), m, \sigma_2, \boldsymbol{reg}) = 1$ **then**
    return 1
  return 0

Fig. 1. Det and DetProve algorithms

Our dynamic CCA-anonymous unique group signature immediately has an *efficient* complete and sound detection algorithm Det coupled with a detection proving algorithm DetProve, as illustrated in Figure 1. We justify the detection algorithm by providing the following theorem (with proof in the full version [15, Appendix C.1]). We also refer to [15] for further discussion and applications.

Theorem 1. *Given a dynamic unique group signature* $\mathcal{DGS}$*, if it is correct and non-colliding, and satisfies CCA-anonymity, uniqueness, traceability, and non-frameability requirements, then the* Det *algorithm given in Figure 1 is complete and sound.* ∎

4   Unique Group Signature Construction – Static Setting

In this section, we first present general constructions for CCA-anonymous unique group signature and for its meaningful relaxations in the static setting. They *together* motivate efficient instantiations by using Groth-Sahai proof system.

A GENERAL CCA-ANONYMOUS UNIQUE GROUP SIGNATURE. Our construction basically follows the general two-level signature constructions of [4]. The difference is that we replace the second-level signature with a verifiable random function, where its public key is signed by the certification key of group manager. We give our general construction using a first-level signature scheme that provides security against random message attacks.[1] Define a verifiable random function $\mathcal{VRF} = (\mathsf{Gen}, \mathsf{Eva}, \mathsf{Prove}, \mathsf{Ver})$ with input domain $\mathcal{X}$ and output range $\mathcal{Y}$. Let $\mathcal{DS} = (\mathsf{Gen}, \mathsf{Sig}, \mathsf{Vrf})$ be a signature scheme. Let $\mathcal{E} = (\mathsf{Gen}, \mathsf{Enc}, \mathsf{Dec})$ be a public key encryption scheme. Let (P_1, V_1) be a NIZK proof system for a language $\mathcal{L}_1 := \{(m, vk, ek, \tau, C) | \exists (r, vk', \nu', \mathsf{cert}) [\mathsf{Vrf}(vk, vk', \mathsf{cert}) = 1, \mathsf{Ver}(vk', m, \tau, \nu') = 1, \text{ and } C = \mathsf{Enc}(ek, r, (vk', \nu', \mathsf{cert}))] \}$ where we write $\mathsf{Enc}(ek, r, M)$ for the encryption of a message M under the public key ek using the randomness r. We define a group signature scheme $\mathcal{SGS}_1$ in Figure 2. We have the following theorem:

---

[1] Informally, a signature is unforgeable against random message attack [14] if it cannot forge a signature on a new message having access to a special oracle that returns signatures on randomly chosen messages.

Alg $\mathsf{GK}(1^\lambda)$

  $R \xleftarrow{\$} \{0,1\}^{p(\lambda)}$

  $(vk, sk) \xleftarrow{\$} \mathcal{DS}.\mathsf{Gen}(1^\lambda)$

  $(ek, dk) \xleftarrow{\$} \mathcal{E}.\mathsf{Gen}(1^\lambda)$

  $gpk \leftarrow (R, ek, vk)$

  for $i \leftarrow 1$ **to** n **do**

    $(sk_i, vk_i) \xleftarrow{\$} \mathcal{VRF}.\mathsf{Gen}(1^\lambda)$

    $\mathsf{cert}_i \xleftarrow{\$} \mathsf{Sig}(sk, vk_i)$

    $gsk[i] \leftarrow (sk_i, vk_i, \mathsf{cert}_i, gpk)$

    $reg[i] \leftarrow vk_i$

  $gmsk \leftarrow (dk, \textbf{reg})$

  return $(gpk, gmsk, \textbf{gsk})$

Alg $\mathsf{GS}(gsk[i], m)$

  $\tau \leftarrow \mathsf{Eva}(sk_i, m); \ \nu \xleftarrow{\$} \mathsf{Prove}(sk_i, m)$

  $C \leftarrow \mathsf{Enc}(ek, r, (vk_i, \nu, \mathsf{cert}_i))$

  $\pi \xleftarrow{\$} P_1(R, (m, vk, ek, \tau, C), (r, vk_i, \nu, \mathsf{cert}_i))$

  $\sigma \leftarrow (\tau, C, \pi)$

  return (m, σ)

Alg $\mathsf{GV}(gpk, m, \sigma)$

  return $V_1(R, (m, vk, ek, \tau, C), \pi)$

Alg $\mathsf{Open}(gpk, gmsk, m, \sigma)$

  if $V_1(R, (m, vk, ek, \tau, C, \pi)) = 0$ **return** $\perp$

  $(vk', \nu', \mathsf{cert}) \leftarrow \mathsf{Dec}(dk, C)$

  if $vk' = reg[i]$ **then return** i

Fig. 2. Static unique group signature (a general construction). We write **reg** to denote $reg[1] \cdots reg[n]$. R is the common reference string for the underlying NIZK proof system (P_1, V_1). $\mathcal{SGS}_1$ is a CCA-anonymous unique group signature, if $\mathcal{DS}$ is unforgeable under random message attacks, $\mathcal{E}$ is CCA-secure, and $\mathcal{VRF}$ is a verifiable random function, and (P_1, V_1) is a simulation-sound NIZK proof system. $\mathcal{SGS}_1$ is CPA-anonymous, if $\mathcal{E}$ is semantically secure and (P_1, V_1) is a regular NIZK proof system.

Theorem 2. *If $\mathcal{VRF}$ is a verifiable random function, $\mathcal{DS}$ is a secure signature against random message attack, scheme, and the underlying NIZK proof system (P_1, V_1) is sound, zero-knowledge, and one-time simulation-sound then the construction $\mathcal{SGS}_1$ in Figure 2 is a secure CCA-anonymous unique group signature in the static setting.* ∎

RELAXATIONS AND SEPARATIONS. The above construction is general but does not seem to immediately give rise to efficient instantiations. This is due, first, to the fact current *simulation-sound* NIZK proof systems are not efficient enough. This is further due to the fact that the VRF proof ν may be incompatible with the efficient proof systems. In light of this, we consider two meaningful relaxations of CCA-anonymous unique group signature. The first natural relaxation is to consider CPA-anonymous unique group signature where the anonymity adversary is never given the opening oracle. This immediately helps avoid using simulation-sound property of NIZK proof system and chosen ciphertext security for the underlying encryption scheme. Namely, we have a group signature the same as illustrated in Figure 2 except that we only use a regular NIZK proof system and a semantic-secure encryption.

Theorem 3. *If $\mathcal{VRF}$ is a verifiable random function, $\mathcal{DS}$ is a secure signature against random message attack, $\mathcal{E}$ is a CPA-secure encryption scheme, and the underlying NIZK proof system (P_1, V_1) is sound and zero-knowledge, then the construction $\mathcal{SGS}_1$ in Figure 2 is a secure CPA-anonymous unique group signature in the static setting.* ∎

The other meaningful relaxation is that we no longer give the uniqueness and traceability adversaries the group manager secret key $gmsk$. This relaxation makes sense as an external adversary usually does not obtain the opening key

Alg $\mathsf{GK}(1^\lambda)$	**Alg** $\mathsf{GS}(gsk[i], m)$
$R \xleftarrow{\$} \{0,1\}^{p(\lambda)}$	$\tau \leftarrow F_{s_i}(m)$
$(vk, sk) \xleftarrow{\$} \mathcal{DS}.\mathsf{Gen}(1^\lambda)$	$C \leftarrow \mathsf{Enc}(ek, r, (s_i, \mathsf{cert}_i))$
$(ek, dk) \xleftarrow{\$} \mathcal{E}.\mathsf{Gen}(1^\lambda)$	$\pi \xleftarrow{\$} P_2(R, (m, vk, ek, \tau, C), (r, s_i, \mathsf{cert}_i))$
$gpk \leftarrow (R, ek, vk, F)$	$\sigma \leftarrow (\tau, C, \pi)$
for $i \leftarrow 1$ **to** n **do**	**return** (m, σ)
$\quad s_i \xleftarrow{\$} \mathcal{S}$	**Alg** $\mathsf{GV}(gpk, m, \sigma)$
$\quad \mathsf{cert}_i \xleftarrow{\$} \mathsf{Sig}(sk, s_i)$	**return** $V_2(R, (m, vk, ek, \tau, C), \pi)$
$\quad gsk[i] \leftarrow (s_i, \mathsf{cert}_i, gpk)$	**Alg** $\mathsf{Open}(gpk, gmsk, m, \sigma)$
$\quad reg[i] \leftarrow s_i$	**if** $V_2(R, (m, vk, ek, \tau, C, \pi)) = 0$ **return** $\bot$
$gmsk \leftarrow (dk, reg)$	$(s', \mathsf{cert}) \leftarrow \mathsf{Dec}(dk, C)$
return $(gpk, gmsk, gsk)$	**if** $s' = reg[i]$ **then return** i

Fig. 3. Static unique group signature $\mathcal{SGS}_2$, with *relaxed* uniqueness and traceability notions, where the adversaries are not given the group manager secret key $gmsk$

of group manager unless it corrupts the group manager which looks less likely. We find that if we restrict the adversary in such a way then we can simply use PRF instead of VRF such that the second problem can be solved.

Define a PRF family $F \colon \mathcal{S} \times \mathcal{X} \to \mathcal{Y}$ where $\mathcal{S}$ is the key space, $\mathcal{X}$ is the message space, and $\mathcal{Y}$ is the range. We write $F_s(\cdot)$ to denote a PRF for every $s \in \mathcal{S}$. Let $\mathcal{DS}$ and $\mathcal{E}$ be a digital signature and a public key encryption scheme respectively. Let (P_2, V_2) be a NIZK proof system for a language $\mathcal{L}_2 := \{(m, vk, ek, \tau, C) | \exists (r, s, \mathsf{cert}) [\tau = F_s(m), \mathsf{Vrf}(vk, s, \mathsf{cert}) = 1, \text{ and } C = \mathsf{Enc}(ek, r, (s, \mathsf{cert}))]\}$. We define a unique group signature scheme $\mathcal{SGS}_2$ as illustrated in Figure 3. The following theorem establishes its security.

Theorem 4. *If F is a PRF, $\mathcal{DS}$ is a secure signature against random message attack, $\mathcal{E}$ is a CCA2 secure encryption scheme, and the underlying NIZK proof system (P_2, V_2) is sound, zero-knowledge, and one-time simulation-sound then the construction $\mathcal{SGS}_2$ given in Figure 3 is a CCA-anonymous unique group signature with relaxed uniqueness and traceability where the adversaries are not given $gmsk$.* ∎

One can verify that $\mathcal{SGS}_1$ (i.e., the CPA-anonymous construction) may be not CCA-anonymous, and $\mathcal{SGS}_2$ may be not secure in the sense of standard uniqueness and traceability. Thus, they give natural separations results for these definitions of security. See [15, Appendix B] for proofs and discussion.

EFFICIENT INSTANTIATIONS. The above concerns do not rule out *ad hoc* constructions in the strongest model. It turns out that we can provide efficient constructions using the Groth-Sahai proof system. The encryption scheme can be replaced with a Groth-Sahai extractable commitment scheme. Given a bilinear group $(q, \mathbb{G}_1, \mathbb{G}_2, \mathbb{G}_T, e, g, h)$, a commitment to $x \in \mathbb{G}$ (either $\mathbb{G}_1$ or $\mathbb{G}_2$) with randomness r_x is denoted $\mathsf{Com}(x, r_x)$, and an extraction algorithm Extr takes as input the extraction key xk and a commitment C to return a group element.

The key component is a PRF that supports efficient NIZK proof that can *degenerate* into a unique signature scheme where they share the *same* tag. In general, the former helps achieve the anonymity security, where the tag has to

Alg GK(1^λ)	**Alg** GS$(gsk[i], m)$
$\quad (\mathsf{crs}, xk) \xleftarrow{\$} \text{Groth-Sahai.Gen}(1^\lambda)$	$\quad \tau \leftarrow g^{1/(s_i + m)}$
$\quad (vk, sk) \xleftarrow{\$} \mathcal{DS}.\text{Gen}(1^\lambda)$	$\quad C_s \xleftarrow{\$} \text{Com}(h^{s_i})$
$\quad gpk \leftarrow (\mathsf{crs}, vk)$	$\quad \theta \xleftarrow{\$} \text{Sig}(sk, h^{s_i})$
$\quad \textbf{for } i \leftarrow 1 \textbf{ to } n \textbf{ do}$	$\quad \textbf{return } (m, \tau, C_s, C_\theta, \pi_1, \pi_2)$
$\qquad s_i \xleftarrow{\$} \mathbb{Z}_q$	**Alg** GV(gpk, m, σ)
$\qquad \mathsf{cert}_i \xleftarrow{\$} \text{Sig}(sk, h^{s_i})$	$\quad \textbf{return } V_3((m, \tau, C_s), \pi_1) \wedge V_4(C_s, C_\theta, vk), \pi_2)$
$\qquad gsk[i] \leftarrow (s_i, \mathsf{cert}_i, gpk)$	**Alg** Open$(gpk, gmsk, m, \sigma)$
$\qquad reg[i] \leftarrow h^{s_i}$	$\quad \textbf{if } \text{GV}(gpk, m, \sigma) = 0 \textbf{ return } \bot$
$\quad gmsk \leftarrow (xk, \boldsymbol{reg})$	$\quad S' \leftarrow \text{Extr}(xk, C_s)$
$\quad \textbf{return } (gpk, gmsk, \boldsymbol{gsk})$	$\quad \textbf{if } S' = reg[i] \textbf{ then return } i$

Fig. 4. Efficient CPA-anonymous unique group signatures. Let V_3 and V_4 be the corresponding verification algorithms for the languages $\mathcal{L}_3$ and $\mathcal{L}_4$. The common reference string crs contains the bilinear map parameter $(q, \mathbb{G}_1, \mathbb{G}_2, \mathbb{G}_T, e, g, h)$ besides the Groth-Sahai proof parameter.

be random, while the latter is used to prove the uniqueness and traceability security, where the tag only needs to be unique and unpredictable.

Specifically, we make use of a *variant* of the PRF with NIZK proof proposed by Belenkiy et al. [3]. We define a language $\mathcal{L}_3 := \{(m, \tau, C_s) | \exists (s, r_s)[\tau = F_s(m)$ and $C_s = \text{Com}(h^s, r_s)]\}$, where $F_s(\cdot) := g^{1/(s + \cdot)}$. The corresponding NIZK proof π_1 is of the form $(C_\tau, \pi_\tau, C'_s, \pi_s, \pi')$, where C_τ is a commitment to τ and π_τ is a NIZK proof for that C_τ is a commitment to τ, C'_s is a commitment to h^s, π_s is a NIZK proof that C_s and C'_s are commitments to the same value, and π' is a witness-indistinguishable proof that C_τ is a commitment to $\bar{\tau}$, C'_s is a commitment to S such that $e(\bar{\tau}, Sh^m) = e(g, h)$. The above proof system is a NIZK proof system for $\mathcal{L}_3$ if DDHI assumption [9,3] holds and Groth-Sahai proof system is secure. As shown above, if we directly let group manager sign each secret key $s \in \mathbb{Z}_q$ (and add each s to $\boldsymbol{reg}$ which is part of $gmsk$) and run a corresponding NIZKPoK then we can get a CPA-anonymous unique group signature yet with relaxed uniqueness and traceability security. Still, this appears hard to find an efficient instantiation in the framework of Groth-Sahai proof system, since the secret s is a scalar rather a group element.

Note that we cannot as well expose the value h^s in the above PRF with NIZK proof system, because neither the above system would be zero-knowledge nor we are able to prove its security based on DDHI assumption. We can, however, degenerate the above PRF with NIZK proof to get a unique signature scheme, where one can view h^s as the public key and $g^{1/(s+m)}$ as the signature of m. Then, the manager can sign each h^s instead of s, and add h^s to $\boldsymbol{reg}$. Fortunately, we can show that uniqueness property and standard unforgeability security (rather than pseudorandomness) suffice to give the security of uniqueness and traceability. This prevents us from using rather strong assumptions such as SDDHI assumption [8] in bilinear groups. In fact, one can prove security of the unforgeability under DHI assumption [13] (with less tight reduction) or SDHI assumption that we formalize where the adversary is only asked to output a new message-signature pair (see the full version [15, Section 2.2]).

It remains to be shown how to choose the first-level signature. Recall that Groth-Sahai commitment, given the extraction trapdoor, can only extract group elements. The first solution is to use the F-unforgeable signature by Belenkiy et al. [2]. They proposed two F-unforgeable signature schemes, one of which has a simple structure, yet using an interactive assumption (i.e., interactive Hidden SDH assumption). We can build our scheme on this signature, while the security can be proven using a weaker and more natural non-interactive q-type assumption. The other is to employ a structure-preserving signature [1] that is only needed secure in the weak random message attack (e.g., one from [17]) to sign h^s directly. To be as general as possible, we let $\mathcal{DS} = (\mathsf{Gen}, \mathsf{Sig}, \mathsf{Vrf})$ be the first-level signature that can sign at least one group element and π_2 is a corresponding Groth-Sahai NIZK proof for the language $\mathcal{L}_4 := \{(C_s, C_\theta, vk) | \exists (S, r_s, \theta, r_\theta)[C_s = \mathsf{Com}(S, r_s)$, and $C_\theta = \mathsf{Com}(\theta, r_\theta)$, and $\mathsf{Vrf}(vk, S, \theta) = 1\}$. The construction is illustrated in Figure 4 and we have the following theorem.

Theorem 5. *The construction in Figure 4 is a CPA-anonymous unique group signature if DDHI and DHI (or SDHI) assumptions hold and Groth-Sahai proof system is secure, and the $\mathcal{DS}$ is structure-preserving and unforgeable under random message attack (or F-unforgeable under random message attack).* ∎

5   Unique Group Signature – Dynamic Setting

Similar to the construction of Section 4, the starting point for a CPA-anonymous unique group signature scheme in the dynamic setting is a two-level certification protocol (with the first-level signature $\mathcal{DS}_1$ and second-level signature $\mathcal{DS}_2$): the issuer signs the verification key of users, and the users can then sign their own messages. This process should be achieved in a zero-knowledge sense.

To make the signature *unique*, one can consider using a PRF F instead of a signature scheme at the second level. Moreover, an interactive protocol is used to get a signature of the secret PRF key s_i of user i under vk, without letting the issuer know the secret. To sign a message m, it computes $\tau := F_{s_i}(m)$, which we would like to use as the unique identifier. It then gets a NIZK proof of knowledge π that there exists a certification chain (s_i, cert_i) such that $\tau = F_{s_i}(m)$ and $\mathcal{DS}_1.\mathsf{Vrf}(vk, s_i, \mathsf{cert}_i) = 1$. The group signature is now (m, τ, π).

It is important that the issuer should not learn the PRF keys that it signs, or the issuer may now attack the CPA-anonymity by simply checking which of the PRF keys could have produced a given unique identifier. In general, we can resort to two-party secure computation. More efficiently, in order for the user i to get cert_i without letting the issuer know s_i (or g^{s_i}, for our construction), they can run a "signing on a committed value" protocol to get a certification of the secret, and user later makes a proof of knowledge of the signature. (They are known as "CL-signatures" [10], and signatures with non-interactive proofs of knowledge are termed as P-signatures [2]). However, this above process does not make the tracing and judging algorithm available. To solve this, we introduce a second chaining of two-level certification; namely, two new signature schemes $\mathcal{DS}_1'$ and $\mathcal{DS}_2'$ are selected. This time, we use Groth-Sahai commitments such

---

Alg GK(1^λ)

  $(vk, sk) \xleftarrow{\$} \mathcal{DS}_1.\text{Gen}(1^\lambda)$

  $(vk', sk') \xleftarrow{\$} \mathcal{DS}_1'\text{Gen}(1^\lambda)$

  $(\text{crs}, xk), (\text{crs}', xk') \xleftarrow{\$} \text{Groth-Sahai.Gen}(1^\lambda)$

  $(X_1, X_2, Y_1, Y_2) \xleftarrow{\$} \mathcal{TE}.\text{Gen}(\text{crs}, 1^\lambda)$

  $ek \leftarrow (X_1, X_2, Y_1, Y_2)$

  $gpk \leftarrow (\text{crs}, \text{crs}', vk, vk', ek, F)$

  $ik \leftarrow (sk, sk'); \; ok \leftarrow xk$

  return (gpk, ik, ok)

Alg Join/Issue (*user i, issuer*)

  $(user\; i : gpk, s_i, vk_i'sk_i')$

  $\leftrightharpoons (issuer : gpk, ik)$

  $gsk[i] \leftarrow (gpk, s_i, \text{cert}_i, sk_i', vk_i', \text{cert}_i')$

  $reg[i] \leftarrow vk_i'$

Alg GS($gsk[i], m$)

  $(vk_o, sk_o) \xleftarrow{\$} \mathcal{OT}.\text{Gen}(1^\lambda)$

  $\tau \leftarrow F_{s_i}(m); \; \phi \xleftarrow{\$} \mathcal{DS}_2'.\text{Sig}(sk_i', vk_o)$

  $\pi_1' \xleftarrow{\$} P_1'(\text{crs}', (gpk, m, \tau), (s_i, \text{cert}_i))$

  $\pi_2' \xleftarrow{\$} P_2'(\text{crs}, (gpk, vk_o), (sk_i', vk_i', \phi, \text{cert}_i'))$

  $C \xleftarrow{\$} \mathcal{TE}.\text{Enc}(ek, vk_o, \phi)$

  $\pi_3' \xleftarrow{\$} P_3'(\text{crs}, (gpk, C, \pi_2'))$

  $\phi_o \xleftarrow{\$} \mathcal{OT}.\text{Sig}(sk_o, (vk_o, m, C, \pi_1', \pi_2', \pi_3'))$

  $\sigma \leftarrow (vk_o, \tau, C, \pi_1', \pi_2', \pi_3', \phi_o)$

  return (m, σ)

Alg GV(gpk, m, σ)

  if $\mathcal{OT}.\text{Vrf}(vk_o, (vk_o, m, C, \pi_1', \pi_2', \pi_3'), \phi_o) = 1$

  and $V_1'(\text{crs}', (gpk, m, \tau), \pi_1') = 1$

  and $V_2'(\text{crs}, (gpk, vk_o), \pi_2') = 1$

  and $V_3'(\text{crs}, (gpk, C, \pi_2'), \pi_3') = 1$ **then**

  return 1

Alg Open($ok, gpk, (m, \sigma)$)

  $(vk^*, \sigma^*, \text{cert}^*) \leftarrow \text{Extr}(xk, \pi_2')$

  $\omega \leftarrow (vk^*, \sigma^*, \text{cert}^*)$

  if $vk^* = reg[i]$ **then return** (i, ω)

  return $(0, \omega)$

Alg Judge($gpk, (m, \sigma), (i, \omega)$)

  if GV(gpk, m, σ) = 1

  and $vk^* = reg[i]$

  and $\mathcal{DS}_1'.\text{Vrf}(vk', vk^*, \text{cert}^*) = 1$

  and $\mathcal{DS}_2'.\text{Vrf}(vk^*, vk_o, \sigma^*) = 1$ **then**

  return 1

Fig. 5. CCA-anonymous unique group signature—Dynamic Setting

that the witnesses can be extracted using the trapdoor given to the opener. Moreover, we can also use this chain to combine the technique of Groth [18] to achieve CCA anonymity. We call this technique "double-chaining certification".

OUR ALGORITHM. The CCA-anonymous unique group signature is illustrated in Figure 5. We define a PRF family $F: \mathcal{S} \times \mathcal{X} \to \mathcal{Y}$ with key space $\mathcal{S}$. Let $\mathcal{DS}_1$, $\mathcal{DS}_1'$, and $\mathcal{DS}_2'$ be three signature schemes, all of which are secure under adaptive chosen message attacks. Issuer runs $(vk, sk) \xleftarrow{\$} \mathcal{DS}_1.\text{Gen}(1^\lambda)$ and $(vk', sk') \xleftarrow{\$} \mathcal{DS}_1'.\text{Gen}(1^\lambda)$, where (vk, sk) is used to certify PRF keys, and (vk', sk') is used for double-chaining certification. Correspondingly, we use two Groth-Sahai proof systems with the same security parameter but with independently generated common reference strings (crs, xk) and (crs', xk')—the former for the double-chaining certification and the latter for certifying the PRF protocol and proving the knowledge of the corresponding signature. Let $\mathcal{OT}$ be a strong one-time signature scheme secure against weak chosen message attacks. Let $\mathcal{TE}$ be Kiltz's selective-tag weakly CCA-secure encryption scheme [20], with the public key compatible with Groth-Sahai proof system setup. (The secret keys of Kiltz's encryption and xk' can be safely discarded.) We write $\text{Enc}(ek, t, M)$ for the encryption of a message M under the public key ek and a tag t. User i and the issuer run an interactive Join/Issue protocol. This includes two steps. First, user i randomly picks its PRF key s_i; the user and issuer run a protocol on signing on committed value s_i, and finally the user gets a signature cert_i on s_i such that $\mathcal{DS}_1.\mathsf{Vrf}(vk, s_i, \mathsf{cert}_i) = 1$. Second, user i runs $(vk_i', sk_i') \overset{\$}{\leftarrow} \mathcal{DS}_2'.\mathsf{Gen}(1^\lambda)$, sends vk_i' to the issuers, and obtains a cert_i' such that $\mathcal{DS}_1'.\mathsf{Vrf}(vk', vk_i', \mathsf{cert}_i') = 1$. After the Join/Issue procedure, user will get its secret key $(s_i, \mathsf{cert}_i, sk_i', vk_i', \mathsf{cert}_i')$, while the issuer puts vk_i' to $reg[i]$. We now specify the three NIZK proof systems in a general NIZK framework. (P_1', V_1') is a NIZK proof system for a language $\mathcal{L}_1' := \{(gpk, m, \tau) | \exists (s, \mathsf{cert}) [\tau = F_s(m) \text{ and } \mathcal{DS}_1.\mathsf{Vrf}(vk, s, \mathsf{cert}) = 1]$. (P_2', V_2') is a NIZK proof system for a language $\mathcal{L}_2' := \{(gpk, vk_o) | \exists (\overline{vk'}, \phi', \mathsf{cert'}) [\mathcal{DS}_1'.\mathsf{Vrf}(vk', \overline{vk'}, \mathsf{cert'}) = 1 \text{ and } \mathcal{DS}_2'.\mathsf{Vrf}(\overline{vk'}, vk_o, \phi') = 1]$. (P_3', V_3') is a NIZK proof system that the plaintext of C and second-level signature in π_3' are the same (see [18]).

All of the primitives used in the above construction can be efficiently instantiated using Groth-Sahai proofs. In particular, the first chaining (including the signing on committed value protocol and $\mathcal{L}_1'$) can be achieved by combining the PRF with NIZK proof [3] and the P-signatures [2] (that relies on F-unforgeability). Clearly, we can use the technique in Section 4 (PRF with NIZK that can degenerate into unique signature) to improve the security as well as achieve extractability. $\mathcal{L}_2'$ can be instantiated using any structure-preserving signature combining any signature whose public keys are group elements. (Please refer the full version [15] for more efficient instantiation with concurrent-join.)

Theorem 6. *The construction illustrated in Figure 5 is a secure unique group signature (CCA-anonymous, dynamic setting).*   ∎

Acknowledgments. The authors would like to thank Sherman Chow and anonymous reviewers for their helpful and insightful comments.

References

1. Abe, M., Fuchsbauer, G., Groth, J., Haralambiev, K., Ohkubo, M.: Structure-Preserving Signatures and Commitments to Group Elements. In: Rabin, T. (ed.) CRYPTO 2010. LNCS, vol. 6223, pp. 209–236. Springer, Heidelberg (2010)
2. Belenkiy, M., Chase, M., Kohlweiss, M., Lysyanskaya, A.: P-signatures and Noninteractive Anonymous Credentials. In: Canetti, R. (ed.) TCC 2008. LNCS, vol. 4948, pp. 356–374. Springer, Heidelberg (2008)
3. Belenkiy, M., Chase, M., Kohlweiss, M., Lysyanskaya, A.: Compact E-Cash and Simulatable VRFs Revisited. In: Shacham, H., Waters, B. (eds.) Pairing 2009. LNCS, vol. 5671, pp. 114–131. Springer, Heidelberg (2009)
4. Bellare, M., Micciancio, D., Warinschi, B.: Foundations of Group Signatures: Formal Definitions, Simplified Requirements, and a Construction Based on General Assumptions. In: Biham, E. (ed.) EUROCRYPT 2003. LNCS, vol. 2656, pp. 614–629. Springer, Heidelberg (2003)
5. Bellare, M., Shi, H., Zhang, C.: Foundations of Group Signatures: The Case of Dynamic Groups. In: Menezes, A. (ed.) CT-RSA 2005. LNCS, vol. 3376, pp. 136–153. Springer, Heidelberg (2005)

6. Boneh, D., Boyen, X.: Short Signatures Without Random Oracles. In: Cachin, C., Camenisch, J.L. (eds.) EUROCRYPT 2004. LNCS, vol. 3027, pp. 56–73. Springer, Heidelberg (2004)

7. Boneh, D., Boyen, X., Shacham, H.: Short Group Signatures. In: Franklin, M. (ed.) CRYPTO 2004. LNCS, vol. 3152, pp. 41–55. Springer, Heidelberg (2004)

8. Camenisch, J., Hohenberger, S., Kohlweiss, M., Lysyanskaya, A., Meyerovich, M.: How to win the clone wars: efficient periodic n-times anonymous authentication. In: ACM CCS 2006, pp. 201–210. ACM (2006)

9. Camenisch, J.L., Hohenberger, S., Lysyanskaya, A.: Compact E-cash. In: Cramer, R. (ed.) EUROCRYPT 2005. LNCS, vol. 3494, pp. 302–321. Springer, Heidelberg (2005)

10. Camenisch, J.L., Lysyanskaya, A.: An Efficient System for Non-transferable Anonymous Credentials with Optional Anonymity Revocation. In: Pfitzmann, B. (ed.) EUROCRYPT 2001. LNCS, vol. 2045, pp. 93–118. Springer, Heidelberg (2001)

11. Chaum, D., van Heyst, E.: Group Signatures. In: Davies, D.W. (ed.) EUROCRYPT 1991. LNCS, vol. 547, pp. 257–265. Springer, Heidelberg (1991)

12. Damgård, I.B., Dupont, K., Pedersen, M.Ø.: Unclonable Group Identification. In: Vaudenay, S. (ed.) EUROCRYPT 2006. LNCS, vol. 4004, pp. 555–572. Springer, Heidelberg (2006)

13. Dodis, Y., Yampolskiy, A.: A Verifiable Random Function with Short Proofs and Keys. In: Vaudenay, S. (ed.) PKC 2005. LNCS, vol. 3386, pp. 416–431. Springer, Heidelberg (2005)

14. Even, S., Goldreich, O., Micali, S.: On-Line/Off-Line Digital Signatures. In: Brassard, G. (ed.) CRYPTO 1989. LNCS, vol. 435, pp. 263–275. Springer, Heidelberg (1990)

15. Franklin, M., Zhang, H.: Unique group signatures. Full version. Cryptology ePrint Archive: Report 2012/204, http://eprint.iacr.org

16. Fuchsbauer, G.: Automorphic signatures in bilinear groups and an application to round-optimal blind signatures. Cryptology ePrint Archive: Report 2009/320

17. Green, M., Hohenberger, S.: Universally Composable Adaptive Oblivious Transfer. In: Pieprzyk, J. (ed.) ASIACRYPT 2008. LNCS, vol. 5350, pp. 179–197. Springer, Heidelberg (2008)

18. Groth, J.: Fully Anonymous Group Signatures Without Random Oracles. In: Kurosawa, K. (ed.) ASIACRYPT 2007. LNCS, vol. 4833, pp. 164–180. Springer, Heidelberg (2007)

19. Groth, J., Sahai, A.: Efficient Non-interactive Proof Systems for Bilinear Groups. In: Smart, N.P. (ed.) EUROCRYPT 2008. LNCS, vol. 4965, pp. 415–432. Springer, Heidelberg (2008)

20. Kiltz, E.: Chosen-Ciphertext Security from Tag-Based Encryption. In: Halevi, S., Rabin, T. (eds.) TCC 2006. LNCS, vol. 3876, pp. 581–600. Springer, Heidelberg (2006)

21. Micali, S., Rabin, M., Vadhan, S.: Verifiable random functions, pp. 120–130. IEEE Computer Society (1999)

22. Nguyen, L., Safavi-Naini, R.: Dynamic k-Times Anonymous Authentication. In: Ioannidis, J., Keromytis, A.D., Yung, M. (eds.) ACNS 2005. LNCS, vol. 3531, pp. 318–333. Springer, Heidelberg (2005)

23. Teranishi, I., Furukawa, J., Sako, K.: k-Times Anonymous Authentication (Extended Abstract). In: Lee, P.J. (ed.) ASIACRYPT 2004. LNCS, vol. 3329, pp. 308–322. Springer, Heidelberg (2004)

24. Teranishi, I., Sako, K.: k-Times Anonymous Authentication with a Constant Proving Cost. In: Yung, M., Dodis, Y., Kiayias, A., Malkin, T. (eds.) PKC 2006. LNCS, vol. 3958, pp. 525–542. Springer, Heidelberg (2006)

Relations among Notions of Privacy for RFID Authentication Protocols

Daisuke Moriyama, Shin'ichiro Matsuo, and Miyako Ohkubo

National Institute of Information and Communications Technology, Japan
{dmoriyam,smatsuo,m.ohkubo}@nict.go.jp

Abstract. In this paper, we present the relationship between privacy definitions for Radio Frequency Identification (RFID) authentication protocols. The security model is necessary for ensuring security or privacy, but many researchers present different privacy concepts for RFID authentication and the technical relationship among them is unclear. We reconsider the zero-knowledge based privacy proposed by Deng et al. at ESORICS 2010 and show that this privacy is equivalent to indistinguishability based privacy proposed by Juels and Weis. We also provide the implication and separation between these privacy definitions and the simulation based privacy proposed by Paise and Vaudenay at AsiaCCS 2008 based on the *public verifiability* of the communication message.

1 Introduction

Radio Frequency Identification (RFID) technology enables the reader to identify objects. RFID systems consist of a reader and many tags. The reader communicates with the tags over the wireless (insecure) channel and checks the identity. RFID is expected to replace barcodes and is now used in many industries (manufacturing, transportation, logistics, etc.). However, the existing low-cost tags only contain the identity with no protection and respond with their identity directly when the reader provides electric power. Many cryptographers have studied the RFID authentication protocol to overcome the privacy problem. This privacy-preserving RFID authentication protocol improves the reliability of the machine-to-machine network system and also ensures the secure transaction.

In cryptography, the security/privacy of each scheme or protocol is evaluated by the security model. There are several security models for RFID authentication protocols [6,5,9,10,12,15,14,18]. All of which define three components: correctness, security and privacy. The correctness and security definitions are almost the same in these models. Correctness ensures that the reader accepts the tag if the reader and tag correctly communicate with each other. Security requires that if a malicious adversary impersonates a valid tag and interferes the communication, the reader rejects the session. However, the privacy notion is not commonly defined and the relationship between them is unclear. In this paper, we concentrate on the privacy definitions for the RFID authentication protocol and investigate the relationship.

S. Foresti, M. Yung, and F. Martinelli (Eds.): ESORICS 2012, LNCS 7459, pp. 661–678, 2012.
© Springer-Verlag Berlin Heidelberg 2012

Our Contributions. Our contributions are twofold:

1. We show that the indistinguishability based privacy definition (IND-privacy) proposed by Juels and Weis [12] and zero-knowledge based privacy definition (ZK-privacy) proposed by Deng et al. [9] are equivalent. Though Deng et al. proved that zero-knowledge based privacy is stronger than indistinguishability based privacy, we show that their argument is inadequate and these privacy definitions are proven to be equivalent.

2. We investigate the relationship between indistinguishability based privacy and simulation based privacy (SIM-privacy) proposed by Paise and Vaudenay [18]. There are many existing RFID authentication protocols that are secure in one of the two security models or its slight variants [11,17], but no one investigates whether there exists a technical difference between [12] and [18], except the trivial separation followed by the corruption timing. These privacy definitions are formalized in a different style and it is hard to present the difference directly. Hence, we consider a variant of the zero-knowledge based privacy proposed in [9] in order to reduce the gap between them (this variant is polynomially equivalent to the Juels-Weis security model). We then compare the resulting privacy definition with [18]. We introduce a notion of public and secret verifiability to the RFID authentication. Roughly speaking, the public verifiability holds if anyone can check the authenticity of an entity from the communication message (note that the tag must be secret verifiable from correctness and privacy). Our result is that there is a technical gap between IND-privacy and SIM-privacy if the communication message is publicly verifiable. Otherwise, we prove that these privacy definitions are equivalent (if the restriction for the tag corruption is equivalent).

Related Work. The privacy definition for RFID authentication is roughly divided into the following: indistinguishability [4,12,11], simulatability [21,18], zero-knowledge [9], unpredictability [10,15] and universal composability [6,5,14] (see [8] for more information). The unpredictability based privacy model [10,15] requires that, at least, the tag's response to the reader is indistinguishable from the random string. Ma et al. [15] showed that (1) the unpredictability based privacy model requires strictly stronger privacy than the indistinguishability based privacy model [12], and (2) the existence of an RFID authentication protocol that satisfies the unpredictability based privacy model equals the existence of a pseudo-random function. This function is used in many lightweight RFID authentication protocols, but we consider unpredictability based privacy too strong to satisfy privacy. For example, if both the reader and tag can perform IND-CCA2 secure public key encryption and all communication is encrypted by each party's public key, then the communication reveals none of the secret information. However, the ciphertext usually consists of group elements and is easily distinguishable from random string.

The universal composability based privacy model [6,5,14] requires a simulator to simulate any actions of the malicious adversary and no external environment should be able to distinguish whether it interacts with the adversary or the simulator. The authors did not describe the relationship between their model and the other privacy model, but Paise and Vaudenay demonstrated the RFID authentication protocol depicted in [6] does not have the narrow-forward privacy present in the Paise-Vaudenay privacy model [18].

2   Existing RFID Security Models

We review security models proposed by Juels-Weis [12], Deng-Li-Yung-Zhao [9] and Paise-Vaudenay [18], respectively. We use the following notations in this paper. We denote by $\mathcal{T}$ the total set of tags in the RFID authentication protocol that is managed by the reader $\mathcal{R}$. The reader runs the Setup algorithm and obtains (pk, sk). The public parameter pk is published and secret key sk is kept as a secret. If the RFID authentication protocol is based on symmetric key cryptography, each tag shares several secret keys with the reader (sk contains the set of these secret keys). In the authentication phase, the reader and the tag communicate with each other via wireless communication. We consider an active adversary $\mathcal{A}$ that can interfere/insert/delete/modify the communication message and its direction. The RFID authentication protocol requires correctness, security and privacy. Roughly speaking, correctness defines that the reader always outputs "accept" if the communication is not modified by the adversary. Security requires that the reader rejects the session if the adversary interferes and modifies the outgoing message. In the following, we concentrate on the privacy definition in the security model and call privacy model.

2.1   Juels-Weis Privacy Model

Juels and Weis proposed a privacy model for RFID authentication protocols based on indistinguishability [12]. We show a slight variant of the privacy model modified by Deng et al. [9]. Based on the IND-CPA definition for public/symmetric key encryption, this model evaluates the probability that an adversary correctly distinguishes the identity of the tag when he interacts with the reader and tags. The privacy game between an adversary $\mathcal{A} := (\mathcal{A}_1, \mathcal{A}_2)$ and challenger is defined as follows:

Setup. The challenger runs the Setup algorithm and obtains (pk, sk) to setup the reader $\mathcal{R}$ and set of tags $\mathcal{T}$. The adversary obtains public parameter pk and $(\mathcal{R}, \mathcal{T})$.

Phase 1. The adversary $\mathcal{A}_1$ can issue oracle queries $\mathcal{O} := \{$Launch, SendReader, SendTag, Result, Corrupt$\}$ and interact with the reader and tags:

   Launch(1^k) — Launch the reader to initiate the session.

   SendReader(m) — Send arbitrary message m to the reader.

   SendTag(t, m) — Send arbitrary message m to the tag $t \in \mathcal{T}$.

   Result(sid) — Output whether the reader accepts the session sid (sid is uniquely determined by the communication message).

   Corrupt(t) — Output the secret key of the tag t.

Challenge. The adversary $\mathcal{A}_1$ sends two tags t_0^* and t_1^* ($t_0^* \neq t_1^*$) to the challenger and outputs state information st_1. st_1 contains all information obtained by $\mathcal{A}_1$ including internal coin tosses of $\mathcal{A}_1$. Then the challenger flips a coin $b \overset{U}{\leftarrow} \{0,1\}$ and sets $\mathcal{T}' := \mathcal{T} \setminus \{t_0^*, t_1^*\}$.

Phase 2. The adversary $\mathcal{A}_2$ obtains st_1 and interacts with the reader $\mathcal{R}$ and tags $(t_b^*, \mathcal{T}')$ with the oracle queries. However, when the adversary interacts with the challenge tag t_b^*, we consider special algorithm $\mathcal{I}$. $\mathcal{I}$ relays the message between $\mathcal{A}$ and t_b^* so that the adversary communicates with t_b^* anonymously.

Guess. The adversary $\mathcal{A}_2$ outputs a guess b'.

We say that the adversary wins the game if $b' = b$ holds and (t_0^*, t_1^*) is not corrupted. The advantage of the adversary in the above game is defined as $\mathsf{Adv}_{\Pi,\mathcal{A}}^{\mathsf{IND}}(k) := |2 \cdot \Pr[b' = b] - 1|$. The following experiment also evaluates this advantage.

$$\underline{\mathsf{Exp}_{\Pi,\mathcal{A}}^{\mathsf{IND}\text{-}b}(k)}$$
$(pk, sk) \overset{R}{\leftarrow} \mathsf{Setup}(1^k);$
$(t_0^*, t_1^*, st_1) \overset{R}{\leftarrow} \mathcal{A}_1^{\mathcal{O}}(pk, \mathcal{R}, \mathcal{T});$
$b \overset{U}{\leftarrow} \{0,1\}, \mathcal{T}' := \mathcal{T} \setminus \{t_0^*, t_1^*\};$
$b' \overset{R}{\leftarrow} \mathcal{A}_2^{\mathcal{O}}(\mathcal{R}, \mathcal{T}', \mathcal{I}(t_b^*), st_1):$
Output b'

We have $\mathsf{Adv}_{\Pi,\mathcal{A}}^{\mathsf{IND}}(k) = |\Pr[\mathsf{Exp}_{\Pi,\mathcal{A}}^{\mathsf{IND}\text{-}0}(k) \to 1] - \Pr[\mathsf{Exp}_{\Pi,\mathcal{A}}^{\mathsf{IND}\text{-}1}(k) \to 1]|$.

Definition 1. *An RFID authentication protocol Π satisfies the privacy in the Juels-Wies security model if for any probabilistic polynomial time (PPT) adversary $\mathcal{A}$, $\mathsf{Adv}_{\Pi,\mathcal{A}}^{\mathsf{IND}}(k)$ is negligible.*

2.2   Deng-Li-Yung-Zhao Privacy Model

The privacy model proposed by Deng et al. is based on a zero-knowledge formulation [9]. The intuition behind this model is that when the communication message does not reveal any tag's identity or secret key, the messages should be simulated even if an algorithm cannot interact with the tag.

We consider two experiments $\mathsf{Exp}_{\mathcal{A},\mathcal{D}}^{\mathsf{ZK}\text{-}0}(k)$ and $\mathsf{Exp}_{\mathcal{S},\mathcal{D}}^{\mathsf{ZK}\text{-}1}(k)$. In the former , the adversary $\mathcal{A}$ interacts with the reader and tags. $\mathcal{A}$ outputs an arbitrary subset of tags $\mathcal{C} \subseteq \mathcal{T}$ and the challenger uniformly chooses a challenge tag $t^* \overset{U}{\leftarrow} \mathcal{C}$ at random. The adversary can then interact with $\mathcal{R}$, tags $\mathcal{T}' := \mathcal{T} \setminus \mathcal{C}$ and the challenge tag t^* anonymously. When the adversary sends message m to $\mathcal{I}$, this algorithm passes m to t^* and responds with the output from t^*. Finally the adversary outputs its view and a distinguisher outputs a bit b with the view. The latter experiment is the same as the former except that the simulator $\mathcal{S}$ cannot interact with the challenge tag. We note that the adversary and simulator cannot issue any corrupt queries to the tags in $\mathcal{C}$ in the experiment. These experiments are depicted as follows:

$\mathsf{Exp}_{\Pi,\mathcal{A},\mathcal{D}}^{\mathsf{ZK\text{-}0}}(k)$	$\mathsf{Exp}_{\Pi,\mathcal{S},\mathcal{D}}^{\mathsf{ZK\text{-}1}}(k)$
$(pk, sk) \xleftarrow{\text{R}} \mathsf{Setup}(1^k);$	$(pk, sk) \xleftarrow{\text{R}} \mathsf{Setup}(1^k);$
$(\mathcal{C}, st_1) \xleftarrow{\text{R}} \mathcal{A}_1^{\mathcal{O}}(pk, \mathcal{R}, \mathcal{T});$	$(\mathcal{C}, st_1) \xleftarrow{\text{R}} \mathcal{S}_1^{\mathcal{O}}(pk, \mathcal{R}, \mathcal{T});$
$t^* \xleftarrow{\text{U}} \mathcal{C}, \mathcal{T}' := \mathcal{T} \setminus \mathcal{C};$	$t^* \xleftarrow{\text{U}} \mathcal{C}, \mathcal{T}' := \mathcal{T} \setminus \mathcal{C};$
$view_{\mathcal{A}} \xleftarrow{\text{R}} \mathcal{A}_2^{\mathcal{O}}(\mathcal{R}, \mathcal{T}', \mathcal{I}(t^*), st_1);$	$view_{\mathcal{S}} \xleftarrow{\text{R}} \mathcal{S}_2^{\mathcal{O}}(\mathcal{R}, \mathcal{T}', st_1);$
$b \xleftarrow{\text{R}} \mathcal{D}(\mathcal{C}, t^*, view_{\mathcal{A}}):$	$b \xleftarrow{\text{R}} \mathcal{D}(\mathcal{C}, t^*, view_{\mathcal{S}}):$
Output b	Output b

The advantage of the adversary in this model is defined by $\mathsf{Adv}_{\Pi,\mathcal{A},\mathcal{S},\mathcal{D}}^{\mathsf{ZK}}(k) = |\Pr[\mathsf{Exp}_{\Pi,\mathcal{A},\mathcal{D}}^{\mathsf{ZK\text{-}0}}(k) \to 1] - \Pr[\mathsf{Exp}_{\Pi,\mathcal{S},\mathcal{D}}^{\mathsf{ZK\text{-}1}}(k) \to 1]|.$

Definition 2. *An RFID authentication protocol Π satisfies the privacy in the Deng et al. security model if for any PPT adversary $\mathcal{A}$, there exists a PPT algorithm $\mathcal{S}$, for any PPT distinguisher $\mathcal{D}$, $\mathsf{Adv}_{\Pi,\mathcal{A},\mathcal{S},\mathcal{D}}^{\mathsf{ZK}}(k)$ is negligible.*

2.3 Paise-Vaudenay Privacy Model

Vaudenay [21] proposed a simulation based privacy model for two-pass RFID authentication protocols. Paise and Vaudenay [18] extended this to satisfy reader authentication. The intuition behind these privacy models is that if the protocol messages are completely simulated by a third party, the privacy of the RFID tag is preserved since the adversary obtains no private information. The privacy game of their model is slightly similar to the Deng et al. privacy model, but the game flow is not explicitly defined. Instead, the adversary can additionally issue the following queries:

CreateTag(ID,s) — Register a free tag to the reader. If the tag is legitimate ($s = 1$), the reader assigns the secret key for this tag and updates the database.
DrawTag($\mathcal{C}$, Dist) — According to the distribution Dist and the arbitrary sets of tags $\mathcal{C} \subseteq \mathcal{T}$, the oracle responds with drawn tags $\mathcal{V} := \{\mathsf{vtag}_1, \ldots\}$. The oracle keeps a list list that maps the drawn tags to the real identity.
Free(vtag) — Change the drawn tag vtag to the free tag.

In their model, the challenger assigns a temporal identity to each drawn tag. The adversary can issue the SendTag query to the drawn tags only, and free tags do not execute the communication to the reader.

Paise and Vaudenay classifies the adversary's capacity into 2×4 categories.

1. Result query for the reader:
   (a) *Wide* — Adversary can issue the result query.
   (b) *Narrow* — Adversary cannot issue the result query.
2. Corrupt query for the tag:
   (a) *Strong* — No restriction for the corrupt query.
   (b) *Destructive* — If the adversary issues the corrupt query to a drawn tag, the tag is destroyed and unusable.

(c) *Forward* — After the corrupt query, the adversary cannot issue any other queries in the experiment.

(d) *Weak* — The adversary cannot issue the corrupt query.

For example, wide-strong privacy is defined as follows. Consider the two sets of the oracle queries $\mathcal{O}_1 := \{\mathsf{CreateTag}, \mathsf{DrawTag}, \mathsf{Free}, \mathsf{Corrupt}\}$ and $\mathcal{O}_2 := \{\mathsf{Launch}, \mathsf{SendReader}, \mathsf{SendTag}, \mathsf{Result}\}$. The wide-strong privacy game in this model is defined by the following experiments:

$\mathsf{Exp}_{\Pi,\mathcal{A}}^{\mathsf{SIM\text{-}0}}(k)$	$\mathsf{Exp}_{\Pi,\mathcal{A},\mathcal{S}}^{\mathsf{SIM\text{-}1}}(k)$
$(pk, sk) \xleftarrow{\mathsf{R}} \mathsf{Setup}(1^k);$	$(pk, sk) \xleftarrow{\mathsf{R}} \mathsf{Setup}(1^k);$
$b \xleftarrow{\mathsf{R}} \mathcal{A}^{\mathcal{O}_1, \mathcal{O}_2}(pk, \mathcal{R}):$	$b \xleftarrow{\mathsf{R}} \mathcal{A}^{\mathcal{O}_1, \mathcal{S}(pk)}(pk):$
Output b	Output b

In the SIM-0 experiment, adversary $\mathcal{A}$ can create tags and interact with the reader and tags through $\mathcal{O}_2$ query. On the contrary, the SIM-1 experiment requires that simulator $\mathcal{S}$ responds to the adversary's oracle queries which correspond to $\mathcal{O}_2$ query. $\mathcal{S}$ can learn any information $\mathcal{A}$ obtains with $\mathcal{O}_1$ query. The advantage of the adversary is defined by $\mathsf{Adv}_{\Pi,\mathcal{A},\mathcal{S}}^{\mathsf{SIM}}(k) := |\Pr[\mathsf{Exp}_{\Pi,\mathcal{A}}^{\mathsf{SIM\text{-}0}}(k) \to 1] - \Pr[\mathsf{Exp}_{\Pi,\mathcal{A},\mathcal{S}}^{\mathsf{SIM\text{-}1}}(k) \to 1]|$. Of course, we can formalize the other types of adversary in the same fashion.

Definition 3. *An RFID authentication protocol Π satisfies the (wide/ narrow)-(strong/destructive/forward/weak) privacy in the Paise- Vaudenay security model if for any PPT adversary $\mathcal{A}$, there exists a PPT algorithm $\mathcal{S}$, $\mathsf{Adv}_{\Pi,\mathcal{A},\mathcal{S}}^{\mathsf{SIM}}(k)$ is negligible.*

In this paper, we slightly modify the restriction on the DrawTag query and assume that the adversary can only input legitimate tags for this query[1].

3   Equivalence between IND and ZK Privacy

The previous section described the three privacy models. Deng et al. [9] showed that their ZK-privacy is stronger than IND-privacy; that is, there exist two examples of the RFID authentication protocols that are secure in the Juels-Weis privacy model but insecure in the zero-knowledge based privacy model. However, we will show that these privacy models are proven to be equivalent. To justify our result, we first review their examples and point out the *flaw* of their argument.

The former example is constructed by a digital signature scheme. In the setup phase, a reader generates signing/verification key pair $(sk_{\mathsf{SIG}}, vk_{\mathsf{SIG}})$ and sends the signature of the tag's identity $\sigma_i \xleftarrow{\mathsf{R}} \mathsf{Sign}(sk_{\mathsf{SIG}}, t_i)$ as a secret key. To authenticate the tag, the reader outputs a request message and the tag responds with

---

[1] Otherwise, the wide-destructive privacy implies the existence of the simulator that can predict the coin tosses of the adversary [21]. To avoid such an unusual situation, Ng et al. formalized another approach s.t. the adversary does not issue oracle queries where the result is predetermined [16].

σ_i itself. Deng et al. argued that *"If the system has only one tag, it is clear to satisfy the IND-privacy but the simulator cannot simulate the signature at Phase 2 in the ZK-privacy"*. But we note that this implication does not make sense. As we explicitly describe in Section 2.1, IND-privacy assumes that the adversary must output two different tags (which is also implicitly assumed in the IND-CPA security for public key encryption). Thus their instantiation is inadequate in considering the IND-privacy. If we consider there are more than two tags in the system, it is clear that the adversary against IND-privacy can distinguish the message since the output of the tag's message is deterministically defined.

The building block of the latter example is the public key encryption scheme (Gen, Enc, Dec) and an RFID authentication protocol Π that holds IND-privacy. Following [9], we assume that when the reader sends a to the tag, it responds with b to the reader in Π. They described the following RFID authentication protocol Π'. In the setup phase, a reader generates a public/secret key pair $(pk_{\mathsf{PKE}}, sk_{\mathsf{PKE}}) \overset{R}{\leftarrow} \mathsf{Gen}(1^k)$ and sends sk_{PKE} to the tags (we remark that all tags in this protocol shares this unique secret key) as a secret key for Π'. When the reader authenticates the tag, it generates a and sends encrypted message $c \overset{R}{\leftarrow} \mathsf{Enc}(pk_{\mathsf{PKE}}, a)$. If the tag receives the message, it decrypts as $a := \mathsf{Dec}(sk_{\mathsf{PKE}}, c)$, generates b with Π and responds $a\|b$ to the reader. Deng et al. said that Π' satisfies IND-privacy and does not satisfy ZK-privacy since no simulator can output the decryption of the ciphertext. However, we found that this argument is also wrong and Π' still holds ZK-privacy. Since the communication message is indistinguishable, simulator $\mathcal{S}_1$ can internally run zero-knowledge adversary $(\mathcal{A}_1, \mathcal{A}_2)$. It is easy to see that $\mathcal{S}_1$ simulates all communication message for $\mathcal{A}_1$. When $\mathcal{A}_1$ outputs $(\mathcal{C}, st_1)$, $\mathcal{S}_1$ uniformly chooses $t_1^* \overset{U}{\leftarrow} \mathcal{C}$ and runs $\mathcal{A}_2$ with input $(pk, \mathcal{R}, \mathcal{T} \setminus \mathcal{C}, \mathcal{I}(t_1^*), st_1)$. Note that t_1^* may not be identical to the challenge tag, but IND-privacy ensures that no adversary can distinguish whether it interacts with the challenge tag or t_1^*. If $\mathcal{A}_2$ sends a message to the challenge tag, $\mathcal{S}_1$ simply sends it to t_1^* and responds with its message. When $\mathcal{A}_2$ outputs $view_{\mathcal{A}}$, then $\mathcal{S}_1$ sets $st_1' := view_{\mathcal{A}}$ and outputs $(\mathcal{C}, st_1')$. Finally, $\mathcal{S}_2$ outputs st_1' as its view regardless of the choice of challenge tag. Since the simulator can continue Phase 1 until the adversary outputs the view (Phase 1 and 2 for the adversary), these outputs are indistinguishable for any distinguisher $\mathcal{D}$. Of course, if we try to simulate the response of the SendTag query issued by $\mathcal{A}_2$ with $\mathcal{S}_2$, it is difficult to construct such a simulator since $\mathcal{S}_2$ must break the security for public key encryption. The key point here is that IND-privacy allows $\mathcal{S}_1$ to simulate the whole behavior of the ZK-privacy adversary $(\mathcal{A}_1, \mathcal{A}_2)$.

We now show that IND-privacy is equivalent to ZK-privacy.

Theorem 1. *The indistinguishability based privacy model is equivalent to the zero-knowledge based privacy model.*

Lemma 1. *If an RFID authentication protocol Π holds IND-privacy, it implies ZK-privacy.*

Proof. We prove the above lemma via the following sequence of games. We gradually change the ZK-0 experiment to ZK-1 experiment which is bounded by IND-privacy. Especially, we show that if for any IND-privacy adversary $\mathcal{B}$, $\mathsf{Adv}_{\Pi,\mathcal{B}}^{\mathsf{IND}}(k)$ is negligible, then for any ZK-privacy adversary $\mathcal{A}$, there exists a simulator $\mathcal{S}$, for any distinguisher $\mathcal{D}$, $\mathsf{Adv}_{\Pi,\mathcal{A},\mathcal{S},\mathcal{D}}^{\mathsf{ZK}}(k)$ is negligible.

For each game, $\Pr[T_j]$ denotes the probability that the distinguisher outputs 1 in Game j.

Game 0: Game 0 is the same as the original ZK-privacy game between a challenger and $\mathcal{A}\mathcal{D}$ Without loss of generality, we assume that $t_0^* \xleftarrow{U} \mathcal{C}$ is chosen as the challenge tag. It is clear that $\Pr[T_0] = \Pr[\mathsf{Exp}_{\Pi,\mathcal{A},\mathcal{D}}^{\mathsf{ZK\text{-}0}}(k) \to 1]$.

Game 1: We modify Game 1 by changing the challenge tag. In addition to t_0^*, we select $t_1^* \xleftarrow{U} \mathcal{C}$ and the adversary (anonymously) interacts with t_1^* instead of t_0^*.

Game 2: Game 2 is the original ZK-privacy game between a challenger and $\mathcal{S}$ under the condition that $\mathcal{S}$ runs $\mathcal{A}$ as in Fig. 1. Note that the challenge tag is chosen as Game 0 and the input to the distinguisher is t_0^*.

$\mathcal{S}_1^{\mathcal{O}}(pk, \mathcal{R}, \mathcal{T})$	$\mathcal{S}_2(\mathcal{R}, \mathcal{T}', st_1')$
$(\mathcal{C}, st_1) \xleftarrow{R} \mathcal{A}_1^{\mathcal{O}}(pk, \mathcal{R}, \mathcal{T});$	$view_{\mathcal{S}} := view_{\mathcal{A}}:$
$t_1^* \xleftarrow{U} \mathcal{C}, \mathcal{T}' := \mathcal{T} \setminus \mathcal{C};$	Output $view_{\mathcal{S}}$
$view_{\mathcal{A}} \xleftarrow{R} \mathcal{A}_2^{\mathcal{O}}(\mathcal{R}, \mathcal{T}', \mathcal{I}(t_1^*), st_1);$	
$st_1' := view_{\mathcal{A}}:$	
Output $(\mathcal{C}, st_1')$	

Fig. 1. Simulation in Game 2

We evaluate the gaps between pairs of advantages with the following claims.

Claim. There exists a PPT algorithm $\mathcal{B}$ such that

$$|\Pr[T_1] - \Pr[T_0]| \leq \mathsf{Adv}_{\Pi,\mathcal{B}}^{\mathsf{IND}}(k).$$

Proof. If $(\mathcal{A}, \mathcal{D})$ distinguishes Game 0 and Game 1 with non-negligible probability, we construct an algorithm $\mathcal{B} := (\mathcal{B}_1, \mathcal{B}_2)$ that can break the IND-privacy. $\mathcal{B}$ internally runs $(\mathcal{A}, \mathcal{D})$ in the IND-privacy game as follows:

$\mathcal{B}_1^{\mathcal{O}}(pk, \mathcal{R}, \mathcal{T})$	$\mathcal{B}_2^{\mathcal{O}}(pk, \mathcal{I}(t_b^*), st_1')$
$(\mathcal{C}, st_1) \xleftarrow{R} \mathcal{A}_1^{\mathcal{O}}(pk, \mathcal{R}, \mathcal{T});$	$view_{\mathcal{A}} \xleftarrow{R} \mathcal{A}_2^{\mathcal{O}}(\mathcal{R}, \mathcal{T}', \mathcal{I}(t_b^*), st_1);$
$t_0^*, t_1^* \xleftarrow{U} \mathcal{C}, \ \mathcal{T}' := \mathcal{T} \setminus \mathcal{C};$	$b' \xleftarrow{R} \mathcal{D}(\mathcal{C}, t_0^*, view_{\mathcal{A}}):$
$st_1' := (\mathcal{T}', t_0^*, st_1):$	Output b'
Output (t_0^*, t_1^*, st_1')	

When the adversary $\mathcal{A}_1$ outputs $\mathcal{C}$, $\mathcal{B}_1$ chooses two tags (t_0^*, t_1^*) in $\mathcal{C}$ and sends it to the challenger. Since the challenger chooses a coin $b \stackrel{U}{\leftarrow} \{0, 1\}$ and $\mathcal{B}_2$ can access $\mathcal{I}(t_b^*)$, the SendTag query that $\mathcal{A}_2$ issues to the challenge tag can be completely simulated. If the flipped coin is $b = 0$, the output distribution is the same as Game 0. Otherwise, this simulation is equivalent to Game 1. Therefore, we obtain

$$|\Pr[T_1] - \Pr[T_0]| \leq \left| \mathsf{Adv}_{\Pi,\mathcal{B}}^{\mathsf{IND}\text{-}1}(k) - \mathsf{Adv}_{\Pi,\mathcal{B}}^{\mathsf{IND}\text{-}0}(k) \right|$$
$$= \mathsf{Adv}_{\Pi,\mathcal{B}}^{\mathsf{IND}}(k).$$

Claim. We have $\Pr[T_2] = \Pr[T_1]$.

Proof. We show that the output distribution of $\mathcal{A}$ in Game 1 is equivalent to that of $\mathcal{S}$ in Game 2. Recall that $\mathcal{S}_2$ cannot interact with the challenge tag in the original ZK-privacy experiment. Nevertheless, the previous claim shows that the anonymous interaction between $\mathcal{A}_2$ and t_0^* can be changed by another tag t_1^*. This means that even if $\mathcal{S}_1$ chooses another tag $t_1^* \in \mathcal{C}$ and replaces the anonymous interaction by $\mathcal{I}(t_1^*)$, $\mathcal{A}_2$ cannot distinguish between the games. Therefore $\mathcal{S}_1$ can simulate $(\mathcal{A}_1, \mathcal{A}_2)$ as in Fig.1 and obtain the view of the adversary $view_{\mathcal{A}}$. Any oracle queries made by $(\mathcal{A}_1, \mathcal{A}_2)$ can be simulated correctly since $\mathcal{S}_1$ can send the same query to $\mathcal{O}$. Thus $\mathcal{A}_2$'s output in Game 1 is equivalent to $\mathcal{S}_2$'s output in Game 2 and it is (information theoretically) indistinguishable for any distinguisher $\mathcal{D}$. Therefore we have $\Pr[T_2] = \Pr[T_1]$.

It is clear that $\Pr[T_2] = \Pr[\mathsf{Exp}_{\Pi,\mathcal{S},\mathcal{D}}^{\mathsf{ZK}\text{-}1}(k) \rightarrow 1]$ and finally we have

$$\mathsf{Adv}_{\Pi,\mathcal{A},\mathcal{S},\mathcal{D}}^{\mathsf{ZK}}(k) = |\mathsf{Exp}_{\Pi,\mathcal{A},\mathcal{D}}^{\mathsf{ZK}\text{-}0}(k) - \mathsf{Exp}_{\Pi,\mathcal{S},\mathcal{D}}^{\mathsf{ZK}\text{-}1}(k)|$$
$$= |\Pr[T_2] - \Pr[T_0]|$$
$$\leq \mathsf{Adv}_{\Pi,\mathcal{B}}^{\mathsf{IND}}(k).$$

Remark. If the zero-knowledge adversary sets $\mathcal{C}$ as only one tag, then we can directly transform Game 0 to Game 2. The strategy of the simulator is the same as in Fig. 1. The simulator issues the SendTag query in Phase 1 until the zero-knowledge adversary finishes the experiment.

Lemma 2. *If an RFID authentication protocol Π holds ZK-privacy, it implies IND-privacy.*

Remark that this lemma has been provided by Deng et al. [9], but their proof is *informal*. So we give the rigorous security proof based on the game transformation technique.

Proof. Again, we prove the above lemma via the following sequence of games. We show that if for any ZK adversary $\mathcal{B}$, there exists a simulator $\mathcal{S}$, for any distinguisher $\mathcal{D}$, $\mathsf{Adv}_{\Pi,\mathcal{B},\mathcal{S},\mathcal{D}}^{\mathsf{ZK}}(k)$ is negligible, then for any IND adversary $\mathcal{A}$, $\mathsf{Adv}_{\Pi,\mathcal{A}}^{\mathsf{IND}}(k)$ is negligible. For each game, $\Pr[T_j]$ denotes the probability that the experiment outputs 1 in Game j.

Game 0: Game 0 is the same as the original IND-0 privacy game between a challenger and $\mathcal{A} := (\mathcal{A}_1, \mathcal{A}_2)$D We consider $\mathcal{A}_1$ outputs two tags (t_0^*, t_1^*) and t_0^* is chosen as the challenge tag in this game. It is clear that $\Pr[T_0] = \Pr[\mathsf{Exp}_{\Pi,\mathcal{A}}^{\mathsf{IND}\text{-}0}(k) \rightarrow 1]$.

Game 1: We modify Game 1 by changing the challenge tag from t_0^* to t_1^*. It is clear that $\Pr[T_1] = \Pr[\mathsf{Exp}_{\Pi,\mathcal{A}}^{\mathsf{IND}\text{-}1}(k) \rightarrow 1]$.

Using $\mathcal{A} = (\mathcal{A}_1, \mathcal{A}_2)$, we construct the following ZK-privacy adversary $\mathcal{B} := (\mathcal{B}_1, \mathcal{B}_2)$ and distinguisher $\mathcal{D}$.

$\mathcal{B}_1^{\mathcal{O}}(pk, \mathcal{R}, \mathcal{T})$	$\mathcal{B}_2^{\mathcal{O}}(\mathcal{R}, \mathcal{T}', \mathcal{I}(t^*), st_1')$	$\mathcal{D}(\mathcal{C}, t^*, view_{\mathcal{B}})$
$(t_0^*, t_1^*, st_1) \xleftarrow{R} \mathcal{A}_1^{\mathcal{O}}(pk, \mathcal{R}, \mathcal{T})$;	$b' \xleftarrow{R} \mathcal{A}_2^{\mathcal{O}}(\mathcal{R}, \mathcal{T}', \mathcal{I}(t^*), st_1)$;	$t^* = view_{\mathcal{B}} \iff b := 1;$
$\mathcal{C} := \{t_0^*, t_1^*\};$	$view_{\mathcal{B}} := t_{b'}:$	$t^* \neq view_{\mathcal{B}} \iff b := 0:$
$st_1' := (st_1, t_0^*, t_1^*):$	Output $view_{\mathcal{B}}$	Output b
Output $(\mathcal{C}, st_1')$		

The adversary $\mathcal{B}_1$ sets two tags (t_0^*, t_1^*) as $\mathcal{C}$ and one of the two tags can be accessed by $\mathcal{B}_2$. If t_0^* is chosen from $\mathcal{C}$, it is equivalent to Game 0 with respect to $\mathcal{A}$ and we obtain

$$\Pr[\mathsf{Exp}_{\Pi,\mathcal{A}}^{\mathsf{IND}\text{-}0}(k) \rightarrow 0] = 1 - \Pr[T_0] = \Pr[\mathsf{Exp}_{\Pi,\mathcal{B},\mathcal{D}}^{\mathsf{ZK}\text{-}0}(k) \rightarrow 1 \mid \mathcal{C} \rightarrow t_0^*].$$

Otherwise, it can be viewed as Game 1 and

$$\Pr[\mathsf{Exp}_{\Pi,\mathcal{A}}^{\mathsf{IND}\text{-}1}(k) \rightarrow 1] = \Pr[T_1] = \Pr[\mathsf{Exp}_{\Pi,\mathcal{B},\mathcal{D}}^{\mathsf{ZK}\text{-}0}(k) \rightarrow 1 \mid \mathcal{C} \rightarrow t_1^*].$$

Of course, the challenger uniformly selects the challenge tag and $\Pr[\mathcal{C} \rightarrow t_0^*] = \Pr[\mathcal{C} \rightarrow t_1^*] = 1/2$. Thus we obtain

$$\Pr[\mathsf{Exp}_{\Pi,\mathcal{B},\mathcal{D}}^{\mathsf{ZK}\text{-}0}(k) \rightarrow 1] = \frac{1}{2} + \frac{1}{2} \cdot (\Pr[T_1] - \Pr[T_0]).$$

Recall that we have assumed that Π is ZK-privacy. Thus, for any adversary $\mathcal{B}$, there exists an algorithm $\mathcal{S}$ such that for any distinguisher $\mathcal{D}$, $|\Pr[\mathsf{Exp}_{\Pi,\mathcal{B},\mathcal{D}}^{\mathsf{ZK}\text{-}0}(k) \rightarrow 1] - \Pr[\mathsf{Exp}_{\Pi,\mathcal{S},\mathcal{D}}^{\mathsf{ZK}\text{-}0}(k) \rightarrow 1]|$ is negligible. However, $\mathcal{S}$ has no information about the flipped coin in the experiment and we have $\Pr[\mathsf{Exp}_{\Pi,\mathcal{S},\mathcal{D}}^{\mathsf{ZK}\text{-}1}(k) \rightarrow 1] = 1/2$. Finally, we obtain

$$
\begin{aligned}
\mathsf{Adv}_{\Pi,\mathcal{A}}^{\mathsf{IND}}(k) &= |\Pr[T_1] - \Pr[T_0]| \\
&= |2 \cdot \Pr[\mathsf{Exp}_{\Pi,\mathcal{B},\mathcal{D}}^{\mathsf{ZK}\text{-}0}(k) \rightarrow 1] - 1| \\
&= 2 \cdot \mathsf{Adv}_{\Pi,\mathcal{B},\mathcal{S},\mathcal{D}}^{\mathsf{ZK}}(k).
\end{aligned}
$$

$\square$

4   Relation between SIM and IND Privacy

4.1   Constraint for Corrupt Query

We revisit the privacy relation between SIM-privacy and IND-privacy. Many researchers have informally analyzed these models and several papers conclude that SIM-privacy is stronger than IND-privacy since a wide-strong adversary can corrupt all tags in the experiment (recall that in the IND-privacy, the adversary must output uncorrupted tags for the challenge phase). However, there are four wide adversaries for SIM-privacy and it is meaningful to consider the other privacy notions. Vaudenay recently showed that the IND-privacy game can be written by the wide-destructive SIM-privacy game [22]. Of course, the condition for the corrupt query in the IND-privacy game is different from that in the SIM-privacy game and we can say that wide-forward SIM-privacy does not imply IND-privacy in the sense of adaptive corruption[2]. However, whether IND-privacy implies wide-weak SIM-privacy is unclear. We can also consider two variants for IND-privacy:

1. Strong IND-privacy — Challenge tags can be corrupted in Phase 1, and
2. Weak IND-privacy — The adversary is prohibited to issue the corrupt query.

Then Strong/weak IND-privacy is comparable to wide-strong/wide-weak SIM-privacy. The actual procedure of the IND experiment is of course different from that of the SIM experiment, but the restriction for the corrupt query in strong (resp. weak) IND-privacy is the same as for wide-strong (resp. wide-weak) SIM-privacy. One can also define these variants for ZK-privacy that are equivalent to the strong/weak IND-privacy, respectively.

One may think that the adaptive registration of the tag is allowed in SIM-privacy through the SetupTag query, but it is not a technical point since we can easily add this query to IND-privacy and ZK-privacy.

4.2   Anonymous Communication with Many Tags in ZK-Privacy

We modify ZK-privacy to minimize the difference between ZK-privacy and SIM-privacy. For simplicity, we consider weak ZK-privacy in the following.

First, we consider a slight variant of weak ZK-privacy such that the adversary can anonymously access any tags in $\mathcal{C}$ in Phase 2. This is done by a slight modification for the intermediate algorithm $\mathcal{I}$. When the adversary outputs $\mathcal{C}$, the challenger randomizes and indexes each tag in $\mathcal{C}$. The challenger keeps the list $\{(i, \mathrm{ID}_j)\}_{i,j}$ where $i \in \{1, \ldots, |\mathcal{C}|\}$ and $\mathrm{ID}_j \in \mathcal{C}$ which is initially empty. When the adversary issues the SendTag query to $\mathcal{I}$ with input (i, m), the challenger checks the list. If the list does not contain index i, the new identity ID in $\mathcal{C}$ is uniformly chosen and the tuple (i, ID) is inserted into the list. The message is sent to the corresponding identity and its response is returned to the adversary. This is a quite natural extension for ZK-privacy but we note that this modification partially interpolates the DrawTag query in SIM-privacy to allow anonymous access. We call the modified privacy as ZK′-privacy. Consider that $\mathcal{O}' := (\mathsf{Launch}, \mathsf{SendReader}, \mathsf{SendTag}, \mathsf{Result})$. Then weak ZK′-privacy is described as follows:

---

[2] If an RFID authentication protocol specifies that the secret key of each tag is initially correlated and always updated, the adversary can obtain the challenge tag's secret key in Phase 1 of the IND-privacy game. However, this protocol can hold wide-forward SIM-privacy due to the key update algorithm.

$$
\begin{array}{l}
\underline{\mathsf{Exp}_{\Pi,\mathcal{A},\mathcal{D}}^{\mathsf{ZK'}\text{-}0}(k)} \\[4pt]
(pk, sk) \xleftarrow{\text{R}} \mathsf{Setup}(1^k); \\
(\mathcal{C}, st_1) \xleftarrow{\text{R}} \mathcal{A}_1^{\mathcal{O}'}(pk, \mathcal{R}, \mathcal{T}); \\
\mathcal{T}' := \mathcal{T} \setminus \mathcal{C}; \\
view_{\mathcal{A}} \xleftarrow{\text{R}} \mathcal{A}_2^{\mathcal{O}'}(\mathcal{R}, \mathcal{T}', \mathcal{I}(\mathcal{C}), st_1); \\
b \xleftarrow{\text{R}} \mathcal{D}(\mathcal{C}, \{i, \mathrm{ID}_j\}_{i,j}, view_{\mathcal{A}}): \\
\text{Output } b
\end{array}
\qquad
\begin{array}{l}
\underline{\mathsf{Exp}_{\Pi,\mathcal{S},\mathcal{D}}^{\mathsf{ZK'}\text{-}1}(k)} \\[4pt]
(pk, sk) \xleftarrow{\text{R}} \mathsf{Setup}(1^k); \\
(\mathcal{C}, st_1) \xleftarrow{\text{R}} \mathcal{S}_1^{\mathcal{O}'}(pk, \mathcal{R}, \mathcal{T}); \\
\mathcal{T}' := \mathcal{T} \setminus \mathcal{C}; \\
view_{\mathcal{S}} \xleftarrow{\text{R}} \mathcal{S}_2^{\mathcal{O}'}(\mathcal{R}, \mathcal{T}', st_1); \\
b \xleftarrow{\text{R}} \mathcal{D}(\mathcal{C}, \{i, \mathrm{ID}_j\}_{i,j}, view_{\mathcal{S}}): \\
\text{Output } b
\end{array}
$$

In this privacy model, the advantage of the adversary is defined by

$$
\mathsf{Adv}_{\Pi,\mathcal{A},\mathcal{S},\mathcal{D}}^{\mathsf{ZK'}}(k) = \left| \begin{array}{l} \Pr[\mathsf{Exp}_{\Pi,\mathcal{A},\mathcal{D}}^{\mathsf{ZK'}\text{-}0}(k) \to 1]- \\ \Pr[\mathsf{Exp}_{\Pi,\mathcal{S},\mathcal{D}}^{\mathsf{ZK'}\text{-}1}(k) \to 1] \end{array} \right|.
$$

Definition 4. *An RFID authentication protocol Π satisfies the ZK'-privacy if for any PPT adversary $\mathcal{A}$, there exists a PPT algorithm $\mathcal{S}$, for any PPT distinguisher $\mathcal{D}$, $\mathsf{Adv}_{\Pi,\mathcal{A},\mathcal{S},\mathcal{D}}^{\mathsf{ZK'}}(k)$ is negligible.*

Theorem 2. *ZK'-privacy is an equivalent privacy notion to ZK-privacy.*

Proof. It is clear that ZK'-privacy implies ZK-privacy. We prove that if an RFID authentication protocol Π satisfies ZK-privacy, Π is also ZK'-privacy. This proof follows from the standard hybrid argument. Assume that the adversary against ZK'-privacy issues the SendTag query at most q_s. Based on the ZK'-0 experiment, we change the output from the SendTag query in Phase 2. The response is simulated by $\mathcal{S}$ for ZK-privacy until j-th invocation and executed by the real tag after j-th invocation. When the adversary issues j-th SendTag query, the challenger flips a coin $b \xleftarrow{\text{U}} \{0,1\}$. If $b = 1$, the challenger activates the real tag, and otherwise it runs the simulator to output the response. The difference between $b = 1$ and $b = 0$ is clearly bounded by $\mathsf{Adv}_{\Pi,\mathcal{A},\mathcal{S},\mathcal{D}}^{\mathsf{ZK}}(k)$. For $1 \le j \le q_s$, we can apply the same argument and finally we obtain an experiment that is identical to the ZK'-1 experiment. Therefore we have $\mathsf{Adv}_{\Pi,\mathcal{A},\mathcal{S},\mathcal{D}}^{\mathsf{ZK'}}(k) \le q_s \cdot \mathsf{Adv}_{\Pi,\mathcal{A},\mathcal{S},\mathcal{D}}^{\mathsf{ZK}}(k)$. $\qquad\square$

Now, recall the simulation strategy in Lemma 1. The simulator $\mathcal{S}$ chooses an arbitrary tag to simulate the anonymous access for the adversary if the RFID authentication holds IND-privacy. ZK'-privacy implies that the simulator can simulate the message between the reader and all tags in $\mathcal{C}$ without any communication with these tags. Even when particular tags are chosen by a distribution (i.e. DrawTag query in SIM-privacy), the tag's behavior is indistinguishable from another tag and simulated by the simulator. Therefore, if the RFID authentication protocol satisfies ZK'-privacy (= IND-privacy), any specific information that corresponds to the tag's identity is not revealed.

4.3 Verifiability in the RFID Authentication Protocols

From the above argument, we can say that the only technical differences between ZK'-privacy and SIM-privacy are: (a) the simulator has the opportunity to interact with the tag, and (b) the simulator can obtain reader's output or not[3]. We explicitly wrote that the simulator takes as input $\mathcal{R}$ and can issue the SendReader and Result queries in ZK'-privacy. On the other hand, SIM-privacy requires that the simulator must simulate the SendReader and Result queries along with the SendTag query. Thus the simulator against SIM-privacy must generate all reader's output which is indistinguishable from the real execution. Whether the output is simulatable or not depends on the protocol, so we define the *verifiability* to classify the protocol:

- Public verifiability: a third party who does not participate in the communication can check the validity of the message with the public parameter
- Secret verifiability: only the party who participates in the communication can check the validity of the message.

In the RFID authentication protocol, any message from the tag must satisfy the secret verifiability. In addition, the reader's output must satisfy at least the secret verifiability if the protocol provides reader authentication. However, we can consider the public verifiability of the reader/tag since any anonymity is not required for the reader and the tag may produce additional message which is not related to its identity. In the following, we provide the relationship among the privacy definitions based on the verifiability of the message.

4.4   Separation in the Presence of Public Verifiability

Theorem 3. *Strong ZK'-privacy does not imply wide-weak SIM-privacy if an RFID authentication protocol provides public verifiability of the communication message.*

Proof. Let Π be an RFID authentication protocol that satisfies strong ZK'-privacy. For simplicity, we assume that $(m_1, m_2, m_3, \ldots)$ is the communication message exchanged by the reader and a tag in this protocol. We describe three examples to clarify the essence of the public verifiability.

First Example Π_1':
  Let (KeyGen, Sign, Verify) be a digital signature algorithm. The reader runs Π to obtain (pk, sk) and shares secret keys with each tag in some cases. Run KeyGen algorithm and obtain signing/verification key pair $(sk_{\mathsf{SIG}}, vk_{\mathsf{SIG}})$. The reader publishes $pk' := (pk, vk_{\mathsf{SIG}})$ and sends sk_{SIG} to all tags in Π_1'. The authentication is executed as follows:
  1. The reader obtains m_1 from Π and sends it to the tag.
  2. When the tag receives the message, it generates m_2 with Π and signs the message as $\sigma \xleftarrow{\mathsf{R}} \mathsf{Sign}(sk_{\mathsf{SIG}}, m_2)$. Then the tag responds (m_2, σ) to the reader.

---

[3] Though the SIM-privacy allows the adversary to activate an illegitimate tag which is not registered to the database of the reader, we can also consider such a tag in the IND/ZK-privacy when the adversary activates a tag $t \notin \mathcal{T}$.

3. Upon receiving m_2, the reader generates m_3 and sends it to the reader. The output message from the tag is publicly verifiable since anyone can check $\mathsf{Verify}(vk_{\mathsf{SIG}}, m_2, \sigma) = 1$ holds or not. However, all tags share the secret key sk_{SIG} and no information about the identity is revealed from this signature.

Second Example Π_2':
Let $(\mathsf{KeyGen}, \mathsf{Sign}, \mathsf{Verify})$ be a digital signature algorithm. The reader run Π to obtain (pk, sk) and shares secret keys with each tag in some cases. Run KeyGen algorithm and obtain signing/verification key pair $(sk_{\mathsf{SIG}}, vk_{\mathsf{SIG}})$. The reader publishes $pk' := (pk, vk_{\mathsf{SIG}})$ and holds sk_{SIG} as its own secret key of the reader in Π_2'. The authentication is executed as follows:
1. The reader obtains m_1 from Π and sends it to the tag.
2. When the tag receives the message, it generates m_2 with Π and responds m_2 to the reader.
3. Upon receiving m_2, the reader generates m_3 and signs the message as $\sigma \xleftarrow{R} \mathsf{Sign}(sk_{\mathsf{SIG}}, m_3)$. Then the reader responds (m_3, σ) to the tag.

It is easy to see that the output message from the reader is publicly verifiable because anyone can check $\mathsf{Verify}(vk_{\mathsf{SIG}}, m_3, \sigma) = 1$ holds or not.

Third Example Π_3':
Let $f : \mathcal{X} \to \mathcal{Y}$ be a one-way function. The reader runs Π to obtain (pk, sk) and shares secret keys with each tag in some cases. Choose $x \xleftarrow{\mathsf{U}} \mathcal{X}$ and compute $y := f(x)$. The reader publishes $pk' := (pk, f, y)$ and holds x as a special secret key of the reader in Π_3'. The authentication is executed as follows:
1. The reader obtains m_1 from Π and sends it to the tag.
2. When the tag receives the message, it generates m_2 with Π and responds $m_2' := 1\|m_2$ to the reader.
3. When the reader receives the message m_2', it is parsed as $b\|m_2$. If $b = 1$, the reader generates m_3 and sends it to the tag (this is the same as the honest execution of Π). If $b = 0$, the reader outputs x as the third message.

It is clear that the above RFID authentication protocols satisfy strong ZK'-privacy. The simulator against ZK'-privacy can issue the SendReader query to obtain reader's signature and internal secret x, respectively. The output from the tag in Π_1' can be simulated based on the proof strategy for Lemma 1. The other messages are trivially simulated by the assumption that Π is strong ZK'-privacy.

In contrast, we can show that these protocols do not satisfy wide-weak SIM-privacy. The SIM adversary $\mathcal{A}$ can obtain the actual message from the party with the SendReader and SendTag query, so we consider the adversary who outputs 1 iff the signature verification holds in Π_1' and Π_2'. On the other hand, the simulator in SIM-privacy cannot output any valid signature to the adversary. If it happens, we can build a forger against the signature algorithm .

In the case of Π_3', the SIM adversary $\mathcal{A}$ launches the reader and sends $0\|m_2$ to the reader to obtain x. $\mathcal{A}$ sets $b := 1$ iff $y = f(x)$ and terminates the experiment by outputting b. It is obvious that $\Pr[\mathsf{Exp}^{\mathsf{SIM\text{-}0}}_{\Pi_3',\mathcal{A}}(k) \to 1] = 1$. However, it is infeasible for any simulator to output x' such that $y = f(x')$ from the assumption that f is a one-way function. Therefore we have $\Pr[\mathsf{Exp}^{\mathsf{SIM\text{-}1}}_{\Pi_3',\mathcal{A},\mathcal{S}}(k) \to 1] \leq \varepsilon$ for a negligible fraction ε. Thus we have $\mathsf{Adv}^{\mathsf{SIM}}_{\Pi_3',\mathcal{A},\mathcal{S}}(k)$ is not negligible.   □

The third example is originally described in Pass, Shelat and Vaikuntanathan to show the gap between their variants of non-malleability definition for public key encryption [19]. We think that it is interesting to show the gap between IND-privacy and SIM-privacy based on the same idea. The main feature of the public verifiability is that the adversary can decide whether the communication message is generated by the actual reader/tag in the protocol.

4.5   Relationship in the Absence of Public Verifiability

We now consider that there is no public verifiability on the communication message. To provide the secret verifiability of the tag, we can think the following two classes:

A1. The consistency of the message (from the tag) is verifiable with the secret key of the tag.
A2. The consistency of the message (from the tag) is not verifiable with the secret key of the tag.

Many previous RFID authentication protocols based on the symmetric key primitives are classified in **A1**. Though, if we add another mechanism like a physically unclonable function, the anonymity of the tag can be ensured after the corruption of the tag [20,13].

Note that we assume the restriction for the corrupt query is the same (unfortunately, we cannot provide any equivalence from the original ZK/IND-privacy [12]) [4].

Theorem 4. *Assume that an RFID authentication protocol Π satisfies security and the communication message in the protocol is not publicly verifiable. Then weak ZK'-privacy is equivalent to wide-weak SIM-privacy. Moreover, if the protocol is classified in A1, strong ZK'-privacy is equivalent to wide-strong SIM-privacy.*

Proof. It is easy to show wide-strong/wide-weak SIM-privacy implies strong/weak ZK'-privacy (see Section 4.3). For simplicity, we prove that weak ZK'-privacy implies wide-weak SIM-privacy. That is, if for any ZK' adversary $\mathcal{A}_1$, there exists $\mathcal{S}_1$, for any $\mathcal{D}$, the protocol Π is weak ZK'-privacy, then we show that for any SIM adversary $\mathcal{A}_2$, there exists $\mathcal{S}_2$ such that Π is also wide-weak SIM-privacy.

Consider that $\mathcal{A}_1$ internally runs $\mathcal{A}_2$ and relays all oracle queries issued by $\mathcal{A}_2$ to the challenger. Since we now assume weak ZK'-privacy, the response to

---

[4] Recall that we assume that the adversary cannot convert any illegitimate tags to the virtual tag. Hence the wide-strong SIM-privacy is achievable (see [16,11]).

the SendTag query is surely simulated by $\mathcal{S}_1$. Therefore $\mathcal{S}_2$ can run $\mathcal{S}_1$ and send the output to $\mathcal{A}_2$ which is indistinguishable from any adversary. The remaining task for $\mathcal{S}_2$ is simulating the SendReader query and Result query. We recall that the output from the reader is not publicly verifiable in this setting and the adversary cannot check the validity of the message. Therefore $\mathcal{S}_2$ can choose arbitrary message which the distribution is identical to the protocol specification and respond it to $\mathcal{A}_2$ as the output of the SendReader query. The simulation for the Result query is as follows. If the communication message between the reader and tag is not modified, $\mathcal{S}_2$ consider that the reader accepts the session. $\mathcal{S}_2$ can consider the remaining sessions are rejected from the reader. Whenever $\mathcal{A}_2$ modifies the communication, these sessions are always rejected by the actual reader until $\mathcal{A}_2$ obtains the secret key of the tag. Otherwise, this contradicts to the fact that the RFID authentication protocol holds security. Remark that in case of the simulation between strong ZK′-privacy and wide-strong SIM-privacy, $\mathcal{S}_2$ can also obtain the tag's secret key along with $\mathcal{A}_2$. Therefore $\mathcal{S}_2$ can correctly simulate the behavior of the corrupted tag and check the validity of the message sent from the adversary, since we now concentrate on the case **A1**.

From the above argument, $\mathcal{S}_2$ can simulate SendTag, SendReader and Result queries whose outputs are indistinguishable from the real interaction. Therefore we can conclude that strong/weak ZK′-privacy is equivalent to wide-strong/wide-weak SIM-privacy, respectively.   □

Theorem 5. *Assume that the communication message of an RFID authentication protocol Π is not publicly verifiable and the protocol is classified in A2. Then the strong ZK′-privacy does not imply the wide-strong SIM-privacy.*

Proof. Contrary to Theorem 4, we cannot provide the equivalence when we consider the case **A2**. We consider the following adversary to show the gap between them.

1. Activate the reader with the Launch query.
2. Obtain the secret key of the tag t with the Corrupt query.
3. Generate a valid message m_1 using the secret key of the tag and a random message m_0 which the distribution is same as the protocol specification whenever the reader waits for the tag's response.
4. Choose a random coin $c \xleftarrow{\mathsf{U}} \{0,1\}$ and send m_c to the reader with the SendReader query.
5. Obtain the authentication result c' of the session with the Result query after the session is finished and output 1 iff $c' = c$ holds.

In the strong ZK′-0 and wide-strong SIM-1 experiments, the adversary always outputs 1. Since the simulator in the strong ZK′-1 experiment can issue the same query as the adversary, Π holds the strong ZK′-privacy. On the other hand, the simulator in the wide-strong SIM-1 experiment cannot issue the Result query. This simulator must guess the authentication result for the adversary, but it is impossible since we now assume that the validity of the message m_c cannot be checked by the tag's secret key. Therefore Π does not satisfy the wide-strong SIM-privacy.   □

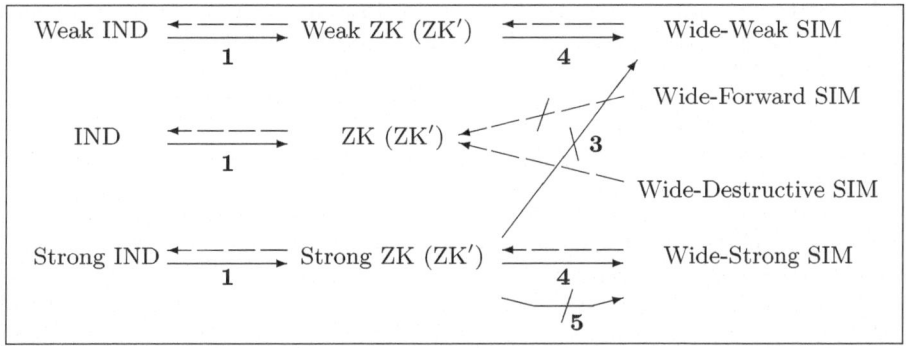

Fig. 2. *A* implies *B* if and only if there is a path from *A* to *B*, and the hatched arrows represent separations. Our result is represented by the solid arrow, and the dashed arrows represent results from prior works. The number on an arrow refers to the theorem in this paper. Recall that the relationship between ZK-privacy and SIM-privacy depends on the public verifiability of the reader and how to verify the tag's message.

We summarize the relationship the privacy notions in Figure 2.

5   Conclusion

We analyzed the three privacy models for RFID authentication protocols. Contrary to the discussion in Deng et al. [9], we showed that IND-privacy is equivalent to ZK-privacy. We also provided a polynomially equivalent variant of ZK-privacy to consider the relation between IND-privacy and SIM-privacy. Depending on the existence of reader's public verifiability, we showed the separation/equivalence between these privacy definitions.

References

1. Avoine, G.: Adversarial model for radio frequency identification. ePrint Archive, 2006/049 (2005)
2. Bellare, M., Desai, A., Pointcheval, D., Rogaway, P.: Relations among Notions of Security for Public-Key Encryption Schemes. In: Krawczyk, H. (ed.) CRYPTO 1998. LNCS, vol. 1462, pp. 26–45. Springer, Heidelberg (1998)
3. Bellare, M., Sahai, A.: Non-malleable Encryption: Equivalence between Two Notions, and an Indistinguishability-Based Characterization. In: Wiener, M. (ed.) CRYPTO 1999. LNCS, vol. 1666, pp. 519–536. Springer, Heidelberg (1999)
4. Billet, O., Etrog, J., Gilbert, H.: Lightweight Privacy Preserving Authentication for RFID Using a Stream Cipher. In: Hong, S., Iwata, T. (eds.) FSE 2010. LNCS, vol. 6147, pp. 55–74. Springer, Heidelberg (2010)
5. Burmester, M., Le, T.V., Medeiros, B.D., Tsudik, G.: Universally composable RFID identification and authentication protocols. ACM TISSEC 2009 12(4), 21:1–21:33 (2009)

678   D. Moriyama, S. Matsuo, and M. Ohkubo

6. Burmester, M., van, Le, T., de Medeiros, B.: Provably secure ubiquitous systems: Universally composable RFID authentication protocols. In: SecureComm 2006, pp. 1–9. IEEE (2006)
7. Canard, S., Coisel, I.: Data synchronization in privacy-preserving RFID authentication schemes. In: RFIDSec 2008 (2008)
8. Coisel, I., Martin, T.: Untangling RFID privacy models. ePrint Archive 2011/636 (2011)
9. Deng, R.H., Li, Y., Yung, M., Zhao, Y.: A New Framework for RFID Privacy. In: Gritzalis, D., Preneel, B., Theoharidou, M. (eds.) ESORICS 2010. LNCS, vol. 6345, pp. 1–18. Springer, Heidelberg (2010)
10. Ha, J., Moon, S.-J., Zhou, J., Ha, J.C.: A New Formal Proof Model for RFID Location Privacy. In: Jajodia, S., Lopez, J. (eds.) ESORICS 2008. LNCS, vol. 5283, pp. 267–281. Springer, Heidelberg (2008)
11. Hermans, J., Pashalidis, A., Vercauteren, F., Preneel, B.: A New RFID Privacy Model. In: Atluri, V., Diaz, C. (eds.) ESORICS 2011. LNCS, vol. 6879, pp. 568–587. Springer, Heidelberg (2011)
12. Juels, A., Weis, S.A.: Defining strong privacy for RFID. ACM Transactions on Information and System Security 13(1) (2009)
13. Kardaş, S., Kiraz, M.S., Bingöl, M.A., Demirci, H.: A Novel RFID Distance Bounding Protocol Based on Physically Unclonable Functions. In: Juels, A., Paar, C. (eds.) RFIDSec 2011. LNCS, vol. 7055, pp. 78–93. Springer, Heidelberg (2012)
14. van Le, T., Burmester, M., de Medeiros, B.: Universally composable and forward-secure RFID authentication and authenticated key exchange. In: ASIACCS 2007, pp. 242–252. ACM (2007)
15. Ma, C., Li, Y., Deng, R.H., Li, T.: RFID privacy: Relation between two notions, minimal condition, and efficient construction. In: ACMCCS 2009, pp. 54–65. ACM (2009)
16. Ng, C.Y., Susilo, W., Mu, Y., Safavi-Naini, R.: RFID Privacy Models Revisited. In: Jajodia, S., Lopez, J. (eds.) ESORICS 2008. LNCS, vol. 5283, pp. 251–266. Springer, Heidelberg (2008)
17. Ouafi, K., Phan, R.C.-W.: Traceable Privacy of Recent Provably-Secure RFID Protocols. In: Bellovin, S.M., Gennaro, R., Keromytis, A.D., Yung, M. (eds.) ACNS 2008. LNCS, vol. 5037, pp. 479–489. Springer, Heidelberg (2008)
18. Paise, R.I., Vaudenay, S.: Mutual authentication in RFID. In: ASIACCS 2008, pp. 292–299. ACM (2008)
19. Pass, R., Shelat, A., Vaikuntanathan, V.: Relations Among Notions of Non-malleability for Encryption. In: Kurosawa, K. (ed.) ASIACRYPT 2007. LNCS, vol. 4833, pp. 519–535. Springer, Heidelberg (2007)
20. Sadeghi, A.R., Visconti, I., Wachsmann, C.: PUF-enhanced RFID security and privacy. In: SECSI 2010 (2010)
21. Vaudenay, S.: On privacy models for RFID. In: Kurosawa, K. (ed.) ASIACRYPT 2007. LNCS, vol. 4833, pp. 68–87. Springer, Heidelberg (2007)
22. Vaudenay, S.: Privacy Models for RFID Schemes. In: Ors Yalcin, S.B. (ed.) RFIDSec 2010. LNCS, vol. 6370, pp. 65–65. Springer, Heidelberg (2010)

PE(AR)^2: Privacy-Enhanced Anonymous Authentication with Reputation and Revocation

Kin Ying Yu[1], Tsz Hon Yuen[1], Sherman S.M. Chow[2],
Siu Ming Yiu[1], and Lucas C.K. Hui[1]

[1] Department of Computer Science, The University of Hong Kong
{kyyu,thyuen,smyiu,hui}@cs.hku.hk
[2] Department of Combinatorics and Optimization
University of Waterloo, Ontario, Canada N2L 3G1
smchow@math.uwaterloo.ca

Abstract. Anonymous authentication schemes allow users to act freely without being tracked. The users may not want to trust a third party in ensuring their privacy, yet a service provider (SP) should have the authority to blacklist a misbehaving user. They are seemingly contradicting requirements. PEREA was the most efficient solution to this problem. However, there are a few drawbacks which make it vulnerable and not practical enough. In this paper, we propose PE(AR)^2, which not only fixes PEREA's vulnerability, but also significantly improves its computation efficiency. Apart from revoking repeated misbehaving users, our system also rewards anonymous users via a built-in reputation system. Our scheme does not require the SP to timely review all previously authenticated sessions, and does not have the dependency on the blacklist size for user-side computation (c.f. EPID/BLAC(R)). Our benchmark on PE(AR)^2 shows that an SP can handle over 160 requests/second – a 460-fold efficiency improvement over PEREA, when the credentials store 1000 single-use tickets.

1 Introduction

It is common nowadays that user identification and authentication are required to perform actions on web applications in the Internet. Some of these applications depend much on users contributing contents or forming a user community to encourage interactions from each other. While most of these web applications require users to register with a self generated login identifier, the true identities of users could actually be revealed by skilled data miners from user-provided information, behavior of consecutive sessions, etc. Privacy concern on the use of these web applications is becoming a more prevailing issue.

Take Wikipedia, a collaboration based encyclopedia website, as an example; anyone could become an editor by contributing contents, or moderating any existing contents. This editing model removes the entry barrier for using the service, thus encourages a lot of content submissions. However, the identities of users who submit contents are traceable, which creates a lot of privacy concerns.

S. Foresti, M. Yung, and F. Martinelli (Eds.): ESORICS 2012, LNCS 7459, pp. 679–696, 2012.

When a user identity is linked to specific document content, reviewers or readers of the document could become biased because they may think that this particular user could be representing a particular organization or community, especially for government organizations or political parties. Another example is Internet discussion forums. Users of common interests on certain topics often express their views on these forums, and other users could further comment on the same threads. In contrast to any verbal conversation which is more transient in nature, users could become much more liable to what they put on the forum. In some cases, lawsuits are resulted. Traceable identities would make users be less liberal in expressing ideas or viewpoints in the worry of censorship.

One trivial solution to the above problem is to allow anonymous users to perform actions without authentications. However this solution creates another problem: misbehaving users could not be stopped. Referencing the Internet discussion forum example again, a misbehaving user could damage the forum by spamming, advertising, or reprimanding threads created by other users. Blacklisting users would not be possible if all users are perfectly anonymous. A forum moderator could only keep removing destructive contents manually.

Anonymous Authentication without Trusted Third Party. Anonymous credential schemes enable anonymous authentications among a set of registered users. These schemes may reduce the number of misbehaving users because the system owner can control who can be registered, and possibly revoke a user's membership when misbehavior is detected. To enable revocation, an intuitive idea is to introduce a trusted third party (TTP) who owns the trapdoor that can reveal the true identity of any user. There are systems based on group signatures (e.g., [1]) or accumulators (e.g., [2]) which use TTP-based revocation.

To enhance users' privacy, or to reduce the trust they need to put, BLAC [3] and EPID [4] eliminate the use of TTP in revocation. A user is required to prove in zero-knowledge that the credential is not listed in the blacklist, and the blacklist can also be constructed from the past authentication transcript without any trapdoor information. However, as the zero-knowledge proof needs to be performed on each of the L entries in the blacklist, the computation complexity for authentication is $O(L)$. These schemes become impractical in practice since the blacklist will keep growing and there is no way to reduce its size, except resetting the system and updating all users' credentials.

To make the authentication process more efficient, PEREA [5] is proposed. In PEREA, a user's credential stores K single-use tickets using a dynamical universal accumulator. After each authentication, the service provider (SP) will certify a new queue of tickets (the used ticket is dequeued and a new one is enqueued in a sliding window manner). Tickets are randomly generated by users which also serve as the identifiers of authenticated sessions. Each authentication spends one ticket, and will then be evaluated (according to certain criteria external to PEREA). If the need of blacklisting arises, the SP will put the corresponding ticket on the blacklist. Revocation check is enforced by a zero-knowledge proof-of-knowledge (ZKPoK) about the possession of a signature on the queued element, and a non-membership proof for each of the queued tickets with respect to the SP side accumulator (storing blacklisted sessions' tickets). While the blacklist size is still $O(L)$, the computation overhead on an authentication step is $O(K)$ since it only needs $O(1)$ time to check each of the K tickets is not in the blacklist using the proof systems provided with the accumulator. Higher efficiency may be obtained by optimizing the parameter K which also governs the time window that the SP must catch any user misbehavior.

Problems with PEREA. The above design appeared to make a significant step towards practical TTP-free revocation in anonymous authentication. However, we observe that this design also has its problems for a practical deployment.

Recall that the SP needs to review authenticated sessions in a timely manner based on the choice of K. Otherwise, a user can quickly get authenticated for K times, get an entirely new queue of tickets, and will not be denied from the service even if all those K sessions are later reviewed as problematic, i.e., the users would be able to "clean" all unreviewed sessions from their queues before they have been published by the SP as revoked sessions. This could only be done by limiting the rate a user can use the service (i.e., a user could only be authenticated for K requests in a predefined period, within that period the blacklisted tickets must be determined). Even if the time window for rate-limiting is synchronized across all users, this still creates a few undesirable properties.

First, if there is no misbehavior whatsoever, the SP might not care much if a user "overuses" the service. Indeed, in applications such as Internet forums, high activity is what an SP wants to see. On the other hand, the SP is now in a stressed situation that all sessions conducted in the predefined period must be reviewed properly, or otherwise a session with misbehavior could not be revoked. Moreover, as blacklisted tickets are required to be published timely, the blacklist accumulator becomes volatile. Consequently, the witness for the non-membership proof for the users' tickets queue also requires updates (even if the tickets queue remains unchanged), which causes user-side overhead. Most importantly, observe that the requirement of *rate-limiting* means we need another kind of protocol (e.g., [6]) which is able to profile the behavior of the *same* user over a period of time. It is not clear how rate-limiting can be tightly coupled with PEREA, *without reducing anonymity*, not to say the additional overhead for such feature.

In terms of performance of deployment, recall that the computational overhead for authentication is dependent on the ticket queue size K. For the SP to achieve practical performance in authentication phase, it was suggested to use $K = 10$ for completing computation under 0.1 seconds using typical hardware. This imposes a very strict requirement for the SP to evaluate each session. Another issue related to realization of an accumulator-based design is that, the proof of non-membership protocol associated with the accumulator is not as "secure" as assumed in PEREA. A recent research [7] has broken the security of the proof of non-membership protocol used [8], which in turns breaks the security of PEREA.

Reputation and Naughtiness. Reputation system is widely used in many online services. (A survey of trust and reputation systems can be found in [9].)

The user reputation is an aggregate (e.g., sum) of the rating of all previously conducted sessions. It can be used as a way to profile a user, and then used for rewarding or punishment upon user's future authentications. For example, in Yahoo! Knowledge[+1], each user is associated with a score, which is an aggregate sum of all individual score gained from the contributed answers. An answer submitted by a user with high score may implicate that the user has been successfully helping many others and hence is considered to be more trustworthy.

PEREA requires the SP to reject authentication once a user has been put on the blacklist. This may be reasonable for applications that only requires an "all or nothing" authentication, but real world applications usually require login session to be associated with different privilege levels such that the SP can provide different access rights to the user. An example could be an abusive user who keeps posting defamation messages to a forum should have the message posting suspended, but still has access right to the forum. Such operation is not possible in the basic setting of PEREA.

In view of this shortcoming, the basic PEREA is extended [5] to revoke users based on "naughtiness", a severity measure of misconducts for a user's K most recently conducted sessions. However, it is not useful in a reputation system since it can only capture the most recent K sessions.

Recently, Au, Kapadia and Susilo [10] proposed BLACR that extended BLAC to support reputation. The basic BLACR subjects to the same inefficiency as BLAC. Their BLACR-Express tries to decouple the blacklist in the past from the performance of authentication, by asking the SP to issue some "express passes" to privileged users. However, the management of these passes costs extra burden on the SP, especially when applied to numerous users in the system.

Our Contribution. We propose $PE(AR)^2$, which preserves the same anonymous authentication functionalities as PEREA, but with a few improvements. Our $PE(AR)^2$ also has a built-in reputation system. Each user can obtain "scores" from the past sessions. Users can also prove (in zero-knowledge) that their scores are higher than a certain threshold. The SP can then provide some privilege services accordingly.

$PE(AR)^2$ has a few advantages. Firstly, it does not require rate-limiting as in PEREA for avoiding any malicious user to shift tickets which will be potentially blacklisted out of the queue. Another advantage is that we no longer require the SP to publish the blacklist in a timely manner for the accuracy of revocation. The SP can then have higher flexibility and better resource scheduling on managing blacklist. Otherwise, the SP might potentially blacklist more sessions than needed, and unblacklist some of them afterwards. say when an "innocent" (and unhappy) user filed a dispute case. As the changes in the blacklist is less volatile, this also helps to achieve better computation efficiency in the user side.

We also remodel the structure of how authentication and blacklisting are done in PEREA to have further improvement in terms of efficiency. In particular, the complexity of SP-side for verifying an authentication in $PE(AR)^2$ does not depend on the ticket queue size K anymore; and for user side, the dependency

---
[1] http://hk.knowledge.yahoo.com

on K is changed from $O(K)$ exponentiations to $O(K)$ divisions, which are much cheaper. We further benchmark the performance of our implementation and show our design is indeed practical and feasible in real world use case.

Regarding reputation, we introduce a score redemption algorithm, such that users are allowed to remove tickets and reclaim the scores associated with the reviewed sessions, thus keeping the ticket queue in a practically small size and making the scores reclaimed aggregatable.

2   Formal Definitions

An anonymous authentication scheme with reputation and revocation, executed between a user $\mathcal{U}$ and a service provider $\mathcal{S}$, consists of the following algorithms:

- KeyGen(1^ℓ) $\rightarrow$ (mpk, msk): KeyGen is the key generation algorithm for the service provider $\mathcal{S}$ that outputs the key pair.
- Reg($\mathcal{U}$(mpk), $\mathcal{S}$(msk)) $\rightarrow$ \{$\mathcal{U}$(cred), $\mathcal{S}$()\}: Reg is the registration protocol that outputs a credential cred to the user, which includes a list of tickets $\mathbb{T}$ not known by $\mathcal{S}$.
- Auth($\mathcal{U}$(mpk, cred, s_{base}), $\mathcal{S}$(msk)) $\rightarrow$ \{$\mathcal{U}$(cred), $\mathcal{S}$(t, s_{base})\}: Auth is the authentication protocol that gives a ticket (session identifier) $t \in \mathbb{T}$ to the SP, where $\mathbb{T}$ is in cred. If the ticket t is not used before, the used tickets in $\mathbb{T}$ are not in the blacklist $\mathbb{B}$, and the score s in cred is larger than s_{base}, then the user is authenticated. The SP stores $(t, 0, \perp)$ in the ticket score list $\mathbb{L}$, and the user refreshes his credential.
- Revoke(t) $\rightarrow$ \{$\mathcal{U}$(t), $\mathcal{S}$(t)\}: Revoke is the procedure for the SP to put a ticket t on the blacklist, which revokes the credential where t is originated.
- Rate(t, s): $\mathcal{S}$ receives score s from the reviewers for the ticket t, updates (t, s, Pf) to the list $\mathbb{L}$, where Pf is a proof of validity of the rating.
- Redeem($\mathcal{U}$(mpk, cred, $\mathbb{L}_s$), $\mathcal{S}$(msk)) $\rightarrow$ \{$\mathcal{U}$(cred), $\mathcal{S}$()\}: Redeem is the algorithm that allows $\mathcal{U}$ to update the score in the credential according to the ticket list $\mathbb{L}_s$. $\mathcal{U}$ proves that some of his tickets in cred are in $\mathbb{L}_s \subseteq \mathbb{L} \setminus \mathbb{B}$. Finally $\mathcal{U}$ obtains an updated credential with new score s_{new}, the summation of the scores in $\mathbb{L}$ for all tickets in $\mathbb{L}_s$, with new tickets refilled, and with the tickets in $\mathbb{L}_s$ removed from the credential.

An anonymous authentication scheme with reputation and revocation should provide the properties *Misauthentication Resistance, Revocability, Anonymity, Unlinkability, Backward Untraceability* and *Identity-Escrow Freeness* as defined in PEREA [5], as well as the following properties:

- **Reputation.** (Completeness:) An honest user who has not been revoked should be able to be authenticated by an honest SP if his score is larger than s_{base}; and (Soundness:) No registered user can authenticate with an honest SP for a score s_{base} if his score is less than or equal to s_{base}.
- **Rating Unforgeability.** The rating is only performed by the honest SP.

Their formal definitions will be given via two main notions to be defined later.

In a reputation system, the unlinkability is guaranteed when the ticket is not redeemed. Some anonymity may be lost during the redeem protocol under some extreme cases. For example, if tickets A and B both have score 100 while the other 5 tickets in the system have score 1. If one redeems his tickets for a total score 200, then we conclude that tickets A and B are used by the same user. This situation would be more noticeable when the user community is small or the distribution of scores are uneven. This kind of unlinkability lost cannot be completely eliminated from reputation system. However, as the number of users and scored tickets gets large, then such issue becomes less likely to occur.

Security Models. We formally define the security notions as games played between the adversary $\mathcal{A}$ and the challenger $\mathcal{C}$. $\mathcal{A}$ can arbitrarily and adaptively query various oracles, which together share a private state st_n that contains counters n, and sets U_P, U_A, U_B, which are initialized to 0 and $\varnothing$, respectively. Here we define a number of oracles, modeling an adversary's attacking power.

Our P-Reg, A-Reg, B-Reg, CorruptU, P-Auth, A-Auth, B-Auth, Add-to-BL, Remove-From-BL Oracles are almost the same as the oracles in PEREA [5]. The meanings of P, A and B in various Reg and Auth oracles are similar to those to be described in three different kinds of Redeem oracles. Below we will highlight the differences between our model and the existing model [5].

- Our private state st_n stores three tuples, including the user counter n and the credential as in [5], and also the refresh counter a which is used to differentiate past and present credentials. We use $\mathsf{cred}_{n,a}$ to represent each credential.
- In A-Reg (resp. A-Auth) Oracle, $\mathcal{A}$ sends all the randomness he wants to use in the Reg (resp. Auth) protocol. The oracle runs it using $\mathcal{A}$'s randomness for the corrupt user. It is because the challenger has to know the credentials of the corrupt users to prevent $\mathcal{A}$ from winning trivially using them.
- In CorruptU Oracle, it also takes the refresh counter a as an extra input, in order to simulate the corruption of past credentials for backward security.

The following oracles are newly introduced in our model:

- Rate Oracle: allows $\mathcal{A}$ to assign scores for tickets. On input a ticket t and a score s, the oracles updates (t, s, Pf) to the list $\mathbb{L}$.
- P-Redeem Oracle (resp. B-Redeem Oracle; A-Redeem Oracle): allows $\mathcal{A}$ to eavesdrop a redemption run between an honest user and an honest SP (resp. an honest user and a corrupt SP; or a corrupt user and an honest SP). The oracle description is similar to the P-Auth Oracle (resp. B-Auth Oracle; A-Auth Oracle), except that we replace the Auth protocol with the Redeem protocol; and the state st_n finally stores the refreshed credential with the new score s_{score} (the summation of scores of tickets in $\mathbb{L}_s$).
- A-Redeem Oracle: allows a corrupt user to redeem with an honest SP. On input i such that $i \in U_A$, the oracle searches for $\langle i, \mathsf{cred}_{i,a}, a \rangle$ from st_n with the largest a, plays the role of the SP and interacts with $\mathcal{A}$ in the Redeem

protocol. $\mathcal{A}$ sends all the randomness he wants to use and the oracles runs the Redeem protocol using them for the corrupt user i. If the redeem is successful, the oracles appends $\langle i, \mathsf{cred}_{i,a+1}, a + 1 \rangle$ to st_n, where $\mathsf{cred}_{i,a+1}$ is the refreshed credential with score s_{score} (the summation of scores of tickets in $\mathbb{L}_s$). The oracle returns $(\pi_a, a, \mathsf{cred}_{i,a+1})$ to $\mathcal{A}$, where π_a is the resulting protocol transcript.

We are now ready to introduce two security games to capture the properties of anonymous authentication [2].

Accountability. We capture the misauthentication resistance, revocability and reputation properties. In this game, the adversary is allowed to act as unregistered users, revoked users, and registered users without sufficient score. No coalition of these users can authenticate with the honest SP. The security game between the challenger $\mathcal{C}$ and the adversary $\mathcal{A}$ is defined as follows.

1. (Setup.) $\mathcal{C}$ runs $(\mathsf{mpk}, \mathsf{msk}) \leftarrow \mathsf{KeyGen}(1^\ell)$ and gives mpk to $\mathcal{A}$.
2. (Query.) $\mathcal{A}$ can issue queries to all the oracles except those start with B-.
3. (End game.) $\mathcal{A}$ runs Auth with $\mathcal{C}$ and $\mathcal{C}$ obtains a ticket t^* and s_{base}^*.

Denote a^* as the largest number such that the ticket t^* is in cred_{n^*,a^*}, for $\langle n^*, \mathsf{cred}_{n^*,a^*}, a^* \rangle$ stored in st_n. $\mathcal{A}$ wins the game if one of the following holds:

- Case 1: (unregistered user) a^* cannot be found since t^* is not in any $\mathsf{cred}_{n,a}$.
- Case 2: (honest-looking user) $n^* \notin U_A$; and t^* is not stored in $\mathbb{L}$.
- Case 3: (malicious registered user): One of the following holds:
  1. ($\mathcal{A}$ reuses old tickets) t^* is stored in $\mathbb{L}$, or
  2. ($\mathcal{A}$ does not have enough score) s_{score} (the score of cred_{n^*,a^*}) $\leq s_{\mathsf{base}}^*$, or
  3. ($\mathcal{A}$ is blacklisted) $\exists \hat{t} \in \mathsf{cred}_{n^*,a^*}$ such that ticket $\hat{t}$ is in the blacklist.

The advantage of $\mathcal{A}$ is the probability that $\mathcal{A}$ wins the game.

Definition 1. *An anonymous authentication scheme is accountable if there is no PPT adversary $\mathcal{A}$ has a non-negligible advantage in the above game.*

The accountability model captures the misauthentication resistance since the adversary can pretend to be an honest user (by setting $n^* \in U_p \cup U_B$ in case 2) or try to authenticate as an unregistered user (by case 1). The model also captures the revocability and reputation, since in case 3 the challenge user is either blacklisted, is reusing old tickets or trying to authenticate with low score.

Privacy. We capture the anonymity, unlinkability and backward untraceability properties in the game below, where the adversary could act as a corrupted SP.

1. (Setup.) $\mathcal{C}$ runs $(\mathsf{mpk}, \mathsf{msk}) \leftarrow \mathsf{KeyGen}(1^\ell)$ and gives $(\mathsf{mpk}, \mathsf{msk})$ to $\mathcal{A}$.
2. (Query 1.) $\mathcal{A}$ is allowed to issue queries to all the oracles except those start with P- and A-.

---

[2] Completeness is easy to define. Rating unforgeability can be easily captured by the standard unforgeability of the Rate protocol. We omit them due to space limit.

3. (Challenge.) $\mathcal{A}$ picks i_0 and i_1 in U_B and sends them to $\mathcal{C}$. Denote the score of i_0 (resp. i_1) in st_n as s_0 (resp. s_1). $\mathcal{C}$ randomly picks a bit $b \in \{0, 1\}$. After that, $\mathcal{A}$ can ask $\mathcal{C}$ to run B-Auth Oracle twice with $s_{\mathsf{base}} > s_0, s_1$, and without specifying the input. $\mathcal{C}$ answers the query assuming the input is i_b and i_{1-b} respectively. Denote the ticket used as t_0^* and t_1^* respectively.

4. (Query 2.) $\mathcal{A}$ is allowed to issue queries to all the oracles except CorruptU Oracle with input i_0 or i_1 and oracles start with P- and A-. $\mathcal{A}$ is allowed to query the B-Redeem Oracle if t_0^* and t_1^* are not involved. Redeeming t_0^* and t_1^* by the B-Redeem Oracle is allowed if and only if all tickets to be redeemed by i_b and i_{1-b} have the same total scores and the same number of tickets.

5. (End game.) $\mathcal{A}$ outputs a guess bit b'. $\mathcal{A}$ wins if $b = b'$.

The advantage of $\mathcal{A}$ is the probability that $\mathcal{A}$ wins the game minus $1/2$.

Definition 2. *An anonymous authentication scheme is private if there is no PPT adversary $\mathcal{A}$ has a non-negligible advantage in the above game.*

The privacy model captures anonymity since the adversary tries to distinguish between two honest users from the challenge authentication instance. It captures unlinkability since the adversary can ask the challenge users to run many instances of Auth with him before and after the challenge phase. It captures backward untraceability since the adversary is allowed to put the tickets of the challenge users on the blacklist, without affecting the other two properties.

3   Building Blocks

We state the notations and constructions of some fundamental cryptographic building blocks used.

Zero-Knowledge Proof-of-Knowledge (ZKPoK). For a language L with witness relation R_L, a proof system is a triplet of algorithms (K, P, V):

- K: on input 1^ℓ, outputs a common reference string crs.
- P: on input crs, x and its witness w, outputs a proof π if $(x, w) \in R_L$.
- V: on input crs, x and its proof π, outputs 1 for accept and 0 for reject.

We use the standard notation (due to Camenisch and Stadler) $PK\{(\alpha, \rho) \colon z = g^\alpha h^\rho\}$, to denote a proof of knowledge of (α, ρ) where $z = g^\alpha h^\rho$ is satisfied.

CL Signature. CL signature [11] is a secure signature scheme which allows signing on (commitments of) a vector of message and proving the possession of valid signatures in zero-knowledge. The algorithm $\mathsf{KeyGen}_{\mathrm{CL}}(1^\ell)$ outputs a public key $\mathsf{pk}_{\mathrm{CL}} = (N, g, h)$ where N is a safe prime product, $g, h \in \mathbb{QR}_N$; and a secret key $\mathsf{sk}_{\mathrm{CL}} = \phi(N)$. For a vector of messages $(\alpha_0, \ldots, \alpha_k)$, the signature on the commitment of $(\alpha_0, \ldots, \alpha_k)$ is denoted as $\sigma \leftarrow \mathsf{Sign}_{\mathrm{CL}}(\{\alpha_i\}_{0\ldots k}, \mathsf{sk}_{\mathrm{CL}})$. The verification algorithm is denoted as $1/0 \leftarrow \mathsf{Verify}_{\mathrm{CL}}(\{\alpha_i\}_{0\ldots k}, \sigma, \mathsf{pk}_{\mathrm{CL}})$ for valid/invalid signature. More details likes its construction can be found in [11].

Dynamically Universal Accumulator (DUA). DUA [8] is a suite of algo-rithms/protocols which allows an accumulation of a set of values into a single accumulator, and the proof of knowledge of a non-membership or membership witness of any value, with respect to an accumulator. We summarize the scheme in [8] as follows. In PE(AR)^2, the tickets are the values to be accumulated.

DUA.Setup. On input the security parameter 1^ℓ, it picks a safe prime product N and $g_{\mathsf{Acc}} \in_R \mathbb{QR}_N$. It compute the public/private key pair $\mathsf{pk}_{\mathsf{Acc}} = (N, g_{\mathsf{Acc}})$, $\mathsf{sk}_{\mathsf{Acc}} = \phi(N)$, and sets the initial accumulator value $c = g_{\mathsf{Acc}}$.

DUA.Accumulating tickets. Denote $\mathsf{Accumulate}(c, \{t_i\}_{0...L})$ as the algorithm to accumulate a list of tickets $\{t_i\}_{0...L}$ to the accumulator value c. It computes $\hat{c} = c^{\Pi_{0 \leqslant i \leqslant L} t_i}$. $\mathcal{S}$ updates $c = \hat{c}$. Note that decumlating tickets can be done similarly by computing $\hat{c} = c^{\Pi_{0 \leqslant i \leqslant L} t_i^{-1} \bmod \phi(N)}$ using $\mathsf{sk}_{\mathsf{Acc}}$.

DUA.Non-membership witness generation.[3] Denote $\mathsf{Compute}_{\mathrm{nmw}}(x, \{t_i\}_{0...L}, \mathsf{sk}_{\mathsf{Acc}})$ as the following algorithm to generate a non-membership witness w, where x is the ticket to be witnessed, $\{t_i\}_{0...L}$ is the list of accumulated tickets.

1. Compute the accumulated ticket product $u = \prod_{i=0}^{L} t_i$.
2. Compute $u' = u \bmod \phi(N)$.
3. Since x is not a factor of u, $\gcd(x, u') = 1$. By Euclidean algorithm, find a and b such that $au' + bx = 1 \bmod \phi(N)$.
4. Output the witness w in the form of $(a, d) = (a, g_{\mathsf{Acc}}^{-b})$.

The accumulator $c = g_{\mathsf{Acc}}^{\Pi_{0 \leqslant i \leqslant L} t_i}$ has the witness $w = (a, d)$ which can be validated by checking if $c^a = d^x g_{\mathsf{Acc}} \bmod N$. Denote this check by $\mathsf{Verify}_{\mathrm{nmw}}(c, x, w, \mathsf{pk}_{\mathsf{Acc}})$. It outputs 1 if the witness is valid, or 0 otherwise.

DUA.Non-membership witness update. Denote $\mathsf{Update}_{\mathrm{nmw}}(w, c, x, \{t_i\}_{L+1...M})$ as the following algorithm to update the non-membership witness $w = (a, d)$, where c is the original accumulator value, x is the ticket to be witnessed, and tickets $t_L + 1, \ldots, t_M$ are the newly accumulated tickets which are absent in c.

1. Compute the new accumulated ticket product $\hat{u} = \prod_{i=L+1}^{M} t_i$.
2. Compute the new accumulator value $\hat{c} = c^{\hat{u}} \bmod N$.
3. Since x is not a factor of $\hat{u}$, by Euclidean algorithm, find $\hat{a}_0$ and r_0 such that $\hat{a}_0 \hat{u} + r_0 x = 1$. Compute $\hat{a} = \hat{a}_0 a \bmod x$.
4. Find r such that $\hat{a}\hat{u} = a + rx$. Output the updated witness $\hat{w}$ in the form of $(\hat{a}, \hat{d}) = (\hat{a}, dc^r \bmod N)$.

The updated witness $\hat{w} = (\hat{a}, \hat{d})$ is valid if $\hat{c}^{\hat{a}} = \hat{d}^x g_{\mathsf{Acc}} \bmod N$ holds.

DUA.Non-membership witness proof-of-knowledge. Setting $\mathsf{pk}_{\mathsf{Acc}} = (N, g_{\mathsf{Acc}}, g, h)$, on a hidden ticket x, a random value r and witness (a, d), a prover runs the ZKPoK with $\mathcal{S}$: $PK_{\mathrm{nmw}}\{(x, r, a, d) : \mathsf{comm}_x = g^x h^r \wedge c^a = d^x g_{\mathsf{Acc}}\}$ to prove the

---

[3] Note that this version of DUA is vulnerable to an attack described in [7]. Our instantiation is described in Section 4.1.

condition $\gcd(x, u) = 1$, where u is the product of all ticket accumulated, is satisfied. Instantiation of such could be found in [8, § 5].

Intractability Assumption. Both CL signature and DUA rely on the *strong RSA assumption*, which is, on input of an RSA modulus N and an element $u \in \mathbb{Z}_N^*$, it is computationally hard to find a pair (v, e) such that $v^e = u \bmod N$ where $e > 1$.

4   A New Scheme: PE(AR)²

In this section, we propose a new anonymous authentication scheme that settles the pitfall and vulnerability of PEREA. We name it as PE(AR)², denoting Privacy-Enhanced Anonymous Authentication with Reputation and Revocation.

4.1   Our Scheme as Improvement to PEREA

Fixing Vulnerability of Dynamic Universal Accumulator (DUA). As stated in [7], the non-membership witness generation algorithm executed by an SP [8] suffers from an attack of extraction of multiple of $\phi(N)$, which is the secret key. The attack is successful because the original scheme [8] makes use of $u' = u \bmod \phi(N)$ in order to efficiently generate a witness $w = (a, d)$ that satisfies $au' + bx = 1 \bmod \phi(N)$ and $d = g_{\mathsf{Acc}}^{-b} \bmod N$.

Yet, the use of $\phi(N)$ to generate witness is not necessary. As stated in the original DUA scheme, users (including SP) can use a less efficient method, without using of $\phi(N)$, to obtain the witness. It can still be generated from $au + bx = 1$ and $d = g_{\mathsf{Acc}}^{-b} \bmod N$ directly. As the computation complexity for the non-membership witness generation is $O(l^2)$, where l is the length of the larger number in u and x, the introduced overhead is negligible as compared with other heavy operations such as large number exponentiations.

Here is the fixed version of the DUA non-membership witness generation, which takes the public key $\mathsf{pk_{Acc}}$ instead of the private key $\mathsf{sk_{Acc}}$.

$\mathsf{Compute_{nmw}}(x, \{t_i\}_{0...L}, \mathsf{pk_{Acc}})$:

1. Compute the accumulated ticket product $u = \prod_{i=0}^{L} t_i$.
2. Find a and b such that $au + bx = 1$ by Euclidean algorithm.
   (Since x is not a factor of u, $\gcd(x, u) = 1$.)
3. Output the witness w in the form of $(a, d) = (a, g_{\mathsf{Acc}}^{-b})$.

Improving Efficiency and Practicability. PEREA relies on a queue based structure of size K in the user side, which mandates the user to generate (or update) K witnesses in every authentication request. Thus the computation overhead is proportional to K times the overhead of DUA witness generation.

PE(AR)² removes the need of the queue, and use the product value of all tickets in all witness generations. Since the accumulator is in the form of $V = g_{\mathsf{Acc}}^X$ where $X = \prod x_i$ and x_i's are prime numbers, we can combine the non-membership witness verification of K tickets $\{t_1, \ldots, t_K\}$ to one single non-membership witness verification of a combined value $T = \prod t_i$.

Notice that now the non-membership witness verification will fail if *any* of the tickets among these K tickets are accumulated in the accumulator, since the underlying accumulator's non-membership proof [8] ensures the fact that $\gcd(X, T) \neq 1$ for the case. This gives another efficiency improvement to PE(AR)^2, as blacklist verification could be done in one operation only, except the cost of multiplying a maximum of K tickets together which can be pre-computed. As a result, the computation complexity shifts from K rounds of non-membership proof to a zero-knowledge proof requiring exponentiation of size $O(K \cdot \ell_t)$, where ℓ_t is the size of one ticket.

We further remove the requirement that tickets are added and deleted from the user side storage for *every* authenticated session. Tickets can only be added in the score redemption protocol after the scores associated with some tickets are redeemed (and of course, some new tickets are initially added in the registration protocol). Users can only delete tickets that have been reviewed in the score redemption protocol. Thus the choice of K no longer has impact to the ticket review time of the SP in our new scheme.

Reputation System. Our reputation mechanism associates a score with the credential. For each past session, there is an external mechanism which assigns score to it. The SP can then authenticate this score. The user can redeem scores from multiple sessions together at any desired time. After validity check, the SP refreshes the user's credential with the new score. The user can later authenticate to the SP and possibly access some special services from the SP when the score is above a certain threshold.

Recall that in PEREA, the SP needs to review each authentication in a timely-manner, and the naughtiness assigned to a credential can only be reflected from its K-most recent authentications. It seems that PE(AR)^2 may run into the same problem of requiring the SP to assign score to each session as quickly as possible, since the user can only delete tickets from the credential for those having the associated past sessions reviewed. It might be possible for a user to have all K tickets in the credential pending to be reviewed, and thus can no longer be authenticated for one more session. However, an importance difference between PE(AR)^2 and PEREA is that not only K affordable by our system is much higher than that of PEREA (which will be demonstrated experimentally in Section 5), but it is just a recommended size instead of a hard limit. A very active user can always store more than K pending tickets in the credential. True, this credential may stand out in the system since the size of ZKPoK must be larger, but the compromise in privacy is minimal since every other attributes (like the linkage of this credential with the past sessions) are hidden. On the other hand, one may consider it as a feature providing some sort of soft rate-limiting.

4.2 Construction

First we establish some notations and convention.

Given a security parameter ℓ, let $\ell_N, \ell_t, \ell_s, \ell_e, K$ be the system parameters. The former four are security parameters.

1. The first one is for the RSA modulus. A typical setting could be $(\ell_N, \ell) = (1024, 160)$.
2. The parameter ℓ_t determines the ticket length, which is also the length of a session identifier. User can pick tickets randomly from a set of ℓ_t-bits prime numbers, denoted as Π_{ℓ_t}. When $\ell_t = 166$, there are at least 2^{160} tickets in this set[4]. For a reasonably large number of tickets randomly picked from Π_{ℓ_t}, probability of having two of them collide is approximately 2^{-80}, due to the birthday paradox.
3. K represents the number of tickets that should be generated during registration, and a typical value could be $K = 1000$.
4. Finally, ℓ_s and ℓ_e determine the domain sizes for the components in the CL signature scheme. For its security we require $\ell_s = \ell_N + \ell_t + \ell$, $\ell_e > \ell_t + 2$.

We use the notation PK with different subscripts to refer to different ZKPoK. Their instantiations are standard and will be described in the full version of this paper. In particular, we use the ZK proof of CL signatures [11] during authentication, and the reputation system is realized by the sum of committed values [5].

KeyGen: The service provider $\mathcal{S}$ generates the keys as follows:

1. $\mathcal{S}$ chooses an ℓ_N-bit safe-prime product $N = pq$ as a special RSA modulus, where p and q are random safe primes.
2. $\mathcal{S}$ chooses $g, h, g_{\mathsf{Acc}}, g_{\mathsf{CL}} \in \mathbb{QR}_N$, the set of quadratic residue modulo N.
3. $\mathcal{S}$ sets $\mathsf{pk}_{\mathsf{CL}} = (N, g, h, g_{\mathsf{CL}})$ and $\mathsf{sk}_{\mathsf{CL}} = \phi(N)$, $\mathsf{pk}_{\mathsf{Acc}} = (N, g, h, g_{\mathsf{Acc}})$ and $\mathsf{sk}_{\mathsf{Acc}} = \phi(N)$, i.e., g_{Acc} and g_{CL} are the exponentiation base used in accumulator and CL-signature respectively.
4. $\mathcal{S}$ maintains and publishes a list $\mathbb{L}$ containing pairs of ticket (or session identifier) and score.
5. $\mathcal{S}$ maintains a public blacklist $\mathbb{B}$, and the corresponding accumulator value c, initialized to g_{Acc}.
6. $\mathcal{S}$ runs $\mathsf{K}(1^\ell)$ for the ZKPoK protocols PK_1, PK_2 and PK_3 (which will be defined below). Denote all the common reference strings generated as crs.
7. Finally $\mathcal{S}$ sets $\mathsf{msk} = \phi(N)$ and $\mathsf{mpk} = (\mathsf{crs}, N, g, h, g_{\mathsf{Acc}}, g_{\mathsf{CL}}, \hat{t}, c)$.

In practice, $\mathcal{S}$ may split the public lists $\mathbb{L}$ and $\mathbb{B}$ into smaller lists for different time periods so users could store and download the smaller set of lists. We omit such construction for simplicity.

Reg: Assuming a user $\mathcal{U}$ and a service provider $\mathcal{S}$ has established a pre-authenticated channel via other means, $\mathcal{U}$ obtains a credential from $\mathcal{S}$ as follows:

1. $\mathcal{U}$ sets ticket $t_0 = \hat{t}$ and picks K tickets $t_i \in_R \Pi_{\ell_t} \setminus \mathbb{B}$ where $0 < i \le K$.
2. $\mathcal{U}$ sets $T = \prod_{i=0}^{K} t_i$, and prepares its commitment.

---

[4] This follows from a result of Dusart [12]: the number of distinct primes less than x is larger than $\frac{x}{\ln x}(1 + \frac{0.992}{\ln x})$ for all $x > 598$.

3. $\mathcal{U}$ prepares t_1's commitment.
4. $\mathcal{U}$ computes $w = \mathsf{Compute}_{\mathrm{nmw}}(T, \mathbb{B}, \mathsf{pk}_{\mathsf{Acc}})$ and its commitment.
5. $\mathcal{U}$ sets the initial score $s = 0$, and prepares its commitment.
6. $\mathcal{U}$ sends $\mathcal{S}$ the ZKPoK:

$$PK_1\{(t_0, t_1, T, w, s) : t_0 t_1 | T \wedge 1 = \mathsf{Verify}_{\mathrm{nmw}}(c, T, w, \mathsf{pk}_{\mathsf{Acc}}) \wedge t_0 = \hat{t} \wedge s = 0\}.$$

It proves that 1) t_0 and t_1 are stored in T, 2) w is a non-membership witness that no ticket in T is in the blacklist accumulator value c, and 3) the initial score s is 0.

7. If $\mathcal{S}$ accepts the ZKPoK, he runs $\sigma \leftarrow \mathsf{Sign}_{\mathsf{CL}}((T, t_1, s), \mathsf{sk}_{\mathsf{CL}})$ with $\mathcal{U}$, by signing on the commitments of T, t_1 and s. As a result, $\mathcal{U}$ obtains σ from $\mathcal{S}$.
8. $\mathcal{U}$ sets $\mathbb{T} = \{t_0, \ldots, t_K\}$, the auxiliary information $\mathbb{J} = (\{g^{T/t_i} : t_i \in \mathbb{T}\}, T, g^T, g^T_{\mathsf{Acc}})$, and stores the credential $\mathsf{cred}_0 = (0, \sigma, w, c, s, \mathbb{T}, \mathbb{B}, \mathbb{J})$.

We will then use the notation c_{cred} and $\mathbb{B}_{\mathsf{cred}}$ to denote the accumulator values stored by $\mathcal{U}$ with the credential, which are the current accumulator value and the current blacklist at the time of ticket generation, and may not be as up-to-date as the public values maintained by $\mathcal{S}$.

Auth: On the i-th round of authentication, where $1 \leq i < K$, the user $\mathcal{U}$ is in possession of $\mathsf{cred}_{i-1} = (i - 1, \sigma, w, c_{\mathsf{cred}}, s, \mathbb{T}, \mathbb{B}_{\mathsf{cred}}, \mathbb{J})$. $\mathcal{U}$ authenticates anonymously with $\mathcal{S}$ and obtains a new credential as follows:

1. $\mathcal{U}$ obtains the current blacklist $\mathbb{B}$ and the corresponding accumulator c via a public channel.
2. $\mathcal{U}$ updates cred_{i-1} with an updated witness $w' = \mathsf{Update}_{\mathrm{nmw}}(w, c_{\mathsf{cred}}, T, \{\hat{t}_j\})$, where $\hat{t}_j \in \mathbb{B} \setminus \mathbb{B}_{\mathsf{cred}}$.
3. $\mathcal{U}$ sends $\mathcal{S}$ the ZKPoK:

$$PK_2\{(t_i, t_{i+1}, T, \sigma, w', s) : \quad s > s_{\mathsf{base}} \quad \wedge \quad t_{i+1} | T$$
$$\wedge \quad 1 = \mathsf{Verify}_{\mathrm{nmw}}(c, T, w', \mathsf{pk}_{\mathsf{Acc}}) \quad \wedge \quad 1 = \mathsf{Verify}_{\mathsf{CL}}((T, t_i, s), \sigma, \mathsf{pk}_{\mathsf{CL}})\}.$$

It proves that 1) $\mathcal{U}$'s score s is high enough when $\mathcal{S}$ expects a base score s_{base}, 2) t_{i+1} is stored in T, 3) w' is a non-membership witness that none of the (previous) sessions in T is in the blacklist accumulator value c, and 4) the tuple (T, t_i, s) is signed by $\mathcal{S}$ in the previous session.

4. If $\mathcal{S}$ accepts the ZKPoK, $\mathcal{U}$ opens the commitment of t_i to $\mathcal{S}$.
5. $\mathcal{S}$ aborts if t_i has been stored on $\mathbb{L}$, the list of used tickets, as an old ticket cannot be reused again.
6. Otherwise, $\mathcal{S}$ authenticates $\mathcal{U}$, appends $(t_i, 0, \perp)$ to $\mathbb{L}$, and executes $\sigma' \leftarrow \mathsf{Sign}_{\mathsf{CL}}((T, t_{i+1}, s), \mathsf{sk}_{\mathsf{CL}})$ with $\mathcal{U}$.
7. $\mathcal{U}$ obtains σ' and stores credentials $\mathsf{cred}_i = (i, \sigma', w', c, s, \mathbb{T}, \mathbb{B}, \mathbb{J})$.

Revoke: $\mathcal{S}$ can revoke a previously authenticated session based on the behavior observed for that session. To revoke a session $t \in \mathbb{L}$, $\mathcal{S}$ adds t to $\mathbb{B}$ and accumulates it by setting $c \leftarrow c^t$. $\mathcal{S}$ publishes $\mathbb{B}$ and c via a public channel[5]. The corresponding $(t, \cdot, \cdot)$ entry should then be removed from $\mathbb{L}$.

---

[5] Multiple tickets can be revoked at once by setting $c \leftarrow c^{\hat{T}}$, where $\hat{T}$ is the product of the tickets to be revoked.

Rate: $\mathcal{S}$ can rate a previously authenticated session based on the behavior observed. To rate a session $t \in \mathbb{L}$ with a score s, $\mathcal{S}$ computes $\sigma_t \leftarrow \mathsf{Sign}_{\mathrm{CL}}((t,s), \mathsf{sk}_{\mathrm{CL}})$ and updates $(t,0,\perp)$ to (t,s,σ_t) in the list $\mathbb{L}$.

Redeem: After the i-th round of authentication, $\mathcal{U}$ attempts to use $\mathsf{cred}_i = (i, \sigma, w, c_{\mathsf{cred}}, s, \mathbb{T}, \mathbb{B}_{\mathsf{cred}}, \mathbb{J})$ to exchange for a new credential with the updated score s' due to a list of redeemable tickets $\mathbb{T}_{\mathsf{old}}$. The protocol runs as follows:

1. $\mathcal{U}$ retrieves the scores of the tickets that he wants to redeem and the associated signatures: $\mathbb{S} = \{(t_j, s_j, \sigma_j) \in \mathbb{L} : t_j \in \mathbb{T}_{\mathsf{old}} \wedge \sigma_j \neq \perp\}$.
2. $\mathcal{U}$ removes t_j from $\mathbb{T}_{\mathsf{old}}$ for every j such that $(t_j, s_j, \perp) \in \mathbb{L}$.
3. $\mathcal{U}$ forms $\mathbb{T}_{\mathsf{new}}$ by picking n random new tickets from Π_{ℓ_t}, where n is the size of $\mathbb{T}_{\mathsf{old}}$.
4. $\mathcal{U}$ sets $T_{\mathsf{old}} = \prod t_j'$ where $t_j' \in \mathbb{T}_{\mathsf{old}}$ and $T_{\mathsf{new}} = \prod \hat{t}_j$ where $\hat{t}_j \in \mathbb{T}_{\mathsf{new}}$.
5. $\mathcal{U}$ sends $\mathcal{S}$ the ZKPoK: (where $t_{i+1} \in \mathbb{T}$ and $T \in \mathbb{J}$)

$$PK_3\{(t_{i+1}, T, T_{\mathsf{old}}, T_{\mathsf{new}}, \sigma, s, s', \mathbb{S}) : \quad T_{\mathsf{old}}|T \quad \wedge \quad s' = s + \sum_{(\cdot, s_j, \cdot) \in \mathbb{S}} s_j$$

$$\bigwedge_{(t_j, s_j, \sigma_j) \in \mathbb{S}} 1 = \mathsf{Verify}_{\mathrm{CL}}((t_j, s_j), \sigma_j, \mathsf{pk}_{\mathrm{CL}}) \wedge 1 = \mathsf{Verify}_{\mathrm{CL}}((T, t_{i+1}, s), \sigma, \mathsf{pk}_{\mathrm{Acc}})\}.$$

It proves that 1) the tickets to be redeemed T_{old} are stored in T, 2) s' is the summation of the old score and the new scores to be redeemed, 3) the score s_j of each ticket t_j is signed by $\mathcal{S}$, and 4) the tuple (T, t_{i+1}, s) is signed by $\mathcal{S}$ in the previous session.

6. If $\mathcal{S}$ accepts the ZKPoK, $\mathcal{U}$ opens t_i from its commitment.
7. $\mathcal{U}$ computes $w' = \mathsf{Compute}_{\mathsf{nmw}}(T \cdot T_{\mathsf{new}}/T_{\mathsf{old}}, \mathbb{B}, \mathsf{pk}_{\mathsf{Acc}})$.
8. $\mathcal{S}$ runs $\sigma' \leftarrow \mathsf{Sign}_{\mathrm{CL}}((T \cdot T_{\mathsf{new}}/T_{\mathsf{old}}, t_i, s'), \mathsf{sk}_{\mathrm{CL}})$ with $\mathcal{U}$.
9. $\mathcal{U}$ obtains σ' from $\mathcal{S}$, recalculates auxiliary information $\mathbb{J}'$ using the new tickets, and stores credential $\mathsf{cred}_{i+1}' = (i+1, \sigma', w', c, s', \{\mathbb{T}\backslash\mathbb{T}_{\mathsf{old}} \cup \mathbb{T}_{\mathsf{new}}\}, \mathbb{B}, \mathbb{J}')$.

Theorem 1. *Our scheme is accountable and private if PK_1, PK_2, PK_3 are ZKPoK, the underlying CL signature scheme and the accumulator system are secure.*

The proof is given in the full version of the paper.

5   Discussions

5.1   Complexity Analysis

Here we present a computation analysis on $\mathrm{PE(AR)}^2$, PEREA [5] and BLACR-Express [10] based on the number of expensive operations, in terms of K (size of user ticket queue), δ_L (number of tickets added to blacklist after the last time when a user retrieved the updated credential) and δ_R (number of tickets to redeem). We also included the **Redeem** protocol for $\mathrm{PE(AR)}^2$ in the comparison

Table 1. Performance analysis in authentication phase

Scheme	Communication		Computation	
	Downlink	Uplink[♠]	User	Service Provider
PE(AR)^2				
Auth	$O(\delta_L)$	$O(K)$	1Eu[♡]+ 14E$_m$	14E$_m$
Redeem	$O(\delta_L + \delta_R)$	$O(K + \delta_R)$	1Eu[♣]+ $(6 + 6\delta_R)$E$_m$	$(6 + 6\delta_R)$E$_m$
PEREA [5]	$O(\delta_L)$	$O(K)$	$[(K + 1)\delta_L + 5K$ $+2\left\lceil\frac{K+1}{3}\right\rceil + \left\lceil\frac{K-1}{3}\right\rceil + 3]E_m$	$(4K + 2\left\lceil\frac{K+1}{3}\right\rceil + 3)E_m$
BLACR [10] (Express)	$O(\delta_L)$	$O(\delta_L)$	$(30\delta_L + 81)$E$_1$[♢] $+ (5\delta_L + 7)$E$_T + (\delta_L + 4)$P	$(12\delta_L + 26)$E$_1$ + $(2\delta_L + 6)$E$_2$ $+ (5\delta_L + 18)$E$_T + (\delta_L + 3)$P

[♠] For PE(AR)^2, $O(K)$-size is due to the product of K tickets, which should be smaller than the $O(K)$ non-membership proof required in PEREA.

[♡] Let $h_1 = \min(\delta_L, K)$. The Euclidean algorithm here require $O(h_1)$ division operations. The performance can be further improved as shown in [13].

[♣] Let $h_2 = \min(L, K)$. The Euclidean algorithm here is running $O(h_2)$ division operations.

[♢] For simplicity, we assume the fraction of tickets that belong to the user is close to zero when there are a lots of tickets in the system, and $\ell = m = 1$ for BLACR-Express.

since it is expected that a user would execute **Redeem** for once after K invocations of **Auth**. In the worst case, users could run **Redeem** after every single instance of **Auth**.

Table 1 outlines the analysis on computation and communication. Denote E$_m$ as the multi-based modular exponentiation that 3 exponentiations could be done simultaneously, Eu as the extended Euclidean algorithm, E$_1$, E$_2$, E$_T$ as the exponentiation of the pairing group $\mathbb{G}_1, \mathbb{G}_2, \mathbb{G}_T$ respectively, and P as the pairing operation. Only BLACR uses E$_1$, E$_2$, E$_T$ and P.

Notice that the main bottleneck of these schemes are on the SP side, PE(AR)^2 has time complexities of $O(1)$ and $O(\delta_R)$ in **Auth** and **Redeem** phase respectively. For PEREA and BLACR-Express, authentication requires $O(K)$ and $O(\delta_L)$ witness verification on SP side respectively. On user side, PE(AR)^2 has time complexities of $O(1)$ and $O(\delta_R)$ multi-base exponentiation E$_m$ in **Auth** and **Redeem** phase respectively. PEREA and BLACR-Express run in $O(K\delta_L)$ and $O(\delta_L)$ respectively on the user side[6]. We remark that PE(AR)^2 uses Eu, with time complexity dominated by the division operation, and the number of division involved is related to L, K, and δ_L. However, the division operation is much more efficient than exponentiation (E$_m$, E$_1$, E$_2$, E$_T$) and pairing P.

5.2 Empirical Result

We benchmarked the time required for authentication on PEREA and BLACR-Express, and both authentication and redemption for PE(AR)^2, for different K, on both SP and user side. We obtained the benchmark from a 2.4GHz Intel Core i5 box with 4GB memory. The result is visualized in Figure 1. We marked the y-axis in *logarithmic scale* so as to capture the benchmark of different magnitude.

---

[6] Here we use the BLACR-Express data without pre-computation. It was claimed that the dependence of δ_L for E$_m$ and P can be removed without details [10], hence we cannot perform benchmark on them here.

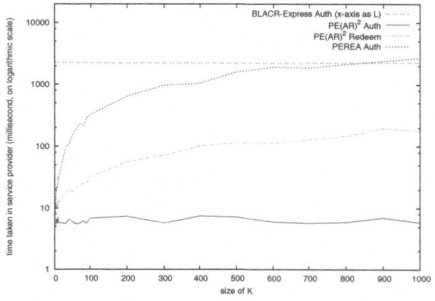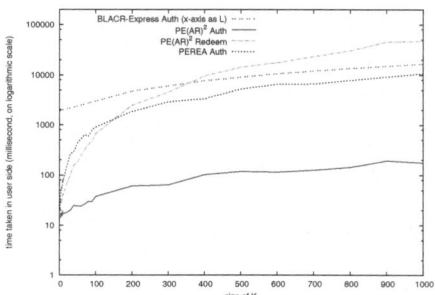

Fig. 1. Benchmark for time taken in service provider and user side

The benchmarks are obtained from averaging the result with repetitive experiments. For PEREA, our benchmark aligns with the result in [5]. The SP takes around 20ms for authentication when $K = 5$, and client takes around 50ms. As K increases to 1000, the SP takes 2758ms and client takes around 10672ms. For BLACR-Express with $\delta_L = 2\%$ of L, SP authentication takes around 2228 ms when $L = 200$ and 2281ms when $L = 1000$. On the other hand, client authentication takes around 4775ms when $L = 200$ and 16539ms when $L = 1000$. For $PE(AR)^2$, the SP takes 6ms and 10ms for Auth and Redeem respectively when $K = 5$, 6ms and 177ms when $K = 1000$. Client takes 15ms and 28ms for Auth and Redeem respectively when $K = 5$, 176ms and 47236ms when $K = 1000$.

Recall the fact that the bottleneck of the scheme should be on the SP side, in particular on authentication part. We look at the traffic statistics of 2channel, one of the most popular internet forum in Japan. They have an average of 2.5 million posts made every day[7], which is about 1736 posts per minute. Our $PE(AR)^2$ on the SP side can handle 10000 posts per minute[8], and hence can handle real traffic for popular internet forums.

5.3   Practical Considerations

Reducing the computation of the Service Provider. Authentication should be made efficient for the SP, since the SP may need to handle multiple user authentication requests simultaneously in real time. $PE(AR)^2$ relaxed the SP computation time requirement as compared with PEREA, such that only one signature verification and witness verification is required. This improvement is done by condensing the witnesses of multiple tickets into one single witness, and the actual computation is shifted from Auth phase to Redeem phase.

---

[7] http://stats.2ch.net/suzume.cgi?yes, in Japanese

[8] BLACR-Express (with pre-computation) is setup to support authentications at the rate of about 25 authentications/minute for active users and about 1 authentication/minute for inactive users [10], based on the traffic of Wikipedia. It is much less than the requirements for popular internet forums.

Pre-computation of Auxiliary Information. As the value to be proved changes from a single ticket to a product of ticket, the proof size can be larger. We thus suggest the use of auxiliary information gathered from Reg and Redeem phase. With terms like g^T, g_{Acc}^T and g^{T/t_i} precomputed and stored as auxiliary information in $\mathbb{J}$, the zero-knowledge proof (PK_2) in the Auth phase can be computed efficiently. For example, CL signature verification requires the computation of g^T, non-membership verification requires the computation of $(z_d)^T$ where $z_d = dg^\rho$, with a random ρ and $d = g_{Acc}^{-b}$. Thus $(z_d)^T = (g^T)^\rho (g_{Acc}^T)^{-b}$ and can be computed efficiently given the auxiliary information $\mathbb{J}$.

Relaxing Mandatory Timely Blacklist Publishing. PE(AR)^2 does not require the SP to publish timely on the tickets that should be blacklisted, as a user could only shift a ticket out of the queue after it is rated. Thus an SP have a higher flexibility in resource management regarding when to review the authenticated sessions, mark them as blacklisted, or give a score rating.

Rate-Limiting Considerations. Our scheme does not require rate-limiting facility. The term rate-limiting refers to the ability to stop abuser from overusing the service over a period of time. In PEREA, rate-limiting is mandatory as an adversary could generate a lot of authentication sessions to shift any potential blacklist session out of the ticket queue before the SP would blacklist them. However, rate-limiting is not provided in the scope of PEREA and could only be integrated using other cryptographic techniques (e.g., see [14]). Our scheme does not have such weakness as the removal of any ticket is checked by the SP in Redeem phase. Our scheme could actually be modified to provide a less-efficient construction for rate-limiting by default as follows. Recall that in Reg and Redeem protocols, a user may attempt to generate more than K number of tickets in the ticket queue. We could modify our construction to have the user to provide zero knowledge proof on the number of tickets generated. Then, a user could no longer authenticate once all the tickets in the queue are used up, and must wait until the SP to participate in Redeem phase.

Types of Scores. Our current construction only considers positive scores to provide rewards for good behavior. It is suitable for a lot of popular Internet sites that use positive scores only, like Facebook (Like) and Google Plus (+1).

Nevertheless, we can extend it to support negative scores like BLACR [10]. For the security model, we need to give a new model which prevents an adversary from not redeeming the negative scores. For the construction, we have to remove the unlinkability of the ticket redeemed in the Redeem protocol, by removing $\mathbb{S}$ from the PK_3. Therefore, the SP can check whether a ticket is redeemed or not. If a ticket with a negative score is not redeemed after a long period of time, the SP can simply add it to the blacklist. Hence, its owner is forced to ask the SP to un-blacklist it by redeeming it, before any further authentication.

6   Conclusion

We presented PE(AR)^2, which preserves the same anonymous authentication functionalities as PEREA, but fixes its vulnerability and incorporates reputation system. $PE(AR)^2$ also eliminated the complexity dependence on the ticket queue size for the SP. The improvement is significant for an active system with many sessions and gives more flexibility to the SP for tickets review. Furthermore, $PE(AR)^2$ avoids the reliance of additional anonymous rate-limiting protocol, which was critical to the operation of PEREA for prevent user from bypassing the misbehavior detection. We believe that $PE(AR)^2$ is more practical for real world use. We presented the construction of our design. We give a brief analysis of the complexity and benchmarks, justifying that $PE(AR)^2$ is efficient for real-world deployment.

References

1. Chow, S.S.M., He, Y.-J., Hui, L.C.K., Yiu, S.M.: SPICE – Simple Privacy-Preserving Identity-Management for Cloud Environment. In: Bao, F., Samarati, P., Zhou, J. (eds.) ACNS 2012. LNCS, vol. 7341, pp. 526–543. Springer, Heidelberg (2012)
2. Camenisch, J., Kohlweiss, M., Soriente, C.: An Accumulator Based on Bilinear Maps and Efficient Revocation for Anonymous Credentials. In: Jarecki, S., Tsudik, G. (eds.) PKC 2009. LNCS, vol. 5443, pp. 481–500. Springer, Heidelberg (2009)
3. Tsang, P.P., Au, M.H., Kapadia, A., Smith, S.W.: BLAC: Revoking repeatedly misbehaving anonymous users without relying on TTPs. ACM Trans. Inf. Syst. Secur. 13(4), 39 (2010)
4. Brickell, E., Li, J.: Enhanced Privacy ID: A Direct Anonymous Attestation Scheme with Enhanced Revocation Capabilities. In: WPES, pp. 21–30. ACM (2007)
5. Au, M.H., Tsang, P.P., Kapadia, A.: PEREA: Practical TTP-free revocation of repeatedly misbehaving anonymous users. ACM Trans. Inf. Syst. Secur. 14(4), 29 (2011)
6. Au, M.H., Susilo, W., Mu, Y., Chow, S.S.M.: Constant-size dynamic k-times anonymous authentication. IEEE Systems Journal (to appear)
7. Peng, K., Bao, F.: Vulnerability of a Non-membership Proof Scheme. In: SECRYPT, pp. 419–422. SciTePress (2010)
8. Li, J., Li, N., Xue, R.: Universal Accumulators with Efficient Nonmembership Proofs. In: Katz, J., Yung, M. (eds.) ACNS 2007. LNCS, vol. 4521, pp. 253–269. Springer, Heidelberg (2007)
9. Jøsang, A., Ismail, R., Boyd, C.: A survey of trust and reputation systems for online service provision. Decis. Support Syst. 43(2), 618–644 (2007)
10. Au, M.H., Kapadia, A., Susilo, W.: BLACR: TTP-Free Blacklistable Anonymous Credentials with Reputation. In: NDSS. The Internet Society (2012)
11. Camenisch, J.L., Lysyanskaya, A.: A Signature Scheme with Efficient Protocols. In: Cimato, S., Galdi, C., Persiano, G. (eds.) SCN 2002. LNCS, vol. 2576, pp. 268–289. Springer, Heidelberg (2003)
12. Dusart, P.: The kth prime is greater than $k(\ln k + \ln \ln k - 1)$ for $k \geq 2$. Math. Comput. 68(225), 411–415 (1999)
13. Möller, N.: On schönhage's algorithm and subquadratic integer gcd computation. Math. Comput. 77(261), 589–607 (2008)
14. Chow, S.S.M.: Real Traceable Signatures. In: Jacobson Jr., M.J., Rijmen, V., Safavi-Naini, R. (eds.) SAC 2009. LNCS, vol. 5867, pp. 92–107. Springer, Heidelberg (2009)

Dismantling iClass and iClass Elite

Flavio D. Garcia[1], Gerhard de Koning Gans[1],
Roel Verdult[1], and Milosch Meriac[2]

[1] Institute for Computing and Information Sciences,
Radboud University Nijmegen, The Netherlands
{flaviog,gkoningg,rverdult}@cs.ru.nl
[2] Bitmanufaktur GmbH, Germany
milosch.meriac@bitmanufaktur.de

Abstract. With more than 300 million cards sold, HID iClass is one of the most popular contactless smart cards on the market. It is widely used for access control, secure login and payment systems. The card uses 64-bit keys to provide authenticity and integrity. The cipher and key diversification algorithms are proprietary and little information about them is publicly available. In this paper we have reverse engineered all security mechanisms in the card including cipher, authentication protocol and key diversification algorithms, which we publish in full detail. Furthermore, we have found six critical weaknesses that we exploit in two attacks, one against iClass Standard and one against iClass Elite (a.k.a., iClass High Security). In order to recover a secret card key, the first attack requires one authentication attempt with a legitimate reader and 2^{22} queries to a card. This attack has a computational complexity of 2^{40} MAC computations. The whole attack can be executed within a day on ordinary hardware. Remarkably, the second attack which is against iClass Elite is significantly faster. It directly recovers the master key from only 15 authentication attempts with a legitimate reader. The computational complexity of this attack is lower than 2^{25} MAC computations, which means that it can be fully executed within 5 seconds on an ordinary laptop.

1 Introduction

iClass is an ISO/IEC 15693 [1] compatible contactless smart card manufactured by HID Global. It was introduced in the market back in 2002 as a secure replacement of the HID Prox card which did not have any cryptographic capabilities. According to the manufacturer, more than 300 million iClass cards have been sold. These cards are widely used in access control of secured buildings such as The Bank of America Merrill Lynch, the International Airport of Mexico City and the United States Navy base of Pearl Harbor [2] among many others[1]. Other applications include secure user authentication such as in the naviGO system included in Dell's Latitude and Precision laptops; e-payment like in the

---

[1] http://hidglobal.com/mediacenter.php?cat2=2

S. Foresti, M. Yung, and F. Martinelli (Eds.): ESORICS 2012, LNCS 7459, pp. 697–715, 2012.

FreedomPay and SmartCentric systems; and billing of electric vehicle charging such as in the Liberty PlugIns system. iClass has also been incorporated into the new BlackBerry phones which support Near Field Communication (NFC).

iClass uses a proprietary cipher to provide data integrity and mutual authentication between card and reader. The cipher uses a 64-bit diversified key which is derived from a 56-bit master key and the serial number of the card. This key diversification algorithm is built into all iClass readers. The technology used in the card is covered by US Patent 6058481 and EP 0890157. The precise description of both the cipher and the key diversification algorithms are kept secret by the manufacturer following the principles of security by obscurity. Remarkably, all iClass Standard cards worldwide share the same master key for the iClass application. This master key is stored in the EEPROM memory of every iClass reader. It is possible though to let HID generate and manage a custom key for your system if you are willing to pay a higher price. The iClass Elite Program (a.k.a., High Security) uses an additional key diversification algorithm and a custom master key per system which according to HID provides "the highest level of security" [3].

Over the last few years, much attention has been paid to the (in)security of the cryptographic mechanisms used in contactless smart cards [4–7]. Experience has shown that the secrecy of proprietary ciphers does not contribute to its cryptographic strength. Most notably the Mifare Classic, which has widespread application in public transport ticketing and access control systems, has been thoroughly broken in the last few years [4, 8–11]. Other prominent examples include KeeLoq [12,13] and Hitag2 [7,14,15] used in car keys and CryptoRF [5, 16,17] used in access control and payment systems. HID proposes iClass as a migration option for systems using Mifare Classic, boosting that iClass provides "improved security, performance and data integrity"[2]. For almost one decade after its introduction to the market, the details of the security mechanisms of iClass remained unknown.

Our Contribution. In this paper we have fully reverse engineered iClass's proprietary cipher and authentication protocol which we publish in full detail. This task is not trivial since it was first necessary to bypass the read protection mechanisms of the microcontroller used in the readers in order to retrieve its firmware. Furthermore we have found serious vulnerabilities in the cipher that enable an attacker to recover the secret key from the card by just wirelessly communicating with it. The potential impact of this attack is vast since other vulnerabilities in the key diversification algorithm allow an adversary to use this secret key to recover the master key, provided that he has mild computational power. Additionally, we have reverse engineered the iClass Elite key diversification algorithm which we describe in full detail. We show that this algorithm has even more serious vulnerabilities than the standard key diversification algorithm, allowing an attacker to directly recover the *master key* by simply communicating with a legitimate iClass reader. Concretely, we propose two attacks: one against iClass Standard and one against iClass Elite. Both attacks allow an adversary to recover the master key.

---
[2] http://www.hidglobal.com/pr.php?id=393

- The first attack exploits a total of *four* weaknesses in the cipher, key diversification algorithm and implementation. In order to execute this attack the adversary first needs to eavesdrop one legitimate authentication session between card and reader. Then it runs 2^{19} key updates and 2^{22} authentication attempts with the card. This takes less than six hours to accomplish when using a Proxmark III as a reader and recovers 24 bits of the card key. Finally, off-line, the attacker needs to search for the remaining 40 bits of the key. Having recovered the card key, the adversary gains full control over the card. Furthermore, computing the master key from the card key is as hard as breaking single DES [18].

- The second attack concerning iClass Elite exploits *two* weaknesses in the key diversification algorithm and recovers the master key directly. In order to run this attack the adversary only needs to run 15 authentication attempts with a legitimate reader. Afterwards, off-line, the adversary needs to compute only 2^{25} DES encryptions in order to recover the master key. This attack, from beginning to end runs within 5 seconds on ordinary hardware.

We have executed both attacks in practice and verified these claims and attack times. For eavesdropping and card emulation we used a Proxmark III (see http://www.proxmark.org) which costs approximately 200 USD.

Related Work. Recently, Meriac proposed a procedure to read out the EEPROM of a PIC microcontroller, like the ones used in iClass readers [19]. The reverse engineering process described here builds upon this work. Garcia, de Koning Gans and Verdult in [18] have reverse engineered the key diversification algorithm of iClass and showed that it is possible to recover a master key when the adversary has full control (i.e., can execute arbitrary commands) over a legitimate iClass reader. They also showed that inverting the key diversification function in iClass is as hard as a chosen plaintext attack on single DES. During the course of our research Kim, Jung, Lee, Jung and Han have made a technical report [20] available online describing independent reverse engineering of the cipher used in iClass. Their research takes a very different, hardware oriented approach. They recovered most of the cipher by slicing the chip and analyzing the circuits with a microscope. Our approach, however, is radically different as our reverse engineering is based on the disassembly of the reader's firmware and the study of the communication behavior of tags and readers. Furthermore, the description of the cipher by Kim et al. is not correct. Concretely, their key byte selection function in the cipher is different from the one used in iClass which results in incompatible keys. Kim et al. have proposed two key recovery attacks. The first one is theoretical, in the sense that it assumes that an attacker has access to a MAC oracle over messages of arbitrary length. This assumption is unrealistic since neither the card nor the reader provide access to such a powerful oracle. Their second attack requires full control over a legitimate reader in order to issue arbitrary commands. Besides this assumption, it requires 2^{42} online authentication queries which, in practice, would take more than 710 years to gather. Our attacks, however, are practical in the sense that they can be executed within a day and require only wireless communication with a genuine iClass card/reader.

Overview. This paper is organized as follows. Section 2 starts with a description of the iClass architecture, the functionality of the card, the cryptographic algorithms. Section 2.6 describes four weakness in the cipher, key diversification algorithm and implementation of iClass. All these weaknesses are exploited in Section 2.7 were we propose a key recovery attack against iClass. Section 3 studies iClass Elite. We first describe its key diversification algorithm and then we describe two weaknesses which are later exploited in Section 3.3 to mount an attack that recovers the master key. Finally, Section 4 gives concluding remarks.

2   iClass

An HID iClass card is in fact a pre-configured and re-branded PicoPass card produced by Inside Secure[3]. HID configures and finalizes the cards so that the configuration settings can no longer be modified. This section describes in detail the functionality and security mechanisms of iClass and it also describes the reverse engineering process. Let us first introduce notation.

Notation 2.1 *Throughout this paper ϵ denotes the empty bitstring. $\oplus$ denotes exclusive or. $\boxplus$ denotes addition modulo 256. Given two bitstrings x and y, xy denotes their concatenation. Sometimes we write this concatenation explicitly with $x \cdot y$ to improve readability. $\bar{x}$ denotes the bitwise complement of x. 0^n denotes a bitstring of n zero-bits. Furthermore, given a bitstring $x \in (\mathbb{F}_2^k)^l$, we denote with $x_{[i]}$ the i-th element $y \in \mathbb{F}_2^k$ of x. We write y_i to denote the i-th bit of y. For example, given the bitstring $x = 0x010203 \in (\mathbb{F}_2^8)^3$ and $y := x_{[2]}$ then $y = 0x03$ and $y_6 = 1$.*

Remark 1 (Byte representation). Throughout this paper, bytes are represented with their most significant bit on the left. However, the least significant bit is transmitted first over the air (compliant with ISO/IEC 15693). This is the same order in which the bits are input to the cryptographic functions. In other words, 0x0a0b0c is transmitted and processed as input 0x50d030.

2.1   Reverse Engineering iClass

In order to reverse engineer the cipher and the key diversification algorithms, we have first recovered the firmware from an iClass reader. For this we used a technique introduced in [19] and later used in [18]. Next we will briefly describe this technique.

iClass readers, as many other embedded devices, rely on the popular PIC microcontroller to perform their computations. These microcontrollers are very versatile and can be flashed with a custom firmware. The (program) memory of the

---

[3] http://www.insidesecure.com/eng/Products/Secure-Solutions/
PicoPass

microcontroller is divided into a number of blocks, each of them having access control bits determining whether this block is readable/writable. Even when the PIC is configured to be non-writable, it is always possible to reset the access control bits by erasing the memory of the chip. At first glance this feature does not seem very helpful to our reverse engineering goals since it erases the data on the memory. Conveniently enough, even when the most common programming environments do not allow it, the microcontroller supports erasure of a single block. After patching the PIC programmer software to support this feature, it is possible to perform the following attack to recover the firmware:

- Buy two iClass RW400 (6121AKN0000) readers.
- Erase block 0 on one of the readers. This resets the access control bits on block 0 to readable, writable.
- Write a small dumper program on block 0 that reads blocks $1, \ldots, n$ and outputs the data via one of the microcontroller's output pins.
- Use the serial port of a computer to record the data. This procedure recovers blocks $1, \ldots, n$.
- Proceed similarly with the other reader, but erasing blocks $1, \ldots, n$. This in fact fills each block with NOP operations.
- At the end of block n write a dumper program for block 0.
- At some point the program will jump to an empty block and then reach dumper program that outputs the missing block 0.

Once we had recovered the firmware, it was possible to use IDA Pro and MPLAB to reverse engineer the algorithms.

2.2   Functionality

iClass cards come in two versions called 2KS and 16KS with respectively 256 and 4096 bytes of memory. The memory of the card is divided into blocks of eight bytes as shown in Figure 2.1. Memory blocks 0, 1, 2 and 5 are publicly readable. They contain the card identifier id, configuration bits, the card challenge c_C and issuer information. Block 3 and 4 contain two diversified cryptographic keys $k1$ and $k2$ which are derived from two different master keys $\mathcal{K}1$ and $\mathcal{K}2$. These master keys are referred to in the documentation as debit key and credit key. The card only stores the diversified keys $k1$ and $k2$. The remaining memory blocks are divided into two areas, so-called applications. The size of these applications is defined by the configuration block.

The first application of an iClass card is the *HID application* which stores the card identifier, PIN code, password and other information used in access control systems. Read and write access to the HID application requires a valid mutual authentication using the cipher to prove knowledge of $k1$. The master key of the HID application is a global key known to all iClass Standard compatible readers. The globally used key $\mathcal{K}1$ is kept secret by HID Global and is not shared with any customer or industrial partner. Recovery of this key undermines the security of all systems using iClass Standard. Two methods have been proposed

Block	Content	Denoted by
0	Card serial number	Identifier id
1	Configuration	
2	e-Purse	Card challenge c_C
3	Key for application 1	Diversified debit key $k1$
4	Key for application 2	Diversified credit key $k2$
5	Application issuer area	
6...18	Application 1	HID application
19...n	Application 2	User defined memory

publicly readable
write-only after authentication
read-write after authentication

Fig. 2.1. Memory layout of an iClass card

[18, 19] to recover this key. To circumvent the obvious limitations of having only a global master key, iClass Elite uses a different key diversification algorithm that allows having custom master keys. The details regarding iClass Elite can be found in Section 3. The second global master key $\mathcal{K}2$ is used in both iClass Standard and Elite systems and it is available to any developer who signs a non-disclosure agreement with HID global. It is possible to extract this key from publicly available software binaries [18]. In addition, the document [21] contains this master key and is available online. This key $\mathcal{K}2$ can be used by developers to protect the second application, although in practice, $\mathcal{K}2$ is hardly ever used or modified.

The card provides basic memory operations like read and write which have some non-standard behavior and therefore we describe them in detail.

- The read command takes as input an application number a and a memory block number n and returns the memory content of this block. This command has the side effect of selecting the corresponding key ($k1$ for application 1 or $k2$ for application 2) in the cipher and then it feeds the content of block n into the internal state of the cipher. Cryptographic keys are not readable. When the block number n corresponds to the address where a cryptographic key is stored, then read returns a bitstring of 64 ones.
- The write command takes as input a block number n, an eight-byte payload p and a MAC of the payload $\mathrm{MAC}(k, n \cdot p)$. When successful, it writes p in memory and it returns a copy of p for verification purposes. This command has the side effect of resetting the internal state of the cipher. In addition, when the block number n corresponds to the address where a cryptographic key k is stored, the payload is XORed to the previous value instead of over-writing it, i.e., it assigns $k := k \oplus p$.

Therefore, in order to update a key k to k', the reader must issue a write command with $k \oplus k'$ as payload. In this way the card will store $k \oplus k \oplus k' = k'$ as the new key. On the one hand, this particular key update procedure has the special feature that in case an adversary eavesdrops a key update he is unable to learn the newly assigned key, provided that he does not know k. On the other hand this introduces a new weakness which we describe in Section 2.6.2.

Before being able to execute read or write commands on the protected memory of a card, the reader needs to get access to the corresponding application by running a successful authentication protocol described in Section 2.3. Cryptographic keys $k1$ and $k2$ can be seen as part of application 1 and 2, respectively. This means that in order to modify a key e.g., $k1$, the reader first needs to run a successful authentication with $k1$.

2.3   Authentication Protocol

This section describes the authentication protocol between an iClass card and reader. This protocol is depicted in Figure 2.2 and an example trace is shown in Figure 2.3. First, during the anti-collision protocol, the reader learns the identity of the card id. Then, the reader chooses an application and issues a read command on the card challenge c_C. This c_C is called 'e-purse' in the iClass documentation [22] and it is a special memory block in the sense that it is intended to provide freshness. In the next step, the reader issues an authenticate command. This command sends to the card a reader nonce n_R and a MAC of the card challenge c_C concatenated with n_R. Finally, the card answers with a MAC of c_C, n_R followed by 32 zero bits. For more details on the MAC function see Section 2.4. After a successful authentication on c_C the reader is granted read and write access within the selected application.

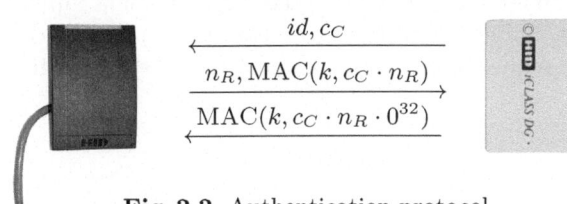

Fig. 2.2. Authentication protocol

Origin	Message	Description
Reader	0C 00 73 33	Read identifier
Tag	47 47 6C 00 F7 FF 12 E0	Card serial number id
Reader	0C 01 FA 22	Read configuration
Tag	12 FF FF FF E9 1F FF 3C	iClass 16KS configuration
Reader	88 02	Read c_C and select $k1$
Tag	FE FF FF FF FF FF FF FF	Card challenge c_C
Reader	05 00 00 00 00 1D 49 C9 DA	Authenticate with $n_R = 0, \mathrm{MAC}(k1, c_C \cdot n_R)$
Tag	5A A2 AF 92	Response $\mathrm{MAC}(k1, c_C \cdot n_R \cdot 0^{32})$
Reader	87 02 FD FF FF FF FF FF FF FF CF 3B D4 6A	Write on block 02, $c_C - 1, \mathrm{MAC}(k1, 02 \cdot c_C - 1)$
Tag	FF FF FF FF FD FF FF FF	Update succesful

Fig. 2.3. Authenticate and decrement card challenge c_C using diversified key $k1 =$ 0xE033CA419AEE43F9

Remark 2. Since the card lacks a pseudo-random generator, the reader should decrement c_C after a successful authentication in order to provide freshness for the next authentication, see Figure 2.3. Note that this is not enforced by the card.

2.4   The Cipher

This section describes the cipher used in iClass. This cipher is interesting from an academic and didactic perspective as it combines two important techniques in the design of stream ciphers from the 80s and beginning of the 90s, i.e., Fibonacci generators and Linear Feedback Shift Registers (LFSRs).

The internal state of the cipher consists of four registers. Two of them, which we call left (l) and right (r) are part of the Fibonacci generator. The other two registers constitute linear feedback shift registers top (t) and bottom (b).

Definition 1 (Cipher state). *A cipher state of iClass s is an element of $\mathbb{F}_2^{40}$ consisting of the following four components: 1. the* left *register* $l = (l_0 \ldots l_7) \in \mathbb{F}_2^8$; *2. the* right *register* $r = (r_0 \ldots r_7) \in \mathbb{F}_2^8$; *3. the* top *register* $t = (t_0 \ldots t_{15}) \in \mathbb{F}_2^{16}$. *4. the* bottom *register* $b = (b_0 \ldots b_7) \in \mathbb{F}_2^8$.

The cipher has an input bit which is used (among others) during authentication to shift in the card challenge c_C and the reader nonce n_R. With every clock tick a cipher state s evolves to a successor state s'. Both LFSRs shift to the right and the Fibonacci generator iterates using one byte of the key (chosen by the $select(\cdot)$ function) and the bottom LFSR as input. During this iteration each of these components is updated, receiving additional input from the other components of the cipher. With each iteration the cipher produces one output bit. The following sequence of definitions describe the cipher in detail; see also Figure 2.4.

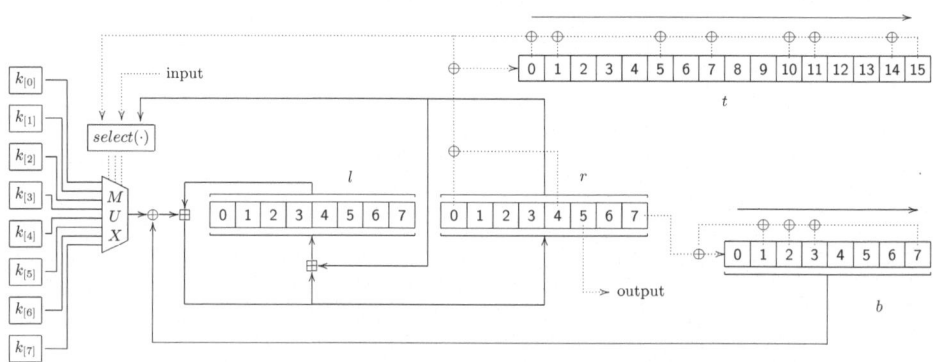

Fig. 2.4. The iClass cipher. Solid lines represent byte operations while dotted lines represent bit operations.

Definition 2. *The feedback function for the top register $T\colon \mathbb{F}_2^{16} \to \mathbb{F}_2$ is defined as $T(x_0x_1\ldots\ldots x_{15}) = x_0 \oplus x_1 \oplus x_5 \oplus x_7 \oplus x_{10} \oplus x_{11} \oplus x_{14} \oplus x_{15}$. Similarly, the feedback function for the bottom register $B\colon \mathbb{F}_2^8 \to \mathbb{F}_2$ is defined as $B(x_0x_1\ldots x_7) = x_1 \oplus x_2 \oplus x_3 \oplus x_7$.*

Definition 3 (Selection function). *The selection function* select $: \mathbb{F}_2 \times \mathbb{F}_2 \times \mathbb{F}_2^8 \to \mathbb{F}_2^3$ *is defined as* $select(x, y, r) = z_0 z_1 z_2$ *where*

$$z_0 = (r_0 \wedge r_2) \oplus (r_1 \wedge \overline{r_3}) \oplus (r_2 \vee r_4)$$
$$z_1 = (r_0 \vee r_2) \oplus (r_5 \vee r_7) \oplus r_1 \oplus r_6 \oplus x \oplus y$$
$$z_2 = (r_3 \wedge \overline{r_5}) \oplus (r_4 \wedge r_6) \oplus r_7 \oplus x$$

Definition 4 (Successor state). *Let* $s = \langle l, r, t, b \rangle$ *be a cipher state,* $k \in (\mathbb{F}_2^8)^8$ *be a key and* $y \in \mathbb{F}_2$ *be the input bit. Then, the successor cipher state* $s' = \langle l', r', t', b' \rangle$ *is defined as*

$$t' := (T(t) \oplus r_0 \oplus r_4)t_0 \ldots t_{14} \qquad l' := (k_{[select(T(t), y, r)]} \oplus b') \boxplus l \boxplus r$$
$$b' := (B(b) \oplus r_7)b_0 \ldots b_6 \qquad r' := (k_{[select(T(t), y, r)]} \oplus b') \boxplus l$$

We define the successor function suc *which takes a key* $k \in (\mathbb{F}_2^8)^8$, *a state* s *and an input* $y \in \mathbb{F}_2$ *and outputs the successor state* s'. *We overload the function* suc *to multiple bit input* $x \in \mathbb{F}_2^n$ *which we define as*

$$\text{suc}(k, s, \epsilon) = s$$
$$\text{suc}(k, s, x_0 \ldots x_n) = \text{suc}(k, \text{suc}(k, s, x_0 \ldots x_{n-1}), x_n)$$

Definition 5 (Output). *Define the function* output *which takes an internal state* $s = <l, r, t, b>$ *and returns the bit* r_5. *We also define the function* output *on multiple bits input which takes a key* k, *a state* s *and an input* $x \in \mathbb{F}_2^n$ *as*

$$output(k, s, \epsilon) = \epsilon$$
$$output(k, s, x_0 \ldots x_n) = output(s) \cdot output(k, s', x_1 \ldots x_n)$$
$$\text{where } s' = \text{suc}(k, s, x_0).$$

Definition 6 (Initial state). *Define the function* init *which takes as input a key* $k \in (\mathbb{F}_2^8)^8$ *and outputs the initial cipher state* $s = <l, r, t, b>$ *where*

$$t := 0\text{xE012} \qquad l := (k_{[0]} \oplus 0\text{x4C}) \boxplus 0\text{xEC}$$
$$b := 0\text{x4C} \qquad r := (k_{[0]} \oplus 0\text{x4C}) \boxplus 0\text{x21}$$

Definition 7. *Define the function* MAC $: (\mathbb{F}_2^8)^8 \times \mathbb{F}_2^n \to \mathbb{F}_2^{32}$ *as*

$$\text{MAC}(k, m) = output(k, \text{suc}(k, init(k), m), 0^{32})$$

2.5   Key Diversification

This section describes in detail the built-in key diversification algorithm of iClass. Besides the obvious purpose of deriving a card key from a master key, this algorithm intends to circumvent weaknesses in the cipher by preventing the usage of certain 'weak' keys. In order to compute a diversified key, the iClass reader first encrypts the card identity *id* with the master key $\mathcal{K}$, using single

DES. The resulting ciphertext is then input to a function called *hash0* which outputs the diversified key k.

$$k = hash0(\text{DES}_{\text{enc}}(id, \mathcal{K}))$$

Here the DES encryption of id with master key $\mathcal{K}$ outputs a cryptogram c of 64 bits. These 64 bits are divided as $c = \langle x, y, z_{[0]}, \ldots, z_{[7]} \rangle \in \mathbb{F}_2^8 \times \mathbb{F}_2^8 \times (\mathbb{F}_2^6)^8$ which is used as input to the *hash0* function. This function introduces some obfuscation by performing a number of permutations, complement and modulo operations, see Figure 2.5. Besides that, it checks for and removes patterns like similar key bytes, which could produce a strong bias in the cipher. Finally, the output of *hash0* is the diversified card key $k = k_{[0]}, \ldots, k_{[7]} \in (\mathbb{F}_2^8)^8$.

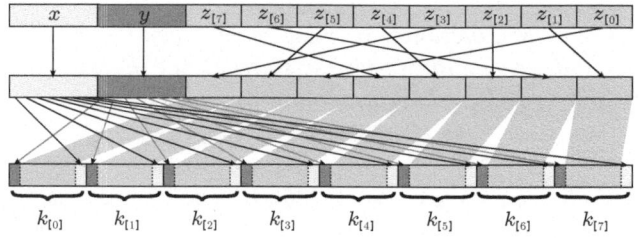

Fig. 2.5. Schematic representation of the function *hash0*

Remark 3. The DES implementation used in iClass is non-compliant with the NIST standard [23] in the way of representing keys. According to the standard, a DES key is of the form $\langle k_0 \ldots k_6 p_0, k_7 \ldots k_{13} p_1, \ldots, k_{47} \ldots k_{55} p_7 \rangle$ where $k_0 \ldots k_{55}$ are the actual key bits and $p_0 \ldots p_7$ are parity bits. Instead, in iClass a DES key is of the form $\langle k_0 \ldots k_{55} p_0 \ldots p_7 \rangle$.

The following sequence of definitions describe the function *hash0* in detail. This function is included here for the sake of completeness. The details over this construction are not necessary to understand the attacks presented in Section 2.7 and Section 3.3.

Definition 8. *Let the function* check: $(\mathbb{F}_2^6)^8 \to (\mathbb{F}_2^6)^8$ *be defined as*

$$check(z_{[0]} \ldots z_{[7]}) = ck(3, 2, z_{[0]} \ldots z_{[3]}) \cdot ck(3, 2, z_{[4]} \ldots z_{[7]})$$

where ck: $\mathbb{N} \times \mathbb{N} \times (\mathbb{F}_2^6)^4 \to (\mathbb{F}_2^6)^4$ *is defined as*

$$ck(1, -1, z_{[0]} \ldots z_{[3]}) = z_{[0]} \ldots z_{[3]}$$
$$ck(i, -1, z_{[0]} \ldots z_{[3]}) = ck(i - 1, i - 2, z_{[0]} \ldots z_{[3]})$$
$$ck(i, j, z_{[0]} \ldots z_{[3]}) = \begin{cases} ck(i, j - 1, z_{[0]} \ldots z_{[i]} \leftarrow j \ldots z_{[3]}), & z_{[i]} = z_{[j]}; \\ ck(i, j - 1, z_{[0]} \ldots z_{[3]}), & otherwise. \end{cases}$$

Definition 9. *Define the function permute:* $\mathbb{F}_2^n \times (\mathbb{F}_2^6)^8 \times \mathbb{N} \times \mathbb{N} \to (\mathbb{F}_2^6)^8$ *as*

$$permute(\epsilon, z, l, r) = \epsilon$$

$$permute(p_0 \ldots p_n, z, l, r) = \begin{cases} (z_{[l]} + 1) \cdot permute(p_0 \ldots p_{n-1}, z, l+1, r), & p_n = 1; \\ z_{[r]} \cdot permute(p_0 \ldots p_{n-1}, z, l, r+1), & otherwise. \end{cases}$$

Definition 10. *Define the bitstring* $\pi \in (\mathbb{F}_2^8)^{35}$ *in hexadecimal notation as*

$$\pi = 0x0F171B1D1E272B2D2E333539363A3C474B$$
$$4D4E535556595A5C636566696A6C71727478$$

Each byte in this sequence is a permutation of the bitstring `00001111`. *Note that this list contains only the half of all possible permutations. The other half can be computed by taking the bit complement of each element in the list.*

Finally, the definition of *hash0* is as follows.

Definition 11. *Let the function hash0:* $\mathbb{F}_2^8 \times \mathbb{F}_2^8 \times (\mathbb{F}_2^6)^8 \to (\mathbb{F}_2^8)^8$ *be defined as* $hash0(x, y, z_{[0]} \ldots z_{[7]}) = k_{[0]} \ldots k_{[7]}$ *where*

$$z'_{[i]} = (z_{[i]} \bmod (63 - i)) + i \qquad\qquad i = 0 \ldots 3$$

$$z'_{[i+4]} = (z_{[i+4]} \bmod (64 - i)) + i \qquad\qquad i = 0 \ldots 3$$

$$\hat{z} = check(z')$$

$$p = \begin{cases} \overline{\pi_{[x \bmod 35]}}, & x_0 = 1; \\ \pi_{[x \bmod 35]}, & otherwise. \end{cases}$$

$$\tilde{z} = permute(p, \hat{z}, 0, 4)$$

$$k_{[i]} = \begin{cases} y_i \cdot \overline{\tilde{z}_{[i]}} \cdot p_i + 1, & y_i = 1; \\ y_i \cdot \tilde{z}_{[i]} \cdot \overline{p_i}, & otherwise. \end{cases} \qquad\qquad i = 0 \ldots 7$$

2.6 Weaknesses

This section describes weaknesses in the design and implementation of iClass that are later exploited in Section 2.7 to mount a key recovery attack.

2.6.1 Weak Keys

The cipher has a clear weakness when the three rightmost bits of each key byte are the same. Let us elaborate on that.

Proposition 1. *Let* β *be a bitstring of length three. Then, for all keys* $k \in \mathbb{F}_2^{64}$ *of the form* $k = \alpha_{[0]}\beta \ldots \alpha_{[7]}\beta$ *with* $\alpha_{[i]} \in \mathbb{F}_2^5$ *the cipher outputs a constant* C_β.

This is due to the fact that only the three rightmost bits of register r define the output of the cipher and only the rightmost bit of r influences register b. But these, in turn, are only influenced by the three rightmost bits of the key bytes. This means that the 5 leftmost bits of r and the 5 leftmost bits of each key byte affect only the key byte selection, but for the key under consideration this does not affect the output. The same holds for c_C and n_R as they are just input to the $select(\cdot)$ function. Figure 2.6 shows the corresponding MAC value for each possible β. The manu-

β	$C_\beta = \mathrm{MAC}(k, c_C \cdot n_R)$
000	BF 5D 67 7F
001	10 ED 6F 11
010	· 53 35 42 0F
011	AB 47 4D A0
100	F6 CF 43 36
101	59 7F 4B 58
110	1A A7 66 46
111	E2 D5 69 E9

Fig. 2.6. Corresponding MAC for each value of β

facturer seems to be aware of this feature of the cipher since the function $hash0$, used in key diversification, prevents such a key from being used. Although, this weakness combined with the weakness described in Section 2.6.2 and 2.6.3 result in a vulnerability exploited in Section 2.7.

2.6.2   XOR Key Update Weakness

In order to update a card key, the iClass reader does not simply send the new key to the card in the clear but instead it sends the XOR of the old and the new key (See Section 2.2). This simple mechanism prevents an attacker from eavesdropping the new key during key update. Although, this key update mechanism introduces a new weakness, namely, it makes it possible to make partial modifications to the existing key. A key update should be an atomic operation. Otherwise, it allows an adversary to split the search space in a time-memory trade-off. Moreover, in case the cipher has some weak keys like the ones described in Section 2.6.1, it allows an adversary to force the usage of one of these keys.

2.6.3   Privilege Escalation Weakness

Several privilege escalation attacks have been described in the literature [24, 25]. The privilege escalation weakness in iClass also concerns the management of access rights over an application within the card. After a successful authentication for application 1 has been executed, the reader is granted read and write access to this application. Then, it is possible to execute a read command for a block within application 2 without loosing the previously acquired access rights. More precisely, when a read command is issued for a block n within application 2, with $n \neq c_C$, this returns a sequence of 64 ones which indicates that permission is denied to read this block. Surprisingly, this read attempt on application 2 does not affect the previously acquired rights on application 1. This read command though, has the side effect of loading the key $k2$ into the internal state of the cipher. In particular, from this moment on the card accepts write commands on application 1 that have a valid MAC computed using key $k2$.

2.6.4 Weak Key Diversification on iClass

The key diversification algorithm of iClass was reverse engineered by Garcia et al. in [18]. This algorithm uses a combination of single DES and a proprietary function called *hash0*, described in Section 2.5. Furthermore, the authors show that the function *hash0* is not one-way nor collision resistant. In fact, it is possible to compute the inverse function $hash0^{-1}$ having a modest amount (on average 4) of candidate pre-images. They also show that once a card key is known, recovering an iClass master key is not harder than a chosen plaintext attack on single DES. After careful inspection of the function *hash0* it becomes clear that this function attempts to fix the weak key weakness presented in Section 2.6.1. The function *hash0* makes sure that, when looking at the last bit of each key byte, exactly four of them are zeros (and the other four of them are ones). Due to this restriction there are only $\frac{8!}{(4!)^2} = 70$ possibilities for the last bits of each key byte, instead of $2^8 = 256$, reducing the entropy of the key by 1.87 bits.

2.7 Key Recovery Attack on iClass

This section shows how the weaknesses described in Section 2.6 can be exploited. Concretely, we propose an attack that allows an adversary to recover a card key by wirelessly communicating with a card and a reader. Once the card key has been recovered, the weak key diversification weakness described in Section 2.6.4 can be exploited in order to recover the master key. Next, we describe the attack on the card key in detail.

In order to recover a target card key $k1$ from application 1, an attacker A proceeds as follows. First, A eavesdrops a legitimate authentication trace on the e-purse with key $k1$, while making sure that the e-purse is not updated. If the reader attempts to update the e-purse, this can be prevented by playing as man-in-the-middle or by simply jamming the e-purse update message. Next, the adversary replays this authentication trace to the card. At this point the adversary gains read and write access to application 1. Although, in order to actually be able to write, the adversary still needs to send a valid MAC with $k1$ of the payload. To circumvent this problem, the adversary proceeds as described in Section 2.6.3, exploiting the privilege escalation weakness. At this point the adversary still has read and write access to application 1 but he is now able to issue `write` commands using MACs generated with the known key $k2$ to write on application 1. In particular, A is now able to modify $k1$ at will. Exploiting the XOR key update weakness described in Section 2.6.2, the adversary modifies the card key $k1$ into a weak key by setting the three rightmost bits of each key byte the same. Concretely, the adversary runs $2^{3 \times 7} = 2^{21}$ key updates on the card with $\Delta = 0^5 \delta_{[0]} \ldots 0^5 \delta_{[6]} 0^8 \in \mathbb{F}_2^{64}$ and $\delta_{[i]} = abc \in \mathbb{F}_2^3$ for all possible bits a, b and c. One of these key updates will produce a weak key, i.e., a key of the form $k = \alpha_{[0]}\beta \ldots \alpha_{[7]}\beta$ with $\alpha_{[i]} \in \mathbb{F}_2^5$. Exploiting the weak key weakness described in Section 2.6.1, after each key update A runs 8 authentication attempts, one for each possible value of β, using the MAC values shown in Figure 2.6. Note that a failed authentication will not affect the previously acquired access rights. As soon as an authentication attempt succeeds the card responds with a MAC value that univocally determines β as stated in Proposition 1. Knowing β the adversary is able to recover the three rightmost bits of $k1_{[i]}$ by computing $\beta \oplus \delta_{[i]}$ for $i = 0 \ldots 6$. Furthermore, the three rightmost bits of $k_{[7]}$ are equal to $\beta \oplus 000 = \beta$. In this way, the attacker recovers $3 \times 8 = 24$ bits of $k1$ and only has to search the remaining 40 bits of the key, using the legitimate trace eavesdropped in the beginning.

This attack can be further optimized. The restriction on the last bit of each byte imposed by *hash0*, described at the end of Section 2.6.4, reduces the number of required key updates from 2^{21} to almost 2^{19}. Therefore, it reduces the total number of authentication attempts to $2^{19} \times 8 = 2^{22}$. Once the attacker has recovered the card key $k1$, as we already mention in Section 2.6.4, recovering the master key is just as hard as breaking single DES.

3   iClass Elite

HID introduces iClass Elite (a.k.a. High Security) as the solution for "those who want a boost in security" [26]. iClass Elite aims to solve the obvious limitations of having just one single world-wide master key for all iClass systems. Instead, iClass Elite allows customers to have a personalized master key for their own system. To this purpose, HID has modified the key diversification algorithm, described in Section 2.5 by adding an extra step to it. This modification only affects the way in which readers compute the corresponding card key but does not change anything on the cards themselves. Section 3.1 describes this key diversification algorithm in detail. Then Section 3.2 describes two weaknesses that are later exploited in Section 3.3.

3.1   Key Diversification on iClass Elite

This section describes the key diversification algorithm of iClass Elite. We first need to introduce a number of auxiliary functions and then we explain this algorithm in detail.

Definition 12 (Auxiliary functions). *Let us define the bit-rotate left function* $rl\colon \mathbb{F}_2^8 \to \mathbb{F}_2^8$ *as* $rl(x_0 \ldots x_7) = x_1 \ldots x_7 x_0$. *Similarly, define the bit-rotate right function* $rr\colon \mathbb{F}_2^8 \to \mathbb{F}_2^8$ *as* $rr(x_0 \ldots x_7) = x_7 x_0 \ldots x_6$. *Furthermore, define the nibble-swap function swap:* $\mathbb{F}_2^8 \to \mathbb{F}_2^8$ *as* $swap(x_0 \ldots x_7) = x_4 \ldots x_7 x_0 \ldots x_3$.

Definition 13. *Let the function hash1:* $(\mathbb{F}_2^8)^8 \to (\mathbb{F}_2^8)^8$ *be defined as* $hash1(id_{[0]} \ldots id_{[7]}) = k_{[0]} \ldots k_{[7]}$ *where*

$$k_{[i]} = k'_{[i]} \bmod 128, \qquad\qquad\qquad i = 0 \ldots 7$$

$$k'_{[0]} = id_{[0]} \oplus \cdots \oplus id_{[7]} \qquad\qquad k'_{[4]} = \overline{rr(id_{[4]} \boxplus k'_{[2]})} + 1$$

$$k'_{[1]} = id_{[0]} \boxplus \ldots \boxplus id_{[7]} \qquad\qquad k'_{[5]} = \overline{rl(id_{[5]} \boxplus k'_{[3]})} + 1$$

$$k'_{[2]} = rr(swap(id_{[2]} \boxplus k'_{[1]})) \qquad k'_{[6]} = rr(id_{[6]} \boxplus (k'_{[4]} \oplus \text{0x3C}))$$

$$k'_{[3]} = rl(swap(id_{[3]} \boxplus k'_{[0]})) \qquad k'_{[7]} = rl(id_{[7]} \boxplus (k'_{[5]} \oplus \text{0xC3}))$$

Definition 14. *Define the rotate key function* $rk\colon (\mathbb{F}_2^8)^8 \times \mathbb{N} \to (\mathbb{F}_2^8)^8$ *as*

$$rk(x_{[0]} \ldots x_{[7]}, 0) = x_{[0]} \ldots x_{[7]}$$
$$rk(x_{[0]} \ldots x_{[7]}, n+1) = rk(rl(x_{[0]}) \ldots rl(x_{[7]}), n)$$

Definition 15. *Let the function hash2*: $(\mathbb{F}_2^8)^8 \to (\mathbb{F}_2^{64})^{16}$ *be defined as* $hash2(k_{[0]} \ldots k_{[7]}) = y_{[0]} z_{[0]} \cdots y_{[7]} z_{[7]}$ *where*

$$z_{[0]} = \text{DES}_{enc}(\mathcal{K}^{cus}, \overline{\mathcal{K}^{cus}}); \quad z_{[i]} = \text{DES}_{dec}(rk(\mathcal{K}^{cus}, i), z_{[i-1]}) \quad i = 1 \ldots 7$$
$$y_{[0]} = \text{DES}_{dec}(z_{[0]}, \overline{\mathcal{K}^{cus}}); \quad y_{[i]} = \text{DES}_{enc}(rk(\mathcal{K}^{cus}, i), y_{[i-1]}) \quad i = 1 \ldots 7$$

Next we introduce the selected key. This key is used as input to the standard iClass key diversification algorithm. It is computed by taking a selection of bytes from $hash2(\mathcal{K}^{cus})$. This selection is determined by each byte of $hash1(id)$ seen as a byte offset within the bitstring $hash2(\mathcal{K}^{cus})$.

Definition 16. *Let* $h \in (\mathbb{F}_2^8)^{128}$. *Let* $k^{sel} \in (\mathbb{F}_2^8)^8$ *be the selected key defined as*

$$h := hash2(\mathcal{K}^{cus}); \qquad k^{sel}_{[i]} := h_{[hash1(id)_{[i]}]} \qquad i = 0 \ldots 7$$

The last step to compute the diversified card key is just like in iClass (see Section 2.5) $k := hash0(\text{DES}_{enc}(k^{sel}, id))$.

3.2 Weaknesses in iClass Elite

This section describes two weaknesses in the key diversification algorithm of iClass Elite. These weaknesses are exploited in Section 3.3 to mount an attack against iClass Elite that recovers the custom master key.

3.2.1 Redundant Key Diversification on iClass Elite

Assume that an adversary somehow learns the first 16 bytes of $hash2(\mathcal{K}^{cus})$, i.e., $y_{[0]}$ and $z_{[0]}$. Then he can simply recover the master custom key $\mathcal{K}^{cus}$ by computing

$$\mathcal{K}^{cus} = \overline{\text{DES}_{enc}(z_{[0]}, y_{[0]})}.$$

Furthermore, the adversary is able to verify that he has the correct $\mathcal{K}^{cus}$ by checking whether $z_{[0]} = \text{DES}_{enc}(\mathcal{K}^{cus}, \overline{\mathcal{K}^{cus}})$.

3.2.2 Weak Key-byte selection on iClass Elite

Yet another weakness within the key diversification algorithm of iClass Elite has to do with the way in which bytes from $hash2(\mathcal{K}^{cus})$ are selected in order to construct the key k^{sel}.

As described in Section 3.1, the selection of key bytes from $hash2(\mathcal{K}^{cus})$ is determined by $hash1(id)$. This means that only the card's identity determines which bytes of $hash2(\mathcal{K}^{cus})$ are used for k^{sel}. This constitutes a serious weakness since no secret is used in the selection of key bytes at all. Especially considering that, for some card identities, the same bytes of $hash2(\mathcal{K}^{cus})$ are chosen multiple times by $hash1(id)$. In particular, this implies that some card keys have significantly lower entropy than others. What is even more worrying, an adversary can compute by himself which card identities have this feature.

3.3   Key Recovery Attack on iClass Elite

In order to recover a master key $\mathcal{K}^{cus}$, an attacker proceeds as follows. First, exploiting the weakness described in Section 3.2.2, the adversary builds a list of chosen card identities like shown in Figure 3.1. This table shows a list of 15 card identities and their corresponding key-byte selection indices $hash1(id)$. These card identities are malicious.

They are chosen such that the resulting key k^{sel} has very low entropy (in fact, it is possible to find several tables with similar characteristics). For the first card identity in the table, the resulting key k^{sel} is build out of only three different bytes from $hash2(\mathcal{K}^{cus})$, namely 0x00, 0x01 and 0x45. Therefore, this key has as little as 24 bits of entropy (instead of 56). Next, the adversary will initiate an authentication protocol run with a legitimate reader, pretending to be a card with identity $id =$ 0x000B0FFFF7FF12E0 as in the table. Following the authentication

card identity id	$hash1(id)$
00 0B 0F FF F7 FF 12 E0	**01 01** 00 00 45 01 45 45
00 04 0E 08 F7 FF 12 E0	**78 02** 00 00 45 01 45 45
00 09 0D 05 F7 FF 12 E0	**7B 03** 00 00 45 01 45 45
00 0A 0C 06 F7 FF 12 E0	**7A 04** 00 00 45 01 45 45
00 0F 0B 03 F7 FF 12 E0	**7D 05** 00 00 45 01 45 45
00 08 0A 0C F7 FF 12 E0	**74 06** 00 00 45 01 45 45
00 0D 09 09 F7 FF 12 E0	**77 07** 00 00 45 01 45 45
00 0E 08 0A F7 FF 12 E0	**76 08** 00 00 45 01 45 45
00 03 07 17 F7 FF 12 E0	**69 09** 00 00 45 01 45 45
00 3C 06 E0 F7 FF 12 E0	**20 0A** 00 00 45 01 45 45
00 01 05 1D F7 FF 12 E0	**63 0B** 00 00 45 01 45 45
00 02 04 1E F7 FF 12 E0	**62 0C** 00 00 45 01 45 45
00 07 03 1B F7 FF 12 E0	**65 0D** 00 00 45 01 45 45
00 00 02 24 F7 FF 12 E0	**5C 0E** 00 00 45 01 45 45
00 05 01 21 F7 FF 12 E0	**5F 0F** 00 00 45 01 45 45

Fig. 3.1. Chosen card identities

protocol, the reader will return a message containing a nonce n_R and a MAC with k. The adversary will repeat this procedure for each card identity in the table, storing a tuple $< id, n_C, n_R, \mathrm{MAC} >$ for each entry. Afterwards, off-line, the adversary tries all 2^{24} possibilities for bytes 0x00, 0x01 and 0x45 for the first key identity. For each try, he computes the resulting k and recomputes the authentication run until he finds a MAC equal to the one he got from the reader. Then he has recovered bytes 0x00, 0x01 and 0x45 from $hash2(\mathcal{K}^{cus})$. The adversary proceeds similarly for the remaining card identities from the table. Although, this time he already knows bytes 0x00, 0x01 and 0x45 and therefore only two bytes per identity need to be explored. This lowers the complexity to 2^{16} for each of the remaining entries in the table. The bytes that need to be explored at each step are highlighted with boldface in the table. At this point the adversary has recovered the first 16 bytes of $hash2(\mathcal{K}^{cus})$. Finally, exploiting the weakness described in Section 3.2.1, the adversary is able to recover the custom master key $\mathcal{K}^{cus}$ with a total computational complexity of 2^{25} DES encryptions.

4   Conclusions

In this paper we have shown that the security of several building blocks of iClass is unsatisfactory. We have found many vulnerabilities in the cryptography and the implementation of iClass that result in two key recovery attacks. Our first attack requires one eavesdropped authentication trace with a genuine reader (which takes about 10ms). Next, the adversary needs 2^{22} authentication attempts with a card, which in practice takes approximately six hours. To conclude the attack, the adversary needs only 2^{40} off-line MAC computations to recover the card key. The whole attack can be executed within a day. For the attack against iClass Elite, an adversary only needs 15 authentication attempts with a genuine reader to recover the custom master key. The computational complexity of this attack is negligible, i.e., 2^{25} DES encryptions. This attack can be executed from beginning to end in less than five seconds. We have successfully executed both attacks in practice and verified the claimed attack times.

This paper reinforces the point that has been made many times: security by obscurity often covers up negligent designs. The built-in key diversification and especially the function *hash0* is advertised as a security feature but in fact it is a patch to circumvent weaknesses in the cipher. The cipher is a basic building block for any secure protocol. Experience shows that once a weakness in a cipher has been found, it is extremely difficult to patch it in a satisfactory manner. Using a well known and community reviewed cipher is a better alternative. The technique described in [27] could be considered as a palliating countermeasure for our first attack. More is not always better: the key diversification algorithm of iClass Elite requires fifteen DES operations more than iClass Standard while it achieves inferior security. Instead, it would have been more secure and efficient to use 3DES than computing 16 single DES operations in an ad hoc manner. NIST have proposed a statistical test suite [28] that can be used to measure the cryptographic strength of a cipher. Although, many weaknesses arise from mistakes in the implementation. Best practice in the development and implementation of security products should incorporate some form of formal verification to prevent that, see for instance [29]. Furthermore, systematic and automated model checking techniques proposed in [30] can help to detect and avoid implementation weaknesses like the privilege escalation in iClass. Alternatively, formalizing the whole design in a theorem prover [31, 32] may reveal additional weaknesses. In line with the principles of responsible disclosure, we have notified the manufacturer HID Global and informed them of our findings back in November 2011. Our collaboration and communication with HID Global is 'open and productive'. HID has established a Product Security Reporting Center to encourage and improve this type of communication.

Acknowledgments. The authors would like to thank Bart Jacobs for his firm support.

References

1. Identification cards – contactless integrated circuit(s) cards – vicinity cards (ISO/IEC 15693), International Organization for Standardization (ISO) (2000)
2. Cummings, N.: Sales training. Slides from HID Technologies (March 2006)

3. HID Global: iClass RW100, RW150, RW300, RW400 readers (2009)
4. Garcia, F.D., de Koning Gans, G., Muijrers, R., van Rossum, P., Verdult, R., Schreur, R.W., Jacobs, B.: Dismantling MIFARE Classic. In: Jajodia, S., Lopez, J. (eds.) ESORICS 2008. LNCS, vol. 5283, pp. 97–114. Springer, Heidelberg (2008)
5. Garcia, F.D., van Rossum, P., Verdult, R., Wichers Schreur, R.: Dismantling SecureMemory, CryptoMemory and CryptoRF. In: 17th ACM Conference on Computer and Communications Security (CCS 2010), ACM/SIGSAC, pp. 250–259 (2010)
6. Plötz, H., Nohl, K.: Peeling Away Layers of an RFID Security System. In: Danezis, G. (ed.) FC 2011. LNCS, vol. 7035, pp. 205–219. Springer, Heidelberg (2012)
7. Verdult, R., Garcia, F.D., Balasch, J.: Gone in 360 seconds: Hijacking with Hitag2. In: 21st USENIX Security Symposium (USENIX Security 2012). USENIX Association (2012)
8. Nohl, K., Evans, D., Starbug, P.H.: Reverse engineering a cryptographic RFID tag. In: 17th USENIX Security Symposium (USENIX Security). USENIX Association, 185–193 (2008)
9. de Koning Gans, G., Hoepman, J.-H., Garcia, F.D.: A Practical Attack on the MIFARE Classic. In: Grimaud, G., Standaert, F.-X. (eds.) CARDIS 2008. LNCS, vol. 5189, pp. 267–282. Springer, Heidelberg (2008)
10. Garcia, F.D., van Rossum, P., Verdult, R., Wichers Schreur, R.: Wirelessly pickpocketing a MIFARE Classic card. In: 30th IEEE Symposium on Security and Privacy (S&P 2009), pp. 3–15. IEEE Computer Society (2009)
11. Courtois, N.T.: The dark side of security by obscurity - and cloning MIFARE Classic rail and building passes, anywhere, anytime. In: 4th International Conference on Security and Cryptography (SECRYPT 2009), pp. 331–338. INSTICC Press (2009)
12. Bogdanov, A.: Linear Slide Attacks on the KeeLoq Block Cipher. In: Pei, D., Yung, M., Lin, D., Wu, C. (eds.) Inscrypt 2007. LNCS, vol. 4990, pp. 66–80. Springer, Heidelberg (2008)
13. Kasper, M., Kasper, T., Moradi, A., Paar, C.: Breaking KEELOQ in a Flash: On Extracting Keys at Lightning Speed. In: Preneel, B. (ed.) AFRICACRYPT 2009. LNCS, vol. 5580, pp. 403–420. Springer, Heidelberg (2009)
14. Courtois, N.T., O'Neil, S., Quisquater, J.-J.: Practical Algebraic Attacks on the Hitag2 Stream Cipher. In: Samarati, P., Yung, M., Martinelli, F., Ardagna, C.A. (eds.) ISC 2009. LNCS, vol. 5735, pp. 167–176. Springer, Heidelberg (2009)
15. Soos, M., Nohl, K., Castelluccia, C.: Extending SAT Solvers to Cryptographic Problems. In: Kullmann, O. (ed.) SAT 2009. LNCS, vol. 5584, pp. 244–257. Springer, Heidelberg (2009)
16. Biryukov, A., Kizhvatov, I., Zhang, B.: Cryptanalysis of the Atmel Cipher in SecureMemory, CryptoMemory and CryptoRF. In: Lopez, J., Tsudik, G. (eds.) ACNS 2011. LNCS, vol. 6715, pp. 91–109. Springer, Heidelberg (2011)
17. Balasch, J., Gierlichs, B., Verdult, R., Batina, L., Verbauwhede, I.: Power Analysis of Atmel CryptoMemory – Recovering Keys from Secure EEPROMs. In: Dunkelman, O. (ed.) CT-RSA 2012. LNCS, vol. 7178, pp. 19–34. Springer, Heidelberg (2012)
18. Garcia, F.D., de Koning Gans, G., Verdult, R.: Exposing iClass key diversification. In: 5th USENIX Workshop on Offensive Technologies (USENIX WOOT), pp. 128–136. USENIX Association (2011)
19. Meriac, M.: Heart of darkness - exploring the uncharted backwaters of HID iClass security. Technical report, Bitmanufaktur GmbH (December 2010); Presentation at the 27th Chaos Computer Congress (27C3)

20. Kim, C., Jung, E.G., Lee, D.H., Jung, C.H., Han, D.: Cryptanalysis of INCrypt32 in HID's iClass systems. Cryptology ePrint Archive, Report 2011/469 (2011)
21. HID Global: HID management key letter (November 2006)
22. Inside Contactless Datasheet PicoPass 2KS (November 2004)
23. FIPS, PUB 46-3, Data Encryption Standard (DES). National Institute for Standards and Technology (NIST), Gaithersburg, MD, USA (1999)
24. Kohno, T., Stubblefield, A., Rubin, A.D., Wallach, D.S.: Analysis of an electronic voting system. In: 25th IEEE Symposium on Security and Privacy (S&P 2004), pp. 27–40. IEEE Computer Society (2004)
25. Davi, L., Dmitrienko, A., Sadeghi, A.-R., Winandy, M.: Privilege Escalation Attacks on Android. In: Burmester, M., Tsudik, G., Magliveras, S., Ilić, I. (eds.) ISC 2010. LNCS, vol. 6531, pp. 346–360. Springer, Heidelberg (2011)
26. Cummings, N.: iClass levels of security (April 2003)
27. Rahmati, A., Salajegheh, M., Holcomb, D., Sorber, J., Burleson, W.P., Fu, K.: TARDIS: Time and remanence decay in SRAM to implement secure protocols on embedded devices without clocks. In: 21st USENIX Security Symposium (USENIX Security 2012). USENIX Association (2012)
28. Rukhin, A., Soto, J., Nechvatal, J., Smid, M., Barker, E., Leigh, S., Levenson, M., Vangel, M., Banks, D., Heckert, A., Dray, J., Vo, S.: A statistical test suite for the validation of random number generators and pseudo random number generators for cryptographic applications. NIST Special Publication, pp. 800–822 (2001)
29. Focardi, R., Luccio, F.L.: Secure Recharge of Disposable RFID Tickets. In: Barthe, G., Datta, A., Etalle, S. (eds.) FAST 2011. LNCS, vol. 7140, pp. 85–99. Springer, Heidelberg (2012)
30. Tretmans, J.: Model Based Testing with Labelled Transition Systems. In: Hierons, R.M., Bowen, J.P., Harman, M. (eds.) FORTEST. LNCS, vol. 4949, pp. 1–38. Springer, Heidelberg (2008)
31. Blanchet, B.: An efficient cryptographic protocol verifier based on prolog rules. In: 14th IEEE workshop on Computer Security Foundations (CSFW 2001), pp. 82–96. IEEE Computer Society (2001)
32. Jacobs, B., Wichers Schreur, R.: Logical Formalisation and Analysis of the Mifare Classic Card in PVS. In: van Eekelen, M., Geuvers, H., Schmaltz, J., Wiedijk, F. (eds.) ITP 2011. LNCS, vol. 6898, pp. 3–17. Springer, Heidelberg (2011)

Evaluation of Standardized Password-Based Key Derivation against Parallel Processing Platforms

Markus Dürmuth, Tim Güneysu, Markus Kasper,
Christof Paar, Tolga Yalcin, and Ralf Zimmermann

Horst Görtz Institute for IT-Security, Ruhr-University Bochum

Abstract. Passwords are still the preferred method of user authentication for a large number of applications. In order to derive cryptographic keys from (human-entered) passwords, key-derivation functions are used. One of the most well-known key-derivation functions is the standardized PBKDF2 (RFC2898), which is used in TrueCrypt, CCMP of WPA2, and many more. In this work, we evaluate the security of PBKDF2 against password guessing attacks using state-of-the-art parallel computing architectures, with the goal to find parameters for the PBKDF2 that protect against today's attacks. In particular we developed fast implementations of the PBKDF2 on FPGA-clusters and GPU-clusters. These two families of platforms both have a better price-performance ratio than PC-clusters and pose, thus, a great threat when running large scale guessing attacks. To the best of our knowledge, we demonstrate the fastest attacks against PBKDF2, and show that we can guess more than 65% of typical passwords in about one week.

1 Introduction

Password-based user authentication is the most widely used form of user authentication, and it will be in the foreseeable future. Alternative technologies such as security-tokens and biometric identification exist but have a number of drawbacks that prevent their wide-spread use outside of specific realms: Security tokens, for example, need to be managed, which is a complicated task for Internet-wide services with millions of users, they can be lost, and there needs to be some standardized interface to connect them to every possible computing device (including desktop computers, mobile phones, tablet PCs, and others). Biometric identification systems require extra hardware to read the biometrics, false-rejects cause user annoyance, and many biometrics are no secret (e.g., we leave fingerprints on many surfaces we touch). Passwords, on the other hand, are highly portable, easy to understand by users, and relatively easy to manage for the administrators. Still, there are a number of problems with passwords. Arguably the central theme is the trade-off between choosing a strong password versus one that is human-rememberable. Various studies and recommendations have been published presenting the imminent threat of insufficiently strong passwords chosen for security systems by humans (see, e.g., [1–3]).

S. Foresti, M. Yung, and F. Martinelli (Eds.): ESORICS 2012, LNCS 7459, pp. 716–733, 2012.
© Springer-Verlag Berlin Heidelberg 2012

Passwords are usually not stored in clear in computer systems but the hash of the password is stored instead. Consequently, *guessing attacks* are the most efficient method of attacking passwords, and studies indicate that a substantial number of passwords can be guessed with moderately fast hardware [4]. One measure to mitigate guessing attacks on passwords is to increase the time required to compute the key derivation function from the human-entered password. The most common approach nowadays is to run the password through a large number of hash function evaluations.

With the release of PKCS #5 v2.0 and RFC 2898 [5], a standard for password key derivation schemes based on a pseudo-random function (PRF) with variable output key size has been established. The specified Password-Based Key Derivation Function #2 (PBKDF2) has been widely employed in many security-related systems, such as TrueCrypt [6], OpenDocument Encryption of OpenOffice [7], and CCMP of WPA2 [8], to name only a few. The PRF typically involves an HMAC construction based on a cryptographic hash function that can be freely chosen by the designer. Besides the password, the PBKDF2 requires a salt S, a parameter for the desired output key length k_{Len}, and an iteration counter value c that specifies the number of repeated invocations of the PRF. While security aspects of salt and key length are quite well understood [9], it remains an open question how large c should be for practical use – especially with respect to adversaries who have access to very powerful computing resources, which have become more widely available in recent years. In particular, an impressive number of parallel computations, and thus password guessing attacks, can be performed with (clusters of) the latest many-core CPUs, highly thread-optimized graphics cards (GPUs), or modern Field-Programmable Gate Arrays (FPGAs). These latest platforms need to be considered when fixing c in practical systems. Note that recent security applications specify c typically to be in the range of 10^3 to 10^4 iterations (e. g., TrueCrypt performs between 1000 and 4000 iterations depending on the hash function applied). Referring to Paragraph 4.2 of RFC 2898, a minimum iteration count of 1000 is recommended in the original release of the standard. We argue that this number should be regularly updated to reflect the performance gains of the most recent high-performance computing platforms. In this work, more than 10 years after the initial release of RFC 2898, we will re-evaluate the security margin provided by PBKDF2 with respect to the password cracking performance of modern computing hardware.

Contribution: In this work we analyze the choice of security parameters for PBKDF2 for real-world systems against state-of-the-art attacks. More precisely, we consider different attack implementations on PBKDF2 using a range of different cluster systems employing recent CPU, GPU, and FPGA devices. As a practical case study, we take the recent security parameters used by TrueCrypt to implement attacks on PBKDF2. We compare the performance of our implementations to identify the most promising computing platform for the attack. To the best of our knowledge, we demonstrate the fastest known attack against PBKDF2. We combine these results with password guessing attacks based on Markov models [2, 10] to show that we can guess more than 65% of typical passwords in about one week. Finally, we derive recommendations how parameters for PBKDF2 should be chosen adequately.

Outline: In Section 2 we introduce some background on password-based key derivation, the PBKDF2 standard, and the state-of-the-art platforms for cracking passwords, followed by an introduction to password security and efficient password guessing in Section 3. In Section 4 we describe the relevant programming techniques of modern GPUs and our GPU implementation of PBKDF2. Likewise, in Section 5 we describe the FPGA cluster RIVYERA, and our implementation on this cluster. We compare the performance of the two implementations in Section 6, and discuss the implications of these results in Section 7.

2   Background and Related Work

With many keyboard-enabled computing systems, passwords are still state-of-the-art for user authentication. The standardized PBKDF2 maps passwords to secret keys that can be used for cryptographic operations. We review the basic operation of PBKDF2 and relevant previous work in the following.

2.1   Password-Based Key Derivation

The Password-Based Key Derivation Function #2 (PBKDF2) takes a user-defined PRF and requires four inputs to generate the output key k_{out} with

$$k_{out} = \text{PBKDF2}_{PRF}(\text{Pwd}, S, c, k_{Len}),$$

where Pwd is the password, S the salt, c the iteration counter, and k_{Len} the desired key output length. By variation of the number of performed iterations c, it is possible to adjust the time needed for computation and thus, by selecting an adequately high number, key strengthening can be achieved rendering password related brute-force attacks less effective. In practice, common values for the applications mentioned above range between the recommended minimum of 1000 [5, 4.2] and 4000 iterations.

Figure 1 shows a simplified block diagram of the PBKDF2 scheme (specifically when using the SHA-512). An HMAC algorithm is repeatedly chained such that the outputs of all HMAC runs are added to the derived key. If the desired output key length is larger than the output of the hash function, the scheme is iterated multiple times, each time with a different counter value CNT. Depending on the input and output length two cases need to be distinguished: If the input length of the hash function is smaller than a padded hash-value, then the HMAC requires at least 6 executions of the compression function. Otherwise, an HMAC value can be computed by means of four executions of the compression function (e.g., RipeMD-160 and SHA-512).

As the password in each chain of the HMAC computations is the same, the outputs of the leftmost compression functions corresponding to the hashing of

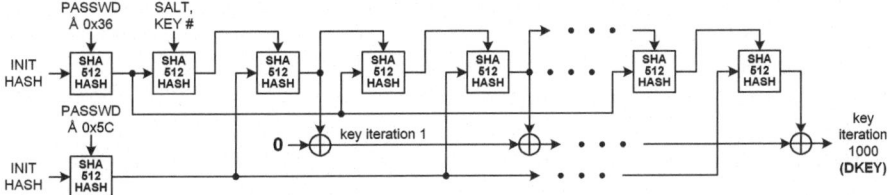

Fig. 1. SHA-512 based PBKDF2 scheme

the password xor 0x36..36 or 0x5C..5C, will not change. Thus they can be computed exactly once per password and then be reused for all subsequent HMAC computations using the same password. Furthermore, the salt value will never change during our brute-force attack, so the hash value corresponding to the hashed salt can be reused when performing the HMAC chain for different counter values. These two measures reduce the required number of computations for a password evaluation to one half and one third for an HMAC with 4 and 6 invocations of the compression function, respectively.

In our evaluation, we have targeted TrueCrypt [6], a free open-source disc encryption software, where the password and salt sizes are fixed to 512 bits. For consistency, we consider TrueCrypt starting with Version 5.0 (released February 5, 2008). Since then, TrueCrypt uses AES-256, Serpent, and Twofish in XTS mode as block ciphers and generates the keys using either RIPEMD-160, SHA-512, or Whirlpool as supported hash functions. The number of HMAC iterations they require are 2000, 1000, and 1000, respectively and the corresponding number of hash runs are 4003, 2002, and 4002. The variation in the number of hash executions is due to the input block sizes of each hash function. TrueCrypt supports combinations of the block cipher algorithms. In the best case, when only one encryption algorithm is used, 512 key bits are required, and 1536 key bits in the worst case.

2.2 Processing Platforms for Password Cracking

Implementing password cracking on general purpose CPUs is straightforward, however, due to the versatility of their architecture, CPUs usually do not achieve an optimal *cost-performance ratio* for a *specific* application. As an example, there exist a number of cracking tools for TrueCrypt compiled for x86 CPUs, but few tools are available that go beyond re-using TrueCrypt-code, most notably True-Crack [11], which reports 15 passwords/sec on an Intel Core-i7 920, 2.67GHz. In the last years, other processing platforms have shown to exceed the performance (and cost-performance ratio) of conventional CPUs, for specific applications.

Modern graphics cards (GPUs) have recently evolved into computation platforms for universal computations. GPUs combine a large number of parallel processor cores (as of today up to 512 atomic cores and more) which allow highly parallel applications using programming models such as OpenCL or CUDA. Their usefulness for password cracking was demonstrated in particular by the Lightning Hash Cracker developed by ElcomSoft, which achieves, for simple MD5-hashed password lists, a throughput rate of up to 680 million passwords per second using an NVIDIA 9800GTX2 [12]. Further work [13, 14] reports similarly impressive numbers with about 230 million SHA-1 (pure) hash operations per second on an NVIDIA 260GTX GPU. TrueCrack reports 330 passwords/sec on an NVIDIA GeForce GTX470, a press release [15] reports 2500 passwords/sec for Passware Kit 10.1, and a presentation [16] states that ElcomSoft software cracks 52400 passwords/sec on a Tesla S1070 with 4 GPUs for WPA-PSK, which essentially is PBKDF2 using only SHA-1.

Another way to tackle the large number of computations for password cracking efficiently is the deployment of special-purpose hardware. Moving applications into hardware usually provides significant savings in terms of costs and provides a boost in performance at the same time, since operations can be specifically tailored for the target application and potentially be highly parallelized. While Application Specific Integrated Circuits (ASIC) are expensive to develop due to their high non-recurring engineering costs, reconfigurable Field-Programmable Gate Arrays, or FPGAs, have been intensively studied by the crypto engineering community over the last 15 years. With today's powerful FPGA devices providing a configurable fabric consisting of millions of gate equivalences, it has become possible to create very fast implementations for specific computational problems. Given that password guessing is amenable to special-purpose hardware architectures and highly parallelizable, FPGAs are a promising platform for password cracking.

A third cost-effective platform for processing parallel applications is Sony's PlayStation 3 (PS3). Bevand [17], for example, presented a Unix crypt password cracker based on the IBM Cell Broadband Engine. However, the Cell processor is slightly outdated when comparing it to recent GPU and FPGA devices. Therefore, we do not expect the Cell processors to achieve a competitive cost-performance ratio, and we don't expect the PowerXCell 8i to become available at comparable prices in subsidized commodity game consoles. Thus, we did not include the Cell processor in our comparison.

3   Password Security

Accepted best practice mandates not to store the password *pwd* on the server in plain, but store the hash $h := H(pwd)$ of the password instead. In an *offline attack* on passwords, an attacker is given access to the value h and tries to recover the password *pwd*. (As opposed to *online guessing attacks*, where the attacker is only given access to a login prompt or similar.)

User-generated passwords usually have a rich structure, e.g., many are simple compositions of words from (English) language and numbers or special characters. Consequently, *guessing attacks*, where the attacker guesses a possible password, hashes it, and compares the hash to the stored value, are usually quite efficient. This has been realized early, and password guessing has been deployed for a long time (see, e.g, [1, 18–20]).

In a *dictionary attack*, the attacker has a list of words that are likely to appear in passwords. He computes the hashes of all these words and compares them with the stored hash. He can use additional *mangling rules*, e.g., appending special characters and numbers. Tools such as John the Ripper implement dictionary attacks and come with large dictionaries of common passwords, often grouped for different languages to better meet a specific site's needs. More recent work by Weir et al. [3] can be seen as generalization of this idea. Here, patterns that constitute extended mangling rules are extracted from real-world passwords using *probabilistic grammars* (context-free grammars with probabilities associated to production rules). These structures are then used to generate passwords, based on these structures and a dictionary as before.

3.1   Attacks Based on Markov Models

Another efficient way to guess passwords, first proposed in [2], is based on *Markov models*. These base on the observation that in human-generated passwords (as well as natural language), adjacent letters are not independently chosen, but follow certain regularities (e.g., the 2-gram th is much more likely than tm, in other words, the letter following a t is more likely an h than an m). In an n-gram Markov model, one models the probability of the next character in a string based on a prefix of length $n - 1$. Hence, for a given string $c_1, \ldots, c_m$, we can write $P(c_1, \ldots, c_m) = P(c_1, \ldots, c_{n-1}) \cdot \prod_{i=n}^{m} P(c_i | c_{i-n+1}, \ldots, c_{i-1})$.

In the *training phase*, the attacker learns the conditional probabilities from lists of leaked plaintext passwords (e.g., the RockYou password list), from available password dictionaries, or from plain English text. In the *attack phase*, the attacker generates passwords that are likely according to the Markov model. Additionally, one filters for certain patterns that typically occur for passwords; one defines finite automata for these patterns, and the algorithm ensures that only passwords that are accepted by one of the automata are tested. (An example for such a pattern is that in alpha-numeric passwords, the numerals are very likely at the end of the password (e.g., password1).

We use an implementation of Markov-based password guessers from [10] to feed our implementation with passwords. This algorithm additionally enumerates passwords in (approximately) decreasing order of likelihood, which substantially speeds up the guessing of frequent passwords, and does not use the hand-crafted patterns from [2]. We train the algorithm with the RockYou dataset, a dataset of 32 Million passwords that was leaked in an SQL injection attack in 2009 in clear. This dataset is publicly available and regularly used for password research. In this work we publish no information about specific passwords from the list, so we do not see ethical problems in using this list.

3.2   Further Related Work

Using precomputations, *rainbow-tables* can be used to speed up the guessing step [21, 22]. An implementation of rainbow-tables in hardware is studied in [23]. A problem closely related to password guessing is that of *estimating the strength of a password*, which is of central importance for the operator of a site to ensure a certain level of security. In the beginning, password cracking was used to find weak passwords [24]. Since then, much more refined methods have been developed. Later, one used so-called pro-active password checkers to exclude weak passwords [1, 25–28]. However, most pro-active password checkers use relatively simple rule-sets to determine password strength, which have been shown to be a rather bad indicator of real-world password strength [29–31]. More recently, Schechter et al. [32] classified password strength by counting the number of times a certain password is present in the password database, and Markov models have been shown to be a very good predictor of password strength and can be implemented in a secure way [31].

4   GPU-Based Attack

Next, we describe our implementation on GPUs as well as the required technical background on GPU programming.

4.1   Introduction to GPU Programming

Within the last decade, the roles of GPUs changed from mere graphic processors to general purpose processing units. Today, there are programming interfaces from all major graphic processor manufacturers, providing easy access to the processors of the graphic hardware, e.g., CUDA [33] developed by NVIDIA or Stream [34] for AMD GPUs. For heterogeneous processor platforms, supporting both CPUs and GPUs, OpenCL [35] has established combining the computational power of recent computer systems. In this section we will focus on NVIDIA GPU devices using the CUDA programming interface.

CUDA Terminology and Code Execution Basics: GPUs execute code in so called *kernels*, which are functions that are executed by many *threads* in parallel. Each thread is member of a block of threads. All threads within a block have access to the same shared memory, which is a kind of user-managed cache area, and can thus interact with each other. Furthermore, threads within a block can be synchronized with each other. Blocks define up to 3 dimensions to index individual threads by x, y, and z coordinates within the kernel code. The dimension of the blocks are provided as a parameter when calling a kernel from host (i.e. CPU) code. The blocks themselves are organized within a grid. During execution, blocks are assigned to *Streaming Multiprocessors* (SMs). An SM then schedules its pending blocks in chunks of 32 threads (a warp) to its hardware, where each thread within a warp executes the same instruction. When threads are scheduled for high-latency memory instructions, the scheduler will execute additional warps while waiting for the memory access to finish. This mechanism of latency hiding is one of the main reasons for the superior performance of GPUs: Whenever there are enough independent instructions on an SM that do not depend on previous results the hardware can completely hide the latency of memory accesses, by meanwhile using the idle computing cores to process the instructions of other warps.

NVIDIA'S Tesla C2070 GPU: For our experiments, we use a machine equipped with four Tesla C2070 GPUs by NVIDIA [36]. A single Tesla C2070 GPU consists of 14 SMs. Each SM has its own set of 32 computing cores, i.e., the architecture provides 448 cores within a single GPU. It provides a high memory bandwidth of 144 GB/s and a low computational overhead to initiate and manage parallel computations. The cores are running at 1.15GHz and can reach a single-precision floating point performance (Peak) of up to 1.03 TFLOPS (NVIDIA [36]). (For comparison: Intel's recent Core i7 980 CPUs running at 3.6GHz are listed at 86 GFLOPS (Intel [37]). We refer to NVIDIA'S website [33] for more detailed information about CUDA and the Tesla GPUs.

4.2 Implementing the KDF

In the following we describe the implementation aspects of our GPU implementation of the PBKDF2 scheme, following the specification of the PBKDF2 as employed by TrueCrypt. To implement the PBKDF2, we decided to aim at an implementation that avoids high-latency accesses to the main memory of the GPU by using only fast registers and shared memory. The other major strategy was to avoid redundant computation as detailed in Section 2.1. In the following we provide an overview of the algorithm specific aspects of the three hash functions RipeMD-160, SHA-512, and Whirlpool.

RipeMD-160: The state of the RipeMD hash function has a size of 320 bit, which is divided into a left and a right part, each consisting of five 32 bit values. Both parts can be processed independently. For this reason, we decided to let two threads team up to process the hashing of one key candidate. Here one thread processes the left part of the RipeMD algorithm and the other one the right part. The state, the intermediate keys, and the two hashes of the passwords are kept in registers. Shared memory is used to synchronize each thread pair and to provide input values (i.e., previous hash and message) to the compression function. The algorithm has been manually unrolled replacing all known inputs by constants residing within the kernel code. The kernel uses an overall of 40 registers and 5376 bytes of shared memory (64 passwords * (16 registers for inputs + 5 registers for outputs) * 4 bytes per 32 bit value) and runs with 128 threads per block. This allows 6 blocks in parallel per SM and an equivalent of 5376 passwords that can be processed in parallel on each GPU.

SHA-512: The state of SHA-512 consists of eight 64 bit values. Compared to the RipeMD-160 state, this complicates the computation of the compression function in two ways: On the one hand, the GPU hardware is a native 32 bit architecture (with some 64 bit extensions), slowing down most computations. On the other hand, many registers and a lot of shared memory is needed to store the state, the two hash values of the password, and the intermediate keys. For this reason our SHA-512 implementation uses only 64 threads per block and compiles to 63 registers per thread and 4096 bytes of shared memory per block. Here 63 registers per thread are the upper bound the hardware can handle. This results in a spill of used variables into the slow device memory. Nevertheless, as the number of spilled variables is small, the device memory should be able to permanently keep them within the still reasonably fast devices memory cache. This kernel again allows 5376 passwords to be processed in parallel.

Whirlpool: The state of Whirlpool has the same size as for SHA-512, which again leads to high register pressure. We implemented the Whirlpool hash function with a table lookup implementation using eight 256×32 bit lookup tables stored in shared memory. We employ 128 threads per block, each using the maximum of 63 registers. The shared memory usage of each block is 16384 bytes per block and only 4 blocks will run in parallel on each SM. Each block processes 128 passwords, such that we achieve 7168 passwords that are processed in parallel.

4.3   Wrapper Implementation

We use a host system powered by two Intel Xeon X5660 six-core CPUs at 2.8GHz with enabled Hyperthreading and AES-NI instruction support. It is equipped with four Tesla C2070 GPUs connected by full PCIe 2.0 16x lanes. We use CUDA Version 4.1 and the CUDA developer driver 286.19 for Windows 7 (x64). The host system generates the passwords in a single threat, writing them to a memory buffer. We schedule passwords in chunks of 21504 passwords, i.e, $14 \cdot 6 \cdot 4 = 336$ blocks for RipeMD-160 and SHA-512 and $14 \cdot 6 \cdot 2 = 168$ blocks for Whirlpool. This number of blocks has been selected to be a small multiple of the maximum number of concurrent blocks on the GPU for all implemented kernels. This way the GPU hardware should always be fully occupied with respect to the number of scheduled blocks for maximum performance. The derived key material is copied back to the host memory to test for the correct decryption of the TrueCrypt header. As the host system is idle during the GPU computations, the password verification (which is much less computationally expensive) can be hidden within the kernel execution time of the GPU computations. For our experiments the implementation on the host system re-uses large parts of the cryptographic primitives from the original TrueCrypt implementation sources. To overlap memory copies between host and GPU with computations, we employed four streams per GPU. Furthermore each stream alternately uses four sets of password and result buffers. This way the GPU can process the next password chunk without having to wait for the host to finish checking the latest generated key material. The implementation is capable of generating both 1536 bits and 512 bits of key material for a password and an HMAC candidate function, according to the worst case in the TrueCrypt specification.

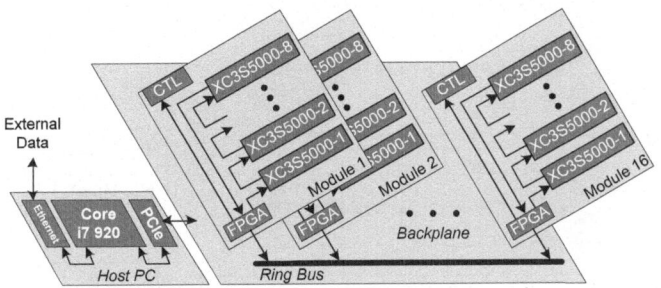

Fig. 2. The RIVYERA cluster architecture

5   FPGA-Based Attack

FPGAs combine the performance of a gate-level hardware implementation with flexibility, simple development, and reconfigurability of a software-based approach. Furthermore, FPGA implementations are truly parallel in nature. Each independent processing task is assigned to a dedicated section of the chip, and can function autonomously. This has made them an ideal choice for cryptanalytic applications, where several instances of the algorithm under test has to be evaluated in parallel with different parameters.

5.1   RIVYERA – An FPGA-Based Cluster System

The RIVYERA FPGA cluster [38], with its 128 Spartan-3 XC3S5000 FPGAs and an optional 32MB memory per FPGA, is a powerful and cost-optimized cryptanalytical machine. All FPGAs are connected with two opposite directed, systolic ring networks that directly interface with the Intel Core i7 based PC (which is integrated in the same housing) via a PCI Express communication controller, as shown in Figure 2.

In our FPGA-based attack on TrueCrypt, we implemented the PBKDF2 scheme on the RIVYERA cluster, balancing the different parts of the algorithm in terms of area and speed. In accordance with the goal of the PBKDF2 algorithm to derive a key using a hash function and perform encryption/decryption afterwards, sufficient key material has to be generated by running the hash function n times. An optimal strategy is to connect several copies of a hash function in a pipelined design in order to get the highest possible throughput. However, the high number of iterations n (1000 to 4000) makes this approach impossible.

The three hash functions used by TrueCrypt need a different amount of clock cycles to complete processing and also have different critical paths, resulting in different processing times. Partitioning parts of an FPGA between these three hash functions would result in a slower and more complex design. Therefore, we chose to implement individual systems for each hash function used and distribute them among multiple FPGAs. This also adds flexibility to implement higher percentage of a favored algorithm, e.g., in case the used algorithm is known or has a higher probability.

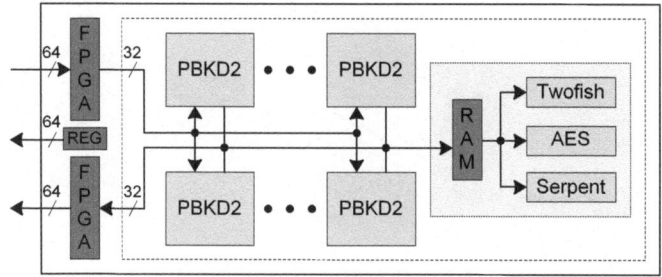

Fig. 3. Top-Level view of the FPGA Design

5.2   Implementing the KDF

Password-based Key Derivation Function #2 relies on repeated executions of a hash function in HMAC construction, where the result of each HMAC is accumulated starting with an initial all-zero key, until the final key is derived at the end of all HMAC runs.

We designed three independent single iteration cores, one for each of the three target hash functions, optimized for time-area product. The other important parameter is the number of key bits that can be generated by each PBKDF module. It is equal to the predefined message digest size of the incorporated hash function, which is 512 bits for both SHA-512 and Whirlpool, but only 160-bits for RipeMD-160. This means that while three instances of either SHA-512 or Whirlpool cores are sufficient to supply the worst case of 1536-bits key (required for Twofish, AES, and Serpent combination), the same can be accomplish with ten instances of the RipeMD-160-based PBKDF core, making it the most critical part of the whole design.

Implementing for FPGAs, the predefined topology of resources is the most limiting and hence the most important factor. It is imperative to come up with a balanced design that uses both registers and block RAMs to the highest possible ratio while losing minimum cycles for additional RAM access. For this purpose, the initial values, constants and hash results are stored in the block RAMs, while registers are utilized for storage of internal iteration variables within each hash function in all our hash cores. As mentioned above, we have developed three different FPGA designs – each targeting one hash function as shown in Figure 3 – and distributed them among the 128 FPGAs on the RIVYERA cluster.

The design uses a 64-to-32 bit input FIFO to split the data from the RIVYERA bus to the local bus architecture and switch between the system clock domain and the computation clock domain. All PBKDF2 units are initialized using the salt from the TrueCrypt header and the passwords are distributed among free units. After receiving a password, each unit immediately starts processing. As soon as a unit finishes its execution, its result is written into a dedicated memory, where the optional cipher blocks can access it and perform the on-chip test phase. An additional 64-bit register stores all information on the current FPGA operations, which the host application can access at any time. Since the additional area taken by the on-chip test is not suitable for all hash functions, the option to read the derived keys read back to the host PC for offline key tests is also supported in order to save resources for more on-chip key derivation units.

The password list, generated by a password derivation program, is transmitted by a host program (running on the Core i7 in the RIVYERA) to the FPGAs using the PCI Express architecture. Each of the three PBKDF units implements the scheme in Figure 1 with minor differences. The basic idea is to first hash the password XORed with IPAD and then with OPAD and store the two results as they will be repeatedly used during further iterations as initial values of the hash function. The next step is to hash the combination of SALT and key number (which is between 1-3 for SHA-512 and Whirlpool, and between 1-10 for RipeMD-160) in order to obtain the input value for the next run of the hash core. In all the following runs, the output of the previous run is the input data, and one of the two stored password hash results (in alternating order) is the initial value. The output of every second hash run (chaining variable) is accumulated (starting with all zero value) to get the final derived key. In the following paragraphs, we present the specific details for each different algorithm.

RipeMD-160: The RipeMD-160 based PBKDF core uses a 512-bit input message and hashes it by mixing with a 160-bit chaining variable which is updated in 80 rounds. At the end of all rounds, the chaining variable is added to the previous hash value. The internal round function is similar to that of SHA-1. However, the RipeMD round function has two parallel paths, whose results are stored in two 160-bit parallel registers, while the final hash result is stored in block RAMs. At the end of each round, the previous hash result, read from the RAM in 32-bit words, is added to the corresponding word of the update value from the current hash run, and then written back to the RAM. While this causes additional cycles, it saves more than 160-bit of registers and 128-bit of adders, resulting in further time-area product optimization. The total cycle count for each hash run is 95 cycles, in comparison to the ideal case of 80 cycles.

The RipeMD-160 core is run twice for the SALT and key number due to its 512-bits input block size. Since the total number of key iterations is defined as 2000 for RipeMD-160, this results in a total of $(5 + 1999 \cdot 2) \cdot 95 = 380285$ cycles for key derivation per core, each of which occupies 1032 slices (461 FF, 1764 LUTs) on a Xilinx Spartan-3 FPGA.

SHA-512: Each SHA-512 PBKDF core operates on 1024-bit message blocks and generates a 512-bit message digest. The intermediate hash values and the internal chaining variables are processed on a 32-bit datapath, which is not only compatible with the existing 32-bit block RAMs, but also minimizes delay paths. The only drawback is the number of cycles per hashing, which is 200 instead of the ideal case of 80. However, this time-area product optimization is well justified with increase in frequency and reduction in area.

Each SHA-512 based key derivation requires 1000 PBKDF iterations, which correspond to a total number of $(4 + 999 \cdot 2) \cdot 200 = 400400$ cycles for key derivation per SHA-512 PBKDF core, each of which occupies 1001 slices (897 FFs, 1500 LUTs) on a Xilinx Spartan-3 FPGA.

Table 1. Implementation Results of PBKDF2 on 4 Tesla C2070 GPUs

Hash	RIPEMD	SHA-512	Whirlpool	RIPEMD SHA-512 Whirlpool	RIPEMD	SHA-512	Whirlpool	RIPEMD SHA-512 Whirlpool
Derived Key Length	512 bits				1536 bits			
Passwords/sec	72786	105351	50686	23366	29330	35246	16980	8268
Passwords/sec (demo tool)	51661	54874	36103	19627	27591	29892	12153	6858

Whirlpool: The structure of Whirlpool [39] significantly differs from the structures of the other two cores. It not only generates a 512-bit message digest, but also processes 512-bit message blocks. The internal structure of Whirlpool resembles a block cipher with two identical datapaths in parallel; one as key expansion module, the other as message processing module. The internal structures of each path are identical. However, the key expansion module uses hash input to generate round keys, while the message processing module uses message inputs together with round keys to generate the next state of the hash.

Whirlpool hashing needs to be executed four times during each iteration due to the equal input and output sizes. However, only 10 iterations allow a word-serial implementation, where the message and the hash (key) are processed in 64-bit chunks, considerably reducing the overall area. The total number of cycles per round becomes 9 and the total number of rounds becomes 11 (including the initial whitening), which results in 99 cycles per round. With a total number of $(6 + 999 \cdot 4) \cdot 99 = 396198$ cycles for key derivation, each Whirlpool PBKDF core occupies 6013 slices (1131 FFs, 10878 LUTs) on a Xilinx Spartan-3 FPGA.

6   Results

In the following we present performance numbers for our experiments.

6.1   Performance Numbers

GPU Implementation: Table 1 gives the performance results for each hash algorithm for the worst case (i. e., 1526 bit of key material) and the fastest case (i. e., 512 bit of key material) of TrueCrypt's password derivation. The latter case corresponds, e. g., to AES-256 in XTS mode, while the first one corresponds to a cascade of all three TrueCrypt ciphers. These numbers clearly show that the implementations scale linearly: The performance boost for the smaller key sizes corresponds to the difference in the number of blocks that need to be hashed to derive the desired output lengths, i. e., 4 vs. 10 rounds for RipeMD and 1 vs. 3 rounds for SHA-512 and Whirlpool.

When deriving 1536 bit of key material per password for each of the three hash algorithms RipeMD-160, Whirlpool, and SHA-512, our fastest implementation

Table 2. Implementation results and performance numbers of PBKDF2 on the RIVY-ERA cluster (Place & Route) without on-chip verification. Please note that the current version is not optimized for speed and uses the lowest clock frequency valid for all designs.

Hash Clock cycles per PBKDF2	RIPE-MD 380,285		SHA-512 400,400		Whirlpool 396,198	
Derived Key Length	1536 bit	512 bit	1536 bit	512 bit	1536 bit	512 bit
PBKDF2 Units	4	9	11	32	3	15
Hash Cores per PBKDF2	10	4	3	1	3	1
FPGA Resources (Slices)	29753	28227	31773	31943	18370	29528
FPGA Resources (%)	89%	84%	95%	95%	55%	88%
Passwords per sec per FPGA	368	828	957	2784	265	1325
Passwords per sec	**47 104**	**105 984**	**122 496**	**356 352**	**33 920**	**169 600**

using a hardcoded salt was able to derive the key material at 8,268 passwords per second, i. e., about 714 million passwords per day and 21.4 billion passwords per month. Using only the TrueCrypt default settings of RipeMD-160 and AES-256 in XTS mode, i. e., 512 bit of key material are generated, the performance boosts to 72,786 passwords per second, 6.29 billion passwords per day and 188 billion passwords per month.

Our fully implemented TrueCrypt cracker tool consists of the password generator, the PBKDF2 and the decryption of the header data to verify the material. We observe a maximum speed limit of around 55,000 passwords per second, which is the speed of the used password generator. This limitation can be leveled by further optimizations. For the sake of completeness, we also provide the performance figures of the full tool. We want to mention that our numbers, as all specific implementations, can only provide a lower bound: implementations using other GPU architectures or further optimized code may improve the results.

FPGA Implementation: In case of the FPGA based key password search, we use different FPGA configurations for the best case (single block cipher) and the worst case (cascade of all three block ciphers).

Figure 2 shows the place and route results. With respect to a single instance, the RIPE-MD design can derive 368 passwords per second for 1536 bit output and up to 828 for 512 bit output on a single FPGA, respectively. This scales to 47,104 and 105,984 passwords per second on RIVYERA, taking only this hash algorithm into account. The SHA-2 implementation is faster and computes 957 and 2,784 passwords per second per FPGA, respectively, and a throughput of 122,496 and 356,352 for the 512 and 1536 bit case on RIVYERA, correspondingly.

Even though the current Whirlpool implementation does not utilize the complete FPGA logic optimally due to the PBKDF2 block size, it is more than 50% faster than the RIPE-MD scheme for 512 bit. In order to test all three hash functions for TrueCrypt, we utilize the full RIVYERA sequentially, as the reprogramming time is negligible. The bottleneck on FPGAs is the host-based password generation and the throughput drops a bit due to offline verification. Hence, with the remaining logic on the FPGA, we built an on-chip verification

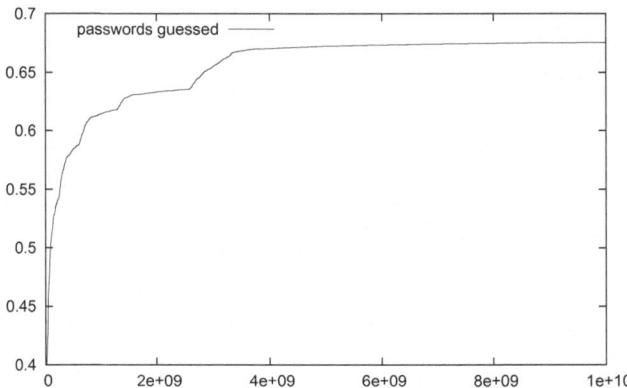

Fig. 4. Fraction of passwords guessed correctly (y-axis) vs. total number of guesses (x-axis)

as the amount of clock cycles necessary to perform a key derivation is large compared to the number of cycles required to compute the ciphers. Hence, all cores of the host CPU can now produce passwords to minimize this bottleneck.

Comparing a single GPU and FPGA device, it turns out that GPUs are significantly better in hashing than FPGAs (e.g., 18,000 vs. 828 RIPE-MD passwords per second). We attribute this result to the high clock frequency and the underlying 32-bit micro-architecture of GPUs that finally provides the distinct advantage with 32-bit-based hash functions. It is difficult to compare the individual device costs, since both platforms cannot be used as a stand-alone device without significant overhead. However, in case we relate the overall financial system costs of our GPU system and the RIVYERA cluster, we yield a scaling factor of 3.3 in favor for the GPU cluster.

6.2 Search Space and Success Rate of an Attack

In order to determine the actual influence of the number of guessed passwords from the last section, we determine the percentage of passwords one can break (on average) with that number of guesses. To this end, we use an implementation of a Markov model based password guesser from [10] (see Section 3 for more details). As *training set* used to derive the Markov model we used a random selection of 90% of the RockYou password list, the test set consists of the remaining 10% of the RockYou list (still more than 3 million passwords).

Figure 4 shows the fraction of passwords guessed correctly (y-axis) for a certain number of guesses made (x-axis). These results were obtained by running the password generator independently of the hashing engine. The reason is that, in order to incorporate the hashing engine, we would need to generate True-Crypt containers for each password in the test set, which is prohibitively time-consuming. From the numbers in the previous section we can estimate that, in the absolutely worst case, we can guess more than 65% of the passwords from the RockYou list in a week and more than 67% in a month.

7   Conclusions and Recommendations

Carefully chosen passwords are essential to protect systems using passwords (for recommendations on choosing good passwords, see, e. g., Appendix A of NIST SP 800-63). But even though PBKDF2 was specifically designed to prevent simple brute-force attacks, we showed that parallel hardware platforms are capable to comb through a significant amount of passwords per second (356,352 passwords per second for SHA-2/512 bit case). Our results indicate that GPU clusters have a better cost/performance ratio than FPGAs, mainly due to the low prices of the wide-spread use of GPUs.

The main parameter of PBKDF2 specifying the level of protection is the iteration counter c. Due to the progress in technology (outlined by Moore's law), we do not consider it sufficient for a secure system to run a constant (minimum) amount of 1000 hash iterations in the lifetime of an application or a system, as defined by RFC 2898 for PBKDF2. We therefore recommend to replace this constant iteration count c with a dynamic variable that is stored in each respective application instance and which is adjusted over time according to technological scaling effects. The iteration count c should be lower-bounded by the computational resources of the least-capable target platform of the application. Note, however, that even recent "low-end" processing device (e.g., smart phones) often provide powerful ARM processors with 1GHz or more so that running 4000-10000 hash iterations is certainly feasible even on these devices.[1] Note that an update of this dynamic iteration count is simple and can take place frequently right after unlocking the application instance with the correct password.

Finally, we like to point out the structural limits of password-based key derivation. Even if we assume a much stronger key derivation function than PBKDF2 being available[2] so that much less passwords can be searched per second, we still achieve with our approach a significant coverage of the password space due to limited selection criteria of human-chosen passwords (see Fig. 4). Although certainly no real news, we need to emphasize the importance of choosing strong passwords, possibly combined with additional security credentials such as cryptographic hardware tokens or biometrics.

References

1. Bishop, M., Klein, D.V.: Improving system security via proactive password checking. Computers & Security 14(3), 233–249 (1995)
2. Narayanan, A., Shmatikov, V.: Fast dictionary attacks on passwords using time-space tradeoff. In: Proc. 12th ACM Conference on Computer and Communications Security, pp. 364–372. ACM, New York (2005)
3. Weir, M., Aggarwal, S., de Medeiros, B., Glodek, B.: Password cracking using probabilistic context-free grammars. In: IEEE Symposium on Security and Privacy, pp. 391–405. IEEE Computer Society (2009)

---

[1] For recent performance figures of hash functions on a wide range of low-cost and high-performance CPUs, see http://bench.cr.yp.to/primitives-hash.html.

[2] For alternative proposals on password-based key derivation, see for example [40].

4. Openwall Community Wiki.: John the Ripper benchmarks (April 2012), http://openwall.info/wiki/john/benchmarks
5. Kaliski, B.: PKCS #5: Password-Based Cryptography Specification Version 2.0. RFC 2898 (September 2000), http://tools.ietf.org/html/rfc2898
6. TrueCrypt - Free Open-Source On-The-Fly Encryption (November 2011), http://www.truecrypt.org/
7. OASIS: Open Document Format for Office Applications (OpenDocument) Version 1.2 (April 2012), http://docs.oasis-open.org/office/v1.2/OpenDocument-v1.2-part3.html
8. IEEE Computer Society: IEEE Standard for Information technology 802.11 - Telecommunications and information exchange between systems - Local and metropolitan area networks - Specific requirements (Jun 2007), http://standards.ieee.org/getieee802/download/802.11-2007.pdf
9. Lenstra, A.K., Verheul, E.R.: Selecting Cryptographic Key Sizes. Journal of Cryptology 14(4), 255–293 (2001)
10. Castelluccia, C., Dürmuth, M., Perito, D.: Personal communication (2012)
11. Truecrack, http://code.google.com/p/truecrack/
12. ElcomSoft: Lightning Hash Cracker (November 2011), http://www.elcomsoft.com/lhc.html
13. Golubev, I.: IGHASHGPU (November 2011), http://www.golubev.com/hashgpu.htm
14. Schober, M.: Efficient password and key recovery using graphics cards. Master's thesis, Ruhr-Universität Bochum (2010)
15. Passware Kit 10.1 – Press Release, http://www.prnewswire.com/news-releases/passware-kit-101-cracks-rar-and-truecrypt-encryption-in-record-time-99539629.html
16. Elcomsoft: GPU assisted password cracking, http://www.slideshare.net/andrey.belenko/gpuassisted-password-cracking
17. Bevand, M.: Breaking UNIX crypt() on the PlayStation 3 (Presentation, ToorCon 10) (September 2008)
18. Wu, T.: A real-world analysis of kerberos password security. In: Network and Distributed System Security Symposium (1999)
19. Zviran, M., Haga, W.J.: Password security: an empirical study. J. Mgt. Info. Sys. 15(4), 161–185 (1999)
20. Kedem, G., Ishihara, Y.: Brute force attack on UNIX passwords with SIMD computer. In: Proceedings of the 3rd USENIX Windows NT Symposium (1999)
21. Hellman, M.: A cryptanalytic time-memory trade-off. IEEE Transactions on Information Theory 26(4), 401–406 (1980)
22. Oechslin, P.: Making a Faster Cryptanalytic Time-Memory Trade-Off. In: Boneh, D. (ed.) CRYPTO 2003. LNCS, vol. 2729, pp. 617–630. Springer, Heidelberg (2003)
23. Mentens, N., Batina, L., Preneel, B., Verbauwhede, I.: Time-Memory Trade-Off Attack on FPGA Platforms: UNIX Password Cracking. In: Bertels, K., Cardoso, J.M.P., Vassiliadis, S. (eds.) ARC 2006. LNCS, vol. 3985, pp. 323–334. Springer, Heidelberg (2006)
24. Morris, R., Thompson, K.: Password security: a case history. Communications. ACM 22(11), 594–597 (1979)
25. Spafford, E.H.: Observing reusable password choices. In: Proceedings of the 3rd Security Symposium, pp. 299–312. USENIX (1992)
26. Klein, D.V.: Foiling the cracker: A survey of, and improvements to, password security. In: Proc. USENIX UNIX Security Workshop (1990)

27. The password meter, http://www.passwordmeter.com/
28. Burr, W.E., Dodson, D.F., Polk, W.T.: Electronic authentication guideline: NIST special publication 800-63 (2006)
29. Weir, M., Aggarwal, S., Collins, M., Stern, H.: Testing metrics for password creation policies by attacking large sets of revealed passwords. In: Proceedings of the 17th ACM Conference on Computer and Communications Security (CCS 2010), pp. 162–175. ACM (2010)
30. Komanduri, S., Shay, R., Kelley, P.G., Mazurek, M.L., Bauer, L., Christin, N., Cranor, L.F., Egelman, S.: Of passwords and people: Measuring the effect of password-composition policies. In: CHI 2011: Conference on Human Factors in Computing Systems (2011)
31. Castelluccia, C., Dürmuth, M., Perito, D.: Adaptive password-strength meters from Markov models. In: Proc. Network and Distributed Systems Security Symposium (NDSS). The Internet Society (2012)
32. Schechter, S., Herley, C., Mitzenmacher, M.: Popularity is everything: a new approach to protecting passwords from statistical-guessing attacks. In: Proceedings of the 5th USENIX Conference on Hot topics in Security, pp. 1–8. USENIX Association (2010)
33. Nvidia: CUDA Developer Zone (Website) (2011), http://developer.nvidia.com/category/zone/cuda-zone
34. AMD: ATI Stream Technology (Website) (2011), http://www.amd.com/US/PRODUCTS/TECHNOLOGIES/STREAM-TECHNOLOGY/Pages/stream-technology.aspx
35. Khronos Group: OpenCL - The open standard for heterogeneous systems (Website) (2011), http://www.khronos.org/opencl/
36. Nvidia: TESLA C2050/C2070 GPU Computing Processor (2010), http://www.nvidia.com/docs/IO/43395/NV_DS_Tesla_C2050_C2070_jul10_lores.pdf
37. Intel: Intel® Core i7-900 Desktop Processor Series (2011), http://download.intel.com/support/processors/corei7/sb/core_i7-900_d.pdf
38. SciEngines GmbH: RIVYERA S3-5000 (2010), http://www.sciengines.com/joomla/index.php?option=com_content&view=article&id=60&Itemid=74
39. Barreto, P., Rijmen, V.: The Whirlpool hashing function. In: First open NESSIE Workshop, Leuven, Belgium, vol. 13, p. 14 (2000)
40. Percival, C.: Stronger key derivation via sequential memory-hard functions. In: BSDCan (2009)

Beyond eCK: Perfect Forward Secrecy under Actor Compromise and Ephemeral-Key Reveal

Cas Cremers and Michèle Feltz[*]

Institute of Information Security
ETH Zurich, Switzerland

Abstract. We show that it is possible to achieve perfect forward secrecy in two-message key exchange (KE) protocols that satisfy even stronger security properties than provided by the extended Canetti-Krawczyk (eCK) security model. In particular, we consider perfect forward secrecy in the presence of adversaries that can reveal the long-term secret keys of the actor of a session and reveal ephemeral secret keys.

We propose two new game-based security models for KE protocols. First, we formalize a slightly stronger variant of the eCK security model that we call eCK^w. Second, we integrate perfect forward secrecy into eCK^w, which gives rise to the even stronger eCK-PFS model. We propose a security-strengthening transformation (i. e., a *compiler*) between our new models. Given a two-message Diffie-Hellman type protocol secure in eCK^w, our transformation yields a two-message protocol that is secure in eCK-PFS. As an example, we show how our transformation can be applied to the NAXOS protocol.

Keywords: Key Exchange, Security Models, Protocol Transformations, Perfect Forward Secrecy, Ephemeral-key reveal, Actor compromise.

1 Introduction

The majority of recently developed key exchange protocols have been proven secure with respect to game-based security models for key exchange protocols [1, 2, 7, 13, 15]. The first such security model was introduced by Bellare and Rogaway [2]. In this model, the adversary is modeled as a probabilistic polynomial-time Turing machine that interacts with the protocol participants through *queries*. The queries specify the capabilities of the adversary. For instance, he can send messages to parties and reveal certain session-keys. The definition of security in the Bellare-Rogaway model requires that (a) two parties who complete *matching sessions* (i. e., the intended communication partners) compute the same session-key and that (b) the adversary does not learn the session-key with more than negligible probability. Building on this work, Canetti and Krawczyk [7] developed a more complex security model that gives the adversary

---

[*] This work was supported by ETH Research Grant ETH-30 09-3 and the National Competence Center in Research on Mobile Information and Communication Systems (NCCR-MICS), which is supported by the Swiss National Science Foundation.

S. Foresti, M. Yung, and F. Martinelli (Eds.): ESORICS 2012, LNCS 7459, pp. 734–751, 2012.

additional powers such as access to a **session-state** query that reveals the internal state of a session. LaMacchia et al. [15] adapted the Canetti-Krawczyk model to capture resilience to key compromise impersonation (KCI) attacks and resilience to the leakage of various combinations of long-term and ephemeral secret keys in a single security model. This model is known as the extended Canetti-Krawczyk (eCK) security model.

One important property of KE protocols that is not guaranteed by the eCK security model is *perfect forward secrecy* (PFS). This property holds if an adversary cannot learn the session-keys of past sessions, even if he learns the long-term secret keys of all the parties [18]. The designers of the eCK model argued that this property cannot be achieved by two-message KE protocols, based on [13]. In particular, in [13, p. 15], Krawczyk sketched a generic PFS attack, for which he claimed that it breaks the security of any implicitly authenticated two-message KE protocol. In the attack, the adversary actively interferes with the communication between the parties by injecting self-constructed messages. This enables him to compute the used session-key if he later learns the long-term secret keys of the parties. To prove a slightly weaker notion of forward secrecy for the HMQV protocol, Krawczyk introduced the notion of *weak perfect forward secrecy* (weak-PFS) [13]. When the long-term keys are compromised, weak perfect forward secrecy guarantees secrecy of previously established session-keys, but only for sessions in which the adversary did not actively interfere. Krawczyk's comments seem to have led to the incorrect belief that the best that can be achieved for two-message KE protocols is weak perfect forward secrecy [5, 9, 13, 15]. As a result, even though the eCK security model [15] guarantees only weak perfect forward secrecy, it is currently described in the literature as the strongest possible security model for two-message KE protocols [8, 15, 17].

Contributions. Our first contribution is to push forward the theoretical limits of key exchange security notions. This contribution has two parts. First, we generalize the eCK security model [15] based on the observation that a restriction on the adversary in the eCK model, whose purpose it is to prevent Krawczyk's PFS attack, is stronger than needed. To weaken this restriction (while still preventing the attack) we introduce the concept of *origin-session*, which relaxes the notion of matching session. The resulting model, which we call eCK^w, specifies a slightly stronger variant of weak perfect forward secrecy than the eCK model. We then integrate perfect forward secrecy into the eCK^w model, which gives rise to the eCK-PFS model. The eCK-PFS model is strictly stronger than eCK^w, and also provides more guarantees than independently considering eCK/eCK^w security and PFS. In particular, security in eCK-PFS implies perfect forward secrecy in the presence of a fully active attacker who can even learn the actor's long-term secret key before the start of the attacked session, or who can learn session-specific ephemeral secret keys (i. e. random coins generated on a per-session basis).

Our second contribution is a generic security-strengthening transformation (a so-called *compiler*) that contributes towards the modular design approach of KE protocols. Given a two-message Diffie-Hellman (DH) type KE protocol that is secure in eCK^w, our transformation yields a two-message protocol that is secure in the eCK-PFS model. We show that NAXOS [15], the first key exchange protocol proven secure in the eCK model, is also secure in eCK^w and use our transformation to construct a protocol that is secure in eCK-PFS. Thus, we demonstrate that it is possible for two-message KE protocols to achieve PFS, even under actor compromise (i. e. disclosure of the long-term secret keys of the actor of a session) and leakage of ephemeral secret keys.

Related Work. The majority of related works claim that perfect forward secrecy cannot be achieved in a two-message KE protocol [5, 9, 13–15]. There are two notable exceptions. First, the two-message modified-Okamoto-Tanaka (mOT) protocol by Gennaro et al. [11] provides perfect forward secrecy in the identity-based setting. Additionally, they sketch variants of the protocol for the PKI-based setting. As noted by the authors [11], the mOT protocol and its variants are not resilient against loss of ephemeral keys, and they are therefore insecure in eCK-like models. Second, in [6], Boyd and Gonzalez suggest a transformation $\mathcal{C}$ based on adding MACs on the message exchange of a key-exchange protocol that satisfies weak perfect forward secrecy, to achieve perfect forward secrecy. However, the MAC transformation does not ensure security in eCK-PFS, because it does not guarantee perfect forward secrecy under actor compromise and leakage of ephemeral secret keys. In Section 4 we show that, e. g., $\mathcal{C}$(NAXOS) [6] is insecure in eCK-PFS. The eCK variant for protocols with more than two messages, defined in [14], guarantees perfect forward secrecy. However, this eCK variant cannot be met by any of the protocols from the class we are considering here because it uses the concept of matching session instead of origin-session.

Organization. In Section 2 we recall some standard definitions used in this paper. In Section 3 we motivate and define our security notions eCK^w and eCK-PFS. In Section 4 we provide a transformation that turns any two-message Diffie-Hellman type KE protocol secure in eCK^w into a two-message KE protocol secure in eCK-PFS. We show how this transformation can be applied to the NAXOS protocol in Section 5. Finally, we conclude in Section 6.

2 Preliminaries

Let $G = \langle g \rangle$ be a finite cyclic group of large prime order p with generator g.

Definition 1 (GAP-CDH Assumption [19]). *The GAP-CDH assumption in G states that, given g^u and g^v, for u, v chosen uniformly at random from $\mathbb{Z}_p$, it is computationally infeasible to compute g^{uv} with the help of a decisional Diffie-Hellman (DDH) oracle (that, for any three elements $g^u, g^v, g^w \in G$, replies whether or not $w = uv \bmod p$).*

Definition 2 (Signature Scheme [12]). *A signature scheme Σ is a tuple of three polynomial-time algorithms (Gen, Sign, Vrfy) satisfying the following:*

1. *The probabilistic key-generation algorithm Gen takes as input a security parameter 1^k and outputs a secret/public key pair (sk, pk).*

2. *The (possibly probabilistic) signing algorithm Sign takes as input a secret key sk and a message $m \in \{0,1\}^*$. It outputs a signature $\sigma := Sign_{sk}(m)$.*

3. *The deterministic verification algorithm Vrfy takes as input a public key pk, a message m, and a signature σ. It outputs a bit b, with $b = 1$ meaning valid and $b = 0$ meaning invalid. We write $b = Vrfy_{pk}(m, \sigma)$.*

Definition 3 (SUF-CMA [4]). *A signature scheme $\Sigma = (Gen, Sign, Vrfy)$ is strongly existentially unforgeable under an adaptive chosen-message attack if for all probabilistic polynomial-time adversaries A, there exists a negligible function negl such that $Adv_A^{Sig}(k) \leq negl(k)$, where $Adv_A^{Sig}(k)$ denotes the probability of successfully forging a valid signature σ on a message m and (m, σ) is not among the pairs (m_i, σ_i) $(i = 1, ..., q)$ generated during the query phase to a signature oracle $\mathcal{O}^{Sign}$ returning a signature for any message m_i of the adversary's choice.*

3   Key Exchange Security Notions

We propose two new eCK-like security models for the analysis of key-exchange protocols. The first model called eCK^w captures a slightly stronger form of weak-PFS than the eCK model. The second model called eCK-PFS integrates PFS directly into eCK^w.

3.1   Motivation for the New Models

eCK^w: Strengthening Weak-PFS. As stated in the introduction, the eCK model captures weak perfect forward secrecy but not perfect forward secrecy, based on Krawczyk's generic PFS attack [13]. We briefly recall the attack. Consider a two-message protocol in which the agents exchange ephemeral public Diffie-Hellman keys, i.e., g^x and g^y, where x and y are chosen at random from $\mathbb{Z}_p$ (for some large prime p). The adversary, impersonating party $\hat{A}$, generates a random value x $(\in \mathbb{Z}_p)$ and sends g^x to a responder session at party $\hat{B}$. $\hat{B}$ responds by sending g^y and computes the session key. The adversary chooses $\hat{B}$'s session as the test-session, i.e. the session under attack, and reveals $\hat{A}$'s long-term secret key after $\hat{B}$'s session ends. Now the adversary can simply follow all protocol steps that an honest party $\hat{A}$ would have performed using x and $\hat{A}$'s long-term secret key. In particular, the adversary can compute the same session-key as the test-session, violating PFS.

Krawczyk's attack works directly for all two-message KE protocols that exchange DH keys of the form g^z, where z does not involve the sender's long-term secret key, such as HMQV [13]. Additionally, the attack also works on protocols like NAXOS [15], where z is a hash of the sender's long-term secret key and a random value. The adversary can just replace this value by an arbitrary value.

To still prove some form of forward secrecy for such protocols, Krawczyk introduced the notion of weak-PFS. In weak-PFS, the adversary is not allowed to actively interfere with the messages exchanged by the test-session. This prevents the attack because the adversary is no longer allowed to insert his own DH exponential. Similarly, in the eCK model, this restriction on interfering with the test-session is modeled by checking if a matching session exists [15, p. 5]. If this is the case, then the adversary must have been passive and he is allowed to reveal the long-term secret keys of the actor and the intended communication partner of a session. If there is no matching session, the adversary is not allowed to reveal the long-term secret key of the intended communication partner.

We observe that Krawczyk's attack only depends on the adversary injecting or modifying the message *received* by the test-session; he does not need to actively interfere with the message *sent* by the test-session. However, eCK models passivity of the adversary in the test-session by checking whether a matching session for the test-session exists, which also prevents the adversary from modifying (or deleting) the message sent by the test-session. In this sense, the restriction on the adversary in eCK is sufficient but not necessary for the prevention of Krawczyk's attack. We therefore relax the notion of matching sessions and introduce the concept of *origin-session*. This allows us to capture the adversary's capability of revealing the long-term secret key of the intended communication partner (i. e. the peer) of the test-session s in case an origin-session s' for s exists even though no session matching to s exists. Thus, in contrast to the eCK model, the adversary may reveal the long-term key of the peer of the test-session s in case an origin-session s' for session s exists and

– actively interfere with the message sent by the test-session (e. g. by modifying it or injecting his own message), or
– replay a message from another session to the test-session (as in [6]), or
– leave session s' incomplete (in case session s' is in the initiator role).

We call our strengthened variant of the eCK model the eCK^w model.

eCK-PFS: Integrating PFS into eCK^w. We extend the eCK^w model by integrating perfect forward secrecy which yields the strictly stronger eCK-PFS model. Perfect forward secrecy is reflected in eCK-PFS by allowing the adversary to reveal the long-term secret keys of all the protocol participants *after* the end of the test-session. These keys can be revealed irrespective of the existence of an origin-session (or a matching session). This attack scenario is neither captured in eCK^w (nor in eCK or [6]) if the origin-session (matching session) does not exist for the test-session.

3.2 Defining eCK^w and eCK-PFS

Terminology. Let $\mathcal{P} = \left\{ \hat{P}_1, \hat{P}_2, ..., \hat{P}_N \right\}$ be a finite set of N parties' identities. Each party can execute multiple instances of a KE protocol, called sessions, concurrently. We denote session i at party $\hat{P}$ as the tuple $(\hat{P}, i) \in \mathcal{P} \times \mathbb{N}$. We associate to each session $s \in \mathcal{P} \times \mathbb{N}$ a quintuple of variables $T_s = (s_{actor}, s_{peer}, s_{role}, s_{sent}, s_{recv}) \in \mathcal{P}^2 \times \{\mathcal{I}, \mathcal{R}\} \times (\{0, 1\}^* \cup \{-\})^2$. The variables s_{actor}, s_{peer} denote the identities of the actor and intended peer of session s, s_{role} denotes the role that the session is executing (either initiator or responder), and s_{sent}, s_{recv} denote the concatenation of timely ordered messages as sent/received by s_{actor} during session s, where "$-$" denotes a special symbol not in $\{0,1\}^*$ that represents the empty sequence. The values of the variables s_{peer} and s_{role} are set upon activation of session s and the values of the variables s_{sent} and s_{recv} are defined by the protocol execution steps. A session can only be activated once.

The notion of *matching sessions* specifies when two sessions are supposed to be intended communication partners. Here we formalize the matching sessions definition from the eCK model [15] which is based on matching conversations.

Definition 4 (matching sessions). *Two completed sessions s and s' are said to be* matching *if*

$$s_{actor} = s'_{peer} \wedge s_{peer} = s'_{actor} \wedge s_{sent} = s'_{recv} \wedge s_{recv} = s'_{sent} \wedge s_{role} \neq s'_{role}.$$

To relate a message received (and accepted) by some session to the session it originates from (if the latter exists), we introduce the concept of origin-session. If an origin-session s' for some session s exists, then the messages received by session s have not been modified or injected (as in Krawczyk's PFS attack [13]) by the adversary.

Definition 5 (origin-session). *We say that a (possibly incomplete) session s' is an* origin-session *for a completed session s when $s'_{sent} = s_{recv}$.*

Note that, if two completed sessions s, s' are matching, then s and s' are origin-sessions for each other. However, if session s is an origin-session for some session s', then it might not necessarily be a matching session for s' (e.g. in case the roles of the sessions are identical). Thus, a session being a matching session for some session is a stronger requirement than a session being an origin-session for some session.

Adversarial capabilities. Similar to the eCK model [15], we model the adversary as a probabilistic polynomial-time (PPT) Turing machine that controls all communications between parties through the following queries:

1. $\mathsf{send}(s, v)$. This query models the adversary sending message v to session s. The adversary is given the response generated by the session according to the protocol. The variables s_{sent} and s_{recv} are updated accordingly (by concatenation). Abusing notation, we allow the adversary to activate an initiator session with peer $\hat{Q}$, via a $\mathsf{send}(s, \hat{Q})$ query and a responder session by sending a message m to session s on behalf of $\hat{Q}$, via a $\mathsf{send}(s, \hat{Q}, m)$ query. In these cases, s_{peer} is set to $\hat{Q}$ and s_{role} is set to $\mathcal{I}$ and $\mathcal{R}$, respectively. The adversary is given the session's response according to the protocol and the variables s_{sent}, s_{recv} are initialized accordingly.
2. $\mathsf{corrupt}(\hat{P})$. This query reveals the long-term keys of party $\hat{P}$.
3. $\mathsf{ephemeral\text{-}key}(s)$. This query reveals the ephemeral secret keys (i.e., the random coins) of session s.
4. $\mathsf{session\text{-}key}(s)$. This query returns the session key for a completed session s (i.e. a session that has accepted/computed a session-key).

5. test-session(s). To respond to this query, a random bit b is chosen. If $b = 0$, then the session-key established in session s is returned. Otherwise, a random key is returned according to the probability distribution of keys generated by the protocol. This query can only be issued to a completed session.

Notions of Freshness. An adversary that can perform the above queries can simply reveal the session key of all sessions, breaking any protocol. The intuition underlying Bellare-Rogaway style KE models is to put minimal restrictions on the adversary with respect to performing these queries, such that there still exist protocols that are secure in the presence of such an adversary. The restrictions on the queries made by the adversary are formalized by the notion of *fresh sessions*.

Definition 6 (Fresh session in eCK^w). *A completed session s in security experiment W is said to be* fresh in eCK^w *if all of the following conditions hold:*

1. *W does not include the query* session-key(s),
2. *for all sessions s^* such that s^* matches s, W does not include* session-key(s^*),
3. *W does not include both* corrupt(s_{actor}) *and* ephemeral-key(s),
4. *for all sessions s' such that s' is an origin-session for session s, W does not include both* corrupt(s_{peer}) *and* ephemeral-key(s'), *and*
5. *if there exists no origin-session for session s, then W does not include a* corrupt(s_{peer}) *query.*

Definition 7 (Fresh session in eCK-PFS). *A completed session s in experiment W is said to be* fresh in eCK-PFS *if all of the following conditions hold:*

1. *W does not include the query* session-key(s),
2. *for all sessions s^* such that s^* matches s, W does not include* session-key(s^*),
3. *W does not include both* corrupt(s_{actor}) *and* ephemeral-key(s),
4. *for all sessions s' such that s' is an origin-session for session s, W does not include both* corrupt(s_{peer}) *and* ephemeral-key(s'), *and*
5. *if there exists no origin-session for session s, then W does not include a* corrupt(s_{peer}) *query before the completion of session s.*

Security Experiment W in model M. Security of a key-exchange protocol Π is defined via a security experiment W (or attack game) played by an adversary E, modeled as a PPT algorithm, against a challenger. Before the experiment starts, each party $\hat{P}$ runs a key-generation algorithm that takes as input a security parameter 1^k and outputs valid static secret/public key pair(s). The public key(s) of each party are distributed in an authenticated way to all other parties. The adversary E is given access to all public data. The setting of the security experiment W can be described in four successive stages, as follows:

1. The adversary E can perform send, corrupt, ephemeral-key, and session-key queries.
2. At some point in the experiment, E issues a test-session query to a completed session that is fresh in model M by the time the query is issued. The challenger chooses a random bit b and provides E with either the real session-key of the test-session (for $b = 0$) or a random key from the key space (for $b = 1$).

3. The adversary may continue with send, corrupt, ephemeral-key and session-key queries, without rendering the test-session un-fresh in model M.
4. Finally, E outputs a bit b' as his guess for b.

The adversary E wins the security experiment W if he correctly guesses the bit b chosen by the challenger during the test-session query (i. e. if $b = b'$ where b' denotes E's guess). Success of E in the experiment is expressed in terms of E's advantage in distinguishing whether he received the real or a random session-key in response to the test-session query. The advantage of adversary E in the above security experiment against a key exchange protocol Π for security parameter k is defined as $Adv_E^{\Pi}(k) = |2P(b = b') - 1|$.

Definition 8. *A key exchange protocol Π is said to be secure in model $M \in \{eCK^w, eCK\text{-}PFS\}$ if, for all PPT adversaries E, it holds that*

- *if two parties successfully complete matching sessions, then they compute the same session key, and*
- *E has no more than a negligible advantage in winning security experiment W in model M, that is, there exists a negligible function negl in the security parameter k such that $Adv_E^{\Pi}(k) \leq negl(k)$.*

Comparison between eCK^w and eCK-PFS. The eCK-PFS model is strictly stronger than eCK^w because it captures more attack scenarios. The eCK-PFS model allows the adversary to corrupt all parties *after* the test-session is completed (regardless of whether an origin-session exists for the test-session), capturing perfect forward secrecy. In contrast, in case there is no origin-session for the test-session, the adversary is not allowed to reveal the long-term secret key of the peer of the test-session in the eCK^w model. As an example, NAXOS is provably secure in eCK^w, as we show in Section 5, but insecure in eCK-PFS due to the PFS attack described in Subsection 3.1.

4 A Transformation from eCK^w to eCK-PFS

We define a class of two-message Diffie-Hellman type key exchange protocols (similar to the class of KE protocols in [6]). Then, we present a security-strengthening transformation (compiler) that can be applied to any such protocol. Finally we show that this transformation turns any KE protocol secure in eCK^w into a KE protocol secure in eCK-PFS.

Let k be a security parameter and let G be a finite cyclic group of prime order p with generator g, where $p = O(2^k)$. Let Ω be static publicly known data such as parties' identities, their long-term public keys or publicly known functions and parameters. Let S be a set of constants from which random values are chosen (e. g. $S = \mathbb{Z}_p$ or $S = \{0, 1\}^k$). We denote by $x \in_R S$ that x is chosen uniformly at random from the set S. In the generic two-message DH type protocol, illustrated in Figure 1, party $\hat{A}$'s long-term secret key is $a \in_R \mathbb{Z}_p$ and $\hat{A}$'s long-term public key is $A = g^a$. The session-specific ephemeral secret key of the session at party

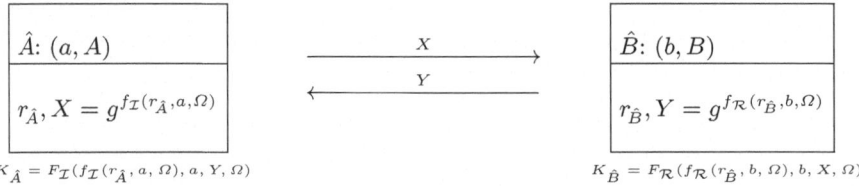

Fig. 1. A generic two-message DH type protocol

$\hat{A}$ is denoted by $r_{\hat{A}} \in_R S$ and the corresponding ephemeral public key is denoted by X. Similarly, party $\hat{B}$'s long-term secret/public key pair is (b, B) and the ephemeral secret/public key pair of the session at $\hat{B}$ is denoted by $(r_{\hat{B}}, Y)$. The public functions $f_{\mathcal{I}}, f_{\mathcal{R}} : \{0,1\}^* \to \mathbb{Z}_p$ depend on the ephemeral secret key and may depend on the long-term secret key or on public information. The public functions $F_{\mathcal{I}}, F_{\mathcal{R}} : \{0,1\}^* \to \{0,1\}^k$ depend on the Diffie-Hellman exponent the long-term secret key, the received Diffie-Hellman exponential and other public information. We assume that the public keys of all parties are known to all other participants in the protocol.

Protocol description. The generic two-message DH type protocol, depicted in Figure 1, proceeds as follows:

1. Upon activation of session $s = (\hat{A}, i) \in \mathcal{P} \times \mathbb{N}$ with peer $\hat{B}$, $\hat{A}$ (the initiator) performs the steps:
   - Choose an ephemeral secret key $r_{\hat{A}} \in_R S$ and compute $X = g^{f_{\mathcal{I}}(r_{\hat{A}}, a, \Omega)}$.
   - Send X (and possibly other public data, e. g. identities of peer and actor of the session) to $\hat{B}$.
   - Initialize T_s to $(\hat{A}, \hat{B}, \mathcal{I}, m, -)$, where m denotes the message sent by session s.
2. Upon activation of session $s' = (\hat{B}, j) \in \mathcal{P} \times \mathbb{N}$ with message X (and possibly other data) on behalf of $\hat{A}$, party $\hat{B}$ (the responder) performs the steps:
   - Check that $X \in G$.
   - Choose an ephemeral secret key $r_{\hat{B}} \in_R S$ and compute $Y = g^{f_{\mathcal{R}}(r_{\hat{B}}, b, \Omega)}$.
   - Compute $K_{\hat{B}} = F_{\mathcal{R}}(f_{\mathcal{R}}(r_{\hat{B}}, b, \Omega), b, X, \Omega)$.
   - Send Y (and possibly other public data) to $\hat{A}$.
   - Set $T_{s'}$ to $(\hat{B}, \hat{A}, \mathcal{R}, m', n')$, where m' denotes the message sent by session s' and n' the message received by session s', and complete the session by accepting $K_{\hat{B}}$ as the session-key.
3. Upon receiving message Y (with possibly other data) in session s , party $\hat{A}$ performs the steps:
   - Check that $Y \in G$.
   - Compute $K_{\hat{A}} = F_{\mathcal{I}}(f_{\mathcal{I}}(r_{\hat{A}}, a, \Omega), a, Y, \Omega)$.
   - Update T_s to $(\hat{A}, \hat{B}, \mathcal{I}, m, n)$ and complete the session by accepting $K_{\hat{A}}$ as the session-key.

The above description also applies to protocols with additional checks, which we omit for clarity. We assume that whenever a check in a session fails, all session-specific data is erased from memory and the session is aborted, i. e., it terminates without establishing a session-key.

Definition 9 (Protocol Class $\mathcal{DH}$-2). *We define $\mathcal{DH}$-2 as the class of all two-message key-exchange protocols that follow the description of a generic DH type protocol and meet the following validity requirement:*

- *in the presence of an eavesdropping adversary, two parties $\hat{A}$ and $\hat{B}$ can complete matching sessions (in the sense of Definition 4), in which case they hold the same session-key.*

The validity requirement requires that if the messages of two parties $\hat{A}$ and $\hat{B}$ are faithfully relayed to each other, then both parties end up with a shared session-key (see also [1–3]). Note that, e. g., the KE protocols NAXOS [15], NAXOS+ [17], NETS [16] and CMQV [21] belong to the class $\mathcal{DH}$-2.

Protocol transformation. We now show how to transform any protocol $\Pi \in \mathcal{DH}$-2 into a two-message protocol SIG(Π), shown in Figure 2, by applying the signature transformation SIG. Party $\hat{A}$ has two *independent* valid long-term secret/public key pairs, one pair (a, A) from protocol Π and one pair $(sk_{\hat{A}}, pk_{\hat{A}})$ for use in a digital signature scheme Σ with security parameter k. Similarly, party $\hat{B}$'s long-term secret/public key pairs are (b, B) and $(sk_{\hat{B}}, pk_{\hat{B}})$. The transformed protocol SIG(Π) in Figure 2 proceeds as protocol Π except that each party needs to additionally sign a message using its secret signature key and check that the received signature on a message is valid with respect to the long-term public key of its peer. The fields between square brackets within the signature are optional.

Security analysis. We show in Theorem 1 below that the SIG transformation is a security-strengthening transformation from the eCK^w model to the stronger model eCK-PFS provided that the digital signature scheme is strongly existentially unforgeable under an adaptive chosen-message attack (SUF-CMA) as well as deterministic. For certain randomized signature schemes, an efficient adversary can compute the secret (signature) key given the corresponding public key, a signature on any message using the secret key, and the random coins involved in the signature generation learned through an **ephemeral-key** query (as noted in [15]).

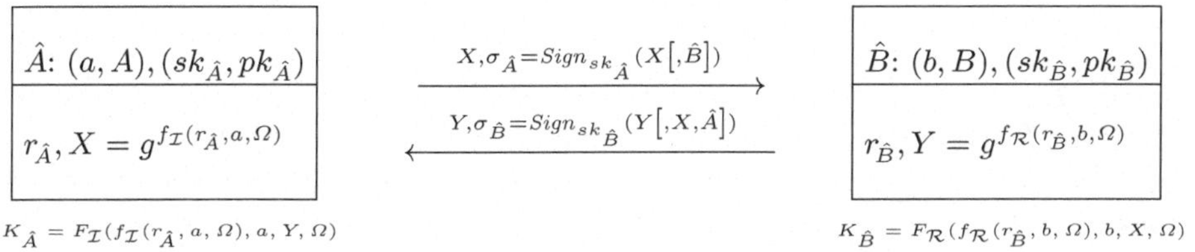

$$\hat{A}: (a, A), (sk_{\hat{A}}, pk_{\hat{A}})$$

$$r_{\hat{A}}, X = g^{f_{\mathcal{I}}(r_{\hat{A}}, a, \Omega)}$$

$$\xrightarrow{X, \sigma_{\hat{A}} = Sign_{sk_{\hat{A}}}(X[, \hat{B}])}$$

$$\xleftarrow{Y, \sigma_{\hat{B}} = Sign_{sk_{\hat{B}}}(Y[, X, \hat{A}])}$$

$$\hat{B}: (b, B), (sk_{\hat{B}}, pk_{\hat{B}})$$

$$r_{\hat{B}}, Y = g^{f_{\mathcal{R}}(r_{\hat{B}}, b, \Omega)}$$

$$K_{\hat{A}} = F_{\mathcal{I}}(f_{\mathcal{I}}(r_{\hat{A}}, a, \Omega), a, Y, \Omega)$$

$$K_{\hat{B}} = F_{\mathcal{R}}(f_{\mathcal{R}}(r_{\hat{B}}, b, \Omega), b, X, \Omega)$$

Fig. 2. A transformed generic protocol SIG(Π)

The following lemma is used in the proof of Theorem 1.

Lemma 1 (Difference Lemma [20]). *Let A, B, F be events defined on some probability space. Suppose that event $A \wedge F^c$ occurs if and only if event $B \wedge F^c$ occurs. Then $|P(A) - P(B)| \leq P(F)$.*

Theorem 1. *Let $\Pi \in \mathcal{DH}\text{-}2$ be a protocol secure in the eCK^w model. Under the assumption that the signature scheme is deterministic and SUF-CMA, the protocol $\mathrm{SIG}(\Pi)$ is a secure key-exchange protocol in the eCK-PFS model.*

Proof. It is straightforward to verify the first condition of Definition 8, i. e., that matching sessions of protocol $\mathrm{SIG}(\Pi)$ compute the same key (since matching sessions of protocol Π compute the same key). We show next that the second condition of Definition 8 holds, i. e., the adversary has no more than a negligible advantage in distinguishing the session key from a random key. We present a security proof structured as a sequence of games, a proof technique introduced in [20]. Let S_i denote the event that the adversary correctly guesses the bit chosen by the challenger to answer the **test-session** query in Game i and let $\alpha_i = |2P(S_i) - 1|$ denote the advantage of the adversary in Game i. Let N, q_s be upper bounds on the number of parties and activated sessions, respectively.

Game 0. This game reflects the security experiment W in model eCK-PFS, as defined in Subsection 3.2, played by a PPT adversary E against the protocol $\mathrm{SIG}(\Pi)$.

Game 1. [Transition based on a small failure event] Let $Coll_{\mathrm{SIG}(\Pi)}$ be the small failure event that a collision for protocol $\mathrm{SIG}(\Pi)$ occurs (e.g. in ephemeral secret keys). As soon as event $Coll_{\mathrm{SIG}(\Pi)}$ occurs, the attack game stops.

Analysis of Game 1. Game 0 is identical to Game 1 up to the point in the experiment where event $Coll_{\mathrm{SIG}(\Pi)}$ occurs for the first time. The Difference Lemma yields that $|P(S_0) - P(S_1)| \leq P(Coll_{\mathrm{SIG}(\Pi)})$. Hence,

$$\alpha_0 = |2P(S_0) - 1| = 2|P(S_0) - P(S_1) + P(S_1) - 1/2|$$
$$\leq 2(|P(S_0) - P(S_1)| + |P(S_1) - 1/2|)$$
$$\leq 2P(Coll_{\mathrm{SIG}(\Pi)}) + \alpha_1.$$

Game 2. [Transition based on a large failure event (see [5, 10])] Before the adversary E starts the attack game, the challenger chooses a random value $m \in_R \{1, 2, ..., q_s\}$. The m-th session activated by E, denoted by s^*, is the session on which the challenger wants the adversary to be tested. Let T be the event that the test-session is not session s^*. If event T occurs, then the attack game halts and the adversary outputs a random bit.

Analysis of Game 2. Event T is non-negligible, the environment can efficiently detect it and T is independent of the output in Game 1 (i.e. $P(S_1|T) = P(S_1)$). If T does not occur, then the attacker E will output the same bit in Game 2 as it did in Game 1 (so that $P(S_2|T^c) = P(S_1|T^c) = P(S_1)$). If event T occurs in Game 2, then the attack game halts and the adversary E outputs a random bit (so that $P(S_2|T) = 1/2$). We have,

$$P(S_2) = P(S_2|T)P(T) + P(S_2|T^c)P(T^c) = \frac{1}{2}P(T) + P(S_1)P(T^c)$$

$$= P(T^c)(P(S_1) - \frac{1}{2}) + \frac{1}{2}.$$

Hence we get, $\alpha_2 = |2P(S_2) - 1| = P(T^c)|2P(S_1) - 1| = \frac{1}{q_s}\alpha_1$.

Suppose w.l.o.g. that $s^*_{role} = \mathcal{I}$ and that protocol Π does not include optional public information in the sent messages. Let F be a forgery event with respect to the long-term public key $pk_{\hat{P}}$ of party $\hat{P}$, that is, adversary E issues a $\mathsf{send}(s^*, V, \sigma)$ query to session s^* being incomplete such that

- σ is a valid signature on message $m = (V, [W, s^*_{actor}])$ with respect to the public key of $\hat{P}$, where W is the Diffie-Hellman exponential contained in message s^*_{sent}, and
- (V, σ) has never been output by party $\hat{P}$ in response to a send query.

Game 3. [Transition based on a small failure event] This game is the same as the previous one except that when a forgery event F with respect to the long-term public key of some party $\hat{P} \in \mathcal{P}$ occurs, the experiment halts and E outputs a random bit.

Analysis of Game 3. The analysis of Game 3 proceeds in several steps. Consider first the following two cases.

1. If E issues a $\mathsf{corrupt}(\hat{P})$ query before the completion of session s^*, then this query would render session s^* un-fresh. This would have caused Game 2 to abort since session s^* would not be the test-session. Recall that the $\mathsf{test\text{-}session}$ query can only be issued to a session that is fresh by the time the query is issued. Hence this case can be excluded.
2. If E does not issue a $\mathsf{corrupt}(\hat{P})$ query before the completion of session s^*, then he can only impersonate party $\hat{P}$ to session s^* by forging a signature on a message with respect to the long-term public key of $\hat{P}$.

Claim. We have $|P(S_2) - P(S_3)| \leq P(F)$.

Proof. If event F does not occur, then Game 2 and 3 proceed identically (i.e. $S_2 \wedge F^c \Leftrightarrow S_3 \wedge F^c$). The Difference Lemma yields that $|P(S_2) - P(S_3)| \leq P(F)$.

Claim. If the deterministic signature scheme is SUF-CMA, then $P(F)$ is negligible. More precisely, $P(F) \leq NAdv_M^{Sign}(k)$, where $Adv_M^{Sign}(k)$ denotes the probability of a successful forgery.

Proof. Consider the following algorithm M using adversary E as a subroutine. M is given a public signature key pk and access to the corresponding signature oracle $\mathcal{O}^{Sign}$. It selects at random one of the N parties and sets its public key to pk. We denote this party by $\hat{P}$ and its signature key pair by $(sk_{\hat{P}}, pk_{\hat{P}})$. Further, the algorithm M chooses signature key pairs (sk_i, pk_i) for all parties $\hat{P}_i \in \mathcal{P}$ with $\hat{P}_i \neq \hat{P}$ and stores the associated secret keys. It also chooses key pairs (c_i, C_i) for all parties $\hat{P}_i \in \mathcal{P}$ as needed for protocol Π and stores the associated secret keys.

ALGORITHM M:

1. Run E on input 1^k and the public keys for all of the N parties.
2. If E issues a send$(z, \hat{Q})$ query to activate session z with peer $\hat{Q} \in \mathcal{P}$, then answer it as follows.
   - If $z_{actor} \neq \hat{P}$, then choose $x \in_R \mathbb{Z}_p$ to get $X = g^x$, compute the signature σ on message $m = (X[, \hat{Q}])$ on behalf of z_{actor} and return the message (X, σ) to E.
   - If $z_{actor} = \hat{P}$, then choose $x \in_R \mathbb{Z}_p$ to get $X = g^x$ and query the signature oracle on message $m = (X[, \hat{Q}])$ which returns the signature σ on message m. Store the pair (m, σ) in a table L, initially empty, and return the message (X, σ) to E.
3. If E issues a send$(z, \hat{Q}, m)$ query to activate session z, then answer it as follows. First check whether message m is of the form (X, σ) for some $X \in G$ and σ a valid signature on message $(X[, z_{actor}])$ with respect to the public key of $\hat{Q}$. If the checks succeed, then:
   - If $z_{actor} \neq \hat{P}$, then choose $y \in_R \mathbb{Z}_p$ to get $Y = g^y$, compute the signature σ on message $m = (Y[, X, \hat{Q}])$ on behalf of z_{actor} and return the message (Y, σ) to E.
   - If $z_{actor} = \hat{P}$, then choose $y \in_R \mathbb{Z}_p$ to get $Y = g^x$ and query the signature oracle on message $m = (Y[, X, \hat{Q}])$ which returns the signature σ on message m. Store the pair (m, σ) in table L (initially empty) and return the message (Y, σ) to E.

   If one of the checks does not succeed, then abort session z.
4. If E issues a send(z, m) query to session z in role $\mathcal{I}$, then check whether message m is of the form (Y, σ) for some $Y \in G$ and σ a valid signature on message $(Y[, X, z_{actor}])$ with respect to the public key of z_{peer} (where $W \in G$ is contained in message s^*_{sent}). If the check fails, then abort session z.
5. If E makes a send(s^*, V, σ) query, where σ is a valid signature with respect to the public key $pk_{\hat{P}}$ of party $\hat{P}$ on message $m = (V[, W, s^*_{actor}])$ (where $W \in G$ is contained in s^*_{sent}), before the completion of the test-session s^* and $(m, \sigma) \notin L$, then stop E and output (m, σ) as a forgery.
6. The queries session-key, ephemeral-key are answered in the appropriate way since M has chosen the ephemeral secret keys for all the sessions and the long-term secret keys for use in protocol Π for all the parties.
7. The queries corrupt$(\hat{P}_i)$, where $\hat{P}_i \in \mathcal{P}$ and $\hat{P}_i \neq \hat{P}$, are answered in the appropriate way since M knows the secret key pairs of the parties $\hat{P}_i \neq \hat{P}$.
8. If E issues the query test-session(s^*), then abort with failure.

Under event F, algorithm M is successful as described in Step 5 and the abortion as in Step 8 does not occur. The probability that E succeeds in forging a signature with respect to the public key of $\hat{P}$ is bounded above by the probability that M outputs a forgery multiplied by the number of parties, that is, $P(F) \le N Adv_M^{Sign}(k)$.

Claim. Let $Adv_E^{\mathrm{SIG}(\Pi),\mathrm{Game\ 3},O}(k) := |2P(S_3|O) - 1|$, where O denotes the event that there is an origin-session for the test-session. It holds that $Adv_E^{\mathrm{SIG}(\Pi),\mathrm{Game\ 3}}(k) = max(0, Adv_E^{\mathrm{SIG}(\Pi),\mathrm{Game\ 3},O}(k))$.

Proof. Note that $|2P(S_3|F) - 1| = |2\frac{1}{2} - 1| = 0$ (since, when event F occurs in Game 3, E outputs a random bit) and that if event F does not occur, then there exists an origin-session for the test-session.

We next establish an upper bound for $Adv_E^{\mathrm{SIG}(\Pi),\mathrm{Game\ 3},O}(k)$ in terms of the security of protocol Π.

Claim. Assume that in Game 3 there exists a unique[1] origin-session s for the test-session s^* with $s_{actor} = s^*_{peer}$. If there is an efficient adversary E in eCK-PFS succeeding in Game 3 against protocol $\mathrm{SIG}(\Pi)$ with non-negligible advantage, then we can construct an efficient adversary E' in eCK^w succeeding in Game 3 against protocol Π with non-negligible advantage using adversary E as a subroutine. Moreover, it holds that $Adv_E^{\mathrm{SIG}(\Pi),\mathrm{Game\ 3},O}(k) \le Adv_{E'}^{\Pi,\mathrm{Game\ 3},O}(k)$.

Proof. Fix an efficient adversary E in eCK-PFS succeeding in Game 3 against protocol $\mathrm{SIG}(\Pi)$ with non-negligible advantage. Let us construct an adversary E' in eCK^w succeeding in Game 3 against protocol Π with non-negligible advantage using adversary E as a subroutine.

ALGORITHM E': E' chooses secret/public signature key pairs for all the parties and stores the associated secret signature keys. It is given all public knowledge, such as public (non-signature) keys for all the parties.

1. Run E against $\mathrm{SIG}(\Pi)$ on input 1^k and the public key pairs for all of the N parties.
2. When E issues a corrupt($\hat{P}$) query to some party $\hat{P}$, E' issues that query to party $\hat{P}$ and returns the answer to that query together with the secret signature key of $\hat{P}$ (that E' has chosen) to E.
3. When E issues an ephemeral-key or a session-key query to some session z, E' issues that query to session z and returns the answer to E.
4. send queries are answered in the following way.
   - If E issues a send($z, \hat{Q}$) query to activate session z with peer $\hat{Q}$, then E' issues the same query to session z. The response is a message $W(\in G)$. Since E' knows the secret signature key of z_{actor}, it can sign the message

---

[1] No collision in the ephemeral secret keys occurs for $\mathrm{SIG}(\Pi)$ (where $\Pi \in \mathcal{DH}$-2) since otherwise Game 1 would have caused the game to abort.

$m = (W[, \hat{Q}])$ on its behalf and then return the message (W, σ) to E, where σ denotes the signature on m with respect to the public key of z_{actor}.

- If E issues a $\mathsf{send}(z, \hat{Q}, m)$ query to activate session z, where message m is of the form (W, σ), then E' first checks whether $W \in G$ and second whether σ is a valid signature on message $(W[, z_{actor}])$ with respect to the public key of $\hat{Q}$. If the checks succeed, then E' issues the query $\mathsf{send}(z, W)$ to session z. The response is a message $V \in G$. Since E' knows the secret signature key of z_{actor}, it can sign the message $m = (V[, W, \hat{Q}])$ on its behalf and then return the message (V, σ) to E, where σ denotes the signature on m with respect to the public key of z_{actor}.

- If E issues a $\mathsf{send}(z, m)$ query, where message m is of the form (V, σ), then E' first checks whether $V \in G$ and second whether σ is a valid signature on message $(V[, W, z_{actor}])$ with respect to the public key of z_{peer}, where W is the Diffie-Hellman exponential contained in z_{sent}. If the checks succeed, then E' issues the query $\mathsf{send}(z, V)$ to session z.

If one of the checks fails, then session z is aborted (i. e. E' aborts session z).

5. In case E issues the test-session query to session s^*, E' issues the test-session query to session s^* and returns the answer to E.

6. At the end of E's execution (after it has output its guess b'), output b' as well.

Thus, it holds that $Adv_E^{\mathrm{SIG}(\Pi),\mathrm{Game}\ 3,O}(k) \le Adv_{E'}^{\Pi,\mathrm{Game}\ 3,O}(k)$.

Finally,

$$Adv_E^{\mathrm{SIG}(\Pi)}(k) \le 2P(Coll_{\mathrm{SIG}(\Pi)}) + 2q_s N Adv_M^{Sign}(k) + q_s Adv_E^{\mathrm{SIG}(\Pi),\mathrm{Game}\ 3,O}(k)$$
$$\le 2P(Coll_{\mathrm{SIG}(\Pi)}) + 2q_s N Adv_M^{Sign}(k) + q_s Adv_{E'}^{\Pi,\mathrm{Game}\ 3,O}(k)$$

Since by assumption protocol Π is secure in eCK^w, there is a negligible function g such that $Adv_{E'}^{\Pi,\mathrm{Game}\ 3,O}(k) \le g(k)$ which completes the proof. $\square$

Remark 1. Let M^w and M-PFS be the security models obtained from eCK^w and eCK-PFS (respectively) by removing the ephemeral-key query and related restrictions in the freshness definitions. Then it can be shown in a similar way as above that for any KE protocol $\Pi \in \mathcal{DH}\text{-}2$ secure in M^w, the transformed protocol $\mathrm{SIG}(\Pi)$ is secure in M-PFS using either a deterministic or a randomized SUF-CMA signature scheme.

Remark 2. In contrast to the SIG transformation, the MAC transformation $\mathcal{C}$ suggested in [6] applied to any protocol $\pi \in \mathcal{DH}\text{-}2$ does not yield a two-message key-exchange protocol secure in eCK-PFS since the transformed protocol is vulnerable to an attack that combines revealing the long-term secret keys of the actor of the test-session with revealing the long-term secret keys of the peer of the test-session after its completion. More precisely, an attacker can impersonate the peer of the test-session by first revealing the long-term secret keys of the actor (which allows him to create valid MACs on messages of his choice) and after the completion of the test-session revealing the long-term secret keys of the peer. For example, this attack shows that $\mathcal{C}(\mathrm{NAXOS})$ [6] is insecure in eCK-PFS.

5   NAXOS Revisited

The NAXOS protocol [15], shown in Figure 3, provides an example of a protocol belonging to the class $\mathcal{DH}$-2, where $H_1 : \{0,1\}^* \to \mathbb{Z}_p$ and $H_2 : \{0,1\}^* \to \{0,1\}^k$ denote two hash functions and $r_{\hat{A}}, r_{\hat{B}} \in_R \{0,1\}^k$. In analogy to Figure 1, note that $f_{\mathcal{I}}(r_{\hat{A}}, a, \Omega) = H_1(r_{\hat{A}}, a)$, $f_{\mathcal{R}}(r_{\hat{B}}, b, \Omega) = H_1(r_{\hat{B}}, b)$, $F_{\mathcal{I}}(f_{\mathcal{I}}(r_{\hat{A}}, a, \Omega), a, Y, \Omega) = H_2(Y^a, B^{H_1(r_{\hat{A}},a)}, Y^{H_1(r_{\hat{A}},a)}, \hat{A}, \hat{B})$, and $F_{\mathcal{R}}(f_{\mathcal{R}}(r_{\hat{B}}, b, \Omega), b, X, \Omega) = H_2(A^{H_1(r_{\hat{B}},b)}, X^b, X^{H_1(r_{\hat{B}},b)}, \hat{A}, \hat{B})$.

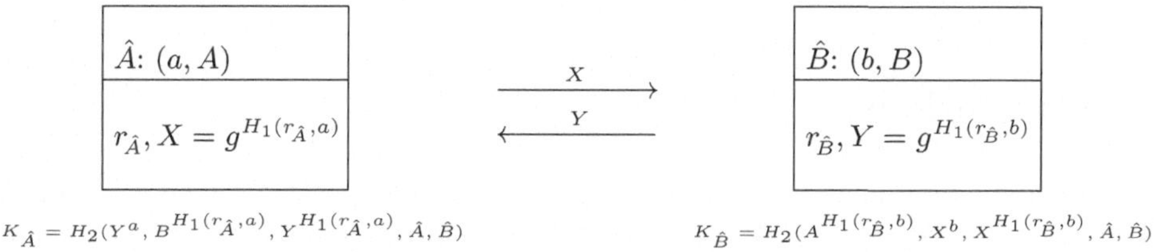

Fig. 3. NAXOS protocol [15]

The following proposition states that the NAXOS protocol is secure in eCK^w.

Proposition 1. *Under the GAP-CDH assumption in the cyclic group G of prime order p, NAXOS is secure in the eCK^w model, when H_1 and H_2 are modeled as independent random oracles.*

In contrast to the proof of NAXOS in the eCK model [15], the proof of Proposition 1 distinguishes between the cases whether or not an origin-session (instead of a matching session) exists for the test-session.

Proof (Sketch). Similar to [15,21], we analyze the following three events:

1. $DL \wedge K$
2. $T_O \wedge DL^c \wedge K$, and
3. $(T_O)^c \wedge DL^c \wedge K$, where

T_O denotes the event that there exists an origin-session for the test-session, DL denotes the event where there exists a party $\hat{C}$ such that the adversary M, during its execution, queries H_1 with $(*, c)$ before issuing a corrupt$(\hat{C})$ query and K denotes the event that M wins the security experiment against NAXOS by querying H_2 with $(\sigma_1, \sigma_2, \sigma_3, \hat{A}, \hat{B})$, where $\sigma_1 = CDH(Y, A), \sigma_2 = CDH(B, X), \sigma_3 = CDH(X, Y)$ given that the test-session is s^* with $T_{s^*} = (\hat{A}, \hat{B}, \mathcal{I}, X, Y)$. $\square$

Applying the SIG transformation on the NAXOS protocol yields the protocol SIG(NAXOS), depicted in Figure 4. Combining Proposition 1 with Theorem 1, we obtain the following result.

Corollary 1. *Under the GAP-CDH assumption in the cyclic group G of prime order p, using a deterministic SUF-CMA signature scheme, the SIG(NAXOS) protocol is secure in the eCK-PFS model, when H_1, H_2 are modeled as independent random oracles.*

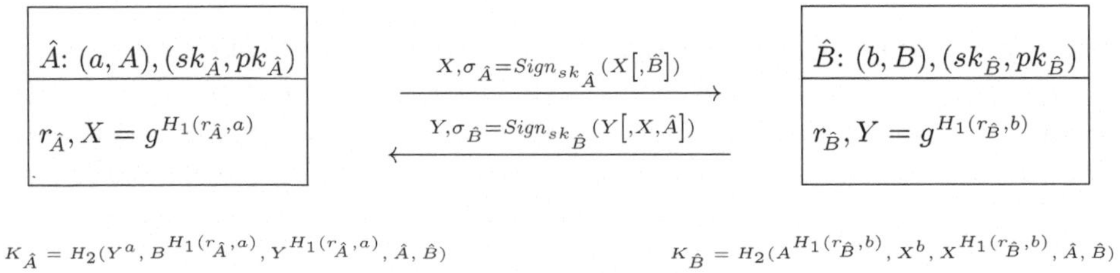

$$\boxed{\begin{array}{l} \hat{A}: (a, A), (sk_{\hat{A}}, pk_{\hat{A}}) \\[6pt] r_{\hat{A}}, X = g^{H_1(r_{\hat{A}}, a)} \end{array}} \quad \begin{array}{c} \xrightarrow{\ X, \sigma_{\hat{A}} = Sign_{sk_{\hat{A}}}(X[,\hat{B}])\ } \\[10pt] \xleftarrow{\ Y, \sigma_{\hat{B}} = Sign_{sk_{\hat{B}}}(Y[,X,\hat{A}])\ } \end{array} \quad \boxed{\begin{array}{l} \hat{B}: (b, B), (sk_{\hat{B}}, pk_{\hat{B}}) \\[6pt] r_{\hat{B}}, Y = g^{H_1(r_{\hat{B}}, b)} \end{array}}$$

$$K_{\hat{A}} = H_2(Y^a, B^{H_1(r_{\hat{A}}, a)}, Y^{H_1(r_{\hat{A}}, a)}, \hat{A}, \hat{B}) \qquad\qquad K_{\hat{B}} = H_2(A^{H_1(r_{\hat{B}}, b)}, X^b, X^{H_1(r_{\hat{B}}, b)}, \hat{A}, \hat{B})$$

Fig. 4. SIG(NAXOS) protocol

6 Conclusions

We provided two new eCK-like security notions, namely eCK^w and eCK-PFS. The eCK^w model slightly strengthens eCK by a more precise modeling of weak-PFS. The stronger eCK-PFS notion guarantees PFS, even in the presence of eCK-like adversaries. Proving security in eCK-PFS provides strictly more guarantees than separately proving eCK^w-security and PFS. Existing two-message KE protocols such as CMQV [21], NAXOS [15], or $\mathcal{C}$(NAXOS) [6] fail to achieve security in eCK-PFS. We specified a security-strengthening transformation that transforms any two-message DH type KE protocol secure in eCK^w into a two-message protocol secure in eCK-PFS. As future work, we would like to specify further transformations on KE protocols that are based on the newly developed security models in this work. It remains an open question whether there exist more efficient transformations that yield two-message KE protocols secure in eCK-PFS.

References

1. Bellare, M., Pointcheval, D., Rogaway, P.: Authenticated Key Exchange Secure against Dictionary Attacks. In: Preneel, B. (ed.) EUROCRYPT 2000. LNCS, vol. 1807, pp. 139–155. Springer, Heidelberg (2000)
2. Bellare, M., Rogaway, P.: Entity Authentication and Key Distribution. In: Stinson, D.R. (ed.) CRYPTO 1993. LNCS, vol. 773, pp. 232–249. Springer, Heidelberg (1994)
3. Bellare, M., Rogaway, P.: Provably secure session key distribution: the three party case. In: 27th Annual ACM Symposium on Theory of Computing, STOC 1995, pp. 57–66. ACM, New York (1995)
4. Boneh, D., Shen, E., Waters, B.: Strongly Unforgeable Signatures Based on Computational Diffie-Hellman. In: Yung, M., Dodis, Y., Kiayias, A., Malkin, T. (eds.) PKC 2006. LNCS, vol. 3958, pp. 229–240. Springer, Heidelberg (2006)
5. Boyd, C., Cliff, Y., Gonzalez Nieto, J.M., Paterson, K.G.: One-round key exchange in the standard model. Int. J. Applied Cryptography 1, 181–199 (2009)
6. Boyd, C., Nieto, J.G.: On Forward Secrecy in One-Round Key Exchange. In: Chen, L. (ed.) IMACC 2011. LNCS, vol. 7089, pp. 451–468. Springer, Heidelberg (2011)

7. Canetti, R., Krawczyk, H.: Analysis of Key-Exchange Protocols and Their Use for Building Secure Channels. In: Pfitzmann, B. (ed.) EUROCRYPT 2001. LNCS, vol. 2045, pp. 453–474. Springer, Heidelberg (2001)

8. Cheng, Q., Ma, C., Hu, X.: A New Strongly Secure Authenticated Key Exchange Protocol. In: Park, J.H., Chen, H.-H., Atiquzzaman, M., Lee, C., Kim, T.-H., Yeo, S.-S. (eds.) ISA 2009. LNCS, vol. 5576, pp. 135–144. Springer, Heidelberg (2009)

9. Chow, S.S.M., Choo, K.-K.R.: Strongly-Secure Identity-Based Key Agreement and Anonymous Extension. In: Garay, J.A., Lenstra, A.K., Mambo, M., Peralta, R. (eds.) ISC 2007. LNCS, vol. 4779, pp. 203–220. Springer, Heidelberg (2007)

10. Dent, A.W.: A note on game-hopping proofs. Cryptology ePrint Archive, Report 2006/260 (2006), http://eprint.iacr.org/2006/260

11. Gennaro, R., Krawczyk, H., Rabin, T.: Okamoto-Tanaka Revisited: Fully Authenticated Diffie-Hellman with Minimal Overhead. In: Zhou, J., Yung, M. (eds.) ACNS 2010. LNCS, vol. 6123, pp. 309–328. Springer, Heidelberg (2010)

12. Katz, J., Lindell, Y.: Introduction to Modern Cryptography. Chapman Hall/CRC (2008)

13. Krawczyk, H.: HMQV: A High-Performance Secure Diffie-Hellman Protocol. In: Shoup, V. (ed.) CRYPTO 2005. LNCS, vol. 3621, pp. 546–566. Springer, Heidelberg (2005)

14. LaMacchia, B.A., Lauter, K., Mityagin, A.: Stronger security of authenticated key exchange. Cryptology ePrint Archive, Report 2006/073 (2006), http://eprint.iacr.org/

15. LaMacchia, B.A., Lauter, K., Mityagin, A.: Stronger Security of Authenticated Key Exchange. In: Susilo, W., Liu, J.K., Mu, Y. (eds.) ProvSec 2007. LNCS, vol. 4784, pp. 1–16. Springer, Heidelberg (2007)

16. Lee, J., Park, C.S.: An efficient authenticated key exchange protocol with a tight security reduction. Cryptology ePrint Archive, Report 2008/345 (2008), http://eprint.iacr.org/

17. Lee, J., Park, J.H.: Authenticated key exchange secure under the computational diffie-hellman assumption. Cryptology ePrint Archive, Report 2008/344 (2008), http://eprint.iacr.org/

18. Menezes, A., van Oorschot, P., Vanstone, S.: Handbook of Applied Cryptography (October 1996)

19. Okamoto, T., Pointcheval, D.: The Gap-problems: A New Class of Problems for the Security of Cryptographic Schemes. In: Kim, K.-C. (ed.) PKC 2001. LNCS, vol. 1992, pp. 104–118. Springer, Heidelberg (2001)

20. Shoup, V.: Sequences of games: a tool for taming complexity in security proofs. Cryptology ePrint Archive, Report 2004/332 (2006), http://eprint.iacr.org/

21. Ustaoglu, B.: Obtaining a secure and efficient key agreement protocol from (H)MQV and NAXOS. Designs, Codes and Cryptography 46(3), 329–342 (2008)

Bleichenbacher's Attack Strikes again: Breaking PKCS#1 v1.5 in XML Encryption

Tibor Jager[1], Sebastian Schinzel[2,*], and Juraj Somorovsky[3]

[1] Karlsruhe Institute of Technology, Germany
tibor.jager@kit.edu
[2] Universität Erlangen-Nürnberg, Germany
sebastian.schinzel@cs.fau.de
[3] Horst-Görtz Institute for IT Security, Germany
juraj.somorovsky@rub.de

Abstract. We describe several attacks against the PKCS#1 v1.5 key transport mechanism of XML Encryption. Our attacks allow to recover the secret key used to encrypt transmitted payload data within a few minutes or several hours, depending on the considered scenario.

The attacks exploit differences in error messages and in the timing behavior of XML frameworks. We show how to attack seemingly invulnerable implementations, by exploiting additional properties of the XML Encryption standard that lead to new side-channels. An interesting novelty of one of our attacks is that it combines a weakness of a public-key scheme (transporting an ephemeral session key) with a different weakness of a symmetric encryption scheme (which transports the payload data, encrypted with the session key).

Recently the XML Encryption standard was updated, in response to an attack presented at CCS 2011. The attacks described in this paper work even against the updated version of XML Encryption. Our work shows once more that legacy cryptosystems have to be used with extreme care, and should be avoided wherever possible, since they may lead to practical attacks.

1 Introduction

In 1998 Bleichenbacher [3] published a chosen-ciphertext attack on the RSA-based PKCS#1 v1.5 encryption scheme specified in RFC 2313 [15]. This attack exploits the availability of an "oracle" that allows to test whether a given ciphertext is PKCS#1 v1.5 conformant. Due to its high relevance, Bleichenbacher's algorithm was well noticed. For instance, it enabled practical attacks on popular implementations of the SSL protocol [17]. These implementations were fixed immediately using a workaround patch, which until today seems to be sufficient to provide security in the context of SSL/TLS. Nonetheless, Bleichenbacher's attack sheds serious doubt on the security of PKCS#1 v1.5, in particular in scenarios where an adversary may issue chosen-ciphertexts to a server and observe the response.

---

* Sebastian Schinzel was supported by Deutsche Forschungsgemeinschaft (DFG) as part of SPP 1496 "Reliably Secure Software Systems".

S. Foresti, M. Yung, and F. Martinelli (Eds.): ESORICS 2012, LNCS 7459, pp. 752–769, 2012.
© Springer-Verlag Berlin Heidelberg 2012

In spite of these negative results, in 2002, four years after publication of the Bleichenbacher attack, the W3C consortium published the XML Encryption standard [6], in which PKCS#1 v1.5 encryption is specified as a *mandatory* key transport mechanism. This standard is implemented in XML frameworks of major commercial and open-source organizations like Apache, redhat, IBM, Microsoft, and SAP and employed world-wide in a large number of major web-based and cloud-based applications, ranging from business communications, e-commerce, and financial services over healthcare applications to governmental and military infrastructures.

The decision to use PKCS#1 v1.5 despite the known criticisms on its security may be partly due to the fact that the *ad hoc* countermeasures against Bleichen-bacher's attack employed in SSL seem to work well – at least for protocols of the SSL family. However, one must not ignore that SSL and XML Encryption are fundamentally different protocols, running in different settings, using a different combination of cryptographic primitives, and providing different side-channels. *Does the use of PKCS#1 v1.5 make XML Encryption vulnerable to attacks?*

CONTRIBUTIONS. We describe different attacks on the key transport mechanism of XML Encryption which is based on PKCS#1 v1.5. Our goal is to turn a given Web Service into a "Bleichenbacher oracle" that allows us to mount the Bleichenbacher attack [3].

We show that it is possible to conduct practical attacks even against Web Services implementations that seem not vulnerable (e.g. since they implement the classical countermeasure against Bleichenbacher's attack, which we describe below). To this end, we exploit two properties of the XML Encryption standard:

1. *The attacker can choose the ciphertext size.* The basic idea is that a larger ciphertext increases the running time of the decryption process. We will show that this allows the attacker to perform very powerful timing attacks, which work even in networks where such attacks can usually not be executed in practice, e.g., in networks with a substantial amount of jitter.
2. *A weak mode-of-operation.* XML Encryption allows the usage of block ci-phers in the *cipher-block chaining* (CBC) mode-of-operation. CBC exhibits a weakness [27] that allows an adversary to make modifications to the en-crypted plaintext, by XORing arbitrary bit strings to the plaintext. We show that it is possible to use this weakness as an alternative way to determine whether a PKCS#1 v1.5 ciphertext is "valid" or not.
   Besides CBC mode, the updated version of the XML Encryption specification allows to use the GCM mode of operation. This mode was introduced to prevent the attacks from [11]. Interestingly, the CBC-attack we describe in this paper *allows to decrypt GCM ciphertexts, too* — if the receiving Web Service *is able to* decrypt CBC ciphertexts, which is mandatory for any standard-compliant implementation. This is due to the fact that we use the PKCS#1 v1.5 weakness in combination with the CBC weakness only to decrypt the session key. After we have obtained this session key, we can decrypt an arbitrary ciphertext, regardless of whether it is encrypted using CBC, GCM, or any other mode-of-operation.

A classical countermeasure against Bleichenbacher's attack is to let the decryption algorithm return a random key, if decryption fails. Then the system proceeds with this random key. We stress that the CBC-based attack described in this paper *can not be prevented* by this countermeasure.

In the full version [10] we also show that it is possible to execute Bleichenbacher's attack *in a straightforward way* against some widely-used Web Services implementations, such as redhat's JBossWS [12]. This is noteworthy, given that Bleichenbacher's attack has received much attention in the computer security community.

We verify our attacks by experimental analyses. Apache Axis2 [26] was used to test the timing-based and CBC-based attacks. The timing-based attack takes 200 minutes on the localhost and less than one week when performed over the Internet. The CBC-based attack takes less than five days. We compare these two attacks and give two realistic scenarios where each attack performs especially well. These attacks are applicable to other systems as well, as we describe below. We stress that all figures are derived using "good" ciphertexts, a property that we describe more precisely in Section 5, and which holds for (heuristically) one out of 80 ciphertexts (see Section 5). We also note that the recent improvements to Bleichenbacher's algorithm by Bardou et al. [1] apply in our case as well.

In general chosen-ciphertext attacks can be avoided by ensuring the integrity of the ciphertext. One would therefore expect our attack can easily be thwarted by using XML Signature [7] to ensure integrity. (Note that XML Signature specifies not only classical public-key signatures, but also "secret-key signatures", i.e., message authentication codes.) However, this is not true, since chosen-ciphertext attacks on XML Encryption can be applied even if either public-key or secret-key XML Signatures over the ciphertext are used, see [11,24] for a detailed description.

FURTHER APPLICATIONS.   In close cooperation with SAP AG, Germany, we furthermore verified that all attacks worked also against the implementation of XML Encryption in Version 7.03 of the SAP ABAP stack. SAP is currently in the process of fixing this issue.

Beyond XML Encryption, the recent JSON Web Encryption (JWE) specification [13] prescribes PKCS#1 v1.5 as a mandatory cipher. This specification is under developement and at the time of writing there existed only one implementation following this specification.[1] We verified that this implementation was vulnerable to two versions of the Bleichenbacher's attack: the direct attack based on error messages and the timing-based attack.

RELATED WORK.   At CCS 2011 [11] an attack on XML Encryption was described which allows to extract the plaintext contained in a given ciphertext. This attack breaks the *symmetric* encryption scheme of XML Encryption (AES-CBC or 3DES-CBC) by submitting modified ciphertexts to a Web Service and observing its response. The attack requires on average $14 \cdot \ell$ chosen-ciphertext queries, where ℓ is the byte-length of the recovered plaintext. Even though this is very

---

[1] Nimbus-JWT: `https://bitbucket.org/nimbusds/nimbus-jwt`

efficient, the complexity grows linearly with the size of the plaintext, thus may become infeasible if the attacker has to decrypt long plaintexts. The W3C has responded to the attack of [11] by updating the XML Encryption standard. Now it recommends the GCM mode instead of CBC, which prevents chosen-ciphertext attacks against the symmetric cipher.

Let us compare the attack of [11] to our work. For efficiency reasons, a typical XML Encryption ciphertext consists of two components. The first component is a public key encryption c_{key} of an ephemeral session key under the public key of the receiver. The second component is a symmetric encryption c_{data} of the actual plaintext data (see Section 3 for a detailed description). Jager and Somorovsky's attack directly decrypts the c_{data} component of the ciphertext to obtain the plaintext. In contrast, the attacks presented in this paper break the public-key encryption part c_{key}, to recover the ephemeral key first. The ephemeral key can then be used to decrypt c_{data} with the symmetric decryption algorithm. This novel approach has two interesting features. First, it is *independent of the symmetric cipher*, so it can also be used to attack XML Encryption ciphertexts that, according to the updated specification, are generated in GCM mode. Second, the attack complexity is *independent of the size of c_{data}*, and thus becomes more efficient than [11] for large c_{data}. Finally, it allows to recover the *session key* instead of only the plaintext, which may in certain scenarios be more serious.

Bleichenbacher's attack [3] on PKCS#1 v1.5 [15] has been published at CRYPTO 1998. This attack has been applied by Klima et al. to popular real-world implementations of the SSL protocol by incorporating an additional side-channel which was a version number check over PKCS#1 plaintext [17]. In [1] Bardou et al. describe several ways to improve the efficiency of Bleichenbacher's attack. At Crypto 2001 Manger [18] has presented an attack on Version 2.0 of PKCS#1 (RSA-OAEP) [16] which is very similar to Bleichenbacher's attack, and applicable to the current Version 2.1 [14] as well. Bauer et al. [2] have shown that PKCS#1 v1.5 is insecure in two non-standard (but realistic) settings, namely broadcast encryption and IND-CPA security in presence of a plaintext validity checking oracle. Smart [23] shows how to apply a Bleichenbacher-style attack to break RSA-based PIN encryption, if a certain side-channel oracle is given. Very recently, Degabriele et al. [4] gave another Bleichenbacher-style attack that allows to forge signatures in an EMV transaction. Both these attacks are rather theoretical, since it is unlikely that the required oracle is given in practice.

In [20] it was noted that valid (symmetric-cipher) padding may lead to a side-channel that allows to mount Bleichenbacher's attack, but without additionally exploiting the plaintext-malleability of the symmetric cipher or giving any concrete application. In contrast, we obtain an oracle which is able to determine wether a given ciphertext is PKCS#1 v1.5-conformant with probability 1 in at most 256 steps, and show that this attack is practically relevant.

Generally, we give a truly practical attack which is directly applicable to a vast number of real-world systems. This shows that using legacy cryptosystems is extremely dangerous, and makes a very strong case for replacing them.

RESPONSIBLE DISCLOSURE. In June 2011 we disclosed our attack to the W3C XML Encryption working group, several developers of well-known Web Services frameworks, and a governmental CERT. All acknowledged the validity of the attack. The W3C XML Encryption working group added a remark to the updated standard [5, Section 6.1.2] which addresses our attack and recommends to use PKCS#1 v2.1 (aka. RSA-OAEP) instead. However, PKCS#1 v1.5 is still contained in the standard, and mandatory for any standard-compliant implementation.

We have also informed the developers of the JWE implementation and the whole JOSE (JSON Object Signing and Encryption) working group about the possible threats.[2] They acknowledged our attack and are reconsidering exclusion of PKCS#1 v1.5 from the standard.

2   Bleichenbacher's Attack

When referring to PKCS#1 in the sequel, then we mean version 1.5, unless specified otherwise. Bleichenbacher's attack [3] on version 1.5 of the PKCS#1 encryption standard [15] exploits properties of the encoding of messages. It requires an attacker who has gained access to an encrypted message and who can send chosen ciphertexts to an "oracle" to determine whether a ciphertext is PKCS#1-conformant. Such an oracle may in practice be given for instance by a server responding with appropriate error messages. We let (N, e) be an RSA [22] public key, with corresponding secret key d. We denote with ℓ the byte-length of N, thus, we have $2^{8(\ell-1)} < N < 2^{8\ell}$.

PKCS#1 v1.5 Padding and Encryption. The basic idea of PKCS#1 v1.5 is to take a message k (a bit string), concatenate this message with a random padding string PS, and then apply the RSA encryption function $m \mapsto m^e \bmod N$.

Let us describe the padding in more detail. In the following, let $a||b$ denote the concatenation of two bit strings a and b. Suppose a message k of byte-length $|k| \leq \ell - 11$ is given. This string is encrypted as follows.

1. Choose a random padding string PS of length $\ell - 3 - |k|$, such that PS contains no 00-byte. Note that the byte length of PS is at least $|PS| \geq 8$.
2. Set $m := 00||02||PS||00||k$. Interpret m as an integer such that $0 < m < N$.
3. Compute the ciphertext as $c = m^e \bmod N$.

The decryption algorithm computes $m' = c^d \bmod N$ and interprets integer m' as a bit string. It tests whether m' has the correct format, i.e., $m' = 00||02||PS||00||k$. If true, it returns k, otherwise it rejects the ciphertext.

In this paper we say that a ciphertext $c \in \mathbb{Z}_N$ is *valid* (PKCS#1 conformant), if the $m = c^d \bmod N$ has the format $m = 00||02||PS||00||k$. Note that this implies in particular that $2B \leq (c^d \bmod N) < 3B$, where $B = 2^{8(\ell-2)}$.

---

[2] See http://www.mail-archive.com/jose@ietf.org/msg00157

A Ciphertext-Validity Oracle. The only necessary prerequisite to execute Bleichenbacher's attack is that an oracle $\mathcal{O}$ is given which tells whether a given ciphertext is valid (PKCS#1 conformant) w.r.t. the target public key (N, e). This oracle takes as input a ciphertext c and responds as follows.

$$\mathcal{O}(c) = \begin{cases} 1 & \text{if } c \text{ is PKCS\#1 conformant w.r.t. } (N, e), \\ 0 & \text{otherwise.} \end{cases}$$

Such an oracle may be given in many practical scenarios, for instance by a web server responding with appropriate error messages. We will show how to construct such an oracle based on properties of XML Encryption.

Bleichenbacher's Algorithm. In this section we sketch the idea of Bleichenbacher's algorithm, which uses the PKCS#1 validity oracle to invert the RSA encryption function $m \mapsto m^e \bmod N$. We give only a high-level description of the attack, and refer to the original paper [3] for details.

Suppose $c = m^e \bmod N$ is given. We assume that c is PKCS#1 conformant. Thus, $m = c^d \bmod N$ lies in the interval $[2B, 3B)$. Bleichenbacher's algorithm proceeds as follows. It chooses a small integer s (see [3] for details on how s is chosen), computes

$$c' = (c \cdot s^e) \bmod N = (ms)^e \bmod N,$$

and queries the oracle with c'. If $\mathcal{O}(c') = 1$, then the algorithm learns that $2B \leq ms - rN < 3B$, for some r, which is equivalent to

$$\frac{2B + rN}{s} \leq m < \frac{3B + rN}{s}.$$

Thus, m must lie in the interval $m \in [\lceil (2B + rN)/s \rceil, \lfloor (3B + rN)/s \rfloor)$. By iteratively choosing new s, the adversary reduces the possible solutions m, until only one is left.

For a 1024-bit modulus and a random ciphertext, the analysis in [3] shows that the attack requires about one million oracle queries to recover a plaintext, plus a small amount of additional computations. Therefore, Bleichenbacher's attack became also known as the "Million Question Attack". The most time-consuming step of the algorithm is to find the first value s such that $\mathcal{O}((c \cdot s^e) \bmod N) = 1$.

We note that very recently Bardou et al. described improvements to Bleichenbacher's algorithm by Bardou et al. [1], which are applicable in our case as well.

3   Web Services

This section summarizes the fundamentals of XML, XML Security, and Web Services, which are relevant to our paper. The reader familiar with these concepts can safely skip this section.

XML and Web Services. Web Services is a W3C standard [9] developed to support interoperable interactions over networks between different software applications. Thereby, the communicating applications use SOAP messages [8]. SOAP messages are XML-based messages generally consisting of *header* and *body*. The header element includes message-specific data (e.g. timestamp, user information, or security data). The body element contains function invocation and response data, which are mainly addressed to the business logic processors.

As the XML documents often contain data whose confidentiality and integrity must be protected, the W3C consortium developed standards describing the XML syntax for applying cryptographic primitives to XML data. These are specified in the XML Encryption [6] and XML Signature [7] standards.

XML Encryption. In order to encrypt XML data, in most scenarios *hybrid encryption* is used, i.e. encryption proceeds in two steps.

1. The encryptor chooses a *session key k*. This key is encrypted using a public-key encryption scheme.
2. The actual payload data is then encrypted with a symmetric cipher.

The XML Encryption standard [6] specifies two public-key encryption schemes, namely PKCS#1 in Versions 1.5 and 2.0. Both are mandatory. Furthermore, the updated version of the standard allows to choose between three symmetric ciphers, namely AES-CBC, AES-GCM, and 3DES-CBC.

```
<Envelope>
 <Header>
  <Security>
   <EncryptedKey Id="EncKeyId">
    <EncryptionMethod Algorithm="...xmlenc#rsa-1_5"/>
    <KeyInfo>...</KeyInfo>
    <CipherData>
     <CipherValue>Y2bh...fPw==</CipherValue>
    </CipherData>
   </EncryptedKey>                          c_key
  </Security>
 </Header>
 <Body>
  <EncryptedData Id="EncDataId-2">
   <EncryptionMethod Algorithm="...xmlenc#aes128-cbc"/>
   <CipherData>
    <CipherValue>3bP...Zx0=</CipherValue>
   </CipherData>
  </EncryptedData>                          c_data
 </Body>
</Envelope>
```

Fig. 1. Example of a SOAP message with encrypted data

Figure 1 gives an example of a SOAP message containing such a hybrid ciphertext. This message consists of the following parts:

1. The EncryptedKey part (c_{key}). The CipherValue element contains the encrypted session key.
2. The EncryptedData part (c_{data}). The CipherValue element contains the payload data, encrypted using the key encapsulated in c_{key}. The symmetric cipher is specified in the EncryptionMethod element.

DECRYPTION PROCESSING AND PARSING. A Web Service processes such an XML document as follows. It parses the document to locate c_{key} and c_{data}. It decrypts c_{key} to obtain the session key k. Then it uses k to decrypt c_{data} to obtain the payload data. Finally, the payload data is parsed as an XML document.

PADDING IN CBC. XML Encryption prescribes usage of block ciphers, namely AES or 3DES. Therefore the payload *data* being encrypted needs to be padded to achieve a length which is a multiple of the cipher's block-size bs of the applied block cipher. XML Encryption specifies the following padding scheme:

1. Compute the smallest integer $p > 0$ such that $|data| + p$ is an integer multiple of bs.
2. Append $(p - 1)$ random bytes to *data*.
3. Append one more byte to *data*, whose integer value equals p.

Let us give an example. Suppose a block-size of $bs = 8$ and payload data consisting of $|data| = 5$ bytes, e.g.

$$data = \text{0x0101010101}.$$

Then we have $p = 8 - 5 = 3$. Thus, the padded payload data would be equal to

$$data = \text{0x0101010101??????03},$$

where the ?? are arbitrary random bytes.

CIPHER BLOCK CHAINING. *Cipher-block chaining* (CBC) [19] is the most popular block cipher mode-of-operation in practice. The XML Encryption standard allows to choose between CBC and GCM mode, both are mandatory. For our application it suffices to describe CBC, but we stress again that both attacks that we present in this paper apply to ciphertexts generated in GCM mode as well.

Suppose a byte string *data*, whose length is an integer multiple $d \cdot bs$ of the block-size of the block cipher (Enc, Dec). Let us write $data = (data^{(1)}, \ldots, data^{(d)})$ to denote individual chunks of *data* of size bs. These chunks are processed as follows.

– An *initialization vector* $iv \in \{0, 1\}^{8 \cdot bs}$ is chosen at random. The first ciphertext block is computed as

$$x := data^{(1)} \oplus iv, \qquad C^{(1)} := \text{Enc}(k, x). \tag{1}$$

– The subsequent ciphertext blocks $C^{(2)}, \ldots, C^{(d)}$ are computed as

$$x := data^{(i)} \oplus C^{(i-1)}, \qquad C^{(i)} := \text{Enc}(k, x) \tag{2}$$

for $i = 2, \ldots, d$.
– The resulting ciphertext is $C = (iv, C^{(1)}, \ldots, C^{(d)})$.

Web Services Frameworks. The rising popularity of Web Services in the recent years led to an emergence of many Web Services frameworks [12,25,26]. A very popular example is the widely-used Apache Axis2 framework. We will execute the bulk of our experimental analyses on Axis2, therefore we describe this framework in more detail.

Apache Axis2 is a Java-based open source framework for deploying Web Services servers and clients. The framework includes several modules implementing various Web Service specifications, such as Apache Rampart. This module enables to utilize XML Encryption. When receiving a SOAP message containing encrypted data, Axis2 locates c_{key} and c_{data} in the XML document structure. In order to decrypt c_{key}, Axis2 performs the PKCS#1-validity checks described in Section 2. In addition, Axis2 tests whether the resulting session key k has a length equal to 16, 24, or 32 bytes. If this fails, then the SOAP error message `security processing failed` is returned. Otherwise, key k is used to decrypt c_{data}, which yields the payload data *data*. Finally, *data* is parsed as an XML message. If this parsing fails, a `security processing failed` SOAP error message (i.e., *the same error message* that is returned if decryption of k fails) is returned. Otherwise, it is forwarded to the next module in the processing chain or to the business application

Now, assume we are given a ciphertext (c_{key}, c_{data}), and we modify the key encapsulation part c_{key} (this is necessary to mount Bleichenbacher's attack). Then we obtain a modified ciphertext (c'_{key}, c_{data}). If we send this ciphertext to the Web Service, then we will receive a `security processing failed` error message, since either processing of c'_{key} or parsing of the payload *data* contained in c_{data} will fail (except for a negligibly small probability). Thus, we are not able to distinguish whether c'_{key} is a valid or an invalid ciphertext. This seems to thwart Bleichenbacher's attack on the first sigh. However, in the next section, we will describe techniques for exploiting side-channels allowing us to determine the validity of c'_{key}.

Remark 1. Though we analyze mainly Apache Axis2, and thus strictly speaking all our experimental results are only valid for Axis2, we stress that the attacks described below are in principle applicable to other frameworks as well (e.g. for SAP). Moreover, as we describe in the full version [10] in detail, it turns out that exploiting certain additional framework-specific side-channels may even lead to dramatically more efficient attacks.

4   Attacks

Imagine an attacker who intercepts a message transferred to the Web Service server and whose goal is to decrypt c_{data}. In order to gain the session key k needed for data decryption, the attacker can apply the Bleichenbacher's attack on c_{key}. In this section, we describe two ways to obtain a side-channel that allows to determine whether a given ciphertext is valid (PKCS#1 conformant), *even though* the server does not respond with error messages allowing to distinguish valid from invalid ciphertexts. Thus, we turn a seamingly secure Web Service server into an oracle $\mathcal{O}$ responding with 1, if the decrypted k is valid, or 0 otherwise. Note that the stateless SOAP message exchange allows us to send an arbitrary amount of requests.

Basic Ideas. Let us first sketch our ideas on a high level. The first idea is to exploit the fact that the server decrypts and parses the payload data if and only if c_{key} is valid. Recall that in principle it is not possible to mount Bleichenbacher's attack, since we need to modify c_{key} in a way that decrypting and parsing c_{data} fails, and thus we receive the same `security processing failed` error message in both cases. However, since c_{data} decryption is executed if and only if c_{key} is valid, the time between sending the ciphertext and receiving the error message depends on the validity of c_{key}. Therefore, we can create a Bleichenbacher oracle by measuring this response time. In practice, this does not always form a practically useful side-channel, since timing measurements in real networks contain jitter introduced by network latency or server workload.

However, here it comes in handy, that the attacker can set c_{data} to any bit string whose length is an multiple of the block-size of the block cipher. Thus, by increasing the length of c_{data}, the attacker can also increase the timing gap between a valid and an invalid c_{key}. The challenge is to keep c_{data} as small as possible (to keep the attack efficient), but as large as necessary (to get distinguishable timing results).

In certain scenarios, the timing approach may become inefficient, for instance if the server workload is extremely unbalanced, or the network connection is not reliable. Therefore we describe a second idea, which exploits a weakness of the CBC mode. Consider a ciphertext encrypting a single (padded) payload data block $data^{(1)}$. Recall that such a ciphertext consists of an iv and a ciphertext block $C^{(1)} := \mathsf{Enc}(k, x)$, where $x := data^{(1)} \oplus iv$. Thus, by flipping bits in iv, we can implicitly flip bits in the plaintext $data^{(1)}$. In particular, we can modify the last byte of $data^{(1)}$, which contains the number of padding bytes. The crucial observation is now, that there exists one modified iv' such that the last byte of $data^{(1)'} = x \oplus iv'$ equals the block-length of the block cipher. In this case, $(iv', C^{(1)})$ corresponds to an encryption of the empty string, and XML parsing of the empty string does *not* fail. We use this property to distinguish a valid from an invalid c_{key}.

In the following sections, we describe how to use these ideas to construct an oracle $\mathcal{O}$ telling whether a given c_{key} is valid. This oracle can then be used to mount Bleichenbacher's attack.

Timing Attack. In this section, we describe a timing oracle $\mathcal{O}_t$ that determines if a given c_{key} is valid. Our observation is that the analyzed Web Service only then decrypts c_{data} if c_{key} is valid. Furthermore, parsing of the clear text does not start until c_{data} was fully decrypted, i.e. filling c_{data} with random data will yield a parsing error *after* the decryption has completed, except for some negligible probability. Another observation is that a larger c_{data} leads to measurably longer decryption times as depicted in Figure 2. This combination makes our attack

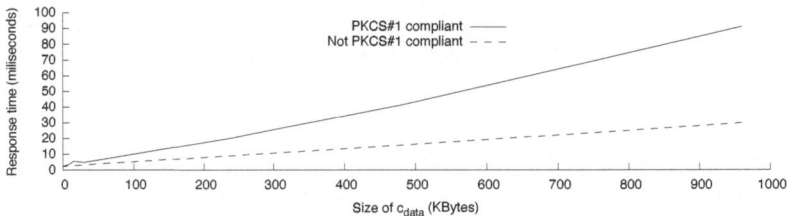

Fig. 2. Timing difference of valid c_{key} and invalid c_{key} in relation to the size of c_{data}, which was decrypted using AES-CBC

well suited for timing attacks across noisy networks, because the attacker can increase the timing differences by changing the size of c_{data}. Note that the actual content of c_{data} is irrelevant, only the size is important for the timing delay. In our experiments we enforced Axis2 to decrypt c_{data} using AES-CBC. Note that 3DES-CBC would bring even larger timing differences because the decryption process in 3DES is less efficient than AES, which would make our attack easier.

By nature, the timing measurements in an adaptive chosen ciphertext attack need to be evaluated during the attack because subsequent requests depend on the answer of the timing oracle of the previous request. We propose a new algorithm which allows this. The algorithm exploits the facts that valid keys have a longer processing time than invalid keys and that any noise in the form of random delays that occur in networks and busy systems is strictly additive. Intuitively, the algorithm determines the minimum response time t_{min} for valid keys. Any measured response time $t < t_{min}$ must be from an invalid key. We call a key a *candidate* for a valid key if the associated response time is above t_{min}. To make sure that this candidate is not actually an invalid key with the random noise pushing it above the timing boundary, we repeat the timing measurement with this key i times, resulting in a set of measurements $T_{c_{key}} = \langle t_1, t_2, \ldots, t_i \rangle$. If any of the repeated measurements is below the boundary, the key is marked as invalid. Note that the attacker can freely choose the size of the timing differences of valid and invalid keys by adjusting the size l of c_{data}. Equation 3 formally defines the timing oracle.

$$\mathcal{O}_t(c_{key}, l) = \begin{cases} 1 \text{ if } min(T_{c_{key}}) \geq t_{min}, \\ 0 \text{ if } \exists t \in T_{c_{key}} : t < t_{min}, \end{cases} \tag{3}$$

The algorithm is split into two phases: First, there is a calibration phase, where the particular timing conditions of the system are determined. The result of this phase is t_{min}, which is fed to the timing oracle in the second phase.

Calibration Phase. The oracle can determine if a given c_{key} is valid by measuring the response time of a request that uses this particular key. Thus, the oracle must be calibrated so that it can distinguish the response time of a valid c_{key} from an invalid c_{key}. For this, we perform i requests with a valid c_{key} and record the set of timings $T_{valid} = \langle t_1, t_2, \ldots, t_i \rangle$. Note that the attacker already has one

```
def is_valid(c_key, n):
    do n times:
            start = now()
            request(c_key, 1)
            end = now()
            t = end - start
            if t < t_min:
                    return 0 // "invalid"
    return 1 // "valid"
```

Fig. 3. Pseudo code sketching the validation routine of candidates of valid keys

valid c_{key} from the message he listened in to. Let $t_{min} = min(T_{valid}) - \epsilon$ where ϵ accounts for the fact that $min(T_{valid})$ is only an approximation for the actual minimum response time t'_{min} of valid keys, because $t'_{min} \leq t_{min}$.

We assume at this stage that the response times for valid and invalid keys remain stable during the attack phase, i.e. t_{min} remains the lower boundary for response times with valid keys for the duration of the attack. If this assumption does not apply for a given system, the attacker can regularly repeat the calibration phase to address fluctuations of t_{min}.

Attack Phase. Now that $\mathcal{O}_t$ is calibrated, the attacker can apply the Bleichenbacher algorithm. Figure 3 describes the procedure of $\mathcal{O}_t$. The Bleichenbacher algorithm calls $\mathcal{O}_t$ and passes c_{key} as a parameter. The oracle copies c_{key} in a SOAP message, sends it to the server and measures the response time t. The oracle answers with 0 if $t < t_{min}$. It repeats the measurement n times if $t \geq t_{min}$ to confirm that c_{key} is indeed valid.[3] The oracle answers with 1 if all measurements resulted in greater response times than t_{min}.

Exploiting a Weakness of CBC. In this section we describe another attack on c_{key}, which is based on the properties of the CBC mode of operation. As described in the previous sections, Axis2 processes XML Encryption as follows. It first decrypts c_{key}. Afterwards, it uses the decrypted session key k to decrypt c_{data}. If an error during the decryption occurs, Axis2 returns an error message that reads `security processing failed`. There are several possible causes for this error:

- c_{key} decryption: the decrypted c_{key} was invalid
- c_{data} decryption: the decrypted data from c_{key} was valid, but the c_{data} decryption or padding processing failed.
- *data* parsing: c_{data} was correctly decrypted and padded, but it contained non-printable characters (e.g. NULL or vertical tab) or a badly placed special character (< or &).

So from this error message, the attacker only then knows that c_{key} is valid if all steps including parsing completed successfully. Therefore, the attacker must find

---

[3] We used $n = 100$ in our measurements.

a way to construct well-formed data that will be parsed successfully. To construct well-formed data, we create c_{data} consisting of two randomly generated 16 bytes long blocks $c_{data} = (iv, C^{(1)})$. Then we submit the ciphertext (c_{key}, c_{data}) to the Web Service, claiming that c_{data} is generated in CBC mode. The latter is possible by simply adjusting the metadata of an XML document containing encrypted parts. The decryption module first decrypts the $C^{(1)}$ block resulting in: $x = Dec_k(C^{(1)})$. The result of decryption x is afterwards XORed with the initialization vector iv, so that the plaintext block becomes $data^{(1)} = iv \oplus x$. The last byte of $data^{(1)}$ is taken as a padding byte and the padding is applied. Again, if the padding byte is not valid or the unpadded bytes result in non-printable characters, an error is returned.

To overcome this problem one can iterate over all the byte values in the last byte of the initialization vector iv and construct 256 different iv' values. As flipping a bit in iv implicitly changes the corresponding bit in the $data^{(1)}$ block, one can iteratively modify the value of the last byte in $data^{(1)'}$. Thereby exactly one pair $(iv', C^{(1)})$ results in a valid padding byte $0x10$, which pads the whole plaintext block. As this special plaintext is empty (0 bytes in length), parsing always succeeds. In this case, the message is passed to the next module in the Axis2 processing chain. Note that errors in other modules result in different error messages.

We can use these observations for constructing an oracle which returns 1 or 0, depending on the validity of the given c_{key}. For each tested c_{key}, the CBC-oracle $\mathcal{O}_{cbc}$ needs to send at most 256 requests with different iv' values, As shown in Equation 4, if Axis2 responds with a `security processing failed` error for a given c_{key} and all possible values of iv, then $\mathcal{O}_{cbc}$ returns that c_{key} was invalid.

$$\mathcal{O}_{cbc}(c_{key}) = \begin{cases} 1 \text{ if } \exists iv_{16} \in \{0, 1, \ldots, 255\} : Dec(c_{key}, iv) = \text{"no error"} \\ 0 \text{ if } \forall iv_{16} \in \{0, 1, \ldots, 255\} : Dec(c_{key}, iv) = \text{"error"} \end{cases} \quad (4)$$

Why this attack cannot be prevented by the classical countermeasure against Bleichenbacher's attack. The classical countermeasure against Bleichenbacher's attack is to let the decryption algorithm return a random key k, if c_{key} is invalid, and then to proceed as if c_{key} was valid.

A first obvious drawback of this countermeasure is that the system has to proceed with the random key *even if it knows that this key is invalid*. This may lead to data inconsistencies at the receiver side.

Even worse, it turns out that this countermeasure cannot prevent our CBC-based attack. Note that if c_{key} is valid, then among all 256 initialization vectors chosen by the attacker there *must exist* at least one iv such that $c_{data} = (iv, C^{(1)})$ returns no error. In particular, if the attacker submits a ciphertext c_{data} that decrypts to well-formed XML repeatedly to the Web Service, then it will always respond that the ciphertext is valid. In contrast, if c_{key} is invalid, and a random key k_0 is chosen by the Web Service for further processing, then even if the Web Service responds once that the tuple $c = (c_{key}, c_{data})$ is decrypted into well-formed XML for k_0, then the attacker can resubmit the same c to the Web

Service. Again, another random key $k_1 \neq k_0$ will be chosen for further processing, and it is unlikely that the same c will decrypt to well-formed XML for k_0 and k_1 simultaneously. By repeating this procedure, the attacker can easily determine whether c_{key} is valid with probability close to 1.

5   Experimental Analysis

In this section, we describe the results of our practical experiments. The timing-based and padding-based attacks were carried out using "good" ciphertexts. We did this to speed up our experiments, which was necessary due to limited computational resources. However, a heuristical analysis shows that it is very likely that a random ciphertext (e.g., encrypting a cryptographic key with correct padding) meets this property: for a 1024-bit modulus a fraction of about 1/80 of all ciphertexts is good in the above sense.

We stress that all timing figures derived from our experiments are valid only for this 1/80 fraction of all PKCS#1 ciphertext, which is however still a significant number. We also note that Bleichenbacher's attack in principle allows to decrypt any ciphertext, but for a 79/80 fraction the running time of the attack will be longer. However, we stress that it is possible to test whether a given ciphertext is good, by issuing at most $N/(3B) - N/(2B) = N/(6B) \approx 10,000$ oracle queries.

In order to evaluate our attacks, we deployed a Web Service secured with XML Encryption and generated a valid SOAP message containing c_{key} in the SOAP header. This element included a symmetric key for c_{data} decryption encrypted with a 1024 bit RSA key. The results of the timing-based and padding-based attacks shown here were all performed against Axis2. Please note that we also got similar results when testing our attack against the other mentionend XML Encryption implementations and other RSA key sizes.

Probability of "Good" Ciphertexts. The first step of Bleichenbacher's algorithm searches for an integer s such that $m \cdot s \bmod N$ is PKCS#1 v1.5 conformant. Note that $m \cdot s \bmod N$ can only be PKCS#1 conformant, if

$$\frac{i \cdot N}{3B} \leq s \leq \frac{i \cdot N}{2B}$$

for some $i \in \mathbb{N}$. Therefore the Bleichenbacher algorithm starts with $s = N/3B$ and increments this value until a suitable s is found. Clearly, this procedure finds s quickly, if m has the property that there exists an s such that

$$\frac{1 \cdot N}{3B} \leq s \leq \frac{1 \cdot N}{2B}$$

and $m \cdot s \bmod N$ is PKCS#1 conformant. Moreover, in our application we will only be able to learn that a ciphertext $c = (ms)^e \bmod N$ is PKCS#1-conformant, if $ms \bmod N$ has the form $ms \bmod N = 00||02||PS||00||k$, where the byte-length of k is equal to 16, 24, or 32. In the sequel, we will say that a ciphertext is a *good* ciphertext, if it satisfies these properties.

In order to save computation time, all our experiments were executed with random *good* ciphertexts. Thus, all our experimental results are meaningful only if the probability that a honestly generated ciphertext meets the above property is sufficiently high. This leads us to the question *what is the probability that a real-world ciphertext is* good?

We ran some additional experiments in order to determine the probability that a random ciphertext is *good*. To this end, the algorithm depicted in Figure 4 was implemented.

We repeated this algorithm 100 times, i.e., we generated 100 random moduli, and tried $\ell = 1,000$ padded plaintexts for each modulus, such that in total 100,000 plaintexts where tested. Among these 100,000 plaintexts there were 1,543 padded plaintext that lead to *good* ciphertexts. Thus, about each 80-th ciphertext is *good*.

Timing-Based Attack. We used the RDTSC assembler instruction of recent Intel Pentium processors to measure the timings with below nanosecond accuracy.

Attack on Local Machine. In this measurement setup, we run the Axis2 server and the attack script on the same computer. This is a very practical attack scenario, e.g. in cloud computing and especially in a *Platform as a Service*, where it is feasible for an attacker to rent a virtual machine that is co-located on the same physical hardware [21] as the victim.

The measurement computer had 2 Intel XEON 2.4 GHz processors. Figure 5a shows the response times measured during the calibration phase with 100KB c_{data} ciphertext and a c_{key} encrypted with an 1024 bit RSA key. The solid line denotes valid requests, the dashed horizontal line marks the learned boundary and the dotted line indicates invalid requests. When compared to the learned timing boundary t_{min}, it becomes clear that most invalid requests are below

---

1. Generate a random 1024-bit RSA modulus N. Set $c = 0$.
2. For i from 1 to ℓ do:
   − Choose a random bit string k
   − Pad k according to PKCS#1 v1.5, such that

   $$m = 00||02||PS||00||k$$

   − If there exists $s \in [N/3B, N/2B]$ such that
     • $m \cdot s \bmod N$ is PKCS#1-conformant,
     • $ms \bmod N = 00||02||PS||00||k$,
       with $|k| \in \{16, 24, 32\}$,
     then set $c = c + 1$.

Fig. 4. Experimental analysis of the distribution of "good" ciphertexts

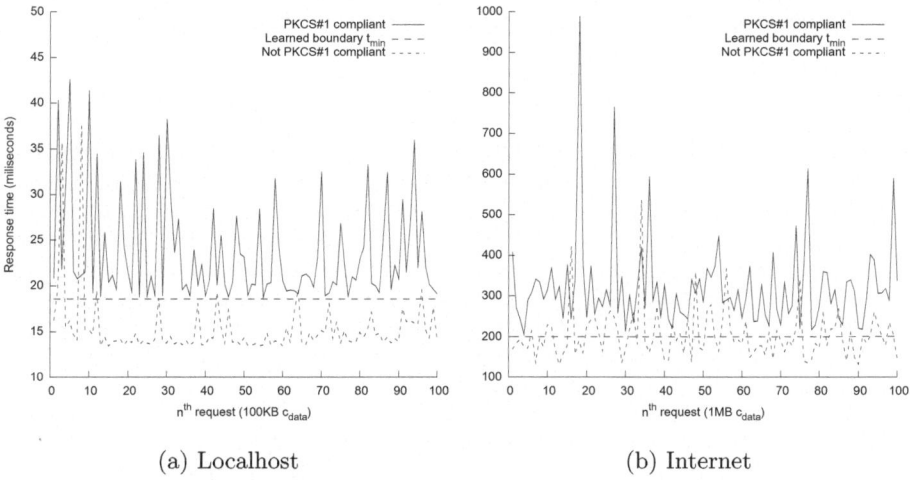

(a) Localhost   (b) Internet

Fig. 5. Response times with valid and invalid c_{key}

t_{min}. Any request above t_{min} is treated as a candidate for a valid request and repeated n times for confirmation. The figure suggests that only few invalid requests slipped above t_{min} leading to a repetion of the request.

As a result, c_{key} could be reconstructed successfully in 200 minutes. Overall, the 321,870 oracle queries resulted in 398,123 queries in our measurement setup, i.e. the oracle needs to perform 1.24 actual Web Service requests per oracle query. On our hardware, we could perform on average 37 Web Service requests per second.

Attack through Internet. Additionally, we evaluated the effectiveness of the timing oracle for a remote attacker who attacks the Web Service through the Internet. For this measurement setup, we chose two Planetlab nodes at universities. The nodes were seven hops apart from each other and the round trip time was approximately 22 milliseconds.

We calibrated the valid/invalid boundary of the timing oracle as shown in Figure 5b and used 1,000KB of random data as c_{data}. In this configuration, the oracle correctly answers approximately 2,000 queries per hour and needs to perform approximately 2,400 actual Web Service requests to the server. Thus, an attacker can learn c_{key} remotely across practical networks in less than one week.

Padding-Based Attack. As the padding-based attack does not depend on the network connection, we tested its functionality on the localhost. The attack execution took less than five days, the attacker sent about 322,000 oracle queries, which resulted in 82,180,000 ($\approx 256 * 322,000$) total server requests.

Acknowledgments. We thank Felix Freiling, Thorsten Holz, Kenny Paterson, Jörg Schwenk, and the anonymous reviewers for their helpful comments.

References

1. Bardou, R., Focardi, R., Kawamoto, Y., Steel, G., Tsay, J.K.: Efficient Padding Oracle Attacks on Cryptographic Hardware. In: Canetti, R., Safavi-Naini, R. (eds.) CRYPTO 2012. LNCS, vol. 7417, pp. 608–625. Springer, Heidelberg (2012)
2. Bauer, A., Coron, J.-S., Naccache, D., Tibouchi, M., Vergnaud, D.: On the Broadcast and Validity-Checking Security of PKCS#1 v1.5 Encryption. In: Zhou, J., Yung, M. (eds.) ACNS 2010. LNCS, vol. 6123, pp. 1–18. Springer, Heidelberg (2010)
3. Bleichenbacher, D.: Chosen Ciphertext Attacks against Protocols Based on the RSA Encryption Standard PKCS #1. In: Krawczyk, H. (ed.) CRYPTO 1998. LNCS, vol. 1462, pp. 1–12. Springer, Heidelberg (1998)
4. Degabriele, J.P., Lehmann, A., Paterson, K.G., Smart, N.P., Strefler, M.: On the Joint Security of Encryption and Signature in EMV. In: Dunkelman, O. (ed.) CT-RSA 2012. LNCS, vol. 7178, pp. 116–135. Springer, Heidelberg (2012)
5. Eastlake, D., Reagle, J., Hirsch, F., Roessler, T., Imamura, T., Dillaway, B., Simon, E., Yiu, K., Nyström, M.: XML Encryption Syntax and Processing 1.1. W3C Candidate Recommendation (2012), http://www.w3.org/TR/2012/CR-xmlenc-core1-20120313
6. Eastlake, D., Reagle, J., Imamura, T., Dillaway, B., Simon, E.: XML Encryption Syntax and Processing. W3C Recommendation (2002), http://www.w3.org/TR/xmlenc-core
7. Eastlake, D., Reagle, J., Solo, D., Hirsch, F., Roessler, T.: XML Signature Syntax and Processing, 2nd edn. W3C Recommendation (2008)
8. Gudgin, M., Hadley, M., Mendelsohn, N., Moreau, J.J., Nielsen, H.F.: SOAP Version 1.2 Part 1: Messaging Framework. W3C Recommendation (2003)
9. Haas, H., Booth, D., Newcomer, E., Champion, M., Orchard, D., Ferris, C., McCabe, F.: Web services architecture. W3C note, W3C (February 2004), http://www.w3.org/TR/2004/NOTE-ws-arch-20040211/
10. Jager, T., Schinzel, S., Somorovsky, J.: Bleichenbacher's attack strikes again: breaking PKCS#1 v1.5 in XML Encryption (full version), http://www.nds.rub.de/research/publications/breaking-xml-encryption-pkcs15
11. Jager, T., Somorovsky, J.: How to break XML encryption. In: Chen, Y., Danezis, G., Shmatikov, V. (eds.) ACM CCS 2011: 18th Conference on Computer and Communications Security, pp. 413–422. ACM Press (October 2011)
12. JBoss Community: JBoss WS (Web Services Framework for JBoss AS), http://www.jboss.org/jbossws
13. Jones, M., Rescorla, E., Hildebrand, J.: JSON Web Encryption (JWE) – draft-jones-json-web-encryption-01 (October 2011), http://tools.ietf.org/html/draft-jones-json-web-encryption-01
14. Jonsson, J., Kaliski, B.: Public-Key Cryptography Standards (PKCS) #1: RSA Cryptography Specifications Version 2.1. RFC 3447 (Informational) (February 2003), http://www.ietf.org/rfc/rfc3447.txt
15. Kaliski, B.: PKCS #1: RSA Encryption Version 1.5. RFC 2313 (Informational) (March 1998), http://www.ietf.org/rfc/rfc2313.txt, obsoleted by RFC 2437
16. Kaliski, B., Staddon, J.: PKCS #1: RSA Cryptography Specifications Version 2.0. RFC 2437 (Informational) (October 1998), http://www.ietf.org/rfc/rfc2437.txt, obsoleted by RFC 3447

17. Klíma, V., Pokorný, O., Rosa, T.: Attacking RSA-Based Sessions in SSL/TLS. In: Walter, C.D., Koç, Ç.K., Paar, C. (eds.) CHES 2003. LNCS, vol. 2779, pp. 426–440. Springer, Heidelberg (2003)
18. Manger, J.: A Chosen Ciphertext Attack on RSA Optimal Asymmetric Encryption Padding (OAEP) as Standardized in PKCS #1 v2.0. In: Kilian, J. (ed.) CRYPTO 2001. LNCS, vol. 2139, pp. 230–238. Springer, Heidelberg (2001)
19. Menezes, A.J., van Oorschot, P.C., Vanstone, S.A.: Handbook of Applied Cryptography. CRC Press, Boca Raton (1996)
20. Rescorla, E.: Preventing the Million Message Attack on Cryptographic Message Syntax. RFC 3218 (Informational) (January 2002),
    http://www.ietf.org/rfc/rfc3218.txt
21. Ristenpart, T., Tromer, E., Shacham, H., Savage, S.: Hey, you, get off of my cloud: exploring information leakage in third-party compute clouds. In: Al-Shaer, E., Jha, S., Keromytis, A.D. (eds.) ACM Conference on Computer and Communications Security, pp. 199–212. ACM (2009),
    http://doi.acm.org/10.1145/1653662.1653687
22. Rivest, R.L., Shamir, A., Adleman, L.M.: A method for obtaining digital signatures and public-key cryptosystems. Communications of the ACM 21, 120–126 (1978)
23. Smart, N.P.: Errors Matter: Breaking RSA-Based PIN Encryption with Thirty Ciphertext Validity Queries. In: Pieprzyk, J. (ed.) CT-RSA 2010. LNCS, vol. 5985, pp. 15–25. Springer, Heidelberg (2010)
24. Somorovsky, J., Schwenk, J.: Technical Analysis of Countermeasures against Attack on XML Encryption – or – Just Another Motivation for Authenticated Encryption. In: SERVICES Workshop on Security and Privacy Engineering (June 2012)
25. Thai, T.L., Lam, H.: NET Framework Essentials, 2nd edn. O'Reilly & Associates, Inc. (2002)
26. The Apache Software Foundation: Apache Axis2, http://axis.apache.org
27. Vaudenay, S.: Security Flaws Induced by CBC Padding - Applications to SSL, IPSEC, WTLS... In: Knudsen, L.R. (ed.) EUROCRYPT 2002. LNCS, vol. 2332, pp. 534–546. Springer, Heidelberg (2002)

On the Security
of Password Manager Database Formats

Paolo Gasti and Kasper B. Rasmussen

Computer Science Department
University of California, Irvine
{pgasti,kbrasmus}@ics.uci.edu

Abstract. Password managers are critical pieces of software relied upon
by users to securely store valuable and sensitive information, from online
banking passwords and login credentials to passport- and social security
numbers. Surprisingly, there has been very little academic research on
the security these applications provide.

This paper presents the first rigorous analysis of storage formats used
by popular password managers. We define two realistic security models,
designed to represent the capabilities of real-world adversaries. We then
show how specific vulnerabilities in our models allow an adversary to
implement practical attacks. Our analysis shows that most password
manager database formats are broken even against weak adversaries.

1 Introduction

As the number of services offered on the Internet continues to increase, the number of passwords an average user is required to remember increases correspondingly, to the point where it is no longer feasible for most people to remember a
new, strong password, for every account.

Users typically solve this problem in one of two ways. A common solution is to
reuse the same password on many different websites [1]. This approach increases
the potential damage if a password is stolen, cracked, or if a service that has
access to it is compromised, since the attacker will be able to reuse it on all
online services that share the password. Another approach is to use a "password
manager" to store strong (random) passwords for each site. A password manager
is a piece of software that requires a user to remember a single strong master
password, used to decrypt the password manager's database. Remembering a
single master password is much more feasible for users, who still get the security
benefits of using a different password for each online service.

Using a password manager has other potential benefits. Full URLs (or at least
domain names) of are typically stored alongside the corresponding passwords,
and used to fill login form automatically. As such, users who rely on password
managers are less susceptible to typo-squatting and phishing attacks [2,3]: even
if a user is directed to a malicious website that is designed to look identical to
the website the user expects, the password manager will not log in automatically,
providing an extra layer of protection.

S. Foresti, M. Yung, and F. Martinelli (Eds.): ESORICS 2012, LNCS 7459, pp. 770–787, 2012.

Due to the sensitivity of the information typically stored in password databases, most password managers protect their content from unauthorized access. Database formats typically rely on encryption for data protection, where the encryption/decryption key is generated from a master password entered by the user.

This protection is also often designed to allow users to store the password manager database on untrusted storage. Several producers of password managers suggest storing password databases on USB sticks [4–6], in the cloud [7,8] or on mobile devices [9–11], to allow convenient access to stored passwords. These storage options however, can also enable potential attackers to get hold of the database. Even when a password database is stored on a local hard drive, it may be possible for an attacker to obtain a copy through other means.

If the password manager database format is insecure, then all the advantages of a good password manager are wasted and the user may actually be less secure and more susceptible to, e.g., leakage of private information: privacy-conscious users may want to keep their browsing habits private and therefore delete cookies, history and cache often. On the contrary, password managers represent long-term storage facilities, storing (ideally) the only copy of passwords, and therefore their content is typically never deleted. If a password manager database leaks information about browsing habits, e.g., by storing URL's unencrypted, then clearing the cache and browsing history does not prevent an attacker from learning sensitive information.

In this paper we analyze the security provided by the database formats of some of the most poplar password managers in use at the moment. We define two different adversaries: a passive attacker that only tries to infer information from a password database, and an active attacker that modifies the content or meta-data. We highlight that using "industry standard practices", such as AES-CBC, is not enough to obtain a secure database format, even assuming the implementation of AES-CBC is correct. Note that we do not attempt to provide an exhaustive list of all possible attacks on all password managers. Rather, we model the security provided by common password manager database formats and provide examples of practical attacks.

The rest of this paper is organized as follows: Section 2 provides a brief overview of password managers used in our study; Section 3 introduces our system- and attacker models, while Section 4 analyzes the various database formats in such models. In Section 5 we discuss various general issues regarding database formats, and Section 6 covers related work. We conclude in Section 7.

2   Overview of Password Managers

Password managers differ in many aspects, including database format, functionality, availability of source code, supported platforms and access to cloud storage. Table 1 summarizes the main features of the password managers we considered. Some popular password managers invent their own database format, used exclusively by them. This is especially true for the password managers embedded

Table 1. This table shows the password managers that where analysed in detail, along with the database format used by the software, the storage options available and the platforms supported. In addition we indicate whether the source code is available and whether the password manager is integrated with a browser.

Password Manager	Database Format	Storage	Open Source	Platform	Browser Integration
Google Chrome [12]	Chrome	local/cloud	✓	Win/Mac/Linux	✓
Mozilla Firefox [13]	Firefox	local/cloud	✓	Win/Mac/Linux	✓
Internet Explorer [14]	MSIE	local	×	Win	✓
1Password [9]	1Password	local/cloud	×	Win/Mac	✓
KeePass 1.x [15]	KDB	local	✓	Win	×
KeePass 2.x [15]	KDB/KDBX4	local	✓	Win/Mono	×
KeePassDroid [11]	KDB/KDBX4	local	✓	Android	×
KyPass [10]	KDB/KDBX4	local	✓	iOS	×
PassDrop [16]	KDB/KDBX4	local	×	iOS	×
PINs [17]	PINs	local	×	Win	×
Password Safe [18]	PasswordSafe	local	✓	Win	×
Password Gorilla [19]	PasswordSafe	local	✓	Win/Mac/Linux	×
Roboform [20]	Roboform	local/cloud	×	Win/Mac/Linux	✓

in major browsers. We include these in our analysis because these password managers are widely used [21]. Several stand-alone password managers share the same database format, so even though each password manager provide a different experience to the user, the underlying storage format is the same.

In the rest of this paper focus solely on database formats and the security they provide, rather than on each password manager implementation. We assume that the password managers themselves correctly implement what the format specifies. As such, we do not consider, e.g., side channel attacks on the cryptographic primitives, or other attacks against the implementation. Rather we investigate the best possible security achievable given a specific storage format. For this reason our analysis focuses primarily on password managers that provide local storage, at least as an option. We leave the analysis of "cloud-only" password managers to future work.

We investigate nine popular password database formats. Three database formats used by in-browser password managers: Google Chrome, Mozilla Firefox and Microsoft Internet Explorer; and six formats used by a large number of stand-alone password managers: 1Password, KDB, KDBX4, PasswordSafe v3, PINs and RoboForm (refer to Table 1.)

3   Adversary and System Model

We consider two efficient adversaries: Adv_r who has read access to the password database, and Adv_{rw} who has read-write access. The goal of both adversaries is to extract as much information as possible and, for $\mathsf{Adv}_{\mathsf{rw}}$, to produce a database that (1) was not created by the user and (2) once opened, will not trigger any warning or error message from the password manager. Clearly, $\mathsf{Adv}_{\mathsf{rw}}$ is strictly stronger than $\mathsf{Adv}_{\mathsf{r}}$: any attack that can be performed by $\mathsf{Adv}_{\mathsf{r}}$ is also available to $\mathsf{Adv}_{\mathsf{rw}}$. Both adversaries are allowed to gather multiple snapshots of the database at different points in time, in order to detect modifications in the database content.

We emphasize that our analysis does not rely on any modification of the user environment, e.g., tampering with the password manager code or installing a key logger. We focus solely on the security provided by the password manager databases, when the password manager software is operated in the "most secure" setting provided. We assume that users choose a strong, high-entropy, master password and that all underlying cryptographic algorithms (e.g., encryption, MAC, etc.) are properly implemented. Additionally, we assume that no additional mechanisms are in place to prevent file tampering. This allows us to compare the security offered by the database formats themselves.

3.1 Untrusted Storage

Consider an adversary who has full access to an encrypted password database, and is able to record different versions of it. Such an adversary can clearly use any of the recorded versions to replace the current database, as long as the master password did not change. This is essentially a replay attack that applies to both cloud-based- and local database formats.

The security notions we define below do not capture this attack, nor do we attempt to address it in any other way. In order to protect against it, a password manager must maintain some local state (e.g., a hash of the latest version of the encrypted database) on a trusted medium. As such, while this attack is clearly relevant when a password database is stored on the cloud or on an unattended USB drive, it cannot be mitigated by the database format alone. Therefore we exclude it from our analysis.

3.2 Security Definitions

We model password managers by defining four algorithms that represent various functionalities: Setup, Create, Open and Valid. These algorithms are defined as follows:

Definition 1. *A password manager $\mathcal{PM}$ consists of the following efficient algorithms:* Setup($\cdot$) *a probabilistic algorithm that, given a security parameter 1^κ, outputs a master password mp;* Create($\cdot, \cdot$) *a probabilistic algorithm that, on input mp and a set of triples $RS = \{(r_1, n_1, v_1), \ldots, (r_\ell, n_\ell, v_\ell)\}$ (which represents a record-set), outputs a database DB;* Open($\cdot, \cdot$) *a deterministic algorithm that, given mp and a database DB, outputs the record-set RS encoded in DB if RS is a valid record-set, i.e, there exist DB' such that $DB' \leftarrow$ Create(mp, RS), and $\perp$ otherwise; and* Valid($\cdot, \cdot$) *a deterministic algorithm that takes as input a master password mp and a database DB and returns 1 if* Open(mp, DB) $\neq \perp$.

In practice, Valid is implemented by password managers within the Open functionality: if validation fails, the password manager returns an error rather than the database content.

We also define two new games, which we call *indistinguishability of databases* game (IND-CDBA) and *malleability of chosen database* game (MAL-CDBA). The former captures the capabilities of a realistic passive adversary, i.e., an adversary that has read-only access to a password database. The latter models and active adversary, which is allowed both read and write access to a password database.

Game 1 (Indistinguishability of databases game IND-CDBA$_{\mathsf{Adv}_r, \mathcal{PM}}(\kappa)$). *A challenger* Ch *running* $\mathcal{PM}$ *interacts with* Adv$_r$ *in as follows:*

- Ch *runs* $mp \leftarrow$ Setup(1^κ).
- Adv$_r$ *outputs two record-sets* RS_0, RS_1
- Ch *selects a bit* b *uniformly at random and the database* $DB_b \leftarrow$ Create(mp, RS_b) *is returned to* Adv$_r$.
- Adv$_r$ *eventually outputs bit* b'; *the game outputs 1 iff* $b = b'$.

We say that Adv$_r$ *wins* the IND-CDBA game if it can cause it to output 1.

Definition 2 (IND-CDBA security). *A password manager* $\mathcal{PM} =$ (Setup, Create, Valid, Open) *is* IND-CDBA-*secure if there exists a negligible function* negl *such that, for any probabilistic polynomial time adversary* Adv$_r$, *we have that* $\Pr[\text{IND-CDBA}_{\mathsf{Adv}_r, \mathcal{PM}}(\kappa) = 1] \leq 1/2 + \mathsf{negl}(\kappa)$.

For most database formats an attacker can trivially win the IND-CDBA game by submitting two record-sets of different sizes. In practice, this corresponds to the fact that the size of the database file is often roughly proportional to the number of records in the database and therefore an adversary may be able to infer information by simply observing the size of an encrypted database. While we do consider this a valid attack, we ignore it in the vulnerability analysis. Database formats that are *only* vulnerable to this attack will be considered secure.

Appendix A shows the relationship between IND-CPA and IND-CDBA. In particular, it shows that IND-CPA-security implies IND-CDBA-security.

Game 2 (Malleability of chosen database game MAL-CDBA$_{\mathsf{Adv}_{rw}, \mathcal{PM}}(\kappa)$). *A challenger* Ch *running* $\mathcal{PM}$ *interacts with* Adv$_{rw}$ *in the following way:*

- Ch *runs* $mp \leftarrow$ Setup(1^κ).
- Adv$_{rw}$ *adaptively outputs* n *record-sets* RS_i *and receives, from* Ch, *the corresponding databases* $DB_i \leftarrow$ Create(mp, RS_i).
- Adv$_{rw}$ *eventually outputs* DB'; *the game outputs 1 iff* Valid(DB') = 1 *and* $DB' \neq DB_i$ *for* $i \leq n$.

We say that Adv$_{rw}$ *wins* the MAL-CDBA game if it can cause it to output 1.

Definition 3 (MAL-CDBA security). *A password manager* $\mathcal{PM} =$ (Setup, Create, Valid, Open) *is* MAL-CDBA-*secure if there exists a negligible function* negl *such that, for any probabilistic polynomial time adversary* Adv$_{rw}$, *we have that* $\Pr[\text{MAL-CDBA}_{\mathsf{Adv}_{rw}, \mathcal{PM}}(\kappa) = 1] \leq \mathsf{negl}(\kappa)$.

Our definition of MAL-CDBA security is equivalent to the notion of "existential unforgeability" of ciphertexts, introduced in [22]. As shown in the same paper, this security notion along with IND-CPA security implies IND-CCA security.

"Integrity of ciphertexts" [23] (also known as INT-CTXT security) is a related security notion. In particular, the main difference between MAL-CDBA and INT-CTXT is that an adversary for INT-CTXT is also given access to the Verify($mp, \cdot$) oracle.

We argue that MAL-CDBA security (together with IND-CDBA security) is an appropriate security notion for a password manager database format in practice. Consider a database format that is not MAL-CDBA-secure, i.e., where Adv_{rw} can compute the encryption of a record-set of its choice, and produce the corresponding valid output DB'. This format would be vulnerable to the following four-step attack:

(1) Adv_{rw} replaces Alice's password database DB with a new database DB' containing the login credentials for an amazon.com account created by Adv_{rw}. (2) Adv_{rw} now induces Alice to go to amazon.com, at which point the password manager automatically logs into the account created by Adv_{rw}. (3) Alice buys something; during checkout, Alice is requested to add her credit card to the account; since she trusts amazon.com, she complies. (4) Adv_{rw} now replaces DB' with Alice's original password database.

Adv_{rw} is now in possession of an account which can be used to purchase goods on Alice's behalf. It is very hard for Alice to detect this attack; she does not receive any warning from her password manager or from amazon.com, since the database is well formed and the login information corresponds to an existing account. Additionally, SSL/TLS does not help since Alice is communicating with amazon.com. Furthermore, Alice may not even be able to find out which username was used in the maliciously crafted account after the adversary restores her original password database.

4   Database Format Vulnerabilities

We now present our analysis, which includes several database formats currently in use by stand-alone and browser-based password managers. For each format, we provide a short description of the relevant features and analyze its security with respect to the security model defined in Section 3. If the format allows for different levels of security, we analyze the most secure configuration.

4.1   Google Chrome

Format Description. Google Chrome stores usernames and passwords in an SQLite database file in the user profile directory. This database provides neither secrecy nor integrity.

Google Chrome can optionally store all browser preferences (including passwords) on Google's servers to allow synchronization between different devices.

Chrome's support pages claim that passwords are stored in encrypted form on Google's servers [24].

Security Analysis. Any user with access to the database file can recover all its content and make arbitrary modifications. As such, users cannot rely on Chrome's password manager for integrity or secrecy of their data, and should implement additional security layers around it.

4.2 Mozilla Firefox

Format Description. Mozilla Firefox stores login data in an SQLite database. Users can specify an (optional) master password that is used to encrypt the database content. URLs are always stored unencrypted regardless of whether a master password is used or not.

Since the database is part of Firefox' user profile, it can be automatically synchronized across multiple devices, either through Firefox Sync [25], manually (e.g., using rsync [26]), or stored on a USB stick and used on different computers.

Security Analysis. Firefox does not provide an effective protection against Adv_r. In order to win in the IND-CDBA game, Adv_r creates two same-size record-sets RS_0, RS_1 which differ in at least one URL field. The encrypted database DB_b can be immediately identified since URLs are not concealed. In practice that means that an attacker can learn a considerable amount of information, such as the websites in which the user has password-protected access, and it can mount effecting phishing attacks based on user information. Moreover, given two different versions of the same database, the attacker can identify which entries have been modified and their corresponding domain name.

Similarly, given any non-empty database DB an active adversary Adv_{rw} can trivially win the MAL-CDBA game by building DB' from DB replacing one or more URLs with a different valid URL. Since the entries are not integrity protected, Firefox cannot detect such an attack. This can be used to mount a very effective man-in-the-middle attack by replacing legitimate domain names with fraudulent ones controlled by Adv_{rw}. In this way, the password manager will automatically submit sensitive information to an adversary-controlled website. The attack is even more effective if Adv_{rw} can also modify Firefox' bookmark database, which is stored in the profile alongside the password database.

4.3 Microsoft Internet Explorer

Format Description. Internet Explorer stores usernames and passwords in the registry. Each record is stored as a separate registry entry and encrypted using the system login credentials. When a user fills-in a password form at address url, Internet Explorer computes $h = \text{SHA-1}(url)$ (where and url uses the unicode character set) and encrypts username and password as $c = E_k(\texttt{metadata} \parallel \texttt{username} \parallel \texttt{0x00} \parallel \texttt{password} \parallel \texttt{0x00})$, where $\texttt{metadata}$ contains additional information such as the size of encrypted elements.

The encryption is performed using the `CryptProtectData` [27] system call, which uses Triple-DES in CBC mode and a hash-based MAC. k is derived from (1) a random salt (also stored in the ciphertext), (2) url and (3) the Windows login credential for the current user. Finally, Internet Explorer creates a new registry entry with key h and value c.

The security of Internet Explorer's password manager depends on the strength of the user account password. As such, accounts with no password provide no protection of the password database.

Security Analysis. Internet explorer is not secure against Adv_r. Similarly to Firefox, Adv_r wins the IND-CDBA game by building two same-size record-sets RS_0, RS_1 which differ in at least one URL.

Say record rec with URL url is in RS_0 but not in RS_1. Adv_r can immediately recognize which record-set corresponds to the challenge DB_b by computing $h =$ SHA-1(url) and verifying whether h is in DB_b.

In practice, a passive adversary can use Internet Explorer's password database to determine whether a user has visited a particular web page and entered his username/password, even if the user deletes his browsing history and cache.

Assuming that `CryptProtectData` uses a secure MAC, an active adversary cannot alter password entries. However, Adv_{rw} can delete password entries by removing the corresponding registry entry, and as such Adv_{rw} can easily win the MAL-CDBA game.

4.4   1Password

Format Description. 1Password stores its database in multiple files. Each file contains a database entry, stored in JavaScript Object Notation (JSON). Entries are listed in an index file called "content.js".

1Password allows users to select a different "security level" for each record [28]. The lowest security level corresponds to unencrypted entries, while the highest level means that sensitive fields, such as username and password, are encrypted with a key derived from the user's master password. Regardless of the security level, some fields, e.g., the title of an entry, are never encrypted. We analyze the protection offered by the highest security level.

The encryption scheme used is AES-128 in CBC mode. Neither the records nor the index file are integrity protected. As a result, database corruption is only detected when the JSON parser fails to process the database.

Security Analysis. 1Password's database format is affected by vulnerabilities that give adversaries a non-negligible advantage in both the IND-CDBA and MAL-CDBA games.

Adv_r can win IND-CDBA with probability 1 as follows: Adv_r builds two same-size record-sets RS_0, RS_1 such that there exist two records r_0, r_1 from RS_0 and RS_1 respectively, which differ in at least one of the following fields: `title`, `location`, `locationKey`, `createdAt`, `updatedAt` or `typeName`. These fields correspond to: the title of the record, the record URL, the URL used by the browser plugin to perform auto-complete, the time of creation and last update and the type of record (e.g., web form, protected note, credit card information). Since these fields are never encrypted, $\mathsf{Adv_r}$ can trivially determine bit b by testing which record belongs to DB_b. In practice this means that an adversary with access to a 1Password database can read these fields and thus gather sensitive information about the user's browsing habits.

$\mathsf{Adv_{rw}}$ can win the MAL-CDBA game with probability 1 as follows. $\mathsf{Adv_{rw}}$ selects an arbitrary record-set RS and receives the corresponding database DB. Then, $\mathsf{Adv_{rw}}$ can (1) alter any of the fields listed above, and/or (2) remove any entry by deleting the corresponding database file and altering the "content.js" index file correspondingly. In general, as long as the database is still composed of a set of correct JSON strings, 1Password will not show any warning. In practice, this means that an adversary can mount phishing attacks by replacing a legitimate URL with one pointing to an adversary-controlled website.

Additionally, if $\mathsf{Adv_{rw}}$ outputs at least two record-sets, say $RS \neq RS'$ and receives the corresponding databases DB, DB' in the MAL-CDBA game, it can construct DB'' selecting records from both DB and DB'. This allows an adversary, among other things, to replace individual records in a database with older versions.

4.5   KDB (aka KeePass 1.x)

Format Description. The KDB database is composed of a single file, divided in two sections: an unencrypted header (hdr) and an encrypted body (bdy). bdy stores the encryption of the various database entries. hdr contains, among other things, the number of groups and entries in the database and the hash of bdy before encryption [15]. This hash is computed every time the database is modified, and is used to check integrity. After decryption, the password manager verifies that the computed plaintext hashes to the same value stored in hdr. If this check fails, the application reports that either the database is corrupted or the master password entered by the user is incorrect.

Security Analysis. Given a database DB, the hash stored (unencrypted) in hdr is computed deterministically from the record-set RS encoded in DB. This allows an adversary $\mathsf{Adv_r}$ to win the IND-CDBA game with probability 1 as follows. $\mathsf{Adv_r}$ selects two same-size record-sets $RS_0 \neq RS_1$ and computes their hash $h_i = H(RS_i)$. Once it receives a challenge database DB_b, $\mathsf{Adv_r}$ checks whether the header of DB_b contains h_0 or h_1 and outputs its choice for b' accordingly.

In practice, given two databases, this allows $\mathsf{Adv_r}$ to determine whether their content is identical even if their corresponding ciphertexts are different. Also, assuming that the record-set encrypted in a database has lower entropy than the database master password, $\mathsf{Adv_r}$ can recover the content of the record-set by simply making a guess and comparing it against the hash value in hdr. In other words, the complexity of breaking the database is a function of $\min(\eta_{mp}, \eta_{RS})$ – where η_{mp} is the entropy of the master password and η_{RS} is the entropy of the record-set – rather than just a function of the master password.

hdr is not authenticated and, as such, is susceptible to malicious modifications. This can be used by $\mathsf{Adv_{rw}}$ to win the MAL-CDBA game with probability 1 by selecting a challenge record-set RS which contains one or more entries. When $\mathsf{Adv_{rw}}$ receives DB he changes the value corresponding to the number of entries (stored in hdr) to a smaller number. Since bdy is not altered, the hash verification does not fail. However, the record-set has been altered since the number of entries shown in the password manager is now the one chosen by $\mathsf{Adv_{rw}}$.

We verified that the latest version of KeePassX (0.4.3) is susceptible to this attack. Moreover, if the victim makes any change in the modified database, KeePassX stores only the entries displayed. This can lead to silent (undetected) corruption of the database.

4.6 KDBX4 (aka KeePass 2.x)

Format Description. The KDBX4 database format is composed of a single password-protected file, divided in two sections: an unencrypted header (hdr) and a main encrypted body (bdy). hdr contains several fields, including `mseed` and `tseed` (used to compute the encryption/decryption key from the user-provided password), `IV`, `pskey` and `ssbytes`, used for secrecy and integrity protection as detailed below.

bdy contains the database records encoded as a single XML string, optionally compressed using the gzip algorithm [29] before encryption. bdy is encrypted using AES-256 in CBC mode, although Twofish is also available. The first 32 bytes of bdy contains the encryption of the `ssbytes` field in order to efficiently verify whether the provided master password is correct. The next 32 bytes of the body contain the hash of the (possibly gzip-compressed) XML string representing the various entries. This hash is used to detect modifications in the database.

In addition, all passwords in the XML string are XOR-ed with a pseudo-random string, computed using Salsa20 [30]. Every time the database is saved, a random 256-bit key k is generated and stored unencrypted in the `pskey` field; each password pwd_i is then encoded as $s_i = pwd_i \oplus \mathrm{Salsa20}(k, IV)$ using a fixed value IV. Each pwd_i uses a different portion of the keystream generated by Salsa20. Passwords are recovered as $pwd_i = s_i \oplus \mathrm{Salsa20}(k, IV)$.

Security Analysis. KDBX4 fixes some of the weaknesses of KDB. hdr does not store the (unauthenticated) number of entries, therefore an adversary cannot alter this value to remove content from the password database. Also, the hash of the unencrypted record-set is now stored in encrypted form. This prevents an adversary from verifying its guesses on the database content and from determining whether two encrypted databases carry the same content. More generally, $\mathsf{Adv_r}$ cannot mount any successful attack on a KDBX4 database except with negligible probability. Due to lack of space, we omit the proof of IND-CDBA security for KDBX4, which is available in the extended version of this paper [31].

Unfortunately, this format introduces new vulnerabilities. Similarly to KDB, the main problem of this format is the lack of authentication of hdr. As such, is it susceptible to modifications. In particular, $\mathsf{Adv_{rw}}$ can win the MAL-CDBA game with probability 1 as follows. $\mathsf{Adv_{rw}}$ outputs a challenge record-set RS. Then, after receiving the corresponding database DB, it replaces the value stored in the pskey field of hdr with an arbitrary 256-bit string and outputs that as DB'. This modification is not detectable by the password manager, i.e., $\mathsf{Valid}(DB') = 1$, since the integrity check on the records is performed *before* the XOR with the output of Salsa20. However, a different pskey value will cause all passwords to appear as pseudo-random data after the decoding process.

It is impossible to recover from this attack unless it is detected immediately, i.e., before the user applies any modification to the record-set. The only way to recover the database content is to restore the original pskey value. However, this value is replaced with a fresh one, and all passwords are "re-scrambled" accordingly, each time the database is modified and saved. For this reason if a user alters, and then saves, a corrupted database, all passwords previously affected by the attack are lost forever.

This attack highlights a remarkable design flaw. Even an accidental bit-flip in the pskey field, e.g., due to a transmission error, cannot be detected, and leads to complete corruption of the database. Such corruption is unlikely to be immediately detected by users, who may subsequently add new entries. Over time, the database will be composed of both correct and corrupted entries, making it difficult to reconstruct the damaged records from a backup.

As an extension to the previous attack, $\mathsf{Adv_{rw}}$ can alter pskey in such a way that an arbitrary (small) number of bits of the first password(s) in the database are not altered. To do that $\mathsf{Adv_{rw}}$ computes a value k' such that the first n bits of Salsa20(k, IV) are equal to the first n bits of Salsa20(k', IV). Then $\mathsf{Adv_{rw}}$ stores k' in pskey. k' can be computed in exponential time in n, and therefore is practical only when n is small. As a proof of concept, we developed an application that implements such attack. The application is available upon request.

Finally, $\mathsf{Adv_{rw}}$ can also win the **MAL-CDBA** game as follows. Given an arbitrary database DB, $\mathsf{Adv_{rw}}$ flips a bit in the first 16 bytes of ssbytes, and then flips the corresponding bit in the IV field of hdr to create DB'. The password manager cannot detect the change, i.e., $\mathsf{Valid}(DB') = 1$, since flipping a bit in IV causes the corresponding bit in the first block of plaintext to be flipped as well (using CBC-mode), and no additional side effect. Since the first block of plaintext corresponds to the first 16 bytes of ssbytes, the modification produces a new correct database. This allows $\mathsf{Adv_{rw}}$, given a database DB, to produce up to $2^{128} - 1$ different databases $DB'_1, \ldots, DB'_{2^{128}-1}$ containing the same record-set as DB.

4.7   PINs

Format Description. The PINs database is stored in a single file, and encrypted using AES in CBC mode. Records are encrypted separately and stored one record per line, using hexadecimal representation written as ASCII text.

The first line of each database defines the version of the software used to create the database, while the second line contains the encryption of the string "#TEST VERIFY" followed by a variable number of up to fifty random bytes. This is used to verify that the user-provided master password is correct. After deriving the database encryption/decryption key from the user's input, PINs decrypts the second line and determines whether the result corresponds to the expected string.

Security Analysis. Each line containing user data is encrypted with AES in CBC mode, which is known to be IND-CPA-secure [32]. As shown in Appendix A, IND-CPA security implies IND-CDBA security. Therefore $\mathsf{Adv_r}$ cannot extract any information from an encrypted database, besides the number of records and their approximate length.

However, PINs' database file does not provide any kind of data integrity. As such, an adversary can exploit the malleability of the CBC mode of operation to modify the content of the database. Since each line is encrypted separately, changes in one record do not affect other records. $\mathsf{Adv_{rw}}$ can exploit this property to win the MAL-CDBA game with probability 1. After receiving a challenge database DB corresponding to an arbitrary record-set RS, $\mathsf{Adv_{rw}}$ flips one bit in any of the records to obtain a new database DB' which is considered correct by PINs, i.e., $\mathsf{Valid}(DB') = 1$. $\mathsf{Adv_{rw}}$ can also remove arbitrary entries, or replace them with versions collected from different challenge databases.

4.8 PasswordSafe v3

Description. The PasswordSafe v3 database is composed of a single file containing all entries [33]. The file can be logically divided into two parts: a header (hdr), an encrypted body (bdy). hdr includes (among other fields) an IV and a pair of 256-bit keys, K and L, which are used to encrypt bdy and to provide authentication using HMAC respectively. K and L are encrypted using Twofish [34] in ECB mode, under a key derived from a user-provided master password. bdy contains the various database entries, and terminates with an HMAC computed over all fields (before encryption) from hdr to the last entry of bdy, only excluding the database version number.

Security Analysis. PasswordSafe v3 is IND-CDBA-secure *and* MAL-CDBA-secure. (Due to lack of space we omit a formal proof of this statement. The proof is available in the extended version of the paper [31].) As such, neither $\mathsf{Adv_r}$ nor $\mathsf{Adv_{rw}}$ can win their respective games with non-negligible probability over $1/2$.

However, we identified a design flaw that, although irrelevant in our security model, should be considered when adopting this format. The PasswordSafe v3 database format stores both the encryption key and the MAC key used to secure the database content in the file header. In this way, if the master password is changed, the database does not need to be re-encrypted. This technique is usually adopted by encrypted file systems (e.g., [35]) to avoid having to re-encrypt all the data if the master password is changed. However, we believe that this choice may not be appropriate for a password database file. In particular, every time the database is modified, IV is changed and therefore the whole database is re-encrypted. For this reason, the reuse of the same values for K and L does not imply any savings.

Additionally, this specification detail opens the door to an attack. Assume that an adversary is able to obtain the master password for an encrypted database. Using the master password, the adversary would also be able to retrieve (and store) K and L. Subsequently, even if the user changes her master password, the adversary can still decrypt and/or modify any new version of the database. The only way to recover from a compromise of the master password is to completely discard the database and create a new one, i.e., changing the master password serves no purpose. It should be noted that some implementations that use the PasswordSafe v3 format are not vulnerable to this attack (e.g., Password Safe [18]), since they choose a new random K and L every time the database is saved. This makes such implementations less efficient than they could be, but secure.

4.9   Roboform

Format Description. Roboform stores its password database in several files. Each file contains a header, which encodes two URLs: `goto`, which is used as a bookmark by Roboform's browser plugin, and `match`, which is used by Roboform's plugin to determine which username/password record should be used on each web form.

The rest of the record is composed of a short header and an encrypted payload. Roboform allows users to choose between AES, Blowfish, DES, Triple-DES and RC6 for payload encryption.

Security Analysis. Roboform's password format is vulnerable to attacks from both $\mathsf{Adv_r}$ and $\mathsf{Adv_{rw}}$ in our security model.

Adversary $\mathsf{Adv_r}$ can win the IND-CDBA game with probability 1 by constructing two same-size record-sets RS_0 and RS_1 which differ in at least one of the URLs in their records. Since neither the `goto` nor the `match` fields are encrypted, $\mathsf{Adv_r}$ can always identify which record-set corresponds to challenge DB_b. As a proof of concept, we wrote a small script that decodes the `goto` and `match` URLs. The script is available upon request.

In practice, this allows $\mathsf{Adv_r}$ to gather recover a list of web site visited by the user even if web cache and history have been deleted.

Similarly, $\mathsf{Adv_{rw}}$ can win the MAL-CDBA game with probability 1, since neither of the URLs stored in Roboform's database are integrity protected. $\mathsf{Adv_{rw}}$ requests a database corresponding to an arbitrary recordset RS, and after receiving the corresponding database DB, creates DB' by altering one or both URLs. The lack of integrity protection means that $\mathsf{Valid}(DB') = 1$.

In practice, an adversary can use this vulnerability to mount a phishing attack by altering URLs and redirecting users to a malicious website designed to capture login credentials.

5   Discussion

Table 2 summarizes the result of our security analysis. Almost all the formats are vulnerable to attack either in the IND-CDBA or MAL-CDBA security model, or

Table 2. Vulnerabilities overview. This table shows, for each format, whether it is secure ($\checkmark$) or broken ($\times$) in the two security games IND-CDBA and MAL-CDBA, defined in Section 3. [1]PasswordSafe v3 is secure in our model but with an interesting design flaw (see Section 4.8).

	Read-Only Attacker (IND-CDBA)	Read-Write Attacker (MAL-CDBA)
Google Chrome	$\times$	$\times$
Mozilla Firefox	$\times$	$\times$
Microsoft Internet Explorer	$\times$	$\times$
1Password	$\times$	$\times$
KDB (aka KeePass 1.x)	$\times$	$\times$
KDBX4 (aka KeePass 2.x)	$\checkmark$	$\times$
PINs	$\checkmark$	$\times$
PasswordSafe v3	$\checkmark$[1]	$\checkmark$[1]
Roboform	$\times$	$\times$

both. What does that mean for the use of these formats in practice? The answer depends on the security provided by the storage mechanism that hosts the password database. We divide the database formats into three classes: *Class I*: those that can be used on an insecure storage medium. According to our analysis, the only format in this class is PasswordSafe v3; *Class II*: those that can be used if the underlying storage mechanism provides integrity and data authenticity. This class contains KDBX4 and PINs; and *Class III*: those that can be used securely only if the underlying storage provides integrity, authenticity and secrecy. This class contains the remaining formats.

Class I password managers can be used safely without any special considerations, except for one caveat with PasswordSafe v3 described in Section 4.8. To safely use Class II password managers in practice, users should make sure never to rely on any information in the database that could have been changed by a malicious adversary. For example, if privacy is not a concern and the password database is kept on, e.g., a read-only smart card, KDBX4 and PINs *can* be used to securely store passwords.

There is nothing inherently wrong with storing passwords in a Class III password manager, e.g., an unencrypted text file, as long as the user is made aware that the format provides no secrecy, integrity or authenticity. In fact, if the user is taking additional steps to store an unencrypted password database on a secure medium (e.g., an encrypted file system) this may be a perfectly safe approach. As an example, Google Chrome stores passwords in a database format that is not designed to provide security. To use the Google Chrome password manager in practice, users should completely prevent access to the database from any unauthorized party (e.g., other users of the same machine).

It seems fair to require that a password manager that asks users to authenticate themselves with a password, at least provides secrecy and data authenticity. This is currently only achieved by a single password database format, namely

PasswordSafe v3. As a general rule, a password manager should be explicit about the security offered by the underlying database format.

6 Related Work

Although the concept of a password manager is well known and used by people all over the world, there is very little scientific literature on the subject.

In 2003 Luo and Henry proposed a method for protecting multiple accounts [36]. Their solution requires a user to remember only one password, called a common password, to access any of a number of accounts. The authors propose a Web based implementation with a password calculator written in JavaScript.

In an attempt to solve the same problem, Blasko published an IBM Research Report in 2005 [37] proposing a Wristwatch-Computer Based Password-Vault. Blasko describes the design and implementation of a wearable computer with wireless connectivity, processing, input, and display capabilities, that is meant to store a users passwords for different services.

A year later, Gaw and Felten published a study of Password Management Strategies for Online Accounts [21]. The authors studied how many passwords 49 undergraduates had, and how often they reused these passwords. At that time about 38% of the people participating in the study used password managers. More than two thirds of those used online, web based password managers. With the inclusion of password managers in popular browsers, that number is presumably significantly higher today.

In 2009 Englert and Shah published a paper on the Design and Implementation of a secure Online Password Vault [38]. This works describes an architecture where encryption and decryption is done locally on the user's machine but storage done online.

Bonneau and Preibusch reported results of, what they claim is, the first large-scale empirical analysis of password implementations deployed on the Internet [39]. This study included 150 websites which offer free user accounts for a variety of purposes, including the most popular destinations on the web and a random sample of e-commerce, news, and communication websites. This work does not deal directly with password managers but the findings support the claim that many online services use poor practices when dealing with user credentials. This serves to highlight the need for password managers and consequently, the need for secure password manager database formats.

In [40], Belenko and Sklyarov analyze the security of several password manager applications running on iOS and BlackBerry smartphones. Their analysis focuses on a passive adversary, who is able to access a password database *at rest*. The goal of the adversary is to determine the database master password, and therefore access the protected data. The authors show that most password managers either force the user to protect the database using a short (four digit) PIN, or do not use expensive key derivation functions to compute the database encryption/decryption key from the master password. This allows an adversary to perform password recovery attacks relatively short time for low-entropy passwords.

7   Conclusion

Password managers are critical pieces of software used to securely store sensitive information. This paper presents the first rigorous analysis of the storage formats used by popular password managers.

We defined two realistic security models, designed to represent the capabilities of real-world attacks. One for passive and one for active attackers. We analyzed popular password manager database formats in our security models; for each vulnerable format, we provided a formal argument for why it is broken. We also showed what the theoretical vulnerability means in terms of practical attacks. Additionally, when a database format was found to be secure, we provided a formal proof.

Unfortunately, most formats turned out to be broken even against very weak adversaries. For this reason, users should carefully consider whether a particular database format is acceptable for storing data in the cloud, on a USB drive or on a machine shared with other users.

Finally, our works shows that it is indeed possible to construct a format that provides security, usability and low computation and storage overhead, using standard cryptographic tools.

References

1. Trusteer: Reused Login Credentials,
   http://www.trusteer.com/sites/default/files/cross-logins-advisory.pdf
2. Herzberg, A.: Why Johnny can't Surf (Safely)? Attacks and Defenses for Web Users. Computers & Security 28(1-2) (2009)
3. Dhamija, R., Tygar, J., Hearst, M.: Why Phishing Works. In: SIGCHI Conference on Human Factors in Computing Systems. ACM, New York (2006)
4. RomanLab Co. Ltd.: USB password manager: When your password database is right where you need it, http://www.anypassword.com/password-database-in-usb-password-manager.html
5. Siber Systems, Inc.: Roboform2go for USB drives,
   http://www.roboform.com/platforms/usb
6. Portable Apps: Keepass password safe portable,
   http://portableapps.com/apps/utilities/keepass_portable
7. 1Password: Automatic Syncing Using Dropbox,
   http://help.agilebits.com/1Password3/cloud_syncing_with_dropbox.html
8. KeePassDroid: Dropbox and KeePassDroid,
   http://blog.keepassdroid.com/2010/06/dropbox-and-keepassdroid.html
9. AgileBits, Inc.: 1password, https://agilebits.com/onepassword
10. Vanhove, M.: Kypass, http://itunes.apple.com/us/app/kypass/id425680960?mt=8
11. Pellin, B.: Keepassdroid, http://www.keepassdroid.com
12. Google: Get a fast, free web browser, https://www.google.com/chrome/
13. Mozilla: Firefox, http://www.mozilla.org/
14. Microsoft: Internet Explorer 9,
    http://windows.microsoft.com/en-us/internet-explorer/products/ie/home
15. KeePass – A Free and Open-source Password Manager, http://keepass.info/

16. Muiznieks, R.: Passdrop,
    http://itunes.apple.com/us/app/passdrop/id431185109?mt=8
17. PINs, Secure Passwords Manager,
    http://www.mirekw.com/winfreeware/pins.html
18. Password Safe – Simple & Secure Password Management,
    http://passwordsafe.sourceforge.net/
19. Pilhofer, F.: Password Gorilla, http://www.fpx.de/fp/Software/Gorilla/
20. Siber Systems, Inc.: RoboForm, http://www.roboform.com/
21. Gaw, S., Felten, E.: Password Management Strategies for Online Accounts. In:
    SOUPS 2006. ACM Press, Pittsburgh (2006)
22. Katz, J., Yung, M.: Unforgeable Encryption and Chosen Ciphertext Secure Modes
    of Operation. In: Schneier, B. (ed.) FSE 2000. LNCS, vol. 1978, pp. 284–299.
    Springer, Heidelberg (2001)
23. Bellare, M., Namprempre, C.: Authenticated Encryption: Relations among Notions
    and Analysis of the Generic Composition Paradigm. J. Cryptology 21(4) (2008)
24. Google: Protect your synced data,
    http://support.google.com/chrome/bin/answer.py?hl=en&answer=1181035
25. Mozilla: Firefox Sync for Mobile, http://www.mozilla.org/en-US/mobile/sync/
26. Frazier, M.: Sync Firefox from the Command Line,
    http://www.linuxjournal.com/content/sync-firefox-command-line
27. Microsoft Dev Center: CryptProtectData function, http://msdn.microsoft.
    com/en-us/library/windows/desktop/aa380261(v=vs.85).aspx
28. AgileBits, Inc.: 1password agile keychain design,
    http://help.agilebits.com/1Password3/agile_keychain_design.html
29. GNU zip: The GZIP homepage, http://www.gzip.org/
30. Bernstein, D.J.: The Salsa20 Family of Stream Ciphers. In: Robshaw, M., Billet,
    O. (eds.) New Stream Cipher Designs. LNCS, vol. 4986, pp. 84–97. Springer, Hei-
    delberg (2008)
31. Gasti, P., Rasmussen, K.: On The Security of Password Manager Database For-
    mats. Technical report, UCI (2012), Available from Cryptology ePrint Archive,
    http://eprint.iacr.org
32. Damgaard, I., Nielsen, J.: Expanding Pseudorandom Functions; or: From Known-
    Plaintext Security to Chosen-Plaintext Security. In: Yung, M. (ed.) CRYPTO 2002.
    LNCS, vol. 2442, pp. 449–464. Springer, Heidelberg (2002)
33. Password Safe V3 Database Format, http://passwordsafe.svn.sourceforge.
    net/viewvc/passwordsafe/trunk/pwsafe/pwsafe/docs/
34. Schneier, B., Kelsey, J., Whiting, D., Wagner, D., Hall, C.: Twofish: A 128-Bit
    Block Cipher. Current 21(1) (1998)
35. Ferguson, N.: AES-CBC + Elephant diffuser A Disk Encryption Algorithm for
    Windows Vista. Technical report, Microsoft Research (2006)
36. Luo, H., Henry, P.: A Common Password Method for Protection of Multiple Ac-
    counts. In: International Symposium on Personal, Indoor and Mobile Radio Com-
    munication (2003)
37. Blasko, G., Narayanaswami, C., Raghunath, M.: A Wristwatch-Computer Based
    Password-Vault. Technical report, IBM Research Division (2005)
38. Englert, B., Shah, P.: On the Design and Implementation of a secure Online Pass-
    word Vault. In: ICHIT 2009. ACM Press (2009)
39. Bonneau, J., Preibusch, S.: The Password Thicket: Technical and Market Failures
    in Human Authentication on the Web. Information Security 8(1) (2010)

40. Belenko, A., Sklyarov, D.: "Secure Password Managers" and "Military-Grade Encryption" on Smartphones: Oh, Really? Technical report, Elcomsoft Co. Ltd. (2012), http://www.elcomsoft.com/WP/BH-EU-2012-WP.pdf
41. Katz, J., Lindell, Y.: Introduction to Modern Cryptography. Chapman & Hall/CRC (2008)

A   Relationship between IND-CPA and IND-CDBA

In this section we shed light on the relationship between our notion of IND-CDBA-security and the standard IND-CPA-security. Let $\Pi = (\mathsf{Setup}, \mathsf{Enc}, \mathsf{Dec})$ be a IND-CPA$_{\mathsf{Adv}, \Pi}(\kappa)$-secure encryption scheme. We recall the standard definition of IND-CPA security [41]:

Game 3 (IND-CPA$_{\mathcal{A}, \Pi}(\kappa)$). *Indistinguishability of chosen plaintext attack. A challenger* Ch *running* Π *interacts with* $\mathcal{A}$ *as follows:*

- Ch *runs* $mp \leftarrow \mathsf{Setup}(1^{\kappa})$.
- $\mathcal{A}$ *is given oracle access to* $\mathsf{Enc}_{mp}(\cdot)$
- *Eventually* $\mathcal{A}$ *outputs two same size messages* RS_0, RS_1
- Ch *selects a bit* b *uniformly at random and the ciphertext* $DB_b \leftarrow \mathsf{Enc}(mp, RS_b)$ *is returned to* $\mathcal{A}$.
- $\mathcal{A}$ *eventually outputs bit* b'; *the game outputs 1 iff* $b = b'$.

Definition 4 (IND-CPA security). *An encryption scheme* $\Pi = (\mathsf{Setup}_{\Pi}, \mathsf{Enc}_{\Pi}, \mathsf{Dec}_{\Pi})$ *has indistinguishable encryptions under chosen plaintext attack if there exists a negligible function* $\mathsf{negl}(\cdot)$ *such that for any efficient adversary* $\mathcal{A}$, $\Pr[\mathsf{IND\text{-}CPA}_{\mathcal{A}, \Pi}(\kappa) = 1] \leq 1/2 + \mathsf{negl}(\kappa)$.

It is easy to see that IND-CPA$_{\mathcal{A}, \Pi}(\kappa)$ security implies IND-CDBA$_{\mathsf{Adv}_r, \mathcal{PM}}(\kappa)$ security. Let $\mathcal{PM} = (\mathsf{Setup}, \mathsf{Create}, \mathsf{Open}, \mathsf{Valid})$ where $\mathsf{Setup} = \mathsf{Setup}_{\Pi}$, $\mathsf{Create} = \mathsf{Enc}_{\Pi}$, $\mathsf{Open} = \mathsf{Dec}_{\Pi}$ and Valid is defined as in Section 3.

Assume Adv_r is an adversary that has a non-negligible advantage in the IND-CDBA game. We show how to build a simulator SIM that uses Adv_r to win the IND-CPA game. SIM lets Adv_r choose RS_0 and RS_1, and forwards these to Ch. Ch returns DB_b which is forwarded to Adv_r. Eventually Adv_r outputs its choice for b', and SIM uses it to answer the challenger. Since $(\mathsf{Setup}, \mathsf{Create}, \mathsf{Open})$ is defined as $(\mathsf{Setup}_{\Pi}, \mathsf{Enc}_{\Pi}, \mathsf{Dec}_{\Pi})$, Sim's advantage is identical to Adv_r's.

Scalable Telemetry Classification for Automated Malware Detection

Jack W. Stokes[1], John C. Platt[1], Helen J. Wang[1], Joe Faulhaber[2],
Jonathan Keller[2], Mady Marinescu[2], Anil Thomas[2], and Marius Gheorghescu[2]

[1] Microsoft Research, Redmond WA 98052, USA
{jstokes,jplatt,helenw}@microsoft.com
[2] Microsoft Corp., Redmond WA 98052, USA
{joefa,jkeller,mady,anilth,mariusg}@microsoft.com

Abstract. Industry reports and blogs have estimated the amount of malware based on *known* malicious files. This paper extends this analysis to the amount of *unknown* malware. The study is based on 26.7 million files referenced in telemetry reports from 50 million computers running commercial anti-malware (AM) products. To estimate the undetected malware, a classifier predicts the underlying nature of unknown files recorded in the telemetry reports. The telemetry classifier predicts that 69.6% (4.27 million) of the unknown files are malicious. Assuming the unknown files predicted to be malicious by the classifier are malware, the telemetry classifier also allows us to estimate the efficacy of the AM system indicating that signatures detected 82.8% (20.6 million) of the malicious files. We have validated our system by conducting a longitudinal study to measure the false positive and false negative rates over a period of thirteen months.

Keywords: malware classification, telemetry, sample collection, prefilter.

1 Introduction

The anti-malware (AM) industry faces two significant problems in the battle to protect their customers' computers from being infected by malware. First these companies are paradoxically confronted by the challenge of trying to discover malware in huge amounts of telemetry data while only having samples (i.e. copies) of a small fraction of the unknown files hosted on their users' computers. Typically, commercial AM products transmit telemetry reports from a large percentage of their client computers when users try to download or install known or potential malware. Although our company receives over 100,000 new file *samples* every day which need to be analyzed, we had previously collected samples from only 3.1% of the files referenced in the set of telemetry reports received in October 2010. Ideally, AM companies would have a copy of every unknown executable file observed on their clients' machines. In this scenario, analysts clearly cannot investigate each new file manually, and anti-malware companies must

S. Foresti, M. Yung, and F. Martinelli (Eds.): ESORICS 2012, LNCS 7459, pp. 788–805, 2012.
© Springer-Verlag Berlin Heidelberg 2012

automate detection of these threats. Researchers have described systems showing great promise on automatically detecting malware [4], [6], [32]. However, in-depth analysis can be time consuming. In some cases, Anubis [4] can require several minutes to analyze each file [2]. Each month, we receive telemetry reports corresponding to tens of millions of files that were not detected as being malicious by the AM system's signature detector. Even with distributed processing and only analyzing new, incoming files, clearly these in-depth malware detection systems will struggle to analyze all of the new, potentially malicious files. Second the companies cannot accurately measure the performance of their systems in detecting the amount of malware in the ecosystem. Consumers often see claims that an anti-malware product detects X% of malware, and industrial reports provide a glimpse of the amount of malware detected on user's machines [13], [24]. However these estimates are based on detections of *known* malware. What is missing is the true detection rate, including the *unknown* files, found in the wild. While it is impossible to measure this malware detection rate exactly, we seek a better estimate of the amount of malware in this study.

To address these problems, we propose a lightweight telemetry report classifier shown in Figure 1. AM clients transmit telemetry reports to the backend system running the telemetry classifier. Each report contains metadata, including file and machine identifiers, associated with the installation or scan of an untrusted portable executable (PE) file including application binaries, screen savers, drivers, and Active X controls. Unlike previous work, we assume that the majority of the executable files cannot be accessed directly since they are either located on remote computers or the installations were blocked by the signature detector. To help manage the collection and analysis of unknown files, the telemetry classifier assigns a probability that the file associated with the report is malicious solving two problems. The reports can be ranked to determine which files are more likely to be malicious for collection from the remote users' computers. In addition, the telemetry classifier output allows the system to prefilter the queue of unknown files for timely processing by an in-depth malware analysis system. Files with the highest malware probability are collected or analyzed first. Recently, several systems have been proposed for prefiltering (i.e. ranking) samples for in-depth analysis [18], [26], [34], but these systems require a sample of the file for classification and clustering on the results of static analysis. In our system, the AM client can perform both static and *dynamic* analysis of the file on the remote computer, and we use this telemetry information for prefiltering. Although we only utilize a simple behavior feature in this study, more sophisticated dynamic execution features could also be detected and reported by the client. Furthermore, the performance of the signature detectors can be measured by the telemetry classifier. Unlike previous work, our estimates include *unknown* files which have not been previously detected. Using the proposed system, we estimate the percentage of malicious files encountered in a large sample of 26.7 million telemetry reports, each corresponding to a unique file, received from a population of over 50 million computers.

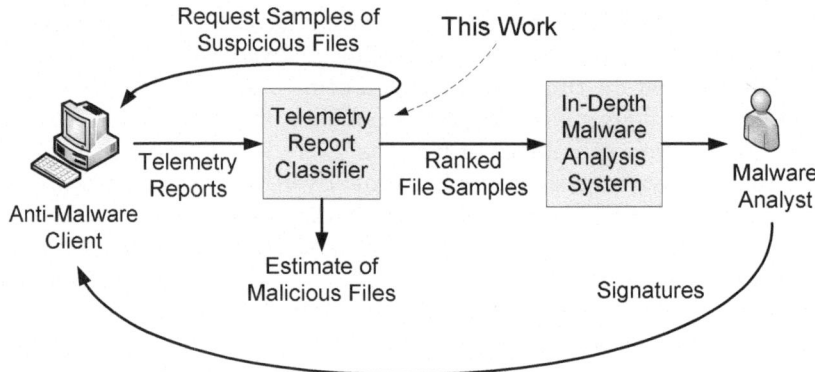

Fig. 1. Classifying malware on the backend based on metadata reports generated by anti-malware clients

A key aspect of this work is to investigate whether *individual* telemetry reports can be accurately classified to predict if an unknown file residing on a remote client is malicious or benign. Previous work [22], [30] proposes various types of malware classifiers, but these systems assume access to the PE file. Recently, commercial products including Symantec's AM products [7], [8] and Microsoft's Internet Explorer have started using reputation data to detect malware or benign files and consider files which have been frequently observed, but not detected as malicious, to be benign. The approach followed in this paper does not rely on file prevalence information. This choice was made explicitly to identify polymorphic and zero-day attacks. In addition, the earlier file-based studies were conducted on small training sets; while these preliminary efforts were promising, it was unclear if the results scale with large numbers of labeled data. In this study, we use over 253 thousand, labeled telemetry reports to train and test the telemetry classifier.

To handle the large number of reports used for training, the system utilizes several technically significant components. The telemetry classifier uses a *limited* combination of features (Section 2) derived from the telemetry data including static features from the binary file and one, simple behavioral feature indicating what action caused the report to be generated. Among these, using trigrams of the file's locality sensitive hash is a novel implementation which scales well. Excluding this feature from our model decreases the accuracy by over 18% (Section 4). We use a feature selection algorithm based on 2x2 contingency tables and the mutual information criterion to create the datasets (Section 3). Next we describe several algorithms used to train both linear and non-linear classifiers for analyzing the telemetry reports and highlight several machine learning algorithms for the security community (Section 4). Logistic regression trained with the L-BFGS algorithm and including L1 and L2 regularization performs best for our task. A boosted decision tree algorithm trained with the MART criteria also performs well. Lastly, an approximation to the SVM using L-BFGS optimization

Table 1. Summary of the telemetry report attributes and additional data aggregated by the backend system

Feature	Description
File Name	Name of the PE file
Original File Name	File name in the original report
File Name Matches Original?	Does the file name in this report match the file name in the original report?
File Type	What type of file is it?
Signer Name	What organization signed the file?
Signing Authority	What certificate authority issued the signature?
Signature Type	Was the file signed or not? If signed, is the signature legitimate or invalid?
Description	What is the description of the file in the header?
Organization	Manufacturer of the binary file
Version	Version number of the binary file
LS Hash	Locality sensitive hash
Behavior Feature	Represents the simple behavior that caused the report to be generated

is competitive and can require much less time to train compared to exact methods (e.g. sequential minimal optimization). We validate the telemetry classifier in a thirteen month longitudinal study to measure the false positive and false negative rates of the samples received one month after training.

We implemented the lightweight telemetry classifier and used it to estimate the number of malicious executable files (Section 5). The telemetry classifier predicts that 69.6% (4.27 million) of the unknown files involved in the reports are malicious. Although biased on the computers which sent the telemetry, this estimate gives a better sense of the total amount of malware. The telemetry classifier also allows us to estimate the efficacy of the signature detector. Assuming all of the unknown files predicted to be malicious by the classifier are indeed malware, the telemetry classifier indicates that signatures detected 82.8% (20.6 million) of the malicious files. A summary of the contributions of this paper includes:

- A large-scale system to classify anti-malware telemetry reports is proposed and implemented, and the results are presented. Using tri-grams of locality sensitive hashes is a novel feature for the system.
- The number of malicious executable files and the effectiveness of a suite of anti-malware products are estimated from a sample of 26.7 million telemetry reports received from over 50 million computers.
- We demonstrate that the lightweight telemetry classification system can be used to prioritize files for sample collection and prefilter these samples for more in-depth analysis.
- Training classifiers based on six different algorithms including logistic regression with L-BFGS optimization and L1 and L2 regularization as well as an approximation of the linear SVM are highlighted for the security community.

2   Telemetry Metadata and Features

This study is based on a large collection of telemetry reports received from a suite of commercial anti-malware products. Our company manufactures these security products which detect and remove spyware (e.g. Windows Defender) as well as viruses and other malware (e.g. Forefront Client Security, Windows Live OneCare, Windows Live Security Scanner, and the Microsoft Malicious Software Removal Tool). Our analysts utilize the reports in our efforts to detect new malware on personal computers (PCs) running the Windows operating system.

The telemetry reports consist of various attributes measured by the AM client running on the remote computer when it detects that a new file is being installed or a previously undetected file is running. To limit the number of reports received at the backend web service, only telemetry reports corresponding to files which have not been signed by a *trusted* certificate authority are transmitted. Additional information can be constructed at the backend by examining the telemetry reports across all of the reporting clients. This local and backend metadata corresponding to the (potential) installation of a file is summarized in Table 1. All of the attributes are extracted by the AM client with the exception of the second and third rows (i.e. original file name and file name matches) which are determined on the backend. In addition to the low-level features discussed in this section, we also construct other features indicating if a particular attribute is blank or null. For example, if the organization is null, a boolean feature is set to true. This high-level metadata is discussed in more detail below and serves as the basis for the low-level features used to train the classifiers in Section 4.

In addition to the metadata listed in Table 1, the telemetry reports also contain several unique file identifiers including the SHA1 and MD5 files hashes. While these hashes cannot serve as features for any classification system since a small change in the executable file leads to a large change in the corresponding hash value, they allow us to assign a label to the incoming telemetry report for files which have previously been collected, investigated and categorized (e.g. malware, benign) by analysts. We could potentially also use files detected by anti-virus signatures and include these in our dataset but we have not done so for the following reason. Training primarily with samples determined by the signature detector may lead to a situation where the telemetry classifier learns to only recognize files we currently detect; doing so may prevent the telemetry classifier from identifying files not currently identified by the signature detector.

While Table 1 illustrates the high-level metadata found in the telemetry reports, we cannot directly use this information as the features for the telemetry classifier described in later sections. There are too many values associated with some of the attributes in the table. For example, we measured over 71 million distinct file names in one month of telemetry data. Next, we describe the methods used to transform this metadata into a set of potential low-level features for the telemetry classifier we train in Section 4. This transformation is just the first step in determining the final classifier features. We further restrict (i.e. filter) this set of low-level features through feature selection in the following section. Only two features may vary when comparing telemetry reports from a unique malware sample, namely, the file name and the behavior which caused the report to be generated (described later). In addition to the file name associated with the report, the telemetry classifier also considers other derived features. All string features are efficiently encoded using 1.5 grams. Given the shear number

Table 2. Most frequent malware signer names

Name	Percentage
Not Signed	95.68%
Freeze.com, LLC	0.26%
Zango	0.21%
WebDevAZ, Inc.	0.16%
WHENU.COM INC	0.15%

Table 3. Most frequent benign signer names

Name	Percentage
Not Signed	78.53%
Microsoft Windows Component Publisher	5.07%
Microsoft Windows	3.54%
Microsoft Corporation	2.50%
Microsoft Windows Publisher	2.50%

of unique strings in the data, we cannot represent each string as a feature. To limit the total number of possible features, we propose a compromise we call 1.5-grams (pronounced one and a half grams). To compute a 1.5-gram set for a unicode string, we first convert the string to a byte array. The initial 1.5-gram for the array is determined as the first 12 consecutive bits (i.e. 3 nibbles). To compute the second 1.5-gram, we slide the index by 4 bits, and the 1.5-gram is the value of next 12 consecutive bits. For standard 8-bit text, this encoding represents a full character and half of the following character. It can also fully represent more obscure non, 8-bit characters. Using the 1.5-gram representation only requires 4096 (2^{12}) possible values for all possible file names. A separate feature identifies if the file name in the report matches the file name associated with the original report of the executable. Furthermore, the type of file (e.g. keyboard driver, printer driver, application, DLL) is also used as a feature.

Two important features of the system are which organization signed the file and which certificate authority granted the certificate. These features were also suggested by Nachenberg et al. [7]. In addition, the certificate is verified for authenticity. The signature type feature indicates whether or not the file was signed. If it was signed, was the signature valid? Tables 2 and 3 provide an example of the most frequent organizations that signed the files associated with malicious and benign reports, respectively; these tables do not necessarily describe the most discriminant (i.e. best) features for the telemetry classifier. For example, since 95% of the malware and 78% of the benign files are not signed, a signature value of "Not Signed" will not be a good feature. While it is not surprising that most malware is not signed, the results for benign files is an artifact of the telemetry reporting process. Reports are not sent by the AM clients for files which are signed by trusted organizations. Thus, the signed, benign files in the head of the distribution are not reflected in this data. The Microsoft signatures in Table 3 are most likely particular signatures used on a small number of files, and therefore, these signatures have not been added to the list of trusted certificates.

Another important feature is the certificate authority (CA) which granted the certificate, and the data for the CA is listed in Tables 4 and 5. Interestingly, a small fraction of malware authors have managed to obtain certificates granted from respectable CAs. The reason is that they are trying to provide assurance to the users that the code is legitimate. This behavior indicating attackers trying to build trust has been studied recently for website certificates [10]. We encoded

Table 4. Most frequent malware certificate authorities

Name	Percentage
No Issuer	95.66%
VeriSign Class 3 Code Signing 2004 CA	1.16%
Thawte Code Signing CA	1.15%
UTN-USERFirst-Object	0.59%
INVALID:Thawte Code Signing CA	0.52%

Table 5. Most frequent benign certificate authorities

Name	Percentage
No Issuer	78.49%
Microsoft Windows Verification Intermediate PCA	7.88%
VeriSign Class 3 Code Signing 2004 CA	4.51%
Microsoft Windows Verification PCA	3.55%
Microsoft Code Signing PCA	2.24%

each distinct value for the signer and certificate authorities in the set of potential features.

All PE files contain information in the header such as the manufacturer, description, and version number. This data is transmitted to the backend in the telemetry reports and encoded as features using 1.5-grams for the telemetry classifier. In addition to the SHA1 hash, a locality sensitive hash (LS hash) is also computed for the file by the AM client and transmitted to the backend. Unlike standard hashes which completely change when a single bit in the file is altered, LS hashes have the property that changing a small amount of code introduces a small change in the resulting hash. Bayer, *et al.* [3] and Jang, *et al.* [19] have utilized the LS hash as a feature for malware clustering. Clustering, however, requires comparing pairs of LS hash values which can be computationally expensive. In our design, the telemetry classifier uses tri-grams of each file's LS hash which is a novel feature representation. The LS hash tri-grams from variants of malware families in the training set increase the likelihood that these tri-grams are associated with malicious files. As a result, training and evaluation are not adversely affected as the scale increases. It should be noted that since the LS hash is composed of hexadecimal digits, only 2^{12} features are required to represent all possible tri-gram values.

The action that caused the report to be generated is also used as a feature for the telemetry classifier. There are roughly 50 distinct behavior actions found in our telemetry reports, and these behavioral actions are indicative of a file being installed on the computer. Table 6 provides the five most frequent behaviors associated with a report generated by malicious files while the five most frequent behaviors associated with benign files are given in Table 7. Example behavior actions include installing an ActiveX control, Browser Helper Object, or driver, adding a Run Key to automatically start a program each time the user logs on, starting a process, or scheduling a task. For both malware and benign files, downloading an ActiveX control is the main behavioral feature associated with the telemetry reports. Surprisingly, only 2.93% of malicious reports were associated with Browser Helper Objects.

Table 6. Most frequent malware behavioral features

Name	Percentage
ActiveX Downloads	73.93%
Run Keys	9.56%
Running Processes	3.77%
Browser Helper Object	2.93%
Task Scheduler	1.96%

Table 7. Most frequent benign behavioral features

Name	Percentage
ActiveX Downloads	70.64%
Services	6.26%
Drivers	5.02%
Run Once Keys	3.91%
Run Keys	3.48%

3   Feature Selection and Dataset Creation

In this section, we describe the process used to create the dataset required to train the telemetry classifier. The anti-malware telemetry classification training system is illustrated in Figure 2. The raw telemetry logs and analyst labels described earlier are input to the system which includes three processing blocks: feature selection, dataset creation, and classifier training. An integral step in the process is feature selection which excludes potential features that are not beneficial during classifier training. In the previous section, we transformed the high-level, telemetry metadata into a large number of potential low-level features, but we cannot use all of these to train the telemetry classifier. The feature selection algorithm determines the most discriminant (i.e. best) subset of all of the features to be used for classification. Based on the selected features, a labeled dataset is next constructed from the analysts' labels and the low-level encoded features derived from the telemetry reports. In the next section, we then use the labeled dataset to train the telemetry classifier using several different algorithms. The output of the training system is a classifier model (i.e. a set of weights or parameters) which can be used to predict if unknown reports were transmitted due to malware or benign files.

Constructing a dataset from all of the encoded data from the previous section can lead to hundreds of thousands of potential features. Using too many low-level features can cause overfitting which is due to training a complex machine learning algorithm with an insufficient number of training examples. If the model is too complex, the results when the system is deployed to production may be significantly worse compared to those observed when trained and tested

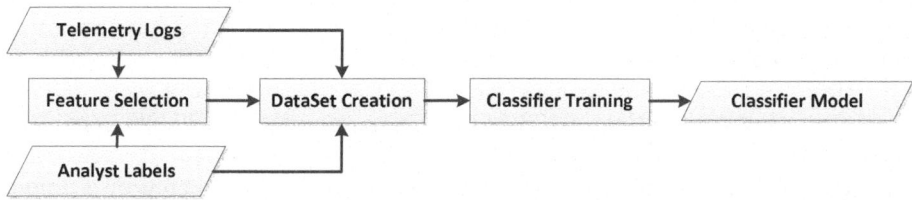

Fig. 2. Anti-Malware telemetry classification training system

on a small labeled dataset. A general rule is to select the number of features F for the system to be the total number of samples divided by a sufficiently large number (e.g. 8-10). The feature selection algorithm we use first computes a 2x2 contingency table for each potential feature based on the mutual information criterion [23]. A maximum likelihood estimate of the mutual information criterion serves as our ranking score $R(f)$:

$$R(f) = \frac{D}{N} \log_2 \frac{N \cdot D}{(\hat{BD})(\hat{CD})} + \frac{B}{N} \log_2 \frac{N \cdot B}{(\hat{AB})(\hat{CD})}$$
$$+ \frac{C}{N} \log_2 \frac{N \cdot C}{(\hat{BD})(\hat{AC})} + \frac{A}{N} \log_2 \frac{N \cdot A}{(\hat{AB})(\hat{AC})}$$

where A is the number of times the potential is not in the reports and the file is determined to be benign, while D is the number of malicious reports which include the potential feature. B (C) similarly is the report count for malicious (benign) files not including (including) the potential feature. In addition, $\hat{AB} = (A + B)$, $\hat{AC} = (A + C)$, $\hat{BD} = (B + D)$, $\hat{CD} = (C + D)$, and $N = A + B + C + D$. Finally, the top F features are selected from the highest ranked mutual information scores.

4 Telemetry Classifier Performance

Now that we have created our labeled dataset in the previous section, we turn to the task of training our telemetry classifier. In this section, we investigate the performance of five, *linear* and one, *nonlinear* classification algorithms. We are particularly interested in linear classifiers because they are fast to train, but more importantly, they can be used to evaluate unknown reports very quickly. Since tens of millions of reports are received every day, evaluation of each unknown report must be fast.

We first consider two forms of logistic regression [5] trained using stochastic gradient descent (LR-SGD) and L-BFGS (LR-L-BFGS) [1] as the optimization methods to learn the model parameters. Next, we train a support vector machine (SVM) [5] with a linear kernel based on the Pegasos [31] algorithm (SVM-Pegasos) as well as an *approximation* of the linear SVM [36] again using L-BFGS (SVM-L-BFGS). The final linear classifier considered in this study is the averaged perceptron [11]. We also train with a nonlinear algorithm employing boosted decision trees using the MART [12] algorithm. Boosting has previously been suggested for malware classification [22], [28].

To train and test the classifiers, we created a labeled dataset from 253,517 telemetry reports consisting of 173,548 malicious reports and 79,969 benign reports collected over a four month period ending January 2012. We selected a single telemetry report to represent each distinct file, as represented by a unique SHA1 hash. To evaluate the performance of the six classification algorithms, we use 5-fold cross validation which is the most fair way to do so. In cross validation, the entire labeled dataset is split equally into N (e.g. 5) sections. For each fold, we use one section as the test data and combine the remaining sections as the training data. After the telemetry classifier has been trained and evaluated for all folds, every sample in the dataset has been independently used in the testing set. To be completely fair, we also rerun the feature selection algorithm for each fold's training data. Consequently, we never do feature selection using samples from the test set. For these experiments, the number of selected features was determined as one-tenth of the number of samples used for training. Using 4/5 of the total 253 thousand samples leads to the selection of 20,281 low-level features.

Since we are dealing with a binary (i.e. two-class, malware versus benign) classification problem, we investigate the performance of the classifiers using detection error trade-off (DET) curves which plot the false negative rate versus the false positive rate for the 5-fold cross validation results. Figure 3 shows the DET curves for the six different classification algorithms. In addition, the equal error rates, where the false positive and false negative rates match, and the training time for one fold of the cross-validation are shown in Table 8. Of the six different algorithms, LR-L-BFGS outperforms the remaining classifiers, particularly at lower false positive rates. This version of logistic regression includes both L1 and L2 regularization terms. For L1 regularization, the algorithm tries to force small weights to have a value equal to zero which helps improve the algorithm's ability to generalize to new telemetry reports. In this case, the L1 and L2 parameters are each set to 1.0. MART is competitive and is slightly better than LR-L-LBGS at higher FP rates. SVMs have been well studied in the machine learning literature [5], [15]. However, training an SVM for large data sets can take a prohibitive amount of time. Zhang, *et al.* [36] proposed an approximation to the linear SVM based on a modified version of logistic regression. The central idea is that the SVM's non-linear hinge loss can be approximated by the logistic regression's smooth log-loss function. We often use this algorithm to approximate the SVM in our work since the datasets tend to be very large. This SVM approximation trained with L-BFGS (SVM-L-BFGS) also performs reasonably well compared to LR-L-LBGS and MART. However, this implementation does not include a separate L1 regularization term which may contribute to the decrease in detection accuracy compared to LR-L-BFGS. The averaged perceptron and LR-SGD are competitive, but the SVM trained using the Pegasos algorithm performed significantly worse compared to the other five algorithms. We conducted another experiment to verify the contribution on the proposed LS Hash features on the LR-L-LBGS model. Removing the LS Hash features from the model increased the CV equal error rate for one particular dataset from 5.76% to 6.81%, an increase of over 18.2%. As Table 8 shows, the classifiers are reasonably fast to train on a large server with dual, 2.0 GHz Intel E7540 processors and 128 GBs of RAM. The best performing algorithm, LR-L-BGGS, requires approximately 11 minutes to train. This training time is approximately one-fourth of the time required to train the second best algorithm, MART, which is significantly more complex.

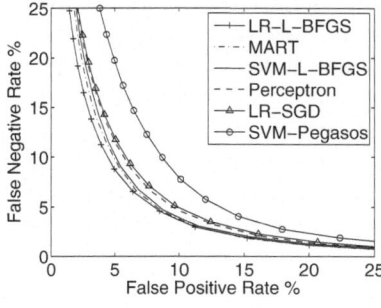
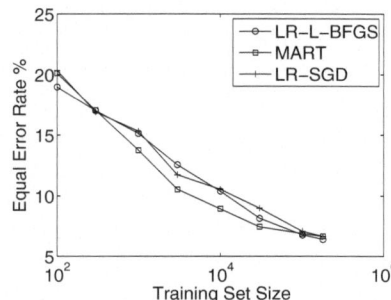

Fig. 3. DET curves for the malware classifiers trained with several different algorithms

Fig. 4. Equal error rates for classifiers trained with various training set sizes

Table 8. Equal error rates and training times for six different telemetry classifier algorithms

Algorithm	Equal Error Rate (%)	Training Time
LR-SGD	7.41	00:07:52.53
LR-L-BFGS	6.45	00:11:13.21
SVM-L-BFGS	6.77	01:59:32.89
SVM-Pegasos	10.34	00:01:12.59
Averaged Perceptron	7.21	00:02:54.15
MART	6.64	00:44:58.39

In Figure 4, we analyze how the telemetry report training set size affects the equal error rate for three of the algorithms: LR-L-LBGS, MART, and LR-SGD. The motivation for studying the effect of the training set size is that the results presented in [22] and [30] are based on small training set sizes of 3622 and 4301, respectively. We would like to understand if a particular classification algorithm is the main factor in determining the classification performance or if the amount of training data is more important. The figure clearly shows that increasing the training set size leads to a significant decrease in the equal error rate for all three models. For many of the different sample sizes, MART performs best but is surpassed by LR-L-BFGS starting at 100 thousand samples. The relative performance of LR-L-LBFGS and LR-SGD depends on the sample size. As the sample size increases, the equal error rates become very close for the different algorithms. One important result from Figure 4 is that the test error is still decreasing even with a training set of 157 thousand samples. Although since the x-axis is on a log scale, achieving better accuracies requires higher and higher numbers of training samples.

Next in Table 9, we evaluated the performance of the telemetry classifier over a period of thirteen months on new, unique reports (i.e. files) received in the month following the classifier training but were not included in the training set. For each test month, the telemetry classifier was trained on the previous five

Table 9. Longitudenal results for the telemetry classifier system over a period of 13 months

Start Training Month	Final Training Month	Test Month	CV Equal Error Rate (%)	Test FP Rate	Test FN Rate
2010_09	2011_01	2011_02	7.66	9.73	9.45
2010_10	2011_02	2011_03	7.52	9.87	8.94
2010_11	2011_03	2011_04	7.43	13.36	6.63
2010_12	2011_04	2011_05	7.37	11.46	8.14
2011_01	2011_05	2011_06	7.43	18.14	16.17
2011_02	2011_06	2011_07	7.29	8.0	10.33
2011_03	2011_07	2011_08	7.23	7.44	11.07
2011_04	2011_08	2011_09	7.40	8.97	10.56
2011_05	2011_09	2011_10	7.13	10.77	14.61
2011_06	2011_10	2011_11	6.37	8.87	7.56
2011_07	2011_11	2011_12	6.33	6.95	9.12
2011_08	2011_12	2012_01	6.17	21.11	6.48
2011_09	2012_01	2012_02	6.78	8.35	6.11

months of unique labeled reports. The files associated with both the training and test reports were previously determined to be malicious or benign by either manual analysis by professional analysts or other automated means. For example, computing the SHA1 hashes of all files in an off-the-shelf program and adding them to a whitelist constitutes an automated method of determining a file's label. As noted earlier, we did not rely on detections based on AV signatures for this validation. The table shows that cross validation rates on the training sets are fairly consistent. However, due to a smaller amount of data, the FP and FN rates for the test month have a larger variance and are almost always higher than the cross-validation error on the training set. This is to be expected because it is the most difficult test on previously unseen data. In January 2012, the FP rate was 21.1% which can happen due to a small number of samples labeled benign for a particular test month. In this case, the number of true positives was 29,836 and true negatives was 5,931. In addition, we found 1,587 false positives and 2,068 false negatives. Overall, there is reasonable agreement between the test and training CV errors. For collecting new samples and sample submission to an in-depth processing system, we believe these error rates are acceptable. In these scenarios, a false positive results in the collection or submission of roughly one benign sample for every nine malicious samples.

5   Malware Estimation

Now that we have trained our malware telemetry classifier to predict the label of the unknown reports, we can use the classification system trained with LR-L-LBFGS to estimate the number of malicious files. The 26.7 million telemetry reports in our sample can be divided into several high-level sets as shown in Figure 5. The figure indicates the number of reports received in October 2010

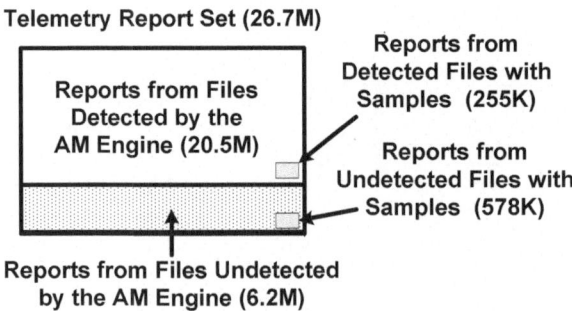

Fig. 5. Anti-malware telemetry report description. All reports represent a distinct executable determined by a unique SHA1 hash.

considering only a single report for each distinct executable file. In other words, we sample the most recent report received for each file and disregard each previous report containing that particular SHA1 file hash. These reports are divided into two sets, namely those for files identified by the signature detector running on the remote computer (20.5 million) and those for unknown files which were not detected (6.2 million). One of the main goals of this paper is to predict the label of these undetected reports in the shaded box. Furthermore, detected reports include 255 thousand reports corresponding to executables where a sample of the file has been previously collected at the backend. Similarly, the file collection system includes 578 thousand file samples found in the undetected reports. From the figure, we see that we have only collected samples of files found in 3.1% ((255K + 578K)/26.7M) of the reports thus providing motivation to analyze reports in the absence of a file sample.

To estimate what percentage of unknown files are predicted to be malicious, we first estimate the percentage of malicious executables from the unknown reports in our sample population. The second and third columns of Table 10 provide the number of reports based on the three detection methods, manual labeling, signature detection, and telemetry classifier prediction. In total, we received reports for 26,749,556 distinct, files during October 2010. Of these 0.27% (72,771) were generated due to files where we have a sample which has been previously labeled as malicious by an analyst. These files are part of the set of 255 thousand file samples in the detected reports in Figure 5. Similarly, we observed that 0.07% (19,952) of the reports correspond to files labeled as benign by analysts from the 578 thousand reports for which we have samples. The vast majority (20,518,412, 76.7%) of reports were due to files that were detected as malicious by the engine but not labeled by the analysts.

For the remaining reports for undetected files, we now use the telemetry classifier to predict how many of these were caused by malware and how many correspond to benign files. Similar to the system described in Section 4, we trained a telemetry classifier using the labeled samples up through October 2010 and then used it to predict the label of the unknown reports. The equal error rate for this

Table 10. Statistics for distinct files associated with telemetry reports received in October 2010

Detection Type	Malicious	Benign
Manual Labeling	72,771 (0.27%)	19,952 (0.07%)
Signature Detection	20,518,412 (76.7%)	Not Applicable
Telemetry Classifier Prediction	**4,270,521** (16.0%)	**1,867,900** (7.00%)
Total	24,861,704 (93.0%)	1,887,852 (7.1%)

version of the telemetry classifier is 5.9%. The third row of Table 10 shows that 16.0% (4,270,521) of the unknown reports are predicted to be malicious, while 7.0% (1,867,900) are predicted to involve benign files. *The telemetry classifier predicts that 69.6% (4,270,521/(4,270,521+1,867,900)) of the reports from undetected files are malicious.* Furthermore, *93% of the total reports correspond to malware.* The telemetry classifier output also allows us to estimate the efficacy of the signature detector. The table indicates that *signatures detected 82.8% (20,591,183/24,861,704) of the malicious files observed on the client computers.*

6   Discussions

We believe the results in Section 4 are quite encouraging. After conducting the experiment to measure how well the telemetry classifier can predict if the file associated with the telemetry report is malicious or benign and reviewing the results, we next set up a research web service for analysts to classify telemetry reports from client machines. The system accomplishes several tasks, namely providing a probability that a specific file is malicious given a report and generating a ranked list of the most malicious items for an analyst to review. For the first instance, the analysts can evaluate the telemetry classifier results for any file based on the SHA1 hash. In addition, the analyst has the option of evaluating the results for reports where we have samples of the file which are labeled as malicious, labeled as benign, or not currently labeled. In the latter case, the status of the file is unknown and the telemetry classifier provides an indication whether or not the file is malicious. For files that are labeled by analysts or the signature detector as malicious, reports which are predicted to be benign should be considered potential false positive (FP) candidates; FPs are particularly problematic for anti-malware products. Similarly, files which are labeled by analysts as benign but the reports are predicted to be malicious are candidates for false negatives and can be analyzed further.

Next we investigate potential methods to defeat the proposed system. The main attack vector is to cause a report to be generated in such a way that the metadata mimics the features associated with benign files (i.e. a mimicry attack), but in some cases, this is not an easy task to accomplish. For example, it would be very difficult to mimic the LS Hash of a benign file. Even if the attacker is able to some create malware with a LS Hash similar to a benign file, other features will help discriminate the malware from the legitimate file. For example, malware often tries to masquerade as legitimate software by copying legitimate signatures and certificate authorities. If the certificates are determined to be invalid by the AM engine, this provides a very strong hint to the telemetry classifier that the file is indeed malicious.

Another issue to consider is the accuracy of the reports analyzed in the previous section. For the results in Table 10, we consider all reports deemed malicious by signature detection to be generated by malware. Although relatively rare, false positives in the signatures lead to an increase in the number of reported detections. In this case, we will overestimate the effectiveness of the signature detection.

7 Related Work

The Microsoft Security Intelligence Report (SIR) [24] provides estimates of the number of detected malicious files for different malware families. The telemetry reports used to make the estimates in the SIR are the same as those used in this paper. As noted earlier, this report is based on known signature detections and does not attempt to estimate the amount of *unknown* malware.

Commercial software vendors have recently started using application and URL reputation to determine if an application or URL is malicious. For example, current versions of Symantec's security products [7], [8] and Microsoft's Internet Explorer [14] both employ telemetry reports to infer a file's reputation. The key observation is that as more users run an application or visit a URL, these entities can be considered more trustworthy. Applications which are only utilized by a few individuals are more likely to be malware. In this paper, we do not use the number of instances a particular SHA1 has been seen in the telemetry data so that we can try to detect zero-day attacks. Waiting some period of time to build a reputation could cause the system to miss many instances of a single polymorphic attack. An alternate version of our system could also be implemented with reputation data to better predict if an application is benign. In addition, earlier systems [7], [8] appear to utilize telemetry reports to build a reputation, but these papers do not attempt to classify the reports directly as proposed in this work.

Security researchers have written many papers on malware classification, and a recent survey of techniques used to detect malware is given in [16]. Most of the features used in the telemetry classifier are determined by static analysis of the file. As such, the telemetry classifier is closely related to early work in static malware classification of executable binaries. Schultz *et al.* [30] train classifiers to distinguish between malware and benign files based on three different feature sets (DLLs, strings, executable byte sequences). In [22], Kolter and Maloof train several different classifiers based on *n*-grams of executable byte code sequences as features, among others.

There have been several in-depth malware analysis systems which have been developed over the years and could be utilized in Figure 1 including Anubis [17],[4], BitBlaze [32], and BAP [6]. Clustering and classification of the results of static analysis of files has been previously proposed for prefiltering for in-depth file analysis [18], [26], [34]. Our work differs in that we classify telemetry reports for files with analyzed on remote computers. Oberheide *et al.* [27] propose running simple clients on remote machines and transmitting the files to a backend service to be analyzed by a suite of commercial malware products. This work differs from the system described in this paper in that the entire file is not transmitted to the backend. Instead malware is detected by classifying the metadata in the telemetry reports.

8   Conclusions

For the first time, we estimate the total number of infected files including unknown files which have been predicted to be malicious using our telemetry report classifier. Based on a sample population of 50 million computers, we estimate that 93% of the files observed in the telemetry in October 2010 are malicious. While this estimate is somewhat biased, it confirms our suspicion that malware is a serious problem. We are somewhat encouraged that the current signatures have identified 82.8% of the known and predicted malware; we feel that this percentage could have been much worse, and the telemetry classifier allows us to measure our progress.

New AV signatures cannot be automatically generated using the proposed system: the false positive rate is too high. However we believe this telemetry classifier can serve several useful purposes including monitoring the current AV signature detection rates, automatically requesting samples, and ranking unknown files for more in-depth automated classification. The consequences of an FP are low: a user may be prompted to submit an unknown file which turns out to be benign or the in-depth analysis system spends a few minutes investigating a benign file. These outcomes can be minimized by only selecting files for analysis which are predicted to be malicious with a high probability.

Acknowledgments.   We   thank   Misha   Bilenko,   Matthew   Richardson, Ofer Dekel, and Galen Andrew for providing some of the machine learning algorithms used in this study. We also thank the anonymous reviewers for their insightful comments.

References

1. Andrew, G., Gao, J.: Scalable training of l1-regularized log-linear models. In: Proc. of the 24th International Conference on Machine Learning (ICML), Corvalis, OR, pp. 33–40. ACM, New York (2007)
2. Bayer, U., Habibi, I., Balzarotti, D., Kirda, E., Kruegel, C.: A view on current malware behaviors. In: Proc. of 2nd USENIX Workshop on Large-Scale Exploits and Emergent Threats (LEET), Boston, MA, USA (2009)
3. Bayer, U., Comparetti, P.M., Hlauschek, C., Kruegel, C., Kirda, E.: Scalable, behavior-based malware clustering. In: Proc. of the 16th Annual Network and Distributed System Security Symposium (NDSS), San Diego, CA (February 2009)

4. Bayer, U., Kruegel, C., Kirda, E.: TTAnalyze: A tool for analyzing malware. In: Proc. of 15th Annual Conference of the European Institute for Computer Antivirus Research, EICAR (2006)
5. Bishop, C.: Pattern Recognition and Machine Learning. Springer (2006)
6. Brumley, D., Jager, I., Avgerinos, T., Schwartz, E.J.: BAP: A Binary Analysis Platform. In: Gopalakrishnan, G., Qadeer, S. (eds.) CAV 2011. LNCS, vol. 6806, pp. 463–469. Springer, Heidelberg (2011)
7. Nachenberg, C., Seshadri, V., Ramzan, Z.: An analysis of real-world effectiveness of reputation-based security. In: Proc. of Virus Bulletin Conference, VB, pp. 178–183 (2010)
8. Chau, D.H., Nachenberg, C., Wilhelm, J., Wright, A., Faloutsos, C.: Polonium: Tera-scale graph mining and inference for malware detection. In: Proc. of SIAM International Conference on Data Mining, SDM (2011)
9. Christodorescu, M., Jha, S., Kruegel, C.: Mining specifications of malicious behavior. In: Proc. of the 6th Joint Meeting of the European Software Engineering Conference and the ACM SIGSOFT Symposium on the Foundations of Software Engineering (ESEC/FSE), pp. 5–14 (2007)
10. Edelman, B.: Adverse selection in online "trust" certifications. In: Fifth Workshop on the Economics of Information Security, pp. 26–28 (2006)
11. Freund, Y., Schapire, R.: Large margin classification using the perceptron algorithm. Machine Learning, 277–296 (1999)
12. Friedman, J.: Greedy function approximation: a gradient boosting machine. Annals of Statistics, 1189–1232 (2001)
13. Group, A.P.W.: Phishing activity trends report, 3rd quarter 2009 (2010), http://www.antiphishing.org/reports/apwg_report_Q3_2009.pdf
14. Haber, J.: Smartscreen application reputation in ie9 (2011), http://blogs.msdn.com/b/ie/archive/2011/05/17/smartscreen-174-application-reputation-in-ie9.aspx
15. Hu, W., Liao, Y., Vemuri, V.R.: Robust support vector machines for anomaly detection. In: Proc. 2003 International Conference on Machine Learning and Applications (ICMLA), pp. 23–24 (2003)
16. Idika, N., Mathur, A.: A survey of malware detection techniques. Tech. rep., Purdue Univ. (February 2007), http://www.eecs.umich.edu/techreports/cse/2007/CSE-TR-530-07.pdf
17. Iseclab: Anubis, analyzing unknown binaries, http://anubis.iseclab.org
18. Jacob, G., Comparetti, P.M., Neugschwandtner, M., Kruegel, C., Vigna, G.: A static, packer-agnostic filter to detect similar malware samples. In: Conference on Detection of Intrusions and Malware & Vulnerability Assessment, DIMVA (2012)
19. Jang, J., Brumley, D., Venkataraman, S.: Bitshred: feature hashing malware for scalable triage and semantic analysis. In: Proc. of the 18th ACM Conference on Computer and Communications Security (CCS), pp. 309–320 (2011)
20. Jiang, X., Wang, X., Xu, D.: Stealthy malware detection through vmm-based "out-of-the-box" semantic view reconstruction. In: Proc. of the ACM Conference on Computer and Communications Security (CCS), pp. 128–138 (2007)
21. Kirda, E., Kruegel, C., Banks, G., Vigna, G., Kemmerer, R.A.: Behavior based spyware detection. In: Proc. of the 15th USENIX Security Symposium, pp. 273–288 (2006)
22. Kolter, J., Maloof, M.: Learning to detect and classify malicious executables in the wild. Journal of Machine Learning Research (JMLR), 2721–2744 (2006)
23. Manning, C.D., Raghavan, P., Schütze, H.: An Introduction to Information Retrieval. Cambridge University Press (2009)

24. Microsoft: Microsoft security intelligence report (July-December 2010) (2011), http://www.microsoft.com/security/sir/default.aspx
25. Moser, A., Kruegel, C., Kirda, E.: Limits of static analysis for malware detection. In: Proc. of the 23rd Annual Computer Security Applications Conference (AC-SAC), pp. 421–430 (2007)
26. Neugschwandtner, M., Comparetti, P.M., Jacob, G., Kruegel, C.: Forecast – skimming off the malware cream. In: 27th Annual Computer Security Applications Conference, ACSAC (2011)
27. Oberheide, J., Cooke, E., Jahanian, F.: Cloudav: N-version antivirus in the network cloud. In: Proc. of the 17th Conference on Security Symposium, pp. 91–106 (2008)
28. Perdisci, R., Lanzi, A., Lee, W.: Mcboost: Boosting scalability in malware collection and analysis using statistical classification of executables. In: Proc. of the 2008 Annual Computer Security Applications Conference (ACSAC), pp. 301–310 (2008)
29. Preda, M., Christodorescu, M., Jha, S., Debray, S.: A semantics-based approach to malware detection. In: Proc. of the 34th Annual ACM SIGPLAN-SIGACT Symposium on Principles of Programming Languages, pp. 377–388 (2007)
30. Schultz, M., Eskin, E., Zadok, E., Stolfo, S.: Data mining methods of detection of new malicious executables. In: Proc. of the 2001 IEEE Symposium on Security and Privacy (SP), pp. 38–49. IEEE Press, New York (2001)
31. Shalev-Shwartz, S., Singer, Y., Srebro, N.: Pegasos: Primal estimated sub-gradient solver for svm. In: Proc. of the 24th International Conference on Machine Learning (ICML), Corvalis, OR, pp. 807–814. ACM, New York (2007)
32. Song, D., Brumley, D., Yin, H., Caballero, J., Jager, I., Kang, M.G., Liang, Z., Newsome, J., Poosankam, P., Saxena, P.: BitBlaze: A New Approach to Computer Security via Binary Analysis. In: Sekar, R., Pujari, A.K. (eds.) ICISS 2008. LNCS, vol. 5352, pp. 1–25. Springer, Heidelberg (2008)
33. Stolfo, S., Wang, K., Li, W.: Towards stealthy malware detection. In: Christodorescu, M., Jha, S., Maughan, D., Song, D., Wang, C. (eds.) Malware Detection. Springer (2007)
34. Wicherski, G.: pehash: A novel approach to fast malware clustering. In: USENIX Workshop Large-Scale Exploits and Emergent Threats, LEET (2009)
35. Zhang, B., Yin, J., Hao, J., Zhang, D., Wang, S.: Malicious Codes Detection Based on Ensemble Learning. In: Xiao, B., Yang, L.T., Ma, J., Muller-Schloer, C., Hua, Y. (eds.) ATC 2007. LNCS, vol. 4610, pp. 468–477. Springer, Heidelberg (2007)
36. Zhang, J., Jin, R., Yang, Y., Hauptmann, A.G.: Modified logistic regression: An approximation to svm and its applications in large-scale text categorization. In: Proc. of the 20th International Conference on Machine Learning (ICML), Menlo Park, pp. 888–895 (2003)

Abstraction-Based Malware Analysis Using Rewriting and Model Checking

Philippe Beaucamps[1], Isabelle Gnaedig[2], and Jean-Yves Marion[1]

[1] Université de Lorraine, LORIA, UMR 7503, Vandoeuvre-lès-Nancy, F-54506, France
[2] Inria, Villers-lès-Nancy, F-54600, France
{Philippe.Beaucamps,Isabelle.Gnaedig,Jean-Yves.Marion}@loria.fr

Abstract. We propose a formal approach for the detection of high-level malware behaviors. Our technique uses a rewriting-based abstraction mechanism, producing abstracted forms of program traces, independent of the program implementation. It then allows us to handle similar behaviors in a generic way and thus to be robust with respect to variants. These behaviors, defined as combinations of patterns given in a signature, are detected by model-checking on the high-level representation of the program. We work on unbounded sets of traces, which makes our technique useful not only for dynamic analysis, considering one trace at a time, but also for static analysis, considering a set of traces inferred from a control flow graph. Abstracting traces with rewriting systems on first order terms with variables allows us in particular to model dataflow and to detect information leak.

Keywords: Malware, behavioral detection, behavior abstraction, trace, term rewriting, model checking, first-order temporal logic, finite state automaton, formal language.

1 Introduction

Behavior analysis was introduced by Cohen's seminal work [1] to detect malware and in particular unknown malware. In general, a behavior is described by a sequence of system calls and recognition uses the formalism of finite state automata [2,3,4,5]. New approaches have been proposed recently. In [6,7], malicious behaviors are specified by temporal logic formulas with parameters and detection is carried out by model-checking. However, these approaches are tightly dependent on the way malicious actions are realized: using any other system facility to realize an action allows a malware to go undetected. This has motivated yet another approach where a malicious behavior is specified as a combination of high-level actions, in order to be independent from the way these actions are realized and to only consider their effect on a system. In [8] and in [9], a captured execution trace is transformed into a higher-level representation capturing its semantic meaning, i.e., the trace is first abstracted before being compared to a malicious behavior. In [10], the authors propose to use attribute automata, at the price of an exponential time complexity detection. These dynamic abstraction-based

S. Foresti, M. Yung, and F. Martinelli (Eds.): ESORICS 2012, LNCS 7459, pp. 806–823, 2012.

approaches, though they can detect unknown viruses whose execution traces exhibit known malicious behaviors, only deal with a single execution trace.

In this paper, we propose a formal approach for high-level behavior analysis, with the following features. Underpinned by language theory, term rewriting and first-order temporal logic, it allows us to determine whether a program exhibits a high-level behavior. Detection is achieved in two steps. First, traces of the program are abstracted in order to reveal the sequences of high-level functionalities they realize. Then, abstracted traces are compared with the behavior formula, using usual model-checking techniques. Functionalities have parameters representing the manipulated data, so our formalism is adapted to the protection against generic threats like the leak of sensitive information.

Our goal here is not to provide a ready-made software to detect behaviors, but to propose a formal framework emphasizing fundamental detection mechanisms, which are independent of implementation-based solutions.

Our approach has two main characteristics. First, we work on an unbounded set of traces representing the behavior of a program, in order to consider a more complete representation of the program than with a single trace. To deal with the infinity of the set of traces, we restrict to regular sets and safely approximate the set of abstract traces, so that we detect in linear time whether a program exhibits a given behavior. Second, we work on abstract forms of traces, in order to only keep the essence of the functions performed by the program, to be independent of their possible implementations and to be generic with respect to behavior mutations. Behavior components are abstracted in program traces, by identifying known functionalities and marking them by inserting abstract functionality symbols.

By working on sets of traces, which may consist of a single trace as well as of an unbounded number of traces, our approach may be used not only for classical, dynamic behavior analysis, but also for static behavior analysis i.e., behavior analysis in a static analysis setting.

Static behavior analysis by abstraction is more challenging than its dynamic counterpart because, precisely, this approach needs to abstract a program behavior potentially representing an infinite set of execution traces. The construction of an exhaustive representation of a program behavior is an intractable problem in general: in particular, a program flow may not be easily followed due to indirect jumps, and a program may use complex code protection, for instance by dynamically modifying its code or by using obfuscation. Self modification is usually tackled by emulating the program long enough to deactivate most code protections. Indirect jumps and obfuscation are usually handled by abstract interpretation [11,12] or symbolic execution [13].

Static behavior analysis has many advantages and applications. First, it allows us to analyze the behavior of a program in a more exhaustive way, as it analyzes the unbounded set of the program execution traces, or an approximation of it. Second, static behavior analysis can complement classical, dynamic, behavior analysis with an analysis of the future behavior, to prevent damages when some critical point is reached in an execution.

An interesting application of static behavior analysis is the audit of programs in high-level technologies, like mobile applications, browser extensions, web page scripts, .NET or Java programs. Auditing these programs is complex and mostly manual, resulting in highly publicized infections [14,15]. In this context, static analysis can provide an appropriate help, because it is usually easier than for usual programs, especially when additionally enforcing a security policy (e.g. prohibiting self-modification [16]) or when enforcing strict development guidelines (e.g. for iPhone applications).

To our knowledge, the use of behavior abstraction on top of static behavior analysis has not been investigated so far. As our detection mechanism relies on satisfaction of temporal logic formulas, it is akin to model checking [17], for which there already exist numerous frameworks and tools [18,19,20]. The specificity of our approach, however, is that, rather than being applied on the set of program traces, verification is applied on the set of abstract forms of these traces, which is not computable in general. Accordingly, we identify a property of practical high-level behaviors allowing us to approximate this set, in a sound and complete way with respect to detection, and then to apply classical verification techniques.

Our abstraction framework can be used in two scenarios:

- *Detection of given behaviors*: signatures of given high-level behaviors are expressed in terms of abstract functionalities. Given some program, we then assess whether one of its execution traces exhibits a sequence of known functionalities, in a way specific to one of the given behaviors. This can be applied to detection of suspicious behaviors. Although detection of such suspicious behaviors may not suffice to label a program as malicious, it can be used to supplement existing detection techniques with additional decision criteria.
- *Analysis of programs*: abstraction provides a simple and high-level representation of a program behavior, which is more suitable than the original traces for manual analysis, or for analysis of behavior similarity with known behaviors, etc. For instance, it could be used to detect not necessarily harmful behaviors, in order to get a basic understanding of the program and to further investigate if deemed necessary. It could also be used to automatically discover sequences of high-level functionalities and their dataflow dependencies, exhibited by a program.

Previous Work. In [21], we already proposed to abstract program sets of traces with respect to behavior patterns, for detection and analysis. We tested our approach on samples of malicious programs collected using a honeypot[1] and identified using Kaspersky Antivirus. These samples belonged to known malware families, like Allaple, Virut, Agent, Rbot, Afcore and Mimail. Most of them were successfully matched to our malware database.

But patterns were defined by string rewriting systems, which did not allow the actions composing a trace to have parameters, precluding dataflow analysis. Moreover, abstraction rules replaced identified patterns by abstraction symbols

---

[1] The honeypot of the Loria's High Security Lab: http://lhs.loria.fr

in the original trace, precluding a further detection of patterns interleaved with the rewritten ones.

The formalism proposed in this paper addresses both issues: first, we handle interleaved patterns by keeping the identified patterns when abstracting them. Second, we extend the rewriting framework to express data constraints on action parameters by using term rewriting systems. An important consequence is that, unlike in [21], using the dataflow, we can detect information leaks in order to prevent unauthorized disclosure or modifications of information.

2   Background

Term Algebras. Let $S = \{Trace, Action, Data\}$ be a set of sorts, $\mathcal{F} = \mathcal{F}_t \cup \mathcal{F}_a$ $\cup \mathcal{F}_d$ be a finite S-sorted signature, where $\mathcal{F}_t$, $\mathcal{F}_a$, $\mathcal{F}_d$ are mutually distinct and:

- $\mathcal{F}_t = \{\epsilon, \cdot\}$ is the set of the trace constructors, where $\epsilon :\to Trace$ denotes the empty trace, . has profile $Data\ Trace \to Trace$;
- $\mathcal{F}_a$ is a set of function symbols or constants, with profile $Data^n \to Action$, $n \in \mathbb{N}$, describing actions;
- $\mathcal{F}_d$ is a set of data constructors, with profile $\to Data$ or $Data^n \to Data$, $n \in \mathbb{N}$.

Let $\mathbb{N}_+^*$ be the set of finite strings of positive natural numbers, called *positions*. The empty string is denoted by λ, and $u \le v$ means that u is prefix of v. Let X be a set of S-sorted variables. A S-sorted *term* over $(\mathcal{F}, X)$ is a partial function $t : \mathbb{N}_+^* \to \mathcal{F} \cup X$, such that the domain of definition of t, denoted by $\mathcal{P}os(t)$, is finite and satisfies, for $w \in \mathbb{N}_+^*$ and $i \in \mathbb{N}$: (1) $wi \in \mathcal{P}os(t) \Rightarrow w \in \mathcal{P}os(t)$, (2) $w \in \mathcal{P}os(t) \Rightarrow t(w) \in \mathcal{F} \cup X$. $\mathcal{P}os(t)$ is called the set of positions of t. We denote by $T(\mathcal{F}, X)$ (resp. $T(\mathcal{F})$) the set of S-sorted terms over $(\mathcal{F}, X)$ (resp. the set of finite ground terms over $\mathcal{F}$). For any sort $s \in S$, and any of the above sets of terms T we denote by T_s *the restriction* of T to terms of sort s and by X_s *the subset of variables* of X of sort s. For a term t with $p \in \mathcal{P}os(t)$, we denote by $t|_p$ the subterm of t at position p. We denote by $t[t']_p$ the term obtained by replacing by t' the *subterm* at position p in t. We use the abbreviated notation $\overline{x}$ for variables $x_1, \dots, x_n$. So $\overline{x} \in X$ stands for $x_1, \dots, x_n \in X$, and if $f \in \mathcal{F}$ is a symbol of arity $n \in \mathbb{N}$, we denote by $f(\overline{x})$ the term $f(x_1, \dots, x_n)$.

The elements of $T_{\text{Trace}}(\mathcal{F})$ are called *traces*, the elements of $T_{\text{Action}}(\mathcal{F})$ are called *actions*. We distinguish the sort Action from the sort Trace but, for a sake of readability, we may denote by a the trace $\cdot(a, \epsilon)$, for some action a. Similarly, we use the $\cdot$ symbol with infix notation and right associativity, and ϵ is understood when the context is unambiguous. For instance, if a, b, c are actions, $a \cdot b \cdot c$ denotes the trace $\cdot(a, \cdot(b, \cdot(c, \epsilon)))$.

We partition $\mathcal{F}_a$ in a set Σ of symbols, denoting concrete program-level actions, and a set Γ, denoting abstract actions identifying abstracted functionalities. To construct purely concrete (resp. abstract) terms, we use $\mathcal{F}_\Sigma = \mathcal{F} \setminus \Gamma$ (resp. $\mathcal{F}_\Gamma = \mathcal{F} \setminus \Sigma$). The *projection* $t|_{\Sigma'}$, also denoted $\pi_{\Sigma'}(t)$, of a trace t on an alphabet $\Sigma' \subseteq \mathcal{F}_a$ corresponds to keeping in a trace only actions from Σ'. If X is a set of variables of sort $Data$, we define the projection on an alphabet $\Sigma' \subseteq \mathcal{F}_a$ of a term $t \in T_{\text{Trace}}(\mathcal{F}, X)$, denoted by $\pi_{\Sigma'}(t)$ or, equivalently, by $t|_{\Sigma'}$, in the following way:

$$\pi_{\Sigma'}(\epsilon) = \epsilon$$
$$\pi_{\Sigma'}(b \cdot u) = \begin{cases} b \cdot \pi_{\Sigma'}(u) & \text{if } b \in T_{\text{Action}}(\mathcal{F}_{\Sigma'}, X) \\ \pi_{\Sigma'}(u) & \text{otherwise} \end{cases}$$

with $b \in T_{\text{Action}}(\mathcal{F}, X)$ and $u \in T_{\text{Trace}}(\mathcal{F}, X)$. The projection is naturally extended to sets of traces.

We define in a natural way the *concatenation* $t \cdot t'$ of two traces t and t'. The concatenation of two terms t and t' of $T_{\text{Trace}}(\mathcal{F}, X)$, where X is a set of S-sorted variables and $t \notin X$, is denoted by $t \cdot t' \in T_{\text{Trace}}(\mathcal{F}, X)$ and defined by $t \cdot t' = t[t']_p$, where p is the position of ϵ in t, i.e., $t|_p = \epsilon$. Projection and concatenation are naturally extended to sets of terms of sort Trace. We also extend concatenation to $2^{T_{\text{Trace}}(\mathcal{F}, X)} \times 2^{T_{\text{Trace}}(\mathcal{F}, X)}$ with $L \cdot L' = \{t \cdot t' \mid t \in L, t' \in L'\}$ and to $2^{T_{\text{Trace}}(\mathcal{F}, X)} \times T_{\text{Action}}(\mathcal{F}, X)$ with $L \cdot a = L \cdot \{a \cdot \epsilon\}$.

Substitutions are defined as usual. A *ground substitution* on a finite set X of S-sorted variables is a mapping $\sigma : X \to T(\mathcal{F})$ such that: $\forall s \in S, \forall x \in X_s, \sigma(x) \in T_s(\mathcal{F})$. σ can be naturally extended to a mapping $T(\mathcal{F}, X) \to T(\mathcal{F})$ in such a way that:

$$\forall f(t_1, \ldots, t_n) \in T(\mathcal{F}, X),$$
$$\sigma(f(t_1, \ldots, t_n)) = f(\sigma(t_1), \ldots, \sigma(t_n)) \ .$$

By convention, we denote by $t\sigma$ or by $\sigma(t)$ the application of a substitution σ to a term $t \in T(\mathcal{F}, X)$ and by $L\sigma$ the application of σ to a set of terms $L \subseteq T(\mathcal{F}, X)$. The *set of ground substitutions* over X is denoted by $Subst_X$.

Program Behavior. The representation of a program is chosen to be its set of traces. When executing a program, the captured data is represented on the alphabets Σ, denoting the concrete actions, and $\mathcal{F}_d$, describing the data. In this paper, we consider that the captured data is the library calls along with their arguments. Σ therefore represents the finite set of library calls, while terms built on $\mathcal{F}_d$ identify the arguments and the return values of these calls. A *program execution trace* then consists of a sequence of library calls and is defined by a term of $T_{\text{Trace}}(\mathcal{F}_\Sigma)$. A *program behavior* is defined by the set of its execution traces, that is a possibly infinite subset of $T_{\text{Trace}}(\mathcal{F}_\Sigma)$. For instance, the term $fopen(1, 2) \cdot fwrite(1, 3)$ represents the execution trace of a file open call $fopen(1, 2)$ followed by a file write call $fwrite(1, 3)$, where $1 \in \mathcal{F}_d$ identifies the file handle returned by $fopen$, $2 \in \mathcal{F}_d$ identifies the file path and $3 \in \mathcal{F}_d$ identifies the written data.

First-Order Linear Temporal Logic (FOLTL).   We consider the First-Order Logic (FOLTL) defined in [17], without the equality predicate, where the set of atomic predicates AP is a set of terms with variables in a set X. FOLTL is an extension of the LTL Logic (see also [17]) such that:

- If φ is an LTL formula, then φ is an FOLTL formula;
- If φ is an FOLTL formula and $Y \subseteq X$ is a set of variables, then: $\exists Y.\varphi$ and $\forall Y.\varphi$ are FOLTL formulas, where as usual: $\forall Y.\varphi \equiv \neg\exists Y.\neg\varphi$.

Notation $\varphi_1 \odot \varphi_2$ stands for $\varphi_1 \wedge \mathbf{X}\left(\top \mathbf{U} \varphi_2\right)$.

We say that a FOLTL formula is *closed* when it has no free variable, i.e., every variable is bound by a quantifier.

Let $Y \subseteq X$ be a set of variables of sort *Data* and $\sigma \in Subst_Y$ be a ground substitution over Y. The *application of* σ to an FOLTL formula φ is naturally defined by the formula $\varphi\sigma$ where any free variable x in φ which is in Y has been replaced by its value $\sigma\left(x\right)$.

A formula φ is *satisfied* on infinite sequences of sets of ground instances of atomic predicates, denoted by $\xi = (\xi_0, \xi_1, \ldots)$. $\xi \models \varphi$ (ξ satisfies φ) is defined in the same way as for the LTL logic, with the additional rule: $\xi \models \exists Y.\varphi$ iff there exists $\sigma \in Subst_Y$ such that $\xi \models \varphi\sigma$.

In our context, a formula is satisfied over traces of $T_{\text{Trace}}\left(\mathcal{F}\right)$ identified with sequences of singleton sets of atomic predicates. A finite trace $t = a_0 \cdots a_n$ is identified with the infinite sequence of sets of atomic predicates $\xi_t = (\{a_0\}, \ldots, \{a_n\}, \{\}, \{\}, \ldots)$, and t satisfies φ, denoted by $t \models \varphi$, iff $\xi_t \models \varphi$.

We consider two distinct instances of this logic, depending on the fact that we consider concrete traces or abstract traces. We denote by FOLTL_Σ the FOLTL logic, where the set of atomic predicates is $AP_\Sigma = T_{\text{Action}}\left(\mathcal{F}_\Sigma, X\right)$ and ξ is in $\left(2^{T_{\text{Action}}(\mathcal{F}_\Sigma)}\right)^\omega$. We denote by FOLTL_Γ the FOLTL logic, where the set of atomic predicates is $AP_\Gamma = T_{\text{Action}}\left(\mathcal{F}_\Gamma, X\right)$ and ξ is in $\left(2^{T_{\text{Action}}(\mathcal{F}_\Gamma)}\right)^\omega$.

Note that in practice, to express behaviors, we only use FOLTL formulas that are negations of safety properties. We do not use properties with liveness aspects, which would note make sense on finite traces. Using FOLTL on finite traces allows us a correct balance between behavior expressivity and decidability.

Tree automata and tree transducers are defined as usual [22].

3   Behavior Patterns

The problem under study can be formalized in the following way. First, using FOLTL formulas, we define a set of behavior patterns, where each pattern represents a (possibly infinite) set of terms from $T_{\text{Trace}}\left(\mathcal{F}_\Sigma\right)$. Second, we need to define a terminating abstraction relation R allowing to schematize a trace by abstracting occurrences of the behavior patterns in that trace. Finally, given some program p coming with an infinite set of traces L (static analysis scenario, for instance by using the control flow graph, see our previous work [21] and [23,24]), we formulate the *detection problem* in the following way. Let $L{\downarrow}_R$ be the set of normal forms of traces of L for R i.e., the set of abstracted traces of L, using R. Given an abstract behavior M defined by an FOLTL formula φ, does there exist a trace t in $L{\downarrow}_R$ such that $t \models \varphi$? Our goal is then to find an effective and efficient method solving this problem.

A behavior pattern describes a functionality we want to recognize in a program trace, like writing to system files, sending a mail or pinging a remote host. Such a functionality can be realized in different ways, depending on which system calls, library calls or programming languages it uses.

We describe a functionality by an FOLTL formula, such that traces satisfying this formula are traces carrying out the functionality.

Example 1. Let us consider the functionality of sending a ping. One way of realizing it consists in calling the *socket* function with the parameter IPPROTO_ICMP describing the network protocol and, then, calling the *sendto* function with the parameter ICMP_ECHOREQ describing the data to be sent. Between these two calls, the socket should not be freed. This is described by the FOLTL formula: $\varphi_1 = \exists x, y.\, socket\,(x, \alpha) \wedge (\neg closesocket\,(x)\; \mathbf{U}\; sendto\,(x, \beta, y))$, where the first parameter of *socket* is the created socket and the second parameter is the network protocol, the first parameter of *sendto* is the used socket, the second parameter is the sent data and the third one is the target, the unique parameter of *closesocket* is the freed socket and constants α and β in $\mathcal{F}_\mathrm{d}$ identify the above parameters IPPROTO_ICMP and ICMP_ECHOREQ.

A ping may also be realized using the function *IcmpSendEcho*, whose parameter represents the ping target. This corresponds to the FOLTL formula: $\varphi_2 = \exists x.\, IcmpSendEcho\,(x)$.

Hence, the ping functionality may be described by the FOLTL formula: $\varphi_\mathrm{ping} = \varphi_1 \vee \varphi_2$.

We then define a behavior pattern as the set of traces carrying out its functionality i.e., satisfying the formula describing the functionality.

Definition 1. *A* behavior pattern *is a set of traces* $B \subseteq T_\mathrm{Trace}\,(\mathcal{F}_\Sigma)$ *satisfying a closed* FOLTL$_\Sigma$ *formula* φ: $B = \{t \in T_\mathrm{Trace}\,(\mathcal{F}_\Sigma) \mid t \models \varphi\}$.

4   Trace Abstraction

As said before, our goal is to be able to detect, in a given set of traces, some predefined behavior composed of combinations of high-level functionalities. For this, we associate to each behavior pattern an abstract symbol λ taken in the alphabet Γ, called abstraction symbol. An abstract behavior is then defined by combinations of abstraction symbols associated to behavior patterns, using an FOLTL formula φ on $AP_\Gamma = T_\mathrm{Action}\,(\mathcal{F}_\Gamma, X)$ instead of $AP_\Sigma = T_\mathrm{Action}\,(\mathcal{F}_\Sigma, X)$.

Definition 2. *An* abstract behavior *is a set of traces* $M \subseteq T_\mathrm{Trace}\,(\mathcal{F}_\Gamma)$ *satisfying a closed* FOLTL$_\Gamma$ *formula* φ_M: $M = \{t \in T_\mathrm{Trace}\,(\mathcal{F}_\Gamma) \mid t \models \varphi_M\}$. *When M is defined by a formula φ_M, we write:* $M := \varphi_M$.

Example 2. The abstract behavior of sending a ping to a remote host can then be trivially defined by the formula: $\varphi_M = \exists x.\, \mathbf{F}\, \lambda_\mathrm{ping}\,(x)$.

In the following, for the sake of simplicity, the initial $\mathbf{F}$ operator is implicit in definitions of abstract behaviors.

Now, let L be the set of program traces we want to analyze. To compare these traces to the given abstract behavior, we have to consider the behavior pattern occurrences they may contain, at the abstract level. For this, we define an abstraction relation R, which marks such occurrences in traces by inserting an abstraction symbol λ_B when an occurrence of the behavior pattern B is identified.

From now on, if a behavior pattern is defined using an FOLTL formula φ and associated to an abstraction symbol λ, we may denote it $\lambda := \varphi$.

The abstraction symbol can have parameters corresponding to those used by the behavior pattern. This allows us to express dataflow constraints in a signature. For instance, the abstraction symbol for the ping behavior pattern can take a parameter denoting the ping target. A signature for a denial of service could then be defined, for example, as a sequence of 100 pings with the same target.

Example 3. The ping behavior pattern in Example 1 is abstracted in traces by inserting the λ_{ping} symbol after the *send* action or after the *IcmpSendEcho* action. Then, the trace $socket(1, \alpha) \cdot gethostbyname(2) \cdot sendto(1, \beta, 3) \cdot closesocket(1)$ can be abstracted into the trace $socket(1, \alpha) \cdot gethostbyname(2) \cdot sendto(1, \beta, 3) \cdot \lambda_{\text{ping}}(3) \cdot closesocket(1)$.

Thus, abstraction of a trace reveals abstract behavior pattern combinations, which may constitute the abstract behavior to be observed. We now formally define the abstraction relation.

As said above, abstracting a trace with respect to some behavior pattern amounts to transforming it when it contains an occurrence of the behavior pattern, by inserting a symbol of Γ in the trace. This symbol is inserted at the position after which the behavior pattern functionality has been performed. This position is the most logical one to stick to the trace semantics. Furthermore, when behavior patterns appear interleaved, this position allows us to define the order in which their functionalities are realized (see the full version of the paper for an example [25]).

As said in the introduction, rather than replace behavior pattern occurrences with abstraction symbols, we preserve them in order to properly handle interleaved behavior patterns occurrences. Now, let us consider the following example.

Example 4. Abstraction of the ping in Example 3 is realized by rewriting using the rule $A_1(x, y) \cdot B_1(x, y) \rightarrow A_1(x, y) \cdot \lambda(y) \cdot B_1(x, y)$, where $A_1(x, y) = socket(x, \alpha) \cdot (T_{\text{Trace}}(\mathcal{F}_\Sigma) \setminus (T_{\text{Trace}}(\mathcal{F}_\Sigma) \cdot closesocket(x) \cdot T_{\text{Trace}}(\mathcal{F}_\Sigma))) \cdot sendto(x, \beta, y)$ and $B_1(x, y) = \{\epsilon\}$, and the rule $A_2(x) \cdot B_2(x) \rightarrow A_2(x) \cdot \lambda(x) \cdot B_2(x)$, where $A_2(x) = \{IcmpSendEcho(x)\}$ and $B_2(x) = \{\epsilon\}$.

As a behavior pattern is a set of possible traces realizing a given functionality, we define the abstraction relation by decomposing the behavior pattern into a finite union of concatenations of sets $A_i(X)$ and $B_i(X)$ such that traces in $A_i(X)$ end with the action effectively performing the behavior pattern functionality. These sets $A_i(X)$ and $B_i(X)$ are composed of concrete traces only, since abstract

actions that may appear in a partially rewritten trace should not impact the
abstraction of an occurrence of the behavior pattern.

Definition 3. *Let $\lambda \in \Gamma$ be an abstraction symbol, X be a set of variables of sort
Data, $\overline{x}$ be a sequence of variables in X. An* abstraction system *on $T_{\text{Trace}}(\mathcal{F}, X)$
is a finite set of rewrite rules of the form: $A_i(X) \cdot B_i(X) \rightarrow A_i(X) \cdot \lambda(\overline{x}) \cdot B_i(X)$
where the sets $A_i(X)$ and $B_i(X)$ are sets of concrete traces of $T_{\text{Trace}}(\mathcal{F}_\Sigma, X)$.*

Dealing with sets as left(right)-hand sides of rules may seem to be heavy. In fact,
this allows us to recognize not only finitely enumerated patterns, but patterns
from languages i.e., patterns among possibly infinite sets of behaviors.

The system of rewrite rules we use generates a reduction relation on $T_{\text{Trace}}(\mathcal{F})$
such that filtering works on traces projected on Σ.

Definition 4. *The* reduction relation *on $T_{\text{Trace}}(\mathcal{F})$ generated by a system of n
rewrite rules $A_i(X) \cdot B_i(X) \rightarrow A_i(X) \cdot \lambda(\overline{x}) \cdot B_i(X)$ is the rewriting relation
$\rightarrow_\mathcal{R}$ such that, for all $t, t' \in T_{\text{Trace}}(\mathcal{F}), t \rightarrow_\mathcal{R} t'$ iff:*

$$\exists \sigma \in Subst_X, \exists p \in \mathcal{P}os(t), \exists i \in [1..n],$$
$$\exists a \in T_{\text{Trace}}(\mathcal{F}) \cdot T_{\text{Action}}(\mathcal{F}_\Sigma), \exists b, u \in T_{\text{Trace}}(\mathcal{F}),$$
$$a|_\Sigma \in A_i(X)\sigma, b|_\Sigma \in B_i(X)\sigma, t|_p = a \cdot b \cdot u$$
$$and \ t' = t[a \cdot \lambda(\overline{x})\sigma \cdot b \cdot u]_p \ .$$

An abstraction relation with respect to a given behavior pattern is thus the
reduction relation of an abstraction system, where left members of the rules
cover the set of the traces realizing the behavior pattern functionality.

Definition 5. *Let B be a behavior pattern associated with an abstraction symbol
$\lambda \in \Gamma$. Let X be a set of variables of sort Data. An* abstraction relation *w.r.t.
this behavior pattern is the reduction relation on $T_{\text{Trace}}(\mathcal{F}_\Sigma)$ generated by an
abstraction system composed of n rules $A_i(X) \cdot B_i(X) \rightarrow A_i(X) \cdot \lambda(\overline{x}) \cdot B_i(X)$
verifying:*

$$B = \bigcup_{i \in [1..n]} \bigcup_{\sigma \in Subst_X} (A_i(X) \cdot B_i(X))\sigma \ .$$

Finally, we generalize the definition of abstraction to a set of behavior patterns.

Definition 6. *Let C be a finite set of behavior patterns. An* abstraction relation
w.r.t C is the union of the abstraction relations w.r.t. the elements of C.

As we will see later, for R to be realizable by a tree transducer, the abstraction
relation R has to be terminating. However, even with a finite set of traces,
abstraction does not terminate in general, since the same occurrence of a pattern
can be abstracted an unbounded number of times. So we require that the same
abstract action is not inserted twice after the same concrete action. In other
words, if $t = t_1 \cdot t_2$ is abstracted into $t' = t_1 \cdot \alpha \cdot t_2$, where α is the inserted abstract
action, then if t_2 starts with a sequence of abstract actions, α does not appear in

this sequence. Formally, we require that: $\forall t_1, t_2 \in T_{\text{Trace}}(\mathcal{F}), \forall \alpha \in T_{\text{Action}}(\mathcal{F}_\Gamma)$, if $t_1 \cdot t_2 \to_R t_1 \cdot \alpha \cdot t_2$, then $\nexists u \in T_{\text{Trace}}(\mathcal{F}_\Gamma)$, $\nexists u' \in T_{\text{Trace}}(\mathcal{F})$, $t_2 = u \cdot \alpha \cdot u'$.

Using the above condition, supposed to be verified from now on, a behavior pattern occurrence can only be abstracted once. Furthermore, abstraction does not create new abstraction opportunities so the relation R is clearly terminating.

Remark 1. A terminating abstraction relation with respect to a set of behavior patterns is not confluent in general. We could adapt the definition of the abstraction relation to make it confluent, for instance by defining an order on the set $T_{\text{Action}}(\mathcal{F}_\Gamma)$. However, as already mentioned, detection works on normal forms. So having several normal forms for a trace does not compromise its mechanism.

In practice, a behavior pattern is regular, along with the set of instances of right-hand sides of its abstraction rules. We show that this is sufficient, with termination of the set of rules, to ensure that the abstraction relation is realizable by a tree transducer, in other words that it is a rational tree transduction. The tree transducer formalism is chosen for its interesting formal (closure by union, composition, preservation of regularity) and computational properties. When $T_{\text{Action}}(\mathcal{F})$ is finite, we can state the following result.

Theorem 1. *Let B be a behavior pattern and R be a terminating abstraction relation w.r.t. B defined by an abstraction system whose set of instances of right-hand sides of rules is recognized by a tree automaton A_R. Then R and R^{-1} are rational and, for any tree automaton A recognizing a trace language L, $R(L)$ is recognized by a tree automaton of size $O(|A| \cdot |A_R|)$.*

5   Detection Problem

Then the detection problem can be formalized as follows.

Definition 7. *A set of traces $L \subseteq T_{\text{Trace}}(\mathcal{F}_\Sigma)$ exhibits an abstract behavior M defined by a formula φ_M, denoted by $L \pitchfork M$, iff: $\exists t \in L{\downarrow}_R|_\Gamma$, $t \models \varphi_M$.*

When L is restricted to a single trace, or to a finite set of traces, like in dynamic analysis, the set $L{\downarrow}_R$ of normal forms of traces i.e., the set of traces that cannot be rewritten anymore with R, is computable since the rewrite system R is terminating. Moreover, as FOLTL quantification is performed over variables in the domain $T_{\text{Data}}(\mathcal{F})$, FOLTL verification is decidable when $T_{\text{Data}}(\mathcal{F})$ is finite. So in this case, it can be decided whether L exhibits M.

For an infinite set of finite traces L however, the computation of $L{\downarrow}_R$ often relies on the computation of the set of descendants $R^*(L)$ of L i.e., the set of all terms that can be rewritten from terms of L. But $R^*(L)$ is computable only for some classes of rewrite systems [26] and when L is regular. Unfortunately, the rewrite systems which implement the abstraction relations and which are described in Sect. 4 do not belong to any of these classes. Hence, we cannot rely on the construction of $L{\downarrow}_R$ to decide whether L exhibits M.

Nevertheless, we will see that, for behaviors considered in practice, a partial abstraction of the set of traces is sufficient i.e., computing the set of normal forms is unnecessary. We therefore propose a detection algorithm relying on a safe approximation of the set of abstract traces. This approximation must be chosen carefully. For instance, it cannot consist in computing, for some n, the set $R^{\leq n}(L)$ of descendants of L until order n, as shown by the following example.

Example 5. Let $\lambda_1 := a$, $\lambda_2 := b$, $\lambda_3 := c$ be three behavior patterns associated to abstraction relations inserting the abstraction symbol after a, b and c respectively. Let $M := \lambda_1 \wedge (\neg \lambda_2 \, \mathbf{U} \, \lambda_3)$ be an abstract behavior. Assume there exists a bound n such that $L{\downarrow}_R$ may be approximated by $R^{\leq n}(L)$ in Definition 7. The trace $t = a^{n-1} \cdot b \cdot c \cdot d$ does not exhibit the behavior M. Yet the trace $t' = (a \cdot \lambda_1)^{n-1} \cdot b \cdot c \cdot \lambda_3 \cdot d$ is in $R^{\leq n}(\{t\})$ and its projection on Γ is in M, so we would wrongly infer that t exhibits M.

The problem comes from the fact that $R^{\leq n}(L)$ contains contradictory traces compromising detection i.e., traces seemingly exhibiting an abstract behavior though a few additional abstraction steps would make them leave the signature.

Consequently, we want to exclude traces unreliably realizing the abstract behavior in $R^{\leq n}(L)$, while not having to reach normal forms. In fact, we identify a fundamental property we call (m, n)-completeness, verified by abstract behaviors in practice in the field of malware detection. This property states that, for a program to exhibit an abstract behavior, a necessary and sufficient condition is the following: there exists a partially abstracted trace, abstracted in at most m abstraction steps, realizing the behavior and whose descendants until the order n still realize it.

Definition 8. *Let M be an abstract behavior defined by a formula φ_M and m and n be positive numbers. M has the property of (m, n)-completeness iff for any set of traces $L \subseteq T_{\mathrm{Trace}}(\mathcal{F}_\Sigma)$:*

$$ L \cap M \quad \Leftrightarrow \quad \exists t' \in R^{\leq m}(L), \forall t'' \in R^{\leq n}(t')\big|_\Gamma, t'' \models \varphi_M \ . $$

We then show in the next section that, when L is regular, there exists a sound and complete detection procedure for every abstract behavior enjoying this property. Moreover, the time and space complexity of this detection procedure is linear in the size of the representation of L.

The following propositions show that the (m, n)-completeness property is realistic for abstract behaviors considered in practice.

We first prove, for particular abstract behaviors describing sequences of abstract actions with no constraints other than dataflow constraints, that we have the property of (m, n)-completeness.

Proposition 1. *Let Y be a set of variables of sort Data.*
Let $\alpha_1, \ldots, \alpha_m \in T_{\mathrm{Action}}(\mathcal{F}_\Gamma, Y)$. Then the abstract behavior $M := \exists Y. \alpha_1 \odot \alpha_2 \odot \ldots \odot \alpha_m$ has the property of $(m, 0)$-completeness.

Proofs of propositions and theorems can be found in [25].

We now show that more complex abstract behaviors, forbidding specific abstract actions, have this property.

For a behavior pattern λ, let R_λ denote the restriction of the abstraction relation R to abstraction with respect to λ. We say that two behavior patterns λ and λ' are *independent* iff: $R_\lambda \circ R_{\lambda'} = R_{\lambda'} \circ R_\lambda$. Then we get the following result.

Proposition 2. *Let* $M := \exists Y. \lambda_1(\overline{x_1}) \wedge \neg(\exists Z. \lambda_2(\overline{x_2}))$ **U** $\lambda_3(\overline{x_3})$ *be an abstract behavior where* Y *and* Z *are two disjoint sets of variables of sort Data,* $\overline{x_1}, \overline{x_3} \in Y$, $\overline{x_2} \in Z$, *and where* $\lambda_2 \neq \lambda_1$, $\lambda_2 \neq \lambda_3$ *and* λ_2 *is independent from* λ_3. *Then* M *has the property of* $(2, 1)$-*completeness.*

In practice, as illustrated in Sect. 7, most signatures are disjunctions of formulas of the form: $\exists Y. \alpha_1 \odot \alpha_2 \odot \ldots \odot \alpha_m$, from Proposition 1, or of the form:

$$\exists Y. \lambda_1\,(\overline{x_1}) \wedge \neg\,(\exists Z_1. \lambda\,(\overline{z_1}))\ \mathbf{U}\ \lambda_2\,(\overline{x_2}) \wedge \neg\,(\exists Z_2. \lambda\,(\overline{z_2}))\ \mathbf{U}\ \ldots \lambda_k\,(\overline{x_k})$$

where λ is independent from λ_2, ..., λ_k. From the proof of Proposition 2, we conjecture that the last formula has the property of $(k, 1)$-completeness.

The independence condition is not necessary in general, in order to guarantee that such abstract behaviors have a property of (m, n)-completeness for some m and n, but absence of this condition results in significantly higher values of m and n.

Fundamentally, by Definition 7, detection of an abstract behavior is decomposed into two independent steps: an abstraction step followed by a verification step. The first step computes the abstract forms of the program traces while the second step applies usual verification techniques in order to decide whether one of the computed traces verifies the FOLTL formula defining the abstract behavior. However, when using the (m, n)-completeness property to bypass the general intractability of the abstraction step, this relies on computing a set $\left\{ t \in T_{\mathrm{Trace}}\,(\mathcal{F}),\ R^{\leq n}(t) \models \varphi_M \right\}$ and then intersecting it with $R^{\leq m}(L)$. So we lose the previous decomposition, thereby preventing us from leveraging powerful techniques from the model checking theory. We therefore show that, in the previous proposition, (m, n)-completeness allows us to nonetheless preserve that decomposition, so that the abstraction step now becomes decidable.

Theorem 2. *Let* M *be an abstract behavior defined by a formula* $\varphi_M = \exists Y.$ $\lambda_1(\overline{x_1}) \wedge \neg(\exists Z. \lambda_2(\overline{x_2}))\,\mathbf{U}\,\lambda_3(\overline{x_3})$ *where* Y *and* Z *are disjoint sets of variables of sort Data,* $\overline{x_1}, \overline{x_3} \in Y$, $\overline{x_2} \in Z$, *and where* $\lambda_2 \neq \lambda_1$, $\lambda_2 \neq \lambda_3$ *and* λ_2 *is independent from* λ_3. *Then, for any set of traces* $L \subseteq T_{\mathrm{Trace}}\,(\mathcal{F}_\Sigma)$, L *exhibits* M *iff:*

$$\exists t \in R_{\lambda_2}\!\downarrow (R^{\leq 2}(L))\big|_\Gamma,\ t \models \varphi_M\ .$$

When both the abstraction relation R and the relation $R_{\lambda_2}\!\downarrow$ are rational, the set $R_{\lambda_2}\!\downarrow (R^{\leq 2}(L))$ is computable and regular, and detection then boils down to a classical model checking problem. In the general case, $R_{\lambda_2}\!\downarrow$ is not *rational*, but in our experimentations, the behavior pattern λ_2 is defined by sets A_i and B_i where A_i contains traces made of a single action and $B_i = \{\epsilon\}$. Thus constructing a transducer realizing the relation $R_{\lambda_2}\!\downarrow$ is straightforward.

Remark 2. An equivalent definition of infection could consist in compiling the abstract behavior, that is computing the set $\pi_\Gamma^{-1}(M)\!\downarrow_{R^{-1}}$ of concrete traces exhibiting M. Then a set of traces L would exhibit M iff one of its traces is in this set. This definition seems more intuitive: rather than abstracting a trace and comparing it to an abstract behavior, we check whether this trace is an implementation of the behavior. However, this approach would require to first compute the compiled form of the abstract behavior, $\pi_\Gamma^{-1}(M)\!\downarrow_{R^{-1}}$, which is not generally computable and whose representation can quickly have a prohibitive complexity stemming from the interleaving of behavior patterns occurrences (especially when traces realizing the behavior patterns are complex) and from the variable instantiations.

6   Detection Complexity

The detection problem, like the more general problem of program analysis, requires computing a partial abstraction of the set of analyzed traces. In practice, in order to manipulate this set, we consider a regular approximation of it i.e., a tree automaton. Moreover, in practice, as seen in Sect. 4, the abstraction relation is rational, which entails the decidability of detection.

Theorem 3. *Let R be an abstraction relation, such that R and R^{-1} are rational. There exists a detection procedure deciding whether L exhibits M, for any regular set of traces $L \subseteq T_{\mathrm{Trace}}(\mathcal{F}_\Sigma)$ and for any regular abstract behavior M having the property of (m,n)-completeness for some positive integers m and n.*

Definition 9. *Let M be an abstract behavior having the property of (m,n)-completeness. The set of traces n-reliably realizing M w.r.t an abstraction relation R is the set $\{t \in T_{\mathrm{Trace}}(\mathcal{F}) \mid \forall t' \in R^{\leq n}(t)|_\Gamma, t' \models \varphi_M\}$.*

Using the set of traces n-reliably realizing M, when $T_{\mathrm{Action}}(\mathcal{F})$ is finite, we get the following detection complexity, which is linear in the size of the automaton recognizing the program set of traces, a major improvement on the exponential complexity bound of [10].

Theorem 4. *Let R be an abstraction relation such that R and R^{-1} are rational. Let τ be a tree transducer realizing R. Let M be a regular abstract behavior with the property of (m,n)-completeness and A_M be a tree automaton recognizing the set of traces n-reliably realizing M w.r.t. R. Deciding whether a regular set of traces L, recognized by a tree automaton A, exhibits M takes $O\left(|\tau|^{m\cdot(m+1)/2} \times |A| \times |A_M|\right)$ time and space.*

7   Information Leak Behaviors

Abstraction can be applied to detection of generic threats, and in particular to detection of sensitive information leak. Such a leak can be decomposed into two steps: capturing sensitive information and sending this information to an exogenous location. The captured data can be keystrokes, passwords or data read from a sensitive network location, while the exogenous location can be the network, a removable device, etc. Thus, we define a behavior pattern $\lambda_{\text{steal}}(x)$, representing the capture of some sensitive data x, and a behavior pattern $\lambda_{\text{leak}}(x)$, representing the transmission of x to an exogenous location. Moreover, since the captured data must not be invalidated before being leaked, we define a behavior pattern $\lambda_{\text{inval}}(x)$, which represents such an invalidation.

Finally, the captured data is usually not leaked in its raw form, so we take into account transformations of this data via the behavior pattern $\lambda_{\text{depends}}(x, y)$ which denotes a dependency of x on y. For instance, x may be a string representation of y, or x may be an encryption or an encoding of y.

Then, in order to account for one such transformation of the stolen data, we define the information leak abstract behavior:

$$M := \exists x, y.\, \lambda_{\text{steal}}(x) \wedge \neg \lambda_{\text{inval}}(x) \, \mathbf{U} \, \lambda_{\text{depends}}(y, x) \wedge \, \mathbf{U} \, \lambda_{\text{leak}}(y) \ .$$

We consider the following definitions of the four behavior patterns involved, after looking at several malware samples, like keyloggers, sms message leaking applications or personal information stealing mobile applications:

– keystroke capture functionality:

$$\lambda_{\text{steal}}(x) := GetAsyncKeyState(x) \vee$$
$$(RegisterDev(\texttt{KBD}, \texttt{SINK}) \odot GetInputData(x, \texttt{INPUT}))$$
$$\vee (\exists y.\, SetWindowsHookEx(y, \texttt{WH\_KEYBOARD\_LL}) \wedge$$
$$\neg UnhookWindowsHookEx(y) \, \mathbf{U} \, HookCalled(y, x))$$
$$\vee \exists y. TelephonyManager\_getDeviceId(x, y)$$

– network send functionality:

$$\lambda_{\text{leak}}(x) := \exists y, z.\, sendto(z, x, y) \vee \exists y, z.\, (connect\,(z, y) \wedge \neg close(z)$$
$$\mathbf{U}\, send(z, x)) \vee \exists c, s.\, HttpURLConnection\_getOutputStream(s, c) \wedge$$
$$\neg OutputStream\_close(s) \mathbf{U}\, OutputStream\_write(s, x)$$

– overwriting or freeing:

$$\lambda_{\text{inval}}(x) := free(x) \vee \exists y.\, sprintf_0(x, y) \vee GetInputData(x, \texttt{INPUT}) \vee \ldots$$

– dependences:

$$\lambda_{\text{depends}}(x, y) := sprintf_0(x, y) \vee \exists s.\, sprintf_1(x, s, y)$$
$$\vee \exists sb.\, StringBuilder\_append(sb, y) \odot SB\_toString(x, sb) \ .$$

8   Experiments

Our goal is to detect the information leak behavior M defined in the previous section. In order to perform behavior pattern abstraction and behavior detection in the presence of data, we use the CADP toolbox [19], which allows us to manipulate and model-check communicating processes written in the LOTOS language. CADP features a verification tool, which allows on-the-fly model checking of formulas expressed in the MCL language, a fragment of the modal mu-calculus extended with data variables, whose FOLTL logic used in this paper is a subset.

We first represent the program set of traces as a CADP process, using a program control flow graph obtained by static analysis (see [21] and [23,24]). Regularity of the set of traces is enforced by limiting recursion and inlining function calls, an approximation that can be deemed safe with respect to the abstract behaviors to detect. Note that there are two shortcomings to regular approximation. First, approximation of conditional branches by nondeterministic branches may result in false positives, especially when the program code is obfuscated. And second, failure to identify data correlations during dataflow analysis can result in false negatives. However, this does not significantly impact our detection results.

Now, as expressed in Theorem 2, detection of the information leak abstract behavior M can be broken down into two steps: abstracting the set of traces L by computing $R_{\lambda_{\mathrm{inval}}} \downarrow \left(R^{\leq 2}(L) \right)$ and then verifying whether an abstracted trace matches the abstract behavior formula.

So, we can simulate the abstraction step in CADP and delegate the verification step to the *evaluator4* module. For this, we represent the set of traces L of a given program by a system of communicating processes expressed in LOTOS, with a particular gate on which communications correspond to library calls. Then, computation of $R^{\leq 2}(L)$ is performed by synchronization with another LOTOS process which simulates the transducer realizing the abstraction. Moreover, the relation $R_{\lambda_{\mathrm{inval}}} \downarrow$ is rational and can also be simulated by process synchronization in CADP.

For each malware sample we tested, we successfully ran *evaluator4* on the resulting process representing $R_{\lambda_{\mathrm{inval}}} \downarrow \left(R^{\leq 2}(L) \right)$, in order to detect the information leak abstract behavior defined in the previous section.

We essentially applied our approach to two case studies. The first one comes from a study on the detection rate of keylogger programs by existing antivirus [27], which shows a high failure rate. For an example of a typical keylogger for test, see [25]. From different keyloggers written in C for Windows, we constructed abstract behaviors of keylogger features. Then, tests we ran on keyloggers to know whether we are able to detect information leaking were successful.

Another example comes from an Android application for cell-phone named `SMS_Replicator_Secret`, which forwards received SMS to the attacker. This application defines a class `SMSReceiver` with a particular method `OnReceive` (`Context context, Intent intent`). It then requests Android systems through its file metadata, to execute `OnReceive` on each SMS received or sent. We extracted from this application abstract behaviors corresponding to SMS leaks. Unlike the previous case study, we ran partial tests because of the difficulty to set up an Android platform. They were successful.

9 Conclusion

We presented an original approach for detecting high-level behaviors in programs, describing combinations of functionalities and defined by first-order temporal logic formulas. Behavior patterns, expressing concrete realizations of functionalities, are also defined by first-order temporal logic formulas. Abstraction of these functionalities in program traces is performed by term rewriting. Validation of the abstracted traces with respect to some high-level behavior is performed via usual model checking techniques. In order to address the general intractability of the problem of constructing the normal form trace set for a given program, we have identified a property of practical high-level behaviors allowing us to avoid computing normal forms and yielding a linear time detection algorithm.

Abstraction is a key notion of our approach. Providing an abstracted form for program traces and behaviors allows us to be independent of the program implementation and to handle similar behaviors in a generic way, making this framework robust with respect to variants. The fact that high-level behaviors are combinations of elementary patterns enables us to efficiently summarize and compact the possible combinations likely to compose suspicious behaviors. Moreover, high-level behaviors and behavior patterns are easy to update since they are expressed in terms of basic blocks.

Our approach is at an early stage. We think that the theoretical results on behavioral analysis presented here are promising. Applicability of our detection technique could be further enhanced by automating construction of reference behavior patterns, for example using mining techniques as in [28].

Acknowledgements. We would like to thank Stephan Merz for fruitful discussions on temporal logics.

References

1. Cohen, F.: Computer viruses: Theory and experiments. Computers and Security 6(1), 22–35 (1987)
2. Le Charlier, B., Mounji, A., Swimmer, M.: Dynamic detection and classification of computer viruses using general behaviour patterns. In: International Virus Bulletin Conference, pp. 1–22 (1995)
3. Sekar, R., Bendre, M., Dhurjati, D., Bollineni, P.: A fast automaton-based method for detecting anomalous program behaviors. In: IEEE Symposium on Security and Privacy, pp. 144–155. IEEE Computer Society (2001)
4. Morales, J., Clarke, P., Deng, Y., Kibria, G.: Characterization of virus replication. Journal in Computer Virology 4(3), 221–234 (2007)

5. Bergeron, J., Debbabi, M., Desharnais, J., Erhioui, M., Lavoie, Y., Tawbi, N.: Static detection of malicious code in executable programs. In: Symposium on Requirements Engineering for Information Security (2001)
6. Kinder, J., Katzenbeisser, S., Schallhart, C., Veith, H.: Detecting Malicious Code by Model Checking. In: Julisch, K., Kruegel, C. (eds.) DIMVA 2005. LNCS, vol. 3548, pp. 174–187. Springer, Heidelberg (2005)
7. Singh, P.K., Lakhotia, A.: Static verification of worm and virus behavior in binary executables using model checking. In: Information Assurance Workshop, pp. 298–300. IEEE Computer Society (2003)
8. Martignoni, L., Stinson, E., Fredrikson, M., Jha, S., Mitchell, J.C.: A Layered Architecture for Detecting Malicious Behaviors. In: Lippmann, R., Kirda, E., Trachtenberg, A. (eds.) RAID 2008. LNCS, vol. 5230, pp. 78–97. Springer, Heidelberg (2008)
9. Bayer, U., Milani Comparetti, P., Hlauscheck, C., Kruegel, C., Kirda, E.: Scalable, Behavior-Based Malware Clustering. In: 16th Symposium on Network and Distributed System Security, NDSS (2009)
10. Jacob, G., Debar, H., Filiol, E.: Malware Behavioral Detection by Attribute-Automata Using Abstraction from Platform and Language. In: Balzarotti, D. (ed.) RAID 2009. LNCS, vol. 5758, pp. 81–100. Springer, Heidelberg (2009)
11. Preda, M.D., Christodorescu, M., Jha, S., Debray, S.: A semantics-based approach to malware detection. In: 34th Annual ACM SIGPLAN-SIGACT Symposium on Principles of Programming Languages, pp. 377–388. ACM (2007)
12. Kinder, J., Zuleger, F., Veith, H.: An Abstract Interpretation-Based Framework for Control Flow Reconstruction from Binaries. In: Jones, N.D., Müller-Olm, M. (eds.) VMCAI 2009. LNCS, vol. 5403, pp. 214–228. Springer, Heidelberg (2009)
13. Brumley, D., Hartwig, C., Kang, M.G., Liang, Z., Newsome, J., Poosankam, P., Song, D.: BitScope: Automatically dissecting malicious binaries. Technical Report CS-07-133, School of Computer Science, Carnegie Mellon University (2007)
14. Security Issue on AMO, http://blog.mozilla.com/addons/2010/02/04/please-read-security-issue-on-amo
15. Aftermath of the Droid Dream Android Market Malware Attack, http://nakedsecurity.sophos.com/2011/03/03/droid-dream-android-market-malware-attack-aftermath/
16. Yee, B., Sehr, D., Dardyk, G., Chen, J.B., Muth, R., Ormandy, T., Okasaka, S., Narula, N., Fullagar, N.: Native client: A sandbox for portable, untrusted x86 native code. In: 30th IEEE Symposium on Security and Privacy (S&P 2009), pp. 79–93. IEEE Computer Society (2009)
17. Kröger, F., Merz, S.: Temporal Logic and State Systems. Texts in Theoretical Computer Science. An EATCS Series. Springer (2008)
18. Holzmann, G.J.: The SPIN Model Checker: Primer and Reference Manual. Addison-Wesley Professional (2003)
19. Garavel, H., Lang, F., Mateescu, R., Serwe, W.: CADP 2010: A Toolbox for the Construction and Analysis of Distributed Processes. In: Abdulla, P.A., Leino, K.R.M. (eds.) TACAS 2011. LNCS, vol. 6605, pp. 372–387. Springer, Heidelberg (2011)
20. Chen, F., Roşu, G.: MOP: An Efficient and Generic Runtime Verification Framework. In: Object-Oriented Programming, Systems, Languages and Applications, pp. 569–588. ACM (2007)

21. Beaucamps, P., Gnaedig, I., Marion, J.-Y.: Behavior Abstraction in Malware Analysis. In: Barringer, H., Falcone, Y., Finkbeiner, B., Havelund, K., Lee, I., Pace, G., Roşu, G., Sokolsky, O., Tillmann, N. (eds.) RV 2010. LNCS, vol. 6418, pp. 168–182. Springer, Heidelberg (2010)
22. Comon, H., Dauchet, M., Gilleron, R., Löding, C., Jacquemard, F., Lugiez, D., Tison, S., Tommasi, M.: Tree automata techniques and applications (2007), http://www.grappa.univ-lille3.fr/tata
23. Christodorescu, M., Jha, S., Seshia, S.A., Song, D., Bryant, R.E.: Semantics-aware malware detection. In: IEEE Symposium on Security and Privacy, pp. 32–46. IEEE Computer Society (2005)
24. Kirda, E., Kruegel, C., Banks, G., Vigna, G., Kemmerer, R.: Behavior-based Spyware Detection. In: Proceedings of the 15th USENIX Security Symposium (2006)
25. Beaucamps, P., Gnaedig, I., Marion, J.Y.: Behavior Analysis of Malware by Rewriting-based Abstraction - Extended Version. HAL-INRIA Open Archive Number inria-00594396 (2011)
26. Gilleron, R., Tison, S.: Regular Tree Languages and Rewrite Systems. Fundamenta Informaticae 24, 157–176 (1995)
27. Devine, C., Richaud, N.: A study of anti-virus' response to unknown threats. In: 18th Conference of the European Institute for Computer Anti-Virus Research, EICAR (2009)
28. Christodorescu, M., Jha, S., Kruegel, C.: Mining specifications of malicious behavior. In: 6th Joint Meeting of the European Software Engineering Conference and the ACM SIGSOFT Symposium on the Foundations of Software Engineering, pp. 5–14. ACM (2007)

Detecting Phishing Emails the Natural Language Way

Rakesh Verma[1], Narasimha Shashidhar[2], and Nabil Hossain[3]

[1] Department of Computer Science, University of Houston
rmverma@cs.uh.edu
[2] Department of Computer Science, Sam Houston State University
karpoor@shsu.edu
[3] Division of Science, Mathematics, and Computing, Bard College
nh1682@bard.edu

Abstract. Phishing causes billions of dollars in damage every year and poses a serious threat to the Internet economy. Email is still the most commonly used medium to launch phishing attacks [1]. In this paper, we present a comprehensive natural language based scheme to detect phishing emails using features that are invariant and fundamentally characterize phishing. Our scheme utilizes all the *information* present in an email, namely, the header, the links and the text in the body. Although it is obvious that a phishing email is designed to elicit an action from the intended victim, none of the existing detection schemes use this fact to identify phishing emails. Our detection protocol is designed specifically to distinguish between "actionable" and "informational" emails. To this end, we incorporate natural language techniques in phishing detection. We also utilize contextual information, when available, to detect phishing: we study the problem of phishing detection within the contextual confines of the user's email box and demonstrate that context plays an important role in detection. To the best of our knowledge, this is the first scheme that utilizes natural language techniques and contextual information to detect phishing. We show that our scheme outperforms existing phishing detection schemes. Finally, our protocol detects phishing at the email level rather than detecting masqueraded websites. This is crucial to prevent the victim from clicking any harmful links in the email. Our implementation called **PhishNet-NLP**, operates between a user's mail transfer agent (MTA) and mail user agent (MUA) and processes each arriving email for phishing attacks even before reaching the inbox.

1 Introduction

Phishing is a social engineering threat aimed at gleaning sensitive information from unsuspecting victims. Attacks are typically carried out via communication channels such as email or instant messaging by attackers masquerading as legitimate and trustworthy entities. In this paper, we focus only on email communication as it is the most popular medium to launch such attacks [1]. As observed

S. Foresti, M. Yung, and F. Martinelli (Eds.): ESORICS 2012, LNCS 7459, pp. 824–841, 2012.

before [2], detecting phishing email messages automatically is a non-trivial task. Our primary contribution in this paper is a comprehensive and effective natural language based phishing detection scheme. Our scheme uses the information present in the email header, text in the email body and the links embedded in the email. We make use of novel techniques to process the header and link information, and deeper natural language techniques to process the text information. To the best of our knowledge, this is the first natural language based scheme for phishing detection.

Natural language processing (NLP) by computers is well-recognized to be a very challenging task because of the inherent ambiguity and rich structure of natural languages. Perhaps this explains why previous researchers have not used NLP techniques for email phishing detection. Despite this difficulty, we show that our scheme outperforms all existing phishing detection strategies in the literature and obtains a phishing detection rate of 97% or better with very low false positives (0.7-0.8%). Our scheme is built on the observation that the fundamental difference between a phishing and a legitimate email lies in its objective. While a legitimate email typically conveys some information to the reader, a phishing email is designed to *elicit* a response. This response often involves making the reader click a link with the intention of obtaining personal sensitive information. None of the detection schemes in the literature make use of this distinction to detect phishing emails. Our scheme is designed specifically to distinguish between "actionable" and "informational" emails. We focus on objectives that are typical of phishing emails - language that intends to create a sense of urgency, threat, worry, concern or offers an incentive to the user to perform an action. Our scheme uses contextual information (when available) to detect phishing. We study the problem of phishing detection within the contextual confines of the user's mail box and show that context plays a significant role in detection. We show that contextual phishing detection outperforms many other non-contextual detection schemes in the literature and is the first contextual scheme to the best of our knowledge. Moreover, the use of context information makes our scheme robust against attacks that are aware of our methods.

Finally, we believe in detecting phishing at the email level rather than detecting fraudulent and masqueraded websites after the website has been visited by the user. Our implementation PhishNet-NLP operates between a user's MTA and MUA and processes each arriving email for phishing attacks. This prevents the user from clicking any harmful link in the email. This approach is in contrast to schemes that analyze the target websites for authenticity. The motivation to operate at the email level is due to the fact that clicking on the link and visiting a phishing website exposes the user to potential malware that could be installed by the website. Furthermore, it is our objective to maximize the *distance* between the user and the phisher - clicking a malicious link puts the user closer to the threat. The added advantage of this approach is that ISPs and email providers may now be able to prevent such emails from being delivered to the user thereby saving precious bandwidth as well.

2 Prior Work

Phishing is primarily a social engineering attack and has attracted a lot of research interest in this context. Different research groups have studied this problem from various perspectives: server-side and browser-side strategies, education/training, evaluation of anti-phishing tools, detection schemes and finally studies that analyze the reasons behind the success of phishing attacks. We note that phishing has been studied extensively. Here, for lack of space, we briefly outline the prior related work on phishing categorized by research objectives.

Phishing Detection Schemes - Email and Web pages. There are two primary classifications of phishing detection schemes: schemes that detect phishing based on analyzing the content of the target web pages (targets of the embedded email links) and schemes that operate directly on the content of the emails. The schemes for detecting phishing attacks (email and web pages) in the literature can be broadly classified into three categories: 1. Schemes based on information retrieval, 2. Machine learning based techniques and 3. String, pattern and visual matching based detection schemes. Before the advent of such schemes, the most popular (and still a widely-deployed solution) was the integration of blacklist-based anti-phishing techniques into browsers. Ludl et al. [3] tested the effectiveness of the blacklists maintained by Google and Microsoft to understand the viability of this approach, and found that blacklist-based solutions are effective and useful components in the fight against phishing. On the other hand, it has also been shown that blacklists are ineffective for protecting users from phishing attacks *initially* and that their effectiveness increases with time [4].

Phishing Detection Over Web page Content. A typical approach to detect phishing using web page content is analyzing the structure of the URLs and validating the authenticity of the content of these target web pages. Cantina [5,6] is one such scheme: a content-based approach to detecting phishing websites based on information retrieval and text mining algorithms. A research team from Google has presented a machine learning technique to accomplish a large scale automatic classification of phishing web pages [7] by analyzing both the URL and the content of the page and achieves 90% accuracy in classifying web pages.

Phishing Detection Using URL analysis. [8] and [9] proposed schemes that identify phishing URLs by analyzing only the structure of the links and not the content of the target web pages. In [8], the authors describe several features that can be used to distinguish a phishing URL from that of a benign URL. They use these features to model a logistic regression filter and show that it has high accuracy in detecting phishing emails. The algorithm of [9], LinkGuard, uses the phishing data provided by the APWG to extract generic characteristics of hyperlinks embedded in phishing emails. It successfully detected 195 out of the 203 phishing attacks.

Phishing Detection Over Email Content. Most phishing detection schemes that operate at the email level use machine learning techniques on a feature set designed to highlight user-targeted deception in electronic communication [10,11,12,13,14,15]. A statistical classifier is trained on a set of features extracted from the email content and structure over the training data. After the training, this classifier is used to detect phishing emails from the email stream. These detection schemes differ both in the number and type of features used in the training process. These statistical filters can either be installed on the server or the client side. One of the important maintenance aspects of a machine learning phishing detection scheme is that these filters need to be updated on a regular basis. [16] presents a comparison of machine learning techniques for phishing detection. PhishCatch is a heuristic algorithm (not based on machine learning) proposed by [17] which performs header, link and a cursory text analysis (scanning for the presence of certain text filters) of incoming emails. In [2], the authors study the evolution of phishing email messages and develop a classification of phishing messages into two groups: *flash* and *non-flash* attacks, and classify phishing features into *transitory* and *pervasive*. For more details on phishing and detection schemes, the reader is encouraged to refer the books by [18,19] and [20].

3   Definitions and Tools

3.1   TF-IDF

In information retrieval, TF-IDF (Term Frequency-Inverse Document Frequency) is a weight used to determine the importance of a word to a document in a collection of documents. The importance of a word increases proportionally to the number of times a word appears in the document (term frequency) and is inversely proportional to the document frequency of the word in the collection. The IDF is a measure of the discriminating power of the term. It measures how common a term is across an entire collection of documents. Thus, a term has a high TF-IDF weight by having a high term frequency in a given document and a low document frequency in the whole collection of documents. For more details about TF-IDF, refer to the book by [21].

3.2   Natural Language Preliminaries

Despite the difficulty of natural language processing on computers, due to the inherent ambiguity and rich structure of natural languages, our approach to email text processing employs the following NLP techniques: lexical analysis, part-of-speech tagging, named entity recognition, normalization of words to lower case, stemming and stopword removal. The goal of lexical analysis is to split the email into sentences and each sentence into words. The part-of-speech tagging phase tags each word with its part-of-speech, viz., noun, verb, etc. Named entity recognition tags the named entities in the email, which are nouns that name either person, location or organization. Words are converted to lower case in a normalization phase. The goal of stemming is to reduce each word form to its root or stem. For example, the verb *acting* is reduced to *act*. A popular program for stemming is the Porter Stemmer [22]. The aim of stopword removal is to remove common words such as *it, a, an, the,* etc. For this purpose a stopword list is used. We also use semantic NLP techniques, viz., word-sense disambiguation and WordNet, as opposed to purely syntactic or statistical ones based on feature counting. The *sense* or meaning of a word depends on its context. For instance the word "plant" could mean a factory in one context and could mean a tree in another context. The goal of word-sense disambiguation is to find the appropriate sense of a word based on the context.

3.3   WordNet

According to Fellbaum [23], WordNet combines features of both a dictionary and a thesaurus. The building block in WordNet is a *synset* (a set of synonyms), which consists of all the words that express a given concept, and the basic semantic relation in WordNet is synonymy. The semantic relation that is the most important in *organizing* nouns into a hierarchy is the hyponymy relation between synsets. Hyponymy is the relation of subordination (or class inclusion or subsumption). For example, the word "poodle" is a hyponym of the word "dog" since a poodle is a kind of dog, and "dog" is the hypernym of "poodle." Miller writes ([23] page 26): "Since a noun usually has a single hypernym, lexicographers include it in the definition." The key point to be noted is that although the hypernymy relation is defined on synsets in WordNet, and hence it could happen that a synset can have more than one hypernym, this situation is not frequent for nouns[1]. However, for verbs the situation is quite different and the hyponymy structure is not even acyclic [24]. The relation between verbs to other verbs is used by PhishNet-NLP.

We use the hyponymy relation between verbs, which is defined as follows: A is a *hypernym* of B if the meaning of A encompasses the meaning of B (B is called the *hyponym*). All nouns in WordNet are stored in a graph (that is close to a tree) that represents the hypernymy hierarchy. The word *entity* is the root of the tree, because it is believed to encompass the meaning of all other nouns. Traversing down the tree manifests more specific nouns as shown in Figure 1 of a small portion of the hypernymy tree. All verbs in WordNet are arranged in a hypernymy graph as well, but for verbs this graph is "forest-like" but not a forest due to the presence of cycles.

---

[1] We do take care of the situation in which there are multiple hypernyms as explained in the Text Analysis subsection 4.1.

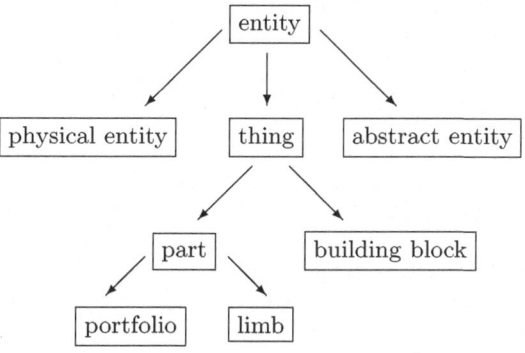

| A | Word A. Nodes are not actually words, but short collections of words, called synsets. |

| A ⟶ B | A is a hypernym of B. B is a hyponym of A. |

Fig. 1. A tiny WordNet hypernymy tree

We need to invoke our word sense disambiguation software before we can call the WordNet program. The reason is that a synset is designed to refer to a single concept and hence we need to disambiguate words in the document to find the correct synset for a noun. As mentioned above, the word "plant" could mean a factory in one context and could mean a tree in another context. Hence the word plant would be found in two different synsets in this case.

4 Phishing Detection Algorithm: PhishNet-NLP

PhishNet-NLP is a comprehensive scheme that makes use of all the information present in an email, except attachments, to ascertain which class it belongs to: phishing or legitimate. The first step in the protocol is parsing: PhishNet-NLP accepts an incoming email from the MTA and proceeds to parse it into its constituent components: header, links and text. If the email is HTML encoded, as indicated by the header, we further decode the HTML email body to plain text to perform further analysis. Having obtained the header, links and text, we proceed to analyze each component through their respective classifiers as discussed below. PhishNet-NLP then proceeds to perform majority voting on the scores obtained from the header, link and text analysis classifiers to determine whether an email is legitimate or phish. The reason for using majority voting as opposed to considering certain weight factors for each of the individual classifiers

Input: SMTP server name, user name, password
Output: Label for each email: Phishing or Legitimate
1 Fetch email from SMTP server
2 **if** *(new email downloaded)* **then**
3   **foreach** *email e* **do**
4   header h = extractHeader();
5   **if** *(h indicates that e is HTML encoded)* **then**
6   decodedEmail dE=HTMLDecode(e);
7   **end**
8   parsedEmail pE = emailParser(dE);
9   headerScore = headerAnalysis(header);
10   linkScore = linkAnalysis(links);
11   textScore = textAnalysis(text);
12   cs = combineScore(headerScore, linkScore, textScore);
13   **if** $cs \geq 2$ **then**
14   Output Label: Phishing
15   **end**
16   **else**
17   Output Label: Legitimate
18   **end**
19   **end**
20 **end**

Algorithm 1. PhishNet-NLP: Phishing Detection Algorithm

is to assign an equal importance to each of the classifiers. The first author has proved that under the assumption of independence, the majority voting approach has better coverage (accuracy) than that of each individual classifier whenever each classifier in the combination has better than a 50% coverage (accuracy). Majority voting also avoids the following two vexing problems: (i) how to compute optimal weights, which requires a training corpus, and (ii) the optimal weight combination is likely to be different for different corpus and users. Algorithm 1 shows an outline of PhishNet-NLP. We begin our discussion of PhishNet-NLP with our novel text analysis classifier and then discuss the header and link analysis classifiers respectively.

4.1 Text Analysis

The goal of email text analysis is to classify the email into two classes: informational and actionable. This is done by analyzing the email text and giving a score to the email called Textscore. The overall approach of PhishNet-NLP is designed for maximum flexibility and efficiency. When the "context" information of an email is available, PhishNet-NLP will use the context to generate a score called Contextscore for the email as well. The context of an email is defined to be the other saved emails of the user, this includes both sent and received emails. For efficiency purposes, the user is given full control over PhishNet-NLP's context analysis option: whether or not to use context analysis, the context size to use for context analysis, and the date at which the context starts. Context size could be specified in two ways: number of emails or a date range. When the context option is used, then the two scores - the Contextscore and the Textscore are combined logically.[2]

To generate the Textscore of the email, we employ a semantics-based method since phishing emails are typically short and designed to hide their sinister purpose and appear innocuous to the user. Hence, applying syntactic techniques, such as sentence position, or purely statistical approaches, such as word frequencies, to email text analysis are likely to prove suboptimal.

Our semantic approach to email text processing employs the following NLP techniques: lexical analysis, part-of-speech (POS) tagging, named entity recognition, normalization of words to lower case, stemming and stopword removal. Stopword removal will include removal of common suffixes such as Jr., Sr., II, etc., after names (named entities) and prefixes such as titles (Dr., Prof., Mr., Ms., etc.). The novelty of PhishNet-NLP consists in deeper word analysis by extracting important words from the email text, tagging them with their senses based on the surrounding contexts of the words, and using these to query Word-Net. These distinguished words are called *keywords*. The sense of the word is used in locating the word in the WordNet hypernymy tree and to generate a score for the word as described below. We employ SenseLearner [25] for word sense disambiguation, and TextRank keyword extraction for identifying the important words of the email text [26]. SenseLearner was trained using the SemCor 2.1 database, which was compiled using WordNet 2.1.

For a user u, let Basic-Names(u) denote the lower-case versions of u's last name, first name, middle name(s) if any, and their common spelling variants. This set can be initialized by the user. Let $Names(u)$ denote all permutations of words from Basic-Names(u) taken two at a time, three at a time, and so on until |Basic-Names(u)| at a time. For an email text, e, let Named-entity(e), denote the set of named entities in e ignoring only the greeting part of the email, which can be identified easily as a sentence fragment using parsing or heuristics such as missing verb and presence of named-entity from $Names(u)$. If |Named-entity(e)$-$Names(u)| = 0, then email e receives a Textscore of 0 (a score of 1 represents phishing and 0 stands for legitimate). The reason is that a phishing email is very likely to mention at least one institution in the body of the email. Now, assume that |Named-entity(e)$-$Names(u)| $\geq$ 1. Since we are interested in determining the extent to which an email is actionable, we score certain verbs in the body of the email. If the email contains no text, we mark it as phishing, since this means the email has either links or attachments only and legitimate email senders usually write a few words to explain the links or attachments that they are sending out.

---

[2] The reason for these options is that the user may wish to restrict context analysis when they have a large mail box with lots of emails unprocessed by our context analysis routine, since for a large unprocessed mail box, context analysis will take more time, which the user may not have. In such a case the user can be warned that the context analysis is using limited information and could be less precise.

Let $V = \{$*click, follow, visit, go, update, apply, submit, confirm, cancel, dispute, enroll*$\}$. To each word in the set V, the appropriate verb sense (denoted by #v at the end of the word in WordNet) is attached. For any set X containing words along with a sense for each word, let $Synset(X) = \{synset(x) \mid x \in X\}$, where $synset(x)$ is the WordNet synset of x for the specified sense. For natural number $i \geq 1$, let $Hypo^i(Synset(V))$ denote the union of all the synsets reached by following up to i hyponymy links from the synsets in $Synset(V)$. We let $SV = Hypo^4(Synset(V))$ be the set of special verbs. Note that the WordNet verb hierarchy is not a tree structure and is not even acyclic [24], which means that following hyponymy links must be done together with cycle detection. Let $SA = Synset(\{$*here, there, herein, therein, hereto, thereto, hither, thither, hitherto, thitherto*$\})$ with each word in this set SA having the adverb sense, $U = \{$*now, nowadays, present, today, instantly, straightaway, straight, directly, once, forthwith, urgently, desperately, immediately, within, inside, soon, shortly, presently, before, ahead, front*$\}$ (words conveying a sense of urgency), and $D = \{$*above, below, under, lower, upper, in, on, into, between, besides, succeeding, trailing, beginning, end, this, that, right, left, east, north, west, south*$\}$, the set of direction words. These words were chosen mainly based on the authors' experience with the phishing emails that they have received in the past, and a scan of about 20 (0.4%) emails in the phishing database.

To motivate the above definitions, consider a phishing email in which the bad link appears in the top right-hand corner of the email and the email (among other things) directs the reader to "click the link above."

The score of verb $v \in SV$,

$$score(v) = \{1 + x(l + a)\}/2^L.$$

The parameter $x = 1$ if the sentence containing v also contains either a word from $SA \cup D$, and, either a link or the word "url," "link," or "links" appears in the same sentence; otherwise, $x = 0$. The parameter $l = 2$ if the email has two or more links, $l = 1$ if the email has one link, and $l = 0$ if there are no links in the email. The parameter $a = 1$ if there is a word from U or a mention of *money* in the sentence containing v, otherwise $a = 0$. We include money since phishers often lure targets by promising them a sum of money if they complete a survey, or by stating that someone tried to withdraw a sum of money from the user's bank account recently, etc. The parameter L is the level of the verb, where *level* of a verb in SV is one more than the least number of hyponymy links followed to reach the verb from a synset in $Synset(V)$.

The reason for weighting the link score of the email (l) and the urgency or incentive score (a) of the sentence with a directive to take action (x) with respect to a link is to reduce the false positives for emails that acknowledge some previous action of the user, or for emails received by user A that are replies to emails sent by A and contain a link in either A's signature included in the reply or in the signature of the sender of the reply. For example, when someone submits a proposal or report to FastLane, an automatic acknowledgment is sent by the website and it usually includes a link. We are aware of several instances in which emails contain links in the signature fields. The reason for the exponential decay with L is the diversity of verbs and the proliferation of their different senses at greater distances from SV, which leads to an increase in the imprecision of word-sense disambiguation. Even without this complexity, word-sense disambiguation is a challenging problem due to the ambiguity inherent in natural languages. The Textscore of an email e is given by $Textscore(e) = Max\{score(v) \mid v \in e\}$. We also experimented with the average score of the scores of all verbs with a nonzero score, but this function gave inferior results in our experiments.

Contextscore. For the Contextscore, we treat the email as a vector of TF-IDF [21] values *in the semantics space as opposed to traditional syntactic techniques* after stopword elimination and stemming. Note that the TF-IDF scheme converts a vector of words to a vector of real values using the product of term frequency and inverse document (for our purposes this is the email) frequency as mentioned above in Section 3. WordNet is again employed for this purpose after POS tagging and word sense disambiguation. Words belonging to the same synset are represented by a common word in the vector. For instance, different forms of the same verb "is", "was", etc. are represented by the common verb "to be" and also different verbs with the same sense and meaning such as "is" and "exists", etc., are also represented by the verb "to be." Then, we perform similarity computation between the email vector ev and the corresponding vector for each email in the context, say ec. For the similarity computation we adopt the cosine measure, $Similarity(ev, ec) = cosine\ \theta$, where θ is the angle between the two vectors. The smaller the θ, the bigger is the similarity between two emails. Finally, $Contextscore(ev) = max_{ec \in C} Similarity(ev, ec)$. We also compute the size of the intersection $|\text{Named-entity}(ev) \cap \text{Named-entity}(ec)|$ for each email ec with similarity of over high-threshold and if this intersection is null, then we lower the *Contextscore* down to 0. If Contextscore is below low-threshold it is rounded down to 0. If it is above high-threshold and the size of the intersection is at least one, then it is rounded up to 1. Low-threshold and high-threshold are initially set to 0.5 (an angle of 60 degrees or higher) and $\sqrt{3}/2$ (an angle of 30 degrees or lower) respectively and can be fine-tuned further, if necessary, based on experiments. No rounding is performed if Contextscore is between low-threshold and high-threshold. For efficiency purposes, PhishNet-NLP saves the vocabulary and named-entity information for the context examined, and the corresponding vectors for the emails examined in a database for subsequent reuse. Multiple indices can be constructed on this information for efficient retrieval based on the context options provided in PhishNet-NLP.

4.2 Combining Textscore and Contextscore

The combination of Textscore(e) and Contextscore(e) is done logically to yield Final-text-score(e). It does not make sense to combine them algebraically. If no context information is available, Final-text-score(e) = 1 if Textscore(e) $\geq$ 1 and 0 otherwise. When context information is available, we proceed as follows.

If Contextscore(e) = 1 and any one of the emails that yield the maximum similarity score is marked as dangerous by the user, the Final-text-score(e) = 1. If Contextscore(e) = 1 and all of the emails that yield the maximum similarity score are marked safe by the user, then Final-text-score(e) = 0. If Contextscore(e) = 0, then the email is not very similar to any email in the context. In this case, Final-text-score(e) = 0 if Textscore(e) < 1 and Final-text-score(e) = 1 otherwise. If low-threshold < Contextscore(e) < high-threshold, then the email has moderate similarity to some email in the context. In this case, if Textscore(e) < 1, then Final-text-score(e) = 0, else Final-text-score(e) = 1.

If user input is an acceptable response, then the user could be queried to determine whether the email has arisen from some past action of the user. This would be useful in two "gray" areas: Contextscore is between low and high threshold and Textscore is less than 0.5 and Contextscore is zero and Textscore is between 0.5 and 1. If $0.5 \leq$ Textscore(e) < 1, the user could be prompted to determine if the email has arisen from some past action of the user. If yes, Final-text-score(e) = 0, otherwise Final-text-score(e) = 1. In our experiments, we simplify the logical combination: rounding down the context score to 0 if it is between 0 to 0.866 (angle greater than 30°) and rounding up to 1 otherwise. These thresholds were not finetuned using the data.

To maintain user's privacy, context analysis can be a separate application that works under user control without downloading user emails into its space.

4.3   Header Analysis

Our header analysis classifier is significantly more advanced than the classifier presented by PhishCatch [17] in several aspects: (i) we deal with email forwarding issues, (ii) we make use of DKIM and SPF information whenever it is available, and (iii) we account for the differences in the headers based on whether the email is sent from a mobile device or relayed by multiple servers in the user's domain. In this classifier, we perform analysis on the data from the extracted headers to determine whether the email is phish. First, the user is asked to input his/her other email addresses that forward emails to this current email address and this information is stored. We assume that these forwarding email accounts and the Local Host also have PhishNet-NLP installed. An in-depth discussion of DKIM/SDID is beyond the scope of this paper and the interested reader is referred to RFC 5585 [27] for an overview of the DKIM service and SDID and to the IETF publication RFC 4408 [28] for more information on SPF. In [29], we present a more detailed treatment of headerAnalysis() and present an interesting discussion on the significance of DKIM signatures and SPF through examples.

Phase 1 - Extracting the data:
We extract the FROM and DELIVERED-TO fields from the header. Then, we extract the RECEIVED FROM field(s) as follows. We look at the received from fields in order, starting with the first such field and then the next such field if present and so on.

- If the Received From section of the email contains a DKIM signature, we store the Signing Domain Identifier [SDID].
- Otherwise, if there is a Received-SPF field below a Received From field, then first we store the Received From field. Additionally, if the SPF query returns "pass," and if the domain in the From Field accepts an IP address as a permitted sender in the Received-SPF field, we perform an NSLOOKUP on this IP address, and store the domain name corresponding to this IP address in the variable SPFQuery.
- Otherwise, we store the RECEIVED FROM field.

Phase 2 - Verifying the data:

- If the first Received From field has the same domain name as the FROM FIELD or LOCALHOST or ANY FORWARDING EMAIL ACCOUNT, or if the NSLOOKUP on the IP address of the permitted sender in the Received-SPF field yields the same domain name stored in the variable SPFQuery, then this email is legitimate.
- Otherwise, if the first Received From field has the same domain name as the user's current email account's domain name, then we look at the next received from field. The justification for this is provided in the security analysis of our scheme.
- Otherwise, we mark the email as phishing.

4.4   Link Analysis

In this classifier, our objective is to determine whether the URLs present in the email point to the legitimate website that the text in the body of the email claims. We extract all domains from the links in the email in an array (let this array be called DOMAINS). The linkAnalysis() classifier assigns an email a score of 1 for phishing and 0 for legitimate as follows:

- If the length of DOMAINS is 0 (no links), the email is legitimate.
- If the email has more than 10 distinct words, we calculate the top four terms in the email using the TF-IDF scores. The IDF value of a word can be obtained by either doing a Google search for the word and obtaining the number of web pages in which it appears, or by using a standard NLP corpus. If the Google search approach is adopted, then the search information, together with the total number of web pages in Google's database, can be used to calculate the IDF value for each word. However, we note that Google returns only a somewhat loose upper bound on the number of web pages containing the word for efficiency purposes, which is progressively refined as the user examines the search results list. For this reason and the fact that Google discourages frequent automated searching (see the Implementation details Section 5.1), we used the email database itself to estimate the IDF value. We Google search each domain together with the top four terms.
- Otherwise, if the total number of distinct words in the email is less than 10, then we Google search each domain. If all domains appear in the top 30

results returned by the Google search, then we mark the email as legitimate, otherwise phishing. The reason for insisting on 10 words as a threshold is the very small likelihood of obtaining at least four content words in a text fragment that is shorter. Cantina's [5] experiments with varying result sizes of Google search justify our choice.

Combining Scores of the Three Classifiers: Recall that a score of 1 represents phishing and 0 stands for legitimate. If the combined score of the three classifiers (header, link and text) is ≥ 2, PhishNet-NLP labels the email phishing, otherwise it labels it legitimate.

5   Analysis and Results

In this section, we present an overview of our results. On a database of 2000 phishing emails (using the same phishing corpus as PhishCatch [30]), the percentage of emails that are marked by PhishNet-NLP as phishing is over 98% compared to PhishCatch's result in low 80%. On 1000 legitimate emails, PhishNet-NLP marked 99.3% of the emails as legitimate compared to 99% for PhishCatch [17]. However, note that the databases are different in this case since the authors of PhishCatch do not mention how they collected their legitimate emails. In this sense, we were able to increase coverage by about 18% for the phishing emails while obtaining higher accuracy. Furthermore, our header analysis classifier is more advanced than PhishCatch [17] in the sense that we also deal with email forwarding issues and also account for the differences in the headers based on whether the email is sent from a mobile device or relayed by multiple servers in the user's domain. Our header analysis goes beyond that of PhishCatch and examines DKIM (DomainKeys Identified Mail) signatures and SPF (Sender Policy Framework) fields when available. Although the phishing corpus emails were collected five to eight years ago, we still feel it is a good test since phishing sites are so short-lived [6] that the link analysis results should not change significantly when run on more recent phishing emails.

Cantina's experiments [5] were on the detection of masqueraded web pages rather than on phishing emails, and they experimented with only 100 websites. Still, they have a much higher false positive rate for legitimate web pages and lower coverage of masqueraded sites. Moreover, their algorithms exhibit a trade-off between coverage and accuracy. In contrast, our first run coverage (without context information) is never lower than 97.7% for the largest 4550 phishing database and simultaneously achieves high accuracy with high coverage.

[10] apply machine learning techniques on a set of 860 phishing emails, and 6950 non-phishing emails, and are able to correctly identify 92% of the phishing emails with 0.1% false positive rate. Using structural properties of emails, [11] were able to detect 95% of phishing emails but did not explicitly state their false positive percentages. Finally, it is important to note that the above mentioned machine learning approaches require a training corpus of emails whereas our approach does not.

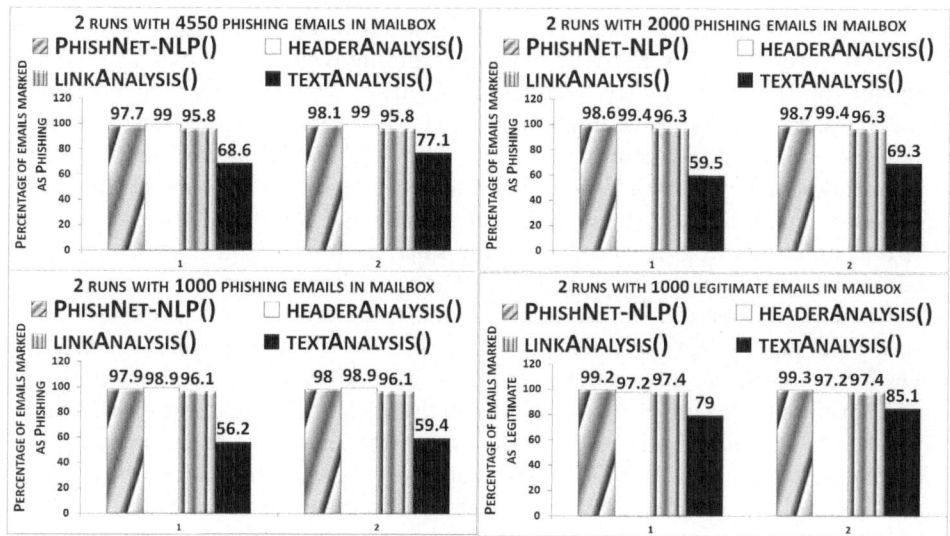

Fig. 2. Results

As explained at the beginning of Section IV, our results show that all three classifiers satisfy the minimum threshold needed for helping to improve the combined classifier since they are all above 50% in coverage and accuracy. However, there is some dependence between the text analysis and link analysis classifiers since one analyzes links and the other uses the presence of links in its scoring. We carefully considered whether to remove even this dependence, but decided against it since links are central to phishing via emails and since text analysis only considers the presence or absence of links and not on analyzing them.

The relatively lower percentage of phishing emails detected by textAnalysis() in the two big mail boxes is explained by the imprecision of NLP tools and the three types of emails: foreign language, emails with unusable text, and emails with tables and pictures and insufficient text that we encountered. Also, in each individual mailbox, the 2nd run produced an increased phishing detection by the textAnalysis() classifier and a small increase in the overall phishing detection. This is a direct consequence of the effect of the Context Score, which was not available in the first runs, but available in the 2nd runs after the first runs assigned scores to each email in the database. We could have obtained a higher detection rate on the first run of textAnalysis() by using the previous context of the first N emails when processing email $N + 1$. However, we preferred to keep a fixed context for analysis of each email rather than a growing context, since in this case our results are insensitive to the order in which emails are processed.

5.1   Implementation Details

We implemented PhishNet-NLP using Perl v5.12.4, WordNet version 2.1 and SenseLearner 2.0. We used the Stanford POS tagger 2006-05-21 and Stanford

Named Entity Recognizer 1.0. Our implementation platform was a core 2 Duo 2.66 GHz processor, 4 GB RAM machine running 32 bit Windows 7. We used Cygwin for the POS tagger, NER, SenseLearner and WordNet. Some of the challenges we faced during implementation were: 1) The Google Search API would not allow us to perform frequent automated searches. We were forced to use a random delay of 10 to 20 seconds after every search to circumvent this issue. 2) Parsing an email into the constituent header and body and then extracting the text and links from it was challenging since most emails are HTML encoded and the headers do not always end with the same line format.

Our method of extracting data from emails relies on the use of regular expressions. From analyzing thousands of emails, we observed that the message headers were formatted differently among them. So we had to study a large number of email formats to design the decoder (which decodes html if present, extracts info from the header and body and removes any attachments). To summarize, our decoder is reliable, but not 100% efficient in extracting the maximum possible data from all the emails. This is an area of improvement that we are working on at this moment. If an attachment is present in an email, then the last portion of the message header contains one of the following: `Content-Disposition: attachment` or `Content-Disposition: inline`. This is followed by the encoded attachment file. We used this information to ignore all attachments. Given that we had to employ a random sleep time between subsequent Google searches, in our future work, we would like to make use of different search engines for consecutive searches to eliminate this problem and possibly obtain better results.

5.2   Security Analysis and Discussion

We now analyze the security of our scheme against several scenarios and discuss some interesting aspects of our approach.

Is textAnalysis() or linkAnalysis() Redundant? Observe that while the headerAnalysis() classifier alone shows very high coverage and high accuracy, the importance of link and text analysis stems from the fact that a sophisticated phisher can manipulate the originating "Received From", "From" and the "Delivered To" information completely (e.g., see Chapter 3 of [18]). To this end, link and text analysis are very important and provide robustness to our scheme. The case of insider attacker discussed below further justifies their inclusion.

Attacks Based on Knowledge of Our Scheme. The reader might think that a phisher can analyze how our detection algorithm works and then design a phishing email to fool PhishNet-NLP. But our results from the LinkAnalysis show that it is very difficult to create a fraudulent link to bypass LinkAnalysis. Moreover, unless the phishers have hacked into the mail server or the user's account, they would not have access to the context of the user's mailbox. Hence, it is likely that Context Analysis will also play a part in detecting such an email.

Insider Attacker. When someone hacks into an account in some domain and uses a friend list to attack any user in the same domain, headerAnalysis() will fail to detect this. But even in such a case, PhishNet-NLP can use the linkAnalysis() and textAnalysis() to mark the email as phishing since the intent of the email is still to steal sensitive information by asking the user to click on a link for a malicious website. This even works for the scenario when user A's account is hacked and user A receives a phishing email, for example, if A's sensitive information is stored in an encrypted form.

Is textAnalysis() Flawed? Observe that as of this implementation, our textAnalysis() classifier will score the following email as phishing: "I found this video to be funny! Click on this link <legitimate link here>". This email will be scored as phishing even when coming from a genuine sender and a legitimate link. We would like to clarify that this is not a limitation of our approach - this is actually a design feature of PhishNet-NLP. The reason is that both header and link analysis will have a high likelihood of returning a score of 0 (indicating legitimate) on such emails and therefore, the majority vote will be legitimate. We also argue that while it may seem counterintuitive, such emails MUST be scored as phishing, since otherwise a sophisticated phisher who could fool headerAnalysis() would escape detection as the majority vote would be legitimate if the header and text score say legitimate and only linkAnalysis() indicates phishing.

Foreign Language Email or Emails with Insufficient Text. As of the present design, emails in foreign languages or emails with insufficient text (only links or attachments) present a challenge to the textAnalysis() classifier which leads to a low phishing detection rate by the textAnalysis() classifier. However, we were able to offset this to a certain extent by using context analysis to correctly identify the email as phishing.

Efficiency Considerations. For efficiency, PhishNet-NLP is designed to first execute headerAnalysis() and linkAnalysis() on the email that is being analyzed. If the sum of the scores of these two classifiers is equal to 1, only then will PhishNet-NLP execute textAnalysis() (because if the combined score is either 0 or 2 from the first two classifiers, then the score from textAnalysis() cannot change the final output label of PhishNet-NLP). But we disabled this feature during our testing phase to obtain the results from each classifier.

Justification of Strategy for Examining Received from Fields. As DKIM becomes widely deployed, sending domains will develop reputations as sources of spam or useful messages. We believe that senders are not able to create covert sub-domains under their main domain (unless an authorized insider attacker is involved which we believe may be unlikely) and cannot manipulate the "Received From" fields of legal intermediate MTAs. We note that it is not very easy to identify whether a "Received From" field is from a genuine intermediate MTA or just added by the phisher to confuse the header analysis. The highest probability for a "Received From" field of truly originating from a genuine intermediate MTA is the one closest to the recipient's domain, justifying our use of the closest MTA in our scheme.

6   Conclusion

In this paper, we presented a phishing detection scheme called PhishNet-NLP. To the best of our knowledge, this is the first scheme to utilize natural language based techniques and context information when available to detect phishing. PhishNet-NLP operates by inferring the "intention" of the email - whether it is informational or actionable. Our phishing detection rate is at least 97% with very low false positives. Another novel feature in PhishNet-NLP is that we utilize all of the information available in an email, namely, the header, links and text of an email. Our scheme operates in the default mode and does phishing detection in the absence of any history. The novelty lies in the fact that when prior history is available, our scheme takes advantage and improves the detection capability. Finally, our scheme is designed to detect phishing at the email level rather than to detect fraudulent, masqueraded websites thereby protecting the user from the start. As future work, we plan to implement PhishNet-NLP to permit the user to be interactive enabling us to understand if a particular email resulted by an action of the user. Processing attachments in emails is also an interesting direction for the future. We have reduced our reliance on Google for link analysis [29].

Acknowledgments. Research of the first author was partially supported by NSF grants DUE 0737404 and CNS 1062954.

References

1. Parno, B., Kuo, C., Perrig, A.: Phoolproof Phishing Prevention. In: Di Crescenzo, G., Rubin, A. (eds.) FC 2006. LNCS, vol. 4107, pp. 1–19. Springer, Heidelberg (2006)
2. Irani, D., Webb, S., Giffin, J., Pu, C.: Evolutionary study of phishing. In: 3rd Anti-Phishing Working Group eCrime Researchers Summit (2008)
3. Ludl, C., McAllister, S., Kirda, E., Kruegel, C.: On the Effectiveness of Techniques to Detect Phishing Sites. In: Hämmerli, B.M., Sommer, R. (eds.) DIMVA 2007. LNCS, vol. 4579, pp. 20–39. Springer, Heidelberg (2007)
4. Sheng, S., Wardman, B., Warner, G., Cranor, L., Hong, J., Zhang, C.: An empirical analysis of phishing blacklists. In: Proc. 6th Conf. on Email and Anti-Spam (2009)
5. Zhang, Y., Hong, J., Cranor, L.: Cantina: a content-based approach to detecting phishing web sites. In: Proc. 16th Int'l Conf. on World Wide Web, pp. 639–648. ACM (2007)
6. Xiang, G., Hong, J., Rose, C.P., Cranor, L.: Cantina+: A feature-rich machine learning framework for detecting phishing web sites. CM Trans. Inf. Syst. Secur. 14, 21:1–21:28 (2011)
7. Whittaker, C., Ryner, B., Nazif, M.: Large-scale automatic classification of phishing pages. In: Proc. of 17th NDSS (2010)
8. Garera, S., Provos, N., Chew, M., Rubin, A.: A framework for detection and measurement of phishing attacks. In: Proc. 2007 ACM Workshop on Recurring Malcode, pp. 1–8 (2007)

9. Chen, J., Guo, C.: Online detection and prevention of phishing attacks. In: First Int'l Conf. on Communications and Networking in China, ChinaCom 2006, pp. 1–7. IEEE (2006)

10. Fette, I., Sadeh, N., Tomasic, A.: Learning to detect phishing emails. In: Proc. 16th Int'l Conf. on World Wide Web, pp. 649–656. ACM (2007)

11. Chandrasekaran, M., Narayanan, K., Upadhyaya, S.: Phishing email detection based on structural properties. In: NYS CyberSecurity Conf. (2006)

12. Bergholz, A., Chang, J., Paaß, G., Reichartz, F., Strobel, S.: Improved phishing detection using model-based features. In: Proc. Conf. on Email and Anti-Spam, CEAS (2008)

13. Basnet, R., Mukkamala, S., Sung, A.: Detection of phishing attacks: A machine learning approach. In: Soft Computing Applications in Industry, pp. 373–383 (2008)

14. Bergholz, A., Beer, J.D., Glahn, S., Moens, M.F., Paaß, G., Strobel, S.: New filtering approaches for phishing email. Journal of Computer Security 18(1), 7–35 (2010)

15. Gansterer, W.N., Pölz, D.: E-Mail Classification for Phishing Defense. In: Boughanem, M., Berrut, C., Mothe, J., Soule-Dupuy, C. (eds.) ECIR 2009. LNCS, vol. 5478, pp. 449–460. Springer, Heidelberg (2009)

16. Abu-Nimeh, S., Nappa, D., Wang, X., Nair, S.: A comparison of machine learning techniques for phishing detection. In: Proc. Anti-phishing Working Group's 2nd Annual eCrime Researchers Summit, pp. 60–69. ACM (2007)

17. Yu, W., Nargundkar, S., Tiruthani, N.: Phishcatch-a phishing detection tool. In: 33rd IEEE Int'l Computer Software and Applications Conf., pp. 451–456 (2009)

18. Jakobsson, M., Myers, S.: Phishing and countermeasures: understanding the increasing problem of electronic identity theft. Wiley-Interscience (2006)

19. James, L.: Phishing exposed. Syngress Publishing (2005)

20. Ollmann, G.: The phishing guide. Next Generation Security Software Ltd. (2004)

21. Salton, G., McGill, M.: Introduction to Modern Information Retrieval. McGraw-Hill, Inc. (1986)

22. Porter, M.: An algorithm for suffix stripping. Program 14(3), 130–137 (1980)

23. Fellbaum, C. (ed.): WordNet An Electronic Lexical Database. MIT Press (1998)

24. Richens, T.: Anomalies in the wordnet verb hierarchy. In: COLING, pp. 729–736 (2008)

25. Mihalcea, R., Csomai, A.: Senselearner: Word sense disambiguation for all words in unrestricted text. In: ACL (2005)

26. Mihalcea, R., Tarau, P.: Textrank: Bringing order into text. In: EMNLP, pp. 404–411 (2004)

27. Hansen, T., Crocker, D., Hallam-Baker, P.: Domainkeys identified mail (dkim) service overview (2009), http://www.dkim.org/specs/rfc5585.html

28. Wong, M., Schlitt, W.: Sender policy framework (spf) for authorizing use of domains in e-mail (2006), http://tools.ietf.org/html/rfc4408

29. Verma, R., Shashidhar, N., Hossain, N.: Two-pronged phish snagging. In: Seventh International Conference on Availability, Reliability and Security, Availability, Reliability and Security (ARES). IEEE (2012)

30. Nazario, J.: The online phishing corpus (2004), http://monkey.org/~jose/wiki/doku.php

JVM-Portable Sandboxing
of Java's Native Libraries

Mengtao Sun and Gang Tan

Lehigh University, Bethlehem, PA 18015, USA
{mes310,gat208}@lehigh.edu

Abstract. Although Java provides strong support for safety and security, native libraries used in a Java application can open security holes.
Previous work, Robusta, puts native libraries in a sandbox to protect the
integrity and security of Java. However, Robusta's implementation modifies the internals of OpenJDK, a particular implementation of a Java
Virtual Machine (JVM). As such, it is not portable to other JVM implementations. This paper shows how to make the idea of sandboxing native
libraries JVM-portable. We present a two-layer approach for sandboxing
without modifying the internals of a JVM. We also discuss our experience of sandboxing Java's core native libraries. Experiments show that
our approach of JVM-portable sandboxing incurs modest performance
overhead on SPECjvm 2008 benchmark programs.

1 Introduction

The Java Native Interface (JNI) [1] is Java's foreign function interface. Through
the JNI, Java code can invoke native libraries developed in low-level languages
such as C, C++, or even assembly languages. The JNI allows Java programmers to reuse legacy code modules without porting them to Java. Furthermore,
performance-critical portions of an application can be developed in C/C++ and
invoked through the JNI.

However, native libraries in Java applications, as the "snake in the grass", is
notoriously unsafe [2]. Native libraries in a Java application reside in the same
address space as a Java Virtual Machine (JVM), but are outside the control of
Java's security model. Java provides strong safety and security support, but once
a Java application incorporates native libraries, there is no assurance about the
safety and security of the whole application. Native libraries with programming
bugs or malicious native libraries may cause an unexpected crash of the JVM,
leak of confidential information, or even a complete takeover of the JVM by
attackers.

To counter the threats of native libraries, our idea is to put them in a sandbox and allow only controlled access from the code in the sandbox to JVM
services. Following this idea, we implemented Robusta [3], a security layer incorporated into a JVM for sandboxing native libraries in Java applications. It
adopts software-based fault isolation (SFI [4]) to isolate untrusted native libraries
from the rest of the JVM. Furthermore, native libraries' access to the outside

S. Foresti, M. Yung, and F. Martinelli (Eds.): ESORICS 2012, LNCS 7459, pp. 842–858, 2012.

world is restricted to the JNI interface and OS system calls, both of which are modulated by Robusta's reference monitor to ensure security. Robusta's design will be briefly described in Sec. 2.

Robusta demonstrated the feasibility of sandboxing native libraries inside the implementation of a JVM. At the same time, a few questions were left unanswered when it was used to evaluate the practicality of sandboxing native libraries.

- **JVM Portability.** Robusta was implemented inside OpenJDK 1.7. Various places in OpenJDK were modified. The JVM-specific implementation makes it hard to evaluate whether the idea of native-library sandboxing can function well in a different JVM implementation, such as IBM's J9 or Kaffe JVM. In fact, since IBM J9 is not open sourced, it is not possible for an outsider to modify its internals. Even for an open-source JVM, a JVM-specific sandboxing framework such as Robusta has to be upgraded whenever the JVM makes an upgrade. Indeed, Robusta was implemented in OpenJDK 1.7, but OpenJDK has upgraded from version 1.7 to 1.8.[1]
- **Java's Core Libraries.** The most common usage of native libraries is actually to support classes in the standard Java Class Library (JCL). Sun's JDK 1.6 has over 800,000 lines of C/C++ code in its native libraries. Robusta did not attempt to sandbox those core Java libraries. It was not clear how difficult it would be to sandbox those core libraries and not clear what the performance slowdown would be for Java applications after the core libraries are sandboxed.
- **Evaluation on Standard Benchmarks.** Robusta's experimental evaluation was performed on a set of handpicked, medium-sized JNI programs. While the experiments were acceptable as preliminary evidence of demonstrating Robusta's practicality, it would be much more convincing if it were evaluated on some standard benchmark programs. However, the challenge is that there are no standard benchmark suites that target the evaluation of JNI applications. Java benchmark suites such as SPECjvm and DaCapo [5] are themselves pure Java programs and cannot directly be used to evaluate Robusta.

In this paper we describe Arabica[2], a newly designed JNI sandboxing framework to further evaluate the practicality of JNI native-code sandboxing. Arabica has a JVM-independent design that requires no changes to a JVM's internals. It relies on a combination of the standard Java Virtual Machine Tool Interface (JVMTI) and a layer of stub libraries. Using Arabica, we have sandboxed several Java's core native libraries. This improves Java's security by reducing the size of trusted native libraries. More importantly, sandboxing core Java libraries enables us to evaluate the performance overhead of native-library sandboxing by running

---

[1] Google engineers are interested in integrating Robusta into Google App Engine. During a discussion, they explicitly mentioned that App Engine uses OpenJDK 1.8, but Robusta was implemented on version 1.7.

[2] Coffee Arabica is a species of coffee with better taste and quality than coffee Robusta.

standard Java benchmark suites, because all Java applications make heavy use of the core libraries.

The rest of the paper is organized as follows. We first introduce necessary background about the JNI and Robusta in Sec. 2. In Sec. 3, Arabica's JVM-independent design and implementation are presented. We then discuss our experience of sandboxing OpenJDK's standard native libraries in Sec. 4. Evaluation of Arabica is presented in Sec. 5. We discuss related work in Sec. 6, future work in Sec. 7, and conclude in Sec. 8.

2 Background: JNI and Robusta

The Java Native Interface (JNI) allows Java code to invoke native methods. A native method is declared in a Java class by adding the `native` modifier. The following code snippet of the `Inflater` class is extracted from the package `java.util.zip` in Sun's JDK. It declares a native `inflateBytes` method. Once declared, native methods are invoked in the same way as how ordinary Java methods are invoked. In the example, the `inflate` Java method invokes `inflateBytes`.

```
public class Inflater {
  ...

  public synchronized int inflate(byte[] b, int off, int len)
    { ...; return inflateBytes(b, off, len);}

  private native int inflateBytes (byte[] b, int off, int len);

  static {System.loadLibrary(''zip''); ...;}
}
```

A native method is implemented in a language such as C, C++, or assembly languages. The JDK implementation of `inflateBytes` above invokes the popular Zlib C library for the inflation (decompression) operation. There is also a small amount of native glue code between Java and the Zlib C library. The glue code uses JNI functions to interact with Java directly. Through these JNI functions, native code can inspect, modify, and create Java objects, invoke Java methods, catch and throw Java exceptions, and so on.

Threats Posed by Native Libraries. We list the most vicious kinds of attacks that can be launched by exploiting vulnerabilities in a native library:

(1) Unconstrained native libraries have access to the entire address space. As native libraries reside in the same address space as a JVM, bugs in native libraries can enable attackers to read and write the JVM's memory.
(2) Abusive JNI calls can cause integrity or confidentiality violations. The JNI interface was not designed with security in mind and does not mandate

any security checks. Native code can steal confidential information from the Java side, for example, by reading a private field of a Java object through the JNI API function `GetObjectField`. Native code can also violate Java's type safety. For instance, it can invoke `SetObjectField` to modify a field of an object to a value whose type is incompatible with the field's declared type, resulting in so-called type-confusion attacks [6].

(3) Native code may invoke an OS system call to read from a system file or send data to the network. This may violate the security policy that JVM imposes on a Java application.

As examples, vulnerabilities have been discovered in the C/C++ modules of Sun's JDK [7–9].

Robusta. We next summarize Robusta's design and implementation; details can be found in the Robusta paper [3]. First, Robusta adopts software-based fault isolation (SFI [4]) to isolate untrusted native libraries from the rest of a JVM. Native libraries are constrained within a sandbox so that direct memory access and control transfers outside of the sandbox are disallowed. The implementation of Robusta extends Google's Native Client (NaCl [10]), a state-of-the-art SFI implementation. Since native libraries are loaded dynamically by the JVM, Robusta extended NaCl with support for dynamic linking and loading. Second, Robusta interposes between Java and native libraries, inserting security checks into the JNI to prevent abusive JNI calls. Finally, Robusta connects to Java's security manager to mediate native libraries' system calls. An OS system call issued by a native library is rerouted to Java's security manager to decide on the system call's safety based on a predefined security policy. This design enables Robusta to place native libraries under the same runtime security restrictions as Java code and reuse much of Java's policy-driven security infrastructure.

The implementation of Robusta modified various places in OpenJDK 1.7. We next summarize these changes. We will use the phrase *Robusta OpenJDK* to refer to the OpenJDK after Robusta's changes.

(a) *Sandbox initialization.* When Robusta OpenJDK starts running, it constructs an SFI sandbox and loads the dynamic linker/loader (`ld.so` in Linux) into the sandbox. The dynamic linker/loader is put into the sandbox to support dynamic loading of native libraries.

(b) *Loading native libraries and symbol resolution.* When Robusta OpenJDK needs to load a native library, it invokes the `dlopen` routine of `ld.so` for loading the library into the sandbox. When Robusta OpenJDK needs to look up a symbol in a native library, it invokes the `dlsym` routine for resolving the symbol's address in the sandbox.

(c) *Calling a native method and returning.* When Java code invokes a native method, Robusta OpenJDK transfers the control to the address of the native method in the sandbox (after copying method arguments into the sandbox). The address is the result of symbol resolution through an invocation of `dlsym`. After the method finishes, Robusta OpenJDK transfers the control back to the Java code and copies out the return value (if there is one).

(d) *Support for Java multi-threading.* Multiple Java threads may be running inside the JVM. Robusta OpenJDK maintains a per-thread data structure to support Java multi-threading.

(e) *JNI safety checking.* Robusta OpenJDK inserts safety checks at the boundary of the JNI. For instance, if native code invokes SetObjectField to update an object's field, Robusta checks that the new value is of the expected type of the field.

3   Arabica: JVM-Portable Sandboxing of Native Libraries

Robusta's JVM-specific implementation limits its applicability. A much better design should provide sandboxing of native libraries as a service to a JVM. This requires the sandboxing functionality be implemented outside of the JVM and be compatible with a variety of JVM implementations.

What made us believe that JVM-portable sandboxing is achievable is because that almost all implementations of JVMs support two standard interfaces: the JNI and the Java Virtual Machine Tool Interface (JVMTI [11]). We have discussed the JNI, the standard interface between Java and native code. The second interface, JVMTI, is the standard JVM interface that allows an external tool to inspect the internal JVM state and control the running of applications in a JVM.

Therefore, our initial idea to achieve JVM portability was to design and implement a JVMTI-based tool. The idea almost worked until we discovered that JVMTI is not fine grained enough to meet all our demands. Sandboxing native libraries requires a greater control over a JVM than what the JVMTI interface allows. In retrospect, this is not surprising as JVMTI was mainly designed to support debuggers and profilers, not security tools.

In the end, Arabica achieves JVM-portable sandboxing through a two-layer approach: a JVMTI-based agent plus a layer of trusted stub libraries. Fig. 1 shows the architecture of Arabica. The first layer is a layer of trusted stub libraries. The stub libraries serve as intermediaries between the JVM and the real native libraries. Its functionalities include native-library loading, symbol resolution, and native-method calling and returning. The second layer is a JVMTI agent library. Its functionalities include sandbox initialization, support for Java multi-threading, and JNI safety checking.

The detailed design of Arabica is presented next in three steps: (1) a brief overview of JVMTI; (2) Arabica's JVMTI agent; (3) Arabica's stub-library layer.

JVMTI Overview. JVMTI provides a programming interface that allows Java programmers to write tools to inspect and control the execution of a JVM. Such a tool, called a *JVMTI agent*, is loaded during initialization of a JVM. A JVMTI agent monitors and controls a JVM by calling JVMTI interface functions. JVMTI supports an *event-driven model*. An agent can register a callback function that is invoked when a certain type of events happens inside a JVM. For instance, a callback function can be registered for the thread-start event, which occurs when the JVM creates a new Java thread. The callback function can perform appropriate actions to support the implementation of a JVM tool.

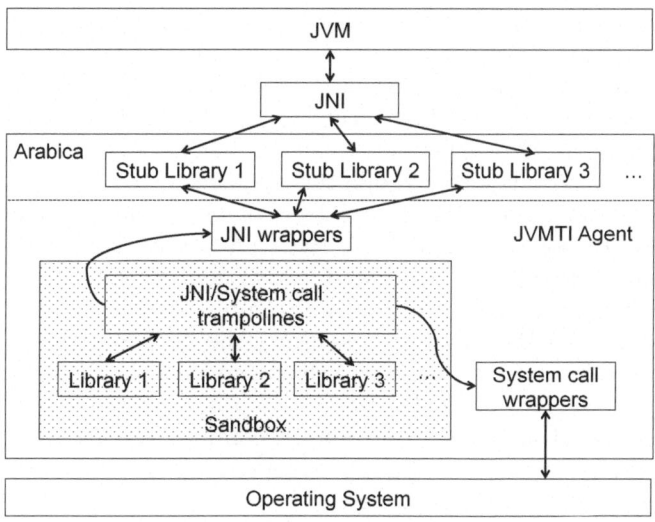

Fig. 1. Architecture of Arabica

Arabica's JVMTI Agent. At a high level, Arabica's JVMTI agent implements those functionalities in items (a), (d), and (e), which were presented when we discussed Robusta's implementation at the end of Sec. 2.

For sandbox initialization, Arabica constructs an SFI sandbox in function Agent_OnLoad, which is part of the JVMTI agent. This function is automatically invoked by the JVM when the agent is loaded during the start of the JVM.

To support Java multi-threading, Arabica registers a callback function for the JVMTI thread-start event and also a callback function for the thread-end event. The callback functions are invoked whenever the JVM creates a new thread and terminates a thread, respectively. In the callback function for the thread-start event, a per-thread data structure is constructed to store information such as the per-thread JNI environment pointer [1]. The data structure is freed in the callback function for the thread-end event.

Finally, JNI safety checks are implemented in the following way. First, Arabica registers a callback function for the native-method-bind event, which occurs when the JVM binds a native method to the address of a native-library function that implements the native method. This callback function initializes the data structures that are necessary for performing JNI safety checks. Second, Arabica adds JNI interface function wrappers, which intercept JNI calls made by native code and perform necessary safety checks before invoking the real JNI functions in the JVM. The implementation of performing JNI safety checks follows the implementation of Jinn [12], a tool for detecting bugs and safety violations in the JNI code.

Arabica's Layer of Stub Libraries. It turns out that a pure JVMTI-based approach is insufficient to achieve JVM-portable sandboxing of native libraries.

The main reason is that JVMTI does not support a "native-library-loading" event. When a native library is loaded, a JVM loads the library into its memory using its own dynamic loader. Without the ability to intercept native-library-loading events, Arabica's JVMTI agent cannot change the process of library loading inside the JVM to allow it to load the native library into the sandbox via the dynamic loader installed inside the sandbox.

Arabica's solution is to introduce a level of indirection through a layer of trusted stub libraries. At a high level, the stub-library layer performs native-library loading, symbol resolution, and native-method calling and returning; that is, it performs functionalities (b) and (c) presented at the end of Sec. 2.

We next illustrate the basic process using the native-method implementation of `inflateBytes` in the library `libzip.so`. The first step is to rename `libzip.so` to `reallibzip.so`. The second step is to create a new `libzip.so`, a stub library for `libzip`. The stub library contains a stub function for each native-method implementation. The following code presents the implementation of the stub function for `inflateBytes`.

```
1  void * _handle = NULL;
2  void * _sym_addr = NULL;

3  jint Java_java_util_zip_Inflater_inflateBytes
4    (JNIEnv *env, jobject this, jarray b, jint off, jint len) {
5    if (_handle == NULL)
6      _handle = (void *) loadLib(env, ''reallibzip.so'');

7    if (_sym_addr == NULL)
8      _sym_addr = (void *)
9        loadSym(_handle, "Java_java_util_zip_Inflater_inflateBytes");

10   return call_in(_sym_addr, env, obj, b, off, len);
11 }
```

The following steps outline what happens when the JVM loads `libzip.so` and invokes the method `inflateBytes`:

(1) When the JVM loads `libzip.so`, it loads the stub version outside the sandbox, not the real one.
(2) When the JVM resolves the address for the native method `inflateBytes`, it finds the address of the stub function for `inflateBytes` in the stub library.
(3) When the JVM invokes the `inflateBytes` native method, the control transfers to the stub function. The stub function (a) uses `loadLib` to load the real library into the sandbox if it has not been loaded (lines 5 and 6); [3] (b) uses `loadSym` to find the address of `inflateBytes` in the real library (lines 7–9); and (c) uses a function `call_in` to copy arguments and perform a function call to the real `inflateBytes` (line 10).

---

[3] Note that the name of a native method in a library is mangled; additional information about package and class names are added to the method name.

For each native library that needs to be sandboxed, a stub library needs to be generated. The stub library can be manually written, but we automated the process of stub-library generation using a stub-library generator. The generator first reads in a configuration file, which specifies the source files for native libraries, the output filename and other options. The stub generator then parses the source files to search for functions that implement native methods. For each native method, the stub generator records the function name, parameter list and return type, and generates the stub function accordingly.

Prototype Implementation. Arabica has been implemented in Linux. Arabica's JVMTI agent is written in around 27,000 lines of C code. The majority of the code is for implementing the JNI function wrappers, which performs safety checks before invoking real JNI functions. When a JVM starts, the agent is loaded into the JVM by specifying the "-agentlib" or the "-agentpath" option. The stub-library generator is implemented in less than 1,000 lines of Java code. The current version of the stub generator works only with native libraries whose source code is available. The stub generator parses a source file, recognizes functions that implement native methods, and generates stub functions. A C function with the JNIEXPORT modifier is recognized by the generator as the implementation of a Java native method. In the future, we will change the stub generator so that it generates stub functions based on Java class files. The benefit of this approach is that it will enable sandboxing of native libraries in a Java package on the fly because stub libraries can be generated online based on the Java class files in the package—no off-line processing will be needed.

4 Sandboxing Standard Libraries in OpenJDK

Sandboxing the standard native libraries in the Java Class Library (JCL) provides multiple benefits. First, it improves a JVM's security. Without constraints, those native libraries are in the TCB. A security vulnerability in the libraries may enable attackers to take over the JVM. In an empirical security study [2], we examined the standard native libraries in Sun's JDK (version 1.6). In 38,000 lines of C code covered by the study, we identified 126 software bugs, of which 59 bugs are security critical. Since Sun's JDK 1.6 has over 800,000 lines of C/C++ code in its native libraries, we expect many more security-critical bugs are there. By sandboxing those libraries and constrain their capability, the size of the TCB is reduced and the JVM's security is improved.

The second benefit of sandboxing JCL's standard libraries is that it enables us to evaluate the performance of native-code sandboxing by running standard Java benchmark suites such as SPECjvm or DaCapo [5]. One difficulty in evaluating JNI-based systems is that there are no standard benchmark suites that target the JNI. As a result, the performance evaluation of Robusta was performed on a set of handpicked JNI applications. With the sandboxing of standard native libraries, a more sound evaluation strategy can be adopted to evaluate Arabica. Since all Java applications make heavy use of JCL's native libraries, we can just sandbox those libraries and run standard Java benchmark suites for the evaluation.

Given the benefits of sandboxing standard native libraries, one natural approach is just to put all code in JCL's native libraries into the sandbox. However, this approach has two disadvantages.

- *Lack of portability.* In the ideal case, the JCL would be portable across JVM implementations. The reality, however, is that each JVM implementation uses its own version of native libraries. For instance, OpenJDK and IBM J9 come with their own JCL packages, which are incompatible with each other. One reason for the incompatibility is that many JCL native libraries may be used for purposes more than just implementing native methods declared in Java classes. Take `libzip` in OpenJDK as an example. Part of its code is invoked directly by OpenJDK's JVM, forming "native-to-native" communication.[4] For instance, the function `ZIP_Open` in `libzip` is directly invoked by OpenJDK during the JVM initialization stage. The second reason for incompatibility is that code in a native library may invoke JVM-specific intrinsics. For instance, native code that supports the `java.io` package in OpenJDK uses JVM intrinsics to manipulate files (e.g., `JVM_Open` for opening a file). Because of these reasons, if all code in a JCL native library were put in the sandbox, then the sandbox interface to Java had to go beyond the JNI interface to allow, for example, functions like `JVM_Open`. This approach would make the sandbox interface dependent on a specific JVM, while our goal is to keep the interface to be the portable JNI interface.
- *Security concerns.* Part of Java security is implemented through standard JCL packages such as `java.lang.SecurityManager`, `java.lang.ClassLoad -er`, and `java.security.AccessController`. Since Arabica has only one sandbox for all native code, putting native code that implements Java security in the same sandbox as other untrusted native libraries might jeopardize security: one vulnerability in untrusted native libraries might allow attackers to disable Java's security manager.[5]

Therefore, we decided to manually separate a native library in JCL into two portions: a portion that is put into the sandbox, and a trusted portion that is outside the sandbox. The sandboxed portion contains the code that implements native methods declared in a JCL class that is not part of Java's security infrastructure; it is JVM-independent and the only way it interacts with a JVM is through the standard JNI interface. The trusted portion contains the rest of the code, including JVM-specific native code and native code that implements Java security. Take `libzip` in package `java.util.zip` as an example. A piece of native code is put into the sandboxed portion if the following conditions hold:

---

[4] We call this "native-to-native" communication because the JVM itself is implemented in native code. By contrast, "Java-to-native" communication includes the cases that Java code invokes a native method.

[5] One solution is to construct multiple sandboxes and put native code of different security levels into separate sandboxes, as discussed in the future-work section.

Table 1. Sandboxed JCL libraries and their descriptions

Library	Description
libjava	The core library that supports java.lang, java.io and part of java.util.
libzip	The library that supports java.util.zip; it includes the ZLib C library for compression/decompression.
libnet	The library that supports java.net.
libnio	The library that supports java.nio.

- There is a Java class in java.util.zip that is not part of Java security and the Java class declares a native method.
- The piece of native code is used to support the implementation of the native method.

Conceptually, the separation process takes out the JVM-independent, Java-security-independent portion from a JCL package. In our view, there is no fundamental reason why JCL packages cannot be reused in multiple JVMs. For instance, regardless of how a JVM is implemented, the standard package java.util.zip should include Java classes and a native library for compression/decompression; the library communicates with the Java side through the standard JNI interface. This would be a welcome design for JVM implementers as they do not need to reinvent those standard packages.

The manual separation process does come with a few complications. First, code occasionally needs to be duplicated in the two portions. For instance, if a function in a native library is both directly invoked by the JVM and used by another native function that implements a Java class's native method, then that function needs to be duplicated in both the sandboxed and the trusted portion of the library. Second, we may make mistakes during the manual separation process. For instance, code that should be sandboxed may be wrongly put into the trusted portion.

Separating JCL Libraries. For the purpose of evaluating the performance of native-library sandboxing, we investigated what JCL libraries are used by benchmark programs in SPECjvm 2008. Table 1 lists these libraries except the AWT library. The AWT library contains over 100k lines of source code and we had difficulty of compiling it through NaCl's toolchain.[6] Fortunately, only one benchmark program, sunflow, in SPECjvm 2008 uses the AWT library and we excluded that program in our performance evaluation.

Table 2 shows the lines of source code of the JCL's libraries we have treated and the sizes after the manual separation process. Note that the total size is not the same as the sum of the sandboxed portion and the trusted portion because some code is duplicated during the separation process. Also note that a relatively

---

[6] Both Robusta and Arabica rely on NaCl's toolchain to create NaCl-compatible modules.

Table 2. JCL library sizes and the sizes of the two portions after manual separation (lines of source code)

Library	Total size	Sandboxed portion	Trusted portion
libnet	6339	6245	192
libnio	3566	3566	0
libzip	8725	8070	1325
libjava	11011	7919	3459

large portion of libjava is not sandboxed because native code that implements Java security such as java.lang.SecurityManager is in that library. In our implementation, the trusted portion is put into the stub library, which was discussed in the previous section. That is, the new "stub library" contains both the stub functions and the trusted portion.

Adding Permissions for the JCL Libraries. Recall that Robusta reroutes system calls issued by native libraries to let Java's security manager decide whether system calls are allowed according to a security policy. Arabica inherited that mechanism from Robusta. For JCL packages, we changed the JVM's policy file to give a minimum set of permissions on a per-package basis. For instance, the package java.util.zip has permission java.io.FilePermission but no other permissions. As another example, the package java.net has permissions java.net.NetPermission and java.net.SocketPermission. Permissions assigned to a package apply to both Java and native code in the package and they are enforced by Java's stack inspection [13]. In particular, in the presence of native method calls, the JVM's method-call stack consists of a mixed Java and native frames. When the security manager performs stack inspection, it can find the right protection domain even for a native frame based on the class where the native method is declared. For instance, if the native code that supports java.util.zip attempted to access the network, the request would be rejected by the security manager since Java classes under java.util.zip do not have networking permissions.

Since Arabica has only one sandbox for all native libraries, one might worry that native code for one package might gain more permissions by exploiting other packages' native code that has a larger permission set. We do not believe this can happen for the following reason. The SFI sandbox for native libraries has separate code and data regions. The code region is immutable; as a result, one package's native code cannot modify other packages' native code. It can modify the data region, which is shared by all native code. But it cannot affect Java's security manager because the security manager stays outside of the sandbox and stack inspection is based on a stack outside of the sandbox. Note that when we sandboxed libjava, we did not put the native code of the security manager in the sandbox because otherwise it would create security-critical data in the data region modifiable by other untrusted native code.

Table 3. Performance overheads of Arabica on a set of JNI programs

Program	Context switches (per millisecond)	Arabica increase (OpenJDK 1.7)	Arabica increase (IBM J9 1.7.0)	Robusta increase
zip (1KB)	18.50	23.90%	19.84%	9.64%
zip (2KB)	9.93	12.26%	10.41%	7.51%
zip (4KB)	5.00	6.36%	5.17%	5.22%
zip (8KB)	2.34	3.10%	2.75%	2.42%
zip (16KB)	0.95	1.31%	1.32%	1.40%
libharu	68.85	59.23%	58.86%	48.22%
libjpeg	0.002	8.43%	11.60%	3.82%
StrictMath	269.57	1588.81%	1647.83%	729.48%

5   Evaluation

We have evaluated Arabica's functionality, portability and performance using a
set of microbenchmarks, a set of handpicked JNI programs, and SPECjvm 2008.
All tests were performed on a system with Ubuntu 8.10 and an Intel Core2
Quad CPU at 2.66GHz. All experimental results we report is the average of
ten runs. To evaluate Arabica's portability, experiments were conducted on two
JVM implementations: OpenJDK 1.7.0 and IBM J9 1.7.0 R26.

Microbenchmarks for Functionality Testing. A set of small programs were
used to test Arabica's basic functionality. The microbenchmarks include programs for testing basic JNI features, such as passing parameters of various
types and sizes from Java to native code, calling back Java functions in native code, synchronization between Java and native code using `MonitorEnter`
and `MonitorExit`, and others. The microbenchmarks also include programs for
testing Arabica's effectiveness for preventing errors such as unsafe JNI calls. All
microbenchmarks performed correctly on both OpenJDK and IBM J9.

A Set of Handpicked JNI Programs. Our previous implementation, Robusta, was evaluated on a set of handpicked JNI programs. For comparison, we
evaluated Arabica also on the same set of JNI programs. Table 3 presents these
programs and the runtime increase of Arabica (on both OpenJDK and IBM J9)
and Robusta.

In Robusta's experiments, we discovered that its runtime overhead is closely
related to *context switch intensity*, which refers to how often an application
makes context switches between the JVM and the sandbox. Since each context
switch comes with the cost of saving and restoring states and other costs such
as JNI safety checks, the intuition is that the higher the context switch intensity, the higher the runtime overhead. This was confirmed by the experiment
on the `zip` program. The Java side of the `zip` program compresses a file of a
fixed size by dividing the file into data segments of small sizes and passing a

Table 4. Performance overheads of Arabica on SPECjvm2008

Benchmark	Context switches (per millisecond)	Arabica increase
compiler	4.38	7.49%
compress	0.10	11.89%
crypto	1.15	3.09%
derby	0.03	4.07%
mpegaudio	19.36	6.33%
scimark	0.02	9.49%
serial	3.10	4.86%
xml	55.60	112.12%

data segment through a buffer to Zlib, which performs the compression and returns the result to the Java side. Then the Java side passes the next buffer of data to Zlib. Therefore, the bigger the buffer size, the smaller the number of context switches between Java and the sandbox, and therefore the smaller the performance overhead. The `zip` program was tested with buffer sizes 1KB, 2KB, 4KB, 8KB, and 16KB. As shown in the table, the runtime increase of Arabica on `zip` demonstrates the same trend as Robusta: as the buffer size increases, the performance overhead decreases. The `StrictMath` experiment is an extreme case. It repeatedly invokes native code for calculating mathematical functions such as `cos`. It stays in the sandbox for only a very short amount of time before switching out. Consequently, it has high context-switch intensity and thus high performance overhead.

Arabica has a higher overhead than Robusta. This is not surprising as Arabica uses JVMTI for portable sandboxing. JVMTI traces events that happen inside the JVM and therefore comes with extra overhead. We believe this is a reasonable price to pay for portability.

SPECjvm 2008. As presented in Section 4, we have manually separated the core JCL libraries used in SPECjvm 2008 (except for the AWT library). This enables a full evaluation of the performance overhead of native-library sandboxing since SPECjvm2008 contains Java benchmarks whose workload resembles realistic Java applications.

Table 4 presents the performance overheads of SPECjvm2008 benchmarks except for `sunflow`. The benchmark `sunflow` is a GUI program that uses the Java AWT library; we have not yet sandboxed the AWT library, as noted before. All benchmarks were run ten times with sandboxed JCL libraries and another ten times with unsandboxed ones to calculate the average performance overhead. All benchmarks were run under the default configuration of SPECjvm 2008 (2-minute warming up time, one iteration with 4-minute iteration time).

On average, Arabica causes moderate overhead on most benchmarks (less than 15% except for `xml`). The `xml` benchmark makes a high number of invocations of the `StrictMath` library and incurs significant performance penalty.

In general, the experiments demonstrate that the idea of native-library sandboxing can be made portable across JVMs and with modest overhead, especially for programs with low context-switch intensity.

6 Related Work

We adopt SFI [4, 10, 14–17] for sandboxing untrusted code in a trusted environment. Sandboxing is an intensively studied topic in computer security and can be achieved in many ways. One natural approach is an *OS-level solution*. A number of systems aimed to address the insufficiency of commodity-OS isolation primitives by implementing new OSes or augmenting OS kernels [18–22]. These systems map protection domains to OS processes. In comparison, SFI sandboxes untrusted code within the same address space and provides faster context switches between untrusted code and the trusted environment. *Virtual-machine based isolation* is both conceptually elegant and practically feasible (e.g., [23]). But it is even more heavyweight in terms of time, space, and communication costs than OS-level abstractions. Another approach is through *language-based isolation*, which is fine-grained, portable, and flexible. For example, languages such as E [24] and Joe-E [25, 26] enforce language-level isolation through an object-capability model. Their downsides are an overall loss of performance, and more importantly, a single language model has to be adopted. Isolation techniques using pure static types (e.g., [27]) have no runtime overhead, but require nontrivial support from developers and compilers. Finally, *hardware-level protection domains* within a single address space have also been explored [28, 29]. This approach is efficient, but is incompatible with commodity hardware on which most user applications run.

Arabica achieves portable sandboxing across JVMs. This is made possible by the availability of two standard interfaces supported by most JVM implementations: the JNI interface and the JVMTI interface. We believe it should be a desirable goal to design portable mechanisms for sandboxing untrusted code in other environments such as web browsers or other language runtimes (e.g., Python). For instance, Native Client [10] does not function in browsers other than Chrome; but if all browsers support some common interface such as the Pepper Plugin API [30], then browser-portable sandboxing should be obtainable with similar ideas we used to construct Arabica.

Sandboxing standard libraries like what we performed on Java's core libraries is always a good way of improving application security since all applications use those libraries. A bug in a common library can impact a large number of applications. Previous work [31] demonstrated the security benefits of decomposing Python's runtime and libraries into a minimal, security-isolated kernel with a set of sandboxed modules for providing basic services such as networking and file I/O, similar to the micro-kernel approach in the operating system domain. Our sandboxing of Java's core libraries puts all native code in one sandbox, but a future direction is to construct one sandbox for each basic service the JVM supports.

7   Future Work

One immediate work we will perform is to support multiple sandboxes. Arabica constructs one sandbox for all native code because we are mainly concerned with protecting the JVM from native code. But the downside is that one native library may interfere with other libraries since they share the data region in the sandbox. Having only one sandbox is also the reason why we cannot put native code that implements Java security into the sandbox. We would like to construct one sandbox for each native library. This would isolate native code of varying trust levels.

We also plan to continue the process of sandboxing those JCL standard native libraries. Our experience for sandboxing the ones used by SPECjvm suggests that putting those native libraries into the sandbox causes only modest performance slowdown. The security benefits are substantial. In the long run, we would like to put most of the JCL's native libraries into the sandbox. The major challenge, as we have experienced, is to define a clear boundary and carve JVM-portable portions out of the libraries. The manual partitioning process we are using is slow and mistakes might be made. The approach of automatic partitioning based on static analysis seems promising.

8   Conclusions

Putting native libraries into a sandbox and constraining their capability is an effective strategy for preventing them from destroying Java's strong support for safety and security. Arabica demonstrates that this idea can be made JVM-portable with modest performance slowdown. Compared to Robusta, Arabica is much easier to be integrated into a Java environment as it does not modify a JVM's internals. We believe our techniques for making the sandboxing portable across environments and our experience of sandboxing core libraries will be helpful in other contexts, including sandboxing native libraries in languages such as Python and OCaml, and sandboxing plugins in web browsers.

Acknowledgments. We thank Martin Hirzel for suggesting the JVMTI approach for native-code sandboxing. This research is supported by US NSF grants CCF-0915157, CCF-1149211, a research award from Google, and in part by National Natural Science Foundation of China grant 61170051.

References

1. Liang, S.: Java Native Interface: Programmer's Guide and Reference. Addison-Wesley Longman Publishing Co., Inc. (1999)
2. Tan, G., Croft, J.: An empirical security study of the native code in the JDK. In: 17th Usenix Security Symposium, pp. 365–377 (2008)
3. Siefers, J., Tan, G., Morrisett, G.: Robusta: Taming the native beast of the JVM. In: 17th ACM Conference on Computer and Communications Security (CCS), pp. 201–211 (2010)

JVM-Portable Sandboxing of Java's Native Libraries   857

4. Wahbe, R., Lucco, S., Anderson, T., Graham, S.: Efficient software-based fault isolation. In: ACM SIGOPS Symposium on Operating Systems Principles (SOSP), pp. 203–216. ACM Press, New York (1993)
5. Blackburn, S.M., Garner, R., Hoffmann, C., Khan, A.M., McKinley, K.S., Bentzur, R., Diwan, A., Feinberg, D., Frampton, D., Guyer, S.Z., Hirzel, M., Hosking, A.L., Jump, M., Lee, H.B., Moss, J.E.B., Phansalkar, A., Stefanovic, D., VanDrunen, T., von Dincklage, D., Wiedermann, B.: The dacapo benchmarks: java benchmarking development and analysis. In: ACM Conference on Object-Oriented Programming, Systems, Languages, and Applications (OOPSLA), pp. 169–190 (2006)
6. McGraw, G., Felten, E.W.: Securing Java: Getting Down to Business with Mobile Code. John Wiley & Sons (1999)
7. Schoenefeld, M.: Denial-of-service holes in JDK 1.3.1 and 1.4.1_01 (2003), http://www.illegalaccess.org/java/ZipBugs.php (retrieved April 26, 2008)
8. US-CERT: Vulnerability note VU#939609: Sun Java JRE vulnerable to arbitrary code execution via an unspecified error, Credit goes to Chris Evans (January 2007)
9. US-CERT: Vulnerability note VU#138545: Java Runtime Environment image parsing code buffer overflow vulnerability, Credit goes to Chris Evans (June 2007)
10. Yee, B., Sehr, D., Dardyk, G., Chen, B., Muth, R., Ormandy, T., Okasaka, S., Narula, N., Fullagar, N.: Native client: A sandbox for portable, untrusted x86 native code. In: IEEE Symposium on Security and Privacy (S&P) (May 2009)
11. Oracle: JVM tool interface, version 1.0, http://docs.oracle.com/javase/1.5.0/docs/guide/jvmti/jvmti.html (2010)
12. Lee, B., Hirzel, M., Grimm, R., Wiedermann, B., McKinley, K.S.: Jinn: Synthesizing a dynamic bug detector for foreign language interfaces. In: ACM Conference on Programming Language Design and Implementation (PLDI), pp. 36–49 (2010)
13. Wallach, D.S., Felten, E.W.: Understanding java stack inspection. In: IEEE Symposium on Security and Privacy, pp. 52–63 (1998)
14. Erlingsson, Ú., Schneider, F.: SASI enforcement of security policies: A retrospective. In: Proceedings of the New Security Paradigms Workshop (NSPW), pp. 87–95. ACM Press (1999)
15. McCamant, S., Morrisett, G.: Evaluating SFI for a CISC architecture. In: 15th Usenix Security Symposium (2006)
16. Ford, B., Cox, R.: Vx32: Lightweight user-level sandboxing on the x86. In: USENIX Annual Technical Conference, pp. 293–306 (2008)
17. Castro, M., Costa, M., Martin, J.P., Peinado, M., Akritidis, P., Donnelly, A., Barham, P., Black, R.: Fast byte-granularity software fault isolation. In: ACM SIGOPS Symposium on Operating Systems Principles (SOSP), pp. 45–58 (2009)
18. Efstathopoulos, P., Krohn, M., Vandebogart, S., Frey, C., Ziegler, D., Kohler, E., Mazières, D., Kaashoek, M.F., Morris, R.: Labels and event processes in the Asbestos operating system. In: ACM SIGOPS Symposium on Operating Systems Principles (SOSP), pp. 17–30 (2005)
19. Zeldovich, N., Boyd-Wickizer, S., Kohler, E., Mazières, D.: Making information flow explicit in HiStar. In: USENIX Symposium on Operating Systems Design and Implementation (OSDI), pp. 263–278 (2006)
20. Krohn, M., Yip, A., Brodsky, M., Cliffer, N., Kaashoek, M.F., Kohler, E., Morris, R.: Information flow control for standard OS abstractions. In: ACM SIGOPS Symposium on Operating Systems Principles (SOSP), pp. 321–334 (2007)
21. Bittau, A., Marchenko, P., Handley, M., Karp, B.: Wedge: splitting applications into reduced-privilege compartments. In: Proceedings of the 5th USENIX Symposium on Networked Systems Design and Implementation, pp. 309–322 (2008)

22. Watson, R., Anderson, J., Laurie, B., Kennaway, K.: Capsicum: Practical capabilities for UNIX. In: 19th Usenix Security Symposium, pp. 29–46 (2010)
23. Cox, R.S., Gribble, S.D., Levy, H.M., Hansen, J.G.: A safety-oriented platform for web applications. In: IEEE Symposium on Security and Privacy (S&P), pp. 350–364 (2006)
24. Miller, M.: Robust composition: towards a unified approach to access control and concurrency control. PhD thesis, Johns Hopkins University, Baltimore, MD (2006)
25. Mettler, A., Wagner, D., Close, T.: Joe-E: A security-oriented subset of Java. In: Network and Distributed Systems Symposium, NDSS (2010)
26. Krishnamurthy, A., Mettler, A., Wagner, D.: Fine-grained privilege separation for web applications. In: Proceedings of the 19th International Conference on World Wide Web (WWW 2010), pp. 551–560 (2010)
27. Morrisett, G., Walker, D., Crary, K., Glew, N.: From System F to typed assembly language. ACM Transactions on Programming Languages and Systems 21(3), 527–568 (1999)
28. Witchel, E., Rhee, J., Asanović, K.: Mondrix: memory isolation for linux using Mondriaan memory protection. In: ACM SIGOPS Symposium on Operating Systems Principles (SOSP), pp. 31–44 (2005)
29. Neumann, P., Watson, R.: Capabilities revisited: A holistic approach to bottom-to-top assurance of trustworthy systems. In: Fourth Layered Assurance Workshop (2010)
30. PPAPI, http://code.google.com/p/ppapi/wiki/Concepts
31. Cappos, J., Dadgar, A., Rasley, J., Samuel, J., Beschastnikh, I., Barsan, C., Krishnamurthy, A., Anderson, T.E.: Retaining sandbox containment despite bugs in privileged memory-safe code. In: 17th ACM Conference on Computer and Communications Security (CCS), pp. 212–223 (2010)

Codejail: Application-Transparent Isolation of Libraries with Tight Program Interactions*

Yongzheng Wu[1], Sai Sathyanarayan[2], Roland H.C. Yap[2], and Zhenkai Liang[2]

[1] Singapore University of Technology and Design
yongzheng_wu@sutd.edu.sg
[2] School of Computing, National University of Singapore
{sathya,ryap,liangzk}@comp.nus.edu.sg

Abstract. Dynamically linked libraries are commonly used in software programs to facilitate code reuse. Once a library is linked into a software program, a bug in the library can lead to compromise of the whole program. Moreover, the library may also contain malicious code. Existing solutions for software component isolation assume simple interactions between a library and the main program, otherwise, they require significant modification of the main program and the library. In this paper, we propose a novel solution, Codejail, which supports a partial isolation of libraries that have tight memory interactions with the main program. Codejail requires no modification to the main program or the library. We demonstrate using a Linux prototype that Codejail can work easily with real-world programs and libraries. The performance is good for a portable implementation with costs commensurate with the degree of tight interaction.

1   Introduction

Software today heavily relies on dynamically-linked libraries. Libraries are usually seen as a necessary step to facilitate code reuse. While the use of libraries can considerably simplify and speedup software development, there is a downside, namely, the libraries can themselves have bugs. In this paper, we distinguish between the code in specific libraries (or simply library) with the code outside the library which we call the *main program*. Once a library is linked into the main program, a bug in the library can lead to compromise of the entire program.

Specifically, there are two main threats posed by third-party libraries to its main program. First, the library may be vulnerable because it contains a bug that can be exploited by an attacker. Typical attacks are through memory corruptions, such as buffer overflow together with code injection or return-oriented programming [1]. Even though the main program contains no vulnerabilities, vulnerabilities in the library may propagate and affect the main program. Second, a library could also be malicious. The extensive use of libraries, i.e. dynamically linked libraries, only exacerbates these problems.

---

* This work has been supported by a DRTech grant R-394-000-054-232.

S. Foresti, M. Yung, and F. Martinelli (Eds.): ESORICS 2012, LNCS 7459, pp. 859–876, 2012.

To mitigate the threats from dynamic libraries, a range of solutions have been proposed to isolate program components to control their privilege [2–5]. Most solutions adopt a separated memory model: a component can only access its own memory, which is mutually exclusive with the memory of the main program. While this model works with simple inter-component interactions, it either does not work or is not efficient for libraries that engage in tight interactions with the main program. Rather, it is more common for programs and libraries to be written with tight interactions, such as sharing global variables, passing references to complex data structures, callbacks, longjmp, etc. It is not practical to assume that such libraries can be rewritten to eliminate the tight interaction, let alone doing so for all software using such libraries. This is even less practical for close-source libraries/programs.

Our goal is to mitigate the threats from dynamic libraries in a transparent fashion. Ideally, we want to reduce or prevent these threats without the need to modify either the libraries or the main program when there are tight interactions between them. Existing solutions, however, are not transparent to the main program and libraries. Often, significant work is needed to port a library and a main program in order to make library execution safe while preserving the functionality. This usually needs source code, thus, preventing reuse of existing binaries. We argue that while existing solutions can provide security, they do not address transparency and hence are of limited applicability.

We use NativeClient (NaCl) [5] as an example to illustrate the need for a transparent library security mechanism. NaCl is designed for isolating *untrusted native browser plugins*. It adopts a separated memory model that ensures an untrusted component can only access its own dedicated memory and code. As a result, communication between the trusted and untrusted components are in a remote-procedure-call style, i.e. parameters and return values are passed by value and data structures are serialized. However, libraries are not typically designed for this model. Instead, most libraries assume that the library and main program share the same memory and by-reference parameter passing is commonly used for efficiency. There are practical difficulties with porting any code that uses such assumptions. Good software engineering practices mean that details of data structures are encapsulated and (mostly) opaque, and thus porting requires reverse engineering the implementation. Many complex libraries employ tight interactions such as callbacks and longjmp, which are not allowed in NaCl because the code segment is isolated, e.g. the popular libpng library uses an opaque structure to keep internal states with longjmp as the error handling mechanism. Thus, NaCl cannot be used to isolate libpng, and libpng is used in a number of web browsers. Many security vulnerabilities have been found in libpng, rendering such browsers vulnerable.

In this paper, we present Codejail, a framework to isolate untrusted libraries. We assume that libraries have well defined APIs, which specify the extent of the tight interactions with the main program. This is reasonable since it is necessary for the user of a library to understand how to make use of it. To prevent bugs in a library from compromising the whole program, Codejail ensures: (i) memory access in the library is sandboxed so that side effects are limited to conform to its API; and (ii) system privileges are controlled to be only what is allowed for its designed tasks. The design goal of Codejail is to provide application-transparent solutions for isolating libraries that have tight interaction with the main program. Unlike the separated memory model, Codejail proposes a semi-shared memory model, which allows common tight interactions while ensuring the integrity of main program's data. In this model, the jailed library has full access to its own memory and read access to other memory. In addition, the main program can selectively allow the jailed library to write to any memory. We support callbacks where the jailed library needs to run a function supplied by the main program using the main program's data and the use of longjmp to return to the main program from the jailed library. As we work at the binary library API level, library source code is not needed and Codejail works with dynamically linked libraries.

Although the overall goal is to support tight interactions of the main program with an untrusted library transparently, we have some restrictions. Codejail ensures that a jailed library is not able to modify arbitrary memory outside its sandbox. This restriction applies even if the library has no vulnerabilities nor is it malicious, so not every library with tight interaction can work transparently with Codejail. Nevertheless, we believe that a much larger class of libraries and software will function with Codejail than with more strongly separated memory models such as software fault isolation.

We have built a portable Unix prototype implementation of Codejail in Linux. We demonstrate the usability of Codejail to transparently sandbox well-known dynamic libraries using the off-the-shelf binaries of standard programs and libraries. Even though our prototype is portable and works in user-mode, the performance impact is still reasonable. Where there are large numbers of calls to a jailed library (or callbacks) and the library needs to write significant data outside its own memory, there will naturally be more overhead. We have tested libpng with the Mozilla Firefox browser and were able to protect against attacks from libpng to Firefox. From a performance standpoint, we did not observe any degradation in the user experience when using Firefox.

In summary, our major contribution is the design and prototype implementation of a novel approach, Codejail, that isolates untrusted libraries. Codejail supports tight program interactions required by a signification portion of libraries. It can also be applied transparently, without modifying the software program or the untrusted library.

2   Related Work

Applying the principle of least privilege by partitioning a program into a number of processes with different privilege has been studied by many researchers. Provos et al. [6] partitioned OpenSSH into two parts, a privileged master to only handle authentication and unprivileged slaves to handle the rest of the work. Kilpatrick [7] proposed Privman, a library to help partition privileged UNIX daemons where the main program talks to a privileged server with the Privman library to perform privileged tasks. This is by replacing privileged function calls to the corresponding Privman wrappers, but a significant amount of manual work is still necessary. Brumley et al. [8] proposed Privtrans to automate the privilege separation work. The programmer manually specifies privileged data and functions. Privtrans automatically separates the program into an untrusted slave and a trusted monitor, each running in a separated process. Access to privileged data and functions only takes place in the trusted monitor. Both Privman and Privtrans adopt a trusted callee model where the main program is untrusted and the privileged operations are performed by a trusted monitor process. In contrast, Codejail addresses the opposite situation with a trusted caller and untrusted callee.

There are other solutions on confining memory access of a software component without separation into different processes. Software Fault Isolation (SFI) [2] ensures all memory accesses of the untrusted component is within the memory dedicated to the component by statically verifying direct memory access instructions and dynamically checking indirect access. Other work [3–5, 9, 10] uses the same idea while using different techniques and hardware features. Vx32 [4] uses the segment register in x86 to confine memory access in hardware. Other solutions [11–13] provide isolation by confining the untrusted component to a memory region assigned to the component, we call such a memory model as a *separated memory model*. There are two problems with this model. Firstly, existing code typically assumes global memory access and has to be recompiled or manually ported. Secondly, inter-component pass-by-reference function calls need to be changed to pass-by-value, as the callee cannot access the memory of the caller. This is not easy or efficient for complex data structures.

Wedge [14] uses tagged memory to restrict memory accesses of software components, where each memory allocation is explicitly associated with a tag. Software is partitioned into least-privilege components, which can only access memory with specific set of tags. Compared to the separated memory model, Wedge allows memory sharing, such as by-reference function parameters, if the memory regions have compatible tags. However, it needs each component to understand how memory is used by other components. This requires understanding the memory access behavior of all components in the software and memory allocation has to be modified to specify the correct tag. When modification is not possible, Wedge provides a way to specify the default tag for all allocations made by a component. This can lead to the confused deputy problem. Consider a malicious component C_1 and a benign component C_2 both using component C_3. C_2 uses C_3 to allocate memory to store critical data. C_1 may be able to tamper with C_2's data by using C_3.

3 Problem Statement

3.1 Motivating Example

We use the libpng library to demonstrate the problem of tight interactions between a main program and a library. It shows the difficulty of supporting such interactions in the separated memory model. Fig. 1 shows a sample main program using libpng. We underline the key points in the listing, and we emphasize whether main or libpng manage the memory of particular data structures, as well as who uses it.

The main data structure for libpng is an opaque structure png_struct pointed by png. It is created at Line 7 with png_create_read_struct (similarly, info at Line 8) – memory allocated by libpng is used in main. This structures pointed by png and info can be thought of as identifying the interaction between main and libpng but as they are not directly accessed by the main program, the details should be considered as private and implementation specific. If libpng is sandboxed using a separated memory model, parameter marshalling of png_struct will break the separation between interface and implementation. Rather than marshalling, png can be treated as a resource handle rather than pointer. However, this can crash the main program if it tries to dereference it. png_destroy_read_struct at Line 10 & 22 is used to free the opaque structure as well as resetting the pointer to NULL – libpng changes png in main.

Due to lack of language-based exception handling in C, setjmp and longjmp are often used in libraries including libpng. At Line 9, setjmp is used to create the error handling code in main, the jmpbuf comes from memory managed by libpng. Such library code does not fit with the separated memory model, e.g. the longjmp branches outside the allowed code range and stack frame in NaCl.

The function main reads the PNG file in a loop. It passes chunks of PNG data to libpng using png_process_data at Line 19 – libpng reads buff managed by main. The main program also passes the function pointer row_callback to libpng at Line 14 – the function resides in main. In png_process_data, row_callback is called by libpng whenever a row of pixels is decoded. The main program then displays the row through its row_callback function. This mechanism is known as *function callback*, where the main program registers a function pointer in the library, which will be called by the library. The callback mechanism will cause a similar problem as longjmp in separated memory model approaches.

3.2 Tight Interactions

We now examine the typical interactions between the main program and a library, including those that are challenging to support under the separated memory model, such as the side effects of library functions and function callbacks:

1. **By-Value Parameter Passing and Return:** The parameters are copied from the caller to the callee and vice versa for return values, e.g. sqrt().

```
1  static void row-callback(png_struct *png, png_bytep new_row,
2        png_uint_32 row_num, int pass) {
3    // display the row
4  }
5  int main (void) {
6    FILE *fp = fopen("foo.png", "rb");
7    png_struct *png = png_create_read_struct(...);
8    png_info *info = png_create_info_struct(png);
9    if (setjmp(png_jmpbuf(png))) {
10      png_destroy_read_struct(&png, &info, NULL);
11      close(fp);
12      return 1;
13    }
14    png_set_progressive_read_fn(ptr, ..., row_callback, ...);
15    while (1) {
16      char buff[1024];
17      size_t len = fread(buff, 1, 1024, fp);
18      if (!len) break;
19      png_process_data(png, info, buff, len);
20    }
21    fclose(fp);
22    png_destroy_read_struct(&png, &info, NULL);
23    return 0;
24  }
```

Fig. 1. Using `libpng` to read a PNG file

2. **By-Reference Parameter Passing and Return:** The caller passes pointers of the parameters, and memory is dereferenced by the callee and possibly modified, e.g. `strlen()` and `asctime_r()`.
3. **Global Variable:** Some libraries export global variables that can be directly accessed by the main program or other libraries, e.g. `errno` from `libc`.
4. **Function Callback:** Library functions may need to call the main program in order to read/write data or signal task completion, e.g. `png_process_data()` makes a callback as described in Sec. 3.1.
5. **Long Jump:** Some libraries, e.g. `libpng`, use `setjmp/longjmp` as an error-handling mechanism. This can cause the library to transfer control to the main program without using the return mechanism.

The first type of interaction involves no tight memory interactions, which can be easily supported by memory isolation models. However, the other types of interactions are not compatible with memory isolation models. They either have implicit shared memory operands, or involve non-standard control transfer between code of the main program and the library.

3.3   Threat Model and Design Goal

Threat Model. In our approach, we aim to mitigate the untrusted library's threat to directly access undesired system resources or memory. Note that the untrusted library can cause indirect threats through the data it returned to the main program, such as returning malicious data to exploit memory errors in the main program. This type of threats is out of the scope of our solution (and the related solutions in Section 2). It can be addressed by the main program through data sanitizing, checking returned data (including updates of by-reference parameters) from the untrusted library.

Design Goal. Under this threat model, an untrusted library must be separated from the main program to prevent it directly accessing the main program's resources and memory. However, the library needs tight interactions with the main program. The goal of Codejail is to isolate untrusted libraries into different execution contexts. The contexts share a flexible memory model which supports close interactions. Specifically, our solution guarantees the following properties:

- The untrusted library cannot execute arbitrary code in the trusted context.
- The untrusted library cannot crash the main process through, for example, null pointer dereference, illegal memory access and deadlock.
- The untrusted library cannot make arbitrary system calls, for example, only system calls explicitly specified by the main process are allowed. The specification can include a set of allowed system calls, a set of files and directories and system resource limits such as memory usage, time limits, etc.

4   The Codejail Approach

We describe Codejail's key techniques showing how they meet our design goals. An untrusted library is typically used in the following fashion. The software consists of a trusted main program, an untrusted library, and a trusted library. The main program uses functions from both libraries; the untrusted library uses the trusted library. The main program only interacts with the untrusted library through the library's API, which specifies functions exported from the libraries with their parameter types and calling conventions. For by-reference parameters, the API should specify whether the callee updates the parameter. The API also specifies exported global variables and their data types. For data types that are directly accessed externally, their data structures have to be specified, e.g., in a header file. We do not assume availability of source code of the main program or the libraries. However, we assume the header file of the library to be available. We have no assumption about the binary of the untrusted library, i.e. it can contain arbitrary code including indirect branches and system calls.

4.1   Codejail Overview

Fig. 2 gives an overview of Codejail. Codejail creates contexts to separate the main program and the untrusted library. The main program runs in the trusted context, while the untrusted library runs in the untrusted context. When the main program calls (Step 2) a function in the untrusted library, Codejail switches execution to the untrusted context. When the untrusted library function returns

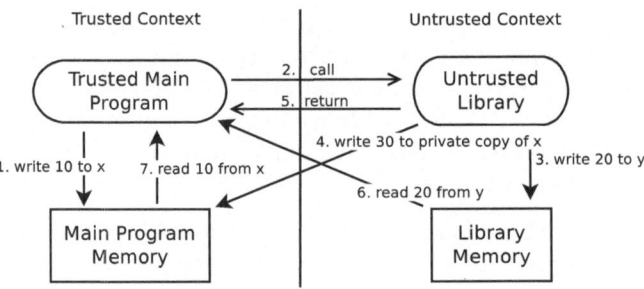

Fig. 2. An overview of Codejail

(Step 5) to the main program, execution switches back to trusted context. Calling functions in the trusted library does not change the context. Calling any function, including functions in the main program, in the untrusted context remains in the untrusted context. However, callbacks can be set up so that the untrusted library can call them to switch from untrusted to trusted context. The untrusted context is unprivileged, and its system resource accesses are sandboxed.

Memory access in the untrusted context is sandboxed. It can write to its own memory. However, for writes to the main program's memory, changes are only observable in the untrusted context but not in the trusted context. In Fig. 2 Step 3, the untrusted library assigns 20 to variable y, which is in its memory. The main program observes this change in Step 6. However, in Step 4, the assignment of 30 to x, which is in the main program, is not observable by the main program in Step 7, where the old value 10 is read. The main program can selectively "commit" changes made in untrusted context, so that it sees the value 30 in x. Other changes are lost in both contexts.

4.2 Memory Access Policies

Codejail classifies writable memory into three types: M_m, memory of the main program; M_j, memory of the untrusted library; and M_l, memory of the trusted library. The semantics of memory access depends on context and memory type.

Table 1 shows the classification of writable memory types. The static allocated memory typically includes global variables and static local variables. In the ELF binary format, such variables reside in the .bss and initialized data segment. The static allocated memory is associated with the code that declares it. In Codejail, we further divided it into three parts: the main program, trusted libraries, and untrusted libraries. Codejail divides the stack into two parts: one used by the trusted context (including the main program and trusted libraries) and the other used by untrusted context. Similarly, the heap is divided into two – different contexts allocate memory in different heaps.

We now describe the policies for memory access on the three types of memory:

- M_m **Memory of Main Program:** Initially, M_m memory in both contexts is synchronized, i.e. memory read gives the same value for the same address.

Table 1. Memory types in Codejail

Memory		Type
	main program	M_m
static allocated memory	untrusted library	M_j
	trusted library	M_l
stack	trusted context	M_m
	untrusted context	M_j
heap	trusted context	M_m
	untrusted context	M_j

After the main context writes to it, the memory is still synchronized. However, after the untrusted context writes to it, the memory is not synchronized. Each context has a different view of the memory, so that the memory writes are only observable in its own context. As a result, after the untrusted library function returns, the main program is not able to observe the change made by the untrusted library. In this way, we prevent the untrusted library from corrupting data of the main program.

In some cases, we want the library to update some data. For example, we want `memcpy(dest, src, n)` to update `[dest, dest+n]`. Codejail provides the API (`cj_recv(void *ptr, size_t size)`) to copy data from the untrusted context to the trusted context.

Before each untrusted function call, M_m memory is re-synchronized to the synchronized state, and changes made by the previous untrusted function, unless committed through `cj_recv`, are discarded.

- M_j **Memory of Untrusted Library:** Both contexts can observe the updates made by each other. As a result, the main program should sanitize it before using its value.
- M_l **Memory of Trusted Library:** Initially M_l memory in both contexts is synchronized. However, memory writes made by either context cause it to be not synchronized, thus the other context is not able to observe the changes. M_l memory is never re-synchronized. For example, if we consider `libc` as the trusted library, the random seed used by `rand()` is in M_l. Thus a different copy of the random seed is kept in each context. The untrusted context cannot modify the trusted context's seed.

4.3 Supporting Tight Interactions

Using the memory types and access policies, Codejail supports tight interactions between the trusted context and the untrusted context.

Pass-by-Reference: The main program passes pointer p to the untrusted library. Memory pointed by p can be allocated in trusted context (M_m) or untrusted context (M_j). In Line 10 & 22 of Fig. 1, `&png` points to memory in the main program's stack, i.e. in M_m. The main program has to call `cj_recv` to "commit" the change made in `libpng`. In Line 19, `png` points to memory allocated

```
png_uint_32 wrapper_png_get_text (png_structp png_ptr,
  png_infop info_ptr, png_textp *text_ptr, int *num_text)
{
  png_uint_32 retval = (png_uint_32) cj_jail(
    real_png_get_text, 4, png_ptr, info_ptr, text_ptr, num_text);
  cj_recv(text_ptr, sizeof(png_textp));
  cj_recv(num_text, sizeof(int));
  return retval;
}
```

Fig. 3. An wrapper function for png_get_text() in libpng

in libpng, i.e. in M_j. The main program does not need to call cj_recv in this case.

Global Variables of the Untrusted Library: The memory model of Codejail allows the main program to transparently read and write global variables exported by the untrusted library. This is because they are in M_j, which allows both contexts to observe changes made by each other.

Callback: Codejail allows the untrusted library to call the main program's functions in a trusted context. To do this, the main program calls Codejail API cj_reg_callback to register a callback function. A function pointer f is passed to cj_reg_callback and another function pointer f' is returned. f' is then passed to the untrusted library. When the untrusted library calls f' in the untrusted context, Codejail will switch to trusted context and call f. After f returns, execution switches back to untrusted context. Both call and return are transparently handled by Codejail. Callbacks can be nested recursively, i.e. during a callback, the main program can call untrusted library functions, which then make more callbacks.

Long Jump: Codejail allows long jumps between different contexts. To prevent the untrusted library from jumping to arbitrary code in the trusted context, Codejail ensures all long jumps are using a jmp_buf registered with setjmp.

We handle typical cases of tight interactions. However, there are cases that Codejail does not support. For example, memory allocation in the trusted context is freed in the untrusted context, which is not allowed to protect M_m. When the interface between the library and the main program is not well defined, Codejail cannot support the interaction. This includes undocumented memory write by the library, undocumented library functions called by the main program, and passing opaque data structures to the library. Such not well defined interactions are less common being not good software engineering practices.

4.4   Codejail Primitives

There are two ways to apply Codejail. One is to write a wrapper library exporting the same set of functions as the untrusted library. The wrapper library calls the

Codejail API. In this way, we do not need to modify the main program. The wrapper library is reusable on any program that uses the untrusted library.

Fig. 3 shows an example of the wrapper function for png_get_text(), which passes back a number of strings to the caller. real_png_get_text is the real libpng function. A string pointer and integer are allocated in the trusted context (M_m). cj_recv is necessary to pass them from the untrusted context. The actual string is allocated in untrusted context (M_j) but it is not necessary to call cj_recv to pass the string. In this example, assuming 32-bits, 20 bytes (one function address and 4 parameters) are passed before the jailed call. 12 bytes (one return value and 2 output parameters) are passed after the jailed call.

The second way is where a general wrapper library is not feasible, or some assumptions in the main program can make Codejail to be more efficient. In these cases, we can modify the main program, to call Codejail API directly.

We list the Codejail API functions which are called from the trusted context:

- void *cj_jail (void *func, int argc, ...)
  It switches the context from trusted to untrusted and calls function func with argc number of integer type[1] arguments and return value.
- void cj_recv (void *data, size_t size)
  It synchronizes M_m and M_l memory from the untrusted context to the trusted context. Note that only one address is specified, because the address space layout is the same in both contexts.
- void *cj_reg_callback (void *mainfunc, int argc)
  It takes a function pointer in the main program and returns another function pointer which can be called from the untrusted context. When it is called, the context is switched from untrusted to trusted.
- void *cj_jail_func (void *libfunc, int argc)
  It takes a function pointer in the untrusted library and returns another function pointer which can be called from the trusted context. When it's called, context is switched from trusted to untrusted.
- FILE *cj_duplicate_file (FILE *fp)
  It takes a file pointer opened in the trusted context and returns a *shadow file* pointer to be used in the untrusted context. The purpose of this function is to allow passing FILE pointers from the trusted context to untrusted context without understanding the internal data structure of the FILE structure. The untrusted context is able to operate on the shadow file which points to the same underling file. The limitation is that the file will be corrupted if both contexts operate on the file after calling this function, because the file pointer in both FILE structures will be out of sync.

4.5   Security Analysis

Although Codejail's design achieves the functionality requirement, attackers may launch attacks targeting Codejail. We consider the following potential attacks.

---

[1] For simplicity, this notation assumes integer type arguments which include char, short, int, long and pointer types but can be extended in a straightforward way.

- **Denial-of-Service**: The untrusted library can refuse to perform its expected function by, for example, infinite looping, infinite memory allocation, segmentation fault. This can be caught by timeout or signal handler and handled appropriately.
- **Return-to-Libc, Return oriented attacks**: Some library APIs allow the libraries to pass function pointers in returned data structure and the main process will call the pointed function. A potential attack is for the untrusted library to pass a pointer to a malicious function and hope the function is invoked in the trusted context. This is prevented by not allowing the library's code to be executed in the trusted context. In case the main program intends to call the function, it can call the Codejail API cj_jail_func described in Sec 4.4 to wrap the function pointer.

  Another attack is to return pointer to code in the main program or trusted library, similar to return-to-libc attack and return-oriented-programming. This is prevented by wrapping all function pointers.
- **Abusing system privileges**: We assume system privileges requested by the untrusted library to be examined by either the programmer of the main program or system administrator, depending on how Codejail is applied.

5   Implementation

Our prototype Codejail is implemented portably in Linux in user mode. We now discuss the implementation choices and challenges.

Context for Isolating Libraries. We choose process as the basic mechanism for implementing the two contexts, a main process for trusted context and a jailed process for untrusted context. Communication across contexts is supported by sending and receiving data through a UNIX socket. In the jailed process, we use etrace [15] as a portable user-mode system call interposition mechanism. (However, kernel-based system call sandboxing mechanisms, e.g. Systrace [16], can be used). When etrace finds a suspicious system call, it sends a signal to the Codejail process. Now, the Codejail process can abort the execution and safely pass the control back to the main program. Thus, Codejail is effective against memory corruption and arbitrary code execution attacks as well as side effects from system calls.

Memory Sharing Across Contexts. Memory of M_m and M_j is shared between two processes using the standard shm_open and mmap API. Codejail creates virtual files to be mapped into both processes. M_j memory is mapped as MAP_SHARED in both processes, so that memory writes can be observed by each other. M_m memory is mapped as MAP_SHARED in the main process and MAP_PRIVATE in jailed process, so that the main process cannot observe jailed process' memory writes. Re-synchronization of M_m memory is done by re-mapping (munmap and mmap) it in the jailed process.

Codejail hooks the memory allocation routines in order to control memory allocation in the M_m for the main process and M_j for the jailed process. This works for most programs using the standard library memory allocator or custom allocators which call the standard allocator.[2]

Since Codejail has to maintain a symmetric memory address layout, mmap performed in one process has to be performed in the other. For readonly mmap, we can simply call mmap with the same parameters in the other process. However, writable mmap has to be handled properly in order to ensure our memory model. The rule is that mmap performed by the main process should be in M_m; while mmap by jailed process should be in M_j. For writable anonymous mmap, we can consider it as a heap allocation. For writable file-backed and MAP_PRIVATE mmap, we can allocate on the heap and read in the file. However, this is inefficient as it breaks the sole purpose of mmap, which is not to read the whole file.

Implementation of Codejail Primitives. The initialization of Codejail is performed after dynamic linking and before calling main. It is implemented transparently by hooking __libc_start_main. Codejail forks a new process and setups the shared memory and the communication channel. After that, the jailed process reads and waits for a message from the socket.

When the main process calls cj_jail, the target function address and arguments are send through the UNIX socket. The jailed process receives them and calls the target function. After the function returns, jailed process sends the return value to the main process through the socket. Callbacks are handled similarly in the reverse direction. To prevent the jailed process from invoking arbitrary internal functions in the main process, a callback table is used (similar to the jump table in related work in control flow integrity [17–19]). When the main process calls cj_recv, the address and size are sent and the memory is received. At the end of the main program, main process sends a termination message and the jailed process exits.

Codejail supports multi-threaded program, but for simplicity we assume only one thread uses the untrusted library at a time. We have one thread in the jailed process servicing multiple threads in the main process. A *pthread* mutex prevents multiple simultaneous library calls.

Application-Transparency Support. To transparently support existing program and libraries, we use a wrapper library exporting the same functions as the isolated library. The LD_PRELOAD environment variable "injects" the wrapper library into a program so that it transparently calls our wrapper functions instead of the real untrusted library functions.[3] Functions in the wrapper library identify the original functions using dlsym(RTLD_NEXT, name), and call the original

---

[2] Some programs use completely custom allocators, e.g. Firefox uses *jemalloc*. In Codejail, the allocated memory will not be shared, but only valid in the allocating process. If the process passes the memory to the other process, it will cause a segmentation fault when it is accessed. We get around this by re-building Firefox and disabling *jemalloc* in the build configuration.

[3] If dynamic loading with dlopen() is used, our wrapper library will be opened when a relative path is used. If an absolute path is used, which is uncommon, the original library will be opened, calling its API has an exception as it is not executable in the main context.

Table 2. Libraries used in evaluation and their types of program interactions

Name	Callback	Shadow File	Modify main's Memory	Pass-by-Reference	longjmp
libpng	Yes	Yes	Yes	Yes	Yes
libexpat	Yes	No	No	Yes	No
libbzip	No	Yes	Yes	Yes	No
libtiff	No	Yes	Yes	Yes	Yes

functions using cj_jail then cj_recv to receive data from the jailed library when necessary.

Attacks targeting the implementation. When the attackers are aware of the Codejail implementation mechanism, they may launch attacks targeting the implementation. We discuss possible attacks and the defenses.

- *Attacking Codejail's internal states*: In the jailed process, the Codejail's internal routines such as heap allocator, signal handler, and RPC handler, execute in the same memory and privilege state as the jailed library routines. Thus, we consider the Codejail's internal routines only as helper routines rather than trusted routines. The security guarantees are not based on the correctness of these routines, thus attacking the internal routines and states does not break the guarantees.
- *Denial-of-service attacks*: Infinite loops and memory allocation can be dealt with by setrlimit, causing an exception in the jailed process. It can then caught by a timeout set in the main process.
- *Controlling the main program using ptrace, /proc/[pid]/mem*: The jail process can use system mechanisms such as ptrace and /proc interface to modify the main process' memory. This is prevented by the system call policy.
- *Library constructor*: The separation into two processes takes place after library loading and before calling main(). Before the separation, the process run with full privilege, thus a malicious library can call system calls in library constructor, which is called before main(). One way to prevent this is to delay the library constructor and call it after the separation.

6   Evaluation

We have evaluated the Codejail prototype using a number of real-world programs using complex real world libraries. The experiments are run on an Intel Core 2 Duo 2.80GHz processor with 4GB of RAM in Linux 2.6.35.

We evaluate the following libraries which exhibit a full range of tight program interactions: libpng (1.4.2) provides handling of Portable Network Graphics (PNG) images; libtiff (3.8.2) provides support for Tag Image File Format (TIFF) images; libexpat (2.0.1) is a XML parser library; and libbzip2 (1.0.4) provides a general purpose compressor/decompressor. The types of program interactions used by the above libraries are shown in Table 2. For example, libtiff does not use callbacks, while libpng and libexpat do. We also chose these libraries for their popularity and because the particular versions have the following known vulnerabilities: CVE-2010-1205, CVE2009-3720, CVE-2008-1372 and CVE-2010-3087.

6.1   Functionality and Usability

We wrote wrappers for all the libraries and evaluated them on the command line utilities listed in Fig. 4. We tested transparency by using the wrappers with executables of each program together with corresponding DLL binary. In all cases, we could transparently deploy Codejail for the program and library with the same functional behavior.

In addition, for libpng, which exhibits the full range of close interaction in Table 2, we tested with several GUI programs that display PNGs using libpng, namely, the eog image viewer, the Mozilla firefox web browser and the xfig and dia graphics editors. All these programs are multi-threaded. The programs all worked and displayed images correctly with Codejail. As these are GUI programs, we did not measure performance, rather their overall usability. We did not find any perceptible delays or other differences in the usage.[4]

As Firefox is a complex program, we show some details of how we jail libpng in Firefox (3.6.4). This version of Firefox is selected as having modern features but still being single process (due to the existing restrictions of the prototype). Normally, Firefox includes its own malloc library, jemalloc, and a special version of libpng. This is because it supports the Animated Portable Network Graphics (APNG) file format which is an unoffical extension to PNG and thus not supported by libpng. However, there is also a patch available to support APNG files with the standard libpng library. While it is feasible to hook the internal Firefox code and redirect them to the appropriate wrappers, we want use Codejail to jail untrusted dynamically linked libraries. Thus, we simply recompiled Firefox, to not use jemalloc and its own internal libpng code so that Codejail can use the APNG patched libpng DLL.

6.2   Performance Evaluation

Fig 4 shows benchmarking Codejail on four command-line programs using the libraries. For each library, we used two input files of different sizes. We measured execution time without Codejail; with Codejail but not jailing any library functions (to see the impact of Codejail on the main program and trusted library); and jailing all library functions. In all the test cases, using Codejail without jailing the library has small overhead.

---

[4] The figures in the paper are drawn using dia with Codejail.

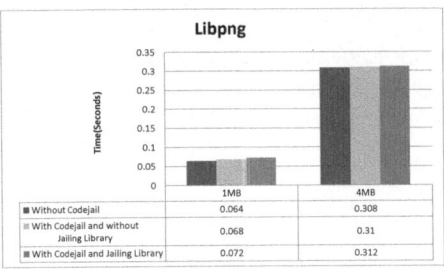

(a) pngtopnm using libpng

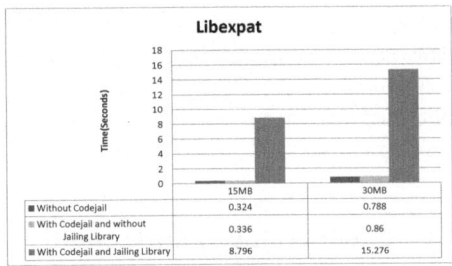

(b) xmlwf using libexpat

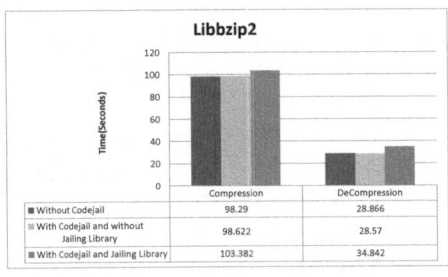

(c) bzip2 using libbzip2 (300MB decompressed)

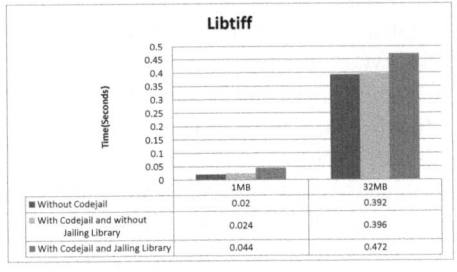

(d) tifftopnm using libtiff

Fig. 4. Performance evaluation: (i) native; (ii) program with Codejail but the library is not jailed; and (iii) program with Codejail and library being jailed

The libpng library, although the most complex, has the best performance. The overhead is low as there are only 15 jailed function calls and no callbacks are used by pngtopnm as it uses file I/O style of using libpng rather than the display function style.[5] The pixel buffer is allocated by libpng thus not copied.

On the other end of the scale is, xmlwf with libexpat. It has large overheads due to the large number[6] of callbacks made. The callbacks have more overhead as they incur context switches.

bzip2 using libbzip2 shows the advantage of the Codejail memory model where the jail can access the main memory. In bzip2, the main program handles I/O to do with decompressed file while the library handles I/O of the compressed file. When compressing, the original data can be accessed directly in the jail which handles the compression and writing of the compressed file, thus, the overheads are small ($\sim 5\%$). Decompression has a higher overhead as the main program allocates the output buffer and ask the library to fill it. Thus, cj_recv is needed to copy the buffer. In total 298.9MB is copied, which is about the same size of the decompressed file.

---

[5] However, eog and firefox use callbacks with libpng.

[6] It registers callbacks which are called for all XML nodes. 425931 callbacks for a 15MB XML and 960961 for 30MB.

The overheads for `tifftopnm` with `libtiff` are due to transferring the pixel buffer processed by the jail process to the main process using `cj_recv`. For a 1MB TIFF file, 1.1MB is copied using `cj_recv`; and 34.3MB for a 32MB file.

7 Discussion

We discuss limitations and other issues of Codejail and its implementation.

Handling the `fork` System Call. `fork` needs to be treated specially. Firstly, both the main process and the jailed process have to be forked. They have to remain in the same state of execution. Secondly, the shared memory and communication socket has to be duplicated. In particular, M_m and M_j should be duplicated into M'_m and M'_j. Modification in M_m should not be reflected in M'_m. For simplicity, our current implementation does not support fork. However, we support multi-threading which does not need to handle new jail processes.

Inline Function and Macros. Inline library functions and macros cause binary code to be generated in the main program which then execute in the trusted context. The simplest solution is to ensure that they stay in the library by turning them into functions and recompiling. This is not totally transparent but is easy to do with source code. Of course, if these functions do not have any security issues, then nothing needs to be done.

Efficient Memory Sharing. The `cj_recv` function is implemented by reading memory in the jailed process, sending it through socket, and writing it to main process' memory. We remark that there are further optimizations which are possible but are not easily doable in a user-mode implementation. A kernel-based implementation only needs to update memory if it has been changed in the jail and copying costs is also more efficient than socket IPC.

Multiple Untrusted Libraries. Codejail can be extended easily to have multiple untrusted contexts for multiple untrusted libraries if they do not interact with each other, i.e., they only directly interact with the main program. Otherwise, it is simpler to place them in the same untrusted context.

8 Conclusion

We presented Codejail, a novel solution that achieves partial isolation of untrusted libraries that require tight interaction with the main program. Codejail transparently supports existing software and library binaries, working without the need to rebuild them. The key techniques of Codejail is to use a separate context to confine untrusted libraries with the Codejail memory model. Our Linux prototype shows that Codejail works with real-world programs and libraries and overheads are small except when there is excessive tight interactions.

References

1. Roemer, R., Buchanan, E., Shacham, H., Savage, S.: Return-oriented programming: Systems, languages, and applications. ACM Trans. Info. & System Security (2012)
2. Wahbe, R., Lucco, S., Anderson, T., Graham, S.: Efficient software-based fault isolation. In: ACM SIGOPS Operating Systems Review (1994)
3. Erlingsson, Ú., Abadi, M., Vrable, M., Budiu, M., Necula, G.C.: Xfi: Software guards for system address spaces. In: Proc. of OSDI (2006)
4. Ford, B., Cox, R.: Vx32: Lightweight user-level sandboxing on the x86. In: Proc. of USENIX Annual Technical Conf. (2008)
5. Yee, B., Sehr, D., Dardyk, G., Chen, J.B., Muth, R., Ormandy, T., Okasaka, S., Narula, N., Fullagar, N.: Native client: A sandbox for portable, untrusted x86 native code. In: Proc. of IEEE S&P (2009)
6. Provos, N., Friedl, M., Honeyman, P.: Preventing privilege escalation. In: Proc. of the USENIX Security Symp. (2003)
7. Kilpatrick, D.: Privman: A library for partitioning applications. In: Proc. of the USENIX Annual Technical Conf. FREENIX track (2003)
8. Brumley, D., Song, D.: Privtrans: Automatically partitioning programs for privilege separation. In: Proc. of the USENIX Security Symp. (2004)
9. McCamant, S., Morrisett, G.: Evaluating sfi for a cisc architecture. In: Proc. of the USENIX Security Symp. (2006)
10. Douceur, J.R., Elson, J., Howell, J., Lorch, J.R.: Leveraging legacy code to deploy desktop applications on the web. In: Proc. of OSDI (2008)
11. Swift, M., Annamalai, M., Bershad, B., Levy, H.: Recovering device drivers. ACM Trans. on Computer Systems (2006)
12. Castro, M., Costa, M., Martin, J.P., Peinado, M., Akritidis, P., Donnelly, A., Barham, P., Black, R.: Fast byte-granularity software fault isolation. In: Proc. of ACM SOSP (2009)
13. Mao, Y., Chen, H., Zhou, D., Wang, X., Zeldovich, N., Kaashoek, M.F.: Software fault isolation with api integrity and multi-principal modules. In: Proc. of ACM SOSP (2011)
14. Bittau, A., Marchenko, P., Handley, M., Karp, B.: Wedge: splitting applications into reduced-privilege compartments. In: Proc. of NSDI (2008)
15. Jain, K., Sekar, R.: User-level infrastructure for system call interposition: A platform for intrusion detection and confinement. In Proc. of NDSS (2000)
16. Provos, N.: Improving host security with system call policies. In: Proc. of the USENIX Security Symp. (2003)
17. Kumar, R., Singhania, A., Castner, A., Kohler, E., Srivastava, M.: A system for coarse grained memory protection in tiny embedded processors. In: Proc. of DAC (2007)
18. Wang, Z., Jiang, X.: Hypersafe: A lightweight approach to provide lifetime hypervisor control-flow integrity. In: Proc. of IEEE S&P (2010)
19. Zeng, B., Tan, G., Morrisett, G.: Combining control-flow integrity and static analysis for efficient and validated data sandboxing. In: Proc. of ACM CCS (2011)

SOCIALIMPACT: Systematic Analysis of Underground Social Dynamics*

Ziming Zhao, Gail-Joon Ahn, Hongxin Hu, and Deepinder Mahi

Laboratory of Security Engineering for Future Computing (SEFCOM)
Arizona State University, Tempe, AZ 85281, USA
{zmzhao,gahn,hxhu,dmahi}@asu.edu

Abstract. Existing research on net-centric attacks has focused on the detection of attack events on network side and the removal of rogue programs from client side. However, such approaches largely overlook the way on how attack tools and unwanted programs are developed and distributed. Recent studies in underground economy reveal that suspicious attackers heavily utilize online social networks to form special interest groups and distribute malicious code. Consequently, examining social dynamics, as a novel way to complement existing research efforts, is imperative to systematically identify attackers and tactically cope with net-centric threats. In this paper, we seek a way to understand and analyze social dynamics relevant to net-centric attacks and propose a suite of measures called SOCIALIMPACT for systematically discovering and mining adversarial evidence. We also demonstrate the feasibility and applicability of our approach by implementing a proof-of-concept prototype *Cassandra* with a case study on real-world data archived from the Internet.

1 Introduction

Today's malware-infected computers are deliberately grouped as large scale destructive botnets to steal sensitive information and attack critical net-centric production systems [1]. The situation keeps getting worse when botnets make use of legitimate social media, such as Facebook and Twitter, to launch botnet attacks [2]. Previous research efforts on countering botnet attacks could be classified into four categories: (i) capturing malware samples [3], (ii) collecting and correlating network and host behaviors of malware [27], (iii) understanding the logic of malware [4], and (iv) infiltrating and taking over botnets [5].

Notably, most studies in the area of countering malware and botnets have been focused on detecting bot deployment, capturing and controlling bot behaviors. However, there is little research on examining how these malicious programs are created, rented and sold by adversaries. Even though preventive solutions

---

* This work was partially supported by the grants from National Science Foundation (NSF-IIS-0900970 and NSF-CNS-0831360). All correspondence should be addressed to Dr. Gail-Joon Ahn, gahn@asu.edu.

S. Foresti, M. Yung, and F. Martinelli (Eds.): ESORICS 2012, LNCS 7459, pp. 877–894, 2012.

against thousands of known bots have been deployed on networked systems, and some botnets were even taken down by law enforcement agencies [6], the majority of adversaries are still at large and keep threatening the Internet by developing more bots and launching more net-centric attacks. The major reason for this phenomenon is that previous malware-related activities–such as developing, renting and selling bots–occurred mostly offline, which were way beyond the scope of security analysts.

In recent years, the pursuit of more profit in underground communities leads to the requirement for global collaboration among adversaries, which tremendously changed the division of labor and means of communication among them [8]. (Un)fortunately, adversaries started to communicate with each other, distribute and improve attack tools with the help of the Internet, which leaves security analysts new clues for evidence acquisition and investigation on unwanted program development and trade. Before the widespread use of online social networks (OSNs), adversaries would communicate via electronic bulletin board systems (BBS), forums, and Email systems [10].

Content-rich Web 2.0, ubiquitous computing equipments, and newly emerging online social networks provide an even bigger arena for adversaries. In particular, the value of OSNs for adversaries is the capability to cooperate with destructive botnets. The role of OSNs in botnet attacks is twofold: first, OSNs are the platforms to form online black markets, release bots, and coordinate attacks [3,9]; second, OSN user accounts act as bots to perform malicious actions [7] or C&C server nodes coordinates other networked bots [2]. Although our efforts in this paper are mainly concerned about the former case, our proposed model for online underground social dynamics and corresponding social metrics can be also utilized to identify compromised and suspicious OSN profiles.

Given the great amount of valuable information in online social dynamics, the investigation of the relationships between online underground social communities and network attack events are imperative to tactically cope with net-centric threats. In this paper, we propose a novel solution using social dynamics analysis to counter malware and botnet attacks as a complement to existing research investments.

The major contributions of this paper are summarized as follows:

- We formulate an online underground social dynamics considering both social relationships and user-generated contents.
- We propose a suite of measures named SOCIALIMPACT to systematically quantify social impacts of individuals and groups along with their online conversations which facilitate adversarial evidence acquisition and investigation.
- We implement a proof-of-concept system based on our proposed model and measures, and evaluate our solution with real-world data archived from the Internet. Our results clearly demonstrate the effectiveness of our approach for understanding, discovering, and mining adversarial behaviors.

The rest of this paper is organized as follows. Section 2 presents our online underground social dynamics model and addresses SOCIALIMPACT, which is a systematic ranking analysis suite for mining adversarial evidence based on the model. In Section 3, we discuss the design and implementation of our proof-of-concept system *Cassandra*. Section 4 presents the evaluation of our approach followed by the related work in Section 5. Section 6 concludes this paper.

2   SocialImpact: Bring Order to Online Underground Social Dynamics

In this section, we first address the modeling approach we utilized to represent online underground social dynamics (OUSDs). Unlike existing OSN models [11] which emphasize on user profile, friendship link, and user group, our model gives attention to user-generated contents due to the fact that a wealth of information resides in online conversations. We also elaborate the design principles of social metrics to identify adversarial behaviors in OUSDs. Then, we present SocialImpact, which consists of nine indices, to bring order to underground social dynamics based on our OUSD model.

2.1   Online Underground Social Dynamics Model

As shown in Figure 1, an OUSD can be represented by six fundamental entities and five basic types of unidirectional relationships between them.

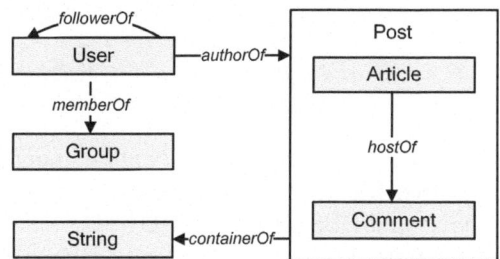

Fig. 1. *OUSD* Model: Entities and Relationships

Users are those who have profiles in the network and have the rights to join groups, post articles, and give comments to others. *Groups* are those to which users can belong. In an OUSD, groups are mainly formed based on common interests. *Articles* are posted by users who want to share them with the society. In an OUSD, articles might introduce the latest technologies, analyze recent vulnerabilities, call for participation of network attacks, and trade newly developed and deployed botnets. In terms of the form of articles, they do not have to be literary. They could also contain multimedia contents, such as photos and melodies. *Comments* are the subsequent posts to articles. *Posts* are the union of articles and comments. *Strings* are the elementary components of articles and comments. Strings are not necessarily meaningful words. They could be names,

URLs, and underground slangs. A user has a relationship *authorOf* with each post s/he creates. A user has a relationship *followerOf* with each user s/he follows. A user has a relationship *memberOf* with each group s/he joins. An article has a relationship *hostOf* with each comment it receives. A post has a relationship *containerOf* with each string it consists of.

The following formal description summarizes the above-mentioned entities and relationships.

Definition 2.1 (*Online Underground Social Dynamics*). *An **OUSD** is modeled with the following components:*

- *U is a set of users;*
- *G is a set of user groups;*
- *A is a set of articles;*
- *C is a set of comments;*
- *P is a set of posts. $P = A \cup C$;*
- *S is a set of strings;*
- *$UP = \{(u,p)|\ u \in U, p \in P$ and u has an* authorOf *relationship with p\} is a one-to-many user-to-post relation denoting a user and her posts;*
- *$FL = \{(u,y)|\ u \in U, y \in U$ and u has a* followerOf *relationship with y\} is a many-to-many user-to-user follow relation;*
- *$MB = \{(u,g)|\ u \in U, g \in G$ and u has a* memberOf *relationship with g\} is a many-to-many user-to-group membership relation;*
- *$AC = \{(a,c)|\ a \in A, c \in C$ and a has a* hostOf *relationship with c\} is a one-to-many article-to-comment relation denoting an article and its following comments; and*
- *$PS = \{(p,s)|\ p \in P, s \in S$ and p has a* containerOf *relationship with s\} is a many-to-many post-to-string relation.*

We focus on the main structure and activities in online underground society and overlook some sophisticated features & functionalities, such as online chatting, provided by specific OSNs and BBS. Hence, our OUSD model is generic and can be a reference model for most real-world OSNs and BBS. As a result, security analysts could easily map real-world social dynamics data archived from any OSNs and BBS to our model for further analysis and investigation.

2.2   Principles of Metric Design and Definitions

We also address the following critical issues related to evidence mining in underground society: How can we identify adversaries among a crowd of social users? Given the additional evidence acquired from other sources, how can we correlate them with underground social dynamics? How can we measure the evolution in underground community? To answer these questions, we articulate several *principles* that the measures for underground social dynamics analysis should follow: 1) The measures should support identifications of interesting adversaries and groups based on both their social relationships and online conversations; 2)

The measures should be able to take external evidence into account and support interactions with security analysts; and 3) The measures should support temporal analysis for the better understanding of the evolution in adversarial groups.

To this end, we introduce several feature vectors to achieve aforementioned goals. For the mathematical notations, we use lower case bold roman letters such as $\mathbf{x}$ to denote vectors, and uppercase bold roman letters such as $\mathbf{V}$ to denote matrices. We assume all vectors to be column vectors and a superscript T to denote the transposition of a matrix or vector. We also define $max()$ as a function to return the maximum value of a set.

Definition 2.2 (Article Influence Vector). *Given an article $a \in A$, the article influence vector of a is defined as $\mathbf{v}_a^T = (v_1, v_2, v_3)$, where v_1 is the length of the article, $v_2 = |\{c \mid c \in C \text{ and } (a, c) \in AC\}|$ is the number of comments received by a, and v_3 is the number of outlinks it has.*

When stacking all articles' influence vector together, we get the **article influence matrix V**. We assess an article's influence by its activity generation, novelty and eloquence [12].

Definition 2.3 (Article Relevance Factor). *Given a set of strings $\mathbf{s} = \{s_1, s_2, ..., s_n\} \subseteq S$ and an article $a \in A$, article relevance factor, denoted as $r(a, \mathbf{s})$, is defined as the number of occurrence of strings $\mathbf{s}$ in the article a.*

The strings $\mathbf{s}$ could represent an external evidence that security analysts acquired from other sources and query keywords in which security analysts are interested.

Definition 2.4 (User Activeness Vector). *The user activeness vector of u is defined as $\mathbf{z}_u^T = (z_1, z_2, z_3)$, where $z_1 = |\{p \mid p \in P \text{ and } (u, p) \in UP\}|$ is the number of articles and comments u posted, $z_2 = |\{y \mid y \in U \text{ and } (u, y) \in FL\}|$ is the number of users u follows, and $z_3 = |\{g \mid g \in G \text{ and } (u, g) \in MB\}|$ is the number of groups u joins.*

We measure a user's activeness by the number of posts s/he sends, users s/he follows, and groups s/he joins. By aggregating all users' $\mathbf{z}_u$, we get **user activeness matrix Z**.

Definition 2.5 (Social Matrix). *Social matrix, denoted as $\mathbf{Q}$, is defined as a $|U| \times |U|$ square matrix with rows and columns corresponding to users. Let v be a user and N_v be the number of users v follows. $\mathbf{Q}_{u,v} = 1/N_v$, if $(v, u) \in FL$ and $\mathbf{Q}_{u,v} = 0$, otherwise.*

Social matrix is similar to transition matrix for hyperlinked webpages in PageRank. The sum of each column in social matrix is either 1 or 0, which depends on whether the vth column user follows any other user.

Definition 2.6 (δ-n Selection Vector). *A δ-n selection vector, denoted as $\mathbf{y}_\delta^n$, is defined as a boolean vector with n components and $\|\mathbf{y}_\delta^n\|_1 = \delta$.*

A δ-n selection vector is used to select a portion of elements for one set. For example, the top 10 influential articles of a user a could be represented by a selection vector $\mathbf{y}_{10}^{|A|}$ over the article set A. By stacking all users' δ-n selection vectors over the same set together, we get the δ-n **selection matrix** $\mathbf{Y}_\delta^n$.

2.3   Ranking Metrics

As shown in Figure 2, SOCIALIMPACT consists of nine indices, which are classified into three categories: string & post indices, user indices, and group indices. Each index in upper categories is computed by the indices from lower categories.

To fulfill *Principle 1*, user and group indices are devised to identify influential, active, and relevant users and groups. We devise personalized PageRank models [13] to calculate UserInfluence and UserRelevance, since it could capture the characteristics of both user-to-user relationships and user-generated contents in social dynamics. To accommodate *Principle 2*, ArticleRelevance, UserRelevance and GroupRelevance are designed to take external strings as inputs, combine them with existing data in social dynamics, and generate more comprehensive results. To fulfill *Principle 3*, all feature vectors and indices could be calculated for a given time window and StringPrevalence could indicate the topic evolution in the society. Moreover, we believe the combination of UserActiveness and UserInfluence could also be used to identify suspicious spam profiles in online social networks.

We consider a weighted additive model [14] when there exist several independent factors to determine one index. To reduce the bias introduced by different size of sets, we use δ-n selection vector to choose a portion of data in calculation. The followings are the detailed descriptions of indices.

ArticleInfluence, *denoted as* $x_1(a)$, *represents the influence of article* a. $x_1(a)$ *is computed as* $\mathbf{v}_a^T \mathbf{w_1}$, *where* $\mathbf{w_1}$ *denotes the weight vector.*

By normalizing $x_1(a)$ to $[0, 1]$ and stacking $x_1(a)$ from all articles together, we get a vector $\mathbf{x_1}$.

$$\mathbf{x_1} = \frac{\mathbf{V}^T \mathbf{w_1}}{max_{b \in A}(x_1(b))} \tag{1}$$

ArticleRelevance, *denoted as* $x_2(a, \mathbf{s})$, *represents the relevance of the article* a *to given strings* $\mathbf{s}$. $x_2(a, \mathbf{s})$ *is proportional to the occurrence of the given strings in the article and the influence of the article.*

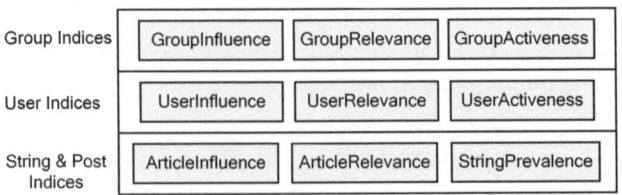

Fig. 2. SOCIALIMPACT: Systematic Ranking Indices

$$x_2(a, \mathbf{s}) = \frac{r(a,\mathbf{s})x_1(a)}{max_{b \in A}(r(b,\mathbf{s})x_1(b))} \tag{2}$$

By stacking $x_2(a, \mathbf{s})$ from all users together, we get a vector $\mathbf{x_2}(\mathbf{s})$ denoting all articles' relevance to $\mathbf{s}$.

UserInfluence, *denoted as* x_3, *represents the influence of a user.* x_3 *can be measured by two parts. One is the impact of the user's opinions, which is modeled by* ArticleInfluence. *The other is the user's social relationships, which is modeled by* $\mathbf{Q}$. x_3 *is devised as a personalized PageRank function to capture both parts.*

By stacking x_3 from all users together, we get a vector $\mathbf{x_3}$.

$$\mathbf{x_3} = d_3 \mathbf{Q} \mathbf{x_3} + (1 - d_3) \mathbf{Y}_\alpha^{|A|} \mathbf{x_1} \tag{3}$$

Where $d_3 \in (0, 1)$ *is the decay factor which makes the linear system stable and convergent.* $\mathbf{Y}_\alpha^{|A|}$ *is the* $\delta - n$ *selection matrix corresponding to all users's top* α *influential articles.*

UserRelevance, *denoted as* $x_4(\mathbf{s})$, *represents the relevance of a user to strings* $\mathbf{s}$.

By stacking $x_4(\mathbf{s})$ from all users together, we get a vector $\mathbf{x_4}$.

$$\mathbf{x_4}(\mathbf{s}) = d_4 \mathbf{Q} \mathbf{x_4}(\mathbf{s}) + (1 - d_4)(\mathbf{Y}_\alpha^{|A|} \mathbf{x_2}(\mathbf{s})) \tag{4}$$

Where $d_4 \in (0, 1)$ *is the decay factor.* $\mathbf{Y}_\alpha^{|A|}$ *is a* $\delta - n$ *selection matrix corresponding to all users's top* α *relevant articles to* $\mathbf{s}$.

UserActiveness, *denoted as* x_5, *represents the activeness of a user.*

$$\mathbf{x_5} = \mathbf{Z}^T \mathbf{w_5} \tag{5}$$

We use the addition of a group's top α members' influence, relevance, and activeness to model its influence, relevance, and activeness, respectively. As mentioned before, this model can reduce the bias caused by the number of members.

GroupInfluence, *denoted as* x_6, *represents the influence of a group.*

By stacking all x_6 together, we get $\mathbf{x_6}$.

$$\mathbf{x_6} = \mathbf{Y}_\alpha^{|U|} \mathbf{x_3} \tag{6}$$

Where $\mathbf{Y}_\alpha^{|U|}$ *is the* δ-n *selection matrix corresponding to all groups' top* α *influential users.*

GroupRelevance, *denoted as* x_7, *represents the relevance of a group to strings* $\mathbf{s}$.

By stacking all x_7 together, we get $\mathbf{x_7}$.

$$\mathbf{x_7} = \mathbf{Y}_\alpha^{|U|} \mathbf{x_4} \tag{7}$$

Where $\mathbf{Y}_\alpha^{|U|}$ *is the* δ-n *selection matrix corresponding to all groups' top* α *relevant users.*

GroupActiveness, *denoted as* x_8, *represents the activeness of a group.*

By stacking all x_8 together, we get $\mathbf{x_8}$.

$$\mathbf{x_8} = \mathbf{Y}_\alpha^{|U|}\mathbf{x_5} \tag{8}$$

Where $\mathbf{Y}_\alpha^{|U|}$ *is the δ-n selection matrix corresponding to all groups' top α active users.*

StringPrevalence, *denoted as* $x_9(s)$, *represents the popularity of a string s.*

$$x_9(s) = \sum_{p_j \in P} ti_{s,p_j} \tag{9}$$

where ti_{s,p_j} is the term frequency-inverse document frequency [15] of a string s in post p_j.

The computations for UserInfluence and UserRelevance are proven to be convergent [16]. And the corresponding time complexity is $O(|H|log(1/\epsilon))$, where $|H|$ is the number of $followerOf$ relationships in the social dynamics and ϵ is a given degree of precision [16]. The time complexity for calculating StringPrevalence is $O(|P||S|)$, where $|P|$ is the number of posts and $|S|$ is the size of string set. The complexities for all other indices are linear if the underlying indices are calculated.

3   *Cassandra*: System Design and Implementation

In this section, we describe the challenges in analyzing real-world underground social dynamics data. We address our efforts to cope with these challenges and present the design and implementation of our proof-of-concept system *Cassandra*.

3.1   Challenges from Real-World Data

The first challenge of real-world data is its multilingual contents. The most effective way of coping with this challenge is to take advantage of machine translation systems. *Cassandra* utilizes Google Translate[1] to detect the language of the contents and translate them into English. However, machine translation systems may fail to generate meaningful English interpretations for the following cases: i) adversaries may use cryptolanguages that no machine translation system could understand. For instance, *Fenya*, a Russian cant language that is usually used in prisons, is identified in online underground society [17]; and ii) both intentional and accidental misspellings are common in online underground society [18]. In order to cope with this challenge, *Cassandra* maintains a dictionary of known jargons, such as *c4n* as *can* and *sUm1* as *someone*.

Another challenge is that the social dynamics data may not be in a consistent format. Different OSNs use different styles in web page design. Even in one OSN, in order to make the web page more personalized, the OSN allows users to

---

[1] http://code.google.com/apis/language/translate/overview.html

customize the format of their posts. Since HTML is not designed to be machine-understandable in the first place, extracting structural information from HTML is a tedious and heavy-labor work. To address this problem, we first cluster data, and then devise an HTML parser for each cluster. We also design a light-weight semi-structure language to store the information extracted from HTML.

Since one major component in social dynamics is the relationships between entities, storing and manipulating social dynamics data in a relational database become relatively time-consuming. We choose a graph database [19] which employs the concepts from graph theory, such as node, property, and edge, to realize faster operations for associative data sets.

3.2   System Architecture and Implementation

Figure 3 shows a high level architecture of *Cassandra*. The upper level of *Cassandra* includes several visualization modules and provides query control for security analysts to provide the additional evidence. In reality, these evidences could be in the format of text, picture, video, audio or any other forms. Yet, representing multimedia contents like pictures and videos in a machine-understandable way is still a difficult challenge. *Cassandra* acts like a modern web search engine in response to keyword queries. Social graph viewer is designed to show social relationships among users and groups. Ranking analysis viewer is used to list the ranking results based on security analysts' queries. Content viewer can show both original and translated English web resources.

The lower level of the architecture realizes underlying functionalities addressed in our framework. After underground community data is crawled from the Internet, the HTML parser module extracts meaningful information from it. If the content is not in English, our translator takes over and generates English translation. All extracted information is stored in a graph database for the efficient retrieval. Analysis modules have two working modes: offline and online. The offline mode generates demographical information with demographical analysis engine (DAE) and intelligence, such as user influence and activeness, with SOCIALIMPACT engine (SIE). When security analysts provide the additional evidence, SOCIALIMPACT engine switches to online mode and generates analysis

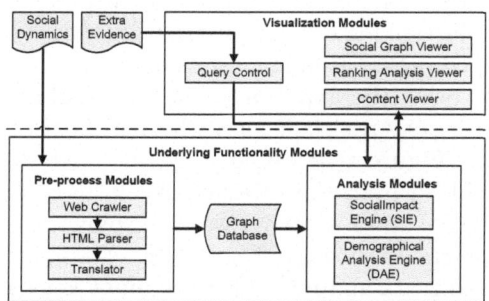

Fig. 3. System Architecture of *Cassandra*

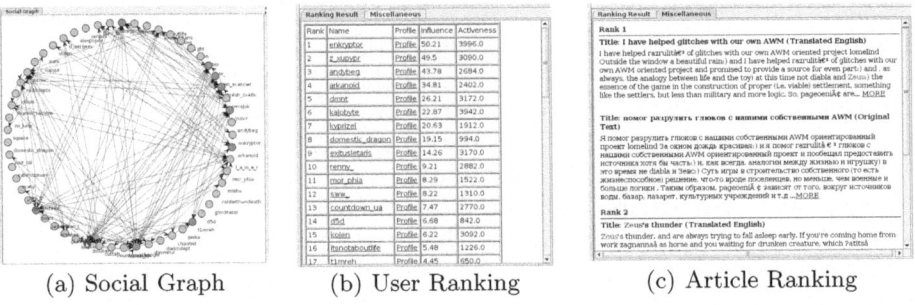

(a) Social Graph   (b) User Ranking   (c) Article Ranking

Fig. 4. Screenshots of *Cassandra*

results, such as user relevance, based on data in the graph database and additional evidence provided by security analysts.

Cassandra was implemented in Java programming language. We took advantage of Java swing and JUNG to realize graphical user interfaces and graph visualization. As we mentioned before, *Cassandra* uses Google Translate API to translate texts. In most cases, Google Translate could output acceptable translations from original texts. *Cassandra* stores user profiles, user-generated contents, and social relationships among users in a Neo4j[2] graph database. For each group, user, article, and comment, *Cassandra* creates a node in the database, stores associated data–such as the birthday of user and the content of article–in each node's properties, and assigns the relationships among nodes.

3.3   Visualization Interfaces of *Cassandra*

Figure 4 depicts interfaces of *Cassandra*. As illustrated in Figure 4(a), all users in a social group are displayed by a circle. And their *followerOf* relationships are displayed with curved arrows. It is clear to view that some users have lots of followers while others do not. By clicking any user in the group, *Cassandra* has the ability to highlight this user in red and all his followers in green. In this way, *Cassandra* helps analysts understand the social impact of any specific user. Another window as shown in Figure 4(b) displays the ranking results. Analysts can specify the ranking metric, such as UserInfluence and UserActiveness, to reorder the displayed rank. Clicking a user's name which is the second column in Figure 4(b) would bring the analysts to the list of all articles posted by the user in descending order of ArticleInfluence. Clicking the user's profile link which is the third column in Figure 4(b) would bring the analysts to the webpage of the user's profile archived from the Internet. Analysts could also specify some keywords in query control and *Cassandra* would display the results in descending order of ArticleRelevance. As shown in Figure 4(c), *Cassandra* displays both the original and translated texts and highlights the input keywords in red.

---

[2] http://neo4j.org/

4   A Case Study on Real-World Online Underground Social Dynamics

In this section, we present our evaluation on real-world social dynamics. We evaluated *Cassandra* on 4GB of data crawled from *Livejournal.com* which is a popular online social network especially in the Russian-speaking countries. We anonymized the group names and user names in this OSN for preserving privacy.

All webpages in this OSN could be roughly divided into two categories in terms of content: i) profile and ii) article. A profile webpage contains basic information of a user or a group, which includes name, biography, location, birthday, friends, and members. Every article has title, author, posted time, content, and several comments by other users. The webpages are mainly *.html* files, along with some *.jpeg*, *.gif*, *.css*, and *.js* files. Our solution only considers text data from *.html* files.

We started to crawl group profiles from six famous underground groups in this OSN [3]. Then we crawled all members' profiles and articles of these six groups. We also collected one-hop friends' articles of these members. Therefore, we ended up with 29,614 articles posted by 6,364 users which are from 4,220 groups. Based on the information in user profiles, we noticed that about 32.7% and 52.7% users were born in early and mid-late 80's. This clearly illustrates the age distribution of active users in this community.

4.1   Post, User and Group Analysis

Cassandra calculated all articles' ArticleInfluence and identified top 50 articles over a time window of 48 months. Since not all of these articles are related to computer security, we checked these articles in descending order of their influences and picked five articles that are highly related to malware. We could observe some popular words related to malware, such as PE (the target and vehicle for Windows software attacks), exploits (a piece of code to trigger system vulnerabilities), hook (a technique to hijack legitimate control flow) and so on.

Table 1. Top Five Influential/Active Users/Groups

Top Five Influential Users		Top Five Active Users		Top Five Influential Groups		Top Five Active Groups	
User	UserInfluence	User	UserActiveness	Group	GroupInfluence	Group	GroupActivenss
z_xx_ur	49.5020	xsbxx_ur	4024	b_gp	344.4807	b_gp	57798
andxx_ur	43.7800	enkxx_ur	3942	c_gp	79.7781	d_gp	28644
arkxx_ur	34.8074	kalxx_ur	3936	d_gp	45.5222	demxx_gp	20846
_moxx_ur	26.7700	exixx_ur	3170	murxx_gp	26.2094	beaxx_gp	20290
kyp_ur	20.6292	kolxx_ur	3092	chrxx_gp	18.6487	_hoxx_gp	19486

Cassandra also generated each user's UserInfluence and UserActiveness and group's GroupInfluence and GroupActiveness over a time window of 48 months.

---

[3] These targeted groups are indicated by law enforcement agency who sponsored this project.

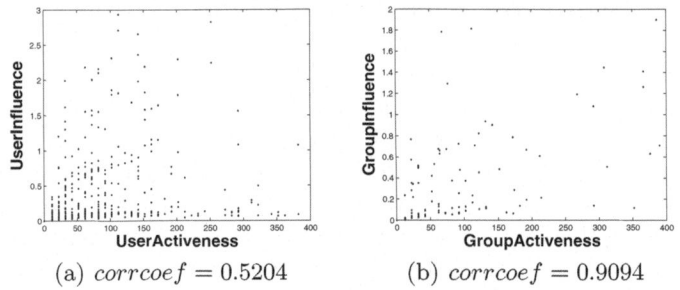

(a) $corrcoef = 0.5204$ (b) $corrcoef = 0.9094$

Fig. 5. Correlation Coefficient of UserActiveness & UserInfluence and GroupActiveness & GroupInfluence

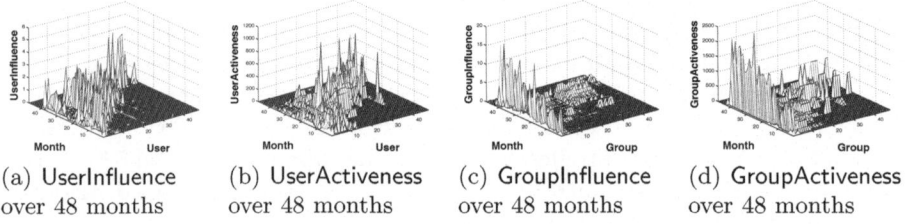

(a) UserInfluence over 48 months   (b) UserActiveness over 48 months   (c) GroupInfluence over 48 months   (d) GroupActiveness over 48 months

Fig. 6. Temporal Pattern Analysis

And, Table 1 shows the top five influential/active users/groups for the entire period of our observation. We can notice that there is no overlap between the top five *influential* users and the top five *active* users, while there exists similarity for the top five *influential* groups and the top five *active* groups.

We calculated the correlation coefficient (*corrcoef*) for the pairs of UserInfluence and UserActivenss, GroupInfluence and GroupActivenss based on the results generated from *Cassandra*. Similar to the phenomenon we identified in Table 1, in Figure 5(a) we observed that the correlation coefficient between UserInfluence and UserActivenss is around 0.52 (the maximum value for correlation coefficient is 1 indicating a perfect positive correlation between two variables), which means one user's influence is not highly correlated to her/his activeness. This phenomenon indicates that talking more does not make a user more influential in a community. On the other hand, as shown in Figure 5(b) we observed that the correlation coefficient between GroupInfluence and GroupActivenss is around 0.90, which indicates a very strong positive correlation between the influence and the activeness of a group. The application of influence and activeness indices is not limited to identify such a social phenomenon. We could also leverage the high UserActivenss and the low UserInfluence as indicators for the analysis of social spammers in any OSN.

The temporal patterns of the influential/active users/groups could be observed in Figure 6, where x-axis denotes the users/groups who were identified

Table 2. Results from *Cassandra* for Queries

(a) Results for Botnet		(b) Results for Identity Theft and Credit Card Fraud		(c) Results for Vulnerability Discovery and Malicious Code Development	
Keywords	Relevant Articles #	Keywords	Relevant Articles #	Keywords	Relevant Articles #
spam	490	pin	129	vulnerability	418
botnet	44	credit card	93	shellcode	169
zeus	9	carding	1	polymorphic	12
rustock	1	credit card sale	0	zero-day	11
mega-d	0	ssn	0	cve	2

as the most influential/active ones for each month. For example, $x = 1$ denotes the most influential/active user/group of the first month in our time window and $x = 48$ denotes the most influential/active user/group of the last month in our time window; y-axis denotes the entire 48 months in the time window; and z-axis denotes user/group's influence/activeness value. As shown in Figure 6(a), some users maintain their influence status for several months. The large plain area in the right part of this figure indicates most users come as the most influential ones suddenly. This observation implies that a user does not need to be a veteran to be an influential one in the community. On the other side, we can see from Figure 6(b) that most active users remain active before they became the most active ones. The plain area in the left portion of Figure 6(b) implies that most users do not always keep active. Normally they keep active for 15 - 30 months, then get relatively silent. While the smaller plain area in the left part of Figure 6(a) shows once a user becomes influential, s/he keeps the status for a long period of time. Figure 6(c) shows that there are 2 or 3 groups who maintain the status of influence during the whole 48 months and get even more influential as time goes on. While, other groups only keep influential for a relatively short period of time and just fade out. Figure 6(d) shows the similar phenomenon.

4.2 Evidence Mining by Correlating Social Dynamics with Adversarial Events

We present our finding with keyword queries on the same dataset in *Cassandra*. For each query, *Cassandra* returns the lists of articles, users, and groups in descending order of ArticleRelevance, UserRelevance and GroupRelevance, respectively. The results we present in this section are with regard to three major adversarial activities: i) botnet; ii) identity theft and credit card fraud; and iii) vulnerability analysis and malicious code development.

Botnet. As we mentioned before, botnet is a serious threat to all networked computers. In order to identify adversaries and their conversations in our dataset related to botnet, we queried the keywords shown in Table 2(a) in *Cassandra*. *Cassandra* was able to identify 490 articles related to 'spam', 44 articles related to 'botnet', 9 articles related to 'zeus' and 1 article about 'rustock'.

Then, we checked the results returned by *Cassandra* carefully and Table 3 shows several interesting articles and their information including the number of comments they received, ArticleRelevance of each article, and authors of these articles. We first noticed one article titled 'Rustock.C' with very high ArticleRevelance and ArticleInfluence. This article presented an original analysis of the C variant of Rustock that once accounted for 40% of the spam emails in the world.

Table 3. Selected Top Relevant Articles

Translated Article Title	# Comments Received	x_2[1]	Author
Rustock.C	13	135.3	swx_ur
On startup failure to sign the drivers in Vista x64	5	59.8	crx_ur
video	3	35.6	zlx_ur
sleepy	3	32.3	crx_ur
FireEye Joins Internet2	2	27.8	eax_ur

[1] ArticleRelevance.

Another article titled 'On startup failure to sign the drivers in Vista x64' returned by *Cassandra* as a top relevant article to 'botnet' attracting our attention as well. In this article, the author crx_ur discussed about how to load unsigned driver to Windows Vista x64 by modifying PE file header. The corresponding author claimed that malware vendors would use this technique to build bots and infect thousands of computers. A further investigation on this user shown in Table 4 reveals that s/he authored several security-related articles. Her/his profile indicated that s/he was very active in malicious code development and interested in several cybercrime topics, such as rootkit, exploits, and shellcode.

Table 4. Selected Articles by crx_ur and Her/His Information

Translated Article Title	# Comments Received	x_1[1]	Translated Interests
The old tale about security	7	79.6	malware, ring0, rootkit, botnets, asm, exploits, cyber terrorism, shellcode, viruses, underground, Kaspersky, paintball
Malcode statistics	6	68.9	
Cold boot attacks on encryption keys	2	37.6	
Wanted Cisco security agent	2	28.1	
Antirootkits bypass	1	18.7	
Syser debugger	0	8.9	
Termorektalny cryptanalysis	0	7.8	

[1] ArticleInfluence.

Identity Theft and Credit Card Fraud. Identity theft and credit card fraud are both serious issues in Internet transactions. Online identity theft includes stealing usernames, passwords, social security numbers (SSNs), personal identification numbers (PINs), account numbers, and other credentials. Credit card fraud also consists of phishing (a process to steal credit card information), carding (a process to verify whether a stolen credit card is still valid), and selling verified credit card information.

Table 2(b) shows results that *Cassandra* returned when these keywords are queried. *Cassandra* identified one article that was authored by a user dx_ur related to 'carding' in the dataset. A further investigation on this user revealed

Table 5. Information about dx_ur

Translated Interests	carding, banking, shells, hacking, freebie, web hack, credit card fraud, security policy, system administrators, live in computer bugs
# Articles Posted	1295
# Comments Posted	7294
# Comments Received	2693

that s/he was a member of a carding interest group, which had more than 20 members around the world. Table 5 shows some basic information of dx_ur. Compared to crx_ur, it is obvious that dx_ur has more interests in financial security issues, such as credit card fraud, web hack, and banking. We could also notice that dx_ur was very active in posting articles and replying others' posts.

Vulnerability Analysis and Malicious Code Development. We analyzed several keywords related to vulnerability analysis and malicious code development, such as polymorphism (a technique widely used in malware to change the appearance of code, but keep the semantics), CVE (a reference-method for publicly-known computer vulnerabilities), shellcode (small piece of code used as the payload in the exploitation of software vulnerabilities), and zero-day (previously-unknown computer vulnerabilities, viruses and other malware).

As shown in Table 2(c), the community is very active in these topics. More than 400 articles related to vulnerabilities were found. However, we noticed most of these articles have low-ArticleInfluence. We checked these low-ArticleInfluence articles and discovered that most of them were articles copied from other research blogs and kept the links to original webpages. Our ArticleInfluence index successfully identified these articles were not very novel, thus calculated low ArticleInfluence for them.

At the same time, as shown in Table 6, *Cassandra* also identified several high-ArticleInfluence vulnerability analysis articles. For example, the article entitled 'Blind spot' authored by arx_ur which analyzed a new Windows Internet Explorer vulnerability even attracted 79 replies.

Table 6. Selected Top Relevant Articles

Translated Article Title	# Comments Received	x_2[1]	Author
Blind spot	79	793.2	arx_ur
Seven thirty-four pm PCR	14	146.4	tix_ur
HeapLib and Shellcode generator under windows	1	15.6	eax_ur
Who fixes vulnerabilities faster, Microsoft or Apple?	0	5.6	bux_ur
FreeBSD OpenSSH Bugfix	0	4.2	sux_ur

[1] ArticleRelevance

4.3 Comparison with HITS Algorithm

In order to evaluate the effectiveness of our approach, we implemented the hubs and authorities algorithm (HITS) [20] in *Cassandra* and compared the results with our SOCIALIMPACT metrics. HITS algorithm is able to calculate the authorities and hubs in a community by examining the topological structure where *authority* means the nodes that are linked by many others and *hub* means the nodes that point to many others. Note that the fundamental difference between SOCIALIMPACT and HITS is that SOCIALIMPACT takes more parameters, such as user-generated content and activity, into account, therefore ranking results are based on a more comprehensive set of social features.

Table 7. Top Five Authorities and Hubs by HITS

Top Five Authorities		Top Five Hubs	
User	auth	User	hub
zhengxx_ur	0.506	zlo_xx_ur	0.265
crx_xx_ur	0.214	zhengxx_ur	0.237
yuz_ur	0.163	crx_xx_ur	0.234
t1mxx_ur	0.148	yuz_ur	0.205
rst_ur	0.143	t1mxx_ur	0.183

Comparing the results for authorities and hubs shown in Table 7 with UserInfluence and UserActiveness (SOCIALIMPACT) in Table 1, we can observe that the authorities and hubs have much overlap with HITS algorithm when online conversations are ignored and the results generated by SOCIALIMPACT are different from HITS counterparts.

5   Related Work

Computer-aided crime analysis (CACA) utilizes the computation and visualization of modern computer to understand the structure and organization of traditional adversarial networks [21]. Although CACA is not designed for the analysis of cybercrime, its methods of relation analysis, and visualization of social network are adopted in our work. Zhou *et al.* [22] studied the organization of United State domestic extremist groups on web by analyzing their hyperlinks. Chau *et al.* [23] mined communities and their relationships in blogs for understanding hate group. Lu *et al.* [24] used four actor centrality measures (degree, betweenness, closeness, and eigenvector) to identify leaders in hacker community. Motoyama *et al.* [29] analyzed six underground forums. In contrast, our proposed solution in this paper considers both social relationships and user-generated contents in identifying interesting posts and users for cybercrime analysis.

Systematically bringing order to a dataset has plenty of applications in both social and computer science. With the development of web, ranking analysis in hyperlinked environment received much attention. Kleinberg [20] proposed HITS by calculating the eigenvectors of certain matrices associated with the link graph. Also, Page and Brin [25] developed PageRank that uses a page's backlinks' sum as its importance index. However, both HITS and PageRank only consider the topological structure of given dataset but ignore its contents [16]. Therefore, we devised a ranking system based on personalized PageRank, which is proposed to efficiently deal with ranking issues in different situations [13].

In order to provide a safer platform for net-centric business and secure the internet experience for end users, huge research efforts have been invested in defeating malware and botnets. Cho *et al.* [26] proposed to infer protocol state machines in botnet C&C protocols. Gu *et al.* analyzed botnet C&C channels for identifying malware infection and botnet organization [27]. Stone-Gross *et al.* [5] took over *Torpig* for a period of ten days and gathered rich and diverse set of data from this infamous botnet. Besides research efforts, legal actions are taken to shutdown certain botnets. *Srizbi* and *Mega-D* botnets were taken down in late 2008 and 2009 [6]. Recently, Microsoft took down *Rustock* by blocking the controller and clearing out the malware infected [28]. Our work focusing on the analysis of malware circulation is complementary to those existing efforts on countering net-centric attacks.

6   Conclusions

In this paper, we have presented a novel approach to help identify adversaries by analyzing social dynamics. We formally modeled online underground social dynamics and proposed SocialImpact as a suite of measures to highlight interesting adversaries, as well as their conversations and groups. The evaluation of our proof-of-concept system on real-world social data has shown the effectiveness of our approach. As part of future work, we would continuosly test the effectiveness and the usability of our system with subject matter experts and broader datasets.

References

1. Anselmi, D., Kuo, J., Santhanam, N., Boscovich, R.: Microsoft Security Intelligence Report, vol. 9
2. Thomas, K.: The Koobface botnet and the rise of social malware. In: Proc. of the 5th IEEE International Conference on Malicious and Unwanted Software (MALWARE), pp. 1–8 (2010)
3. Bächer, P., Holz, T., Kötter, M., Wicherski, G.: Know your Enemy: Tracking Botnets–Using honeynets to learn more about Bots (2005)
4. Chiang, K., Lloyd, L.: A case study of the rustock rootkit and spam bot. In: Proc. of Usenix Workshop on Hot Topics in Understanding Botnets (2007)
5. Stone-Gross, B., Cova, M., Cavallaro, L., Gilbert, B., Szydlowski, M., Kemmerer, R., Kruegel, C., Vigna, G.: Your botnet is my botnet: Analysis of a botnet takeover. In: Proc. of Computer and Communications Security (CCS). ACM (2009)
6. Mushtaq, A.: Smashing the Mega-d/Ozdok botnet in 24 hours, http://blog.fireeye.com/research/2009/11/smashing-the-ozdok.html
7. Athanasopoulos, E., Makridakis, A., Antonatos, S., Antoniades, D., Ioannidis, S., Anagnostakis, K.G., Markatos, E.P.: Antisocial Networks: Turning a Social Network into a Botnet. In: Wu, T.-C., Lei, C.-L., Rijmen, V., Lee, D.-T. (eds.) ISC 2008. LNCS, vol. 5222, pp. 146–160. Springer, Heidelberg (2008)
8. Dunham, K., Melnick, J.: Malicious bots: an inside look into the cyber-criminal underground of the internet. Auerbach Pub. (2008)

9. Holt, G.W.B., Thomas, J., Bossler, A.M.: Social Learning and Cyber Deviance: Examining the Importance of a Full Social Learning Model in the Virtual World. Journal of Crime and Justice, 33 (2010)

10. Goodin, D.: Online crime gangs embrace open source ethos, http://www.theregister.co.uk/2008/01/17/globalization-of-crimeware

11. Zheleva, E., Getoor, L.: To join or not to join: the illusion of privacy in social networks with mixed public and private user profiles. In: Proc. of the 18th International Conference on World Wide Web (WWW), pp. 531–540. ACM (2009)

12. Agarwal, N., Liu, H., Tang, L., Yu, P.: Identifying the influential bloggers in a community. In: Proc. of the 1st International Conference on Web Search and Web Data Mining (WSDM). ACM (2008)

13. Chakrabarti, S.: Dynamic personalized pagerank in entity-relation graphs. In: Proc. of World Wide Web, WWW (2007)

14. Keeney, R., Raiffa, H.: Decisions with multiple objectives. Cambridge Books (1993)

15. Salton, G., Buckley, C.: Term-weighting approaches in automatic text retrieval. Information Processing & Management 24(5), 513–523 (1988)

16. Bianchini, M., Gori, M., Scarselli, F.: Inside pagerank. ACM Transactions on Internet Technology (TOIT) 5(1), 92–128 (2005)

17. Yarochki, F.V.: From Russia with love.exe, http://www.seacure.it/archive/2009/stuff/Seacure2009FyodorYarochkin-FromRussiaWithLove.pdf

18. Raymond, E.: The new hacker's dictionary. The MIT Press (1996)

19. Angles, R., Gutierrez, C.: Survey of graph database models. ACM Computing Surveys (CSUR) 40(1), 1–39 (2008)

20. Kleinberg, J.: Authoritative sources in a hyperlinked environment. Journal of the ACM (JACM) 46(5), 604–632 (1999)

21. Xu, J., Chen, H.: CrimeNet explorer: a framework for criminal network knowledge discovery. ACM Transactions on Information Systems (TOIS) 23(2), 201–226 (2005)

22. Zhou, Y., Reid, E., Qin, J., Chen, H., Lai, G.: US domestic extremist groups on the Web: link and content analysis. In: IEEE Intelligent Systems, pp. 44–51 (2005)

23. Chau, M., Xu, J.: Mining communities and their relationships in blogs: A study of online hate groups. International Journal of Human-Computer Studies 65(1), 57–70 (2007)

24. Lu, Y., Polgar, M., Luo, X., Cao, Y.: Social Network Analysis of a Criminal Hacker Community. Journal of Computer Information Systems, 31–42 (2010)

25. Page, L., Brin, S., Motwani, R., Winograd, T.: The PageRank Citation Ranking: Bringing Order to the Web (1999)

26. Cho, C., et al.: Inference and analysis of formal models of botnet command and control protocols. In: Proc. of the 17th ACM Conference on Computer and Communications Security (CCS), pp. 426–439. ACM (2010)

27. Gu, G., Porras, P., Yegneswaran, V., Fong, M., Lee, W.: Bothunter: Detecting malware infection through ids-driven dialog correlation. In: Proc. of USENIX Security Symposium. USENIX Association (2007)

28. Prince, B.: Microsoft takes down a botnet responsible for 39 percentage of global spam, http://www.pcmag.com/article2/0,2817,2368935,00.asp

29. Motoyama, M., McCoy, D., Levchenko, K., Savage, S., Voelker, G.M.: An analysis of underground forums. In: Proceedings of the 2011 ACM SIGCOMM Conference on Internet Measurement Conference. ACM (2011)

Author Index